Let Freedom Ring:

A Collection of Documents from the Movements to Free U.S. Political Prisoners

KER
SPL
EBE
DEB

PM

Let Freedom Ring:

A Collection of Documents from the Movements to Free U.S. Political Prisoners

foreword by Adolfo Pérez Esquivel
afterwords by Lynne Stewart and Ashanti Omowali Alston

edited by Matt Meyer

KER SPL EBE DED PM

Let Freedom Ring: A Collection of Documents from the Movements
to Free U.S. Political Prisoners

Edited by Matt Meyer

ISBN: 978-1-60486-035-1
Library of Congress Control Number: 2008931786

Kersplebedeb Publishing and Distribution
CP 63560
CCCP Van Horne
Montreal, Quebec
Canada H3W 3H8
www.kersplebedeb.com

PM Press
PO Box 23912
Oakland, CA 94623
www.pmpress.org

Layout and Index by Kersplebedeb

Cover Design: Josh Macphee/justseeds.org
Cover image originally from flyer to free political prisoners.

Printed in the U.S.A.

Contents

Acknowledgments

First and foremost, this book would never have been completed without the hard work of my unindicted coconspirator, Betsy Mickel. Betsy's support and vision—on technical, political, and personal levels—made the book both stronger and made my work much easier. Much more than just the best copy editor on the left, Betsy's own input has ensured that various details and wordings appear clear to the reader. I think of all the praise given to progressive doctors and lawyers, whose "pro bono" work does, indeed, contribute to the cause. But our movements, more than anything, must be vehicles for communication—and our copy editors deserve special praise for making our communications understandable to a wide audience.

Another co-conspirator, Bob Lederer deserves thanks for his detailed review and edits of the text, research and added historical notes, and compilation of the contributors' profiles and political prisoner support organizations at the end. This book would not be as accurate or complete without his hard work and watchful eye. Elspeth Meyer contributed her own, underutilized artwork and helped assemble the art of some of the others whose work appears on these pages. Meg Starr, my life partner, leadership, and general inspiration, had the initial idea for this collection and convinced a number of us that it was of vital importance at this time. All the above names also share the distinction of being part of my home base—my grassroots political collective, Resistance in Brooklyn (RnB). Some of the works herein were first published in pamphlet form by RnB or through RnB's coalition work. I remain forever indebted to all the members of RnB for their support, critique, and work to make the world a better place.

My main mentor and guide to the movements to free U.S. political prisoners has always been Puerto Rican educator, lawyer, and organizer Dr. Luis Nieves Falcón. Words cannot adequately express the wealth of knowledge, skills, strategies, and support that he has shared and imparted on whole generations of activists. I am honored to be one amongst them. Comrade Alejandro Molina and I shared important moments working side by side some decades ago, and those lessons stay fresh with me to this day. More recently, I have been privileged to call Ashanti Alston both colleague and friend, as the work to free political prisoners enters a new phase of U.S. imperial history. All three of these great men have shaped my understanding of this work and have given support to bringing together the documents presented in this book.

Laura Whitehorn is not only an indefatigable spokesperson for the freedom movement, she is also a stalwart behind-the-scenes agitator. Her early comments on the contents of this volume have made it a more well rounded affair. Similarly, tireless Jill Soffiyah Elijah offered some early suggestions and support, for which I am most grateful. My basement full of file cabinets and old papers help supply the lion's share of what is presented here, but where they failed, the diligent efforts of Dawn Reel helped complete an important section. Jenny Radtke assisted with late night copyediting. These and many other women warriors have provided me with so much more than I can thank them for here; their work continues to serve as a guide to how we must go forward.

I am indebted to all whose writings appear in this book. I especially want to thank those who wrote significant new pieces or were interviewed just for this anthology: Dan Berger, B♀ (rita d. brown), Bill Dunne, Ryme Katkhouda, Bob Lederer, Margie Lincita, Suzanne Ross, Jane Segal, Brendan Story, Linda Thurston, and Barbara Zeller. I am deeply indebted to the incredibly hard-working and meticulous Karl of Kersplebedeb, who has done much more than any publisher is supposed to (including the entire index). His commitment to the freedom of all political prisoners, and to making this book work as a movement resource, has been nothing less than breathtaking. I must also thank the good folks at PM Press, whose own political and organizational vision and network have made this a more exciting and significant endeavor. Eric Drooker contributed several beautiful illustrations and photographs were generously provided by Hans Bennett, Diane Greene Lent, Lallan Schoenstein and JEB (Joan Biren). Significant sensational services were provided, in the last moments of production, by Mbet Umanah of UbiQus, Beverly Keene of Jubilee South, Anne Lamb of National Jericho, Josh MacPhee (cover artist extraordinaire) of JustSeeds.com, Kai Lumumba Barrrow and Linda Thurston of Critical Resistance, Suzanne Ross of the Free Mumia Abu-Jamal Coalition, and John Riley of ACT UP. Sara Falconer of Anarchist Black Cross/Toronto and Paulette D'Aueteuil of New York City Jericho were of great help in assembling the political prisoner support organization list.

Finally, the suggestions, support, and inspiration I receive in every letter and call from a political prisoner remind me on a regular basis of the urgent nature of this work. I must especially thank David Gilbert, whose friendship and mentoring has enriched so many aspects of my life. In addition, ongoing correspondence and conversations over the years with Marilyn Buck, Herman Bell, Seth Hayes, Sundiata Acoli, Oscar López Rivera, Mututu Shakur, and Jalil Muntaqim, amongst others, continue to shape my understanding of the world. I am privileged to live in a city and at a time when I can regularly be at meetings with former political prisoner Herman Ferguson and the amazing Iyaluua Ferguson. And those who have passed on—most especially Safiya Bukhari, Dave Dellinger, and Standing Deer—need mention for the indelible mark they have made on my consciousness, and on the work. The errors and omissions in this book are, ultimately, solely my responsibility. The work to free all political prisoners remains, however, the responsibility of us all.

Matt Meyer, August 1, 2008

Foreword

Adolfo Pérez Esquivel
recipient, 1980 Nobel Peace Prize
founder, Servicio Paz y Justicia

As a political prisoner jailed by the Argentine dictatorship in 1977, I started out my jail time in what we called "the pipe"—a very narrow, L-shaped cell just long enough to lie down in, with a little space at the door where one could just about stand up. I was in "the pipe" at La Plata Prison for 32 days, followed by another 13 months with no access to books, even a Bible. That is what imprisonment in general—and political imprisonment in particular— is all about: making sure that we do not stand up for our rights or the rights of others, for our spirituality, for freedom itself.

What is the purpose of putting someone in prison? In most cases, it is simply to destroy a person psychologically and physically. In Argentina, we were treated severely—with constant body searches, blows, and all manner of torture. But the worst inhumanity of all was to hear the screams of ones comrades and fellow prisoners—being beaten and forced to denounce God and themselves. If not for my own friends and family, I would not have been a political prisoner, but instead one of the disappeared... lost and made invisible by a repressive regime.

In the more than 25 years since my release from prison, in the more than 25 years since I was awarded the Nobel Peace Prize that I accepted on behalf of the poor people of Latin America, many things have changed, and not all for the better. As I stated at the start of the 2003 war in Iraq, the U.S. is the chief danger in the world today. With continued interference in Colombia, Venezuela, Panama, and elsewhere, it is clear that the U.S. is trying to control the world. The Latin American reaction has been equally clear; despite high points and low ones, the people of the South are rising up to say *no* to U.S.-based globalization. It is no surprise, then, that when people rise up within the U.S., they face repression and imprisonment. Though the U.S. government may try to deny it, it is a barely concealed fact that the U.S. holds many political prisoners.

Matt Meyer's *Let Freedom Ring* is a welcome and important addition to the growing literature on U.S. human rights abuses and the question of political imprisonment. By bringing together documents of the last quarter century, Meyer provides tools for today's activists, while placing contemporary legal cases in their historic context. A longtime member of the War Resisters International, Meyer—in a spirit akin to the Peace and Justice Service, the Latin American organization I helped found —takes a nonviolent approach to radical social change. That means he is also a coalition-builder, and the documents in this book reflect the broad range of dissent found throughout U.S.-based movements.

When, in the late 1980s, I joined the Call for the release of 15 Puerto Rican independence activists jailed in the U.S. on conspiracy charges, it was clear that that case had significant international human rights repercussions. More recently, in 2007, I added my name on similar grounds to the Call for the release of five Cuban representatives held in the U.S. All of the cases presented in this vital book deserve greater international attention. Our task is clear, as set forth in the teachings of the prophet Isaiah: We must work together to set free those who are bound, to turn our swords and spears into plowshares.

Let Freedom Ring:
An Introduction

Matt Meyer

"Face Reality!" The poster screams out at you. Forty-eight faces, men and women of every racial and ethnic group, look determined and active and strong. They stare out, they reach out, of the black-bordered design, stark and clean, with bold white lettering proclaiming the message. "There *are* political prisoners in the U.S.A."

When the coalition known as Freedom Now! first produced that poster in the late 1980s, many in the U.S. left were unaware of most of the names attached to those faces and of the fact that over 100 people who could easily be classified as political prisoners by the standards of the Geneva Convention or the United Nations languished in U.S. jails. Even figures who now serve as icons in the struggle against the death penalty, such as death row journalist Mumia Abu-Jamal, or respected leaders of the American Indian Movement, such as Leonard Peltier—who has had petitions calling for his release signed by literally millions of people across the globe—were not easily recognizable amongst progressives in their own country. Twenty years later, that situation is somewhat improved; the existence of U.S. political prisoners is readily accepted throughout movement circles. And, in what may be surprising news even to ardent antiprison campaigners who face depressing conditions every day, no fewer than 27 of the men and women on that Face Reality poster are now out of jail, living productive lives back in their communities. There has been progress, born of struggle, over these two decades.

But three of those pictured are dead. Albert Nuh Washington and Richard Williams died in prison, away from their families, of cancerous cells and infections that ate away at their bodies with a speed indicative of their deadly surroundings. They were denied humanitarian release, even in the late stages of the disease—when freedom would have simply meant the ability to lie in a nonprison hospital bed, surrounded by family and friends. Filiberto Ojeda Ríos, also on the original poster, did not die in prison. As is known throughout the island of Puerto Rico, Filiberto—who had been living a quiet, clandestine life in the years since escaping the jailer's grasp—was gunned down at his home by the same FBI that is largely responsible for the unjust and illegal incarceration of his comrades. That the FBI selected to assassinate the 72-year-old Filiberto on *Grito de Lares,* the traditional day of celebration of Puerto Rico's short-lived independence from Spain (before the U.S. Marines showed up), is further indication of the provocative and hateful manner that U.S. authorities have dealt with these "enemies of the state." Nuh, Richard, and Filiberto, along with Merle Africa, are dead, and 18 others on that critical old poster are still imprisoned. And new faces continue to be jailed, taking the place of some of those now free.

This book is being put together as a guide to the past 20 years of campaigning for the release of political prisoners, prisoners of war, and prisoners of conscience held in U.S. jails. We are doing so at this time because we believe it to be a crucial moment to redouble our efforts for justice for all. We want to look clearly and strategically at some of the successes we've had; we do not for a moment believe that the release of political prisoners in this past period was merely a matter of luck or good timing, or the act of benevolent politicians. We want to examine, without undue pride or remorse, the strengths and weaknesses in our own movements that have helped bring about the condition we face today. Most of all, we want to make available some of the documents, and some of the thinking that went behind the tactics and strategies used, that produced—in our evaluations—some of the strongest results. We want to push the level of dialogue and work. If you were involved, what efforts have we left out? What critiques have we overlooked? What analysis is shaky? If you were not involved, did you think the issue didn't touch your own work for social justice and peace?

Why political prisoners?

The history of the world—from before the days of Jesus of Nazareth till long after any alleged combatant is held by the U.S. military at Guantánamo Bay—can be rightly told by the prominent examples of people held unjustly because of their beliefs. Many of those now considered political prisoners are jailed because of their participation in various movements for social change. Since the end of World War Two, in an effort to ensure that the policies and practices leading to and executed by the Fascists of Nazi Germany would never again rip the heart of humankind, the international community established regulations to serve as global guideposts. Though too often ignored by the governments of the world, these guidelines regarding the waging of war, the treatment of prisoners, and the rights of all peoples nevertheless serve to remind us all of some basic standards, internationally discussed and ratified, during the worst of times. The definitions of who qualifies as a political prisoner may be long debated and cause for disagreement; the International Declaration of Human Rights may be a far from perfect document, administered unevenly in a far from perfect world. As we campaign for a peace based upon justice, however, it helps to hold to some standards that can be easily communicated no matter what the date and place and time.

In contemporary world history, few would deny that much of the moral leadership of our age has come from political prisoners. Indian independence leader Mohandas Gandhi made going to jail a rite of passage for those campaigning for his country's freedom; Pan Africanist Kwame Nkrumah of Ghana followed suit. Rev. Dr. Martin Luther King, Jr., wrote some of his most famous words while jailed for his political beliefs and actions, and Malcolm X left his cell so energized, he built a Nation upon release. Puerto Rican freedom fighter Lolita Lebrón, one of the first 20th-century Latin American women who took up arms for their people, found God in her prison cell and remains today the conscience of her nation. Nonviolent human rights fighter Aung San Suu Kyi of Burma was awarded the Nobel Peace Prize in 1991 for her work against the Burmese dictatorship, though she still remains under house arrest for her efforts. Her Nobel Prize-winning colleague, Nelson Mandela—African National Congress leader who spent 27 years under lock and key for his refusal to give up his principles or his tactical beliefs—is probably the most recognized and respected person on the face of our planet today. Mandela spent his quarter-century in jail for refusing to renounce the right of oppressed people to wage armed struggle for liberation, though now is correctly viewed as a great force of nonviolence.

The current U.S. political prisoners have received no Nobel honors and scant little attention from the human rights community. But they share many similarities to their above-named predecessors, playing leadership roles for progressive social change, standing fast in their beliefs that a better world is possible. This is true whether we are talking about Dr. Mutulu Shakur, a proponent of New Afrikan independence in the Black Belt south, who pioneered acupuncture techniques for intravenous drug users in Harlem trying to free themselves from substance abuse, or about Oscar López Rivera, a decorated Vietnam Veteran from the Puerto Rican community of Chicago, who has found out the hard way that one does not receive commendations for fighting for one's own people here at home. This is certainly true of Native elder Leonard Peltier, whose main crime was a commitment to defend his community against FBI military attack. This commitment, though real and undeniable, must be understood in the light of mountains of legal evidence that suggests that Peltier never took any action that resulted in any harm to anyone. It is true for the many former Black Panthers, who had the audacity to want to defend themselves against police violence, and it is true for the Cuban 5, who may be considered terrorists simply because of the country of their birth—and whose nonviolent actions were clearly in the cause of peace. It is true for white activists Marilyn Buck and David Gilbert, who wanted to demonstrate by their actions that some would stand in solidarity when attacks were waged against the Black Panther Party, their allies, and their offshoots. It is true for the many Plowshares campaigners, who beat their hammers on real, not imagined, weapons of mass destruction, and for the new wave of animal rights and environmental defenders. It is true for the growing number of U.S. military resisters, whose political act is refusing to fight and be killed in a war that most would agree (now even in Congress!) is unjust and unnecessary. Taken together, the current U.S. political prisoners represent the heart of people's movements, past and present. They symbolize the unfinished legacy of recent struggles for humanity. Their freedom represents nothing less than claiming our history with pride, proclaiming our certainty that the struggle, indeed, does continue.

Why now?

When the PATRIOT Act informed all U.S. citizens that the price of freedom was freedom itself, Orwellian double-speak surpassed even Reagan-era standards. With habeas corpus and the First Amendment under attack, it was clearly time to act. When the atrocities of Abu Ghraib sparked a public discussion about the effectiveness of torture, it was clearly time to act. When Filiberto was murdered, six years after 11 Puerto Rican Prisoners of War were granted clemency, to provoke angry *independentistas* to take actions that might lead to a new generation of *presos políticos*, it was clearly a time to take action. When governmental representatives met in guarded General Assembly quarters, and the new Latin American radical momentum enabled the president of Venezuela to laughingly call the president of the United States "the devil," there was not just time, but opportunity for us to act. When nongovernmental representatives meet in open tents at World Social Forums in Brazil and Venezuela, Mali and Kenya, India and Pakistan, calling for grassroots U.S. activists to focus energy on the social justice issues in our own backyard, there was—and is—clearly a responsibility for us to act.

When, during the summer of 2006, five men in their fifties and sixties—all former members or associates of the Black Panther Party—were called before a San Francisco-based grand jury allegedly investigating a crime committed over three decades previously, the state threw down a gauntlet. When it became clear that the investigations were reopening cases based on evidence obtained primarily through torture, the message was unmistakable: Be afraid, be very afraid, and don't even think of fighting back. When these same men stood strong, firm on the principle that they would not take part in a new, government-sponsored witch hunt, they sent a counter-message on behalf of us all: We will *not* allow our struggles, our communities, our very lives to be criminalized by a corrupt and racist criminal justice system. When, in the first weeks of 2007, indictments were handed down for eight former Panthers—including four of the five previously mentioned and two political prisoners, Jalil Muntaqim and Herman Bell, who have already served more than 30 years behind bars—the responsibility to speak out became that much more urgent. We must speak out not only for the San Francisco 8 and for the movements they symbolically represent. We speak out for ourselves, as the legacy of those movements and the growing interest in them among younger generations today help inform a new wave of struggle that learns from the mistakes of the past. We speak out for tomorrow.

Enough is enough! The message we must send is a simple one: Never again. Never again will progressive people in the U.S.—liberals and radicals, Black, white, Latino, Asian, and Indigenous—remain divided or inactive as government agents jail our leaders, criminalize our movements, and terrorize the people. Never again will we allow torture, abroad or here at home. Never again will we allow illegal wars and immoral laws used as excuses to roll back hard-earned human rights that are considered basic in most of the world. Never another political prisoner; never another colony.

The means of achieving these goals are not so simple, but the task is clear. It's not enough to pledge that the building of empire must end; Puerto Rico must be freed of its colonial status, and the neo-colonies and internal colonies must be granted sovereignty as well. It's not enough that the members of the San Francisco 8 not yet convicted of any crimes must be kept out of prison. Herman Bell and Jalil Muntaqim (and all the political prisoners) must be immediately released and returned to the communities they have worked so hard to enrich. The tactics and even some of the strategies can and must be varied. Some of us must engage in genuine, respectful, interactive meetings with those in power; others of us will be chanting and getting arrested on the other side of those same meetings—involved in massive and disciplined direct actions that will demonstrate by our deeds that we are prepared to shut the system down if our demands are not met. Many of us must hand out petitions, send out e-mails and mailings, organize educational events, and make telephone calls to let new people learn about our work in ways that they are ready to hear. And all of us will have to learn that most basic of acts of communication and dialogue; we must knock on a neighbor's door, introduce ourselves politely, and begin telling the story of our buddies behind bars. Whether at our places of work or our local schools, the place we do our laundry or the places we go to relax, we must talk about the real people whom the U.S. government would like to make disappear.

This book was quickly thrown together, chronologically and thematically arranged as a resource guide for organizers. It is filled with old documents and speeches, essays, and calls to action, from a variety of the campaigns over the past 20 years. There are a few new pieces as well, and joined together they give us a sense of where we've been, what we've done, and where we might be heading. As you read through these resources, you will find some information that is dated and some that was written for a particular audience or event. They are included not simply to give one a sense of the time, but to help frame the context for certain strategies utilized in the various campaigns described. We hope that they are all informative and inspiring. But more than that, we hope that when put together as a whole, they can inform our collective thinking about the movements we must build today. They are not all-inclusive; there are examples of good work done for the release of U.S. political prisoners that are only briefly referred to, or not reproduced at all. We present the texts we do with an eye toward what we consider particularly strategic. We present them for review in reference to the next steps we feel need to be taken in building the next broad campaign—to let freedom ring for all the remaining U.S. political prisoners.

For many peoples, from a broad historical perspective, liberty has never truly been won. Let us begin today, freeing those who are bound.

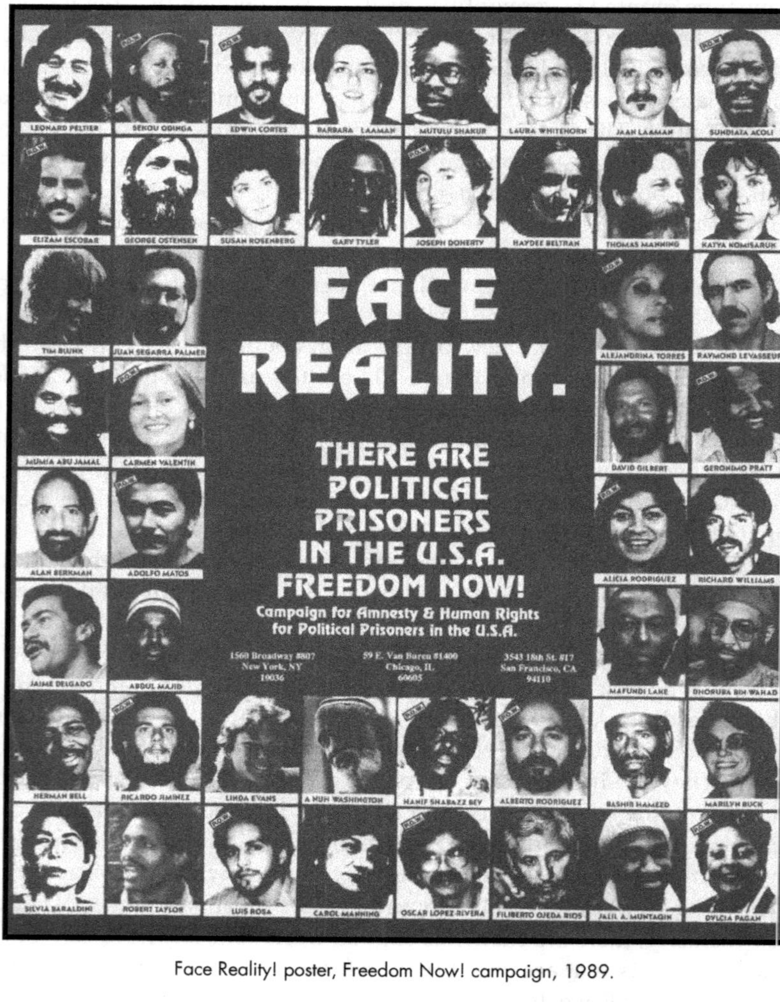

Face Reality! poster, Freedom Now! campaign, 1989.

Gearing Up: A Guide to This Collection

Matt Meyer

First and foremost, it is important to understand this book as a resource manual. It is not intended to be read cover to cover and is also not intended as a comprehensive set of materials from the period in question. What it *is* is a political selection of some of the strategic opportunities set forth over the past 20 years to bring the issue of U.S. political prisoners, prisoners of conscience, and prisoners of war to a wider audience than a "preaching to the choir" left. In the process of making this selection, we have tried to avoid sectarianism and regionalism, but recognize that this is an ongoing process of struggle of which we, too, are a part. So the sense of what is important to emphasize and what is considered strategic is, ultimately, the perspective (and fault) of the editor.

That said, there are some basic assumptions that derive from collective political history, not simply individual preference. That the work to free U.S. political prisoners has its modern roots in the Black liberation movement in general, and the Black Panther Party in particular, is evidenced in their pioneering work to repopularize the concept of the political prisoner and to raise consciousness around prison issues in general.

It is beyond the chronological scope of this collection to include some documents from campaigns that we nevertheless feel compelled to acknowledge. We stand proudly on the shoulders of the movement to free the Soledad Brothers, the campaigns to free Angela, and the many struggles to get folks to realize that Attica is *all* of us. In looking at the many decades of support work for Black Panthers like Sundiata and Geronimo, we recognize that the poster "Assata Is Welcome Here" continues to have meaning today. As the New Jersey police and government put nothing less than a million-dollar bounty on her head, we are called to proclaim: Keep Assata Free!

This collection brings together many efforts to understand in international context both the issue of political prisoners and the reality of internal colonialism faced by the Black/New Afrikan, Puerto Rican, Mexican/Chican@, and Native Nations. We would therefore be remiss in not citing some precedents for our imperfect, 20-year retrospective. In 1978, Lennox Hinds of the International Association of Democratic Lawyers presented an important petition to the United Nations citing human rights abuses regarding political prisoners. This petition, presented on behalf of the National Conference of Black Lawyers, the National Alliance Against Racism and Political Repression, and the Commission for Racial Justice of the United Church of Christ, led to a significant international inquiry into the conditions of confinement of our comrades. The international campaign to free the five Puerto Rican Nationalists, taking place during the same period of 1970s upsurge, brought such pressure on the Carter administration that the president was forced to commute the sentences of Lolita Lebrón, Rafael Cancel Miranda, Irvin Flores, and Oscar Collazo. Bitter irony strikes again that one of the remaining Puerto Rican *independentistas* in prison today after more than 25 years is Oscar López Rivera, who was, among other things, an activist with the campaign to Free the Five.

There is not enough information on these pages about the myriad of grand jury resisters who faced intense jail time for refusing to collaborate with prosecutors' "fishing expeditions" attempting to criminalize radical thought and activity. And the efforts to close down control units and super-maximum security house units, once known by their less stylized name—dungeons—are not as focused on as we'd have liked. The fact that the infamous Lexington Control Unit, which tortured political prisoners Alejandrina Torres, Susan Rosenberg, and Silvia Baraldini, was successfully shut down in the 1980s is little comfort in light of the fact that new federal and state-based control units have been built at an alarming rate ever since.

There is much to be done, and the documents included herein suggest that much work has, in fact, already been done. For this collection to serve its purpose, the active reader will think about how these efforts can be built upon. Together, we must figure out how a new and more united movement can emerge that will understand that a future worthy of winning cannot be built if we ignore our past.

The Real Dragons:
A Brief History of Political Militancy and Incarceration, 1960s to 2000s

The Real Dragons:
A Brief History of Political Militancy and Incarceration, 1960s to 2000s

Dan Berger
2008

"When the prison doors are opened, the real dragon will fly out."

Ho Chi Minh

Governments have long used incarceration and execution to crush dissent. Political prisoners occupy a crucial position in liberation struggles around the world; their incarceration signals the terror of state repression, and their activism defines the principled, long-term commitments of our movements. Working for their full freedom constitutes a vital element in building, defending, and sustaining the revolutionary traditions for which they have fought. In ways political and personal, fighting for their release grounds radicalism in its layered history: it puts long-term activists who have borne the brunt of repression in public view, connects younger radicals with older generations, and, in the West, exposes the contradictions of liberal democracy. As such, freeing political prisoners always comprises a giant victory for the left, just as work on their behalf offers much-needed opportunities to learn from the strengths and weaknesses of previous struggles and to build coalition among the many communities in struggle. Working for their freedom provides the chance to improve people's material conditions, to free people from the state's clutches before medical neglect, long sentences, or open execution can take their lives. It also enables us, ideally, to build on the best of those traditions while avoiding some of their pitfalls.

The connection to movement history generated by working to free political prisoners is multifaceted: just as participation in the struggle expands one's knowledge of history, so too is our organizing strengthened through at least a provisional awareness of the movements and conditions, ideologies and strategies, that produced the revolutionaries who have served or are now serving time in American gulags. What follows is just such a cursory introduction; though it is by nature partial and incomplete, I trace some of the foundational cases and contexts of political incarceration in the United States since the 1960s. The state uses the imprisonment of political leaders and rank-and-file activists as a bludgeon against movement victories. Their incarceration is a reminder of the strength, potential, and, just as crucially, the weaknesses and vulnerabilities of radical mass movements. As a result, political prisoners serve collective prison time for all those who participated in the movements from which they emerged. And because, as James Baldwin once wrote, "[a] people who trust their history do not find themselves immobilized in it," we have a responsibility to know where we come from. Grounding our

3

actions in our histories enables us to build mental and physical resistance to the state assaults on our memories and our victories. It is a safeguard, perhaps the only one, against the politics of repression and annihilation.

Militancy and Raising the Stakes

The liberal international human rights community often defines political internees as those incarcerated for their beliefs, not necessarily their actions. While such instances abound, they are not the only or even the best examples of politically motivated incarceration. Whether someone "did it" ought not to determine fully who receives our support. Instead, political prisoners are best conceived as active participants in resistance movements. International law established the rights and treatment of political prisoners and prisoners of war; the latter category includes not only formal armies but guerrilla fighters of recognized liberation struggles. Attuned to ongoing injustice and wary of repeating the horrors of Nazism, the United Nations sanctioned struggle (including by force of arms) against racist and repressive regimes. While the framework of international law still leaves much to be desired, its stipulations—supposed to be the highest law of the land—are still more progressive than normal policy in the United States.

Thus the central issue for thinking about political prisoners is not whether they did it but what movements did they come from and what are the broader circumstances surrounding their arrest. Most of those incarcerated participated in radical movements seeking fundamental overhauls of structures of power. Some of these, most notably death row journalist Mumia Abu-Jamal as well as several other former members of the Black Panther Party, are victims of state frame-ups. But many others were active participants in liberation struggles that included involvement in illegal activities. Regardless of which side of the law their actions fell on, however, America's political prisoners participated in movements presenting revolutionary left challenges to the capitalist state; for many, these politics emerged out of an explicit commitment to fighting white supremacy (and, for some, patriarchy). These politics necessitated direct, confrontational responses to the violence of U.S. imperialism and corporate hegemony—from war overseas to murderous attacks on people of color in the United States, from environmental destruction to the stark repression of incarceration. Political prisoners emerged from movements seeking to stop, to overturn, to develop alternatives to the violence of the system. All of America's political internees did something; some resisted with force, some put their bodies on the line, and others used words and propagated ideas the state deemed too powerful to let slide as just so much free speech. Supporting political prisoners is defending the radical left's ability to wage resistance.

Of those incarcerated for engaging in illegal, often clandestine actions, most followed a similar path: several years of legal activism led to a determined belief in the need to raise the stakes. Their backgrounds are varied; prior to

4

being activists, they were good-hearted liberals or class-conscious workers, apolitical moderates or red-diaper babies. They spent years protesting, petitioning, organizing, and engaging in civil disobedience. But, time after time, frustration at the limited possibilities of available (i.e., legal) remedies to such entrenched injustice led many activists to seek—and many more to support— alternative options of resistance. This search for alternatives emerged from a desperation, it is true, but also from a palpable belief in the possibility for a more successful revolutionary politics. Building a movement, many have argued, requires an infrastructure outside the eyes and ears of the state— especially as state repression becomes more intense against revolutionary currents. Although it often meant a turn to armed struggle, the search for new mechanisms of engaging in political action did not necessarily lead to violence. What it did mean, across the board, was a belief in raising the stakes of resistance to imperial rule. Upping the ante through militant, often clandestine, tactics was not intended to stand in for organizing a mass movement (although sectarianism and different strategic priorities have often yielded this in effect if not in intent). Rather, militancy meant an ongoing commitment to develop a revolutionary movement that looked to create opportunities for expanded resistance in the context of concrete conditions.

There are several, somewhat overlapping communities of struggle from which America's political prisoners have emerged in recent decades. I will focus below on the most significant: the national liberation struggles of Black/New Afrikan, Puerto Rican, Indigenous, and Chicano people; antiracist solidarity and opposition to U.S. imperialism; revolutionary nonviolence against the state's ability to wage war; and, more recently, activists incarcerated for their actions on behalf of earth and animal liberation. While my focus is on those facing the most severe sentences and tied to established political movements, readers should keep in mind that the United States has always had more political prisoners than can be summarized in one essay or book. Each wave of repression has not only targeted those who end up serving long sentences, but also many activists who go to jail rather than cooperate with grand jury investigations or who are targeted for their support of radical actions. Many people have passed in and out of prison on a variety of politically motivated charges and not always based on longstanding connection to social movements. The 2007 convictions of four young Black lesbians in New York City for defending themselves from a homophobic attack is surely a case in point, as are the many examples of women and trans people being incarcerated for fighting back against or killing their abusers. The urgency of many acts of resistance makes hard and fast rules a risky endeavor. What follows, then, is an introductory sketch of the revolutionary struggles that have found themselves facing stiff repression. It is lengthy but by necessity incomplete. For ease of reading, the below essay is not footnoted; while the other contributions in this collection should provide some relevant historical markers, I also include a list of some additional sources as an epilogue for those eager to read more.

1

National Liberation on U.S. Soil
The three decades following World War II, roughly 1945 to 1975, witnessed
an array of upheavals around the world. These immense changes—political,
economic, social, cultural—continue to structure and inform the contemporary world. Perhaps the most important development internationally was the
success of anticolonialism. With European colonial powers stretched thin by
a costly global war, radical and revolutionary movements throughout the
Third World of Africa, Asia, and Latin America began achieving independence or emerging triumphant against U.S.-supported dictators in their own
countries. In most cases, these movements attempted to replace the corrupt
regime with some form of socialism. Most of these Third World liberation
movements struggled for independence from the colonial regimes or the overturning of neocolonial regimes that had controlled their countries for decades
or generations. The list of victories was impressive and seemed permanently
expanding: beginning with China in 1948, there were successful revolutions or
triumphs by popular movements in Ghana (1957); Cuba (1959); Algeria (1962);
Chile (1970); Guinea Bissau (1974); Angola and Mozambique (1975); Vietnam,
Cambodia, and Laos (1975); Grenada (1979); Nicaragua (1979); Zimbabwe (1980);
Namibia (1991); South Africa (1994); and dozens of other Third World nations.
Such sweeping radical change defined the Third World, unaligned with
either the capitalist First World or the bureaucratic communism of the Second
World (although the Soviet Union and/or China did provide much-needed
material aid to several revolutionary struggles). Refusing to choose sides in
the interimperialist rivalry of the Cold War, these movements united revolutionary nationalism with some form of socialism and an eclectic range of
tactics to achieve independence. While recent history has shown capitalism's
ability to colonize without formal armies, as well as the corruption of even
leftist authoritarian rule, the sweeping tide of revolution seemed to leave no
country unaffected in the several-decade period known as "the Sixties."

Part 1: The Black Liberation Movement and Settler Colonialism
Within the United States, the politics of national liberation were most forcefully articulated by the Black liberation struggle. Through the internationalist politics of many leaders and rank-and-file activists, Black liberationists
identified their cause with anticolonial resistance overseas. More than affinity, however, this unity was born of a similar designated status. As the Sixties
wore on, many radicals began to speak of peoples of color in the United States
as "internal colonies," captive nations within U.S. boundaries. This analysis
was predicated on the abject poverty, state repression, and racist attitudes
faced by colonized people overseas; this triad was especially prevalent in
other "settler colonial" societies. Rather than a colonial government serving a faraway power, settler colonies are those countries—the United States,
Israel, Canada, South Africa, Australia, New Zealand—established through
the settlement of foreign populations as dominant classes and the imposition

2

of institutions and structures upon a displaced and marginalized indigenous population. Settler colonialism in the Americas is based on both the slaughter and containment of the indigenous population, as well as imported African slave labor.

Viewing the situation of African Americans and other peoples of color as one of internal colonialism was a natural complement to the militant politics already developing within the movement. This analysis joined race and class as constituent elements of colonial rule: the nations internal to the United States were the most oppressed populations, where race served as a marker of class distinction. The goal was to liberate the captive nations—and, as Black Liberation Army soldier Mtayari Shabaka Sundiata once put it, every nation has an army. While the armed actions of the 1970s marked a different phase of the Black liberation movement, this shift was not as decisive as some have suggested. The civil rights movement was never as nonviolent as it has been traditionally depicted; sections of it were always armed (most famously the Deacons for Defense), and even the unarmed aspects were constantly seeking to raise the stakes of resistance to white supremacy. Groups like the Revolutionary Action Movement worked behind the scenes in the early to mid-1960s to develop both Black nationalist consciousness and the capacity for armed resistance. As civil rights activists were more effective and with the quick growth of a self-consciously Black Power movement, the struggle for Black liberation clashed with an entrenched white supremacist power structure and increasingly repressive state.

The Black Panther Party was the most well known of the revolutionary nationalist formations in the late 1960s. Born in Oakland in 1966, the Panthers had grown to a nationwide organization in just two years. Panther chapters in cities across the country built a series of community programs; the most well known entailed community defense, whereby Party members would observe police officers making arrests in an attempt to thwart brutality or stop the arrest altogether. The Panthers also engaged in free community health care and breakfast for children programs, among other "survival pending revolution" operations. With the full weight of state repression against them, the Panthers soon began racking up political prisoners on charges big and small. And the repression wasn't just prison-based; part of the FBI's campaign against the Panthers, as codified in the Counterintelligence Program (COINTELPRO), entailed spreading distrust within the group and between the Panthers and other radical groups. Sometimes these FBI-fostered hostilities degenerated into violence; for instance, the shooting deaths of Panther activists John Huggins and Bunchy Carter in early 1969, ostensibly by members of a rival organization, were in fact provoked by the police. Police had already killed Bobby Hutton, one of the first to join the Panthers, on April 6, 1968, and a dozen other Panthers were felled by police by 1970. In addition to the murder of Panther activists, both leaders and rank-and-file activists found themselves facing trumped-up charges.

3

Such repression bred a climate of fear and distrust internally, as well as a push toward clandestine armed struggle. Black communities had been increasingly in open revolt against the state, especially the police; there were hundreds of rebellions in cities across the country between 1964 and 1968. In that climate, several police officers were killed, and the government increasingly looked to blame Black Panther activists for any attack against police or, for that matter, white people in general. This climate made it easy for the state to frame Black radicals. Just to name a few cases: Panther leaders Dhoruba Bin-Wahad in New York and Geronimo ji Jaga Pratt in California both served time in prison (19 and 27 years, respectively) for attacks of which the state knew they were innocent. Mondo we Langa (s/n David Rice) and Ed Poindexter in Nebraska continue to serve time on trumped-up charges, as do Marshall Eddie Conway in Maryland and Herman Bell and Jalil Muntaqim of the New York 3. (Their codefendant, Albert "Nuh" Washington, died of cancer in prison in April 2000 after almost 30 years inside.)

Two instances of repression particularly stand out in the formation of a Black underground: in a predawn raid on December 4, 1969, Chicago police murdered Mark Clark and Fred Hampton, the 21-year-old leader of that city's Panther chapter. Police fired almost 100 bullets into the apartment, unprovoked, seriously wounding Hampton as he slept (a police informant had drugged him to ensure his slumber) and then finishing him off with two execution-style bullets to the head, fired at point-blank range. Given the climate in which these murders happened, the message was unmistakable: the government was bent on destroying the Black Panther Party by any means necessary. The other key incident at this time was the April 1969 indictment of 21 Black Panthers from the BPP's New York chapter for a host of fabricated, violent conspiracies. Although all were acquitted by the jury in less than an hour, the trial lasted two years, during which time most of the accused remained in prison, as bail had been set at $100,000 each. Even without securing convictions, the government had managed to remove most of the leadership and key activists of the New York chapter. And during those two years, internal divisions within the Panthers had become unbridgeable, as Huey Newton expelled many members of the New York 21, as they were collectively known, for questioning his leadership. Many of the defendants from that case either went into exile with the international chapter of the Panthers or they went underground to help form the Black Liberation Army (BLA).

The BLA emerged in the climate of heightened police repression, not only against Black liberation activists, but against the Black community at large. Police shootings and killings of unarmed civilians, including children, had become a regular feature of urban life by the late 1960s. Viewing the police as an occupying army, the BLA crafted a response of guerrilla warfare. While the idea, and perhaps even the infrastructure, for the BLA had long been in the making, the organization announced its presence through armed attacks against police as retaliation, not against individual officers but against police

4

violence in general. In 1971 alone, the FBI claimed that the BLA carried out more than a dozen attacks on officers in California, Georgia, New Jersey, New York, and Pennsylvania. The BLA claimed responsibility for several of these in communiqués sent to the media. Between 1971 and 1981, at least eight people alleged to be BLA members were killed in shootouts with police, and more than two dozen were arrested. In many cases, the shooting was initiated by police, and the alleged BLA members were then falsely accused of wounding or killing their attackers. Most notorious were the murder charges brought against Assata Shakur and Sundiata Acoli following their arrests on the New Jersey Turnpike in 1973; despite evidence showing their innocence, they were convicted (in separate trials) and sentenced to life. In addition to engaging the police in combat, the BLA also had a campaign against drug dealers in the ghettoes, whom they saw as sapping the strength and vitality of Black communities; BLA prisoner Teddy Jah Heath, who died in prison in 2001, served 28 years for the kidnapping of a drug dealer in which no one was hurt.

Lacking wealthy benefactors or steady access to resources, BLA cells often relied on bank robberies to secure funds (a tactic known as expropriations, for they involved revolutionaries taking money from capitalist institutions to further liberatory ends). In a phenomenon other revolutionary groups would also experience, many BLA soldiers were captured engaging in these high-risk actions.

As members of a clandestine army fighting to free a colonized people, most captured BLA combatants have defined themselves as prisoners of war, not just political prisoners. Several attempted to escape from prison, often with the help of units on the outside—sometimes successfully, at least for short periods of time. Among those still incarcerated for alleged BLA activities (and not mentioned here) are Russell "Maroon" Shoats, Kojo Sababu, Joe-Joe Bowen, Bashir Hameed, and Abdul Majid. Meanwhile, after their release, former BLA soldiers and POW's, such as Ashanti Alston and Safiya Bukhari, became stalwart organizers for the freedom of remaining prisoners. (Bukhari founded the Free Mumia Abu-Jamal Coalition and was a central figure in the Jericho Amnesty Movement until her untimely death in 2003; Alston is the former Northeast regional coordinator for Critical Resistance and now co-chairs the National Jericho Movement.)

By 1975, there was a lull in BLA activity, as many participants were on trial or in prison and whose attention turned toward consolidating the political ideology of the BLA through small-scale newsletters, a study manual, and communiqués. On the outside, however, others began rebuilding the BLA's capacity to carry out even grander actions than had been undertaken to date.

In November 1979, the BLA made a most auspicious public reentry, helping Assata Shakur break out of prison in New Jersey; it was a daring escape, made more impressive by the fact that it succeeded without anyone getting hurt. Shakur ultimately went into exile in Cuba, but this unit of the BLA continued. (Besides Shakur, ex-Panther Nehanda Abiodun remains in exile there, as does Puerto Rican *independentista* William Morales. News reports estimate that Cuba is home to 90 U.S. fugitives, although it is unclear how many of them fled political persecution, nor is Cuba the only place housing U.S. exiles. Indeed, former Panthers Donald Cox and Pete and Charlotte O'Neal are exiled in France and Tanzania, respectively.)

Two years after Shakur's escape, in October 1981, several people attempted to rob a Brink's armored car in Nyack, New York, about 30 miles north of New York City. The expropriation would have netted $1.6 million which, according to a communiqué issued two weeks later under the name Revolutionary Armed Task Force of the BLA, was to have helped fund continued clandestine endeavors and other Black community programs. But the action went awry: a shootout near the Brink's truck left a security guard dead, and two police officers were killed at a roadblock in an exchange of gunfire a few miles away, as the radicals attempted to flee. Four militants were captured at the scene, including BLA member Sam Brown and three white allies—Kathy Boudin, David Gilbert, and Judy Clark. The whites were not at the scene of the robbery; they were arrested at the police roadblock. A shootout in Queens, New York, two days later left BLA soldier Mtayari Shabaka Sundiata dead and Sekou Odinga in police custody; police tortured Odinga, burning him with cigarettes, removing his toenails, and rupturing his pancreas during long beatings that left him hospitalized for six months.

In the weeks that followed, an FBI dragnet created a climate of hysteria, sweeping up many other activists, some of whom had nothing to do with the Brink's incident (and several of whom were ultimately acquitted of all charges). All told, more than a dozen people were arrested leading to multiple trials, at both the state and federal levels, emanating from the Brink's robbery and the escape of Assata Shakur. Additionally, several aboveground supporters and friends, both Black and white, served time for refusing to testify before grand juries investigating these matters. While many from these assorted trials have since been released, several remain in prison with what, for most of them, amount to life sentences. Clark, Gilbert, and BLA member Kuwasi Balagoon were convicted on state felony murder charges in 1983 and sentenced to 75 years to life. In another state trial, BLA member Sekou Odinga was convicted of attempted murder and sentenced to 25 years to life for returning fire against the cops shooting at him prior to his arrest. In a move that would be repeated in later cases brought against left-wing radicals, federal prosecutors in the Brink's case used the RICO (Racketeer Influenced and Corrupt Organizations) Act, originally intended for prosecuting the Mafia, to try those they claimed were involved in illegal underground activity. (RICO allows guilt-by-association "conspiracies" to be prosecuted as criminal enterprises). In the 1983 federal trial, Odinga and white anti-imperialist Silvia Baraldini were found guilty of racketeering and conspiracy in connection with an attempted bank expropriation and Assata Shakur's escape, receiving 40-year sentences each. Three codefendants facing robbery-murder charges, former Panthers Chui Ferguson and Jamal Joseph and Republic of New Afrika activist Bilal Sunni-Ali, were acquitted, although Ferguson and Joseph were convicted of accessory charges and received 12-year sentences. Balagoon and Odinga had attempted to be tried together to collectively mount a POW defense, but the state tried them separately. Still, both invoked international law in claiming the right to resist unjust rule by force. Balagoon died in prison of AIDS on December 13, 1986, and Odinga remains incarcerated. Brown was convicted in 1984. (Brown and Clark are not considered political prisoners: Brown was tortured after his arrest and denied medical care until he cooperated with authorities, yet he still received a life sentence, which he serves under protective custody for being a government witness. In the mid-1980s, Clark asked to be removed from political prisoner lists.) Kathy Boudin, who pled guilty in 1984 to felony murder and robbery, was sentenced to 20 years to life; she was granted parole and released from prison in 2003. Marilyn Buck and Mutulu Shakur were convicted of racketeering and conspiracy in a federal trial in 1988; Buck received 50 years (on top of 20 years for an earlier conviction), Shakur 60 years.

A later case that the FBI falsely dubbed "Son of Brink's" and a "successor" to the BLA involved an attack on another group of Black revolutionary nationalists: In October 1984, eight members of the aboveground Sunrise Collective—Lateefah Carter, Coltrane Chimurenga, Omowale Clay, Yvette Kelley, Colette Pean, Viola Plummer, Robert Taylor, and Roger Wareham—were arrested in a set of massive, military-style police raids around New York City. They were charged with conspiracy to rob banks and break out Balagoon and Odinga from prison. Using a new "preventive detention" law pushed through Congress by then-President Reagan supposedly to combat the Mafia, prosecutors led by U.S. Attorney Rudolph Giuliani convinced a judge to deny bail to the activists—none of whom had any criminal record—as "dangers to the community" and they were all held for several months. The case became known as the New York Eight+ (a ninth, Latino activist José Ríos, was charged later), and it sparked major headlines, mass organizing, and a packed trial. Despite extensive video and audio surveillance and testimony by an informant in the group, in August 1985 the jury acquitted all defendants of the major charges. They were convicted only of minor charges—seven of possession of illegal weapons and one of possession of false IDs; Ríos was acquitted on all counts. In interviews afterwards, jurors condemned the FBI surveillance and the prosecutors' "guilt by association" tactics. One defendant (Pean) received three months' jail time; the others got probation and community service. (These activists later became the core of the December 12th Movement, which has done much work internationally and at the United Nations to highlight the human rights violations against Black political prisoners and the demand for reparations for Black people.) The New York Eight+ case also led to an investigative grand jury that sub-

7

poenaed many Black community members and jailed several who refused to cooperate for months.

Several of those tried for alleged involvement in the second generation of the BLA—including the Assata escape and Brink's debacle, but also several other robberies and attacks during the late 1970s—were citizens of the Republic of New Afrika (RNA), a Black nationalist group formed in 1968. The RNA took the internal colonialism thesis a step further, proclaiming Alabama, Georgia, Louisiana, Mississippi, and South Carolina as the territory of the Black Nation. The RNA developed the governmental apparatus of the Black Nation and organized for independence, choosing Mississippi as its base. Following Brink's, the Joint Terrorism Task Force (a collaborative effort of various police agencies and the FBI) raided RNA territory in Mississippi to arrest several activists. Some were brought to a federal trial emanating from Brink's; others refused to cooperate with grand jury investigations. These arrests were not the first time RNA activists found themselves behind bars. Most famously, 11 RNA citizens were arrested in 1971 in the first (but clearly not the last) military assault on the group's headquarters, which coincided with arrests at a residence where several members lived. While the government had a warrant to arrest one person (who, it turned out, wasn't even there), police officials fired 300 rounds into the RNA government office. RNA officials returned fire, and in the melee, a police officer was killed. All 11 were charged with his death, even though four of the 11 were arrested at an entirely different location. Two RNA activists also served five years for gun possession at the 1972 Democratic National Convention in Miami; authorities speciously claimed the pair was there to assassinate the Democratic nominee.

New Afrikan politics have permeated America's prisons, with dozens of Black men who may not have been previously active or incarcerated for political offenses declaring themselves citizens of New Afrika committed to various forms of revolutionary Black nationalism. (Khalfani Khaldun, Shaka N'Zinga, and Sanyika Shakur are among the better-known examples). Insurgent politics have long held sway among imprisoned populations. Even before New Afrikan politics held such sway, the revolutionary potential of Black Power energized thousands behind prison walls. The most famous example was George Jackson; arrested for participating in a petty robbery as a teenager, Jackson was given the brutally vague sentence of one year to life. Jackson discovered politics while in prison, studying voraciously and ultimately becoming a Field Marshal of the Black Panther Party. His book *Soledad Brother* became a bestseller, and Jackson became a symbol and strategist of revolutionary opposition. His second book, *Blood in My Eye*, was viewed as a manual for Black guerrilla activity. Along with John Clutchette and Fleeta Drumgo, Jackson was charged in January 1970 with killing a corrections officer in retaliation for guards having shot and killed three prisoners in the yard. Defense committees for the "Soledad Brothers," as they were known, sprouted up across the country, bringing together nationalists, communists, and assorted radicals. On August 7, 1970, Jackson's 17-year-old brother, Jonathan, attempted a daring raid at Marin County Courthouse. Although George was not in court that day, Jonathan equipped prisoners William Christmas and James McClain with guns and invited Ruchell Magee to join them. The group took the judge, prosecutor, and several jurors hostage, demanding the state free George and other political prisoners. As they attempted to escape in a van, police opened fire, killing Jackson, Christmas, McClain, and the judge, and seriously wounding Magee and the prosecutor. Magee was acquitted on the most serious charges against him. Yet this 69-year-old man, who was first incarcerated in the 1950s, remains in prison, in large part because of his politics.

Angela Davis, Black communist leader and close friend of George Jackson, was arrested in conjunction with Jonathan's raid, after it was discovered that some of the guns Jonathan used were licensed in her name. (The younger Jackson had been serving as Davis's bodyguard at the time.) She was ultimately acquitted, though her case and Jackson's brought increased attention to the plight and politics of prisoners. On August 21, 1971, George Jackson was shot in the back by San Quentin prison guards in what they insisted was an escape attempt, but which considerable evidence suggests was an assassination. The fightback that August day against mistreatment in the sensory-deprivation unit resulted not only in Jackson's death but also the deaths of two other prisoners and three particularly vicious guards. Afterward, six of the most activist prisoners were charged with conspiracy and murder. Three of the six were convicted in the late 1970s; one of them, Hugo Pinell, who had also become a revolutionary while in prison, remains incarcerated although he was convicted only of assault.

These events helped spark one of the most famous prison rebellions in this period. Hearing of Jackson's murder, prisoners at Attica Correctional Facility in western New York State held a silent protest and fast. This demonstration followed steady organizing that prisoners had been doing to improve their conditions, and the show of solidarity among the prisoners frightened the authorities. The increasing tension boiled over weeks later, when prisoners seized control of the prison in what started as an inchoate riot but quickly turned into a highly political rebellion. Prisoners maintained control of Attica for four days, holding negotiations with the state to not only end the standoff but improve conditions in the prison and advance a revolutionary response to state power. It ended brutally, however, when Governor Nelson Rockefeller ordered troops to retake the prison, leaving 43 people dead (10 guards who had been held as hostages and 29 prisoners were murdered, all by police gunfire; four others died over the course of the rebellion).

The Attica rebellion reflected a growing radicalism among prisoners that had yielded increased pressure, both inside and out, on the prison system as a whole. The late 1960s and early 1970s witnessed a rising prison movement, including dozens of riots, work strikes, escape attempts, and the formation of prisoner labor unions. Following Jackson's example, Herman Wallace, Robert Wilkerson, and Albert Woodfox formed a prison chapter of the Black Panther Party in Louisiana's notoriously brutal Angola prison (the site is a former plantation). The trio had a history of involvement with the Panthers, though they were serving time on separate robbery charges. To stop their organizing, prison officials charged them with murder, won convictions based on concocted evidence, and placed them in solitary confinement. Wilkerson was released in 2001, having been found innocent of the charges for which he served almost 30 years. Wallace and Woodfox remain incarcerated; after 36 years of isolation, legal appeals, and an international pressure campaign succeeded in removing them from solitary confinement in March 2008, and Woodfox's conviction was overturned in July 2008, although he remains incarcerated. A massive campaign, in which Wilkerson plays a leading role, continues to work for their release.

Not all radical Black groups who have found themselves under attack have espoused politics of national liberation. The Philadelphia-based MOVE organization is an almost all-Black naturalist group—some would say family. MOVE began in the 1970s around the philosophy of a working-class Black man named John Africa. Members of the group chose the last name Africa and lived collectively, ate vegan, and staged militant protests against both police violence and animal abuse. The notoriously racist Philadelphia police, under the leadership of police commissioner-turned-mayor Frank Rizzo, developed an instant distaste for MOVE. Through public protest and a loudspeaker attached to their communal West Philadelphia home, MOVE members challenged police authority. The police, meanwhile, routinely attacked MOVE demonstrations. The situation first came to a head in 1978, when police attempted to enforce a court order mandating MOVE to vacate its house. MOVE refused the order, and by August, police had laid siege to the house in an effort to drive a resource-strapped MOVE out. On August 8, the efforts to remove MOVE erupted in violence: 600 police officers used guns and fire hoses to drive the activists from the basement where they were hiding. Officer James Ramp was shot and killed in the melee; although Ramp was standing in front of the house and was shot from behind and even though MOVE members were in the basement of the house, the nine adults inside were arrested, tried, and collectively sentenced to 30 to 100 years for Ramp's death. Police officers also bulldozed the house and destroyed any evidence that might exculpate MOVE members. (Before doing that, however, three officers savagely beat Delbert Africa as he surrendered to them clearly unarmed.) Merle Africa died of cancer in prison in 1998, , and seven of the other eight MOVE prisoners were denied parole in spring 2008, a decision expected to be replicated when the last one, Chuck Africa comes up for parole in October 2008. As is typical in political prisoner cases, part of the reason the MOVE members were supposedly denied parole is the "severity of their crime"—which never changes and thus becomes a convenient excuse for indefinitely prolonging incarceration.

Standoffs between police and MOVE continued; tensions spilled over again in 1985, when another siege of the new MOVE home culminated in city police dropping a bomb on the house, killing 11 people, including MOVE founder John Africa, and destroying much of the block.

Even before the bombing, however, successive mayoral administrations from Frank Rizzo to Wilson Goode virulently chastised anyone, including reporters, who challenged its authority or decision to act violently against MOVE. A radio journalist named Mumia Abu-Jamal, a former leader of the city's Panther chapter and sympathetic to MOVE, particularly attracted the city's ire. Late at night on December 9, 1981, while driving a taxi to supplement his income, Abu-Jamal saw his brother being beaten by police officer Daniel Faulkner. He stepped out of his cab to intervene, at which point both he and Faulkner were shot. Although several witnesses claim they saw others flee the scene, Abu-Jamal was the only person seriously considered as a suspect and was quickly charged with Faulkner's murder. At trial, Judge Albert Sabo denied Abu-Jamal the right to have an attorney of his choosing (MOVE founder John Africa) and also denied Abu-Jamal the right to defend himself, even removing him from the courtroom during most of the proceedings. Witnesses heard Judge Sabo, notoriously eager to send people to the electric chair, utter a racial slur and a commitment to "fry" Abu-Jamal. The prosecutor, in a practice later found unconstitutional by the U.S. Supreme Court in another case, used Abu-Jamal's past political affiliation with the Black Panthers as an argument to the jury for the death penalty. In July 1982, Abu-Jamal was sentenced to death; from death row, he has become the country's most well-known political prisoner.

Mumia's international support movement has succeeded in preventing his execution and has even extracted momentary legal openings. Each level of appeal within the judiciary system has, however, quickly closed those openings by reaffirming Mumia's conviction, despite significant evidence of prosecutorial, police, and judicial misconduct, and adamantly denied him the new and fair trial that Amnesty International and many other legal organizations have demanded. In 2001, U.S. District Court Judge William Yohn affirmed Mumia's conviction but voided his death sentence, citing "irregularities" in the original sentencing. The judge converted the sentence to life without parole and gave the prosecution the option to conduct a new sentencing hearing in accordance with legal procedures to determine whether Mumia would be sentenced to death. Both sides appealed. In March 2008, the U.S. Third Circuit Court of Appeals again upheld Mumia's conviction and in July 2008 the full Third Circuit rejected his request to rehear the appeal. But there still remains the possibility of a new trial if the U.S. Supreme Court accepts the case and if it overturns the conviction. The Appeals Court also affirmed the lower court's voiding of Mumia's death sentence. But he is not out of danger of judicially sanctioned killing: If the prosecution continues to fight for execution, it could either ask the U.S. Supreme Court to reverse this part of the Appeals Court ruling or it could insist on a new jury hearing on that issue, and there is a possibility that such a jury could reimpose the death sentence. For now, Mumia remains housed on death row.

Part 2: The American Indian Movement

While the Black liberation struggle provides a necessary narrative arc to understanding the clandestine militancy and political incarceration of the time period, it is not the only such struggle. The American Indian Movement (AIM) formed in Minnesota in 1968 and was always strongest in the western half of the country. Founded by four Indigenous activists, two of whom were former prisoners, AIM set out to apply the militant community organizing model of the Black Panthers to Indigenous communities and conditions in cities and reservations. AIM's focus on sovereignty and daring political action quickly earned the group its fair share of publicity. One of its first actions was the 19-month occupation of Alcatraz, the abandoned island prison off the coast of San Francisco, to draw attention to the colonial conditions Indigenous people faced. The proclamation announcing the occupation declared that reservations already resembled abandoned prisons. The group also launched daring marches, such as the Trail of Broken Treaties, a national caravan that ended in Washington, DC, in 1972 with a 20-point plan to improve the status of First Nations people in the United States. A similar march in 1978, the Longest Walk, stretched from Alcatraz to the capital.

By the early 1970s, as the Panthers declined, in part due to state violence, AIM had become the FBI's new number one enemy. Dozens of AIM activists were murdered, some openly by police or vigilantes employed by corrupt tribal leaders, and the group was similarly disrupted through a web of informants and misinformation. Most of the leadership—Dennis Banks, Vernon and Clyde Bellecourt, Leonard Crow Dog, Russell Means, John Trudell, and others—found themselves in and out of jail for participating in civil disobedience actions or simply for being outspoken in their opposition to U.S. colonialism. Their houses were routinely raided, and police openly surveilled their actions.

Besides the FBI, a state-sanctioned paramilitary outfit known as the Guardians of the Oglala Nation (GOON's) became the vanguard counterinsurgency force. Head GOON Dick Wilson called for an all-out war against AIM, and he did his part to deliver it, using the GOON's as an unofficial death squad in the Pine Ridge area. The repression was stark. People affiliated with the GOON's were suspected of murdering several AIM activists and supporters, presumably with the collusion of police and other law enforcement officials. For instance, on October 17, 1973, leader of the Independent Oglala Nation, Pedro Bissonnette was murdered by a GOON at a Bureau of Indian Affairs roadblock.

Anna Mae Aquash was an artist and a talented organizer; she helped establish AIM chapters across the country, raised funds to support a variety of AIM programs, and had been organizing to quell anti-Indian racism in the white communities surrounding Indian Country. She was murdered in February 1976 after rebuffing the FBI's attempts to make her an informant and for challenging the character of an AIM activist who really was an informant.

In another incident, longtime AIM activist Tina Trudell, her mother, and her three children were burned to death in an arson attack on their Nevada home on February 11, 1979. The attack occurred 12 hours after her husband, fellow AIM activist John Trudell, burned an upside-down American flag outside FBI headquarters during a rally in support of Leonard Peltier. There was no official investigation into the attack. A fiery spokesman for AIM, Trudell and his family had long been targets of state harassment.

In 1973, AIM occupied the hamlet of Wounded Knee, the site of an infamous massacre of Indigenous people in 1890. The occupation lasted from February to May, during which time AIM operated an autonomous territory despite being surrounded by several federal law enforcement agencies and GOON vigilantes. The action generated solidarity from activists across the country seeking to assist AIM by breaking through the police blockade meant to eliminate any resources or attention into Wounded Knee; in one of the most auspicious attempts, a group of activists (including many from Vietnam Veterans Against the War) chartered a plane to airdrop supplies. During the 71-day occupation, there was constant gunfire exchanged between the state and AIM, leaving two AIM members dead. GOON's also "disappeared" 12 community members during this time. By May, AIM negotiated with the government to end the occupation. But it was hardly over.

Twelve hundred people were arrested in the immediate aftermath of Wounded Knee, and 500 more were arrested over the next two years. Between 1973 and 1975, federal officials and GOON's engaged in an immense crackdown on Red Power. In the immediate aftermath of the occupation, the government charged seven activists with conspiracy. Much of AIM's top leadership was indicted. Two of them, Dennis Banks and Russell Means, had their case separated from the others (Clyde Bellecourt, Carter Camp, Leonard Crow Dog, Stan Holder, and Pedro Bissonnette). Both men were acquitted in 1974. The depths of FBI malice against the Wounded Knee occupation were so prevalent that seven jurors involved in the trial publicly petitioned for any remaining cases to be dismissed. Several judges in other cases did dismiss most of the other cases, and most of those who went to trial were acquitted. In the other conspiracy case, Camp, Crow Dog, and Holder were convicted on reduced charges in 1975 and served brief jail terms. The case against Bellecourt was dismissed for lack of evidence, and Bissonnette was murdered before he could stand trial.

The repression continued. In June 1975, two FBI agents, driving in separate and unmarked cars, entered Pine Ridge reservation in search of a man wanted for questioning. The agents were fired upon; they radioed for backup but engaged in a firefight on the reservation. Both agents and an Indian man were killed as a result. Four months later, police arrested two AIM activists, Dino Butler and Bob Robideau, for the murders. A grand jury refused to indict Butler and Robideau on grounds of self-defense. Leonard Peltier, also suspected in the defensive effort, was found in Canada, where he had fled in fear of reprisals stemming from the firefight. Peltier had served as bodyguard for AIM cofounder Dennis Banks, participating in the group's Trail of Broken Treaties in 1972 and moving to the Pine Ridge reservation in 1973 to help in the defense of Wounded Knee. Peltier was extradited to the United States and tried a year later. The government changed its strategy to ensure a conviction of Peltier. The new approach included a change of venue to a town known for its prejudice against Native people, a conservative judge, and ample new evidence—much of it perjured or otherwise questionable. The FBI also assigned agents to "protect" the judge and jury; similar actions were used later in one of the Brink's trials to the same effect. While there had been no threats against jurors and never an instance where radicals had tampered with trials, the state used such tactics to instill fear among the very people who have to sit in judgment against the accused.

As a result, Peltier has become one of the most well-known and longest-held political prisoners in the world.

Peltier's time in prison has not been without controversy. Standing Deer, an Indigenous prisoner at Marion (a control-unit prison in Illinois), exposed a government plot to kill Peltier in 1978 and worked to protect Peltier's safety. Six years later, the pair entered a 42-day fast to win protections for Native spiritual practice in prison. The hunger strike received international attention and won some concessions, though it also resulted in both men being placed in solitary confinement for 15 months with nothing but a bed and a toilet. His principled commitments throughout his time in prison earned Standing Deer much respect and admiration as a politically conscious and active prisoner. Standing Deer was released on September 4, 2001, after 25 years in prison, and immediately jumped into organizing to free Peltier and other political prisoners. He was murdered in his apartment on January 20, 2003, by a houseguest with whom he had argued.

Of course, not all Indigenous political prisoners have been affiliated with AIM. Eddie Hatcher, a community activist in Robeson County, North Carolina, took over the offices of a local newspaper in 1988 to protest corruption in the area. Specifically, Hatcher and his comrade, Timothy Jacobs, took 20 journalists hostage to protest rampant police murder, the local government's involvement in drug trafficking, and the silence surrounding these issues. The men released their hostages unharmed when the governor agreed to their demand to establish an independent investigation on these issues. Hatcher was acquitted by a jury for the action, but was indicted a second time, on federal kidnapping charges. After a brief stint underground, he was captured and sentenced to 18 years in prison. He was given early parole in 1995, however, after being stabbed four times with an ice pick and contracting HIV in prison. He was arrested again, this time for murder, and sentenced to life in prison in early 2001 in an incident for which he maintains his innocence.

Part 3: The Puerto Rican Independence Movement
Through centuries of Spanish colonialism, Puerto Rico generated a vibrant and militant independence movement that nearly drove out the Spanish before the U.S. invasion and occupation of 1898. With the arrival of a new colonizer, the resistance continued, providing as deep an opposition as any that U.S. settler colonialism has yet faced. There have been successive generations of struggle over the century since then. As under the Spanish, pro-independence activism has been continually and often brutally repressed. Throughout the 1930s and in the early 1950s, there were several uprisings against U.S. colonial rule. The Puerto Rican Nationalist Party—led by its president, Don Pedro Albizu Campos—played a fundamental role in organizing this resistance, met by police assassinations (for instance, a 1937 massacre in the town of Ponce killed 19 and wounded 200), jailings, and blacklistings. Albizu was one of many Nationalists who did long stints as political prisoners on U.S. soil; he died of cancer in prison in 1964 after deliberate radiation poisoning by the authorities. On October 30, 1950, after an islandwide uprising headquartered in the town of Jayuya against U.S. colonial rule, the colonial government declared martial law throughout Puerto Rico, and the U.S. brought in Air Force planes to bomb the temporarily liberated towns. Many activists were killed and hundreds were jailed. In response, seeking to bring world attention to this repression, U.S.-based Nationalist Party activists Oscar Collazo and Griselio Torresola attempted two days later to assassinate President Harry Truman. One of Truman's bodyguards was shot and killed, several others were wounded, Torresola was killed, and Collazo wounded, arrested, and ultimately sentenced to death. In response to an international campaign that gathered 100,000 signatures on Collazo's behalf, Truman later commuted the sentence to life in prison.

In March 1954, four other U.S.-based Nationalist Party activists, seeking to hold the U.S. Congress accountable for its direct role in colonial rule, unfurled a Puerto Rican flag inside the U.S. House gallery and opened fire, wounding five Congress members. Led by Lolita Lebrón, the action also involved Rafael Cancel Miranda, Irvin Flores, and Andrés Figueroa Cordero. It was timed to coincide with the Inter-American Conference in Caracas, Venezuela. The four were arrested and sentenced to life in prison. With a climate of terror and reprisals against *independentistas* both on the island and in the United States, the five Nationalists received limited open support throughout the 1950s and early 1960s.

The successful revolution in Cuba in 1959 helped create a rising tide of militancy within Puerto Rico starting in the early 1960s, which snowballed through the decade and made its way throughout the United States. Forced migration had created large communities of Puerto Ricans living in the

United States who, influenced by the civil rights movement and developments within Puerto Rico, grew more radical as the decade wore on. The end of the 1960s witnessed a visible spike in Puerto Rican radicalism, which particularly took the form of antiwar, especially antidraft, resistance, and the upsurge in the pro-independence movement. A major pro-independence force in the United States at the time was the Young Lords Party. Inspired by the example of the Black Panthers, the Young Lords, initially a Chicago street gang turned political, initiated a host of community programs in the barrios of New York and Chicago. The organization combined a militant politics of community self-defense with radical service (helping Spanish Harlem get garbage service and proper health care, for instance) and a diasporic strategy that connected Puerto Ricans in the United States to those on the island. The Young Lords articulated a strong position against male chauvinism and for women's liberation. The group was part of a wave of Puerto Rican militancy at the time. The Puerto Rican left was a vibrant force throughout the 1960s and 1970s. Among the active organizations were, on the island, the *Liga Socialista Puertorriqueña* (LSP; Puerto Rican Socialist League) and the *Partido Socialista Puertorriqueña* (PSP; Puerto Rican Socialist Party), which also had a U.S. presence, and, in the United States, *El Comité* and, later, the *Movimiento de Liberación Nacional* (MLN; Movement for National Liberation).

Armed struggle featured prominently in the Puerto Rican militancy of the 1960s and 1970s, both in the States and on the island. Juan Antonio Corretjer, a brilliant strategist of the independence movement and former leader of both the Nationalist Party and the Puerto Rican Communist Party as well as a former political prisoner and one of the island's most well-known poets, had already outlined a vision of people's war to build an independent and socialist Puerto Rico. As secretary-general of the LSP, Corretjer situated Puerto Rican people's war as part of a long tradition of Puerto Rican radicalism, as part of the anticolonial revolutions then sweeping the globe, and as part of unraveling the United States from within as well as from without. Corretjer's influence is manifest throughout the Puerto Rican left at this time, both aboveground and under.

As early as 1964, clandestine groups emerged in Puerto Rico, followed several years later by similar formations in the United States. These included the *Comandos Armados de Liberación* (CAL, Armed Commandos of Liberation), *Movimiento Independentista Revolucionario Armado* (MIRA, Armed Revolutionary Independence Movement), and then, starting in the mid-70s, the *Comandos Revolucionarios del Pueblo* (CRP, People's Revolutionary Commandos), the *Fuerzas Armadas de Resistencia Popular* (the Armed Forces of Popular Resistance), and the *Organización de Voluntarios por la Revolución Puertorriqueña* (OVRP, Organization of Volunteers for the Puerto Rican Revolution). The two most active, however, were the *Fuerzas Armadas de Liberación Nacional* (FALN; Armed Forces of National Liberation) and the *Ejercito Popular Boricua* (Puerto Rican Popular Army), also known as *Los Macheteros*, the Machete-Wielders.

16

All of these underground organizations targeted U.S. military installations, police stations, federal agencies, U.S. banks, and department stores, among other sites selected for their role in helping uphold U.S. colonialism. In some cases they mounted joint actions.

The *Macheteros* were active almost exclusively in Puerto Rico; the FALN, in the United States. Between 1974 and 1983, by which time more than a dozen alleged members of the group had been arrested, the FALN claimed responsibility for more than 120 bombings against U.S. corporate or military targets. These attacks targeted property in all but one case: In January 1975, the FALN detonated a bomb during lunch hour at Fraunces Tavern, a New York City restaurant popular with Wall Street executives. The bomb killed four and wounded 50 people. (No one was ever charged with this bombing.) The accompanying communiqué claimed the bombing as a response to a restaurant bombing in Puerto Rico by CIA-connected right-wing Cubans that killed two *independentistas* and maimed 10 other people—just the most recent in a wave of anti-independence terrorist attacks. Indeed, there would later be other U.S.-directed death-squad actions. Most notoriously, in July 1978, Puerto Rican police lured two young *independentistas,* whom they had recruited into a government-created underground group, to the top of a mountain called Cerro Maravilla, where they were executed in cold blood. After years of *independentista* campaigning that forced Watergate-style hearings by the colonial legislature (after the U.S. Justice Department refused to act), in 1984, 10 police officers, including the head of the Intelligence Division, were indicted, tried, convicted of various charges related to the killings and their cover-up, and sentenced to prison time. Two years later, the undercover agent who lured the young men to their deaths—and who was never prosecuted—was assassinated in an action claimed by the clandestine OVRP.

In the 1970s, the campaign to end the lengthy incarceration of the five Puerto Rican Nationalists went into high gear: The independence movement and its allies in the United States and the Nonaligned Movement of Third World nations and liberation movements mounted a well-organized international campaign for their release. The organizations involved used tactics as wide-ranging as petitions, lobbying, mass demonstrations, civil disobedience, and bombings (all communiqués accompanying armed actions in this period included calls to "Free the Five"). In 1974, a diverse group of independence activists and their North American supporters, led by the Puerto Rican Socialist Party, held a rally at Madison Square Garden with 20,000 people that identified Puerto Rican independence and the freeing of the five Nationalists as central to a progressive agenda for the U.S. left. In one of the most attention-grabbing actions done as part of the campaign, more than two dozen activists seized the Statue of Liberty and hung a Puerto Rican flag on its crown on October 30, 1977 (the anniversary of the thwarted 1950 uprising), using the media coverage to draw attention to the ongoing incarceration of the Nationalists. Finally, in 1979, feeling the pressure of this international campaign, President Jimmy Carter granted unconditional release to Collazo, Lebrón, Cancel Miranda, and Flores. (Carter had released Andrés Figueroa Cordero in 1977; he was suffering from cancer and passed away 18 months after his release.) They returned to Puerto Rico triumphant, though the ordeal of Puerto Rican political incarceration was far from over.

By the time of the four Nationalists' freedom, the first of what was soon to prove a new wave of arrests of Puerto Rican independence fighters had occurred. In July 1978, William Morales was arrested at the site of a bomb explosion in Queens, New York, in which he lost part of both hands and sight in one eye. While in custody, Morales was tortured by FBI agents. A long-time pro-independence activist, he was accused of membership in the FALN and indicted on federal and state charges of possession of illegal weapons. Morales became the first of a new generation of imprisoned *independentistas* to refuse to participate in their own trials, asserting the position of prisoner of war, thus not subject to the colonial courts of the United States. Judges rejected that claim, and Morales was convicted and sentenced to a total of 99 years. After a successful community pressure campaign to transfer him to a prison hospital for treatment of his eye and fitting his hands for prosthetic devices, Morales audaciously escaped, in an action claimed by the FALN. In 1983, Interpol agents rearrested him in Mexico, and he served five years in prison there until a successful international campaign by the Puerto Rican independence movement and its Mexican and North American allies forced the Mexican government to defy the United States, which was seeking his extradition, and instead to fly him to Cuba, where he received political asylum and has been living ever since.

On April 4, 1980, 11 people suspected of involvement with the FALN were arrested outside Chicago. At least four others would be arrested over the next three years to also stand trial for alleged FALN involvement. The accused also refused to participate in their own trials, asserting their position as prisoners of war not subject to the colonial courts of the United States. As with Morales, the courts rejected these claims without a hearing and proceeded to try the defendants against their wishes and, therefore, often in their absence. Most were convicted of "seditious conspiracy"—organizing to overthrow the government—and given lengthy sentences amounting to life in prison. The youngest of the group, Luis Rosa, received the longest sentence: 108 years, for federal and state charges, along with a contempt sentence. None of the alleged FALN members was convicted of harming or killing anyone.

Throughout the 1980s, other Puerto Rican independence groups continued to target U.S. colonialism. In 1981, the *Macheteros* blew up 11 U.S. military planes in Puerto Rico that were destined for use in El Salvador. But it was a daring bank expropriation for which they received the most attention. It occurred in Hartford, Connecticut, in 1983, when members of the group, including a bank employee, took $7.2 million from Wells Fargo without injury or arrest. On August 30, 1985, in a massive military operation that activists dubbed "the second invasion of Puerto Rico," 13 *independentistas* were swept up, charged with planning or participating in the robbery, the biggest in U.S. history. Ultimately, 19 people faced charges. They went through a series of trials in various groups; outcomes varied, including some convictions, some acquittals, some negotiated agreements, and some charges dismissed due to government misconduct. Several of these activists spent numerous years in prison, the longest terms of which were served by Antonio Camacho Negrón (15 years) and Juan Segarra Palmer (19 years).

As with the earlier efforts to free the five Nationalists and William Morales, a lengthy and far-ranging international campaign finally proved successful in winning release of many of the remaining Puerto Rican political prisoners. In September 1999, President Bill Clinton offered clemency to more than a dozen, including 14 people still incarcerated after 14 to 19 years and several *Macheteros* activists who still had fines pending. Twelve of those still in prison accepted the terms, under which 11 (Edwin Cortés, Elizam Escobar, Ricardo Jiménez, Adolfo Matos, Dylcia Pagán, Alberto Rodríguez, Alicia Rodríguez, Lucy Rodríguez, Luis Rosa, Alejandrina Torres, and Carmen Valentín) were immediately released and another (Segarra Palmer) had to serve five more years before being freed. Camacho Negrón was not offered a shortened term; he was released in 2004. Three of the alleged FALN members remain in prison today. Oscar López Rivera rejected the terms offered; he is serving 55 years on the FALN charges and 15 for an alleged conspiracy to escape. Carlos Alberto Torres was not included in the clemency offer and is serving a 78-year sentence. Haydée Beltrán Torres chose not to apply for clemency and is serving a life sentence. *Independentistas* and other activists continue working for their release; Carlos and Oscar have also been prodigious artists since their incarceration, and their artwork has traveled repeatedly throughout the United States and Puerto Rico to raise awareness about their case and the ongoing colonial domination of Puerto Rico.

The repression of the *Macheteros* has also continued up to the present. One of the defendants in the Wells Fargo case was Filiberto Ojeda Ríos, a co-founder of the *Macheteros* and a well-respected fighter in the struggle for Puerto Rican independence. Ojeda Ríos was captured in 1985 after an attack on his house by FBI agents. Following Ojeda Ríos's successful campaign to win bail, with the requirement that he wear an electronic ankle bracelet to monitor his whereabouts, federal authorities—desperate to incarcerate him—charged him with shooting an FBI agent during his arrest. But, in a trial where he represented himself, the Puerto Rican jury accepted his self-defense argument and acquitted him. In 1990, Ojeda Ríos removed his ankle bracelet and once again went underground. The U.S. government then tried him in *absentia in* Connecticut on the Wells Fargo charges, this time securing a conviction and a 55-year sentence.

In the intervening years, Ojeda Ríos periodically released communiqués from the *Macheteros*. At the age of 72, Ojeda Ríos was killed at his rural home by an FBI sniper on September 23, 2005—the 15th anniversary of his return to clandestinity. It was also *Grito de Lares*, a Puerto Rican holiday of resistance. The FBI surrounded his house, opened fire, and denied him medical assistance after shooting him in the neck. He bled to death.

Ojeda Ríos's murder led to large protests and broad calls to investigate the FBI and also kicked off a new wave of repression against the Puerto Rican movement. Five months later, FBI officials raided the homes of several independence activists, and more than two years later the independence movement remains under attack. Three Puerto Ricans in their 20s and 30s were called before grand juries in January 2008, and two others were subpoenaed later in the year. In February 2008, another alleged *Machetero* leader, Avelino González Claudio, who had also been living underground for more than 20 years, was arrested in Puerto Rico and extradited to Connecticut to stand trial for the Wells Fargo robbery. As of July 2008, he remains in custody awaiting trial.

The 2008 grand jury was a revival of a federal tactic that between 1976 and 1990 had led to numerous activists unaffiliated with the underground— not only Puerto Ricans, but also Mexicano, Venezuelan, and white North American allies—being subpoenaed to grand juries and, in most cases, jailed for refusing to cooperate. The state frequently used the grand jury system as fishing expeditions to fragment the movement and remove vocal supporters of underground actions from public organizing. The government had done this many times since at least the late 1960s. The grand jury repression emanating from the FALN investigations, however, was fiercer. Determined to crush the strong position of noncollaboration with government inquisitions pioneered by Juan Antonio Corretjer in 1936 and pursued by many later *independentistas*, prosecutors charged several resisters with criminal contempt, which carries an unlimited sentence, as opposed to the 18-month maximum for those found in civil contempt. In the end, mass pressure limited the criminal contempt sentences to three years. (Grand juries were not only directed against the Puerto Rican movement and its allies: throughout the 1970s and 1980s, dozens of people also served anywhere from weeks to years in prison for refusing to cooperate with grand juries investigating the BLA, American Indian Movement, Weather Underground, and other militant organizations.)

One more aspect of the Puerto Rican anticolonial movement bears mentioning here: the struggle over Vieques. For decades, this tiny island, which is part of Puerto Rico, was used by the U.S. military for weapons training after the Navy appropriated two-thirds of the island in the 1940s. In the late 1970s, after a successful campaign stopped similar war games in the neighboring island of Culebra, the Navy increased its bombing practice on Vieques; in turn, Viequensans and other Puerto Ricans dramatically increased their protests. Surrounded by Navy facilities and chemically laden weaponry, the people of Vieques demanded the expulsion of the Navy to protect their lives, their livelihoods (especially fishing), and the environment—and for many, to advance the freeing of Puerto Rico from U.S. colonial rule. Not only had the Navy occupied most of the island, but the weapons had led to very high cancer rates for people who lived there.

With the support of people and organizations in the United States, including several prominent activists and celebrities, Puerto Rican activists staged a series of blockades and demonstrations against the Navy's presence. The first round of protest occurred between 1978 and 1983, and there was a subsequent spike in Vieques activism following the death of Vieques resident David Sanes Rodríguez in April 1999 by two stray bombs. In both phases of the campaign, which succeeded in removing the Navy in 2003, high-risk civil disobedience actions (such as using flotillas to prevent practice bombings) generated several political prisoners. While these sentences were often less than a year, they were disproportionate to the nonviolent nature of the actions.

Further, prison sentences have not been the only risk of working against U.S. militarism in Vieques: In November 1979, while serving a six-month sentence for trespassing on military land in Vieques as part of a nonviolent mass occupation, *La Liga Socialista Puertorriqueña* leader Angel Rodríguez Cristóbal was found beaten to death and hanged in his jail cell in Florida. A month later, a joint commando of the *Macheteros*, OVRP, and CRP opened fire on a U.S. Navy bus in Puerto Rico, killing two Naval personnel and wounding nine; their communiqué declared that the action was in response to Rodriguez Cristóbal's murder. His death confirmed for independence activists, those engaged in both legal and clandestine organizing, the depths to which the state would go to crush dissent. And yet it strengthened their resolve to fight for a free Puerto Rico.

Part 4: The Chicano Liberation Movement
As with Indigenous and Puerto Rican resistance, the Chicano movement also displayed great initiative in the late 1960s. The Chicano liberation movement has always been strongly rooted in historic Aztlán, the colonized parts of Mexico taken as part of the 1848 war and what is now the Southwest United States (Texas, New Mexico, Arizona, and California). The Chicano movement has taken several forms; catalyzed by the Black Power movement, organizations like the Brown Berets formed with a similar program of community-based revolutionary nationalism. The grassroots struggles of Chicano youth have been particularly powerful, as students have led walkouts from schools in California and elsewhere in the Southwest against a variety of racist and antiyouth ballot initiatives over the years. The *Movimiento Estudiantil Chicano de Aztlán* (MEChA) has been a particularly potent force in these struggles—leading Arizona lawmakers to propose a statewide bill in April 2008 that would deny funding to any school with organizations whose membership is based on race.

Led by César Chávez, the United Farm Workers proved an inspiring example of organizing Chicano workers throughout the 1970s. UFW activists, including Chávez and Dolores Huerta, staged several hunger strikes and other dramatic actions against both corporate farms and government immigration policies, leading them and several of their comrades to serve brief stints in jail for their participation in assorted civil disobedience actions. And, partly due to the machismo of male radicals, Chicana feminism became a spearhead of women of color feminism, Cherríe Moraga and Gloria Anzáldua, editors of *This Bridge Called My Back*, being the most well-known examples.

The Chicano movement has not yet produced an underground the way other movements have, although sectors of the Chicano national liberation movement did team up with the Puerto Rican independence movement for a time in the 1980s, a coalition that vocally supported clandestine actions by Latino groups. The militancy of the Chicano struggle, and the ensuing state repression, has been no less fierce.

Two examples from California testify to the growing militancy of the Chicano movement in the time period.

On Mayday 1969, seven youth were arrested in the Mission District in San Francisco after an altercation with two plainclothes police officers left one dead. Police reinforcements then arrived, firing automatic weapons and flooding the house with tear gas. The group was dubbed *Los Siete de la Raza*, despite the fact that the men were of Central American rather than Chicano descent. Still, the case became a rallying cry for Chicano, Latino, and people of color organizations more generally, as the seven were defended by leftist attorneys and supported by a range of radical groups. The defense committees that sprung up to support them became leading entities in Chicano radicalism following their 1971 acquittal.

The other example typifies a Chicano internationalism. On December 20, 1969, about 70 Brown Berets staged an antiwar march in Los Angeles. Eighteen months later, on August 29, 1970, more than 20,000 Chicanos marched in Los Angeles against the Vietnam War. The Chicano Moratorium March was the largest antiwar demonstration by an oppressed national community in the U.S., and it reflected a growing radicalization of Chicanos, particularly young people, connecting the history of U.S. colonialism against Mexico to the war. A broad gathering of progressive and radical Chicanos, the Moratorium signaled a growing movement in which opposition to police brutality was a cornerstone. As was true in Black ghettoes and Indigenous reservations, the Mexican barrios viewed the police as an army occupying their communities. The Chicano Moratorium was a community resisting such colonial control.

After a peaceful, joyous march, the protesters were attacked as police charged the park where the rally was concluding. Many of the young people there fought back, lobbing tear gas canisters and rocks back at the police. Dozens were hurt; 150 were arrested in the resulting battles that caused more than $1 million in damage. Most significantly, three were killed: a 15-year-old

Brown Beret named Lynn Ward was thrown through a plate glass window from an explosion in a trash can, most likely a tear gas canister; Angel Gilberto Díaz was shot in the head while driving; and Ruben Salazar, a sympathetic Chicano journalist who was covering the march for the *Los Angeles Times*, was killed when police stormed into a bar where Salazar and other journalists were sitting after the march. Salazar was killed by a tear gas canister projectile that hit him in the head.

In the face of rampant police violence and a legacy of disenfranchisement, a series of organizations sprouted up to provide political alternatives for Chicano communities at the time. Two of the most famous and most militant were *La Alianza Federal de Pueblos Libre* and the Crusade for Justice. *La Alianza* was led by Reies López Tijerina and was in many ways the model for Chicano radicalism. Bridging traditional Chicano land claims with a fighting spirit, *La Alianza* was founded in 1963 to pursue the treaties the United States had signed after annexing northern Mexico in 1848 (*La Alianza* was founded on the anniversary of the 1848 treaty). The group sought land grants for the Mexican farmers living in northern New Mexico.

Upon its founding, *La Alianza* began petitioning the U.S. government for their lands. Not waiting for the American state to accede, *La Alianza* began reclaiming the land and establishing a governing apparatus. When two forest rangers attempted to evict *La Alianza* activists in 1966, 300 people participated in arresting the rangers, trying them in a people's court, and convicting them of trespass. They were released with a suspended sentence. This confident approach became a hallmark of *La Alianza*, leading to repeated altercations with law enforcement. Tijerina and four others were arrested for the action and ultimately sentenced to between 30 days and two years in prison. But *La Alianza* was undeterred; Tijerina issued a citizen's arrest warrant, even filing it with the Supreme Court, for Judge Warren Burger when the latter man was appointed by Nixon to head the Supreme Court as a law-and-order justice.

The most famous *Alianza* action occurred on June 5, 1967. Two days earlier, police had preemptively arrested 11 *Alianza* activists in an attempt to shut down the organization. In response, Tijerina led an armed raid on the Rio Arriba County Courthouse in Tierra Amarilla, New Mexico. The action was twofold: to free the captured comrades and to place the district attorney under citizen's arrest for the repression. The prosecutor didn't show up, but two officers were shot in the melee. The *Alianza* activists, including those arrested on June 3, left the courthouse victorious. In response, the governor launched the biggest manhunt in New Mexico's history to capture anyone who participated in the attack. Tijerina eventually turned himself in, using the attention generated from his case to boost Chicano demands. Defending himself at trial, Tijerina was acquitted of all charges. Upon release, he resumed his organizing activities, becoming a leader in Martin Luther King, Jr.'s initiative, the Poor People's Campaign.

Through the Crusade for Justice, Denver became an epicenter of the Chicano movement. Rudolfo "Corky" González, who founded the Crusade as a youth conference in 1966, is also credited with having popularized the notion of a distinctly Chicano identity as Indigenous, European, Mexican, and American through his poem "Yo Soy Joaquín." Like Tijerina, González built an organization guided by revolutionary nationalism and a commitment to self-defense. González also became a leader in the Poor People's Campaign; his increasing visibility led the FBI to consider charging him as part of the Chicago conspiracy trial, though they knew he wasn't present during the Democratic National Convention protests. The Crusade held protests against the brutality of police and white supremacists, demonstrated in solidarity with both *La Alianza* and with Black Power activists, and engaged in a variety of actions opposing the Vietnam War and racism against Chicano high school students. The Crusade occupied Columbus Park, renaming it *La Raza*.

Given their high profile and militant style, the Crusade found itself increasingly targeted by surveillance and repression. Because the Crusade helped coordinate an impressive Pan-Latino display of solidarity with the Wounded Knee occupation, the FBI suspected it of running guns to AIM and publicly accused the Crusade of conspiring to kill police officers. In 1973, police arrested a man for jaywalking in front of an apartment building that served as the Crusade headquarters, sparking a bigger, armed conflagration between police and the Chicano community. Crusade member Luis Martínez, 20, was killed in the fracas that injured a dozen police officers (four from gunfire). An explosion, which Crusade activists say police set off but which police say was the Crusade's doing, destroyed much of the upstairs apartment. City officials had the apartment, and any evidence therein, destroyed. More than 60 people were arrested, with four being prosecuted for felony assault.

Police killed several Chicano activists in the Denver area and beyond, including some associated with the Crusade. Later in the 1970s, Crusade activists were subpoenaed to appear before grand juries investigating the FALN.

This repression targeted people throughout the Chicano movement. For instance, Francisco Eugenio "Kiko" Martínez, a Chicano activist who served as attorney for the Crusade (and other radical groups), was indicted in 1973 on charges of mailing three bombs to various targets in Denver. Fearing for his life, he fled to Mexico but was arrested trying to reenter the United States in 1980. He then faced separate trials for each bombing; the first was thrown out after it was discovered that the trial judge had met with prosecutors and witnesses to devise a plan for Martínez's conviction. He was acquitted at the second trial; charges were dropped in the third after police destroyed physical evidence. He was ultimately convicted in 1986 for trying to reenter the country with false identification, though this conviction was overturned on appeal and Martínez was reinstated to the bar. Others were not so lucky. Six Chicano activists in their 20s and 30s in Boulder were killed in May 1974 when two car bombs exploded on two successive nights. Police charged that the two sets of three activists were transporting bombs that exploded prematurely, though others dispute this claim. A grand jury was convened on the "Boulder 6" but passed down no indictments and was not made public.

The most prominent Chicano political prisoner today is Alvaro Hernandez Luna. A longtime community organizer in both Houston and Alpine, Texas, Hernández Luna has a history of defending political prisoners; he was the national coordinator of the Ricardo Aldape Guerra Defense Committee, which fought to free a Mexican national who had been sent to Texas's death row on trumped-up charges. Hernández Luna's lengthy political involvement also included his work with the National Movement of *La Raza*, Stop the Violence Youth Committee, and the Prisoners Solidarity Committee. He spent more than a decade in prison for crimes he did not commit, ultimately being released after newspaper reports helped prove his innocence. He was organizing against police brutality in Chicano communities when an officer came to his house on July 18, 1996, to arrest him on a spurious robbery charge. The officer drew his gun when Hernández Luna questioned his arrest; he disarmed the officer without hurting him and received a 50-year sentence for "threatening" the officer. He has become a valuable and successful jailhouse lawyer since his incarceration.

Anti-Imperialist Solidarity and the White Working Class

Part 1: The Politics of Solidarity

As the above sketch illustrates, militancy became an increasingly pervasive phenomenon among the U.S. left by the end of the 1960s, with some sectors pushing for coordinated armed struggle. The sector of the left that was predominantly white followed a somewhat similar trajectory, though its roots and development differed in key ways.

The biggest and most famous, primarily white New Left organization of the 1960s was Students for a Democratic Society, a youth- and student-based group that had an estimated membership of 100,000 people by the time it collapsed in 1969. Originally the student wing of the anticommunist social democratic League for Industrial Democracy, SDS became an independent and multitendency organization in 1962. It was particularly catalyzed by the Student Nonviolent Coordinating Committee and the civil rights movement, as well as the war in Vietnam. SDS sponsored the first antiwar march in 1965, which brought 20,000 people to Washington, DC. The group continued to grow exponentially throughout the decade, becoming home to an assorted radical agenda broadly united in opposition to war and racism and celebration of counterculture. The reasons for its collapse were varied, but included unbridgeable fissures over organizational strategy and direction amidst what seemed to many a revolutionary era.

Out of SDS's collapse emerged many groups, including the Weatherman, later the Weather Underground. Taking its name from a line in a Bob Dylan song, the Weather Underground included some of the most well-known SDS leaders at the time, articulated a politics that defined Black people and other people of color as colonized populations, and saw the role of white people as opening another front of struggle in the fight against imperialism. Such militant solidarity, argued Weather, would overextend the state and its ability to repress revolutionary struggles and therefore hasten the pace and success of revolutionaries around the globe.

Weatherman was the most visible, vocal, and organized expression of white left militancy, but it was far from the only one. One month after Weather led a few hundred people in a violent demonstration in Chicago, 10,000 people during an antiwar protest formed a breakaway march to trash the U.S. Justice Department. A significant minority of New Leftists were turning to bombs, targeting banks and recruiting stations, while many more fought back against police at demonstrations and called for armed struggle. A map of the United States printed in a (temporarily censored) 1971 special issue of the radical *Scanlan's Monthly* on guerrilla war listed thousands of acts of political violence between 1965 and 1970; according to journalist Kirkpatrick Sale, from September 1969 to May 1970, there was at least one bombing or attempted bombing somewhere in the United States every day by the progressive and radical movements. Such a widespread turn to violence was hardly limited to white leftists; communities of color were often the most militant, as evidenced by the ghetto rebellions of the mid-1960s. But by the end of the decade, many white radicals were also joining in the fray.

Some such expressions of militancy were more organized than others. A New York City cell organized by a man named Sam Melville bombed several targets in 1969: an induction center, two banks, two corporate headquarters, a courthouse, and the federal building. The group was set up by an FBI informant, and several of its members were arrested. The main person to stand trial, Melville died when police violently crushed the Attica prison rebellion. His partner and collaborator, Jane Alpert, skipped bail and lived underground for several years before turning herself in and cooperating with the state.

In Madison, Wisconsin, a small group calling itself the New Year's Gang bombed an on-campus army research facility in August 1970. Although they had taken precautions to avoid injury, a postdoctoral student working late into the night was killed in the blast. A month later, a Boston bank robbery intended to fund further clandestine activities, and carried out with weapons expropriated from a National Guard armory, went awry when the radicals killed a police officer. Susan Saxe and Kathy Power fled the scene and remained underground for years. The two Brandeis students—Saxe had graduated the previous spring, Power was still enrolled at the time of the robbery—had teamed up with three former prisoners to commit the robbery. One of them, William Gilday, was captured shortly after the robbery and has been incarcerated ever since. Saxe received significant support from the lesbian feminist community, bridging antiwar militancy with the burgeoning radical women's movement as several women went to jail rather than cooperate with grand juries investigating her whereabouts. Captured in 1975, Saxe served eight years. Power stayed underground until 1993, when she turned herself in and served six years in prison.

Although Weather had been the most vocal adherent of armed struggle, its path changed in March 1970, when three members of the group died when a bomb they were building exploded. Because that bomb had been intended for human targets, the deaths compelled Weather leadership to declare that the group would continue to pursue a clandestine strategy but one that would refrain from causing any injury. It changed its name to the Weather Underground, deepened the clandestine infrastructure it had developed, and at its best moments looked to engage creatively with aboveground struggles rather than act as vanguard. Over the next seven years, the group claimed credit for more than two dozen bombings of high-profile targets such as the Pentagon, numerous courthouses and police stations, the U.S. Agency for International Development, and several corporations involved in the coup in Chile or colonialism in Angola. Weather articulated a politics of solidarity that demanded a high level of sacrifice by whites in support of Black and other revolutionary people of color. This support emanated from a strategic belief, pioneered by Che Guevara, that U.S. imperialism could be defeated through overextension; bombings were an attempt to pierce the myth of government invincibility and draw repressive attention away from the Panthers and similar groups. It also reflected a political position that said white people had to side with Third World struggles against the U.S. government—and had to do so in a similarly dramatic way.

The end of the Vietnam War, which dried up some of Weather's hippie base, brought a crisis of direction. With the Black and Native liberation movements facing stiff repression, with the Puerto Rican independence movement gaining traction, with the National Liberation Front of Vietnam emerging victorious against U.S. colonialism, and with much less motion among white Americans, the Weather Underground was lost. Through its aboveground support organization, the Prairie Fire Organizing Committee, Weather initiated the Hard Times conference in 1976. The conference brought a multiracial group of approximately 2,000 people to Chicago—where it then fell apart, as various Black and women's groups present sharply criticized its agenda, which they saw as significantly diluted from the approach that had been Weather's calling card. The failure of the conference brought other internal contradictions to light, and the group was torn apart among bitter factionalism in 1976-1977. A group calling itself the Revolutionary Committee of the Weather Underground expelled the Central Committee and attempted to rebuild armed struggle but was caught in an FBI sting operation. Five people served between two to four years as a result.

The end of Weather was significant, but it did not signal the end of armed struggle among white radicals. Most people in the group surfaced, especially after the Revolutionary Committee busts. Upon surfacing, people generally found their way to other radical groups, especially the Prairie Fire Organizing Committee (PFOC), which had always maintained public support for clandestine actions. PFOC was also rocked by the failure of Hard Times, with a shakeup of leadership—especially after one of the leaders was arrested for being part of the Revolutionary Committee.

In 1980, a group of West Coast Prairie Fire activists (including a former member of Weather) went underground in an attempt to continue armed struggle and help some political prisoners escape. They were unsuccessful, but eluded capture until turning themselves in to police in 1994; two people, Claude Marks and Donna Wilmott, served several years in prison.

On the East Coast, the PFOC maintained a stronger relationship with the Black liberation movement, particularly with the seeming revival of the BLA in the late 1970s. A split, born more of sectarian infighting than substantive political differences, tore PFOC apart; while the group on the West Coast kept the name, the New York City group became the May 19th Communist Organization, named after the birthdate of Malcolm X and Ho Chi Minh. May 19th was small and severe; it had significant lesbian leadership and employed a variety of strategies to aid Third World liberation struggles in the United States and abroad. The group pledged its support to the BLA and various Third World liberation struggles, and it, too, led many militant demonstrations in which activists faced off with police. While it had long been the subject of police harassment as a result of its protests—several people served jail time for a militant demonstration against the South African Springboks rugby team's 1980 U.S. tour, for instance, and the group was no stranger to physically standing off against police—May 19th was ultimately crushed by the wave of repression that followed the failed Brink's robbery in 1981.

As we have seen, on October 20, 1981, a BLA unit working with white supporters attempted to rob a Brink's armored car. Arrested at the scene of the failed, tragic robbery were two former members of the Weather Underground who had remained underground (Kathy Boudin and David Gilbert) and Judy Clark, who was a public activist and known leader of May 19th. Indeed, Clark was a lead plaintiff in the lawsuit May 19th helped file with New Afrikan leader Mutulu Shakur against the FBI for COINTELPRO. Clark's arrest brought immense pressure on May 19th activists and supporters, along with numerous Black activists, who were harassed, intimidated, arrested, and called before grand juries in the three years following Brink's. As mentioned earlier, some of those charged were ultimately exonerated, while others went to jail. The longest sentence for the aboveground white activists—40 years—was given to May 19th leader Silvia Baraldini (along with her codefendant, BLA member Sekou Odinga) in the 1983 RICO case. The following year, Baraldini was given an additional three years, along with Puerto Rico solidarity activist Shelley Miller, for resisting a grand jury investigating the Puerto Rican

independence movement. An Italian national, Baraldini fought to be repatri-
ated to her home country; after a long campaign by her and her supporters,
including a large movement in Italy, she was returned there in 1999 and set
free in 2006.

The climate of constant arrests and intimidation following the Brink's fiasco
put May 19th on the defensive as it tried to protect itself and support those
incarcerated. Several of the group's active members felt unable to continue
working politically as they had been, and as a result they went underground.
Others joined them, trying to raise the level of struggle or hoping to deflect
the repression against Black and Puerto Rican clandestine groups by mounting additional actions.

Operating in cells alternately called Red Guerrilla Resistance and the
Armed Resistance Unit, these groupings were responsible for more than half
a dozen bombings between 1983 and 1985 against U.S. military installations
(a DC military base and a navy yard), the U.S. Capitol, the New York offices of
Israeli Aircraft Industries, the South African consulate, and the Patrolmen's
Benevolent Association. These actions were done in opposition to rampant
police murder in Black communities, U.S. imperialism in Latin America
and support for apartheid, the invasion of Grenada, and Israeli attacks on
Palestine and Lebanon.

While these actions contributed to a climate of militant opposition under
Reagan's rule, the newly bolstered security forces clamped down on the
persisting underground. Susan Rosenberg and Tim Blunk were arrested in
November 1984, and Alan Berkman, Marilyn Buck, Linda Evans, and Laura
Whitehorn were arrested in May 1985. All except Buck had previously been
involved in May 19th, working in public formations such as the John Brown
Anti-Klan Committee against police brutality, South African apartheid, and
white supremacy and the New Movement in Solidarity with Puerto Rican
Independence and Socialism. (Years before, Evans and Whitehorn had been
members of Weather.) Buck was a longtime, stalwart supporter of the Black
liberation struggle in a variety of formations; in 1973 she had been arrested
and sentenced to 10 years for purchasing two boxes of bullets, which the government alleged were for the Black Liberation Army. She had been wanted
since 1977, when she was let out from federal prison on furlough and never
returned.

Arrested at a storage unit where they had been storing explosives, Blunk
and Rosenberg were tried on charges of weapons and explosives possession
and given an unprecedented sentence of 58 years. (By comparison, Michael
Donald Bray, a far-right reactionary, served less than four years for bombing 10 occupied abortion clinics.) Berkman was jailed for a year in 1982 for
resisting a grand jury; a doctor, he went underground rather than face trial
on charges of providing medical care to Marilyn Buck while she was underground. He was ultimately convicted of possession of weapons, explosives
and false IDs, as well as bail jumping, and sentenced to 12 years. Evans

received 35 years for illegally obtaining handguns and false ID, and for harboring Buck. Whitehorn, held for more than two years in "preventive detention," was convicted of possession of false IDs and contempt of court. Besides facing individual charges emanating from the circumstances of their arrest, the six were ultimately indicted together as part of what became known as the Resistance Conspiracy case. They were charged with "conspiracy to oppose, protest, and change the policies and practices of the U.S. government in domestic and international matters by violent and illegal means." On top of the lengthy sentences most of them were already serving, this conspiracy charge covered many of the bombings claimed by the Armed Resistance Unit and Red Guerrilla Resistance.

In 1990, to secure a faster release for Berkman, who was being denied adequate medical care for a life-threatening recurrence of Hodgkin's lymphoma, Buck, Evans, and Whitehorn pleaded guilty to various charges, including the Capitol bombing; conspiracy charges against Berkman, Blunk, and Rosenberg were dropped. Berkman was released on parole in 1992 and recovered. Whitehorn, sentenced to 20 additional years, served a total of 14 years (counting her earlier jail time) and was released in 1999. Blunk was released on parole in 1996. A campaign pressuring Bill Clinton to pardon Leonard Peltier and other political prisoners before Clinton left office did not win Peltier's release, though he did grant clemency to Evans and Rosenberg; they were released on his last day in office in 2001. Buck, meanwhile, was the subject of several trials in the 1980s. In addition to the 10 years she received in the Resistance Conspiracy case, she was already serving time from previous trials relating to the Brink's robbery and Assata Shakur's escape. All told, Buck was sentenced to 80 years in prison.

Part 2: Militants of the White Working Class
The use of conspiracy charges was a particularly potent tool against political militancy in the 1980s. Besides the cases outlined above, RICO charges were ultimately used against accused members of one of the other primary clandestine organizations of the period: the United Freedom Front (UFF). Unlike many of the other white people discussed above, those accused of belonging to the United Freedom Front came from solidly working-class backgrounds. (While the Weather Underground is sometimes disparaged as the offspring of the bourgeoisie, the class status of its membership was mixed and similar to the dominant sectors of the white New Left overall: some poor, some rich, but overwhelmingly middle class in background.)

The UFF claimed credit for 19 bombings in the Northeast in the 1980s against assorted U.S. military installations and corporate headquarters, such as General Electric, Motorola, and IBM. These actions were done expressly in solidarity with the revolutionary struggles against racism and U.S. imperialism in El Salvador, Nicaragua, and South Africa. Like many of its comrades, the UFF took precautions to ensure that no one was killed in any of its bombing attacks. Like most other groups, the UFF relied on bank robberies to secure funding for its activities.

Police ultimately charged Barbara Curzi Laaman, Patricia Gros Levasseur, Jaan Laaman, Ray Luc Levasseur, Carol Manning, Tom Manning, and Richard Williams with participation in the UFF. Ray Levasseur and Tom Manning were both Vietnam veterans and accused of previously participating in a similar group called the Sam Melville-Jonathan Jackson Unit.

Each of the men had spent time in prison in the late 1960s or early 1970s, for drugs or apolitical robberies—not unheard of circumstances for veterans and other working-class men—which became formative experiences in their political development. By 1971, all of them had committed themselves to revolutionary politics. This included, centrally, working with prisoners and their families, supporting Black resistance movements domestically and in South Africa, and joining with other antiwar soldiers. Levasseur ran a radical bookstore in Portland, Maine, which served as a hub for many of these activities. Facing increased repression personally and through the bookstore, Levasseur went underground by 1974. Curzi Laaman, Laaman, and Williams, along with New Afrikan activist Kazi Toure, helped organize the 1979 Amandla concert against apartheid featuring Bob Marley, among others. But repression and the desire to build a movement away from the eyes and ears of the state forced the others underground by 1981.

On November 4, 1984, federal agents captured Curzi Laaman, Laaman, Gros Levasseur, Levasseur, and Williams in Ohio. The following year, Carol and Tom Manning were captured. Tried together, they were dubbed the Ohio 7, although legal battles took some of them from Ohio to New York, New Jersey, and Massachusetts. These legal battles weren't the only troubles greeting these revolutionaries: except for Williams, whose wife and children did not accompany him underground, the other six were couples who lived and raised their families underground. After the arrest, the government attempted to use the nine children, most of them under 10 and all of them minors, as bargaining chips against their parents. The state offered the Levasseurs' eight-year-old daughter $20 and some pizza to cooperate with the government against her family. The Mannings' children were held incommunicado for two months after the parents were first arrested; they had to go on hunger strike to force the government to disclose the whereabouts of their children.

As with the Brink's case, the severity of the charges and the intensity of the search for the accused led to multiple court cases. In assorted trials, all of the Ohio 7, along with Kazi Toure, were convicted on bombing charges: Pat Gros Levasseur received a five-year sentence for harboring a fugitive, her husband; Barbara Curzi Laaman and Carol Manning each received a sentence of 15 years. Ray Luc Levasseur and Richard Williams were sentenced to 45 years each for their role in UFF bombings, and Jaan Laaman received a sentence of 53 years. Besides a 53-year sentence for bombing charges, Tom Manning was sentenced to life in prison during an additional trial for the 1981 self-defense shooting death of a New Jersey trooper. Even though Tom Manning admitted shooting the trooper, claiming he opened fire only after being fired upon, the state of New Jersey also tried Richard Williams for the murder. It took two trials, but Williams was ultimately sentenced to 35 years to life on the murder charge. In two separate trials, Kazi Toure was sentenced to 11 years for gun possession (six years on federal charges, up to five years on state charges) and seven years for "seditious conspiracy."

In 1989, after all members of the Ohio 7 had already been convicted on other charges, the government recharged Gros Levasseur, Levasseur, and Williams with racketeering and seditious conspiracy—functionally a charge of treason and gangsterism. Despite the state spending $10 million and calling more than 200 witnesses, the jury acquitted the defendants of sedition, and the court was forced to drop the RICO charges when the jury could not reach a verdict on them. Barbara Curzi Laaman, Carol Manning, and Pat Gros Levasseur were all released in the 1990s, as was Kazi Toure. Ray Levasseur was paroled in 2004. After being put in isolation after the September 11 attacks, Richard Williams suffered increasing medical problems. He died in prison in December 2005.

Jaan Laaman and Tom Manning remain in prison. Although he suffers from injuries and medical neglect, Manning continues to paint. Laaman is the founding editor of *4Struggle* magazine, a revolutionary (mostly) online journal of and for political prisoners and their allies (www.4strugglemag.org).

The UFF was not the first clandestine organization composed primarily of white working-class revolutionaries. Indeed, the West Coast political scene in the 1970s, especially in and around Seattle, yielded several insurrectionary underground actions. To be sure, this region contributed more than a few members and supporters of the Weather Underground and its aboveground support groups, but it also bred more local expressions of clandestine militancy, informed by a more anarchist (if still strongly Marxist and generally eclectic) orientation.

The most well known group to emerge out of this milieu was the George Jackson Brigade (GJB). Named after the murdered Black Panther and imprisoned intellectual, the GJB brought together seven militants from the Seattle area. The group had explicitly queer leadership—Bo Brown achieved a degree of notoriety as "the gentleman bank robber" for her daring drag expropriations—and was multiracial due to the involvement of Mark Cook, an ex-Panther and former prisoner who had helped organize inspiring and effective protests from behind prison walls. The group took responsibility for about 10 bombings, together with bank robberies to fund their activities and a daring prison escape. More so than any of the groups discussed above, the George Jackson Brigade provided clear, armed underground support to public struggles domestic to the United States, often local to the Pacific Northwest. The group was still internationalist—for instance, it bombed a BMW dealership in protest of the 1977 murders of Red Army Faction leaders in Germany—but its actions were designed primarily to support rebelling prisoners and striking workers in Washington State. The group bombed the Washington Department of Corrections, the corporate offices of the Safeway grocery store chain during a labor dispute, two banks, the state capitol, and several targets connected to the demands of striking autoworkers. Like many other clandestine formations at the time, the Brigade took its media seriously, releasing communiqués explaining their actions as well as statements of support or clarification to unions, poems in honor of captured comrades, and political tracts outlining its practice, beliefs, and (self)criticisms. The Brigade's political statement included essays upholding anarchism and Marxism-Leninism, and it tried to dialogue with other radicals based on its commitment to a variety of left schools of thought.

Coming almost entirely from working-class backgrounds and with lengthy personal run-ins with the law, members of the George Jackson Brigade were as reliant on bank expropriations as the Black Liberation Army and United Freedom Front. During its first attempt in January 1976, police quickly arrived and opened fire on the members inside, killing Bruce Siedel and wounding John Sherman. Ed Mead was also captured at the scene. (He would spend the next 18 years in prison, becoming a bold jailhouse lawyer, a prolific author, and an organizer of the first Men Against Sexism prison chapter to combat rape and sexual slavery inside.) Other members of the Brigade attempted a daring rescue of Sherman from a prison hospital on March 8, 1976; they succeeded in freeing Sherman, wounding a police officer in the process. This action ultimately landed Brigadista Mark Cook, new to the group and the only nonwhite member, in prison for 30 years—by far the longest anyone served for Brigade actions. Between November 1977 and March 1978, the remaining members of the Brigade were arrested. All served some time in prison and were released in the 1980s and 1990s.

Most revolutionaries in this time period, especially those engaged in armed struggle, identified prisons as a bulwark of state repression. As such, radicals pledged their solidarity with prison struggles, often leading to a revolving door between incarceration and revolutionary activities. Prison became both a breeding ground for and a target of insurgency. All of the groups discussed above—the Black Liberation Army, FALN, and AIM; the Weather Underground, United Freedom Front, and George Jackson Brigade—and dozens of other organizations directed their actions in various ways against prisons as a fundamental site of racist and ruling-class exploitation. But it was not just formalized groups who targeted the prison system. The insurrectionary anarchist approach percolating especially on the West Coast also gave rise to militant actions against the state as represented by prisons.

On August 21, 1971—the same day George Jackson was murdered—anarchist Larry Giddings was arrested in Los Angeles with a small group attempting to expropriate weapons for revolutionary action. He was paroled in 1978, at which point he moved to the Bay Area and began working with a radical collective doing prisoner support, among other activities. Released from parole in 1979, Giddings resumed clandestine activities, this time in Seattle, with other antiauthoritarians, including Bill Dunne, a former airplane mechanic. The two were arrested in October 1979 attempting to free a jailed comrade who was killed in the melee. At trial, the pair was also charged with using bank robberies and stolen weapons to carry out the attack. Although he was subject to the post-9/11 temporary disappearance many political prisoners in federal institutions faced, Giddings was paroled in 2004. Dunne, who was sentenced to 90 years at trial plus 15 years for an attempted escape in 1983, remains incarcerated in super-maximum prisons without much hope of release. An antiauthoritarian militant, Dunne considers himself a prisoner of the class war.

Revolutionary Nonviolence
Although armed actions have attracted the most media attention, revolutionary militancy has never been limited to guns and bombs. Hundreds of political prisoners in recent years have come from pacifist circles, both secular and religious. While these activists are generally imprisoned on shorter sentences than those described above, their political actions are no less vital, their commitments no less revolutionary. Just as those who engaged in armed struggle never comprised the majority of the movements from which they came, most nonviolent activists who serve prison time for acts of civil disobedience are not revolutionaries. Yet many of them are, and their work provides a vital point through which to build strategic unity among those who differ on questions of tactical importance. It was, in fact, revolutionary nonviolent activists who maintained dialogue and critical support for armed revolutionaries in the 1970s when other sectors of the left, who were often theoretically supportive of armed struggle in Third World countries, were decidedly hostile to its domestic iterations.

As prisoners from this tradition tend to serve shorter sentences and have often lacked solid relations with groups defending armed revolutionary activity, they remain largely absent from the documents compiled in this book. Nevertheless, they merit mention, as they have represented an ongoing subsection of those incarcerated for their progressive political activities over the past 40 years.

Beginning in the late 1960s, some activists managed to establish illegal, clandestine structures committed to nonviolent action. While no one knows for sure, it is believed that persons affiliated with this tendency were responsible for the break-in at the Media, Pennsylvania, FBI office that led to the exposure of COINTELPRO. This nonviolent underground had several expressions to aid those in danger: the two most common were to help ferry draft resisters and antiwar soldiers out of the country and to provide safe abortions for women in need before the practice was legalized in 1973. In the 1980s, much of this infrastructure was revived and expanded to provide sanctuary for refugees fleeing repressive, U.S.-backed military regimes in Latin America.

The experiences of these nonviolent revolutionaries disentangle militancy from violence and violence from clandestinity. After all, Dave Dellinger—who served time for resisting conscription in World War II—was the only one of the Chicago 8 defendants to intervene when police bound and gagged Panther leader Bobby Seale during the infamous conspiracy case in 1969, despite the fact that the other defendants were much more publicly in favor of militant confrontation. Likewise, Dellinger was among the most high profile of a small group of older pacifist radicals who continued to maintain a public dialogue with members of the Weather Underground and others throughout the 1970s and beyond.

Such militancy also manifested itself in clandestine actions. Perhaps the most famous nonviolent militants of the time were Daniel and Philip Berrigan, Jesuit priests and tested pacifist warriors. The Berrigan brothers and seven other Catholic leftists burned almost 400 draft files in Catonsville, Maryland, on May 17, 1968, using homemade napalm to protest its widespread use in Vietnam. Regarding the attack, Daniel Berrigan said, "Our apologies, good friends, for the fracture of good order, the burning of paper instead of children, the angering of the orderlies in the front parlor of the charnel house. We could not, so help us God, do otherwise."

All of the Catonsville 9, as they were known, were convicted of destroying government property and interfering with the Selective Service Act. Catonsville was not the first time Catholic leftists had destroyed draft files; a year earlier, Catonsville 9 activists Philip Berrigan and Thomas Lewis, along with two others, ruined hundreds of draft records in Baltimore by pouring blood over them. (They were, in fact, out on bail but sentenced to serve six years for this action when they went to the Catonsville draft board.) The Catonsville attack, however, raised the stakes through the use of arson. "We do this because everything else has failed," one of the defendants said during the action itself.

The Catonsville fire helped spark a more militant style of antiwar protest, as thousands of radicals, religious and secular alike, began attacking draft offices and destroying draft files. Catholic leftists found themselves facing political trials for their stiff resistance to the war, including the outlandish charge against seven pacifists (including Philip Berrigan and his wife, Elizabeth McAlister) for supposedly conspiring to kidnap Henry Kissinger in 1972.

The Catonsville action upped the ante in another way as well: after being convicted and sentenced to serve two to three years, five of the nine went underground rather than go to jail. Most of those who went underground did not stay long, either turning themselves in or being captured. Three days after releasing an audiotaped message of solidarity and constructive criticism to the Weather Underground, one of many public appearances he made while underground, Daniel Berrigan was arrested in August 1970. But Mary Moylan, a former nun, evaded capture altogether. She eventually joined the Weather Underground, pursuing a clandestine strategy until 1978, when the group had fallen apart and she turned herself in to serve a three-year sentence from the Catonsville action.

This sector of the Catholic left—with roots dating back to Dorothy Day and the Catholic Worker Movement, as well as the War Resisters League, World War II draft resistance, and bohemian anarchist circles of the 1950s—has continued its uncompromising organizing against empire. This has included everything from war tax resistance to attempts at shutting down the School of the Americas counterinsurgency training center to ongoing civil disobedience against U.S. wars. Whereas political prisoners of the armed-struggle left are often distinguished by serving lengthy sentences, radical pacifists are more known for the sheer number of times they find themselves behind bars for civil disobedience. For more than 40 years, it has been the political tendency among the most oriented toward civil disobedience, and adherents have served sentences of several months or several years for resisting the apparatuses of war through nonviolent confrontation, including direct action.

In 1980, the Berrigan brothers helped found the Plowshares movement, which became one of the most well known expressions of radical pacifism in the decade. The name comes from an injunction in the Bible, to "beat swords into plowshares"—that is, convert weapons of war to peaceful uses or get rid of them altogether. It was a movement targeting the use and proliferation of nuclear power and weapons. In the first Plowshares action, eight activists went to a General Electric plant in King of Prussia, Pennsylvania, and destroyed missile reentry nosecones designed for a first-strike nuclear system and poured blood on documents. Activists affiliated with the Plowshares movement were responsible for at least 30 attacks throughout the decade. At the height of the Cold War arms race, Plowshares activists dismantled several nuclear weapons, submarines, helicopters, and other military equipment, often with implements as simple as a common hammer and by pouring their own blood over the weapons. Their actions were effective at actually dismantling aspects of the military.

Unlike other high-risk radical actions, Plowshares activists did not adopt a hit-and-run strategy. Their project was one of moral and spiritual witness. As such, they awaited their capture at the scene of an action, using the trial and surrounding publicity, even jail time, as further opportunity to spread their political message. During these trials, Plowshares and other pacifist radicals (including, for instance, antiwar civil disobedience during Gulf Wars I and II) have cited international law and the necessity defense as justification for their actions—often resulting in lower sentences or even acquittals. While most of Plowshares activists came from a religious background, the antinuclear and antiauthoritarian politics were much more salient; for instance, Jewish secular anarcho-feminist Katya Komisaruk dismantled a military computer designed to guide nuclear missiles as part of her involvement in Plowshares. She served five years in prison.

The average Plowshares sentence hovered around two years in prison, although several activists received longer sentences. The longest Plowshares sentence occurred in Missouri for four activists who used a jackhammer and air compressor to damage the cover lid of a missile silo at an air force base. Larry Cloud Morgan received an 8-year sentence; Paul Kabat, 10 years; Helen Woodson, 18 years (reduced to 12 on appeal); and Carl Kabat, who had participated in two earlier Plowshares actions, 18 years.

Revolutionary nonviolence in the 1970s and 1980s overlapped considerably with radical feminism, especially lesbian feminism. The Women's Pentagon Actions in 1980 and 1981 attempted to use civil disobedience to shut down the heart of American militarism, and there were dozens of such actions at weapons plants and military offices across the country. Many of these organizers, including Barbara Deming, one of the most well known theorists and practitioners of revolutionary nonviolence, helped build the 1983 Seneca Women's Encampment for a Future of Justice and Peace. The camp, which involved thousands of women challenging imperialism and militarism as patriarchal endeavors, attempted to stop the deployment of nuclear weapons from a nearby army depot. The camp was both an intentional community of feminists (including many lesbians) and a constant exercise in civil disobedience. Fifty-four women were arrested when Marines attempted to break up the camp. It was disbanded after four months.

Militant Catholic leftists, anarchist-pacifists, and radical feminists helped rewrite the script of radical action—making it both politically deeper and more fun. Radicals affiliated with these tendencies valued direct democracy as well as direct action. They emphasized anarchist organizing processes: decentralized, consensus-based affinity groups were the model of action. This style helped inform the actions that shut down of the World Trade Organization in Seattle in November 1999 and subsequent global justice demonstrations. But the fusion of anarchism, spirituality, and direct action expressed itself well before then. Since the 1980s, perhaps the most visible expression of this approach came from the environmental movement.

Earth and Animal Liberation
The 1970s inaugurated many things, including the first Earth Day celebration, on April 22, 1970. While the celebration has, by and large, become just another kitschy, corporate-sponsored festival, it also signals a growing concern with environmentalism and sustainability. The interest in protecting the earth and its resources has found many expressions in recent decades, ranging from communal living and recycling to civil disobedience and sabotage. All of these activities, in fact, have increased as scientists, farmers, and others around the world call attention to the crisis of global climate change.

While liberal nonprofits attempted to steer the new-found environmental concern to more watered-down ends, radical environmentalists began to congregate around a group and political framework called Earth First! (EF!). Inspired in part by the "ecotage" novels of Edward Abbey, EF! formed in 1979-1980 in the Southwest under the banner "No Compromise in Defense of Mother Earth." Behind its single focus on the environment, the group brought together a politically diverse range of activists, including some reactionary and even racist elements in its earlier years. By the mid-'80s, tensions between reactionaries and others were causing more and more conflicts within the organization, until a 1990 split led to the group being grounded more firmly in the anarchist milieu. While formally rejecting the state, EF! politics have tended to target corporate power as the greatest threat to environmental sustainability.

Activists associated with Earth First! have been responsible for direct action environmentalism against logging, dam and other hazardous development, pollution, and genetic engineering. It has embraced a direct-action and, since 1990, more explicitly anarchist organizing style and placed high value on tree sits, roadblocks, and monkey wrenching. Indeed, many credit Earth First! with helping develop a variety of creative forms of civil disobedience that are both high profile and successful.

The most well known main target of government repression against EF! was Judi Bari, a former labor organizer turned environmentalist. More than anyone else, Bari bridged environmental and economic concerns—a vital task at a time when the timber industry tried to position economic necessity as the reason for deforestation. Bari flipped the script, organizing workers and environmentalists to seize corporate property and eliminate corporate power. Bari also added a strong feminist presence to Earth First! leadership and activism, helping to displace the negative image the group had developed in the 1980s.

With the help of Earth First! troubadour Darryl Cherney, Bari organized Redwood Summer in 1990, an effort self-consciously indebted to SNCC's Mississippi Summer in 1964 and similarly attempting to bring thousands of young people and national attention to fight for justice—this time, California's redwood forests. While organizing for the summer program in Oakland in May 1990, a bomb placed under the driver's seat in Bari's car exploded, shattering her pelvis and wounding Cherney. Three hours later, while still at the hospital, Bari and Cherney were placed under arrest, as local and federal law enforcement agents said the pair were terrorists and were the only suspects in the bombing. The prosecutor's office dropped the charges two months later for lack of evidence. Bari and Cherney then sued the FBI for placing the bomb, ultimately winning a $4.4 million settlement in 2002. Bari died of cancer in 1997.

Bari's skill for building coalition extended to other elements of Earth First! activism. Although aspects of the environmental movement have exhibited racist Malthusian and anti-immigrant politics, the deep ecology framework has also enabled inroads with land-based struggles of Indigenous sovereignty. In Minnesota, for instance, radical environmentalists teamed up with the Mendota Mdewakanton Dakota tribe to block road construction through a park the Dakotas held sacred. Together, the radicals built the "Minnehaha Free State," a four-month-long land occupation in 1998. Destroying the free state was the largest police action in Minnesota history, involving 800 police officers evicting several dozen activists from six squatted homes. These and similar actions have often ended in jail time for participants—though, as with Plowshares, the charges tend to be lower and the sentences shorter.

Since the mid-1990s, autonomous groups and individuals operating under the banner of the Earth Liberation Front (ELF) have been carrying out more and more militant, clandestine acts of sabotage against a variety of targets—universities, corporations, real estate developments—accused of endangering the planet through genetic engineering, overdevelopment, pollution, and conspicuous consumption. ELF actions (and those of the related Animal Liberation Front, ALF) have caused millions of dollars in damages in more than 1,000 acts of arson across the country. As a result, the state has clamped down on the earth and animal liberation movements.

Particularly since 9/11, public animal rights and eco-activists have been called in front of grand juries, especially along the West Coast but also in the Midwest. Far more troubling, more than two dozen people have been arrested for suspected ALF or ELF activities. Eco-activists have dubbed this repressive trend "the Green Scare." The most chilling aspect of the Green Scare arrests occurred as part of what the FBI called "Operation Backfire." A case involving conspiracy and multiple arsons over a five-year period, Operation Backfire was frightening not just because it swept up more than a dozen people in its dragnet, but because the case was built almost entirely on informants. Through threatening life in prison, the government successfully pressured eight defendants to cooperate (people who themselves were arrested based on the extensive testimony of one person, an alleged member of several ELF cells). And yet, because the collaborators were often the most involved in illegal activity, most of them ended up with longer sentences than those who maintained their principles.

Déjà Vu

The early 21st century has witnessed a certain political déjà vu in political trials. Emboldened by the broad powers enabled through "fighting terrorism," the state has not only targeted a new crop of dissidents; it has arrested some old ones as well. Several cases stand out here.

Perhaps most notorious is the case of eight former Black Panthers who were arrested on January 23, 2007, for the 1971 shooting death of a San Francisco police officer. Several of the men had already been arrested in New Orleans in the 1970s, and a judge had dismissed the charges when he found that their basis lay in confessions garnered through torture. In the post-9/11 environment, however, the San Francisco agents who oversaw the original investigation and torture came out of retirement to reprosecute the case.

Five men were called in front of grand juries in 2005—and then thrown in jail when they refused to cooperate. The grand jury ultimately faded away, and the men were released, only to be arrested with others a year later. (One of the five grand jury resisters, John Bowman, died of cancer shortly before the big arrests.) The eight were Herman Bell, Ray Boudreaux, Richard Brown, Hank Jones, Jalil Muntaqim, Richard O'Neal, Harold Taylor, and Francisco Torres. Bell and Muntaqim had already been in prison since 1971, being the two surviving members of the New York 3 who were framed for the murder of a New York City police officer that year.

The state was initially charging the men not only with the murder but with participating in a hazy conspiracy of Black militancy between 1968 and 1973. The conspiracy charge has been dropped against all but Torres, Bell, and Muntaqim. Because he was only charged with conspiracy, charges against O'Neal have been dropped entirely. The others, however, still face a murder indictment in a case that has no known new evidence and has already cost millions of dollars without going to trial.

In other revived cases, former BLA soldier Kamau Sadiki was sentenced to life in prison in 2003 for the 1971 death of a police officer in Georgia. Sadiki was arrested in New York in early 2001 on separate, but contemporary, charges that were subsequently dismissed. Once in custody, though, police officers tried to get his help in solving other BLA-suspected cases. That proved futile, but FBI files listed him as a suspect in the Atlanta killing and he was transferred to Georgia. The timing was a bit odd: the district attorney refused to prosecute the case in 1972 for insufficient evidence, there was no new evidence, and Sadiki had been living a quiet but nonetheless public life working for the phone company in New York City.

Besides the Panthers, the other organization to be most subject to the politics of retrospective justice is the Symbionese Liberation Army (SLA). Perhaps the most controversial armed struggle organization of the 1970s, the SLA was a mostly white group based in California and formed under the leadership of a Black former prisoner who took the name Cinque, after the leader of a 19th-century slave rebellion. Several members of the group were lesbians; "symbionese" came from the word "symbiosis," as the group believed it was bringing together diverse elements of revolutionary thought. The group is best remembered for two actions: the murder of Oakland's superintendent of schools and the kidnapping of newspaper heiress Patty Hearst. The SLA assassinated Marc Foster, a well-liked Black administrator, for proposing a controversial student ID system. The group then kidnapped Patty Hearst, using her as ransom to force her wealthy family to provide food to Oakland's poor and to get their statements publicized. In an unexpected twist, Hearst later joined the group and participated in bank robberies to fund the group's activities (including one robbery gone awry, where a bystander was killed).

Five hundred Los Angeles police, FBI, and U.S. Treasury agents surrounded a house in Compton on May 17, 1974, where SLA members had been staying. Police fired tear gas and 9,000 bullets into the house, ultimately using an incendiary device to kill the six SLA members inside. Those remaining, and those who joined after the "Compton massacre," fled Los Angeles and eluded capture at least for another year. Patty Hearst was arrested in 1975; she disassociated herself from the SLA and claimed her participation was a result of being brainwashed. She was convicted, though President Carter commuted her sentence. Other members of the group also served several years in prison throughout the 1970s and 1980s.

In recent years, however, five former members of the group have also found themselves in court for charges emanating from their activities in the 1970s. The SLA arrests include the extradition of James Kilgore from South Africa, where he had been living and working as a well-respected academic for years, and the arrest and trial of Kathy Soliah, who had been living a quiet life as Sara Jane Olson in Minnesota. Kilgore received a six-year sentence. Arrested shortly before 9/11, Soliah initially planned to fight her charges, but pled after the crumbling World Trade Center towers smashed her hopes of a fair trial. Sentenced to 14 years, Olson was released on March 17, 2008, and rearrested on March 18, after being ordered to serve another year of her sentence.

Emily Montague, Bill Harris, and Michael Bortin have also been arrested in recent years for their involvement in the SLA three decades earlier; they pled guilty in 2002 and were sentenced to eight, seven, and six years, respectively, for the accidental death of Myrna Opsahl in the failed bank robbery.

Two other post-9/11 prosecutions of 1960s-era radicals bear mentioning: H. Rap Brown, who famously declared violence to be "as American as cherry pie," was sentenced to life in prison in 2002 for the shooting death of a Fulton County sheriff's deputy two years earlier. The former leader of the Student Nonviolent Coordinating Committee had become imam of a Muslim community in Atlanta, changing his name to Jamil Al-Amin. As with Sadiki, Al-Amin denied any involvement in the shooting for which he was charged; he and his supporters allege the case to be the culmination of decades of harassment made possible by post-9/11 legal shifts.

Gary Freeman, born Joseph Pannell, was arrested in Canada in 2004, after living there for 35 years. He was arrested for the 1969 shooting of a white police officer in Chicago. The officer survived, but police claim Freeman was a Black Panther carrying out a politically motivated attack. After fighting extradition for several years, Freeman pleaded guilty in February 2008 to the shooting under an agreement that saw him serve just 30 days and pay restitution to a scholarship fund for the children of slain police officers. Given the vengeful tone characterizing other retrospective cases, Freeman's is a relatively successful tale.

Conclusion: Toward Amnesty

While the United States denies the existence of political prisoners, it pursues a vengeful policy of lifelong incarceration. To acknowledge the political basis of their incarceration would further expose the depths of social problems that these militants have committed their lives to fighting. The veneer of U.S. democracy and tolerance requires that dissidents be branded as criminals, or terrorists. Working to free political prisoners goes hand in hand with exposing the façade that the U.S. is a country where injustice is minimal and solved through electoral politics—one point necessitates the other. The fact that so many political prisoners have been charged with treason or sedition demonstrates that the government fears this precise point; resistance is criminalized, deemed a threat to "the American way of life." The ubiquity of state repression affords an opportunity to forge solidarity among multiple revolutionary movements. Seizing this opportunity does not mean ignoring contradictions (e.g., the difference between pacifism and armed struggle, anarchism and Marxism-Leninism, secularism and faith-based organizing, or the struggles within particular movements over racism and patriarchy). Instead, it offers a chance for serious radicals to work with one another, addressing differences in ways that build alliances and strengthen the potential for revolutionary opposition. The fact that most political prisoners have continued their political work in prison—through writing, mentoring younger activists, conducting peer education with other prisoners, and fighting AIDS, misogyny, and homophobia—provides a worthy example to follow.

Most governments routinely release political prisoners every decade or so, and political internees are often incarcerated together or allowed increased family visits, in tacit recognition of the political nature of their "crimes." Not so in the United States, where amnesty is a forbidden term. The FBI, Police Benevolent Associations, U.S. Parole Commission, and similar entities have routinely lobbied hard to prevent parole, even when people meet all standards for release (e.g., good records, jobs available upon release, community support). In the most frightening example, former Panther Veronza Bowers has been kept in prison more than four years past his mandatory release date, without cause or indication of when he will get out. The government has regularly pointed to the serious charges and prior political affiliations of the prisoners as reasons for ongoing incarceration—even where it contradicts the normal functioning of parole and release from prison. Thus, building an amnesty movement becomes a priority: the issue of political incarceration needs to be framed as a fundamental question of building and defending our movements. Amnesty is the position holding prisoner support as vital to looking out for each other and defending our victories from state attacks.

Prison can be seen as an extension of the repression that drove many of these people to undertake militant action in the first place. It is part of the government's arsenal to destroy revolutionaries. The state has sometimes made this explicit by housing radicals in control unit prisons, prisons-within-prisons that are based on solitary confinement and sensory deprivation. The prisons in Florence, Colorado, and Marion, Illinois, are the best examples of this, and those institutions have housed Ray Luc Levasseur, Mutulu Shakur, Bill Dunne, and Yu Kikumura, among others. The most famous example of a political prison was the Lexington Control Unit, a basement prison in Kentucky that held former May 19th activists Silvia Baraldini and Susan Rosenberg and Puerto Rican *independentista* Alejandrina Torres from 1986 to 1988. The prison was so oriented toward inducing physical and psychological ailments that Amnesty International declared it cruel and unusual punishment; a grassroots campaign succeeded in closing the unit, but supermax prisons remain.

The bulk of such repression is meted out against revolutionary people of color, particularly Black, Native American, and Puerto Rican radicals. The reasons for this are complex—they involve not just white privilege but the fact that the government has taken a firm position against the release of any political prisoner with a murder conviction. Due to the open levels of confrontation between police and communities of color, these liberation movements often adopted different tactics than white militants. But the state's intransigence on paroling those with murder convictions has repercussions for political prisoners regardless of race—several white anti-imperialists are also imprisoned for the deaths of law enforcement agents, seemingly with no chance of release.

The political incarceration of people who became active in the 1960s is inextricably tied to state repression. Even when they committed illegal acts or acts of which they themselves are now critical, their continuing incarceration cannot be separated from the legacy of COINTELPRO. Even now, movement veterans captured as a result of movement work in the 1960s are paying for the state's crimes through continued incarceration. The ongoing imprisonment of '60s-era activists—together with a new breed of political prisoners coming from an array of contemporary movements—presents a direct connection between the struggles of yesterday and those of today.

There are serious challenges to this work, including limited resources, a strategy that must deal with the legal system, public fear of "terrorists," and the difficulty of building working relationships among the various movements who find themselves experiencing state repression. But combating political incarceration and supporting those in the crosshairs of state repression remain central to creating a better future. After all, the government remembers who joins and organizes in the movement—and we cannot afford to forget.

A Note on Sources

The best source on political prisoners are the prisoners themselves; reading their words—in interviews, essays, pamphlets, books, videos, and through correspondence—is vital. But there are many perspectives on political movements, and additional sources are necessary to provide a more rounded examination. Below I provide some of the key texts used in preparing this article and in thinking about political prisoners. The list is, at best, woefully incomplete and focused only on books rather than pamphlets, of which there have been many dealing with relevant issues. (Please note: some of these books are out of print.) Still, the following bibliography should provide a good start to those curious for more reading.

The politics of incarceration: Tim Blunk and Ray Luc Levasseur (eds.), *Hauling Up the Morning: Writings and Art by Political Prisoners and Prisoners of War in the U.S.* (The Red Sea Press, 1990); Committee to End the Marion Lockdown, *Can't Jail the Spirit: Biographies of U.S. Political Prisoners* (2002 or other editions); Ruth Wilson Gilmore, *Golden Gulag: Prisons, Surplus, Crisis, and Opposition in Globalizing California* (University of California Press, 2007); Marie Gottschalk, *The Prison and the Gallows: The Politics of Mass Incarceration in America* (Oxford University Press, 2006); Joy James, ed., *The Angela Y. Davis Reader* (Blackwell Publishers, 1998); Joy James, ed., *Imprisoned Intellectuals: America's Political Prisoners Write on Life, Liberation and Rebellions* (Rowman and Littlefield, 2003); Christian Parenti, *Lockdown America: Police and Prisons in an Age of Crisis* (Verso, 2000); Elihu Rosenblatt, ed., *Criminal Injustice: Confronting the Prison Crisis* (South End Press, 1996).

Repression: Ward Churchill and Jim Vander Wall, *Agents of Repression: The FBI's Secret Wars Against the Black Panther Party and the American Indian Movement* (South End Press, 1988); Ward Churchill and Jim Vander Wall, *The COINTELPRO Papers: Documents from the FBI's Secret War Against Dissent in the United States* (South End Press, 1990); David Cunningham, *There's Something Happening Here: The New Left, the Klan and FBI Counterintelligence* (University of California Press, 2005); Joy James, ed., *States of Confinement: Policing, Detention, and Prisons* (Palgrave McMillan, 2002).

Revolutionary nationalism and independence movements: Mumia Abu-Jamal, *We Want Freedom: A Life in the Black Panther Party* (South End Press, 2006); Kuwasi Balagoon, *A Soldier's Story* (Kersplebedeb, 2003); Terry Bisson, *On a MOVE: The Story of Mumia Abu-Jamal* (Litmus Books, 2000); Patricia Bell Blawis, *Tijerina and the Land Grants: Mexican Americans in Struggle for their Heritage* (International Publishers, 1971); Kathleen Cleaver and George Katsiaficas, eds., *Liberation, Imagination, and the Black Panther Party* (Routledge, 2001); *Angela Davis: An Autobiography* (International Publishers, 1989); Charles

Jones, ed., *The Black Panther Party Reconsidered* (Black Classics Press, 1998); Peter Matthiessen, *In the Spirit of Crazy Horse* (New York: Penguin, 1991); MOVE, *Twenty-Five Years on the MOVE* (self-published); Lorena Oropeza, *Raza Si! Guerra No! Chicano Protest and Patriotism During the Viet Nam War Era* (University of California Press, 2005); Vijay Prashad, *The Darker Nations: A People's History of the Third World* (New Press, 2007); Laura Pulido, *Black, Brown, Yellow, & Left: Radical Activism in Los Angeles* (University of California Press, 2006); J. Sakai, *Settlers: The Mythology of the White Proletariat* (Chicago: Morningstar, 1989); Assata Shakur, *Assata* (Laurence Hill Books, 2001); E. Tani and Kae Sera, *False Nationalism, False Internationalism: Class Contradictions in the Armed Struggle* (Seeds Beneath the Snow, 1985); Andrés Torres and José E. Velázquez, eds., *The Puerto Rican Movement: Voices from the Diaspora* (Temple University Press, 1998); Ernesto B. Vigil, *The Crusade for Justice: Chicano Militancy and the Government's War on Dissent* (University of Wisconsin Press, 1999); Cynthia Young, *Soul Power: Culture, Radicalism, and the Making of a U.S. Third World Left* (Duke University Press, 2006).

Anti-imperialism: Bill Ayers, Bernardine Dohrn, and Jeff Jones, eds., *Sing a Battle Song: The Revolutionary Poetry, Statements, and Communiques of the Weather Underground 1970-1974* (Seven Stories Press, 2007); Dan Berger, *Outlaws of America: The Weather Underground and the Politics of Solidarity* (AK Press, 2006); Ward Churchill with Mike Ryan, *Pacifism as Pathology: Reflections on the Role of Armed Struggle in North America* (AK Press, 2007); Roxanne Dunbar-Ortiz, *Outlaw Woman: A Memoir of the War Years, 1960-1975* (City Lights, 2004); Abbie Hoffman, *The Autobiography of Abbie Hoffman* (New York: De Capo Press, 2000); George Katsiaficas, *The Imagination of the New Left* (South End Press, 1987); The New Yippie Book Collective, *Blacklisted News, Secret Histories: From Chicago to 1984* (Berkeley: Bleecker Publishing, 1983); Becky Thompson, *A Promise and a Way of Life: White Antiracist Activism* (University of Minnesota Press, 2000); Jeremy Varon, *Bringing the War Home: The Weather Underground, the Red Army Faction, and Revolutionary Violence in the Sixties and Seventies* (University of California Press, 2004).

Revolutionary nonviolence: Scott H. Bennett, *Radical Pacifism: The War Resisters League and Gandhian Nonviolence in America, 1915-1963* (Syracuse University Press, 2003); Daniel Berrigan, *The Trial of the Catonsville 9* (Fordham University Press, 2004); Dave Dellinger, *More Power Than We Know: The People's Movement for Democracy* (Anchor Press/Doubleday, 1975); Dave Dellinger, *From Yale to Jail: The Life of a Moral Dissenter* (Rose Hill Books, 1993); Barbara Deming, *Remembering Who We Are* (Pagoda, 1981); Barbara Epstein, *Political Protest and Cultural Revolution: Nonviolent Direct Action in the 1970s and 1980s* (University of California Press, 1991); Arthur J. Laffin and Anne Montgomery, eds., *Swords into Plowshares: Nonviolent Direct Action for Disarmament* (Harper & Row, 1987); Staughton and Alice Lynd, *Nonviolence in America: A Documentary*

History (Orbis, 1995); Pam McAllister, ed., *Reweaving the Web of Life: Feminism and Nonviolence* (New Society Publishers, 1982); Pam McAllister, *You Can't Kill the Spirit: Stories of Women and Nonviolent Action* (New Society Publishers, 1988); Jane Meyerding, ed., *We Are All Part of One Another: A Barbara Deming Reader* (New Society Publishers, 1984); Murray Polner, *Disarmed and Dangerous: The Radical Life and Times of Daniel and Philip Berrigan (Westview Press, 1997); James Tracy, Direct Action: Radical Pacifism from the Union Eight to the Chicago Seven (University of Chicago Press, 1996).*

Earth and animal liberation: Steve Best and Anthony Nocella, *Igniting a Revolution: Voices in Defense of the Earth* (AK Press, 2006); Direct Action Manual Collective, *Earth First! Direct Action Manual* (1997); Dave Foreman, *Ecodefense: A Field Guide to Monkeywrenching* (Abbzug Press, 1997); Derrick Jensen, *Endgame* [2 volumes] (Seven Stories Press, 2006); Christopher Manes, *Green Rage: Radical Environmentalism and the Unmaking of Civilization* (Back Bay Books, 1991); Leslie James Pickering, *Earth Liberation Front, 1997-2002* (Arissa Media Group, 2007); Craig Rosebraugh, *Burning Rage of a Dying Planet: Speaking for the Earth Liberation Front* (Lantern Books, 2004).

Section I.

Putting
Political Prisoners
on the Map

*I*n the early and mid-1980s, an upsurge in militant activity by U.S. revolutionary movements led to a series of arrests and renewed waves of repression, producing a whole new batch of political prisoners. Both the newer and the longer-term prisoners from each national movement, drawing on successful campaigns of the 1970s, pushed outside organizations to reassess their efforts, devise broader and more creative outreach methods, and build unity with one another. The result was that those organizations resumed working in a more coordinated way within the U.S. left and oppressed communities to put the issue of political prisoners squarely on the activist map. One of the strategies of choice was the use of People's Tribunals.

Not only did these organizations make the case that, contrary to U.S. government denial, there were more than 100 political prisoners, but also that authorities had programs scientifically designed to break the will of those prisoners through isolation, sensory deprivation, and brutality in specialized control units. Most notorious were the federal prison for men in Marion, Illinois, and for women in Lexington, Kentucky. Jailed revolutionaries like Bill Dunne (at Marion); Alejandrina Torres, Susan Rosenberg, and Silvia Baraldini (at Lexington); and Black political prisoners in the Research Committee on International Law and Black Freedom Fighters played key roles in documenting and exposing conditions in these and other units and in galvanizing outside activists to fight against them. A large-scale, multi-tactic campaign, including a federal lawsuit, pressured the government to shut down the Lexington Control Unit in 1988, but the Marion Control Unit would remain open for many more years. Ultimately, new and more sophisticated federal control units – particularly Florence, Colorado, for men and Marianna, Florida, for women – replaced them (although because of the struggle, conditions in Marianna have never matched the extreme abusiveness of Lexington), and horrendous clones now exist in virtually every state.

Despite these setbacks, the campaigns and events by the political prisoner support movements of the late '80s and early '90s paved the way for the broader popular support, and many of the victories, that mounted throughout the '90s.

Political Prisoners in the U.S.?

Freedom Now!
1989

Freedom Now!

Campaign
for
Amnesty and
Human Rights
for
Political
Prisoners
in the
United States

The government denies it. Yet today there are more than 100 people locked up in U.S. prisons because of their political actions or beliefs.

The U.S. alone among the world's governments maintains the fiction that it holds no political prisoners. The official position is that all those jailed for politically motivated actions are "criminals." The U.S. tries to hide the existence of political prisoners because they challenge the image that the U.S. is a truly democratic and humane society. These prisoners expose the fact that there are political resistance

This was the text of a flier produced by Freedom Now!, an effort to pull together in a single organization representatives of all the U.S. political prisoners and leaders of all the internal national liberation movements.

movements of such influential impact that the government is compelled to use repression against them.

By labeling political prisoners as criminals, the U.S. government has also been able to shield from view serious human rights violations against them. These include:

- excessive prison sentences—example: 8 Black political prisoners will soon begin their third decade behind bars;
- psychological torture;
- assault—example: one Puerto Rican prisoner of war was beaten to death by guards and his death labeled a suicide;
- sexual assault—example: under the guise of security, male prison staff forcibly conducted cavity searches on two women political prisoners at F.C.I. Tucson;
- denial of medical care;
- placement in control units—example: the men's federal prison in Marion, Illinois, which includes several political prisoners among its 400 inmates, has been condemned by Amnesty International for violating international standards on the minimum treatment of prisoners. The men in Marion are locked in their cells 23 hours per day and are sometimes chained spread-eagle to their beds for days at a time. The control unit for women at Lexington, Kentucky, was an experimental underground political prison that practiced isolation and sensory deprivation. It was finally closed by a federal judge after two years of protest by religious and human rights groups.

Human Rights Must Begin at Home!

Who are America's political prisoners? Like the four women and men pictured on the facing page—Alejandrina Torres, Leonard Peltier, Geronimo Pratt and Susan Rosenberg—they represent many movements for freedom and social justice.

People of color are most often targeted. Black activists participating in the fight for Black Liberation and against racism are the largest group represented, with well ever 50 political prisoners. Many of them, like Geronimo Pratt, have been in jail nearly 20 years.

The movement for Puerto Rican independence has also been heavily attacked with the imprisonment of many of its members. These include 14 women and men such as Alejandrina Torres who consider themselves prisoners of war. They have taken this position because they believe that as colonized people they have the right to fight for independence, and their captor, the United States, has no right to criminalize them.

Other political prisoners in the United States include more than thirty white North American activists. These militants are accused of various actions opposing the foreign, domestic and military policies of the U.S. government. Their protests have been directed against symbols of U.S. support for the apartheid regime in South Africa, military intervention in Central America, and the continued colonial oppression of Blacks and Puerto Ricans. Among these prisoners are women and men from the religious peace community who have received long sentences for direct actions against U.S. nuclear installations.

Revealing the existence of all of these political prisoners is of extra importance now because greater world attention is being focused on human rights. Many countries, including the Soviet Union and Cuba, have released most of their political prisoners. They have also started to raise questions about human rights problems here in the U.S.A. Now is the time to break through the wall of silence that has surrounded these political prisoners in the United States. We in the Freedom Now! campaign are making information available on all their cases to the people of the U.S. and the world. While the government will continue to deny holding political prisoners, we seek to make their existence common knowledge in every American community.

At the same time, all of us can begin to speak out against the terrible human rights violations taking place against political prisoners and all prisoners in the U.S. Jails and prisons have abandoned all pretenses of "rehabilitating" inmates, and have become concentration camps for warehousing the youth from the ghettos and barrios of America. We must especially denounce the spread of prison control units, which attempt to rob prisoners of their humanity, sanity and even their lives.

Ultimately we must seek the freedom of all political prisoners in the U.S. Other countries are doing it. Why not here? Freedom Now! is initiating a campaign for amnesty for all the women and men imprisoned in this country as a consequence of their political actions. Officials of the U.S. government have signed many international laws and treaties governing political repression. We must hold them to those standards!

The Freedom Now! campaign is about real people, women and men behind bars who care deeply about justice and humanity. The government has sought to isolate them, not only from their friends and families but from their ability to influence and lead political movements.

Our campaign is breaking that isolation. We are bridging the walls with a common effort that includes the active participation of the prisoners and their families, along with political activists, clergy and professionals. We welcome your participation! Join us in stopping the continued imprisonment and mistreatment of political activists in the United States. Human rights must begin at home.

Amnesty for Political Prisoners!

Political Prisoners and International Law

Research Committee on International Law and
Black Freedom Fighters in the U.S.
1990

> The only alternative that Black [people] have in America today
> is to take it out of [U.S.] jurisdiction and take it before that body
> [United Nations]... which represents International Law and let them
> know that the human rights of Black people are being violated in a
> country that professes to be the moral leader of the free world.
>
> Malcolm X, April 8, 1964

The quality and nature of the struggle waged in this country by Black people must be viewed in a historical context. First, it must be recognized that we were brought here against our will, thereby making us, en masse, political prisoners.

The initial laws of this country, the Constitution, and the Bill of Rights, did nothing to change this status. They inherently stated that the laws of inclusion did not apply to us, and we have essentially remained outside to the present. This lack of legal parity has demanded that our struggle develop from one of civil rights to human rights.

We must always look at our situation differently from those who have been included within the American society. Ours has been a continuous struggle starting with the capture, the middle passage, slave revolts, and each successive generation of revolutionaries. The Black Freedom Fighters who resisted militarily in the 1960s, '70s and '80s follow in the tradition of Denmark Vesey, Nat Turner and Malcolm X.

Their struggle—our struggle—is similar to that of other peoples in the world striving for human rights and self-determination. Today, these world struggles are gaining legal recognition and protection in the growing body of international law vitalized by the Third World. Part of our task now is to have the International Law and international community recognize and protect the just struggle of Black Freedom Fighters within the United States.

Dr. John Henrik Clarke
Professor Emeritus, African World History
Hunter College, New York, NY

Committee Purpose

The purpose of the Research Committee is to increase awareness of the relevance of International Law to the situation of Black political prisoners and prisoners of war in the U.S. For nearly four centuries, Afrikans in the United States have been denied the power over their own destinies and, in return, have been fighting for self-determination. This struggle has taken many forms. In the 1960s, responding to the Civil Rights and Black Liberation Movements, a low-intensity war was undertaken by the U.S. government through the Federal Bureau of Investigation's Counterintelligence Program and local police intelligence units. As in any war, this war has had its combatants, noncombatant support units, casualties, and prisoners.

It is crucial that the local and international communities understand how International Law, including the 1949 Geneva Accords and Protocols I and II, apply to the cases of Black Freedom Fighters who are an essential and inseparable part of the Black Liberation Movement in its struggle for self-determination.

Statement of International Law

> International norms and principles for the treatment of national minorities have become a part of international law through treaties and membership in the United Nations and hence part of the laws of all states.
>
> Dr. Y. N. Kly, *International Law and the Black Minority in the U.S.*

Among the international documents that guarantee the right to self-determination and protect those who fight to exercise the right are the following:

- 1949 Geneva Convention
- 1977, Protocol I (to 1949 Geneva Convention)
- 1/29/87, Protocol II (to the 1949 Geneva Convention)
- Universal Declaration of Human Rights, General Assembly Resolution No. 217 (III), December 10, 1948
- Convention on the Prevention and Punishment of the Crime of Genocide, 78 UNTS 277
- International Covenant on Civil and Political Rights, 1966
- Political Offense Exception to Extradition

Board of Advisors: Haywood Burns (Chair Emeritus of the National Conference Board of Black Lawyers); Joy James, Ph.D. (Associate Professor, University of Massachusetts, Amherst); Duma Ndlovu (Political Poet/Playwright, in exile from Southern Africa); Father Lawrence Lucas (Liberation Theologist, Resurrection Roman Catholic Church); Professor James Turner (Founding Director, Professor, African Studies & Research Center, Cornell University); Yuri Kochiyama (Activist); Judge Bruce Wright (Author of *Black Robes, White Justice*); Curtis Powell, Ph.D. (Immunologist). Organizations listed for identification only.

Political Prisoners: Guilty Until Proven Innocent

Susie Day
1989

> People are so afraid of us, they don't want to hear. Like thy say we
> believe in violence. That's been said of me every time I was moved
> from one institution to another.... Hollywood believes in violence; this
> country believes in violence. But we don't.

Laura Whitehorn has spent nearly four years in eleven different jails and
prisons since she was arrested in May 1985. Held under "preventive detention," the 43-year-old Whitehorn has been denied bail, although her record
shows no previous criminal charges and only three arrests for demonstrating
against the Vietnam War and forced sterilization.

Now Whitehorn and six others—Alan Berkman, Timothy Blunk, Marilyn
Buck, Linda Evans, Susan Rosenberg, and Elizabeth Duke (who remains
free)—stand accused by the federal government of the 1983 bombing of the
U.S. Capitol and three military buildings in the District of Columbia. Although
no one was killed or injured in these bombings, which protested the invasion
of Grenada and other U.S. foreign aggression, the defendants could receive as
many as 45 years in prison, if convicted. The Resistance Conspiracy trial, as
the defendants call it, will likely begin in March of this year, and promises to
be one of the most important political cases of the decade.

In November 1988, I traveled to the Detention Facility in Washington, DC,
and talked to the four women awaiting trial. Their words in this article are
drawn from those interviews. Here, Susan Rosenberg speaks:

> Most people don't think there are forms of political oppression in this
> country, but there are. And I think we're a very good example of it,
> you know?... When you go to jail because of conscious acts, it doesn't
> mean that being in prison is easier. I mean, the most fundamental
> deprivation is to lose your liberty.... Short of death, it's probably the
> most profound loss a person can have.

In 1985, at the age of 30, Rosenberg was sentenced, with Tim Blunk, to 58
years in prison for weapons possession and fake identification. She spent 20

Reprinted from *Sojourner: The Women's Forum*, February 1989.

months in the Lexington High Security Unit, a notorious behavior modification facility for "violence prone" women.

Although the United States refuses to acknowledge them as political prisoners, Rosenberg and her codefendants are part of some 200 people with left-wing views now in federal prisons for alleged crimes against the government. This figure includes "prisoners of war" such as Puerto Rican Nationalists, who see themselves as part of oppressed nations within the United States. The psychological toll of years in confinement is incalculable to these prisoners—25 percent of whom are women. Says Marilyn Buck:

> I haven't worked in three and one-half years. Even if I didn't work a job where I brought home a paycheck before, I did work that was organized, that was directed.... I see women sitting in jail, idle, doing nothing. Take Marion [men's prison in Illinois] or Lexington, where there's no work, no productive labor.... It really tears you apart.

Buck was convicted in 1988, with Dr. Mutulu Shakur, a New Afrikan freedom fighter, for alleged conspiracy in actions attributed to the Black Liberation Army, including the 1979 prison escape of Black activist Assata Shakur. Before the Resistance Conspiracy trial begins, Buck at 41, already faces 70 years in prison.

Like her codefendants, all of whom are white, Buck has devoted her life and political work to fighting racism. Perhaps it is the alliance of these six North Americans with people of color, and with radical black and Puerto Rican groups in particular, that has motivated the prosecution in the Resistance Conspiracy case to erect a massive, bullet-proof plexiglass wall—the kind often seen in South African trials—to separate the defendants from the rest of the courtroom. As an extra "precaution," special cameras have been installed to monitor the defense table as well as courtroom spectators.

Ironically, at about the same time and in the same building, Oliver North is scheduled to be tried, without shields or cameras. Unlike Laura Whitehorn, neither North nor his colleagues have spent time in preventive detention. There is also wide speculation that these men will not go to prison, even in the unlikely event that they are convicted. These legal discrepancies are not unusual, according to Linda

Marilyn Buck (© 2008 JEB (Joan E. Biren))

55

Evans; convicted right-wing defendants generally receive lighter sentences than those who disagree with government policy:

> I ended up getting five years in New York... for being a felon in posses-
> sion of a gun when I was arrested. And then 40 years in Louisiana for
> making false statements.... And, of course, the thing that's interesting
> about the Louisiana case is that it's the same jurisdiction where the Ku
> Klux Klan tried to mount an invasion of Dominica, a Black island in the
> Caribbean. You might have heard about it, in '81? It was Don Black.
> And he had ten other men with him; he had almost a million dollars in
> cash; they had a boatful of illegal weapons, machine guns and stuff.
> And he received a total of ten years and was out in 24 months.

Evans is a vibrant woman in her early forties, whose identity as a lesbian is intrinsic to her politics. "I love women," she says, "and I really believe that we should be completely free to develop our full potential with no barriers at all.... And I know that because I identify my own oppression, both as a woman and a lesbian, it means that I have a real stake in winning."

"Winning," to Evans and to the other women, means the eventual restruc-turing of a society that nourishes itself on inequality. Their will to win comes from the fact that they are women. Susan Rosenberg explains:

> We very much see our liberation as women tied into the structure of
> this system as necessary... I'm involved in social change and radical
> action and revolutionary movements because I'm a woman, you know?
> I didn't feel this system had too much to offer me as a woman in terms
> of real liberation.

Susan Rosenberg (© 2008 JEB (Joan E. Biren))

All six Resistance Conspiracy defendants base their political work on anti-imperialist principles, which allow them to see the U.S.-dominated corporate/military structure as responsible for a range of international atrocities, from apartheid to nuclear weaponry. They also call themselves internationalists, grounding much of their thought in the 1948 Universal Declaration of Human Rights, which guarantees everyone the right to a chosen nationality. Rosenberg continues:

> I see the world not only through North American eyes. And so I know, for example, that the people of South Africa are going to be free in my lifetime. And I know that when the people of South Africa are free, it's going to change the nature of the world.

These are views held by thousands of activists and thinkers across the country. Why, then, does the government consider these six people so threatening? Why has it set up a courtroom security system that will make a fair trial by jury all but impossible? And why is it bothering to subject prisoners with virtual life sentences (all but Berkman and Whitehorn already carry at least 45 years) to another four decades in prison?

"They want to make an example of us," answers Linda Evans, "by burying us in prison.... The fact that there are white people—women, lesbians—fighting against racism and fighting to fundamentally change the system is very threatening to them." Mary O'Melveny, attorney for Susan Rosenberg, agrees:

> I think this is a government that hasn't hesitated to strike out at people who it thinks have the potential to encourage people to join in... more than just the conventional picket signs.... Why subject Susan Rosenberg to another 40 years? Why [spend] the taxpayers' money—it's going to cost millions of dollars to try this case—why? To make a point. To make a point that says to people, "Shut up. And don't even consider stepping out of very narrow bounds of protest." That's what I think this case is all about.

According to O'Melveny, the government does not know who carried out the bombings, and has no evidence that any of the six were directly involved in them. Susan Rosenberg, in fact, states that she and other defendants were in prison at the time some of the bombings occurred. The defendants' direct guilt or innocence, then, appears immaterial to the government, which has constructed an indictment to convict the six on charges of aiding and abetting and of conspiracy "to influence, change, and protest policies and practices of the United States government... through the use of violent and illegal means."

These are alarmingly elastic charges, which define guilt for an illegal action as anything from directly participating in the action to simply being a member of a group that is accused of carrying it out. "Convictions on charges of conspiracy and of aiding and abetting, moreover, are often easy to obtain; once the prosecution establishes an accused's political sympathies, the charges can be proven on simple circumstantial evidence. Mary O'Melveny observes that the prosecution in this case need merely establish that, at different times in their lives, the defendants knew each other and held similar political objectives.

This criminalizing of association makes it difficult to protect defendants using their First Amendment right of free speech. "In other words," says Laura Whitehorn, "If you belong to such and such an organization, that means that you must have done these illegal acts.... It's no longer just a question of what you believe. It's not that different from McCarthyism."

If the government can convict the six, it could convict others on similar charges, simply because of what groups they may have joined in the past. Increasing numbers of people would be frightened to develop, let alone act on, progressive opinions, at seeing activists sentenced to years in prison.

Besides being a form of political control, prisons in the United States are used increasingly to warehouse unwanted segments of the population. The Bureau of Justice reported in April 1987 that prisoners in this country numbered 546,659. This is the largest prison population of any country in the world, and the figure is likely to double in the next decade to over one million. Five percent of U.S. prisoners are women, and about 80 percent are people of color—Blacks, Latinos, Native Americans—who, outside prison, comprise only 20 percent of the population. The imprisonment rate for Blacks alone is the highest in the world—twice the rate of Black imprisonment in South Africa.

It is now widely conceded that the purpose of prison is not rehabilitation but dehumanization. Prisoners incarcerated for social crimes are randomly brutalized as a matter of course; political prisoners are usually isolated from the general prison population and abused, explicitly because they hold progressive or leftist ideas. Like most prisoners, the majority of political prisoners and those who identify as prisoners of war are people of color.

As a rule, male prisoners are treated with more overt physical violence than female prisoners. Tim Blunk spent two years and Alan Berkman several months in the Marion high security prison for men. There, says Laura Whitehorn,

> ...the guards walk up and down the units, hitting their nightsticks against their hands, and if you refuse to obey a direct order... you get the shit beaten out of you.... They don't do that to women as much. But what they do against us is the threat of sexual attack.... By their rules, they are permitted to do just about anything to us. And so the number of rapes, which have not been "normal" rapes but rapes with a speculum or with a hand, searching for contraband, is a particularity toward women.

Susan Rosenberg and Alejandrina Torres, a Puerto Rican prisoner of war, were each raped in a Tucson prison by a male administrator, in the presence of female guards. Eve Rosahn, a paralegal at Prisoners' Legal Services of New York, states:

> The issue of privacy, of control, of having your will as a grown up human being taken away from you is really typical, partly of how all women prisoners are treated, and then when it's very focused in that way, how women political prisoners are treated.

Lesbians can experience an additional level of sexual degradation. Whitehorn recalls, "I was in Pleasanton, where the male pat-searches are a regular thing... and knowing they were going to look at me and say, 'This is a lesbian,' and be pat-searching me really gave me the roaring creeps."

Designated "special handling" by the Bureau of Prisons, both male and female political prisoners have been kept for years at a time in "lock down," a modified form of solitary confinement, by which they are isolated in tiny, often windowless cells, for 23 ½ hours each day. Prisoners are allowed out of their cells, in handcuffs and leg shackles, for one half-hour, to shower and make phone calls. All six Resistance Conspiracy defendants were locked down for months in the DC Detention Facility, until a recently successful campaign alleviated their conditions.

The Bureau of Prisons has gone to great lengths to rationalize its abusive "special handling" of leftist prisoners. Gilda Zwerman, associate professor at the State University of New York, cites "experts" who claim that conventional punishment for political prisoners is useless and may even reinforce their self-concept as "threats to the state." Since these prisoners do not respond to "normal treatment," officials reason, they must be incapacitated, their individual and political identities erased. By these neoconservative standards, notes Zwerman, in an article in *Social Justice*, women political prisoners are believed to be more dangerous than the men.

It is no accident, then, that the Bureau of Prisons has seen fit to build two high-security detention centers specifically for women. The Lexington High Security Unit (HSU) is now infamous. There, political prisoners Susan Rosenberg and Silvia Baraldini and prisoner of war Alejandrina Torres were intentionally placed in a state of almost infantile subservience.

As part of an experiment to observe long-term effects of sensory deprivation, fluorescent lights at the HSU were left on 24 hours a day, windows were covered, and cameras continuously surveyed the stagnant air conditioned cells. The women's actions and spoken words were written down by male guards, who also observed them taking showers and sitting on the toilet. Although designated "violence prone" by prison officials, and strip searched each time they re-entered the Unit, not one of those women was convicted of assaulting or injuring another person. The cost to taxpayers of keeping each of them in this concentrated misery was $55,000 a year.

Although the HSU was closed by judicial decree in July 1988, after an international protest that included the efforts of Amnesty International, its purpose will likely be carried on elsewhere. The Shawnee Unit at the Federal Correctional Institution in Marianna, Florida, has been opened recently for medium- to high-security women prisoners. So far, it has given every indication that it intends to duplicate, if not intensify, conditions at Lexington. If Buck, Rosenberg, and Whitehorn are convicted, speculates Mary O'Melveny, they will spend most of their sentence at Marianna, while Berkman and Blunk will be returned to Marion, which is under permanent lock down.

If these are the conditions under which political prisoners are sentenced to live for years of their lives, why is there not an outcry from feminist and progressive communities? One reason may be the fact that these six political prisoners, and others like them, support armed struggle as a people's right to resist oppression. This view is translated by the U.S. government to mean "terrorism." Says Marilyn Buck:

> The issue is resistance against an illegal government, against a government that is engaged in violence on such a grand scale that we could talk about it for years and not even go through all it's doing. And then look at the fact that... anyone who fights back is called a "terrorist."

Coming of age during the liberation movements of the '60s, the women in the Resistance Conspiracy case remain inspired by the activism of the women of Southeast Asia and the Black Power uprisings in the United States. Susan Rosenberg remembers:

> I saw the women of Vietnam rise up as part of their nation to say, "We're going to have our own destiny." I had never seen anything like that. And I wanted to be like that.

Yet there is something fundamentally shocking to the public about the image of a woman who picks up a gun to fight for her people. "I think the prospect of women fighting the system is particularly threatening," says Laura Whitehorn, "because they see what women have done for the struggles in all other countries. Until the majority of women are involved in a people's war or in a revolutionary movement, the movement doesn't have as much chance for success."

All six defendants criticize the United States' "antiterrorist" campaign, which, they say, holds the lopsided view that a few scattered revolutionaries are somehow more dangerous than a government possessing the world's largest nuclear arsenal. According to this stultifying mentality, they observe, homelessness, lack of money for AIDS research, the ruin of the ecosystem

Linda Evans (l) and Susie Day (© 2008 JEB (Joan E. Biren))

are not considered dangerous since they are not "violent." Anti-imperialist prisoners, on the other hand, deserve their sentences, since, by affirming armed struggle as one means of resistance, they have asked to be seen as terrorists. "The problem," says Linda Evans,

> ...is that I think our movement—and I include the women's movement—has been so influenced by government limitations, by our relative privilege in the world... that they're willing to allow the government to write people like us off from the movement that we've struggled as a part of for our whole lives.

Looking beyond the Resistance Conspiracy trial to other political cases, however, violence ceases to be the issue. Draft resisters, sanctuary workers, and Plowshares activists are now in U.S. prisons for nonviolent acts against the government. They have been given as long as 18 years behind bars, and their sentences are getting longer.

In the past eight years, the government has worked to insure that more and more people are seen as dangerous. Under the Reagan administration, there has been an escalation of grand jury investigations, in which progressives who refuse to testify are jailed, often for indeterminate lengths of time. The Congress has also passed a series of repressive laws, such as the Bail Reform Act of 1984, used to hold Laura Whitehorn; and the Racketeer Influenced and Corrupt Organizations (RICO) Law, used to indict Marilyn Buck and Mutulu Shakur and sentence them, respectively, to 50 and 60 years in prison. According to Gilda Zwerman's article, more than 150 activists in the Black liberation, Puerto Rican independence, and North American anti-imperialist movements were tried under these statutes and are now serving long sentences.

An astounding assault on civil liberties comes with the intensification of security initiatives by the Federal Emergency Management Agency (FEMA), whose plans, in the event of an "emergency," now include legal suspension of the Constitution; imposition of martial law on U.S. citizens; government censorship of the media; and—in a horrifying leap backwards—the establishment of detention camps for illegal "aliens," troublesome racial groups, and political dissidents. Again, the Oliver North case makes an ironic entrance: it was North and his colleagues who devised these plans.

Even more astounding is the fact that the public knows as little about these restrictive measures as it does about the growing number of political prisoners. (There are cases now being prosecuted that merit as much attention as the Resistance Conspiracy trial. The trial of the Puerto Rican 16, for example, begun in September 1988, in Hartford, Connecticut, involves a large number of videotapes illegally obtained by the FBI to prosecute a group of Puerto Rican *independentistas* on bank robbery charges. Another trial, begun in January 1989 in Springfield, Massachusetts, concerns three working-class people charged with politically motivated bombings.) The mainstream media, sensitive to government interests, chooses to keep virtually silent about political cases and the laws that will engender more prisoners. And political prisoners remain isolated, not only from human contact, but also from contact with the outside world.

Isolation, lethal because of its silence, may finally prove the most effective government weapon against individual will as well as political coalitions. In Part Three of *The Origin of Totalitarianism*, Hannah Arendt writes:

> It has frequently been observed that terror can rule absolutely only over [people] who are isolated from each other and that, therefore, one of the primary concerns of all tyrannical government is to bring this isolation about. Isolation may be the beginning of terror....

Meanwhile, the Resistance Conspiracy defendants await trial. If they were to recant their politics, name names, tell the government what, if anything, they know of other radical groups, would they be treated better, even, in Laura Whitehorn's case, released? "Oh, I bet, in a second," answers Whitehorn, "I mean, one of the things they hate about us is that they can't get any of us to turn even the littlest things."

Women of political conscience would do well to find out what lies behind such commitment. "Probably every single political prisoner in the United States has a history as an organizer in some movement or another, and would have a lot to offer the people," says Eve Rosahn. Susan Rosenberg was an acupuncturist in a Bronx hospital; Linda Evans was in a women's band and started a women's press collective in Texas; Marilyn Buck was among the first to introduce women's liberation into the SDS agenda; Laura Whitehorn helped start the Boston/Cambridge Women's School and was active in the John Brown Anti-Klan Committee. "These are people," reflects Mary O'Melveny, "with enormous skills and compassion and desires to help people." We have much to learn from them. And they need to hear from us.

Glasnost Abroad, Gulags at Home:
Political Prisoners in the U.S.

Matt Meyer
1990

"Jail is a kind of warehouse for the poor." So states the faded Peg Averill poster lining the walls of the War Resisters League's national office, along with our supply of antimilitary and antinuclear designs. In its history, WRL has had its share of imprisoned members, been involved in prisoner support, and called for the abolition of prisons.

But in recent years, prison issues do not often get introduced into our own analysis of domestic militarism, and the reality of political prisoners within the U.S. seems an even more distant concern. In 1989, some questioned WRL's endorsement of the new Freedom Now!! campaign, fighting for amnesty and the release of political prisoners in the U.S.

However, the imprisonment of Plowshares people has drawn many peace activists to greater understanding about prisons and the fate of political prisoners. Some Plowshares, such as Carl Kabat and Helen Woodson, received over ten-year sentences for throwing blood and hammering on nuclear missiles. While others have gotten lighter terms, it is clear that they are imprisoned for purely political actions. The Plowshares are actively involved in Freedom Now!; they find themselves working along with the many political prisoners whose horrifying conditions in prison must be brought to the attention of the wider movement and the public.

All Prisoners Are Political
Elmer Maas, one of the original Plowshares Eight, states that in the coming period "our consciousness has to be tuned to the very deep connections that exist between the various levels of potential violence, in the cafeteria of violence, that keeps a structure of imperial system intact."

"I'm very aware, being in jail, of the levels of injustice in this society that tend to result in a disproportionate and unfair singling out of the poor and people of color. Our national attitude towards crime, rather than bringing about justice, simply increases the level of injustice in our culture. Nothing is going to be solved by doubling the number of prisons; there is a sense in which everyone in prison is, to some degree, a political prisoner."

Reprinted from *Nonviolent Activist*, September 1990.

Katya Komisaruk served twenty-five months of a five-year sentence for her one-person Plowshares action at Vandenburg Air Force Base (California). Katya did define herself as a political prisoner, and she looks at defense of political prisoners as a key civil rights issue. "If the Gandhian-oriented peace activists say, 'We want civil rights for us, but we don't care so much about the civil rights for people engaged in militant activism,' then we kiss them goodbye. Then, when it is our turn next, the government has all the precedent to say, 'Well, we denied their rights, and now we're going to deny your rights.' When it comes to political prisoners, each of us is at risk," explains Katya.

Elmer Maas is reluctant to classify himself as a political prisoner, but he acknowledges that technically when one does an action in good conscience while maintaining that that action is "not criminal," there is a "certain sense" in which Plowshares prisoners are political prisoners. He distinguishes himself, however, from prisoners in the Black liberation or Puerto Rican independence movements, Maas sees these prisoners as "definitely political prisoners." Their sentences are so outrageous, and they often faced government campaigns such as the Counter Intelligence Program (COINTELPRO), specifically aimed at criminalizing a group because of its politics. Elmer added, "There are very strong linkages politically between movements that address injustice. That does not necessarily mean that everyone has the same philosophical or religious or spiritual starting point.... But there is a very broad spectrum of agreement that does address injustice and violence."

Freedom Now! (FN), the Campaign for Amnesty and Human Rights of Political Prisoners in the U.S., seeks to draw upon these linkages and build a support movement that will raise awareness about the over 100 political prisoners currently in U.S. jails. With the slogan, "Human Rights Must Begin at Home," Freedom Now! is developing an Urgent Action Network to respond to specific emergency legal and medical needs of the prisoners and has developed an international working group, which has brought the issue of U.S. political prisoners to the United Nations Commission on Human Rights in Geneva. Along with providing legal and political support, FN initiated an International Tribunal, to take place in New York City, on December 6-9, 1990, just following Human Rights Week.

One of the leading forces within Freedom Now! is the National Committee to Free Puerto Rican Prisoners of War. Committed to the independence of Puerto Rico, the National Committee defends those Puerto Ricans charged with "seditious conspiracy to overthrow the authority of the U.S. government" and related charges as heroes and patriots. Asserting that their nation is at war with the U.S., they conclude that they have the right to be tried by an international court and not by the courts of the U.S. or the colonial courts controlled by the U.S. Therefore, the *independentistas* have applied the term POW.

"As POW's, we represent the strategy that will liberate our people," states Lucy Rodríguez. "It is our responsibility, not only to the people of Puerto Rico, but to humanity as a whole that is struggling, to maintain our strength." And for their special political status, they have been given special treatment—and a special kind of repression. "In Alderson [federal women's prison in West Virginia], there was a prison within a prison—there was a unit specifically created to house us as Puerto Rican POW's... It is not accepted that we think for ourselves. When we reassert our political identity, the iron hand comes down."

Alejandrina Torres, though not convicted of any acts of violence or guilty of any "misconduct" while in prison, was sent to the Female High Security Unit commonly known as the Lexington Control Unit [Kentucky]. Along with political prisoners Silvia Baraldini and Susan Rosenberg, Alejandrina was subjected to small group isolation, sensory deprivation and daily strip searches. Once told to repeat the search she refused, and a male guard was called who handcuffed her and shoved her into a room with four other guards. "I felt a blow to my rib cage, and he forcefully pushed my face onto the floor, which caused tremendous pain, " she testifies. "I felt my legs being spread forcefully, my panties lowered, and the spread search consummated by his orders and in his presence, with total disregard for my continuous pleas."

Oscar López Rivera is housed at the infamous federal prison at Marion, which is on constant "lock down." After almost four years spent in isolation, López was due for transfer to a regular maximum security prison, but last June he was taken back into segregation, supposedly because a home-made knife was found in his cell. Actually, López is a danger to the system because his political spirits and ideals have not yet been broken. Writing from prison, he noted: "For Bush and his cohorts to have appropriated $25 billion for prison construction at a time when the same government claims that it has no money for housing for the homeless, for children's education or even for victims of natural disasters, is to make a very powerful and dangerous statement. It is telling this society that the gulags are fast becoming the final solution to the social ills that it is suffering.

Mumia Abu-Jamal is a former Black Panther Party member and activist with MOVE in Philadelphia. Despite a trial with many irregularities (i.e., the judge questioned character witness Sonia Sanchez, who had written a foreword to Assata Shakur's book, suggesting that Sanchez seemed "to get involved with people who were cop killers"), Abu-Jamal is currently on death row.

"Prisoners in America jeer at the rhetoric of liberty espoused by those who now applaud Eastern Europe's glasnost, for capital's elite guardian, the U.S. Supreme Court, has welded prison doors shut, blacked out and shuttered windows, closing off any 'opening,' any notion of the rights of free press, religion or civil rights....Indeed, in the late 1980s, the term 'prisoners' rights' became oxymoronic," concludes Mumia.

COINTELPRO Revisited

Abu-Jamal is one of dozens of political prisoners from the Black liberation/ New Afrikan independence movements. Including Geronimo ji-Jaga Pratt, Sekou Odinga, Abdul Majid and Bashir Hameed, the New York 3 and others, many Black prisoners are those who were involved in the Black Panther Party (BPP). Former Field Secretary of the New York BPP and political prisoner for nineteen years, Dhoruba al-Mujahid Bin-Wahad was released last spring after his conviction was overturned on the grounds that the prosecution had withheld crucial statements of key witnesses. The "dirty tricks" used to frame militant Black activists, however, should be of no surprise twenty years later, as full documentation of the illegal COINTELPRO operation has been described.

"The BPP principle," states Dhoruba, "that Black people had a right to defend themselves against white aggression was the idea that had to be destroyed….

"The white left of the Vietnam era did not fully appreciate that U.S. domestic policy informs U.S. foreign policy, that racism at home informs a racist foreign policy.

"The massive mobilizations to 'End The War' and 'Bring The Boys Home' didn't highlight the many parallels between the Vietnam War and the war on the Black community. The Phoenix program, which aimed at destroying the infrastructure of the national liberation movement in Vietnam, was an equivalent program to COINTELPRO, or the Houston plan, which aimed at destroying the infrastructure of the Black movement in the U.S. The Law Enforcement Assistance Act (LEAA) was created to militarize local police agencies, with trainings to put down domestic rebellions. Many who got LEAA training had taken one- to two-year leaves of absence to work in Phoenix."

Criticizing the antinuclear and solidarity movements for being too Eurocentric, Dhoruba asserts: "I seriously doubted that the white folks in Moscow were going to destroy the white folks in Washington, DC, based upon ideology, and thereby destroy their control over the world and the resources of the world, including the infrastructure that they've meticulously built up over the last 1100 years." One way of dealing with this Eurocentric attitude is to deal with issues that concern people of color, such as the issues of the prisoners. The anti-intervention movement, for example, with all its concern for sanctuary and refugees from abroad, is weaker because it hasn't clearly defined the terms of political imprisonment, or understood the importance of

Leonard Peltier

66

U.S.-based activists, fighting for their liberation, who have been "banned," killed or imprisoned. "Violation of human rights is a universal thing."

Probably the most universally recognized U.S. political prisoner, one who is charged with a violent crime and who was arrested fighting for the liberation of his people, is American Indian Movement leader Leonard Peltier. In jail for fourteen years, there have recently been some high-level discussions between Senator Daniel Inouye, attorney William Kunstler and State Department officials about a possible Presidential pardon for Peltier.

"Leonard is a symbol of the natural world in the indigenous community," noted Antonio Gonzales, Information Director of the International Indian Treaty Council. "He was defending indigenous people's ways of life, against the collusion of the U.S. government and the U.S. corporations to take uranium which was under the Pine Ridge reservation.... As Leonard is held prisoner, the natural world is held prisoner and North American people are also held prisoners behind an administration and a law enforcement that upholds itself on a double standard."

"The history of COINTELPRO," states Ingrid Washinawatok of the Indigenous Women's Network. "proves that it could be any one of us...but it's been Leonard, and that's a real heavy burden to carry. It's always on our minds—what could happen if we do any work for people's empowerment." Ingrid made clear that, in a sense, all Native Americans in U.S. society are prisoners—"where indigenous people feel trapped. The whole denial of our culture puts us in the prison of who we are, trying to survive in both worlds."

Defending All, Defending Ourselves

The fights for survival and cultural identity, for liberation and independence, for an end to racism and nuclear madness are some of the threads that unite these activists and political prisoners. Their resistance of not just the symptoms but the cause of what Elmer Maas called "this imperialist system" is what unites them in the Freedom Now! campaign and in their ongoing work.

Washington, DC, area WRL member Paul Magno, who is also active in the Catholic Worker and Plowshares communities, noted that "the government has initiated a struggle to ascribe the terrorist label to all resistance politics of the left, and significantly, away from itself while it develops more sophisticated forms of state terrorism under such policies as low-intensity conflict." Speaking of an increasing development of a political police force, Paul argues that it is urgent that we work together to fight against these state initiatives. The work in support of political prisoners is central to that fight.

As Dhoruba Bin-Wahad put it, "The issue of U.S. political prisoners is something that should cause us as conscientious and progressive people to question things on a very fundamental level. Because we are approaching a historical moment in time, we must realize that our ability to defend political prisoners is directly related to our ability to defend our movements and our rights in this country."

A Scientific Form of Genocide

Dr. Mutulu Shakur, Anthony X. Bradshaw, Malik Dinguswa, Terry D. Long,
Mark Cook, Adolfo Matos, James Haskins
1990

This is a research paper on genocide waged against the Black Nation through behavior modification in the United States penal system. It was initially drafted in December 1988 and distributed to several political prisoners in the state and federal prisons to encourage support and participation for an in-depth development of this issue for the Research Committee on International Law and Black Freedom Fighters in the United States for input to the human rights campaign.

This paper was developed by a team of Black prisoners who experienced behavior modification inside the prisons and who desire to expose the immediate but prolonged and historical effects of this government's efforts to control the Black Nation. We do not suggest that the techniques employed are exclusively implemented on the Black Nation, but there is no denying that the Black Nation is the government's paramount target.

Before going on we want to extend our thanks to our supporters and to those who have contributed to this paper because this paper was especially developed to bring about a broader unity on this issue so that we might collectively expose these human rights violations to the world through the human rights conference of non-governmental organizations in Zurich, Switzerland.

We specifically charge that the government of the United States is practicing genocide through behavior modification and counterinsurgency and low-intensity warfare techniques

Presented for Consideration by the Research Committee on International Law and Black Freedom Fighters in the United States. The original full title of this document was "Genocide Waged Against the Black Nation Through Behavior Modification Orchestrated by Counterinsurgency and Low-Intensity Warfare in the U.S. Penal System."

in its penal system, i.e., the state and federal prisons.

We submit that behavior modification as practiced in United States prisons incorporates techniques from both counterinsurgency—low-intensity warfare and the science of psychology in the interest of political and military objectives. The implementation of this strategy in the United States penal system is the result of research conducted by government scientists and counterinsurgency agents who studied the theories and works of past experts in the distinct fields of behavior therapy (synonymous with behavior modification), insurgency, and low-intensity warfare.

Every aspect of this behavior modification program violates the human rights of those persons subjected to it and it is this treatment that is vehemently complained about by political prisoners and POW's. This program involves a scientific approach in targeting special prisoners with the aim of achieving political objectives. Each targeted prisoner is observed to determine his or her leadership potential, religious beliefs, aspirations, and most importantly, to record his or her reaction to the experiments being implemented. The sole purpose of the program is for government agents to learn lessons from experimenting with political prisoners, how they suffered and reacted, then use those findings to formulate a broad plan to be implemented against the people in society at large who are the ultimate targets.

The oppressive conditions and the experiments conducted in the United States penal system, as implemented by this government through prison officials, are the evidence of a psychological war being waged against political prisoners* who come from a people who are involved in a struggle of resistance against oppression in all forms. When the behavior modification program conducted by the government is viewed in the light of the mandates contained in the "Geneva Accord," one can only conclude that the United States Government's actions are criminal and specifically violate the international laws concerning the rights of human beings. Accordingly, the United States Government's acts should be regarded as war crimes.

Specifically, the U.S. Government is in violation of Article I of the Geneva Convention on the prevention and punishment of the crime of genocide, which was approved by the United Nations General Assembly on December 9, 1948, and the U.S. Government is in violation of resolution 260, III, which entered into force on January 12, 1951. In this resolution, "the contracting parties confirmed that genocide, whether committed in time of peace or in time of war, is a crime under international law which they undertake to prevent and punish." According to Article II, genocide is defined as any of the following

---

* When the term "political prisoner" is used in this paper, it is not limited to those who are incarcerated as a result of their political beliefs, actions, or affiliations. The term includes persons in prison for social crimes who became politicized inside prison walls and who oriented their lives around the struggle for social justice and national liberation. Such persons as Malcolm X, George Jackson, the Attica Warriors, and the many other men and women of yesterday and today's struggle would be and are encompassed in the term.

acts committed with the intent to destroy, in whole or in part, a national, ethnical, racial, or religious group; such as:

    (a) Killing members of the group;
    (b) Causing serious bodily or mental harm to members of the group;
    (c) Deliberately inflicting on the group conditions of life calculated to bring about its destruction in whole or in part;
    (d) Imposing measures intended to prevent births within the group;
    (e) Forcibly transferring children of the group to another group.

The Law of Nations, ed. Herbert W. Briggs

Subsequent to having reviewed the above list of acts that constitute the crime of genocide, as set forth by the Geneva Convention, we submit that the behavior modification program being carried out in the United States penal system is a scientific form of genocide waged against the Black Nation, and it is a continuance of the nefarious tactics employed by the government over the years to keep the Black Nation subjugated.

On learning of the use of behavior modification techniques in furtherance of counterinsurgency and low-intensity warfare objectives, especially in light of the government's intended broad application, all caring people in any society should be shocked.

The Theory and Practice of Behavior Modification

Behavior modification is a highly complex science composed of information from various sciences such as psychology, sociology, philosophy, anthropology, and even some aspects of biology. By definition, "behavior modification" broadly refers to the systematic manipulation of one's environment for the purpose of creating a change in the individual's behavior.

It involves a "systematic effort to influence the frequency, intensity, and duration of specified target behavior." (From notes of Michael S. Rubin that appeared in the *Arizona Law Review*, Vol. 18.)

During our research, we discovered that the behavior scientists and counterinsurgency agents of the government learned many of their tactics from studying the works of John B. Watson and B. F. Skinner, two United States psychologists who are leading authorities in the field of behavior modification.* We have also learned that there are three basic types of behavior modification techniques recognized today—operant conditioning, classical conditioning, and aversion therapy.

---

* John B. Watson was the founder of behaviorism in the United States in the early 1900s. He rejected mentalism and introspection and advocated a purely objective psychology...
B. F. Skinner was a pivotal figure in psychological behaviorism. Much of his work has centered on the process of operant conditioning.

Operant Conditioning

Operant conditioning is based largely on the work of B. F. Skinner and involves the presentation of a reinforcer, usually called a reward, upon the production of a desirable behavior in order to increase the probability that the particular behavior will be repeated. A classic example of operant conditioning is that of a rat being trained to depress a lever in his cage that releases food pellets. A reinforcer, such as the food pellet, is something that increases the rate of the behavior. (See Durland's *Illustrated Medical Dictionary*, 25th edition, 1938).

Classical Conditioning

Classical conditioning utilizes a stimulus to elicit an involuntary response or a reflex. At the beginning of the program, an "unconditioned" stimulus, such as food, is employed to elicit the reflex, such as salivation. A second stimulus, which by itself would not produce the involuntary or unconditioned response, is paired with the unconditioned stimulus. After continued pairing of unconditioned and conditioned stimuli, the same response is obtained from the presentation of the neutral stimulus—as was produced by the unconditioned stimulus. Thus, Pavlov in his now famous experiments was able to elicit a dog's salivation upon the hearing of a bell by the repeated pairing of the sound of the bell—conditioned stimulus—with the presentation of food—unconditioned stimulus.*

Aversion Therapy

Aversion therapy has been defined as an attempt to associate an undesirable behavior pattern with unpleasant stimulation or to make the unpleasant stimulation a consequence of the undesirable behavior. In either case it is hoped that an acquired connection between the behavior and the unpleasantness will develop. There is further hope that the development of such a connection will be followed by a cessation of the target behavior. (See S. Rachman and J. Teasdale, *Aversion Therapy and Behavior Disorders*.)

Even though all three of the above techniques are used by prison officials in the United States penal system, aversion therapy seems to be the most preferred technique used in connection with counterinsurgency and low-intensity warfare. Many behavior therapists have confirmed that there are many adverse side effects associated with aversion therapy, e.g., pain, frustration, increased aggressiveness, arousal, general and specific anxieties, somatic and physiological malfunctions, and development of various unexpected and often pathological operant behaviors. (See F. Kanfer and J. Phillips, *Learning Foundation of Behavior Therapy*.)

For the most part, we should not overlook the fact that all behavior modification techniques are intrusive to the individual, whether the effects of the behavior modification experiment are felt physically or psychologically. In

---

* See G. Kimble and N. Garmezy, *Principles of General Psychology*, 1968.

short, individuals in the experiment are subjected to the tampering with their mind, or their body, or both.

As history shows us, behavior modification is no new phenomenon in the United States penal system. However, in earlier years prison officials used more of a "hands-on" approach in manipulating prisoners' behavior. During our investigation of the past experiences of many prisoners and ex-prisoners, we learned that in earlier years those persons who resisted the oppressive measures perpetrated by prison officials, or those persons who complained of oppressive conditions, or those persons who were labeled incorrigibles were arbitrarily confined to mental wards inside the prison, or transferred to mental institutions for the criminally insane where they experienced the severe effects of mind-altering drugs, electric shock treatment, or psychosurgery, which were the ultimate weapons used by prison officials in carrying out their behavior modification strategy.

However, these measures had proved to be virtually ineffective in the United States penal system by the end of the '60s or early '70s as prison demonstrations and uprisings occurred in rapid succession throughout the United States and coincided with the liberation movement happening outside prison walls. Accordingly, the government became concerned about group control inside the prisons, and to address this concern the government resorted to the use of psychological warfare. Consequently, prisoners of strong religious and cultural beliefs who had organized prisoners to resist and those prisoners who put up independent resistance were singled out and met with extreme oppression as the targets of experimental behavior modification.*

We submit that Black people were in fact the first experimental targets of group behavior modification. Furthermore, current data and statistics on the prison situation support our contention that Black people inside the state and federal prisons today remain the prime targets of the government's program.

Moreover, we discovered during our research that the psychological warfare being waged in the U.S. penal system was planned as far back as the early '60s

Source: Prison News Service

---

* We want to emphasize that prisoners who resist outside of an organization framework are expressing dissatisfaction with the social situation although their expressed reason for having done so does not include the use of terms commonly articulated by a conscious resister.
As one writer stated while addressing this issue, "criminality itself is a form of unconscious protest, reflecting the distortions of an imperfect society, and in a revolutionary situation, the criminal, the psychopath, may become as good a revolutionary as the idealist." (See *War of the Flea*, p.113, by R. Tabor).

because the government foresaw that Black people would revolt against being oppressed, even in prison. Black people's conduct, like that of many people throughout history, validates the axiom that "oppression breeds resistance."

Significantly, in 1961 a social scientist named Dr. Edward Schein presented his ideas on brainwashing at a meeting held in Washington, DC, that was convened by James V. Bennett, then director of the Federal Bureau of Prisons Systems, and was attended by numerous social scientists and prison wardens.* Dr. Schein suggested to the wardens that brainwashing techniques were natural for use in their institutions. In his address on the topic "Man Against Man," he explained that in order to produce marked changes of behavior and/or attitude it is necessary to weaken, undermine, or remove the supports of old patterns of behavior and old attitudes. "Because most of these supports are the face-to-face confirmation of present behavior and attitudes, which are provided by those with whom close emotional ties exist." This can be done by either "removing the individual physically and preventing any communication with those whom he cares about, or by proving to him that those whom he respects are not worthy of it, and indeed should be actively mistrusted." Dr. Schein then provided the group with a list of specific examples such as:

1. Physical removal of prisoners to areas sufficiently isolated to effectively break or seriously weaken close emotional ties.
2. Segregation of all natural leaders.
3. Use of cooperative prisoners as leaders.
4. Prohibition of group activities not in the line with brainwashing objectives.
5. Spying on the prisoners and reporting back private material.
6. Tricking men into written statements which are then shown to others.
7. Exploitation of opportunists and informers.
8. Convincing the prisoners that they can trust no one.
9. Treating those who are willing to collaborate in far more lenient ways than those who are not.
10. Punishing those who show uncooperative attitudes.
11. Systematic withholding of mail.
12. Preventing contact with anyone nonsympathetic to the method of treatment and regimen of the captive populace.
13. Building a group conviction among the prisoners that they have been abandoned by and totally isolated from the social order.
14. Disorganization of all group standards among the prisoners.
15. Undermining of all emotional supports.

* Information concerning that historic meeting was found in the *The Mind Manipulators* by Alan W. Scheflin (see Library of Congress cataloging-in-publication data); additional information was found in a pamphlet on "Breaking Men's Minds," behavior control in Marion, Illinois.

16. Preventing prisoners from writing home or to friends in the community regarding the conditions of their confinement.
17. Making available and permitting access to only those publications and books that contain materials which are neutral to or supportive of the desired new attitudes.
18. Placing individuals into new and ambiguous situations for which the standards are kept deliberately unclear and then putting pressure on them to conform to what is desired in order to win favor and a reprieve from the pressure.
19. Placing individuals whose willpower has been severely weakened or eroded into a living situation with several others who are more advanced in their thought reform and whose job it is to further the undermining of the individuals' emotional supports which were begun by isolating them from family and friends.
20. Using techniques of character invalidation, e.g., humiliations, revilement, shouting to induce feelings of guilt, fear and suggestibility, coupled with sleeplessness, an exacting prison regimen and periodic interrogational interviews.
21. Meeting all insincere attempts to comply with cellmates' pressures with renewed hostility.
22. Repeated pointing out to prisoner by cellmates of where he was in the past, or is in the present, not even living up to his own standards or values.
23. Rewarding of submission and subservience to the attitudes encompassing the brainwashing objective with a lifting of pressure and acceptance as a human being.
24. Providing social emotional supports which reinforce the new attitudes.

Following Dr. Schein's address, James Bennett commented, "We can perhaps undertake some of the techniques Dr. Schein discussed and do things on your own. Undertake a little experiment with what you can do with the Muslims. There is a lot of research to do. Do it as groups and let us know the results."

Approximately 11 years after that historical meeting, it was confirmed that Dr. Schein's ideas and objectives were in fact being implemented inside the prisons. In July 1972, the Federal Prisoners' Coalition, in a petition to the United Nations Economic and Social Council, asserted that the Asklepieion program conducted at the Marion, Illinois, federal penitentiary was directly modeled on Chinese methods of thought reform. The petition contains a point-by-point comparison between Dr. Schein's address and the written description of the goals and structure of the Asklepieion program. (See *The Mind Manipulators* by Alan W. Scheflin.)

Although the tactics introduced by Dr. Schein when viewed individually may not necessarily shock the conscience of society, the tactics, when executed singularly or in total, are nevertheless very deleterious to those persons subjected to them. We charge that the execution of the tactics are a violation of the prisoner-victim's human rights, violations which are prohibited under international law.

Many writers today who have done articles on prison behavior modification usually leave their readers with the inaccurate impression that the experiments are only implemented in isolated units of a prison. The writers usually mention the infamous control unit at the U.S. Penitentiary located at Marion, Illinois, as a prime example. However, we want to make it very clear that the experiments are conducted nationwide and that there is close collaboration between the state and federal prison systems. Moreover, the results obtained from having conducted these experiments are used by government agents to formulate a broader plan that will be implemented against people in society at large. One of the objectives of the broader plan is altering the behavior of young people by creating conditions and situations that incline them in the direction of deviant and self-destructive behavior and that derail them from a course which would incline them to resist being oppressed.*

Subsequent to having examined B. F. Skinner's analysis of behavior, one would readily conclude that United States penologists heavily borrowed information from Skinner's works in formulating their behavior modification program and in devising its specific techniques. In his book, *Beyond Freedom and Dignity*, Skinner explains that "a culture is very much like the experimental space used in the analysis of behavior. Both are sets of contingencies reinforcement. A child is born into a culture as an organism is placed in an experimental space. Designing a culture is like designing an experiment; contingencies are arranged and effects noted. In an experiment we are interested in what happens, in designing a culture with whether it will work. This is the difference between science and technology."

In unequivocal terms, Skinner's theory relates to a prison environment and society at large. If we imagine a prisoner replacing the child in the situations spoken of above and imagine a prison as the experimental space, then one can clearly see that the experiments carried out inside prisons are done with the experimenters having in mind the ultimate objective of altering the culture of an entire people. The placing of a person in a designed situation for the purpose of tearing him or her down then rebuilding him or her according to the specification of an alien group is a clear act of genocide.

As Black psychologist Bobby E. Wright perfectly stated in his view of Skinner's theory, "any Black with a cursory knowledge of B. F. Skinner's experimental analysis of behavior should recognize its potential danger to our community, where every institution is under the control of the White race." (See *Black Suicide*, by Bobby E. Wright, Ph.D., 1980).

---

* Many behavior scientists will attest to the fact that situations can be contrived in such a manner that they will influence people to engage in self-destructive behavior. Therefore, the U.S. Government must be held accountable for contributing to the behavior of the oppressed.

We want to emphasize that it would be very difficult for a Black psychologist or any other psychologist not to draw a parallel between Skinner's theory and Dr. Schein's objectives as it pertains to the agenda implemented against the Black Nation.

Nevertheless, in further discussion of the many tactics implemented under this behavior modification program, we should not overlook the fact that prison officials will use drugs as a method of control. In fact, we have discovered that most of the drugs used by prison officials today are far more detrimental in their relative potency than those used in earlier years.* It is not unusual inside the prisons today to see prisoners exhibiting "Zombie-like behavior" as a result of the type of drugs administered to them against or with their consent. In many prisons it is a prerequisite for some prisoners to take certain prescribed drugs in order to be released from solitary confinement. There are several courts that support the forcible use of drugs by prison officials, thus leaving the way open for the use of drugs as a hands-on tactic.

In a recent tour of the Soviet mental institutions by the American Psychiatric Association, which included numerous interviews with detainees, it was found that most of those being detained were for political reasons and that they were being administered psychotropic drugs as part of a clear program to neutralize political dissent. Furthermore, it was reported that Soviet doctors still use the "broad brush diagnosis schizophrenic" to lock people up.

The "broad brush diagnosis schizophrenic," which is still commonly used in America, is a smoke screen appellation used in the government's political-military strategy to contain and isolate individuals perceived to be a potential threat to the status quo.

The APA specifically alleged that patients are treated with massive doses of pain-causing psychotropic drugs that Western doctors consider to have no medical value. This position gives rise to the very serious question of the intent of the APA, especially when the light is cast on the empirical investigation of the value and efficiency of the drugs. (See *New York Times* article, March 3, 1989, which is an exhibit in support of the above.)

We submit that the APA tour to and reported findings about Soviet institutions clearly represent the height of hypocrisy on the part of the United States Government, because we make the same contentions about the practices in the United States penal system that the APA alleges with respect to the Soviet Union. If the past and present tactics implemented in the United States penal system are not acknowledged, and the objectives clearly recognized

---

* The drug thorazine (chlorpromazine) was the first antischizophrenia drug used in the United States and was generally given to prisoners in earlier years. This drug clearly produces a "Zombie-like behavior" in the individual. Furthermore, it is used as the standard against which the newer drugs are compared. (See *Multimodal Behavior Therapy*, by Arnold A. Lazarus.) Although, thorazine is still being used by prison officials today, new drugs called prolixin (fluphenazine) and haldol (haloperidol) are more preferably prescribed. Prolixin has a relative milligram potency of 70:1 to thorazine, and haldol has a potency of 100:1 to thorazine. Both drugs produce drastic mental and physical side effects.

and understood, then we simply make way for these abuses to continue in the future, thereby, furthering the program of genocide.

It is our position that whether or not one's response is a shocked conscience on learning of the behavior modification experiments, one should not consider the measure of one's feelings as the acid test in deciding that the experimenters have exceeded the legal criterion of what constitutes violative practices. One should merely bear in mind that the behavior modification experiments are conducted to achieve nefarious counterinsurgency and low-intensity warfare objectives. Nevertheless, the judicial branch of government continues to support the daily abuses arising out of the behavior modification program carried out in the United States penal system by not intervening to order the executive branch to cease their deleterious program and practices.

Moreover, many of the programs carried out by the Reagan administration and continued by the Bush administration that focus on the suppression of the Black Nation would immediately be condemned were they exposed to public scrutiny. Of course, one such program that would meet with public condemnation if it were given wide public exposure is the behavior modification program under discussion.

The Use of Behavior Modification to Achieve
Counterinsurgency and Low-Intensity Warfare Objectives
Counterinsurgency tactics are the political-military actions undertaken to forestall the inevitable fire of resistance before it is strikingly manifested. Of course, the use of such tactics demonstrates a clear recognition on the part of those governing the state that unjust conditions exist and will continue to exist into the foreseeable future. Additionally, once resistance has been manifested, counterinsurgency tactics are used to effectively destroy it.

Low-intensity warfare involves the use of political-military strategy to achieve political, social, economic, and psychological objectives. Such wars are often of a protracted nature and many of the major battles are fought in the diplomatic, economic, and social arenas in an effort to apply psychobiological pressure on the resisters. Equally important is the fact that low-intensity wars have as their main features the constraint on weaponry used and the intermittent eruptions of violence. Accordingly, low-intensity warfare is suited for the use of subtle and sophisticated techniques. The use of such techniques is aimed at keeping the conflict disguised (e.g., using such techniques enables the state authorities to label a military action a police action), preventing scrutiny by relevant in-country and out-of-country parties, and preventing the introduction into the conflict of international standards governing warfare and/or acts of genocide.

During our research we discovered that the application of counterinsurgency and low-intensity warfare techniques in the United States is derived from the strategies formulated by Frank Kitson and Robin Evelegh.

The government has effectively managed to pursue this two-track strategy through the military, law enforcement agencies, and prison officials.*

It is our contention that judging by all the standards of what constitutes a low-intensity war, we, the rising Black Nation, are in fact the targeted insurgents in the United States, because our people have not been standing still in response to the permanent oppression perpetrated against us by the government. Moreover, we should not forget the infamous J. E. Hoover's COINTELPRO of the 60s era during which time he directed counterinsurgency measures against the "Black Nationalist Movement" to prevent the rise of a "Mau Mau"-like group and to prevent the ascent of a "Black Messiah." The diction contained in the above-quoted passages were taken from documents detailing Hoover's plan and serves as unequivocal testimony that the government formed its strategy against the Black Nation after having read about Kitson's experience, particularly in Kenya, fighting the "Mau Mau" and after having read about Kitson's use of gangs and counter gangs. Specifically, Hoover's cointel program contained the following five objectives:

1. To prevent the coalition of militant Black Nationalist groups, which might be the first step toward a real "Mau Mau" in America.
2. To prevent the rise of a "Messiah" who could unify and electrify the movement.
3. To prevent violence on the part of Black Nationalist groups by pinpointing potential trouble makers and neutralizing them before they exercise their potential violence.
4. To prevent groups and leaders from gaining respectability by discrediting them to the responsible Negro community, to the White community (both the responsible community and the liberals—the distinction is the Bureau's), and to Negro radicals.
5. To prevent the long-range growth of these organizations, especially among the youth, by developing specific tactics to prevent those groups from recruiting young people.

Political Legacy of Malcolm X, Oba T. Shaka, pp. 225-26

---

* Frank Kitson was the commander of the British counterinsurgency force in Northern Ireland for many years, and before that he was an officer in many of Britain's lost colonial wars, e.g., Kenya, Aden and Cyprus. Most of his examples of low-intensity operations are drawn from Britain's war in Ireland and the U.S. war in Indochina. One of his strategic techniques was the use of gangs. The rise of gangs in the oppressed communities in America partially reflects the successful use of his strategy by past administrations. The corollary to the use of gangs is the emergence of an increasing clamor for law and order. Kitson's book, which is entitled *Low-Intensity Operations* (1971), is the basic manual of counterinsurgency methods used in Western Europe and North America. Robin Evelegh has written a book that forms the basis of the revised British strategy used in Ireland. His approach is also widely favored by the secret police in the United States. However, Evelegh's suggested methods for smothering an insurrection are presently being hotly debated in ruling-class circles. (See Evelegh's *Peace Keeping in a Democratic Society: The Lessons of Northern Ireland* (1978))

Even the Church committee report on urban unrest in the '60s era labeled the participants, the disenfranchised who took part in the riots, rebellions, and skirmishes, as insurgents. It should be remembered that the urban unrest and Church's labeling of those who participated as insurgents occurred during the developments of the Black Liberation Movement. Many of the people of that period who participated in the struggle on various levels became social prisoners, political prisoners, and prisoner of war.* However, it should be pointed out that in many cases those who were imprisoned were jailed as a result of tactical maneuvers carried out by the government in their effort to suppress the resistance of the people in society at large. As one prisoner of war stated, "Prisons are a fundamental pillar of state power. Their main function is the suppression of all internal threats to the State." (See *Sun Views* by Sundiata Acoli.) The implementing of counterinsurgency and low-intensity warfare through behavior modification is geared to destroy the captive Black Nation.

Over the years we have seen many of our brothers and sisters in the struggle placed in prison for their political beliefs and affiliations. These imprisonments resulted from a wicked conspiracy perpetrated by this government through their law enforcement agents and agencies. All this was done for the purpose of suppressing the liberation movement of Black people. We have also seen our people assassinated for the same reasons.

We submit that the captured Black Nation was, and remains, a prime target of the government's strategy of behavior modification counterinsurgency and low-intensity warfare. The evidence of the implementing of the government's strategy is evinced by the exceptionally harsh treatment inflicted on Black prisoners in the United States penal system—especially those prisoners who are committed to the Black Liberation Movement—the struggle for self-determination.

We want to point out, and it is important to understand the fact that the prisons in the United States have always been operated primarily by White administrators and supplied with predominantly White prison guards. This combination of factors renders the Black prisoner excessively vulnerable to and a prime target of unbridled racism and brutality. In addition, there is the fact that the government itself is deeply rooted in racism.

Also, we must not overlook the fact that there are prisoners from other oppressed Nations inside the United States and from the Caribbean Islands who, as they fight for their national liberation, are also targeted by this government's strategy of counterinsurgency and low-intensity warfare. One indication of the commitment and determination possessed by these brothers is reflected by the fact of the many political prisoners and POW's from their struggles locked inside the bowels of the United States penal system.

---

* A committee chaired by Senator Frank Church made an overall evaluation of the riots and rebellion that swept the United States during the development of the Liberation Movement in the '60s era.

The Puerto Rican National Liberation Movement in Puerto Rico and in the United States of America has been a prime target of the United States Government, and the government has used the most severe tactics of counterinsurgency and low-intensity warfare against them for a half century or more. Since United States troops invaded the island in 1898, the people have used every method within their reach to terminate the colonial-type structure designed and imposed on them by the colonizers, specifically the United States Congress.

Again the United States has violated the most basic principles of a people. The United States is cognizant of its wrongfulness and it is aware that people of the world, airing their views through their representatives in the United Nations General Assembly, side with the struggling Puerto Rican people. In fact, "The General Assembly... reaffirms the legitimacy of the people's struggle for liberation from colonial and foreign domination and alien subjugation by all available means, including armed struggle."*

The American government has assassinated certain members of the Puerto Rican Movement; it has tortured and maimed political prisoners; it has used frame-ups resulting in imprisonment; it has transferred the Puerto Rican leadership from the Island of Puerto Rico to prisons deep inside the continent of the United States. Thus, denying the leadership the opportunity for community with persons in the ongoing movement.†

An example of United States imperialism and the United States efforts to control and alter the behavior of people resisting oppression becomes startlingly clear when we observe the handling of Black and Latin freedom fighters from the Caribbean Islands who are incarcerated inside the U.S. penal system. Many of these prisoners are politically opposed to the "puppet regimes in their Caribbean Islands that America controls."

Consequently, these dissident prisoners also become targets of the government's counterinsurgency and low-intensity warfare.

It should also be understood that because of the geo-political and economic objectives the United States is carrying out in these underdeveloped and developing nations, many social crimes are committed on these islands and these crimes are a direct result of America's intervention. After arriving on United States soil, though, the prisoners from the Caribbean Islands become socially, politically, and culturally active in the United States prison system and their experiences incline them to create unbreakable bonds between

---

* See U.N. General Assembly Resolution 3030 [xxviii].

† Again, the U.S. Government is clearly violating international standards by transferring Puerto Rican and Caribbean political prisoners into prisons deep inside the United States. The United Nations has established clear provisions against this sort of practice. On March 3, 1989, the U.N. General Assembly passed into effect resolution 43/173, which is called, "Body of principles for the protection of all persons under any form of detention or imprisonment." Under its listing of principles, specifically U.N. resolution 43/173, principle 20, the following is stated: "If a detained or imprisoned person so requests, he shall, if possible, be kept in a place of detention or imprisonment reasonably near his usual place of residence."

themselves and the other Black freedom fighters inside the United States.

To fully appreciate the overall effect of behavior modification and low-intensity warfare on those prisoners subjected to it, more research will have to be done. But we feel that it is safe to say, in view of the incarceration of freedom fighters from the Caribbean in the United States prison system, which results in their political and cultural isolation, that they are very, very much enmeshed in the United States Government's counterinsurgency, low-intensity warfare, and behavior modification programs.*

When White Anti-Imperialists Participate in the Resistance
The mentioning of Blacks from the United States continent and the Caribbean Islands, the mentioning of Puerto Ricans from the United States and from the Island of Puerto Rico—all of whom are freedom fighters of color, gives rise to the question: are White anti-imperialist prisoners also targeted by the government's programs?

When White anti-imperialists are charged and brought before judicial tribunals, many American judicial members suggest that because the White anti-imperialists are not victims of oppression, they have no justification for participating in the resistance. This position is clearly a nullification of the "Nuremberg principle."

Furthermore, we submit that it is natural for a caring human being to sympathize with, support, or align with those who resist being oppressed. However, when the White anti-imperialists do get involved in the resistance and are thereafter placed in prison because this government is deeply rooted in racism and feels compelled to discourage Whites from aligning themselves with Blacks, the treatment inflicted on anti-imperialists are just as severe as that meted out to Blacks and the treatment is sometimes exceptionally cruel. These tactics are aimed at sending the message to North American Whites to stay clear of the struggle.

But the strategy goes further than merely preventing Whites from entering the struggle. The government is concerned with determining why this phenomenon exists, and in altering the behavior patterns of captured White anti-imperialists. The government seeks thereby to achieve one prong of their multiprong objectives by preventing the growth of the ranks of White people who fight against oppression.

Another tactic used by this government that we must not overlook and that we have seen used in most of the liberation movements is the imprisonment and the inflicting of harsh treatment on grand jury resisters. These comrades are clearly not guilty of or even charged with any crime. These comrades are

---

* The exploitative and brutal control the United States wields over the Caribbean Islands is evinced by the cowardly attack on Grenada, the intervention in Manley's government during the election in Jamaica, and the continual colonization of the Virgin Islands. One salient consequence of the U.S. exploitative and brutal control over the Caribbean is the major influx of Rastafarian and progressive prisoners from the Islands into the United States penal system.

incarcerated because they refuse to violate their principles that prohibit them from collaborating with the government. On this issue, like we have done at the close of other issues discussed in this paper, we charge the United States Government with violating accepted international standards.*

Many times grand jury resisters are not members of a particular movement. They are usually the friends or relatives of the revolutionary who is being inquired about or they are sympathizers of the cause. So their imprisonment is clearly a tactic designed to intimidate. Moreover, what we see here is another aspect of the counterinsurgency strategy that encompasses the objectives of determining the resisters' leadership capabilities and level of political development and dedication. All the obtained information is essential to the government for use in conducting counterinsurgency operations.

In short, grand jury resisters are given a subpoena, are thrown into jails and prisons, and are subjected to psychological and emotional distress... all this is done in order to facilitate the breaking of the mind of the revolutionary inquired about and to suppress the movement. For the government to execute all the above-mentioned measures actually consummates the marriage between behavior modification and counterinsurgency low-intensity warfare.

What really needs to be considered and is truly of paramount importance, is the totally licentious fashion [in which] the United States Government officials so effectively utilize their penal system as the primary tool in repressing and crushing all dissent, mercilessly destroying the minds of countless people, and their souls, after a slow death, are offered on the altar of "real politic."

To examine this question in its proper context, we must first of all endeavor to understand the actual mechanism that the state employs to achieve its nefarious ends.

We submit that, first of all, the science of politics is not truly grounded in morality. Political scientists and politicians in general simply utilize a lot of false laudatory moralizing to build a convenient facade behind which to cleverly conceal their real designs.

In the politician-oppressor's dealings with the oppressed, when the question is raised regarding what guiding precept to embrace, morality loses out to expediency, doing that which, not surprisingly, conforms to the cynical spirit of Machiavelli. History speaks all too clearly in confirmation of this.

So, it is against the backdrop of these brutal realities that we examine the question of imprisonment in general and isolation and sensory deprivation

---

* By the American government taking punitive measures against grand jury resisters, it violates accepted standards that were enacted prohibiting the use of such measures. On March 19, 1989, the United Nations General Assembly passed into effect resolution 43/173, entitled "Body of Principles" for the protection of all persons under any form of detention or imprisonment. Under its listing of principles, U.N. resolution (A/Res/43/1 73), principle 21, number 1, the following is stated: It shall be prohibited to take undue advantage of the situation of a detained or imprisoned person for the purpose of compelling him to confess, to incriminate himself otherwise or to testify against any other person.

in particular. What are isolation and sensory deprivation, and how do they impact upon its victimized subjects?

This is a deep question that encompasses very subtle and deep emotional, psychological, and physiological realities.

We charge that at present, and for some time now, there is and has been a very clear and systematic program of low-intensity warfare perpetually in motion in the prisons across America. Also, this program, brutally alive and well, is no mere accident, no loosely controlled haphazard affair. No, it is part of a precise, coordinated, careful, well-thought-out program that embraces the most scientific and subtle techniques of brainwashing, of psychological infiltration, of menticide. It is a program for the ruthless manipulation of people's minds for forcing them to conform with scientific and archetypal patterns of broken subjects.* Their scientists have very meticulously worked out the intricate details of this practice through experimentation, deduction, and inference.

They have worked out the details on how to create a controlled environment, on how to impregnate the environment with certain subtle messages in order to trigger certain thoughts and behavior patterns in their controlled subjects, all based upon their knowledge of the laws of the workings of the mind.

Isolation and sensory deprivation as they are practiced in the Auschwitzes and Dachaus scattered across America are a definite aspect of the oppressor's controlled environment. They know that through isolation, through the systematic removal, inclusion, or manipulation of key sensory stimuli they can attack a prisoner's mind and reduce him or her to a warped, subservient state characterized by feelings of lethargy, listlessness and hopelessness... in short, a prisoner develops the feeling of being more dead than alive.†

They combine the practice of tampering with sensory stimuli with a deficient diet, a diet lacking key nutrients indispensable to the proper functioning of a well-integrated personality. The diet consists of meals that have acceptable appearances, but are nutritiously deficient, and after having eaten a few meals one finds oneself getting hungrier and feeling lethargic. Being on such a diet promotes depression and ultimately gives rise to thoughts of self-destruction. All of this is intentional and all of this is based upon a very clear, scientific program, one of the best programs their "think tanks" could devise. On this, as in all other areas, they know exactly what they are doing;

---

* Through experimentation, deduction, and inference, all of which is empirically verifiable through repeated experimentation and arriving at the same results in conformance with the projected model or worked-out archetype, their scientists are able to work out and develop the precise formula that will enable them to direct and control people's behavior with mathematical precision.

† See *Covert Action Information Bulletin,* issue number 31, wherein Susan Rosenberg speaks about the horrendous conditions she, Silvia Baraldini and Alejandrina Torres were confined under the Lexington High-Security Unit.

they know precisely what their experiments, their scientific applications, will entail. In this, as in other areas, they are again in violation of international standards.*

It is clear, unequivocally clear, that this is a most cruel brand of psychological and emotional torture that is a violation of human rights and violates the U.S. Constitution's prohibition against cruel and unusual punishment. These measures rival even the methods used by Nazi Germany. Right now there are literally thousands of people being subjected to this program. It is an essential feature of the American penal system.

The penal system is designed to break minds, to create warped and aberrated personalities, and isolation and sensory deprivation play a most singular and unique role in this.†

In general, all prisoners are targeted. Even the staff themselves become victimized by the same system they blindly seek to uphold. You cannot dehumanize people without yourself becoming dehumanized in the process. Yes, all prisoners are targeted, and the harshness of their treatment varies only in degree with the most severe treatment being meted out to those with some political consciousness or to those who are in prison for political offenses.

They concentrate extra hard on the political prisoner because the political prisoner has the clearest understanding about the true nature of things, about the exploitative relationships that prevail. Accordingly, they concentrate extra hard on the political prisoner because she or he has the greatest potential for awakening and organizing the rest of the prisoners.

So, isolation and sensory deprivation have always played a unique role in the government's perennial war on the political prisoner. Through isolation and sensory deprivation, through being confined within a limited space, through the denial of privacy, lack of natural light and fresh air, through the lack of intellectual stimulation, lack of comradeship, through the lack of undisturbed sleep, lack of proper health care, lack of educational and recreational outlets—the lack of these things that contribute to fueling life reduces one to an existence of lifelessness.

This is war. This is a war of attrition and it is designed to reduce prisoners to a state of submission essential for their ideological conversion. That failing, the next option, in deadly sequence, is to reduce the prisoners to a state of psychological incompetence sufficient to neutralize them as efficient, self-directing antagonists. That failing, the only option left is to destroy the prisoners, preferably by making them desperate enough to destroy themselves.

---

* U.N. Resolution 43/173, principle 22, passed into effect on December 9, 1988, states the following: No detained or imprisoned person shall, even with his consent, be subjected to any medical or scientific experimentation which may be detrimental to his health.
† See *The Mind Manipulators* by Alan Scheflin. It contains information on some of the techniques used on prisoners. Here is a telling list of the chapters: Assaulting the Mind; Tampering with the Mind (II); Ruling the Mind; Amputating the Mind; Pruning the Mind; Rewiring the Mind; Blowing the Mind; Castrating the Mind; Robotizing the Mind.

The purpose of this isolation and sensory deprivation is to disrupt one's balance, one's inner equilibrium, to dehumanize the prisoner, to depersonalize him, to strip him of his unique individuality, pliant in the hands of his vicious captors.

We note that amongst the many effects of the process is the disruption of the biological time clock, neuropathic disorders, bio-chemical degeneration, depression, apathy, chronic rage reaction, defensive psychological withdrawal, loss of appetite (or the opposite extreme), weight loss, and the exacerbation of pre-existing medical problems.

These things are real, frighteningly real, as many, many documented cases prove. All of these things are part of a very clear, scientific program operated by the government, and it is designed to crush, dehumanize, and decimate those held captive.

This implacable, relentless attack by the United States Government is a very clear violation of fundamental human rights. These violations constitute an issue we must all hasten to confront. This terrible malady is already in its most advanced state, and everyone is affected by it. In addition, it is to the peril of the whole nation the longer people procrastinate on taking a just stand on this issue.

There are relevant international bodies that exist to uncover and redress human rights violations... all of which are highly salutatory.* But what we ask, those of us who have been victimized, is where are the stringent voices of those international bodies as day in and day out, our rights, our dignity, are offended and trampled on over and over again? Is everyone so inexorably chained to partisan politics that they refrain from applying their conscience until given the nod by party bigwigs? The world can see what goes on in the tomb of America as Black people are being slowly strangled and suffocated to death and are reeling drunkenly under the tyrannical whip of oppression.

Yes, the world can see what goes on. Yet there remains a deadly chorus of silence, a conspiracy of silence.

We charge the American government with genocide. In clear, unequivocal terms, we charge the American government with genocide against the captive Black people in America who are perpetually under siege. We charge genocide, infanticide, and menticide, which is perpetrated via institutionalized racism.

The voracious jaws of oppression and exploitation constantly feast upon our people. Additionally, every aspect of our existence is determined and controlled by another people, by a brutal enemy intent upon our total annihila-

---

* We do not mean to imply that these international bodies have not done some outstanding work. We acknowledge that these bodies have monitored certain regions and countries and they have called attention to human rights abuses occurring in those areas. What we do charge, however, and feel most strongly about, is that these same international bodies have been virtually silent with regard to the brutal treatment of Blacks in America, a people who have never had any real rights in America. We are calling attention to this neglect.

tion. We see the emissaries of death wreaking havoc in our ravaged communities by further eroding the quality of life (already at a subhuman level) and by further contributing to the horrendous deficiency of life-supporting stimuli.

The funeral pyre burns on and on. Our youth stumble through the wilderness of confusion, hopelessness, and feelings of insignificance. Their young and vulnerable bellies are bloated with the plague of self-destruction, miseducation, rejection, feelings of worthlessness. Our youths are the denizens of a defective social system that was not designed with the best interest of our people at heart.

The government of America knows exactly what it is doing; it has mastered the techniques of mass control. It knows how to build into an environment certain stimuli that will set into motion a desired process that takes on a life of its own, with the hand that originated the process becoming less and less visible. The withdrawing of the hand results in the people mistaking the effect for the cause.

Before this process can be properly cultivated to fruition, it first of all becomes necessary for the oppressor to develop ways to determine what the oppressed will think and when they will act. The first step in determining these things is to systematically destroy anything and anybody which or who might provide an alternate frame of reference, which means first of all attacking and destroying that people's history and culture and, second, giving the oppressed something warped and twisted in place of that which has been destroyed. Keep in mind that the oppressor knows what negative experiences the oppressed are subjected to and the oppressor knows what trashy ideas are stuffed into the heads of the oppressed.

In connection with this, Brother Amilcar Cabral noted "that oppression or domination of a people is only secured when the cultural life of a people is destroyed, paralyzed, or at least neutralized." Parenthetically, it may, in fact, be the case that the different forms of oppression experienced by African peoples are determined by the emphasis placed on destroying, paralyzing, or neutralizing the culture of the people under domination.

We hold this government responsible for the conditions of our people. In places like Chile, Argentina, Paraguay, and South Africa, they have done it blatantly (and we must not forget that it was, and is, the United States Government that finances and trains practically all of these oppressive regimes); they do it crudely, and blatantly with gun and truncheon.

In America, they do it through psychology, theology, philosophy, biology, through the refinement of sophisticated behavioral sciences, and we see the evidence of its effectiveness. All of the institutions of America serve to further uphold and perpetuate this oppressive order; all of their sciences are drawn into this nefarious enterprise and are subordinated to it.

Brother Wade Nobles has expounded on this saying, "The ideas of science do not develop in empty space, or even abstract space where there is supposedly nothing but ideas. The ideas, interests, application and definition of science goes on in a human world, and human life is social. There is, therefore, no science which is not some part of a social science. Similarly, when the social reality is defined by racism and oppression, there can be no science which is not, in part, oppressive and racist. Just as science and technology have gone hand-and-hand in the last three hundred years to assist in the development of the Western World, so, too, does it seem apparent that social science, as a political institution, now serves to maintain the advantages obtained by technological superiority of the Western World. Where the connection between science and society once was in science's devotion to the creation and use of technical and industrial power, science now serves Western society in the creation and use of theories and ideas designed to control the use of power in general by oppressed people. In fact, where power before was defined by the creation of ideas and the ability to have people respond to one's ideas as if they represented the respondent's reality."*

The allegations we make are very clear; even many of their own establishment figures admit as much. Statistics always fall short of fully conveying the entire picture, but even the ones that are out present a most bleak and shocking picture of what is happening to our people. Cited here are just a few of these statistics.

It is estimated that one-third to one-half of Black men up to the age 24 are unemployed; many are caught in a cycle of drugs, homicide and suicide. They say that employment among Black men was 84 percent in 1940, but only 67 percent in 1980. Today one-third of all Black men are either unemployed or completely out of the labor market. This is more serious than during the great depression. In the past 25 years, the employment rate of young White men has remained constant, while Blacks dropped from 52 to 26 percent in the 16 to 19 age group and from 77 to 55 percent in the 20 to 24 age group.

It is estimated that a young Black man has one chance in 21 of dying from homicide while the typical American has a 1 in 133 chance. More Black men died from homicide in the single year 1977, for instance, than died in the entire Vietnam War, and we believe there has been many such years.

In 1987, the Bureau of Justice estimated that the number of prisoners in this country reached 546,659—over one half-million people. It has been estimated that from 1975 to the year 2000 the total prison population will quadruple, and the number of Black prisoners is expected to increase tenfold.

Moreover, on closer inspection of the statistics, one clearly sees that the rates of imprisonment began accelerating after the social upheavals of the late 1960s era. In 1969, 120 cities burned during the Black rebellion. In 1983, the imprisonment rate per one hundred thousand people was 713 for Black people (even greater now), compared to 114 for White people, and it goes on and on ad infinitum.

---

* Wade Noble,"African Consciousness and Liberation Struggles: Implications for the Development and Construction of Scientific Paradigms."

The Further Erosion of Constitutional Protection

We submit that it would be a meaningless exercise to litigate the charge of human rights violations in the United States Courts, especially in view of the fact that the executive branch has virtually usurped the discretionary powers of the judicial branch, thus making it impossible for us to receive relief.

Even the Supreme Court of the United States has closed its eyes and ears to these human rights violations. As Alvin J. Bronstein states in his introduction to *Prisoner's Litigation Manual*, "The courts have returned to the handoff doctrine."

Over the years, prisoners have put forth the effort to engage in legal battles regarding constitutional violations and prison conditions and treatment. (Moreover, it was hoped that the occasion of being in court could be used to expose the United States penal system to the international community.)

The courts, for a brief period, listened to the prisoners' complaints and at times sustained their allegations of constitutional rights violations. However, as the result of the pressure applied on the courts by the executive branch, the independence of the judicial branch was erased, and consequently, prisoners were left deprived of the institutional guarantor of the protection of their constitutional rights, which really means prisoners exist in a constitutional void.

Conclusion

In every stage of these oppressions, we have petitioned for redress in the most humble terms. Our repeated petitions have been answered mainly by repeated injury. A nation, whose character is thus marked by every act that may define a racially oppressive regime, is unfit to receive the respect of a free people.

America's national mentality demonstrates poor judgment and irresponsibility in dealing with people at both a domestic and foreign level. America appears self-centered in her search for immediate gratification and failure to make long-range goals that benefit humanity.

As we note the 1962 meeting with Dr. Schein and his objectives, and recall the infamous J. E. Hoover memo, therein directing counterinsurgency against the Black Nationalist Liberation movement, it is evident that Kitson's experience in Kenya, fighting against the "Mau Mau," emerged as a strategy of the U.S. Government's counterinsurgency objectives....

Again, this paper is to encourage an investigation by the United Nations Human Rights Commission.

1.6

The People's Tribunal to Expose Control Units

Committee to End the Marion Lockdown
1987

The Control Unit is a relatively new technique developed by the U.S. Bureau of Prisons. These units, which are unmatched in terms of their calculated brutality, are used as an attack on all prisoners in the giant U.S. prison system—the largest in the world. They are used particularly to single out, as an example of what is in store for those who fight for a society that is humane, political leaders and others who dare to speak against the system. As the number of political prisoners in this country increases rapidly, it is becoming clear to the U.S. government that even prison will not frighten many people away from pursuing their vision of a new society. And so the government has created Marion and Lexington in an effort to halt organized opposition to its policies at home and abroad. Control Unit prisons must be closed!

This was the background piece for this Tribunal, which occurred on October 24, 1987, in Chicago. Following this document are excerpts from the transcript of the indictment and the verdict.

The Marion Control Facility

Marion was opened in 1963 to replace Alcatraz Prison, which was closed that same year. Marion is the most maximum security prison in the country. It is the experimental laboratory and trendsetter for the whole federal prison system. Here, the Bureau of Prisons established the Control Unit, a "prison within a prison," where prisoners were and still are subjected to sensory deprivation and solitary confinement. In the early years at Marion, prison officials experimented with the use of drugs on Control Unit prisoners. Marion also uses "boxcars"—small, enclosed, soundproof boxes in which prisoners are placed—as a means of psychological torture.

In October 1983, two guards were killed in isolated incidents by two prisoners. Although there was no prison riot, authorities seized this pretext to violently repress the entire prison population. They turned the prison into one huge Control Unit. Since that date, the 350 men imprisoned at Marion have experienced brutal, dehumanizing conditions:

- For 23 hours a day, prisoners are locked in individual cells, denied contact with each other and forced into total idleness.
- During the initial stage of the lockdown, 60 guards equipped with riot gear were shipped in from other prisons, and assisted Marion guards in systematically beating approximately 100 handcuffed and defenseless prisoners.
- All Control Unit prisoners are subjected to humiliating finger probes of the rectum every time they leave the unit for a court date, hospital visit, etc.
- All contact visits have been ended—no prisoner can touch or be touched by family or loved ones.
- Prison authorities shut down work programs, group educational activities and congregational religious services.

Although one or another of these conditions have existed in some prisons from time to time, Marion is the first place where they have all been imposed as part of a strategy selected deliberately by the Bureau of Prisons. These conditions are not the result of a whim of some backward warden. They are the result of policy constructed by the highest offices of the U.S. government.

In its efforts to justify such brutality, the Bureau of Prisons tries to perpetrate the myth that Marion contains "the most vicious, predatory prisoners in the system." Although some infamous felons are placed at Marion, the prison also houses people sentenced to short terms for victimless crimes and people imprisoned for their political beliefs and activities. In addition, many prisoners are told they will be transferred out of Marion if they will drop their lawsuits against the prison. Also, several political prisoners have been sent directly from conviction to Marion, without ever having spent any time in prison, let alone causing trouble or being violent in prison. The fact is that the criteria for placement at Marion are intentionally vague, and that, according to the government's own report, 80% of the men there are eligible for placement at less restrictive prisons.

The Marion Control Unit was never really designed to contain "vicious, predatory prisoners." The Bureau of Prisons established the Control Unit in July 1972, in response to a peaceful prisoner protest against the guard beating of a Mexican prisoner. About 60 prisoners were placed in isolated, sensory deprivation cells. With the Marion Control Unit, prison officials hoped to extinguish their spirit of protest, resistance, and solidarity.

As predicted from its inception, the Control Unit produces in prisoners feelings of intense rage and helplessness that often are expressed in violence—either against themselves or against others. Over the years, many prisoners have committed suicide or have turned on other prisoners or guards. Since the entire prison was locked down in 1983, three prisoners have been killed by other prisoners and several stabbings have occurred. The Marion prison lockdown is a bloody failure; it promotes the very violence it claims to be trying to prevent.

Top prison officials have made it clear they intend to permanently maintain the lockdown status, in spite of congressional and church inquiries and a class action lawsuit by the prisoners. A recent report condemning Marion was issued by Amnesty International, the Nobel Prize-winning organization that monitors human rights abuses throughout the world. This is the first time that Amnesty has ever criticized a U.S. prison. Amnesty concluded that Marion's policies appear to violate the United Nations' standard minimum rules for the treatment of prisoners. In fact, Amnesty went so far as to send to the Director of the Bureau of Prisons a copy of another of its reports entitled "Safeguards Against Torture." It added that conditions at Marion, in their totality, amount to "cruel, inhuman, and degrading treatment."

The Lexington Control Unit for Women

Taking lessons learned from Marion, the Bureau of Prisons has built a 16-cell maximum security unit for women prisoners in the Lexington, Kentucky, Federal Prison. It is located in the basement of a high-security building, totally separate from the rest of the prison. It is literally a dungeon.

The Control Unit at Lexington is the first of its kind in the country—a special unit designed with the express purpose of breaking women political prisoners.

What are conditions like in Lexington?

- The women are never allowed contact with other prisoners.
- The cells were initially painted bright white to produce feelings of disorientation, until a demonstration at the prison resulted in the Unit being repainted a drab beige.
- The few windows in the unit are covered with screens to prevent the women from seeing the outside.
- The women are never free from the eyes of either guards or video cameras.
- Visits are restricted to family members and attorneys; no friends are allowed to visit.
- Visiting takes place in a "special" room and is of shorter duration than visits allowed to other prisoners at Lexington.
- The women are required to wear special uniforms to identify them at all times as "high-security" prisoners.
- The women are guarded by twice as many guards as other prisoners.

Placement in the Lexington Control Unit, as with Marion, has already proven to be completely arbitrary. There is one significant difference—the head of the entire prison system makes the final decision about who is designated for Lexington. He has already decided, without any justification, to imprison Puerto Rican Prisoner of War Alejandrina Torres, North American Political Prisoner Susan Rosenberg, and Italian national Silvia Baraldini, already the subjects of special abuse, in the Lexington Control Unit.

Lexington presents us with a qualitative change in the repression of women, and a very substantial protest has already been mounted against the brutality. In addition to a great deal of church protest, hundreds of phone calls and letters, and two large demonstrations at the gates of the prison, the ACLU has issued a stinging attack on the Control Unit. As a result, the Bureau of Prisons has recently announced that it will close the Lexington Control Unit and open a special prison for women in Marianna, Florida, with over 100 cells. This outrageous plan indicates once again that the BOP is incapable of understanding what is at issue here. They have been embarrassed and exposed in their torture plans at Lexington, and so their response is to make it larger (increasing from 16 cells—although only five at Lexington are now being used—to over 100 cells) and move it to Florida.

Prisons and Society

Fyodor Dostoevsky once wrote that to understand a society, one should look within its prisons. What does a glimpse behind U.S. prison walls tell us about our society?

U.S. prisons hold a vast number of people of color. Black people are incarcerated at a rate of 714 per 100,000 population, six times the rate for white people in this country. While white people go to prison about as often as people in European countries, Black people in the U.S. go to prison at a rate that is almost twice as high as the rate for Black people in South Africa! This rate is the highest in the world. In fact, the probability that a Black man in the U.S. will go to prison in his lifetime is about 25%, or one out of every four! And the situation is even worse than it sounds, for we use the word "prison" here in its precise meaning. Thus, these figures do not include jail, probation, or any of the other criminal justice categories.

Such a large number of incarcerated people constitute a well-defined system of population control. It is predicted that U.S. prisons (this does not include jails) will hold over 1,000,000 people by the year 2000 and that more than half will be people of color. This growth is taking place with devastating rapidity. For example, during the period of January-June, 1986, the number of prisoners in the U.S. increased by 25,630—or more than 1,000 per week! It is the case now, and has always been the case, that such increases in the imprisonment rate have little to do with the crime rate, but rather reflect the ideological and economic realities of the times. This is not meant to imply that crime is not a major problem, but merely to recognize that imprisonment occurs as a result of elite policy rather than as a direct response to "crime."

A growing disparity exists in this country between those who enjoy a comfortable life and those who must struggle to survive. It is these "have-nots" who fill the U.S. prisons. The society that delivers such a disproportionate number of Third World people to the prison doors is one that has produced a generation of Black youth—75% of whom are unemployed—who are trapped in deteriorating public housing projects, who drop out of schools at alarming rates, who lose their lives to drugs, crime, and violence.

A glance at some recent data provides some insight into living conditions for Black people. All of the following data come from government publications or professional journals. Data are all from 1980 or later. In every case, the conditions are getting worse for Black people, so that the more recent the data, theworse the situation.

- 10% of white people live below the poverty line compared with 25% of Latino people and 32% of Black people.
- Black median family income is about half (54%) that of white families.
- The median net worth is $40,000 for white families and $3,000 for Black families.
- A government study predicts that by the year 2000, 70% of Black men will be unemployed
- The Black infant mortality rate is two times the white infant mortality rate.
- The Black maternal mortality rate is three times the white maternal mortality rate.

- White people live, on the average, about six years longer than Black people. The average Black man will not even live long enough to collect his Social Security.
- Of doctoral candidates, 4% are Black; 4% of college faculty are Black.
- Of medical students, 7% are Black and this percent has been decreasing since 1972; 2% of physicians are Black; 2% of medical school faculty are Black; 2% of dentists are Black.
- Of law school students, 5% are Black; 2% of law school faculty are Black 1% of lawyers are Black.

(All of the information about education includes the Black colleges, at which virtually all students and faculty members are Black. If these were omitted from the calculations, the percentages in the last three items would decrease much further.)

Finally, there is the death penalty, used to murder Black people at a rate six times greater than white people. According to a recent study, 7.5% of Black people convicted of killing a white person in Illinois were sentenced to death while none of the 56 white people convicted of killing a Black person received the death penalty. Although Blacks and Hispanics make up about 15% of the population of Illinois, they comprise 70% of death row.

Taken together, we assert that this set of conditions constitutes genocide. This is a word that is emotionally charged, yet we nevertheless maintain that we are using it in a manner consistent with the United Nations definition. This definition states that "genocide" takes place when one group deliberately inflicts upon another group the "conditions of life calculated to bring about its physical destruction in whole or part."

Through its actions, the U.S. makes a clear statement: It will not grant Third World people their human rights. It will not provide them with job opportunities, schools that teach, or medical care. It will, however, spend billions of dollars to build bigger and more repressive prisons—prisons that are certain to house swelling numbers of unemployed Black and other Third Work people.

What makes this government's program for social "stability" work? Law and order. Longer prison terms. The death penalty. More prisons. More police. In the 1980s, prisons no longer pretend to rehabilitate—they are simply warehouses. While prisons spend money on more guard towers, barbed wire, and new maximum security units, they cut the educational/vocational programs. The message is that crime is caused by bad individuals. Will society be healed by caging and electrocuting them?

Attention turns away from the social, political, and economic roots of crime. Instead, the individual is blamed—and since most of the blame is directed toward Black people, this leads to the criminalization of an entire people. As William Nagel, a leading criminologist, states: "The causes of crime in this country are deeply rooted in its economic and social injustices.

The massive use of incarceration has not contributed and will not contribute significantly to the abatement of crime or to the correction of flaws in the social fabric."

If prisons reflect the structure of society, they also reflect the nature of the struggle against that structure. In the '60s, as the Civil Rights and Black Power movements grew, the number of Black political prisoners swelled and the prison struggle became a major part of the Black liberation movement. Political prisoners like George Jackson stated clearly that prisons are an important tool in the government's effort to contain and destroy Black people's freedom. The rebellion at Attica in 1971 was a defining event in U.S. history. The demands of the prisoners, their eloquence and dignity, and the mass murder of 41 of them by the governor of New York, Nelson Rockefeller, all revealed to the world what the United States was about and at the same time proclaimed what the movement for a new society would be about.

Although the government refuses to admit it, there are well over 100 political prisoners and prisoners of war in U.S. prisons today. They come from the Puerto Rican, Black/New Afrikan, and Native American liberation movements. They include progressive Christians, white anti-imperialists, draft resisters, grand jury resisters, and members of anti-intervention and sanctuary forces. The movements that these people represent honor, love, and respect them. Yet the government contends that they are criminals or terrorists. Although the government denies the existence of political prisoners in this country, it often reserves the harshest treatment for these very people. Control Units are designed to break every prisoner's spirit. In the case of political prisoners and prisoners of war, the Control Units are part of a calculated strategy to weaken these movements and to intimidate others from taking a stand.

Normal Channels Unresponsive
The Marion lockdown continues despite two U.S. congressional hearings (at one of them only two members of Congress attended), and the recommendation of congressional consultants that the lockdown end. The lockdown continues despite a class action lawsuit by the prisoners seeking an injunction to end it, and months of hearings in which prisoner after prisoner testified that guards have beaten them or forced them to undergo finger probes of the rectum, which the men likened to rape. The lockdown continues—and it appears that neither Congress nor the courts will provide a remedy to the prisoners from the inhumane Control Unit at Marion. In a similar manner, these same channels have also been unresponsive to the women placed in the Lexington Control Unit who are seeking an end to the barbaric conditions they are forced to endure.

Our experiences participating in the anti-intervention, antiapartheid, antinuclear, and disarmament movements have shown us that we cannot rely on Congress or the courts to recognize or protect the rights of people when these rights are in conflict with the aims of the government of the United States. We have thus taken to the streets and demonstrated in order to expose human rights abuses caused by U.S. intervention in Central America and U.S. support for the apartheid regime of South Africa and the murderous Israeli occupation of Palestine.

For the same reasons we must take to the streets and demonstrate to expose and protest the human rights abuses that occur in U.S. prisons. These abuses occur most regularly to Third World prisoners who represent the sectors most often targeted by government repression. Over the years, Marion has been a holding place for leaders of the Black/New Afrikan, Puerto Rican, and Native American struggles: leaders like Rafael Cancel Miranda, Imari Obadele, and Leonard Peltier. In the past few months, Oscar López Rivera and Kojo Bomani Sababu (slave name, Grailing Brown) have been transferred to Marion, joining Richard Thompson-El. (Sundiata Acoli and Sekou Odinga have recently been transferred out of Marion, in part as a result of our protests.) Also transferred to Marion recently have been Tim Blunk, Alan Berkman, and Ray Levasseur, three North American anti-imperialist resistance fighters.

We Can Make a Difference

The Bureau of Prisons intentionally builds a wall of silence around its prisons in hopes that the public will never learn about its brutal policies. Largely for this reason, Marion, like so many other prisons, is tucked away in a rural and not easily accessible area. However, when the public calls on government and prison officials to account for their abuses, they become extremely uncomfortable and are often pressured into allowing some changes.

For example, from a small group of people who began to protest the continued imprisonment of the Puerto Rican Nationalists grew a movement that led to their unconditional release in 1979. In another instance, when several hundred people demonstrated in 1983 at Alderson federal prison in West Virginia against the punitive segregation conditions of Haydée [Beltrán] Torres and Lucy Rodríguez, two Puerto Rican Prisoners of War, Torres and Rodríguez were transferred out of isolation. In 1984, public attention to Leonard Peltier, the Native American leader who was incarcerated at Marion, resulted in his transfer out of Marion to a less restrictive prison, and the same thing happened to New Afrikans Sekou Odinga and Sundiata Acoli.

Furthermore, we can already see the Bureau of Prisons frantically trying to gain control of the situation around Lexington. As we described above, small improvements have been made there from time to time as the result of continuing protest. Now the BOP says they will shut down the Control Unit! This is a great victory, but it will have even greater impact if we assure that no replacement is ever opened—not at Marianna or anywhere else.

Prisons and the Movement

Since prisons reflect both the structure of society and the nature of the struggle against that structure, when we work to minimize the brutality of the prison system, we simultaneously work to support those, like political prisoners and prisoners of war, who have been a dynamic catalyst in the movement for a changed, humane society.

It may be that very few of us will go to prison or even know someone who goes to prison, so it may not be apparent why we should be concerned with this issue. But if we are to be part of the solution, and not part of the problem, we must fight against these racist warehouses. Only by dealing with these stark realities, only by making these kinds of sacrifices, can we build a movement that will some day be an alternative to this system and its repression.

The wall of silence around prisons will work only if we let it—out of sight, out of mind. Historically, most of us have become aware of prisons only after some terrible, violent event occurs, such as after the 1971 massacre at Attica Prison. Yet, right now the prisoners at Marion and Lexington are experiencing physical and psychological violence on a daily basis. Many of us now know about these conditions. The question is, what will we do with this awareness? As Rafael Cancel Miranda, who spent many years in Marion, admonished us at a conference about Marion Prison, "we cannot just feel bad or sad, we must do something."

The Committee to End the Marion Lockdown

The Committee to End the Marion Lockdown is trying to generate concern and action in the white community over the issues of Control Units in specific and the prison system in general.

Black/New Afrikan and Puerto Rican organizations are going to their communities with similar appeals. We can only succeed with the broad support of many people working long and hard at this issue. We ask you to join with us to fight against Marion, Lexington, and the entire concept of Control Units for three reasons. First, they are the ultimate barbarity, and their existence not only brutalizes those they incarcerate, but those of us in whose name Marion and Lexington were built. Second, Marion and Lexington are models that will be continued and expanded unless they are stopped, and stopped soon. Third, Marion and Lexington represent one of the most explicit manifestations of the attempt of white supremacy to sustain itself.

This is a difficult historic period for people who are seeking a new way of living, who are seeking a world free of exploitation. But it is not a hopeless time. We have choices. We can act in the pursuit of our vision. This is what the Committee to End the Marion Lockdown is all about. We hope you will join us.

97

PRISONS:
FORTRESSES OF REPRESSION

Stop the Control Units: Shut Down Marion & Lexington!

DEMONSTRATE: Saturday, April 19

New York City: Metropolitan Corr. Center

Rally at 11:00 am at Brooklyn House of Detention, march to MCC, then rally at City Hall Park

1. End the Marion Lockdown; Close the Marion Control Unit; Immediately transfer New Afrikan Freedom Fighters Sekou Odinga and Sundiata Acoli.
2. Stop the Control Unit at Lexington.
3. Uphold the right of political association; immediate transfer of all Puerto Rican, New Afrikan and Native American Prisoners of War to the same prison so as to enable them to prepare their international cases.
4. Immediately transfer all political prisoners to prisons near their homes.
5. End grand jury repression and political internment;

6. Repatriate all Puerto Rican political prisoners.
7. Release North American political prisoner Dr. Alan Berkman so as to insure proper treatment to recover from cancer.
8. Repatriate political prisoner Julio Veras-Delgadillo to his native Dominican Republic.
9. Stop religious harrassment; Allow prisoners to practice religious principles and rites.
10 Stop sexual harrassment of women POWs and political prisoners

I.6.A
Partial Transcript from the Tribunal on Control Units

1987

Moderator: I would like to officially call this People's Tribunal to order. Here to present us with the indictment is José López, National Coordinator of the *Movimiento de Liberación Nacional*. José is a historian, scholar, activist, and international leader of the Puerto Rican independence movement.

José López: Today we are gathered here to issue an indictment—it's interesting because we are not usually the ones who are issuing indictments, so it feels good to be on the other side—against the U.S. government and particularly the Attorney General, Edwin Meese, the FBI, and the Bureau of Prisons.

Before I begin formal issuance of the indictment, I think it is important for us to note certain things about the question of prisons in this society. We cannot really speak of prisons as a place where the surplus labor force is put away within the context that, somehow, prisons in relationship to people are just another government manifestation of political repression. We have to look at the role of prisons as a reflection of what has happened, particularly in the United States, in the past generation.

Paralleling the growing crisis of the economic structure of the U.S. has been the increasing focus on the problem of crime during the past two decades. By the mid-1960s, as we all know, the U.S. was embroiled in a costly war in Vietnam and faced stiff economic competition from its allies. At that very juncture, crime became the number one domestic problem.

In 1965, President Johnson launched his war on crime. He said, "We must arrest and reverse the trend toward lawlessness because crime has become a malignant enemy in America's midst." Congress responded by adopting the Omnibus Crime Control and Safe Streets Act. The adoption of this law ushered in a new form of crime control. Not only would the war on crime be fought by legislation, presidential commissions, policy research, etc., but a new strategy of domestic population control was now being instituted. Ever since then, billions of dollars have been poured into this war under the Orwellian doublespeak of the criminal justice system, because, of course, they have couched this repression within a new terminology—now you speak of a "criminal justice system" instead of the "penal system," you do not speak of "prisoners," you speak of "inmates," you don't speak of "penitentiaries," you speak of "federal correctional facilities," and so on. This law has profoundly impacted almost every facet of life in America. Everyone has become involved in combating crime, from the major corporations, reaching to the highest level of government, and even to every livingroom in America's homes. A criminal justice/industrial complex has even emerged. Everyone from the Justice Department to the neighborhood beat representative program (read: spy-on-your-neighbor network) has been mobilized to fight "crime." Thus, a full infrastructure of population control has begun to take shape. Therefore, in some respects the character of prisons and jails in America has been profoundly altered.

Today we are here to charge the U.S. with the crime of using prisons as a tool of population control, particularly for people of color. With the initiation of the war on crime, America's growing prison population has literally made it a nation of prison-houses. According to the figures of the Bureau of Justice, in April of 1987, the number of prisoners in this country reached 546,659—over one-half million people in prison. No other country in the world has that many prisoners.

A close look reveals that from 1980 to 1984 there was an increase of over 40% in the prison population. It is also very interesting to note that the number of incarcerated women has increased 138% in the last 10 years; about 27,000 women were in federal or state custody in 1986—an increase of about 15% over the year before.

But what is probably most significant is that the largest number of inmates are Blacks/New Afrikans, Mexicans, Puerto Ricans, and Native Americans. The imprisonment rate for Blacks/New Afrikans is much higher than any other segment of the population in this society. In a recent article in Time magazine, it stated that: "While black men account for only 6% of the American population, they make up half of its male prisoners." They have a "1 in 21 chance of becoming murder victims—more than 6 times greater than the population as a whole." Understanding, of course, that Black on Black crime has been derived from the colonial condition Black people have been subjected to, as Frantz Fanon clearly stated, "The colonized man will first manifest his aggressiveness, which has been deposited in his home, against his own people. This is the period when the niggers beat each other up...." The article goes on to say that while the national unemployment rate is 6.9%, for Blacks it is 15% and for Black youth it is more than 40%. "Some 18% of black males drop out of high school. This hard-core segment of the community, dominated by young men who are both the victims of broken families and perpetrators of new ones, has evolved into an entrenched subculture, where poverty and despair and crime are recycled from one generation to the next." I hope you will keep those words in mind because they are the words of Time magazine, not a rabble-rousing communist.

We are here, today, to charge the U.S. government with a crime of turning prisons into America's future concentration camps for oppressed nationalities. There is little doubt that if the spiraling prison population growth continues at the present rate, within the next decade or less there will be one million people in prison in this country, not to speak of people in jails, principally people of color. Given the cutbacks in social programs, as America's decline is evident in the growing deficit, an unfavorable balance of trade, and an ever-expanding foreign debt of developing nations, the government cannot continue the same rate of social expenses in the war on crime, particularly the growing costs of prisons.

Presently, it costs more to imprison a person for one year than to send him or her to Harvard University. New formulas are being experimented with. The prison-for-profit option is being implemented. Within the next generation, we may see factories, textile plants, foundries, and even high-tech industries springing forth in and around prisons. These industries will guarantee the necessary industrial production still needed in this postindustrial society, yielding super-profits and using super-exploitative slave wages. Of course, we must understand this development within the greater context of the plan, the counterinsurgency plan of population control, and particularly what the Trilateralist Samuel Huntington has called in his book, *Crisis in Democracy,* the "ungovernable sector" (read: Blacks/New Afrikans, Mexicans, Puerto Ricans, and Native Americans). Included among these programs is the project of spatial deconcentration—a concept developed by Anthony Downs, a member of the Kerner Commission, which calls for a process whereby the ghettos are deconcentrated and their populations dispersed to the outskirts of the cities, far away from the financial and commercial centers.

All you have to do is look at what is happening in places like Harlem in New York or the Wicker Park Community of Chicago. Look at this neighborhood right where we are. Fifteen years ago this was a Puerto Rican neighborhood. Today, where three Puerto Rican families lived, a yuppie lives with a live-in lover and two German shepherds. An added dimension to the spatial deconcentration proposal are tax-free enterprise zones to be established in the outskirts of America's cities, thus assuring super-profits by paying wages below minimum level and creating future Bantustans à la South Africa. If on the outskirts of America's urban centers future Bantustans are to emerge, then surely from America's prisons will rise future concentration camps.

Today, the evidence will show that as conditions worsen for Third World people and all poor people within U.S. borders, as the government continues to carry on "little" wars abroad to stave off the lingering and growing economic crisis that it entered two decades ago, the system is realizing that discontent at home and national liberation struggles everywhere are inevitable. They have thus begun to draw up plans for a strategy of a new state repression based on the political framework of counterinsurgency models utilized in other parts of the world, particularly theorized in the writings of British Colonels Evelegh and Kitson.

Today, U.S. prisons hold more than one hundred political prisoners: some, using international law, assert a Prisoner of War (POW) stand; others are political prisoners or prisoners of conscience, members of the Black/New Afrikan, Puerto Rican, and Native American struggles, as well as white anti-imperialists, antimilitarist activists, and progressive Christians. In implementing counter-

101

insurgency policies within the prison, the Bureau of Prisons carries out one of its most important aspects—developed and enunciated in a secret conference that was held in Puerto Rico in 1978—the policy of the denial system, which seeks to isolate political prisoners from their community and families, also constantly moving them from one prison to another, in some cases thousands of miles away from families and loved ones, restricting correspondence and visits, censorship of political literature, controlled movement within the prison, central monitoring, maximum security level, and even the denial of adequate medical care. Some of the political prisoners are in jail for exercising their human rights to silence—those were the cases of those who a few years ago refused to speak before the grand jury. A more vicious and sophisticated form that seeks to psychologically destroy those accused of violence against the U.S. state is the use of the maxi-maxi unit to house these anti-imperialist revolutionaries so as to break their spirit of resistance.

You will hear the evidence about Marion and Lexington. The evidence will show that Alejandrina Torres, Puerto Rican Prisoner of War, and anti-imperialist North American Susan Rosenberg and Italian national anti-imperialist Silvia Baraldini are buried alive in the Lexington Control Unit. The evidence will show that hundreds of prisoners are being kept in practically total isolation in the dungeon that is called Marion Prison.

Today, our witnesses will bring forth a great deal of evidence that will demonstrate clearly that America, for those of us who are a little bit different in terms of the color of our skin; for those of us who pose a problem in the ability of the U.S. to carry out its warlike policies; for those of us who in any way, shape, or form do not conform to its diabolical and belligerent plans, that those of us who constitute the "ungovernable sectors"—that those of us who pose any threat or in any way are not part of its scheme—the evidence will show that there definitely is a counterinsurgency strategy that will move against us and that is being defined and refined in Marion and Lexington.

What is important today is that you who participate in this People's Tribunal, that you must keep in mind that you are not dealing with prisons as "something that is bad, but we have to have them"; but rather that we see prisons as institutions that are becoming America's concentration camps, particularly for people of color. As we hear the evidence today, as we listen to the comments and the conclusions of the justices, it is important to keep in mind that in many ways, prisons and jails are a reflection of the society in which we live. The conditions in those prisons reflect the condition of America. And those who believe that racism has ended and those who believe that because there is a Black mayor in Chicago and Black congressmen, that Black people are better off, look at the statistics for the Black masses, and look at the statistics in terms of prisons and jails.

Finally, it is important for us to keep in mind the slogan that was developed around Attica—"Attica is all of us." I think Lexington and Marion are also in all of us—and let's keep that in mind this afternoon.

Moderator: The next judge is Dave Dellinger. He is a longtime peace and anti-intervention activist. Many people may remember that he was one of the main organizers of the demonstrations here at the Democratic Convention in 1968 and consequently became part of one of the most well-known trials of the era, the Chicago Eight. He will be going on trial in Langley, Virginia, for a protest last April at CIA headquarters.

Dave Dellinger: It has been both painful and inspiring to hear the testimony today. Painful to be reminded of the atrocities that are committed against human beings in the name of "justice." Inspiring to be reminded that there are people—prisoners, friends, parents, lawyers, and others—who refuse to tolerate these atrocities and are determined to put an end to them. And inspiring to see that this determination extends to a commitment to do away with the gross injustices that, directly or indirectly, lead people to do things that cause a backward and vengeful society to put them in prison. Sometimes the things they do are acts of desperation that are antisocial and self-defeating. But this does not justify excluding them from the human family and treating them as the inmates of our prisons are treated. Sometimes the things they do are exemplary acts—or at least reflect an exemplary motivation. Their offense is to oppose the institutional crimes of a society that disrespects, disempowers, and despoils millions of its members for the sake of the private privileges, profits, and power of a few. They work for a society of human solidarity in which the guiding principle will no longer be competition to rise above one's fellows in a ceaseless war of all against all, but cooperation to rise together. Archbishop Romero, another offender, spoke of a new society that will encourage "the generous… contributions of all to the good of all."

The invitation to serve on this Tribunal couldn't have come at a worse time for me. I was seriously overcommitted and had made a firm decision not to accept any more outside engagements of any kind. But prisoners are the untouchables of our society. They come in disproportionate numbers from the victims of race and class oppression. They become doubly untouchable once they have been convicted by a criminal "criminal justice" system and sent to prison. There aren't enough tribunals like this one. So here I am, experiencing not only pain and inspiration, but also a flood of memories from my own prison experiences.

Shortly after graduating from college, I went to prison as a war objector. When I got out I use to say that I went from Yale to jail and got a better education in three years of jail than in six years at Yale. Yet I had gotten a relatively good education at Yale. Dostoyevsky is right: If you want to understand a society, you have to look inside its prisons. That is where the laws are "writ large"; where the kid gloves are off—all gloves are off—and you see the underlying violence that enforces the injustices of the society.

I especially appreciate the comments today by a number of witnesses, that prisons play a key role in racial genocide; that a lot of what once happened to

Black people on the plantations now takes place in prisons. When I went to Cook County Jail in 1970, over 90% of the prisoners were people of color—of various colors other than the pink that more accurately describes the people we usually call white. Faced by such facts, you have to conclude either that there is something wrong with Black people—that they are criminally inclined— or that the society is racist. My own conclusion is that there is something drastically wrong with the society and right about a lot of Black people. What is right shone forth in the late '50s and early '60s, when the Black-led struggle for civil rights broke the spell of McCarthyism and inspired and energized what became known as "The '60s." And today, more and more Black people are in jail because one way or another they are rebelling; refusing to accept the cruel and destructive lot that a racist society assigns them. As Ashanti said, the forms of their revolt are not always pretty—and, I would add, not always productive. But they are attempts at self-assertion, tortured ways of trying to survive, to get quick relief, or in some cases to get some of what other people have and society unfairly denies them.

Speaking of Cook County Jail, one of my joys today—and I hope that Alan will forgive me—that I met my friend Alan, who was in the same tier as I was in that jail in 1970. I got out after a month, but Alan didn't get out for 15 years, and I congratulate him for being here today fighting for prisoners' rights. Stand up, Alan.

When I first met Alan, I was in jail as one of the Chicago Eight—Seven at the time, because Bobby Seale's case had been severed from ours. The judge had denied us bail, saying that we were too dangerous to be on the streets. That, I thought was the biggest compliment I had ever received. Anyway, I don't believe that the amount of money a person can come up with should determine whether or not that person stays in jail. Once I stayed in for six weeks before trial rather than accept bail. However, when we were in Cook County jail, the Appeals Court decided that we could be released on bail. Supporters raised the money and said, "Come on out." We thanked them and said that we would not come out until they raised an equal amount to release other prisoners who were not known as political prisoners—and they did. At the time, getting them out was more important to me than making an issue of opposition to the bail system. It was a simple act of the kind of elementary solidarity with all prisoners that we have to develop much further.

To continue on a personal note that has implications for the issues raised today, the first time I went to federal prison, antiwar people began a campaign to have me and six fellow war objectors treated as political prisoners. We sent out word that we had spent a month with the other prisoners and didn't want to be treated any differently than they were. To us they were political prisoners, too, whatever they had done and whatever they were called. They deserved to be treated with intelligence and compassion rather than with cruelty and contempt. And we wanted to rise or fall with them rather than to be treated as a privileged elite.

Here's another story that tells something about the prison system. When I got to federal prison, I found that it was racially segregated. The only place that wasn't segregated was quarantine, where you spent your first 30 days being examined, cataloged, etc. My first Saturday night out of quarantine, I walked into the weekly movie with a Black man. Guards ushered him into the Black section and pointed me toward the white section. But I followed my friend and sat down next to him. Hardly had the lights gone out and the movie begun when I was blinded by half a dozen searchlights in my eyes. I was taken out and put in solitary confinement.

It is preposterous to think that a prison system that reflects the worst attitudes and practices of society and backs them with violence is capable of rehabilitating people. We should be atoning for the injustices and oppressions that they have suffered by acting toward them in the best ways that human beings can interact—giving them positive "strokes," as Ted Blunk told us—rather than trying to break their spirits in ways that have been described today.

The '60s gave birth to some good things and also went wrong in a number of ways. One of the worst slogans of the late '60s was "The duty of a revolutionary organizer is to stay out of jail by any means necessary." But I was lucky. By then I had spent enough time in jail to know that jail is a great place to organize people and be organized by them. A great place to gain a deeper understanding of the realities of human nature and of the role of a cynical view of human nature in producing a corrupt and corrupting society. If, as George Bernard Shaw maintained, false patriotism is the last refuge of scoundrels, propagating a false view of human nature is the first line of attack against those who think that human beings are capable of doing away with injustice, oppression, and war.

Some of the people I lived with had committed horrendous crimes. Yet there was an awesome reality to their life experience and a basic, if partially repressed, instinct to love and be loved that was able to express itself if you treated them with the kind of respect every human being deserves. Like everyone, they needed to feel and be useful; to be forgiven rather than guilt-tripped, valued as persons of equal worth rather than patronized. If they slipped into prison bullshit, they needed to be challenged, but other than that, they needed patient listeners who believed that they could become their best selves rather than their worst. They needed to be encouraged to love themselves, no matter what they had done or society had done to them.

Usually those who had committed the most atrocious crimes were the most open to these kinds of influences, not because they had the longest sentences but because they were unhappy with—at some level even revolted by—what they had done. My judgment is that removing such people from the environment and context in which they have committed such crimes is often necessary, for their sake and sometimes for the sake of possible future victims. But putting them in one of our U.S. prisons cannot possibly heal them. Nor can it deter others who are wrestling with similar problems—insecurity, oppression, repressed explosive anger, socially induced negative self-images—from committing similar crimes. From these prisoners in particular, I learned about human nature and absolutely everyone's potential for both good and evil, lessons that have stayed with me to this day.

I guess I'll give one more personal example of what happens in prison, how those in authority try to divide and rule, much as they do outside prison. One time when I was on a long hunger strike, the doctors told me that if I didn't eat I would die. It was about the 60th day, and I was being force-fed through the nose with liquids. I believe that they put something in the liquid to frighten me, because the first thing that happened was that I felt a tremor and an overwhelming sensation that I was about to die. I didn't have time to tell anyone, even if I had wanted to, because I looked up to see two doctors and the warden entering my hospital cell. They gave me a cardiogram and announced that my heart had been damaged by going without food. I would die unless I ate. I've never in my life had any heart problems, before or after that incident. Anyway, I didn't eat, and as you can see, I didn't die.

A week later, after we had won a partial victory and gone off the strike, we were not given any time to recover. I was thrown, weak, dizzy, and with a ringing in my ears that made me hard of hearing, into the fuck-up dorm. It was populated almost exclusively by Southern white military prisoners. The guards said to them: "This is one of the guys who spits on the flag and says he is too good to be in prison with the rest of you." They were trading on the claims of two or three war objectors that they should be treated as political prisoners, a position I always opposed. Then they said, "He's a nigger lover who wants to force you guys to eat and sleep with niggers and shit in the same toilet. We don't care what you do to him. Bring him out with his head in his hands, if you want to." Then they left.

The only way I survived was that I was god-damned lucky. Earlier, before the hunger strike, someone had been assaulted by a guard, and I stepped out of line and defended him. So I was able to say to them, "I was fighting for your rights when I was on that hunger strike, and I'm the guy who was put in the hole for defending Joe Snedecker when the motherfuckin' hacks were beating the shit out of him. Who are you going to side with, the hacks or me?" Luckily it was my second sentence, and I had learned a little the first time around about how to appeal to some basic feelings that are strong in most prisoners.

Let me end by extending what I have already said about Blacks to two other groups. It was an inspiration to hear witnesses from the movement for Puerto Rican independence. I was lucky, again, because when I was in federal prison, I met Puerto Rican *independentistas* who opened my eyes to some things that I didn't understand deeply enough. I knew something about imperialism and colonialism and thought I was against them. But I wasn't nearly sensitive enough to what goes down in Puerto Rico. As a result of what they taught me, when I got out I worked with the Puerto Rican Independence movement, and some years later I attended the funeral of Albizu Campos in Puerto Rico and stood honor guard by his casket. [Applause] I don't deserve the applause. I haven't done nearly enough. But being here today will help me.

And I want to say how happy I am for the presentations by women. Anybody who thinks that the movement for justice is not advancing, deepening, and becoming more vital, for all its inevitable confusions and setbacks, ought to compare the role of women here today with the way it would have been a few years ago. Imagine, today there were three women lawyers making superb presentations. And all those other women, talking about what's being done to women as women in prison—finger probes of their vaginas by male guards, and all the rest. Never forget that in the civil rights struggle in the late '50s and early '60s, men were doing heroic things and treating women as shit. And women were doing heroic things and being treated like shit. It was in that context that the women's movement got a fresh start. Like every movement, it has its periods of energy, growth, and at least partial triumphs and its periods of decline. But when women in the civil rights movement—and later in the anti-Vietnam War movement—began refusing to be treated as shit, the women's movement got new energy and insights. And that's just as important for men as it is for women.

Finally, I will respond specifically to the indictment. Can you guess whom I find guilty? I find the government guilty of monstrous crimes. And I find the American people guilty for not having paid enough attention to the crimes, in and out of prison, against the victims of class, racial, and other prejudices. Finally, I indict myself for not doing enough to help expose and put an end to these crimes. I don't want to overstate it, but when I go back to Vermont, I'm going to do more—and a lot more intelligently—as a result of these hearings.

Moderator: Sister Jean Hughes is a member of the Eighth Day Center for Peace and Justice. She is an activist in the Pledge of Resistance and the Sanctuary Movement here in Chicago. She is an integral part of the anti-intervention movement here. Please welcome Jean Hughes.

Jean Hughes: Today has been a privilege as well as a difficult experience. What I have seen and heard has touched the very core of being human. Therefore, I am forced to respond—will try to articulate—not out of the political strategy perspective at which I function daily, but rather out of the motivation for that activity, the belief system. In fact, the only level out of which I can begin to deal at all with human torture is at a faith level. It is a faith that has been chipped and honed through 17 years in Latin America, where I learned from the people how to be a community person. It is a faith that brought me back here to my own country hoping to live with people in a new way.

107

I find Edwin Meese, Ronald Reagan, the economic system, the educational system, our churches, the media, every facet of acculturation in our country, guilty. I find them guilty of living out and promulgating the myth that individual wealth and/or power is a value to be sought and cherished above all else. Within this framework and in order to ensure that value, the victimization of whole nations, whole races, communities, and individuals is not only tolerated but institutionalized. Within this framework and in order to ensure that value, any other world view must quickly and brutally be expunged. Within this framework and in order to ensure that value, Lexington and Marion exist.

I believe that we are all sisters and brothers, children of the same God. I believe that life is a covenant in which each community with its unique gifts contributes to the development of all of humankind. Within my framework, how could I not find the entire system, especially those responsible for Lexington and Marion, guilty of crimes against humanity? By their own admissions, Lexington and Marion exist to break down the human personality, reconstructing personalities "compatible" with the system... historical amnesiacs, economic illiterates, and/or fatalists. The message is that until those women and men become "compatible," they will continue to be subjected to the experiment which translates into inhuman, sadistic treatment. Most insidious is the fact that the authorities, knowing that these inmates will not choose "compatibility," are therefore trying to destroy them. It is a crime against all of humanity.

Besides finding the above system, foundational structures, administrators, and supporters guilty, it is necessary to ask myself and all of you what we are going to do about it? This is not the first time we have heard about Lexington and Marion... or U.S. intervention in Nicaragua, or $1.5 million a day in military aid to El Salvador, or the systematic extermination of the Indians in Guatemala, or the military build-up in Honduras, the continuing struggles for liberation and self-determination in Puerto Rico, the Philippines, South Africa, Chile, the Middle East, to name a few.

I struggle with what to do about all of these issues. They are pieces in the groaning, wrenching, weaving fabric of the human family struggling to become. I do know what I will not do. I will not write letters to my congressperson. It costs so much to get elected in this country, it would be absurd to suppose that someone who truly represented the interests of the poor would be elected. Why would I write to someone asking her/him to change the very system that put him/her in power? No, I won't call my congressperson or the president or anyone like that. It reinforces the system. It creates the impression that the system, with the right people and/or votes, would work. This is not true. It is fatally flawed, because the basic value supposes throwaway people. It establishes an economic elite whose choices mandate life or death for other communities.

What I am telling you here tonight is that, although I do not have any answers, I'm open to the possibilities. We must do something. Besides the testimony of the relatives, one of the things that struck me powerfully today was the slide show on the Stanford prison experiment. It frightened me badly. Watching those young, well-meaning people turn into not only supporters but promoters of an arbitrary, oppressive system made me ask myself how co-opted I have become without even realizing it. It is a fair guess that each of you could ask yourself the same question. So, what should we do? What can we do? I learned a great deal today from each and every participant. I will commit to the degree that I can, but I am asking, begging for some creative suggestions. We need to do something that will make a difference. If we want a new world, we have to build it… and not on the bodies of our sisters and brothers.

Credit: Miriam Klein Stahl
(Reproduce y Rebélate/Reproduce & Revolt, Soft Skull 2008)

"I struggle with what to do about all of these issues. They are pieces in the groaning, wrenching, weaving fabric of the human family struggling to become…"

Strings Attached in the Age of Authority

Bill Dunne
2008

On 27 October 1983, the U.S. Penitentiary at Marion, Illinois, was slammed into full lockdown mode. Officialdom claimed the lockdown and the wave of brutality with which it was implemented were the last-resort emergency response to a crisis in which prisoners were purportedly on the verge of taking over the already maximum security facility. In reality, the lockdown was the deliberate and long-planned expansion of the one-block control unit into the country's first control unit prison. Control unit Marion was subsequently supplemented and then supplanted by the Administrative Maximum control unit prison at Florence, Colorado, and similar facilities in many other states. Verily, the control unitization of U.S.P. Marion inaugurated an age of escalating ruling class resort to this qualitatively higher level of repression aimed at more class-interest effective use of the prison system, the leading edge of the apparatus of social control.

I was relegated to dungeon Marion in February of 1985. The Federal Bureau of Prisons (BOP) had somehow concluded I did not enjoy its hospitality and was inclined to fulfill the first duty of the POW. The worst of the atrocities with which Marion was control-unitized was over by then. Mass goonings in the course of pointless cell moves, beatings, and chainings to bunks no longer demonstrated power with the frequency of the six months immediately following the lockdown; by my arrival they required at least the slightest pretext. The windows had been fixed and heat turned on, more clothing and bedding supplied, and food quality and quantity improved, so cold, hunger, and physical abuse were no longer the immediately dominant aspects of prisoners' lives. Memories of the months-long guard riot that ushered in the new regime were still fresh, however, and there were still plenty of problems with the gratuitously oppressive nonprogram.

Prisoners were locked in their cells 23 hours per day, getting only an hour per day on the tier in small groups, five days per week. One day each week, prisoners were afforded two hours on the yard instead of the hour on the tier. Another day they were offered two hours in a gym. Many prisoners did not participate in the out-of-unit recreation due to the chaining and driving by a gang of hostile, club-wielding guards the movement entailed, not to mention the risks of any interaction with staff. A prisoner was never allowed outside the cell without being manacled with at least one club wielder and one other guard present; movements of multiple prisoners thus drew out lines of guards. Prisoners who did not return to their cells or "cuff up" fast enough when the ends of these "rec" periods were decreed were subject to verbal and physical abuse and a trip to the hole. This had the salutary result of making it a tenet of tier rec lock-in etiquette that prisoners on a rec group would stand in front of the open cell doors but not enter the cell until everyone was there to step in together. That way guards could not lock someone out to be singled out for abuse.

Virtually everything was against the rules at control unit Marion, and guards used that fact to pursue prisoners into the very corners of their cells. Nothing could be put on the bars. Nothing could be hung in the cells (as to dry). Nothing off the food tray could be retained in the cell (so the salt and pepper packets and milk cartons had better be on the returned tray). Nothing on the walls. Nothing on the floor. Stand for count. No body parts outside the bars. Ad nauseam. Orders by itinerant guards to undo cell felonies had to be obeyed quickly and with the proper attitude on pain of having one's indeterminate sentence to Marion extended. And a hand outside the bars might get clubbed. Violations of the slightest proscription or prescription could result in an "incident report" and/or a cell extraction and/or another *year* more at control unit Marion.

All of the prohibitions and draconian punishments and attendant inse-curity were designed to be psychologically oppressive and make prisoners dependent on their oppressors. My second warden at Marion, a Ph.D. in administrative systems, characterized official intent on local TV as "taking all their decisions away." The idea was to give prisoners not the slightest sanctu-ary from the mailed fist of the state. Even in the dark and quiet predawn solitude at one of many small cells, the bureau was on his case. In whatever refuge a prisoner might find in the pages of a book, study of a personally transporting subject, or in some other way, the agency of repression was with him. In the solitary details of his life with himself, big brother was a lurking, threatening observer and potential actor. Every action thus became a risk and a stressor. Every intrusion by roving authority raised a spike of angry resent-ment that could rip a fella out of his diversion and prevent slipping back into its flow for hours. And the confiscation of decisions and self-determination inherent in the enforced dependence required prisoners to solicit or at least acquiesce in many such intrusions.

All of that made it apparent to me and other prisoners, not to mention outside lawyers and activists who knew the situation and were active in opposing the lockdown, that the lockdown was counterproductive... verily, a reactionary nightmare. It could not possibly (and did not) do what the Marion and BOP administrations were alleging for it. It could not be (and was not) a repository for "the worst of the worst," "bad apples" who had committed acts of violence in other prisons. It could not (and did not) allow other prisons to be operated in a more open manner by "concentrating" all the ne'er-do-wells in one place.

It could not (and did not) reprogram anyone into a more tractable condition; it did, in fact, the reverse. And it could not and did not improve public safety; instead, it did the opposite on two counts: increased the probability of crime and gave the state another instrument of oppression to wield against the people.

But what could we do? The one thing about which the empire's storm troopers were right was that "resistance is futile," at least in the physical sense, for us. A lot of litigating was already being done and done ably, and many prisoners were exercising the futility of administrative remedy requests and reaping retaliation toward documenting official depredations for future reference.

The one thing I did not see being done was informational outreach. I was and remain convinced that if people generally—the citizenry; the body politic; we, the people—could see behind the razor wire and concrete curtain of penological WMD and al Qaeda connections and the mythology of infinite and irrevocable prisoner nastiness, they would never approve of what was being perpetrated in their name. Apparently just such information gleaned directly by local reporters changed their judgments radically from the straight administrative line to acceptance of the prisoners' version of control unit Marion and its genesis. The concomitant change in their reporting led the then warden and executive assistant (and later warden) to personally pressure the local newspaper, *The Southern Illinoisan*, to sever its contacts with prisoners, which it did.

Prisoncrats and the "law enforcement" interest group as well as the bourgeois beneficiaries of police power may well have been content not to look too closely at the rationales and justifications for and actual practice of lockdown Marion. The interest groups have a gang mentality toward prisoners that disposes them to abusive treatment and other violence as a solution for whatever problems they may perceive, whether or not they are the best solution. They feel the public is little more than sentimental potential "perps" inclined to be sympathetic to the gratuitously oppressed and should, therefore, be kept as much out of the loop as possible. And the bourgeoisie tend to rely on their "experts" to keep the rabble in its place and protect them from the have-nots. How that is done concerns the ruling class little; indeed, they do not want to see that sausage being made, as is demonstrated by all the procedural ploys to keep prisoners out of court enacted since the age of control unit prisons spawned. That unaccountable elite is insulated from the results of bad penal policy because its members are infrequently crime victims, are disconnected from victims of the penal system, and do not need the social services whose funding is squandered on purported criminal justice.

The prisoners themselves, however, their families and social infrastructures, communities, and the segment of society that is adversely impacted by crime and does need the social services foregone in the name of "fighting" crime, as well as people actually interested in justice as a social good, have an interest in being able to make judgments about the tactical use of institutions such as control unit Marion on the basis of full, accurate information. Was generalizing and hyperbolic propaganda about the need to virtually totally isolate thoroughly dangerous men sufficient to explain and justify the result and any liabilities that may accrue to these groups through it? Were other prisons operated more openly? Did violence decline because all the baddies were locked down? Were communities safer and happier? Was the penological toll on prisoners compensated by any salutary effect? Did the outcome warrant the sacrifices or the benefits, the consequences? Did the ends justify the means? We knew the answers to these questions were all *"No!"* and wanted to give everyone the true picture of control unit Marion so they could and would reach the same conclusion.

Institutions such as prisons have a responsibility to those in whose names they deprive others of liberty, the pursuit of happiness, and sometimes even life, and whose opportunities and living standard they circumscribe by allocating social wealth to corrections, punishment, retribution, rehabilitation, socialization. We saw that control unit Marion was not fulfilling that responsibility, indeed, was shirking and operating counter to it. We felt our own oppression, but also saw it in the larger context in which we were peons on the field of class control—a context in which control unit Marion could not and would not fulfill its responsibility to the whole people. We also saw the mainstream media was owned and operated by the part of the people control unitization was intended to serve, leaving letters to the editor and seeking news coverage unlikely to provide the requisite reach (though we did that, too). So what, with all that motivation, was a fella to do?

Enter *The Marionette*. I had learned a little about prison journalism from reading the writings of and other involvement with luminaries in the field. I also had some experience in that area with *Washington Prison News Service* (WPNS), for which I was banished into internal exile in the federal prison system in 1982. Since we and our supporters did not have the resources to launch a direct-to-the-people publication, as with WPNS, we opted for a model more like that of the *Pacific News Service*. Through it, we hoped to reach out more to progressive groups than individuals, particularly those with their own media. The theory was that that would intensify what light we could shine into the dark concrete corners of "the swamp," as many knew control unit Marion, not only for its location near the polluted, shallow, and besilted end of Crab Orchard Lake. The title said that though the puppet master could make us dance to a lockdown, cell-time beat, its strings of chain could only attach to the outside.

The Marionette was launched in May of 1985. I wrote some of the material, and other prisoners contributed the rest of the writing and virtually all of the artwork. On the last mail day of every month, I sent my handwritten version thereof to some local activists who had formed the Marion Prisoners' Support Group to distribute it. They would type it and mail it to an unfortunately

Marion Prisoners' Newsletter

The Marionette

January, 1988   Number 33

Big Juju, Big Harassment

On 12/Jan/88, unit manager Brooks came down the A/C side of F block insisting with particular vehemence on adherence to every absurd detail of his desires of the moment for cell arrangement. Characteristically, some of his demands differed from those of previous weeks. Other staff agreed (outside his presence) that it was impossible to keep up with the inane pettiness of this needless annoyance of prisoners, but felt compelled to do his bidding. Brooks was so driven by this particular crusade of harassment that he threw socks and books on or near cell bars onto sleeping prisoners, something that would be considered armed assault if done by a prisoner to a staff member. According to some reports, Brooks was in an alcohol induced altered state at the time. No other explanation for his particularly arcane though not novel behaviour could be determined.

This behaviour expanded when a clean up of unprecedented scope was undertaken the next day. Recreation schedules were interrupted and orderlies were made to clean more thoroughly than ever since the lockdown was imposed over four years ago. Later, blowers were brought in to blow the dirt out of the holes in the steel sheets over the windows in the units, also a unique occurrence. On 15/Jan/88, a bunch of administration officials toured, all of them acting harried, the new associate warden True so much so that he would not speak to prisoners. They behaved as if something secret and monumental and at least a little threatening to them were in the offing.

The next week, the apparent reason surfaced; a visitation by CBS news. But that was not it, executive assistant George Wilson claimed on 18/Jan. It was that the big juju from Washington, new BOP director Michael Quinlan had been planning to tour. He made his appearance on 15/Jan. apparently making it OK to lift the veil of secrecy around the obsessive concern with appearances on 18/Jan. The administration must have been trying to impress him in order to prevent any of the liberalization with which he is reputed to have toyed in the past. The tension that induced in them was, of course, taken out on prisoners via the chain of minions. As one staff member put it ruefully: "You know how it is; they tell us and we tell you." Only the big powers apparently don't let the middle exactly what is expected. They let the underlings twist in uncertainty of having to figure it out. Warden Henman admitted on 29/Jan that he doesn't ask the big guys much, seemingly in the belief that the closed mouth catches no flies.

That psychological beating is passed on with some mark-up until it gets down to those without power, the prisoners. Unfortunately, prisoners are not in the loop by choice. Moreover, many demands on them are irrational and therefore impossible to figure out. And this binge of neurotic senselessness has not yet run down, with at least one prisoner being taken to the hole for failure to comply fast enough on 29/Jan.∞

short list. Time and money were in short supply (as always!). Eventually, I got into hand printing copy-ready copy. That is the big picture. Some of the details of how *The Marionette* played out are hazy to me, however, and my journal of the time has fallen victim to the vicissitudes of porcine persons' shuffling me and my stuff from island to island in the U.S. gulag archipelago over the years. The reliance on the vagaries of imperfect memory that necessitates may leave some of those details somewhat vague (though that might not be the only reason for vagueness!).

The Marion Prisoners' Support Group could not expand the distribution and even had trouble with the regularity and consistency that are so critical to a credible and successful news publication. Southern Illinois is not a very progressive area, so the time and resources were just not there to do the needful—and would have had plenty of other demands on them had they been. Hence, we had to look farther afield. The Bulldozer Collective of Toronto, Ontario, Canada, came to the rescue as our publisher and distributor, while I remained editor. Bulldozer's astute organization of the format, layout, printing, and distribution enabled the technical quality to improve dramatically. Particularly after we went to a tabloid format, circulation grew markedly, ultimately exceeding 1,000, including a great many prisoners.

Eventually, we concluded that even if control unit Marion was the crest of oppression's new wave, it was not enough by itself to sustain more than a small niche publication. Plus, it was distorting not to see Marion and control unitization in its broader context of the wider U.S. and, indeed, the world gulag archipelago. In addition, many of our prisoner subscribers wanted to see more news of the gulag archipelago generally and had important information to contribute to prison struggle as well. Accordingly, *The Prison News Service* (PNS) was joined to *The Marionette* as a co-publication. I edited both efforts. PNS's brief was imprisonment generally and how it played out as an instrument of repression and class control and counterinsurgency around the world. PNS carried articles from and about all over, but focused on the U.S. and Canada, where most of our writers and readers were and were on the front lines. But *The Marionette* remained a separate entity within the larger publication. The situation was that unique.

As editor of *The Marionette*, I would develop information for stories that would shed light on the character of subsistence at U.S.P. Marion. That included helping others get their information into their own voices and a coherent form because our perspectives and experience were not monolithic. Marion staff were also sources: they would treat prisoners as inanimate hazardous waste and so say things around them as if they had no ears (or it would not matter if they did). Sometimes these loose lips would provide useful information upon request. After a time, though, guards because very, well, guarded in what they said around or to me, so I had to rely on alternative sources (such as their radios and literal eavesdropping—for example: few prisoners came out for early morning tier rec, so guards who were supposed to be watching us would go into their office around the corner and chew the fat, which often carried to an ear 20 still and silent feet and a set of bars away) and the ears and eyes (though we didn't get to see much) of other prisoners. The executive staff were frequently not so guarded, apparently thinking a scruffy prisoner in a pair of drawers in a small cell behind bars could not possibly wheedle anything useful from their besuited majesties. They often just dug the hole deeper when asked about this or that new (or old) needless abuse of their virtually absolute authority over prisoners' lives. Even local media provided occasional grist for *The Marionette*'s mill.

When the first edition (actually the third edition, but the first to be sent in on a big enough scale to be noticed) of *The Marionette* arrived at the institution, I was taken to the hole and put on an empty range. That was somewhat disquieting because it is in such isolated situations that bad things happen. I was relieved to discover the following day that a serial killer who was too hot to be kept in local facilities was being stashed there, too. Bad things are less likely in the presence of witnesses, and I did not think it likely *he* was the bad thing 'cause he was small and scrawny.

The charge against me was "misuse of the mails" because a cartoon allegedly showed the making of weapons. The cartoon has a few fat pigs bursting out of cop uniforms and crammed behind little school desks. In front of them was a lieutenant pig straining the buttons of his cop shirt and aiming a pointer at an easel, sternly instructing the little piggies on what the caption said was "attack sock," of which three were depicted. You see, prisoners had been engaging in the deadly terroristic practice of hanging socks on the cell bars to dry. Of course, this was forbidden, so prisoners caught perpetrating the horrible crime would be found guilty of an infraction and have their sentences to Marion extended for *a year* and perhaps more. I was released from the SHU (Special Housing Unit) after a few days, and the incident report was never processed. My property, however, had been thoroughly "rednecked," and every handwritten piece of paper in the cell had been seized. I did not get the writing back for three weeks. But *The Marionette* remained banned in control unit Marion for the next three years.

The powers that were did not engage in further direct and overt action specifically aimed at suppressing *The Marionette*, though I was required to stay at dungeon Marion twice as long as the average. I recall only one time my handwritten version did not arrive at its destination. (And *The Marionette* had to be handwritten; I received an infraction for typing it on the legal material typewriter after receiving permission to do so via an administrative remedy request—indeed, I got *two* infractions; the guard who held the heat transfer typewriter tape up to a mirror and read it and the counselor who was alerted by the mail room that I was mailing out nonlegal typing each wrote one.) I cannot remember why the missing edition did not arrive, but do recall it was something not likely attributable to the officialdom. The replacement copy I sent did make it, as did every other copy for the entire seven-year run. Nor did the guards search the cell looking for the rough draft around mailing time, as did Washington State Penitentiary guards trying to impede the WPNS.

The absence of direct suppression of *The Marionette* may have come under the heading of giving a fella rope (but surely not enough for scaling!). Marion's executive assistant to the warden (less than an associate warden but more than a department head, this official is usually the prison's media liaison person) did, however, tell an author he was conducting on a tour of the prison that he had a file of every *Marionette* and was monitoring them closely to ensure I violated no rules. Various officials and others friendly to the BOP were frequently given tours of U.S.P. Marion. I used to accost the ones I saw to see who they were, what their interest in Marion was, and what kind of official lies they were being told. I was always looking for muck for *The Marionette* to rake. I also kept argument and copies of pertinent propaganda on tap for just such occasions; only bad decisions could have been made on the swill the swine spouted, and most of the tourists were some sort of decision makers or their observers. The author said—and the executive assistant did not contradict him—that he had been hired to write a history of the BOP and had been a director of corrections in five state prison systems. I think it unlikely that any of *The Marionette*'s history made it into his history, the executive assistant's file notwithstanding.

In *The Marionette*'s second year of publication, another prisoner and comrade, Ron Del Raine, sued the Marion administration about the ban on the publication entering the prison. No case could be made for excluding it: it did not advocate violence, unrest, or rebellion; it did not amount to correspondence between prisoners; it did not show the making of weapons; it did not include any deliberately false information (and I often challenged the officials to come up with any error, which they never could do). At a deposition to which I was called regarding this suit, the Assistant U.S. Attorney representing the prison attempted to elicit from me some ulterior motive for *The Marionette* that would justify the ban on it. Her tactic seemed to be to "prove" *The Marionette* was written by outside agitators to foment resistance at control unit Marion and that I was just their cat's paw. (The Washington State Assistant Attorney General charged with representing the state's corrections bureaucracy made similar allegations about the WPNS.)

Given the level of mail scrutiny at Marion, the difficulty of any such proof may suggest an effort to get me to admit a rule violation upon which suppression could be justified. Acting as a reporter and writing under a byline is forbidden by BOP regulations, as is circulating a manuscript. Since that was the era of the Iran-contra hearings in the U.S. Congress, I was well-schooled in the means and methods of asserting my right not to incriminate myself and to remain silent. Moreover, it was part of my editorial function to protect the identities of sources and those who chose to write in *The Marionette* and, later, *The Prison News Service* under a *nom de guerre*. I was not charged with anything in the wake of the lawsuit, and I suspect that suit was responsible for the elimination of the ban on *The Prison News Service/Marionette* after three years. It certainly was not any editorial change!

Of course, that prosecutor's questions may have been just evidence of a more generalized official thrashing about trying to create some—any!—justification for the Marion administration's and BOP's indefensible control unit policy she was job-bound to defend. Official avoidance of a demonstrable pattern and practice of retaliation directly and specifically for participation in *The Marionette* may have been related to the difficulty of that task. Policy and, indeed, law give prison administrators discretion to ban reading material they deem a security threat or facilitator of criminality. Accordingly, the Marion prisoncrats apparently felt secure in excluding *The Marionette* as a means of limiting unfavorable commentary because allowing it would have stimulated contributions and because they felt it an affront to their exaltednesses. Political sensitivity, however, circumscribes the discretion of the official stick, and involvement of the U.S. Attorney and federal court may have persuaded the prisoncrats to back away from a potentially controversial and untenable interpretation and treatment of *The Marionette* and its makers. They may have thought that suppressing us would give us credibility and undermine officialdom's with media workers sensitive to the trampling of free speech; jackbooted thugs just can't get a fair break, they probably felt. The

Marion staff thus had to be at least somewhat subtle and indirect about action against their pencil paparazzi. Known major participants in *The Marionette* were thus more subject to the petty infractions that extended people's stays at lockdown Marion and other annoyance—but always with a purported reason other than *The Marionette*.

Nevertheless, control unit Marion stimulated a lot of controversy and even more attention—which undoubtedly contributed to that protective effect for *The Marionette*, at least to the extent that the administration(s) could not shut it down directly (though one could argue that its ultimate demise was the result of the swine having made involvement with it too risky). The agency of repression was, therefore, forced to exercise spin control in the maelstrom of scrutiny its escalation of repression had engendered. Toward that end, it fostered and facilitated dissemination of its tortuous view of control unit Marion's operation in favorable venues. Aside from hack flacks telling the press what the BOP thought it could get printed and trotting out two psycho-killers, the only prisoners it could use to bolster its position, many information management tours were permitted entry. States contemplating their own control unit/supermax facilities sent contingents. Other countries with internal debates about control unitization sent investigators. Various minions of the "just-us" system such as judges, prosecutors, cops, lawyers (though none representing prisoners), and even a couple congresspersons were squired through. Many mainstream media outlets, including ABC, BBC, CBS, NPR, *The New York Times*, French TV, and *The Southern Illinoisan* sent reporting teams. Local TV and authors like the aforementioned "historian" also made the trek through the swamp and its morass of official disinformation. And there were undoubtedly many others of which I was not aware or have forgotten.

The intent and goal of *The Marionette* was to ensure all that controversy and attention did not play out solely on the basis of the official version, which was substantively false and would thus render conclusions regarding the future of Marion in particular and control unitization more broadly erroneous. Our voice, however, was too small and weak and the class connection of the Marion and BOP administrators to the mainstream media's operatives and certainly to the minions of other government entities weighing their own control unit nightmares too strong for *The Marionette* to compete adequately. At least the rapid proliferation of control units so suggests. Despite the sending of many copies of *The Marionette* and many of its articles to multitudinous media on multitudinous occasions, including directly giving the material to reporters getting the official tour and/or conducting interviews, I do not recall a single instance of one being cited as a source. But we could not abandon the field!

Indeed, an ABC "20/20" interviewer had a whole fan of issues (and I do not recall ABC TV being on our regular mailing list). But he used them only to demand an explanation of the administration's claim *The Marionette* was inflammatory. Probably short on preparation—or, more likely, prepped only in and uncritical of the official version—an article entitled "Fork U" caught his attention as an example. That article, however, detailed a grotesque overreaction to what turned out to be a case of guards miscounting plastic forks. Accordingly, it could only corroborate a prisoner's statement about the situation: "I'd say we'd been forked. Wouldn't you?" Apparently because it exposed a circumstance inconsistent with official disinformation, the segment was banished to the cutting room floor.

That, however, does not mean *The Marionette* had no impact. We received requests for copies from as far away as Israel, Japan, and Taiwan. And we did receive a request to archive the entire run from The State Historical Society of Wisconsin, which apparently has one of the most extensive collections of prison publications in existence. The information did go forth and multiply and at least gave thousands of individuals a picture of what "control unit" means in actual human experience rather than the official abstraction. It may have slowed the goose-step of Marion-style repression an iota, a heartbeat, a micrometer from the draconian extreme it might have reached without the opposition. If it did that, it did well, considering the circumstances. Verily, perhaps we contributed to the feds never building another control unit prison after ADX despite the closure of U.S.P. Marion and roughly doubling their prison population. Mainstream attention seemed to crest in 1988. Alternative progressive attention was more difficult to quantify and opposition was still necessary, so we soldiered on. We would have used and did use the mainstream to the extent we were able, but we were not in it for that; we were under no illusion that we could foment revolution via the mainstream, or that it would not try to use us to our detriment.

The Marionette ran for seven years even, from May of 1985 to April of 1992. At first, it was a monthly publication, but as resources became strained due to our inability to draw sufficient support from our constituency and clientele—and, I must admit, our own mistakes—a bimonthly. Eventually, I was transferred from U.S.P. Marion to U.S.P. Terre Haute. Though I tried to secure a successor-in-office, so to speak, by the time I left Marion, none had materialized. I did not think *The Marionette* editor could fulfill that role credibly without being there, and given the communication difficulties imposed by the Bureau of Prisons, content would be exceedingly difficult to organize. So a month after I left Marion, *The Marionette* joined *The Guardian*, *The Red Dragon*, *Tug*, *The Torch*, and a thousand other flowers of the movement for the most equitable social reality untimely uprooted from the vale of struggle.

Twenty-two years after the birth of *The Marionette*, and 15 years after its demise, it is even more apparent that its underlying message was and remains correct: that Marion-style repression, i.e., the control unit prison, is not merely needless and costly abuse, it is actively counterproductive from any rational sociological perspective. This is especially true if correction is to be the goal and justification of penology. Socialization would be a better word and goal if the intent is to have social institutions that are effective at criminal justice rather than merely cosmetically appealing, because no one goes out deliberately to wreak evil, virtually everyone having a rationalization. But that is a digression into another rant! *The Marionette* directly and circumstantially exposed the deliberate falsity of official propaganda about the theory and practice of control unit Marion and thus also indicated that officialdom knew the prospective result and had ulterior motives that made it willing to accept/impose those negative consequences. The years have corroborated *The Marionette*'s debunking of that propaganda as the few brief paragraphs below illustrate; they have also blown away some of the official smoke and mirrors obscuring what those ulterior motives might be.

Control unit Marion was not (and could not be) a repository for "the worst of the worst." First, there was the very subjective question of who fit into that category. Accepting, *ad arguendo*, the version of "the worst of the worst" the prisoncrats quoted to various media as "prisoners who have committed acts of violence in other prisons," Marion was not such a repository. Various counts I conducted during my decade in the dungeon never found a majority confined there for such reasons. Further, my observation when I was not there was that people were sent there for drug use, gang affiliation, escape suspicions, and directly from court without a chance to act violently in other prisons. Litigators, the politically active, and the attitudinally impaired were at greater risk of going there than the violent. Moreover, the number of perpetrators of violence who did not go there (or, later, ADX) while nonviolent prisoners did provides further evidence that official claims that Marion was for the "worst of the worst who had committed violence in other prisons" was not true and thus a cover for another motive.

Control unit Marion did not (and could not) allow other prisons to operate more openly. Presumably, people were expected to believe that "concentrating" all the "bad apples" would mean the resources required to guard against assault, murder, riot, et cetera, could be devoted to more constructive programs like academic education, vocational training, and recreational and other "treatment" programs at other places. Well, they were not. Right about the time Marion was converted to a control unit prison, programming opportunities for prisoners began to evaporate. Outside groups that used to bring cultural and social events into prisons began to be excluded to the point at which only the occasional religious visitor is permitted to enter federal penitentiaries to bring programming to prisoners. Vocational programs began to disappear as well, and there are now no postsecondary programs other than the largely joke-style adult continuing education offerings in penitentiaries. Some penitentiaries no longer even have libraries or have some cardboard-cutout substitute. Hobby programs have been reduced. Social visiting has been cut back from five days per week to as little as two, and its conditions have deteriorated as well. Control unit Marion apparently informed the swine that isolated and cut-off prisoners were easier to manipulate and control. Enforced regimentation has also become more common, and penitentiary prisoners are now pressured about inanities like wearing uniforms, not wearing hats inside, tucking in shirts, and walking on this or that side of lines painted on the floor. Cell and unit time has been significantly increased with bizarre movement schedules that make it difficult to access what opportunities may be available. And access to noncustodial staff for services such as visiting and phone list processing, administrative remedy requests (grievances), custody and classification concerns, and housing problems has diminished markedly. All that means that prisons are now more closed and restrictive with a harder and sharper line drawn between staff and prisoners. This was despite the fact that control unit Marion existed and had been supplemented (though now replaced) by control unit Florence.

Control unit Marion did not (and could not) "correct" its victims. It has not worked as some sort of "treatment" that would, in effect, beat people into not misbehaving—either actually or as a threat. The holes in all the penitentiaries are now so chronically overcrowded that the staff has had to stop enforcing or enforcing so rigidly many rules. Instead, prisoners are punished in other ways such as denying phone and visiting and commissary privileges. That increases the incentive to violate rules to get around the denial of these privileges where most people have them. It also further cuts prisoners off and penalizes their families and friends—and often confers the freedom of nothing left to lose. In addition, neither the threat nor the actuality of hole or lockdown time dissuades prisoners from "doin' what a fella has to do"; verily, they can promote it. If a prisoner feels s/he is being taken advantage of as in, say, being pressured for sex or robbed or assaulted, that prisoner must and is expected to respond violently; one may not acquiesce in his or her own oppression and one may not rat. Doing what one must is widely approved in the prison society—especially if the unavoidable consequences are severe. This fullness of the holes, the absolute and per capita increase in violence and other rule violation in penitentiaries (the higher threshold for the writing of infractions notwithstanding), and the impossibility of sending all of those involved in violence to a control unit all show control unit Marion has not worked in the behavior modification way intended, or at least stated. Though I would be surprised if such records were kept, I think they would show the incidence of incident (misbehavior) reports for control units Marion and Administrative Maximum alumni would be greater after the experience than for others and not reduced in a before versus after comparison, except, maybe, to an extent that could be attributed to other factors.

Verily, rather than correct or rehabilitate, U.S.P. Marion alienated and embittered. The most it taught anyone was to be more careful to avoid detection of chosen proscribed activity. It inculcated the lesson that power is the only arbiter or right and wrong, so it is correct to do whatever one has the power to do as long as it can be concealed from anyone more powerful who might object. Of course, the psychological damage control unitization inflicted on some rendered them incapable of incorporating that lesson into their behavior. Consider the volume of the current debate about the pervasiveness of

Post-Traumatic Stress Disorder (PTSD) among U.S. soldiers returning from Iraq. They all signed on knowing the probability of such duty, are stationed there only briefly (and, like prisoners, with high probability of return engagements), have a huge social and material support infrastructure, yet are still plagued by a host of debilitating psychological symptoms from having been exposed to periods of random violence and insecurity. (Imagine the symptoms Iraqis must be experiencing, then, in their permanent predicament of perpetual violence on a shock and awe scale!) Imagine, then, prisoners also exposed to random violence (including the potentially deadly), not only while out on patrol in armored convoys, but 24/7 indefinitely, with no support infrastructure—indeed, an antisupport infrastructure that has them all having an unassailably incorrigible gangster mentality that only age can ameliorate. But prisoners cannot be mentally ill, only bad and evil, and are thus not worthy of treatment, just punishment. The circumstances of control unit Marion thus ensured that even Marion victims who did not leave with an identifiable psychological injury left with some damage; any improvement was despite rather than due to the "program" and not nearly what it could have been.

As a result, Marion could not (and did not) improve public safety. Though few prisoners were released directly from Marion, most prisoners are released eventually to some community, maybe yours. Most control unit prisoners go to other prisons, however, which are also de facto communities. They bring with them the attitudes gestated during their experience in lockdown. So do guards or all ranks that spread the infection of control unit treatment attitudes laterally when they transfer. That conditions the required attitudes and resulting experience for both prisoners and staff in supposedly more open prisons. The end is a winterization of the environment in which the atmosphere tends to become cold, hard, edgy, gray, and threatening. Hence, not only Marion prisoners, but those at prisons whose regimes are toughened due to control units as well, are released to communities in conditions that make them less likely to be good neighbors. While it is also unlikely that this statistic is kept officially, from my observation, the recidivism rate of victims of control unit prisons is higher than for other ex-prisoners.

Control unitization undermines public safety not only by increasing the probability of crime by opportunist and psychologically impaired elements of the lumpen proletariat, but also by increasing the probability of crime by the apparatus of repression itself. It puts a powerful tool to use in suppressing progressive movements in the hands of the protectors of ruling-class interests. People in control unit prisons are virtually cut off from the outside world, and what communication is permitted is closely monitored. And even that can be cut off if the BOP decides to impose "Special Administrative Measures," which amount to holding someone virtually incommunicado. Political prisoners are most likely to be thus victimized—and may be sent to control units without passing through another prison, as control unit Marion has shown. In this way, the apparatus may attack social justice undertakings by sequestering and stigmatizing their activists at crucial times during the initiatives' development.

Moreover, aside from the instruments of control themselves, control unitization changes official attitudes toward what is acceptable in dealing with the public, which the apparatus increasingly sees as something to be dominated and controlled rather than protected and served. Before control unit Marion, the deviation was from maximum security to lockdown as in a hole or one-unit control unit. Now it is from lockdown to extraordinary rendition, total isolation, enemy combatant status (and when will the wars on crime and drugs join the "war on terror" in conferring that status?), water boarding, sleep deprivation, stress positions, and all the other tortures Bush the Lesser insists are not tortures and not used by his administration. The mere existence of debate about these tactics suggests they will infiltrate the civilian domain soon; some of them already have, as the scandals regarding the use of tasers and stun belts, restraint chairs, four-pointing, and police torture scandals from Chicago to New Orleans and New York to Los Angeles, among myriad other "civilian" instances of abuse morphed into policy attest.

That suggests the ulterior motives for control unit Marion and control unitization generally. Control units are laboratories for experimentation in social manipulation and control as well as a stick to wield against the politically disfavored. As far back as 1961, the BOP's psychology apparatus made the point to its minions in the far-flung isles of the U.S. gulag archipelago that they were in a unique position to perform such experiments on their captive populations and exhorted them to do so and report back to the center. The lessons thus gleaned will ultimately translate to the outside where ruling-class interests lie in exploiting rather than incarcerating or killing labor (though history is replete with demonstrations that it will do both the latter on a grand scale upon feeling threatened; and we are on the verge of a big surplus of labor). Those lessons (and a huge gulag archipelago) to contain that 2 to 4 percent who will not be manipulated or controlled will help contain resistance and rebellion fomented by depression of the proletariat's living standards as global capital forces a race to the bottom in labor compensation. Increasingly, things that used to be made in the U.S. and Europe only are now also made in Asia at much lower labor costs. So Western living standards will have to come down (or wealth will have to be redistributed in a more equitable manner, and even so). The developing world's standards are rising, which will contribute to its stability, and people are less likely to buck not getting what they want than losing what they have in any event. The ruling class has to handle that—with a huge and powerful apparatus of repression. And it will have to ensure that apparatus does not become a university of struggle; prisons have been for other revolutions. It also has to demonize and vilify its opposition, to make them like the Abu Ghraib prisoners in the eyes of their jailers and others serving the apparatus, so the agents of repression will do the needful (for the ruling class) to what are essentially their class sistren and brethren.

Yes, *The Marionette* is gone—and so, for that matter, is U.S.P. Marion as the first control unit prison. (It is now an F.C.I.—medium security "Federal Correctional Institution.") But its clones are still in business, and the turning of the screws here at U.S.P. Big Sandy suggests there is a competition afoot between a group of the new federal penitentiaries for which one will be the replacement. *The Marionette* shot its paper bullets in furtherance of the most equitable social reality in which all people will have the greatest possible freedom to develop their full human potential. I like to think that my comrades and I did not suffer the slings and arrows of prisoncrat wrath in vain. The problem of control unit prisons remains, however. Perhaps we can claim a modicum of success in contributing to the fact that though there are now many control unit prisons, the feds only have one (permanent and acknowledged; there have been several temporary ones billed as "pilot programs" here and there) and every state does not have one. But the issue is still live. Control unitization is a cancer that may not currently be metastasizing rapidly. That might not be true tomorrow. It might not even be true today: because Marion is the only control unit I have heard was closed and because I have not seen news of many new ones does not mean they are not a-building. So attention to, examination of, and resistance against the control unitization of the U.S. gulag archipelago is still in order.

The future holds promise!

Section II.

International Tribunal on Political Prisoners/ Prisoners of War in the U.S.A.

*T*he December 1990 International Tribunal at Hunter College in New York City, led by Dr. Luis Nieves Falcón, brought together over a thousand participants from around the world and groups and leaders from various national liberation movements within the U.S. The Tribunal was a serious political-judicial undertaking: Legal documents were carefully drawn up in accordance with international law. An indictment was written and delivered to U.S. officials, who were invited to attend and defend. An international panel of judges with distinguished legal and civic credentials was assembled. And the Tribunal itself was only the capstone of a carefully orchestrated set of multifaceted events throughout 1990. A large-scale poetry reading was held at New York's prestigious Society for Ethical Culture; an art show was presented at Charas, a progressive community center. An Interfaith Summit was convened at the American Indian Community House. The Tribunal itself became a hot-ticket, public political event. By the end of it all, the issue of political prisoners was more clearly and definitively on the agenda of the U.S. left, and a verdict was available for the various movements to use in their base-building work.

This section brings to print for the first time many of the key documents of that effort, preceded by a summary and history of precursor efforts written the next year. Erring on the side of inclusion, we have kept the lists of various individuals signing onto or serving as part of these events in order to suggest the possibilities before us. Look at the denominations and stature of people listed on the Interfaith Religious Call. We must rebuild. But we can only do that if we are able to break through our own assorted isolations and recognize that the issues we hold dear are not so far away from those of our neighbors next door. Sometimes we just have to knock.

Introduction and Historical Context for the International Tribunal on U.S. Political Prisoners and P.O.W.'s

Bob Lederer
(with assistance from Dhoruba Bin-Wahad and Tanaquil Jones)
1991

Around the world, 1990 was a year in which political prisoners and prisoners of war (POW's) were spotlighted—and in some cases freed. The most celebrated case was that of African National Congress leader Nelson Mandela, released after 27 years, along with seven other antiapartheid guerrillas. Many other dissidents and resistance fighters—from SWAPO's POW's in newly independent Namibia to antifascist activists in a nominally "democratic" Chile to dissenters in the former East Bloc European nations—also gained freedom. The U.S. government often cynically applauded the releases, while chastising other regimes—particularly those on the left—for continuing to hold political prisoners.

Yet that same government continues its longstanding refusal to acknowledge the vast numbers of political prisoners and POW's inside its own borders. The sensitivity with which U.S. officials—Democratic and Republican alike—view this allegation can be seen in the treatment of then-United Nations Ambassador Andrew Young (under President Jimmy Carter), whose 1978 statement that the U.S. holds "hundreds of political prisoners" brought an instant, sharp Administration rebuke and played a role in his firing several months later.

Unfortunately, many progressive activists, journalists and diplomats, both within and outside this country, have tended to believe U.S. government denials. Some think that political repression in the sophisticated "democratic" United States takes milder forms than outright jailing for radical dissent, while others simply lack knowledge of more than the one or two cases that have gained some international notoriety.

Yet by at least two counts, there are over 100 political prisoners and POW's in U.S. detention—many serving virtual life sentences and some already held for as long as 20 years (thereby probably earning the U.S. the distinction of having the world's longest-held political prisoners). Those incarcer-

This article was written for, but never published by, a major U.S. progressive magazine shortly after the conclusion of the International Tribunal on Political Prisoners/POWs in the U.S. It has remained unpublished until now.

ated include Black and New Afrikan liberation activists (by far the largest category), Puerto Rican *independentistas* (independence supporters), Native American fighters for sovereignty, Mexicano-Chicano freedom activists, Euro-American (white) anti-imperialists and "Plowshares" antinuclear religious protesters. In recent years, the U.S. has also at times jailed draft registration resisters and providers of sanctuary to Central American refugees. (Meanwhile, at various times U.S. authorities have jailed or held in immigration detention centers scores of militant activists fleeing persecution—individually or en masse—by U.S.-backed repressive regimes. Among these have been Palestinians, Salvadorans, Haitians and Irish.)

It was precisely to counter the lack of awareness of these cases that Freedom Now! The Campaign for Amnesty and Human Rights of Political Prisoners in the U.S.—a broad coalition formed in 1988 by individuals and groups defending jailed activists—called for an International Tribunal on this issue. In the tradition of the various Bertrand Russell Tribunals on such questions as the Western-sponsored wars of conquest against Vietnam, East Timor and Western Sahara, a panel of distinguished human rights lawyers and experts from eight countries was assembled to hear a detailed exposition of evidence of U.S. violations of international law. After obtaining 88 organizational sponsors and endorsers—representing a broad cross-section of the U.S. progressive and religious community—the *Special International Tribunal on Violations of Human Rights of Political Prisoners and Prisoners of War in United States Prisons and Jails* convened from December 7-10, 1990, at New York City's Hunter College.

Historical Background

Since the first brutal armed assaults by European settlers against Native Americans and their land, there have been struggles—employing both armed and nonviolent tactics—for self-determination by oppressed peoples in North America. For centuries, indigenous peoples of many nations (so-called "Indian tribes") militarily fought the ever-larger land grabs by insatiable Euro-Americans, forcing the British colonies and later the U.S. government to sign a total of 371 treaties granting sovereignty. All have been systematically violated by the U.S., spurring further resistance activities. Despite the mass genocide leading to the final defeat of Native peoples in the Western U.S. during the 1890s, many-sided opposition to colonialism has continued, dramatically revived by the American Indian Movement in the late 1960s and still very much alive.

After the U.S. seized 50 percent of Mexico's territory in the war of 1846-48, the occupation was enforced by state-backed vigilante "policing" and lynchings, which sparked organized Mexicanos resistance. In the early 1900s, several armed clandestine Mexicano organizations emerged to fight for self-determination, only to be crushed by military force. Among these was a group led by Juan Nepomucemo Cortina (who led a 15-year guerrilla war in Texas) and the *Plan de San Diego* (which in 1915 carried out a pro-independence uprising). The 1960s saw a renewed flowering of both armed and peaceful resistance groups of great diversity, some of which continue today.

When the U.S. invaded and seized Puerto Rico in 1898, guerrilla forces fought the military until two years of martial law—enforced with brutal assassinations and jailings—exterminated all resistance. Years of unsuccessful electoral struggle for independence followed. From the 1930s through the early 1950s, the Nationalist Party led mass street protests and armed resistance. This campaign culminated in the paramilitary Jayuya Uprising of 1950 and the proclamation of a Republic in several rural towns crushed with U.S. aerial bombardment, street killings, and hundreds of' imprisonments. Since the early 1960s, guerrilla and mass protest movements have re-emerged, fighting both in Puerto Rico and among the large displaced population of islanders living in the U.S.

The legacy of Black people's struggle for freedom in the U.S. goes back to the many armed revolts during the entire slavery period and has included many ideological approaches. Among these were (just to cite a few) the Pan-Africanist movement of the early 1800s, the Black town movement led by Pap Singleton in the 1860s, the huge United Negro Improvement Association led by Marcus Garvey in the 1910s and 1920s, the Nation of Islam beginning in the 1930s and the modern Black liberation movement with its many organizations, both armed and nonviolent, in the 1960s and 1970s—with continuing struggles today.

Through much of U.S. history, Euro-American opposition to government suppression of people of color (either domestically or internationally) has been sporadic and inconsistent. But since the 1960s, a broad range of antiracist, anti-war and solidarity movements have developed, using many tactics, including armed resistance. Meanwhile, many Euro-Americans have participated in a variety of social protest movements alongside people of color, against other injustices such as worker exploitation, nuclear weapons, women's oppression, homophobia, poor health care and environmental destruction.

Whenever militant resistance movements have developed, multisided repression has been soon to follow and with it, the arrest and detention of activists and fighters. Thus, the phenomenon of detaining U.S. political prisoners and prisoners of war is by no means new. But in recent years it has become more carefully planned and scientific as part of a broader scheme of counterinsurgency.

Internationalizing the Human Rights Issue

In recent decades, people of color fighting for self-determination—targets of the most sustained and intense repression—have worked hard to bring these abuses into the international arena. Black activists have been among those at the forefront of such efforts. In 1951, William Patterson of the Civil Rights Congress brought a historic petition called *We Charge Genocide* to the

United Nations, accusing the U.S. of a range of human rights violations against Black people.* In the early 1960s, Malcolm X, the Black nationalist leader, called upon the Black community to again seek to bring the U.S. before the U.N. on human rights violations charges. He was killed, most likely by assassins working for the Federal Bureau of Investigation, before he could accomplish this. In 1976, Jalil Muntaqim became the first political prisoner to take up this banner.† Muntaqim organized other jailed activists into a National Prisoners' Campaign, which submitted a petition to the U.N. Human Rights Commission in Geneva. Spurred by this effort, a group of progressive organizations, coordinated by Lennox Hinds of the National Conference of Black Lawyers, invited an international delegation of jurists to tour numerous U.S. prisons and interview political prisoners in August 1979. Their findings raised serious questions about the treatment and reasons for confinement of the many political prisoners they interviewed.‡ In November 1979, a coalition of Black liberation groups led a march by 5,000 people to the United Nations in New York, accompanying the filing of another such petition. However, until the 1990 Tribunal, none of these efforts produced a finding by any international body that Blacks in the U.S. constitute a people legitimately fighting for self-determination.

Meanwhile, since the early 1960s, Puerto Rican independence organizations had been making presentations before the United Nations Decolonization Committee and later to the Non-Aligned Movement, raising the political prisoner issue along with broader issues of colonialism and repression. By the 1970s, those bodies began adopting annual resolutions (reiterated as recently as 1990) calling on the U.S. to decolonize Puerto Rico, at times specifically urging the release of all jailed *independentistas*. These efforts dramatically bore fruit in 1979, when after a many-year international campaign, four Puerto Rican Nationalists jailed over 25 years for bringing symbolic armed resistance to the colonizer's capital—and viewed on the island as national heroes—were unconditionally freed by President Jimmy Carter. Perhaps the most thorough airing of the issues of Puerto Rico's colonial status occurred at the Permanent Peoples' Tribunal on Puerto Rico, a successor to the Bertrand

* William Patterson, *We Charge Genocide: The Historic Petition to the United Nations for Relief from A Crime of the U S Government Against the Negro People* (New York: International Publishers, 1970).

† One of the Black activists known as the "New York 3," Muntaqim is still in a New York State prison serving 25 years to life. An active community campaign is under way to reverse the New York 3's questionable conviction on murder charges.

‡ J. Soffiyah Elijah, Research Committee on International Law and Black Freedom Fighters, "Conditions of Confinement" (previously unpublished paper submitted to 1990 International Tribunal and included here as II.7.B, page 191); see also "Report of International Jurists—Visit with Human Rights Petitioners in the United States." August 3-20, 1979, filed with the U.N. Commission on Human, Sub-Commission on Prevention of Discrimination and Protection of Minorities; and Lennox S. Hinds, "Illusions of Justice: Human Rights Violations in the United States," University of Iowa School of Social Work, 1979, for text of U.N. petition filed by Hinds on behalf of numerous organizations.

Russell Tribunals, meeting in Barcelona, Spain, from January 27-29, 1989, which joined the growing international chorus for decolonization and prisoner release.

Organizations working for Native American sovereignty, notably the International Indian Treaty Council, a U.N.-recognized Non-Governmental Organization, have similarly made presentations before various U.N. bodies since the 1970s. These have included the question of jailed activists.

Meanwhile, various movements worked for several years to urge Amnesty International to investigate U.S. political prisoners. Since the early 1980s, Amnesty has taken up only a handful of individual cases, although in 1987 and 1988, it took a strong stand against brutal U.S. prison control units using behavior modification mainly or partly against activists.*

One of those special sub-prisons, the Lexington (Kentucky) High Security Unit, which housed three women revolutionaries for two years under conditions of isolation and sensory deprivation, was closed in 1988 after an international campaign, led by some of the activists who later formed Freedom Now! and supported by numerous legal, religious, human rights, women's, and lesbians' organizations. (In May 1988, at the height of the effort, Soviet President Mikhail Gorbachev raised the issue with U.S. President Ronald Reagan at a summit meeting.)

In 1989 and 1990, joint delegations of Blacks, Puerto Ricans, Native Americans and Euro-Americans submitted material on political prisoners and POW's to the U.N. Human Rights Commission in Geneva. So far, no governmental member of the Commission has been bold enough to place these issues on the agenda.

1990 Tribunal Convened

All of these efforts laid the groundwork for the 1990 International Tribunal in New York. A five-count indictment of responsible federal and state officials was brought on behalf of 92 political prisoners and POW's (joined by 88 progressive organizations and scores of individuals). Count I, denial of the right to self-determination, enumerated numerous acts of repression directed against the Black/New Afrikan, Mexicano, Native American and Puerto Rican peoples. Count II, criminalization of Euro-Americans for behavior protected by international law, covered repression of those in solidarity with national liberation movements, as well as those working against nuclear weapons, militarism, racism, sexism and antigay oppression. Count III, genocide,

---

* Amnesty International,"The High Security Unit: Lexington Federal Prison, Kentucky U.S.A.," August 1988; Amnesty International,"Allegations of Ill Treatment in Marion Prison, Illinois, U.S.A.,"May 1987. Amnesty's policy against adopting as prisoners of conscience those who "advocate or practice violence"has excluded many dedicated activists from consideration In recent years; however, Amnesty has criticized the trial procedures leading to the convictions of, among others, the Wilmington 10 (Black civil rights activists in North Carolina freed in the early 1980s), Native American leader Leonard Peltier, and Black Panther leader Geronimo ji Jaga Pratt. Regarding Pratt, see Amnesty International 1989 Report, pp. 151-52.

applied the U.N. definition of that term to people of color in the U.S. Count IV, deprivation of fundamental rights, listed numerous methods used to convict activists of criminal charges and impose lengthy sentences. Finally, Count V, cruel, inhuman and degrading treatment, details the "variety of conditions in prison designed to break [activists'] will to resist, intimidate them from or punish them for persisting in their beliefs and affiliations with movements and/or organizations which resulted in their incarceration." A long list of violations of international law and U.S. constitutional provisions, with citations, was provided.

This indictment was served by mail on all the charged officials with an invitation to offer a defense. Predictably, none responded.* The Tribunal convened on December 7, attended by over 1,000 people from around the U.S. and numerous foreign observers (including several United Nations diplomats). Five special prosecutors and two counsel (all noted attorneys who have defended numerous political prisoners and POW's) presented the indictment.

Over a two-day period, 22 witnesses testified in person or by videotape, representing the diverse movements from which the prisoners are drawn. Among these were many former political prisoners (including two political exiles testifying by video from Cuba, Puerto Rican guerrilla William Morales and former Black Panther member Assata Shakur). Many audience members were especially shocked and moved by the testimony of such ex-prisoners as Alberta Africa, a member of the MOVE organization, who narrated the years of Philadelphia police beatings and murders of her organization's members and families (including the 1985 bombing which killed six adults and five children); Rafael Cancel Miranda, the Puerto Rican Nationalist fighter who served 25 years in prison, long stretches of it in solitary at Alcatraz and Marion Federal Penitentiaries, and Dhoruba Bin-Wahad, the Black Panther activist whose 19 years of incarceration, many in isolation, ended in 1990 with the overturning of his conviction due to prosecutorial misconduct. In addition, several attorneys and a psychiatrist served as expert witnesses presenting the array of legal and psychological abuses and international law violations that have occurred.† Over 1,500 pages of detailed written documentation

---

* In response to the Tribunal's telephoned invitation to the U.S. Mission to the United Nations to send an observer, Neal Waldrop, adviser to the Mission and a member of the U.N.'s Third Commission (which includes human rights concerns), angrily told a Tribunal staffer, "I would never insult my government by attending such a thing. The U.S. has no political prisoners. There are people in prison for violent acts, but no one who's a prisoner because of political conscience."

† Issues of international law concerning political prisoners and resistance to state crimes ware presented by Francis A. Boyle, Professor of Law, University of Illinois College of Law. For general background see his articles, "Preserving the Rule of Law in the War Against International Terrorism," 8 *Whittier Law Review* 735 (1986); "The Right of Citizen Resistance to State Crimes" (1990); and "The Hypocrisy and Racism Behind the Formulation of U.S. Human Rights Foreign Policy in Honor of Clyde Ferguson," 16 *Social Justice* 71 (1988).

were also provided, including "dossiers" prepared by Freedom Now! with the cooperation of many political prisoners.

The eight distinguished jurists—most of whom were not experts on U.S. politics—listened attentively and asked numerous questions. They spent the entire day of December 9 deliberating privately over their verdict. On December 10, International Human Rights Day, the jurists presented their findings at a press conference. (Predictably, no mainstream media covered any portion of the proceedings, despite ample notification.)

After reviewing the testimony and the voluminous but far-from-complete documentation, the judges expressed their shock at learning of what they deemed racist and inhumane government policies. They determined that such a tribunal indeed had jurisdiction over this issue under international law. Their findings, presented in a 26-page verdict, upheld the major contentions of the indictment. The judges found that the Black, Puerto Rican, Mexicano-Chicano and Native American peoples each constituted a unique people with the right to self-determination. For Blacks and Mexicanos, this was the first time any international body had ever made such a finding. The decision on Black people, after decades of unsuccessful activist efforts to gain United Nations recognition of the colonial nature of Black oppression in the U.S., was a particularly historic breakthrough. In terms of both Blacks and Native Americans, the Tribunal found the U.S. guilty of genocide, as defined by international law. In accordance with previous U.N. resolutions finding Puerto Rico to be a U.S. colony, the jurists agreed that Puerto Rican combatants should be treated as prisoners of war.

Significantly, this tribunal was the first international body to acknowledge the existence of political prisoners and POW's from a variety of nationalities in the U.S. Without reservation, the jurists called for the release of all U.S.-held activists from any nationality working for self-determination or protesting U.S. violations of international law.

The Tribunal's verdict may be presented to the U.N. Human Rights Commission at its February 1991 hearings, the International Human Rights Conference (sponsored by U.S. and U.S.S.R. governments) in Moscow in July, and other international fora. In addition, it will be the basis for an intensified campaign by Freedom Now! and other organizations to broaden public awareness and media coverage among diverse communities in the U.S., Puerto Rico and abroad.

Most important will be the effort to reconnect the jailed activists with the movements and communities from which they emerged and to which they have devoted their lives. With the 1979 freedom of the Puerto Rican Nationalists in mind as a model of grassroots international organizing, activists believe that even those facing life sentences may yet see the light of day.

Political Prisoners in the U.S.A.
A Year of Consciousness-Raising Activities

Dr. Luis Nieves Falcón
1990

There are political prisoners in the United States! Though the government denies it, this is the shocking reality. More than 100 persons are incarcerated in U.S. prisons for their political actions or beliefs.

The official position is that they are "common criminals," but this conclusion does not stand any serious analysis. To the contrary, the accumulated evidence on each and every one of the cases reveals systematic harassment and persecution of selected persons for opposing the U.S. government and its policies with regard to colonialism, militarism, and social justice.

These persons are known and respected for their longstanding activism in struggles for Native American sovereignty, Black liberation, Puerto Rican independence, and for their struggles against racism, imperialism, women's oppression, and nuclear weapons. They have challenged U.S. policies through a variety of forms, including civil disobedience, armed political actions, and grand jury resistance.

The arrests, trial procedures, sentencing, and incarceration reveal a continuous violation of their human rights ranging from isolation, sensory deprivation, and psychological torture to physical aggression and sexual abuse. The situation of political prisoners, and those who claim Prisoner of War status, is flagrantly inconsistent with the basic norms of international law as accepted by all states, including the United States.

The problem of the prisoners is most severely aggravated by the denial of the United States that it holds political prisoners, thus keeping their condition hidden from normal forms of international scrutiny. In fact, the U.S. government has taken elaborate steps to confuse world public opinion as to the true character of these prisoners, because their existence exposes deep injustices in U.S. society. Furthermore, behind the screen of secrecy the jailers hope to break the prisoners' bodies and spirits before an international conscience moves in a solidary effort to demand an end to these abuses and for their immediate freedom.

A group of concerned organizations and individuals in the U.S. and

---

This was an account written in the fall of 1990 to summarize the year of activities aimed at raising awareness of U.S. political prisoners and to promote the culminating event, the International Tribunal that would be held in December of that year.

Puerto Rico have pledged themselves to bring to the attention of the North American and international communities, the human rights violations which are routinely perpetrated by the U.S. government against these prisoners. They have joined forces to organize consciousness-raising activities on the issue. The culmination of this process will be a Tribunal, including an international panel of people of universally recognized moral reputation, who will judge the validity of the charges against the United States of persistent violations of human rights contained in the indictment.

Three activities antecede the Tribunal: a Symposium on human rights violations of political prisoner/Prisoners of War in U.S. North American jails, a Religious National Summit to examine the problem from a theological point of view, and a Literary Reading in solidarity with the prisoners. The Symposium took place last April at the Borough of Manhattan Community College. More than 200 persons attended the all-day activity. Some of the participants are actively involved in working for the Tribunal.

The Religious National Summit took place on July 28, 1990. Its goal was to bring together distinguished religious leaders to examine the present conditions of the prisoners from a theological perspective and the responsibility of religious institutions in eliminating inequities and violations (see II.5, page 152).

The Literary Reading in solidarity with political/POW prisoners will take place on October 24, 1990. Its goal is to bring together a group of distinguished North American and Third World writers to express, through their creative participation, solidarity with the prisoners (see page 148).

The culmination of these consciousness-raising activities will be the Tribunal, to be held at Hunter College from December 7-10, 1990.

A group of 11 persons of internationally recognized moral standing will examine the grievances of the prisoner/POW's and concerned human rights organizations against the government of the United States. They will pass judgment on the evidence presented to substantiate the charges of human rights violations against the United States, and they will deliver a verdict based on the factual legal foundations presented.

The Tribunal will be attended by national and international observers from human rights organizations. The diplomatic corps accredited in Washington will be invited as well as selected members of the United Nations and grassroots organizations concerned with human rights in the United States.

International Symposium on Human Rights Violations on Political Prisoners and Prisoners of War in the United States

The International Symposium, held at Borough of Manhattan Community College in April 1990, served both as a regional mobilizing opportunity for Tribunal organizers and an initial working session for key constituents from the various national liberation movements. Observers from the Philippines, Japan, and Germany took part, suggesting both formally and informally ways in which a full tribunal looking into U.S. abuses of basic international human rights standards could strengthen global anti-imperialist campaigns. The three pieces that follow—by Puerto Rican former political prisoner Pablo Marcano García, former Black Panther political prisoner Dhoruba Bin-Wahad, and Filipina former political prisoner and noted author Ninotchka Rosca—are transcripts of their remarks that give just a flavor of that impressive event. Dhoruba's presentation was notable as his first major public address since his release weeks earlier from 19 years of unjust incarceration.

II.3.A

In the Final Analysis, Prison Is a Reflection of the Society It Is a Part Of

Pablo Marcano García
1990

I would like to begin my testimony by quoting Don Pedro Albizu Campos*, who said: "I dedicated myself to politics because I was born in an enslaved country. If I had been born in a free nation, I would have dedicated my life to the arts, to the sciences."

On July 4, 1978, Nydia Cuevas Rivera and I took possession of the Chilean Consulate in Puerto Rico. This act occurred in a very particular moment. This was the period when the United States government, under a Democratic Party administration, decided to repair its worn image at both the national and international level, using the human rights issue as its magic wand. This was a very intense period in the struggle for the sovereignty of nations, in the fight to abolish ancestral dictatorships, and in the civil rights struggle to achieve equal and better conditions in Asia, the Middle East, Africa, Latin America, and the United States.

For the Puerto Rican people this was a very special moment because regardless of our political differences, we were able to rise up as a single entity to give support to the demand for the unconditional freedom of the Puerto Rican nationalist patriots. Religious, labor, cultural, political, student and community groups joined together to demand the freedom of the Puerto Rican Nationalist heroes. At that moment Oscar Collazo, Lolita Lebrón, Irvin Flores, Andrés Figueroa Cordero, and Rafael Cancel Miranda had spent 28 and 25 years, respectively, in prison. Our action was then an attempt to dramatize that broad and general demand of the Puerto Rican people over the deaf ears of a government that centered its foreign policy in the supposed respect for human rights. Additionally, this act was an attempt to impact on the conscience of our people and the international community, the sad reality of a nation that is induced to celebrate the independence of the same country that, till that time, had spent 80 years denying and criminalizing the legitimate right of the Puerto Rican people to fight for our independence. Lastly, the takeover of the Chilean consulate was a feat in which we joined in a solidarious embrace with our brother Chilean people and their organized resistance, victims themselves of the weapons that the U.S. government supplied to the repressive institutions of Augusto Pinochet.

That particular 4th of July, more than four hundred members of the FBI, the U.S. Intelligence Services, the National Guard and the police force of the

---

* The great Puerto Rican Nationalist leader and former political prisoner who died in 1964

137

Commonwealth, took by assault old San Juan to create an atmosphere of terror and criminalize this action. Despite the fact that this action took place in Chilean territory, since everything occurred in the embassy's interior, and was recognized as such by the consul who didn't want to press any charges against us, the North American federal government claimed jurisdiction and immediately denied our right for bail by imposing a disproportionate sum in relation to the crime charged and our economic situation. The judicial farce materialized in the language of the metropolitan power: English. In Puerto Rico, contrary to the belief that a large percentage of our population master English, only a small group, about 15 percent, actually speak the language. We were submitted to a judicial process where the principle of representation, or trial by one's peers, was nonexistent. We were sentenced to twelve years in prison for the takeover of the Chilean consulate with an additional penalty: Exile. Punishment that, according to Linda Backiel and other attorneys, constitutes, in the case of those condemned in Puerto Rico, an unlegislated penalty. Whereas my comrade Nydia was sent to California, almost 6,000 miles from her homeland, I was placed 3,000 miles away from my family and friends.

When a group of Puerto Ricans and North Americans in solidarity with Puerto Rican independence exerted their constitutional right to protest the imprisonment of the Puerto Rican Patriots in the United States, my case was used again to exemplify the apprehensiveness and all the cruelty of a prison system whose main political function, in the Puerto Rican situation, has been to contain and break, under a veil of legality, the emancipation and class struggle that prevails within the framework of imperialistic-colonial relations. That's how I was transferred, or better yet kidnapped, from a minimum security prison, like Danbury, Connecticut, within an hour's drive from New York, where all my family had previously moved and where I was given an out-custody classification, to a maximum security prison where my personal well-being worsened and where both the communication with my family and contact with the community outside would be reduced. In this prison, I was placed in the "most aggressive behavior unit" (MAB unit) without any explanation or reason.

And it's precisely here where I wish to take time to make a reflection that goes beyond what we ordinarily know of the prison and the insanity and limitations of a system whose rehabilitation policy is none other than military discipline, where the Black Puerto Rican is discriminated against, not only for being Puerto Rican, but also for being Caribbean-Hispanic, Black, and of course, for being an independence supporter. Of everything that I could speak to you about—the vicissitude of the families, the privations, of what 15 minutes per week for phone calls implies, of the physical violence that I was subjected to—I am sure you already have heard. We know of that reality through other means, since it isn't different from the Latin American capitalist universe where prison takes identical and sinister forms of expression. In the final analysis, prison is a reflection of the society it is a part of.

Roque Dalton, a Salvadorean poet and fighter who personally experienced the atrocities of prison, shared the following from a fragment of one of his poems:

> The jail does everything possible to cause pain.
> It is the iron night that suddenly falls over us,
> The well without stars where one forgets even the oblivion.
> Where the sound of silence is like a desperate strong drum.
> But even then, jail can be Loved,
> When one has sufficient heart.

I learned to love prison, as Dalton did, in the sense of perceiving it as a repressive element that needs to be challenged in order to transform the society that sustains it, from the same prison experience. I learned to love prison from the unconditional solidarity extended to me by a liberation movement that made it possible to go beyond that objective and crushing reality of the federal prison and made me feel like a privileged person. That experience, of being imprisoned in different penal institutions in this country for seven years, allowed me to conceive prison not as a mere discrimination center, forced sexual abstention, or privation of a quantum of liberty, but as another battleground for freedom. In the case of the Puerto Rican prisoners of war and the political prisoners, this has definitively meant several years of political struggle at diverse levels, intensities, and, surely, many sacrifices. The MAB unit, where the inmates who had very long sentences and who could supposedly endanger my physical and moral life [but] turned out to be my most loyal and noble bodyguards, is a good example. The Puerto Rican nationalists had already been at the worst North American prisons; Alcatraz, Marion, Leavenworth and, through them, prisoners knew of our struggle for independence, of the reason for my imprisonment, and consequently, I was given special consideration.

If I learned anything from that privileged condition, it was that no matter how far one might be from one's country, or even if one is secluded or locked up in the dungeons of the prison, one is able to achieve unimaginable ways of communication. For example, my parents, who didn't speak English, who had to travel by car, armed themselves with more love and determination and drove two, three times per month, under the snow, the rain, discovering at the same time, all the injustice around them. In that correlation of forces between the imperialist state and the patriotic movement, we were able to witness how organizations from Puerto Rico like the United Committee Against Repression and for the Defense of Political Prisoners (CUCRE), as well as neighbors and countrymen surpassed those obstacles and visited me. Here in the United States, several comrades, lawyers, friends, members of the

Movimiento de Liberación Nacional Puertorriqueño (MLN), from the Puerto Rican Nationalist Party, as well as different cultural entities overcame the isolation politic of exile imprisonment. The written communication was surprising; especially, when that correspondence came from people who did not necessarily think like you or share your own political ideology or beliefs, but they showed you respect by their treatment. What I am sharing with you today might not carry a lot of weight, yet it is precisely what made me see prison as another frontier of struggle and battleground for the liberation of my country. It was through the combination of all these factors, including solidarity work such as demonstrations, picketing in front of the prison, sending telegrams, addressing international forums such as United Nations, Geneva, or in a symposium like this one, that allows us—the Puerto Rican political prisoners and prisoners of war—to defeat the prison system and transcend its political function.

That individual and organized disposition led me to embrace, at the age of 30, a part of me that is able to speak in a painting both the cruelty as well as the beauty of life; an artistic expression that allows me today to dedicate myself fully to painting as a way of living. Whereas Carlos Irizarry, a well-known Puerto Rican painter, goes to prison as a consequence of his art, I reach the arts through prison. Two Afro-American comrades were able to understand that political bond well, and they endowed me with their immense talent in the plastic arts.

It was that organized, systematic, solidarious and militant engagement that helped me to research and publish a book about criminality in Puerto Rico and the reason for the prison system in a capitalist colonial country like ours. All of this, in the long run, leads me to better understand Dr. Pedro Albizu Campos when he explained why we had to dedicate ourselves to politics in the colony when our aspirations are such that conditions should exist where repression and the violation of human rights are things of the past, and in turn, dedicate ourselves to superior and more constructive things. This is why we still struggle in this, the other side of prison.

II.3.B

Our Fight Is Essentially a Work of the Heart and Spirit...

Dhoruba Bin-Wahad
1990

I really appreciate the warm and loving welcome you all have just expressed, this emotional outpouring from progressive people of color, and especially my own people. It is an awesome responsibility to realize how much a victory can mean to an oppressed person. It leaves me without words, and anyone who knows me knows that I am very seldom without words.

I vividly recall the day I was sentenced, almost 20 years ago. The courtroom was filled with district attorneys, police, detectives, all wall-to-wall cops. There was only one person in the courtroom besides my attorney, Robert Bloom, that was there for me. There was my former wife, Kisha, and my little baby boy, who is now 18 years old. They were the only ones in court. I refused to come into the courtroom. I told them to kiss my behind, I was not coming out. I stayed in the bullpen. I told them they could send me my time in an envelope. That is exactly what they did. I had to struggle from there. A month ago when I was released, there were over 100 people in court, people like you, who supported me, who came out when it counted, and my wife, Tanaquil, who worked her fingers to the bone for my release. She fainted afterwards. The courtroom was filled with wall-to-wall people this time. When I was returned to the bullpen to await the bureaucratic rigamarole to release me, there was a Latino brother in the bullpen. A totally apolitical brother, and I did not know what to do. I was just pacing up and down the length of the bull pen. I kept saying I won, I won, I won. This guy was looking at me and saying, man, they put a bug in this cell. He's a bug out. So the dude is standing alone in the corner. I looked him in the eye and I said, man, I won. He said, you did! I said, yeah, I beat them. He said, that's great, man, shook my

Dhoruba Bin-Wahad *(Source: Jericho Amnesty Movement)*

141

hand. I told him how long I had been imprisoned. He did not believe it. He said, you know, I was thinking about copping out. I said, well, you must do what you think is best. But, if you are right, and you know you are right, don't give up. He said I gave him a whole different perspective on this. He thought, I don't have a chance, I had a legal aid attorney. But you were imprisoned 19 years? I said, yep. He said, that's hard to believe.

When I walked into that courtroom and I saw all of you folks out there, a lot of you were there in spirit, a lot of you were watching on TV, or whatever the case may be, I knew it was going to be like this. I knew I was going to beat them because I'm Muslim and the law says: Never will he cause falsehood to triumph over truth. Your presence here today is a testimony to that. I had a few people in my corner for a very, very long time. They did not have much to work with. I was a lunatic. They had to deal with me. I was stark raving mad. On top of that, they had to deal with the courts. That would drive anybody crazy. They had to deal with each other because they were all eccentrics. Before I go any further, I want to acknowledge two of my attorneys here tonight. These are two people who fought for me and I want to give them a little bit of recognition. You all should give them a round of applause.

There are some people here, too, that I have not seen in a long time. There are two comrades here who were part of the Panther 21 case with me. In their own way, they continue to struggle and I just want people to acknowledge that there are other people from the Panther 21 case here. Two of them are doctors, one studied the tsetse fly into oblivion in Africa; he is the foremost authority on that species. And there is another brother here who turns out to be a doctor and a professor of Afrikan studies. So, I want you all to know Dr. Curtis Powell and Dr. Kwando Kinshasa.

The Panther 21 case was a very significant case in the late '60s because it represented for the first time a coming together of forces around a clearly political case in New York City. There were other political cases in New York City as well. I am quite sure a lot of us are familiar with the Harlem 5 and cases like that. But, they had not grown out of a movement for national liberation and a movement against class oppression like the Black Panther Party had evolved. So, the Panther 21 was a significant case. It caused the FBI a great deal of problems. It really did because people from every spectrum of American society, from doctors and lawyers to actors and actresses came out to support the Panther 21. Most of those brothers spent over a year in prison, and they were targets of a very vicious counterintelligence program. They endured even with their fallibilities. We all know that no one is perfect, but we need to understand that our enemy capitalizes on our imperfections. That when we do not carry out our struggle in a principled fashion, they will destroy us with those imperfections. Principle must lead to struggle. In the struggle for human rights, for human dignity, we must put principle in the leadership. This is very, very important. It is something the counter-intelligence program has taught me very, very well. We cannot abdicate our principles; we cannot give up what we believe in. We must be principled with each other, and although it may be hard, we must be principled in our opposition to our enemy. Because if we stoop to his level, in essence we are no better than he is.

When J. Edgar Hoover launched the counterintelligence program he stated that one of the primary objectives of COINTELPRO was to prevent the rise of the Messiah in the Afrikan American community that would galvanize the nationalist movement and unify them. They succeeded. They succeeded beyond their wildest imaginations. The destruction of principle and militant leadership in the Afrikan American community left a terrible vacuum in our communities, a vacuum that we still struggle against today. So, in building a support movement for political prisoners in the United States, we have to struggle mightily to overcome sectarianism, to overcome our individual weaknesses, and to build a principled, ethical, and moral movement. One thing that I learned from the Rev. Dr. Martin Luther King was this: that the day they assassinated him, I realized that the United States of America could not deal in any way whatsoever with the ethics and the morality of truth. So, I figured that when they killed Martin Luther King, they deserved Dhoruba Bin-Wahad. I think that's when I joined the Black Panther Party, and, of course, my life has been whacked out ever since. I think most of the brothers that were in the Black Panther Party in the '60s to one degree or another essentially felt the same way. Like the old song goes...we were young and we were strong and we were running against the wind. I'm much older now, but still running against the wind.

The issue of political prisoners in the United States has not been brought to the attention of the American public. It is because we have failed to build a movement in the United States for human rights that is principled and that connects the issue of political imprisonment with all of the other relevant social issues that afflict our people in this country. There can be no movement for social change or political empowerment that ignores the contradiction of political prisoners. Those years I spent up north in places like Attica, Quentin, in isolation, forced me into a very combative state of mind. I had to live next to my enemy 24 hours a day. Every day he changed shifts, while I couldn't change shifts at all. I had to sleep with one eye open like a junk yard dog. I learned something. I may have my faults, but I learned this—never to compromise with a principled behavior, never give in to opportunism, never, never surrender your integrity. Some people would say to me, Dhoruba, you know, you can't go around here just talking crazy to folks and expect to get support. Well, I have learned also that those people who are going to support the truth are going to support it no matter what, and those people who are in opposition to the truth are going to compromise no matter what. I would rather be with those that support the truth and tell those that oppose it to kiss my behind.

Now, of course, I wouldn't quite put it like that some times, but it is very important that we take the time out to really analyze the state of disorganization around the issue of political prisoners, the conditions that led to it, and begin to formulate strategies and organizational methods that would strengthen us in the future. I think this symposium is a good beginning. I think that the turn out at this symposium has been very, very good. You can believe that the police department and the various law enforcement agencies of New York State and New York City realize that there is a potential in the issue of political prisoners that could blow their boots off. They are going to come at you from every angle, from below, from the top, from behind, from front. They are going to be right in our ranks whispering in our ears strategies and ideas, but if you stick to principles, they can do nothing to you. They cannot disunify you, they cannot divide you, and they cannot stop you from success. One of the things that I have learned when I had nothing else to rely on, I had to visualize myself walking down those court stairs. I had to imagine myself hugging my attorneys. I had to visualize it, and like Liz Fink told me, ever since she met me, I've been coming home. Dhoruba, ever since I met you 15 years ago, you've been getting out of prison. I said, you know something Liz, you're right. Every year I was coming home and this year I did.

We have over 100 political prisoners who remain in prison today. Their day has to come. That day will come when we make it come. I have always said to myself in prison, the only person that can get my comrades out of prison is me. Nobody else could do it but me. I am saying that you have to feel that way, too. Nobody can get them out of prison except you, because if three attorneys could fight for 13 years to finally beat the state, if one woman can call all of her friends and say, if you do not come to court for my husband, I will never speak to you, and fill the courtroom, multiply that by everyone in this room, imagine what we could do.

You know, the question is not always a question of leadership, it is also a question of followship. We have to learn how to follow as well as accept the responsibilities of leadership. If there is a program that presents an analysis and that analysis moves you to action, then you should give up some of your time to furthering that program. So, my message to you tonight is essentially this—not only must principle lead to movement or any struggle, but analysis has to inform them. And, if a leader cannot present an analysis of a situation to you, then you shouldn't deal with him or her. That's very, very important because we are in a situation today that is critical. We are living in a time of monumental historical transitions all over the world. And it can be confusing. A lot of myths are crumbling and new ones are being erected. One monster is being put to rest—the monster of communism, the specter of communist control is being put to rest and another bogey man is being erected, the bogey man of Islamic fundamentalism. You don't understand it. You don't know it. It is alien to you so you should be afraid of it.

I say to you today that any ideology or any way of life that opposes racist imperialism, that opposes European hegemony over the majority of the world, that opposes the class oppression of people is an ideology and methodology of revolutionary change, is one you must understand before you can criticize it. I bring this message to you because in the future I hope to begin to work around putting together a national human rights campaign for the freedom of Afrikan American political prisoners and there are a lot of brothers here who have struggled and labored incessantly in the vineyards of this discrepancy. I think now things are beginning to come together on a spiritual level as well, because one of the failures of the movement of the '6os was not that our hearts were in the wrong place, it was not that we were just completely repressed and murdered out of existence, although that was a part of it, but it was our failure to tap into the energy and the soul of the human spirit, to realize that we are not just material physical beings, we are people with a spirit and a heart. People get involved in struggles because of what is in their hearts. We need to address the heart. We cannot change our conditions as a people, as a movement, until we first change the condition of our hearts.

So, look inside yourself and imagine yourself on death row with Mumia Abu-Jamal, and get mad, get angry, feel desperate just like he must feel and make him strong and freer. I want to ask all of you not to leave here today without committing yourself to do work around the issues that are being raised by Freedom Now! and the coalitions of organizations and groups that are trying to free political prisoners and prisoners of war. Addressing envelopes, pass out leaflets in your building, put yourself on a mailing list, do something. Don't let this historical moment pass you by. When your children say, hey mom, pops, what were you doing at the turn of the century when the world was going to hell in a handbasket? Well, I was working for the man, trying to make me a living. He says, mom, is that all you did, pops, that's all you did? Be one of those who said, I used to work with those crazy radicals of Freedom Now!, I used to address envelopes.

Our fight is essentially a work of the heart and spirit. I remember in the Black Panther Party whenever a criticism was given to a brother or sister, the first thing out of their mouths used to be: that's subjective, sister, that's subjective, brother. You have to be objective. I used to sit back and reflect on that and one day I was picking on Nuh Washington in Green Haven. I said, you know something, Nuh, back in the days of the party we used to always talk about how everything was subjective and Nuh says, you're right. What we didn't realize then is that it was the subjective factor that was the dynamic factor. Before we could move ourselves, we have to change our hearts, and if we change our hearts, we can move other people because the human heart is universal, the human spirit is universal and those that do not want to move with us, we can leave behind.

I want to say one of the things that will confront us time and time again in the armed struggle for liberation and in the freeing of our people, whether we are dealing with the liberation of Puerto Rico, the anticolonial struggle in Latin America, Central America, or the oppression with national minorities in the U.S., and that is racism. There is not a segment of American society untainted by racism. America is a eurocentric society, and it bases all of its values upon a European ethic and standard. We need to examine that because historically the left and the various European nations in the United States have been unable to deal with their own racist attitudes. There are people who would rather save whales than human beings. We could look at people who are against the use of animals for clothes and I am not with that.

When I say these things, it is not that I am antiwhale or that I would want to pollute the environment. I just want you to reflect for a minute. We have people sleeping on sidewalk crates right around us. One of the things that appalled me when I stepped out one night were the walls lined with homeless people sleeping, like something out of the Village of the Damned. I mean, it was unreal. It was not like this when I left the streets, so I was hit by future shock. Meanwhile, there are houses standing abandoned. You walk in New York City and where are we? Back in the 60s we would have taken over the building and volunteers would have fought for water rights. But what has happened to us is that we have become complacent. We used to get angry that someone was starving. We used to get angry if someone did not have a place to sleep. And that was alright.

Maybe I am a throwback. I still get mad, and I still get angry. Let's rely on the attorney to fight the legal fight, let's rely on the young warriors that we have to man the barricades, and let's rely on the brothers and sisters who churn out the papers and perform all the tasks that no one wants to do. Those are the people who are the heroes. Those are the ones who make things work. I stand before you because Robert Boyle read thousands and thousands and thousands of documents over and over again, until he could read them in his sleep. Liz Fink would come in and rewrite everything in the middle of the night, nonstop for three days and then pass out. Robert Bloom would fly in from the West Coast, stand up in the court and give his appeal. I would rant and rave and scream and holler about how none of this reflected my politics. But we all played a part, we all did our thing, and I am saying we should do that again. That's what movements are made of. Those who are articulate enough to present the script should speak and those who are hip enough to write should script. Those who can do nothing but pass out leaflets should pass out leaflets, and in the final analysis, the person who passes out the leaflet will be the one who gets the greatest reward. There is much to the axiom that the last shall be first and the first shall be last, because those people who are humble enough, those people who are human enough to stop and pass out leaflets and touch people where they need to be touched, those are the foot soldiers who win this struggle and we need every foot soldier we can get.

So, I want to say as I close now, free all political prisoners, free all political prisoners, free all political prisoners.

II.3.C

Marketing War

Ninotchka Rosca
1990

In 1986, when I returned to the Philippines after many years of exile, I attended a national conference of SELDA, the association of former Filipino political prisoners. In this conference and in informal gatherings afterward, it was noticeable how a subculture based on the detention experience had evolved. The former political prisoners had an idiom of their own, a slang-language referring to various aspects of being imprisoned that the daily languages of my country, 150 of them, could not encompass. Songs, poems, paintings, and poster art referring to this experience were in abundance. One noted, as well, that the term "XD" (for ex-detainee) had crept into the popular lexicon.

These are testaments that human rights violations, which we are inclined to view as individual experiences, are actually felt societally and communally. They are a social experience, commonly felt, and affect the national consciousness. It may be difficult to trace the general breakdown of norms of conduct in the Philippines directly to the oppression of a single individual. However, there exists such a correlation, no matter how tenuous. The rise in human rights violations in the Philippines was paralleled by an erosion in ethical norms and by a debasement of the value given by society to human life. We can state then that the violation of one individual's human rights leads to a general violation of all and everyone's human rights. This is, of course, a paraphrase of Martin Luther King's words: "Injustice anywhere threatens justice everywhere."

Ninotchka Rosca's contribution to the symposium was important, not only as a prominent author, but also because her observations as a Filipina former political prisoner reminded attendees of the universality of human rights violations and the importance of fighting them globally. Her remarks were particularly poignant coming from a citizen of a former U.S. colony and current neocolony. To quote the Philippines Research Center:

> Between 1900 and 1902, over 100,000 [U.S.] troops fought a war of imperialist suppression against the Filipino people through this war, the U.S. perfected antiguerrilla and antipeople practices that have been universally condemned, such as physical dismemberment....

> The U.S. legally dominated the Philippines until 1946, at which point nominal independence was gained. Then, through economic, political and military maneuvers, the U.S. continued its domination of the Philippines in a barely concealed manner. During this long period of both direct and indirect rule of their homeland, the Filipino people have continued to resist the United States, the Japanese during World War II, and finally the several pro-U.S. neocolonial regimes since the war.

Literary Reading to Benefit the International Tribunal

Wednesday, October 24, 1990
2 West 64th Street (corner of Central Park West)

...true contemplation is resistance: and poetry, gazing at the clouds is resistance, I found out in jail...

Ernesto Cardenal

That no degree of pressure ever will cause us to repudiate our principles, does not in any way lessen the heartbreak we suffer.

Ethel Rosenberg

Any struggle is first that deep feeling that grows from the center of a person, a people. The poem is not separate from me, from the person that I am...

Susan Sherman

the day they hung the poet for crimes against the state his mother stood outside the prison gates, bells tolled, a policeman looked out and said "you can go home now, he's dead"

Gale Jackson

The colonized person who writes for her/his people ought to use the past with the intention of opening the future, as an invitation to action and a basis for hope. But to ensure that hope and to give it form, he/she must take part in action...

Frantz Fanon

All of life is a struggle to obtain desired freedom. The rest is nothing, but surface and style.

Juan Antonio Corretjer

First Part • Primera Parte
Luis Nieves Falcón
Susan Sherman
José Yglesias
Daniel Berrigan
Amiri Baraka

Intermission • Intermedio

Second Part • Segunda parte
Piri Thomas
Giannina Braschi
Terry Bisson
Ninotchka Rosca
Ernesto Cardenal

In solidarity • En solidaridad

The Creative Process as a Form of Resistance

Dr. Luis Nieves Falcón
1990

The creative process is perhaps the single criterion that best attests to the basic humanity inherent in every person. It's fundamental for oppressed people anywhere in the world since the dominating classes, through the ideology of domination, tend to question the human condition of the dominated person. In consequence, creativity becomes for the dispossessed of the world an instrument for individual and collective recuperation. Why is this so?

On the one hand, the dominating ideology espouses the idea of a subhuman condition for the oppressed peoples as a way of justifying the socioeconomic disadvantaged position in which they are placed. From this categorization flow the myths developed about exploited people: dominated people like to be dominated; dominated people are basically responsible for their own situation; dominated people need an overseer to guide them; dominated people are like small children, they really never grow up; dominated people act only at the most instinctual levels: eat, sleep and fornicate. This effort to dehumanize the oppressed is socially reproduced by the principal ideological instruments of power. These persistently emphasize a negative depicting of the oppressed and of any social or cultural element attached to him/her. No element is allowed to enhance the image of the dominated person.

In opposition to this perverted image arises the process of creative imagination. The threatening relationship posed by creativity goes more or less like this: Creative imagination is a human attribute. There are elements of creativity in the oppressed. The oppressor is human. In consequence, there is an essential equality between the oppressor and the oppressed. That unavoidable finding regarding the mutuality of the human essence between the dominator and the dominated threatens the whole oppressive condition, because it disrupts the scheme of inherent inequality that gives support to oppression and its accompanying elements of racism, sexism, and subordination.

In addition to his role as coordinator of the International Tribunal, and as a leading educator and human rights lawyer, Dr. Luis Nieves Falcón has always been an ardent supporter and collector of political art. It was never a question that among the multi-faceted aspects of the International Tribunal, a literary reading and art show would be included. This essay by Dr. Nieves Falcón served as the basis for understanding the importance of art in building the work around political prisoners.

The process of creative imagination has other disturbing effects on the oppressive condition: it allows the subordinated person to shatter the world of rigid absolutes that engulfs him/her; it allows him/her to destroy the myth that there is no way of breaking away from the world of oppression. In fact, creative imagination becomes a significant contradiction to the inalterability of fate, of *el sino, el destino irrevocable*. The truth is that through the creative imagination the individual can rethink anew his/her situation; new ways can be invented to destroy the constraints around the subjugated person, and those alternatives creatively developed may become behavior-oriented goals against the condition of oppression.

From the above, it may be clearly seen why any creative person is basically a subversive person. The creative process involves a basic challenge to the official world, to the world of the status quo. And the objects of creation are the most obvious manifestation of the opposition to the contested world.

The political prisoners and Prisoners of War are subversive persons because they dared to challenge existing norms supporting the prevailing system of exploitation and oppression in present U.S.A. They imaginatively created alternatives to challenge the system of injustice and inequality. They were captured and put away for life in isolated cells with the express purpose of destroying them physically and emotionally. The prisoners responded with new avenues of creative imagination to support themselves spiritually against the jailors, but also to make incarceration another space for the continuation of the political struggle. The net result has been the conquest of the prison environment, the conquest of the isolation milieu by the prisoners rather than the decimation of the prisoners by their incarceration for life.

The transformation of the prison condition is equivalent to the transformation of the dominated condition outside. The prison condition confirms to the prisoners the importance of creative imagination in our lives, because it is a dimension of freedom. They realize that it is not only an important instrument to advance social and economic change, but also indispensable to understand the real needs and the real meaning of individual and collective freedom. Its development during incarceration, in various forms, provides the prisoner with the opportunity to link political struggle and survival in a hostile environment. It offers the prisoner the opportunity to go beyond the static and inflexible parameters imposed by the jailers. In fact, the subversive element of creative imagination allows prisoners to go beyond the wire, to go beyond the bars to join the comrades who are outside the reach of the oppressors, also fighting for the destruction of the oppressive condition and the recuperation of the human being. In that sense, creative imagination from the cell, from the isolation unit, from the prison in the prison, is a form of resistance. To resist the degradation imposed by the jailors; to resist the dehumanization of the prisoner; to reaffirm his or her indomitable spirit. The true meaning of the dimension of liberation inherent in creative imagination is admirably presented by Susan Rosenberg from the literary perspective. She says, in talking about poems from the jail:

> Poems are a gift for me in the late time.
> My time for myself. I think of night
> and how it draws its knees up near me,
> and settles in, singing its light and its mysteries.
> I think of the countless numbers
> of us who put down the pen to pick up
> other tools, and how of necessity we are
> returned to the pen.
> I think of the poet who said
> "I curse the poetry of those who do not take sides."
> I think the torture, the degradation, and the
> humiliation that the enemy inflicts on us all
> is to teach us, to force us to lose the memory of ourselves.
> So, in that, poetry becomes a weapon that guides
> us to the future.
> Opening the heart to love, to justice, to dignity,
> and to a freedom the enemy knows nothing of
> To be willing to give everything to achieve
> that/allows poetry/to course through all
> of us
> like a revolutionary elixir.

It can be seen, the resistance in words, in the spirit which they communicate and which forces us to conclude that there is but only one fate: *Venceremos, we shall overcome!*

II.5

A Call to Liberation

Interfaith Religious Summit on Political Prisoners
1990

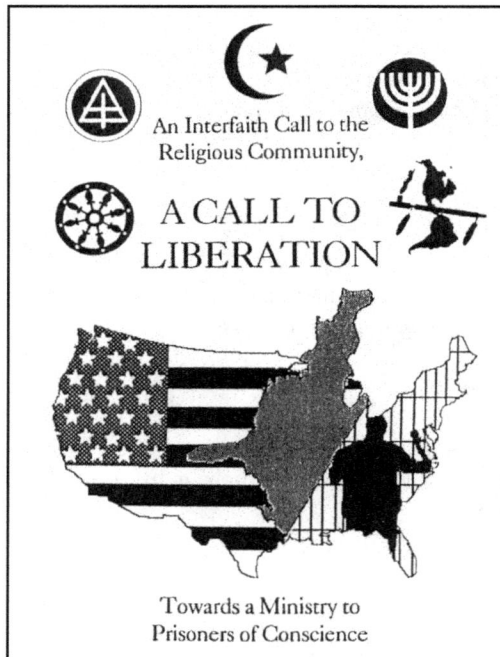

An Interfaith Call to the Religious Community,

A CALL TO LIBERATION

Towards a Ministry to Prisoners of Conscience

Held in New York's American Indian Community House on July 28, 1990, the Interfaith Religious Summit on Political Prisoners was organized out of the national headquarters of the United Church of Christ. In partnership with the National Council of Churches Racial Justice Working Group, the Summit was an important building event for the International Tribunal planned for later that year. It brought together Protestant and Catholic, Muslim and Jewish, Native and Africanist religious and spiritual leaders, including the Rev. Dr. Benjamin Chavis, Sister Anne Montgomery of the Plowshares 8, and Indigenous Women's Network founder Ingrid Washinawatok (later killed by Colombia's FARC guerrillas). The Call to Liberation, signed by a score of these leaders—including several bishops and heads of national denominations—was one of the first major documents to show that the issue of U.S. political prisoners need not be consigned to a narrow part of the left.

On July 28, 1990, at the American Indian Community House in New York City, an Interfaith Religious Summit on Political Prisoners was convened. Attended by more than 40 national theologians, clergy, and lay people from the Catholic, Jewish, Muslim, Native Spiritual, and Protestant communities, the Summit reviewed the conditions and terms of imprisonment of the more than 100 persons currently in jail for their political beliefs and actions. The Summit, a project of the International Tribunal on the Human Rights Violations of Political Prisoners/POW's in the U.S., was sponsored by the Racial Justice Working Group of the National Council of Churches (NCC), the Interfaith Prisoners of Conscience Project of the Prophetic Justice Unit (IPOC), the NCC Commission on Justice and Liberation, the United Church Board for Homeland Ministries, and Clergy and Laity Concerned.

The issue of political prisoners in the U.S. is a crucial one for our time. All those concerned with human rights in the world must, we believe, bear witness, and take action on behalf of those prophetic voices who now find themselves behind bars. It is ironic that just as U.S. governmental officials welcome the release of former South African political prisoner Nelson Mandela, so too do the same officials deny the existence of political prisoners here at home. It is a testimony that as we approach the 500th anniversary of European colonialism in the Americas, the U.S. government still holds in prison indigenous American activists whose chief crime is fighting for the land that is rightfully theirs.

The Interfaith Religious Summit hoped to continue a process of education and inspiration on this issue among people of faith in the U.S. Our session began with reflections from five former political prisoners, individuals whose leadership in their various communities moved them to take action. They inspired us with their example of the work that they had done and with the courage and strength they showed with their resistance to the repression brought down on them. Mr. Ted Means of the Heart of the Earth Survival School and the Prison Project graphically explained the plight of the Native American in the U.S. and challenged us to struggle for greater understanding and justice. Sister Anne Montgomery, one of the original Plowshares Eight and a participant in six additional Plowshares disarmament actions, told us of her experiences in building communities against the arms race.

Mr. Dhoruba Bin-Wahad, a former member of the Black Panther Party, discussed his 19 years behind bars for a crime that he did not commit. Mr. Bin-Wahad examined the interreligious basis for work on issues of amnesty and human rights and reflected on the points of unity between the prisoners of conscience, prisoners of war, and political prisoners. Ms. Maria Cueto, an Episcopalian activist from the Mexican community, shared with us her two experiences as a grand jury resister. Proclaiming the importance of the position of noncollaboration with state repression, Ms. Cueto affirmed the support of the church in the past and called for continued responsiveness to issues of true justice. Finally, Rev. Dr. Benjamin Chavis, Executive Director of the Commission on Racial Justice, United Church of Christ, reminded us that support for political prisoners is not simply about supporting individuals in jail, but is primarily about defending the movements for peace and justice in which we all work. A movement that does not defend its leaders, he asserted, cannot expect people to want to join and be part of it. Dr. Chavis, the first U.S. citizen to be proclaimed a political prisoner by Amnesty International, reminded us of the special role and responsibility that religious people must take on.

The Summit discussed a variety of strategies for advocacy and mission work on the prisoners. The Interfaith Religious Call on Political Prisoners, a Call to Liberation, was seen as one concrete way of informing our constituencies and building material and spiritual support. As we looked over a draft of the Call, we solicited input on how the Call might be made most appropriate for the diverse sectors from which we come together. Using the sacred texts and writings of our various faiths, we hoped to create a truly unifying document to religious leaders and to the grassroots, a Call for mercy and for human rights, for education and inspiration, for justice, a Call to Action.

We also discussed the need for support of the International Tribunal on Political Prisoners, to be held during United Nations Human Rights Week, December 7 through 10, 1990 at New York's Hunter College/CUNY. The Tribunal will bring together nine prominent judges from five continents, to review testimony from legal experts, former prisoners, family members, and the prisoners themselves. The verdict of the judges will be an instructional tool for our own support work for years to come. The testimony itself provides us with the information necessary to make our advocacy most effective. The need for both mobilization and financial assistance, for the Tribunal and for the work beyond it, was stressed, even as we realized our limits in a conservative environment.

And so, we present to you this Call. It is our sincere hope that you may be moved to use it in worship and in contemplation, to use it as a study tool and as a resource for future work. We do not consider the Call to be a finished document; we must have active input and response for it to be a success. We hope for more and more congregations and individuals to sign on to the Call, until there is a national consensus that justice must be done. We must carry on the vision of a liberating theology and practice a redemptive lifestyle of justice, "until the captives are set free...."

Ms. Lois M. Dauway (NCC Commission on Justice and Liberation)
Imam Khalid Abdul Fattah-Griggs (Institute for Islamic Involvement)
Rev. Alfonso Roman (United Church Board for Homeland Ministries; NCC Racial Justice Working Group)
Ms. Suzanne Ross (Coordinator of Jewish Issues, Clergy and Laity Concerned)
Ms. Ingrid Washinawatok (Indigenous Women's Network; American Indian Movement)
Rev. Michael Yasutake (Interfaith Prisoners of Conscience Project)

A Call to Liberation

That thou may say to the prisoners,
Go Forth; to them that are in darkness,
Show yourselves.... Even the captives of
the mighty shall be set free.

Isaiah 49:9, 25

The Spirit of the Lord is upon me, he
hath anointed me to... set at liberty they
who are oppressed.

Luke 4:18

Righteousness does not go east or west,
but sets the captives free.

Holy Qu'ran

Through the ages, communities of faith have been concerned with the well-being of those who have been incarcerated. It has been accepted that one of God's given gifts to us is our freedom.

In the U.S. today, the growing prison population now represents over half a million persons. As people of faith we are concerned about all of those imprisoned, but take particular note of those jailed for uniquely political reasons, of those political prisoners that the U.S. government denies the existence of. These prisoners represent a population often forgotten and usually subjected to inhumane conditions, worse than the rest of the inmate populations.

Political prisoners in the U.S. include prisoners of conscience, such as the Plowshares community, who are led by their faith to act against the false idols of militarism and who act in strict nonviolence to dismantle the bombs and carry out real disarmament. Political prisoners include those who call themselves Prisoners of War, whose struggles for justice and freedom have led them to struggle against those forces who have waged genocide against their people. From the Puerto Rican, Native American, and Black/New Afrikan communities, these POW's represent a militant and patriotic grouping, who struggle for peace within the context of independence and sovereignty. Political prisoners also include a wide range of people who, as a consequence of their active involvement in political movements and organizations, have been targeted by the government for repression, harassment, and jail. In short, they share in common the fact that their time behind bars has more to do with their beliefs than with the alleged "criminal" acts for which they have been charged.

The more than 100 political prisoners in U.S. jails today face human rights abuses and conditions condemned by the United Nations Standard Minimum Rules for the Treatment of Prisoners. They have been faced with arbitrary arrest, detention, and imprisonment; they have been subjected to preventative detention and political internment through the grand jury. Many have been denied a fair trial and face cruel and degrading treatment, including physical and psychological torture, sexual abuse, and racism. Their plight is the plight of all those concerned with human rights.

The Road to Imprisonment

Trouble no person about their religion—respect their views and demand that they respect yours... seek to make your life long and of service to your people.

Teachings of Tecumseh

O You who believe: Be steadfast witnesses for Allah in equity and let not hatred of any people seduce you that you deal not justly. Be just; that is nearer to piety.

Qu'ran 5:8

For I was hungry, and you gave me meat; I was thirsty and you gave me drink; I was a stranger and you took me in; I was in prison and you visited me... And the Lord shall answer and say unto them, Inasmuch as you have done it unto one of the least of these my brethren, you have done it unto me.

Matthew 25:35-40

And they shall beat swords into plowshares, and their spears into pruning hooks; nation shall not lift up sword against nation, neither shall they learn war any more.

Isaiah 2:4

The political prisoners respond to a deep sense of dissatisfaction with a social and political order that is characterized by racism and colonialism.

The political prisoners object to the mindset of cultural and national superiority that, no less than 500 years ago in 1492, led to the foundation of an apartheid system in the New World.

The political prisoners resist the policies that feed a military industrial complex, while depleting the resources available to sustain a better quality of life for millions of poor people in the world.

The political prisoners question a national security ideology that subordinates every social value to the hegemony of the interests of the dominant political and economic elite.

The political prisoners' dissenting activities are interpreted by the dominant society as insurrectionary, and so they are considered terrorists. Their cases are judicially criminalized as an attempt to silence their voices of ideological protest.

The political prisoners thus become scapegoats for an increasingly dehumanized state apparatus, seeking new human sacrifices.

The New Idols

As people of faith, we see the suffering caused by the violent institutions of our society that perpetuate racism and colonialism, and we especially identify the status of our present U.S. society as the manifestation of new idols trying to usurp the heart of the nation. As they take possession of the institutional fiber of the country, signs of death thrive; life and all creation seem to be in danger. Those new idols tempting our global life and claiming our spiritual loyalty are:

- the idols of greed and materialism
- the idol of power over another
- the idols of Eurocentricity, white supremacy, racism, and sexism
- the idols of borders, and man's possession of land for profit
- the idols of self-centeredness and "thingness"
- the idols of national security and nuclearism

In our sacred writings, we find admonitions against this kind of idolatry. Some of these texts call us to repentance and obedience to a God of justice and mercy; others call us to a new and interdependent relationship with all life. As we follow these paths, new life flourishes and peace abounds.

The wrongs? The selfish pride of birth, the massing of power and wealth in the hands of the few, the slaughter of female infants, the orgies of gambling and drunkenness, the frauds of temples and idols and priests, the feuds and arrogance of tribes and races, the separation of the sacred and profane, as if the unity of All Life and All Truth did not flow from the unity of God Most High.

Qu'ran c. 36

You ask me to cut grass and make hay and sell it to the rich like the white man…. But how dare I cut off my mother's hair?

Smohalla, Nez Perce

Is not the sky a father and the earth a mother and are not all living things, with feet and wings or roots their children?

Black Elk's vision, Oglala

Even as a mother, at the risk of her life, watches over and protects her only child, so with a boundless mind should one cherish over all living things.

Metta Sutra, Buddhist scripture

If your heart turns away and you give no heed, and are lured into the worship and service of other Gods, I declare to you this day that you shall certainly perish…. Choose life—so that you and your children may live.

Deuteronomy 30:17-19

Many false prophets shall rise, and shall deceive many. And because inequity shall abound, the love of many shall grow cold. But those that shall endure unto the end, the same shall be saved.

Matthew 24:11-13

New Prophecy for a Troubled Time

We must understand these prisoners, heralding a new prophecy of a troubled time, in concrete human terms:

There is Jean Gump, 61-year-old Irish Catholic and mother of 12, who in 1986 entered a nuclear weapons silo in Holden, Missouri, and with four other Catholic Workers, cut the electrical sensor equipment, poured blood on the silo covers in the form of a cross, painted "Disarm and Live for the Children" on the silo lid, and left indictments charging the U.S. government with committing crimes against the laws of God and humanity. She decided that she had to "get serious" about stopping the arms race after the birth of her first grandchild in 1983.

There is Abdul Majid, a Muslim leader and former member of the Black Panther Party. An organizer of the free breakfast programs, free clothing programs, and liberation schools for youth, he became a target of the U.S. government Counter Intelligence Program (COINTELPRO) against the Black Panthers. After two mistrials and deliberate attempts to hide evidence helpful to the defense, the government was able to jail Majid for attempted murder. In 1990, after the holy month of Ramadan, Majid was placed in solitary confinement at Great Meadow Prison in New York. Claiming that he had spoken to a Muslim cook about not preparing meals during the holy fast times, the prison charged him with "demonstrating." Though these claims were never substantiated, the prison report reveals their real reasons for isolating Majid: "he is part of the Muslim hierarchy."

There is Leonard Peltier, a member of the Anishinabe/Lakota nation, born in North Dakota. During the early 1970s, at a time when COINTELPRO activity against the American Indian Movement and activists at reservations was particularly heavy, Oglala organizers and traditional elders set up an encampment on the land of the Jumping Bull family. The Jumping Bull Camp, on the Pine Ridge reservation was put together to protect the community from FBI operatives. After a U.S. military "invasion" of the camp, Peltier and two others were charged with the murder of two federal troops. In 1984, along with Standing Deer and Albert Garza, Peltier began a spiritual fast to call attention to the systematic denial of religious rights at the "super-maximum" security prison at Marion. For defending his people and their traditional spiritual ways, Peltier remains in prison despite petitions from millions worldwide, including the Archbishop of Canterbury, Archbishop Desmond Tutu, and fifty members of the U.S. Congress. After 500 years of colonialism, the U.S. government still denies indigenous people the right to land, and still denies Peltier his freedom.

There is Alejandrina Torres, a model church and community activist from the Puerto Rican section of Chicago. As a teacher at an alternative Puerto Rican high school and secretary of the First Congregational Church (United Church of Christ), she became a leader of the National Committee to Free Puerto Rican Prisoners of War. In prison, she has suffered a heart attack

158

due to the daily trauma of her environment, and she has been denied proper medical care. At the infamous Lexington Control Unit, she was not permitted to participate in recreational activities or to attend religious services. In 1984, Alejandrina experienced a brutal physical assault, when a male guard forced her to submit to a second strip search after a visit from her daughter. Yet, Alejandrina's spirit remains strong: for her own freedom and the freedom of her people.

Dr. Alan Berkman was raised in a Jewish household, where involvement in the synagogue meant involvement with the community. Active in the civil rights and antiwar movements of the 1960s, he used his medical skills to build solidarity with the Black Liberation and Puerto Rican independence movements, with Native Americans, and with oppressed communities in New York, Alabama, and Boston. Though diagnosed with Hodgkin's disease, he was held in preventative detention awaiting trial for two years. He has been eligible for parole since 1987 and just had all charges dropped relating to the DC Resistance Conspiracy case. Bishop Browning, head of the Episcopal Church in the U.S., stated that he has reviewed the case in depth and found that Berkman's continued incarceration is both "inappropriate and without justification." No action has been taken, however, and Alan's cancer keeps getting worse.

Mumia Abu-Jamal was a young Black Panther Party member, and has been a reporter in media: print and broadcast. Following the MOVE bombings in Philadelphia, on which Mumia reported, a shoot-out occurred, where Mumia ended up beaten and shot and an officer was killed. In a trial where Mumia tried to defend himself, and with a racially imbalanced jury, much evidence centered around the activities of the Black Panther Party. These documents were meant to incite fear among the white jurors, who delivered a guilty verdict with death penalty attached. He still awaits the possibility of cruel state murder.

These are but a few of the prisoners of conscience, prisoners of war, and political prisoners. As we reflect upon their road to imprisonment, we must also project our own work on the road toward building a more just society. Defending political prisoners does not simply mean engaging in defense of an individual, but rather calls us to defend the movements of peace and justice in which we work.

I wanted to stand true to the old traditions that are sacred to me, and I found before me a door open to a jail...

Chief Dan Katchangua,
Hopi Sovereign Nation

Fighting in defense of truth and right is not to be undertaken light heartedly, nor to be evaded as a duty.

Qu'ran c. 51

A Call to a Ministry for Freedom

As interfaith members of the United States religious community, we commit ourselves to respond in faith to the conditions in which our brothers and sisters in prison endure. As such, we renew our engagement in the world of the suffering and covenant among us to:

- engage in a process that will help us to have a clear analysis of the situation facing each one of the political prisoners.
- make an effort to understand their struggle and the root causes that brought about their incarceration.
- disseminate true information on the specific cases, unmasking the myths regarding political prisoners.
- facilitate and be engaged in religious services as needed by the prisoners.
- participate actively in efforts supporting their struggle for peace with justice, for human rights and amnesty.

Stand out firmly for justice to all, even against yourself or your nearest of kin. Remain firm in faith.

Qu'ran c. 67

For hatred does not cease by hatred at any time, hatred ceases by love. This is an ancient law.

Dhammapada,
verse 5, Buddhist scripture

The Spirit of the Lord God is upon me, because the Lord hath anointed me to preach good tidings unto the meek... to proclaim liberty to the captives and the opening of the prisons to those who are bound.

Isaiah 61:1

The following national organizations have endorsed this call:

Christian Church (Disciples of Christ), Church Action for Safe and Just Communities

Clergy and Laity Concerned

The General Board of Church and Society, United Methodist Church

Interfaith Prisoners of Conscience Project of the Prophetic Justice Unit, National Council of Churches

National Assembly of Religious Women

Metodistas Asociados Representando La Causa Hispano-Americana (MARCHA), *Iglesia Unida Metodista*

National Interfaith Task Force on Criminal Justice

Racial Justice Working Group of the National Council of Churches

United Church Board for Homeland Ministries, United Church of Christ

United Church Board for World Ministries, World Issues Office, United Church of Christ

The following individual religious leaders have signed the call with organizations listed for identification purposes.

Bishop Philip Cousin
11th Episcopal District
African Methodist
Episcopal Church

The Right Rev.
Walter D. Dennis,
Suffragan Bishop
Episcopal Diocese of
New York City

Bishop Lowell G. Erdahl,
St. Paul Synod
Evangelical Lutheran
Church in America

The Most Rev.
Thomas J. Gumbleton,
Aux. Bishop
Catholic Archdiocese
of Detroit

The Right Rev.
Barbara C. Harris,
Suffragan Bishop
Episcopal Diocese
of Massachusetts

The Rev. Dr. John Humbert,
General Minister and
President
Christian Church
(Disciples of Christ)

The Right Rev.
J. Antonio Mama,
Episcopal Bishop

The Right Rev.
Dr. Roy I. Sano, Bishop
Denver area,
United Methodist Church

The Most Rev. Walter
T. Sullivan, Bishop,
Catholic Archdiocese of
Richmond, Virginia

Rev. M. William Howard,
Past President
National Council of
Churches, U.S.A.

Rev. Tyrone Pius,
General Secretary
Progressive National
Baptist Convention

Ms. Diane Porter
Presiding Bishop's
Dep. for Public Ministries
Episcopal Church, U.S.A.

Dr. Jean Sindab,
Executive Secretary
Program to Combat Racism
World Council of Churches

Rev. Jovelino Ramos.
Associate Director
Racial Justice Ministries
Presbyterian Church. U.S.A.

Rev. Esdras Rodriguez Diaz
Gen. Commission on
Religion and Race
United Methodist Church

Dr. Pat Rumer,
General Director
Church Women United

Dr. Loretta Williams
National Interreligious
Commission on Civil Rights

Rev. Jew Don Boney
National Black
United Front

Rev. Lucius Walker,
Director
Interfaith Foundation on
Community Organization

Bishop C. Dale White
New York area,
United Methodist Church

Mr. Dwaine C. Epps,
Director, Global Issues and
Programs
Church World Service and
Witness
National Council of
Churches of Christ, U.S.A.

Father Brian J. Grieves
Presiding Bishop's
Office on Peace and Justice
Episcopal Church, U.S.A.

Mr. William Davis, Director
Christic Institute (West)

Sister Marie D. Grasso,
National Chairperson
Pax Christi, U.S.A.

Sister Mary Kownacki, OSB,
Executive Director
Pax Christi, U.S.A.

Rev. Dr. Joseph E. Lowry,
President
Southern Christian
Leadership Conference

Mr. Daniel Levitas,
Executive Director
Center for Democratic
Renewal

Mr. Matt Meyer
War Resisters League

Mr. Ed Nakawatasc
American Friends
Service Committee

Ms. Barbara Owl
International Indian
Treaty Council

Ms. Carmen Rivera, Director
Office on Racial Justice
Young Women's
Christian Association

Mr. Andres Thomas
United Methodist Seminars

Ramsey Clark, Esq.,
Former U.S. Attorney General
Plowshares Defense Fund

Rev. William Sloane Coffin,
President, SANE / FREEZE
Campaign for Global Security

Rev. Herbert Daughtry
African People's
Christian Organization
House of the Lord
Church (NY)

Mr. Douglas Hostetter,
Executive Director
Fellowship of Reconciliation

Mr. Dale Aukerman
Brethren Peace Fellowship

Rabbi Philip Bentley,
President, Jewish
Peace Fellowship

Ms. Sharon Bishop,
Chair,
Unitarian Universalist
Peace Fellowship

Mr. A. Garnett Day,
Executive Secretary
Disciples Peace Fellowship

Ms. Margaret Howe,
National Coordinator
Buddhist Peace Fellowship

Mr. Bill Ofenloch
Catholic Peace Fellowship

Rev. L. William Yolton,
Executive Director
National Interreligious
Service Board on
Conscientious Objection;
Presbyterian Peace
Fellowship

Puerto Rico

Rev. Parilla Bonilla
Iglesia Bautista de Roosevelt

Rev. José M. Vilar
Parroquia la Encarnación
Iglesia Episcopal
Puertorriqueña

Local

Imam Jamil Abdullah Al-
Amin
Community Mosque
of Atlanta (GA)

Father Dan Berrigan

Father Philip Berrigan and
Liz MacAllister
Jonah House (MD)

Rev. Elizabeth Butler
Salvation Baptist
Church (NY)

Rev. Calvin Butts
Abyssinian Baptist
Church (NY)

Brother John T. Conway
Order of Friars Minor,
Capuchin (WI)

Sister Darlene Cuccinello
Intercommunity Center for
Justice and Peace (NY)

Mr. Jerry Ebner
Plowshares activist (WI)

Rev.
Graylon Scott Ellis-Hagler,
Pastor,
Church of the United
Community (MA)
Assoc. Regional Minister,
Christian Church
(Disciple), Northeast

Ms. Rowena General
Mohawk Warrior
Society (NY)

Angelica and
Richard Harter
United Church of
Christ (MA)

Sister Jean Hughes
Eighth Day Center for
Peace and Justice (IL)

Father Paul Kabat
Plowshares activist (IL)

Ms. Katya Komisaruk
White Rose Disarmament/
Plowshares activist (CA)

Imam Al Amir, A. Latif
Masjid Al Muminin (NY)

Rev. Lawrence Lucas
Resurrection Roman
Catholic Church (NY)

Mr. Paul Magno
Olive Branch Catholic
Worker (Washington, DC)

Mr. Elmer Maas,
Mr. John Munves, and the
members of the Kairos
community (NY)

Mr. Imani Mahdi
New Afrikan Network
in Defense of Political
Prisoners and POWS
(Washington, DC)

Ms. Wende E. Marshall
Black Women's Caucus,
Union Theological
Seminary (NY)

Rabbi Robert J. Marx
Congregation Hafaka (IL)

Ms. Julia Matsui-Estrella
Pacific and Asian-American
Center for Theology
and Training (CA)

Rabbi Marshall Meyer
Congregation B'nai
Jeshurun (NY)

Minister Ernest Mohammed,
Mosque #45
Nation of Islam (TX)

Minister Kevin Mohammad
Representative of the
Hon. Louis Farrakhan,
Mohammad Mosque #7,
Nation of Islam (NY)

Rev. Roberto Morales
St. Ann's Church
Episcopalian (NY)

Ms. Donna Nevel
Jews for Economic and
acial Justice (NY)

Imam Ali Rashid
Masjid Malcolm
Shabazz (NY)

Dr. Mark Ridley-Thomas
Southern Christian
Leadership Conference of
Greater Los Angeles (CA)

Mr. Philip M. Runkel
Catholic Worker Archives,
Marquette University (WI)

Father William Starr
Episcopal Chaplain,
Columbia University (NY)

Rev. José Alberto Torres
First Congregational
Church, UCC (IL)

Ms. Majorie Van Cleef
Pledge of Resistance (CT)

Imam Siraj Wahaj
Masjid at-Taqwa (NY)

Mr. Art Woolsey
Native American
Indian Inmates Support
Project (NY)

II.6

Special International Tribunal on the Violation of Human Rights of Political Prisoners and Prisoners of War in United States Prisons and Jails

December 7-10, 1990
Hunter College
New York, New York

The International Tribunal was not only a political/educational event, it was also a semi-formal judicial proceeding. The pages that follow include a small sampling of key documents from that proceeding—which together provide a landmark body of documentation still applicable to political prisoners and prisoners of war held today:

1. the indictment of the U.S. government drawn up by longtime movement attorneys Lennox S. Hinds and Jan Susler on behalf of 95 political prisoners and POW's then held in the U.S.;
2. a paper by attorneys Michael Deutsch and Jan Susler laying out the repressive U.S. government strategy and policies that led to the incarceration of the political prisoners and POW's;
3. a paper by attorney J. Soffiyah Elijah analyzing the sentencing and abusive conditions of confinement to which New Afrikan/Black political prisoners and POW's were subjected;
4. a similar analysis by Tribunal coordinator Luis Nieves Falcón as to the Puerto Rican political prisoners and POW's;
5. an analysis by attorney Elizabeth Fink of the conditions of confinement of the North American anti-imperialist political prisoners; and
6. the verdict delivered by the eight judges of the Special International Tribunal after due deliberation, based on all the written, oral and videotaped evidence presented before them.

II.6.A
Tribunal Indictment

Before the Special International Tribunal on the Violation of Human Rights of Political Prisoners and Prisoners of War Held in United States Prisons and Jails

Mumia Abu-Jamal	Edwin Cortés	Ruchell Cinque Magee
Sundiata Acoli	Barbara Curzi-Laaman	Abdul Majid
Alberta Wicker Africa	Jaime Delgado	Carol Saucier Manning
Carlos Perez Africa	Joseph Doherty	Thomas Manning
Charles Sims Africa	Dorothy Eber	Adolfo Matos
Consuella Dodson Africa	Jerry Ebner	Dan McGuire
Debbie Sims Africa	Malik El-Amin	Edward Mead
Delbert Orr Africa	Elizam Escobar	Jalil Muntaqim
Edward Goodman Africa	Linda Evans	Sababu Na Uhuru
Janet Holloway Africa	Herman Ferguson	Sekou Odinga
Janine Phillips Africa	David Gilbert	Dylcia Pagán
Merle Austin Africa	Jean Gump	Leonard Peltier
Michael Africa	Jennifer Haines	Richard Picarello
Ramona Johnson Africa	Bashir A. Hameed	Hugo Pinell
Sue Leon Africa	Abdul Haqq	Alberto Rodríguez
William Phillips Africa	Eddie Hatcher	Alicia Rodríguez
Abdul Aziz	Robert "Seth" Hayes	Lucy Rodríguez
Silvia Baraldini	Teddy Jah Heath	Luis Rosa
Marya Barr	Geronimo ji Jaga (Pratt)	Juan Segarra Palmer
Duane Bean	Ricardo Jiménez	Mutulu Shakur
Herman Bell	Raphael Kwesi Joseph	Standing Deer
Haydée Beltrán	Carl Kabat	Robert Taylor
Alan Berkman	Yu Kikumura	Alejandrina Torres
Luz María Berrios	Geuka Mohannan Koti	Carlos Alberto Torres
Hanif Shabazz Bey	Jaan Laaman	Kazi Toure
Timothy Blunk	Richard Mafundi Lake	Gary Tyler
Kathy Boudin	Mondo Langa	Carmen Valentín
Marilyn Buck	Maliki Shakur Latine	Albert Nuh Washington
Antonio Camacho Negrón	Ray Levasseur	Laura Whitehorn
Judy Clark	Oscar López Rivera	Richard Williams
Mark Cook	Elmer Maas	Jerry Zawada

POLITICAL PRISONERS AND PRISONERS
OF WAR IN THE UNITED STATES,
Petitioners,
-versus-

THE GOVERNMENT OF THE UNITED STATES OF AMERICA;
GEORGE BUSH, President
RICHARD THORNBURGH, Attorney General
WILLIAM SESSIONS, Director, FBI
WILLIAM WEBSTER, Director, CIA
MICHAEL QUINLAN, Director, Bureau of Prisons
and the Governors of each state which holds Political Prisoners
Defendants.

Indictment

This is a criminal indictment charging the United States government, through
the President and its highest law enforcement officials, with conspiring to
violate the fundamental human rights of political activists and opponents of
the U.S. government. The indictment charges the defendants, *inter alia*, with
arbitrary arrests and detentions, denial of fair trials, and cruel, degrading
and inhumane treatment of those imprisoned.

The indictment alleges the existence of a special FBI counterintelligence
program designed to destroy the Black, Puerto Rican, Mexican and Native
American liberation movements pursuant to which many political activists were imprisoned, victims of false, politically motivated and framed up
charges. The indictment also alleges that others have been illegally imprisoned for associations and acts of resistance as part of or in support of libera-
tion/independence movements opposing U.S. colonial domination.

Jurisdiction

1. This case is brought before a special tribunal of distinguished
   international jurists mandated to investigate the situation in regard
   to Political Prisoners and Prisoners of War held in U.S. prisons. The
   Special Tribunal will apply the law of international human rights as
   well as the U.S. Constitution.

I. Factual Allegations

2. Throughout its history the United States government has denied
   fundamental human rights to groups defined by race, sex/gender,
   nationality and class. As part of this long record of human rights violations, political movements, particularly those for self-determination
   by people of color, have been continuously repressed by judicial and
   extra-judicial methods.

3. The United States government, and its state and municipal governments, criminalize these political movements as part of its ongoing
effort to destroy the more militant forms of resistance to injustice and
oppression. Actions taken in furtherance of the movements for self-
determination or in opposition to the U.S. government are punished as
criminal offenses, and not recognized as political offenses. This policy
of criminalization denies the political status of more than 100 known
political activists presently held in United States prisons and jails.
4. As part of its criminalization policy, the United States government
refuses to recognize the legitimacy under International Law of the
national liberation struggles of the Black, Puerto Rican, Mexican and
Native people and utilizes its "criminal" justice system to incarcerate
freedom fighters and other activists participating in the struggle for
liberation, human rights and peace.
5. The political prisoners/prisoners of war in the United States include:
    a. Political activists who by working for self-determination and
liberation, violate the criminal laws of the U.S. government.
These political offenses range from nonviolent acts of civil disobedience to clandestine armed struggle in support of national
liberation and/or against colonialism;
    b. Political activists who, in a government effort to disrupt and
destroy their political work, have been falsely charged for
offenses they did not commit;
    c. Prisoners who were initially incarcerated for nonpolitical
actions who are eligible for release but denied their freedom
due to their political activism against racism, sexism, and brutality inside the prisons.

II. The Movements and Political Prisoners

A. Black/New Afrikan Political Prisoners and POW's

6. The resistance of Africans in America (Black people) to the genocidal
policies and practices of the United States government and its criminalization of the Black community has a long, continuous history
from the middle passage to the slave rebellions up to the present day
struggle for liberation and equality. Some were repressed for struggling for control of their community and other means of self-determination. Others were repressed for working for the establishment of
an independent New Afrikan nation-state in the Southeast Blackbelt
within the geographic borders of the United States. The United States
government's response, especially to those organizations advocating
self-determination and national liberation, has been to criminalize
these movements and kill or imprison their leaders.

7. Many of the Black political prisoners imprisoned today began their political activity in the 1960s and early 1970s as members and/or supporters of the Black Panther Party (BPP). The BPP was a political organization that advocated Black community control of institutions affecting the Black community and the right of Black people to defend themselves against racist attack.

8. The Black Panther Party, along with other organizations such as the Student Nonviolent Coordinating Committee, the Southern Christian Leadership Conference, the Nation of Islam, the Revolutionary Action Movement and the Republic of New Afrika, organized millions of Black people to demand basic human rights.

9. The U.S. government's response was to initiate overt and covert programs of repression. One such program instituted by the Federal Bureau of Investigation (FBI) was known as COINTELPRO.

    a. According to the FBI, the goals of COINTELPRO were to "expose," "disrupt" and otherwise "neutralize" the movement of Black people for fundamental social change.

    b. One aspect of COINTELPRO was to eliminate effective leadership by murdering and/or incarcerating key leaders. Some, such as BPP leaders Fred Hampton and Mark Clark, were murdered by law enforcement officials in staged "raids." Others were killed in factional violence instigated by government informants and infiltrators. False criminal charges were brought against other leaders who were given life terms and remain imprisoned today.

10. Many who were not killed or incarcerated under COINTELPRO were forced underground and engaged in resistance as part of the Black Liberation Army. Between 1971 and 1982, numerous BLA members and suspected BLA members were killed in confrontations with police, and others arrested and incarcerated for life on false criminal charges or for engaging in acts of expropriation or other forms of armed resistance.

11. There are approximately 50 Black political prisoners and prisoners of war incarcerated in the United States.

B. The Puerto Rican Independence Movement

12. Since 1898, when the island of Puerto Rico was invaded by the United States, it has been held as a colony in violation of international law. Despite the United States assertion that its domination of Puerto Rico is an "internal matter," the United Nations Decolonization Committee confirms annually by resolution that General Assembly Resolution 1514 (XV) on self-determination and independence applies to Puerto Rico.

13. Throughout the 92 years of colonial occupation, there have been numerous activists and freedom fighters for the independence of Puerto Rico who have been murdered and/or jailed for their political activity. Among these freedom fighters are the five Nationalists, Rafael Cancel Miranda, Lolita Lebrón, Irvin Flores, Oscar Collazo, and Andrés Figueroa Cordero who each spent over 25 years in United States prisons until they were freed in 1979 as the result of an international campaign.

14. In the 1960s the Federal Bureau of Investigation initiated a counter-intelligence campaign against "Groups Seeking Independence of Puerto Rico" calling for the disruption of those organizations both inside the United States and in Puerto Rico.

15. Today there are 18 Puerto Rican women and men incarcerated in the United States for their active participation in the Puerto Rican anticolonial struggle. Thirteen of these 18 Puerto Rican prisoners are serving sentences for "seditious conspiracy," i.e., opposing the authority of the United States by force. At their trials these *independentistas* assumed the position of "prisoner of war" pursuant to the 1977 Protocols to the Geneva Convention and the United Nations General Assembly resolutions. They asserted that the domestic proceedings against them were illegal, as the United States government had no right to criminalize their resistance to colonialism, and they refused to offer a legal defense to the charges against them.

16. In 1989, a Bertrand Russell Tribunal sitting in Barcelona, Spain, issued a verdict condemning the United States' colonial domination of Puerto Rico and demanding that all Puerto Rican political prisoners and prisoners of war be freed.

C. The Native American Movement

17. When Europeans first came to what is now the United States, there were 10 million inhabitants who shared the natural resources of this land. The Europeans stole the Native Americans' land, rendering them homeless and threatening the social, political, and economic infrastructures of Native American society.

18. The policy of the United States concerning the Native American people was one of genocide. Their numbers have been reduced from 10 million to approximately one million, most living on "reservations" under conditions of extreme poverty and social devastation.

19. Through organizations such as the American Indian Movement (AIM), Native Americans have resisted the genocidal policies of the United States government and fought for the return of land and resources. The 71-day siege in 1973 at Wounded Knee Reservation demanded, *inler alia*, investigation into the violations of the hundreds of treaties between Native American nations and the United States.

20. By 1975, the FBI declared AIM "one of the most dangerous organizations" in the United States and embarked upon a paramilitary strategy to destroy the movement. In one confrontation at Pine Ridge in June 1975, two FBI agents and one AIM member were killed. Although no one was ever charged in the death of the Native American, AIM activist Leonard Peltier was tried, convicted, and given two life sentences in the deaths of the FBI agents. FBI documents obtained after his conviction showed that the FBI falsified key evidence in order to secure Peltier's conviction. The case of Leonard Peltier has been condemned by Amnesty International and numerous international human rights organizations and remains a symbol of the struggle of Native Americans for national liberation.

D. White/North American Political Prisoners

21. There are approximately 20 political prisoners who are white North Americans. These political prisoners are primarily from the anti-imperialist and peace/religious movements.
22. The peace/religious political prisoners, mainly Catholic, are sometimes called "Plowshares prisoners" from the biblical mandate to "beat swords into plowshares." They are imprisoned for actions such as criminal trespass and/or malicious destruction of government property, i.e., military/nuclear equipment. Many have refused to put forward a "legal" defense at trial, arguing that their actions were required under international law and/or religious principles.
23. The anti-imperialist political prisoners have been prosecuted for armed, clandestine actions taken in solidarity with national liberation movements inside the United States and throughout the world. In accordance with international law, they unequivocally support national liberation struggles and fight for an end to racism, sexism, and economic exploitation and for social justice.
24. These women and men come from a variety of backgrounds: Students for a Democratic Society, Vietnam Veterans Against the War, the women's movement and prisoners support groups. Some were targets of covert and overt government repression as public activists and were forced to go underground for survival. The actions for which they are convicted include possession of weapons and explosives, "conspiracy," and the bombing of unoccupied government installations and corporate offices.

The Defendants and their agents have conspired to deny arrested political activists their rights guaranteed under international human rights declarations and covenants and the United States Constitution.

Count I: Arbitrary Arrest, Detention, and Imprisonment

25. The Defendants have arrested and/or detained hundreds of political activists, in some cases without specific charge or providing reasonable bail. In the case of many political prisoners, they have been subjected to political internment through the grand jury or to exorbitant bail or denied bail punitively because of the political nature of their case.

   a. Preventive Detention: Arrested members of organized resistance groups are often detained indefinitely without bail upon a determination that they pose a "danger to the community." This law has been used to confine individuals alleged to be associated with clandestine liberation movements for years prior to trial.

   b. Political Internment Through the Grand Jury: United States law permits incarceration for a refusal to cooperate with a federal "investigation" through a secret proceeding called a grand jury. This law has been used to incarcerate and re-incarcerate public political activists who support movements for national liberation and refuse to collaborate with government witch hunts.

Count II: Denial of a Fair Trial Before an Independent Tribunal

26. Political activists are often charged with vague and far-reaching accusations of criminal conspiracy, which allows the government to greatly expand the scope of admissible evidence. The use of special conspiracy laws (RICO and seditious conspiracy) against political people allows the government to criminalize associations with, or membership in, resistance organizations.

27. In numerous cases, political activists have been framed up with false charges in order to destroy their political work in opposition to the United States government. In these cases, favorable evidence was suppressed, physical evidence fabricated, and witnesses given undisclosed favorable treatment. Despite the disclosure after conviction of evidence showing government misconduct and suppression of evidence, in all but a few cases, United States courts have refused to reverse these convictions and release these prisoners.

28. The trial procedures of political prosecutions are designed to prejudice the accused before the jury and the public and maximize the possibilities of convictions.

   a. Anonymous Juries: Recent United States court rulings have upheld a procedure denying to those on trial the names, addresses, and work places of jurors. This use of a secret jury has been routinely permitted in prosecutions of political activists where the government claims the accused is associated with militant resistance movements. The anonymous jury strongly suggests to the jury and the public-at-large that the person on trial is "dangerous" and should be convicted.

b. Prejudicial "Security": In the cases of political activists, especially those connected to clandestine movements, the courthouse/courtroom has been militarized. In one instance, an eight-foot shield has been ordered constructed between the spectators and defendants; in another, a concrete bunker was installed in front of the courthouse. In most political prosecutions, armed police require all who enter court buildings to submit to a search. The courtroom itself is filled with law enforcement, sometimes armed with electronic "stun guns" or other weapons. Supporters of those charged are often harassed or denied entry. These and other "security" measures are often highlighted in the media, prejudicing prospective jurors and discouraging the community of supporters from attending the trial.

c. Access to Counsel: Those charged in political cases have been denied their right to counsel and/or their attorney of choice. In addition, the isolated punitive conditions under which those political prisoners awaiting trial are detained, prevents meaningful counsel. There has been documented evidence of illegal surveillance of privileged attorney-client communications, and attorneys who represent political prisoners have themselves been subjected to harassment, disbarment, and false criminal charges.

d. Denial of a Right to a Defense: In trials where political activists choose to put forward a defense, the government and courts have been successful in preventing the jury from hearing the evidence/testimony. The courts force the person charged to disclose defense matters prior to their presentation so that a court may rule upon its admissibility. "Justification" defenses based upon international law have been routinely denied. In other cases the government has been successful in precluding any evidence concerning the political background/motivation of the person charged. Also in many political cases, under the guise of security, the prosecution submits secret information to the court without providing it to the defense. These *ex parte* contacts between the court and prosecutor often contain false or exaggerated information harmful to the accused.

e. Denial of Proper Venue: With few limitations, the government may choose the location in which to try a case. In broad "conspiracy" prosecutions, the case may be tried in any location where any "act" is allegedly committed. Taking advantage of this rule, the government has tried Puerto Rican *independentistas,* not in Puerto Rico, but in North American courts thousands of miles from their homeland and families, before jurors unfamiliar with, and hostile to, the Puerto Rican reality.

29. Disproportionate Sentencing: Political activists regularly receive sentences much longer than those imposed on nonpolitical defendants convicted of the same, or similar, offense. They also have received sentences that far exceed those called for by statutory "guidelines." Further, political prisoners are often prosecuted in different jurisdictions, and consecutive sentences imposed until the aggregate sentence is one of life imprisonment.

30. Death Penalty: The United States Supreme Court has ruled that the racially discriminatory imposition of the death penalty does not violate the Constitution. A grossly disproportionate number of people of color are on death row. At present, Mumia Abu-Jamal, a Black journalist and former leader of the Black Panther Party and member of MOVE, is on death row in a case where the prosecutor argued that his past political affiliations warranted the imposition of capital punishment.

31. Denial of Parole/Conditional Release: "Parole" is discretionary and is determined in administrative proceedings in which a prisoner has few, if any rights. Although the parole authorities have "guidelines" recommending early release under established criteria, the political background and/or associations of a prisoner are usually used to deny a prisoner release until the maximum sentence has been served. Some parole boards have stated that a prisoner must change his/her political beliefs before he/she is released.

Count III: Cruel, Inhumane, and Degrading Treatment

32. The conditions of all prisoners in United States prisons and penitentiaries are generally brutal and onerous. Even so, the political prisoners/prisoners of war are housed under conditions which are qualitatively worse than the average prisoner. Some examples include the following:

    a. Physical Torture: Upon arrest, and throughout confinement, the political prisoner/prisoner of war is subject to arbitrary physical beatings and torture, which have resulted in permanent physical and psychological harm to the prisoner. Although complaints have been made and lawsuits filed in state and federal courts, few prisoners have received any redress.

b. Psychological Torture: The political prisoner's confinement is often designed to break his/her spirit and/or force him/her to renounce his/her political beliefs. Long periods in segregation (solitary confinement), both pretrial and postconviction, are routinely imposed upon political prisoners. In addition, "control units" have been built and prisoners are assigned to them solely due to their political beliefs and/or associations. Other forms of psychological torture include sensory deprivation, denial and restriction of visitation, harassment of families, and the detention and interrogation of the prisoners' children.

c. Sexual Abuse and Harassment: Women political prisoners and prisoners of war have been subjected to particularly cruel treatment. This treatment includes cavity and strip searches by male guards and denial of medical care.

d. Racism: The large majority of prisoners in the United States are Black, Puerto Rican, Mexican, and/or Native American. The overwhelming majority of prison guards are white. Prisons are often located in white, rural areas and provide much needed economic support to these areas. Prisoners must cope daily with racial attitudes and discrimination imposed upon them. Political prisoners who attempt to focus attention upon these issues and to organize to fight against them, are punished physically and/or isolated from the population.

e. Retaliatory Transfers: Political prisoners, including those who have become politicized since their incarceration, are transferred from one prison to another in retaliation for the exercise of their right to free speech and/or association in the prisons, and/or to isolate them from outside friends and supporters. Most states and the federal government are now parties to an interstate compact permitting a prisoner in one state to serve his/her sentence thousands of miles away from home and family.

f. Denial of Political Identity: In attempting to break the resistance and coerce renunciation of political beliefs and association, prison officials deny the prisoners their political identity. Authorities deny permission for visits from supporters, censor political literature and correspondence, and refuse to allow prisoners to associate with each other.

g. Administrative Segregation/Spurious Disciplinary Charges: Prisoners in state and federal prisons may be placed for long periods in segregation for alleged violations of prison "rules." There is little, if any, judicial review of prison disciplinary proceedings. Prison guards preside at these proceedings and determine all issues of fact and law. These proceedings are highly subject to abuse and have been used to house politically active political prisoners in segregation for years at a time. "Due process" now even permits indefinite housing in "administrative" segregation, even if no violation of prison regulations is established.

h. Religious Discrimination: The right of a political prisoner to practice his/her religion is often totally denied, based upon the custodial status of the prisoner. Muslim and Native American prisoners, in particular, are singled out for racist harassment and denied their right to observe their religion.

i. Control Units: The federal prison system and many states have built high security "control units" to permanently house prisoners they consider a threat. Many political prisoners have been placed in control units indefinitely, solely due to their political beliefs and/or outside political associations. In control units, prisoners are usually housed in their cell for 23 hours per day, outside recreation is severely restricted, and all contact with the outside, including reading material, is scrutinized and often denied.

j. Health Care: Medical care for all prisoners is grossly inadequate. For a political prisoner who becomes ill, this can mean a death sentence. Political prisoners are routinely denied even emergency treatment. In one case, Alan Berkman, a political prisoner with recurrent cancer, was denied timely treatment solely due to the political nature of his case.

Charges

33. Based upon the above enumerated politically motivated acts, which are in violation of fundamental principles and guarantees of international and United States constitutional law, the United States Government, through its highest officials, federal and state, is hereby charged with the following criminal counts:

a. Count I: Conspiring to violate the right of all people to be free from arbitrary arrest, detention, and imprisonment as guaranteed by the Universal Declaration of Human Rights (UDHR) Art. 9 (G.A. Res. 217 (III 1948)); International Covenant on Civil and Political Rights (ICCPR), Art. 9 (999 UNTS 171, 1969); American Convention on Human Rights (ACHR), Art. 783; U.S. Constitution, 4th, 5th and 8th Amendments.

b. Count II: Conspiracy to violate the right of the accused to a fair and prompt trial before an independent tribunal, to a presumption of innocence and the right to bail while awaiting trial, as guaranteed by the UDHR, Art. 10; ICCPR, Art. 9 §2;

Art. 14 §§2 and 3; U.S. Constitution, 5th and 6th Amendments; ACHR, Art. 8.

c. Count III: Conspiracy to violate the right to be free from torture and other cruel, inhumane, or degrading treatment or punishment, as guaranteed by the G.A. Res. 3452 (XXX 9 Dec. 1975) Art 1-4; G.A. Res. 39/46 (10 Dec. 1984); ACHR, Art. 5; Standard Minimum Rules for Treatment of Prisoners (MSTP); UDHR, Art. 5; U.S. Constitution, 1st and 8th Amendments.

d. Count IV: Conspiracy to violate the right guaranteed to all people to freedom of political thought, expression, and association as guaranteed by UDHR, Art. 18, 19, 20; ICCPR, Art. 18. 19. 21; ACHR, Art. 12, 13, 15, 16; U.S. Constitution, Art. 1.

e. Count V: Conspiracy to violate the right to nationality and right to self-determination and to use all available means to resist colonialism, as guaranteed by UDHR, Art. 15; ICCPR, Art. 1; G.A. Res. 1514.

Sanctions Requested

WHEREFORE, based upon the foregoing violations of international and domestic law, it is hereby requested that this distinguished Tribunal:

1. Declare that the government of the United States, and the several states, are guilty of gross violations of the human rights of political prisoners in this country;
2. Condemn the aforementioned human rights violations;
3. Demand that the United States government cease and desist existing violative practices;
4. Demand the immediate, unconditional release of all political prisoners/prisoners of war;
5. Request that the United Nations General Assembly Commission on Human Rights investigate the violations of human rights of political prisoners in the United States.

Dated: July 31, 1990
New York, New York

Lennox S. Hinds, Esquire
Jan Susler, Esquire

II.6.B

Political Prisoners in the United States: The Hidden Reality

Michael E. Deutsch and Jan Susler

1990

Geronimo ji Jaga Pratt, a former leader of the Black Panther Party, an African-American organization fighting for self-determination in the 1960s, has served 22 years in prison for a murder the U.S. government knows he did not commit. FBI documents reveal the agency considered him a prime target of COINTELPRO, a U.S. government secret program to destroy the Black liberation movement. The victim's wife identified another man as the killer and was later coached by police to identify Pratt. The FBI withheld surveillance documents that established Pratt's presence at the time of the murder at a meeting 350 miles away from the scene of the murder. Denied parole several times, the state explains he is being kept in prison not because he is thought to be a murderer but because he is still a revolutionary.

Dhoruba al-Mujahid Bin-Wahad, another Black Panther Party leader and target of COINTELPRO, is serving a term of 25 years to life, falsely accused of the attempted murder of a New York City policeman. The FBI withheld documents revealing that the prosecutor (now a federal judge) suppressed evidence that the key prosecution witness had initially reported Bin-Wahad was not involved and only changed her testimony after extreme pressure by government agents. Twenty years later, after the discovery of the suppressed documents, Bin-Wahad is fighting to reopen his case.*

Alejandrina Torres, a 50-year-old Puerto Rican woman, is serving a 35-year sentence for seditious conspiracy—"opposing the U.S. government's authority over Puerto Rico by force." The FBI collected evidence against her and other *independentistas* by planting hidden video cameras in private dwellings and secretly recording all activity. Since her imprisonment, U.S. prison authorities have carried out a six-year campaign to break her spirit, including numerous assaults, denial of medical care, sensory deprivation, and small group isolation in an experimental Women's High Security Unit.

Leonard Peltier, a member of the American Indian Movement, also a COINTELPRO target, has spent 13 years in prison convicted of killing two FBI agents. In spite of the prosecution's concession that it could not prove who shot the agents and in spite of the acquittal of his codefendants on the basis of self-defense, Peltier has been denied all legal attempts for freedom. The government fraudulently extradited Peltier from Canada and put him through a trial fraught with manufactured evidence and perjured FBI testimony. Serving two consecutive life sentences, he spent several years at

---

* Released shortly after this was written, after 19 years in jail due to prosecutorial misconduct.

U.S.P. Marion, the most maximum security prison in the United States.

Jean Gump, a mother of 12 and a grandmother, with four other disarmament activists entered an isolated Minuteman II nuclear weapon silo where they used sledgehammers to try to split and disarm the track used to open the 120-ton missile covers. They cut the electrical sensor equipment, poured blood on the silo covers in the form of a cross, and spray painted "Disarm and Live for the Children" on the silo cover, leaving at the site indictments charging the U.S. government with crimes against humanity and the law of God, for its complicity in the arms race. Sentenced to six years in federal custody for this nonviolent protest act, Gump was recently placed in segregation for refusing a humiliating drug urinalysis when staff would not assure her privacy from male guards.

Despite its numerous and vociferous denials, the public record clearly shows that the United States government holds numerous political prisoners in its jails and penitentiaries. These men and women, African-Americans, Puerto Ricans, Native Americans, Chicano-Mexicanos, white citizens, and even foreign nationals, have been targeted for their political activities within the borders of the U.S. as well as abroad and victimized by purposeful, harsh, discriminatory treatment in the U.S. judicial system. In the process of employing the U.S. legal system—including prosecutors, police, courts, judges, and the prisons—for political ends, the legal system has adopted counterinsurgency methods and has become more repressive and undemocratic.

U.S. political prisoners can be roughly divided into three categories: (1) foreign nationals whose political status or political activities against allies of U.S. imperialism (e.g., Israel, Great Britain, El Salvador) result in detention or imprisonment; (2) members of U.S. oppressed nationalities (African-Americans, Puerto Ricans, Chicano/Mexicanos, and Native Americans) who are prosecuted and imprisoned for political activities in furtherance of their movements for liberation and justice.* Included in this group are anticolonial combatants or Prisoners of War—members of national liberation movements who as part of clandestine organizations have employed armed struggle as a means to achieve self-determination and independence for their nation and upon capture have the right, under the Additional Protocols of the Geneva Convention and the U.N. General Assembly Resolutions, to POW status and not to be tried as domestic criminals; (3) white people who have acted in solidarity with the liberation movements of oppressed nationalities and/or in opposition to U.S. foreign or domestic policies.

As to each of these groups, the U.S. judicial system has operated to accommodate the political interests of the U.S. government and has detained or imprisoned scores of men and women.

* The U.S. has one of the largest prison populations in the world, made up almost entirely of oppressed nationalities and poor people. From this same population comes almost exclusively those given the death penalty. The warehousing in overcrowded and inhumane conditions is part of the government's strategy to control potentially insurgent populations.

Who Are the Political Prisoners and Prisoners of War?
Oppressed Nationalities

In the 1960s in many oppressed communities within the United States there emerged a more militant resistance to racial and economic oppression that culminated in organized efforts toward national liberation. Mass organizations demonstrated in the streets, and clandestine organizations and armed self-defense groups began to function in the Black community,* in the Puerto Rican barrios,† among Mexican people in the southwest U.S.,‡ and on Native American reservations.§

It is the militancy and fundamental anticolonial character of these movements that have been the primary impetus for the implementation of counterinsurgency methods of repression, including special restrictive procedures during trials and the creation of high-security isolation prison units. These liberation movements, which emerge from the struggles for the fundamental rights of survival of the oppressed communities of the United States, pose

---

* The Black liberation movement of the 1960s and early 1970s, from Martin Luther King to Malcolm X to the Black Panther Party ("BPP"), the Republic of New Afrika (RNA) and the Nation of Islam, was targeted by the FBI's COINTELPRO program, in a design to "expose, disrupt, misdirect, discredit, or otherwise neutralize the activities of black nationalist hate-type organizations and groupings, their leadership, spokesmen, membership, and supporters." The then FBI director, J. Edgar Hoover, viewed the BPP as the "single greatest threat," which should become the subject "of imaginative and hard-hitting counterintelligence measures aimed at crippling the BPP." An FBI memo spelled out the goals of destroying the self-determination efforts of Black people, including "preventing the rise of a messiah," preventing leaders from gaining respectability by discrediting them, and preventing the development of organizations, especially among youth.

Pursuant to the COINTELPRO program, Panther leaders were murdered and many were framed with criminal charges that have resulted in two [today almost four] decades of imprisonment. In the 1970s emerged clandestine formations of African-American freedom fighters including the Black Liberation Army (BLA). Many of these cadre were also killed or captured and given long prison sentences.

† The U.S. has a long history of attempts to crush the Puerto Rican independence movement. The independence movement has been a focus of government repression since the U.S. invaded that island nation in 1898. Within the last several years, Puerto Rico has been considered by the government to be "the Achilles heel of the United States." Over the last 30 years there has emerged a clandestine movement in complement to the mass movement for independence. Numbers of these anticolonial combatants have been captured, many asserting POW status and refusing to recognize the U.S. courts, others assuming the position of political prisoners.

‡ Chicano/Mexicano people and their organizations seeking liberty and justice for Mexican people living in occupied northern Mexico have been subjected to a history of discrimination and repression for their demand for human rights. In the early 1970s, seven leaders of the Chicano/Mexicano movement in the Southwest were killed and numerous others were imprisoned on politically motivated charges.

§ Native American activists likewise have experienced, since the Europeans came to North America, a repression to their resistance that has been of genocidal magnitude. In the 1960s and 1970s, the U.S. government escalated its attack on organized Native forces, the American Indian Movement (AIM), killing and jailing its leadership, and infiltrating its chapters pursuant to the FBI COINTELPRO program, attempting to crush the growing insurgency.

the greatest potential threat to the U.S. ruling class, which has engendered qualitative repressive changes in the U.S. legal system.

White U.S. Citizens—Solidarity and Resistance

Activists in this category have in common that they are white citizens of the U.S. who cannot stand by as the United States pursues its unjust and oppressive domestic and foreign policies. Beyond these commonalities, the movement is rich in its diversity, ranging from faith-based nonviolence to armed resistance. Among the groups and individuals who have been repressed and imprisoned for their political actions are the Plowshare protesters*: nonviolent religious activists who have carried out direct symbolic action against war materials, hammering bombers, computers, or missile nosecones and pouring blood on documents; the Sanctuary movement: clergy, lay church workers, and political activists who have worked with illegal Central American refugees who enter the U.S. without immigration documents and provided them sanctuary from capture and a forum from which to speak out about the war in their homeland†; those who refuse to register for the U.S. military service as required by law‡; and clandestine cells of anti-imperialist fighters who have employed armed resistance in solidarity with liberation struggles here and abroad.§

---

* The name comes from the biblical passage to "beat swords into plowshares."

† In hopes of breaking the sanctuary network, in a series of arrests the government charged clergy and lay workers with harboring, smuggling, and transporting "illegal aliens" and with conspiring to do so. In one arrest, the government swept up 12 prominent sanctuary workers, including two priests, a nun, and a minister, following an investigation that included a government informant infiltrating Bible study groups. The court refused to allow the defendants to present evidence that their work with the refugees was necessary to save lives and to prevent imprisonment, persecution, torture, and death. In sentencing convicted sanctuary workers, some courts imposed alternative sentences—a defendant could choose probation, with the conditions that s/he stop working with Central American refugees and stop speaking about the sanctuary movement to the press or public, or s/he could go to prison.

‡ Gilliam Kerley was sentenced to three years in prison plus a $10,000 fine, not merely for the acts of refusing to register but because he persisted in organizing against registration and the draft.

§ Two of these groups have been particularly targeted and victimized by the counterinsurgency strategy. The Ohio 7 is a group of working-class men and women accused of membership in a clandestine organization that carried out numerous bombings in opposition to U.S. policy in Central America and in solidarity with the worldwide movement against apartheid. They were arrested following a massive counterinsurgency hunt coordinating local, state and federal law enforcement. Their young children were also captured, isolated, and interrogated about their parents' activities. In a series of trials, the seven faced accusations of political bombings, murder, and attempted murder of police. They were then charged with seditious conspiracy, in spite of the fact that most of them were already serving sentences of over 45 years. The other group is charged with conspiracy to bomb the U.S. Capitol in protest of the U.S. foreign policies, including the invasion of Grenada. These six men and women are longtime political activists, virtually all of whom are already serving long prison terms for their acts of resistance and solidarity.

Foreign Nationals in the U.S.

The U.S. legal system is used not merely to quell domestic dissent and destroy national liberation movements within its borders. It also serves the government's allies in effecting their own counterinsurgency programs. In so doing, it echoes and enforces U.S. foreign policy.

For the last six, years Joseph Doherty has been held in U.S. custody, although he is not awaiting trial in the U.S. and has never been convicted of a crime in the U.S. This Irish citizen, a member of the Irish Republican Army, served three periods of imprisonment in Ireland for his activity in support of self-determination. During his trial for the death of a Special Air Service counterintelligence unit soldier, he escaped from British custody. He was captured in the U.S. three years later. The British government has consistently sought his extradition. Mr. Doherty is not safe from extradition in spite of numerous U.S. federal court and immigration court decisions finding he is nonextraditable.* After every decision in Doherty's favor, the U.S. Attorney General has intervened and ordered his extradition.

Using immigration laws as a means of implementing its hegemonist foreign policy,† the United States detains in large numbers refugees from El Salvador and Guatemala, fleeing repression and war financed by U.S. dollars. Those who make it across the militarized U.S. borders are treated as criminals; those men, women, and children who seek political asylum are locked up behind bars and barbed wire fences, barring them from access to legal counsel, preventing detained family members from seeing each other.‡ As of February 1989, close to 4,000 refugees were being held in Texas. Immigration and Naturalization Service (INS) documents explicitly acknowledge "the purpose of detention as deterrent."§ A U.S. court has found that detention is "inherently coercive and often deliberately intimidating."¶

In March of 1986, the United States opened in Oakdale, Louisiana, a federal alien detention center, with a capacity to house 5,000. It is the largest detention center of its kind in the United States. (Before it was destroyed by a pris-

---

* See, e.g., Matter of Doherty by the Government of the United Kingdom, 599 Supp. 270, 276 (S.D.N.Y. 1984). ("The facts of this case present the assertion of the political offense exception in its most classic form.").

† The U.S. policy is reflected in the percentage rate for approval of asylum applicants. From June 1983 to September 1988: from El Salvador, 2.7%, from Guatemala, 2.1%. In contrast, 61.7% of Iranians and 61.4% of Romanians were granted asylum for the same period. U.S. policy is also reflected in the INS Enhancement Plan for the Southern Border (February 16, 1989): "The INS Intelligence Program will continue ongoing liaison with other government agencies, particularly the CIA, Drug Enforcement Administration, and the Department of State..."

‡ The government reactivated a facility in Arizona that had served as a concentration camp for detaining Japanese Americans during World War II. On the Texas border, the main camp at Port Isabel is known as the "Corralon" (the great corral).

§ INS Enhancement Plan for the Southern Border, February 16, 1989, at p. 8.

¶ Orantes-Hernandez v. Meese, F. Supp. (D.TX., 4/28/88). See also, Helsinki Watch, "Detained, Denied and Deported: Asylum Seekers in the United States" (New York: June 1989).

oner rebellion in 1987, Oakdale housed 1,000 Cuban "undocumented aliens" and 60 U.S. prisoners. The Cubans, who arrived on the Mariel boatlift, have either completed service of the sentences they received for criminal conduct within the U.S. or have never been brought to trial or sentenced. The detention capacity of Oakdale has since been shifted to Port Isabel, Texas.)

As for Haitian refugees, some are detained in seriously overcrowded facilities, while most are interdicted, that is to say, intercepted before they set foot on U.S. soil, and rejected. Interdiction, which occurs outside the jurisdiction of the U.S., permits the government to avoid the obligations of its own law.*

In early 1987 the INS arrested seven Jordanian citizens and one Kenyan citizen, all residents of the United States. The FBI had surveilled the eight for 10 months and detected not a single substantive law violation. Instead, they were arrested on immigration charges seeking their deportation based on their alleged membership in or affiliation with a group (the Palestine Liberation Organization and the Popular Front for the Liberation of Palestine)† the U.S. government charges advocates world communism or unlawful destruction of property. The essence of the charge was that the eight read and distributed pro-Palestinian literature. Though they had no prior criminal records, they were treated as maximum security cases, held in preventive detention and isolation, later to be released on bond.

Discovery revealed that the case was a dry run for a secret, interdepartmental "Alien Terrorists and Undesirables: A Contingency Plan," which focused on citizens from seven Arab nations and Iran and which provided for massive roundups and detentions and summary deportation.

The Criminalization of Political Activists: The New Repression
Over the last 10 years, the U.S. government has begun to employ a counterinsurgency strategy‡ of repression against movements of oppressed U.S. nationalities and other political movements and activists.

The law-enforcement implementation of this strategy occurs primarily through the police power of the Federal Bureau of Investigation (FBI), the prosecutorial powers of the U.S. Justice Department, and within the U.S. federal courts and prisons. As a result, judicial counterinsurgency methods are gradually appearing within U.S. federal law and judicial procedures. Many

---

* The U.S. Committee for Refugees, "Refugees at Our Border: The U.S. Response to Asylum Seekers, September 1989, at pp. 12-13.
† Later amendments to the anticommunist legislation protect all foreign nationals from exclusion and deportation based on beliefs and expression except the PLO.
‡ The United States Pentagon has provided the following definition of counterinsurgency, which is generally accepted among so-called experts in the field: "Those military, para-military, political, economic, psychological and civic actions taken by a government to defeat subversive insurgency. Insurgency is defined as: a condition resulting from revolt or insurrection against a constituted government that falls short of civil war. In the current context subversive insurgency is primarily communist inspired, supported or exploited." *Dictionary of the United States—Military Terms for Joint Usage.*

of these new judicial developments parallel repressive measures by other Western "democracies" faced with insurgent political movements.* This new "repression" has the following defining components:

A) Surveillance and Intelligence Gathering

A key ingredient to the success of any counterinsurgency program is the ability of law enforcement to have sufficient powers to identify potential participants and supporters of insurgency, and to thoroughly surveil the activities of these targets.†

U.S. FBI guidelines released in 1983 by the then Attorney-General William French Smith greatly expanded the power of the FBI to gather political intelligence and infiltrate political groups. Referring specifically to its use in "Domestic Security/ Terrorism Investigations," [he said,] "We must ensure that the criminal intelligence sources which have been brought to bear so effectively on organized crime are effectively employed in domestic security/terrorism cases."

The Smith guidelines allow the FBI to investigate and

---

* A key defining characteristic of a counterinsurgency strategy is the assumption that the resistance of oppressed sectors of the population is inevitable and continuing. Therefore, the strategy of security forces, rather than react to individual acts or periods of heightened resistance, must be one of permanent repression directed against broad public sectors of a political movement. Even in periods of relative calm or inactivity, counterinsurgency principles mandate that the repressive forces be active identifying potential leaders and supporters of resistance, gathering information, and building dossiers about them, as well as infiltrating political and community organizations. In subsequent periods, as insurgent activities begin to emerge, counterinsurgency tactics suggest the use of law and the legal system as a key tool to attack and destroy the insurgent movements, while at the same time maintaining the appearance of the law as impartial and nonpolitical.

† In his treatise "Peace Keeping in a Democratic Society," Lt. Col. Robin Evelegh, former commander of British occupation forces in Northern Ireland, argues that "population surveillance, including the right to question, photograph, fingerprint all members of a population affected by insurgency are the fundamental legal powers necessary for the police and army engaged in the suppression of insurrection. Evelegh also advocates that the population carry identity cards and the development of a computerized intelligence system linking all the identity cards.

infiltrate groups that merely advocate unlawful activities without evidence of criminal wrongdoing. These new guidelines provide legal justification for full-scale spying and intelligence gathering on all sectors of political movements organizing against the U.S. government and its policies.

As part of this expanded intelligence gathering, U.S. government law enforcers have employed sophisticated technology, including miniature cameras and microphones secretly planted in activists' homes, cars, and workplaces* and computers to catalog and cross-reference data obtained from intelligence gathering.

B) Compulsory Police Questioning and Political Internment

Directly related to law enforcement intelligence gathering and political surveillance is the power to compel citizens to submit to questioning.†

While U.S. security forces have not moved for the right to compel interviews of citizens, the investigatory methods of the FBI and the use of the federal grand jury's subpoena and coercive contempt power have created a de facto compulsory interviewing power. In efforts to investigate and identify antigovernment activists, the FBI has carried out an extensive program of surveillance and of visiting people's homes and workplaces to carry out interviews. The tactic of repeated visits to homes and workplaces, including the questioning of neighbors and co-workers, has a strong coercive effect, forcing people to submit to FBI questioning.

The Justice Department and FBI have also repeatedly usurped the U.S. federal grand jury subpoena power‡ to compel information in secret proceedings for investigative purposes. After the grant of "limited use" immunity, which strips the subject of all rights to remain silent, the subpoenee must essentially answer all questions, regardless of their political or personal nature or relevancy, or go to jail. This gives the government a power to

---

* See, e.g., U.S. v. Alejandrina Torres, et al., 83 CR 494 (ND Ill.); U.S. v. Victor Manuel Gerena, et al., Crim. No. H-85-50 (D. Conn); U.S. v. Oscar Lopez, et al., 86 CR 513 (ND Ill.).

† In "Peace Keeping in a Democratic Society," Evelegh argues that the power to conduct "compulsory interviews" is an essential tool of counterinsurgency programs: "What then would be the objects of such an interview? They would be first the simple ones of finding out who lived in the terrorist-affected area, where they lived and what they looked like. These compulsory interviews would also enable the Security Forces, with a certain degree of error, to categorize the population into 'pro-government', 'neutral' and 'antigovernment'. In security operations, as in most human activities, it is important to know who are your friends and who are your enemies. This information would be valuable not only from the point of view of security operations, but also as an indication to the government of what policies would be acceptable or unacceptable." (p. 21)

‡ The U.S. federal grand jury, composed of 23 private citizens and modeled after a similar body in England, theoretically decides whether the government has sufficient evidence to require an accused to stand trial. While it is supposed to act as a protection to the accused, the grand jury has been transformed into a rubber stamp of the prosecutor and used as a tool of investigation with the power to compel cooperation. See Deutsch, "The Improper Use of the Federal Grand Jury: An Instrument for the Internment of Political Activists," 75 *Journal of Criminal Law and Criminology* 1159 (Winter 1984).

politically intern political activists who will not provide information about their movements.*

Another new power of political internment prior to criminal conviction is provided by the Bail Reform Act of 1984. Under this new law, the government can hold people in prison awaiting trial indefinitely without any bail if they are found to be a danger to their community or a risk of flight.[†]

C) Special Laws and the Criminalization of Organizations

The U.S. government has recently employed the seldom-used criminal statute of seditious conspiracy against political activists—the charge of agreeing to oppose or overthrow the government of the U.S. by force. In the case of the Puerto Rican Independence Movement, the charge is to oppose by force the U.S. authority—and therefore criminalizes membership in groups that fight for the legitimate right of the people of Puerto Rico to self-determination and independence.

The RICO statute (Racketeer Influenced Corrupt Organization Act), a law originally passed to address organized crime influence in the labor field, has also been turned against political activists and their organizations. The law has now been applied to designate as criminal enterprises organizations with political aims and to try members of such groups under broad conspiracy rules that allow for up to 40 years in prison.[‡] Using the shibboleth of fighting terrorism, U.S. counterinsurgency experts are also planning new substantive laws to criminalize political association and activity.[§]

D) The Rights of Political Defendants on Trial

A whole series of serious repressive measures has been instituted and/or refined in the course of recent criminal prosecutions of political activists.

1) Anonymous Petit Jury: While first appearing in several cases involving jury tampering in organized crime prosecutions, the use of the anonymous

---

* See, e.g., U.S. v. Julio Rosado, et al., 728 F.2d 89 (2nd Cir. 1984); in re Cueto, 443 F.Supp. 1081 (S.D.N.Y. 1977); U.S. v. Watani Tyehimba (Los Angeles, CA 1986).

† Puerto Rican independence leader Filiberto Ojeda Ríos was detained over four years without trial, and anti-imperialist activist Laura Whitehorn has been detained over three years.

‡ See, e.g., U.S. v. Sekou Odinga, Silvia Baraldini, et al., 82 CR 312 (S.D.N.Y.)

§ Already a very expansive definition of terrorism has been placed in the U.S. federal law. In a statute providing for rewards to informers about terrorism, the law defines terrorism as an "act of violence" (including violence against property as well as persons) that violates criminal law "and appears to be intended… to influence the policy of a government by intimidation and coercion." With this broad definition of terrorism, further federal laws directly criminalizing other political conduct as terrorist is much more likely. One statute proposed several years ago, but withdrawn in the face of strong opposition, was an effort to punish anyone providing aid to or soliciting aid for a terrorist movement, organization, or nation. Under the legislation, the designation of a terrorist movement, organization, or nation would be determined by the Secretary of State, and the defense to a charge of aiding or soliciting aid would permit no challenge to this designation.

trial jury in the prosecutions of political activists is greatly increasing, particularly where the defendants are accused of associations with clandestine groups.* The juror, given a number to replace his/her name, is told s/he will not be asked to identify his/her workplace or address, because of violence associated with the case. Such a juror can only be seriously prejudiced against the accused by this procedure.

The process of influencing or restricting the independence of the jury—the only real hope for those charged in political cases—is critical to an effective counterinsurgency program. The complete elimination of jury trials for so-called political offenses is a common factor in countries engaged in counterinsurgency campaigns.

2) Courtroom Security: The trials of many political activists in the United States courts have been accompanied by extraordinary courtroom security procedures, which are not related to any real threat, but are calculated to create the public impression that the defendants are dangerous terrorists who should be feared by the jury and the general public.

Metal detectors, concrete bunkers, armed U.S. marshals, sharp shooters on roofs surrounding the courthouse, multiple searches and the requirement of spectators showing identification before entering the courtroom are the usual practices.†

3) Motions in Limine and Ex Parte Submissions: While motions in limine are a traditional trial tool to restrict the introduction of irrelevant evidence, in recent political cases they have been used to prevent the jury from hearing any of the political ideas of the accused. Puerto Rican *independentistas* charged with opposing U.S. authority over Puerto Rico have been disallowed from presenting any evidence about the illegal colonial domination of the U.S. over Puerto Rico.‡

Also, in these trials, the prosecution frequently submits documents and other matters to the court, in camera and exparte, for unspecified "security" reasons. In almost all cases, there is no valid security reason for these submissions, but the courts accept them without any meaningful opportunity for the defense to challenge.

---

* See, e.g., U.S. v. Julio Rosado, 728 F.2d 89 (2nd Cir. 1984).

† In a District of Columbia federal courtroom, where six white anti-imperialists will be tried for conspiracy to use force to alter U.S. foreign policy, the government constructed a thick plexiglass wall between the well of the courtroom, where the defendants will sit, and the spectator area. Cameras have been installed to monitor and record all conduct in the courtroom. U.S. v. Whitehorn, et al., No. 88-145 (U.S. Dist. Ct., DC).

‡ In a trial of clergy and lay religious workers of the sanctuary movement charged with smuggling and harboring "illegal aliens," the defendants were forbidden from mentioning a host of terms that would have exposed the Unites States' war against the people of Central America as the basis for the flow of refugees and the need for the church to provide sanctuary. U.S. v. Maria del Socorro Pardo de Aguilar, et al., CR 85-008 (D.AZ.)

4) Sentencing—Informants: Political activists convicted in U.S. courts have routinely received draconian sentences, demonstrably higher than nonpolitical defendants and often designed to hold them for life.* Counts are run consecutively with maximum time on each. In some cases in which the accused have claimed Prisoner of War status, refusing to submit to the court's jurisdiction, illegal sentences have been imposed.

5) Attacks on Lawyers: As part of the counterinsurgency and use of media strategy to isolate political prisoners, the government has also targeted their lawyers and legal workers. Attorney-client meetings in U.S. prisons have been secretly taped, lawyers' cars and hotel rooms bugged, and the briefcase of a legal worker seized pursuant to a search warrant after a visit with her client.†

In addition, lawyers have been accused, without any proof or formal charge, of assisting clients in escape plots and acting as couriers. This tactic is designed to discourage lawyers from fighting the government counterinsurgency program and vigorously representing their clients. Those who are not intimidated are then subject to attack and criminalization themselves.

6) Special Prisons and Special Treatment of Prisoners: The special and punitive treatment of incarcerated political activists in U.S. prisons clearly underscores their status as political prisoners. Through special, brutal conditions, the government seeks to punish imprisoned political people and make examples of them in such a way as to intimidate others from following in their footsteps, in spite of the basic principle of the United Nations Standard Minimum Rules for the Treatment of Prisoners [Rule A I 6 (1)], which proscribes discrimination on grounds of political opinion. The U.S. seeks to punish and destroy the revolutionary spirit, the will, the resistance of the prisoners and, through them, their movements.

Emboldened by government inspired antiterrorist hysteria, and the virtual abdication of oversight responsibilities on the part of U.S. Congress and the U.S. courts, prison authorities act with impunity generally, but especially toward the POW's and political prisoners. The arsenal of tactics

---

* Susan Rosenberg and Timothy Blunk, white anti-imperialists and clandestine fighters were both sentenced to 58 years in prison for conspiracy and possession (not use) of a quantity of weapons and explosives and false identification. Their sentence is 16 times longer than the average sentence meted out in federal court to weapons-possession offenders and twice in the average for first-degree murderers. Oscar López Rivera, Puerto Rican prisoner of war, received his 55-year sentence for seditious conspiracy from the same judge who, in an earlier case sentencing López's codefendants to terms of 55 to 90 years, had stated that he would have given them the death penalty if he could have under the law. See also, Marilyn Buck (50 years); Mutulu Shakur (60 years); Silvia Baraldini and Sekou Odinga (40 years); Leonard Peltier (two consecutive lives); and Dhoruba Moore (25 to life).

† U.S. v. Oscar López, et al., 86 CR 513 (ND Ill.)

includes a denial system that uses isolation and special prisons,* destabilization through numerous prison transfers, humiliation, denial of medical treatment, physical and sexual assault, and continual harassment and
vigilance.

A less subtle form of isolation is the Control Unit, which describes Marion
Federal Prison, the most maximum security prison in the U.S. In such Control
Units or prisons, the policy is to totally control not merely the prisoner's body,
but also the mind. Prisoners are typically confined, indefinitely, to a small
single cell or to small group isolation for 22-24 hours a day in an environment
devoid of human contact and sensory stimulation.

The federal appellate court that upheld the constitutionality of the Marion
regime described the conditions thusly:

> As a result of the permanent lockdown, each inmate at Marion is con-
> fined to a one man cell (there are no female inmates in the prison)
> round the clock, except for brief periods outside the cell for recre-
> ation (between 7 and 11 hours a week), for a shower, for a visit to the
> infirmary, to the law library, etc... Recreation means pacing in a small
> enclosure—sometimes just in the corridor between rows of cells. The
> inmate is fed in his cell, on a tray shoved in between the bars. The cells
> are modern and roomy (8'x10') and contain a television set as well as
> a bed, toilet, and sink, but there is no other furniture and when an
> inmate is outside his cell he is handcuffed and a box is placed over
> the handcuffs to prevent the lock from being picked; his legs may also
> be shackled. Inmates are forbidden to socialize with each other or to
> participate in group religious services. Inmates who throw food or
> otherwise misbehave in their cells are sometimes tied spreadeagled
> on their beds, often for hours at a stretch, while inmates returning to
> their cells are often (inmates of the control unit, always) subjected to
> a rectal search: a paramedic inserts a gloved finger into the inmate's
> rectum and feels around for a knife or other weapon or contraband.
>
> Bruscino v. Carlson, 854 F.2d 162, 164 (7th Cir. 1988)

---

* The government intentionally places the prisoners in prisons far away from their families
and communities and has banished Puerto Rican independence activists, taking those
convicted of pro-independence activity from their country and forcing service of prison
sentences inside the U.S.

There is further isolation from attorneys, ranging from denying legal visits to opening mail
that is, by U.S. law, confidential between attorney and client, to electronically eavesdropping
on supposed confidential legal visits. At Marion prison (see *infra*), video cameras monitor all
legal visits, and another camera on the ceiling directly above focuses on the table to capture
images of papers exchanged and notes written.

In addition to seeking to demoralize them in this way, the U.S. also seeks to preclude
the prisoners from effectively preparing their cases for presentation to domestic courts,
international tribunals, and other forums.

The Women's High Security Unit (HSU) at the federal prison in Lexington, Kentucky, a special small group isolation prison for political women, was designed specifically to destroy the three women political prisoners placed there; Alejandrina Torres, Susan Rosenberg, and Silvia Baraldini:

> This program sets up a hierarchy of objectives. The first of these is to reduce prisoners to the state of submission essential for their ideological conversion. That failing, the next objective is to reduce them to a state of psychological incompetence sufficient to neutralize them as efficient, self-directing antagonists. That failing, the only alternative is to destroy them, preferably by making them desperate enough to destroy themselves.*

The objectives were to be accomplished by the conditions in this underground prison: a restricted sensory environment, small group isolation, ill-fitting clothing, limited and censored reading material, shackling and handcuffing, strict limitation on telephone calls and visitors, as well as multiple daily strip searches, patdown searches by male officers, voyeurism, and general harassment by staff.

Amnesty International was moved by the similarity of the HSU to the Federal Republic of Germany's dead wings and white cells to accomplish the same goals with respect to the Red Army Faction (RAF). Amnesty's observer noted of the HSU:

> The conditions and regime are deliberately and gratuitously oppressive. The constant and unjustified use of security chains, the repeated strip searching, the almost total lack of privacy, the claustrophobic lack of sensory stimuli, freedom of movement, possessions, choice of activities and incestuously small range of contacts cannot be other than debilitating…. There is no need for these prisoners to be at HSU. There is overwhelming evidence that the prisoners at HSU have deteriorated physically and psychologically during their custody there. There has to be a prospect that one or more will finally resort to suicide should their custody at HSU be prolonged. I conclude therefore that HSU should close forthwith.†

---

* The development of psychological syndromes resulting from isolation has been documented in the 19th and early 20th centuries in Europe and with U.S. prisoners of war in Korea. See Stuart Grassian, "A Review and Delineation of a Clinical Syndrome" (unpublished). Such brainwashing techniques have also been used in Korean and Chinese prisons. See Richard Korn, "The Effects of Confinement in HSU, August 1987," 15 *Social Justice* 8-19 (Spring 1988).
† Amnesty International, "The High Security Unit, Lexington Federal Prison, KY," August 1988. See also Baraldini v. Meese, 691 F. Supp. 432 (DC 1988), rev'd. 884 F.2d 615 (D.D.C Cir. 1989).

Amnesty found:

> the conditions and placement of the women on the basis of their politics... constitute cruel, inhuman and degrading treatment in violation of the Universal Declaration of Human Rights. A critical aspect of the entire counter-insurgency strategy is the use of the mass media to discredit and dehumanize the political activists. The inflammatory use of "terrorist" and "terrorism" replaces any rational discussion of the issues underlying the actions of those targeted. The government seeks to place the media under its discipline when covering issues concerning political opposition to the government.[*]

Conclusion

While the U.S. has tried to hide the reality of its political prisoners and its politically repressive legal system, the truth cannot be denied. Today, throughout the United States, people who are part of the movements these prisoners represent are organizing, educating, and making demands for the human rights of the prisoners as well as for their unconditional amnesty. The U.S. holds political prisoners in violation of international law and its own domestic law. Progressive lawyers, because of the protected right of access to the prisoners, have a special responsibility to monitor and expose their human rights violations. These prisoners should be immediately released and allowed to return to their political work on behalf of freedom, justice, and equality.

---

[*] The government also affirmatively uses the media to put out its own propaganda. Immediately after the 1985 arrest of 13 Puerto Rican Independence activists, the head of the FBI and the Attorney General of the U.S. held press conferences denouncing the accused as terrorists and claiming that they were assisted by the government of Cuba. Public statements equating the independence movement as Cuban controlled and terrorist are constantly being made by government officials.

II.7.B

New Afrikan/Black Political Prisoners and Prisoners of War: Conditions of Confinement

J. Soffiyah Elijah
Research Committee on International Law and Black Freedom Fighters
1990

In our review of the conditions of confinement for New Afrikan/Black* political prisoners and prisoners of war, it is important to remember the reasons that the United States government wants them confined. The U.S. will not allow Black people to exercise their right to self-determination. All of these freedom fighters have committed their lives to fighting for the liberation of Black people. U.S. intolerance of this political position held by Black people is historical. There have been many Black political prisoners throughout the history of the United States, all of whom have been jailed as a part of the government's attempt to silence resistance.

One of the most notable early political prisoners and someone who may not immediately come to mind in this context is Marcus Garvey. As his movement, the United Negro Improvement Association (UNIA), spread throughout the country and his call for self-determination was heeded by more and more Black people, the government's plan to destroy him was implemented. He was jailed on charges of mail fraud and deported.

We find that during the past three decades there has been a steady increase in the number of people imprisoned because of their political views and actions. Many of the New Afrikan political prisoners and prisoners of war came from the Black Panther Party and/or the Black Liberation Army (BLA). The FBI's notorious COINTELPRO effort to destroy the Black liberation movement is primarily responsible for the imprisonment of numerous former Panthers and BLA members.

We also find that as the prison population became more politicized, the level of repression to which it was subjected was heightened. Prison rebellions increased and many prisoners who were targeted as organizers or leaders within the prisons were subjected to beatings and lengthy periods of total isolation. Such is the case of the Reidsville Brothers, who in 1978 participated in a rebellion by Black prisoners at Reidsville Prison and demanded an end to guard brutality, degrading living conditions and racist attacks from white inmates. The prison officials retaliated with beatings and solitary confinement.

Stark in its illustration of this heightened repression is the Attica Prison Rebellion, which occurred in 1971. In response to demands from prisoners who

---

* Throughout this paper, the terms New Afrikan and Black were used interchangeably.

had taken over Attica seeking more humane treatment, Nelson Rockefeller, governor of New York State, ordered that state troopers retake the prison by force. This order was given despite ongoing negotiations for a peaceful resolution of the Attica situation. In essence, Gov. Rockefeller ordered the mass murder of 43 people: 34 prisoners and 9 guards. Rockefeller's barbarism was rewarded when he was selected to serve as vice-president to Gerald Ford.

So we see that the attitude of the U.S. government toward prisoners' concerns is one of intolerance and indifference. And, with respect to political prisoners, the imposition of egregious conditions is part of a systematic effort to destroy any visible signs of resistance. The intent of the government in imposing these conditions is two-fold; destroy the will of the political prisoner and send a strong message to supporters and followers that their resistance will be met in kind.

The United States government continues to deny to the world that there are political prisoners within its borders. It maintains this position at whatever cost necessary. Recall the almost immediate removal from office of U.S. Ambassador to the United Nations, Andrew Young, when he publicly acknowledged the existence of political prisoners within the U.S.

Back in the 1970s, Jalil Bottom, one of the New York 3, recognized the significance of raising the issue of political prisoners held within the U.S. in the international arena. Thus, in 1976, he launched the National Prisoners Campaign to Petition the United Nations. This effort was widely supported by political and progressive prisoners, resulting in a petition being submitted and discussed in Geneva, Switzerland. This work formed the impetus for Lennox Hinds and the National Conference of Black Lawyers to invite the U.N. International Commission of Jurists to tour numerous U.S. prisons and interview political prisoners. Their findings raised serious questions about the treatment and reasons for confinement of the many political prisoners they interviewed.

Type of Sentence

As a general rule, political prisoners have been given the harshest sentences possible. Journalist Mumia Abu-Jamal, a former Panther and staunch supporter of the MOVE members who were bombed by Philadelphia police, is on death row in Pennsylvania for defending himself and his brother from a vicious beating by local Philadelphia police.

After years of court battles, Gary Tyler finally had his death sentence commuted to life imprisonment.

Johnny Imani Harris, who was originally serving 5 consecutive life sentences at the infamous Atmore Prison at the time a rebellion broke out, was subsequently sentenced to death in 1974, because of his participation in a rebellion during which a prison guard died.

Oscar "Gamba" Johnson, also an Atmore inmate convicted of participating in the rebellion, is serving a 148-year sentence.

Geronimo ji Jaga Pratt, was sentenced to life and, despite his exemplary prison record, has been denied parole 9 times.

Sekou Odinga was sentenced to life plus 40 years with a recommendation of no parole.

Assata Shakur and Sundiata Acoli were sentenced to life plus 30 years. Fortunately, in 1979, Assata was liberated from prison and she is now living in exile in Cuba. This was the only way to put an end to the horrendous conditions under which she had been confined.

Each of the nine MOVE defendants was sentenced to 100 years.

Bashir Hameed and Abdul Majid were both sentenced to 25 years to life.

Seth Hayes and Teddy (Jah) Heath are also serving 25-years-to-life sentences.

Baba Odinga is serving a 25-years-to-life sentence.

Donald Taylor, a former member of De Mau Mau, which was a clandestine self-defense formation within the U.S. Marine Corps in Vietnam formed to defend against racist attacks from white troops, was sentenced to 150 to 200 years without parole.

The New York 3 (Herman Bell, Jalil Bottom and Albert Nuh Washington) were each sentenced to 25 years to life.

Mutulu Shakur was sentenced to 60 years.

Kuwasi Balagoon was sentenced to 75 years to life.

Jihad Abdul-Mumit, a former Panther and BLA member, was sentenced to 14 years for a parole violation that did not involve a new arrest.

Prior to his recent release due to prosecutorial misconduct, Dhoruba Bin-Wahad was serving a life sentence.

Solitary Confinement and Administrative Detention

In the early '60s, a meeting of social scientists and prison wardens was convened by director of the Federal Bureau of Prisons, James V. Bennett. The main speaker was Dr. Edward Schein, a social scientist. He presented his theories on brainwashing and the application of such techniques to achieve behavior modification with the prison population. Among the twenty-four techniques suggested by Dr. Schein were the following:

1. physically remove the prisoner to an area sufficiently isolated in order to break or seriously weaken close emotional ties;
2. segregate all natural leaders;
3. prohibit group activities that do not fit brainwashing objectives;
4. systematic withholding of mail;
5. create a feeling among the isolated group of prisoners that they have been abandoned by and totally isolated from the community;
6. undermine all emotional supports; and
7. preclude access to literature which does not aid in the brainwashing process.

193

James Bennett urged the participants in the meeting to experiment with Dr. Schein's theories within their respective institutions.

Approximately a decade later, the "experiments" that grew out of that meeting in 1961 began cropping up all around the country. The glaring similarities between Dr. Schein's techniques and the treatment received by the vast majority of Black political prisoners serve to enforce the belief that there is a thinly disguised attempt on the part of the U.S. government to psychologically destroy political prisoners.

Marion Penitentiary in Illinois is the highest level security prison in the country. This is where the first control unit was established. Its main focus is sensory deprivation and solitary confinement. A disproportionately high number of political prisoners have been sent to Marion. Many of them have had lengthy stays in the control unit there. The control unit consists of small soundproof box-type cells. Since 1983, the entire prison has been on lockdown status. This means that all prisoners are locked in their cells 23 hours a day. They are permitted only one hour outside the cells to shower and take recreation on the tier. Twice a week, for two hours at a time, outdoor recreation in a small, fence-enclosed area is permitted at the whim of the guards.

The cells at Marion consist of a stone bed and a toilet/wash bowl. No contact visits are allowed with social visitors. All legal visits are monitored by video camera and guards. All meals are taken in the cell. No phone access to lawyers is permitted unless the prisoner can prove that his lawyer wants him to call. Only two ten minute calls per month are permitted to family and friends. Marion is the epitome of the implementation of Dr. Schein's theories on isolation and segregation.

Sekou Odinga was immediately designated to Marion upon being sentenced to 40 years plus life. After spending three years at Marion in lockdown status, he was transferred to Leavenworth in general population. When a bogus investigation of escape charges commenced, he was snatched during the early morning hours and thrown in administrative segregation. Shortly thereafter, he was moved to a new special housing unit (SHU) modeled after Marion. Sekou remained in the SHU after the investigation cleared him of the escape allegations. After 9 months of being held in solitary confinement at Leavenworth, Sekou was returned to Marion. He spent a month in the control unit there, and then was moved to D Block, which is also under 23-hour lockdown as previously described.

Sundiata Acoli spent 5 years in the Management Control Unit (MCU) of Trenton State Prison. He was the first prisoner sent there. At MCU, Sundiata was locked down 24 hours a day in a cell that was smaller than the space requirement for a German shepherd dog set by the Society for the Prevention of Cruelty to Animals. No contact visits were allowed. All meals were taken in the cell. Strip searches were required every time he left the cell for any reason. Cavity searches were frequently imposed. In 1979, just months before the liberation of his codefendant, Assata Shakur, he was secretly transferred during the middle of the night to federal custody at Marion. (He was a New Jersey state prisoner.) Sundiata remained at Marion for 8 ½ years before he was transferred to Leavenworth. Like Sekou, he was also placed in administrative segregation during an investigation of the same bogus escape charges. He spent 6 months in SHU before being returned to general population.

James "Blood" Miller spent over 6 years at Marion before his eventual release last year.

Geronimo ji Jaga Pratt spent 8 of his 20 years of incarceration in solitary confinement.

Hugo A. Dahariki Pinell, one of the Soledad Brothers, spent 20 years in solitary confinement.

Prior to her liberation, Assata Shakur spent over 20 months in solitary confinement, often housed in men's facilities.

Oscar (Gamba) Johnson, Gary Tyler and Johnny Imani Harris have all spent over 5 years in solitary confinement.

Chui Ferguson-El spent 8 years in federal custody in general population without any disciplinary infractions. Last year, upon his transfer to Pennsylvania, he was immediately thrown in solitary confinement (the "hole"). In response to his attorney's inquiry, the state prison officials stated that Ferguson-El would spend the balance of his sentence in the hole because "he had previously been shown to be a threat to security while in federal custody at Lewisburg Penitentiary."

In late 1988, Bashir Hameed, a member of the BLA and a well-respected Muslim leader among the prisoners, was placed in solitary confinement at Shawangunk Prison in New York State because of his leadership and organizing abilities.

Source: Prison News Service

In early April of 1990, Abdul Majid, a member of the BLA, was put in solitary confinement (the box) because of "his status in the Muslim hierarchy." The official "charge" made against Abdul was for demonstrating. It was alleged that he urged a cook not to prepare food for the Ramadan evening meals. Despite the fact that the cook testified at his hearing that no such conversation had taken place, Abdul was condemned to a year in the box at Great Meadows Correctional Facility in Comstock, New York. The box consists of a 6'×8' cell where Abdul is locked in for 23 hours a day. Recreation is twice a week alone in

195

a fenced cage that is 6'x9' feet. Showers are allowed twice a week unless a social visit is to occur. Visits are allowed once a week.

New York State has recently passed legislation that implemented more lenient guidelines for the use of administrative segregation.

In the '70s, a group formed in Pennsylvania State Prison known as the Black Liberation Front. They sought religious freedom and protection from human rights violations. They were labeled as terrorists by the prison administration and singled out for punishment. Joseph "Joe Joe" Bowen was held in a control unit for 5 years. Russell "Maroon" Shoats, a BLA member, was held in solitary confinement for 3 years and Clifford "Lumumba" Futch was held in a control unit for 14 years.

Distance from Family and Supporters

In keeping with Dr. Schein's suggestion that behavior modification can be achieved by separating a prisoner to weaken or break emotional ties, most of the New Afrikan political prisoners and prisoners of war have been confined far away from their families and supporters. For instance, Geronimo had been incarcerated in northern California at San Quentin for many years. He had a large base of support including his defense committee located in the Bay Area of California. Last year, in retaliation for his offer to testify on behalf of Filiberto Ojeda Ríos who was on trial in Puerto Rico, Geronimo was transferred to Tehachapi Prison, which is located in Southern California.

Nuh Washington is confined at Wende Correctional Facility in Alden, New York. This facility is located in the far northwestern corner of the state. Nuh's lawyers and primary base of support are in New York City.

Mutulu Shakur is confined at Lompoc Penitentiary in Lompoc, California. His family, friends, lawyers and support committee are all located in New York. Despite these factors, he was immediately designated to Lompoc by the Bureau of Prisons.

Punitive Transfers

In order to understand the punitive nature of a transfer, we must first appreciate the disruption in routine that a transfer causes. When a prisoner is transferred, he/she is placed in administrative segregation, usually for one month. During this time they cannot work, and whatever work status they had previously achieved is lost. No educational program can be pursued during this time, and prior educational credits are seldom transferable. Personal items are frequently "lost," and many weeks may pass before a new visitors' list is established for the prisoner. During this waiting time, visitors are frequently frustrated by

Source: Prison News Service

196

being refused visits even though they were previously approved on another facility's list. Additionally, friendships and contact with other inmates are destroyed.

Herman Ferguson has been moved all over New York State in the past two years. Punitive transfers have been extensively used against the New York 3. Nuh Washington has been transferred 10 different times in the past 17 ½ years. Jalil Bottom has been in six different New York State facilities in the past 12 years.

Before Geronimo ji Jaga Pratt was transferred to Tehachapi, it took a court order to keep him from being transferred to Folsom Prison, where it was clear that his life would be endangered.

Torture

Upon being arrested, most of the Black political prisoners and prisoners of war were beaten and tortured. Abdul Majid suffered several damaging blows to the head when he was beaten at the time of his arrest. Jamal Joseph, Kazi Toure (he was brutally beaten while handcuffed), Chui Ferguson, Sundiata Acoli, Sam Brown (his neck was broken and medical attention withheld), Assata Shakur (she was refused adequate medical attention for a gunshot wound), Nuh Washington (he was also refused medical attention for gun shot wounds to the face) and Sekou Odinga were all subjected to brutality when arrested.

Sekou was captured after a shoot-out with police. During the shoot-out, his companion, Mtayari Shabaka Sundiata, was murdered by the police while he was lying on the ground wounded and unarmed. Sekou was then arrested and tortured for many hours while the police attempted to interrogate him. He was beaten so badly that he was unrecognizable, and his pancreas was almost destroyed. During the torture sessions, Sekou's head was repeatedly flushed in the toilet, his toenails and fingernails were ripped out and cigarettes were snuffed out all over his body. He was hospitalized for three months and his eyesight was damaged as a result of this beating.

Dhoruba Bin-Wahad was set-up for an armed attack from another inmate by guards. His lawyers had to seek an order of transfer from the court in order to avoid further incidents at that facility.

Psychological torture is also employed against Black political prisoners. James "Tarif" Haskins, a BLA member, has been subjected to tactics of mind manipulation and drugs, from which he suffered hallucinations.

Forced Labor

The labor of prisoners is used to maintain the prisons. Refusal to work is one way to guarantee receipt of an incident report and disciplinary action. Sometimes, as a form of punishment, groups of prisoners are taken to the fields and forced to work under the threat of guns. Upon his arrest in California, Mutulu Shakur was held at Florida State Prison in the East Unit.

The East Unit was a replica of Marion. Here, prisoners were forced to work in the fields as punishment for various disciplinary infractions.

Health and Medical Care

In general, the health and medical care provided to prisoners is abhorrent. Bashir Hameed suffers from acute hypertension. His medication must be increased regularly. His prison doctor has determined that continued confinement in the box creates a substantial danger of a stroke. Despite his doctor's request that he be removed from the box, the Shawangunk administrators have refused to move him. Sometimes Bashir's blood pressure is so high that medication does not bring it back down.

Ahmed Evans was a Black nationalist leader from Cleveland, Ohio, who was incarcerated in the infamous Southern Ohio Correctional Facility. Due to medical neglect, he died of cancer at the facility.

When Sundiata Acoli was transferred from the MCU at Trenton State Prison to Marion, his entrance physical exam revealed that he had been heavily exposed to tuberculosis while at MCU

Kuwasi Balagoon, a member of the BLA who was serving 75 years to life for the attempted Brink's armored car expropriation in 1981, died in a New York State correctional facility due to gross medical negligence. Despite exhibiting all the tell-tale signs of AIDS, Kuwasi was not transferred to a hospital for medical care until 10 days before his death.

Visitation, Religious Freedom, Legal Access, Personal Hygiene

Extensive background checks are done on all visitors of political prisoners. This includes legal and social visitors. These visits are closely monitored by prison officials and are sometimes denied for fabricated reasons.

Legal and social visitors are usually harassed by prison officials in an effort to discourage them from visiting. Frequently, family members, friends and lawyers travel many miles to visit a prisoner only to be denied a visit because they have not followed some procedure that either does not exist or has already been complied with to the letter. Social visiting time is reduced with no explanation. Legal visiting rooms often times are not supplied to lawyers and paralegals. Without notice to the prisoner or the visitor, the visitor's name is removed from the prisoner's visiting list, preventing the visitor from gaining access to the prison until a new background check is completed. Although the check can be completed in less than 24 hours, visitors and inmates are usually told that it will take 6 to 8 weeks to complete a background check.

Without explanation or rationale, rules are imposed that infringe on the religious freedom of political prisoners. Particular targets of this sort of harassment are Muslims, MOVE members and prisoners who wear their hair in long locks. For instance, despite his religious practices, Chui Ferguson-El was placed in administrative segregation because of his refusal to cut his hair. There has been frequent and widespread interference in the attempt by Muslim prisoners to observe Ramadan in accordance with their religious beliefs. This type of harassment resulted in Abdul Majid being sent to the box for a year.

It is very difficult for political prisoners to remain in regular contact with lawyers if they are in solitary confinement. Phone access to lawyers is extremely limited. Sekou Odinga must present a letter from his attorney stating that the attorney wants him to call the office in order to make the collect phone call. All phone calls are monitored. When an attorney calls the prison requesting that a political prisoner be allowed to call back to their office, the message is not given to the prisoner except in extremely rare instances.

Censorship

Prisoners in federal custody are only allowed to correspond with their attorneys, immediate family and those individuals with whom they were friends prior to their incarceration. The obvious hardship this works on political prisoners serving lengthy sentences is that with each passing year, they grow further away from developing new friendships.

All social mail is read and for political prisoners, most, if not all, is photocopied. Although the prison authorities do not admit it, it is the belief of this author and many others that the legal mail of political prisoners is also read and photocopied.

Reading material is sanctioned according to the whim of the institution. Political materials come under heavy scrutiny. I understand that the Freedom Now! literature is being banned from some institutions. At Wende Correctional Facility, Nuh Washington is not allowed to receive any books, hard cover or paperback, unless they come from the publisher or a bookstore. However, he can receive photocopies of books. There's no rationale for this rule.

Surveillance While Incarcerated

The growing trend in the incarceration of political prisoners is to place them in small monitoring units within or adjacent to a larger correctional facility. As a result, "mini-Marions" are cropping up around the country. MCU's and SHU's are the "popular" choice of prison officials when it comes to political prisoners and prisoners of war.

At Shawangunk, a Close Supervision Unit has been opened that is separate and apart from the main facility. The CSU prisoners take their recreation separate from the rest of the prison population in a separate recreation space except for two times a week. All recreation for the entire prison is done after 6PM. They have a separate mess hall. There is a low guard-to-inmate ratio. Every single move made by an inmate is monitored and logged on a daily activity sheet. Each inmate must be in a program 8 hours a day.

The prisoners who are housed there are told that there is no way that they can be transferred out. The position of the New York State Department of

Corrections is that once a prisoner is placed in the CSU, that is where they will serve the balance of their time. Since October 5, 1988, the prisoners in the CSU have staged a shut down of the unit and they have been locked in their cells. Some of the political prisoners in the CSU are Maliki Shakur Latine, Herman Bell, Al Musadig Yusef of the Williamsburg 4 and Bashir Hameed prior to his removal to the box where he has remained for the past 20 months.

Another form of surveillance used against political prisoners is that of an escort. The prisoner is not allowed to move anywhere in the prison without an escort. This is the method used for Nuh at Wende. He is not even allowed to come to legal visits without his escort pacing back and forth just outside of the legal visiting room.

Conclusion
Through this discussion, I have attempted to give you a comprehensive view of the conditions under which New Afrikan/Black political prisoners are incarcerated. Some of these conditions are not unique to Blacks or political prisoners. However, in light of the large number of Black political prisoners and prisoners of war, an analysis of the treatment they receive will aid in an understanding of the plight of all political prisoners and prisoners of war.

II.7.C

Criminalization and Persecution of Opponents to the Colonial Status of Puerto Rico Human Rights Violations

Dr. Luis Nieves Falcón, President, Puerto Rico National Chapter,
International League for the Rights and Liberation of Peoples
1990

The permanent People's Tribunal, at its Session on Puerto Rico, in Barcelona, from 27-29 January 1989 concluded that the United States of America is criminalizing and persecuting opponents of the colonial status of Puerto Rico. The sentence further concluded that "the U.S. has used a variety of dubious tactics to attack the activities of Puerto Rican activists, including conspiratory charges, wide ranging grand-jury investigations, paramilitary arrest procedures, assassinations by 'death squads,' and repeated police brutality. Puerto Ricans are, however, treated as common criminals, not as political prisoners... Conspiracy charges and indictments have been used to intimidate the whole nationalist community."

Today, I bring before you the case of 19 Puerto Rican men and women, anticolonial combatants, convicted for opposing U.S. authority over Puerto Rico.* These patriots are serving draconian prison sentences of 35-90 years and are being subjected to special inhuman conditions of isolation and selective punishment. These men and women share unique characteristics. They are not "criminals"—they have no criminal records and, in the eyes of the independence movement and international law, have committed no crimes.

The special and punitive treatment of these men and women falls short of meeting the United Nations Standard Minimum Rules for the Treatment of Prisoners (UNSMRTP), beginning with the proscription against discrimination on grounds of political opinion—a basic principle of Rule A 161.

The arsenal of tactics includes a denial system which includes isolation, destabilization, criminalization, humiliation, denial of medical treatment, physical and sexual assault, and continued harassment and vigilance. The denial system connotes not just denial of human rights, but denial of the essence of the person's political being and existence. The very existence of

---

* Thirteen men and women Puerto Rican Prisoners of War (POW's) are currently held in U.S. prisons: Edwin Cortés, Elizam Escobar, Ricardo Jiménez, Oscar López Rivera, Adolfo Matos, Dylcia Pagán, Alberto Rodríguez, Alicia Rodríguez, Ida Luz Rodríguez, Luis Rosa, Alejandrina Torres, Carlos Alberto Torres, and Carmen Valentín. Political prisoners held in jails and prisons for their pro-independence beliefs and actions: Lucy Berrios Berrios, Jaime Delgado, Dora García (out 4/18/90—served three out of a five-year sentence), Fiiberto Ojeda Ríos (out on bond pending trial, almost three years in preventive detention), Haydée Beltrán, and Julio Antonio Veras y Delgadillo (served 11 years of a 25-year sentence). Also incarcerated at this point are Juan E. Segarra Palmer, 75 years, and Antonio Camacho Negrón, 15 years.

this governmental political campaign to destroy these prisoners violates the guiding principles of the UNSMRTP, which prohibits the aggravation of suffering inherent in imprisonment (Rule A II 57) and prescribes "minimizing any differences between prison life and life at liberty which tend to lessen the responsibility of the prisoners or the respect due to their dignity as human beings" (Rule A II 60 [1]). The rules also mandate that for persons under sentence "the treatment shall be such as will encourage their self respect..." (Rule A II 65).

Isolation
The U.S. government intentionally places the prisoners far away from their families and communities. The isolation from political support is accomplished not only by assignment to distant and inaccessible prisons but also by restrictions on contact. Oscar López, Carlos Alberto Torres, Ida Luz Rodríguez, and Alejandrina Torres have each endured periods of months to years, prohibited from corresponding with anyone outside the immediate family. In each case, the restriction was imposed for absolutely no valid reason and in violation of Rule A I 37.

A dramatic example of isolation is reflected in the visiting restrictions, which include denial of contact visiting all together (Oscar López at U.S.P. Marion and Alejandrina Torres at the Lexington Women's Control Unit), to denial of all social visits (nonimmediate family) (Oscar López, Alejandrina Torres, Carlos A. Torres). The UNSMRTP clearly provides for communication of prisoners, including visits, with family and friends (Rule A I 37) and that prison staff be responsible for maintaining and improving the prisoners' relationships with their families (Rule A II 61). See also Rule A II 79, that special attention should be paid to maintenance and improvement of prisoner-family relationships.

Another manifestation of isolation is the assignment of the sentenced prisoners to pretrial detention centers, which are ill equipped to provide programs or services to people with lengthy sentences, in disregard for the provisions of Rule A II 66 (1). Dylcia Pagán, Ida Luz Rodríguez, Haydée Beltrán, and Alejandrina Torres have all spent periods of months to years in such settings, often at great expense to their physical well-being.* Oscar López Rivera was kept in such a jail for over one year. He was held in a solid steel, closed-front sensory deprivation cell 23 to 24 hours a day, equipped with plumbing that brought his neighbor's excrement into the toilet in his cell (Rule A I 12), with absolutely no ventilation (Rule A I 10, 11 [a]), no access to fresh air or sunshine (Rule A I 21 [1]), denied all interaction with other prisoners, and shackled upon leaving for any purpose (Rule A I 33). Recreational opportunities consisted of being placed in a corridor outside the cell, where there is nothing to do (Rule A II 78).

---

* This punishment by close confinement violates Rule A I, 30,32.

A less subtle form of isolation in the Control Unit, which describes Marion Federal Prison,* where following a year in pretrial jail, Oscar López Rivera was confined alone to a cell 23 hours daily; F.C.I. Alderson's Davis Hall, where Ida Luz Rodríguez and Haydée Beltrán were held for 10 months, the only two prisoners in the unit, prohibited from seeing other prisoners; and the Women's Control Unit at Lexington, where Alejandrina Torres was prohibited from contact with other prisoners. With regard to Marion Prison, it is pertinent to point out that it was the first prison in the United States to be observed and condemned by Amnesty International.† Using the United Nations Standard Minimum Rules for the Treatment of Prisoners as an international norm, Amnesty's observer concluded:

> Within Marion, violations of the Standard Minimum Rules are common. Although this report deals only with some facts of life at Marion, a comparison of the Standard Minimum Rules with the conditions at Marion... shows there is hardly a rule in the Standard Minimum Rules that is not infringed in some way or other. The reason has to do with the purpose of Marion. According to the Standard Minimum Rules, treatment of persons shall have as its purpose encouraging self-respect and developing a sense of responsibility amongst inmates. The purpose of Marion, however, is security. All other considerations are secondary.

The effects of living under the "sordid and horrible" conditions reveal the human toll. Says POW López:

> The last few months have been rather lethargic for me. The intellectual and spiritual stimulation is lacking. I don't like to feel that the environment is stagnating or stifling me, yet that's the reality.

The government also seeks to isolate the prisoners from their attorneys and legal advisers. Tactics range from denying legal visits to opening mail that is, by U.S. law, confidential between attorney and client to electronically eavesdropping on confidential legal visits.

A final example of isolation is to prevent these men and women from communicating with each other. In addition to seeking to demoralize them, the U.S. also seeks to preclude the prisoners from effectively preparing their case for presentation to international tribunals and other global forums, such as this one.

---

* Marion is the only prison in the history of the United States to be observed by Amnesty International, whose report on that prison facility is highly critical.
† Amnesty International, "Allegations of Ill-Treatment in Marion Prison, Illinois, U.S.A.," May 1987.

Destabilization

To ensure that no one gets too "comfortable," prison officials maintain a practice of program assignment, changes, moves from one cell or unit to another, and transfers between prisons—sometimes frequent and sometimes infrequent, always without notice or legitimate reason. While the concrete act itself is disruptive to the individual, resulting in lost property (Rule A I 43), unforwarded mail, and severed friendships with social prisoners; the anticipation of abrupt changes is itself unsettling. The transport of the prisoners has often been dangerous for them, traveling at break-neck speed or being escorted by drunken prison guards, in violation of Rule A I 45 (2). Transfers are generally carried out in military fashion, sometimes complete with convoy and helicopters accompanying. On occasion the timing of the transfers has been calculated to maximize the destabilizing effects. Elizam Escobar's family came on their annual visit from Puerto Rico to see their son and spent a day with him in the prison in which he had been for one year. The following day they returned to the prison, only to be told he had been transferred to another prison hundreds of miles away. (See Rules A II 61, A I 37.) Years later, this same man was transferred at the Thanksgiving/Christmas holidays, a difficult time for many people in prison, and then held incommunicado in segregation over Christmas and New Year's. This transfer was to punish this artist for painting—timed to coincide with the publication of a catalog of his work and the opening of an exhibit to commence a national tour of his paintings and drawings. He was placed in a prison where he was prohibited from painting for almost a year.

Criminalization

Officials have accused the prisoners of prison rule violations for several purposes, none of which are legitimate. Rules A I 27032 establishes a due process regimen calling for rules, notices of violation thereof, the opportunity for self-defense, and proscribing "all cruel, inhuman or degrading punishments." In spite of these international minimum standards, and though the U.S. has a set of rules that on paper meet the minimum standards, the government's political motivation to destroy these prisoners, and through them, their movement, dictates abuse of the disciplinary process. First, accusations result in disciplinary segregation, allowing physical isolation and disruption of the prisoner's routine. Second, the arbitrary invoking of rules, castigating previously unpunished conduct, assists in destabilization. Third, criminalization is calculated to defame and demoralize. "Dirty" urine has supposedly resulted from "random" testing, as occurred with Carlos Alberto Torres, clearly meant to slur this man and the movement, who politically reject the use of drugs because of the devastation they wreak on the Puerto Rican community. Finally, and most significantly, officials create adverse disciplinary records by these means, which they then use to "justify" higher security classifications and transfers to maximum security prisons or Control Units.

Humiliation and Degradation

To belittle the prisoners and the movement they represent, official actions run the gamut. They have assigned demeaning tasks to POW's. (Ricardo Jiménez was ordered to pick cigarette butts out of the cracks in the sidewalk) (Rule A II 71) and illegally denied them privileges afforded to social prisoners (Rule A II 70).

The UNSMRTP expressly prohibits disrespect for the human dignity of prisoners (Rules A II 60 [1], A II 65). Yet the U.S. prisons' use for the "strip search," loudly condemned by Irish political prisoners, parallels and may even surpass its use by the British government. The procedure is not a search at all, for it is invoked without even a suspicion that the person is carrying contraband. Rather, it is an occasion to dehumanize, a nonconsensual disrobing when guards usually require the men to lift their scrotum, the women to lift their breasts, and both to bend over and spread their gluteal cheeks. Examples of its use are instructive. Oscar López Rivera was made to disrobe before guards who recorded the procedure on videotape. Prison staff invoked the strip search so often that one day he was made to strip seven times: Carmen Valentín was recently searched three times in a row following a visit with her teenage son.

Physical Assault and Sexual Abuse

Taking humiliation and degradation one step further, prison authorities have made the prisoners targets of physical and sexual assaults. The UNSMRTP prohibits aggravating the suffering inherent in imprisonment (Rule A II 57) as well as officers' use of force except in rare and clearly delineated circumstances (Rule A I 54 [1]).

Flaunting the Minimum Standards, officials have placed an inordinate focus on Alejandrina Torres, with whom they have consistently experimented in this regard. In three different prisons, guards have attacked her physical and psychological integrity. The first assault was the most indirect—locking her in an all-male unit, in violation of Rule A I 8 (a), and permitting men to expose themselves to her. Prison staff then took a more active role, when a male lieutenant wrenched her arm behind her back, costing her the use of her arm for two years, and then forcefully held her head between his knees watching as female guards tore off her clothes and exposed her naked body to this man. In another prison, a male guard conducted regular pat-down searches, fondling her breasts. See Rule A I 53 (3). And, before taking her to the Women's Control Unit, as four women guards held her down, a male prison employee rammed his fingers up her vagina and anus, painfully invading her body cavities in a "search," though devoid of even a suspicion that she had secreted contraband. And most recently four male guards ogled at her naked chest, refusing to allow her to receive a needed electrocardiogram in private.

Other political prisoners and POW's have also been assaulted—Orlando González Claudio, choked unconscious and beaten for the "heinous crime" of wearing a small cloth Puerto Rican flag on his shirt; Elizam Escobar, beaten during a hunger strike as officials sought to impose medical intervention; Haydée Beltrán, weighing 90 pounds, severely beaten while exemplars of her hair were forcibly taken.

Denial of Medical Treatment

The UNSMRTP applicable to prisoners under sentence provide for diagnosis and treatment of any medical problem "which may hamper a prisoner's rehabilitation. All necessary medical (and) surgical... services shall be provided to that end" (Rule A II 62).

Disregarding the Minimum Rules, prison staff and health care providers alike routinely inform the POW's that, in spite of their serious medical needs, they are "security cases," not "medical cases." This label leads not only to serious adverse physical consequences but is also a means of government psychological gamesmanship, in its announcement to intentionally deprive needed medical attention to these men and women whose sentences would keep them in custody virtually all of their lives. It also ignores the mandate of Rules A I 22-26 that adequate medical services be provided.

Haydée Beltrán is sterile today because for five years prison officials refused to treat her pelvic inflammatory disease, ignoring her episodes of drastic weight loss and pelvic pain so severe she could not stand up. Felix Rosa's entire arm swelled from an infection in his finger, left unattended by officials who refused to take him to a nearby hospital. Oscar López Rivera's rectal bleeding for eight months was aggravated by an intrusive examination and then ignored. It took officials three months to take Alejandrina Torres to the third floor of the same building that houses the Control Unit for needed eye and cardiac examinations. Alicia Rodríguez, undergoing surgery for a large uterine tumor, was disappeared to an undisclosed hospital, where she remained shackled to the bed throughout surgery, recovery, and recuperation.

Assassination

Angel Rodríguez Cristóbal, a young family man active in the independence movement on the island, took part in a 1979 demonstration to protest the presence of the U.S. navy on the tiny island of Vieques. Along with twenty others, he was arrested and charged with a misdemeanor. Following conviction, he was taken to prison in the U.S. The government placed him in F.C.I. Tallahassee in Florida to serve a six-month sentence. There he was forcibly injected with thorazine. Nevertheless, he enjoyed a visit from his attorney, talked of continuing proindependence work and returning to his family and country upon his imminent release. Hours later he was dead. The gash on his head belies government claims that he committed suicide by hanging.

Sensory Deprivation

In October 1986, the U.S. opened the Women's Control Unit, a prison within a prison and the only one of its kind in the United States. This small unit, which is underground, housed only POW Alejandrina Torres and four other women, two of whom (anti-imperialists Susan Rosenberg and Silvia Baraldini) are also in prison for political activity against the U.S. government. Its capacity is 16 women, and it is ill equipped to provide for the needs of the women interned therein (Rule A II 63 [4]). The special conditions that apply in no other prison in the U.S. embody the "denial system," and include:

- placement of political prisoners and POW's in the Unit solely because of political associations;
- indefinite length of stay in the Unit, with no stated policy of how one earns one's way out (except possibly renouncing one 's political association);
- performances of nonconsensual vaginal and rectal cavity "searches" conducted by male prison employees prior to placement in the Unit. The prison officials denied them the option of x-rays, an option offered to men housed at the only other federal Control Unit, Marion Federal Prison;
- a policy of no contact visits with family or lawyers, which, for a time, was not enforced with them;
- no visits whatsoever with people other than immediate family (Rule A I 37);
- limited visiting hours (Rule A I 37, A II 61, A II 79);
- an initial restriction on correspondence, limited to 15 people, who must first submit to FBI and prison screening and approval (Rule A I 37);
- censorship or rejection of all political literature (Rules A I 39,40);
- visitors—family and attorneys—will be denied unless they submit to being photographed twice by officials before entering;
- denial of religious services and congregational worship, as well as denial of religious visits from any non-prison-employed clergy (Rules A I 41 [3], 42, A II 59);
- denial of interaction with any other prisoner;
- denial of participation in normal work and recreation activities (Rule A II 71-75);
- denial of haircuts (Rule A I 16);
- limited recreation in a small outside yard surrounded by a tall wooden fence to prevent sensory stimulation (Rule A II 78);
- strip "searches" every time they return from recreation in the outside yard;
- special uniforms purportedly designed to keep the women "feminine" (Rule A I 17 [1]);
- virtually no natural light or ventilation (Rule A I 11 (a));

207

- denial of all privacy—guards and video cameras are present at all times, including a camera aimed at the shower, which has no curtain or provides no privacy;
- placement in closed front cells painted stark white, in a unit painted stark white*;
- limitation of personal property to 5 books and 10 photographs.

The government asserts that placement in the unit is merely a classification and is not for discipline or punishment. Yet the conditions approximate those of disciplinary custody, in total disregard for the provisions of Rule A I 30. Bureau of Prisons documents reveal that all three political prisoners were assigned to the unit because of their political beliefs and associations (Baraldini v. Meese, 691 F. Supp. 432 [Wash., DC, 1988]). Neither Alejandrina Torres nor any of the women in the Control Unit have been notified of, tried for, or found guilty of a prison rule violation. Furthermore, officials have announced policies here distinct from those at other maximum security prisons: media are prohibited from bringing cameras into the Unit.

The women began to experience some of the predictable psychopathological effects of long-term solitary confinement,† including lethargy, inability to concentrate, memory lapses, loss of appetite, and problems with eyesight (see Rule A 1 32).

So unusual is this Unit that Amnesty International has determined that the allegations of human rights violations meet its criteria and has concluded:

> The conditions and regime are deliberately and gratuitously oppressive. The constant and unjustified use of security chains, the repeated strip searching, lack of sensory stimuli, freedom of movement, possessions, choice of activities and incestuously small range of contacts cannot be other than debilitating.... There is overwhelming evidence that the prisoners at HSU have deteriorated physically and psychologically during their custody there. There has to be a prospect that one or more will finally resort to suicide should their custody at HSU be prolonged.‡

Even the United States federal court concurred that the unit "in many respects measures below acceptable standard for federal prisons," noting prison offi-

---

* Public pressure has resulted in a change of wall color, now a drab, institutional beige.

† See, e.g., Stuart Grassian, "The Psychopathological Effects of Solitary Confinement," 140 *American Journal of Psychiatry*, pp. 1450-54 (November 1983); Amnesty International's "Work on Prison Conditions of Persons Suspected or Convicted of Isolation and Solitary Confinement," May, 1980; Amnesty International's "Current Work on the Federal Republic of Germany," February 20, 1986.

‡ Amnesty International, "The High Security Unit, Lexington Federal Prison, Kentucky, U.S.A.," August 1988, at p. 15.

cials' "gross insensitivity" and operation of a unit that "has skirted elemental standards of human decency" (691 F. Supp. at 447).

After months of public pressure, the Bureau of Prisons announced it would close the Lexington High Security Unit in favor of a larger unit, to which it would "transfer the mission" of the HSU Soon after the August 1988 opening of the Marianna [Florida] Unit, the Bureau of Prisons stated its intention to place there four Puerto Rican Prisoners of War, if it could get around the court order prohibiting placement of women based on their political beliefs and affiliations. Three of the cited women—Dylcia Pagán, Carmen Valentín, and Ida Luz Rodríguez—have served several years of exemplary conduct, without incident, in the general population of an open, co-ed prison in Pleasanton, California. The fourth woman is Alejandrina Torres. The government has acknowledged that the only basis for such placement is the women's affiliations with the FALN (*Fuerzas Armadas de Liberación Nacional*—Armed Forces for Puerto Rican National Liberation)* (Rule A 1 6 [1], UNSMRTP).

The government asserted that "their FALN affiliation and their participation in the seditious conspiracy were virtually co-extensive" (Id.). This virtual recognition of the status of political prisoners, accompanied by the harsh and discriminatory treatment of the Puerto Rican prisoners of war and political prisoners, flies in the face of the U.S. government's denial that it has no political prisoners.

Conclusion

In concluding, we wish to bring to your attention the part of the judgment of the Permanent People's Tribunal related to the actual criminalizing and persecuting of opponents of the colonial status of Puerto Rico:

> This Tribunal is convinced that Puerto Rican nationalists deserve to be treated as political prisoners and given protection as "prisoners of war" in accordance with the Geneva Conventions of 1949 and the Geneva Protocols of 1977. As such, all Puerto Rican political figures, currently in custody, should be released forthwith or, at minimum, should be sent into exile in a country whose government is prepared to grant asylum.

We ask that the United Nations Human Rights Commission send representatives to the United States to interview the political prisoners and Prisoners of War, particularly Oscar López Rivera at Marion, Illinois and Alejandrina Torres at M.C.C. San Diego, California, since transferred to Pleasanton Federal Correctional Institution in California, and report on their conditions. We further ask that the Commission establish a committee to review and monitor their prison conditions.

---

* Baraldini v. Thornburgh, No. 88-5275 (DC Cir.), defendants' motion to expedite appeal.

II.7.D

North American Anti-Imperialists and U.S. Government Repression

Elizabeth Fink

1990

My topic is the North American anti-imperialists, but I should clarify that and say that I will speak about one North American and one European anti-imperialist, because Silvia Baraldini is not a North American. She lived here and carried out her political activities here, but she is European and hopefully in the near future, she will return to Europe.

What Soffiyah says is absolutely correct; the vast majority of people in prison are Third World people, but there are any number of white people who are political prisoners in the U.S. Once having made that decision and having had the entire wrath of the U.S. on their backs, they face the same conditions that every political prisoner faces. These people made a choice to do what they did. They all have a history of community activism and primarily had a history of support for national liberation struggles. Marilyn Buck, who was a member of the Students for a Democratic Society in the '60s, an editor of *New Left Notes*, went to San Francisco and became a support person for the Black Panther Party. She received a sentence for purchasing ammunition in the early '70s that she is still serving today in 1990. It is that history that has given her the kind of sentence she has now, which is a ridiculous 70 years. Not only is she already doing 70 years, but she faces another 45 in the Washington Resistance Case. After it is over, she will have served what they want to give her—over 100 years in prison. What they want to do to her and the rest of the Resistance people is never let them see the light of day. Marilyn has been in the DC jail with the others since her arrest. They occasionally receive "recreational periods" during the weekend, but they never get to see the sun. These people have not seen the sun for five years.

Ray Levasseur is another person who never gets to see the sun, because he is imprisoned in Marion. He began his activist career as a mill worker in the mills of Maine, went to Vietnam; after his tour of duty he worked for the Students Organizing Committee in Tennessee and then returned to Maine where he was a member of the Vietnam Veterans Against the War. He did community activism work in Maine and founded an organization called SCAR, which dealt with prison reform. In 1975 he made a decision, along with others, that, based on the repression against him, based on the existence of a death squad in Portland, Maine, he would go underground. He was captured in 1984 and received a 45-year sentence. The government wanted to give him a 105-year sentence, but they did not get what they wanted. Thank you, Ray Levasseur.

Many of us have seen *Through the Wire;* we have seen the pictures of Susan Rosenberg on the picket line when she was only 14. These people have a long history of political activism. Silvia and I met in December of 1966. At that time, she was an organizer in Madison, Wisconsin, doing antiwar activity. She came to New York, worked in support of the Black liberation movement, and found herself in prison. Because, once you align yourself with these kinds of struggles, that is what happens when the wrath of the U.S. government falls on your shoulders. Soffiyah talked about the disparity of sentencing and the enormously long prison terms. This is true for these people as well. The disparity of sentencing between the right wing and the left wing in this country is well known. If you possess 2,000 pounds of dynamite in Pennsylvania and you are a member of the Order of the Posse Comitatis you are going to do six months in jail. If you bomb a series of abortion centers in Florida, and you stand up in court and say, "I'm proud of what I did," you are going to get five years and your wife will receive probation. If you do the most outrageous of criminal offenses and you are a member of the right wing, you are going to get out of prison. However, if you are Linda Evans and purchase 3 guns, you can expect a 40-year sentence. If you are found to be in possession of weapons, which under a normal situation will get you 10 years, you will receive 56 years if you are Tim Blunk and Susan Rosenberg. The U.S. will want you to receive the maximum sentence, but how long you actually serve in prison depends on us and the fight that has to be waged.

The same thing occurred in Silvia Baraldini's case. The Circuit Court considered her conviction a closed question, and the judge gave her maximum time. She then went to Brooklyn and refused to cooperate with the grand jury investigating the Puerto Rican independence, and the judge added an additional three years to her sentence.

These people all suffer under the worst conditions of confinement, too, the conditions of political prisoners in America. All of them are primarily in federal custody, although Judy Clark, Kathy Boudin, and David Gilbert are in state custody in New York State. There have been a number of serious struggles that have been waged against the federal government around their custody. One that we must all take some pride in is the fight that we made around Lexington. When you watch the movie *Through the Wire,* you get the feeling that it was the lawsuit that closed Lexington down. That is a lie. Lexington was closed down by all of you. It was going to be closed down even before we filed that lawsuit. They told us they were going to open another prison in New Mexico. They were going to open another prison in Marianna [Florida] because they did not want to deal with Lexington. Certainly, the lawsuit pushed them over the line, but we were at the line when we filed that lawsuit. Silvia Baraldini was transferred to Marianna four days ago, and I have been in contact with her. Because of our campaign against Lexington, Marianna, though it is a terrible prison and we hate it, is not a control unit. It does not have the social and sensory deprivation that Lexington did and that Marion does. Soffiyah talked about Marion. I do not want to say any more. It is a nightmare. It is the incarnate of evil. I was there last week. It chills your bones to walk into that place. I saw some people who had traveled from Chicago; they had a five-month-old baby with them. They would not let them visit because the baby was not on the visitors' list. They had driven nine hours. They were not even going to have a contact visit but they still would not let that little baby in. These people were crying and the guards just didn't care.

The worst thing in prison is to be ill. It is the one thing that everybody hates and, in a political situation, is even worse. A great number of political prisoners have had serious medical problems. Marilyn had a tumor on her neck, which was not treated properly. Silvia requested to see a gynecologist for eight months before she was allowed to see a doctor, only to discover that she had contracted cancer of the uterus. She required two operations and radiation therapy. Laura, who probably has nonspecific non-A, non-B hepatitis, is constantly sick and has not received treatment.

However, the most serious case is that of Alan Berkman. Alan Berkman received only a twelve-year sentence, and the U.S. government was very upset about that. Alan was diagnosed as having Hodgkin's disease. It was only because he had a judge who was a humane person that he was treated properly. But now, he has suffered a relapse. The government knows he is sick, but instead of transferring him to the Mayo Clinic Hospital in Rochester, the Bureau of Prisons has announced that they are going to transfer him to Marion. Marion, where the water is contaminated, where he will sit in a cell and wait for maybe three weeks, even though he has a relapse of cancer, before they send a doctor to examine him. The doctor will sit around, maybe wait a month and a half, maybe two, and then say, "Oh, well, you have cancer now. We will take you to Springfield." Springfield is a morgue. It is not a hospital. It is a morgue where they put people and kill them. Rather than take him to Rochester, rather than have another judge order that Alan receive medical care and be taken to Georgetown or some hospital, they are going to put him away, lock him up and hope that he dies. Since they were not able to give him the maximum sentence, they want to give him a death sentence instead. The situation with Alan is really critical. We must organize a letter-writing campaign right now and demand that Alan receive proper medical care. We must do everything in our power to prevent the government from murdering Alan—which is exactly what they intend to do.

Verdict
of the International Tribunal on
Political Prisoners/Prisoners of War

1990

Members of the Special International Tribunal

Frank Badohu
Barrister and solicitor

Jawad Boulus
Attorney, Palestine

Lord Anthony Gifford
Barrister in London and a member of the
Northern Ireland Bar and Jamaican Bar;
Member of the House of
Lords, United Kingdom

Norman Paech
Professor of Public International
Law and Constitutional Law at the
University of Hamburg, Germany

José Roberto Rendón Vásquez
Attorney and Professor,
Faculty of Law and Political Science,
Universidad Nacional Mayor
de San Marcos, Peru

Celina Romany
Professor of Jurisprudence,
Constitutional Law, and Human Rights,
City University of New York Law School.

Toshi Yuki Tanaka
Professor of Political Science at
Melbourne University, Australia.

George Wald
Professor Emeritus of Biology at
Harvard University;
Nobel Prize Winner for Biology, U.S.A.

Coordinator:
Dr. Luis Nieves Falcón

Special Prosecutors:
Lennox S. Hinds, Esq.
Jan Susler, Esq.
Robert Boyle, Esq.
Bruce Ellison, Esq.
Roger Wareham, Esq.

Counsel to the Tribunal:
Daniel Nina
Richard Harvey

I. Constitution of the Tribunal

The Special Tribunal on Violations of Human Rights of Political Prisoners and Prisoners of War in United States Prisons and Jails was convened by 88 sponsoring and endorsing organizations from all parts of the United States. The members of the Special Tribunal assumed jurisdiction pursuant to accepted principles of international law approved and adopted by the world community under the United Nations Charter, in accordance with the precedents of the Nuremburg and Tokyo Tribunals and following procedures approved by the Economic and Social Council of the United Nations (Resolution 1503 [XLVIII]).

The Tribunal received extensive written and oral evidence from political activists and experts testifying in support of a detailed indictment of the United States Government, alleging, *inter alia*, the denial of the right of peoples in the United States and Puerto Rico to self-determination; the criminalization of the legitimate struggle against illegal acts committed by the Government of the United States; the denial of the rule of law to those engaged in such struggles and the use against them of torture, inhuman and degrading treatment.

The Special Tribunal does not sit as a court of law but, like the Bertrand Russell Tribunals on the U.S. war against the Vietnamese people, this Tribunal applies principles of customary international human rights law. Article 38 of the Statutes of the International Court of Justice recognizes the authoritative effect of the findings of such tribunals on contemporary standards of international law.

The Defendant Government and its agencies are bound to respect international human rights law, not least because Article VI of the Constitution of the United States provides that treaties and other international agreements are "the supreme law of the land."

Although customary principles of law require Petitioners to exhaust the domestic remedies before having recourse to international fora, the overwhelming weight of testimony presented to the Tribunal showed that the courts and judicial officers of the United States routinely refuse to allow Petitioners to raise defenses based on international law and that relief under the law is routinely denied. Therefore we find that Petitioners have in fact exhausted all domestic remedies and that the Special Tribunal is entitled to review all of the cases presented for its consideration.

The Tribunal is satisfied that all appropriate steps were taken by Petitioners to inform the Defendant Government and its agencies of the nature and purposes of the Tribunal hearings, including the service of the indictment on President George Bush and other appropriate federal and state officials, and that every opportunity was given to Defendants to attend and present testimony. Although Defendants failed to avail themselves of the opportunity to testify, many of the documents and expert witnesses indicated fairly the basis of the Government's opposition to Petitioners' claims, and the Tribunal has duly noted Defendants' views in reaching its findings.

In examining the evidence and reaching its conclusions, the Tribunal has taken and employed the following definitions:

"Self-Determination": the right by virtue of which all peoples are entitled freely to determine their political status and to pursue their economic, social and cultural development. All peoples may, for their own ends, freely dispose of their natural wealth and resources without prejudice to any obligations arising out of international economic co-operation, based upon the principle of mutual benefit and international law. In no case may a people be deprived of its own means of subsistence. (Common Article 1 (1) of the International Human Rights Covenants, 1966)

"Prisoner of War": those combatants struggling against colonial and alien domination and racist regimes captured as prisoners are to be accorded the status of prisoners of war and their treatment should be in accordance with the provisions of the Geneva Conventions Relative to the Treatment of Prisoners of War, of 12 August 1949. (General Assembly Resolution 3103 [XXVIII])

"Genocide": any of the following acts committed with intent to destroy, in whole or in part, a national, ethnical, racial or religious groups as such:

a. Killing members of the group;
b. Causing serious bodily or mental harm to members of the groups;
c. Deliberately inflicting on the group conditions of life calculated to bring about its physical destruction in whole or in part;
d. Imposing measures intended to prevent births within the group;
e. Forcibly transferring children of the group to another group.[*]

"Political Prisoner": a person incarcerated for actions carried out in support of legitimate struggles for self-determination or for opposing the illegal policies of the United States government and/or its political sub-divisions.

II. Overview
1990 has been a landmark year in the worldwide campaign for the recognition and freedom of political prisoners. The release of Nelson Mandela, Walter Sisulu and other antiapartheid fighters, and the negotiations for the release of all South African political prisoners, have shown that even the most repressive and intransigent regimes must at some point acknowledge the existence of political prisoners and account for their treatment and continuing imprisonment. For decades the South African government denied the existence of political prisoners, branding imprisoned antiapartheid fighters

---

[*] International Convention on the Prevention and Punishment of the Crime of Genocide, 1948 [Article 2].

as criminals and terrorists. However, the growing liberation struggle of the people of South Africa and worldwide solidarity forced the government of South Africa to abandon this farcical denial of political prisoners. Similarly, the triumph of the liberation struggle of the Namibian people led by SWAPO resulted in the independence and self-determination of Namibia, constituting a resounding affirmation of customary principles of international human rights law.

Ironically, the U.S. government has expressed strong support, albeit selective, for the freeing of political prisoners throughout the world. At the same time, however, the U.S. government vociferously denies the existence of political prisoners at home and resolutely echoes a familiar refrain that those who claim to be political prisoners and prisoners of war are simply terrorists and criminals.

This Tribunal presents a unique and important opportunity to review carefully Petitioners' contention that the U.S. does indeed hold political prisoners and Prisoners of War.

The Tribunal members have approached this responsibility with the utmost of seriousness and careful scrutiny. The U.S. government must be held to the same standard of international law and human rights safeguards that it subscribes to for the other nations of the world. The denial of the existence of political prisoners and the consequent failure to afford such prisoners the fundamental protections of humanitarian international law constitute serious violations of human rights which, if found to be true, would require the immediate attention of world public opinion and rectification by the U.S. government.

Numerous supporting documents which are delineated in the appendix were also submitted. Of particular interest were documents of the Counter-Intelligence Program (COINTELPRO) of the U.S. Federal Bureau of Investigation (FBI) showing its program to disrupt and neutralize leaders and organizations of the African-American, Puerto Rican, Mexicano-Chicano and Native American self-determination struggles.

As we will spell out in more detail in the body of this document, the Tribunal finds that the U.S. judicial system (state and federal) has been used in a harsh and discriminatory manner against people struggling for self-determination within its borders and Puerto Rico, as well as against other political opponents of the U.S. government. Some have been falsely accused and had evidence favorable to their defense destroyed or suppressed, others have been tried on overbroad conspiracy charges which rely on associations and beliefs as an essential element, and many have been tried in an armed camp atmosphere saturated with prejudicial publicity designed to intimidate and prejudice the juries before whom they were tried. Most of the Petitioners have also received draconian disproportionate sentences and have been subjected to torture, cruel, discriminatory and degrading punishment.

We also find that the Black and Mexican people living within the borders of the United States and Native American and Puerto Rican people have the fundamental right to exercise self-determination and to seek and receive support from other opponents of repression, and that the U.S. government has carried out a consistent pattern and policy of repression against these peoples, their leaders and supporters.

We further find that captured combatants in a legitimate national liberation movement are entitled to the special protected status of Prisoner of War and should not be tried and imprisoned by the U.S. government as criminals. Rather, these captured national liberation fighters must be held separately under conditions in accordance with the Geneva Convention and immediate steps taken to transfer these combatants to neutral countries until all hostilities cease between their movements and the U.S. government.

We are mindful that the U.S. judicial system is promoted by many here and throughout the world as one of the most progressive and protective of individual rights. The claim that the U.S. does not have political prisoners has gone generally unchallenged. We believe that the evidence presented at the Tribunal overwhelmingly established the opposite case. The U.S. government uses its judicial system to repress the legitimate political movements opposing the government.

It is of critical importance for the international human rights community as well as all freedom-loving people to bring to world attention the plight of U.S. political prisoners.

III. The Right to Self-Determination
Over the last 30 years, since the passage in 1960 of the historic United Nations General Assembly Declaration on the Granting of Independence to Colonial Countries and Peoples (Resolution 1514 [XV]) which called for the "speedy and unconditional end to colonialism in all its forms and manifestations," the right to self-determination has evolved to a peremptory norm of International Law—a norm accepted and recognized by the international community of states as a whole from which no derogation is permitted.

Of particular importance to the codification of this fundamental right is the Universal Declaration of the Rights of People ("Algiers Declaration") which affirms that the peoples of the world "have an equal right to liberty, the right to free themselves from any foreign interference and to choose their own government, (and) the right, if they are under subjection, to fight for their liberation." This assurance is specified in Article 1, "Every people has the right to existence," and Article 6, "Every people has the right to break free from any colonial or foreign domination, whether direct or indirect, and from any racist regime."

In addition, U.N. Resolution 2625 (XXV) known as "The Declaration on the Principles of International Law Concerning Friendly Relations and Co-Operation Among States in Accordance with the Charter of the

United Nations," adopted by consensus in 1970, provides authoritative clarity to the character and importance of the right to self-determination. Its preamble affirms that "the principle of equal rights and self-determination of peoples constitutes a significant contribution to contemporary law, and its effective application is of paramount importance for the promotion of friendly relations among States."

The Declaration mandates that every state has a duty to promote the principle of self-determination and to assist the United Nations in its realization so as to improve relations among states and "to bring a speedy end to colonialism, having due regard to the freely expressed will of the peoples concerned." The right of self-determination as a peremptory norm of international law has been confirmed by the International Court of Justice in its Advisory Opinion on Namibia (ICJ Reports 1971) and in its decision in the Western Sahara case (ICJ Reports 1975). As the Vienna Convention on the Law of Treaties provides, a peremptory norm of international law (*Jus Cogens*) cannot be abridged or superseded by any act of sovereign will, including a treaty.

Finally the two international covenants on human rights (International Covenant on Economic, Social, and Cultural Rights and International Covenant on Civil and Political Rights [which the United States has refused to endorse]) are initiated by a common Article 1 (1) indicating a place of primacy for self-determination: "All peoples have the right of self-determination. By virtue of that right they freely determine their political status and freely pursue their economic, social and cultural development."

The Tribunal heard evidence by Puerto Rican, Native American, Black and Mexicano witnesses of their peoples' national development, characteristics, and continuing history of oppression. Witnesses also testified to the long train of repression against the organizations and leaders of their people. Each of these peoples satisfies the objective and subjective criteria for self-determination. Each perceives themselves as separate people and each suffers special targeting and oppression by the U.S. Government.

III. 1 Native Americans

This Tribunal received ample evidence on the history of the Native American People's struggle for their right to self-determination and on the genocide committed against this people by the United States Government.

The history of European and Native American relations reveals theft of 99% of the land base and genocidal practices of war, disease, alcohol, starvation and deculturalization which reduced the indigenous population from approximately 12.5 million to less than 227,000 by 1890.

Meeting substantial resistance, if not outright defeat, at times seeking alliances against others, what became the United States Government entered into some 371 treaties with the indigenous people of North America during the 18th and 19th centuries. The importance of these treaties was embodied in Article VI of the U.S. Constitution as the "supreme law of the land."

By this principle, the United States Government has incorporated into its domestic law the content of the treaties signed with the Native American people. However, as was pointed out consistently in the evidence presented to the Tribunal, the U.S. Government has systematically violated or refused to respect the terms of the agreements reached with the Native American people.

Therefore, this Tribunal recognizes that, first, the Native Americans constitute a people within international law definitions who are carrying out a struggle for self-determination. Moreover, this Tribunal takes notice that, despite all the treaties signed by the U.S. Government with the Native American peoples, the U.S. has consistently denied those treaty rights to these peoples. In decisions of the U.S. Supreme Court such as *Cherokee Nation v. Georgia*, 30 U.S. 5 Pet. 1 (1831) and *Worcester v. Georgia*, 31 U.S. 6 Pet. 515 (1832), the Court established the principle that Native American people are domestic and dependent on the U.S. Government, thus denying their right to self-determination. After these two Supreme Court decisions, the so-called "plenary power" doctrine was initiated by the U.S. Government which denied the right of the Native American people to organize and govern themselves. This, for example, is the pattern followed by the enactment in 1924 of the U.S. Congress's Indian Citizenship Act (8 USCA Sec. 1401). Through this Act U.S. citizenship was imposed upon the Native American people. In addition, in 1934 the U.S. Congress enacted the Indian Reorganization Act (25 USCA Sec. 461) by which the U.S. Government decided to organize "tribal" councils to resemble corporate boards. The intention behind this was to reduce the autonomy of the Native American peoples to govern their own affairs.

Thus, this Tribunal after carefully hearing various witnesses and taking judicial notice of many historical aspects of U.S. Government policies toward the Native American peoples, considers that the practices of the U.S. Government are in breach of Common Article 1 of the United Nations International Covenants of 1966 (on Economic, Social and Cultural Rights and on Civil and Political Rights) guaranteeing, amongst other things, the right of the people to self-determination.

Second, this Tribunal considers that the U.S. Government has also conducted a policy of genocide against these people. The Tribunal follows the definition of Genocide as established by Article 2 of the Convention on the Prevention and Punishment of the Crime of Genocide, 1948. This Tribunal recognizes the most cruel policies occurred in the early years of the U.S. republic, when a plan of physical extermination was conducted against the Native American people. After failing to completely exterminate them, a new policy was designed to impose compulsory assimilation, so as to destroy the history and culture of the Native American people.

Tactics employed to achieve this end include the criminalization of Native religious practices, forced transfer of children through mandatory indoctrination at boarding schools for extended periods, adoption by non-Indians, enactment of laws designed to destroy traditional culture, e.g., by prohibiting the holding of land in common. Implementation of policies such as "termination" (where the Federal government literally dissolved selected indigenous populations) and "relocation" (systematic dispersal of Native populations) were combined by the U.S. Government with declarations that certain groups of living peoples were "extinct." Systematic involuntary and uninformed sterilization of Native American women has compounded these genocidal policies, as has the use of the "blood quantum" method of identification to statistically manipulate out of existence certain groups of Native Americans.

Native Americans are the poorest population group in North America with the highest incidence of infant mortality, death by exposure, tuberculosis, plague disease, malnutrition and teen suicide. The average life expectancy of an American Indian male is 44.6 years, and for females it is less than three years longer. For white males the figure is 74 years.

The policy of genocide has been legitimized by different laws approved by the U.S. Congress, for example, the General Allotment Act (25 USCA sec. 331 [1887]) used to deprive the Native American people of the land that they consider common and sacred.

In addition, this Tribunal has taken notice of documents that proved the collaboration by the Bureau of Indian Affairs during the 1970s, together with the Indian Health Service, in the systematic performance of involuntary sterilization on Native women. This particular practice, in conjunction with other practices of the U.S. Government, clearly manifests a pattern of committing genocide against the Native American people.

III. 2 Puerto Ricans

Of the four peoples represented before the Tribunal, the right to self-determination for the people of Puerto Rico is the clearest and most recognized by the international community. With a separate territory, language and culture, the plight of Puerto Rico constitutes one of the last remaining classic colonial cases in the world.

Beginning in 1973 and 1976 and then in each succeeding year, the United Nations Special Committee on Decolonization has reviewed the case of Puerto Rico, reaffirmed the right of the Puerto Rican people to self-determination and called upon the United States to stop all interference with the free and full exercise of that right. The U.S. has refused to follow these mandates and has consistently used all its coercive powers to block the case of Puerto Rico from being considered by the entire General Assembly.

The Decolonisation Committee resolutions, plus pronouncements from the non-aligned countries and the International Association of Democratic Lawyers, provide authoritative support for Puerto Rico's right to self-determination. Even the President of the United States, George Bush, in his recent call for a referendum on the island's status, has acknowledged that the Puerto Rican people have not chosen freely their present relationship with the U.S.

This Tribunal also adopts the findings and verdict of the Permanent Peoples' Tribunal on Puerto Rico (Barcelona, January 27-29, 1989), which declared in part:

(1) That Puerto Rico and its people have the right to freely determine their political, economic, social and cultural condition in accordance with the Algiers Declaration and the principles of International Law.

(2) That the Constitution of the Commonwealth of Puerto Rico is not the proper way for the Puerto Rican people to exercise their self-determination right, whereas in the referenda which have been carried out on the Island, the required guarantees which govern the true exercise of said right, in accordance with the Resolutions of the U.N., have not been observed.

(3) That the U.S. has an international duty to respect the Right of Puerto Rico to its self-determination, in accordance with the obligations it has conventionally and customarily assumed.

Regrettably, the United States Government refused to participate in the Barcelona Tribunal and has ignored its findings.

As clear as the Puerto Rican people's right to self-determination is the historical record that such right has been denied to that people. Testimony established a military, political, psychological, economic, ideological, cultural and linguistic domination by U.S. colonial power over Puerto Rico since the beginning of the U.S. invasion and occupation. The evidence also was compelling as to the use of repression against the national movement for independence, its leaders and organizations. The Nationalist Party and its supporters were fiercely repressed in the 1930s and again in the 1950s when a mass resistance to U.S. attempts to eliminate the independence movement resulted in the killing and arrest of hundreds of people.

Today that repression continues. Seventeen Prisoners of War or political prisoners are serving draconian sentences, exiled from their homeland to jails in the United States. The FBI and the grand jury system are used to investigate, intimidate and intern independence activists and supporters. Thousands of others have been placed under surveillance and on "subversive lists" for their pro-independence sentiments. Presently nine more independence activists and leaders face conspiracy charges in Hartford, Connecticut, hundreds of miles from their homeland.

It should also be noted that some of the colonial conditions imposed on the people of Puerto Rico have genocidal characteristics. These include the forced sterilization of 33% of Puerto Rican women of child-bearing age; the economically forced migration to the United States of one half of Puerto Rico's population; the consequent deculturalization of the population; and one of the world's highest rates of suicide, drug abuse and mental illness.

We again quote from the verdict of the Barcelona Tribunal as to the obligation of the U.S. government to:

(a) acknowledge the political prisoner status of those Puerto Ricans incarcerated due to their work and militancy in favor of Puerto Rico's independence and to grant a general amnesty to all Puerto Ricans currently incarcerated because of their involvement in the struggle against colonialism.

(b) relinquish the current powers the U.S. Congress has to amend and approve the decisions made by the representative bodies and government of Puerto Rico.

(c) completely transfer any power the U.S. Congress or the U.S. government may have over Puerto Rico, to a deliberative body with constitutional character, made up of representatives from all the political and social forces of Puerto Rico chosen on an equal elective basis.

(d) negotiate such measures, as a transitional status of the juridical and political condition of Puerto Rico, until the self-determination right is effectively exercised.

We further call upon the United States government to accord Prisoner of War status to those Puerto Rican prisoners captured as anticolonial combatants.

III. 3. Black People in the United States

It is an uncontested historical fact that Africans, forcibly brought to the area which would become the United States, came from various tribes and regions of Africa. In addition, these kidnapped Africans spoke many tongues and were forged into a new and distinct people, with distinct problems, requiring unique solutions, during the three-century ordeal of chattel slavery. It is also historically documented that these Africans and their descendants were considered "three-fifths" of a human being, thereby necessitating an elaborate system of laws, cultural norms and religious canons to deprive people of African descent of their rights as human beings and, by extension, to deprive them of their right to self-determination.

In 1865 at the end of the U.S. Civil War, the U.S. government abolished slavery (13th Amendment), freeing the kidnapped African slaves. Rather than allowing this freed people to choose or reject citizenship and to freely exercise the right to self-determination, the 14th Amendment imposed citizenship upon them, as the Jones Act of 1917 would later do to Puerto Ricans and as the Indian Citizenship Act did to the Native Americans in 1924.

There have been various strategies, necessitated by a system of white supremacy, pursued by Black organizations in the United States in their efforts to obtain freedom and justice for their people. The main strategies at work today within the Black movement are the struggle for independent political power; forms of community control and autonomy; and some groups who advocate independence of the New Afrikan nation. U.N. General Assembly Resolution 2625 expresses the options available to a people entitled to exercise the right to self-determination:

> the establishment of a sovereign and independent state, the free association or integration with an independent state or the emergence of any other political status freely determined by a people, constitute modes of implementing the right of self-determination by that people.

Whichever strategy prevails that brings about genuine self-determination is for Black people in the United States to decide. However, it is clear that the Black people of the U.S. have not been allowed to freely exercise their right to self-determination. The evidence overwhelmingly established an unbroken pattern of repression against Black organizations and activists fighting for their human, political, economic and civil rights.

While the Tribunal recognizes that the right of self-determination for Black people in the U.S. has not previously been established by international bodies or tribunals, we do not feel that this lack of precedent is determinative of the issue. Rather, this Tribunal believes that the evidence presented before us strongly supports the claim that Black people living within the borders of the United States are a distinct people entitled to self-determination.

Equally compelling is the evidence that Black people in the U.S. have been forcibly denied the freedom to exercise that right. From the inhuman outrage of slavery up to the present circumstance of attacks on community and political organizations, Black people in the United States have never been given the opportunity to choose their destiny. The documents submitted which establish this conclusion are the FBI Counter-Intelligence Program and the testimony on the targeting and repression of the Black Panther Party (BPP), Republic of New Afrika (RNA), Student Nonviolent Coordinating Committee (SNCC), Southern Christian Leadership Conference (SCLC), the MOVE organization and the Black Men's Movement against Crack. The evidence also established that the Ku Klux Klan and other white supremacist hate groups functioned with impunity and often with the complicity of the government in committing acts of violence and intimidation against the Black community.

The history and treatment of Black people in the United States also supports a claim that the U.S. Government is guilty of the crime of genocide against the Black people. There is no question that during the kidnapping of Africans in the slave trade, and in the barbaric Middle Passage to North America, millions of Blacks were killed. In addition, during the more than 200 years of chattel slavery, Black people were wantonly murdered, savagely brutalized and denied all basic human rights.

The condition of Black people living in the United States today strongly suggests that policies of the U.S. Government are designed to lead to the elimination of Black people. The Tribunal was presented with evidence that:

1. the infant mortality rate for Black people is double that for whites;
2. Black women, regardless of class, are twice as likely to bear low-weight babies than white women;
3. The gap in life-expectancy rates between Blacks and whites has recently widened from 5.6 to 6.2 years, and "Blacks today have a life expectancy already reached by whites in the 1950s or a lag of about 30 years";
4. The rate of survival for Black males over 40 years old in Harlem, New York City, is lower than for men in Bangladesh;
5. Dangerously high blood pressure is a hidden cost of racial prejudice at least for some Blacks;
6. In New York City "increasingly large numbers of women of child bearing age are dying... combined with the deaths of men in the same age group, the result is the destruction of families and the orphaning of tens of thousands of children, most in low-income African-American neighborhoods" ;
7. AIDS is "more and more becoming a disease of poor, Black and Hispanic heterosexuals in the inner city." It is the leading killer of Black women in the 15-44 year age group in New York and New Jersey;
8. Unemployment for Blacks is double the rate for whites and nearly 50% of Black teenagers are unable to find work;
9. White families earn 45.5% more than Black families.

III. 4 Mexican People (Chicanos) Living in the United States
Mexican people living in the north of their country came under the authority of the U.S. government after the Mexican-American War of 1841, a war generally recognized as expansionist and unjust and which deprived Mexico of 50% of its territory.

After the conquest and occupation, there was a continuing policy of brutal repression and exploitation of Mexican people throughout the occupied territories, including numerous lynchings and other killings.

Mexicano people organized resistance to, and have fought against, this occupation. Among the most famous Mexicano resistance fighters are Tiburcio Vásquez, Joaquin Murietta and the Cortez and Espinoza brothers. Also, Juan Nepomuceno Cortina from Texas who for fifteen years waged guerrilla warfare against the U.S. government. Armed clandestine organizations also emerged like *La Mano Negra* and *Las Gorras Blancas*. In 1915, the *Plan de San Diego* was another armed uprising calling for self-determination and independence of the occupied territories. It was violently repressed.

Armed Rangers and other law enforcement agencies that formed in California, New Mexico, Texas and Arizona were essentially private vigilantes organized to repress Mexicanos with the consent of the U.S. government. Between 1915 and 1920, about 5,000 Mexicanos were killed along the border by the Texas Rangers, who have also been used to police migratory labor, striking unions, civil rights activists and organizations and to beat up Mexicano-Chicano candidates running for elected positions.

The FBI and grand jury have been used to repress the Mexicano/Chicano resistance movement. Beginning in the late 1930s, the FBI has consistently investigated and monitored Mexicano/Chicano organizations such as LULAC, the GI Forum, the *Associación Nacional Mexico-Americano*. In the 1950s the FBI created the Border Coverage Program (BOCOV) as part of COINTELPRO. It maintained offices both in the occupied territories and Mexico. Additionally, the Border Patrol and the Immigration and Naturalization Service are special police agencies created primarily to be used against the Mexicano people.

All these repressive actions are supplemented by the terrorist activities of the Ku Klux Klan against Mexicanos/Chicanos.

The homes of Mexicano/Chicano resistance fighters have been bombed and many have been killed. Among the latter are Ricardo Falcon, Rito Canales, Antonio Cordova and *Los Seis de Boulder*.

The Tribunal heard that a United States border separates the Mexicano/Chicano people and that since the 1850s *"Los Rinches"* (the Texas Rangers), a police terror force, have killed 20,000 Mexicano/Chicanos. There have also been countless lynchings by North Americans. There is a high incidence of poverty, malnutrition and a proliferation of drugs (50% of incarcerated Mexicano/Chicanos are held for drug offenses). Not only is there a high rate of premature births but although Mexicano/Chicanos comprise 8% of the U.S. population, 25% of all pediatric AIDS cases are found among Mexican/Chicano children. Overall, there is a grossly disproportionate incidence of AIDS infection compared with the general population.

Mexicano/Chicanos have also been subjected to a policy of cultural assimilation, principally directed toward their Spanish language. The issue has become more acute with the newly imposed legislation compelling the use of the English language only and forbidding the use of Spanish in all official activities including schooling of Mexicano children.

The Tribunal recognizes the claim that the Mexicano/Chicano people living within the borders of the United States are a people entitled to exercise their right to self-determination.

IV. Puerto Rican Prisoners of War
Among the Petitioners are 13 Puerto Rican women and men (Carlos Torres, Adolfo Matos, Dylcia Pagán, Ida Luz Rodríguez, Carmen Valentín, Elizam Escobar, Alejandrina Torres, Ricardo Jiménez, Alicia Rodríguez, Luis Rosa, Edwin Cortés, Alberto Rodríguez and Oscar López Rivera) most of whom have been held in U.S. prisons since 1980. They are serving literal life sentences for their involvement with a clandestine Puerto Rican independence

liberation group, *Fuerzas Armadas de Liberación Nacional* (FALN). They are combatants in a struggle against colonialism and for national liberation in accordance with Article I, Paragraph 4, of Additional Protocol I to the 1949 Geneva Conventions, extending POW protections to "include armed conflicts in which peoples are fighting against colonial domination and alien occupation and against racist regimes, in the exercise of their right of self-determination." Pursuant to the Resolutions of the United Nations General Assembly on the Rights of Colonial People and the Legal Status of Combatants Struggling Against Colonial and Alien Domination of Racist Regimes, which provides that combatants struggling against colonialism "are to be accorded the status of prisoners of war and their treatment should be in accordance with the Geneva Convention" (Resolution 3103 [XXVIII], 12 December 1973), these Puerto Rican combatants are entitled to be treated as Prisoners of War.

The U.S. has refused POW status to these anticolonial fighters, claiming that it is not a signatory to the Additional Protocols. This refusal to accept universally recognized humanitarian protections for peoples fighting colonialism, apartheid and alien domination should not and does not preclude the according of these protections.

Colonialism has been identified as a crime for over three decades. The U.N. General Assembly has consistently asserted that colonized and dependent people have the right to use all means available including armed struggle to resist colonialism. And, since the General Assembly Resolution 3103 was passed in 1973, captured anticolonialism combatants have been entitled to POW status. This protected status for people fighting colonialism is specifically designed to assist the customary international law right to self-determination and to deter the colonial power from perpetuating the crime of colonialism.

The expansion of the definition of international conflicts in the Additional Protocols to the Geneva Convention, to include those struggling for national liberation, also constituted recognition by the international community that the protection of anticolonial fighters was to be elevated to a customary norm of international law.

Clearly today, if not in 1977 when the Additional Protocols were first enacted, now that colonialism has been universally condemned and almost eradicated from the world, those who fight against colonialism are entitled to special protection and should not be criminalized by the colonial power.

We find, therefore, that Puerto Rican combatants who have asserted their right to POW status are entitled not to be tried in the U.S. courts but to be protected under the Geneva Convention. We believe that these prisoners who have been illegally incarcerated and criminalized for over 10 years should be unconditionally released or at the very least, transferred to a neutral country.

Certain other Petitioners who are people struggling for self-determination for Black people in the United States and Native American people have also asserted the right to be considered as Prisoners of War. We believe that these claims have merit as these are peoples fighting against alien occupation or racist regimes. However, the evidence before the Tribunal does not allow us to reach a defmitive conclusion at this time, and we recommend that there be further investigation into these claims.

V. White North American Opponents of United States Government Policies
Testimony was presented on behalf of white North Americans who have been imprisoned for protesting U.S. foreign and domestic policies and against militarism, war and nuclear armaments. The actions of these Petitioners have taken a variety of forms, from symbolic acts of sabotage of weapons of war by the Plowshares group, to armed actions against U.S. military or corporate targets supporting apartheid and intervention in Central America.

The Petitioners involved in these activities share a common belief that it is their responsibility as citizens of the United States to engage in acts of resistance intended to prevent or impede ongoing criminal activity in the conduct of the policies of the U.S. Government.

At the trials of these petitioners, United States courts have routinely denied them the opportunity to present a defense based upon a citizen's right to resist illegal state conduct and based upon their religious and/or political motivations. The Tribunal heard from an expert witness on international law that these defenses are well grounded in the First Amendment to the United States Constitution as well as the Tokyo and Nuremberg War Crimes Tribunals.

We conclude that the United States Government has criminalized and imprisoned white North Americans who have struggled in solidarity with national liberation movements and other peoples struggling for self-determination, for peace and against nuclear armaments and against racism, sexism and other forms of discrimination.

VI. Criminalization and Denial of the Rule of Law

> Whereas it is essential, if man is not to be compelled to have recourse, as a last resort, to rebellion against tyranny and oppression, that human rights should be protected by the rule of law....
>
> Preamble to the Universal Declaration of Human Rights
> December 10, 1948

It is a violation of international law for a state to attempt to criminalize the struggle of peoples to achieve self-determination. According to the authoritative United Nations Resolution 2625 (XXV) of 1970: "Every State has the duty to refrain from any forcible action which deprives peoples... of their right to self-determination and freedom and independence" and Resolutions 33/22 and 33/24 (1978), which condemn the imprisonment and detention of people fighting colonialism.

We have heard testimony of the development of a system of repression in the United States which uses the courts and judicial system as a key element to deny peoples' rights to self-determination and to disrupt people organizing to oppose illegal U.S. government policies.

The evidence shows that the U.S. Government is using a strategy which parallels certain other states (e.g., South Africa, Israel and British administration in the North of Ireland) confronting insurgent movements, through the creation of repressive and antidemocratic modifications to the legal system aimed at the suppression of radical political opposition. This counterinsurgency strategy allows for the enhancement of the power of law enforcement to surveil and infiltrate political groups as well as to coerce cooperation with police investigations and to criminalize political association.

The testimony showed that federal agents are authorized to spy on and infiltrate political, community and religious groups, and substantial evidence was received of such activity. In addition, the Tribunal was informed of the use of highly sophisticated electronic technology to carry out video and audio surveillance at the homes and workplaces of members and supporters of the Puerto Rican liberation movement.

Additionally, litigation in Puerto Rico has recently revealed the existence of more than 100,000 dossiers collected by the police on activists and supporters of the cause of independence who have been labeled "subversives" by the police because of their legitimate desire and work to end colonization.

The FBI also uses an internment power through the Federal grand jury to force cooperation with investigations into political activities under pain of imprisonment for refusal. The grand jury, a secret proceeding under the direction and control of the government, is used as a tool to intern political people. The government issues subpoenas to a secret hearing where there is no judge and where defense counsel is barred from attending. The coerced witness can be stripped of his/her fundamental right to remain silent and forced to answer all questions about political associations and activities. A refusal to appear or answer results in civil contempt penalties of up to 18 months or criminal contempt, which has no maximum limit of sentence.

Scores of activists in political movements have been imprisoned over the last fifteen years through this process. The government has even re-subpoenaed activists who have already served time in prison for refusing to collaborate with grand juries, in full knowledge that the person has not collaborated and will not do so in future. This effectively constitutes internment without trial or just cause.

Political activists are often charged with violations of broad conspiracy laws which rely on evidence of political associations and beliefs to prove "criminal" agreements. Two special statutes, Seditious Conspiracy and the Racketeer Influenced Corrupt Organizations (RICO) Act, specifically allow for the criminalization of membership in political organizations and national liberation movements. These statutes have been used to incarcerate political activists with lengthy sentences. The Seditious Conspiracy law specifically criminalizes opposition to U.S. governmental authority and has been used particularly against the Puerto Rican independence movement to criminalize its resistance to colonialism. Under this law a mere agreement to oppose U.S. authority with force, without proof of any act taken in furtherance of that agreement, is subject to a twenty-year sentence.

Political prisoners in the U.S. are also victims of false charges and prosecutions in which evidence favorable to the accused is deliberately suppressed. The Tribunal was presented with evidence of three particularly serious cases: Geronimo ji Jaga Pratt, Leonard Peltier and Dhoruba Bin-Wahad, in which the government deliberately destroyed and concealed evidence which would have established their innocence.

Those charged with politically motivated offenses are frequently held in preventive detention. Specifically, the evidence showed that the U.S. government's use of the Bail Reform Act of 1984 violates international law by designating as "dangerous to the community" persons who struggle for self-determination. This statute enables the government to jail its opponents for years without trial by means of indefinite preventive detention, thus denying the right to speedy trial or to release pending trial. When the FBI arrested fifteen Puerto Rican independentists on August 30, 1985, the government invoked this law to detain every accused. In spite of the community's clamor for these activists to be released, the courts found almost all of those arrested to be a "danger" to the community and held them under punitive isolation for periods between 18 months to almost four years without trial. The last to be released, Filiberto Ojeda Ríos, who had triple by-pass open heart surgery, was released only because the U.S. courts held that his lengthy pretrial custody had become an embarrassment to U.S. democracy. Ojeda was redetained for another year within three months of his release, as a result of a three-year-old charge arising out of his original arrest.

Excessive pretrial detention violates international law provisions Article II (1) of the Universal Declaration of Human Rights and Article 9 (3) of the International Covenant on Civil and Political Rights, as well as Article 8 (1) of the American Convention on Human Rights, 1969.

The Tribunal also received evidence of a series of repressive measures employed in political trials. Of particular concern was the evidence indicating a deliberate attack by the U.S. government on the independence and impartiality of the trial jury. The media have been used to poison attitudes in the community from which that jury will be selected. Just as disturbing is the use of "anonymous" trial juries. Under the latter system, by declaring the necessity to keep jurors' identities secret, those same jurors are inevitably prejudiced into believing that they have cause to fear the political defendants. This fear is further exacerbated by the intentional and excessive militarization of courtroom security employed to turn political trial courts into armed encampments. The Tribunal was informed of the use of multiple metal detectors, concrete bunkers, armed marshals, sharp-shooters on roofs adjacent to courthouses and, in one case, the erection of a special bullet-proof glass partition to separate the accused from the public.

The Tribunal also heard that trial venues are manipulated, particularly in the case of Puerto Rican activists, to deny them a trial in their homeland by their peers. Also, politically accused persons are routinely denied the right to present a full defense, including issues of necessity and justification under international law.

The use of the judicial system to repress political activists violates Articles 6, 7, 8, 9 and 10 of the Universal Declaration of Human Rights and Articles 9 and 14 of the International Covenant on Civil and Political Rights. Such conduct further violates Article 5 of the International Convention on the Elimination of All Forms of Racial Discrimination, 1966.

We find most disturbing that the U.S. government continues to incarcerate certain Petitioners despite documentary and other proof, disclosed after conviction, conclusively establishing that they did not commit the offenses for which they have been tried.

Excessive and Inhumane Sentences

The evidence showed that the United States government metes out the longest sentences of any country in the world to its political prisoners. Such excessive and disproportionate sentences imposed on persons active in self-determination struggles and in support of those struggles constitute torture, inhuman and degrading treatment in violation of Article 1 of U.N. Resolution 3452 (XXX), the Declaration on Protection from Torture, 1975.

Most of the political prisoners and Prisoners of War are serving the equivalent of natural life in prison. The Puerto Rican POW's, many of whom have already spent more than ten years in prison, have sentences averaging sixty-seven years. The judge who sentenced them stated that he would have given them the death penalty if it had been within his power.

Mumia Abu-Jamal currently sits on Pennsylvania's death row under sentence of death. Leonard Peltier has served over thirteen years of two consecutive life sentences; Sundiata Acoli is serving life plus thirty years; Herman Bell, Nuh Washington and Jalil Bottom are each serving twenty-five years to life.

Evidence was presented demonstrating that the political beliefs of Petitioners have been used as a basis to impose, in many instances, sentences of life imprisonment. Moreover, it is clear that the sentences imposed upon Petitioners are grossly disproportionate to sanctions imposed upon members of right wing and/or racist organizations convicted of similar offenses. For example, an assassin of Chilean diplomat Orlando Letelier was permitted in a plea agreement, wherein most charges were dropped, to receive a sentence of twelve years. Conversely, Petitioner Yu Kikumura, arrested with three pipe bombs in his car, was charged with twelve separate offenses and received an aggregate sentence of thirty years.

In 1986, a man convicted for planning and carrying out bombings, without making warning calls, of ten occupied health clinics where abortions were performed received a sentence of ten years and was paroled after 46 months. By contrast, Petitioner Raymond Levasseur was convicted of bombing four unoccupied military targets in protest against U.S. foreign policies and received a total sentence of forty-five years.

Another acknowledged abortion clinic bomber received seven years following his arrest in possession of over 100 pounds of explosives in a populous Manhattan apartment building. Petitioners Tim Blunk and Susan Rosenberg, charged with possession of explosives in a storage facility, each received sentences of fifty-eight years.

A Ku Klux Klansman, charged with violations of the Neutrality Act and with possessing a boatload of explosives and weapons to be used in an invasion of Dominica, received an eight-year sentence. Petitioner Linda Evans was convicted of purchasing four weapons with false identification and was sentenced to forty years, the longest sentence ever imposed for this offense in U.S. history.

The evidence also established that Petitioners have been denied parole as a penalty for refusing to renounce their political beliefs and associations.

VII. Torture and Cruel, Inhuman and Degrading Treatment

As part of the system of repression in the United States, we heard testimony that the government uses the prisons as a key element in its efforts to deny peoples the right to exercise self-determination and disrupt people organizing to oppose U.S. policies. The evidence established that the defendants use political beliefs and associations as a basis for classification and placement in highly punitive and restrictive isolation units.

The testimony of Dr. Stuart Grassian, a psychiatric expert on the serious and harmful effects of long-term isolation and solitary confinement, made a profound impression on the Tribunal. Evidence was also received which showed that in the early 1960s the U.S. prisons adopted a policy to put into effect brainwashing practices to "modify" the behavior of political prisoners and resisters.

Further, with full knowledge that conditions of solitary confinement, "small group isolation," and restricted sensory stimulation cause adverse psychopathological effects, the evidence also showed that the defendants have created and maintained prisons and control units embodying these conditions, such as the U.S. Federal Penitentiary at Marion, Illinois; the Women's High Security Unit at Lexington, Kentucky; and New York State's Shawangunk Correctional Facility.

The U.S. penitentiary at Marion, condemned by Amnesty International as violating virtually every one of the United Nations Standard Minimum Rules for the Treatment of Prisoners, holds more political prisoners and Prisoners of War than any other prison in the United States. Prison officials place political prisoners at Marion and retain them there for years although they do not meet the stated criteria for assignment there. A U.S. court which found the conditions at Marion to pass constitutional muster was nonetheless forced to describe them as "sordid" and "depressing in the extreme." Locked in their cells over 22 hours daily, the prisoners at Marion are denied meaningful human interaction and essential sensory stimulation. Their visits are noncontact through glass, and they are required to submit to a strip-search before and after visits. Their only source of drinking water is contaminated with carcinogenic chloroform and is reliably suspected of containing dangerous levels of toxins.

The Women's High Security Unit at Lexington, Kentucky, which was closed in 1988 as the result of a national and international human rights campaign, was also condemned by Amnesty International, which found that the Federal Bureau of Prisons deliberately placed political prisoners there in cruel, inhuman and degrading conditions because of their political beliefs. The conditions included two years of isolation in subterranean cells, daily strip-searches, sleep deprivation and denial of privacy to the extent that male guards were able to observe the women bathing. Expert medical testimony demonstrated that the conditions were calculated to destroy the women psychologically and physically.

We find that the defendants place political prisoners and prisoners of war in such prisons, and under such conditions, as part of their efforts to destroy them and to repress the struggles which they represent.

The evidence showed that in addition to the use of isolation in control unit prisons, the defendants also use other prison conditions as a means of breaking political prisoners and prisoners of war. These conditions include assassination; torture; sexual assault; strip and cavity searches, including such searches by male staff on women prisoners; punitive transfers; false accusations of violating prison rules; censorship; denial of religious worship; harassment of families; limitation of visits; and denial of necessary medical care.

Several political prisoners with cancer have been subjected to lengthy and punitive delays in diagnosis and treatment. Alan Berkman, suffering from Hodgkin's disease, has nearly died several times because prison officials have withheld necessary medical treatment and refused to place him in an appropriate medical facility. Kuwasi Balagoon, suffering with AIDS, was not diagnosed until ten days before his death. Silvia Baraldini's palpable abdominal lumps were ignored for months, only to reveal that she had an aggressive form of uterine cancer.

The evidence also showed that the courts of the U.S. have consistently condoned and sanctioned the application of such punitive and harmful conditions and their application to political prisoners and prisoners of war.

We find that the defendants' treatment of political prisoners and prisoners of war constitutes torture, cruel, inhuman and degrading treatment in violation of Article 6 the Universal Declaration of Human Rights and contravenes most of the United Nations Standard Minimum Rules for the Treatment of Prisoners. The U.S. Government is also in breach of the First, Eighth and Fourteenth Amendments to the Constitution of the United States and their equivalent provisions in the various state constitutions; the Declaration on the Protection of All Persons from Being Subjected to Torture and Other Cruel, Inhuman or Degrading Treatment or Punishment; the Convention Against Torture and Other Cruel, Inhuman or Degrading Treatment or Punishment; the International Covenant on Civil and Political Rights; the American Declaration of Human Rights; and the Geneva Convention and the protocols thereto.

Verdict
Based on the factual and legal foundations stated above, the Special Tribunal declares:

1. Within the prisons and jails of the United States exist substantial numbers of Political Prisoners and Prisoners of War.
2. These prisoners have been incarcerated for their opposition to U.S. government policies and actions that are illegal under domestic and international law, including the denial of the right to self-determination, and resistance to genocide, colonialism, racism and militarism.
3. The U.S. government criminalizes and imprisons persons involved in the struggles for self-determination of Native Americans, Puerto Ricans, and Black and Mexicano-Chicano activists within the borders of the United States.
4. Those peoples legitimately struggling for national liberation are not to be treated as criminals, but must be afforded the status of Prisoners of War under the Additional Protocol I to the Geneva Convention.
5. The U.S. government also criminalizes and imprisons white North-Americans and others who have worked in solidarity with struggles for self-determination as well as for peace and against nuclear arms, against racism, sexism and other forms of discrimination.
6. The criminal justice system of the U.S. is being used in a harsh and discriminatory way against political activists in the U.S.
7. The use of surveillance, infiltration, grand juries, preventive detention, politically motivated criminal conspiracy charges, prejudicial security and anonymous trial juries deprive political activists of fair trials guaranteed under domestic and international law.
8. Political people have been subjected to disproportionately lengthy prison sentences and to torture, cruel, inhumane and degrading treatment within the U.S. prison system.

Further the Tribunal calls on the U.S. government to:

1. Release all prisoners who have been incarcerated for the legitimate exercise of their rights of self-determination or in opposition to U.S. policies and practices illegal under international law.
2. Cease all acts of interference and repression against political movements struggling for self-determination or against policies and practices illegal under international law.

Source: Prison News Service

The Special International Tribunal on Political Prisoners and Prisoners of War in the United States received testimony from the following witnesses:

Dr. Imari Obadele
Representative of the
Black Movement

Ms. Assata Shakur
Former political prisoner
(videotape deposition)

Ms. Eve Rosahn
Representative of the
White North American
anti-imperialists

Sister Anne Montgomery
Former political prisoner
and representative of the
Plowshares Communities

Ms. Elizabeth Murillo
Representative of the
Mexican people living within
the borders of the U.S.

Ms. Rita Zengotita
Representative of the
Puerto Rican National
Liberation Movement

Mr. Jorge Farinacci
Puerto Rican activist in
the National Liberation
Movement, and on bond
awaiting criminal trial

Mr. Bobby Castillo
Former political prisoner
and representative of
the Native Americans

Mr. Ward Churchill
Representative of the
Native Americans

Mr. Michael E. Deutsch
Expert on U.S. repressive
strategy against movements
opposing U.S. policy and
seeking self-determination

List of Witnesses continued

Ms. Mary O'Melveny
Expert on disparate
sentencing

Ms. Patricia Levasseur
Former political prisoner

Mr. Majid Barnes
Representative of the
Black Movement

Ms. Alberta Africa
Former political prisoner
and member of MOVE

Dr. Stuart Grassian
Expert on the
pyschopathological
effects of long-term
solitary confinement

Mr. Rafael Cancel Miranda
Former political prisoner
and representative of the
Puerto Rican National
Liberation Movement

Mr. Dhoruba Bin-Wahad
Former political prisoner
and representative of the
Black Movement in the U.S.

Mr. Bob Robideau
Former political prisoner
and member of the Native
American Movement

Professor Francis Boyle
Expert on international law

Mr. Jaime Delgado
Former political prisoner
and representative of the
Puerto Rican National
Liberation Movement

Ms. J. Soffiyah Elijah
Expert on conditions
of confinement of
political prisoners and
POWs in the U.S.

Mr. William Morales
Former prisoner of war
(videotape deposition)

Documents Submitted by the Movements

Brief in Support of New Afrikan Political
Prisoners and Prisoners of War, Imari
Obadele, Kwame Afah,
Chokwe Lumumba, and Ahmed Obafemi

Report of the International
Indian Treaty Council

"We Will Remember," Leonard
Peltier Defense Committee

Memorandum of Support and
Clarification, American Indian
Movement of Colorado

Agents of Repression,
Ward Churchill and Jim Vander Wall

The COINTELPRO Papers, Ward
Churchill and Jim Vander Wall

FBI COINTELPRO documents on
the Puerto Rican independence,
Black, Native American, Mexican,
and anti-imperialist movements

Statement of Eve Rosahn

*Los Medios de Represión Utilizados por el
Gobierno de los Estados Unidos en Control
del Pueblo de Puerto Rico y Sus Medios
de Liberación Nacional y los Intentos de
Criminalizar la Lucha Puertorriqueña
por la Independencia, Comité Unitario
Contra la Represión y por la Defensa
de los Presos Políticos* (CUCRE)

(Repressive Measures Used by the U.S.
Government to Control the People
of Puerto Rico and Their Means of
National Liberation and the Attempts to
Criminalize the Struggle for Puerto Rican
Independence, the Unitary Committee
Against Repression and for the Defense
of Political Prisoners) (CUCRE).

Alvaro Hernandez and Alberto
Aranda, Chicano Political Prisoners;
Committee to Free Álvaro Hernández
and Alberto Aranda and the *Movimiento
de Liberación Nacional Mexicano*

Statement of Sister Anne Montgomery

Documents Submitted by Former Political Prisoners

Statement of Majid Barnes

Overview of the Black Struggle in the United States as It Relates to Political Repression and United States Domestic Policies of Genocide, Dhoruba Bin-Wahad

"The Case of Dhoruba BinWahad and the Existence of Black Political Prisoners in the United States," Dhoruba Bin-Wahad and Robert J. Boyle

Affidavit of Dhoruba Al-Mujahid Bin-Wahad

The State of Black America 1990, The Urban League

Statement of Alberta Africa

Statement of Jorge Farinacci

Leonard Peltier Writ of Habeas Corpus

Affidavit of Attorney Bruce Ellison

Statement of Patricia Helen Levasseur

Transcript of Interrogation of Jeremy Manning

Legal Dossiers of Political Prisoners and Prisoners of War Held in the United States, Submitted by Freedom Now! Campaign for Amnesty and Human Rights for Political Prisoners in the United States

Documents Submitted by Expert Witnesses

"Political Prisoners and the Denial of Fair Trials," Michael E. Deutsch.

"The Improper Use of the Federal Grand Jury: An Instrument for the Internment of Political Activists," Michael Deutsch, 75 *Journal of Criminal Law and Criminology*, 1159 (1984).

"New Developments in U.S. Judicial Repression: The Use of Counter-Insurgency Methods Against the Puerto Rican Independence Movement," Michael Deutsch, *The National Lawyers Guild Practitioner* (Winter 1988).

"Memorandum on Disparate Treatment of Political Prisoners and Prisoners of War by United States Authorities on Sentencing and Parole Eligibility," Mary O'Melveny.

"Conditions in Confinement," J. Soffiyah Elijah.

"Report of International Jurists' Visit with Human Rights Petitioners in the United States" (1979), Report and Findings.

"Report of Amnesty International on the United States Penitentiary at Marion, Il" (1987).

"Report of Amnesty International on the Women's High Security Unit at Lexington, KY" (1988).

"The Right of Citizen Resistance to State Crimes," Francis Boyle (1990).

"Preserving the Rule of Law in the War Against International Terrorism," Francis Boyle, 8 *Whittier Law Review* 735 (1986).

"The Hypocrisy and Racism Behind the Formulation of U.S. Human Rights Foreign Policy: In Honor of Clyde Ferguson," Francis Boyle, 16 *Social Justice* 71 (1988).

Written statements by individual petitioners

Section III.

The Quincentenary:
Diss'ing the "Discovery"

As the U.S. and Spain prepared to make a major spectacle of the fact that in 1492 a drunken sailor was discovered by a sophisticated group of peoples indigenous to what is now known as the Americas, many in the U.S. prepared to use the opportunity to focus on the plight of oppressed nationalities in general and native nations in particular. The selections in this section focus mostly upon work produced during this year that had an emphasis on political imprisonment.

One cannot look at indigenous issues in the U.S. without significant mention of the case of Leonard Peltier. Leonard Peltier was a member of the American Indian Movement who, in 1977, was convicted and sentenced to two consecutive terms of life imprisonment for the murder of two FBI agents. These agents were killed during a 1975 shoot-out on the Pine Ridge Indian Reservation. Even often-conservative Amnesty International has stated that "although Peltier has not been adopted as a prisoner of conscience, there is concern about the fairness of the proceedings leading to his conviction." Post-1992 documents on Peltier, especially from the International Indian Treaty Council, are also included here.

Weeding

Chrystos
2006

My garden in Autumn I want to send you this wind
Dancing through Madronas
Alder trees going gold
Sun piercing fog as the buoy sings her bells
These 2 Geese going south who cause me to pause
root in muddy hands
For their hoarse calls to everybody else
As they circle over the sound
This heat soothing my sweaty shoulders
Smell of Lavender I've gathered for winter letters
This Birch who brings me home
Moment of no walls no locks no guards no torture
No lonely cruel years
These two Apples
.. not quite "ready to pick"
who hang pale yellow blushed in dapples
They're the only ones & the first to grow
After years of tent caterpillar infestations
I refused to spray with poison
I planted this tree about the time they locked you up
Next year I pray for a better crop
& you
biting into one
on the way
to visit your mother
or go fishing
anyplace you can smell the wind

   for Leonard Peltier

239

Conference on the Oppressed Nationalities Within the U.S.

1492-1992: A Quincentenary of Continual Resistance to Genocide, Colonialism, Racism and Political Internment

December 6 and 7, 1991
in Celebration of International Human Rights Day, December 10, 1991
University of Illinois at Champaign-Urbana

On October 12, 1992, the eyes of the world will be upon the Americas and particularly on the United States. On that date, many in Europe and their Euro-American descendants will celebrate the 500th Anniversary of the "discovery" of the Americas by the "Admiral of the Ocean Sea," Christopher Columbus. Most of the rest of the world will remember 500 years of oppression, 500 years of genocide, racism, and colonialism—in reality, 500 years of resistance.

In the United States, the official circles will look upon that day as the day of their real birthday. As the great Caribbean thinker Frantz Fanon so ably observed in his book *The Wretched of the Earth*: "Two centuries ago, a former European colony decided to catch up with Europe. It succeeded so well that the United States of America became a monster, in which the taints, the sickness and the inhumanity of Europe have grown to appalling dimensions." Like their European forebears (who introduced to the Americas an avaricious system of capitalist exploitation, which sank to the lowest depths imaginable, even to the point of enslaving their own kind through indentured servitude), the Euro-American settlers in the U.S. set upon a course of stealing the land from Native Peoples first and, later, that of Mexicans and Puerto Ricans; of

---

This Chicago-based event, held after the dissolution of Freedom Now! but prior to the broad activities around the Quincentenary, brought together many of the key leaders involved with the 1990 Tribunal on U.S. Political Prisoners. Discussing historic and contemporary analysis about the nature of colonialism within the U.S., including the conquering of Native Nations as well as the continued occupation of the internal colonies of Puerto Rico, the Mexicano/ Chicano nation, and the New Afrikan nation, the conference centered around a call for united action in 1992. With the political prisoners as a centerpoint for this call, the conference succeeded in bringing together several hundred participants from diverse political, geographic, and national backgrounds. The event was sponsored by the African-American Cultural Center, *Casa Cultural Latina, La Raza* Movement, *Frente Estudiantil de Liberación Nacional,* If Not Now Movement, Progressive Resource/Action Cooperative, and the Student Government Association.

forcibly extracting labor from the Africans and, even worse, of attempting to strip all peoples of color of their humanity; of attempting to objectify these people to the point where they would lose their sense of self-worth, their sense of human dignity—where all they would see in their cradles was a "strong armed... sharp-eye... chain gang captain" as the great poet from Martinique Aimé Césaire would poetically describe.

In a period of world history when many of the progressive forces seem to be in disarray, when the West has proclaimed that "it has won," and that "history has ended," and that a "new world order" is being ushered into guarantee the continual control by Euro-Americans, we are called upon, not to celebrate the past 500 years of European domination. A domination that was initiated half a millennium ago with the onslaught of the European menace, which through pillage, plunder, violence, and hatred guaranteed the development of their region of the world (the North), and forced upon the rest of humanity a course of underdevelopment and self-hatred (the South.)

We are called upon, instead, to study the roots of the resistance of the forebears of New Afrikans (Blacks), Native Americans, Mulattoes, and Mestizos. It is imperative to learn the mysteries of their persistence and presence in these Americas 500 years after the Europeans, attempted to annihilate these populations with the only superior thing they possessed—their instruments of war.

It is against this backdrop of the two legacies of the Columbian Quincentenary—the legacy of pillage, and genocide, and of oppression, on the one hand, and the legacy of the continual resistance of peoples of color on this continent on the other—that a Conference on the Oppressed Nationalities Within the U.S. is scheduled to be held at the University of Illinois at Champaign-Urbana.

Goals and Objectives of the Conference:
The conference will seek to bring together experts as well as activists from the various national liberation struggles within the U.S. to delve into and reflect upon the two legacies of Columbus for people of color within the U.S. frontiers and to explore ways and means of confronting the 1992 Columbus Quicentenial Celebrations; this Conference will have the following specific objectives:

- To undo the myth of the "European Discovery" of the Americas and Columbus as the embodiment of the European Spirit of Adventure and of rugged individualism—Columbus and the Europeans who accompanied and later followed him were conquerors and not discoverers of a new world.
- To understand that one of the true legacies of Columbus was that he initiated the process of objectification and dehumanization of people of color through the introduction of the Chattel System in the Americas.

- To understand the true history of the U.S. as the country that became the depositor of the worst features of the European legacies of colonialism, genocide, and racism, which were institutionalized in its Constitution, a Constitution that provides for a Federalist System based upon the incorporation of land, but the marginalization, exclusion, and even destruction of the inhabitants of those lands. For example, in Article I, Section II, of the U.S. Constitution, it is stated that representation "...shall be apportioned among the several states... according to their respective numbers, which shall be determined by adding to the whole number of free persons, ... and excluding Indians... three fifths of all other persons." In other words, Indians were to be excluded as historical subjects—as Human Beings. As persons, Blacks were to constitute 3/5 of a Human Being. Some may point to the fact that this was changed by the 13th and 14th Amendments, but it should be noted that the 13th Amendment reads: "Neither slavery nor Involuntary servitude, except as a punishment whereby the party shall have been duly convicted, shall exist in the United States." One look at the racial makeup of today's penal population will suffice to indicate what groups of people held as wards of the state who have no rights. The prison population is overwhelmingly people of color.

- To understand the true legacy of genocide, colonialism, and racism, so in the words of Native American activist, Suzan Sharon Hoijo, we can "...turn our attention to making the next 500 years different from the past ones; to enter into a time of grace and healing. In order to do so, we must first involve ourselves in educating the colonizing nations, which are investing a lot, not only in silly plans, but in serious efforts to further revise history, to justify the bloodshed and destruction, to deny that genocide was committed here and to revive failed politics of assimilation as to the answer to progress. These societies must come to grips with the past, acknowledge responsibility for the present and do something about the future. It does no good to gloss over the history of excesses of Western Civilization, especially when the excesses are the cause of deplorable conditions today." (*Newsweek, Special Issue* (Fall/Winter 1991), p. 32.)

- To rediscover, analyze, and celebrate the heritage of a culture of resistance that grew and developed alongside, and in spite of, the dominant Euro-American culture of domination. A legacy that dates from the heroic resistance fighters, such as Urayoán, Cuauhtémoc, Toussaint L'Ouverture, Sojourner Truth, Denmark Vesey, Betances, Lolita Lebrón, Tiburcio Vásquez, Ricardo Falcon, Chief Joseph, Crazy Horse, Malcolm X, to the embodiment of that tradition today, the jailed or exiled patriots Leonard Peltier, Geronimo Pratt, Assata Shakur, Alejandrina Torres, Oscar López Rivera, as well their allies such as Silvia Baraldini, Alan Berkman, and Susan Rosenberg.

Diss'ing the "Discovery":
Political Prisoners and Prisoners of War in U.S. Prisons De-Celebrate the Columbus Quincentenary and Affirm 500 Years of Resistance

Meg Starr, Barbara Zeller
Co-editors of "Diss'ing the 'Discovery'"
1992

From the first Native American warriors captured by Columbus's soldiers, political prisoners have been both part of and a result of resistance to imperialism and genocide.

In the spring of 1992, several of us who have done defense work in support of political prisoners and prisoners of war in the u.s. wrote and asked the prisoners to comment on the Columbus madness. This booklet represents the unedited complete text of all the responses we got. As such, this collection is not reflective of the breadth of national struggle within these borders, nor of the proportion of revolutionary women spending their lives behind bars. To the prisoners who responded: Thanks! To those who didn't, we hope that our letters reached you through the prison censors.

What a year this has been. Smirking at the end of the war on Iraq, the imperialists started celebrating 500 years of genocide, rape, racism, and conquest. All over the world, their celebrations have been met with resistance. Wherever the replicas of the Niña, Pinta and Santa María have landed, Native American activists and others have demonstrated and disrupted. Right now, the corporation that contracted to bring the boats over is nearly bankrupt, and some of their engagements have been canceled.

An activist from the American Indian Movement (AIM) poured blood on himself in the strangely bloodless "Encounter" exhibit that has been touring the u.s. In Guatemala, Indigenous leaders from throughout the continent converged and marched on October 12, 1991. The ties between Indigenous Peoples of the Americas has been strengthened as 500 years of Resistance has been celebrated throughout the continent. The rebellion in Los Angeles

---

As a part of the campaign around the 500th anniversary of Columbus getting lost at sea, Resistance in Brooklyn co-founder Meg Starr and longtime anti-imperialist activist Barbara Zeller put together a booklet of writings by U.S. political prisoners. Several hundred copies of "Diss'ing the 'Discovery'" were distributed, mainly in New York City. It was part of an ongoing effort to give the political prisoners an active voice at all major U.S. radical and progressive events.

shook the complacency of u.s. imperialism. In Washington Heights, where the Dominican community rebelled against police violence and murder, one of the chants linked today's rebellions to the history of militancy dating back to the Taino struggles against the original conquistadors.

If we knew and could name all the acts of resistance committed this year, it would have an empowering effect upon us. The impact of all that shared feeling and action would dent the sense of powerlessness and isolation that imperialism creates and depends on.

This is why we wanted to bring you the voices of our prisoners. They were taken from us in the first place to attack our movements and intimidate activists. Now they are held under the ultimate conditions of isolation and disempowerment, yet they continue to resist. This fact can strengthen us all—if we keep in contact with them.

We ask all of you to think of your own creative ways to keep the political prisoners and prisoners of war with us in our lives and campaigns. We have printed the authors' addresses; write to them! We have also printed a partial listing of groups that do support work around PP's and POW's.

Finally, we dedicate this booklet to the millions of people over five centuries who were imprisoned or gave their lives to the fight against imperialism. We are highlighting Leonard Peltier and Mumia Abu-Jamal, two comrades whose cases deserve particular attention this year.

Free Them Now!

Diss'ing the "Discovery"

Political Prisoners and Prisoners of War in U.S. Prisons
De-Celebrate
the Columbus Quincentennary
and affirm
500 Years Of Resistance

with contributions from
* Sundiata Acoli * Marilyn Buck * Mark Cook * Edwin Cortés *
* Elizam Escobar * Larry Giddings * David Gilbert *
* Jaan Laaman * Mondo Langa * Ray Levasseaur * Alberto Rodríguez *
and updates on
* Mumia Abu-Jamal * Norma Jean Croy * Leonard Peltier *

III.3.A
The Real Columbus
A Book Review of Hans Koning's
Columbus: His Enterprise (Monthly Review)

David Gilbert

1992 is the quincentennial of Columbus' landing in America. It will be a year marked by lavish celebrations—and strong protests—peaking on Oct. 12.

Hans Koning's iconoclastic *Columbus: His Enterprise* presents the historical Columbus, "a man greedy in large ways and cruel on a continental scale," as opposed to the hagiography we were taught in school. The main section of this book was first published in 1976; Monthly Review Press issued this 1991 edition with a new introduction and a useful afterward by Bill Bigelow on using this book to help teach critical thinking in the high school classroom.

Contrary to the myth, Columbus was not unique or even unusual in holding that the world was round—this was the predominant understanding among educated Europeans at the time. Where he bucked the conventional wisdom was in his firm belief that the world was much smaller and Asia much more extensive than the prevailing estimates. Thus Columbus mistakenly calculated the westward distance from Europe to Japan to be only ¼ of what is actually is. This miscalculation was the basis for his staunch belief that the trip was within the range of the ships of his day.

What was extraordinary about his character, in Koning's view, was his fierce determination to effect his vision and his ability to convince others to support him. Also, Columbus did have the good luck and the sailing knack to start from the Canary Islands, much farther south than the Portuguese sailors who had tried the western route before him. Thus his three ships picked up the strong trade winds blowing west that could carry them to America before their provisions ran out.

Columbus professed a fervent Catholicism and wrote passionately of his mission to "convert the heathens." Before setting sail, Columbus demanded and obtained for himself and his heirs the extravagant terms of 10% of all the wealth that would arrive by this new route to Asia, forever more.

On Oct. 12, 1492, Columbus made his first contact with Native Americans, the Arawaks, in the Bahamas. He described them in his log: "Some brought us water, others food." "They later swam out to the ships... and brought us [gifts]. They willingly trade everything they own." "They do not bear arms, and do not know them." "I believe they could easily be made Christians...."

But none of these Arawaks ever was converted. The Spaniards' insistence on seizing captives, their forcing of Arawak women to be sex slaves, and their

---

Originally reprinted with permission from *Downtown* magazine.

245

thirst for gold caused a deterioration in relations. All the 10 Commandments were rolled into one for Columbus: Profit. On the second voyage, still having failed to find the fabled Asian wealth by 1495, Columbus seized 1,500 Arawaks and picked the 500 strongest to cram into his ships returning to Spain. Three hundred souls survived the journey to be sold into servitude, but so many of them died in captivity that his version of the slave trade could not prosper. Columbus intensified his obsession for gold.

The quest centered on the island of Hispaniola (now Haiti and the Dominican Republic). There, a few gold ornaments and various confused myths about Asia led Columbus to convince himself that he had found the fabled land of overflowing fields of gold. In reality, Hispaniola just had a few rivers carrying grains of gold in alluvial form.

Koning's passage, "Death of a Nation," vividly presents the unbridled gold lust and unspeakable human cruelty at the heart of the enterprise. It is worth quoting at length:

> Every man and woman, every boy or girl of fourteen or older, in the province of Cibao (of the imaginary gold fields) had to collect gold for the Spaniards.... Every three months, every Indian had to bring to one of the forts a hawks' bell filled with gold dust. The chiefs had to bring in about ten times that amount. In the other provinces of Hispaniola, twenty-five pounds of spun cotton took the place of gold.

> Whoever was caught without a token (proving payment) was killed by having his or her hands cut off. There are old Spanish prints... that show this being done: the Indians stumble away staring with surprise at their arm stumps pulsing out blood.

> There were no gold fields, and thus, once the Indians had handed in whatever they still had in gold ornaments, their only hope was to work all day in the streams, washing out gold dust from pebbles. It was an impossible task, but those Indians who tried to flee into the mountains were systematically hunted down with dogs and killed, to set an example for the others to keep trying.

> By that time there was no longer a possibility of mass resistance... The island was so well pacified that a Spaniard could go anywhere and take any woman or girl, take anything, and have the Indians carry him on their backs as if they were mules. Thus it was at this time that the mass suicide began: the Arawaks killed themselves with cassava poison. During those two years of the administration of the brothers Columbus, an estimated one half of the entire population of Hispaniola was killed or killed themselves.

By 1540 the entire Arawak nation on Hispaniola, perhaps up to one million people, had vanished in a total genocide. The killing off of the Native Americans also became the impetus for the massive trade in African flesh to provide slave labor in the Americas. While not the focus of his book, Koning does mention that, for example, in Haiti in 1804 there were only 600,000 surviving descendants of the estimated two million Africans that had been imported into that area throughout the slave trade.

As we approach the quincentennial, Columbus' individual character is not really that important. Even if he personally had been a saint, what matters is the nature of the era he ushered in; the glorification of Columbus has been used as a perfume to cover the stench of the ensuing conquest. As it happens, Columbus was indeed a fitting representative of a much larger enterprise based in colossal greed, unprecedented genocide, and the horror of slavery. The standard textbook version of Columbus is nothing but the unabashed propaganda of the conquerors.

CHRISTOPHER COLUMBUS

WANTED:
FOR CRIMES AGAINST HUMANITY

III.3.B

If Columbus Had Not Come

Sundiata Acoli

Every now and then i catch myself daydreaming of what i'd be, or have been, if Columbus had not come. Frankly, i can only conjure up fuzzy images of being surrounded by kids somewhere on a sunny beach—in Afrika. I guess that proves that Assata knew me better than i knew myself, or that perhaps 20 years of imprisonment has somewhat clouded my childhood ambitions. In any event, i would have been perfectly happy to have been simply "left alone," that is, left "undiscovered" by European explorers, left free to live my life as i chose (as long as i didn't transgress others), and left free to depart this world peaceably, hopefully having left it a little better place than when i entered.

But the reality is that Columbus came—and he came as a conqueror, a murderer, a robber, and a racist. It changed my life forever, altho yet unborn. Wherever Columbus and other European explorers went, they murdered, raped, robbed, kidnapped, enslaved, cheated and lied. They called it many names—"discovering the New World," "spreading christianity and Western Civilization," and "pioneering," but reduced to its lowest term it was simply "Murder, Incorporated." They murdered in Afrika, Asia, Oceania, and in the Americas. And whenever they went, people resisted. They fought. Even when defeated and enslaved, people continued to resist. They slacked in their work, sabotaged, ran away, stole, cheated, lied, mugged, robbed, rioted, and rebelled.

U.S. imperialism today continues the tradition of Columbus, but in a more sophisticated manner, and under a different set of banners—"stopping Communism," "protecting Human Rights," and "spreading Democracy and the Free Market System." Now they murder thru the U.S. Army, Third World proxy armies and death squads, paid assassins, the police, and the death penalty. They rob thru "taxation without representation," high prices for shoddy goods and services, starvation wages, and thru unjust fines and penalties. They kidnap thru Children's Courts that rule mothers unfit and then send their children to detention centers and orphanages for adoption. They cheat by supplying inadequate health care, inadequate schools, and inadequate housing. They lie thru their mass media rife with stories and innuendoes which paint non-white people as nothing but a bunch of "welfare queens," "Willie Horton" rapists, crackheads, street criminals, Black racists, whiners, slackers, and polluters of the world with "illegitimate" babies.

So it's not too surprising that there are people who still resist today. Nor is it surprising that instead of individual and anarchistic acts of resistance— slacking work, stealing, mugging, robbing, and rioting—there would be those who sought/seek to organize the individual acts of resistance into a coherent mass—Marcus Garvey of the UNIA, W. E. B. Du Bois of the NAACP, Martin Luther King of SCLC, Malcolm X of the NOI/OAAU, Huey P. Newton of the BPP, and Assata Shakur of the BLA.

In response to such resistance (organized and unorganized) America cranks up its "Big Lie" machine and sends in its police to murder, maim, suppress, and imprison them as common criminals, thugs, bandits, cop killers, and the like.

And so goes the cycle, from one generation to the next. There are over 150 Political Prisoners and Prisoners of War (PP's/POW's) from the last generation still imprisoned today. They are PP's/POW's because they are imprisoned for organizing mass resistance to, and for resisting themselves, the colonization and genocide, and modern-day enslavement of oppressed nationalities here in America, by U.S. imperialism. The next generation will do no less and is already beginning to stir itself against the legacy of Columbus. They carry on a 500 (and more) years' tradition that will never end until today's "Columbus," and all his admirers, wish that he had not come.

III.3.C

Autopsy

Wopashitwe Mondo Eyen we Langa

five-pointed skulls on a field of blue
razor-edged lines in a bone-white land and
blood-red
running long as rows of cotton
as forced marches from tribal lands
to reservations
a cloth haunted
by the ghosts of dred scott
chief joseph
emmet till
and others whose spirits do not lie still
but wail
in the night of this seamless weave.

III.3.D

In History's Back Pages:
The African/Native American Alliances

Wopashitwe Mondo Eyen we Langa

The pages of history are replete with testimonies, by European explorers, traders, etc., of the grand levels of the advanced civilizations of both "Indians" (the indigenous peoples of the "Americas") and Africans. Often it was the case that these civilizations, which Europeans encountered, contrasted with conditions of widespread barbarism in their own countries of Europe. And typically, though not without exception, the native peoples of both Africa and the Americas greeted their European "discoverers" with friendliness and hospitality. We know, however, how this friendliness and hospitality came to be "rewarded."...

The agents of death of Africans were the same as and similar to those employed in the slaughter of Native Americans.

Both of these texts by Wopashitwe Mondo Eyen we Langa originally reprinted with permission from *mObetter news*.

III.3.E

A Short Story Still Untitled

Alberto Rodríguez

Ixquin stared into the phantom's eyes as lightning entered her, tearing out her entrails. As she lay down, her life pouring out of her, she could see the people of her yacayeque (village) vanishing, no one escaped.

The old bohite (mystic) woke from her herb-induced trance, exhausted.

Huasyoan, the yacayeque's cacique (chief), sat on his dujo (low stool) surrounded by nitainos (wise men).

"I saw what looked like men," said the cacique, "but they covered their white skin. They came in three large canoes, but came onto the shore in smaller canoes. They have set up a camp near the shore and are there now. They did not see me for I did not want them to."

"They are gods," interrupted one of the nitainos. "We must go and pay homage to them." "No!" said Ixquin. "They come to kill and enslave us." All the nitainos began to talk softly among themselves. Many of them did not like her because they felt that the yacayeque's bohite should be a man. Their fear of her powers and their cacique's great respect for her kept them from voicing their opposition. The cacique listened quietly and patiently to the chatter of the nitainos. Finally he stood up and said: "We must stay away from these strangers until we know why they come."

Soon the whole yacayeque was talking about the strangers:

"They are gods."

"No! They are not. Ixquin says that they come to destroy us."

"That old woman does not know of what she speaks."

251

"Our bohite has always been truthful to us."

'Tomorrow some of us are going to gather some yucca, maize, batata and yahutia and give them to the strangers as offerings to pay homage to them."

"I will only give offerings and pay homage to our god Yocahu and our cemis (lesser gods)."

The next morning Huasyoan, his wife, Suguax, and Ixquin watched as a small procession left the yacayeque toward the stranger's camp. They never returned.

Several days later the cacique called together his bravest warriors—Agueymaca, Guarioyoan and Uradamaca. He told them, "We must go and find out what happened to our people who went to the strangers' camp."

The cacique put on his guanin (gold plate worn as a necklace to demonstrate power and authority). All of them carried macanas (wooden clubs) as well as bows and arrows.

They quietly approached the strangers' camp, and what they saw filled their eyes with horror. Some of the nitainos had been tied to trees, their bodies flayed. Most were dead; those who were alive prayed to Yocahu to let them die to end their pain and suffering. Some women lay dead on the ground, their bodies spread grotesquely in pools of blood. Those who were still alive were tied up. The children wept openly.

Without hesitation Huasyoan, Agueymaca, Guarioyoan and Uradamaca hurled themselves against the strangers. They fought valiantly, but their wooden macanas were no match for the strangers' weaponry. Several of the white strangers were injured, but all the Taino warriors were quickly killed. During the struggle Carmaj, one of the children, was able to free herself from her bonds and escape into the forest. This was soon discovered and a search party set out to recapture her.

Carmaj ran as quickly as she could. Upon reaching her yacayeque, she fell from exhaustion. Carmaj soon woke and found herself in Suguax's bohio (hut). Ixquin poured cool water over her brow.

"What happened, little Carmaj?" asked Suguax. For a moment she could not respond, for it all seemed a fantasy.

"Please," insisted Suguax. "What happened to the nitainos, your father and mother, your brothers, all those who went to the strangers' camp? Where is Huasyoan?"

Carmaj sat up and rubbed her eyes with her hands. She then began to speak:

"We all marched right into the strangers' camp. At first they were friendly, smiling, laughing and eating the food we brought them. They were especially interested in the gold of the nitainos. Several of the strangers went into the forest with one of the nitainos. Soon they returned without the nitaino. They were very angry." Carmaj lowered her head and began to cry. Suguax embraced the girl and began to softly caress her hair.

"Please, Carmaj, tell us what happened," pleaded Suguax.

"When the strangers returned," continued Carmaj, "they were very angry. They spoke to their cacique who they called the admiral. Then the white-skinned men turned on us. The nitainos and the all the men were captured and tied up. Many fought back and were killed or tied to trees and cut with shiny blades. Some of the women were killed because they fought back. Those who didn't had terrible things done to them and then they were tied up."

"We must leave the yacayeque right now," said Ixquin. "The strangers will come here and destroy us. We must flee into the mountains."

"Where is Huasyoan, my husband, our cacique?" asked Suguax.

"Dead!" cried Carmaj.

Suguax stood silently for a moment. She then walked out of her bohio into a brilliant sun. All the Tainos of the yacayeque were in the batey (space for games, meetings and fiestas) in front of the cacique's bohio.

Suguax began to speak in a strong, vibrant voice:

"Our cacique is dead. The white strangers have come to destroy us. They will come to our yacayeque to kill or enslave us. If we are to live, we must go into the mountains."

The people were confused and began to talk among themselves. Several of the surviving nitainos as well as several young boys not yet old enough to be warriors stared at Suguax, but when she looked straight into their eyes, they looked away.

Ixquin and Carmaj came out of the bohio and each stood at Suguax's side. Ixquin placed a cacique's guanin on Suguax's neck while Carmaj placed a macana in her hand. The women Aliquin, Sudee and Sumaj went to their bohios and returned armed with their now dead husband's weapons, to stand by Suguax.

Later when the invaders marched into the yacayeque it was completely abandoned.

The Tainas found a redoubt in the forest. All learned how to use weapons and all searched for food. Late into the night, Ixquin sat with Suguax.

"The one called the admiral," said Ixquin, "wants the shiny metal we use to make the guanin and the nitainos' ornaments. He cares nothing of how many of us he kills."

"Then we will hide forever," said Suguax.

"No, my cacique!" replied Ixquin. "We cannot hide forever, for the admiral will never stop searching for us until he destroys us all."

"What are we to do?" asked Suguax.

"Kill the admiral," said Ixquin.

The next day Ixquin and several others went into the forest in search of berries. As she bent over to pick the little fruit to satisfy her hunger, she heard a noise behind her. She turned around as quickly as her old body would allow her. Ixquin stared into the bearded white phantom's empty pale eyes as a cold blade entered her, tearing out her entrails. As she laid on the ground, her life bleeding away from her, she could see the people of her yacayeque being slaughtered or captured. Suguax, Alguin, Sudee and Sumaj shot arrows at the white invaders, giving some of the children a chance to escape. They all fled deeper into the forest.

Suguax realized the futility of running away. She gathered all that remained of her yacayeque and together silently marched to the white invaders camp. When they finally reached it, the invaders had boarded their canoes and were rowing toward their large canoes.

Suguax knew where Huasyoan had a war canoe hidden. It was still there when they reached it. They pushed it into the water, climbed in and started to row toward the white men's canoe. The admiral watched the Tainos' canoe approach with both curiosity and suspicion.

Suguax stood at the head of the canoe waving her macana over her head. As the war canoe approached the admiral's ship, she shouted: "Please Yocahu, give us the strength to kill the admiral, so that you good people can live!"

Dear Sir,

As I know, many will be rejoiced at the glorious success in my voyage. I have discovered a great many islands inhabited by numberless people, and of all I have taken possession without opposition. The people are so unsuspicious and so generous with what they possess, that no one who has not seen it would believe it. They never refuse anything that is asked for. They even offer themselves, and show so much love they would give their very hearts.

I was very attentive to them, and strove to learn if they had any gold, seeing some of them with little bits of metal hanging at their noses. I took by force some of the natives, that from them we might gain some information. They are still with me and still believe that I come from heaven.

As for monsters, I found none except in one village inhabited by a people considered in all the isle as most ferocious. They possess many canoes. The women have no feminine occupation, but use bows and arrows of cane, and eat human flesh.

Many other things of value will be discovered by the men I left behind me, as I stayed nowhere when the wind allowed me to pursue my voyage.

Thus I record what has happened written on board the Caravel, off the Island of San Juan, on the 15th of October 1493.

Yours to command
The Admiral
Christopher Columbus

III.3.F

The Uprising

Raymond Luc Levasseur

The Los Angeles uprising isn't about a free lunch or integrated lunch counters. It's about those whose lives have been diss'd: disinherited, displaced, discriminated against, and disenfranchised. It's about 500 years of European-exported genocide. The entire state of California sits on stolen Indian and Mexican land. There is nothing legitimate about this kind of theft, nor the institutional racism and violent repression that accompanies it.

The most intense flames of this uprising have burned in predominantly Black South Central LA. This community is one of many emanating from the African Diaspora and its historically developed land base in the Black Belt south. Today's resistance draws its lifeblood from the earliest slave rebellions and is embodied in the descendants of Malcolm X. There is no "middle of the road" after the Middle Passage.

There are common threads between the LA uprising and the Palestinian Intifada. Both defy overwhelming superior police and military forces. Both constitute dispossessed nations fighting for basic human rights. And at the heart of their struggles is the right to national identity and land. The LA uprising has broken through one of oppression's fundamental realities: its disarming effectiveness at turning its victims against each other instead of their oppressors. The rising has redirected the rage of its participants against the moral bankruptcy of capitalism and white supremacy.

As of this writing, the battleground has claimed 50 lives in four days, most by police gunfire. In the usual course of events, LA's killing grounds would take two weeks to claim as many lives. The significant difference is that instead of passively waiting for death to stalk them, the people went on the offensive. Or what might be considered a vigorous self-defense, since they were going to die anyway through police violence, internecine warfare, alcohol and drug poisoning, and social neglect.

The uprising resulted in extensive property damage. While there was some needless destruction, the people's firebombs were strikingly accurate at rooting out capitalism's ghetto infrastructure. For the most part people avoided damaging schools, mosques, churches, and housing. Most damaged property was corporate and absentee owned. More than one Bank of Amerikkka branch was torched into oblivion. These are the businesses that bleed the community with overpriced staples of life, then take the money and run. These are the purveyors of unlimited supplies of alcohol. It was like pouring salt on leeches as the profiteers squirmed in their suburban enclaves.

When faced with uprising and mass resistance, the government has historically responded with military intervention. From one decade and century to another: Watts, East St. Louis, Chicago, New York—the police and military have combined to exact a fearful death toll. It was during the 1965 Watts rebellion that Darryl Gates—the Bull Connor of LA—drew his first blood as a police commander. From Watts, Black rage swept through Cleveland in '66, and Newark, Detroit, and other cities in 1967. After returning from Viet Nam, I traveled to Detroit and saw the immense destruction. In Viet Nam I've seen extensive bomb damage from the door of a helicopter; in Detroit, I saw it from the asphalt. Both areas burned in wars for self-determination. The deployment of federal troops is predictable, but uprisings that trigger deployment demand attention and demonstrate the potential power of the people.

This is not a time for apology and accommodation. If I began writing all the names of those murdered and beaten senseless by the police, I'd be writing until forever. I could never catch up with the reality. With each death is a killer cop who walks free. I know I've written this before, but it's something I can't forget. It shouldn't be forgotten. I will write but two: Philip Pannell, a Black teenager from Teaneck, New Jersey, who died from a police officer's bullet as his hands were raised over his head. And Ralph Canady, a personal friend, who was murdered in cold blood by police in Baltimore, Maryland. No civil rights enquiries were initiated into these murders. There rarely are. It took 50 deaths in LA and the U.S. Government's embarrassment in the court of world opinion to legitimize a federal inquiry into the Rodney King case.

Thousands have been arrested in LA, and the federal and state governments have formed a special task force to prosecute them. Steal a pair of shoes and go to jail; rip off the livelihood of a people and you're rewarded with profits and high office. These prosecutions will be punitive and vindictive. Years after the Watts rebellion, some of its participants are still in California prisons. Black Nationalist Ahmed Evans was sentenced to death following the Cleveland uprising. I first met Ralph Canady after he'd been railroaded to prison in the wake of the 1968 rebellion in Nashville's Black community. Colonial rebellions strike fear in the bowels of American capitalism, and it'll spare no effort to imprison the most rebellious. Still in prison, some for decades, are those women and men who represent their peoples aspirations to be free: Leonard Peltier, Geronimo Pratt, Mumia Abu-Jamal, Gary Tyler, Alejandrina Torres, Abdul Haqq, and many others. As Mandela put it—there's no easy walk to freedom.

The federal deployment in LA includes elements of the U.S. Marshall's Service, who made their notorious mark in history tracking fugitive slaves, the racist dogs of the Border Patrol, and the Bureau of Prisons. The presence of the latter is a further indication of what lies in store for the rebellious poor: more prisons in a country that's already choking with them. The U.S. has more steel cages than any country on earth, and imprisons more Blacks per capita than South Africa. I live in this compressed nightmare of a gulag. Each year of my imprisonment, I've endured the exile with those from Amerikkkas' barrios and ghettos, including South Central and East LA. There's no denying this apartheid reality or the necessity to break its chains.

Nat Turner said that the struggle for freedom was not a war for robbery or to satisfy passions. Opportunists exist everywhere, but most of that unleashed the power of mass resistance did not act with criminal intent. They are pursuing their very survival. Their intent is to demand respect and gain some measure of control over their lives and community. What criminal intent exists is primarily represented by police violence and a system that fosters and protects the real criminals: that rotten element that lives in bourgeois splendor derived from exploiting and defrauding societies' most vulnerable. Their rapacity is exceeded only by their ruthlessness and disregard for the value of human life. The rule of class and white supremacy ensures they can operate with impunity.

No doubt the system will attempt some band-aid application to problems reflected in the uprising. This has been attempted before, but hasn't worked. That's one of the messages from the streets—government money, with all its bureaucratic strings, may alleviate some conditions in the short term, but it cannot deal with the basic causes that underlie a people's subjugation. There's only one serious context in which to discuss money, and that is reparations. Billions of dollars in reparations. Millions of acres of land in reparations. However, a government and general population that applauds the agonizing death of Iraqi children caused by U.S. bombing raids will not seriously consider reparations simply to quell the impact of 50 death and property destruction in LA.

The situation is desperate but not hopeless. To rise from ashes and bondage requires a well-organized and militant resistance that's willing and prepared to take it to the limit. For amerikkka's most oppressed, there's no viable alternative to revolutionary nationalism and socialism.

There was widespread participation by Mexicans in the LA uprising, though the media has manipulated coverage to keep them voiceless. Their involvement is understandable given the conditions of survival and the fact the amerikkka occupies their land. Los Angeles was forcibly taken from the Mexicans in 1846.

There was marginal participation by young whites in LA as well as in actions in other cities. This is encouraging, but it is not enough. Historically, white people have laid claim to privilege based on race. There are exceptions, but they're not the rule. White power rules in amerikkka, as is clearly evident in the presidency, congress, supreme court, and corporate boardrooms. You can see it in the faces of the swine wearing the badge of the LAPD. You see it in celebrations of Columbus. There are those that embrace the racist ideology that permeates this country; others are simply complacent when confronted with its effects. Both are part of the problem.

For the predominantly white Left and broader groupings of "progressives," there exists a heightened call to action. Where are the millions who created a vibrant antiapartheid movement? Where are all those that provided political support and material aid to Nicaragua and El Salvador? Where are the near million strong that attended the recent pro-choice demonstration in Washington? And where the hell is organized labor? It's time for this conspiracy of silence to end.

For poor and working-class whites, the choice is clear: collaboration with a system based on white supremacy, or combating it. When John Brown was asked why he fought to end slavery, he replied, "I act from principle. My objective is to restore human rights." When Malcolm X was asked what whites who care about Black people's struggle could do to support them, he replied, "Do as John Brown did." It's time to get down to dismantling the apartheid legacy of slavery. It's time to organize a 20th-century abolition movement, and to provide aid and assistance to freedom fighters. It's way beyond the time of no return.

III.3.G

A Letter from Mark Cook

Mark Cook

Dear Friends,

I sincerely believe in the abolition of all economic, social and political double-standards. These are the bases for violations of human rights.

I find no pleasure in celebrating the invasion of the Afrikan continent and the carrying away of the Afrikan Tribes to the Americas for purpose of slavery. I adopt no double-standard to support the 1992 U.S. celebration of the invasion and 500-year colonization of the Americas.

True, the invasion of the Americas was a historical turning point for many people, but that event in history extended into unaccountable, disgraceful acts which violated—and continue to violate—the human rights of the Native Tribes in the Americas. Unwarranted invasions of lands and acts of genocide against the peoples are not to be celebrated. Such celebration gives credence to overt violations of human rights. I join the Native Tribes in the Americas in memorializing this day as a permanent day of mourning for the Native Tribes in America and as a permanent day of repentance for those who benefited from that invasion 500 years ago.

We must now and forever assert ourselves as abolitionists against violations of human rights throughout the world. We shall very likely be criminalized for being the activist conscience of the world but we are needed to make clear that barbarism has no place in a civilized world.

Be an abolitionist for a better future for us all.

Love and Struggle!

III.3.H

Prayer from the Americas

Marilyn Buck
1988

after reading Eduardo Galeano's La Memoria del Fuego

Oh my God
so gold and pure
my golden God
in whose name
I offer blood
washing the new world red.

My God of gold
more brilliant than the sun
(oh, but the one God is not
the Sun god
of the Aztecs or the Mayas)

I say to you
the son of the one God
died to save our sins
not their sins
and they must pay.

My God
Praise him with gold
Cultures must fail
Destruction must rain
on all who would stop
my holy mission
I, man of the Inquisitions.

III.3.I

Rejecting White Supremacy:
Thoughts from a North American Brother

Jaan Laaman

Repression breeds resistance—Resistance means struggle—Struggle brings results—Unity leads to victory.... These are only slogans, easily and often tossed around, yet they are widely understood because they are grounded in reality. Any political activist, and certainly any revolutionary, has spent at least some serious time considering resistance, struggle, unity and methods to victory. A minimum level of unity among the exploited and oppressed, among the victims of all sorts, is a prerequisite for achieving any positive results and of course total victory.

The u.s. is a country wracked by racial, class and gender inequalities. The recent uprising in LA gave Bush's new world order a very public and well-deserved black eye. The good people of Los Angeles put the issues of forceful struggle and rebellion back on the front burner.

The central issue in the LA rebellion was racism. The racism of the white cops who savagely beat Rodney King, of the judge and prosecutor who sent the trial to the white suburb of Simi Valley, of the white police-oriented jury who sided with the cops and generally of the miserable conditions of life that millions of African people live in, in South Central Los Angeles and around the country. The u.s. was founded and built on genocide and theft of the lands and lives of people of color: the indigenous Native Americans, the Africans brought here as slaves, the Mexican and Puerto Rican people whose land was taken and incorporated as states or colonies. Since those times, immigrants of color, Asian, African, Latino, have continued to face discrimination and prejudice, including vigilante-klan-type attacks.

Jaan Laaman

260

DISS'ING THE "DISCOVERY" • III

From the founding of the u.s.a., its major institutions have been and are inherently racist, and by racist is meant white supremacist. White supremacy is both an ongoing ideology and day to day reality. It is permeated throughout the culture and life of this country. Any number of examples can be drawn from all areas of life to show this and it's hard to believe that anyone living here could not be aware of it. In fact feigning ignorance or "wondering what Black people want" is but another manifestation of white supremacy. Certainly all Blacks and other people of color have no doubt that racism is a reality of life in america.

The left and progressive community and movements are not immune to racism. This isn't to say that any credible or sincere progressive, let alone revolutionary group or movement tolerates overt white supremacy, but as products of this society, even the opposition movements are affected by this most central flaw of u.s. society.

Raising this issue is not meant to illicit some kind of liberal guilt tripping or despair. As leftists and revolutionaries and particularly those of us who rely on the insight of marxist tools of analysis, it does mean that we should renew our efforts at understanding the pervasive and insidious role that racism plays, so as to continue to expose it and root it out. The fight against racism is a moral, social, political, economic and just struggle. But most importantly, without recognizing, confronting and overcoming white supremacy, revolution in america will never succeed.

Our, that is, People's, history in the u.s. is replete with examples of strong struggles being sabotaged and defeated because racism was effectively used to split the people. On the positive side, there have always been organizations and individuals who have fought against white supremacy. In the mid 1800s, the Workingman's Party and the Knights of Labor organized Black workers and class unity. John Brown and his people used force and arms to battle racism and racists. The IWW stood for and defended all labor. The CIO and communists organized Blacks and white. In the '50s and '60s, whites joined in civil rights efforts and supported Black Liberation. Support for national liberation and anti-imperialism is understood by many today as an essential part of fighting for socialist revolution within the multinational reality that is the u.s. of a.

All these positive examples, unfortunately, are outweighed by the more usual practices of racial discrimination and prejudice. Whites are taught early and often to fear and dislike people of color, especially Blacks. Not all white people go for this or go for it forever. Rejection of racist attitudes is a positive first step, but must be followed up with a broader understanding.

White supremacy isn't just a twisted ideology based on ignorance and falsehoods about culture, history, etc.; it is also a means and justification for denying the right of nationhood to people of color. The u.s. is a multicultural and multinational entity. People from just about every nation and culture have come to live here, with most retaining some of their customs. More substantially, the u.s. consists of several actual nations. By nation here is meant the historically accepted and internationally required basis of people having a common history, language, culture, land and economic relations. The dominant u.s.a. nation originated from European settlers. This nation was founded and is still largely ruled by wealthy white males. Although genocide was committed against the indigenous people of the Americas, nations of Native Americans still exist. Africans, kidnapped and carried to this continent as slaves, have by their long history and reality evolved into a separate new African nation. Puerto Rico, lying far from u.s. shores, but politically, economically and militarily controlled by the u.s., is clearly a nation in bondage. The battle against white supremacy has to recognize and take up support for the right of nations to self-determination. This is a crucial basis for building multinational unity among all those victimized in one way or another by the u.s. By recognizing a people's right to determine their own national destiny, lay the foundation for the unity of equals. In a similar way, men recognizing women's right and need for equality and an end to sexist stereotyping and activities, is a necessary basis for a united effort of men and women in the Freedom Struggle.

Serious and lasting unity only comes about through recognizing and understanding other people and their realities. This means differences and similarities, so we can see each other as equals, perhaps different but with a mutually shared basis for joining in the face of a common enemy. Not all exploitation and oppression is the same, yet we all can join together in the effort to deal with our different levels and types of oppression. It makes sense to do so and in fact success depends on it.

The various attempts at putting forth theories of the "end of history," the "merging of classes" and the "this is as good as society gets" (speaking of western u.s. capitalism!), by apologists of this new world order aside, reality in the u.s., as we know it from our own lives, is and always has been a class-divided and class-clashing society. The government tries very hard to get as many whites as possible to identify with the interests of the ruling class— with imperialism. Material incentives and ideology (white supremacy) are both used to deceive and mislead the majority of white people; the poor and working class—including most of what's called the middle class. Too often they have been successful in swaying a lot of our people to reject their own working-class interests and support imperialism.

White revolutionaries today need to look back historically to people like John Brown. We need to take an active role in opposing the violence and oppression of both the State and any racist or fascist groups. We need to win over our people ideologically and practically. We need to and we can do this. It is in our own class interests to oppose most everything that Washington does and stands for. It is in the interests of the white working class (as well as the entire multinational working class in this country) to flat out oppose white supremacy, to support the right of nations to self-determination and progressive national liberation. This is the necessary basis for multinational working-class unity in the u.s. Further, it's the foundation for an even broader progressive unity of various classes and groups who all could and need to be part of the Freedom Struggle right here in the midst of america.

What a post-imperialist america would look like is too early to call. Supporting a people's right to self-determination doesn't automatically translate to a series of small states with rigid borders, though. There could be separate new states, a confederation or new single state. As a socialist and internationalist, i can envision our being able to give birth to a truly democratic, just, multinational society, based on social equality and mutual cooperation, free of war and harsh economic disparities, committed to improving the health of our planet for the sake of our children and all humanity. These are some beautiful and bold concepts. They are also fully achievable, necessitating only that we continue in our Freedom Struggle—striking down white supremacy, rejecting the centuries-long abomination of racism and genocide; instead, reaching for and pushing forth the tradition of John Brown and the Wobblies, militant multinational struggle based on support for national liberation and unity in the battle for socialist revolution.

III.3.J

Maroon Tunes

Larry Giddings

History, Herstory, Ourstory
reflected in our eyes
reflected in our hair
reflected in our skin
not like a mirror
more like music
and rhythm

Credit: Eric Drooker (www.drooker.com)

Half-breed, quarter-breed
   octoroon, metis
   mestizo, cross-breed, dog-blood
     "a bit of the tar brush"
     "_____ in the wood pile"
     "with a Moorish tint"

Race-mixin', House-mixin'
   world Beat
the language of love, hate, war
   and more
     red, black, yellow and white

500 years of swimmin' in the pool
  cymbals clangin'
     heartbeats bangin'
       an Oriental love song
         an African chant
           an Arawak brew
             with a Celtic crew,
              a Maroon tune,
                fires in the night!!

Riding in the maelstrom of conquest
   rebellion in the blood
     we are the New World
       and we ain't lookin' for
       no Order
       no myth of purity
       no genetic border

Outlaws, out-lawed, runaways, wild
   livin' on the run
     Osceoloa drinks in
       the sound of the drum
       and smiles
        the child lives
       and so,
        he's won

Fires burn
   in our hearts
      with knowledge of
        our past
500 years of runnin'
   to an equation
      that claims:
         "You are not who you are."

A chain of slavery,
   ancient,
     passed by caste and class,
       aristocratic "blue-bloods"
         your time has come at last,
          your fears are alive
          and singing:
            WE KNOW WHO WE ARE!!!

500 years they helped us
   to grow upon these shores
     they hid us in their valleys
       fed us with their knowledge
       visions and lore,
     they took us in their families.
      so the children would live,
         they showed us it was stronger, by far
        to give

500 years of slavery, genocide and war
   and still we hear the drums beat,
     the songs grow

We are the children of your future,
   WE KNOW WHO WE ARE!
This is Turtle Island,
   our memory is alive
     we have joined with those
       that help us
         to see this future come,
          we are the colors of the rainbow
           we will be here when it's done

Mixed, like you: mixed, like me
    we are the New World
        the Iroquois could see

500 years of slavery, genocide and war
    the Native People of this land
        have brought us together
            over their dead bodies

A hemisphere is waiting
    to hear our song of life,
        reflected in our eyes
        reflected in our hair
        reflected in our skin
            dancing to the rhythm

We are the New World,
    WE KNOW WHO WE ARE!
        riding in the maelstrom
        of conquest,
            rebellion in our blood

We are the New World
    and we ain't lookin' for
        no Order
        no myth of purity
        no genetic border.

Credit: Eric Drooker (www.drooker.com)

III.3.K

What Are We Celebrating?

Edwin Cortés

500 Years of Amerikkka!
I make my plea;
It has been 500 years of misery.

Columbus set sail in the Niña, Santa
María, and Pinta:
and conquered the Aztecs, Tainos, and
Incas.
Conquista became a household word;
In order to satisfy the King's lust for
gold.

Colonialism led to mercantilist/capitalist
penetration;
in complete opposition to native
civilization.
Our forefathers were cleverly out-foxed;
subsequently exterminated by small-pox.

Africans were forced to endure
indentured servitude;
to labor on foreign soils by the
multitudes.
Slavery is genocide;
which some escaped by suicide.

The Mexicano people taught them land
cultivation;
which the European transformed by
brutal mutilation.
Mexico was invaded by military fleets;
and its northern borders incorporated by
the U.S. colonial elite.

Imperialism, an accursed damnation;
invaded my nation.
And to invoke your resistance tradition;
is to be labeled a terrorist and accused of
sedition.

Struggling for freedom's sake;
incarceration becomes your fate.
Once, again, I make my pleas;
because I witness this misery.

The imposition of capitalist/imperialist
construction;
has led to 500 years of
environmental destruction,
Is Science and Technology for liberation?
or for our extermination.

Do we continue our lives in desperation?
or take the risk of liberation.
Let's do away with exploitation;
and create a system that will last for
generations.

There will be no classes;
only the liberated masses.
Let's regain our patrimony;
in order to live once again in harmony.

While imperialism perpetuates its lie;
our nations are forced to die.
For those who fight,
armed struggle will be their might.

Let's begin a new era for justice and
human rights;
which could be just as powerful as
dynamite.
Let's undo the 500 years of
misery;
and become the makers of our own
history.

III.3.L

1992

Elizam Escobar

We must understand history as a live process. In today's debates and polemics about the events of 1492, more than a longtime dead man (Columbus), or a longtime dead empire (the Spanish one), one must judge and condemn those who continue in the present the injustices and atrocities of the past. Yesterday's "adventure of discovery" is today's "misadventure of concealment." In this sense, while hypocrisy reigns in the celebrations of "500 years of the discovery," the United States keeps Puerto Rico under a direct colonial subordination, postponing for eternity our decolonization process while it champions conveniently the independence of other countries. It is easy to judge and condemn yesterday's Columbuses but difficult to do it with today's colonists and neo-colonists.

1992 is not just a symbolic date but a real historical opportunity to reconceive independence and self-determination—for peoples and nations, as well as the individual.

But these processes of liberation will not necessarily lead to a mature freedom unless they are transformed into total processes strong enough to defeat the alienated fragmentation of the "postmodern" individual and the apoliticalness of serial collectivism (the make-believe "people" who "enjoy" a fictional democracy).

This alienated fragmentation of the individual and the apoliticalness of serial collectivism conform a kind of *mental colonialism* (a global mental subordination to the media, first worldist structures and ideologies) that is epidemic and very difficult to defeat.

We—the progressive and revolutionary forces—must oppose this extraordinary force with the power of truth. And this power must be headed at all possible levels by the power of the imagination.

Through this political power of the creative minds we must rediscover and re-invent new and necessary ways of cultural resistance that could lead to total processes of liberation. This means, for example, that at the cultural level we should look for the ways to transform the pseudodemocratization process into a real one and push it to its limit. And, simultaneously, to provide an immediate content to the liberation of the human spirit through the work of art. This immediate content provided by the creative process is essential to maintain the necessary amount of faith not only of the future but of the present. It is also necessary, in order to oppose the plagues of global capitalism, the mistakes of manqué (bureaucratic) socialism, and all postponements of revolution.

Those plagues unraveled by capitalist lechery cannot be detained by merely taking state power or by merely going through a national liberation process. Revolution must be a total event dealing not only with problems of political-direct power, but with all aspects of our spiritual and material existence. And any form of liberation must be understood as a process leading us to a responsible and mature praxis of independence and liberty, where there should be no antagonistic contradiction between the individual and the collective, between difference and egalitarian society.

Specifically the renovation of Marxist thought (instead of the mere application of Marxism to the particular conditions) and the incorporation of the radical existential experience of the excluded into the new political conceptions of reality and views of the future are of vital importance in order to keep liberation struggles and revolution alive.

The artist, then, must incorporate, somehow, directly or indirectly, or both, the reality of this future that is already here with us.

self-portrait: 1980-1992 June 1992, by Elizam Escobar

Freedom Now!

Matt Meyer
1993

Every major social change movement throughout U.S. history has included leaders who have been jailed at some point during the struggle. These political prisoners, from backgrounds as diverse as the movements they worked for, have often played pivotal roles in pushing society toward greater justice and peace.

In the 1700s there was Thomas Paine; in the 1800s, Nat Turner and John Brown. A list of past U.S. political prisoners must include Sacco and Vanzetti, Crazy Horse, Emma Goldman, Mother Jones, Lolita Lebrón, and Rosa Parks. Socialist Eugene V. Debs ran for president while in prison for opposing WWI; he stated that "while there is a soul in prison, I am not free."

Today there are over 100 political prisoners, serving long sentences in U.S. prisons. Though the names of former Black Panther Sekou Odinga, white anti-imperialist and lesbian feminist Linda Evans, or Puerto Rican patriot Dylcia Pagán are hardly household words, their struggles for liberation are as significant as any waged in the decades before them.

Many of today's political prisoners, like those in the past, belong to what are considered by the government to be "fringe" groups. Some are radical pacifists who accompany their prayer vigils with hammering on nuclear weapons until those weapons are inoperable. Some are Native Americans struggling for self-defense and autonomy after 501 years of broken treaties and genocide. Others are Black nationalists fighting to liberate their people from economic and social oppression forged by centuries of slavery. Over a dozen of the political prisoners in jail today are Puerto Ricans struggling for independence against the colonial status that even the United Nations recognizes. Still others are radical environmentalists who believe that protecting Mother Earth will take much more than lobbying. Military resisters, who believe that in addition to filing for conscientious objection, one must also refuse to fight in war, are also included among the ranks of modern political prisoners. A quick review of these "fringe groups" should reveal that a common factor among them is a deep commitment to not just talk about political change, but to take action.

This text first appeared in the Nov./Dec. 1993 issue of the *Nonviolent Activist,* magazine of the War Resisters League.

The groups and movements mentioned above have long been the targets of government harassment due to their "radical" political stance and actions. It is often for the very effectiveness of these actions and wide appeal of their messages that the government considers these activists a threat. The Counterintelligence Program (COINTELPRO) of the 1960s and '70s used infiltration, wiretapping, forgery, agents provocateurs, and assassination to "divide and conquer" various groups, most notably the Black Panther Party, the American Indian Movement, and the Puerto Rican Independence Movement. As documented in Ward Churchill and Jim Vander Wall's *Agents of Repression* (South End Press), illegal U.S. government activity resulted in the murder of dozens of Black Nationalist and Native American activists. In addition, some leaders were forced underground, some escaped into exile, and still others were framed and are now in prison. Targeted political prisoners commonly received blatantly prejudiced trials, unusually harsh prison sentences, and severe prison conditions. Well over half the current political prisoners are a direct or indirect result of COINTELPRO, the government's hope being to destroy existing movements and to dissuade new activists from social change movements through fear. Forgetting or ignoring the plight of political prisoners is one clear way that progressives may inadvertently bolster that hope.

Defining "Political" and "Prisoner of War"
There are many variations and definitions of what a political prisoner is. Clearly there are those who think that, due to the criminal nature of poverty and racism in the U.S., all people imprisoned for "petty crimes" in the larger capitalist context should be considered political prisoners. Arguments have been made, for example, that all Blacks in U.S. prisons are political prisoners due to the relationship between the U.S. government and people of African descent. It can also be argued that all Puerto Ricans living in the U.S., in and out of jail cells, should be considered imprisoned by Puerto Rico's colonial status. Some Plowshares activists, many coming from a radical Catholic perspective of not separating oneself from the poor, have felt uncomfortable being placed in special categories apart from the rest of the prison population.

There are also prisoners who have committed clearly nonpolitical criminal acts, but who have become politicized while in prison. Lawyers and former prisoners speak of many examples of "social" prisoners who claimed to have taken on a revolutionary ideology in order to get attention and support from the outside world, only to shed their ideology once on the outside themselves. Of course, countless examples can also be provided of politicized social prisoners whose commitment to progressive change was unwavering: leaders such as Malcolm X and George Jackson were developed in the Jail House University. Most commonly, however, political prisoners are defined as those who have been imprisoned due to political work or associations that they had before being imprisoned.

For most people in the U.S., the letters POW are inextricably linked to MIA

(Missing In Action) and relate to captured U.S. soldiers of the war in south-east Asia. For oppressed nationalities organizing for justice, however, the POW's who are among the political prisoners in U.S. prisons are revolution-ary heroes. According to the U.N. protocols set forth in Geneva, a prisoner can qualify for internationally recognized POW status if s/he is a combat-ant struggling against "colonial and alien domination and racist regimes." Special treatment standards have been set for such prisoners by various U.N. agencies. Those who have claimed POW status have most often been active in underground or semi-clandestine groups, such as the Black Liberation Army or in armed self-defense groups, such as the security wing of the American Indian Movement (AIM). Not every POW claim, however, is associated with an armed action. Leonard Peltier, for example, though openly admitting his membership in AIM and commitment to self-defense, has steadfastly denied involvement in the murder of two FBI agents, for which he was convicted and is serving two life sentences. Many of the Puerto Ricans claiming POW status (such as Edwin Cortés or Alejandrina Torres) were charged with nothing more than membership in the Armed Forces of National Liberation (FALN). Though the FALN claimed responsibility for several armed attacks, and some of the individuals accused did have weapons or the wherewithal to construct them, many of the Puerto Rican POW's are combatants in association only. Charged and found guilty of seditious conspiracy, they proudly admit their involvement in the movement to free Puerto Rico of colonialism though no charge or proof of violence has ever been executed.

The basis for the POW claim lies in the position that the U.S. has waged and is waging a war against these oppressed nations. Dr. Imari Obadele, a colleague of Malcolm X, articulated this theory in a classic pamphlet entitled *War in America*, as did Puerto Rican Nationalist lawyer Pedro Albizu Campos, who cited the illegality of the 1898 U.S. takeover of Puerto Rico.

Some political prisoners do not assume POW status. These include members of oppressed nationalities who were never associated with armed groups, or whose politics differed from this interpretation of the U.S. at war, and non-combatants struggling for self-determination or against illegal policies of the U.S. government. Supporters of liberation movements are included in this group, such as Silvia Baraldini—an Italian national whose case has prompted Italian parliamentarians to demand her extradition back to Europe.

Prisoners of conscience typically refers to the Plowshares and disarmament prisoners, who often face less severe sentences but who occasionally, such as in the case of Helen Woodson, get slapped with an extraordinary 18 years for a nonviolent action. Radical environmentalists, such as the Earth First! activ-ists who carry out nonviolent direct action to protect all species also fit into this category, as do military resisters. The last military resister, Hawaiian Keli'i Carmack, refused to report for duty after the centennial of the U.S. overthrow of Hawaiian Queen Lili'uokalani at which 15,000 sovereignty sup-porters marched. He was released in July.

Freedom Now

Since there have been political prisoners, there have been support networks working for their release. Ranging from friends and family members to community, state, national and international religious and political organizations such as Amnesty International, to radical lawyers to government officials domestically and abroad, political prisoners count on supporters on the outside to voice their bid for freedom. In 1989, a coalition of religious activists, artists, pacifists, Black Nationalists, Native American organizers, Puerto Rican *independentistas,* anti-imperialists, Chicano, and others came together to form a campaign entitled Freedom Now! Two major goals of the Freedom Now! campaign were to bring the issue of political prisoners to a place of prominence within the various movements represented in the coalition and to bring the human rights issues rebating to the prisoners to an international audience. The Special Tribunal was seen as a vehicle that could accomplish both of these objectives and be used as a stepping stone to presentations at the United Nations, World Court, and other international assemblies. By December of 1990, when the Tribunal took place in New York City, an initial list of 95 political prisoners had been generated. Over 1,000 observers from all 50 states and many countries attended. Eminent sociologist, educator and lawyer Dr. Luis Nieves Falcón coordinated the four-day proceedings. The judges, including British Lord Anthony Gifford, U.S. Nobel Prize recipient Dr. George Wald, and African jurist Frank Badohu, issued a powerful call for the release of all political prisoners.

Many of the groups involved with Freedom Now! helped coordinate activities at the time of the Columbus Quincentenary, raising the issues of political prisoners alongside the issues of colonialism. A second tribunal, the International Tribunal of Indigenous Peoples and Oppressed Nations, was put together in October 1992, building upon the themes of the 1990 testimony.

More recently, grassroots educational work is increasing with the development of a letter-writing and postcard campaign on the part of the National Committee to Free Puerto Rican POW's, and the publication of a new book by the Campaign to Free Black Political Prisoners/POW's. The Interfaith Prisoners of Conscience Project of the National Council of Churches has launched the Sponsor-a-Prisoner project, whereby local congregations can link up with prisoners and help break down the dehumanizing process of prison. Myriad other community groups continue their efforts. Of course, much work and education remains to be done

Political prisoners are the conscience of the left. They come from diverse political and social backgrounds yet share a deep commitment to justice. Their struggles for a more just world have landed them in the place most representative of the hypocrisy of our "free and just" society. As activists, our responsibility is not only to carry on their struggles but also to continue to struggle for their release.

International Tribunal of Indigenous Peoples and Oppressed Nations in the U.S.A.

October 2-4, 1992
San Francisco, California

III.5.A

That Everyone Resist... That No One Stay Behind... the Legend of Popul-Vuh

On October 2-4, 1992, the eve of the 500th anniversary of Columbus's invasion of the Americas, a historic International Tribunal of Indigenous Peoples and Oppressed Nations convened in San Francisco, California, U.S.A. Initiated by the American Indian Movement (AIM) and joined by representatives of the Puerto Rican, New Afrikan, and Mexicano movements as well as progressive white North Americans, the Tribunal placed the U.S. Federal Government on trial for grave crimes against humanity. As the contemporary inheritors of the Columbus legacy of colonialism, genocide, and political internment, representatives of the U.S. government—Attorney General William Barr in Washington, DC, and John Méndez, the U.S. attorney in San Francisco—were formally served with the indictment on September 23, 1992. In a published statement to Reuters News Service, the U.S. government acknowledged receipt of the indictment and stated that it refused to avail itself of the opportunity to offer a defense of the Federal Government.

During the weekend of October 2, over one thousand people from every region of the U.S., as well as Canada, Spain, the Philippines, Germany, Puerto Rico, Hawaii, Haiti, South Africa, and Peru, attended or participated in the Tribunal. A distinguished panel of international judges, each with long experience in human rights, heard testimony, deliberated for 12 hours and rendered the preliminary verdict contained in this volume. Following the tradition of other International Tribunals, such as the Bertrand Russell Tribunal, which judged U.S. war crimes during the Vietnam war, this Tribunal's findings will be brought before the United Nations and other international bodies. It is important to underscore that the authority of the Tribunal and its verdict rests in its scrupulous adherence to international law and the urgent demand by our peoples that the U.S. government be held accountable for its historical and present-day crimes. With 1993 designated by the United Nations as the Year of Indigenous Peoples, it is our hope that this verdict will make a serious contribution to our peoples' effort to assume our rightful place in the international community.

From the outset of this process more than a year ago, the aims of the Tribunal were defined as:

- To destroy the myth of the "European Discovery" of the Americas and make clear that Columbus and the Europeans who later followed him were conquerors and not discoverers of a new world.
- To provide a forum for a broader understanding of the human right to self-determination for Native Americans, Puerto Ricans, New Afrikans (Blacks), and Mexicans. To understand the history of the U.S. as a country that became the inheritor of the European legacies of colonialism, genocide, and racism.
- To demand the immediate, unconditional release of the more than 100 political prisoners and prisoners of war from the different movements, such as Leonard Peltier, Eddie Hatcher, Norma Jean Croy, Alejandrina Torres, Oscar López, Geronimo ji Jaga, Mumia Abu-Jamal, Silvia Baraldini, and many others presently in U.S. prisons.

For our Peoples and Nations, the common experience of 500 years of resistance teaches us all too well that the U.S. has never respected moral principles, treaties, or international law. From the regime first imposed upon us in the Caribbean by Columbus five hundred years ago, up to the present day "New World Order" proclaimed by the U.S. government—the pursuit of wealth and domination has brought only genocide and ruin to our sacred Mother Earth. Now that the end of the 20th century is nearly upon us, it is time for this predatory way of life to end. This criminal system is driving us all, from every part of this planet, into the 11th hour of global crisis. With the urgent need to restore justice, balance, mutual respect, and dignity foremost in our minds, our movements humbly bring this indictment and verdict to our peoples and the world.

Preliminary Finding of Fact and Order

Distinguished Jurors Composing the International Tribunal

Francisca Villalba Merino, JD
Attorney and expert on international
law and political prisoners from Spain

Dale Marie Standing Alone
Leader of the Blood Tribe, member
of the Blackfoot Nation in Canada

Norbert Georg
Member, Board of Directors of the
Society for Threatened Peoples,
the second largest human rights
organization in the world

Mitsuye Yamada
Poet and author, formerly on the
National Board of Directors of
Amnesty International USA,
interned in Idaho during World War II

Dr. Rae Richardson
Professor emerita, Black History; cofounder and co-owner of
Marcus Bookstores, specializing in books
by and about Black people;
and well-respected elder in
the Black community

Adora Faye de Vera
Former political prisoner from the
Philippines; poet and founding
member of KAIBA, the Philippines'
only women's political party

Rory Snow Arrow Fausett, JD
Professor, Native American Studies,
University of California at Berkeley

Distinguished Witnesses Appearing Before the International Tribunal

Charge of Genocide

Native Americans

Dr. Kekuni Blaisdell
Pro-Hawaii Sovereignty Working Group

Professor Elizabeth Parent
Head of Native American Studies,
San Francisco State University

New Afrikans

Oba T'chaka
Professor, San Francisco State University

Daramola Cabral-Evins
Epidemiologist, Hartford Hospital

Mexicans

María Ortíz
Mexican Democratic Forum,
San Jose, California

Puerto Ricans

Deborah Santana
Puerto Rican environmentalist

Rafael Cancel Miranda
Puerto Rican national hero

Charge of Human Rights Violations

Native Americans

Sage La Peña
Wintu-Nomtipom; human rights activist

Tom Goldtooth
Environmental coordinator from the
Red Lake Band of Chippewa;
acting co-director,
ndigenous Environmental Network

New Afrikans

Emory Douglas
Founding member, Black Panther Party

Muhjah Shakir
Co-coordinator, International Campaign
to Free Geronimo ji Jaga (Pratt)

Mexicans

Ricardo García
Regeneración Human Rights Group

José Rico
Co-founder,
Frente Estudiantil de Liberación Nacional

Puerto Ricans

Carmen Vázquez
Board of Directors,
National Gay and Lesbian Task Force

Piri Thomas
Poet and author of
Down These Mean Streets

Charge of Political Prisoners and Prisoners of War

Native Americans

Bob Robideau
Co-defendant of Leonard Peltier;
national coordinator,
Leonard Pettier Defense Committee

Ward Churchill
Professor, University of Colorado;
noted author and co-director,
Colorado American Indian Movement

New Afrikans

Watani Tyehimba
Former political prisoner;
national secretary of the
New Afrikan People's Organization

Mexicans

Ricardo Sánchez
Former political prisoner; professor,
Washington State University

Puerto Ricans

Carlos Ortíz
National coordinator of the National
Committee to Free Puerto Rican
Prisoners of War and Political Prisoners

White North Americans

Rita "Bo" Brown
Former political prisoner

279

III.5.B

Indictment of the Federal Government of the
United States of America for the Commission of
International Crimes and Petition for Orders Mandating
Its Proscription and Dissolution as an International
Criminal Conspiracy and a Criminal Organization

All citizens of the World Community have both the right and the duty under public international law to sit in judgment over a gross and consistent pattern of violations of the most fundamental norms of international criminal law committed by any member state of that same World Community. Such is the case for the International Tribunal of Indigenous Peoples and Oppressed Nations in the United States of America that convenes in San Francisco during the weekend of October 2-4, 1992. Its weighty but important task is to examine the long history of international criminal activity that has been perpetrated by the Federal Government of the United States of America against the Indigenous Peoples and Peoples of Color living in North America since it was founded in 1787.

Toward that end, I have the honor to present to the Members of this Tribunal the following charges against the Federal Government of the United States of America under international criminal law. In light of the gravity, severity, and longstanding nature of these international crimes and also in light of the fact that the Federal Government appears to be irrevocably committed to continuing down this path of lawlessness and criminality against Indigenous Peoples and Peoples of Color living in North America and elsewhere, I hereby petition the Members of this Tribunal to issue and order proscribing the Federal Government of the United States of America as an International Criminal Conspiracy and a Criminal Organization under the Nuremberg Charter, Judgment, and Principles as well as other sources of public international law specified below. For that reason, I also request that the Members of the Tribunal issue an Order dissolving the Federal Government of the United States of America as a legal and political entity. Finally, I ask this Tribunal to declare that international legal sovereignty over the Territories principally inhabited by the Native American Peoples, the New Afrikan People, the Mexicano People, and the People of Puerto Rico resides in the hands of these respective Peoples Themselves.

In this regard, I should point out that the final Decision of this Tribunal will qualify as a "judicial decision" within the meaning of article 38 (1) (d) of the Statute of the International Court of Justice and will therefore constitute a "subsidiary means for the determination of rules of law" for international law and practice. The Statute of the International Court of Justice is an "integral part of the United Nations Charter under article 92 thereof. Thus, this Tribunal's

Decision can be relied upon by some future International Criminal Court or Tribunal, as well as by any People or State of the World Community that desires to initiate criminal proceedings against named individual for the commission of the following international crimes. The Decision of this Tribunal shall serve as adequate notice to the appropriate officials in the United States Federal Government that they bear personal responsibility under international law and the domestic legal systems of all Peoples and States in the World Community for designing and implementing these illegal, criminal, and reprehensible policies and practices against Indigenous Peoples and Peoples of Color living in North America. Hereinafter, the Federal Government of the United States of America will be referred to as the "Defendant."

Bill of Particulars Against the Federal Government
of the United States of America

The Native American Peoples
1. The Defendant has perpetrated innumerable Crimes against Peace, Crimes against Humanity, and War Crimes against Native American Peoples as recognized by the Nuremberg Charter, Judgment, and Principles.
2. The Defendant has perpetrated the International Crime of Genocide against Native American Peoples as recognized by the 1948 Convention on the Prevention and Punishment of the Crime of Genocide.
3. The Defendant has perpetrated the International Crime of Apartheid against Native American Peoples as recognized by the 1973 International Convention on the Suppression and Punishment of the Crime of Apartheid.
4. The Defendant has perpetrated a gross and consistent pattern of violations of the most fundamental human rights of Native American Peoples as recognized by the 1948 Universal Declaration of Human Rights.
5. The Defendant has perpetrated numerous and repeated violations of the 1965 International Convention on the Elimination of All Forms of Racial Discrimination against Native American Peoples.
6. The Defendant has systematically violated 371 treaties it concluded with the Native American Peoples in wanton disregard of the basic principle of public international law and practice dictating *pacta sunt servanda.*
7. The Defendant has denied and violated the international legal right of Native American Peoples to self-determination as recognized by the 1945 United Nations Charter; the 1966 International Covenant on Civil and Political Rights; the 1966 International Covenant on Economic, Social, and Cultural Rights; fundamental principles of customary international law; and *jus cogens.*

281

8. Defendant has violated the seminal United Nations Declaration of the Granting of Independence to Colonial Countries and Territories of 1960 with respect to Native American Peoples and Territories. Pursuant thereto, the Defendant has an absolute international legal obligation to decolonize Native American Territories immediately and to transfer all powers it currently exercises there to the Native American Peoples.

9. The Defendant has illegally refused to accord full-scope protections as Prisoners-of-War to captured Native American independence fighters in violation of the Third Geneva Convention of 1949 and Additional Protocol I thereto of 1977. The Defendant's treatment of captured Native American independence fighters as "common criminals" and "terrorists" constitutes a "grave breach" of the Geneva Accords and thus a serious war crime.

10. The Defendant has deliberately and systematically permitted, aided and abetted, solicited and conspired to commit the dumping, transportation, and location of nuclear, toxic, medical, and otherwise hazardous waste materials on Native American Territories across North America and has thus created a clear and present danger to the lives, health, safety, and physical and mental well-being of Native American Peoples in gross violation of article 3 and article 2 (c) of the 1948 Genocide Convention, *inter alia:* "Deliberately inflicting on the group conditions of life calculated to bring about its physical destruction in whole or in part...."

The New Afrikan People

11. The Defendant has perpetrated the International Crime of Slavery upon the New Afrikan People as recognized in part by the 1926 Slavery Convention and the 1956 Supplementary Convention on the Abolition of Slavery, the Slave Trade, and Institutions and Practices Similar to Slavery. The Defendant has illegally refused to pay reparations to the New Afrikan People for the commission of the International Crime of Slavery against Them in violation of basic norms of customary international law requiring such reparations to be paid.

12. The Defendant has perpetrated innumerable Crimes against Humanity against the New Afrikan People as recognized by the Nuremberg Charter, Judgment, and Principles.

13. The Defendant has perpetrated the International Crime of Genocide against the New Afrikan People as recognized by the 1948 Genocide Convention.

14. The Defendant has perpetrated the International Crime of Apartheid against the New Afrikan People as recognized by the 1973 Apartheid Convention.

15. The Defendant has perpetrated a gross and consistent pattern of violations of the most fundamental human rights of the New Afrikan People as recognized by the 1948 Universal Declaration of Human Rights and the two aforementioned United Nations Human Rights Covenants of 1966.
16. The Defendant has perpetrated a gross and consistent pattern of violations of the 1965 Racism Convention against the New Afrikan People. The Defendant is the paradigmatic example of an irremediably racist state in international relations today.
17. The Defendant has denied and violated the international legal right of the New Afrikan People to self-determination as recognized by the United Nations Charter, the two United Nations Human Rights Covenants of 1966, customary international law, and *jus cogens*.
18. The Defendant has illegally refused to apply the United Nations Decolonization Resolution of 1960 to the New Afrikan People and to the Territories that they principally inhabit. Pursuant thereto, the Defendant has an absolute international legal obligation to decolonize New Afrikan Territories immediately and to transfer all powers it currently exercises there to the New Afrikan People.
19. The Defendant has illegally refused to accord full-scope protections as Prisoners-of-War to captured New Afrikan independence fighters in violation of the Third Geneva Convention of 1949 and Additional Protocol I thereto of 1977. The Defendant's treatment of captured New Afrikan independence fighters as "common criminals" and "terrorists" constitutes a "grave breach" of the Geneva Accords and thus a serious war crime.

The Mexicano People
20. In 1821, Mexico obtained its independence from Spain as a sovereign Mestizo State, extending from Yucatán and Chiapas in the south, to the northern territories of California and New Mexico, which areas the Defendant today calls the "states" of Texas, California, Arizona, Nevada, Utah, New Mexico, and Colorado. Nevertheless, in 1836 so-called "settlers" under the sponsorship of the Defendant began the division of the Mexicano People and State by causing the division of the Mexican state of Coahuila-Texas into the Mexican state of Coahuila and the so-called "republic" of Texas.
21. In 1846, the Defendant perpetrated an unjust, illegal, and unjustifiable war upon the remainder of the sovereign People and State of Mexico that violated every known principle of public international law in existence at that time, including, but not limited to, the Christian Doctrine of "just war," which was the reigning standard of customary international law. As a result thereof, the Defendant illegally annexed close to 51% of the territories of the sovereign

State of Mexico by means of forcing it to conclude the 1848 Treaty of Guadalupe-Hidalgo under military duress. For these reasons, this Treaty was and still is null and void *ab initio* as a matter of public international law. The Defendant acquired more Mexican territory through the Gadsen Treaty (Purchase) of 1854.

22. Since these 1848 and 1854 Treaties, the Defendant has perpetrated the International Crime of Genocide against the Mexicano People living within these occupied territories, as recognized by the 1948 Genocide Convention.

23. The Defendant has perpetrated the International Crime of Apartheid against the Mexicano People living within these occupied territories, as recognized by the 1973 Apartheid Convention.

24. The Defendant has perpetrated a gross and consistent pattern of violations of the most fundamental human rights of the Mexicano people living within these occupied territories, as recognized by the 1948 Universal Declaration of Human Rights and the two aforementioned United Nations Human Rights Covenants of 1966.

25. The Defendant has perpetrated a gross and consistent pattern of violations of the 1965 Racism Convention against the Mexicano People living within these occupied territories.

26. The Defendant has denied and violated the international legal right of the Mexicano People living within these occupied territories to self-determination as recognized by the United Nations Charter, the two United Nations Human Rights Covenants of 1966, customary international law, and *jus cogens.*

27. Since the militarily imposed division of the Mexican State, the Defendant and its agents have militarily occupied other portions of the Mexican State, have sought to influence the outcome of the Mexican Revolution of 1910, have practiced a consistent pattern of intervention into Mexico's internal affairs, all of which have resulted in the arresting distortion and deformation of the Mexican social and economic order. In this regard, Defendant's so-called "North American Free Trade Agreement (NAFTA)" constitutes nothing more than an attempt to impose its hegemonial imperialism, economic colonialism, and human exploitation upon the People and State of Mexico.

28. The Defendant has illegally refused to apply the United Nations Decolonization Resolution of 1960 to the Mexicano People and to these occupied territories that they inhabit. Pursuant thereto, the Defendant has an absolute international legal obligation to decolonize both the Mexican occupied territories and the Republic of Mexico immediately, and to transfer all powers it currently exercises there to the Mexicano People.

The People and State of Puerto Rico

29. Since its illegal invasion of Puerto Rico in 1898, Defendant has perpetrated innumerable Crimes against Peace, Crimes against Humanity, and War Crimes against the People and State of Puerto Rico as recognized by the Nuremberg Charter, Judgment, and Principles.

30. The Defendant has perpetrated the International Crime of Genocide against the Puerto Rican People as recognized by the 1948 Genocide Convention.

31. The Defendant has perpetrated the International Crime of Apartheid against the Puerto Rican People as recognized by the 1973 Apartheid Convention.

32. The Defendant has perpetrated a gross and consistent pattern of violations of the most fundamental human rights of the Puerto Rican People as recognized by the 1948 Universal Declaration of Human Rights and the two aforementioned United Nations Human Rights Covenants of 1966.

33. The Defendant has perpetrated a gross and consistent pattern of violations of the 1965 Racism Convention against the Puerto Rican People.

34. The Defendant has denied and violated the international legal right of the Puerto Rican People to self-determination as recognized by the United Nations Charter, the two United Nations Human Rights Covenants of 1966, customary international law, and *jus cogens.*

35. The Defendant has illegally refused to apply the United Nations Decolonization Resolution of 1960 to Puerto Rico. Pursuant thereto, the Defendant has an absolute international legal obligation to decolonize Puerto Rico immediately and to transfer all powers it currently exercises there to the Puerto Rican People.

36. The Defendant has illegally refused to accord full-scope protections as Prisoners-of-War to captured Puerto Rican independence fighters in violation of the Third Geneva Convention of 1949 and Additional Protocol I thereto of 1977. The Defendant's treatment of captured Puerto Rican independence fighters as "common criminals" and "terrorists" constitutes a "grave breach" of the Geneva Accords and thus a serious war crime.

An International Criminal Conspiracy and a Criminal Organization

37. In light of the foregoing international crimes, the Defendant constitutes a Criminal Conspiracy and a Criminal Organization in accordance with the Nuremberg Charter, Judgment, and Principles and the other sources of public international law specified above. The Federal Government of the United States of America is similar to the Nazi government of World War II Germany. Indeed, the Defendant's President, George Bush, has proclaimed a so-called "New World Order" that sounds and looks strikingly similar to the "New Order" proclaimed by Adolph Hitler over 50 years ago.

Conclusion

Like unto a pirate, the Defendant is *hostis humani generis*: The enemy of all humankind! For the good of all humanity, this Tribunal must condemn and repudiate the Federal Government of the United States of America and its grotesque vision of a "New World Order" that is constructed upon warfare, bloodshed, violence, criminality, genocide, racism, colonialism, apartheid, massive violations of fundamental human rights, and the denial of the international legal right of self-determination to the Indigenous Peoples and Peoples of Color living in North America and elsewhere around the world. Consequently, this Tribunal must find the Defendant guilty as charged on all counts specified above beyond a reasonable doubt. This Tribunal must also issue an Order that formally proscribes the Federal Government of the United States of America as a Criminal Conspiracy and a Criminal Organization. This Tribunal must also issue a separate Order mandating the dissolution of the Federal Government of the United States of America as a legal and political entity. Finally, this Tribunal must declare that international legal sovereignty over the Territories inhabited by the Native American Peoples, the New Afrikan Peoples, the Mexicano People, and the People of Puerto Rico, resides, respectively, in the hands of these Peoples Themselves. The very lives, well-being, health, welfare, and safety of the Indigenous Peoples and Peoples of Color living in North America and elsewhere around the world depend upon the ultimate success of your deliberations.

Respecifully submitted by

    Francis A. Boyle
    Professor of International Law
    Special Prosecutor

    Dated: September 18, 1992

III.5.C

Verdict of the
International Tribunal of Indigenous Peoples and
Oppressed Nations in the United States of America,
San Francisco, California

NATIVE AMERICAN PEOPLES, NEW AFRIKAN PEOPLE,
MEXICANO PEOPLE, AND PUERTO RICAN PEOPLE
Plaintiffs,
-versus-

THE FEDERAL GOVERNMENT OF THE UNITED STATES OF AMERICA
Defendant.

Preliminary Findings and Order
This matter having come before the International Tribunal of Indigenous Peoples and Oppressed Nations in the United States of America, hereinafter "Tribunal" by request of representatives of the Native American Peoples, the New Afrikan People, the Mexicano People, and the Puerto Rican People; the Indictment of the Federal Government of the United States of America for the Commission of International Crimes and Petition for Orders Mandating its Proscription and Dissolution as an International Criminal Conspiracy and a Criminal Organization having been presented by Special Prosecutor Francis Boyle; the Native American Peoples having appeared personally and by counsel, Bryan Savage; the New Afrikan People having appeared personally and by counsel, James Simmons; the Mexicano People having appeared personally and by counsel, Guillermo Suárez; the Puerto Rican People having appeared personally and by counsel, Dennis Cunningham and Rachel Lederman; the white North American People having appeared on the issue of political prisoners personally and by counsel, Marilyn Kalman; the United States Government having failed to appear personally or by counsel; the Tribunal having completed its preliminary consideration of the testimonial evidence, the documentary evidence, the argument of counsel, and otherwise being fully informed of the premises, finds that:

1. The Defendant, the Federal Government of the United States of America, has been duly served with summons and process.
2. This Tribunal has jurisdiction over the parties, in the name of the Peoples whom the Plaintiffs represent.
3. The Plaintiff parties consider that the judgments of this Tribunal qualify as "judicial decisions" within the meaning of Article 38 [1] [d] of the Statute of the International Court of Justice.

4. The following sources and principles of law are applicable:
    a. the Nuremberg Charter, Judgment, and Principles;
    b. the 1948 Convention on the Prevention and Punishment of the Crime of Genocide;
    c. the 1973 International Convention on the Suppression and Punishment of the Crime of Apartheid;
    d. the 1948 Universal Declaration of Human Rights;
    e. the 1965 International Convention on the Elimination of All Forms of Racial Discrimination;
    f. the 1945 United Nations Charter;
    g. the 1966 International Covenant on Civil and Political Rights;
    h. the 1966 International Covenant on Economic, Social, and Cultural Rights;
    i. the 1960 United Nations Declaration of the Granting of Independence to Colonial Countries and Territories;
    j. the Third Geneva Convention of 1949 and Additional Protocol I thereto of 1977, and United Nations Resolution 3103 XV;
    k. the 1926 Slavery Convention;
    l. the 1956 Supplementary Convention on the Abolition of Slavery, the Slave Trade, and Institutions and Practices Similar to Slavery;
    m. the 1960 United Nations Decolonization Resolution;
    n. the 1969 American Convention on Human Rights;
    o. the 1981 United Nations Declaration on the Elimination of All Forms of Intolerance and of Discrimination Based on Religion or Belief;
    p. the 1984 United Nations Declaration on the Right of Peoples to Peace;
    q. the 1989 United Nations Convention on the Rights of the Child;
    r. the 1987 United Nations Convention against Torture and Other Cruel, Inhuman, or Degrading Treatment or Punishment;
    s. the principles of the Common Law;
    t. the principles of the Civil Law;
    u. international custom;
    v. the general principles of law recognized by civilized nations; and
    w. judicial decisions and the teachings of the most highly qualified publicists of the various nations of the world.

Native Americans

5. With respect to the charges brought by the Native American Peoples, the Tribunal finds, by unanimous vote, the Defendant, the Federal Government of the United States of America, is guilty as charged in:

The Defendant has perpetrated innumerable Crimes against Peace, Crimes against Humanity, and War Crimes against Native American Peoples as recognized by the Nuremberg Charter, Judgment, and Principles.

The Defendant has perpetrated the International Crime of Genocide against Native American Peoples as recognized by the 1948 Convention on the Prevention and Punishment of the Crime of Genocide.

The Defendant has perpetrated the International Crime of Apartheid against Native American Peoples as recognized by the 1973 International Convention on the Suppression and Punishment of the Crime of Apartheid.

The Defendant has perpetrated a gross and consistent pattern of violations of the most fundamental human rights of Native American Peoples as recognized by the 1948 Universal Declaration of Human Rights.

The Defendant has perpetrated numerous and repeated violations of the 1965 International Convention on the Elimination of All Forms of Racial Discrimination against Native American Peoples.

The Defendant has denied and violated the international legal right of Native American Peoples to self-determination as recognized by the 1945 United Nations Charter; the 1966 International Covenant on Civil and Political Rights; the 1966 International Covenant on Economic, Social, and Cultural Rights; fundamental principles of customary international law; and *jus cogens*.

The Defendant has violated the United Nations Declaration of the Granting of Independence to Colonial Countries and Territories of 1960 with respect to Native American Peoples and Territories. Pursuant thereto, the Defendant has an absolute international legal obligation to decolonize Native American Territories immediately and to transfer all powers it currently exercises there to the Native American Peoples.

The Defendant has deliberately and systematically permitted, aided and abetted, solicited and conspired to commit the dumping, transportation, and location of nuclear, toxic, medical, and otherwise hazardous waste materials on Native American Territories across North America and has thus created a clear and present danger to the lives, health, safety, and physical and mental well-being of Native American Peoples in gross violation of article 3 and article 2 (c) of the 1948 Genocide Convention, *inter alia*: "Deliberately inflicting on the group conditions of life calculated to bring about its physical destruction in whole or in part...."

Hawaiian Peoples

6. The Tribunal further accepts a motion by the Prosecutor for the Native American Peoples to amend the face of the Indictment to include the following allegation, which the Tribunal unanimously finds has been sufficiently proved by the evidence it has received:

> The Federal Government of the United States of America has perpetrated crimes of genocide against the Kanaka Maoli (the Indigenous Hawaiian People) and has engaged in actions constituting gross violations of their human rights and their right to self-determination, all of which threaten to render the Kanaka Maoli extinct.

New Afrikans

7. With respect to the charges brought by the New Afrikan People, the Defendant, the federal Government of the United States of America, is, by unanimous vote, guilty as charged in:

> The Defendant has perpetrated the International Crime of Slavery upon the New Afrikan People as recognized in part by the 1926 Slavery Convention and the 1956 Supplementary Convention on the Abolition of Slavery, the Slave Trade, and Institutions and Practices Similar to Slavery.
>
> The Defendant has perpetrated innumerable Crimes against Humanity against the New Afrikan People as recognized by the Nuremberg Charter, Judgment, and Principles.
>
> The Defendant has perpetrated the International Crime of Genocide against the New Afrikan People as recognized by the 1948 Genocide Convention.

The Defendant has perpetrated the International Crime of Apartheid against the New Afrikan People as recognized by the 1973 Apartheid Convention.

The Defendant has perpetrated a gross and consistent pattern of violations of the most fundamental human rights of the New Afrikan People as recognized by the 1948 Universal Declaration of Human Rights and the two aforementioned United Nations Human Rights Covenants of 1966.

The Defendant has perpetrated a gross and consistent pattern of violations of the 1965 Racism Convention against the New Afrikan People. The Defendant is the paradigmatic example of an irremediably racist state in international relations today.

The Defendant has denied and violated the international legal right of the New Afrikan People to self-determination as recognized by the United Nations Charter, the two United Nations Human Rights Covenants of 1966, customary international law, and *jus cogens*.

The Defendant has illegally refused to accord full-scope protections as Prisoners-of-War to captured New Afrikan independence fighters in violation of the Third Geneva Convention of 1949 and Additional Protocol I thereto of 1977. The Defendant's treatment of captured New Afrikan independence fighters as "common criminals" and "terrorists" constitutes a "grave breach" of the Geneva Accords and thus a serious war crime.

Mexicano People
8. With respect to the charges brought by the Mexicano People, the Defendant, the Federal Government of the United States of America, is guilty as charged in:

> Since these 1848 and 1854 Treaties, the Defendant has perpetrated the International Crime of Genocide against the Mexicano People living within these occupied territories, as recognized by the 1948 Genocide Convention.

> The Defendant has perpetrated the International Crime of Apartheid against the Mexicano People living within these

occupied territories, as recognized by the 1973 Apartheid Convention.

The Defendant has perpetrated a gross and consistent pattern of violations of the most fundamental human rights of the Mexicano People living within these occupied territories, as recognized by the 1948 Universal Declaration of Human Rights and the two aforementioned United Nations Human Rights Covenants of 1966.

The Defendant has perpetrated a gross and consistent pattern of violations of the 1965 Racism Convention against the Mexicano People living within these occupied territories.

Puerto Rican People

9. With respect to the charges brought by the Puerto Rican People, the Defendant, the Federal Government of the United States of America, is, by unanimous vote, guilty as charged in:

Since its illegal invasion of Puerto Rico in 1898, Defendant has perpetrated innumerable Crimes Against Peace, Crimes Against Humanity and War Crimes against the People and State of Puerto Rico as recognized by the Nuremberg Charter, Judgment, and Principles.

The Defendant has perpetrated the International Crime of Genocide against the Puerto Rican People as recognized by the 1948 Genocide Convention.

The Defendant has perpetrated the International Crime of Apartheid against the Puerto Rican People as recognized by the 1973 Apartheid Convention.

The Defendant has perpetrated a gross and consistent pattern of violations of the most fundamental human rights of the Puerto Rican People as recognized by the 1948 Universal Declaration of Human Rights and the two aforementioned United Nations Human Rights Covenants of 1966.

The Defendant has perpetrated a gross and consistent pattern of violations of the 1965 Racism Convention against the Puerto Rican People.

The Defendant has denied and violated the international legal right of the Puerto Rican People to self-determination as recognized by the United Nations Charter, the two United Nations Human Rights Covenants of 1966, customary international law, and *jus cogens*.

The Defendant has illegally refused to apply the United Nations Decolonization Resolution of 1960 to Puerto Rico. Pursuant thereto, the Defendant has an absolute international legal obligation to decolonize Puerto Rico immediately and to transfer all powers it currently exercises there to the Puerto Rican People.

The Defendant has illegally refused to accord full-scope protections as Prisoners-of-War to captured Puerto Rican independence fighters in violation of the Third Geneva Convention of 1949 and Additional Protocol I thereto of 1977. The Defendant's treatment of captured Puerto Rican independence fighters as "common criminals" and "terrorists" constitutes a "grave breach" of the Geneva Accords and thus a serious war crime.

White North American Political Prisoners
10. With respect to the charges brought by the white people of North America, the Defendant is, by unanimous vote, guilty of holding white North Americans as political prisoners.

Additional Findings
11. In light of the foregoing findings, this Tribunal also, by unanimous vote, finds the Defendant guilty as charged in paragraph 37, which, as amended, reads:

In light of the foregoing international crimes, the Defendant constitutes a Criminal Conspiracy and a Criminal Organization in accordance with the Nuremberg Charter, Judgment, and Principles and the other sources of public international law specified above, and the Federal Government of the United States of America is similar to the Nazi government of World War II Germany.

12. With respect to the following charges brought by the Native American Peoples:

    a. six members of the Tribunal find the Defendant guilty as charged in paragraph 6, which reads:

> The Defendant has systematically violated 371 treaties it concluded with the Native American Peoples in wanton disregard of the basic principle of public international law and practice dictating *pacta sunt servanda*.

> One member of the Tribunal reserves the right to consider the documentary evidence further before making a final determination.

    b. four members of the Tribunal find the Defendant guilty as charged in paragraph 9, which reads:

> The Defendant has illegally refused to accord full-scope protections as Prisoners-of-War to captured Native American independence fighters in violation of the Third Geneva Convention of 1949 and Additional Protocol I thereto of 1977. The Defendant's treatment of captured Native American independence fighters as "common criminals" and "terrorists" constitutes a "grave breach" of the Geneva Accords and thus a serious war crime.

> Three members of the Tribunal reserve the right to consider the documentary evidence further before making a final determination.

13. With respect to the following charges brought by the New Afrikan People:

    a. four members of the Tribunal find the Defendant guilty as charged in paragraph 11, which, as amended, reads:

> The Defendant has illegally refused to pay reparations to the New Afrikan People for the commission of the International Crime of Slavery against Them in violation of basic norms of customary international law requiring such reparations to be paid.

> Three members of the Tribunal reserve the right to consider the documentary evidence further before making a final determination.

b. three members of the Tribunal find the Defendant guilty as charged in paragraph 18, which reads:

> The Defendant has illegally refused to apply the United Nations Decolonization Resolution of 1960 to the New Afrikan People and to the Territories that they principally inhabit. Pursuant thereto, the Defendant has an absolute international legal obligation to decolonize New Afrikan Territories immediately and to transfer all powers it currently exercises there to the New Afrikan People.

Four members of the Tribunal reserve the right to consider the documentary evidence further before making a final determination.

14. With respect to the following charges brought by the Mexicano People:
a. six members of the Tribunal find the Defendant guilty as charged in paragraph 20, which reads:

> In 1821, Mexico obtained its independence from colonial Spain as a sovereign Mestizo State, extending from Yucatán and Chiapas in the south, to the northern territories of California and New Mexico, which areas the Defendant today calls the "states" of Texas, California, Arizona, Nevada, Utah, New Mexico, and Colorado. Nevertheless, in 1836 so-called "settlers" under the sponsorship of the Defendant began the division of the Mexicano People and State by causing the division of the Mexican state of Coahuila-Texas into the Mexican state of Coahuila and the so-called "republic" of Texas.

One member of the Tribunal reserves the right to consider the documentary evidence further before making a final determination.

b. six members of the Tribunal find the Defendant guilty as charged in paragraph 21, which reads:

> In 1846, the Defendant perpetrated an unjust, illegal, and unjustifiable war upon the remainder of the sovereign People and State of Mexico that violated every known principle of public international law in existence at that time, including, but not limited to, the Christian Doctrine

of "just war," which was the reigning standard of customary international law. As a result thereof, the Defendant illegally annexed close to 51% of the territories of the sovereign State of Mexico by means of forcing it to conclude the 1848 Treaty of Guadalupe-Hidalgo under military duress. For these reasons, this Treaty was and still is null and void *ab initio* as a matter of public international law. The Defendant acquired more Mexican territory through the Gadsen Treaty (Purchase) of 1854.

One member of the Tribunal reserves the right to consider the documentary evidence further before making a final determination.

c. five members of the Tribunal find the Defendant guilty as charged in paragraph 26, which reads:

The Defendant has denied and violated the international legal right of the Mexicano People living within these occupied territories to self-determination as recognized by the United Nations Charter, the two United Nations Human Rights Covenants of 1966, customary international law, and *jus cogens*.

Two members of the Tribunal reserve the right to consider the documentary evidence further before making a final determination.

d. six members of the Tribunal find the Defendant guilty as charged in paragraph 27, which reads:

Since the militarily imposed division of the Mexican State, the Defendant and its agents have militarily occupied other portions of the Mexican State, have sought to influence the outcome of the Mexican Revolution of 1910, have practiced a consistent pattern of intervention into Mexico's internal affairs, all of which have resulted in the arresting distortion and deformation of the Mexican social and economic order. In this regard, Defendant's so-called "North American Free Trade Agreement (NAFTA)" constitutes nothing more than an attempt to impose its hegemonic imperialism, economic colonialism, and human exploitation upon the People and State of Mexico.

One member of the Tribunal reserves the right to consider the documentary evidence further before making a final determination.

e. six members of the Tribunal find the Defendant guilty as charged in paragraph 28, which reads:

The Defendant has illegally refused to apply the United Nations Decolonization Resolution of 1960 to the Mexicano People and to these occupied territories that they inhabit. Pursuant thereto, the Defendant has an absolute international legal obligation to decolonize both the Mexican occupied territories and the Republic of Mexico immediately, and to transfer all powers it currently exercises there to the Mexicano People.

One member of the Tribunal reserves the right to consider the documentary evidence further before making a final determination.

NOW THEREFORE, it is ordered, adjudged and decreed that the Defendant cease and desist from the commission of the crimes it has been found guilty of herein. This Tribunal reserves the right to issue further relief after full consideration of the evidence.

Shasta Woman:
The Story of Norma Jean Croy

B♀ (rita d. brown)
2008

The saga of Norma Jean Croy is but one of many in the ongoing racism and genocide endured by the indigenous people of this stolen land we so-called modern ones call the u.s.a. Norma Jean was 24 and had known for some time that she liked women, but that's another story. This one begins July 16, 1978. It was another hot summer in Yreka, a northern California town full of deadly gold rush history. On this day, she, along with friends and relatives, was enjoying a weekend street fair filled with dancing and home visits and, of course, drinking. They all decided to go to grandma's house in the country, but first they needed to stop at the local mini-mart for cigarettes and other supplies.

It was near midnight, and the clerk became verbally abusive with Hooty (Norma's brother), accusing them of short changing him. This was merely life as usual for Indian youth who were treated everyday in this way by the locals and their cowboy mentality. There was a scuffle of sorts, when the clerk became physical in his abuse. Just as Norma and her friends ran out of the store, a police squad car rolled by and the clerk yelled *"Get them!"* Thus began the chase.

The police radio squawked about a "car load of injuns." One cousin woke up from a nap in the back seat and tried to shoot the headlights out of the pursuing "night riders." His single shot didn't even hit the road. When they got to grandma's, three took their chances by running into the darkness. Two surrendered and were handcuffed, beaten, and strategically placed in the direct line of fire. Norma Jean and one cousin ran up a hill covered in sage-brush. She was shot in the back (this bullet remains in her body today). The cousin was shot in the groin as he raised his hands in surrender. The cops also committed friendly fire and got one their own in the hand. Hooty had managed to get to the back of grandma's cabin to check on her. An off-duty cop, Hittson, who had also been drinking, opened fire on Hooty without warning. One bullet entered the buttocks and traveled down the leg (this bullet remains in his body). The second bullet tore through the rear upper arm, exiting out the front. Hooty took the old single-shot .22 rifle, turned and fired. Hittson died immediately. More than 200 automatic weapon rounds were fired by the police.

The ensuing trial and ridiculous sentences were but further proof of the history of fear and racism directed at Shasta and Yorok and Karuk Native people of northern California. Hooty got the death penalty and Norma Jean got life. Years later this same history (a **Red** twist to the **Black Rage** defense used by Clarence Darrow in 1925) would be brilliantly used by San Francisco Attorney Tony Serra as grounds for self-defense in Hooty's bid for a new trial in 1985. It was culturally and logically proven beyond the shadow of a doubt that a Native person from this region should expect to be murdered by a policeman who was repeatedly shooting him/her in the back. He was found "not guilty" in May 1990. However, even though they were codefendants, Norma Jean received no benefit from this decision. His was a death penalty case that afforded him mandatory appeals. She got none of that and so remained in prison. The obvious lesbian butch Shasta Native Woman, Norma Jean Croy, was also denied parole at least four or five times.

While working on a San Francisco 1992 International Tribunal focusing on 500 years of colonialism and political prisoners in the u.s.a., i was approached by Hooty, who had a hard time saying it, but got it done, "My sister is a lesbian and she needs your help." And this was the birth of the Norma Jean Croy Defense Committee that became an amazing grassroots co-operative working group of mostly women. White activist dykes and Native women, their families and communities, came together with no funding (as usual). Attorney Diana Samuelson was the legal expert who worked out of Tony Serra's office with access to all the pertinent files. Nylak Butler who survived Wounded Knee, Johnella LaRose, Yvonne Wanrow, and several other Women of All Red Nations did amazing jobs within their community. We became regular visitors at chowchilla prison for women in the almond orchards of California. Many benefits were held wherever possible; most being within the lesbian/gay community of the SF Bay Area; artists donated their time. Out of Control Lesbian Committee to support women political prisoners placed Norma Jean on its list for commissary funding and included her regularly in the *Out of Time* newspaper. Hundreds of speaking gigs were held. Many, many, many envelopes were stuffed and many potlucks were eaten. Information was regularly presented at the Lesbian and Gay Pride events in the SF area and beyond. Every opportunity that could be found was used to spread the word.

In 1993 the International Indigenous Peoples Conference declared Norma Jean Croy a political prisoner and declared her case evidence of the government's continuing assault on Native peoples that followed the FBI incident at Ogala, North Dakota. Two films were made about the case: *Shasta Woman*, by me, was made totally by volunteers and was shown at the SF International Lesbian and Gay Film Festival in 1994. I did receive some funding from the Paul Robeson Fund for distribution and was able to send a few hundred copies across the country and some to Europe. Steve Patapoff did a longer film, *Reasons to Fear: the Cultural Defense of Hooty Croy*, which was released

299

after Norma's release in 1998. People understood this case instantly; it was the epitome of racism and classism and homophobia for thousands to easily recognize and realize. It transcended any simple definition of "political prisoner." It was the reflection of all colonialism that could not be denied. It was the base for all the murder and rape and enslavement and oppression that is amerikkkan history.

Norma Jean Croy was released and credited with time served in February 1997. Many celebrations were held. Norm stayed around the bay area for a few years trying to work and love and live. But really she ain't no urban Indian. She lives in the country of northern California and is a very happy farmer now. Some folks see her from time to time and she is not drinking and is in good health, doing well and smiling. We wish her continued good health and happiness.

United Nations Draft Declaration on the Rights of Indigenous People

Leonard Peltier
November 30, 2004

Sisters, Brothers, Friends and Supporters,

Indigenous Peoples of the United States are no strangers to hardship and abuse at the hands of the oppressor. We also are no strangers to treaty negotiation and betrayal. Between 1778, when the first treaty was signed with the Delawares, and 1868, when the final one was completed with the Nez Perces, there were hundreds of treaties between the U.S. government and the Indian Nations. Not one of these treaties was honored by the government.

The United Nations itself says that human rights must be applied to all Peoples without discrimination. Accordingly, the United Nations Draft Declaration for the Rights of Indigenous Peoples was adopted by the U.N. Subcommission for the Prevention of Discrimination and Protection of Minorities in 1994. The text of the Declaration has been endorsed and supported by hundreds of Indigenous Peoples and organizations around the world as the *minimum* standard required for the recognition and protection of Indigenous Peoples' rights internationally.

However, there have been continued attempts by some states to undermine efforts to protect the human rights of the Indigenous Peoples. We cannot allow our rights to be negotiated, compromised or diminished by the oppressor or by the U.N. process, which was initiated more than 20 years ago.

Yesterday, the Indigenous Peoples' delegates declared a hunger strike and spiritual fast inside the United Nations Palais des Nations in Geneva, Switzerland, to call the world's attention to these attempts to weaken the Draft Declaration on the Rights of Indigenous Peoples.

This week, I urge you to send expressions of solidarity to our brave sisters and brothers and letters of support for the adoption of the current text of the U.N. Draft Declaration on the Rights of Indigenous Peoples.

Thank you for caring.
Mitakuye Oyasin.
In the Spirit of Crazy Horse

The International Indian Treaty Council and Indigenous Prisoners' Struggles

The work for American Indian Movement political prisoner Leonard Peltier has taken many forms over many years. On the international level, the International Indian Treaty Council has long been a leader of the work, especially relating to the United Nations and official inter-governmental bodies. The documents included over the following pages include some significant IITC resources. The IITC had also actively attempted to bring attention to the ongoing persecution of Indigenous prisoners who try to practice their religious beliefs in U.S. prisons. (For more on the IITC, see page 826.) The documents included over the following pages are some examples of this work.

III.8.A

excerpt from a written Intervention to the United Nations Commission on Human Rights,

60th Session, March 15-April 23, 2003
Agenda item 11, Civil and Political Rights

a) Detention

The Justice Department as a branch of the United States government, has a legally binding trust responsibility to protect traditional Native religions, spiritual and cultural practices. The international community recognizes that persons under detention are not exempt from human rights protections and accords this vulnerable population special protections.

In January 2003 testimony was presented at U.S. Civil Rights Commission Hearings in Albuquerque, New Mexico, addressing violations of the spiritual, cultural and religious rights of Native Prisoners in the U.S. federal and state prison systems. Leonard Foster, Coordinator of the National Native American Prisoners Rights Advocacy Coalition, Director of the Navajo Nation

Corrections Project and Board Member of the IITC, testified that prisons in Arizona, California, Texas, South Dakota, Montana, Kansas, Colorado, Utah, Minnesota and New Mexico continued to violate religious freedom provisions mandated for American Indian prisoners by both U.S. and international law. In November 2002, Mr. Foster presented similar violations to the U.S. Department of Justice Civil Rights Division in Washington, DC, including:

a) denials of access to traditional ceremonies; b) lack of equal access to religious and spiritual leaders; c) lack of equal access to religious items; d) denial of the right to wear long hair or traditional hair style according to the religious customs of respective Indian Nations; e) denials of access to ceremonial foods; f) transfer to state facilities where American Indian religious practices are prohibited; and g) denial of access to traditional counseling and ceremonies, including requested last rites ceremonies for American Indian inmates on Death Row.

Both Federal Agencies committed to investigate and address these problems, but to the knowledge of those involved, nothing has been done to date. Since that time, the IITC and the National Native American Prisoners Rights Advocacy Coalition have received reports of new and continuing violations, including State of California Department of Corrections "grooming regulations" mandating forced hair-cutting, despite requests for religious exemptions for Native prisoners, and continued denial of sweat lodge ceremonies by the Texas Department of Corrections.

Recent court cases filed by Native prisoners and their advocates have upheld these denials, confirming the lack of effective redress through domestic remedies. Prison officials sited "security" concerns, which seems to be all that is required for the Justice Department, now a part of the new U.S. "Department of Homeland Security," to forgo civil and human rights protections, including freedom of religion guaranteed by its own Constitution.

These violations of federally and internationally protected rights have been presented at Congressional Hearings in 1978, 1992, and 1994. Similar testimony has been presented by the IITC to this Commission in various past sessions, as well as at the World Conference Against Racism in 2001 and to the U.N. Special Rapporteur on Religious Intolerance, Mr. Abdelfattah Amor, on his visit to the U.S. in 1999.

These policies directly affect the spiritual well-being and cultural survival of virtually every Indian Nation because of the high population of incarcerated Indian prisoners. The adoption and enforcement by state and federal prison systems of policies and regulations to protect against Religious Intolerance and Racial Discrimination is essential to ensure Native American prisoners access to healing and recovery through traditional religious practices and worship. We call upon this Commission to recognize the urgent need for international oversight and further investigation of these serious ongoing human rights violations in order to ensure that the freedom of religion for Native Prisoners is protected.

III.8.B
Written intervention submitted to the United Nations Commission on Human Rights Regarding the New Restrictions of Religious Practices in U.S. State and Federal Prisons

61st session, 14 March-22 April 2005
Agenda Item 11: Civil and Political Rights
including the questions of: (b) Religious intolerance

Read by Lenny Foster
IITC Board Member (Dine)

The American Indian prisoners in the United States Prison System are facing new restrictive policies on their religious and spiritual practices that make healing and rehabilitation in the traditional manner virtually impossible.

These new restrictions include:

a. Four-hour time limit on the Sweat Lodge ceremony that includes the heating of the stones, which takes two hours and two hours for the actual ceremony, rushing through an ancient old ceremony is not proper because the ceremony is very sacred. The deliberate attempt to shorten the hours and circumvent the ceremony is sacrilegious and undermining the seriousness and sacredness of the spiritual healing and blessings;

b. Supervision of the sweat lodge by the Chaplain is not necessary because it takes away time from other spiritual and cultural activities such as the Talking Circle, Drumming Sessions and Pipe Ceremonies that also mandate the presence of the Chaplain;

c. Rationing of the firewood has deliberately undermined the heating of the stones because the stones need to heated for at least two hours or else the stones are cold and the Sweat Lodge is not complete and/or beneficial to the healing and prayers;

d. Mandating the English-only requirement for the ceremony is discrimination and racist because the Native language is used and needed for the songs and prayers to be blessed by the Creator.

When the traditional ceremonies are held in the ancient and sacred way and manner, the Native prisoners receive the beneficial rehabilitation and spiritual healing. The Sweat Lodge ceremony has been the foundation of the healing and recovery from alcohol and drugs, and it has been a very positive therapy for the Native prisoners. All the traditional practices and beliefs are very important for the rehabilitation and recovery or the experience of incarceration becomes nothing more than warehousing human beings.

Leonard Peltier, who has been incarcerated in the United States Penitentiary—Leavenworth, Kansas for twenty-eight years, is a traditional practitioner of these practices and beliefs and is a beneficiary of this religious freedom struggle.

All American Indian Nations and Spiritual Leaders need to be consulted to rectify these new policies.

To deny these basic human rights and show indifference to a dignified spiritual healing is tantamount to a cultural genocide of a young generation of American Indian prisoners.

Thank you.

Source: Prison News Service

III.8.C

Urgent Appeal to United Nations
Working Group on Arbitrary Detentions, Part IV.C:
Leonard Peltier, AIM Activist and Human Rights Defender

July 6, 2005

Dear Members of the Working Group on Arbitrary Detentions,

Please receive the respectful greetings of the International Indian Treaty Council (IITC).

On 12 September 2004, the IITC submitted a communication to the United Nations Working Group on Arbitrary Detentions regarding the conviction and imprisonment of Leonard Peltier, considered by the IITC and many others throughout the world as a political prisoner of the United States government. The Working Group acknowledged this communication by telefax, dated 7 October 2004, also informing that the communication had been sent to the government of the United States with a formal letter concerning Mr. Peltier's detention. We understand that the Working Group has not received any response from them.

It has been reported to us that on the morning of July 1, 2005, Cyrus Peltier went to visit his grandfather at the United States Prison at Leavenworth, Kansas, as he has for the last 13 years. He was stopped at the visiting area and was told, "he's gone." Upon further inquiry, the grandson was told that Mr. Peltier had been transferred to the United States Prison at Terre Haute, Indiana, U.S.A..

As the attached letter from the Leonard Peltier Defense Committee (LPDC) informs*, Mr. Peltier was transferred on June 30th, without notice to his family or attorneys. He is being kept in indefinite solitary confinement, without fresh air, without telephone privileges, without stamps for letters out. He is now 60 years old, a respected elder, and in frail health. He has many health problems including diabetes and will be without medication soon.

We also understand that he is being denied access to his spiritual guide and practice.

Mr. Peltier is and has been a model prisoner throughout his incarceration, in spite of its injustice. The authorities have not explained the reasons for the transfer or their callous treatment. As reported by our communication of September, 2004, the Federal Bureau of Investigation spent a great deal of money to lobby against Mr. Peltier's receiving clemency and release from President Clinton during Mr. Clinton's last year in office. In another communication to the IITC, the LPDC also informs that although the Bureau of Prisons may argue that the placing of a transferred prisoner in solitary

---

* See III.8.D on page 308.

confinement is a routine procedure until all the appropriate paperwork is processed, the timing of this action adds to its cruelty since it was carried out right before the long weekend preceding this 4th of July. [U.S. Independence Day, a four-day holiday.] That solitary confinement, without human contact, continues to this day.

We urge the Working Group on Arbitrary Detentions exercise its mandate under Urgent Appeals, part IV.C in the case of Leonard Peltier. We again urge the Working Group to visit Mr. Peltier in prison. He is now located in solitary confinement at U.S. Penitentiary Terre Haute (Indiana).

As the attached letter from the LPDC requests, we are sending this communication to other relevant human rights mechanisms including the Special Representatives of the Secretary General on Human Rights Defenders, Mr. Rodolfo Stavenhagen, the Special Rapporteur on the Human Rights of Indigenous Peoples, and Mr. Wilton Littlechild, Member of the Permanent Forum on Indigenous Issues. We hope that they will join with you and your efforts on behalf of Mr. Peltier.

If you have any questions or comment, please do not hesitate to communicate with us at the addresses found in the letterhead. We would very much appreciate acknowledgement of receipt of this urgent communication and updates on its progress.

For all our relations,
Alberto Saldamando
IITC General Counsel

III.8.D

Letter from Leonard Peltier Defense Committee to International Indian Treaty Council

July 6, 2005

We are appealing to you on behalf of Leonard Peltier, an internationally known Native American political prisoner who has been in prison in the United States for almost thirty years. We recognize the work of the International Indian Treaty Council over many years to present the profound miscarriage of justice and human rights violations to which he has been subjected by the United States government at United Nations, in particular to the U.N. Commission on Human Rights and its Working Group on Arbitrary Detentions.

We are requesting your urgent assistance in response to a new crisis situation which has further violated his rights and is currently threatening his health. Last Thursday, June 30th, Mr. Peltier was moved without notice to his attorneys or his family from United States Federal Prison at Leavenworth, Kansas, to United States Prison at Terre Haute, Indiana. He is arbitrarily being held there in solitary confinement indefinitely. He was a well-respected model prisoner at Leavenworth. He is an elder, has many serious health problems, and poses no threat to the system. There is no basis for subjecting him to this kind of treatment. At Terre Haute he gets no fresh air, no phone privileges; he cannot write out because they give him ho stamps; his medications will run out in a couple of days (he is a diabetic). U.S.P. Terre Haute does not have a good record of taking care of prisoners' medical needs. We are asking with great urgency that you pass on this report on his status and ask for intervention on his behalf to the United Nations Commission on Human Rights, the Working Group on Arbitrary Detentions, and any other Human Rights bodies or Rapporteurs you deem relevant.

Thank you in advance for your efforts.

III.8.E

Resolution on Leonard Peltier

Commission on Prisoners' Rights
August 3-7, 2005

Whereas, the International Indian Treaty Council has consistently continued
to support Leonard Peltier, his human rights and his immediate release;

Whereas, a new crisis situation has arisen in which Peltier has and may be
successively transferred to different prisons without the knowledge of his
Defense Committee, Family, and attorney and held in solitary confinement
indefinitely without his basic human and prisoner rights;

Whereas, the International Indian Treaty Council has taken the case of
Leonard Peltier to the international arena, including the United Nations
Commission on Human Rights as recently as July 2005; and

Whereas, the Leonard Peltier Defense Committee respects and appreciates
this work of the International Indian Treaty Council; and

Now therefore be it resolved that the International Indian Treaty Council reaffirms its support of Leonard Peltier and will continue its work in support
of his freedom on the international level; and that it will continue to appeal
to the United Nations High Commissioner for Human Rights, its Working
Group on Arbitrary Detentions, Special Rapporteur on Indigenous Human
Rights, the Special Representatives of the Secretary General on Human
Rights Defenders, members of the Permanent Forum on Indigenous Issues,
the Office of Multi-Lateral Affairs, Democracy, Human Rights and Labor of
the United States State Department, Amnesty International, Human Rights
Watch, the United States Bureau of Prisons and any other National and
International Agencies it deems useful to safeguard his human and prisoner
rights; and

Be it further resolved that the International Indian Treaty Council will have a
direct and structured process of communication with Leonard Peltier and
his Defense Committee where the two entities will report to each other on
a regular basis; that Leonard Peltier personally and through his designated
representatives to be determined by Leonard Peltier, will have an active
role in the International Indian Treaty Council's work at the U.N. on behalf

This resolution was adopted by consensus at the 31st Anniversary International Indian Treaty
Council Conference hosted by the Confederacy of Treaty 6 First Nations, at Ermineskin
Cree Nation, Alberta, Canada.

of Leonard Peltier; and all claiming to represent Leonard Peltier will be verified by Leonard Peltier personally and by his Defense Committee Headquarters wherever they may be located; and

Be it finally resolved that this resolution shall be the policy of the International Indian Treaty Council.

Guatemala City, July 8, 2005

U.S.P. Terre Haute
Director

Dear Director:

With great concern I have received the news about Mr. Leonard Peltier's situation in the Terre Haute prison, in Indiana.

There is no need to adopt such measures – solitary confinement, no post mail or phone calls, lack of medicines – with him. He is elder, he was a model intern in the Leavenworth jail and he is sick.

I appeal to your conscience, to your sense of humanity, so that the basic human rights of Mr. Peltier are fully respected. Moreover, it is necessary that Mr. Peltier, a very well known and respected Native American leader, be transferred to a better penitentiary.

Many indigenous leaders and members of indigenous peoples all around the world are very worried about Mr. Peltier's treatment, which we have found very indignant and inhumane. We send you a call to urgently revise the conditions in which Mr. Peltier remains in jail.

I do hope that the authorities hear of this humanitarian call. The entire world, especially the Indigenous Peoples, will thank you.

Rigoberta Menchú Tum
Nobel Peace Prize Laureate

Section IV.

Campaigning to End Colonialism in Puerto Rico

*I*n the early 1980s, when many of the Puerto Rican political prisoners discussed in this chapter were first arrested, they were demonized in the popular press as terrorists; even some progressive forces suggested that they were crazies. By the 1990 Tribunal, there was more widespread support, especially from within the Puerto Rican community, but those who suggested that most of them would be released within 10 years were considered utopian and unrealistic at best. In 1999, the majority of the Puerto Rican patriots were granted clemency and set free.

The full story of the steadfast vision, leadership, and commitment of the architects of that successful campaign cannot be told here in a few documents and pages. That effort achieved what it did because of an understanding of the material conditions and sentiments of the masses of the Puerto Rican people—at home and in the U.S. A strategic analysis coupled with hard work brought that campaign across class, race, and traditional political divisions, to form alliances that, for a time, characterized the identity of the Puerto Rican nation. What is presented here are primarily some of the papers that helped to bring the campaign beyond its original and most dynamic base. Also presented are efforts, as the campaign was nearing success, to link the issue of the Puerto Rican prisoners to the issue of U.S. militarism and colonialism as practiced by the U.S. Navy occupation and bombing of the island of Vieques. This linking of peoples and issues should provide a signpost for future possibilities. Clearly the U.S. continues to try to silence the Puerto Rican shout for freedom, as evidenced by the 2005 assassination of 72-year-old *independentista* radical Filiberto Ojeda Ríos, the 2008 arrest of alleged Machetero leader Avelino González Claudio, and the continued grand jury investigations calling on testimony from prominent Puerto Rican activists in New York. The struggle must also continue.

This articles in the following pages were included in the booklet *Puerto Rico: The Cost of Colonialism,* published in 1992 by the Fellowship of Reconciliation's Task Force on Latin America and the Caribbean. The booklet was offered, the Task Force wrote, as one remedy to the lack of general information available about the Puerto Rican colonial reality, and particularly to deal with the North American progressive movement's lack of support and solidarity with the Puerto Rican people's struggle for self-determination.

IV.2.A

Why Focus on Puerto Rico?
Matt Meyer
1992

The 1990s began with the United Nations calling upon all nations and peoples to use this decade to finally remove the blight of colonialism from the face of the earth. They felt that this may be a realizable goal.

Since 1981, however, the U.N. Decolonization Committee has recommended that the General Assembly consider Puerto Rico a "non-self-governing territory," which obliges the U.S. to submit an annual report regarding its treatment of Puerto Rico. Several years ago, a process began that was intended to lead to a Puerto Rican plebiscite resolving its colonial status. As that process has been forestalled by the U.S. Congress and events around the world have led to independence of former republics and colonies, Puerto Rico remains a glaring example of justice denied. Yet a great outcry from the progressive community, in the U.S. or around the world, has yet to be heard.

Rather than answer the question, Why focus on Puerto Rico? I find it more useful to ask, why not? Given the outpouring of material and political church support for a decolonization process in southern Africa, why not focus on the last major remaining colony of the Americas? Given the United Nations call for a decade to end colonialism, and the 1992 quincentenary call of Indigenous Nations to celebrate 500 years of resistance and work toward a future of reconciliation, why not focus attention on what is now the world's oldest direct colony? Given the wealth of solidarity offered over the last decade to our sisters and brothers in various Latin American countries, why not develop massive and mainstream solidarity for the Latin American nation that, along with Mexico, is interwoven into the very fabric of U.S. life and history? Given the consistent pacifist leadership in opposing militarism, intervention, and weapons of mass destruction, why not put significant resources toward the elimination of the major foreign military base in our own hemisphere, the Puerto Rican staging ground for all major regional interventions? In so many ways, Puerto Rico seems to be a perfect point of progressive unity.

Why, then, have so few peace and justice groups made Puerto Rico work a priority, especially in light of the U.S. State Department's priority maintenance of Puerto Rican colonial status? One reason is simple to understand, but difficult to deal with: oppression that is close to home is always harder to combat than oppression that is at a "safe" distance. This truism may espe-

This article was the introduction to the booklet *Puerto Rico: The Cost of Colonialism,* published by the Fellowship of Reconciliation's Task Force on Latin America and the Caribbean.

cially challenge us in these times of harsh economic depression, as we walk over homeless people on our way to vigils protesting some injustice overseas. For most North American progressives, however, it is an exercise of race and class privilege to seek "elsewhere" for that moral activist work; most of us are not faced with the stark realities of survival that dictates bread-and-butter politics based in our own neighborhoods, communities, nationalities. It is, in fact, our primary moral task to overcome our personal and institutional racism and classism by understanding the struggles of those just down the block, of those who live "across the tracks," yet whose experiences within U.S. society are qualitatively different. Puerto Rico offers us the unique opportunity to engage on two levels of struggle, for Puerto Rico is both within and outside of the United States, and Puerto Ricans in each place experience unique forms of colonialism.

Perhaps a reason for reluctant support of Puerto Rican progressive movements stems from the fact that concrete resistance already exists, though in an indigenous and hard-to-define form. A strong sense of self-determination, autonomy, and self-definition, added to a shrewd sophistication regarding the nature of U.S. society, has placed Puerto Rican activists in a position of leadership under which some white activists may feel uncomfortable working. Anticolonial resistance movements, furthermore, have not come together under a single consistent organization or "united front" banner, making solidarity subject to sectarianism, inconsistency, and short-term interest. These movements have also faced significant repression, with leaders jailed, killed, and blacklisted by Puerto Rican and U.S. intelligence and police agencies. Fear of repression among North American supporters is not unwarranted, as several have faced similar, though less severe, hardships.

For those of us who are nonviolent activists, it is always important to examine the nature of any struggle we wish to support; though our aims may be similar, for us the means are as important as the ends. A brief overview of the current Puerto Rican community may find no quick Gandhi or King substitute. Looking closely at Puerto Rican anticolonial politics, we will, however, find a great deal of creative, persistent nonviolent actions. The squatter communities of Villa Sin Miedo may remind one of the Gandhian campaigns of land give-backs, or the University of Puerto Rico student strikes, of the tactics of SNCC. From the educational conferences against war toys to the nonviolent direct action of the people of Vieques resisting the U.S. military, the large mass of Puerto Rican activism has been as pacifist-oriented as any found in the U.S.

Of course, it is also necessary to note that armed actions have played a part in Puerto Rican resistance and that most Puerto Rican progressives will not disavow those actions or dismiss them as counterproductive. The absence of absolutist pacifism on the part of most of the Puerto Rican movement can hardly be used as an excuse, however, for withholding support from the entire freedom movement! At the very least, we have a moral responsibility to actively support those nonviolent actions and campaigns that make up the majority of anticolonial work.

At best, we need to understand how distancing ourselves from activists advocating the importance of armed struggle violates our very own principles of dialogue and reconciliation. We cannot treat these militant activists with a missionary attitude, preaching the "truth of nonviolence." We must understand, as Gandhi did, that we are all "experimenting with truth," with no progressive having a monopoly on tactics or strategies, especially in these tumultuous times. Our inactivity bespeaks our own doubts about the effectiveness of nonviolence against the oppressive nature of direct U.S. colonial power. We must meet the challenge of armed struggle with our own militant, nonviolent support actions.

One problem raised by some North Americans is how to support a Puerto Rican movement for self-determination when it is not clear what the majority of Puerto Ricans "want for themselves." The complications of the three status options facing Puerto Rico—continued or enhanced commonwealth status, statehood (incorporation into the U.S.), or complete independence—have caused some potential supporters to hesitate. And while neither this booklet nor the Fellowship of Reconciliation directly advocates any one option at this time, it is clear that the current commonwealth status as it is practiced today amounts to colonialism. The leading political parties that represent each of the three options have pushed the U.S. Congress to allow some type of plebiscite or referendum to take place, because they are united in the understanding that the current realities are not the result of a real choice on the part of the Puerto Rican people.

Progressive people must take up a position, similar to the United Nations position previously cited, that calls for decolonization according to the international conditions set forth by the U.N. "Committee of 22." This demands that all powers—including the courts, police, etc.—be handed over to Puerto Rican authorities, all colonial military powers be removed, all anticolonial prisoners be released, and repression be ended. If these conditions are met, and the U.N. determines that a sufficient length of time has elapsed for a free and open U.N.-supervised vote, then we may all witness what self-determination means. Until that time, however, it is crucial to understand that U.S.-supervised plebiscites are no more genuine than the South African-administered "freedoms" of South West Africa before the independence of Namibia.

The question of "independence," however, continues to present a controversial issue for some, since many Puerto Ricans equate an end to colonialism with independence. And while those of us who are not part of the Puerto Rican nation must not presuppose to choose a status option for them, we should also not be surprised that so many of the Puerto Ricans working with us for an end to colonialism are also advocating independence. We must take great care not to be hypocritical about our own support: we did not wait until 51 percent of the U.S. people called for an end to nuclear weapons before we called for an end to the production of these warheads. Most of us base our politics not on simple majoritarianism, but on morality. If independence is seen by most of our progressive brethren as the moral solution to the colonial problem, we must struggle to respect and understand that position. We must also take great care not to be racist in our support: we did not dare say to Gandhi, "Yes, Mahatma, we see the truth to your teachings about nonviolence, but could you tone down your talk about British colonialism… we'd really like to meet one of your pacifist colleagues who does not support independence for India." Gandhi's *satyagraha*, though much more than strategy or tactic, was borne of the struggle for independence as the principal means for an end to British colonialism. Though independence may take many diverse forms, there was little room for compromise on the need for an end to paternalistic foreign rule.

IV.2.B

The Costs of Colonialism

Dr. Luis Nieves Falcón

1991

History helps us understand why colonialism has been called a crime against humanity. The original people who inhabited Puerto Rico no longer exist; indeed they were so rapidly exterminated by the Spanish that we must turn to archaeologists and anthropologists to know our forebears.

The Spanish were haunted by the delusion that Puerto Rico was rich with gold. They hoped to extract and export the gold to Europe, using native peoples as slaves in the mines and exploiting them as a completely expendable resource. The resistance to this first genocidal phase of colonialism turned to organized rebellion by 1511, but by the middle of the 16th century, the entire Taino nation—spread throughout Puerto Rico, Cuba, and the Dominican Republic—had been devastated by forced labor, starvation, disease, and warfare.

In 1582 the Spanish royal inspector general lamented that farming had "practically stopped for lack of Indians and the high price of blacks" and begged for a thousand slaves to be sent at once. The Africans sent as slaves proved to be both the workhorses of the economy and a constant source of concern for the colonial masters as they conspired, ran away into the mountains, and organized guerrilla bands.

The first modern rebellion against Spanish colonialism was organized simultaneously in Puerto Rico and Cuba in 1868. The Puerto Rican uprising, known as the *Grito de Lares*, proclaimed the first Republic of Puerto Rico and placed the abolition of slavery as the first of its commandments.

The first Republic was brutally quelled, but as the result of this popular agitation, Puerto Rican deputies were sent to the Spanish Court for the first time in 1869. Slavery was abolished on April 21, 1873 (a date that is still celebrated as an official holiday), and the autonomy of Puerto Rico recognized in 1897. In 1898, however, the United States invaded Puerto Rico, abolishing all previously established rights of the Puerto Rican people and substituting for it, in the words of Commanding U.S. Army Major General Nelson A. Miles, "the largest measure of liberty consistent with military occupation."

Neither the reality of military occupation nor the yardstick by which lib-

---

This paper was adapted from a presentation given at the Summit of Seven of the World's Poorest Peoples, held in in Houston in 1990, to coincide with a meeting of the G7. The Summit's description noted, "Even within the legal borders of the U.S.A. there is a 45% poverty rate on Native American reservations and a 39% poverty rate in Puerto Rico." This gathering of witnesses was part of The Other Economic Summit (TOES). Dr. Nieves Falcón's paper was included, with permission, in *Puerto Rico: The Cost of Colonialism*.

erty is measured in our country has changed greatly, although appearances have. Today, at least thirteen percent of the best arable land in Puerto Rico is occupied by United States military bases, including one of the largest U.S. military bases outside of the United States at Roosevelt Roads (37,000 acres), located in Ceiba, Puerto Rico. Reported to be one of 13 U.S. military facilities on the island to have nuclear capability, the Roosevelt Roads base is in violation of the Treaty of Tlatelolco, which declared Central and Latin America to be a nuclear-free zone.

There are, according to the Caribbean Project on Justice and Peace, an additional 69 United States military installations in Puerto Rico, including the base at Fort Allen, which contains the presidential communications system known as "Mystic Star," to be used in case of nuclear emergency. Two-thirds of the island community of Vieques has been declared "off limits" to its residents so that the U.S. Navy can practice bombing, low-intensity warfare in tropical and mountainous climates, sea landings, and other tactics essential to its military strategy for Latin America in the coming decade and century.

With the approach of the expiration of both the Guantánamo Bay and Panama Canal contracts, the importance of securing Puerto Rico as a safe harbor for United States military action in the Caribbean and Central and Latin America increases, as does the concern of the United States military and financial interests in controlling "their" hemisphere. With these anxieties comes intolerance for all those who do not accept the idea that United States military interests should determine the degree of freedom they enjoy.

Those who have actively opposed the United States exploitation of Puerto Rico often find themselves judged in an English-language tribunal of the United States.

Currently 18 Puerto Ricans are incarcerated with exceedingly long sentences—e.g., ninety-eight years—under conditions designed to break their spirits, if not their bodies. And an additional 11 face sentences in excess of 160 years.

Repression has been a constant in our history, because it is impossible to maintain colonialism by consent, no matter how attractive the prize for the privileged few. In Puerto Rico, this repression has served three complementary functions: first, to protect the enormous U.S. economic interests and infrastructure in Puerto Rico; second, to protect the symbols of U.S. executive and military power; and finally, to control the levels of rebellion and protest endemic to the deprivation of liberty and the economic hardship that are visited upon colonized peoples.

Hand-in-hand with military occupation came economic occupation, making Puerto Rico a paradise for North American business interests. This exploitation relies on two devices: the depopulation of Puerto Rico and the transculturation and ideological assimilation of those Puerto Ricans who remained so that they would identify with "American" consumer goods, tastes, and political objectives. Depopulation has been accomplished largely through massive, economically compelled migration to the United States on the one hand, and the forced sterilization of more than 40 percent of all women of child-bearing age, on the other.

Mass migration represents more than a simple loss of population. It is also evidence of a profound transformation in the relation between the working people of Puerto Rico and their land, which in turn, has profound effects on feelings of collective and individual self-worth and self-sufficiency. In the first decades after the invasion, the economy was reoriented not to feeding the people of Puerto Rico, but to the manufacture of sugar for export. In the second half of the 20th century, light industry, especially the manufacturing of textiles, petrochemicals, and pharmaceuticals, replaced sugar production as the primary economic activity. But the fundamental character of an economy had important cultural and psychological consequences. Rather than an expression of an encounter between our people and our land, work became a mechanism for squeezing profits out of those who did not flee the destruction of independent agriculture and could adapt to large-scale agriculture or the assembly line. Forceful and continuous repression of the work force was imposed in an effort to cultivate attitudes of conformity and dependence, rather that individual or collective initiative and independence.

In order to convert Puerto Rican farmers, small business owners, housewives, clerics, and independent professionals into loyal employees of large foreign corporations, an ambitious program of cultural assimilation was undertaken. For the first two generations after the invasion, English was the official language of instruction in public schools. Teachers who dared speak to children in their shared native language were fired. The policy was abolished in 1948 following a long and militant strike by teachers and students.

As the "English only" movement suggests, every effort to implant "American" values and identities was made, and the public instruction system was viewed as the most appropriate vehicle for transforming cultural values. For those too old to learn to pledge allegiance to the flag of the United States every morning, it was made a crime to display the flag of Puerto Rico, even at home. All gatherings of nationalist character were persecuted as "seditious parties," and the first of the interminable lists of suspected "subversives"—a practice confirmed and declared illegal in 1989, but which continues to this day—was compiled.

The legalization of the invasion and occupation of Puerto Rico has been critical to the process of Americanization and transculturation. Between 1898 and 1900, Puerto Rico was frankly and formally a militarily occupied territory. In 1900, the first civilian government was installed by the United States. In 1917, three weeks before the United States entered World War I, Puerto Ricans were declared to be its citizens, subject to the military draft. They were still not permitted to select the judges of their own Supreme Court or even the president of their own university, let alone those who declared war.

Between 1950 and 1952, a series of steps were taken culminating in the implementation of a new official title, *Estado Libre Asociado* (Free Associated State, or Commonwealth). During this period, an armed uprising by the Nationalist Party in 1950, designed to call attention to the imminent peril of assimilation and declaring a Second Republic of Puerto Rico, was put down only by jailing over 5,000 men, women, and children who participated in or were suspected of aiding the rebellion.

Another widely boycotted effort to manufacture consent to colonialism was made in 1967. This misnamed "plebiscite" of 1967 was likewise so clearly invalid that in 1989, President Bush felt obliged to acknowledge that Puerto Ricans had been treated "unfairly" by the United States and offered to hold another plebiscite, which has subsequently been canceled by the U.S. Congress. But in none of these successive efforts to legitimize colonialism has the United States been willing to comply with international law and transfer all the powers to the people of Puerto Rico prior to making any binding decision on their political status.

To survive, Puerto Ricans must create a modern nation consistent with the real needs and priorities of Latin America and the Caribbean in the 21st century. It is a task that we cannot undertake alone, without the collective wisdom, experience, and support of other nations who have struggled to overcome colonialism and of others more experienced in nationhood in our region. We recognize the growing interdependence of the world today and look forward to participating in an international economic and social order based on cooperation, not conflict. Our first contribution to this new order is the abolition of colonialism in one of its last outposts in the modern world.

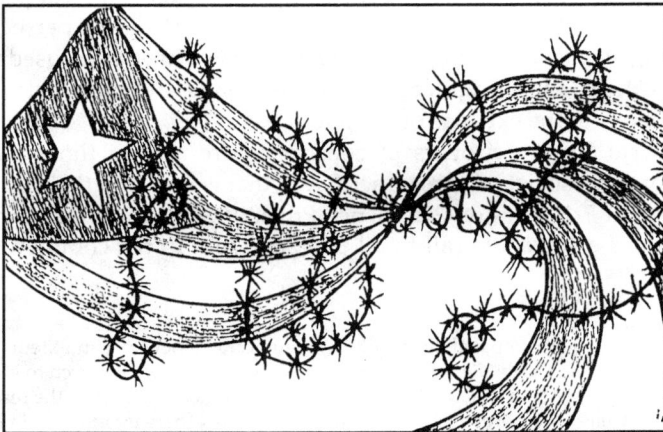

Proclaim Release: A Call to Conscience and Action for the Release of Puerto Rican Political Prisoners

Interfaith Prisoners of Conscience Project
1997

The Rev. Dr. S. Michael Yasutake, Executive Director:
Charity projects, providing direct services to the needy, are worthy and valuable. But we also need systemic change which eliminates poverty and the need for charity work altogether.

Prisoners of conscience, more commonly known as "political prisoners," have sided with the powerless and the poor. They are being persecuted for challenging systemic injustice. In many cases, laws have been used illegally to convict them. More frightening, laws are made and enforced to benefit those in power at the expense of the powerless.

The Puerto Rican prisoners of conscience are among those who have worked for a just society, at great sacrifice to themselves and their loved ones. The Interfaith Prisoners of Conscience Project (IPOC) and other supporting organizations extend this call to all people to join in the common struggle for justice.

After years of grassroots campaigning, mainly in United Church of Christ and Methodist congregations, the national bodies of both of these denominations were moved to issue statements in support of the release of the Puerto Rican prisoners. Pressuring the rest of the Protestants, as well as mainstream Catholic church hierarchies, these efforts were in large part coordinated and motivated by the Interfaith Prisoner of Conscience Project (IPOC). This booklet, produced by IPOC as an international affirmation of this work, helped shift the consensus toward release in the last years before clemancy was granted.

The Rev. C. Nozomi Ikuta, Chair:

Although work with "political prisoners" was among the expectations when I began my ministry at the United Church Board for Homeland Ministries, it took me over a year to summon the courage to find out how to visit a political prisoner. Driving up to a compound surrounded by razor wire and stepping through a gate which clangs behind one is not an easy thing to do. Frankly, I wasn't sure what to expect. What I found changed my life.

My first visit was with four Puerto Rican women at the Federal Correctional Institution (F.C.I.) in Dublin, California—Dylcia Pagán, Lucy Rodríguez, Carmen Valentín, and United Church of Christ member Alejandrina Torres. These were profoundly impressive women of gentle courage, strength, and integrity. My visit with them moved me to meet some of their compatriots— Edwin Cortés at the United States Penitentiary (U.S.P.) in Terre Haute, Indiana; Oscar López Rivera at the super-maximum prison in Florence, Colorado; Adolfo Matos at the U.S.P. in Lompoc, California; Ricardo Jiménez and Alberto Rodríguez at U.S.P. Lewisburg in Pennsylvania; Antonio Camacho Negrón at F.C.I. Allenwood in Pennsylvania; Alicia Rodríguez at Dwight Correctional Center in Illinois; and Luis Rosa at Stateville Prison in Illinois. In each case, I encountered men and women vibrant with life and love, whose eyes sparkle with vision and hope despite all they have already suffered and the terribly long sentences—as long as 105 years for Luis—which they are continuing to serve. Although these sentences seem harsh in the abstract form of the printed page, they are simply horrifying for those who have been privileged to meet the actual people who are enduring them. A peculiar form of outrage seeps into one's bones, calling forth a commitment to do all one can to secure their release.

These prisoners' friends, families, and community have mounted an energetic campaign for their freedom. They have sent thousands of letters and faxes to the President, urging him to grant them amnesty, and have been joined in this appeal by legislators, artists and religious leaders, including, most recently, Coretta Scott King and Desmond Tutu. With all their hearts, they—and I—urge you to join in the effort to free these remarkable men and women.

> The Spirit of the Lord is upon me, because he has anointed me to bring good news to the poor. He has sent me to proclaim release to the captives and recovery of sight to the blind, to let the oppressed go free, to proclaim the year of the Lord's favor.
>
> Luke 4:18-19

For over seventeen years, Puerto Rican men and women have been imprisoned throughout the U.S. because of their beliefs and actions in support of Puerto Rican independence. They are serving extremely long sentences (35-105 years)—far longer than the sentences meted out to others for heinous activities*—and many of them have suffered unusually harsh treatment while in prison, including physical assault and extended periods of solitary confinement—conditions condemned by Amnesty International. Puerto Ricans throughout the U.S. and Puerto Rico from all political sectors have called for their release. Now these prisoners—and the families and communities they have left behind—appeal to us, as Christians, to join in the growing effort to "proclaim release to the captives."

In 1991, the Eighteenth General Synod of the United Church of Christ said:

> The Scriptures commit us to bring to your attention the cry for justice and mercy from our Puerto Rican prisoners who are subjected to discriminatory treatment from the prison officials. Because we are called by Christ to bring the good news to the captives and to preach release to the oppressed, we have a responsibility to improve the prison conditions of the Puerto Rican prisoners and to eliminate the colonial condition of the Puerto Rican people. ... The Eighteenth General Synod demands that President Bush and the Congress undertake a process for Puerto Ricans to achieve self-determination and, as a gesture of good will, take the following steps, which are part of any legitimate process of self-determination: grant immediate and unconditional amnesty to all Puerto Rican prisoners of conscience and political prisoners. ...

This resolution was the fifth of six statements supporting Puerto Rican and other political prisoners adopted by the General Synod of the United Church of Christ from 1979-1995.

In 1996, the General Conference of the United Methodist Church said:

> The United Nations' resolutions on decolonization have clearly established that colonialism is a crime and recognize a colonized people's right to end colonialism. The United Nations also recognizes that these resolutions and laws apply to Puerto Rico. For many years,

---

* Their average sentence is 65.4 years—or about six times longer than the average murder sentence. The disproportionate sentencing is discussed further on page 332.

the United Nations Decolonization Committee has approved resolutions recognizing the inalienable right of Puerto Rico's people to
independence and self-determination. The injustice suffered under
Puerto Rico's colonial reality cannot be overlooked. President Bush
admitted that the people of Puerto Rico have never been consulted as
equals on their political status. ...

Therefore, be it resolved, that the General Conference of the
United Methodist Church advocate for justice and freedom for the
Puerto Rican political prisoners. Furthermore, that a letter from
the General Conference Secretary be sent to the President of the
United States asking him to grant pardon, because they have more
than sufficiently served their sentence.

In 1995, the Baptist Peace Fellowship said:

In the spirit of reconciliation throughout the world we call upon the
President of the United States to exercise the constitutional power
of pardon to grant immediate and unconditional release to the many
Puerto Rican women and men in U.S. prisons for their actions in favor
of self-determination and independence.

Also in 1995, the Episcopal Church of Puerto Rico said:

Whereas, political action and the struggle for self-determination of the
peoples respond, in our national case, to an unresolved problem...

Therefore, be it resolved that the 88th Annual Diocesan Assembly of
the Episcopal Church of Puerto Rico, the Sixteenth as an Autonomous
Church,

Ask the Honorable William Jefferson Clinton, President of the
United States of North America, to grant unconditional and imme-
diate amnesty to the Puerto Rican patriots imprisoned in the
United States. ...

In the January-February 1995 issue of *The Witness,* an independent journal
owned by the Episcopal Church Publishing Company, editor/publisher
Jeanie Wylie-Kellerman wrote:

In this issue, we raise the names of several political prisoners. We raise
them as icons into the injustice and cruelty that are woven through our
American way of life. We raise them as people willing to move past
liberalism to activism with cost.

325

Who are these prisoners?
Their names are Antonio Camacho Negrón, Edwin Cortés, Elizam Escobar, Ricardo Jiménez, Oscar López Rivera, Adolfo Matos, Dylcia Pagán, Alberto Rodríguez, Alicia Rodríguez, Lucy Rodríguez, Luis Rosa, Juan Segarra Palmer, Alejandrina Torres, Carlos Alberto Torres, and Carmen Valentín.

Most are parents; some are grandparents. Prior to their incarceration, they were workers, professionals, teachers, community organizers, and activists. They labored in their communities for quality education, child care facilities, health services, and against drug abuse. In prison, they have done artwork, developed child care and AIDS awareness and prevention programs, and taught literacy, high school equivalency (GED), and English as a Second Language (ESL) classes.

Church leaders who have met some of them in person have said:

> I found myself very moved... They are women of great character and are... in the midst of very difficult circumstances, holding fast to their own sense of who they are and who they want to be.
>
> Rev. Dr. Paul H. Sherry, President, United Church of Christ

> The personal impact that they had on me as Latina sisters is the personal integrity that they demonstrate, their spirit of dignity, and their gentleness about what they believe in.
>
> Ms. Linda Jaramillo, President,
> Council for Hispanic Ministries of the United Church of Christ

> You almost feel, after a visit like this, that you should speak in lower voice than you usually do. These were three very gentle people whose vision, even after all these years of incarceration, is anything but dimmed, and that does something to anybody who makes a visit like this.
>
> Rev. Dr. Thomas E. Dipko, Executive Vice-President,
> United Church Board for Homeland Ministries,
> United Church of Christ

> Meeting the women... was a profound honor. Their dedication, their serenity, their compassion, their commitment, and their humility—along with their inner and outer beauty—combine to make them exactly what they say they are not: role models.
>
> Ms. Sammy Toineeta, Lakota; Associate for Racial Justice,
> National Council of the Churches of Christ

My visit with Alejandrina Torres and the other political prisoners in September was my first such visit, and I was very, very impressed with what they had to say, with their integrity, with their commitment, and with all the injustices their people have endured. I was moved by the strength they have maintained despite all the hardship and suffering they have endured, and by Alejandrina's strong religious convictions.

Rev. Helen Locklear, Associate,
Racial Justice Leadership, Presbyterian Church

Visiting Alejandrina was a most powerful experience—she is an incredible woman of faith. She sets a tremendous example of the willingness to confront oppression, going the road to Jerusalem, as Jesus did, regardless of the cost.

Rev. Annie Gonzalez, Pastor, Northlake United Methodist Church

Why are they in prison?

These 15 men and women were convicted as members of organizations involved in armed actions against corporate and military targets maintaining the ongoing colonial situation of Puerto Rico. None of the 15 was ever charged with any action resulting in bloodshed.

The *Macheteros*: Two of the 15 (Antonio Camacho Negrón and Juan Segarra Palmer) were convicted of conspiracy and related charges as members of the *Macheteros*, a clandestine group based in Puerto Rico. The *Macheteros* took responsibility for a series of military actions, including bombings, the destruction of nine National Guard planes, attacks on military personnel based in Puerto Rico, and the taking of $7.5 million of government-insured money. The charges against these two prisoners included taking the money and transporting it out of the U.S.

The Armed Forces for National Liberation (FALN): The other 13 prisoners were convicted of seditious conspiracy and related charges as members of the Armed Forces for National Liberation (FALN), a clandestine group based in the United States. The FALN took responsibility for a series of bombings of government, corporate, and military sites. The charges against these men and women included possession and transportation of firearms, armed robbery, and transportation of stolen vehicles. Invoking international law, they claimed prisoner of war status, refused to recognize the jurisdiction of state and U.S. courts, did not defend themselves, did not challenge the government evidence against them, and received particularly long sentences of 35 to 105 years.

What is "seditious conspiracy"?
Webster's Dictionary defines sedition as "a stirring up of rebellion against the government." Seditious conspiracy is the charge for which Nelson Mandela was convicted and imprisoned in South Africa for so many years. In the U.S., it has been used primarily against Puerto Rican *independentista*s, proponents of Puerto Rican independence (from the 1930s to the 1980s, it was used exclusively against them), for conspiring to use force against the lawful authority of the United States of America over Puerto Rico. It does not reflect a distinct "crime," but serves as an "umbrella" charge which ties together all other charges. Like the charge of conspiracy, it also enables the government to charge members of an organization for actions of everyone else in the organization, regardless of their actual involvement in the specific action. For example, Luis Rosa was about 12 years old when the first bombing occurred in the conspiracy with which he is charged.

How can their actions be explained?
A brief history: On November 19, 1493, Christopher Columbus landed on an island called Borinquén by its people, the Tainos. Most of the Tainos soon died from slavery, disease, and murder; the Spanish brought Africans to replace them as slaves. On November 25, 1897, Puerto Rico negotiated a Charter of Autonomy with Spain requiring the consultation of the Puerto Rican people before the island's status could be changed. On July 25, 1898, at the end of the Spanish American War, the U.S. invaded Puerto Rico. In the Treaty of Paris, Spain ceded Puerto Rico to the U.S. as "war boooty" without consulting the Puerto Rican people regarding their status, in violation of the Charter of Autonomy.

U.S. presence in Puerto Rico severely altered every aspect of Puerto Rican life. It shifted the economy, first from subsistence agriculture to sugar for export, and then to light industries, such as textiles and pharmaceuticals, resulting in significant environmental degradation. The government imposed U.S. citizenship, the teaching of U.S. history and the English language, outlawed the display of the Puerto Rican flag, persecuted *independentistas* as "subversives," and sterilized 40% of the women of child-bearing age.* And although Spanish has been the official language of instruction since 1948, English remains the official language of the courts, and U.S. cultural influence continues through the official and popular media and through the presence of U.S. corporations on the island.

Today, the U.S. maintains numerous military installations, including 11 military bases, which cover 13% of the island. Throughout the history of Puerto Rico, there have been numerous incidents of violence against the people, including more recent times. On July 25, 1978—the 80th anniver-

---

* Luis Nieves Falcón, "Puerto Rico: The Costs of Colonialism," reprinted in this volume as IV.2.B, page 318.

sary of the U.S. invasion of Puerto Rico—two *independentistas,* Carlos Soto Arriví and Arnaldo Darío Rosado, were murdered by government agents. In 1982, then Governor Carlos Romero Barcelo ordered the National Guard to bulldoze Villa Sin Miedo (Village Without Fear), a squatters' village on idle government lands. In 1985, over 300 FBI agents and members of the U.S. Special Forces armed with automatic weapons invaded the homes of dozens of student activists and trade unionists, without informing the Puerto Rican government. The island of Vieques, a fishing site, has been used for decades for bombing practice, destroying the livelihood of the people. Those who protested were imprisoned as "criminals." Today, new military radar facilities are being constructed, generating massive protests among the people. In short, the U.S. colonial relationship with Puerto Rico has affected every aspect of Puerto Rican life and continues to be maintained by U.S. military occupation and corporate influence.

If we call for the release of these prisoners, aren't we supporting a particular political perspective? What political status do Puerto Ricans support?
Of course, *independentistas* are among those working most intensively to secure the release of these prisoners. But people of all political sectors in Puerto Rico have joined the call for their release in light of how much time they have already served and in the recognition that the release of political prisoners must be part of any genuine resolution of conflict in a colonial situation.[*]

The U.N. affirmations were more fully spelled out in U.N. Resolution 3103, adopted by the General Assembly on December 12, 1973, which

- outlawed attempts to suppress struggles against colonial and alien domination,
- recognized anticolonial conflicts as international armed conflicts, and
- recognized prisoners captured in such conflicts as prisoners of war.

International law outlawing colonialism has been explicitly applied to the case of Puerto Rico by the United Nations Decolonization Committee. Although the U.S. has consistently denied it, the United Nations and both the pro-independence and pro-statehood political sectors in Puerto Rico have recognized that Puerto Rico is a colony of the U.S., lacking political, economic, or cultural self-determination. Like the American colonists, the Puerto Rican prisoners see themselves as part of an anticolonial struggle, and place their actions—however the U.S. may criminalize them—in the context of this international law. They argue that in the context of international law, the real crime is the U.S. occupation of Puerto Rico, and not their actions to resist it.

---

[*] See, for example, the open letter to President Clinton, signed by people from all political sectors.

In Puerto Rico today, the pro-commonwealth Popular Democratic Party (PPD) and the pro-statehood New Progressive Party (PNP) each usually win approximately 45% of the vote, and the pro-independence Puerto Rican Independence Party (PIP) wins approximately 5% of the vote. The relatively low electoral support for the independence position leads some people in the U.S. to discount the independence movement. Independence advocates point out, however, that support for independence has been seriously weakened by criminalization and persecution of the independence movement, such as in the exclusion of *independentistas* from public-sector jobs. They also say that the significance of such referenda is devalued by the U.S. Congress's repeated statements that the results of votes concerning Puerto Rico's status are not binding. Such self-perpetuating effects of the colonial relationship have been recognized by the United Nations, which provides for the complete with-drawal of the colonial establishment, including the military apparatus, prior to a decision regarding political status.* In addition, it should be noted that many *independentistas* boycott elections and referenda because of the failure of such processes to meet international standards.

What do the Scriptures say?
The Scriptures show that Jesus' battles were ideological and spiritual rather than military—but they did involve profound conflict with the colonial ruling powers. The arrest of John the Baptist propelled Jesus to begin his public ministry (Mk. 1:14), and Jesus' clearing of the temple (Mt. 21:12-17, Mk. 11:15-19, Lk. 19:45-58, Jn. 2:13-22) dramatically challenged the economic, political, and religious control of the authorities over the people. Like the political prisoners of our day, Jesus was clearly considered a threat by the state, charged with "perverting our nation" (Lk. 23:2) and "stirring up the people" (Lk. 23:5). He endured both "state" and "federal" trials, where he refused to defend himself (Mt. 27:1-2, 11-14; Mk. 15:1-5; Lk. 23:1-12; Jn. 18:28-38, although John's account differs somewhat from the others). By his silence, he may have been refusing to recognize the jurisdiction of the colonial courts over him—or he may have simply recognized the futility of a legal defense in courts run by the very forces whose authority he rejected. Like today's political prisoners, who are repeatedly strip searched, he was stripped and humiliated, and ultimately received the harshest possible sentence—the sort reserved for political dissidents.

Scholars have suggested that the two "bandits" crucified with him were militant revolutionaries, who, like him, were considered a threat to the state.

---

* U.N. Resolution 1514.

Jesus said to "Turn the other cheek."
Shouldn't Christians insist on nonviolence, too?
Throughout history, Christians have, at times, felt compelled to break the law in pursuit of justice. In the U.S., Henry David Thoreau, the underground railroad, draft resisters, Martin Luther King and the Civil Rights movement, Dorothy Day, and the nuclear disarmament movement are all examples of inspiring, nonviolent courage and witness. But from the founding of the United States as a nation, people of conscience have, at times, also taken up arms in the quest for freedom. The American patriots, for example, were church members and used the churches to prepare for armed resistance against British colonialism. Other examples of armed resistance include slave rebellions and the indigenous resistance to the western expansion of the U.S.

In the same issue of *The Witness* quoted above, Interfaith Prisoners of Conscience Project director Rev. Michael Yasutake responds to the question of violence:

> The so-called radical movements that would resort to armed defense or resistance against forces of injustice are not any more violent than any nation that resorts to armed conflict for national security. International laws such as of the U.N. maintain that the oppressed may use any means necessary for liberation, including the use of arms.

> The prevalent view of the dominant society in the U.S. is that nonviolent methods are the only appropriate means of social change. ...[even though] many in the dominant society, including religious institutions, are not pacifists themselves—fully relying on armed police power for protection or on the... armed services in the name of national security.

As Lourdes Garcia, United Church Board for World Ministries staff person, wrote more bluntly in the Fellowship of Reconciliation's resource, *Puerto Rico: the Cost of Colonialism*:

> The oppressed have repeatedly been told by the church that salvation lies in their capacity to passively accept their fate and turn the other cheek... It is not difficult to imagine, therefore, why a call for nonviolence put forth by some North American Christians is hard to take. What challenges are North American Christians prepared to confront regarding the power structures of their society that operate in Puerto Rico?

The international community has recognized that in the case of Puerto Rico, as in other situations of colonial conflict, the release of political prisoners is

331

critical to the reconciliation process. Because as Christians we are called to be agents of justice and reconciliation, whether we are pacifists or not, we are called to join the international community in its reconciling call for the release of these men and women.

I thought the U.S. didn't have any political prisoners;
aren't these prisoners just common criminals?
When the international community—including the U.S. and President Clinton—has called for the release of "political prisoners" as part of a reconciliation process, it has clearly included people imprisoned for their participation in armed conflicts. In the case of Puerto Rico, however, the U.S. has resisted acknowledging that it has political prisoners by insisting that people who affirm the right to resort to arms are "criminals," not "political prisoners." But if we apply the same standards used in the cases of South Africa, Cuba, Northern Ireland, and the Middle East, these Puerto Rican women and men would indeed be considered political prisoners.

Of course, many people will disagree with—or condemn outright—the activities for which these prisoners were convicted. But it should be noted that the actions for which they were imprisoned were motivated not (as with "common criminals") for personal gain, but rather, for the sake of their nation. They accepted the risk of imprisonment or death because of their commitment to independence.

Further, the U.S. government has treated these cases more severely than those of common criminals. Government statistics show that common criminals receive far shorter sentences than the Puerto Rican prisoners did. As mentioned above, their average sentence is 65.4 years—or about six times longer than the average murder sentence. And their sentences are far longer than those meted out to police convicted of anti-independence activity.

Former Puerto Rican police colonel Alejo Maldonado, an admitted assassin, is soon to be paroled after serving less time than the *independentista* prisoners, despite press reports that he took part in police death squads involved in kidnapping, robbery, extortion, weapons trafficking, torture, and murder. The five Puerto Rican police who were convicted of the 1978 Cerro Maravilla murders of two *independentistas* received sentences of 10-30 years—far shorter than Luis Rosa's sentence of 105 years—and the commander of the intelligence unit was released on parole after six years in prison.[*]

---

[*] Ortiz Luquis,"Ignacio Rivera: Un agente encubierto de abogado," *Claridad,* Nov. 29-Dec. 5, 1991, p. 3. For other articles concerning disproportionate sentencing, see: U.S. v. Moreno Morales et al., 815F.2d 725 (1st Cir. 1987); Ortiz Luquis,"Carta ajena desmiente a Romero involucra al FBI," *Claridad,* Nov. 29-Dec. 5, 1991, p. 5;"Acuerdo esclareceria caso Muñoz Varela," *Claridad,* August 4-10, 1995, p. 3; Marilyn Perez Cotto,"Justicia no puede descansar en testirnonio Alejo," *Claridad,* Aug. 11-17, 1995, p. 3.

If we call for the release of these prisoners, aren't we condoning violence?
No. In calling for their release, we are not making a judgment about the use of
arms. We are joining people from Puerto Rico, the U.S., and around the world
who are calling for the release of these prisoners in light of the 14 to 17 years
most of them have already served and in the recognition that the release of
political prisoners must be part of any genuine resolution of conflict in a colonial situation.

Shouldn't they have to show remorse before they are released?
Although none of the Puerto Rican Nationalist prisoners pardoned by
President Carter in 1979 renounced the principle of the right to engage in
armed struggle, in fact none ever engaged in it after their release. Neither
were expressions of remorse required of Nelson Mandela, Irish nationalists,
nor Palestinians prior to their release. Rather, the United Nations regards the
release of such prisoners as a part of the process of reconciliation and resolution of the conflicted or colonial situation.

Credit: Elspeth Meyer

Puerto Rican Bishops' Conference
April 24, 1996

Dear President Clinton:

"The Spirit of the Lord is upon me, because he has anointed me to bring good news to the poor. He has sent me to proclaim release to the captives and recovery of sight to the blind, to let the oppressed go free, to proclaim the year of the Lord's favor." (Luke 4:18-19)

We write to urge you to grant the pending application for the immediate and unconditional release of the fifteen Puerto Rican women and men in prison for their pro-independence activities.

This expression of support comes as a result of exploring not only the theological aspect, but the historical and human rights aspects, and included a pastoral visit, conducted at the behest of one of our bishops, with one of these prisoners. This visit, along with our reflections, has led to our discernment that both justice and mercy place upon us a moral claim.

The Scriptures commit us to hear the cry for justice and mercy for our imprisoned brothers and sisters, and to preach release for the oppressed.

We therefore stand among the many other denominations, civic and religious groups, elected officials, and community leaders ready and willing to embrace these fifteen men and women in the spirit of reconciliation.

May the God of justice and compassion guide you in making this significant moral decision. Respectfully,

S.E.R. Luis Cardenal Aponte Martínez,
Archbishop of San Juan

Mons. Iñaki Mallona, CP
 Bishop of Arecibo, President

Mons. Ulises Casiano,
Bishop of Mayaguez, Vice President

Mons. Fremiot Tories Oliver,
Bishop of Ponce

Mons. Enrique Hernández,
Bishop of Caguas

Mons. Ricardo Suriñach,
Auxiliary Bishop of Ponce

Mons. Héctor Rivera,
Auxiliary Bishop of San Juan

Mons. Hermín Negrón Santana,
Auxiliary Bishop of San Juan,
Secretary

INTERNATIONAL CALL TO CONSCIENCE
To U.S. President William Clinton & U.S. Attorney General Janet Reno
On the Puerto Rican Political Prisoners

We join our voices with those of other people of conscience by asking for unconditional amnesty for the Puerto Rican political prisoners confined in prisons and jails within the United States. Before their incarceration, these men and women were individuals who functioned as vital members of their community. Comprised of students, artists, lawyers, secretaries, scholars, journalists, community activists, trades people and teachers, many are also mothers and fathers who have spent over a decade in prison while their children have grown up without them.

These men and women have been imprisoned, and many given virtual life sentences, for their activities on behalf of the struggle for the independence of Puerto Rico. In reaffirming the Puerto Rican people's right to self-determination, the United Nations Special Committee on Decolonization has passed resolutions every year since 1972 on the vital necessity for the decolonization of Puerto Rico.

The conditions of their confinement have violated generally accepted human rights standards. For example, in disregard of explicit federal regulations mandating that prisoners be placed in prisons as close to their families as possible, these prisoners have been imprisoned unnecessarily far from their homes. Their disproportionately large sentences, when compared to social prisoners sentenced during the same time frame, indicate the politica nature of their incarceration.

Given the above considerations, we ask that you grant all of them unconditional amnesty.

Adolfo Pérez Esquivel
founder, Servicio Paz Y Justicia, Argentina;
recipient, 1974 Nobel Peace Prize

Tandi Luthuli Gcabashe
SA Director, American Friends Service
Committee * (recipient, 1947 Nobel Peace Prize);
daughter of South African Chief Albert Luthuli
(recipient, 1960 Nobel Peace Prize)

Rev. Monsignor Bruce Kent
past president, Bureau International Permanent
de la Paix/International Peace Bureau *
(recipient, 1910 Nobel Peace Prize)

Mrs. Coretta Scott King
Director, Dr. Martin Luther King Jr. Center
for Nonviolent Social Change;
widow of Martin Luther King
(recipient, 1964 Nobel Peace Prize)

Mairead Corrigan Maguire
Community of Peace People, N. Ireland;
recipient, 1976 Nobel Peace Prize

Rigoberta Menchú Tum
UNESCO Goodwill Ambassador;
recipient, 1992 Nobel Peace Prize

José Ramos-Horta
Special Rep. of the Maubere (East Timor);
recipient, 1996 Nobel Peace Prize

Dr. Victor W. Sidel
Co-President, International Physicians
for the Prevention of Nuclear War *
(recipient, 1985 Nobel Peace Prize)

The Most Reverend Desmond Mpilo Tutu
Archbishop of Cape Town, South Africa;
recipient, 1984 Nobel Peace Prize

Dr. George Wald
recipient, 1967 Nobel Prize in Medicine

William C. Wardlaw
Executive Director's Leadership Council, Amnesty
International *
(recipient, 1977 Nobel Peace Prize)

Dr. Elise Boulding, former Secretary General, International Peace Research Association; **Doreen Boyd**, Deputy General Secretary, Young Women's Christian Association; **Etienne De Jonghe**, International Secretary, Pax Christi International; **Bishop Federico Pagura**, President, Consejo Internacional de Iglesias; **Wendy Singh**, Vice President, Penal Reform International; **Dr. Aaron Tolen**, President, World Council of Churches.

The above was published as a full-page advertisement in the *Washington Post* on Friday, December 20, 1996.

IV.5

A Day Without the Pentagon

Resistance in Brooklyn
1998

We dedicate our participation in this War Resisters League 75th anniversary Pentagon action to the Puerto Rican Political Prisoners and Prisoners of War. At this very moment, the legal case for their pardon rests on the President's desk. President Clinton, hear our voices: pardon all of these dedicated women and men.

At the same time, behind the very walls of the Pentagon, military advisors are holding discussions about adding substantial personnel and bases in Puerto Rico, to counteract the diminishing forces that are in the process of withdrawing from Panama. Now is the time for universal military downsizing: we demand that the U.S. remove all of its military from Puerto Rico.

Although the U.S. denies it holds political prisoners and prisoners of war, there are over 100 incarcerated freedom fighters in this country. Of these, there are 5 women and 10 men who languish in U.S. prisons for their activity in the struggle toward decolonizing and demilitarizing Puerto Rico. These 15 *independentistas* have been, as substantiated by international law, illegally imprisoned for over 18 years. Their sentences are over 6 times longer than the average murder sentence, yet none of them was charged with any action resulting in bloodshed. The real crime is U.S. occupation of Puerto Rico, *not* actions taken to resist this brutal colonial relationship.

Since its 1898 invasion of Puerto Rico, the U.S. has systematically destroyed the island's agrarian-based economy and has, through strident military occupation, wrought extreme environmental, cultural, social and political devastation. Puerto Rico has been used by the U.S. for its geopolitical positioning. Strategically, the island has served as the center of U.S. naval control for the entire Caribbean and South Atlantic. The U.S. has operated its antirevolu-

---

For its 75th anniversary, the War Resisters League organized a blockade of the Pentagon. As a part of that campaign, Resistance in Brooklyn decided to link the issue of antimilitarism in general to the U.S. Navy bombing and occupation of the Puerto Rican island of Vieques, and to the U.S. holding of Puerto Rican political prisoners. Dr. Luis Nieves Falcón, who was president of the Puerto Rican Human Rights Campaign at the time, addressed the preceeding WRL conference and Pentagon demonstration as a plenary speaker, and served as a consultant to RnB's affinity group presence. Veteran peace activist Dave Dellinger joined RnB for the action itself, in which 10 of us were arrested at an entrance to the building. The following leaflet was handed out at the conference and demonstration, to fellow demonstrators, WRL members, and curious onlookers.

tionary activity in the region from its military bases in Puerto Rico and has conducted its recruitment, training and attacks from the island, including the contra war against Nicaragua and the invasion of Grenada. There are over 20 military bases on 15% of Puerto Rico's most arable land. U.S. military and corporations, acting with virtually no restrictions, have caused deforestation as well as river, soil and forest contamination resulting from agent orange testing and mercury poisoning. There is a water crisis due to sand and rock quarrying. The island of Vieques (considered part of Puerto Rico) has been decimated by bombing maneuvers that have led to soaring rates of cancer and leukemia, sterile animals and dead fish, making sustainability impossible. Puerto Rico has functioned as a source of cheap labor for American corporations, ultimately inducing extreme poverty and unemployment. The U.S. sterilized 40% of Puerto Rico's women and has continuously forced its men to participate in fighting U.S. wars. Puerto Rico's history has been erased in U.S. education. Reflexively, systemic and compulsory acculturation has foisted U.S. history and English on Puerto Rico's people in their schools, courts and media.

Concurrent with this century-old system of imperialism and control, there has existed a tireless Puerto Rican liberation movement—on the island and in the U.S.—challenging and resisting this repressive apparatus and fighting for economic and political self-determination by every possible means—from rallies, armed propaganda actions, civil disobedience and educational reform to religious services and independent trade unions. Most recently, the August 1998 general strike brought 50% of all Puerto Rican workers into a movement to prevent privatization of the National Phone Company. The military, local police, national guard, FBI and the judicial system are all used to crush this movement. As *independentistas* have protested, they have been imprisoned. The 15 prisoners that are presently being held are severely repressed, suffering abuse, solitary confinement, frequent transfers, medical neglect and denial of furloughs to pay last respects to dying or deceased parents. These tactics are imposed to intimidate them and are an attempt to break the spirits of the prisoners and activists. There has also been an increase in FBI attacks to prevent organizing for release of the political prisoners and to destabilize the independence movement.

The United Nations has declared the 1990s as the decade to end colonialism. Year after year, the U.N.'s Decolonization Committee has heard testimony from representatives of all three political status options, who disagree on much but agree on one fact: Puerto Rico's current status amounts to little more than traditional colonialism. The U.N. Decolonization Committee has agreed, recognizing that no true decolonization process can take place without a complete withdrawal of foreign (U.S.) military, police and judicial personnel; without the releasing of all political prisoners; and without an independent plebiscite or referendum monitored by an impartial international group. No future vote, such as the one proposed at the end of this year, can be deemed legitimate if the U.S. colonial power administers and reviews the entire process from start to finish, and if the other conditions have not been met.

Calls for the release of the Puerto Rican prisoners have come from 11 Nobel Laureates, from members of Congress, from leaders of all three Puerto Rican political parties, and from tens of thousands of Puerto Ricans on the island and in the U.S. Former President Jimmy Carter has also called upon Clinton to exercise his constitutional power of pardon, granting immediate and unconditional release to the Puerto Rican men and women detained in U.S. prisons for their work toward Puerto Rican autonomy. We add our voices and bodies to this Call, and urge all U.S. activists committed to social justice and peace to join us at this crucial moment.

From a Day Without the Pentagon to a Century Without Colonialism!
Free Them All!
Amnesty for All Puerto Rican Political Prisoners/P.O.W.'s!
Pentagon Presence Out of Puerto Rico!
Puerto Rico 1998: 100 Years of U.S. Colonialism, 100 Years of Resistance
Free All Political Prisoners!

The Ones Left Behind

Matt Meyer
1999

After 19 years in prison, serving a 78-year sentence for the political thought crime of "seditious conspiracy," Adolfo Matos's first steps into JFK's International Airport in New York bring tears to everyone present. The tears are mainly of relief—after the intense campaigns, the long meetings and multiple strategies, and *(oh my!)* Adolfo looks so good *(almost younger than when he went in!)*. But they're also tears of political shock, tears of rage at the injustice of it all. Adolfo's time in New York is brief—a one-hour stop-over with his extended family and supporters, between the prison in California and the land he'll now call his home: Puerto Rico, the land whose freedom he was conspiring for.

The struggle against the U.S. occupation of Puerto Rico goes back to 1898, when U.S. troops invaded the island at the end of the Spanish-American War. Since that time, a steady movement of resistance has developed, weathering both harsh colonial conditions as well as draconian measures to keep down progressive and independence activists. Puerto Rico continues to be used as the main U.S. military base in Latin America, with over 14 sub-bases located throughout the small island, and with both of the two tiny but populated islands connected to Puerto Rico—Vieques and Culebra—used at times as bombing ranges. Puerto Ricans were granted a nominal form of U.S. citizenship just prior to World War I, facilitating the conscription of Puerto Rican men while disallowing Puerto Ricans not living within the U.S. to even vote for president or governmental representatives. Sent to the front in numbers widely disproportional to their percentage in the population, Puerto Ricans have also led U.S. statistics in the area of draft resistance and evasion. When not facing conventional conflicts, colonial violence has been imposed through the forced sterilization of large numbers of Puerto Rican women, in experiments to further the interests of multinational pharmaceuticals. Economic exploitation has allowed U.S. corporations to operate in Puerto Rico tax-free, while poverty levels continue to increase in a country stripped of its natural resources. The English-language court system in this Spanish-speaking nation presides over the "security" work of various departments of the FBI, military police, and domestic forces. Truly resisters of these conditions—

Originally published in *Peace News: Newsletter of War Resisters International*, December 1999.

from student activists, to environmentalists, to feminists or trade unionists or nationalists—qualify as those resisting war during wartime. Colonialism itself has always been a form of war, and Puerto Rico remains—at the beginning of the century the U.N. had hoped to declare an era without colonies— one of the world's last direct colonial enclaves.

The Puerto Rican political prisoners—technically acknowledged as being prisoners of war by a number of independent international tribunals—grew out of this context of resistance and repression. All had been connected to community-based improvement efforts, including church groups, alternative schools, cultural centers, and anti-U.S. Navy efforts. The U.S. government's conspiracy charge, made when they were arrested throughout the early 1980s, united them conceptually as being members of one or another clandestine group that was engaged in symbolic bombings, bank robberies and the like. And while a few of the 15 were found in possession of some weapons, none were ever linked to actual acts resulting in death or destruction. Nevertheless, the sentences handed down for possibly belonging to an organization that possibly could be proven responsible for militaristic acts far outweighed the sentences typically given for the proven crimes of murder, kidnapping or rape. These terms—in some individuals' cases totaling as many as 105 years—were carried out under tortuous conditions often condemned by human rights groups, in jails spread out across the U.S., far away from the prisoners' families or support networks. The outrageous sentences and treatment, along with the stalwart ways in which the prisoners continued to assert their justice and peace politics, led them to become symbols for the entire Puerto Rican people. It was on this basis that an amnesty campaign was waged.

The Puerto Rican Human Rights Campaign, under the direction of sociologist and educator Dr. Luis Nieves Falcón, organized a multifaceted strategy that understood the need for both massive grassroots momentum and for well-placed international solidarity. Modeling the life of a tireless activist, Falcón retired from a prestigious position as head of the Department of Caribbean and Latin American Studies at the University of Puerto Rico to get a law degree so he could better understand the cases and support his imprisoned compatriots. Once the legal basis for amnesty was clearly established— at conferences in Barcelona, New York, San Francisco, and Geneva—teams of students were trained to go to every town and municipality, knocking on doors and getting people to write letters, sign petitions, and pressure politicians. Careful to respect the issues that the prisoners stood for, the campaign was also committed to making the fact and conditions of their imprisonment (an outgrowth of the colonial condition facing all Puerto Ricans) the central political concern. Thus, in time, leaders of virtually every Puerto Rican trade union, church, and legal association joined in the call for amnesty; representatives of every political party from left to center to right added their names. On the eve of a huge march held on 29 August, a dinner was held to gather supporters; the keynote addresses were made by Catholic Archbishop

Roberto González Nieves and Episcopal Bishop David Álvarez. The slogan of the march, which attracted well over 100,000 people in what has been called the largest demonstration in Puerto Rican history, had gone beyond the more common "freedom for the political prisoners" to "Liberty for Our Own: It's time to bring them home."

On the international level, educational work became an early priority, along with mobilizing the large sectors of Puerto Ricans living in the continental U.S. By the end of last year, almost every Latino elected official in the U.S. had joined in the amnesty efforts, and the letter-writing campaign had reached groups and individuals throughout Europe, Latin America, Africa, Asia and the Pacific. The international pacifist and peace movements played a significant role, and—under the coordination of the Puerto Rican Human Rights Campaign and with the assistance of the local Resistance in Brooklyn (RnB) affinity group—a Call from the Nobel Peace Prize community was developed. Ultimately, 11 Nobel laureates or those representing Nobel-winning organizations signed the Call, including Archbishop Tutu, Mairead Corrigan Maguire, José Ramos-Horta, Coretta Scott King, and Adolfo Pérez Esquivel (who helped initiate the Call at War Resisters International's Brazilian Triennial). With this type of solidarity growing, the prisoners' lawyers initiated a series of meetings with the White House pardon attorney and White House Hispanic Affairs chief, to open a channel of communication.

Never relying on the honesty of politicians, the Campaign believed that a subjective connection was, in fact, necessary, and the children and parents of those imprisoned began direct appeals to the very center of political power. Over the past year, after a number of implied promises of release were broken, the tactical flexibility of the campaign was also revealed: a series of nonviolent civil disobedience actions began. First, at the October 1998 Day Without the Pentagon actions commemorating WRL's 75th anniversary, RnB—joined by some Plowshares activists and by veteran pacifist Dave Dellinger—dedicated their arrests to the Puerto Rican prisoners and to the people of Vieques, who deserved freedom from the Pentagon's bombing raids. Then, last July—on the 101st anniversary of the U.S. Marines invasion of Puerto Rico—the U.S.-based National Committee to Free Puerto Rican Political Prisoners/POW's (supported by RnB and by the Interfaith Prisoners of Conscience Project of the National Council of Churches), staged a civil disobedience action in front of the White House. Although a civil and courteous meeting (between the President's attorneys, the prisoners' attorney Jan Susler, and Pax Christi supporter Bishop Thomas Gumbleton) had just taken place moments earlier inside the White House, the Campaign had matured to the point of understanding that a strategic use of multiple tactics and approaches, of the objective need to mobilize masses of people as well as the subjective need to speak truth to the powerful, could ultimately end in success.

In spite of all this, the events of August and September 1999 sped by like a blur for most amnesty workers. When, on August 11, William Clinton offered a conditional clemency to 14 of the 15 (also extending a reduction in fines to two already-released prisoners), campaigners were both overjoyed and outraged. Under the conditions, 12 could be released immediately and two others could spend five and 10 additional years (still a sentence reduction) in prison. An oath of nonviolence would have to be signed by all those accepting the offer, despite the fact that the Campaign had already submitted documents from the prisoners agreeing to participate in the legal, nonviolent movement for independence. Another condition stipulated that no prisoner could visit or see another convicted felon, despite the fact that two of the prisoners are sisters who have been bunked together in jail, and another is the husband of a previously released *independentista*.

The movement shifted focus toward a call for unconditional freedom, as the prisoners themselves tried to find a way to respond to the offer as a group, despite their geographic separation. A conference was held in San Juan in late August, with presenters including this author and WRL staff person Roberta Bacic, speaking on the reintegration of the prisoners of conscience of Chile following the ouster of Pinochet. At the grand march following the conference, the key speaker was not a Puerto Rican nationalist or independentist hero, but Chicago Congressman Luis Gutiérrez, who delivered a fiery condemnation of the President's conditions. Back in the U.S., the Republican Party was waging an attack of its own, focusing on the electoral aspirations of Hillary Clinton and Al Gore and the importance of the Latino vote. When Hillary noted, in early September, that the prisoners were taking a long time to decide what to do, and that perhaps the offer should be rescinded, a furious New York Congressman, José Serrano, fired back that the U.S. had been taking over 100 years to decide upon the fate of Puerto Rico. Several days later, 12 of the 14 agreed to accept the clemency, resulting in the almost immediate release of 11. After two decades of uphill struggle, a real victory had been won.

Alejandrina Torres is one of those 11, now surrounded by family and friends. A teacher and officer of the First Congregational Church of Chicago (where her husband is the retired pastor), her engaging smile, soft demeanor, and strong spirit belie the 16 years of hellish conditions she endured. Immediately upon arrest, Torres was placed on special administrative detention on an all-male unit, and in 1984 experienced a brutal physical assault and double strip search at the hands of one male and four female guards. One of three political prisoners placed in the experimental Lexington Control Unit, she faced 24-hour-a-day surveillance, sensory and sleep deprivation, and various forms of psychological and physical torture—before the Control Unit was closed due to grassroots pressures and an Amnesty International investigation. Despite suffering a heart attack and several chronic medical conditions, Torres was never allowed proper medical treatment. In an exclusive conversation with *Peace News*, Alejandrina characteristically turned the discussion away from her personal suffering and toward the conditions facing her people. Her affect is one not of bitterness, but of beauty.

"We decided at this particular time that we needed to respond to the people," she began, speaking of the decision to accept the clemency offer. "We owed a response that would be reasonable to them, and many leaders were saying that it's been long enough. It would be better, they argued, for us to be outside, to work together and deal collectively with the ones left behind."

Four of those included in the amnesty campaign remain behind bars, including Alejandrina's stepson, Carlos Alberto Torres (who was not offered any clemency deal). Juan Segarra Palmer, who accepted the Clinton offer, must serve another five years, and Antonio Camacho Negrón—who was out on parole two years ago but re-imprisoned when he violated parole conditions by traveling extensively and speaking out politically—refused the offer and has several more years to serve. Oscar López Rivera, who also refused the government's offer (to release him conditionally after serving an additional 10 years), has 52 years left to serve. A Vietnam veteran and lifelong community organizer, Oscar's steadfast noncooperation with the government's machinations didn't stop him from supporting the decisions of his comrades. Oscar's commitment was mirrored in the statements of the 11 upon release, who vowed to continue work for the freedom of all.

"Our years in prison have not made our focus wane," continued Alejandrina, responding to a question about their ability to remain united. "I think that's been part of the victory. The White House thought we would just run as individuals to sign the offer. They were surprised when we decided that we wanted to somehow meet. I suggested a telephone conference call, which we eventually were able to have. They weren't expecting that we would do it so collectively. We had some interesting conversations and came to the conclusion during some of them that what we have conceded is what they had already been in control of for most of our lives. Yes, to some extent they put the prison on our shoulders; we're carrying our chains with us onto the street. There were some very strict limitations imposed, but really it is just part and parcel of the overall U.S. outlook on the case of Puerto Rico. It is a struggle for average working people just to survive."

When asked about the historical context for the conditions, especially the hypocritical call for a pledge of nonviolence while the Navy continues to bomb Vieques, Alejandrina responded by stating: "We are Vieques and Vieques is us. Vieques is struggling for their life, their rights, their freedom... and at this point it is a formidable issue to be brought out. Vieques seems to be a catalyst right now, as people are opposing the U.S. military all over the world. It's an issue that people can relate to—getting the military out and getting the U.S. out of Puerto Rico. Vieques shows how clearly the issue is colonialism, and they can't just sweep it under the rug.

"As for us, every historical period goes through phases," Torres continued, "and we have to grow and develop in response to the times. The Puerto Rican independence movement was never a violent movement. It had its periods in history where its resistance was expressed and manifested in a more aggressive manner, but the movement itself is not a violent movement."

So how do you deal with the greatest power in the world at this particular point? "When the whole issue of people occupying the bombing ranges of Vieques came up, and the whole issue of nonviolence was raised—of civil disobedience, which is another aspect of nonviolence—I thought that we should run with it. This is something that the people respond to; our people will never respond totally to violence. We are not a violent people, and the U.S. should be really thankful for that—as there are over three million Puerto Ricans living within the U.S.! I think that the struggle of the 1990s had been one of civil disobedience."

There are few enough moments when progressives have cause to celebrate, and undoubtedly the freeing of Alejandrina Torres and her fellow defendants should be heralded by all of us working for peace. The struggle of the next period—for the release of the remaining four and loosening of the parole conditions, for a permanent end to the use of Vieques by the U.S. military, for an end to colonialism and political imprisonment everywhere—must be met with creativity and a determination fueled by the lessons of the Puerto Ricans' campaign. As we learn from one another, and learn to work together, the struggle will, indeed, continue.

Credit: Elspeth Meyer

International Tribunal on Human Rights Violations in Puerto Rico and Vieques by the United States of America

2000

THE PEOPLE OF PUERTO RICO
-versus-
UNITED STATES OF AMERICA

Judgment

I. Precedential Background

In January of 1989, a special session of a Permanent People's Tribunal was convened in Barcelona, Spain, to determine whether the U.S. government was in violation of human rights treaties and obligations under international law in relation to Puerto Rico and its people. After considering three days of testimony from experts, and reviewing numerous documents on varied aspects of the U.S.-Puerto Rico relations and their effect on the lives of the Puerto Rican people, the Tribunal found that the U.S. government was denying the People of Puerto Rico their most fundamental human right: the right to self-determination.

In arriving at this legal conclusion, our colleagues of the Barcelona Tribunal issued the following verdict. Based on the factual and legal foundations presented, the Permanent People's Tribunal *declares*

1. That Puerto Rico and its people have the right to freely determine their political, economic, social and cultural condition in accordance with the Algiers Declaration and principles of International Law.

2. That the Constitution of the Commonwealth of Puerto Rico is not the proper way for the Puerto Rican people to exercise their self-determi-

---

Held on the island of Vieques in November 2000, the International Tribunal was a critical attempt at bridging the movement to free the Puerto Rican political prisoners with the movement to end U.S. Navy occupation of Puerto Rico. In addition to collecting testimony from many international experts and local survivors of the assorted human rights abuses associated with these pillars of colonialism, this Tribunal was also significant in that it took place after eleven of the Puerto Ricans had been released. With almost all of them in attendance (though sitting apart from one another, as proscribed by their parole conditions), the Tribunal was both joyous and reflective of the fact that some of the Puerto Rican prisoners were still, alas, in jail.

nation right, whereas in the referenda that have been carried out on the Island, the required guarantees which govern the true exercise of such right, in accordance with the Resolutions and practices of the United Nations, have not been observed.

3. That the U.S. has an international duty to respect the Right of Puerto Rico to its self-determination, in accordance with the obligations it has conventionally and customarily assumed.

4. That the actual U.S. military policy in Puerto Rico constitutes an obstacle for self-determination of the island and it threatens the peace and security conditions of the Caribbean region.

In returning their verdict, our predecessor Tribunal called upon the U.S. government to take the following steps to ensure the self-determination rights of the People of Puerto Rico:

> To implement through all political, economic and administrative means available to them, the conditions that would make possible for the Puerto Rican People to exercise their self-determination right, and especially to:
>
> (a) acknowledge the political prisoner status of those Puerto Ricans incarcerated due to their work and militancy in favor of Puerto Rico's independence and to grant a general amnesty to all Puerto Ricans currently incarcerated because of their involvement in the struggle against colonialism.
>
> (b) relinquish the current powers the U.S. Congress has to amend and approve the decisions made by the representative bodies and government of Puerto Rico.
>
> (c) completely transfer any power the U.S. Congress or the U.S. government may have over Puerto Rico, to a deliberative body with constitutional character made up of representatives from all the political and social forces of Puerto Rico chosen on an elective basis.
>
> (d) negotiate such measures, as a transitional status of the juridical and political condition of Puerto Rico, until the self-determination right is effectively exercised.
>
> (e) guarantee that the U.S. military forces currently stationed in Puerto Rico will not interfere directly or indirectly in the free exercise of the right of self-determination by the People of Puerto Rico.

II. Findings and Legal Foundations

1. Introduction

This International Tribunal on Violations of Human Rights in Puerto Rico and Vieques by the United States of America has been convened to examine what steps, if any, the U.S. government has taken to follow the directives of the Barcelona Tribunal and end its colonial domination over Puerto Rico and its people. Reaffirming the principles of self-determination set out by the Barcelona Tribunal, we sought to reexamine all the areas of Puerto Rican life that were the subject of inquiry in 1989, to determine whether the U.S. government had made any efforts to comply with its obligations under international law.

What we have found, as will be discussed more fully within this document, is the absence of any movement toward the decolonization of Puerto Rico. Rather, the evidence, as comprised of the testimony of numerous experts and lay witnesses, supported by a voluminous amount of documents (many authored by U.S. government officials), show a continuation of colonial domination over the Puerto Rican nation.

Harm caused by this continuing colonial domination is particularly acute in Vieques, an island municipality of Puerto Rico, three-fourths of which is occupied by the U.S. Navy that persists, since 1941, in using the island for military exercises and aerial bombardment, thus destroying the environment, ecology, health, and life of its people. Despite the nearly unanimous sentiment of the people of Vieques and Puerto Rico—expressed, amongst other ways, in demonstrations by hundreds of thousands on the streets of San Juan, and by hundreds of acts of civil disobedience on the U.S. military base at the firing range of Vieques—the U.S. government refuses to stop its bombing and withdraw its military force from Vieques.

At this time, the colonial situation of the Puerto Rican people has not improved. What has changed is the massive support across ideological lines for the U.S. Navy to leave Vieques (fully and completely compensating the population for losses and damages, and repairing any and all damages caused by their presence on and around the island) and to free the Puerto Rican political prisoners.

This is a propitious moment for world opinion, particularly within the human rights community, to join with the people of Puerto Rico to demand that the U.S. government immediately initiate the process of decolonization. This process must begin with the complete transfer of all power in the hands of the U.S. Congress and other branches of the U.S. government, so as to allow for the creation of a constituent body of the Puerto Rican people representing all political and social forces.

We want our findings and verdict contained herein to help serve as a catalyst to marshal the pressure of public opinion to support the inalienable right of the Puerto Rican people to self-determination.

347

2. The U.S. Government Is Found Guilty for the Continuation of the Denial of the Right to Self-Determination

Despite the annual resolutions of the United Nations Decolonization Committee, reaffirming the right of the people of Puerto Rico to self-determination and independence in conformity with Resolution 1514 (XV), the U.S. Congress and other branches of government continue to refuse to take the necessary steps to transfer all its illegally held power back to the people of Puerto Rico. Without following in full the United Nations Decolonization protocols, no process of decolonization can be deemed genuine or complete. In July 2000, the Special Decolonization Committee again called upon the United States government to assume the responsibility of expediting a process that would allow the Puerto Rican people to fully exercise their inalienable right to self-determination and independence.

Despite these directives mandated by the United Nations to eradicate colonialism, the U.S. Congress continues to put forth schemes designed to appear as some form of self-determination, but in reality intended to maintain the colonial status. In 1993 and 1998, referenda, denominated as plebiscites, were held in Puerto Rico, but even the colonial political parties and their U.S. government sponsors could not claim that international legal requirements for decolonization were satisfied. Neither of these votes were accompanied by the guarantee of acceptance by the U.S. Congress; neither allowed for the participation of Puerto Ricans living in the United States or clearly defined the consequences of the proposed status options, all elements required by international law.

Most importantly, the voting was not conducted under the United Nations or other independent auspices, or held subsequently to full transfer of power to the Puerto Rican people and the removal of the U.S. military and other U.S. influences.

2.1 The Continuing Effect of Colonialism on the Economic Situation in Puerto Rico

For the U.S., Puerto Rico often appears to be little more than a military base and an economic enclave. As established before, the U.S. military complex in Puerto Rico has increased. On the other hand, since the U.S. invasion in 1898, Puerto Rico has been treated as an economic enclave, with an institutional structure favorable to the extraction of surplus, resulting in economic disadvantage to the island. U.S. capital prevails over Puerto Rican capital. Most of the wealth generated in the Puerto Rican enclave does not remain there. About 70% of the Net Domestic Income generated in Puerto Rico leaves the island.

During fiscal year 1999, the Gross Domestic Product was $59,946 million while Gross National Product rose to $38,299 million. The difference, $21,717 million, represents a payment for external factors, basically, earnings remissions. From 1991 to 1999 the remissions totaled the amount of $139,695 million. One third of the total value of the productive activity in Puerto Rico turns into payments that the residents of Puerto Rico never see. The net U.S. government transfers—$8,315 million in 1999, most of them vested rights of the people as Social Security or Veterans Pensions—pale compared to earnings remissions toward the U.S. for $21,717 million in the same year. This comparison does not take into consideration that the U.S. military forces in Puerto Rico do not pay any rent for the bases and the 12% of the land occupied.

The employees' compensation component of the Net Domestic Income has dropped from 61.1% in 1977 to 48.7% in 1987 to 40.8% in 1999. In contrast, in the U.S. over 70% of the total income accrues to the workers. According to the 1990 census, 58.9% of the Puerto Rican population falls under the poverty level. There will probably be no significant variations for the year 2000. In Vieques, as in the other 24 municipalities, the poverty level exceeds 70%.

Since 1900, the U.S. imposed maritime laws in which all Puerto Rican commercial maritime transportation has to be carried out using transport from the U.S., the most expensive in the world. If this law did not apply to Puerto Rico, transportation costs would decrease by 40%, the cost of exported goods would diminish considerably, and the competitiveness of the Puerto Rican products in the international market would greatly increase.

As of 1999, over three million Puerto Ricans live in the U.S. Their unemployment rate is the highest of all ethnic groups in the U.S. and three times the number of Puerto Ricans live below the poverty level as white citizens. Puerto Ricans, through numerous devious methods, have been driven from their homeland, forced to leave under impoverished conditions, and subjected to racial discrimination, police brutality and other forms of oppression. The situation of the Puerto Ricans in the diaspora is the direct result of the colonial situation of Puerto Rico and can only be resolved by the end to colonialism.

2.2 The Increased Militarization of Puerto Rico

The military presence of the U.S. in Puerto Rico has been a major dimension of U.S. rule over the island since its military invasion in 1898. The military occupies the 12% of the land of Puerto Rico.

Roosevelt Roads Base, together with other installations in the island, makes Puerto Rico the center of the United States military presence in the Caribbean. There has been an increase of militarization in the island in the last decade.

Recently, with the closing of the United States military installations in Panama, installations and units were transferred to Puerto Rico, thereby becoming home to the highest concentration of United States military forces in Latin America. The headquarters of Army South and Navy South and part of the Air Force South of the United States Southern Command were all transferred to Puerto Rico.

The United States military installations in Puerto Rico have had an important role in illegal United States direct and indirect interventions in other countries.

*2.3 The Continuing Assaults on the Culture, Language
and Legal Traditions of the Puerto Rican People*

The invasion and conquest of Puerto Rico in 1898 initiates a policy of Americanization that, in effect, starts a process of acculturation characterized by the following. English is made the mandatory language of instruction; elimination of Puerto Rican history as part of the school curriculum; criminalization of the singing of the Puerto Rican anthem and displaying of the Puerto Rican flag.

While these impositions have been removed, English is the official language in all government transactions; there has been a substitution of the Puerto Rican criminal code for the U.S. code; creation of a U.S. court that may override Puerto Rican courts: extension to Puerto Rico of laws contrary to its customs and traditions and in direct contradiction with the Puerto Rican Constitution: i.e., the death penalty.

The above impositions violate the Declaration and Action Program of the International Conference of Human Rights, June 25, 1993, which among other things affirms the rights of peoples to freely develop their culture. It also adds that democracy and the respect for human rights are interdependent with the enjoyment of linguistic rights and its own cultures. This cultural imposition also violates the Declaration on the Rights of Persons Belonging to Minority, National, Ethnic, Religious and Linguistic Groups, which recognizes, promotes and stimulates respect for [these persons'] human rights; linguistic rights in absolute conditions of equality; and the enjoyment and development of their culture.

Credit: Luz María González

2.4 The Continuation of Repression and Criminalization
of the Independence Movement

Ever since the U.S. military invaded Puerto Rico in 1898, there has been a continuous history of repression against those who resisted U.S. intervention. This Tribunal heard testimony from former political prisoners and independence leaders verifying this history. The conditions of release of the eleven independence fighters in September 1999—after nineteen years imprisonment—underscores the political nature of their imprisonment. The prisoners' release was the result of overwhelming support amongst the Puerto Rican people, and a massive international campaign.

We echo the most recent resolution of the Decolonization Committee and call for the immediate release of all incarcerated Puerto Rican political prisoners. We further condemn the continued repression against the independence movement activists in Chicago, who have been the target of an over two-decade campaign of harassment, disruption and criminalization by the FBI and U.S. Justice Department.

3. The Violations of the Human Rights of the People of Vieques

In 1941, 75% of the land in the island of Vieques—26,000 acres—was expropriated by the U.S. Navy for military maneuvers in the eastern part of the island and munitions depots in the western part. The Vieques expropriations impacted most severely tenant farmers and poor people who, under coercive conditions, were paid $12 to $25 for their homes.

For years, the U.S. Navy conspired to force Viequenses off the remaining lands, in order to occupy the whole island for their war games. Viequenses, who numbered 20,000 to 25,000 inhabitants at the time of the expropriations, have been reduced to 9,300 inhabitants, with more than 15,000 people forced to migrate to the nearby islands of St. Thomas and St. Croix. Many others now live in the main island of Puerto Rico, or the United States.

As stressed by former Governor of Puerto Rico Luis Muñoz Marín in a letter dated December 28, 1961, to President of the United States John F. Kennedy, in response to a U.S. plan to expropriate the remaining part of the island:

> The project involves the destruction of a community, which is a political and juridical entity to which people have strong emotional attachments. The people of Vieques regard themselves as Puerto Ricans, but they also regard themselves as especially identifiable on the basis of residence in Vieques. Obviously, the political and human dismemberment, which the project involves, will be a fundamental shock. We know of no truly comparable action in American history. I believe that it is the kind of action which arouses instinctive disapproval.

After 1975, when the U.S. military stopped its maneuvers in the island municipality of Culebra, maneuvers in Vieques were intensified. The U.S. military and its NATO allies use the eastern part of Vieques, known as the Live Impact Area, and its adjacent waters for their military practices and weapons testings. Moreover, the U.S. has rented the firing range to the private sector and other countries for testing most conventional and nonconventional weapons. Such arrangements generate $80 million annually for the U.S.

Extensive contamination of the land, waters and air of Vieques has resulted from the U.S. military practices and maneuvers, including a large submarine wasteland of ordinance, exploded and unexploded, and ammunition depots in western Vieques, causing an ecological disaster.

Some areas have been bombed for so long and often that there is no soil there. What is left is the underlying rock, which is being broken down into small pieces by the persistent bombing. Thus, unexploded bombs and shrapnel are buried deeper every time as they hit the loose rock. Some of the off-shore keys have been bombed into disappearance, and the hillsides facing the Caribbean Sea are crumbling. This causes erosion and sedimentation of the seagrass beds and coral reefs, which facilitate the entry of toxic substances into the food chain.

After having denied for years that it was using depleted uranium in Vieques, the U.S. Navy was forced to admit the use of such toxic materials. In its letter, the Navy confirmed the use of depleted uranium in Vieques.

Heavy metals, cyanide and explosives have been found in the Vieques soil. Under natural conditions, heavy metals should not be present in these soils; yet, laboratory analyses indicated high concentrations of heavy metals, substances that could only be explained by human activities occurring in the area. The metals found include arsenic (metalloid), barium, cadmium, cobalt, copper, chromium, lead, nickel, vanadium, and zinc, all of which are highly toxic and most carcinogenic. Many accumulate in the food chain and the fish, mollusks, birds and humans.

The spread of these toxic substances by the Navy explosions, including depleted uranium and other radioactive and chemical materials, has caused serious health problems including cancer, breathing and nervous system disorders to the Viequense population.

The people of Vieques have substantially poorer health than the rest of the Puerto Ricans. In 1997, the mortality rate for the people of Vieques was 141% in relation to the rest of Puerto Rico. This rate has been steadily increasing.

It is indisputable that the right of the people of Vieques to life, to a wholesome environment and to health, as well as to economic, social and cultural development, is threatened by the military presence and activities of the U.S. Navy.

The situation of the people of Vieques created by the U.S. Government, and particularly the U.S. Navy, is the result of the intention to destroy in whole or in part the inhabitants of this island, that have caused death and serious bodily and mental harm.

The Tribunal heard moving testimony from women who had suffered harassment, rape, and abusive treatment and who lived in fear under conditions of great hardship for many years since the occupation of the island by the U.S. Navy.

The above findings of fact constitute multiple and gross violations of the human rights of the people of Puerto Rico and particularly the population of the island of Vieques. See International Convenant on Civil and Political Rights, Articles 1, 2, 6, 7, 9, 17, 24, 26 and 47; GA/SPD/30, October 11, 1994; GA/8841, A/AC.109/2039, August 21, 1995; G.A. Res. 2105 (XX), p. 12; G.A. Res. 2023 (XX); Teheran Proclamation, May 13, 1968; the Declaration of Algiers of Universal Rights of People; G.A. Res. 1803 (VIII); the International Convention on the Elimination of All Forms of Racial Discrimination (1965), Preamble and Articles 1, 5, 6 and 15; the Convention Against Torture and Other Cruel, Inhuman or Degrading Treatment or Punishment, Articles 13, 14 and 16; the Universal Declaration of Human Rights (1948), Articles 2, 3, 5, 13, 22, 23, 25, 26 and 28; the International Covenant on Economic, Social and Cultural Rights.

III. Verdict

According to the evidence presented before this Tribunal through direct testimonies and expert witnesses, this Tribunal concludes that the United States has committed systematic violations of human rights regarding Puerto Rico's right to self-determination; has persecuted opponents to United States colonial policies; has increased militarization on the islands and, thereby, threatened peace in the region; has continued the economic exploitation; has forced the displacement of much of the population of Vieques; has caused the economic and political repression of Puerto Ricans in the diaspora; has caused a general degradation of the environment; has committed abuses against women and against the cultural rights of the population.

This Tribunal urges that the United States of America take the following steps without any further delay.

1. Transfer all sovereign powers to the People of Puerto Rico, without any conditions or reservations, to enable Puerto Ricans to exercise peacefully and freely their right to self-determination, in the manner Puerto Ricans deem most appropriate, and to secure the integrity of their national territory.
2. Release the remaining political prisoners and cease all forms of repression against those working against colonialism.
3. Take immediate steps to end the military exploitation and colonial oppression of the people of Puerto Rico, including the immediate cessation of bombing in and around Vieques and the removal of all military installations from the territory of Puerto Rico.
4. Redress all damages caused to the natural wealth and resources of Puerto Rico and Vieques, caused by the military activities of the United States, and to provide for full reparations for the injuries caused to the people of Vieques, and the damage to their environment,

including all measures for the complete decontamination of the island, and surrounding air and waters, and for the economic recovery and development of the island.

Only in this manner will the People of Puerto Rico be in a situation to fully exercise their right to self-determination and freely pursue their economic social and cultural development.

In Vieques and San Juan, Puerto Rico, November 21, 2000.

Dr. Dennis Brutus
President

Dr. Grahame Russell
Vice-President

Dr. Manuel Ramon Alarcón Caracuel
Vice-President

The Most Rev. Walter F. Sullivan, Bishop
Vice-President

Attorney Aderito de Jesus Solares
Vice-President

Dr. Antonia Pantoja
Vice-President

Dr. Rainer Hulhe
Vice-President

Chief's Designee F. Ryan Malonson
Vice-President

Witnesses' Testimonies and Documents
Declaraciones de Testigos y Documentos

Noel Colón Martínez, Esquire

Juan Mari Brás, Esquire

Fernando Martín, Vice-President
Partido Independentista Puertorriqueño

Lolita Lebrón

Dr. Ronald Fernández

Jan Susler, Esquire

Alicia Rodríguez

Elizam Escobar

Rafael Cancel Miranda

José Solis Jordan

Juan A. Giusti-Cordero, Ph.D.

Letter dated August 8, 1947,
from I. W. Silverman

Letter dated December 28, 1961,
from Governor L. Muñoz Marín

Letter dated January 16, 1962, from
President John F. Kennedy

Dr. Francisco Catalá, Economist

Eduardo Morales Coll, Esquire

Radamés Tirado Guevara

Ismael Guadalupe

Carlos Ventura

Alvaro Corrada del Río, Bishop
(Ricardo Díaz, Esq.)

Cristina Garay

Miriam Sobá

AFWTF Internet Page

Yabureibo Zenón

Lirio Marquéz & Jorge Fernández Porto

Rev. Héctor Soto Vélez

Carlos (Taso) Zenón

Dr. Rafael Rivera Castaño

Dra. Cruz María Nazario

Robert L. Rabin

Elen Sciater

José López

Luis Gutiérrez

Ana Rivera Lassen

Credit: Elspeth Meyer

More Than 25 Years: Puerto Rican Political Prisoners

Jan Susler
2007

In 1999, President Bill Clinton commuted the prison sentences of 12 of 15 Puerto Rican men and women arrested in the early 1980s, all of them long considered political prisoners and prisoners of war. Convicted of seditious conspiracy (that is, of conspiring to use force against the authority of the United States over Puerto Rico), they had served 16 and 19 years of prison sentences ranging from 35 to 90 years. Most were convicted of being members of the *Fuerzas Armadas de Liberación Nacional* (Armed Forces of National Liberation), a militant, clandestine pro-independence group that between 1974 and 1980 claimed responsibility for more than 100 bombings, mainly in Chicago and New York, aimed at corporate, military, and government targets. None of the 15 were charged with or convicted of hurting anyone. As a 1980 *Chicago Tribune* editorial noted, they had been "out to call attention to their cause rather than shed blood." Nonetheless, their sentences averaged together amounted to 70.2 years—about seven times the average murder sentence at the time. That is why the president said he was moved to act: because they were "serving extremely lengthy sentences... which were out of proportion to their crimes."* Their supporters said then, and continue to say now, that they were punished not for what they did but for who they are and what they represent.

Puerto Ricans have fought and gone to jail for their resistance to colonialism since the days of the Spanish empire. Under U.S. rule beginning in 1898, there have been some 2,000 political prisoners whose sentences added together come to 11,116 years.† And there have always been campaigns for the release of those in custody. In the 20th century, successful campaigns led the 1952 presidential commutation of the death sentence given to Nationalist Party member Oscar Collazo, convicted after the 1950 attack on Blair House in Washington; the release of hundreds of Nationalist Party members detained

Originally published in *Third World Resurgence*, Nov./Dec. 2007.

* Robert Friedman, "Clinton: Clemency Was Humanitarian Act," *San Juan Star*, September 22, 1999, p. 5, citing President Clinton's letter to U.S. Congressional Representative Henry Waxman.
† Jose F. Paralitici, *Sentencia Impuesta: 100 Anos de encarcelamientos por la independencia de Puerto Rico* (San Juan, Puerto Rico: Ediciones Puerto Historico, 2004).

as a result of the 1950 uprising; the 1979 presidential commutations of the Nationalist Party prisoners Lolita Lebrón, Rafael Cancel Miranda, Irvin Flores, and Andrés Figueroa Cordero, convicted after the 1954 attack on the U.S. Congress and held in prison for 25 years, and Oscar Collazo, who served 29 years; and finally the 1999 presidential commutations. Puerto Rico has welcomed the former prisoners with open arms, and each has not only successfully integrated into civil society, but has joined the ongoing campaign for the release of those who remain imprisoned.

Today, two of the original 15 pro-independence militants arrested in the early 1980s remain in prison: Carlos Alberto Torres and Oscar López Rivera, who have now served 27 and 26 years of their 70-year sentences. They have broken every record for the longest-held Puerto Rican political prisoners, except one: that of Collazo, who served 29 years. When they and the others were arrested and charged, they immediately invoked international law, which provides that colonialism is a crime, that a colonized people may use any means at its disposal to combat this crime, and that the courts of the colonizing country may not criminalize anticolonial militants. They thus claimed prisoner-of-war status and refused to recognize the courts' jurisdiction. They mounted no defense and did not challenge the government evidence against them. Neither the state nor the federal authorities recognized this argument. At sentencing, one of the accused pointed out to the court that the hearing was taking place on the U.S. holiday commemorating George Washington's birthday and likened the cause of Puerto Rican independence to that of Washington and his anticolonial efforts. The judge retorted that if the British had captured Washington, they would have killed him on the spot, adding that he regretted there was no federal death penalty in effect, since this would have been his preferred sentence.

During their time in prison, both Torres and López Rivera have endured mistreatment, including sleep deprivation and total isolation. From 1986 to 1998, López Rivera was held in the highest-security facilities in the federal prison system, in conditions not unlike those at Guantánamo under which "enemy combatants" are held, conditions the International Red Cross, among other human rights organizations, have called tantamount to torture. In 1988, he was convicted of conspiracy to escape in an FBI sting operation. His additional 15-year sentence is more than eight times longer than the average sentence for actual escape. At long last he was transferred to a general-population maximum-security prison, only to be moved seven years later to a new, harsher penitentiary that houses death row inmates and the federal execution chamber.

After the September 11 attacks, Torres was segregated from the rest of the medium-security prison population, which puzzled the prison staff, given his spotless record. But they said they were unable to do anything, since the order came from Washington. Personnel made it quite clear that his segregation had nothing to do with his prison conduct and everything to

357

do with "national security" and his being convicted of seditious conspiracy. The Bureau of Prisons uses the same justification each time they deny them something other prisoners are entitled to, like family visits and attendance at funerals.

Despite these hardships, both men, thirsting to express themselves, found art. Never having painted, drawn, or worked with ceramics before prison, they taught themselves the skills and patiently worked to hone them. In anticipation of the 25th anniversaries of their arrest and imprisonment, Torres conceived "Not Enough Space," a traveling exhibit of his ceramics and paintings and López Rivera's paintings and drawings, as a way to once again call attention to the case of the Puerto Rican political prisoners. The colorful portraits, as well as the masks, bowls, and plates, draw on Puerto Rican folkloric images and draw attention to the island's rich history, as well as to its continuing colonial status. But beyond that, the works also say to us, unequivocally, *"Estamos vivos y coleand"* (we are alive and well), and 25 years of prison cannot rob us of our culture or extinguish our commitment to our people and their right to determine their own destiny.

The National Boricua Human Rights Network (NBHRN) is coordinating "Not Enough Space," which has already opened in Chicago, Cleveland, Los Angeles, New York City, Philadelphia, San Francisco, and Morelia, Mexico, as well as in several cities in Puerto Rico, sponsored by the *Comité Pro Derechos Humanos*. "Not Enough Space" will also travel to Venezuela, then return to Puerto Rico for additional exhibitions. The Comite, working nationally and internationally, is actively garnering support for their release. In addition to sponsoring the exhibit, the work includes collecting signatures on letters to President Bush; advocating with religious, civic, labor, and governmental entities to pass resolutions supporting their release; convening educational seminars and conferences; holding vigils, marches, and pickets; and presenting at international forums, including the United Nations.

Puerto Rican Independence Movement Under Attack in New York and San Juan

Jan Susler
2008

> It appears to us to be a reinitiation of the harassment of
> independentists.
>
> U.S. Congressman José Serrano,
> speaking to FBI director Robert Mueller[*]

An unexpected knock on the door… men in trench coats handing you a grand jury subpoena… If you're involved in the movement for the independence of Puerto Rico, this isn't just a not-so-fond memory of the COINTELPRO era. It's 2008 in New York City, and you are Christopher Torres, a young social worker; Tania Frontera, a young graphic designer; or Julio Pabón, Jr., a young filmmaker from the Bronx.

Their subpoenas have aroused vigorous support for them, not just in New York, but also in cities across the U.S. and in Puerto Rico. On the island, over 40 organizations united to condemn this latest wave of repression and convened a demonstration on January 11 where over a thousand people participated under the theme "In the Face of Repression, Unity and Struggle," with placards and banners calling for the FBI and the federal courts to leave the island. Simultaneous activities took place in Brooklyn, Hartford, Chicago, San Francisco, Los Angeles, Philadelphia, Orlando, Fitchburg, Massachusetts, and Cleveland. As resolutions condemning the repression emanated from the National Lawyers Guild New York City Chapter, the American Association of Jurists, the Interfaith Prisoners of Conscience Project, and the Latin America Solidarity Coalition, the New York Spanish language daily *El Diario/La Prensa* published an editorial ringing the alarm bell, and U.S. congressman José Serrano telephoned FBI director Mueller to voice his concern.

Why the subpoenas? Why now? And why the resounding, unified denunciations?

Originally published in *Monthly Review Zine* (http://mrzine.monthlyreview.org), January 28, 2008.

[*] José Delgado, "Habla con el jefe del FBI," *El Nuevo Día*, January 9, 2008.

Dating back to the era of Spanish colonial control over Puerto Rico, Puerto Rican people have organized to wrest their sovereignty from foreign domination. That resistance continued after the U.S. invasion and occupation in 1898. When the colonizers repressed and criminalized public organizing for independence, clandestine organizations formed, including the Popular Boricua Army—*Macheteros*—in the 1980s. In 1985, the FBI arrested and almost killed its leader, Filiberto Ojeda Ríos, accusing him of participation in the 1983 expropriation of $7.5 million U.S. government-insured dollars from a Wells Fargo depot in Hartford, Connecticut. After his release on bail, Ojeda returned to clandestine existence. In spite of the FBI's ever-increasing reward for information leading to his capture, he remained underground for some 15 years. On September 23, 2005, however, a squad of FBI assassins circled his home, shot him, and left him to bleed to death.* The assassination outraged the entire nation, and the FBI became a pariah.

Hoping to distract public attention from their own criminal conduct and justify their presence on the island, particularly in the post-9/11 era, the FBI soon went on the offensive. On February 10, 2006, allegedly in a continuing investigation of the *Macheteros*, they raided the homes and businesses of several independence activists and in the process pepper-sprayed the nation's journalists who were covering the FBI's paramilitary incursions. Again, the entire country expressed its outrage. Since then, activists have been stopped, searched, and harassed, with the homes and offices of many others, including attorneys and movement leaders, mysteriously broken into in events reminiscent of the infamous black-bag COINTELPRO jobs: computers, digital cameras, and cell phones are taken, while other valuable items remain untouched.

Recent rumors are that the head of the FBI in San Juan, Luis Fraticelli, is close to the end of his tenure and has given instructions to accelerate efforts to neutralize the remains of the clandestine group.†

For Fernando Martín, a leader of the Puerto Rican Independence Party, the FBI "wants to clean up its image after the assassination of Filiberto (Ojeda Ríos), because they want to be able to say that in Puerto Rico, they investigate people of all parties (and) somehow salvage their image after their selective attacks."‡

Julio Muriente, a leader of the National Hostos Independence Movement, stated, "The legal facade of this repressive operation is directed against the

---

* In the white papers designed to avoid criminal liability, the government blamed some of the errors in the operation on Luis Fraticelli, the Puerto Rican special agent in charge of its San Juan field office. Not coincidentally, Fraticelli had also participated in the 1985 near assassination of Ojeda Ríos. See: U.S. Department of Justice, Office of the Inspector General, "A Review of the September 2005 Shooting Incident Involving the Federal Bureau of Investigations and Filiberto Ojeda Ríos," August 2006, available at www.usdoj.gov/oig/special/index.htm.

† José Delgado, "El caso de Nueva York," *El Nuevo Día*, January 14, 2008.

‡ Combined Services, "Denunciation of persecution of independentists: Fernando Martín criticized the newspaper *El Nuevo Día* for articles published December 23," *El Nuevo Día*, January 4, 2008.

Macheteros, but the real intention is against the entire independentist movement, including against the people of Puerto Rico," calling it "an attack which is not against any particular organization, but against a political, social, patriotic movement, and against a people."*

U.S. Congressman José Serrano (D-NY), who was instrumental in getting the FBI to disclose thousands of pages of records documenting its illegal surveillance of and intervention in the independence movement,† said of these subpoenas, "It certainly appears to be a fishing expedition,"‡ which, he noted, harkens back to the days when, according to FBI director Freeh, the agency engaged in "egregious illegal action, maybe criminal action."§

The subpoenas, initially returnable on January 11, were continued to February 1. Attorneys announced they would file motions to quash the subpoenas. Frontera's attorney, Martin Stolar, noted that "if the motion is denied, Tania will have to appear before the grand jury, and may decide not to testify, invoking her constitutional rights."¶

Organizations in Puerto Rico have announced they will protest in various towns of the island on February 1 in defense and support of the three young people subpoenaed, with the themes "Wake Up, Boricua, Defend Your Own!" and "The Grand Jury Is Illegal!" Additional protests are being planned in U.S. cities as well.

The consequences of not collaborating with the grand jury are well known to those who support independence. Norberto Cintrón Fiallo, whose home was searched during the February 10, 2006, FBI incursion, and who participated in the January 11 protest in San Juan, refused to collaborate with various grand juries investigating the independence movement in both Puerto Rico and New York in 1981 and 1982 and served close to three years in prison as a result.** Julio Rosado, who participated in the January 11 protest in New York, resisted grand juries investigating the Puerto Rican independence movement, serving nine months for civil contempt in 1977, and later much of his three-year sentence for criminal contempt. "They have always been there, whenever they want to intimidate," he said, adding that he is convinced there will be more subpoenas to come.††

* AP, "Repudio *independentista* a citaciones a Gran Jurado," *El Vocero*, January 7, 2008.

† The disclosed documents are being classified at Center for Puerto Rican Studies of the City University of New York at Hunter College. See: www.pr-secretfiles.net/.

‡ José Delgado, "Habla con el jefe del FBI: José Serrano le expresó a Robert Mueller el malestar que existe entre los boricuas en Nueva York por la citación de tres jóvenes," *El Nuevo Día*, January 9, 2008.

§ Matthew Hay Brown, "Puerto Rico Files Show FBI's Zeal; For Decades, Secret U.S. Dossiers Targeted Suspected," *Orlando Sentinel*, November 6, 2003.

¶ Ruth E. Hernández Beltrán / Agencia EFE, "Posponen citación a *independentista*s de Nueva York," *Primera Hora*, January 11, 2008.

** José "Ché" Paralitici, *Sentencia Impuesta: 100 Años de Encarcelamientos por la Independencia de Puerto Rico*, Ediciones Puerto Histórico (San Juan, Puerto Rico: 2004), pp. 339-41.

†† Ruth E. Hernández Beltrán / Agencia EFE, "Posponen citación a *independentista*s de Nueva

A New York daily Spanish language newspaper expressed editorial concern over the political witch hunt, in words which should give us all pause:

> Because of laws initiated by the Bush Administration and passed by our Congress, the legal protections that would give political dissidents a right to due process have been eroded. The net is wide for casting someone with "suspicious" political beliefs, without having been charged, tried or convicted of a crime, as a threat. [...] Because the attacks on civil liberties and human rights and the historical intimidation and repression of Puerto Rican independence supporters are interrelated, activists must make those links.

That's all the more urgent considering the silence of most elected leaders and the virtual media blackout on the subpoenas. In the context of secret prisons, torture, detention without trial, and warrantless wiretapping, the FBI's fishing should be a concern for anyone interested in rescuing this country from a rising police state.*

York,"Primera Hora, January 11, 2008. Rosado was one of five supporters of independence so imprisoned. Ricardo Romero, Steven Guerra, María Cueto, who are Mexican, and Rosado's brother Andres, simultaneously served time for criminal contempt of the same grand jury. See: United States v. Rosado et al., 728 F.2d 89 (2nd Cir. 1984).
* "Constructing an Enemy,"Editorial, El Diario/La Prensa, January 17, 2008.

Section V.

Resisting Repression: Out and Proud

During the last 25 years, a strategic linking of peoples and struggles has also taken place between the lesbian, gay, bisexual, and transgender liberation movement and communities and the movements to free U.S. political prisoners. These links were not hurt by the fact that many key activists working for the freedom of these prisoners were, themselves, members of the LGBT movement. Also significant, especially given the extreme homophobia present in much discussion about prison life, is the fact that several political prisoners were out lesbians, and one (the late Kuwasi Balagoon) was a bisexual man. This section includes some of the published documents of this work, as well as a couple of newly written or published pieces reflecting on these links.

After the Confiscation of Gay Community News

Laura Whitehorn
1992

© 2008 JEB (Joan E. Biren)

There's been a terrible mistake
You've just informed me that
homosexuality is not permitted
in this institution

I now inform you
that I am a homosexual
Therefore, I am not permitted
in this institution
and must be
immediately
released.

Not Something That We Can Postpone

Dhoruba Bin-Wahad
1991

I've been looking forward to speaking to a predominantly gay and lesbian gathering around the issue of repression. It's very difficult to deal with the issue of misogyny and sexism and homophobia in a society that is premised upon white skin male privilege. The issue of political repression, of course, is an ethical issue. It's an issue that touches all of us, regardless of our particular ideological tendency within the progressive movement, regardless of our sexual orientation. It is an issue informed by a system of racist class privilege that determines our relationships to one another.

It has been a struggle for me, since my release, to arrive at a principled position around the issue of homophobia and sexism. It is an ongoing struggle on my part. I'm still learning. I feel that it is very important, if we are to build a movement, to deal concretely and in a principled way with the issues of sexism and homophobia.

As a Black revolutionary who has struggled and continues to struggle on the core issues of Black liberation, I cannot but conclude that if we are to be successful, we have to deal with sexism head on. It is not something that can be swept under the rug. It is not something that we can postpone until tomorrow, pending revolutionary victory.

This is important, because as my comrade and companion and wife, Tanaquil Jones, has often said: the personal is political and the political is personal. I'm kind of taken aback that she's not here addressing you instead of me.

I think that her analysis of sexism, misogyny, and homophobia is much more developed than mine. She attempted to point out to me one evening, while we were struggling over the issue of homophobia in the Black movement, how we often shy away from dealing with sexism because of the establishment of a heterosexual standard of conduct, of set behaviors and of social relationships. We seldom (and when I say we here, I mean heterosexuals), we seldom question certain assumptions that we make. After long and arduous

Excerpts from a talk given at a New York City forum on the case of Mumia Abu-Jamal sponsored by Lesbian and Gay Folks Supporting Political Prisoners, a group later renamed QUISP (Queers United in Support of Political Prisoners). The speech was widely acclaimed as a groundbreaking statement by a Black Muslim revolutionary, and the sponsoring group later sold tapes of it at LGBT events and arranged to have it played on Pacifica radio station WBAI.

struggle with Tanaquil, I could only conclude that the issue of misogyny and the issue of homophobia are very much interwoven. The hatred and fear of women is part and parcel of the whole edifice of homophobic behavior and conduct in the society. Therefore, it is impossible to struggle against sexism—against Black women or white women, or in society at large—without simultaneously struggling against homophobia.

I now find myself constantly struggling with brothers in the Black movement in this respect. Very few of them see the issue of homophobia as being an issue that has to be addressed with principle. Surely we cannot build a new society if we premise that society on the oppression of other people. And in the course of building a new society and struggling for empowerment in our communities, it becomes clear that we have to establish the basis for our relationships with each other as we struggle. In other words, we cannot—for instance—build an organization that claims to liberate Black people and yet instills in that organization sexist or misogynist behaviors. We cannot build an organization based on projection of male egos. Historically, we have seen that the majority of wars—if not all of the wars that humanity has faced—have been launched and initiated by men. Very few women have started cataclysmic wars. Of course there are exemptions; there are the Margaret Thatchers of the world. But I am not trying to deal with the exceptions. I'm trying to deal with the rules!

I was in Europe recently, and I sat with the old comrade by the name of Donald Cox, DC. And DC had a very interesting proposition. "You know the rule book?" he asked. "We have to build an organization and make sure that the men do not read it." I said, now, homeboy, that's a little strong. How can we build an organization where men don't participate in the leadership? DC said: "No, I'm not saying that men should be excluded from the leadership per se. I'm just saying that we should experiment with a new type of organization. An organization that empowers women and ensures that women are the primary leaders of the organization." The rules suggest that we have been socialized over a millennium to react and deal with things a certain way as men. We take male privilege for granted. And the majority of the power struggles that occur in organizations occur as a consequence of male egos... as a consequence of certain presumptions that we make as men. We can see this when we look at our history, including our recent history in the Black Panther Party.

We cannot have an organization with big eyes and little views. We can never have an organization that is founded upon one leader. This doesn't necessarily mean that men and women who are qualified to lead a particular struggle or a particular program at a particular time cannot be empowered by the collective to carry something forward which the collective has agreed upon. But we have to have collective leadership.

It's not easy to struggle with your own privilege. As a male, it's not easy to struggle with your own privilege. It therefore should proceed, and I think everyone here can agree, that it is not easy for white people to struggle with their own racism. It's very difficult to struggle with white skin privilege in a racist society. White folks take a lot of things for granted. One thing they take for granted is that what they have to say is important. They always assume that. And men do the same thing. Men believe that what they have to say is important and what women have to say is somewhat less important. Even the most advanced men who are struggling actively and sincerely with their own sexism show some signs of this.

So how do we deal with these things that we take for granted in this society? I know, for instance, that there's a predominantly gay male organization called the AIDS Coalition to Unleash Power (ACT UP). Here's a group that in many respects has carried out some of the most militant actions around the AIDS crisis, around homophobia, through direct action. They have carried out some very good struggles that have advanced the consciousness, the mass consciousness, of many people. But they have not principally struggled with their own racism. They have not principally struggled with their own white skin privilege and white skin male privilege, even though it's a gay organization. And we have to ask ourselves how it is that an organization like ACT UP has no people of color in leadership? How is that they do not have a principled position around the issue of political repression and political prisoners? How is it they do not support the liberation struggles of people of color? How is that they have not yet formed any operational coalitions with grassroots Black, Puerto Rican, or Asian organizations?

Another example to look at is that of the Irish movement. Just about every Irish organization in New York City is an advocate for the freedom of IRA political prisoner Joe Doherty. His cause has been put at the head of the St. Patrick's Day parade. The Negro mayor of New York City has seen fit to visit Joe Doherty in prison, to pay his respects and wear a freedom button. David Dinkins has said that Joe is a freedom fighter. Now I believe that Joe Doherty should be supported by every one of us. Joe is a man who has struggled mightily against British domination and British imperialism in Northern Ireland. He deserves our principled support. But Joe's freedom is not the issue. The issue is, how can all of these Irish groups support Joe Doherty and the right of the Irish people to wage armed struggle, but find it reprehensible when the Puerto Rican nationalists wage the same armed struggle against U.S. domination in Puerto Rico? How is it that the Irish policemen find it admirable when the IRA slay British soldiers, but find it difficult to believe that Black people have an equal right to slay their oppressor? You see, they're a one-issue community. The only issue that they're dealing with is Northern Ireland. The only issue that they're dealing with is the freedom of Joe Doherty, and they don't even understand that the IRA itself expresses solidarity with Puerto Rico and with other oppressed people with color!

We have gay and lesbian organizations that support gay and lesbian issues, antisexist issues, but they do not support freedom for Black political prisoners. And I come to you this evening to ask you to put on more affairs like this, to reach out into the gay and lesbian community and accept Black leadership. When a Black man who is gay is attacked by the police, he is attacked for two reasons. He is attacked because he is Black and he is attacked because he is gay. And I, as a revolutionary involved in trying to build a principled movement, can no more deny that Black man the right to struggle for liberation of his people than you can deny that gay man the opportunity to lead in the gay and lesbian movement.

Now I get a lot of flack from Muslims, and I myself am a Muslim. I say that, as Muslims, we cannot endorse the oppression of anyone. In the Qu'ran, we are enjoined to stand up for the truth, even if it is against our own self. We are told that there should arise from amongst us a band of people who enjoin the good and forbid the wrong. That's the bottom line in Islam: to enjoin the good and forbid the wrong. And so I would always ask the Islamic scholars who challenged me: how can you enter into a coalition with people who are reactionaries and who carry out policies that are contrary to interests of our community, yet condemn me for working with gay and lesbian groups who have never oppressed one Muslim, who have never killed one Muslim? Those movements that identify the same enemy as ours, those movements who establish the right and forbid the wrong, we should align ourselves with them. And if you're telling me that we shouldn't do this because of the individual sexual orientation, I would beg to differ.

So you see, I have a problem in the Muslim community, but it's nothing I can't handle! You'd be surprised how a principled struggle with well-meaning individuals can bring about some significant changes in how they deal with people.

I remember when I was in prison we got word through the VooDoo
Communiciations network through Kuwasi (and others whom I can't
name), that if we needed help in raising up on outta that high
walled prison to let them know. We did. That was Kuwasi, for whom
RISKS were like the air he breathed. You breathe, you take risks.
I risk, therefore I AM. And though it made no sense to me then
that he was also The Anarchist, I thoroughly understood it now.
When the BPP could no longer serve his spirit, the Black Liberation
Army's anarchistic style could. And he obviously liked the vision
of a Republic of New Afrika, free from Babylonian control and
self-determining.

Ashanti Omowali Alston

We say that the U.S. has no right to
confine New Afrikan people to red-lined
reservations and that we have a right
to live on our own terms in a common
land area and to govern ourselves,
free of occupation forces such
as the police, national guard
or GIs who have invaded
our colonies from time
to time. We have a
right to control our
own economy, print
our own money, trade
with other nations
and enter a work
force where we are
not excluded by
design and where
our wages and the
wages of all workers
can not be manipulated
by a ruling class that
controls the wealth.
We have a right to build
our own educational
institutions and systems
where our children will
not be indoctrinated
by aliens to suffer the
destructive designs of the U.S.
government.

—Kuwasi Balagoon
Brinks Opening Trial Statement

Kuwasi Balagoon

December 22, 1946 - December 13, 1986

"He was an anarchist in a Black nationalist movement, he was queer in a straight dominated movement, he was a guerrilla fighter after it was 'chic,' and he never backed down from his ideals, his beliefs, the struggle or himself. And he demanded to be seen not as a revolutionary icon, but as a person, beautiful and flawed."
— Walidah Imarisha
revolutionary poet

The following is an excerpt from a previously unpublished letter Kuwasi wrote to a supporter on November 17, 1983:

it's a strange
night a lot of singing—
especially, bongo fury on the
metal sink upstairs; the pigs came to
move a guy to population! Last sunday,
a guy gave the "i've been to the mountaintop"
speech, seemingly verbatim, it sound so much like
Martin Luther King that i thought it was a record until i
remembered that the guys are in the hole back there, didn't have
tape recorders or radios; and then they started singing "we shall overcome" - but that was last sunday. This sunday they are telling me
for the second time that i can't make a call because some clerk
jerk didn't send a card over with my name and phone
numbers to call. Every day since they've told me
that i've been classified for population and i
sit out here is stranger and stranger, and
i consider them intending to keep
me here indefinitely. starting
tomorrow i am stepping
up my opposition to
this bullshit.

Love, Power & Peace by Piece
Kuwitsi

Kuwasi at the time of his capture

Kuwasi Balagoon died of AIDS-related pneumonia in 1986, while in his fifth year of a seventy five year prison sentence. For more writings by and about Kuwasi Balagoon, see *Kuwasi Balagoon, A Soldier's Story: writings by a revolutionary New Afrikan anarchist* Kersplebedeb, 2003). Also visit: www.urbanguerrilla.org/kuwasibalagoon.html

Dykes and Fags Want to Know:
Interview with Lesbian Political Prisoners

Queers United in Support of Political Prisoners,
Linda Evans, Laura Whitehorn, and Susan Rosenberg
1991

QUISP: I'm an activist. Why haven't I heard of you before ?

Laura: I think it's because there's been a long time during which the "left" and progressive movements haven't really tried to know who's in prison— including but not limited to political prisoners and POW's. For instance, how many AIDS activists know about the many PWA's in prison and the horrible conditions they live in? Aside from Mike Riegle at *Gay Community News*, how many writers and media folks in our movements try to reach into the prisons to support lesbian and gay prisoners, whose lives are often made pretty rough by the pigs. In general, this country tries to shut prisoners away and make people outside forget about us. In the case of political prisoners, multiply that times X for the simple fact that our existence is a danger to the smooth, quiet running of the system: our existence shows that this great demokkkracy is a lie. The government doesn't want you to know who we are—that's why they try so hard to label us "terrorists" and "criminals."

Linda: Political prisoners have been purposely "disappeared" by the U.S. government, whose official position is that "there are no political prisoners inside the U.S." This is the way that the government denies both that the motivations for our actions were political and that the movements we come from are legitimate, popular movements for social change. The prison system isolates all prisoners from their communities, but especially harsh isolation is instituted against political prisoners: restricted visiting lists, frequent transfers to prisons far away from our home communities, mail censorship, "maximum security conditions," long periods of time in solitary confinement. But our

---

Dykes and Fags Want to Know was a compilation of three separate interviews conducted by mail with lesbian political prisoners Laura Whitehorn, Linda Evans and Susan Rosenberg in 1991, when all three were held at DC Jail awaiting trial in the Resistance Conspiracy 6 case, referred to herein as the RCC 6. The interviews were conducted and released as a booklet by the New York City solidarity group called Queers United in Support of Political Prisoners (QUISP). It was published by Arm the Spirit Press in Toronto in 1995. The language of "dykes and fags" reflects usage among some LGBT people, then and now, aiming to reclaim those terms from their status as hateful epithets and make them badges of pride for their own use.

372

own political movement, too, has ignored the existence of political prisoners. I think this has largely been a product of racism—most U.S. political prisoners/ POW's are Black and Puerto Rican comrades who have been locked up for over a decade. Unfortunately there has never been widespread support among progressive white people for the Black Liberation struggle, for Puerto Rican independence, or for Native American sovereignty struggles—and these are the movements that the Black/Puerto Rican/Native American political prisoners/POW's come from. Also, many political activists have actually withheld support for political prisoners/POW's because of disagreements with tactics that were employed or with actions of which the political prisoners have been accused or convicted. These disagreements are tactical in nature and shouldn't be allowed to obscure the fact that we all have been fighting for justice and social change. This withdrawal of support leads to false divisions amongst us and actually helps the state in its strategy to isolate political prisoners/POW's from our communities and political movements.

Susan: The activists/radicals of the late 1980s and 1990s have to reclaim the history of resistance that emerged and continued through the 1970s and '80s. As long as the government and mass media get to define who and what is important, then the real lessons contained in ours and others' experiences will get lost. People haven't heard of us (except as a vague memory of a headline—if that) because there is a very serious government counterinsurgency strategy to bury the revolutionaries who have been captured in prison. I have been in prison six years, and over half of that time was spent in solitary confinement or small-group isolation thousands of miles away from my community and family. My experience is similar to the 100-150 other political prisoners in the U.S. If the individuals from different movements (i.e., the Black, Puerto Rican, Native American, and white movements who have seen the need for organized resistance to oppression) are destroyed, it is a way to delegitimize the demands of the movements.

QUISP: Did you do it? Did the government misrepresent what you did? If so, how?

Laura: Yes, I did it! I did (do) resist racism, sexism, imperialism with every fiber of my queer being, and I believe we need to fight for justice. The government's "version" of what I/we did is a complete lie, though, in that they call resistance a crime. It's sort of like the way Jesse Helms calls us "sick"—he's as sick as you can get. On the morality meter, he doesn't even make the needle move. Same way the U.S. government, a genocidal system, calls acts of revolutionary struggle "terrorist violence," and their system of law, "justice."

Linda: Yes, I'm proud that I've been part of the struggle to build an armed clandestine resistance movement that can fight to support national liberation

373

struggles and that will fight for revolution in the U.S. Of course the government misrepresented what we did first of all by calling us "terrorists" to make people think we were a danger to the community, as if our purpose was to terrorize or kill people. Quite the contrary: all the armed actions of the last twenty years have been planned to minimize any risk to human life. This, of course, is in stark contrast to the actions of the terrorist government, which is responsible worldwide for supporting death squads and mercenary armies like the contras and Savimbi's UNITA in Angola, which supports the Israeli war of genocide against the Palestinians and the brutal system of apartheid, and which supports daily police brutality in Black and Third World communities here, even such acts as the aerial bombing of MOVE in Philadelphia in 1985, which killed 11 people and created a firestorm that left over 250 people homeless.

Susan: I have been a revolutionary for much of my life—a revolutionary in the sense that I believe in the need for profound social change that goes to the roots of the problem, which I believe is systemic. Consequently I have, along with others, tried many methods of struggle to enact a strategy to win liberation and attack the state (government) as representative of the system, first as a peace activist in the late '60s, then as a political activist in the '70s, and then in joining the armed clandestine resistance movement that was developing in the '80s. I am guilty of revolutionary anti-imperialist resistance. Of course, the government has misrepresented me and all of us. The main form that has taken is to call us terrorists, which is something that couldn't be further from the truth. Just as all opposition to the cold war of the '50s was labeled communist, the '80s equivalent is terrorist. Now there are all kinds of terrorists according to the U.S.—all of it bullshit. I don't mean to beg the question in the specific. I believe that no revolutionary captured comrade says what they have or haven't done within their revolutionary work.

QUISP: Audre Lorde says the master's tools (violence) will never dismantle the master's house (the state). How do you react to this?

Laura: I don't think "violence" is just one thing, so I don't think it's necessarily "the master's tool." If revolutionaries were as vicious and careless of humanity and innocent human lives as the U.S. government is, then I think we'd be doing wrong. But when oppressed people fight for freedom, using "violent" means among others, I think we should support them. Would you have condemned African slaves in the U.S. for killing their slave masters or for using violence in a struggle for freedom? To me, the issue is how do we fight effectively—and humanely—for liberation. As we build the struggle, we have to be very self-critical, very self-conscious about how we struggle as well as what we struggle for. But I think we also need to fight to win—and I think that means engaging in a fight for power. For the past five plus years,

I've witnessed close up the violence—slow, brutal, heartless—of genocide against African American women. To refuse to fight to change that (and I don't believe we can fight for power completely "nonviolently") would, I think, be to accept the violence of the state in the name of rejecting the violence of revolutionary struggle.

Linda: I disagree with posing the issue in the way she does. I don't think the issue is violence, but rather politics and power. Around the world, imperialism maintains itself—keeps itself in power—through military power and the threat of violence wherever people struggle for change. Liberation movements have the right to use every means available to defeat the system that is oppressing and killing people. This means fighting back in self-defense, and it means an offensive struggle for people's power and self-determination. But reducing it to a tactical question of "violent means" doesn't recognize all the aspects of building a revolutionary movement that are crucial to actually mobilizing people, developing popular organizations, empowering oppressed groups within the people's movement like women and indigenous people, developing a revolutionary program that can really meet people's needs and that people will fight to make real. A slogan that embodies this for me comes from the Chinese Revolution: "Without mass struggle, there can be no revolution. Without armed struggle, there can be no victory."

Susan: I always took the quote from Audre Lorde to mean the opposite of what you say. Funny, no? I always interpreted her saying that to mean the masters' tools being electoral/slow change. Well—there you go!

QUISP: Why is it important to support political as opposed to nonpolitical prisoners? Shouldn't we be concerned about all prisoners?

Laura: I think we should be concerned about all prisoners, and I don't think it's ever been us political prisoners who have promoted any irresolvable contradiction between us and the rest of the prisoners in the U.S. But within that, I think there is a particular need for progressive movements to defend political prisoners, because it's a part of fighting for the movements we come from. If you are fighting racism and homophobia, and there are people serving long sentences in prison for fighting those things, I think you advance the goals by supporting the prisoners. I also think that support for political prisoners helps expose how repressive and unjust the whole system is. That can also be an avenue to supporting all prisoners. Support for political prisoners is a concrete act of resistance to the control the government keeps over all our minds: it fights the isolation and silencing of political prisoners and POW's. It asserts the legitimacy of resistance. And in my experience it is a major way that people outside become aware of the purpose and nature of the prison system as a whole.

Linda: Yes—it's important for our movement to be concerned about all prisoners, and I think it's especially important for the lesbian and gay movement to concern ourselves with combating attacks on lesbian/gay prisoners and supporting all prisoners with AIDS. Concerning ourselves with all prisoners and with the repressive, warehousing role of prisons in our society is another way of fighting racism, since the majority of prisoners are from Third World communities. Prisoners get locked away—out of sight, out of mind—and the few prisoners' rights that were won in prison struggles are being undermined and cut back. Human rights are nearly nonexistent in prison, and without community support and awareness, the government can continue to escalate its repressive policies, and conditions will just steadily worsen. This is especially true for prisoners with AIDS, since the stigma attached to AIDS in society generally is heightened in prison. Prisoners with AIDS die at an even faster rate than PWA's on the outside because treatment is so sporadic and limited and conditions are so bad. So I would never say for people to support political prisoners as opposed to nonpolitical prisoners. Our interests inside prison are definitely not in opposition to each other. All the political prisoners/POW's actively fight for prisoners' rights and for changes in conditions that will benefit all prisoners. But it's important to build support specifically for political prisoners because we represent our movements, and it's a way for us to protect and defend the political movements we come from against government repression. For the movement on the outside to embrace and support political prisoners/POW's makes it possible for us to continue to participate in and contribute to the movement we come from and it makes it impossible for the government to isolate and repress us in their efforts to destroy our political identities.

Susan: All prisoners are in desperate need of support, and as the (prison) population gets greater and the repression gets heavier, the prisons will become a major confrontation within the society. If the prisons are to become a social front of struggle, then there must be a consciousness developed to fight the dehumanization and criminalization that prison intends. Political prisoners are important to support because we are in prison for explicitly social/political/progressive goals. Our lack of freedom does affect how free you are. If we can be violated, so can you. There is no contradiction between political and social prisoners.

QUISP: How does being a lesbian fit in with your work?

Laura: The same way it fits into my life—it is a basic, crucial part of my character, my outlook on things, my personality. Because I'm a lesbian, the fight against homophobia and sexism take on particular importance. But really I think my lesbianism helps me care about the oppression of others by the imperialist system. So I think my lesbianism makes me a better anti-imperialist—it makes me fight all the harder. Being a lesbian in prison is often very hard, but being "out" gives me a lot of strength. I have to say that I am very proud when I hear or read about the struggles queers are waging out there.

Linda: Being a lesbian has always been an important part of the reasons why I'm a revolutionary—even before I was self-conscious about how important this is to me! I don't separate "being a lesbian" from any other part of my life, or from my politics. Because I experience real oppression as a lesbian and as a woman, I am personally committed from the very core of my being— to winning liberation for women, lesbians, and all oppressed people. This makes me more willing to take risks and to fight, because I have a vision of a society I want to live in and to win for future generations, where these forms of oppression don't exist. I think being a lesbian has also helped me recognize the importance of mutual solidarity and support between the struggles of oppressed people, despite the sexism, heterosexism, and racism that often interfere in the process of building these alliances. I really believe that we have a common enemy—the imperialist system—and that we have to sup- port each other in all the forms our struggles against that enemy may take. These alliances need to be built in a way that respects the integrity of our various movements.

Susan: Well! Being a lesbian is part of the very fabric of my being—so the question is not really how it fits into my work, but rather how conscious do I make my lesbianism in living in prison or in the life of resistance I lead. It alternates depending on what the conditions are. Recently I have "come out" because at this point I have chosen to be more consciously lesbian-identified. I have done this because I believe that as gay people we need more revolu- tionary visions and strategies if our movement is to become significant in linking the overturning of sexual oppression with other forms of oppres- sion. The other reason I have felt compelled to be out is that my tightest, most important women in the community we live in are the butches. It is the butches who suffer most for their choices/existence in prison. In recognition of Pete, Cowboy, JuJu, Slimie, and all the other sisters, it seems only right. Finally—Laura and Linda have been out since the RCC6 began, and it has been a very important political and personal experience for them and for us all. They have through their struggles created an environment of love and solidarity that enabled me to subsequently "come out" as well.

QUISP: How have you struggled with sexism and heterosexism in the groups with which you have worked?

Laura: Mostly by confronting people when I think they are being sexist or heterosexist and by fighting for women's liberation and lesbian and gay lib- eration to be included not just as words but as real goals. The saddest times for me have been those times when I was in groups where we didn't do this. I think it's very important for people to be able to struggle for a variety of goals without setting up a hierarchy or exclusive list. I will continue to join groups whose main program is, for example, antiracism or support for Palestine or Puerto Rico, because those things are just as necessary for my liberation as women's and lesbian liberation are. And I won't demand that my liberation be made a part of every agenda. But I won't ever deny my identity, my right to be respected, and the urgency and legitimacy of lesbian, gay, and women's liberation, either.

Susan: I have become much more of a feminist over the last number of years—and by that I mean ideologically and politically I believe we have to examine the position of women, the structures of the society and how male dominance defines women's position in all things. I don't think in the past I fought against the subjugation of women and gay people enough. I substituted my own independence as a woman with actively struggling against political and social forms of oppression. For example: in Nicaragua now, the women militants of the FSLN are reevaluating their practice of struggling against sexism, and some of them are self-critical, and they subordinate the struggle of women to the needs of the so-called greater societal good. What it means now is that abortion and the struggle for reproductive rights under the new nonrevolutionary society are being set back generations, and the level of consciousness among women is not (at this point) strong enough to effectively challenge this development. I believe that to subordinate either women or gay people and our demands is a big mistake.

QUISP: What is the connection between the primarily white middle-class gay rights movement and the struggles of other oppressed people? How do we envision a gay movement that encompasses other struggles?

Laura: I believe that any struggle of "primarily white middle-class" people has the danger of being irrelevant to real social change unless it allies itself with the struggles of oppressed people. This country has a great track record for buying off sectors that have privilege. Once that happens, not only do things stay the same, they get worse. But even more than that, I feel that we cannot be full human beings unless we fight for all the oppressed. Otherwise, our struggle is just as individualist and racist as the dominant society. In that case, we'll never win anything worth fighting for. I think the queer movement needs to talk to other movements and communities in order to work out common strategies and figure out how to support one another. I think we need to talk to groups in the national liberation struggles in order to figure out how to set our agenda and strategy—like what demands can we raise in the fights about AIDS that can help other communities fighting AIDS? It's a struggle, not necessarily an easy process, but it's crucial. It's also true that our movement has already adopted lessons from other movements—often without even realizing or rec-ognizing it. We've especially incorporated strategic concepts developed (at a high cost!) by the Black Liberation struggle from the Civil Rights movement to the Black Power and human rights struggle. It's no accident that Stonewall's leadership was Third World gay men and lesbians. So I think it's important to recognize whenever we pose the question of alliances and coalitions, that we don't need to "encompass" other people—we need to ally with them, learn from, and struggle side by side with them. We need to support them. And we need to fight for them as well as for ourselves, because the second we accept divisions or ignore the urgency of fighting racism, we lose.

Linda: I don't think that struggles against sexism or homophobia or racism can be delayed, because these are forms of discrimination/oppression that actively disempower individuals and groups of people who can be mobilized to actively participate in the struggle. Racism, sexism, and heterosexism cannot be tolerated in our movement or in our alliances because we don't want to duplicate the oppression that we're fighting against. Of course the process of building these alliances is difficult and long-term, because build-ing trust and respect requires building relationships that are really differ-ent from those that exist in society in general. So I don't think the primarily white middle-class gay rights movement can, or should, "encompass" other struggles. White middle-class gay men and women cannot set the agenda for other movements or for other communities. Rather, I think that this move-ment should actively support struggles against other forms of oppression as a way of making our own movement stronger, more revolutionary, less self-centered, and more supportive of the goal of liberation and self-determination for all oppressed people.

Susan: This is a big question and has many aspects to it. I can only offer a small answer, as I believe that prisoners who have no social practice in a movement because of being locked up have a warped or limited understand-ing of the real dynamics in the free world movements. The gay movement as it is currently constituted has re-emerged since I have been in prison, so I have not been a part of its development. I don't think the gay movement can be relevant to other oppressed peoples and their struggles without an anti-imperialist analysis of the roots of gay oppression and then, correspond-ingly, a practice to implement change. In other words a movement that is led by white middle-class men—even those oppressed because of their sexual identification/orientation—without ceding power (within the movement) to Third World women and men, and dealing with their agendas, will never be anything but reform-oriented. To only struggle for gay rights without strug-gling for the rights (human and democratic) of all those in need, and specifi-cally those who are nationally oppressed, sets up a competing struggle rather than a cohesive radical opposition to the government.

QUISP: What was going on in your life that led you to participate in or support armed struggle?

Laura: I began supporting armed struggle in the late '60s, when I realized the government would keep on killing Third World people if left to its own devices. The murder of Fred Hampton (chairman of the Illinois BPP) by the Chicago pigs and FBI was a turning point, not only because it was an assassination, not only because the state tried to cover it up, but also because it made me understand that the U.S. would never agree to "give" oppressed nations their human rights. That's why the government had to kill Fred, and Malcolm X, and so many other leaders. I'd hated the injustice of this society for years, but it was in the '60s, when I supported the Vietnamese, Native American struggles, the Black struggle, Puerto Rico, and saw those nations waging struggles for freedom that included armed struggle—that I started to see that there could be a struggle to win. Once I began supporting Third World nations' right to use armed struggle to win self-determination, it made sense to me that I should be willing to use many forms of struggle to fight, too. Mostly, I think that it's my vision of what a wonderful thing it would be to live in a just, humane, creative world that motivates me to embrace armed struggle as one part of what it takes to fight for a new society.

Linda: When I first became a political activist, I was a pacifist. I had never experienced real violence in my own life and naively hoped that the changes I envisioned could come about nonviolently. Then, I got beat over the head and teargassed by cops guarding the Pentagon at my first major demonstration. I came "head-to-head" with the fact that this system maintains its power through violence on every level—from beating up protesters, to genocide against internally colonized nations, to waging war against nationally colonized nations, to waging war against the people of Vietnam. I became an activist in a time that was defined by the victories and development of national liberation struggles around the world and inside the U.S. I was especially inspired by the Vietnamese and by Black people struggling for civil rights and then for Black Power/Black Liberation. Vietnamese women fighters and Black women in the struggle were role models for me—because they were dedicated to fighting until victory was won. Their courage and dedication, their willingness to risk everything for freedom, the fact that women were being empowered by the process of struggle—all were exemplary. So by supporting these national liberation struggles, I came to support the right of oppressed people to fight for liberation by any means necessary. Malcolm X, Che Guevara, and Ho Chi Minh were important influences in my life and political development. But I actually became determined to participate in armed struggle because of the rage I felt after the FBI/police raids on Black Panther Party offices and homes all over the U.S. and particularly the murder of Fred Hampton and Mark Clark by Chicago police. The intensity of this police terrorism against the

Black community in so many cities made me realize that whenever a political movement even begins to threaten the stability of the status quo, the state will act in whatever ways it must to destroy it. In order for a revolutionary movement and vision to prevail, therefore, it's necessary for us to defend ourselves and our comrades and to build our own capacities toward a day when we can seriously challenge the repressive power of the state, so that state power can be taken out of the hands of those who use it to oppress, taken over, instead, by the people themselves. I know this sounds idealistic, yet it is a struggle that has succeeded in many countries around the world. I believed then—as I do now—that U.S. imperialism was the main enemy of the people of the world, and I wanted to fight on the side of the oppressed to build a better world for all. This was the era of Che Guevara's call for "two, three, many Vietnams," and I recognized that the U.S. government depends on the "domestic tranquillity" of its population to allow for imperialist interventions around the world. This is one reason the Black Liberation struggle was such a threat and why white people fighting in solidarity with national liberation struggles were threatening as well. That's part of the reason that the repression of the internal liberation movements was so immediate and devastating and why there were such efforts to divide off white struggles from these struggles.

Susan: The war against the Black Liberation movement by the FBI/U.S. government was most influential for me in seeing the necessity for armed self-defense. The challenge placed on us who were in a position of solidarity with revolutionary nationalist Black organizations was to uphold self-determination and to fight for it. The other element that most personally propelled me into armed clandestine resistance was witnessing the genocide of the chemical war being waged in the South Bronx against Black and Puerto Rican people. As a doctor of acupuncture and community health worker, I watched us fail to stop the plague.

QUISP: What do you do all day?

Laura: My time is divided among: fighting for decent conditions and against the prison's denial of those things (a daily necessity!), working on my political and legal work, communicating with people via letters and phone calls, talking to other prisoners (and working with them to try to deal with legal issues, health issues, etc.), meeting with my codefendants, trying to find out how my comrade Alan is (he's engaged in a hard, life-and-death battle with cancer, shackled to a bed in the ICU oncology unit at DC General Hospital). I spend a lot of time talking to women about AIDS—by one estimate, 40-50 percent of the women in here are HIV+, yet there is no program, no education, no counseling provided. Like my other comrades, I spend a lot of time doing informal counseling and education on this.

Linda: Work and work out.

Susan: Because I am a doctor of acupuncture and a conscious person, I have become (in addition to a political prisoner) a peer advocate/AIDS counselor. It is not recognized by the jail, but I spend 75 percent of my time counseling people—women who are HIV+. The other time is spent doing my other work and talking with others. We spend a lot of the day locked down in our cells. Because of the overcrowding and lack of programs, the administration keeps us locked down an enormous amount of time.

QUISP: How do you deal with your white privilege in jail?

Laura: I struggle to be aware of it; I fight racism actively and organize for that fight; I try to make the resources that I have access to, available to others. Educating people about how to fight AIDS is another way, because that's information that the gay and lesbian movement have that women in the DC Jail lack—and it means that women are continuing to contract HIV every day. That is a crime.

Linda: I try to use the resources and education I've had access to as a result of my white privilege to benefit all the prisoners I live with and to fight for our interests. This takes many forms, from struggling as a prisoner for the institution of AIDS education and counseling programs, to helping individual women with legal problems or abuses of their rights by the jail. When I was in jail in Louisiana, we were able to win a jailhouse lawyer's legal suit forcing the jail to give women glasses and false teeth. (All jail dental care amounts to is pulling teeth, and few jails replace them.) One of the conflicts I confront is between dealing with immediate needs and crises as an individual counselor/agitator/jailhouse lawyer and always pushing the institution to provide the services and programs that prisoners should be entitled to as a basic human right—education, medical care, exercise, mental health, and AIDS counseling.

Susan: Well! I struggle against racism in every way I can. I have learned patience, and how to be quiet, and how to really listen to who is talking, and what they are saying.

QUISP: What observations or advice do you have for lesbian/gay and AIDS activists as we start to experience police surveillance, harassment, and abuse?

Laura: Fight it. Don't back away. Develop clandestine ways of operating so that the state won't know everything that you're doing. Support one another so that when anyone is targeted for state attack, they can resist—that resistance will build us all. Don't ever give information—even if you think it's "safe" information—to the state. Don't let the state divide the movement by calling some groups "legitimate" and others not. Unity is our strength. Support other movements and people who are also targets of state attack. When the state calls someone a "terrorist," or "violent," or "crazy," or anything, think hard before ever believing it to be true. Resist. Resist. Resist.

Linda: Be cool. Develop a clandestine consciousness. Value your work enough that you don't talk to the enemy about it (like over tapped phones). Don't underestimate the power and viciousness of the state, and don't expect white privilege to make you exempt from repression. Take the lessons of past repression against political movements seriously—not to demobilize you or make you afraid, but to safeguard and defend your work. Remember you're building for the future, not just for today, and keep struggling to broaden your vision. Remember that reforms are only temporary concessions, that they're neither permanent nor do they really solve fundamental problems.

Susan: Study other movements here and around the world and examine the state's methods in order to develop tactics that allow you to keep functioning—very important, if one self-consciously is building a movement that knows the state will destroy it if the movement begins to pose a real or perceived threat.

QUISP: What is your position on go-go girls in women's bars ?

Laura: Take me to a bar and we'll have a scintillating discussion of this issue, Okay?

Linda: Take me to a bar and I'll let you know!

Susan: I think that anything that objectifies women as sexual objects (versus sexual beings) is antiwoman. Even in an all-woman context. Being lesbian is subversive because women loving women is a crime against the state and against the bourgeois patriarchal morality of this society—but being subversive doesn't necessarily mean it's about liberation. If nothing else, I have learned that liberation and the need for it begin in oneself—objectification/sexual stereotypes/misogyny not only destroy us in the world, they corrode our own hearts. I am not interested in a society that promotes those things—although I don't believe that they will be ended until we decide to end them—they cannot be overturned through the law of this state.

QUEERS
We won't be free until everyone is.

FREE LINDA EVANS!

There are over 150 political prisoners in the United State

Linda Evans is a North American anti-imperialist and out lesbian. Charged with conspiring to "infl
change and protest policies and practices of the U.S. government," she is serving 5 years for bombi
Capitol in protest of the U.S. invasion of Grenada. She is also serving 35 years for illegally buying thr

QUISP (queer women & men united in support of political prison
380 Bleecker St., Suite 134, New York NY 10014 • (212) 969-85

Three Decades of Queer Solidarity and Radical Struggle: A Rich History

Bob Lederer
Lesbian/Gay Community Center, New York City
1999

Tonight's forum is an important step toward mobilizing queers to take our rightful place in the fight to free Mumia, and it comes out of a long history. Sexual outlaws of all sorts have always fought for the radical transformation of society. For example, black gay men were key leaders and participants for civil rights, from Bayard Rustin to James Baldwin. And since the 1969 Stonewall rebellion, thousands of out lesbians, gay men, bisexuals, transgendered and two-spirited people have participated in every major struggle for social justice. From the anti-Vietnam war and women's liberation movements of the '60s and '70s to the antiapartheid and Puerto Rican independence movements of the '80s and '90s, just to name a few, queers have been there, both as individuals and in groups, proudly proclaiming our sexualities.

Our persistence has raised consciousness and broken down barriers in every progressive movement. Over and over, we've found that the true path to our liberation lies in participating in radical movements that have the capacity to totally transform society, while at the same time being completely out and grappling with homophobia in the movement. Key to our effectiveness is recognizing two things: that racism is the fundamental issue to confront for anyone seeking radical change in the U.S., and that all of us who are serious about change will eventually come up against the issues of police brutality and/or political imprisonment, and therefore we all need to support those who are fighting those forms of oppression. The April 24 mobilization for Mumia is a critical opportunity to bring together all of these issues.

So let's go back to the Stonewall rebellion: It was fundamentally a revolt against police brutality. Queers of all sorts, with drag queens of color playing a major role, said enough is enough and fought back with their voices, their bodies and with rocks and bottles. Some leaders were leftists who later formed the Gay Liberation Front, which organized the first gay contingents in antiwar protests and marches to free Black Panther political prisoners. Those marchers paid a price in verbal and even physical attacks by homophobic

---

This is the text of a speech given at a forum on March 18, 1999, to build a "Rainbow Flags for Mumia" Contingent at the April 24, 1999, "Millions for Mumia" March in Philadelphia.

activists. But their efforts, and those of white and Black gay groups nation-wide, led a Black Panther leader, Huey Newton, to criticize homophobia by other Panthers and to invite the new gay movement to attend a massive People's Constitutional Convention in 1970, which adopted a strong gay lib-eration plank written by a white gay leftist.

Among the many places that queers participated in radical politics were the underground resistance movements against genocidal wars at home and abroad. And so, inevitably, some became political prisoners. In the 1970s, lesbian and gay communities in Connecticut and Kentucky withstood fierce FBI sweeps and grand jury fishing expeditions seeking to find underground lesbian Susan Saxe and her colleague Kathy Power—who had been part of group that robbed a bank to raise money for clandestine antiwar resistance. Several lesbians went to jail rather than become informants to the grand jury, but by 1976 the FBI tracked down Saxe, who was then sentenced to several years in prison. Other queer underground fighters arrested and given long sentences in this period included West Coast anarchist Bø Brown, a lesbian, and Ed Mead, a gay man, both part of the George Jackson Brigade that bombed federal buildings and corporate headquarters to resist U.S. aggres-sion internationally. Another West Coast fighter, lesbian communist Judy Siff, was part of a spin-off of the Weather Underground Organization busted for planning to bomb the office of a California senator who was heavily promot-ing antigay legislation.

The period I know best begins after I came on the New York radical scene in the late '70s as a part of a sector of the left that focused on building militant support among whites for revolutionary groups of color at home and abroad. In particular, I worked mainly in a group in solidarity with independence for Puerto Rico, and I also briefly participated in a group supporting liberation movements in Southern Africa. Many people I knew ended up as political prisoners; numerous queers were among them. In the early '80s, Judy Clark, a white lesbian communist, and Kuwasi Balagoon, a Black bisexual anarchist, were among six activists working with the Black Liberation Army who were arrested and charged with participating in the robbery of a Brink's truck—during which one cop and two Brink's guards were killed—to raise money for Black community armed self-defense, alternative health care and anti-Klan infiltration. All the activists got life sentences. Judy and the others remain in prison today, but for Kuwasi his penalty turned out to be a death sentence, as he died four years later of AIDS after gross neglect of his health needs by the New York State prison authorities. Another white lesbian activist, Eve Rosahn, was falsely charged as an accessory to the Brink's robbery and finally got her charges dropped, only to then face a subpoena to testify before a grand jury, which she refused, earning her fifteen months in prison. Today, Eve is a lawyer who often represents queers and AIDS activists, among many other fighters, who commit civil disobedience. And while mentioning courageous queer lawyers, another person who faced huge pressures and persecution from the state in this period was Susan Tipograph, another white lesbian. She faced all sorts of attempts to jail and defame her for her vigorous representation of radical clients of color, yet she beat back those efforts and is still in the trenches today. Finally, I must pay tribute to another speaker tonight, Joan Gibbs, revolutionary Black lesbian lawyer, who has been a consistent defender of countless political prisoners, as well as activists arrested for civil disobedience, for many years. She is active in the Free Mumia campaign.

In the early '80s, an underground group of white revolutionaries called the Red Guerrilla Resistance began a campaign to heighten struggle against government repression here and military aggression abroad. This group carried out a string of bombings of U.S. military, government and corporate offices in which no one was injured. Among their targets was the Capitol building in Washington, to protest the invasion of Grenada, and a Naval headquarters, protesting attacks on Nicaragua and support for the contras. The group's final bombing was at the office of the Patrolmen's Benevolent Association here in New York, to protest their efforts to get manslaughter charges dropped against a racist cop who had killed an unarmed Black grandmother, Eleanor Bumpers. (The Black community had mobilized after the murder, thus forcing the prosecutor to obtain the very rare indictment of a cop for a killing; it was this indictment that had so enraged the PBA that they mobilized thousands of "off-duty" cops to march against the prosecutor.)

A month after the PBA bombing, I and novelist/activist Terry Bisson became the fifth and sixth people subpoenaed before a federal grand jury attempting to track down the members of the Red Guerrilla Resistance. Terry and I, like four colleagues before us, refused to name names or answer any questions. The prosecutor asked the judge to hold us in contempt of court and be jailed. We held a press conference and burned our subpoenas in front of the FBI building in Washington. I said publicly that I would never cooperate with a government that committed crimes like the recent FBI and Philadelphia Police bombing of the MOVE organization, a radical Black collective. That police bombing, which killed eleven people, including five children, was undertaken because MOVE upheld the right to armed self-defense. Seven years earlier, other police attacks on MOVE had been bravely exposed by crusading journalist Mumia Abu-Jamal, undoubtedly setting him up to be targeted by the police. In my public statement (in front of the "J. Edgar Hoover Building"—how fitting!), I also said that as a gay man, part of my commitment to fight this government came from my determination to help create a society free of antigay oppression.

Meanwhile, in the preceding year, I had become involved in the gay movement, joining Men of All Colors Together, including helping organize a forum on police abuse against the gay community, particularly gays/lesbians of color. So in my few remaining weeks before going to jail, I decided to use the time to travel to several cities, speaking to lesbian/gay forums and doing interviews with gay newspapers. My message was that queers should fight

387

government repression because the same weapons used against other movements will be used against our movements—and because we all have a stake in a more just society. For whites, that means that solidarity with people of color is key. Lesbians and gays rallied behind my case and against repression. Nonetheless, after several weeks of legal battles—including our unsuccessful argument that international law protected us from punishment for resisting our government's criminal acts—Terry and I were jailed without trial on civil contempt charges. We served three months in federal prison; many others in that period served much longer terms.

Just before our jailing, the FBI arrested several longtime activists, former colleagues of ours who had gone underground with the Red Guerrilla Resistance. Among them were two out lesbians, Laura Whitehorn and Linda Evans. Members of their group got draconian sentences—20, 30, 40 years— for charges that are not usually punished so harshly—illegal gun purchase, harboring a fugitive, or possession of guns and bombs. But three years later, the feds piled on an extra charge against seven of them: "conspiring to alter U.S. foreign policy by force and violence." By this time, around 1989, I had become active in ACT UP [the AIDS Coalition to Unleash Power], and several of us nationwide published an open letter to the queer community supporting the call that the charges be dropped. We noted that two defendants were lesbians, that all had supported ACT UP's militant actions and that such draconian charges posed a threat to all our movements. ACT UP itself was facing government repression, and many queers worked around this case. Laura and Linda, along with their colleague Marilyn Buck, ended up pleading guilty to the Capitol bombing, for which they got stiff added sentences. All three remain in prison. And Laura just called me today with the bad news that her scheduled release this month to a halfway house was rejected by higher-ups, so she won't be home till August. But back to 1990: another codefendant serving a 58-year sentence on earlier charges, Susan Rosenberg, was so inspired by the widespread queer support that she came out as a lesbian for the first time since her incarceration.

Out of this support campaign, queers in my group, the Free Puerto Rico Committee, joined with others to form QUISP—Queers United in Support of Political Prisoners. Launched in 1990 in the heyday of Queer Nation and a revived spirit of queer liberation, QUISP worked from the simple premise that no one can be free until everyone is free. For several years, we sponsored forums and cultural events to educate the community and raise funds around particular cases of political prisoners. We also joined with queers of color when key issues were being fought out in the community, like the 1991 demo led by Asian American queer groups to protest several gay organizations' benefit showing of the racist and sexist play *Miss Saigon*.

Eight years ago next month, we held a forum in support of Mumia—perhaps the first such New York event for a mostly white audience. Mumia had just lost his last round of appeals, and the situation looked grim. We wrote him to ask how he felt about our holding a forum. He thanked us profusely, said he welcomed support from all, but revealed that his philosophy, following that of the MOVE organization, was that "heterosexual hookups are the most natural." He added that he sincerely hoped he hadn't offended us. After some debate, we agreed to share his response at the forum, so the community could understand the importance of defending all political prisoners who fight for justice, even if we disagree with some of their views. As one member noted, "Once Mumia is free, we'll have plenty of time to argue with him on this issue. But that won't happen if we allow the state to execute him." [Note: Since the night of this speech, Mumia has issued a statement from death row strongly condemning antigay violence.]

At the forum that night, our invited speaker was former Black Panther Dhoruba Bin-Wahad, who had been recently released after nineteen years in prison fighting to overturn an FBI frame-up. Frankly, we didn't know what to expect from this straight male Black nationalist, but we were richly rewarded. Dhoruba made a passionate appeal not only for us to help free Mumia and all political prisoners, but also for radical movements including his own Black nationalists to embrace the struggles against sexism and homophobia as integral to revolution. He also called for white lesbians and gays to respect the leadership of lesbians and gays of color. Dhoruba attributed much of his new political consciousness to his comrade and wife, long-time activist Tanaquil Jones. This speech was a crucial moment in building cross-movement solidarity.

And if I can add a personal note, it was this speech that later led me to my lover of seven years, John Riley. Nine months after Dhoruba's speech, our least favorite prosecutor, Robert Morgenthau, was trying to rejail Dhoruba on the old bogus charges. The Black movement had set a rally for his court date. I was so inspired by his incredible QUISP speech that I leafleted all 500 people at that week's ACT UP meeting (yes, it was that big every week back then!). Suddenly, this cute, very tall, pony-tailed guy takes a flier and says, "Great! I've been wondering when Dhoruba's court date was! I just moved here from Iowa and want to hear all about the gay left!" Well, folks, the rest is history, and John and I have since maintained our romance and revolutionary commitment through many actions by ACT UP and the Free Mumia Coalition. So I can thank Dhoruba, and for that matter, Mumia, for bringing me the love of my life. Queer liberation in practice!

It was in fact John who suggested QUISP's first street action in 1992 against Pennsylvania's then-Governor Robert Casey, a so-called pro-lifer with the gall to both oppose abortion and support the death penalty. When the *Village Voice* invited Casey to Cooper Union to discuss abortion, we helped form a broad coalition, including members of WHAM, the Women's Health Action Mobilization, to protest Casey's policies on both issues and demand that he stop Mumia's execution. It was the first large New York demo about Mumia, and it got lots of publicity. Over the years, QUISP also organized queer contingents in several Washington marches to free Puerto Rican political prisoners and in the now-annual Philadelphia marches to free Mumia. In addition, QUISP continued to hold forums, video showings and fundraisers for the case of Mumia and other political prisoners in the U.S.

Today, unfortunately, QUISP no longer exists. But the spirit behind QUISP has lived on in many individuals, including all of tonight's speakers, and in several organizations. It lived on in 1997, after New York's finest assaulted ACT UP members committing civil disobedience on Wall Street, illegally strip-searching several women and seriously injuring one man with AIDS when cops beat his head into the concrete six times shouting, "Die, diseased faggot." Days later, ACT UP members joined the Audre Lorde Project, a center for queers of color, and numerous Black, Latino and Asian community groups in a broad march against police brutality. That spirit lived on last fall, after police brutally attacked the October 19 political funeral for Matthew Shepard. Days later, dozens of queers joined a massive coalition march against police brutality. That spirit lived on three weeks ago, when eight members of the affinity group Fed Up Queers lay down in the street next to the mass rally demanding justice for Amadou Diallo, in a brave act of solidarity. They became the first of what's now become a tidal wave of civil disobedience. And that spirit lived on earlier today, when a much larger group of queers was arrested at 1 Police Plaza in the continuing campaign against police brutality.

Let's keep that spirit of resistance alive and continue our rich queer history of fighting to end police brutality and free political prisoners, by pulling out all the stops to build this Rainbow Flags for Mumia Contingent at the April 24 march as large as we possibly can. Because remember, as we fight to free Mumia, we're also fighting to free ourselves.

Queer Activists Join Massive Civil Disobedience Protests Demanding Liberty and New Trial for Death Row Journalist Mumia Abu-Jamal

Simon Nkoli Queer Crusaders in Support of Political Prisoners
1999

Dozens of queer activists from around the country joined coordinated nonviolent civil disobedience protests and actions on both coasts July 3, demanding liberty, a new trial and urgent medical attention for award-winning African-American journalist and Pennsylvania death-row inmate Mumia Abu-Jamal. At Philadelphia's Liberty Bell, amidst 100-degree heat, 95 protesters disrupted business as usual and closed the building for the afternoon, during a weekend with the heaviest tourist presence of the year. In San Francisco, after a mass march from the Federal Building to Union Square, 27 activists blocked the street and were arrested.

Taken together, the demonstrations amounted to the largest civil disobedience action against the death penalty in U.S. history. The unprecedented actions, accompanied by support vigils of hundreds nearby, were sponsored by broad coalitions of progressive groups (including ACT UP/NEW YORK) and marked 17 years to the day after Abu-Jamal's death sentence was imposed in a trial deemed grossly unfair by Amnesty International and many other observers worldwide.

One of the most visible parts of the Philadelphia protest occurred when the "Simon Nkoli Queer Crusaders for Mumia" took the front position in blockading one entrance to the Liberty Bell Pavilion. Brandishing a banner reading "Queers Say: Stop the Execution of Mumia Abu-Jamal," the group— ten lesbians, gay men, bisexuals and allies—joined other activists in front of the door, to which two people had chained themselves, while U.S. Park Police looked on helplessly. (Simon Nkoli was a proudly gay, Black South African antiapartheid activist who narrowly escaped execution on treason charges in the 1980s, then went on to form gay/lesbian rights and AIDS advocacy groups. He was a leader in the successful effort to make South Africa the first

---

This press release accompanied the civil disobedience action for Mumia Abu-Jamal held at Philadelphia's Liberty Bell on July 3, 1999, in which the Simon Nkoli affinity group was one of many whose members were arrested. The release was circulated to the Lgbt media. See also, VI.7.A "How Freedom Rang," by Matt Meyer (page 432), VI.7.B "Why We Are Demonstrating at the Liberty Bell" (page 438), and "An Urgent Message from Dennis Brutus and Friends" (page 440).

country to include sexual orientation in its constitutional protections against discrimination. Nkoli died of AIDS earlier this year.)

ACT UP/NEW YORK member Bob Lederer, organizer of the Simon Nkoli group and one of those arrested, said, "Anyone concerned about the future of queer and AIDS activism should be outraged by Mumia's impending execution. Many of us have experienced or witnessed vicious homophobic, AIDSphobic police brutality against our movements. The injustice against Mumia springs from his history as a journalist and activist against police brutality, and his prior membership in the Black Panther Party was used to inflame the jury to sentence him to death. That makes this a bellweather case. If Mumia can be executed without ever having had a fair trial, it sets a dangerous precedent that would make it easier to heighten repression against all types of activists. That's one reason groups which rarely work together united in action today. In addition, many of us oppose the use of the death penalty against anyone."

The Philadelphia protest was made up of sixteen affinity groups from queer, AIDS, peace, anti-intervention, African-American, Latino, student and leftist groups. Before the door-blocking action, four people went inside the Liberty Bell Pavilion and unfurled a banner reading "Let Freedom Ring for Mumia" next to the historic icon. Two student activists clambered onto the building's awning and held a banner reading "Liberty for Mumia" for three hours, until they were removed by police using a forklift. It took police several hours to clear all 95 protesters, including two blind people and a woman in a wheelchair. All were released within ten hours after being charged with failure to obey a lawful order. They are now facing fines of $250 each, which will be contested.

Along with the Philadelphia and San Francisco protests, over 100 people attended a Providence, Rhode Island prayer vigil and rally against the death penalty and in support of Abu-Jamal, held in conjunction with the national General Synod of the United Church of Christ. Two weeks earlier, 23 activists were arrested in Paris after storming the American Library, demanding a new trial and health care for Abu-Jamal.

Last October, Pennsylvania's Supreme Court denied Abu-Jamal's bid for a new trial, upholding the ruling of Judge Albert Sabo, the original trial judge. Abu-Jamal, an author and activist, was convicted in 1982 of the shooting death of a Philadelphia police officer in a trial tainted by the flagrant bias of Judge Sabo, by the deliberate exclusion of 11 Black potential jurors and by a court-appointed lawyer who, by his own admission, was inexperienced in criminal law. In addition, witnesses came forward during the 1995 Post-Conviction Relief Appeal hearings, saying they were coerced by police to lie, suppress or change their initial accounts of the December 9, 1981 incident. In recent weeks, Abu-Jamal has suffered from troublesome pain, swelling and discoloration in his feet, and has yet to be examined by an independent physician.

Lesbian activist Dawn Reel, another arrestee from the Simon Nkoli group and a member of New York's Free Mumia Abu-Jamal Coalition, said that the July 3 actions are only the beginning of a campaign of civil disobedience demanding a new trial for Abu-Jamal. "At this point," she said, "despite all efforts by the legal team, the system has denied Mumia his due-process rights. That's why we have to take this matter to the streets for the Court of the People to judge."

Interest in Abu-Jamal's case has been growing in LGBT communities nationally. This past April, hundreds joined "Rainbow Flags for Mumia" contingents of two massive pro-Mumia marches in Philadelphia and San Francisco. Last month, large contingents supporting Abu-Jamal marched in LGBT pride parades in New York and San Francisco. Among the prominent endorsers of the July 3 civil disobedience action was bisexual musician Ani DiFranco and New York lesbian activist Leslie Cagan, co-chair of the 1987 March on Washington. Other endorsers included South African poet laureate and antiapartheid former political prisoner Dennis Brutus, African-American educator/writer Professor Manning Marable, Puerto Rican independence leader Rafael Cancel Miranda, longtime antiwar activist David Dellinger, and Rev. Lucius Walker, director of Pastors for Peace (who was one of those arrested).

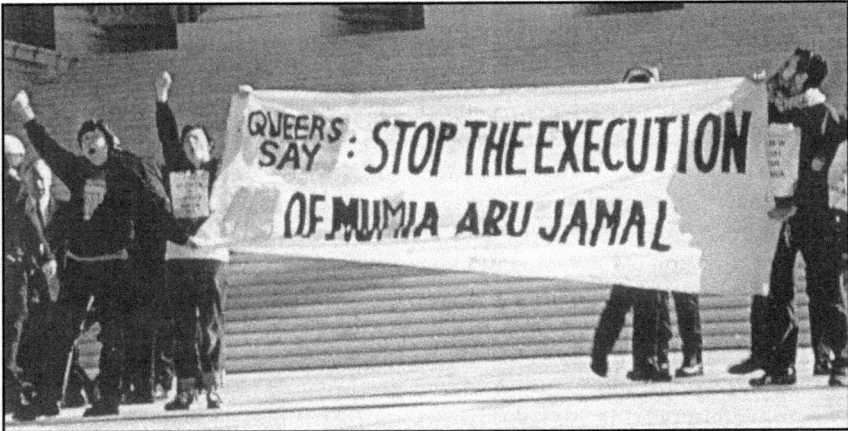

Credit: Diane Greene Lent

One Herstory of Out of Control:
Lesbian Committee to Support Women Political Prisoners and Prisoners of War, 1986-2008

B♀ (rita d. brown) and Jane Segal
2008

Chapter #1

The u.s. bureau of prisons has always had some sort of extra-secure lockup for women they could identify as somehow notorious, and therefore in need of "closer custody." For many years, Davis hall at Alderson, West Virginia, was that place. In the '40s Billie Holiday was held there. Puerto Rican Nationalist Lolita Lebrón was there in the late '50s and early '60s. In the late '70s it was actually called the "maximum security unit" and held New York Black Liberation Army political prisoner Assata Shakur; and B♀ (rita d. brown), a white dyke anti-imperialist political prisoner of the George Jackson Brigade from Seattle, Washington. In the '80s the immigrant Cuban and Haitian women prisoners were housed in the same building. This prison within a prison exists in every prison in this country. It has always been a secret place where every kind of torture imaginable can go on undetected. They are now everywhere and called "control units."

In 1986 the u.s. bureau of prisons opened its next version, the LHSU. The first official "high-security unit" for women prisoners. It was built in a basement at Lexington, Kentucky, federal correctional institution that once housed a hospital designed to help prisoners addicted to drugs. Now held in undeniable sensory deprivation conditions were Alejandrina Torres, a Puerto Rican nationalist from Chicago, and Susan Rosenberg, a political prisoner from New York. Both of these sisters came directly from kourt to the new subterranean, small group isolation facility. This was a clear violation of the b.o.p.'s own policies since they had never been in general population and therefore had violated no institutional rules. Italian national Silvia Baraldini, another anti-imperialist political prisoner from New York, was transferred in from f.c.i. Dublin, California. where she had been held for several years without incident. In fact her custody had recently been lowered because she had no infractions and was considered no threat or risk. All three of these women were moved into LHSU because of their political beliefs and politi-

---

This piece was a collaboration by two of the founding mothers of *Out Of Control*: B♀ (r.d.brown) and Jane Segal, who were ½ of the four women who first met in "*that*" SF Mission District kitchen in 1986.

cal associations. There were also two social prisoners who were doing long terms. They appeared to be the cover that allowed the b.o.p. to deny this unit was specifically built for women political prisoners.

Daily mental torture was clearly the basic program in effect here: All walls were painted white. The all-male guard staff controlled all the lights. No visitors were allowed except attorneys of record. Property was extremely limited, including books, letters and personal hygiene items (the women had to ask for kotex). Locked in cells 23 hours a day. All meals were brought from outside the building and eaten alone in their cells. No education programs of any type, and certainly there was no clear plan or method for ever being released out of the unit. That was a primary point of abuse—no way out. The diabolical design was to create despair and depression and thus break the spirits of these women prisoners. The social prisoners would simply be considered as casualties of this ongoing war against the women political prisoners.

Shortly after the third political prisoner, Silvia Baraldini, arrived at LHSU, four women who knew and loved her met in a San Francisco Mission District kitchen to brainstorm ways to protest her abrupt transfer and to stop this outrageous control unit. We formed a women's committee to shut down the LHSU and sent out a call to other sisters in the Bay Area. The group grew instantly, and we quickly became Out of Control Committee to Support Women Political Prisoners and Prisoners of War. We joined a national grass roots campaign of activists to expose the brutality at Lexington and demanded that it be immediately shut down. This national struggle included very broad-based support from the national Puerto Rican independence movement, the prison abolitionists, the civil rights and women's communities, the American Indian

Alejandrina Torres, Susan Rosenberg and Silvia Baraldini inside the Lexington High Security Unit. *(Source: Daedalus Productions)*

Movement, many unaffiliated individuals, the progressive churches and pacifists, as well as Susan's mother and father.

Psychological torture experts were brought on board to define and document and evaluate the conditions. The ACLU National Prison Project, the Center for Constitutional Rights, the People's Law Office and other experienced movement attorneys provided their expertise. A lawsuit was filed against the b.o.p. to close the LHSU. They did a great job and we thank them all for their good work. The evidence was so overwhelming from the beginning that the only reason Alejandrina, Silvia, and Susan were held under these conditions was because of their politics. The kourts could only rule in favor of the women political prisoners and barred the b.o.p. from "considering a prisoner's past political associations or personal political beliefs " when deciding to transfer prisoners into federal prisons. The LHSU was shut down after a relatively short 18 months. We had ourselves a well-deserved little victory! However, it was short lived, as the decision was overturned on appeal and the torture continued in other ways.

In October 1988 all three political women prisoners were moved back to jails. Two were placed in Metropolitan Correctional Centers (federal high-rise jailhouses): Silvia in New York and Alejandrina in San Diego. Susan went back to the Washington, DC, jail. This madness continued for two more years while a small new women's prison was opened in Marianna, Florida. All movement was controlled in the Shawnee Unit there, and it was just a little bit bigger kind of small group isolation. It was a women's prison contained within a larger men's prison opened in 1988, and the mission was pretty much the same. To control, isolate and neutralize the women sent there who, for varying reasons, pose either a political, escape, or disruption threat to be defined by the masters of unreason within the b.o.p. The goal was to destroy the ability of the women prisoners to function in anything other than an institutional setting. It was 1994 before they would make it to a general population in Danbury, Connecticut.

Chapter #2

In 1989 there just wasn't much information or support for political prisoners, especially the women. So after the LHSU closed, some of us decided to continue our work on behalf of the 25 women political prisoners and Prisoners of War being held in amerika's prisons. We knew it was our job to focus on these women because if we didn't no one would. It was that simple. Our political prisoner sisters would be shipped throughout the federal prison system. We knew this would keep information coming from the inside about basic conditions around the country because the political prisoners would experience it and speak out. Having survived many years of typical leftist coalitions, we had come to understand the importance of choosing the correct name for our group. So, we morphed a bit (before morphing was even popular) and became *Out Of Control: Lesbian Committee To Support Women*

Political Prisoners And Prisoners Of War. Thus, we were assured that our community, the prisoners, and the world would know that lesbians were doing this work to support our sisters and to expose the myth that political prisoners did not exist in the usa.

Our most important job was to help make it known that there were political prisoners in amerika, and many were women and some of them were lesbians. Over the years we painted several powerful banners and took them to a wide variety of demonstrations and other progressive events. One year we made these great black and silver *Dykes Out Of Control* T-shirts that were immediately sold out before we ever got to the Pride Parade. We had enough money then to make a second run and sold it out, too. But then a local leather shop created a knock-off that was white with small black letters and cost twice as much, and they sold them for many years. That's ok because there ain't nothing wrong with having some dykes out of control. We had a small contingent in *Dykes On Bykes* one year, complete with the lesbian political prisoners names on the back of my bike. Lots of people gave us support as we rode down Market Street that year. Maybe it was that bare-breasted young sister on the back of another bike with *Free All Political Prisoners* written on her back in bright red lipstick. Or, maybe it was cuz we were doing a good job at raising the consciousness of those who attended the Pride Parade events. We shared a table space with LAGAI—QUEER INSURRECTION every year at the Pride Parades, where we had a sandwich board with pictures and current info on our sister political prisoners. People actually came to find us and ask about the prisoners. One year we marched along side the Fat Dyke Float carrying thousands of a lavender ½ sheet featuring an Alison Bechdel—"Dykes to Watch Out For"—cartoon strip about the lesbian political prisoners. We almost gave them all away before we got to our table. We did house parties, spoke on local college campuses; we were on KPFA and several college radio shows. We got to travel on occasion to speak at college campuses. B̶ was asked to speak in the basement of some church in New York with other longtime queer activists during the 25-year anniversary of the *Stonewall Riots*.

In 1990 we created a women political prisoner commissary fund with LAGAI, supported by an annual garage sale in the Castro where many expert/recycler interior designers regularly shopped and cruised very early on Saturday mornings. In cooperation with many local sisters, we also began producing *Sparks Fly*, an amazing event that happened mostly at the *Women's Building*. This was a not-to-be-missed annual cultural/educational event, where we continued to bring updates on the prisoners and build community support. Many local artists donated their time and craft to help raise those commissary funds. It wood be impossible to name everyone, so i'll just mention a few of the favorites: Jewelle Gomez, Cherríe Moraga, Chrystos, Dorothy Allison, Melanie DeMore, Elizabeth Summers, Carolyn Brandy, Tom Ammiano, Gwen Avery and Mary Watkins w/ Judy G & Diva as backup, and we had our drag kings with Fresh White as Barry White, and a very convincing Frida Kahlo and Che were even the MC's one year. *Out Of Control* was able to provide a reasonable stipend to 11 women political prisoners, including the MOVE sisters in Pennsylvania (who still remain in prison after 30+ years). This was a very successful and fun grassroots-community way of creating/involving/building ways to have effect. We packed the house year after year after year. How many years? We think it was somewhere between 10 to 12 years. We were part of a very strong political queer activist community in the SF Bay Area, and our people supported our work just as we supported theirs.

In 1992, OOC participated in the International Tribunal of Indigenous Peoples and Oppressed Nations in the usa. We provided testimony on behalf of the white north amerikan political prisoners and offered legal counsel. All testimony was presented to a panel of international judges and was presented to the United Nations. During this time we were also introduced to the case of Norma Jean Croy, a Shasta Native woman whose case we supported and included in our daily work.*

In October 1995, we provided more testimony; this time at the Ecumenical National Conference on Racism for the United Nations. We presented the case of Norma Jean Croy and the cases of the North American Political prisoners engaged in antiracist and antiapartheid struggle.

During the winter of 1996-97, OOC worked with the Mumia Art Show Women's Group to bring the Mumia Art Show to the SF Bay area. The show was a collection of visual and written pieces from over 90 political prisoners from around the world. The money raised went directly to Mumia's defense fund.

In winter and spring of 1997-98, OOC worked in coalition with Jericho '98. This national effort was spearheaded by African American activists and brought attention to the specific issue of political prisoners. Calling for amnesty for all political prisoners, that campaign culminated with a major demonstration in Washington, DC, with a walk out at Berkeley High School and a demonstration in Oakland, Ca.

Out Of Control was a part of the organizing committee for *Critical Resistance—Beyond The Prison Industrial Complex*, a monumental prison/prisoner-focused conference held at U.C. Berkeley in September 1998. OOC presented a two-hour workshop about women political prisoners where some of our sisters being held locally were able to call in with a live feed to KPFA radio. In total, we think we participated either individually or collectively in at least 5 different workshops over the course of the 2-day event.

There are a few other things we somehow managed to get done in the '90s. They include *Sparks Fly: Women Political Prisoners in the u.s.a.*; a brochure used to introduce the issue of our sisters and their stories; "Celebrate Resistance," a collection of biographies, photos, poetry, writings and artwork by the women political prisoners, giving voice to the voiceless; and *Sparks Fly*, a 20-minute

---

* See Bᕯ's article on this sister that appears earlier in this book at III.6, page 298.

video featuring 10 women (5 Puerto Rican nationals and 5 white north americans) political prisoners. We created a dissolve of photos of the women political prisoners and voice over with telephone-recorded messages from jail. High-tech shit for that time period.

Since 1989 we have published a newsletter, *Out Of Time*. We are the only newsletters of this kind in the usa, with a primary focus on women political prisoners. It began as one photocopied double-sided sheet. Within a few short years, it became a 4-page tabloid on newsprint. Of the 1,000 we currently print, 600 are sent inside the walls of mostly women's prisons around the country. Various activist groups here and in Europe receive multiple copies. *Out Of Time* is also an insert in *Ultra Violet*, the newsletter of LAGAI—QUEER INSURRECTION, which prints 1,500 copies to be mailed as well as distributed to a variety of bookstores and coffee houses in San Francisco. Copies of current issues can be viewed on the LAGAI website. This remains our primary work, and hopefully it will outlive all of us. We continue to support Marilyn Buck and the MOVE Women and to focus on amerika's political prisoners. We have expanded to include more international coverage by reporting on prisoner-related human rights violations as well as the ever-growing war on women in war-torn countries around the world. There is clearly an international increase in the torture of women and the number of women political prisoners. Rape and mutilation of women and children is not new but even more hideous in the 21st century, when the rich ruling parties of the so-called world leaders certainly know and consciously ignore these crimes.

Several of us work regularly with other prison abolitionist projects. These include: All of Us or None, California Coalition for Women Prisoners, Prison Activist Resource Center, and Center for Young Women's Development, and we are working in various ways on the Critical Resistance 10 conference slated for September 2008. All these groups are in need of your support and have websites that you can check out for more information.

Chapter #3

The nineties were amazing! There was ACT UP actions, lots of antiwar demos (desert storm era), calls for bank of america and shell oil to divest in South Africa; political activism was strong and evident everywhere. Through it all we continued our work to build support for the concrete demands of the growing prison abolition movement. This included compassionate release for prisoners with HIV/AIDS and an end to the death penalty, as well as the closing of all control units. And even political lesbians started saying fem and butch and top and bottom out loud without fear of being ostracized. We could even find a place to live in SF for under $500, and we could still eat and get around to check out all the political things going on all over the city. It was great times filled with good politics and good work and some good victories.

399

Our M.O. has not really changed much. We live our politics and function as best we can with our personal practice being as honest a reflection of our theoretical beliefs as possible. We remain a small, grassroots group with no formal board and no paid staff.

We do have a 501 (c) (3) fiscal sponsor. And many of the women political prisoners have served in advisory capacity. For years we met at least once a month and maybe more depending on what work was happening. Some of us still work with others on broader issues, and all major decisions are made by consensus as much as possible. As we get older and older (i think most of us are in our 60s + now), we meet less and work on fewer things, but we are far from done.

Section VI.

Pulling Out the Stops to Free Mumia Abu-Jamal

So much important work has been done around the case of death row prisoner Mumia Abu-Jamal, it has been a difficult task determining what to include in this section. In addition to wanting to include campaigns for Mumia initiated by other political prisoners, we have also decided to focus on those actions that the editors of this volume were personally closest to. Though we harbor no illusions that these were the best or most important examples of work on behalf of Mumia, we do believe that the documents and articles presented in this section shine light on a convergence of previously unaligned individuals and groups in our attempt to broaden the tactics available to the overall campaign. Insofar as the actions cited helped to bring Mumia's message to folks who hadn't heard it before, we believe that they were important successes. Insofar as Mumia is still on death row as of this writing, those successes were clearly limited ones.

Besides the above areas of work, we have included documents from the important international, legislative, and judicial efforts to free Mumia. All of these aspects of the Mumia movement derive their strength from the grassroots, day-to-day, community-based organizing that continues to this day.

A Brief History/Herstory
of the Movement to Free Mumia

Suzanne Ross
2008

This presentation of the history of the Free Mumia movement, now 27 years in existence, is in no way comprehensive. It is meant to give a sense of its breadth, consistency, and international dimensions, as well as its leadership. Cities such as Pittsburgh, Chicago, and Atlanta, and the state of Vermont are not even mentioned, and each of these, as well as others, has played a very important role in different ways. Also, while it is appropriately heavily focused on Philadelphia, the focus on New York City as well, is partly a reflection my living in New York. In Europe, several cities that honored Mumia were also not included, not to mention dozens of demonstrations around the world that ultimately included tens of thousands of people that were not mentioned. And, finally, perhaps most important, the role of the Fraternal Order of Police, as well as that of other repressive institutions and operations in trying to destroy the movement and assure the conspiracy to execute Mumia, is only referred to superficially.

Time, space, and availability of information account for most of these omissions. Hopefully, the amazing spirit and longevity of this movement, inspired by a quite remarkable Black revolutionary whom the U.S. powers have been determined to not only execute but also silence, will nonetheless emerge.

Mumia Abu-Jamal was arrested and charged with the murder of Police Officer Daniel Faulkner on December 9, 1981. But before that, he had already been in close contact with the MOVE organization in Philadelphia, covering their struggles as a radio journalist. MOVE, in turn, had defended him when he refused to comply with his radio stations' demand that he change his hair and his overall appearance and tone. In protest, MOVE supporters and Mumia's wife, Wadiya, created the West Philadelphia Committee for Mumia Abu-Jamal. Once Mumia was arrested, that committee became the West Philadelphia Support Committee to Free Mumia Abu-Jamal.

MOVE and its supporters monitored Mumia's hospital and prison situation, raised money for his legal defense, and organized protests. John Africa appointed Pam Africa to lead the support work for Mumia. At that time and through the '80s, it was primarily the Black community of Philadelphia and surrounding areas that supported these protests. Former Black Panthers

Reggie Schell and Barbara Easley Cox, for example, were in the courtroom throughout the trial. After the bombing of MOVE in 1985, the Partisan Defense Committee (established by the Spartacist League, a Trotskyist organization) also became involved, working to raise money and help MOVE supporters organize yearly indoor events focused on Mumia.

In 1993, Equal Justice USA published an ad in the *Nation* magazine and began producing educational materials about Mumia's case. Left parties began writing columns in their papers supporting Mumia. Support began to be organized in France and Germany. In 1994, when the West Philadelphia Committee to Free Mumia was told that Governor Robert Casey was about to sign a death warrant, the organization became the International Concerned Family and Friends of Mumia Abu-Jamal, with Pam Africa in leadership. ICFFMAJ and Pam Africa in particular continue to be at the heart of the Mumia solidarity movement today, leading it in collaboration with different organizations and individuals.

Upon learning of the impending death warrant, ICFFMAJ began an intensive organizing effort to build broad-based support from Black politicians, Black churches, and Black lawyers as well as from activists across ethnic lines. There were now frequent demonstrations, some of significant size, many taking place in Harrisburg, the state capital. As a result, ICFFMAJ and its allies, including several Black politicians—David Richardson, Vincent Hughes, and Roxanne Jones—and Lois Williamson of Citizens United for the Rehabilitation of Errants, gained enough visibility and recognition to get a hearing before Governor Casey, where (to the surprise of many) they succeeded in dissuading him from signing Mumia's death warrant.

When Governor Tom Ridge was inaugurated in 1995, after promising the Fraternal Order of Police (FOP) that he would sign Mumia's death warrant, a

Demonstrating for Mumia, Philadelphia 1992.
Credit: Workers World

huge demonstration was held in Harrisburg by ICFFMAJ and other Mumia supporters. Representatives from France and Germany began coming to support the struggle here.

When Ridge signed Mumia's death warrant on June 1, the movement went into full swing, both in this country and abroad. Close to one thousand people demonstrated at Philadelphia's City Hall. In New York City, the same number showed up for a street demonstration within 24 hours of the signing—this was organized under the leadership of former political prisoner, Black Panther, and BLA member Safiya Bukhari, who along with Sally O'Brien had founded the Free Mumia Abu-Jamal Coalition (FMAJC) in New York City in 1992. (Bukhari would later lead the founding of the Jericho Movement, but to her last days—she passed away in 2003—would remain completely committed to the Mumia support work.) Herman and Iyaluua Ferguson, attorney Joan Gibbs, Black Panther and friend of Mumia Rosemari Mealy, noted Pan-Africanist Elombe Brath, attorney Michael Tarif Warren, and many other leaders of the Black movement were present and contributed support, as were Puerto Rican, Asian, and white activists and organizations. Longstanding leader of the political prisoner movement and revered Asian-American friend of Malcolm X Yuri Kochiyama—who even when ill came to New York, Philadelphia, and even Washington, DC, demonstrations for Mumia—formed Asians for Mumia; and members of the Latino community formed Latino@s for Mumia. The political prisoners and, from exile, Assata Shakur, themselves in such a vulnerable position, spoke out loudly in support of Mumia, urging activists to focus on preventing his execution.

In San Francisco, a demonstration of nearly 1,000 people was held on June 26, and 250 demonstrators were arrested. In Minneapolis, 200 people tied up traffic in a university neighborhood. They were attacked by police using mace and horses and suffered nine arrests. By June 10, 40,000 petition signatures had been collected, and people from many sectors were mobilized. In Los Angeles, the coalition included actor Mike Farrell. The City Councils of Detroit, Los Angeles, and Madison, Wisconsin, passed resolutions of support. Op-ed pieces appeared in the New York Times, USA Today, and the Washington Post, including a very widely distributed one by E. L. Doctorow. The international support was loud and effective. It was in this context that the Congressional Black Caucus (CBC) called for a stay of execution, the removal of Judge Albert Sabo from the case, and a new trial (see pages 415, 416). Mumia support groups and organizations were formed across the country. Trade unionists, artists, academics, lawyers, students, and many others began to write letters, pass resolutions, take out ads, contribute money, attend meetings, and hold teach-ins and conferences. Academics for Mumia took out an ad in the Philadelphia Daily News with more than 500 signatures, demanding a stay of execution, the removal of Judge Sabo from the case, and a new trial. (Led by Professor Mark Taylor, the group continues its work today under the name of Educators for Mumia.)

Anti-death penalty organizations were energized by the tremendous attention Mumia brought to death row, especially after the publication of his powerful book, *Live from Death Row,* in which he gave voice and humanity to the condemned. Mumia's commentaries were to have been broadcast on National Public Radio, but this was canceled under pressure from the Fraternal Order of Police (see page 413). The determination of those who wield power not only to kill Mumia but also to silence him became apparent.

Hans Bennett, Abu-Jamal-News.com

In July and August 1995, Mumia's Post-Conviction Relief Appeal hearings took place in Philadelphia, with Mumia present in the courtroom. Thousands of people, including international representatives and well-known public figures, came to attend the hearings in Judge Albert Sabo's court. Sabo was the judge in the original, very flawed case and was now reviewing the very trial over which he had presided. Observers were shocked by his courtroom behavior—his obvious racism, his intense animosity toward Mumia and his attorneys, and his consistent rulings in favor of the prosecution. Pressure to have Sabo recuse himself intensified, but to no avail. Rallies in which demonstrators shouted "Sabo must go" echoed through the streets, and legal updates from the lawyers were taking place on a daily basis outside City Hall. The United African Movement, led by Alton Maddox, and the National Action Network, led by the Reverend Al Sharpton, brought busloads of supporters to the courtroom and rallies. Activists came from all communities.

A huge national demonstration was planned in Philadelphia for August 12, five days before the scheduled execution, by the International Action Center (IAC) in collaboration with ICFFMAJ and many other organizations. By August 7, the execution was stayed, but the 10,000-person demonstration took place as a victory for the people and a consolidation of the determination to continue the struggle.

Still, despite the massive outcry and powerful legal arguments pointing to violations of due process, racial bias, and prosecutorial and police misconduct, Sabo rejected all the arguments of Mumia's lawyers and reaffirmed both the conviction and the death sentence.

The case next went to the Pennsylvania State Supreme Court, a body that was strongly connected to the Fraternal Order of Police. Additionally, one of the judges, Ronald Castille, had played a major role in Mumia's original conviction and in some of its violations of due process. But when a legal and grassroots effort to have him recuse himself was mounted, he, like Sabo, refused. On October 30, 1998, the Pennsylvania Supreme Court denied Mumia's appeal and essentially rubberstamped the decisions made in Sabo's court.

Over the years, from 1996 to the present, Jeff Mackler with the Mobilization to Free Mumia Abu-Jamal in San Francisco organized rallies that included Angela Davis, Ossie Davis, Alice Walker, Danny Glover, and Michael Franti, among others. These efforts raised a total of $250,000 to pay for the legal work. There were yearly demonstrations in Philadelphia on April 24, Mumia's birthday; July 4, the day after the date when Mumia was sentenced to death; and December 9, the day in 1981 when Mumia was arrested. There were visible efforts to confront media distortions, such as ABC's hatchet job on "20/20" in 1998 and later *Vanity Fair*'s publication of yet another fabricated "confession." The International Tribunal putting the U.S. government and all the agencies involved in Mumia's conviction on trial in December 1997 in Philadelphia (see page 424), which had its parallel in San Francisco, mobilized the movement internationally. And the movement began to prepare for the signing of yet another death warrant by Governor Ridge.

Also in the period following 1995, the FMAJC developed a strategy to call for a civil rights investigation, the argument being that the statute of limitations did not apply, as the conspiracy to deny Mumia his rights was ongoing. This was supported by the Million Letters for Mumia campaign, an international effort whereby 100,000 letters were collected from around the world—in France, Spain, Italy, Portugal, Holland, Japan, and Israel, among other places—calling on Clinton's attorney general Janet Reno to initiate such an investigation. The letters were finally delivered by hundreds of demonstrators who marched to the Justice Department from Howard University on May 20, 1997.

In January 1999, 20,000 young people attended a sold-out concert at the Meadowlands in New Jersey featuring Rage Against the Machine, the Beastie Boys, Bad Religion, and Black Star, with MC's from Chumbawamba—this despite the Fraternal Order of Police trying to have the concert canceled and threatening that participants would be arrested if they distributed literature. About 75 activists received complimentary tickets to the show and distributed thousands of fliers while educating the young concert audience about Mumia's case. The special appeal Mumia holds for young people, those in the hip-hop community in particular, but so many others around the world, is a pivotal aspect of the continuity of this movement, which now reaches people who were not even born when Mumia was first arrested and charged.

A month later, the IAC in conjunction with ICFFMAJ, FMAJC, Refuse and Resist, WBAI/Pacifica Radio, and other groups organized a 1,700-person solidarity event at New York City's prestigious Town Hall. Speakers included the former political prisoner Puerto Rican Revolutionary Nationalist Rafael Cancel Miranda, Dennis Rivera of 1199 Health and Human Services Union/Service Employees, Dick Gregory, Ossie Davis, Ramsey Clark, and former political prisoner Geronimo ji Jaga Pratt.

By April 1999, Mumia's lawyers were expecting another death warrant. It was in that context that IAC, ICFFMAJ, the New Afrikan Liberation Front, Academics for Mumia, the FMAJC, the Jericho Movement, the Million Woman March, the Bruderhoff (a communal Christian organization), the Black Radical Congress, the Mobilization to Free Mumia Abu-Jamal, Refuse and Resist, the Campaign to End the Death Penalty, Critical Resistance... and dozens of other organizations and networks brought together tens of thousands of people in Philadelphia. With a delegation of 50 people from France plus a representative of the European Parliament, the rally began with contingents marching dramatically from different starting points: the people of African descent contingent led by long-time activists such as Herman and Iyaluua Ferguson, the Latin@s for Mumia contingent led by Rafael Cancel Miranda, the Asians for Mumia contingent, and the Rainbow Flags for Mumia contingent (lesbian and gay supporters) all came together at City Hall, as powerful expressions of the diversity of this movement. Kathleen Cleaver and other former Black Panther Party Sisters were very visible participants.

At the same time, among the many demonstrations that took place across the country and around the world, there was a huge rally of 20,000 people in San Francisco, led by a contingent of 250 members of the International Longshore and Warehouse Union. Members of this union had on that day closed down all West Coast ports from Canada to Mexico, demanding Mumia's freedom in one of the most powerful demonstrations of solidarity we have seen to date.

Two months later, Mumia gave the first of his commencement speeches, amid much protest from the Fraternal Order of Police, at Evergreen College (see page 510). One year later, he did the same at Antioch University, as well as at the Brooklyn Friends High School graduation. Mumia might be on death row, where they may refuse to allow cameras, tape recorders, and video equipment, and NPR might be intimidated into breaking a contract— but Mumia's voice would not be silenced.

Related was the regular broadcasting of Mumia's powerful weekly commentaries through the work of Noelle Hanrahan's Prison Radio Project. Sally O'Brien, longtime host of WBAI's *Where We Live*, has been providing updates on Mumia on her show since the late '80s and, once Prison Radio recordings became available, has opened all her shows with one of Mumia's recorded commentaries. Journalist Kiilu Nyasha, a former Black Panther, has provided information about Mumia on her radio show on KPFA/ Pacifica (Berkeley) since the early '90s. Currently, also on Pacifica Radio, J.R., minister of information for the Prisoners of Conscience Committee, regularly broadcasts recorded interviews with Mumia, conducted by J.R.

himself, Chairman Fred Hampton, Jr., and occasionally other members of the hip-hop community.

In 1999 and 2000, Resistance in Brooklyn, in collaboration with members of the Black Liberation Movement, organized two very large and effective civil disobedience actions, the first on July 3 at the Liberty Bell in Philadelphia and the second on February 28 at the U.S. Supreme Court in Washington, DC (See pages 431-444.)

At the same time, on January 12, 2000, an international delegation of trade union and political leaders met with a Justice Department representative and demanded that the department conduct a federal investigation of documented violations of Mumia's civil and constitutional rights. Echoing the demands of the Million Letters for Mumia campaign, this initiative was organized by Labor for Mumia and chaired by Baldemar Velásquez, president of the Farm Labor Organizing Committee (FLOC/AFL-CIO). One year later, the Justice Department gave its answer: no civil rights investigation. Once again, the Clinton administration refused to conduct an investigation, arguing that this was the domain of the courts, when it was precisely the courts' misconduct that needed to be investigated.

September 11, 1999, dubbed "Mumia 911," was organized by dozens of artists—with an active role played by Refuse and Resist—as a National Day of Art to Stop the Execution of Mumia Abu-Jamal. Well-known hip-hop artists Chuck D, M-1 of Dead Prez, Mumia's daughter Goldii Lokks, Channel Live, and Zack de la Rocha participated on both coasts, and artists such as Don Byron, Oscar Brown, Jr., Ed Asner, Hugh Masekela, and Alice Walker expressed their support. In different venues and on different days, "Mumia 911" had a significant presence and excitement.

To this day, artists continue to play a very important role in the movement to free Mumia, while facing threats from the FOP and inspiring thousands. Just to name a few, Sonia Sanchez (who had testified in Mumia's 1982 trial), Danny Glover, Harry Belafonte, Amiri and Amina Baraka, and the next generation(s), KRS-1, Immortal Technique, Will Calhoun, Michael Franti, the Welfare Poets, and Rebel Diaz, among many others.

On May 7, 2000, 6,000 Mumia supporters packed a sold-out Madison Square Garden theater event organized by a coalition of groups including the ICFFMAJ, FMAJC, and Refuse and Resist, led by the IAC, and MC'd by Ossie Davis and Ed Asner. Attorneys Johnnie Cochran and Ramsey Clark, former New York City mayor David Dinkins, and hip-hop artists Mos Def and Will Villainova, as well as mothers of those who had been victims of police killings were among the participants in the dramatic program. On that same day, Academics for Mumia bought an ad in the New York Times with over 600 signers, including Toni Morison, Jonathan Kozol, Patricia Williams, Cornel West, and Noam Chomsky, stating that many of the signers felt Mumia was innocent; all agreed that he should get a new trial. On that day, it was hard to ignore Mumia!

Credit: Joe Piette/Workers World

In August 2001, Mumia's attorneys were finally able to present their request for a new appeals process (PCRA) to the Philadelphia Court of Common Pleas, based on all the violations of due process in the 1995 PCRA. Mumia was prevented at the last moment from being present, allegedly due to security concerns. Nonetheless, a loud and angry crowd of 2,000 people gathered outside the courtroom and were addressed by Ossie Davis, Dick Gregory, Jesse Jackson, Sonia Sanchez, and others. Judge Pamela Dembe was to deny all the issues raised, including the significance of the racism involved in Judge Sabo's alleged comment, "I'm going to help them fry that n-----," overheard by a court stenographer who had signed an affidavit to that effect.

Now the case went to Federal Court, where some lawyers had placed their hopes. In December 2001, came Judge William Yohn's ruling in Federal Court affirming Mumia's guilt but giving him life in prison without parole. The wheels of injustice were now moving quickly to deny Mumia's freedom. This ruling was (probably intentionally) confusing and weakening to the movement. Many thought Mumia was now off death row. Others felt he was no longer in danger if he was not about to be executed. The reality was that Mumia was never removed from death row, that the prosecution appealed the decision and remained determined to see him executed, and that the doors to proving his innocence and gaining his freedom were shutting tighter.

The movement had to face this challenge and also the dissent in some sectors that resulted from Mumia's firing of his attorney. In New York City, the FMAJC concentrated its work more specifically in the Black community, particularly in Harlem, hoping to consolidate Mumia's support where it was strongest. These solidarity events attracted Black and Latino church leaders and politicians as well as community activists. The work of raising funds for the attorneys, having cultural events and book parties, and distributing Mumia's books continued.

In 2004, the French support escalated, with honorary citizenships and street namings and seriously challenged those who wanted to see Mumia executed—the FOP and its supporters in the governmental and social struc-

410

ture. Our movement drew strength and inspiration from the French initiatives (see pages 445-451) and from their and our refusal to be intimidated by the FOP attacks. We would not back down. We went to the Philadelphia City Council to denounce the resolution they had passed attacking the Saint-Denis street naming and then held a press conference in front of the FOP headquarters to rebut the press conference the House of Representatives initiators of Resolution 407 had held. (Two U.S. Congress members from Pennsylvania had introduced this resolution to demand that the city of Saint-Denis reverse its decision to name a street after Mumia, proposing to sanction Saint-Denis or call for a U.S. boycott of the city should it not submit to their pressure.)

The FOP has regularly threatened, intimidated, and terrorized those who support Mumia. In 2007, they targeted a Philadelphia jazz club where Danny Glover was supposed to speak and a New York City hip-hop club where a benefit for Mumia was scheduled. The FOP's unofficial website talked openly of the violence they would inflict on our movement, but we never canceled an event. When the clubs were forced to cancel, we simply changed the location. Through resisting this FOP terrorism, the Mumia campaign became an important antifascist front.

We also went to visit Philadelphia officials and regularly sat in at the mayor's office. Mayor John Street had supported the NAACP's pro-Mumia resolution and had once worked closely with Pam Africa—yet he now refused to challenge a statement attributed to him by Maureen Faulkner (the widow of Daniel Faulkner, the police officer whose murder Mumia has been framed for); Faulkner claimed that Street had said that he thought Mumia was guilty. Street tried to avoid meeting with us and even avoided meeting with the French deputy mayor, a representative to the French Parliament who had been very instrumental in getting the street in Saint-Denis named in honor of Mumia.

Finally, in May 2007, the Third Circuit Court of Appeals announced that it would hold an open hearing for oral arguments to be presented as to why Mumia should get a new trial. Close to 200 Mumia supporters filled the courtroom, with former Congresswoman Cynthia McKinney, Kathleen Cleaver, Ward Churchill, Lynne Stewart, several international representatives, and many other movement leaders and activists present. A thousand demonstrators were outside the courthouse with Chairman Fred Hampton, Jr., joining Pam Africa to prevent the plainclothes FOP hecklers from endangering the crowd. Twenty-six years after Mumia's initial arrest, 1,000 people were in the streets supporting him, among them many new, young supporters who had initially had been attracted to a concert the night before featuring Immortal Technique.

One year later, in April 2008, after the Third Circuit ruled that Mumia would not get a new trial, a thousand angry protestors once again came to Philadelphia in a very militant and spirited demonstration, led by young drummers and including members of a Washington Heights (New York) liberation church, *Iglesia San Romero de las Américas*, who marched alongside longtime Puerto Rican Mumia supporter Esperanza Martell.

In the meantime, in May 2007, Journalists for Mumia held a press conference to publicize explosive new evidence discovered and analyzed by German professor Michael Schiffman—photographs long available to the prosecution that strongly contradicted the prosecution's version of what had happened on December 9, 1981. In December 2007, NBC's *Today Show* announced plans to invite Maureen Faulkner (widow of the slain officer) and Michael Smirconish (right-wing radio show host) on to promote their new book, *Murdered by Mumia*, arguing for Mumia's execution. Through an impressive campaign—Journalists for Mumia holding another press conference and getting information to the *Today Show*, a national telephone campaign to get the program to present Mumia's side, and FMAJC organizing a loud and visible picket line right outside the NBC studio early in the morning on a freezing day—we actually succeeded in getting coverage of the photographs and in getting a balanced presentation of the controversy around Mumia's case, But this evidence of Mumia's innocence, as with the additional extensive evidence of violations of law, precedent, and due process, has still not entered the legal record.

The future remains in question. Few legal options remain for Mumia. All appeals before the Third Circuit Court of Appeals have been exhausted—the only court left is the U.S. Supreme Court. But this movement, which has lasted so long, been so strong and committed, will surely continue the fight to not allow this injustice to stand. Immediately following the Third Circuit's refusal, plans were set in motion for the next steps.

The struggle to free Mumia is one of freeing all our political prisoners. It is about standing up to the police racism and terrorism that millions of disenfranchised young people of color, in particular, are subjected to on a daily basis. It is about abolishing the racist prison industrial complex and the death penalty once and for all.

The Free Mumia Movement has both highlighted those struggles because of the "fame" of Mumia's case and, at the same time, been part of them. We have joined forces around these issues in our common struggle for justice.

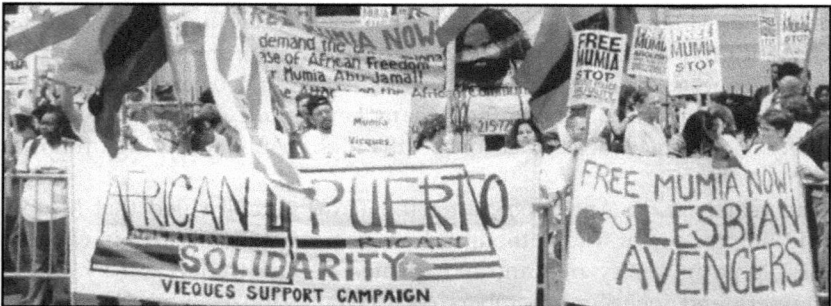

Credit: Hans Bennett, AbuJamal-News.com

Death-Row Journalist Barred
from National Public Radio

Bob Lederer
1994

Amidst a wave of "anticrime" hysteria, National Public Radio has cancelled a planned commentary series by an internationally known Black journalist on death row in Pennsylvania. Media activists are calling the decision one of NPR's most blatant acts of censorship. Before his arrest in 1981, Mumia Abu-Jamal was well known for investigative coverage of police brutality, particularly against the MOVE organization. He won a Corporation for Public Broadcasting award for his reporting on NPR-affiliated WUHY, and he was elected president of the Philadelphia chapter of the Association of Black Journalists. Later, from prison, he was published in the *Yale Law Review*, *The Nation* and *The Philadelphia Inquirer*.

In April 1994, NPR contracted with Abu-Jamal to be a monthly commentator on criminal justice, and several tapes were recorded. The opinion pieces specifically excluded his own case—a death penalty conviction for the 1981 killing of a police officer. Abu-Jamal maintains his innocence, and a worldwide support movement charges his trial was filled with blatant violations of his constitutional rights. Amnesty International expressed "grave concern" about the inflammatory introduction into his sentencing hearing of statements he had made as a young Black Panther leader. (His death warrant can be signed by the Governor at any moment.)

A month of intense promotion for the series by NPR created media interest, prompting a May 13 announcement of a May 16 air date on "All Things Considered," which led to the first wire story. The Philadelphia Fraternal Order of Police then launched a furious campaign denouncing the network for giving a platform to a "cop killer." Police officials went on local commercial radio urging listeners to withdraw support from NPR. Within 48 hours, NPR reversed itself. Managing Editor Bruce Drake cited "serious misgivings

---

A shorter version of this article was published in the July/August 1994 edition of *Extra!*, the magazine of Fairness and Accuracy in Reporting (FAIR). The feared signing of Mumia's death warrant by then-Gov. Robert Casey was staved off by activist pressure, but only temporarily, as his successor, Tom Ridge, did the deed in 1995, only to have it stayed by court order inspired by an intense international uproar. For an update on Mumia's legal situation as of July 2008, see VI.10 "This Is No Victory: Analysis of Appeals Court Ruling on Mumia Abu-Jamal's Case," on page 457.

about the appropriateness of using as a commentator a convicted murderer seeking a new trial, especially since we had not arranged for other commentaries… that provided context or contrasting points of view."

The next day, Sen. Robert Dole attacked NPR from the floor of the Senate for even considering running Abu-Jamal's commentaries (*Current* magazine, 5/23/94). "The last time I checked, we were trying to fight crime, not promote the fortunes of convicted murderers through taxpayer-supported public broadcasting," he said. He noted ominously that this "mistake" showed the need for "closer oversight by Congress."

But in a letter to NPR, FAIR commented, "Abu-Jamal's contributions would have provoked and enriched NPR listeners, helping the network fulfill its mission of providing challenging programming that goes beyond 'conventional sources.' The move to cancel the series is a disturbing signal of timidity at NPR and threatens to have a dangerous chilling effect."

2008 Update: After NPR reneged on its contact with Mumia, various producers throughout the progressive Pacifica Radio Network picked up Mumia's recorded commentaries, which he gradually was able to produce more frequently, thanks to the Herculean efforts of Noelle Hanrahan, founder of Prison Radio, who has recorded nearly all of them. Today these recordings can be heard weekly on Sally O'Brien's program "Where We Live" on WBAI/Pacifica Radio, 99.5FM in New York City (streaming and archived for 90 days at www.wbai.org), and periodically on Free Speech Radio News, which airs on many community radio stations (archived on www.fsrn.org). An archive of many of the commentaries is kept at the website of Prison Radio, www.prisonradio.org.

Graphic: Eric Drooker, www.drooker.com

The Congressional Black Caucus Letter

Suzanne Ross
2008

The following letter was initiated by Congress member Chaka Fattah, who represents the district in which Mumia lived prior to his incarceration and who had a long history of political collaboration with Pam Africa of the International Concerned Family and Friends of Mumia Abu-Jamal. When the Free Mumia Abu-Jamal Coalition (FMAJC) contacted him to urge him to initiate such a letter to Attorney General Janet Reno, Fattah responded promptly and positively. Equal Justice informational packets were sent to all the members of the Congressional Black Caucus (CBC). The letter that emerged demanding a civil rights investigation circulated around the world six weeks before Mumia's scheduled August 17, 1995, execution. It became part of the massive international pressure that was exerted against all branches of the U.S. government that forced Judge Albert Sabo to grant a stay of execution.

Other CBC members added their names in the following months: John Lewis, Major Owens, Floyd Flake, James Clyburn, Kweisi Mfume, and Eleanor Holmes Norton. Others, mostly outside the Congressional Black Caucus, later added their names as well: Congressional Representatives Jerrold Nadler, Albert Russell Wynn, Patsy Mink, José Serrano, Henry B. González, Edolphus Towns, and Harold B. Ford. Representative Nadler had been contacted in the beginning, and it was he who suggested that a civil rights investigation, as had occurred in the '60s in the South, might be very effective.

Subsequently, the FMAJC led an international grassroots campaign, the Million Letters Campaign, that also called for a civil rights investigation, While no civil rights investigation ever happened, the fact that so many congressional representatives had agreed that Sabo's kangaroo court had been a travesty, had demanded a new trial, and had added that Mumia might even be innocent, all lent great "legitimacy" and credibility to the movement.

Sadly, by 2006, when the House of Representatives voted on the anti-Mumia House Resolution 1082 (a revised version of H.R. 407), which denounced the naming of a street after Mumia in St.-Denis, France, Chaka Fattah abstained. He had been publicly threatened on the "unofficial" website of the Fraternal Order of Police, who declared they would be present in the Congress when the vote took place to observe how he voted. Fattah was then running for mayor of Philadelphia. He abstained on this important test of standing up to police terrorism to defend an innocent man.

VI.3.A

"A Grave Injustice Is About to Be Committed..."
Congress member Chaka Fattah
1995

Dear Ms. Reno:

A grave injustice is about to committed. We are rushing to execute someone in the face of ample evidence that his constitutional rights have been
denied, that he did not receive a fair trial, and most importantly, that he
may be innocent. Passionate and documented racial biases, both personal
and societal, surrounded this man's arrest, his trial, his conviction and his
sentencing. Because we understand our history, we understand how we got
to this point; but as legislators and as persons concerned with the processes
of justice in this country, we cannot sit silently by and allow this travesty of
justice to proceed.

Mumia Abu-Jamal is an outstanding African-American journalist from
Philadelphia known for his reporting of police brutality in the 1970s and 80s.
In 1982 he was sentenced to death for the murder of a white police officer.
Testimony of eyewitnesses was suppressed, a witness was bribed to testify
against Abu-Jamal, the ballistics evidence did not match the circumstances
of the case, there is no physical evidence linking Abu-Jamal to the crime, and
tests which could have been done to prove his guilt or innocence were not
ordered. At the trial, Mr. Abu-Jamal, a most powerful orator, was denied the
right to represent himself. His court-appointed attorney—a man who was
later disbarred on unrelated matters—failed to object to 11 of 15 peremptory
challenges to remove African-American jurors, and consented to the judge's
replacing an African-American juror who had been chosen, with an older
white male who admitted that he could not be fair to both sides. Abu-Jamal
was even denied the right to confront his accuser. The judge used his insistence on his right to represent himself as an excuse to remove him from the
trial. No audio transmission of the trial was provided, so Mr. Abu-Jamal did
not hear most of the prosecution's case.

It is apparent that these outcomes were not accidental. The presiding Judge,
Judge Albert Sabo, has sentenced more people to death than any other Judge
in this country, all but two of whom were persons of color. Judge Sabo is
a lifetime member of the Fraternal Order of Police ruling this instance on
the killing of a police officer. No fewer than nineteen instances of unconstitutional error and legal impropriety have been documented in the this (sic)
trial, including the use of Abu-Jamal's political affiliation as evidence in the
sentencing phase of the trial. In a case regarding a member of the Aryan
Brotherhood complaining of similar prosecutorial improprieties that same
year, the Supreme Court ruled that the defendant's First Amendment rights

barred the use of his political associations against him in the penalty phase of the trial.

The appeals process through the Pennsylvania Supreme Court was similarly flawed. For example, in his summation, the prosecutor in the Abu-Jamal case insisted to the jury that they were not being "asked to kill anyone," that the defendant would have "appeal after appeal after appeal," incorrectly implying that the responsibility for determining a death sentence does not ultimately rest with the jury. Such implications by the prosecution were determined to be "fatally misleading" by courts in New York, Georgia, California, and other states and the United States Supreme Court, providing reason to overturn the death sentence. In a 1986 Pennsylvania case prosecuted by the same prosecutor (McNiel (sic)), and presided over by the same judge (Sabo), the Pennsylvania Supreme Court ruled that language which "minimized the jury's sense of responsibility for the verdict of death" provided reason to overturn the sentence. Yet in Abu-Jamal's case, the court ruled otherwise. All relief was denied in the appeals process and this decision was made by fewer judges than in any other case in Pennsylvania's history. One of the judges who upheld the death penalty had actually engaged in a direct and bitter verbal exchange with Abu-Jamal, leading some to question his impartiality.

It is clear that the treatment of evidence and the application of justice in this instance have been at best arbitrary and capricious. Even if Mumia Abu-Jamal were guilty, we would deserve to have more solid assurance of that before we put him to death. If he is innocent, to put him to death on the basis of the evidence at hand is to make of us the very murderers against whom we seek relief. Governor Ridge's signing Mr. Abu-Jamal's death warrant on June 1st was particularly ill-timed in view of the fact that his lawyers were scheduled to appear in court on June 5th to file a petition for post-conviction relief.

In light of all we have presented to you, we urge you first, to have Judge Sabo recuse himself from this case. We are convinced that Mumia Abu-Jamal cannot get a fair hearing before Judge Sabo. Further we urge you to do all in your power—and we feel it is particularly important for you, Attorney General Reno, to become actively involved—to insure that Mumia Abu-Jamal is not executed on August 17 as is now scheduled, and that he is granted a new trial.

Signed by the following:

Chaka Fattah	Bobby Scott	Charles Rangel
John Conyers	Eva M. Clayton	Donald M. Payne
Ronald Dellums	Bennie G. Thompson	Cardiss Collins
Cynthia McKinney	Carrie P. Meek	Walter R. Tucker, III
Maxine Waters	Corrine Brown	Earl F. Hilliard
Bobby L. Rush	Alcee L. Hastings	William Clay
Melvin L. Watt	Barbara-Rose Collins	Sanford Bishop

Art Against Death:
Political Prisoners Unite for Mumia

Laura Whitehorn
2008

The creation of art in prison is the statement that I am still a human being. I am being packaged, I am being dehumanized, I am being abused, but as long as I can speak creatively and express my humanity, I am still a human being. I think that so many prisoners discover their ability to draw, paint, or engage in whatever creative form is because it's an act of resistance.

For those of us in the Resistance Conspiracy Case, when we were all together in the DC jail for three years (1988-1990), we all discovered that we had an interest in doing a lot of art for our case. One of the RCC codefendants, Alan Berkman, had been in prison in Philadelphia earlier in the decade with a former Black Panther named Mumia Abu-Jamal. At this point, Mumia's name was not so well known, and

**MUMIA ART SHOW
COMES TO THE
BAY AREA**

his case was hardly talked about at all outside of Philadelphia. Mumia is a very modest man, and he hadn't spent a lot of time saying "Hey, pay attention to me, I'm on Death Row." Alan, however, was horrified. Mumia had helped to take care of Alan when he was undergoing cancer treatment at Holmesburg Prison. At that point Mumia's risk of being executed was fairly imminent, and there was very little resistance to it.

After we were all sentenced and sent to other prisons, Tim Blunk went to Lewisburg, where Puerto Rican political prisoner Alberto Rodríguez was being held. They began engaging in all kinds of art projects at Lewisburg, including music and performances. And they came up with the idea to do

an art show that would include art exclusively made by prisoners, primarily political prisoners. We were quite aware that people on the outside would be moved by the fact that people who were themselves in prison had this idea of something to do in solidarity with another prisoner. We wanted to move people on the outside, who had more resources and more ability to resist, to intensify work on behalf of Mumia.

I have to emphasize that when you are in prison, you have very little control over your voice. You don't have the ability to talk to a group of people about what you think about what's going on in the world. The prison system tries to block communication from inside prison to the outside, especially for political prisoners. At that point in history, in the early to mid 1990s, there was not a huge recognition of the fact that there are political prisoners in the United States. So for us to have a voice was threatening to the government and to the prison administration. To say that we would be producing something that would, in turn, be shown and spoken about on the outside, was itself an act of resistance.

All of us were also strongly opposed to the death penalty. And we felt that Mumia had not gotten a fair trial. This seems so obvious on the face of it; he should at least get a new trial if not a complete exoneration. Certainly the death penalty should be lifted. That was why we named the exhibit Art Against the Death Penalty and Art for Mumia, Art Against Death.

One of the things that made this project so powerful was that there has always been a struggle, internationally and in the U.S., for the right of association between political prisoners who share basic beliefs. Knowing that there were prisoners in other units working on this, some even in isolation units not able to see anyone except for prison guards, was a high point of this project. To sit in your cell and produce a piece of art that you knew was going to go out beyond the walls and express your heart to people—it kept you alive, it kept you political and active.

We were able to stand together in this way, and to actually organize people on the outside. In the beginning, there were just a few outside supporters, but as time went on, there were committees throughout the U.S. that put this show on. The first show was at the Harlem State office building in New York City in 1994. When that show was reported on in Z Magazine, some artists involved with a gallery space in SoHo put together a special exhibition that featured all kinds of speakers and panels on the death penalty and on political prisoners. That then reached a much broader audience and led to another showing out in California. At that point, there were a number of women political prisoners in the correctional institution at Dublin, California. Because we had pretty good visiting opportunities there, and the prison was located close to San Francisco and Oakland, we had a lot of visitors from the progressive community and were able to work very closely with the activists on the outside who were mounting that show.

There is a constant, hopefully creative, tension between those on the inside and out, often relating to how much control prisoners have on the way our work and politics are presented. In California, I was in direct contact on an almost daily basis with the women who put that show together. And there was a constant push and pull. One of us on the inside would say "We want this issue highlighted" and the people from the outside would say "Well, it might not work the best way," and they would describe to us the material conditions that they faced. I consider myself a socialist and a Marxist, so we begin with trying to analyze the situation and how we can effect change in a given historical moment. So if someone says to me, "Laura, those words don't mean anything to anyone, you have to say that differently," then I have to listen to that. What's the point of just spouting off something that people won't understand, especially when the folks on the outside who I trust and love are telling me that I need to say it differently.

One of the things that used to drive me nuts and still does from the other side now, is when people on the outside act as yes-men for political prisoners, based on the principle that the prisoners are the political leadership. There needs to be interaction and dialogue, where people can give their ideas, and also say "Let me tell you what I think would work better." I guess the main issue is respect in both directions and trying to strive for a high level of political communication. It is so important for political prisoners especially to have some avenues for political expression. So they must be treated as human beings who deserve to be talked to with honesty and respect.

Reaching a broader audience is my number one priority for this work. So these successful shows, which had people coming together and talking about Mumia, the death penalty, and political prisoners in general, were—to me—a major, very exciting achievement.

Our job as activists supporting political prisoners today is to go broader. There is now a whole new generation of political prisoners from different movements. This is an opening, where people should be talking to a broader sector of people. I still go to sleep thinking about comrades who have been in jail for 30 years, like Herman Bell and Jalil Muntaqim. But we can't rely on the old guard to keep this issue alive, especially at a time when things have become more repressive. But the struggles that we came out of, that turned us into political prisoners or for which we became political prisoners, should never have been isolated from the progressive movements in this country. We were struggling against racism, against killer cops, against colonialism, against the U.S. government invading other countries and going to war. And all of those issues are still urgent problems. There are other issues that we were concerned about on a deeper level than in past generations, such as environmental racism and the environment in general. The increasing crisis in the economy, and the increasing incarceration of poor people, are also particular to this period.

If we cannot make the issue of political prisoners relevant to people in all progressive movements, I don't think we are doing our job. I don't think we should view the question as "Why isn't the rest of the movement paying attention to political prisoners?" I think that we haven't tried well enough to make this an issue that relates to everyone else's work. Prisoners are put in prison in order to repress any social change. We have to be able to talk about that. My personal goal is that every major progressive or left organization in this country should add to their program a position calling for the freedom of all political prisoners. There are many movements around the world that automatically have that, because they understand that in the course of struggle people go to prison for their political actions and beliefs. For those of us whose hearts are in the struggle for social change, we must recognize that part of our hearts are in prison. The struggle for liberation, for peace with justice, is broader than the issue of amnesty for political prisoners, but political prisoners are a central part of the struggle.

VI.4.A

Mumia Abu-Jamal

Susie Day
1995

For years, Mumia Abu-Jamal, a Black man in Philadelphia, tried to speak of injustice as a radio journalist.

He is now struggling to speak from death row.

Sentenced to death for killing a police officer, Jamal has spent nearly 15 years in Pennsylvania prisons, continuously maintaining his innocence. In order to prevent his execution, over 70 political prisoners around the world, along with numerous artists and community activists, have joined forces to produce Art and Writings Against the Death Penalty, a traveling art exhibit that opened in Harlem, New York, December 1994.

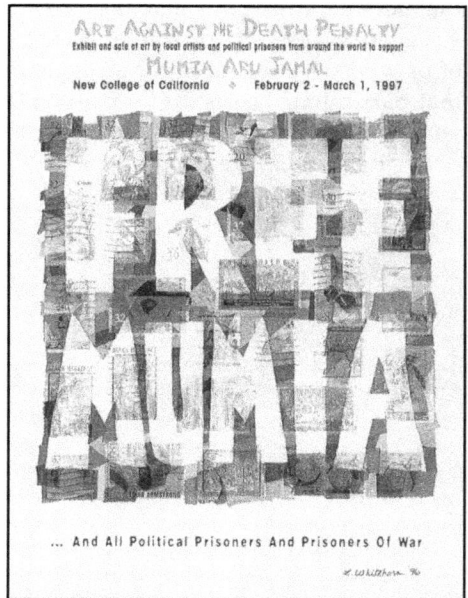

Jamal was a reporter at Philadelphia station WUHY and other local stations. His stories were usually about people without money or power: in fact, they often questioned those whose power devastated the black community—notably, the Philadelphia police force. Jamal's coverage of a police raid on the Black naturalist group MOVE in 1978 had much to do with the *Philadelphia Inquirer's* calling him the "Voice of the voiceless." It was also a probable catalyst for then-mayor Frank Rizzo to denounce a "new breed of advocacy journalism" that bred dangerous contempt for local authority. "I simply did what any so-called 'objective' reporter was trained to do," writes Jamal. "I got both sides—the system's and MOVE's." Because his work was so controversial, Jamal was forced to work freelance, and drove a cab to supplement his income.

In December 1981, at about four in the morning, while driving his cab, Jamal caught sight of a police officer beating a Black man. Rushing to the scene, Jamal recognized the beaten man as his own brother, Bill, who had been stopped for a traffic violation. What happened next is unclear, except

This article was published in Z *Magazine*, March 1995.

that the officer was shot and killed and Jamal took a bullet in his abdomen. When more police arrived, they badly beat Jamal at the roadside, and again after he was taken to a hospital.

One of the many reasons that events of the shooting remain hazy is that State prosecutors prevented over 125 eyewitnesses from testifying at Jamal's trial—even though some bystanders claim to have seen a man, not answering Jamal's description, shoot the officer, then flee. Although the prosecution identified the murder weapon as Jamal's legally registered gun, the police ballistics expert testified that the bullets that killed the officer belonged to another—as yet unrecovered—weapon.

But concrete proof was probably unnecessary for the predominantly white jury, which appeared to have been persuaded of his guilt by the prosecution's characterization of Jamal as a "dangerous" former Panther, with current radical affiliations. Seemingly oblivious to the First Amendment right of free speech and association, the State selected one of Jamal's political comments—made over 10 years before, when he was 16—to the effect that "all power grows out of the barrel of a gun," as evidence that Jamal had only been waiting for his chance to kill a cop.

Jamal—who had no previous criminal record—has for years spent 22 hours of each day locked in a tiny cell. He is given two hours outdoors every weekend—in a 20 x 8 foot cage. With scant prospect of a new trial, legal appeals are all but exhausted. Already, Tom Ridge, newly elected governor of Pennsylvania, has promised to make Jamal's swift execution a priority for his administration.

The idea of Art and Writings Against the Death Penalty came from Pennsylvania's Lewisburg Prison, where a collective of inmates decided to draw attention to Jamal's case and to the escalation of the death penalty in the U.S. The collective also wanted to heighten public awareness that there are now about 150 leftists and progressives in U.S. prisons, convicted for various antigovernment protests, from peaceful antinuclear demonstrations to acts of armed struggle. Scores of these political—and some social—prisoners have painted, drawn, or sculpted art for Jamal's campaign. Most of the artwork is for sale, the proceeds going to replenish Jamal's legal campaign. From Harlem, Art and Writings Against the Death Penalty will move to various locations in New York, and throughout the country.

Word has it that the governor of Pennsylvania plans to sign Abu-Jamal's death warrant by March 16 [1995], at the latest.

The People's International Tribunal for Justice for Mumia Abu-Jamal

1998

The People's International Tribunal For Justice For Mumia Abu-Jamal convened in Philadelphia on December 6, 1997, to investigate the facts surrounding Mumia's conviction and death sentence and to call attention to the ongoing effort to save Mumia's life. The tribunal examined the denial of Mumia's civil and human rights and the actions of: Pennsylvania Governor Thomas Ridge, the Pennsylvania Department of Corrections, the Philadelphia Police Department, Judge Albert Sabo, as well as, the FBI and the Counter Intelligence Program (COINTELPRO).

Internationally renowned jurists, political leaders, artists and community activists reviewed testimony concerning the effort to execute Mumia, and at the end of the day they rendered a verdict. The international team of judges, organized through the office of Stevens, Hinds & White, included: Walter Brooks (now known as Sundiata Sadiq) of the NAACP; Gamal Nkrumah, International Editor of Cairo's *Al Ahram,* and son of the late Pan-Africanist President of Ghana, Kwame Nkrumah; Yuri Kochiyama, the revered Japanese-American activist, and Julia Wright, Parisian journalist, activist, and daughter of famed author Richard Wright. The prosecution was led by attorney Michael Tarif Warren in consultation with Mumia's attorney, Leonard Weinglass.

The Tribunal for Justice for Mumia Abu-Jamal, like the Bertrand Russell Tribunals on the United States war against the Vietnamese people, applied principles of customary international humanitarian law. Article 38 of the Statute of the International Court of Justice recognizes the authoritative effect of the findings of such tribunals on contemporary standards on international law.

A verdict of guilty was delivered by a distinguished panel of 25 International judges (a list of judges is attached) who also proposed several remedies including the United Nations assignment of a Special Rapporteur to investigate the human rights violations in the case of Mumia Abu-Jamal.

This report was published in 1998 by the Tribunal's initiators, International Concerned Family and Friends of Mumia Abu-Jamal and the Ad Hoc Coalition for a People's International Tribunal for Justice for Mumia Abu-Jamal. Attorneys Lennox Hinds and Richard Harvey played a key role in organizing the team of judges.

Complete Tribunal Findings:
We find as a fact that those charged are guilty of a criminal conspiracy to deny Mumia Abu-Jamal's human rights and we call for his immediate release, exoneration and compensation.

We find as a fact that the human and constitutional rights of Mumia Abu-Jamal were blatantly violated in numerous and systematic ways, resulting in his unjust conviction, unlawful incarceration and illegal death sentence.

We recommend that a thorough, independent, international and impartial judicial investigation, with full subpoena powers, should be conducted into:

- the historical and current operations of the Philadelphia Police Department, particularly in relation to its treatment of people of color; and
- into the FBI's Counter-Intelligence Program (COINTELPRO), and all similar repressive programs, particularly in relation to their treatment of the Black Panther Party, MOVE and other political organizations led by people of color; and into the actions of all Federal, State and City elective, judicial and law enforcement officials that had any role in relation to the bombing of MOVE headquarters in 1985; and
- that all public officials found responsible for the deprivation of Mumia Abu-Jamal's human rights should be removed from office and declared unfit to hold such office in future by reason of their breach of public trust;

We therefore urge the Secretary-General of the United Nations and the U.N. High Commissioner for Human Rights to call for reports on the case of Mumia Abu-Jamal from U.N. Special Rapporteurs, especially those with jurisdiction over:

1. extra judicial, summary and arbitrary executions;
2. torture, cruel, inhuman and degrading treatment and punishment; and
3. independence of the judiciary.

signed,*

Tribunal Judges: Francése Araneu (Spain), Christoph Arnold, Barbara Nimri Aziz, John Black, Dennis Brutus (South Africa), Gilma Camargo, Philé Chinosesu, Asia Coney, Myriam Falco-Mairat (France), Herman Ferguson, Marita Golden, Rev. Cecil Gray, Martha Grevatt, Mattie Humphrey, John Judge, Yuri Kochiyama, Pierre Leroy (Haiti), Jim Lester, Gamal Nkrumah (Egypt), Ulf Panzer (Germany), Queen Ivory, Father Paul Washington, and Julia Wright.

---

* In the listing of Tribunal judges, all those whose nationality is not stated are from the United States.

Rationale for Organizing United Nations Support:
The Tribunal, and the critical international follow-up effort to bring to fruition the judges' verdict, comes at a crucial stage in Mumia's legal battle. The decision to call for the Tribunal was made last fall in an effort to maintain momentum for resisting the planned execution of Mumia during the seemingly endless wait for the Supreme Court of the State Pennsylvania to rule on Mumia's motion for a new trial. The Tribunal has educate and continues to educate the public about the egregious violations of commonly recognized due process and basic international human rights in Mumia's case.

The prospects for a new trial are grim. First, Judge Albert Sabo's consistent rulings that all of the powerful new evidence submitted by the defense since 1995 is irrelevant severely hampers Mumia's ability to have a fair review of his case. Second, since President Clinton signed the Antiterrorism and Effective Death Penalty Act the availability of Federal habeas corpus review has been severely curtailed. Given these circumstances the Tribunal, and the ability to implement the judges' recommendations, is critical to our ability to impact the decision of the State Supreme Court, subsequent appeals to the Federal Courts, as well as international opinion.

There is considerable potential for exerting moral and political pressure on the various institutional structures of the United States through the delegation's presentation of the Tribunal's verdict to the United Nations. The delegation will present the verdict of the distinguished and international body of jurists which ruled that "human and constitutional rights of Mumia Abu-Jamal were blatantly violated in numerous and systematic ways, resulting in his unjust conviction, unlawful incarceration and illegal death sentence." Additionally the delegation will formally present the judges' recommendations that the U.N. assign a Special Rapporteur who will investigate issues such as "extra-judicial, summary and arbitrary executions; torture, cruel, inhuman, and degrading punishment; and independence of the judiciary" (judges verdict) which is a crucial step in documenting the myriad ways in which international and U.S. Constitutional laws have been violated in the case of Mumia Abu-Jamal.

We will also be able to highlight how many other political prisoners and death row prisoners have been, in direct violation of Constitutional guarantees, denied a "fair trial." We intend to expose how the U.S. government's counterintelligence program (COINTELPRO), which aimed to neutralize Black and other progressive political leaders, resulted in the incarceration, exile and murder of some of the most effective leaders of the 60s and 70s.

We expect that the delegation's presentation at the United Nations hearings will encourage mainstream organizations such as lawyers' groups and human rights groups to take more forthright positions in the case of Mumia Abu-Jamal, as well as, in other cases involving prosecutorial and judicial misconduct. The U.N. hearings will also add weight to the mounting opposition to the death penalty. Finally, it is our hope, through this process, not only to gain Mumia Abu-Jamal's freedom, but to create a more democratic climate in this country so that those who are critical of government policy can express their views without risking illegal arrests, trials, convictions and even death.

In addition to the presentation to the Human Rights Commission, we wish to send at least one member of the delegation to Germany, France, Belgium, Spain & Italy while in Europe, to report to Mumia Coalitions and Mumia Supporters in those countries. European support of Mumia Abu-Jamal has been extremely effective in pressuring the Governor of Pennsylvania and other U.S. officials. In 1995 European efforts played a key role in gaining a stay of execution from Governor Ridge. Tens of thousands of Europeans demonstrated in the streets in support of Mumia and thousands sent letters to Governor Ridge, to Attorney General Janet Reno and to President Clinton. We want to support the international nature of this movement as it has maximized the pressure to free Mumia.

Human Rights Day Presentation:
Our follow up work began immediately after the Tribunal. On December 10th— Human Rights Day—a delegation from the People's Tribunal delivered the Tribunal's Indictment and the Judges' Verdict to the United Nations High Commissioner for Human Rights Office in New York. Dr. Purificacion Quisumbing, Director of the New York Office of the High Commissioner for Human Rights greeted the delegation which included, Gamal Nkrumah, International Editor of Cairo's *Al Ahram*, Julia Wright, author and political analyst and Ramona Africa of MOVE.

Dr. Quisumbing accepted the findings of the Tribunal and made several recommendations regarding international action on the findings.

Veronica Jones, a key prosecution witness in Mumia's original trial, testified in the 1996 Post-Conviction Relief Hearings that in 1982 she had been working as a prostitute, and was threatened with losing her children and ten years' imprisonment, if she did not change her story to suit the police. While recanting her forced 1982 testimony, Jones was threatened by Judge Sabo with five to ten years' imprisonment for perjury if she continued. He then allowed her to be arrested, while being cross-examined, for writing a bad check years earlier. With tears streaming down her face, Jones declared, "This is not going to change my testimony." She was introduced at the tribunal by Michael Tarif Warren and received a standing ovation.

427

Specifically Dr. Quisumbing recommended that the findings of the Tribunal and a complete package of materials concerning Mumia's legal case should be presented to: Mary Robinson (U.N. High Commissioner for Human Rights, Geneva), Kofi Annan (Secretary General of the United Nations), Bill Richardson (United States Ambassador to the United Nations), and Gaye MacDougal (recently nominated as a U.S. member of the U.N. Committee on the Elimination of all Forms of Racial Discrimination; Ms. MacDougal is also Director of the International Human Rights Law Group).

The 30 minute meeting was filmed and has already aired on public access channels.

The delegation is presently working to secure the support of several NGO's in advance of its presentation to the U.N. High Commission. The delegation will include: Michael Warren, lead prosecutor for the Tribunal, Ramona Africa and Sue Africa of International Concerned Family and Friends of Mumia Abu-Jamal and MOVE, and Linda Thurston, former Director of the Program to Abolish the Death Penalty of Amnesty International USA.

The Tribunal for Justice for Mumia Abu-Jamal and the follow up work required to activate the Tribunal's findings, is a truly international endeavor. On the day of the Tribunal, December 6th, there were solidarity rallies in San Francisco and Vancouver. Solidarity Messages were sent to the Tribunal from around the world, including messages from Ramsey Clark, former U.S. Attorney General, Leoluco Orlando, Mayor of Palermo and long-time death penalty opponent, Assata Shakur, exiled leader of the Black Liberation Movement, and Leonard Peltier of the American Indian Movement.

The 1998 People's International Tribunal for Justice for Mumia Abu-Jamal in Philadelphia
(Source: Workers World Photos)

An Appeal from U.S. Political Prisoners/P.O.W.'s: Mobilize to Save Mumia Abu-Jamal!

Herman Bell, David Gilbert, Abdul Majid, Bill Dunne, Jihad Abdul Mumit,
Marilyn Buck, Dr. Mutulu Shakur, Jaan Laaman, Tom Manning,
Richard Williams, Ray Luc Levasseur, Linda Evans, Edward Africa,
Sundiata Acoli, Chuckie Africa, Teddy Jah Heath, Phil Africa,
Larry Giddings, Robert "Seth" Hayes, Russell "Maroon" Shoats,
Yu Kikumura, Janine Africa, Janet Africa, Debbie Africa,
Juan Segarra Palmer, Oscar López Rivera, Jalil Muntaqim,
Leonard Peltier, Veronza Bowers, Nuh Washington
1999

We are Prisoners of War and Political Prisoners (POW/PP's) within the United States. We were variously imprisoned for a range of activities: struggle against white supremacy and colonialism, opposition to the economics of global plunder and class exploitation, efforts against sexism and discrimination, a general unwillingness to abide the multiple ways human beings are demeaned and delimited in this society. We stand for self-determination for all oppressed peoples, for an end to racism, for women's liberation (equality), for economics centered on human need rather than corporate greed.

The reason for this unprecedented collective statement is the urgent situation of fellow political prisoner Mumia Abu-Jamal on death row in Pennsylvania. His legal challenge has now moved to the federal courts, the final arena available to him, and these proceedings could be completed within months. While there is overwhelming evidence of his innocence, most of it has been excluded from judicial review. Many of you who have worked hard to save Mumia's life are to be commended. Without your hard work the state probably would have already executed him, but we need to alert you to the urgency of the situation. A measure of the importance of this case can be taken from the recent "big lie" slanders of Mumia by ABC's "20/20" on TV and by *Vanity Fair* magazine. The Fraternal Order of Police, the reactionary criminal justice system, and the corporate media are determined to execute this articulate and courageous brother. It will take a very determined and strong movement to stop the plans for cold-blooded murder.

This appeal was circulated nationally among POWs/political prisoners for sign-ons. It was then published by various political prisoner support organizations.

The urgency is not just because a precious life is at stake, but also because of the implications for political and social movements. Mumia has been a singularly eloquent and effective "voice of the voiceless." He has spoken and written powerfully for more than 3,000 persons on death row within the U.S. about the fundamental flaws of the criminal justice system, on the foundations of racism and injustice. We want to encourage the range of activist and social justice groups to make Mumia's case their lead project, their key example, in the coming months. Such a focus would not at all mean abandoning broader politics and programs. Mumia's case can powerfully illustrate the general issues of the death penalty, of POW/PP's, of the criminal justice system, and of racism and injustice. He can personify these crucial concerns and help energize each area of work. We call upon all people who care about life and social justice to mobilize for Mumia.

Free Mumia!

End the Death Penalty!

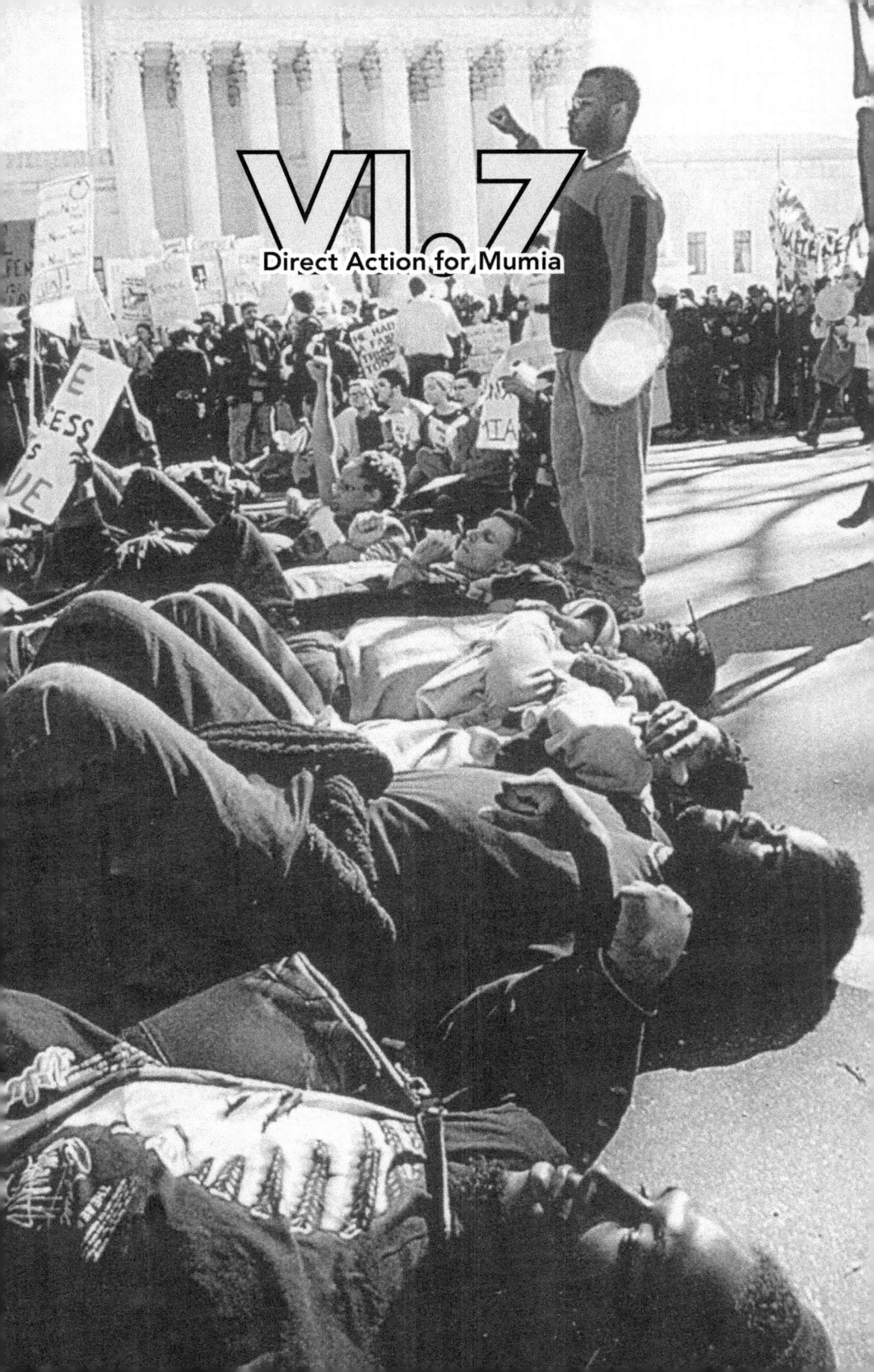

VI.7
Direct Action for Mumia

VI.7.A

How Freedom Rang

Matt Meyer

1999

When actor-activist Ossie Davis proclaimed early this year, "Every generation has its historic task, and ours is to free Mumia Abu-Jamal," he was not simply calling for increased attention to the case of one Death Row inmate. Mumia, a former member of the Black Panther Party and a distinguished Philadelphia-based journalist, has become an international symbol of much of what is wrong with the U.S. criminal justice system, from unfair courtroom practices disproportionately affecting poor defendants, to imprisonment based upon political beliefs, to racially unequal application of the death penalty.

The prison industry, which has begun to overshadow even the military-industrial complex as far as U.S. economic growth priorities are concerned, has only recently received significant attention from peace movement and pacifist groups, despite the grim cycle of violence that the building of jails implies. One recent action—a nationally coordinated civil disobedience held at the Liberty Bell in Philadelphia this past July—saw significant peace movement participation and the seeds of coalition work that could lead not only to a new trial for Mumia, but also to a new linking of issues and organizations calling for justice.

July 3, 1999, was 17 years to the day after Mumia's death sentence at the end of a trial deemed grossly unfair by Amnesty International, and one day before President Clinton visited Philadelphia's Independence Mall to award a freedom medal to the president of South Korea (himself, ironically, a former political prisoner). That day, 96 activists from across the country, holding banners reading "Freedom Rings for Mumia," shut down the Liberty Bell. In 100-degree heat, on one of the busiest tourist days of the year, protesters from 12 affinity groups representing diverse sectors of progressive thought asserted their conviction that "so long as Mumia is on Death Row, there is no true liberty in Pennsylvania." In nonviolent waves, demonstrators handed out leaflets inside the Liberty Bell pavilion, unfurled a banner on the pavilion's roof, and formed a semicircle around the bell, blocking its entrance doors, while a legal vigil held across the street shouted words of encouragement and solidarity. One affinity group, which linked Mumia's case to that of Native American political prisoner Leonard Peltier, performed street theater for demonstrators and passers-by.

A simultaneous prayer vigil took place in Providence, Rhode Island, at the

This article was published in *The Nonviolent Activist*, the magazine of the War Resisters League, Sept./Oct. 1999.
Photo credit previous page: Diane Greene Lent

site of the annual General Synod of the United Church of Christ, a major national Protestant denomination. The vigil, focusing both on Mumia and on the immorality of the death penalty itself, marked a unique moment in church-based coordination with secular civil disobedience campaigns. In San Francisco, 27 additional people were arrested in conjunction with the direct action efforts. Taken together, the demonstrations constituted the largest civil disobedience action against the death penalty in U.S. history.

Countering a Setback
The idea of a national civil disobedience campaign around Mumia's case developed late last year after the Pennsylvania Supreme Court upheld a decision by Judge Albert Sabo—one of the nation's most notorious "hanging" judges—upholding his own original 1982 trial decision. The setback in Mumia's bid for a new trial, despite substantial evidence of police coercion of witnesses presented at a 1995 post-conviction relief appeal hearing and legal irregularities also noted at that hearing, enraged many long-term Mumia supporters. Emergency demonstrations were organized by the Free Mumia Abu-Jamal Coalition, and the New Afrikan Liberation Front called for increased militancy—including the possibility of civil disobedience—in Mumia's name.

At that point, small groups of primarily New York-based activists, including the local Resistance in Brooklyn affinity group, began discussing the possibilities of pulling together a broad coalition for civil disobedience, creating a bridge between leaders of the Black liberation movements and Mumia activists on the one hand, and potential Mumia supporters from the peace movement, church organizations, gay and lesbian groups, and anti-death penalty activists on the other. Student organizations, some affiliated with the Hunter College-based Student Liberation Action Movement known as SLAM, were also discussing possible civil disobedience scenarios. Hosted by the War Resisters League and WRL staffer Chris Ney at New York City's "peace pentagon," SLAM, Resistance in Brooklyn, the New Afrikan Liberation Front and others formed a Free Mumia Abu-Jamal Coalition civil disobedience subcommittee, which quickly consulted with the International Concerned Family and Friends of Mumia Abu-Jamal [ICFFMAJ], the major group coordinating work around Mumia's case. Pam Africa of ICFFMAJ agreed to cooperate with and assist these efforts; however, because of both heightened police repression against the Philadelphia-based MOVE organization and the International Concerned Family and Friends' own annual call for July 4 demonstrations, the decision was made to keep the July 3 and July 4 coalitions separate and distinct. Thus, a positive model for collaboration and cooperation was developed, and the national call for a civil disobedience action was put forward.

The first step in putting together the civil disobedience coalition was to solicit political support from diverse individuals and organizations. From those who had already called for Mumia's release or for a new trial, a list was developed of people who would be willing to risk arrest. Some, such as Columbia University's Dr. Manning Marable, a spokesperson for the Black Radical Congress and the Committees of Correspondence, added their names even though they could not attend the action. Marable wrote about the historic and strategic importance of civil disobedience in his nationally syndicated column, and Ossie Davis did several radio spots on the same topic. Author Julia Wright, daughter of novelist Richard Wright, got arrested at a civil disobedience action for Mumia in Paris two weeks before the Philadelphia actions. Folk/rock artist Ani DiFranco, who was scheduled to be on tour at the time of the protests, lent her name and gave a generous contribution for possible bail costs for those arrested. Organizations not directly connected to Mumia or death penalty work, but with substantial civil disobedience experience, like the Committee in Solidarity with the People of El Salvador and the AIDS Coalition to Unleash Power (ACT UP), also joined the coalition at this time, along with activists from the Green Party, Women for Justice, Westchester People's Action Coalition and the Kairos/Catholic Worker/Plowshares movement. Ron Daniels, director of the Center for Constitutional Rights, agreed to speak at the legal rally, and Rev. Lucius Walker, director of the Interreligious Foundation for Community Organization, just back from leading a Pastors for Peace delegation to Cuba, agreed to be in the lead group blocking the Liberty Bell.

With initial endorsements in place, the task of building a working coalition began. As in all coalition work, an array of ideological perspectives had to be included, and representatives of most of the left's political parties, from communist to anarchist, ended up taking part and playing some role in the action. The central coordination, however, came not from the national parties but from grassroots activists with their own philosophical and tactical differences.

"I've never given myself voluntarily to the police," noted Zayid Muhammad, a New Afrikan Liberation Front member and founder of Frontline Artists. Although coming more from the tradition of Malcolm X than Martin Luther King, Muhammad nonetheless organized a full nonviolence training to prepare for July 3 in his home base in Newark, New Jersey. He concluded, "If this is what folks are doing to raise the stakes for Mumia, then we have got to participate."

Militance vs. Militarism

On the other hand, said longtime Kairos/Plowshares activist Dr. Anna Brown, "Many within the pacifist movement have felt that the rhetoric at recent demonstrations for Mumia has gotten dangerously militaristic." Brown, a professor at New Jersey's St. Peter's College and a leader of Academics for Mumia Abu-Jamal, added, "But this moment is crucial for all justice-loving people to come together, both to take a principled stand against the violence of state-sanctioned murder, as well as to stand in solidarity with our brethren in the Black liberation movement, especially those such as Mumia, who have spoken out so eloquently despite decades of repression."

The nonviolence trainings—always a crucial element of building for any successful civil disobedience—also provided key opportunities for discussing the role of nonviolence and militance, between people not often in contact with one another. Each of the pre-action trainings took on a different character based on the participants involved; as the trainings took place, the need to allocate a full day of time and to schedule frequent small group discussions became clear to the CD organizers. Civil disobedience coordinator Meg Starr of Resistance in Brooklyn reflected, "Even many of those leading the trainings had not done so for some years, and an intensive effort was made to ensure that the coalition nature of the event be reflected in the team of trainers."

Despite some moments of confusion, participants did get practice in working together, in making quick and disciplined affinity group-based decisions, in building for nonviolent civil disobedience. Commented War Resisters International Chair Joanne Sheehan, who conducted one pre-action training with both Brown and former Black Panther political prisoner Ashanti Alston, "We carried the banner together, coming from different places and politics, but working together for the same goals."

One controversial issue, raised squarely at several trainings but not fully resolved there, was the nature of affinity groups' relations to the police. The agreed-upon guidelines for the action, modified from WRL's guidelines for the 1998 Day Without the Pentagon, required that participants act with "dignity toward"—but not necessarily "respect for"—the authorities who would be handling them. And though there was clear agreement that no violent provocation would be allowed, the gray areas of what constituted "verbal abuse" led to some important, fascinating and sometimes difficult discussions. To avoid alienating any constituency and because many potential participants were coming from communities under constant police attack, coalition leaders decided that affinity groups should be able to exercise autonomy regarding the slogans or banners they wanted to carry, as long as both fit the broad guidelines. Did, then, calling the police "pigs"—as the Black Panthers often do—violate the guidelines regarding verbal confrontation? Debates took place regarding political appropriateness, the difference between singling out an individual cop versus critiquing the overall system of policing and questions of safety and de-escalation. Ultimately, one affinity group from an organization that has always chanted Panther slogans decided, after many of its members attended a nonviolence training, not to not use the word "pig" in its chants on July 3. This spirit of real dialogue and a commitment to coalition consciousness is part of what made the day so powerful. In hindsight, perhaps the guidelines from the coordinators could have been sharper or spelled out more clearly, but the openness and commitment to autonomy undoubtedly allowed the greatest number of participants to feel empowered by, and part of, the process that made the action possible.

Singing in the Cells

When July 3 came, the good feelings carried on well after the protesters were carried off, with singing and discussions continuing in the federal holding cells. Media work also continued, with coordinator John Riley of ACT UP sending audio, video, and still photo clips to news agencies well into the night. Ultimately, the story of the action was carried around the world, from a color photo of the action on the cover of Sunday's *Philadelphia Inquirer*, to

Credit: Diane Greene Lent

articles in Italy's daily newspapers, to an Associated Press piece published in Puerto Rico. There was mention on every local television station as well as on CBS-TV and radio news, BBC radio, and national Pacifica stories; New York's *Daily Challenge*, a newspaper reporting on events relating to the African-American community, gave the story two days of full coverage with numerous color photos, terming the action "A Force of July." Philadelphia activist Marie Bloom noted that the action garnered some of the best coverage ever for a Mumia demonstration.

All 95 protesters. including a woman in a wheelchair from California who singlehandedly blocked the doors to the Liberty Bell long after most demonstrators had been carted away, were ticketed out of detention within 10 hours, having already called for a follow-up meeting based on conversations in the cells! The high spirit of resistance was exemplified by coordinator Kai Lumumba Barrow of SLAM who, after being admonished by the federal judge not to return to the Liberty Bell and to "go in peace," responded firmly with the call, "Free Mumia!"

Tomorrow Will Be Too Late

The power of the July 3 action lay not in any major celebrity participation, nor any major funding or national staff effort, but in the strength of genuine local organizing, linking issues and a willingness of people to truly listen to one another. Civil disobedience, in this instance, was used as a catalyst to build bridges and movements. Contrary to a sectarian but all too common notion, civil disobedience can be used to both raise the stakes and broaden the work. A young woman from Refuse and Resist, who did not get arrested but was part of the legal support vigil, reported to her organization that July 3 "was a once-in-a-lifetime experience. Everyone was so emotional, intensive and supportive... everyone in the movement was supporting each other regardless of factions, which is new."

South African poet laureate and former political prisoner Dennis Brutus, inspired by this spirit, has called for an ongoing campaign of civil disobedience against the death penalty and for Mumia's release. "In struggling for justice," Brutus remarked, "we are discovering that our voices are not heard, our efforts are ignored, and in fact what is confronting us is injustice. We have to take this matter to the streets for the Court of the People to judge." Brutus is part of building for new national civil disobedience actions, to take place some time in late October and November.

This fall, in fact, is a crucial period in Mumia's legal efforts. Under constant threat of a renewal of Mumia's death warrant, his lawyers are awaiting a Supreme Court ruling on the appeal of the previous Pennsylvania Court's decision. Both the Supreme Court case and another federal procedure based on one of Mumia's motions are expected to be heard as early as October, with the ultimate appeal process after that lasting only several months. History suggests that the judicial system does, in fact, respond to political pressures—and also that political executions, such as those of Sacco and Vanzetti or Julius and Ethel Rosenberg, do take a great toll on the entire progressive movement.

Thus, we now face a historic opportunity. Now is the time to take the words of Puerto Rican leader Rafael Cancel Miranda to heart. "Our silence would be complicity," he said, in a special message sent to the July 3 action. "Let us fight for Mumia today because tomorrow may be too late for all of us. By fighting for Mumia, we are fighting for ourselves. All of us are on Death Row with him. Mumia is everyone who cares for one another; Mumia is all of us. Stay strong and united. We are but one people. Together we are powerful."

VI.7.B

Why We Are Demonstrating at the Liberty Bell

Ad Hoc Coalition for the Liberty Bell Action
1999

Let Freedom Ring for Mumia Abu-Jamal! New Trial for Mumia!
Medical Care for Mumia and All Death Row Inmates! Free Mumia!

Many come to Philadelphia on the July 4 weekend to visit the Liberty Bell. This is an affirmation of essential values like liberty, justice, and freedom. We share these values, as do most people in the United States. We are demonstrating here today to affirm, but even more to deepen our commitment to liberty, justice, and freedom in this country. We insist that these ideas must become more than mere words on paper. They must be put into practice.

Today prisons incarcerate more people than ever before in our nation's history. The U.S. prison population is the highest, per capita, in the world. Many have been jailed simply because they could not afford a proper legal defense, or because as people of color they faced a racist court system. (Of 126 sent to Death Row from Philadelphia, for example, 112 are Black, Latino, or other people of color.) For these, and others unjustly imprisoned, the promise of freedom and liberty in the United States is a hollow fraud.

We therefore choose this symbol as an appropriate location for us to call attention to that fraud and, in particular, to point out the plight of an award-winning journalist who has now been on death row for 17 years as a result of a completely unjust trial, for a crime that growing numbers around the world are convinced he did not commit: Mumia Abu-Jamal.

Mumia was convicted in 1982 for the killing of a Philadelphia police officer and sentenced to death. He faced a racist judge, Albert Sabo, who holds the U.S. record for death sentences handed down, and in whose court (according to a group of Philadelphia assistant district attorneys) no defendant could get a fair trial. Mumia had no money to hire crucial experts to investigate on his behalf and testify in court. An incompetent attorney was forced upon him, and he was denied the right to represent himself.

It has now been well documented that the pretrial investigation and the trial itself were rife with improper actions by the police, prosecuting attorney, and judge. Tens of thousands of people have protested worldwide demanding a new trial for Mumia—including such figures as the former first lady of France, Danielle Mitterrand, and that country's current president Jacques Chirac, Nelson Mandela of South Africa, along with Hollywood celebrities like Ed Asner and Mike Farrell.

This was the flyer distributed in Philadelphia on July 3, 1999, to accompany the rally and civil disobedience action at the Liberty Bell.

The European Parliament passed a resolution last year demanding a review of the case and a new trial for Mumia. Dozens of unions have also endorsed the same call, including the International Longshore and Warehouse Union, which organized a one-day work stoppage in support of Mumia along the entire West Coast of the U.S. on April 24, 1999.

Despite all of the facts and protests, in October last year Mumia's conviction was upheld by the Pennsylvania Supreme Court. His appeal for a new trial is now before the federal courts. However, legislation passed by Congress in 1996 ("The Antiterrorism and Effective Death Penalty Act") means that it is possible, even likely, the federal courts will simply rubber-stamp decisions made at the state level, without ever undertaking an independent review of the facts in this case. We cannot allow this to happen.

We therefore take this nonviolent, militant action to demand: "Let Freedom Ring for Mumia Abu-Jamal!" We hereby express our outrage at what has been done to Mumia and to all the other death-row inmates who find themselves trapped in a legal quagmire, where the word "justice" has lost all meaning. Join us! We are here today—and tomorrow beginning at 9 am.

Credit: Diane Greene Lent

439

An Urgent Message from Dennis Brutus and friends . . .

February 2000

We join together at this crucial moment to alert you to an important action that will send a strong message to the decision-makers in Washington DC.

On Monday, February 28, a legal demonstration and a nonviolent act of civil disobedience will take place at the steps of the U.S. Supreme Court, at 9:30 am. These actions will be preceded by an inter-faith prayer service across the street at the Chapel of the United Methodist Building, 100 Maryland Avenue, at 9 am. The focus of these acts will be our unconditional opposition to the death penalty, and our particular concern for the case of journalist Mumia Abu-Jamal. The many irregularities in Abu-Jamal's case, unfortunately typical in so many death penalty cases, necessitate our call for a new trial–even as Pennsylvania's Governor and Police Associations increase their pressure to put an end to Abu-Jamal's life. The recent moratorium on executions called by Governor Ryan of Illinois must only strengthen our efforts.

February 28 is a significant day for our cause, in part because the case of Williams v. Taylor (#996615) is being reviewed by the high court. This case, coming about in reaction to the Effective Death Penalty Act, could strip the federal government of it's ability to hold fact-finding hearings in the cases of inmates who failed to develop successful habeas corpus briefs on the state level. As the Supreme Court conducts it's session, we must stand up for those whose lives are on the line, and make our voices heard as we cry out for justice.

Some of us will be praying that morning, others speaking at the legal rally, others of us risking arrest in a nonviolent sit-in on the steps of the Court, and some of us doing all three. We ask that you join us–in spirit and in person–to help build our movement and let freedom ring.

In Peace,

Dennis Brutus, South African poet and former Robben Island political prisoner
Jennifer Harbury, attorney, activist, author of <u>Bridge of Courage</u>
Stephen Hawkins, Director, National Coalition to Abolish the Death Penalty
Rev. Nozomi Ikuta, President, National Interreligious Task Force on Criminal Justice
Sam Jordan, Death Penalty coordinator, Amnesty International USA
Dr. Manning Marable, Professor, Columbia University; Black Radical Congress
Bishop Walter Sullivan, President, Pax Christi USA
Rev. S. Michael Yasutake, Director, Interfaith Prisoners of Conscience Project

for information on Feb. 28 DC logistics, on pre-action nonviolence trainings, or to make a contribution, contact: mumiacd@hotmail.com; 202-722-4783; 914-353-5032

VI.7.C

Face Reality!
Mumia Is One of Over 100 Political Prisoners in the U.S.A.

Resistance in Brooklyn
2000

Though the U.S. government has always denied it, there are well over 100 political prisoners held across the country. Mumia Abu-Jamal, whose case has catapulted the racist nature of the U.S. criminal justice system and of the death penalty itself to a position of international concern, has always linked his own struggle to that of the other U.S. political prisoners. It's time for the movement to do the same!

Today, as we face the steps of the "highest court in the land," Resistance in Brooklyn (RnB) affinity group members will don the masks of heroes and sheroes, whose faces represent a history of repression and resistance. These faces—from past and present, jailed and free, and from a variety of movements—are meant to remind us to face reality: all U.S. political prisoners must be free!

U.S. Political Prisoners and Repression of Our Movements
The majority of political prisoners today come out of the movements of the 1960s and 1970s. At that time, as the civil rights movement and liberation struggles threatened the status quo in America, the FBI developed a program called COINTELPRO (Counterintelligence Program). COINTELPRO's mission was to destroy liberation struggles and eliminate political opposition in the U.S. Methods of disruption included surveillance, infiltration, intimidation, harassment, violence, and even murder.

The government's Counterintelligence Program actively harassed, framed, and murdered political activists, resulting in incarceration or death. In 1971, COINTELPRO was exposed to the public, and Congress slapped the FBI on the wrist. However, no reparation was awarded to any of the victims of COINTELPRO, and many of them continue to sit in prison after more than two decades—framed on charges of crimes they did not commit. The government continues its own criminal activities; though COINTELPRO, in name, has been shut down, similar government campaigns of disruption, intimidation, and

---

Though RnB helped initiate and organize the Supreme Court direct action for Mumia, we also maintained an independent affinity group presence at the demonstration. As some chose to highlight Mumia as part of the larger anti-death penalty movement, RnB linked Mumia's cause to that of all the U.S. political prisoners—currently and through history. With placards and poster-board images of Leonard Peltier, Marilyn Buck, Assata Shakur, Rev. Martin Luther King, Jr., Abbie Hoffman, and many others, we handed out this flyer to help make the connections.

441

LET FREEDOM RING

infiltration attempt to target radical movements today. The drive to execute Mumia is only the most drastic example of U.S. intentions to silence us.

Today, the masks we wear represent the following faces of resistance:

Mumia Abu-Jamal: death row journalist, former Black Panther Party leader

Anna Mae Pictou Aquash: American Indian Movement activist, killed as a result of an FBI COINTELPRO smear campaign

John Brown: militant abolitionist, hanged by the state on December 2, 1859—but his spirit lives on in this 200th anniversary year of his birth

Marilyn Buck: current anti-imperialist political prisoner, antiracist ally of the Black liberation movement

Standing Deer: current Native American political prisoner

Abbie Hoffman: peace activist and former prisoner of conscience, hounded by FBI COINTELPRO sting operations throughout the 1960s and '70s

Martin Luther King, Jr.: civil rights leader, target of one of the FBI's most extensive "red-baiting" efforts

Oscar López Rivera: current Puerto Rican prisoner of war

Assata Shakur: leader of the Black Liberation Army, former political prisoner, and FBI's "Most Wanted"—escaped and now in exile in Cuba

Alejandrina Torres: recently released Puerto Rican political prisoner, granted clemency after close to 20 years of intensive amnesty campaigning

Bartolomeo Vanzetti: Italian anarchist and labor activist, executed by electric chair in 1927: Never Again!!

VI.7.D

Supreme Court and Weekend Actions United Press Release

Free Mumia Abu-Jamal Coalition
2000

FOR IMMEDIATE RELEASE: One hundred eighty-five arrested at U.S. Supreme Court as it hears landmark death penalty case. Three hundred fourty-eight arrests nationwide. Activists demand new trial for death row journalist Mumia Abu-Jamal and abolition of the death penalty.

WASHINGTON, DC—"Grant a New Trial/Abolish the Death Penalty" was the call Monday morning at 10AM February 28 as one hundred eighty-five people, including former South African political prisoner Dennis Brutus and Jennifer Harbury, lawyer and widow of a slain Guatemalan resistance leader, were arrested during a dramatic, nonviolent civil disobedience action at the U.S. Supreme Court. This action and its companion support vigil called for a new trial for award-winning journalist and death row inmate Mumia Abu-Jamal. The three thousand strong demonstration also demanded abolition of capital punishment in the U.S. All of the arrested protestors were charged with unlawful conduct and impeding traffic on the Supreme Court grounds. Rev. Nozomi Ikuta, President of the National Interreligious Task Force on Criminal Justice, and Rev. Michael Yasutake, an officer of the National Council of Churches Racial Justice Working Group, were also arrested.

The CD and companion vigil brought together renowned labor leaders, religious figures, entertainers, human rights activists and academicians. Among human rights leaders speaking at the support vigil were Sam Jordan, Director of Amnesty International's Program to Abolish the Death Penalty; Stephen Hawkins, Executive Director of the National Coalition to Abolish the Death Penalty; and Pam Africa, Director of International Concerned Family and Friends of Mumia Abu-Jamal. At a simultaneous demonstration in San Francisco, one hundred sixty-three people were arrested for blocking the front entrances of the U.S. Court of Appeals. The arrest total for the day was three hundred forty-eight for the two civil disobedience demonstrations. Demonstrations were also slated for Los Angeles, Toronto and other cities in the U.S. and Canada.

As people were arrested outside, the U.S. Supreme Court was considering "Williams v. Taylor (99-6615)"—a landmark case challenging restrictions to habeas corpus law by the 1996 Antiterrorism and Effective Death Penalty Act. "This decision will greatly impact Mumia's case because it will set the

---

This press release was distributed shortly after the Supreme Court civil disobedience action on February 28, 2000.

boundaries for federal judges—either they will be able to conduct independent reviews of state cases or they are going to be severely restricted in independent reviews in what they do," said Abu-Jamal's lead attorney Leonard Weinglass, "What Williams is about is whether or not federal judges have to accept the findings of state court judges or whether or not they are independent—habeas corpus is our most valued human right."

Mumia Abu-Jamal's case has shone an international spotlight on the arbitrary use of the death penalty in the U.S. On January 31, Illinois Republican Governor George Ryan instituted a temporary halt to executions in his state after 13 Illinois death row inmates were found innocent. Two weeks later, on February 10, the Philadelphia City Council joined many other municipalities nationwide in passing a resolution calling for a moratorium on their state's executions. And on February 22, the Judiciary Committee of Pennsylvania's Senate held hearings on Senate Bill 952, which calls for a two-year moratorium on executions in Pennsylvania. At present, Pennsylvania Federal District Judge William Yohn is reviewing Abu-Jamal's petition for habeas corpus to overturn his conviction based on 29 constitutional violations during the initial trial.

Noting that this celebrated author has thus far failed in the courts, educator Herman Ferguson, co-chair of the New York-based Free Mumia Abu-Jamal Coalition said, "Civil disobedience is as American as apple pie, from the Boston Tea Party to the labor movement, from the civil rights sit-ins, antiwar and antinuclear activism, right up to the recent police brutality protests, civil disobedience has always shown the people's willingness to prevail against injustice."

Today's actions followed a July 3, 1999, action at the Liberty Bell and a simultaneous one in San Francisco where one hundred twenty-two people were arrested. That was the first action of a civil disobedience campaign that organizers plan to continue until Mr. Abu-Jamal gets a new trial. The cumulative arrest total for the two actions is four hundred seventy. The demonstration was organized by the Free Mumia Abu-Jamal Coalition and the February 28th Coalition for Mumia.

In October 1998, Pennsylvania's Supreme Court denied Mumia's bid for a new trial, upholding the original trial judge's ruling. The journalist, MOVE supporter, and former member of the Black Panther Party, was convicted in 1981 of the shooting death of a Philadelphia police officer in a trial tainted by the flagrant bias of that judge, the deliberate exclusion of 11 Black jurors and a court-appointed lawyer who, by his own admission, was inexperienced in criminal law. In addition, witnesses came forward during the 1995 Post-Conviction Relief Appeal hearing saying they were coerced by police to lie, suppress or change their initial account of the December 9, 1981, incident.

Worldwide Solidarity with Mumia

Suzanne Ross
2008

The international component of the Free Mumia movement has been strategic in exerting political pressure. Its activity peaked in 1995 and 1999, when death warrants for Mumia were signed, with highly publicized demonstrations in Europe, Asia, Latin America, and South Africa, and official government statements in France, Germany, Japan, and Cuba. There were also delegations from France, Japan, Germany, Spain/Catalonia, Denmark and Egypt who came to attend court hearings, visit Mumia, meet with government officials, participate in events, or join street demonstrations. Some of the international visitors to Mumia were Danielle Mitterrand, wife of the former French president; numerous French mayors; French Communist Party officials; Julia Wright, daughter of author Richard Wright; and Mireille Mendès-France, daughter of Frantz Fanon; and most recently the Archbishop Desmond Tutu.

In 1995, the African National Congress and President Nelson Mandela urged Governor Tom Ridge to grant Mumia a new trial, while the Congress of South African Trade Unions (COSATU) requested clemency. Within days of the signing of the warrant, there were protest actions in London, Berlin, Paris, Frankfurt, Amsterdam, Tokyo, Toronto, and Vancouver. A year later, in a meeting of church leaders in Guatemala, 51 of them, including four Catholic bishops, formally joined the international campaign for a civil rights investigation. The Zapatista National Front called for a stop to the execution, Amnesty International demanded a new and fair trial, members of Workers Russia called for commutation of the death sentence, and unions in Britain, Australia, the French *Confédération générale du travail* (CGT), the Metro Toronto Labor Council, the Vancouver Public Employees, Section 10 of the Mexican Teachers Union, and the Brazil National Confederation of Educational Workers all gave support to Mumia. Demonstrations in Europe and Latin America continued. In 2001, at the World Conference Against Racism in Durban, South Africa, support was again expressed for Mumia. As late as April 2008, when there was an angry protest in Philadelphia against the Third Circuit Court of Appeals' rejection of Mumia's appeal for a new trial, demonstrations were reported in Mexico City, London, Dublin, Vienna, Paris, and Saint-Denis, and on July 4, there were "die-ins" in Marseille and Paris.

The French support has been particularly notable because the grassroots work never stopped. Weekly vigils at the U.S. Consulate in Paris were started by Julia Wright and Catherine Grupper in 1995. The focus was on Mumia embodying the arbitrary nature of the U.S. death penalty and grew to include all political prisoners, particularly Leonard Peltier. That same year, the Unified Collective to Save Mumia was formed. It continues its work to this day. Smaller solidarity groups were created throughout France. About twenty Communist Party-led "suburbs" surrounding Paris, with working-class and primarily African immigrant populations, presented honorary citizenship to Mumia, Bobigny and its famous late mayor being the most well known. Marseille, in Southern France, began a yearly street naming in honor of Mumia, which though not official because of the right wing mayor's opposition, involves putting up the Mumia street sign across the street from the U.S. Consulate. It was partly these smaller solidarity actions that led to the two big French events: the granting of honorary citizenship of Paris to Mumia in 2004 and the naming of a newly built street in the largely immigrant, working-class city of Saint-Denis in 2006.

Approached by the Unified Collective, the Socialist mayor of Paris agreed to grant Mumia honorary citizenship, the first such awarding since 1971 when Pablo Picasso was its recipient. At a very prestigious event at City Hall in 2004, with International Concerned Family and Friends of Mumia Abu-Jamal's Pam Africa and Free Mumia Abu-Jamal Coalition's Suzanne Ross present, Angela Davis accepted the award on behalf of Mumia. Hundreds were present, including many African immigrants and ex-patriot Black Americans, who were very eager to meet with both Pam Africa and Angela Davis.

In 2006, after much preparation, the mayor and other officials of Saint-Denis, a town adjacent to Paris, worked with the Saint-Denis Mumia Committee to name a street in Mumia's honor. This modest street on Human Rights Square was named with fanfare, linking it to the Spanish Civil War, the South African liberation struggle, and other antifascist struggles. Young Mumia supporters followed with an international arts festival of music, dance, and food cooked by African immigrant women. U.S. activists, led by Pam and Ramona Africa, attended. Despite the ensuing blistering denunciations from four U.S. legislative bodies, Saint-Denis refused to back down, stood strong, and had an anniversary celebration with city officials, and another U.S. delegation, a year later.

VI.8.A

Conscious of His Own Destiny

Angela Y. Davis
2004

The movement for the liberation of Mumia Abu-Jamal, who has been on death row for more than 20 years, has taken on new meaning in light of American unilateralism, the aggression against the Iraqi people, and the racist attacks against immigrants, all of which merely erode even further the vestiges of democracy in America.

Mumia was our guide and showed us the best possible way to mourn the victims of September 11: a mourning not stamped with nationalism, xeno-phobia and violence, but rather with a spirit of peace and world-wide soli-darity. Mumia showed us how to denounce the war and the state-supported violence which is the complement to the epidemic of violence done to the bodies of women...

In my opinion, what has touched us the most in Mumia Abu-Jamal is his profound sense of humanity, the fact that he is conscious that his own destiny is tied to that of thousands of men and women who are in death row in the United States and around the world...

Pam Africa, Angela Davis and Julia Wright (l-r) in Paris, France, 2004.

Mumia Abu-Jamal was made an honorary citizen of Paris in October 2004. Bertrand Delanoë, socialist mayor of Paris, praised the occasion as the first of its kind since 1971, when Pablo Picasso received the honor. Delanoë added his denunciation of "this barbarity called the death penalty." Angela Davis attended the ceremony on Mumia's behalf. Speaking in French, she made these remarks in her speech.

VI.8.B

Regarding U.S. Resolutions Condemning the Naming of a Street for Mumia Abu-Jamal by the French City of Saint-Denis

Patrick Braouezec

2006

Concerning Resolution 407, introduced by persons close to the FOP [Fraternal Order of Police], I first want to say that I condemn the murder of the police officer. I believe that everyone must condemn this act. That is clear.

This draft resolution claims that the murder was undoubtedly committed by Mumia. But everybody knows that the point of naming a street in Saint-Denis in honor of Mumia Abu-Jamal is to underscore the fact that Mumia has always maintained his innocence and has always demanded a fair trial. These are entirely two different matters: condemning the murder of a police officer is one thing, but the absence of a fair trial for Mumia is an entirely different matter. Finally, it seems outrageous to me [that this resolution] demands that the French government force the city of Saint-Denis to reverse its decision.

Cities in France have the right to name streets in honor of individuals. We have experienced in our recent history many unnamings linked to political change. It is true that in choosing the name of Mumia Abu-Jamal we made a choice, a political choice, a choice aimed to show that we stand at his side in the struggle he is waging to obtain legal recognition of his innocence—and we proclaim our choice for all to hear. In the same manner, a few years ago, we named a street for Bobby Sands, who had resisted the British occupation of Ireland. We have also named other streets in honor of other resisters, other individuals who fought unconditionally against the bullying established orders that refuse to acknowledge injustice.

One last thing concerning the proposed resolution's third paragraph, commending all American and police officers worldwide: I must tell you that, while I recognize the role played by the police today, under certain circumstances, I am not willing to consider all police officers of equal valor whether those officers are American or hail from other parts of this planet. Because I know for a fact that many of them do not act in the constitutional way we would expect of them under all circumstances, especially as far as minorities are concerned. This is so whether we are speaking about the United States or certain other countries where the police abuse their power and do not play the role we expect of them as custodians of the equal treatment of all citizens. So let us not put the entire police force in the same basket. Statements such as those made in the proposed resolution regarding police forces as a whole constitute a false generalization—since it holds these police forces immune from any suggestion that they are capable of breaking or abusing rules.

Concerning the current situation confronting Pam Africa and the movement in Philadelphia, I have two reactions. First, when one is reduced to resorting to fear, to imposing the law of silence, it means that somehow there is a degree of uneasiness, somehow there is a lack of confidence, somehow there are those who are afraid of the final verdict of truth. So my first reaction is that when a group of individuals tries to impose the law of silence in this way, it means that the final truth is not what we are led to think nor is it what is made to appear as such. And my second reaction is to say that one should definitely not allow oneself to be intimidated. Beyond the struggle Mumia is waging to gain recognition of his innocence, he is also waging another struggle to abolish the death penalty, and this struggle should be waged by all democrats worldwide. Also, it is obvious that by exerting this type of pressure, very strong almost physical pressure, a certain number of police unions, not to mention rightwing or extreme rightwing unions, are intimidating all those who are waging a struggle today against the death penalty, whether it be in the United States or in other countries.

This struggle against the death penalty is a vital one. In my opinion, it is not permissible to play games with the lives of people. There are too many examples in the world, and first and foremost in the United States, of people who were sentenced unjustly. Sometimes they have been condemned to death or to very heavy prison sentences while proof of their innocence is established either after execution or after they have spent a great many years in prison. So we must not allow ourselves to be intimidated by these types of actions but rather recognize that the show of pressure is more a form of weakness than a demonstration of force.

Credit: Lallan Schoenstein

449

As far as raising the FOP's proposed resolution in the French National Assembly, I believe that we must work on some type of action at that level. I do not know at this stage whether it can be a "current events" issue like the ones we raise every week, which take the form of a written question to the government. It is necessary that we elected representatives initiate action against the death penalty at both the national and other levels. I am speaking also of those who, as elected representatives, support Mumia in his struggle, for example, by adopting him as honorary citizen or conferring other tokens of support.

I believe that all these people should raise the issue with the French government in a very direct manner, including a request that our government should react explicitly even if in the end the American government does not challenge the French government in response to the proposed draft resolution that some are attempting to introduce today. But this would be an opportunity for the French government to take a clearcut positon concerning this affair and cut through any ambiguity there might be. So I am completely in favor of raising the issue in one form or another through the voices of a certain number of elected representatives—*députés,* mayors or municipal councillors—because there is also within cities governed by the political opposition a great deal of political mobilisation for the defense of Mumia. I think raising the issue at government level today would be useful.

Concerning the question from a youth as to whether we should take orders from American capitalism, I say *no,* I take orders from no capitalist even if we are compelled to accept capitalism as part of our lives, even if we have to make accommodation at this juncture with the situation it creates. We know perfectly well that we are living in a capitalist system, but the issue is much larger than the American capitalist order. I believe that there are American democrats, as well as democrats throughout the world, who fail to question capitalism but who nonetheless adhere to certain human rights and that, even in the absence of challenging capitalism, there are still many citizens in the world who are probably against the death penalty and consider that Mumia Abu-Jamal has the right to an honest trial.

As far as our media notoriety in the U.S. is concerned, as mayors who named a street in honor of Mumia Abu-Jamal, our only objective as far as any media interest is concerned (whether the media be American or not) is to enhance the fairness of our claim. What is our claim today? We are among the many people who simply ask that Mumia be granted a new trial so that the evidence of his innocence can be heard. That is all we ask and I think that all the exposure we can obtain in the media should establish the claim concerning this issue. So let us make efficient use of the mikes or cameras that seek us out to validate our claim.

My thoughts are very much today with Mumia Abu-Jamal and the situation that entraps him. I am currently reading the most recent book by Michael Connelly, *The Lincoln Trial,* which exposes all the blemishes, all the abuse at the core of America's legal procedures, including the ways a trial can be manipulated. And we are made to see that it is money that fuels the neuro-logical system of American justice—and that is a fact we can only condemn. If our statements, my statements, are known throughout a number of radio stations and their networks—so much the better. I think it is useful, useful for Mumia, useful for the issue of abolition, useful for the totality of democracy whether it be in the United States or other countries that call themselves democracies today but are really undemocratic.

VI.8.C

South African Robben Island Press Release
Dennis Brutus
2000

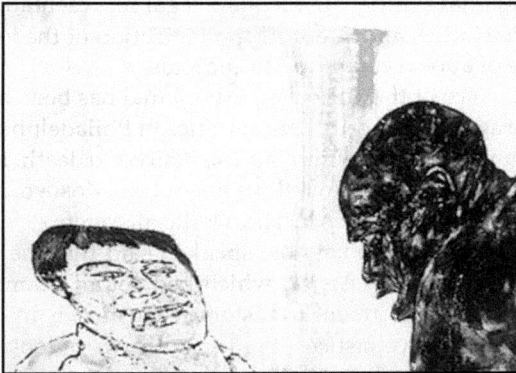

Encounter, by Leon Golub

South African Archbishop calls for new trial for U.S. prisoner Mumia Abu-Jamal on "Freedom Day"; Robben Island service to focus on death row prisoner and human rights

An inter-faith church service on Robben Island, South Africa on April 26 will focus on the escalating call for a halt to the execution of Philadelphian death-row prisoner, Mumia Abu-Jamal and on a global need to commit to

Following Dennis Brutus's participation in the Liberty Bell and Supreme Court actions, he was eager to bring the message of Mumia's plight to his native South Africa. At this time, the infamous South African prison fortress, Robben Island, was being converted into a pubic museum. Robben Island was the site that held Brutus, along with Nelson Mandela and scores of other antiapartheid prisoners, as well as (in a previous era) Mohandas Gandhi. In conjunction with the South African Anglican archdiocese, and with the U.S.-based Art Against Death, a showing of artwork by U.S. political prisoners accompanied a press conference on Mumia at a special opening on the island.

restorative justice. Robben Island, the internationally infamous former high security island prison, has been converted into a symbol of justice and peaceful transitions—and includes a museum and a newly renovated Chapel. The Church of the Good Shepherd is administered by the Anglican Church of Southern Africa, whose presiding Archbishop has recently joined the campaign for a new trial for Abu-Jamal.

The service will coincide with the opening of a poster exhibition of art dedicated to Abu-Jamal. The aim of this show—which is traveling to galleries throughout South Africa, Europe and the U.S.A.—is to escalate international pressure for a retrial. Announcing the service and the art show, Anglican Archbishop Njongonkulu Ndugane said it had been organized in association with Amnesty International, at the request of South African poet laureate and former political prisoner Prof. Dennis Brutus and recently released U.S. political prisoner Laura Whitehorn.

Very serious questions have arisen about Abu-Jamal's trial and the evidence used against him. A February 2000 Amnesty International report raised concerns about Abu-Jamal's initial "inadequate legal representation," about the fairness of the trial judge, and about the politicization of the judicial process and possible bias of appeal courts in Mumia's case.

Known as "the voice of the voiceless," Abu-Jamal has been a leading critic of police violence against minority communities in Philadelphia. He was convicted of killing a white police officer, and sentenced to death. He has written extensively from his jail cell against the wars in Iraq, Kosovo, and Colombia, and also about the racism of the American judicial system.

The Archbishop, who is the keynote speaker, said that the matter was of grave concern because South Africa, which had set an example to the rest of the world with its commitment to restorative justice, is in dire danger of shifting towards retributive justice. "We in South Africa look in horror and great sadness at the United States," stated Archbishop Ndugane, "which historically has made tremendous contributions towards the achievement of universal human rights, yet where 27 states now apply the death penalty. Apartheid South Africa applied the death penalty. The culture of violence that still grips South Africa is without doubt a consequence of the apartheid era, and its depraved contempt for other human beings. From that experience, we have learned of the brutalization of society which results when the State resorts to killing as a deterrent to killing."

In noting particular concern regarding the case of Abu-Jamal, the Archbishop continued, "We remind our friends in the United States that Nelson Mandela and many other South Africans were saved from the gallows only because of the outrage expressed during the 1960s by the international community. Here on Robben Island we remember the brutality of the past, and commit ourselves that never, never again will such acts of inhumanity be repeated." During the apartheid era, both Ndugane and Dennis Brutus served time as political prisoners on Robben Island, along with former South African President Mandela.

The service begins at 10:00AM, and the participants include Methodist Bishop James Gribble, Prof. Brutus, and Judge Dennis Davis. Prayers will be led by Guru Krishna, and Imam Rashid Omar and Peter John Pearson, of the Roman Catholic parliamentary office, will read from the Qu'ran and from the Bible. An Amnesty International candle will be lit by former political prisoners who had been held on Robben Island.

April 27 marks "Freedom Day" in South Africa—a national holiday commemorating the transition to democratic rule. At that time, the poster exhibition—taken in part from a collection of the Los Angeles-based Center for the Study of Political Graphics—will open at Cape Town's St. George's Cathedral. In addition, prominent U.S. artists Leon Golub and Nancy Spero have contributed works to the show, as have Art Against Apartheid founder Cliff Joseph and former prisoner Laura Whitehorn. In a statement by Golub and Spero accompanying their work, they comment: "Mumia is symbolic of the innumerable situations where justice has been denied. When one such imprisoned individual is brought to international light, perhaps that helps ignite local and world attention to so many nameless prisoners in so many different countries. The fight for Mumia is a fight for all such prisoners, that essential vigilance that freedom demands."

The show, Robben Island ceremony, and Freedom Day activities come at a crucial time in Mumia Abu-Jamal's proceedings. It is expected that an announcement from Federal District Court Judge Yohn could come at any time, possibly summoning Abu-Jamal into court in Philadelphia for the first time in many years. These efforts coincide with an Appeal from U.S. political prisoners to intensify work around Abu-Jamal's case.

VI.9

Confronting the NAACP

Suzanne Ross
2008

Two years of grassroots struggle to get the NAACP to take a pro-Mumia position, focused on its highly publicized annual July national conventions, preceded the passing of this resolution. In 2003, at the Miami Convention, Sundiata Sadiq, former president of the Ossining NAACP chapter, made his first attempt to pass such a resolution. The proposed resolution was informally approved but later squashed by Ben Andrews, national resolutions chairman, and Hazel Dukes, leader of the New York State NAACP, and others in national leadership.

In 2004, the Ossining Chapter once again tried to have the resolution raised at the national convention, scheduled that year for Philadelphia. Activists insisted that the NAACP could not ignore Mumia in the city where he was framed and sentenced to death and where the MOVE organization was bombed and members were murdered. With media and heavy security present on the first day of the convention, activists held a rally in front of the convention hotel and distributed fliers to all who entered. Having announced in advance that they would attend the death penalty workshop, which ICFFMAJ's Pam Africa was promised she could attend, the activists now protested the NAACP's cancellation of that workshop, explained the significance of Mumia's case, and asked for support in passing the resolution.

On the day presidential nominee John Kerry was addressing the convention, Mumia activists returned for the third time and insisted that they would be peacefully protesting the NAACP's refusal to budge. With a letter of rebuke to Julian Bond from the son of legendary NAACP founder, W. E. B. Du Bois, support from Mayor John Street, and members of the more progressive chapters, the resolution crafted by the NAACP with FMAJC's Bill Bachmann, was passed just hours after Kerry spoke, with only one dissent! Word spread around the world of this victory, and Mumia thanked the organization.

Unfortunately, the NAACP has done nothing since that day to implement this resolution, and within a short time of its passing, the Ossining Chapter that initiated the struggle was suspended indefinitely from the organization and continues to be suspended to this day, despite endless unfulfilled promises of reinstatement. Still, the resolution stands as an example to other organizations and remains as a basis for challenging the NAACP again.

A luta continua!

VI.9.A

Emergency Resolution Reaffirming
Opposition to the Death Penalty

National Association for the Advancement of Colored People
2004

Whereas the NAACP adopted a resolution in 2001 re-affirming our opposition to the death penalty due to its racially disparate application; and

Whereas the NAACP has re-affirmed its 1975 resolution opposing the death penalty on the grounds that it constitutes cruel and unusual punishment in violation of the Eighth Amendment of the United States Constitution; and

Whereas many people, including Mumia Abu-Jamal, are incarcerated on death row and face possible execution; and

Whereas more than 320 people on death row have been exonerated; and

Whereas though African Americans make up only 12.4% of the U.S. population, we make up 38% of all the Americans that were sentenced to death and later freed after being found innocent; and

Whereas African Americans make up 35% of those being found innocent after being executed; and

Whereas African Americans make up over 80% of those awaiting execution on federal death row; and

Whereas 145 people have been exonerated based upon DNA evidence; and

Whereas there is no possible way of restoring the life of an innocent person killed by the death penalty; and

Whereas the implementation of the death penalty raises concerns regarding bias identification, police and prosecutorial misconduct, judicial apathy in protecting the rights of the accused, faulty evidence, inadequate defense representation, coerced confessions, and fabricated testimony, and,

---

Text of NAACP Resolution for a New Trial for Mumia Abu-Jamal and a National Death Penalty Moratorium, adopted at the NAACP National Convention, Philadelphia, Pennsylvania, July 15, 2004.

455

Therefore be it resolved that the National Association for the Advancement of Colored People reiterates its strong opposition to the death penalty; and

Be it further resolved that the NAACP calls on its units throughout the United States and the world to support the international call for Mumia Abu-Jamal to be released from death row; and

Be it further resolved that the NAACP reiterate its support of the international movement for a new and fair trial for Mumia Abu-Jamal; and

Be it finally resolved that the NAACP renew its call for new nation wide studies on racial discrimination, the adequacy of counsel, access to modern research technology such as DNA analysis, the sentencing of children and women to the death penalty and that the NAACP reiterate its call for a national moratorium on all executions.

(signed)

> Kweisi Mfume
> President and CEO
>
> Julian Bond
> Chairman of the Board of Directors

VI.10

This Is No Victory:
Analysis of Appeals Court Ruling on
Mumia Abu-Jamal's Case

Linn Washington, Jr.
2008

The long-awaited ruling by the Third Circuit Court of Appeals in the Mumia Abu-Jamal case released on March 27, 2008, again displays the dismaying pattern of U.S. courts ignoring precedent to deny relief to this death row journalist whose plight generates international support.

Precedent in American law means courts following previous court rulings when determining specific legal issues.

Precedent is the bedrock of American law.

America law requires courts to follow precedent unless significant evidence and/or compelling rationales necessitate changing precedent.

This Third Circuit ruling changes precedent. This ruling changes precedent by applying legal procedures in a highly questionable manner to dismiss compelling evidence of injustice against Abu-Jamal.

The Third Circuit did uphold the elimination of Abu-Jamal's death sentence. This is no victory because the ruling upheld his conviction, thus condemning Abu-Jamal to life in prison.

This ruling refused to grant Abu-Jamal a new hearing or new trial on three compelling issues: prosecutors using racism to exclude African Americans from the jury during Abu-Jamal's 1982 trial; the prosecutor making improper comments to that '82 jury at the end of the trial; and pro-prosecution bias by the '82 trial judge during a 1995 appeals hearing.

The Third Circuit previously granted relief to persons convicted of murder in Philadelphia after ruling that Philadelphia prosecutors had illegally excluded African Americans from juries.

However, in this Abu-Jamal case ruling, the court found no fault in evidence of exclusion of African Americans from the jury in his 1982 trial.

Curiously, the evidence of exclusion at Abu-Jamal's trial is of equal or greater magnitude than proof of exclusion previously found acceptable for relief by the Third Circuit.

This article was published on the website of the Philadelphia Independent Media Center, www.phillyimc.org, on March 29, 2008.

These previous rulings on jury discrimination formed the precedent on that issue for the Third Circuit.

That precedent stated it is wrong for prosecutors to discriminate against even one black potential juror. Additionally, that precedent stated defendants did not have to object to jury selection discrimination by prosecutors immediately when it occurred.

Yet, this ruling reversed precedent on those two points of legal procedure.

A week before this Abu-Jamal ruling, the U.S. Supreme Court granted relief to a death row inmate in Louisiana because of a discriminatory jury selection process. That Supreme Court ruling was written by a Justice on that court who formerly served on the Third Circuit.

That Justice, Samuel Alito, had approved relief to Philadelphia murder defendants due to discriminatory jury selection practices by prosecutors. Alito, in a February 2005 Third Circuit ruling, stated prosecutors commit a violation by removing "any black juror because" of their race—a position similar to the position contained in that recent U.S. Supreme Court ruling he authored.

Third Circuit Ruling

The Third Circuit's ruling rested on a procedural finding by two of the three judges on this appeal's court panel. This finding stated that lawyers for Abu-Jamal during the 1982 trial and the 1995 appeal hearing failed to follow the procedures legally required to properly raise the issue of prosecutors improperly using racism during the jury selection process.

The panel's majority asserted that "Abu-Jamal has forfeited his Batson claim by failing to make a timely objection" to improper procedures by prosecutors referencing the U.S. Supreme Court's 1986 Batson ruling that outlaws the exclusion of black jurors for reasons rooted in racism.

Philadelphia area author and investigative reporter Dave Lindorff notes the absurdity of holding Abu-Jamal's lawyer responsible for not strictly following procedures during the 1982 trial that the U.S. Supreme Court did not create until four years later in that 1986 Batson case.

No lawyer (or judge) in the United States could have predicted what procedure the U.S. Supreme Court would order four years in the future, observes Lindorff, author of the seminal 2003 book on the Abu-Jamal case: *Killing Time* (Common Courage, 2002).

In reaching this conclusion against Abu-Jamal's jury discrimination claim, that Third Circuit panel's majority created a new standard for persons raising Batson claims in that court.

This standard requires that a Batson violation claim must be raised at the time of jury selection—a contemporaneous objection.

Interestingly, in reaching this conclusion of procedural errors by Abu-Jamal's attorney, the panel's majority failed to note that this lawyer at

1982 trial was unfairly thrust into the jury selection process after that process was underway without the opportunity to do any preparation.

The trial judge granted the prosecutor's request to remove Abu-Jamal from selecting his own jury, a decision without merit that unfairly benefited the prosecutor and stripped Abu-Jamal of his right to represent himself. Plus, this action aggravated tensions between Abu-Jamal and his attorney.

Further, the panel's majority faulted an Abu-Jamal lawyer for not properly raising the jury selection racism issue during Abu-Jamal's first appeal in the late 1980s to the Pennsylvania Supreme Court without acknowledging a major error committed by the lawyer who filed that appeal.

That attorney prepared that appeal without ever reviewing the trial transcript.

There is no way that attorney could have prepared a legally valid appeal without knowing what specifically had happened at trial. (That appeal attorney was also suffering from what proved to be a fatal brain tumor, a medical condition that impaired that attorney's cognitive abilities.)

In creating this new standard, the panel's majority makes it harder to prove Batson violations. Plus, this standard changes that court's precedent on procedures needed to raise Batson claims.

The judge who dissented from his two colleagues faulted them for creating this new standard, a standard not ordered by the U.S. Supreme Court.

"This case's newly created contemporaneous objection rule…goes against the grain of our prior actions, as our Court has addressed Batson challenges on the merits without requiring that an objection be made during jury selection in order to preserve future appellate review," the dissenter said.

This judge, speaking specifically to changing precedent, said since Third Circuit precedent did "…not have a federal contemporaneous objection rule… I see no reason why we should not afford Abu-Jamal the courtesy of our precedents."

Additionally, this dissenter stated that jury discrimination practices displayed in a now infamous videotaped training session at the Philadelphia DA's Office gave "a view of the culture" of that office during the 1980s when Abu-Jamal was tried.

This dissenter criticized his two colleagues for failing to make the obvious connection between the discrimination instruction given at the taped session and discriminatory practices used by Philadelphia prosecutors before, during and after the 1980s.

"Indeed, given that Abu-Jamal's trial preceded Batson, it is not far-fetched to argue that the culture of discrimination was even worse," the dissenter declared.

Previously, the Third Circuit ordered new federal trial court hearings to collect more evidence to enable full and fair determinations on jury discrimination claims.

The Third Circuit's ruling rejected that procedure for Abu-Jamal.

Major Flaws in Court Rulings

This practice of creating new court standards to only apply to Abu-Jamal was criticized in an Amnesty International report of the Abu-Jamal case controversy released in 2001.

Amnesty International criticized the Pennsylvania Supreme Court for altering its prior rulings—precedents—to reach results against Abu-Jamal.

In 1986, for example, the Pennsylvania Supreme Court overturned a Philadelphia death sentence after ruling that a prosecutor named Joseph McGill made improper comments to the jury during a trial presided over by Judge Albert Sabo.

McGill prosecuted Abu-Jamal in a 1982 trial presided over by Judge Sabo.

Abu-Jamal's attorneys had alleged that McGill engaged in jury selection discrimination—a claim documented by evidence but a claim that the Third Circuit panel's majority rejected. Sabo's rulings during that 1982 trial aided this documentable discrimination.

During Abu-Jamal's 1982 trial, McGill made the same comments to the jury that the Pennsylvania high court faulted in its 1986 ruling. But when the Court upheld Abu-Jamal's conviction in 1989, it refused to find any fault with McGill making the same comments it had faulted him for in its ruling three years before.

Then, in 1990, the Pennsylvania Supreme Court reinstated its 1986 standard regarding prosecutors making improper comments like McGill made.

The Pennsylvania Supreme Court's flip-flopping on this form of prosecutorial misconduct led Amnesty International to state in its 2001 report that: "This contradictory series of precedents leaves the disturbing impression that the Court invented a new standard of procedure to apply it to one case only: that of Mumia Abu-Jamal."

McGill's improper comments to the jury faulted by the Pennsylvania Supreme Court in 1986 were an appeal issue before the Third Circuit Court. That federal court panel found no fault in McGill's comments, denying Abu-Jamal relief he should have received if those federal appeals judges fairly followed established law.

The Third Circuit panel also rejected allegations that Judge Sabo was biased during a major 1995 appeals hearing.

Sabo's biased antics during that 1995 proceeding were so outrageous this misconduct provoked strong, caustic criticisms from even Philadelphia's normally anti-Abu-Jamal media. An August 1995 editorial in the *Philadelphia Inquirer* blasted Sabo's "injudicious conduct" that included verbally badgering Abu-Jamal's attorneys and even briefly jailing one of those attorneys for objecting to one of his improper rulings.

Scores of newspaper articles from the *New York Times* to the ultra-conservative law-&-order *Washington Times* reported on Sabo's pro-prosecution bias at that '95 appeal hearing.

The Pennsylvania Supreme Court curtly dismissed this widespread journalistic criticism by contending that the "view of a handful of journalists" did not convince that Court of Sabo's bias.

Five of the seven Pennsylvania Supreme Court justices that upheld Abu-Jamal's conviction in 1998 received campaign contributions from the lead group seeking Abu-Jamal's execution, Philadelphia's police union, the Fraternal Order of Police (FOP). One of those '98 justices was the ex-DA of Philadelphia who as DA fought to execute Abu-Jamal.

The Third Circuit agreed with the Pennsylvania Supreme Court's 1998 ruling that no evidence exists showing a "settled bias" by Sabo against Abu-Jamal. The Third Circuit panel made this assertion despite noting Sabo making a series of "intemperate remarks" against Abu-Jamal and his defense attorneys during that 1995 appeal hearing.

In another flip-flop ruling, the Pennsylvania Supreme Court in March 1988 found that a single statement uttered by the judge during the murder trial of a former Pennsylvania state trooper "was extremely prejudicial" to this trooper who killed a woman inside a judge's office.

Where the Pennsylvania Supreme Court granted a new trial to that killer cop because of that judge's one improper comment, one year later the same Court found no fault in numerous opinion-laden statements Judge Sabo made during the Abu-Jamal trial.

Sabo rejected requests to remove himself from hearing that '95 appeal made by Abu-Jamal attorneys citing his pro-prosecution bias during the 1982 trial. News articles, editorials and commentaries all faulted Sabo for not removing himself, stating his failure to recuse himself graphically displayed unfairness in a proceeding where fairness was desperately needed.

Journalistic watch-dogs normally hostile to Abu-Jamal sought the face of fairness in that '95 proceeding both to follow established law and to quell critics claiming Sabo's unfairness against Abu-Jamal undermined fairness.

The federal panel's majority employed a legal procedure to sidestep Sabo's clear and illegal bias—an Achilles heel of that federal ruling and this entire case.

It is incredible to contend that the widely condemned Judge Sabo who presided during most trial court proceedings in Abu-Jamal's case did not violate any of Abu-Jamal's rights at any time—despite his history of violating rights in this case and other cases.

Judge Sabo handled 32 murder trials that ended in death sentences before his retirement. But 24 of those sentences in Sabo's courtroom had been vacated for errors as of June 2007 according to the American Civil Liberties Union (ACLU). Some of those death sentences were reversed due to misconduct and/or mistakes by Sabo.

Sabo had once ordered prosecutors to pursue a death penalty when the death penalty had been ruled illegal in Pennsylvania. Sabo's ordering that illegal procedure led to overturning that death sentence.

What Next?

This March 2008 Third Circuit ruling leaves Abu-Jamal with few legal options to challenge his conviction.

Abu-Jamal can appeal the panel's ruling to the entire Third Circuit Court hoping for that full Court to overturn the panel's ruling. Further, he can appeal any Third Circuit ruling to the U.S. Supreme Court.

There is a slight prospect of new action in Pennsylvania state courts.

The Third Circuit issued an order stating Abu-Jamal will receive a life sentence unless Philadelphia prosecutors hold a new penalty phase hearing seeking to reinstate his death sentence within six months.

This mini-trial style hearing would allow Abu-Jamal to present evidence, including new evidence of innocence that has emerged like a flood since his first trial.

But it is unclear if prosecutors will pursue this route that could create evidence and procedure that could secure a new round of federal appeals for Abu-Jamal.

Overlooked Crux of the Case

Sadly, the federal judges at the trial and appellate court levels, like judges in Pennsylvania state courts, have refused to uphold the most fundamental issue in the contentious Abu-Jamal case: the right to a fair trial.

Critics of Abu-Jamal's conviction from Philadelphia's Francisville section to France all feel he was denied a fair trial.

Police and prosecutors blatantly engaging in misconduct to secure a conviction destroys fair trial rights. A trial judge openly biased toward police and prosecutors destroys fair trial rights. Courts applying the law in the Abu-Jamal case differently than they do in other cases destroys equal justice rights.

The Pennsylvania Supreme Court declared in a 1959 ruling involving a Philadelphia murder case that every defendant is entitled "to all the safeguards of a fair trial...even if evidence of guilt piles as high a Mt Everest..."

Abu-Jamal was four-years-old when the Pennsylvania Supreme Court issued that 1959 ruling against judges and prosecutors' cutting corners during a trial.

Abundant evidence documents that corners cut by the prosecutor and judge during Abu-Jamal's trial and by judges during his appeals corrupted his rights to a fair trial and equal justice—rights guaranteed by the U.S. Constitution.

In June 2007, state courts in Pennsylvania overturned the 200th death penalty case since 1978 when that state reinstated executions, the ACLU stated.

It is incredible to contend that 200 death penalty cases contained errors egregious enough to be vacated but not a single element in the Abu-Jamal case warrants either a new hearing or a new trial.

Section VII.
John Brown and Beyond

In the heat of the work around Mumia Abu-Jamal and the Puerto Rican political prisoners, Resistance in Brooklyn felt it important to bring together as many activists in the white antiracist left as possible, along with leading members of domestic national liberation movements. The occasion of the 200th birthday of radical abolitionist John Brown seemed an appropriate opportunity for such a gathering. With national leadership from the newly developing Jericho Movement seeking amnesty for political prisoners, local cosponsorship from City University of New York's people of color-led Student Liberation Action Movement, and involvement of other white antiracist activists in the planning, a major national John Brown 2000 Conference was held at Hunter College on May 12-14, 2000. What follows are a short political recounting of John Brown's antislavery struggle, the transcript of a preparatory panel discussion held six months earlier, original writings by 21 political prisoners for the conference, and early Jericho resources, all of which were distributed at the event. Wrapping up the section is a recent interview with Dr. Barbara Zeller on the ongoing medical work to protect the health needs of political prisoners, so often purposely neglected by the jailers.

Who Was John Brown?

Terry Bisson
2000

One dark night in 1856 in Kansas Territory, in a remote area known as the Swamp of the Swan, five men appeared at the door of the leader of the pro-slaver "Border Ruffians" that were terrorizing the antislavery settlers. They beat on the door and awakened the man, in this case a federal judge. While his wife and children watched in horror they led him into the night and killed him with swords. Four other pro-slavery ringleaders were killed the same way that night in what radical Black historian W. E. B. Du Bois called "a bold act of terror" that laid to rest forever the notion that only the slaveowners would fight, and Kansas must fall to their will.

John Brown, who led this midnight raid, is one of the most controversial figures in U.S. history. Born in 1800, he committed his life to destroying slavery. Brown believed that no one would be free until Black people were free and wanted to see a society organized on a "less selfish basis." Because he preferred action to words and fought against the slaveocracy as well as U.S. federal troops, he was—and in some circles, still is—considered a fanatic. Yet, among Black people and abolitionist whites, Brown was honored as a great warrior and antislavery hero.

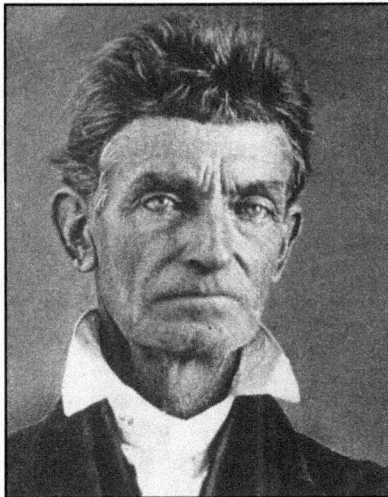

Much of Brown's early work against slavery was with Black people. In 1851, he helped organize an armed self-defense group in Springfield, Massachusetts, in response to the 1850 Fugitive Slave Law. This law, which said that any alleged runaway slave could be seized and re-enslaved without trial or defense, extended the power of the slave owners and endangered all Black people. Brown called his group the League of Gileadites and wrote their principles:

> Hold on to your weapons, and never be persuaded to leave them, part with them, or have them far from you. Stand by one another and by your friends, while a drop of blood remains, and be hanged if you must but tell no tales out of school. Make no confession. Union is strength.

In the 1850s there were two vital questions facing all people in the U.S.: the political/economic conflict between the southern slaveocracy and northern industrialists, and the future of 8 million enslaved Africans. The Southern planters were trying to expand the slave system into the newly conquered territories—Texas and New Mexico, stolen from Mexico, and Arkansas, stolen from Native Americans. Northern capitalists and free (white) labor were against this, not primarily because they believed in freedom for Black people, but because they wanted to develop the land differently for the growth of industrial capitalism.

In 1854, Congress passed the infamous Kansas-Nebraska Act; this strengthened the pro-slavery forces by revoking the Missouri Compromise of 1824, which had made Kansas a "free" state. The Act included a plan for "white popular sovereignty"—which meant that the white people living in the territory would vote to decide its political and economic future. This wasn't democracy; it was a set-up for war! Moving to Kansas became a partisan political act.

In 1854, five of Brown's sons moved their families to Kansas to help claim the land for the antislavery settlers. At first they, like others, thought this could be accomplished through voting and negotiations.

The free state settlers, as they were known, were largely unprepared for the fight ahead of them. When elections were held in March 1854, thousands of pro-slavery residents of Missouri poured into Kansas and took control of the polls. A total of 831 legal voters cast ballots, but a total of 6,320 votes were counted! All the members of the legislature were pro-slavery, except two. When the free state settlers rejected the outcome of the bogus election, armed pro-slavery mobs came in to "enforce order." Despite the readiness of the Missourians to use violence and ignore legality, the majority of antislavery settlers hesitated to go beyond peaceful appeals to Congress.

John Brown, Jr., wrote to his father asking him to raise money for arms so that the settlers could defend themselves against the Missouri Border Ruffians—a southern pro-slavery mercenary army, 3,000 strong, that raided across the border from Missouri to burn, pillage and terrorize antislavery settlements in Kansas. Brown's sons hoped he could win the support of the abolitionist movement in the North.

In 1855, Brown went to the abolitionists' Syracuse Convention to make a plea for money and arms. He told what his sons and other antislavery farmers were facing in Kansas. Writing home, Brown said of the convention,

> I have met with a warm reception from all, so far as I know, and except by a few sincere, honest peace friends, a most hearty approval of my intentions of arming my sons and other friends in Kansas.

Brown then decided to "strike a blow for freedom" and take the supplies to Kansas himself, disguised as a surveyor. This disguise enabled him to walk unnoticed through pro-slavery bands and overhear their conversations.

The free state movement that Brown found in Kansas reflected the same struggles and conflicts as the entire antislavery movement. There were those, like himself, who hated slavery and respected the humanity of Black people. There were those who saw slavery as a competitive threat to free (white) labor, but also were prejudiced against Black people. There were those who believed that they could appeal to the Southern slaveowners to change their ways, or thought that Congress would intervene if only petitioned urgently enough.

These were precisely the issues that Black people had been debating for 200 years. In 1829, David Walker's Appeal attacked the economic system of slavery as the basis of white supremacy. Walker called for resistance and self-determination for Black people. His fiery writings were smuggled into the South, causing slaveowners to panic.

> Our sufferings will come to an end in spite of all the Americans this side of eternity. Then we will want all the learning and talents among ourselves and perhaps more, to govern ourselves.

In 1843, another Black leader, Reverend Henry Highland Garnet, echoed Walker's call for rebellion:

> Brethren, arise, arise. Strike for your lives and liberties. Now is the day and the hour. Let every slave throughout the land do this, and the days of slavery are numbered. You cannot be more oppressed than you have been—you cannot suffer greater cruelties than you have already. Rather die freemen than live to be slaves. Remember that you are FOUR Million.

Brown was influenced by these and other Black leaders who argued that freedom for Black people demanded the complete destruction of the slave system. Further, Brown was committed to setting an example and creating an alternative for white people who did not want to be part of the slave system.

Brown came to Kansas with the view that slavery itself was a state of war, and that slaveholders would never give up their slaves "until they felt a big stick about their heads."

On many issues, Brown found himself in disagreement with the other Kansas freemen settlers, and sometimes horrified by their racism. Yet because Brown was a serious political and military leader, they united in the goal of making Kansas a free state. Brown commanded defense patrols and was a respected member of the community.

In December 1855, when a treaty was made between the government representatives of both sides, Brown publicly denounced it as a compromise with slavery. Though he initially won many supporters to this view, they were pacified by the politicians who made grand assurances that nothing had been conceded.

However, when Brown saw that government troops were being put under the command of the slave supporters, and armed bands from the South were camped directly outside his own settlement, he began to move. Donning his old surveyor's disguise, he coolly walked into their camp and overheard their plans to "whip, drive out or kill" all the abolitionists. They named Brown and others as their targets.

Brown warned his allies and they finally began to question their passive resistance. But it was too late for this battle. On May 21, the Border Ruffians burned the town of Lawrence to the ground. There was virtually no resistance or defense because the false hopes and pacifism of the settlers had left them unprepared. Brown knew that the time had come for decisive action, or the free state forces would be wiped out and their movement destroyed.

Gathering a small army, including four of his sons, he made a plan to bring the war home to the slave owners. In the words of W. E. B. Du Bois:

> The men condemned were among the worst of their kind. One was a liquor dealer in whose disreputable dive the U.S. court was held. His brother, a giant of six feet four, was a thief and a bully whose pastime was insulting free state women. The third was the postmaster, who managed to avoid direct complicity in the crime, but shared the spoils. Next came the probate judge who harried the free state men with warrants of all sorts and lastly, three miserable drunken fools, formerly slave chasers, who had come to Kansas with their bloodhounds and were ready for any kind of evil.

Brown's band left late in the night. They visited each man at his home and knocking on the door, roused him from bed. Five pro-slavery terrorists were brought to the woods, shot and stabbed with broadswords that night.

The Pottawatomie murders, as they were called, ended the uneasy peace and influenced the entire country. No longer was there even discussion of winning a vote; the question of slavery was going to be settled on the battlefield.

Some free state people condemned the executions and loudly disassociated themselves from them. Others switched sides. Others took up arms and joined John Brown. Kansas was plunged into Civil War. The war spread, creating clear terms for white people to participate in the struggle against slavery. In Missouri, the homeland of the slave owners, the slaves staged an insurrection armed with scythes and other farm tools.

Though Brown never claimed the Pottawatomie slayings, he became a hunted fugitive. He took 35 followers deep into the woods to train for war. As the pro-slavery forces mobilized, the free state towns began to ask Brown's guerrillas to defend them. He refused to do this without their own active participation in fighting slavery. "I am not willing to sacrifice my men without having some hope of accomplishing something."

Brown became a legend as he appeared here and there, striking, then swiftly retreating. By August 1856, the free state forces were clearly winning. The slave-staters gathered their forces for a massive attack on the town of Osawatomie in an effort to turn the tide.

Though newspaper reports of the Battle of Osawatomie on August 30 put the numbers at 250 slavers to 200 abolitionists, the truth was that Brown, leading no more than 30 fighters, was able to fight off 400 enemy troops and kill or wound 70 of them. Five free state men were lost, including Frederick Brown, and John Brown was injured, but all agreed it had been a decisive battle. A rumor was spread that Brown had been killed, but when he emerged very much alive, he became known as "Osawatomie Brown."

In September, John Brown left Kansas to begin work on a new idea he was developing. He began to meet with some of the most prominent abolitionists of the day: Thomas Wentworth Higginson, Samuel Gridley Howe, Theodore Parker, Franklin B. Sanborn, Gerrit Smith and George L. Stearns, who became known as the Secret Six for their clandestine financial support of Brown. He traveled extensively to speak to abolitionist groups, Black and white, about his plan to strike slavery a death blow. His plan was to seize an arsenal and to arm the slaves throughout the mountains of the South. He hoped a successful slave insurrection would destroy the slave system and lead to the establishment of an independent Black state. He even had the target picked out—a small town in Virginia where the Shenandoah and Potomac Rivers cut through the Blue Ridge Mountains.

It was called Harper's Ferry.

A long continuous mountain range from 2,000 to 5,000 feet high, running south and west from Pennsylvania to Tennessee, the Blue Ridge is aimed like a spear into the heart of the South.

The town of Harper's Ferry is situated inside the point of a "V" where the Potomac and Shenandoah Rivers join and then plunge through the mountains, which are here about 1,800 feet in elevation and, as everywhere, rocky, steep and thickly wooded. In 1859 there was a railroad bridge connecting the town to the Maryland shore, and a rifle factory and a federal arsenal in the town.

John Brown came to Harper's Ferry fresh from his victories in Kansas—a controversial figure widely known as "Osawatomie Brown," already a wanted man by the federal government and a hero to abolitionists, who funded and sheltered him; and respected even by those who didn't agree with his conviction that only armed struggle could defeat the slave system.

Brown's plan in the raid on Harper's Ferry was to launch a guerrilla force which would move along the Blue Ridge, using the mountains as a base of operations to strike at slave owners and draw off slaves. Harper's Ferry was chosen because of its strategic position at a mountain gap; because Brown hoped to deny the Hall's federal rifles to the slave catchers and local militias; and because he hoped that a lightning attack on a federal position in the South would heighten the antislavery debate already raging in the U.S. government.

His friend Frederick Douglass had urged him to gather his force and slip into the mountains, but Brown had political as well as military goals, and he wanted to start things off with a bang, knowing that a daring raid would embolden the slaves; inspire the abolitionist movement "in spite of itself" (for John Brown was well aware of the reformist and pacifist trends in the movement); and strike terror into the hearts of the slaveholders.

The raid was not aimed, as some historians have mistakenly claimed, to get rifles. Brown's abolitionist fighters were already equipped with the most sophisticated weapons of the day—the breech-loading sharps carbine. These rifles, brought from Kansas, were faster firing and more accurate than the weapons used by federal troops, and far outgunned the musket-carrying local Virginia militias. Ironically, the sharps, which was to help make possible the genocide of the Plains Indians, was first used as a weapon of liberation.

Brown's force also had 10,000 pikes (spears), for they knew that most slaves had been prevented from knowing how to use rifles.

On the night of October 17, 1859, after months of preparation and training in which two of his daughters played a major role, gathering and hiding the men and weapons, a column of 20 men marched into town, their carbines hidden under their long coats. Their captain wore a "lucky" hat given to him by an Indian friend in Kansas.

Taking the town with little bloodshed, the abolitionists seized hostages such as the grandson of George Washington, a local slaveowner, and forced him to turn over the sword presented to Washington by Frederick the Great to one of the Black freedom fighters. Brown took other prominent hostages, hoping to use them to bargain with the governor of Virginia and the federal authorities.

His mistake was he put far too much emphasis on these propaganda moves and lost sight of the military objectives. The hostages, in particular, kept his force pinned down long after his men had urged him to pull out. Out of concern for the hostages' safety, faced with the drunken trigger-happy Virginia militia sniping from barrooms and rooftops, he missed his chance to shoot his way out and get his men up the mountain.

Meanwhile the federal forces gathered—Marines led by a U.S. officer named Robert E. Lee, later to become commander of the Confederate Army. His second in command was a young officer later to be known as "Stonewall" Jackson.

Brown's most trusted lieutenants, John Kagi and Aaron Stevens, both seasoned Kansas fighters, urged him to pull out. But their captain hesitated. Why didn't Brown strike and withdraw as planned? His hostages were distinguished white slaveowners, and Brown treated them politely and tried to justify his actions to them. He mistakenly came to think he could use them to bargain his way out of town. Because of the white supremacy in him as in all white people, even the most antiracist, he wavered between the war that would arm the slaves and the vain hope that he could negotiate "peacefully" with the slaveowners' government. In the end, he put more value on his hostages than on his objective or the lives of his men.

It was his fatal error and his defeat is still felt today. It is often said that even in death John Brown was victorious, and it's true that he and his men inspired millions; the Black Union troops used "John Brown's Body" as a marching song five years later.

Yet history would look different if he had succeeded. Even a small army of abolitionists and freed slaves, in those days before the helicopter, would have been untouchable in the laurel thickets of the southern Appalachians. Others might have sprung up, arming the Black masses the U.S. was afraid to arm, hastening the beginning of the Civil War, hurrying its end, and ultimately saving thousands of lives.

And a war fought on abolitionist terms, with Black liberation the explicit aim, would have changed the balance of power after the war. John Brown went into battle with a constitution drawn up by Black abolitionists calling for a free state for Black people. Instead, the war was fought to unify the white nation rather than free the Black nation. Black soldiers were disarmed after the war, the Klan rode and slavery was exchanged for the new domination of Jim Crow, sharecropping and segregation.

John Brown hesitated too long. The Marines attacked and after a fierce fight the abolitionists were killed or captured. After a spectacular show trial, which gained worldwide attention, all were sentenced to hang for treason. Robert E. Lee, who two years later led a much larger army against the U.S., is of course still honored for his "treason."

The Fighters

Most of Brown's men were in their twenties—fifteen white and five Black freedom fighters. They were not zealots or religious fanatics as many historians pretend. They were revolutionaries, almost to a man—conscious and proud participants in the worldwide struggle for freedom that was shaking the old order of Europe, Latin America and the Caribbean as well as the U.S. In Europe, their counterparts fought with Garibaldi (who refused to aid Lincoln in the Civil War until he freed the slaves) or manned the barricades of revolutionary Paris. In America, the fight was against slavery. Most, including Brown's own sons, were freethinkers, not fundamentalists. Their Captain read them the Bible but they quoted him back Tom Paine, David Walker and Victor Hugo.

Among the Black fighters, Leary and Copeland, educated young craftsmen from Ohio, had fought bounty hunters and U.S. marshals to defend escaped slaves. Dangerfield Newby and Shields Green had worked with Frederick Douglass and left him to join Brown. Osborne Anderson, who escaped and wrote the best account of the raid, was a Black intellectual. He was offered a leadership position but turned it down in favor of Kagi and Stevens, who were more experienced. Harriet Tubman was supposed to be Brown's second-in-command, but she got sick at the last minute.

Among the whites, Aaron Stevens was a former U.S. Army officer who had been imprisoned for defending an enlisted man from a beating; escaping, he had lived several years with the Delaware Indians. Will Leeman was a "wild, reckless" factory worker. The Coppoc brothers were Quaker idealists. Brown's own sons were veterans of Kansas.

These men followed Captain Brown because of his proven ability as a military leader. After Kansas, it was widely believed that if anyone in the U.S. had the ability and the will to strike at slavery successfully it was "Osawatomie Brown."

Today these men are maligned as fanatics or, at best, misguided idealists. What a lie! They were revolutionaries, the fighting youth of a revolutionary age, among the best their day had to offer.

The Response

Their raid electrified the country as few acts before or since. John Brown and his men were seen as martyrs for freedom, or traitors to the human (white) race. Among abolitionists, the reaction was split between those who stood fast in support and those who fled or shut up. For the most part (though not completely), the split broke down along national and racial lines. Black people liked and understood John Brown and his men. White people had problems supporting them.

In the first weeks after Harper's Ferry, the abolitionist *Liberator*, a white-owned reformist newspaper, called the raid "misguided, wild and apparently insane, though disinterested and well-intended." They did admit that Brown had "struck terror into all Virginia." The racism of this white-centered view was coolly exposed in the leading Black paper, the *Weekly Anglo-African*: "John Brown did not frighten all Virginia. There were in that state some half million of slaves and we have no reports that they were terrified...."

Radical Black ministers such as Henry Highland Garnet spoke out immediately. Garnett told his congregation that anyone who could not support the captured raiders had "better keep still."

Others were apparently more timid. An open letter to Black ministers from

New Haven reminded: "You are expected to do your duty in pressing this matter home to the hearts and consciences of our people. Do not let us hear any uncertain sound from you on this point..."

The highest form of support was, of course, a rescue attempt, and this was actually planned. Blueprints of the jail were printed in northern newspapers to encourage the idea. A spy was sent to Virginia as part of Brown's legal team. An armed force was gathered, including 100 European socialists, exiled veterans of the 1848 revolutions. But Brown knew how closely he and his men were guarded and discouraged the plan.

Another form of material support was raising money for the widows and orphans of the fallen fighters. Black women led this work, and thousands of dollars were raised at church suppers and socials around the country. White people also contributed. A white man named Hyatt raised $6,150 in six months selling photographs of "Old Captain John Brown." He explained his work, saying: "It places in the hands of every contributor a likeness of one of the great men of the world—the man of the 19th century. Secondly, (it places) the family of the noble old man beyond the place of want, so that the icy finger of tyranny may point at them in vain."

Hyatt was also a grand jury resister of his day, spending a year in prison for refusing to cooperate with a Senate Committee investigation into Harper's Ferry.

At first the Brown family received almost all the relief funds, but this was criticized by the *Weekly Anglo-African*, and funds were distributed to the families of the Black fighters and others as well. Ten years after the raid, supporters were financing Leary's daughters' education at a private school.

December 2, 1859, the day John Brown was hanged was called Martyr's Day and ceremonies were held in twelve cities and Canada. Black people were the main organizers; businesses were closed and black armbands were worn in mourning. At Yale, students broke into the chapel and draped it in black, too late for school officials to remove it before Saturday service. In Albany, New York, thousands gathered and a four-minute ovation greeted the declaration that in a just society the Virginia governor, and not John Brown, would hang. In Detroit the church bells tolled all day.

The day was also observed by the slaves. In Virginia three plantations were torched, and three of the jurors that found Brown guilty were poisoned.

Two thousand troops surrounded the scaffolds as the abolitionists were hung. The only voice to break the silence was that of an old Black woman, the only civilian allowed within miles, perhaps unnoticed because she was so old. "God bless you, Old Man," she shouted defiantly. "If I could help you, I would."

One of the burning issues of the day was the question of Black participation in the rebellion. Osborne Anderson wrote that several slaves joined them. Some were able to escape and melt back into the population; others pretended they were "kidnapped." Those killed were secretly buried in a common grave, since it was vital to the South to maintain the lie that no slave wanted, or would fight for, freedom.

The Black abolitionist press took on directly the lies of the white media:

> The early boast of Judge Parker that not a slave or a free man of color had joined John Brown is contradicted by the fact that Colonel Washington's coachmen were found among the slain insurgents; and Virginia's Governor Wise, who knows much more than he publishes, has been ominously silent on this point of late; and the many slave owners who no longer dare sleep on the plantations, the many who have fled all the way to New York and may be seen any day on Broadway; and more than all, the selling off south within the next six months of nearly all the slaves from Jefferson and the adjoining counties in Virginia...

For 125 years history has been rewritten to make us think John Brown was mad and his men were misguided fanatics. Why? Because nothing is more subversive to imperialist law and racist order than the idea that white and Black people, oppressor and oppressed, could share a common humanity based on revolutionary ideals. It undermines the whole structure of white supremacy built so carefully in every white American youth from the time he or she first learns to play "cowboys and indians."

John Brown was far from mad. Frederick Douglass, the greatest and most influential Black abolitionist of the day, disagreed with Brown often and heartily, but defended his comrade in a famous essay, "Captain John Brown Not Insane":

> Not only is it true that Brown's whole movement proves him perfectly sane and free from merely vengeful passion, but he has struck the bottom of the philosophy which underlies the abolitionist movement. He has attacked slavery with the very weapons precisely adapted to bring it to the death. Moral considerations have long been exhausted upon slaveholders. It is vain to reason with them.

One hundred years later, another great Black leader, and one of the leading anti-imperialists of our century, agreed:

> If a white person wants to help our cause, ask him what he thinks of John Brown. Do you know what Brown did? He went to war.
>
> Malcolm X

Far from being mad, John Brown and his men represented the revolutionary ideals and practices that flourish in times of change, for their age like this one was a revolutionary time. Then as now, revolutionaries were slandered by the ruling powers as fanatics and criminals. Then as now, white people who fought in solidarity with the Black struggle were seen as "traitors." Then as now, revolutionaries are humankind's future.

This is why we honor them.

We are here to celebrate a life, not a death. John Brown is most famous for his martyrdom. After an unsuccessful raid on a federal arsenal in slave Virginia, he and his small band of abolitionists were convicted of treason and hanged. The courage with which Brown faced his death, the humanity with which he defended the rights of African people, and the eloquence with which he attacked slavery inspired people around the world—including Henry David Thoreau, Harriet Tubman, and Victor Hugo. The union soldiers who defeated the South in the Civil War carried his name into battle with the song, "John Brown's Body."

But it is important to remember that Brown's defeat at Harper's Ferry came after years of successful struggle. Brown lived and worked with Black people, when most whites, even abolitionists, were racist. In New England, his League of Gileadites defended the Underground Railway from bounty hunters tracking runaway slaves. In the Adirondacks he organized a farming community for freed Africans. In Boston he raised money for the "Free Staters" fighting to keep Kansas from becoming a slave state. When they were attacked by "Border Ruffians," Brown smuggled a wagon filled with guns into Kansas and joined the fight himself.

John Brown was a man of action. His midnight assassination of five pro-slavery thugs in the Swamp of the Swan horrified many abolitionists but turned the tide in Kansas. "Captain Brown" led the free state guerrillas to victory at Black Jack and Osawatomie. Disguised as a surveyor, he penetrated enemy camps to spy. Twice he led raids into Missouri to "steal" slaves. With a price on his head, he traveled to Niagara, New York, and helped write an abolitionist constitution. Recruiting in secret throughout the North, he raised men and money for a daring raid into Virginia that he hoped would inspire abolitionists everywhere to action.

Brown's followers included educated free Blacks, escaped slaves, social reformers, free thinkers and Quakers. The most influential abolitionists of the day, including Frederick Douglass, Harriet Tubman and Gerrit Smith, knew of and supported his plan—though Douglass feared it was doomed to failure.

Douglass was right. Brown was wounded and captured, his men brutally murdered. But the raid on Harper's Ferry terrified the South and made the Civil War inevitable. Church bells rang all across the North the day he was hanged.

Let us remember John Brown today, not only for the courage with which he faced his death, but for the ingenuity, audacity and principle with which he led the abolitionist cause. Brown was far more than just a martyr. He was a seasoned, successful, and celebrated antislavery warrior who fought many battles, and lost only one.

The Meaning of John Brown,
Mumia Abu-Jamal, and All Political Prisoners

a panel discussion organized by
Jericho Movement & Resistance in Brooklyn
December 3, 1999

Safiya Bukhari: Hello. My name is Safiya Bukhari. I'm the National Co-chair of the Jericho Movement. The Jericho movement was founded on March 27, 1998, to win amnesty and freedom for all political prisoners inside the U.S. We recognize that the U.S. government does not recognize the existence of political prisoners inside this country. All around the world, they're talking about human rights violations and freeing political prisoners in all the other countries. But when asked about whether political prisoners exist in this country, they answer an unequivocal no. We know different. And a lot of other people of other countries around the world, who have supported people like Leonard Peltier, Geronimo ji Jaga, Angela Davis, and others over the years, recognize the existence of political prisoners inside this country.

It is our responsibility, those of us who are involved in struggle in this country, to make sure to educate people about the fact that U.S. political prisoners exist. Some of our political prisoners have been in prison for over 30 years. And one of the things that I say often is that we have a tendency to go to trials and support them while they're on trial. But as soon as the trial's over and they're sent off to the institutions, within a year or two that they're even there, they may be forgotten. Some of our political prisoners have not gotten visits in years. We have one in Pennsylvania who is dead—who died in prison—and the vast majority of the community doesn't even know he's dead. His name still appears on some lists as Thomas Water, out of Pennsylvania, who was one of the Philadelphia Five. And how many of you knew this? It is

This is the transcript of a panel organized by the National Jericho Movement on December 4, 1999, at Manhattan's Brecht Forum, to commemorate the anniversaries of John Brown's hanging (1859) and the assassination of Black Panther Party leaders Fred Hampton and Mark Clark (1969). Linking those historic anniversaries with the campaigns to free Mumia Abu-Jamal and all political prisoners, the event brought together a distinguished grouping of speakers to discuss the state of repression and resistance—past, present, and future. Their remarks are presented here, in their complete and unabridged form. This transcript was subsequently published in booklet form by National Jericho, copublished by Resistance in Brooklyn.

because we have a tendency not to keep up with our political prisoners. We have known for years that if our political prisoners are left in a vacuum, and if people don't keep up with them, if they don't get visits, they fall prey to the system itself. The main reason the system gives these long sentences is so that they can break the political prisoners—their morale, their consciousness, their will to struggle. Finally they put them in a position where the state can even kill them. Thomas Water, in Pennsylvania, is dead.

There are four components of the Jericho Movement.

One is to educate people about the existence of political prisoners in this country.

Two is to form a Jericho Legal Defense Fund so that political prisoners can have legal representation, not just during the trial period but throughout their incarceration period. Once inside prison, many of our political prisoners get set up, like New York's Robert "Seth" Hayes recently did. In his case, this happened so that he could not be eligible for parole at a time when they knew he was fighting his parole denial. They set him up and gave him a year in the hole. And so when he goes in now, he's in a Special Housing Unit that's totally locked down, twenty-three and a half hours a day. Right here in the state of New York. Legal defense is necessary every step of the way while they're incarcerated. Sometimes, just to get educational programs that all other prisoners routinely get, the political prisoners have to fight in the courts.

The third aspect of the Jericho Movement is our Medical Project, for the medical needs of all political prisoners. Right now, at least three of the political prisoners across the country are dealing with serious medical issues. We sent out a notice about Albert Nuh Washington, who was recently diagnosed with serious cancer, and what was happening with him. Right now he's in a wheelchair. He's now being given necessary medical care. But he had gotten to the point where he had no feeling on the left side of his body. He could not walk without the aid of crutches, and he was in pain constantly, till his leg numbed out. We did a letter writing campaign. We notified people. And now he's in the hospital, in a wheelchair, but he's had an MRI and he's getting the medical care he has needed.

Thomas Manning needed hip replacement surgery for years. And it took a campaign, a concerted effort on the part of lawyers and people who knew about his situation, to make sure he got moved and finally got the hip replacement surgery he needed. Now he's undergoing physical therapy. We recently found out that Seth Hayes was sick. No one knew why. And finally he was able to get care, and they found out he's diabetic. The same with Mutulu Shakur. Some may remember Mutulu's eye problems, which were eventually diagnosed as glaucoma. The Medical Project is very much needed. Dr. Barbara Zeller is heading that up. One of our panelists today is the head of the Jericho Legal Defense Fund.

The fourth aspect of Jericho is the Amnesty Campaign. And that Amnesty Campaign is not just about one political prisoner, it's about all the political prisoners. If we're clear about the fact that the U.S. government has waged war on our communities and we're involved in a war of liberation, then what happens is *not* about court, and parole. For our political prisoners to be freed, we need an amnesty campaign. If they say we have made a difference and there's no war going on here, then free our political prisoners. Deal with amnesty. An Amnesty Campaign cannot just happen on a federal level, because a lot of our political prisoners are held on a state level.

There has been no organization recently that's been dealing with all these issues, affecting all the political prisoners. These issues we're dealing with affect political prisoners across the board, across the gamut. One other thing we in the Jericho Movement understand is that sometimes political prisoners get to prison when they've been involved in organizations. The organizations on the street, on the ground, that they were from—organizations to support them—in many cases just don't exist any longer. But the political prisoners are still there. So we have to deal with this! We have to deal with a unified effort around the issue of freedom and amnesty for all our political prisoners. And that's what the Jericho movement is all about.

This is our first forum that the Jericho Movement has done on the national level, since we came into being on March 27 at the March on Washington. That demonstration was to let the U.S. know, to serve notice, that there's a new commitment to the freedom of our political prisoners. And this is our first forum, because we have been in the midst of building, consolidating, and getting the job done that we started to do to make these things a reality. Mumia Abu-Jamal had a new death warrant signed on October 13, 1999, and the date for execution was set for December 2. We looked at the archives, and we found... but wait—let me go back a minute.

When Mumia had his first "death warrant" signed in 1995, they set his execution date for August 17, 1995. We found that August 17 was in fact the birth date of Marcus Garvey. And so, around the African world there was outcry that you can't do this. You can't use the date of the birth of one of our heroes to assassinate, to martyr, to execute another one of them. And there was a major coming together of people to not just stop the execution of Mumia, but to say you can't slap us in the face with an execution on August 17. And it didn't happen. That death warrant was stayed.

When they signed the new warrant, they really picked another date!—a date that was not only important for the African community, but also important for our allies. December 2, 1999, was the hundred-fortieth commemoration of the lynching, the murder, of radical abolitionist John Brown. How many people know John Brown? The Black community sure knows John Brown! Because I remember the first ditty I ever heard was "John Brown's body lies a-mouldering in his grave and his truth is marching on." That's the first time I heard the name John Brown, when I was just a child. Then, as we grew up, we learned what happened at Harper's Ferry, what happened in Virginia, what happened in terms of a white activist who didn't just talk of freeing the slaves, but who actually led people to take up arms in defense of the slaves, fighting the slave system. And so we said, December 2? It can't be!

Two days following December 2—December 4, 1999—was the thirtieth anniversary of the murder of two Black Panthers: Fred Hampton and Mark Clark. When the state moved off December 2, and Mumia got another stay of execution, we in the Jericho Movement decided that this was a date we had to do something on. We've decided to put together this forum on John Brown, Mumia Abu-Jamal and all political prisoners. There is a connection between all of this.

Our panelists today are:

- Gilda Sherrod-Ali, our lead attorney. She's the acting attorney of Jericho Legal Defense Fund.
- Laura Whitehorn, former political prisoner, after doing, how many years, Laura? *["Fourteen and change—and the change counts!", Laura replies, to rousing applause.]*
- Meg Starr of Resistance in Brooklyn (RnB), who's also organizing John Brown 2000—a conference around John Brown and what we can do today in the spirit of John Brown.
- Elombe Brath, the people's historian, host of WBAI Radio's *Afrikaleidoscope.*
- Rosemari Mealy, activist and former Black Panther Party member.

Meg Starr: Resistance in Brooklyn (RnB), my collective, wanted to do something to commemorate the 200th birthday of John Brown in May this year, and when we were putting together our ideas about it, one of the things that motivated us was a story from the Puerto Rican independence movement. The Puerto Rican movement had a minor revolution in the 1950s—which was actually rather major—and over five thousand people went to jail. Almost none of us know about these events here in the U.S., but the Jayuya Rebellion is a significant part of contemporary Puerto Rican resistance history. The longest held of those five thousand political prisoners were the "five Nationalists," and most of us do know at least some of their names: Lolita Lebrón, Rafael Cancel Miranda, Oscar Collazo, Irvin Flores and Andrés Figueroa. That they were joined by five thousand other folk on the island, some of them doing fairly lengthy time, a lot of people don't know. In the wreckage of the movement that fell apart after that revolution was over, and as the intense repression and jailing was occurring, two leaders emerged who were, coincidentally, married to each other—Juan Antonio Corretjer and Consuela Lee Corretjer.

One of the first things that the Corretjers started doing was an annual com-memoration of the 1950s Jayuya Rebellion. These commemorations started with the two of them going to the mountain town of Jayuya, putting some flowers on the graves of the martyrs who were buried there. Eventually, the annual events became a rallying point, as the independence movement re-emerged in the 1970s and grew strong again. When we claim history for ourselves, and don't let the powers that be lie about it, we claim it as a point of consciousness for ourselves and a rallying point for the movement. That's why we wanted to rescue John Brown in the two hundredth year of his birth.

Over the last couple of years, RnB has been holding events at the time of John Brown's birthday. At each one of those events, we've taken one of the white anti-imperialist political prisoners and we've commemorated their life, putting it in a historical context, making the connections with John Brown and his life. We've done this as a way of claiming our prisoners at this current time period, showing that they come out of a particular movement context, and showing that we can educate about them in new ways. We've focused thus far on David Gilbert and Marilyn Buck, two anti-Vietnam war activists who were involved with Students for a Democratic Society and who became antiracist allies of the Black Liberation Army.

There are two ways that John Brown is seen in history that are incorrect. One of the ways they take away our power is to lie to us about history. A common caricature is to see John Brown as this fanatic who was just crazed, who went out on his own and did stuff. This, I think, is the worst interpreta-tion of Brown's life. The other way people often see him is as this lone, very brave, guy—who was sort of ahead of his times. Neither of these two inter-pretations is really true.

When I was in college, I just adored the white abolitionists, fighting against slavery. Every course I took, I made it a point to try to turn the course around so I could do all my research, and write all my papers, about the Grimké Sisters and all those folks. It wasn't until I got out of college and I got to New York City (thank goodness!), and heard from leaders of the Black lib-eration movement and the white anti-imperialist movement, that I realized that the white abolitionist movement of the 1800s was an outgrowth of the Black movement of that time. The abolitionists were profoundly influenced and related to the very real war that Black people were waging for their own liberation. Despite all my studies at a "top" university, I didn't realize this basic fact until after I got out of college. That's just one example of how racist, bourgeois historians take us away from the truth of what's going on.

If you look at John Brown in the context of the Black movement of that time, he was one brave soldier out of many brave soldiers. Some of the steps that he took may have been tactical errors, but they were part of an ongoing war that was being waged. Yes, he was one of the martyrs of that movement (and important because he was a white activist who was willing to go beyond talk and take militant action), but there were many unsung martyrs of that movement. We all know of Harriet Tubman, and the uprisings around the Underground Railroad, and undoubtedly Tubman was more successful at clandestinity than John Brown. But we must understand—as they themselves understood—that they were all part of this larger war, in which Brown becomes one brave soldier among many. Brown should be significant to us not because he was "one great white man," but because he saw what the Black movement's overall strategy was, and he wanted to participate in it. He wasn't diverging from it, he wasn't going off on his own, he wasn't telling the Black movement, "Well you're really doing things the wrong way, and we should be doing things some this other way." Brown wanted to participate, in the most serious way possible, in the larger freedom struggle.

I'd be glad to answer more questions on John Brown from a historical point of view, but I really wanted to talk a little bit about being white allies right now, about how we draw together "white allies" in this current period of time. How do we make a more significant mark in what's happening now with imperialism at this moment in time? How can we best support the struggles of the oppressed nations within the U.S., and outside of U.S. borders, at this moment in history?

One of the things I've been thinking about in that context is that Mumia has triggered an amazing international movement, both by the quality of his resistance on death row and by the quality of his life. I think one of our tasks is to make people aware of what he represents as an individual, but beyond being an individual, as a part of an oppressed nation with a real history of struggle. When you look at Mumia, he was a brilliant teenager and a Minister of Communications for the Black Panther Party before he was even in his twenties. Then, there was a lull in the movement (after a period of intense government Counter Intelligence Program/COINTELPRO repression), and Mumia starts working for a newspaper that's fairly mainstream, and he's very successful really. Nevertheless, he can't stop "teachin'" from the traditional sense of the word. He can't stop teaching, he has to write about the incredible corruption of the Philadelphia police at that time, even though that was dangerous to do. He has to teach about what's going on with MOVE. He can't leave his people behind him, and he must have known at some point that he was going to face consequences for that. He knew that there would be consequences for him, as well as his family, and those consequences could change his life.

When you listen to tapes of Fred Hampton's speeches, you can understand that that man knew that he could face consequences. Hampton's saying that whatever consequences he faced, he was part of a movement that went beyond the consequences, and that his strength could also go beyond. As an individual you think you want to protect yourself, but if you think of yourself as part of this incredible movement, you can go beyond certain kinds of things. And Mumia has gone beyond these things in his life. His revolutionary character, I think, is what draws people to him. Here he is on death row, yet he never makes a statement that is just personal. His statements are about himself, but they are also always teaching about the entire world of oppressed peoples. He never doesn't do that! I think that this is one of the key reasons why he has motivated so many people to want to work on his case.

When you look at the white community in particular, we have the white radicals—white revolutionaries who want to be allies of the Black movement and movements around the world right now. We have a responsibility to take his case and make the people who are moved by Mumia understand they're not just moved because he's a victim of tremendous insults, which he is. He's a victim in a certain sense of the word, but also he's incredibly strong, and part of a larger movement. The strength of the Black liberation movement is exemplified by this soldier, this one soldier who's on death row right now. We have to challenge people to see the strength of that entire movement. And in a very specific way, I want to challenge people to build the Jericho Movement as part of building our work around Mumia.

This is something that the political prisoners themselves have been talking about. There's a concern from one of the anti-imperialist prisoners and one of the Black Liberation movement prisoners, from David Gilbert and Herman Bell, that we make these links. They sent out a call, along with many political prisoners under the banner of the Jericho Movement, urging people to say that this is the year, 2000-2001, for all campaigns around political prisoners to have a focus on Mumia, because his life is at stake.

There have been calls from people like Native American political prisoner Standing Deer, who's got bad health and has been in prison for twenty-five years, who have said that what's important right now is that Mumia might lose his life. And if the community of political prisoners is prioritizing Mumia in a certain way right now, I think we on the outside should also, while at the same time remembering all the political prisoners and remembering that he comes from a movement. The Black liberation movement, the New Afrikan independence movement, has the major number of political prisoners held in the U.S.—dozens and dozens and dozens who have been jailed for many many years. There are the Native American prisoners, and white anti-imperialists, and still some Puerto Rican prisoners of war, in spite of the great victories of this fall when eleven of them were released. We must remember all this in the building of Jericho. If one looks around for the unified strategies of the Black radical movement at this time, Jericho is a unified strategy.

We need to try to draw people into an understanding of that. Yet we also need the help of people, whether or not they're going to understand the full revolutionary context of the political prisoners and the power of the Black movement. We still need to get something from them. Sometimes I think we get very oversimplified. We want only the people with the full radical commitment; we don't reach out to everybody. We have to reach out to everybody on their level. I met a revolutionary white clandestine member of the African National Congress during the period of the rise of the South African liberation movement in the 1980s, just before they won power. And one of the things he talked about was splitting the white community. They weren't trying to just get revolutionary white people over to the ANC. They were also trying to neutralize white people and to split communities where there were people they were never going to win over. They did, for example, manage to persuade a lot of white people in South Africa that they didn't want to join the army, that they didn't want to go into the Black communities and fight in there. Some of the reasons white people resisted the South African Defense Forces were for self-preservation and self-interest, not for good, principled, antiracist reasons. But we have to be able to reach out, to have a multi-level strategy, where we're working on many different levels to free the prisoners.

Not everybody has to agree with everything to be involved in some level of these efforts. As white revolutionaries, we've got to argue for a broad, historical picture that understands the need for militant action. But we also have to have levels that we argue for that are not so militant, but mass. We must say, simply: no one can be a responsible anti-death penalty advocate without doing something around Mumia this year. There are simple levels as well as broad levels. These are some of our considerations.

When we're trying to fight white supremacy, we believe it has to be a dialogue between white activists and people of color activists all the time. Because I don't think white people can fight white supremacy on their own. We've been brought up and educated in a tremendously white supremacist system, and white privileges are part of our everyday lives no matter how we resist them. We have to keep that dialogue open and keep being aware of the things that affect us. That's why I call on white people to look at strategy, building Jericho in a certain kind of context. We have friends, for example, who have done some great work in the *Race Traitor* movement, talking about "abolishing the concept of whiteness." They've also been doing commemorations of John Brown, though from a somewhat more academic viewpoint. Well, *Race Traitor* wrote a paper in 1999 in which they had questions for the Mumia movement, such as "How is the Mumia movement reinforcing whiteness," and "Why isn't the Mumia movement doing this and that." The thing is, for the most part *Race Traitor* hasn't been working in the Mumia movement, or in the movement to free all U.S. political prisoners. Yes, it's important to raise questions about strategy, and to talk within a movement about strategy and tactics. But to stand on the outside, as white activists looking in at an effort that has been led by the Black movement... this is what reinforces white supremacy.

We may not be where we want to be around the movement to free political prisoners in this country, but we've got to look at certain realities. The 1998 Jericho rally itself was the biggest demonstration for a generation around the general issue of U.S. political prisoners. The freedom this year of the eleven Puerto Rican prisoners wasn't under the terms they would have liked, but it was a major triumph of the movement. It empowered people in Puerto Rico to continue their resistance and win, at this moment, another strategic victory around Vieques. Clinton's recent announcement that he is not going to bomb Vieques [editor's note: this agreement was subsequently, and not surprisingly, retracted] is only because of the unity on the part of the Puerto Rican people. We know that the minute something changes, the U.S. could continue bombing, but there is still a victory in this period. We've had some victories, and we have some strengths.

And I'm just in admiration of the level of unity in the Black movement that's led to some of these victories and strengths. I'm hoping we can look at these often obscured realities, and recognize them at the moment they're happening. That's what will give us the power to go on, to form respectful alliances and to do our necessary work. By working for and with the liberations movements, we can break through our feelings of disempowerment that are developed by bourgeois society, the feelings of invisibility of the power of the Black community that's fostered by bourgeois society. We have to break through it, to see how it's affecting our daily activism, and rebuild our own movements stronger than ever.

Gilda Sherrod-Ali (Jericho Legal Defense Fund): I am the acting director of the Jericho Legal Defense Fund and also the co-chair of the Criminal Justice Conference of the National Conference of Black Lawyers. I want to talk about the legal challenges that we face in this movement. I read a quote by one of the political prisoners (Ojore Lutalo), who indicated that, and I'm going to loosely quote him, that "any movement which does not revere and support its political prisoners and prisoners of war is a sham movement." And I agree with that wholeheartedly. Because the people who are incarcerated, jailed, in captivity, in the U.S. penitentiaries and state penitentiaries across the country, are people who have never given up the idea of a free and just society, be they anti-imperialists, Puerto Rican nationalists, Afrikan nationalists.

I want to talk a little bit about some of the legal challenges that are faced by our heroes and sheroes (because that's what they are) and why there is this absolute necessity, not only for Jericho, but for the Jericho Legal Defense Fund. Because there is nothing worse than to have one of our brothers or sisters in prison serving eighty years—like Marilyn Buck and Mutulu Shakur—received eighty years imprisonment. And while they're there, they're confronted with a legal issue, they have to do the work themselves. They have to do their own paper work. You know about this. So what are we doing out here? Benefiting, really. Because there wouldn't have been any civil rights without the Black Power movement. That's a fact... benefiting from their sacrifice, and not giving them the support and energy that they deserve and need.

The Jericho Legal Defense Fund is necessary to provide legal assistance, for those who need it. I just work pro bono, and there are lawyers who work without a fee, pro bono. Some lawyers need some compensation; we need to provide the compensation to them. It is also needed to pay legal expenses, travel expenses where necessary, and travel expenses can be huge because they scatter political prisoners all across the country, and not only that, but they move them constantly. We need to raise the issue nationally, and consistently, about political prisoners and prisoners of war. So how does legal defense raise the issue? Whenever you are litigating any issue, you get a heightened degree of publicity. It happens all the time, and though it does not happen as much with political prisoners' cases, it still does happen, and we can make it happen even more.

The Jericho Legal Defense Fund is necessary, now and in the foreseeable future. Why do I say that? I say that, in part, based on the correspondence that I receive from political prisoners/POW's, such as Marilyn Buck. She's one of the two political prisoners who serve on the board of Jericho Legal Defense Fund. The other is Sundiata Acoli. Marilyn Buck indicated in her correspondence to me that she disagreed with one of the statements about defining what a political prisoner is, because we were talking about just those that exist right now. Marilyn Buck said, "Oh, no, no, no. This thing has to be an ongoing entity. Given the nature of the ongoing state of the union, and the ever-rising up vision of resistance and liberation struggle, there will be more political prisoners." When you know that the battle is an ongoing one, you have to prove that something's going to be around to give that assistance.

Legal challenges that are presented to political prisoners are very, very unique—you heard Safiya say it, and it's true. The U.S. does not recognize political prisoners and POW's inside its borders. Now how can they get away with that? They get away with that because the people who are imprisoned for their political beliefs and political activities are there because they were charged with a violation of a state or federal crime. They went to trial, were found guilty of those charges, and so the U.S. says, "They're just common criminals in jail, they're not political prisoners. They broke the law." So that's how they get away with it. They create this fiction.

Political prisoners don't get treated the same way other criminals do. Take my word for it, I know from my representation of political prisoners, the U.S. doesn't treat them the same way. They treat them very distinctly. And it is highly, highly, highly oppressive. I want you to think now, everybody in here, just take a minute to think about this. What state of mind would you be in, if you were kept in solitary confinement locked in a room, only let out for an hour day, year after year, after your fifteenth and sixteenth and seventeenth and eighteenth year on end? What state of mind would be you in? Could you be as strong as Russell "Maroon" Shoats? That's the question. And that is why we have to come to the aid of our political prisoners and POW's. They are treated differently.

They are kept, not only in solitary confinement, but housed in the most secure and maximum units in the country. Many of our political prisoners have been held for many years in Marion, Illinois, or in Florence, Colorado, in "MDX," a maximum prison inside a maximum prison. It's a control center, a behavior modification center. The U.S. government is involved in behavior modification, and they do it to political prisoners and POW's. They are moved constantly from one institution to another, particularly when a political prisoner/POW becomes involved in organizing from within the institution, or becomes a legal assistant to other prisoners inside of the institution. Or even begins legal actions on his or her own behalf. The prison gets wind of it, and right away for "administrative reasons" they find a way to transfer them. They can transfer them within a facility, or from one facility to another. Political prisoners are specially monitored by the Bureau of Prisons in Washington, DC, at a central monitoring unit. If you're a political prisoner/POW, the warden of the prison where you are cannot authorize your move. Your move is authorized from Washington. They give them this different treatment, but they say "Oh no, you're not a political prisoner."

When they're moved, it's disruptive. It is terribly, terribly disruptive. It has a disruptive effect on the political prisoners/POW's, and on their legal advisors, and their families. Once again, the prisoner becomes separated from their family and their supporters. It takes sometimes a week before people know where they are and can catch up with them. Their mail gets interrupted; it has to be rerouted. Their magazines have to be rerouted. Their property gets separated from them. And when their property gets separated from them, their legal papers get separated from them. If you're in the middle of litigation, you've got to chase down your client's legal papers. I know when I was working on a case with Dr. Mutulu Shakur, it was just a horror story, when we had to chase his papers down. His moves took him from Atlanta to Springfield, Missouri. Then his papers were shipped someplace else. It was not even Atlanta or Springfield, so it was really a horror story. The contacts made within a prison by a political prisoner/POW are disrupted when there is a move. They have contacts that they make. Imagine you, if you moved around a lot as a kid, or moved around a lot, now as an adult, you make contacts in your community, where you live. When you move, those contacts get disrupted.

When they are moved, the lawyer has to go through a situation of reestablishing connections with the people in the prison. Now it's not easy dealing with these people, I'm going to tell you. You have to deal with their legal staff, you've got to deal with their lawyers, you've got to deal with any number of counselors who are supposed to be working with your client. [Laughter] Laura is laughing, because some counselors work only in the day time, other counselors work only at night. And another counselor comes in only on the weekends. And you have this whole plethora of people, none of whom seem to know who the other one is. When your client gets moved, you've got to deal with a whole new group, some of whom are almost human, and some of whom haven't got a clue as to how to be nice, even on a good day. So it becomes even more of a challenge just to connect with your client, to keep your client's paperwork intact, and to make sure that you and your client can communicate while you're litigating the case.

When political prisoners/POW's are moved, from one institution to another, they are kept in segregation, called Segregated Housing Units or SHU's, or what I like to call the box. Because that's what it is, it's a little box. I mean they can barely lay out. If you're really tall, like some of them are, you can barely stretch out from end to end inside this little cramped cell that they put you in. And you are totally segregated. They take you out twice a week for a shower. They let you run around in an enclosed area for an hour a day, if they give you that, an enclosed area for recreation purposes. This is not outside! This is enclosed inside the prison. This is also supposed to be where you go so they can do a medical exam of you and a psychological, and they have to run some other tests and they have to do this and that. It's just a lot of b.s. to keep a man or woman separated from the population until they decide whether they're going to put them in population or keep them in isolation.

Every time a political prisoner/POW is moved, they are moved into a SHU. They don't just go right into population in new prison. That doesn't happen. And if you are a lawyer advocating for your client, you've got to be on top of that, otherwise they'll keep your client in that SHU for months. When they're in the SHU, they have limited or no phone contact. The lawyer may be able to have some phone contact, but they don't have any phone contact with anybody else. No phone contact. Everything is monitored, and as a lawyer you really have to stay on top of that. And it takes a lot of time. It takes a lot of effort, and it takes a lot of work. And oftentimes, just a phone call or a letter won't work. You've got to send a certain kind of letter to let them know that if they don't do something real quick you're going to sue them in court... and have the papers ready to sue them in court. Don't just have an empty threat out there. Be ready. So that when what is supposed to happen doesn't happen, you file it in court, and all of a sudden they say, "Oh, we were going to do that! ... We were going to do that, we were going to move him... Ms. Ali, you didn't have to sue us." But you didn't move him by the deadline date! You have to be ready, and that takes time and that takes commitment on the behalf of the attorneys who do this.

While they're in the SHU (or even when they're not in the SHU), political prisoners—who are not supposed to be monitored illegally—often have their legal connection violated; their private attorney/client mail is often "accidentally" opened. [Laura adds here, "more often than not."] Their telephone calls are monitored, and they're not supposed to be monitored. You get into the habit, when you're talking to your client, of saying "If there's anybody else on this line that's listening to this phone call they better not use anything we say or we will have to sue them in court." Monitoring calls between attorney and client violates basic attorney/client privilege.

In addition to these obvious challenges that I have just told you, when you start litigating the case, when you start trying to prove your client's case, you see all the differences in how political prisoners and other prisoners are treated. For the ordinary person who's in prison for a social crime, it might be quite easy to begin litigation. Even if it's difficult, you don't have to jump through the hurdles and hoops that you would as a political prisoner. I'm going to give you an example, then I'll stop after this. I'm one of the attorneys, along with Karl Franklin, who's working on "Rule 78" for Robert "Seth" Hayes. This is a petition challenging the parole board's decision to deny him parole. In order to make that denial, the board used some things that were outside their guidelines. Well, we cite some really good case law that's on point in terms of Seth's case. In fact, one of the cases that we cite in his petition is a case involving the parole board talking about the political affiliation of the prisoner. And it talks about something to do with the Republican Party vs. the Democratic Party. When, in the case of this precedent, the person was denied parole after a brief discussion of their political affiliation, the courts found that that was enough to grant that prisoner a *de novo* hearing, a new hearing before a judge independent of the parole board. That conversation was egregious enough, talking about somebody's political beliefs.

With a political prisoner, that would not be enough. I'm telling you flat out. We argued the "political belief" issue for Seth, plus other stuff, truly egregious stuff. And we haven't heard anything from the court. It's been almost two months. I'm very optimistic, but when we're arguing a case for a political prisoner, we have to say not only that they used this information about his political beliefs to deny him parole, but a whole bunch of other stuff. They don't use the same standard, so we have to work harder. We need more help, greater access to materials, to assistance. We need more money, we need more researchers, we need more assistance to help our political prisoners. And until we get that more, we're not going to be able to do all the things we need to do. So I'm glad that you are here, I hope that more people will support the Jericho Movement, and also support the Jericho Legal Defense Fund, so that we can provide this "more" for the political prisoners/POW's.

If we don't do this for them, they're not going to get what they deserve, they're not going to get the kind of help that they need. It would be truly a wrongful act for us to continue to have our political prisoners working on their own behalf trying to litigate these cases. Even though some of them are really good in terms of their abilities to learn new stuff about the legalities and the law, they're not lawyers. And those of us who are lawyers, and some of us are pretty good lawyers, if we're going to do this, we need to make sacrifices. Like my grandmother always said, you don't gain anything in life without sacrifice. You can't imagine going from Point A to Point B without making some sacrifice. So, we want to make this sacrifice, but we need everybody to make some sacrifices and support the Jericho Legal Defense Fund and the Jericho Movement.

Laura Whitehorn: I'm really glad to be here, and I mean that on a lot of different levels! I want to thank the people who do the Jericho work, I've got to tell you, because when we first got the word that Jericho was going to happen... the idea first came from Jalil Muntaqim, a New Afrikan political prisoner. And anyone who's been in the anti-imperialist movement or the Black liberation movement for a lot of years knows that Jalil has had a lot of good ideas over the years and some of them have been taken up and some of them haven't. I remember in 1979, when he came up with the idea of a petition to the U.N. saying that the situation of Black people in the U.S. is a human rights violation in and of itself, not just because of slavery. The petition would note that the West has never made up for that, and also note the oppression that exists right up to today. That petition was taken up a few days before Assata Shakur was liberated. When the Jericho idea was taken up too, we all celebrated!

Until the fact that there are political prisoners in this country is recognized by every progressive person and then on into the communities, the government is never going to say a word or do a thing. I could give examples of all the things that Gilda said, because it's all true and it all happened to me, it happened to my comrades. I want to tell just one thing that just happened to me a couple of days ago. I was on the train riding to my sister's house for Thanksgiving. She lives in New Jersey and I was with my girlfriend. And all of a sudden she heard me go "Huh!" and she said "What happened?" I looked out the window and saw these cages outside; I thought it was a prison. And as we're looking, as the train is pulling away, it was a kennel. I said, "Yeah, that's right, that's what you feel like when you're in one of those cages, when you're in the hole." I was held in solitary confinement for a year, and that's the kind of place I had to exercise. We used to go out there and bark, kidding around, ha ha. Everything Gilda said is true.

I want to talk about three things, and I will be brief. I was really happy to be asked to speak today because Fred Hampton and John Brown and Mumia and all the rest of the political prisoners are my heroes. First I want to talk about Fred Hampton a little bit. And I guess the context for talking about Fred Hampton is to talk about the 1960s. In prison, I was in a very tight collective of women political prisoners, most recently with Marilyn Buck and Linda Evans, Carmen Valentín, Dylcia Pagán and Lucy and Alicia Rodríguez. And we all came out of the 60s. We had a certain language together, and as I got out I realized we speak a language about the 60s that is probably spoken by some people in this room and not by others. What we talk about, when we're talking about the 60s, is not just about the level of demonstrations, important as they were. We're not just talking about the Black Panther Party as a mass movement that captured the imagination and the passion and the aspirations of thousands and thousands of people in this country, important as that was. We're not just talking about the antiwar movement, and the fact that young people in this country said, for a variety of reasons: "No. We're not going to allow our government to do this to the people of another country." All of those things are part of the 60s. When I talk about the 60s, what I'm talking about is the fact that it was the high tide of national liberation around the world. All of those things that we saw in the 60s were an expression of that.

Underneath it all, what that period meant was that all the injustices that we have grown up with—and that we still see today that I hated as a kid even though I didn't really understand them—those things could be changed. People around the world, oppressed nations, were wising up and overthrowing colonialist regimes. That's what was happening in the 1960s, and it was a very significant change in the nature of the world. It meant that the imperialists, the colonialists, the ruling class—whatever you want to call them—couldn't hold on to their properties and their nations of people. It meant that there was something called People's War, which was put into effect not only in Vietnam, but in nations in Africa and in Latin America. Finally, to someone like me—to someone who had grown up just dissatisfied with the nature of this country, and particularly disliking racism—it became clear that there were people out there fighting for change.

For some reason, I can't explain it, but as a little kid before I knew anything about anything, I just hated that what I saw in front of me was lies—that we lived in a democratic system and then I would go into Harlem and see that people in Harlem didn't have the same opportunities that people in white communities had. It was just as plain as that. So all of a sudden, to me and to other people around the world, there was this strategy and there was something happening that was changing things. Instead of just thinking, "We've got to fight racism, we've got to fight racism forever and ever and ever," all of a sudden there was this strategy that could actually overturn the system that produced racism. That's what the Panthers were a part of, to me.

My own relationship to the whole thing, to the murder of Fred Hampton, was very personal—because he was the person who organized me to go from being kind of a liberal to being a revolutionary. In study groups that I was part of with the Panthers in Chicago, he heard things that I was saying which he took a step further. Fred said to me, "You know, you're not going to like this because it's going to mean a big change in your life, but I think you really mean what you're saying. You've got to become a revolutionary, and not just a progressive, good-hearted person." And I took that seriously. He inspired me, and the Panthers inspired me and hundreds of other people. Marilyn Buck could sit here and tell you a very similar thing. For her it wasn't Chicago, it was California. Linda Evans could tell you a similar thing; it wasn't Chicago, it was Michigan. For Susan Rosenberg, a similar thing; she was ten years younger than me but it happened to her here in New York. And I think that this is true for all the anti-imperialist political prisoners—the Ohio 7, Tommy Manning and Ray Levasseur could tell you a similar thing coming out of the Army. To me, that's the continuity between the fact that we're commemorating the 30th anniversary of the assassinations of Fred Hampton and Mark Clark and we're celebrating political prisoners, because that's where we come from.

There was a sense of power that was available if people were willing to sacrifice and struggle and fight to take it. There was a sense of fury at the government, because when Fred was murdered, some things became clear. People would remember, if anyone has had the chance to see the movie *The Murder of Fred Hampton*. I used to say to friends of mine who weren't in the movement, "The FBI is watching us. They're infiltrating. This guy who came to a meeting the other day—I can't tell you why but I know he's an agent. This thing is happening, my phone is tapped." My parents would say, "Right, yeah. And there are UFO's arriving from Mars, too." But twenty years later it's all out on paper, it all was happening. When Fred was killed, everybody knew immediately that he had been set up. We knew that it wasn't just the Chicago police that set him up. It was the FBI—and sure enough after months and months, it was finally exposed that the FBI had put an informant and an agent into Fred's security circle. On the very night that Fred was killed, he was kind of drugged, and couldn't get up out of the bed. His kool-aid had been drugged by this FBI agent William O'Neal, who later killed himself after admitting his involvement.

I'm going to say something now that, if my lawyer were here, she'd probably kill me! When Fred Hampton was killed, I wasn't in Chicago anymore—I was in Weatherman. I was in Cleveland, and it was the first time that I tried to engage in active armed struggle, because I was so infuriated. Once again, Malcolm X had been killed; that's how I saw it. Once again, someone who was a leader... you can't tell just from tapes of Fred speaking. You would go to a church on the west side of Chicago. The church would be packed, wall to wall people, and it wasn't "the left," it wasn't students, it was the entire Black community. There'd be a bunch of young white people and a bunch of Puerto Rican people too. In Chicago, there were Puerto Rican gangs and Black gangs, and the Puerto Rican gangs became united with the Young Lords Party and the Black gangs became united with the Black Panther Party. That's one of the reasons the police were so terrified. And Fred would open his mouth and you could see on everyone's face that he was saying things that all of us had felt in our hearts and in our guts. He was articulating them. I can say this as an antiracist white person; for the Black people there, it must have been even more true. Fred was twenty-one, maybe twenty-two years old. He had been a leader since he was in high school right outside of Chicago. That's just who he was. When he was killed, I just said, "They killed Malcolm X again."

Fred's assassination made me understand on a deeper level what this government is capable of and what it's going to take to win justice. What were people really asking for? The Black Panthers were asking for a basic program of land, independence, freedom, bread, food, housing. You know, basic democratic rights. What it took to put them down was murders and assassinations and putting people in prison. On the other hand, the Panthers held out that hope that I was talking about before, the hope of taking power. That's why we still say to each other "Power to the People" when we leave a message on each other's phone machines. And it still does mean something.

I agree with what Meg said in the beginning about Mumia. The government trying to murder Mumia is not so different from the government that murdered Malcolm X and Fred Hampton. We couldn't stop it the other times. We couldn't stop them from murdering Martin Luther King. But this time we've got a lot of lead time, and we've got to do whatever we can to stop them from murdering Mumia.

One last thing—I just want to say that, even though I "maxed out" of prison, I'm still on parole. Go figure! I never went to the parole board, but somehow I ended up on parole. I did all of my time, and I had "good days," under the law that folks used to be tried under before 1987. I had loads of good days accumulated, that I would lose every time I would get in trouble, then I would get them back. But despite all that, I'm not allowed to speak to Linda or Marilyn or Susan or David Gilbert or Sundiata Acoli or Mutulu or anyone. I do know, once you've been in prison with people and in clandestinity with people, you kind of know what they're thinking even if they don't tell you. I know that they send their solidarity, and that they say: "Free Mumia! Free all Political Prisoners!"

When Gilda said that Marilyn Buck said that there were going to be more political prisoners, she really knows that because Marilyn was in prison first in 1972 or '73. She was arrested in California for buying two boxes of ammunition... just some little bullets which were for the Black Panther Party! It wasn't like cop-killer bullets or dum-dums. Yet she went to prison, and she got ten years. She was given a furlough, because in those days people were allowed out. When she was in prison, she was there with Assata. And she was in prison with Lolita Lebrón, who was one of the five Puerto Rican nationalists that Meg was talking about in the beginning. When Marilyn went on a furlough, she didn't go back to prison—so they considered that an escape. And what she did then wasn't to high tail it out of the country and go find a place to live a life of ease. She came right back into the struggle. Which is how she ended up being arrested the same day I was in 1985. Marilyn was in prison when there were a handful of women political prisoners, and then she was in prison again when there were a lot more women political prisoners. She knows from her own experience that there are political prisoners from different struggles and different years. And the struggle continues.

Elombe Brath: It's a great pleasure to be once again at the Brecht Forum, this time with the Jericho Movement to deal with the question of John Brown, Mumia, Fred Hampton and all political prisoners. I wanted to piggyback on what Gilda said before about Marilyn Buck. Given the nature of the ongoing struggle, there's going to be a lot more political prisoners... I testified for Mutulu in his case. I was there when Mutulu and Marilyn got their time. And I think one of the things that we really need in this movement is some time to be able to document what people say. If the people who we're trying to attract could have just heard both Mutulu and Marilyn as they stood before the judge, with the fine spirit to talk about what they believed in and why they felt no shame for what they were charged with having done. They were ready to go on into prison. Of course, I can't repeat it verbatim; one of the things we need to do is go back and get some of those transcripts and print them out so people can see the kind of character that the political prisoners we're talking about have. When people see that, they'd have to ask themselves what they would have done in that particular case.

The fact is, when you start to look at what happened 140 years ago with John Brown, we should lay down the paradigm for what African peoples expected of European people in the society, and the kind of person you'd have to be in order to show that you should be anti-imperialist and antiracist. Because John Brown was not alone.

He took some of his sons with him. For a man to give up his sons, to get his sons involved and then see them die, it shows the tremendous commitment of that particular person. That's the reason why, when people say John Brown, many Black people who happen to be nationalists get up and salute. They realize what he was all about.

If you look at what the *Village Voice* did a couple of weeks ago on their cover, in a photo-realism painting of Mumia on a gurney, you see them really trying to project a mind set of acceptance of Mumia being killed. To me, in a certain way, although Peter Noel, who I understand had something to do with that cover, said yesterday that it was for the shock value, I think that it's just as slimy as TV commentator Sam Donaldson. Sam Donaldson is more outright trying to say that Mumia should die. That was kind-of the artist's suggestion... projecting the killing of Mumia as acceptable for most people. As if that's a foregone conclusion, that it was going to happen.

We have to be able to discern those nuances that people put out, claiming they're doing something for us while really at the same time trying to undermine us in our efforts for our people. We talk about COINTELPRO, and we go back to when J. Edgar Hoover first started out with Marcus Garvey, the first case. Look at the way that Hoover set that case up before there was even a Federal Bureau of Investigation, just a Bureau of Investigation at that time. It was a classic COINTEL-Program that again, as Laura pointed out (and this was pointed out many years ago when the ANC got busted and rounded up in those big South African dragnets), we're "shocked" and we say these people are "diabolical" ... when, in reality, we know all along this is what they want to do. In the case of Fred Hampton and Mark Clark, which took place thirty years ago, we heard all the sordid details. The fact is that, later on, they can still take Fred Hampton, Jr. (Fred's son), and frame him up for causing a fire that torched a Korean shop during the Rodney King uprisings. Fred Hampton, Jr. is carrying on his father's role, not just in trying to organize the gangs as he was doing in Chicago, but also struggling in prison under false charges. I know yesterday they had a big party in Chicago for sister Akua Njeri, Fred Hampton's widow, and I think it's fantastic that you can be witness to a horror that took place thirty years ago, and still engage in struggle. Then they take away your son, and put him away, and you continue to struggle on.

What I'm saying is that there's a particular type of character, that people who are committed to liberation find themselves unable to restrain, and they might become a political prisoner. Although we don't want more political prisoners, we want to have more political victories, and the fact is that we can't worry about imprisonment if we intend to live out the action of liberation.

We have now the demand for reparations. There are some who are trying to put on the indigenous African population the idea that they are responsible for slavery themselves! That Africans engaged in slavery organizing, which is a lie. The Africans didn't have penitentiaries. Penitentiaries are something you see in Europe. One of the ways they finally got rid of prisoners in Europe was to send them off to penal colonies, like the U.S. or New Zealand or Australia. All of these places became penal colonies, and even in this particular place—the U.S.—a lot of people were sent over here. The Africans, while they did take political prisoners, would usually put them in some kind of indentured servitude, or they would even initiate them into their own ethnic group and have them carry on the traditions of that particular ethnicity. They didn't have any problem with letting some of those people be sent away, because they had no idea what was happening on the other side of the Atlantic.

That's not to actually apologize... to give a defense that would be just total. But you do have to realize, in all kinds of struggle, that there are class dimensions. That's what people have to learn today, the fact that class is inextricably intertwined with race. That's one of the things that actually makes a difference in the Black liberation movement. More and more people have understood that it's not simply just racial... there's a class dynamic that starts to give you a new perspective on who your friends are and who your enemies are. And that's one of the things that the Panthers came to acknowledge and were able to make a lot of people around them understand.

I don't know if anyone saw what happened yesterday with this young man, Johnson, an eighteen-year-old that was just getting convicted in Staten Island for killing a policeman. He was convicted of killing a policeman last year when he was seventeen, and the policeman was black. Johnson has a striking resemblance to Mumia... these long dreads; he looks like Mumia. You had to see the media orchestrate this thing. There were all these white cops from Staten Island, and a Black mother, who of course is mourning for her son who got killed. But there's this lasting impression in your mind, and a transfer of identification of this guy and how one cop said, "Because he was seventeen years old when he committed the crime, we couldn't convict him of first degree;" they got him on second degree which means he'll get twenty-five-to-life. One cop was saying about the cop that was killed, "Our dear brother," and "This guy should be getting the death penalty." So the idea is sent out again, that these guys who kill cops or are convicted of killing cops need to get the death penalty. Exactly as Sam Donaldson was arguing.

We have a tremendous responsibility. You realize that the U.S. is the biggest death penalty advocate and practitioner. George Bush is riding high with a whole lot of money behind him to put him into the executive mansion. And you can only imagine if he has about 500 people on death row in Texas, he's actually doing more than Ann Richards. Ann Richards was no slouch either. George Bush's theme was that he'd actually killed more people than Ann Richards! That was his campaign. There's a build-up of people moving into position to concretize these death camps, which is what these prisons have come to be. The U.S. at the World Trade Organization (WTO) argues against China. The rest of them were forced to take a position against China, because China was supposed to be using slave labor. China is a society of a billion people. How many people there are actually involved with this particular "slave" labor? And what about the United States? The United States has the fastest growing prison industry, not just incarcerating people for political crimes, but for any crimes. Many of the "crimes" people are doing are also political, from a social point of view. For a lot of these crimes, people are being framed up. If you look at what's going on in New York State, and you get into the Rockefeller laws, a lot of people who are in prison and get a record should never have been there in the first place. In many cases, if it weren't for race, they wouldn't be in there. There's a subliminal feeling, by a lot of people who have never been in prison, that anyone who's ever been in prison deserved to be there. "After all, they got convicted." They don't look at the machinations of the trial, of the jury selection. They don't look at how the judges are put into position to be hanging judges. Sabo should never have been on Mumia's trial. We had heard about him; when we first went out to see this guy it looked like we were looking at a movie. It was out of a movie of down South. This judge Sabo came out of central casting! So we know that the deck is stacked.

The fact is that at this particular time in history, we are seeing that people are trying to get organized. Who was there, eighty years after the first general strike in this country, that took place in Seattle, with 60,000 workers who walked off? We were going to go in there and shake them up and embarrass them, and make sure the WTO delegates couldn't get in there! We actually put the question of world trade in a place where no one had even thought about, and now people are thinking about it.

Of course, the first "globalization" was slavery. That was a very successful enterprise, enslaving one group of people and misappropriating lands from another group of people—a group of people who showed their charity. Carlos Cook used to say that the African and the Indian were both victims of their own charity. A lot of these societies had legends that one day, over the horizon, were going to come a strange group of people. They argued over whether they should kill them on the beach. There was a big debate, and, of course, the radical people lost out. Therein lies the rub. A lot of people "fell into" imperialism and colonialism. The fact is, we do have a situation where we have to make our people realize that there's a war going on. Twenty years ago, we were arguing that the New York State prison system was the biggest housing project for Blacks and Latinos. This is not new stuff people are talking about. But now, more people are saying it... people are saying, "We know about this prison industrial complex." We're talking about fascism.

We saw this case the other day. Steven Johnson, a graffiti painter who was on WLIB radio, on the Khalid Muhammad show, said he was going to make this painting that replicated Chris Ofili's Madonna [The Holy Virgin Mary]. Chris Ofili was the Nigerian painter based in London that caused the whole controversy with the "Sensation" show. What Steven Johnson has done is to take a picture of [New York Mayor] Giuliani's head, and put it on his painting, and today—to raise money for Housing Works—he was going to charge a dollar a person to throw elephant dung on Giuliani! He had some elephant dung, and a glove to use. The next day, the New York City Police broke into his house, downloaded things off of his computer, took everything they could get out of there including some brass knuckles he had up on a wall (like the old ceremonial swords), and charged him with having a weapon. I'm telling you what's happening right now in New York City! They got a judge to sign a search warrant... but what kind of law are we coming to? When we talked about fascism before, people thought we were outrageous.

Fascism doesn't have to come like it came in Europe. This is a unique society. And, of course, within a unique society there will be new ways to deal with this thing. A couple of weeks ago, Clinton was surrounded by all of these Republicans and Democrats, all of them agreeing on the new Latin American relations in banking. They all agree that this is a good thing. Isn't Clinton the same guy we were trying to lynch over his sexual proclivities? They're all smiling together, because this is something they realize is the business of America: global trade, and utilizing slave labor all over the world. They're the ones who are actually creating the systems that have other people brutalizing their own people in order for them to get into the game. What we have now is a unipolar world, with the U.S. at the top. Of course, you have these slight skirmishes within it, within the European allies, but for the most part we're looking at a very dangerous situation.

I just wanted to close out in saying, the Native American people feel (though they don't talk about it much) that the Europeans who came here—though under the aristocrats and land owners—didn't come from a democratic society and didn't use the word democracy. They learned about democracy from the Iroquois, the Great Law of Peace. Benjamin Franklin and Jefferson, all the laws from the Great Law of Peace showed them how to set up the United States of America. So Europeans didn't just steal the land, they even stole the governing principles that were already here at that time. You really see how callous these people are who govern society. At the same time that they were saying "We hold these truths to be self-evident, that all men are created equal, that they are endowed by the creator, with certain inalienable rights, among them life, liberty and the pursuit of happiness," George Washington had four hundred slaves on his cotton plantation in Mt. Vernon. Thomas Jefferson had slaves at his plantation in Monticello, Virginia. Benjamin Franklin was arguing that he didn't want the sons of Guinea being born any more in this country, because they were darkening the country too much. Already the native population was "too tawny." Some of the Europeans, such as Swedes and Germans, were too swarthy and could not be compared to Englishmen. So there were these kinds of dynamics. For them to go outside and talk about the paradigm of democracy and freedom is the biggest joke in the world.

Because we don't have an education about what really happened to us, we go along with it. We're taught to say that Columbus discovered America and we can't pass kindergarten if we say something different. In reality, it was the Indian's that discovered Columbus on the beach!

We have a mandate. When we start talking about the Jericho Movement, and we start talking about a person like Jalil—who is a brilliant theoretician... We used to go up to Green Haven prison a lot, when both Jalil and Robert "Seth" Hayes were there. When you sit down and talk with Seth, he is so calm—even though he's done all that time. You would not believe the spirit of the people who have been convicted as political prisoners. The people who cry the most are the real criminals who should be in jail. As Richard Pryor said, they need some penitentiaries for some of these people because some of them are just out here, off the hook. But the political prisoners, the people who can make a decisive change, have decided to make that contribution in Jericho. That's why you have the New Afrikan Liberation Front. These kinds of things are coming up because there's no more division between those people inside who were incarcerated... they're still a part of this movement. They are not alienated, they're not disrespected. They have the highest respect. When someone comes out from inside, people listen. Because they're speaking from experience of what they've undergone, being totally under control of the state.

We have to take ourselves a little more seriously. We're going to have to figure out how to make this movement grow bigger, because we're going into the year 2000. The state has already established what it's going to do. And they know they're going to have a big fight. If they'd done what they said they were going to do on Thursday, December 2 (Mumia's execution date), a lot of this country would have been in smoke. A lot of people are very serious about different ways they want to act and respond. They know that if what they were dealing with was embarrassing in Seattle, try killing Mumia. We have to consolidate our movement to be much stronger than it is now, because we're fighting against a very formidable enemy and one that is not taking any prisoners—no pun intended. Peace.

Safiya Bukhari: In the very beginning of the major work around Mumia, the political prisoners started "Art and Writings against the Death Penalty: Political Prisoners Unite to Save Mumia." They sent out their writings and their artwork, and it was out on tour across the country, raising awareness about Mumia's condition. One of the things over the years that has been done by the political prisoners, who are in terrible conditions themselves, has been to push us to focus work around Mumia. I know, I was working on the New York 3 case—was one of the few working on it—and I literally got a waiver from them to start working on Mumia's case before there got to be as much work being done on it.

People must recognize that Mumia's case is not just about Mumia; it's about all political prisoners. And it's not just about the political prisoners, it's about those of us who are involved in political work in general. If the government of the U.S. is allowed to get away with using the death penalty as a means of political repression, then that's the way it's going to go for all of us. If they can continue to keep political prisoners isolated from their communities, they're going to do that. And if they can keep the idea of political action, of people being involved in a revolutionary struggle, out of the minds of people, they'll do that by keeping political prisoners in prison and by using the death penalty for political repression too. That's the message we have to get out here.

This is why John Brown is important. He took political action in the form of militant action. You can't just talk about revolution, you can't just talk about what needs to be done, you've got to take the steps to make sure it happens. This is also why Mumia is so important. One of the things that people say all the time is, "How come you can't just write about it, use the pen? Why do you have to deal with armed struggle?" If nothing else, we've learned from Mumia's case, from Mumia as a revolutionary journalist. He was a major threat because he did not take a back-step. He worked to expose and educate people about what was going on. Frank Rizzo said about him, "You're the kind of journalist that creates a problem. Be careful that this does not come back to haunt you." And it haunted him.

On the night the incident occurred, he was there and he became a target because he was on the scene, and they wanted to find a way to silence Mumia. If we're not careful… if we don't champion the issue of political prisoners/POW's and don't build a movement that recognizes the contributions of these people and the fact that they're in there because of the work they've done, then they'll try to silence us all. Not just because of the ideas… the ideas are threatening enough… but because many of the political prisoners acted on their ideas. They were willing to put their lives on the line, to open the doors that many of us don't even realize were opened by the work of political prisoners/POW's. That's why this forum is on the meaning of John Brown, Mumia and all political prisoners.

Sally O'Brien (producer, WBAI/Pacifica Radio): When we talk about political prisoners and the fact that there will be new political prisoners, we can see that in Seattle there were about a thousand people arrested. I just a minute ago spoke with someone in Seattle who got back from two days outside the prison where they're still holding people, where some five hundred people still haven't spoken to a lawyer. They haven't had phone calls out. Some of them are sick and they're not getting their medication. So the woman I spoke with urged people to please call or fax or write the mayor of Seattle, who two days ago invited people to go down for a peaceful demonstration and then he arrested them. Those people are still in jail, and we must demand that the mayor let them go, and let doctors and lawyers in.

Matt Meyer (Resistance in Brooklyn): What are we thinking of doing at the John Brown 2000 conference, and what are the next steps for the Mumia movement, beyond the next day and the next time to go to Philly. What are the panelists' thoughts about linking Mumia and the Jericho Movement? What are the strategies and tactics that need to be employed in this next period for all political prisoners?

Meg: The John Brown 2000 Conference is going to be at Hunter College, from May 12 through 14, and we need to have a lot of dialogue, workshops and events there. There will also be an action at the U.S. Supreme Court Building on February 28 that will include civil disobedience and direct action, in terms of linking the issue of "legal lynching"—the death penalty—and Mumia's case. There are also plans—with South African poet and former political prisoner Dennis Brutus—for a show of U.S. political prisoner posters and other art for Mumia, that will open at South Africa's notorious Robben Island, where Mandela and so many others were held. The idea here is to continue pushing Mumia work internationally, to broaden the international issue of Mumia's case.

Safiya: I know that there's going to be a meeting of Black legislators in Pennsylvania, and we'll be putting Mumia on the agenda, trying to pass a resolution in the Philadelphia legislature, calling for a new trial. Then there's going to be a major conference to try to pull together people who are doing the work around Mumia. In order to save Mumia's life, it's going to take a bunch of people from many different places; we have to broaden the basis for this work. We have to get the religious community out en masse. We have to get some people in the corporate world who are straddling the fence. We have to get the teachers. We have to get all of those people involved.

Folks should call the Mumia hot line to keep up on these activities. There are also local Jericho Committees. The one in New York meets at the Center for Constitutional Rights, on several Thursday evenings a month. They're working very hard, focusing on the nine political prisoners held in New York State. They try to keep visits with them, to make sure they get what they need, and to begin to build a base around the amnesty question.

Here now is our final panelist—author, activist, and former Black Panther Party member Rosemari Mealy:

Rosemari Mealy: Good afternoon, Brothers and Sisters.

It was a cold, cold winter day in December, and we were driving through the Pennsylvania Turnpike, on through Ohio. The mountains were forlorn, lonely. I remember we stopped, in a little gray Saab, and we couldn't get any attendants to wait on us because we were a Black and while team... somewhere in the Western hills of Pennsylvania. Our car was the type of car, some of you remember, that in order for it to move swiftly you had to mix the oil with the gas. Remember that? So we were able to coast on for awhile, but the atmosphere in the car was one of great sadness and trepidation. Finally, after what seemed like endless hours, we arrived in Chicago.

Everybody was to meet in this church. I remember when we got there, it seemed like there were thousands and thousands of people. To this day, I don't know exactly the number. There were the embraces of meeting comrades, but there was also a sadness and stillness hanging over us, as we assembled to march. When we finally began to march the lonely path of those Chicago streets, to the little house, we walked inside and we saw the blood spattered all over the room. We saw the bed where they lay. That was the bed where Fred Hampton had been murdered.

I remember returning back to Philadelphia. Before that I had lived in a commune—a resistance commune of white folks and Black folks. It was unusual during this period. John Brown's photo hung in the rooms of the house that we lived in, and in the basement a printing press pumped out leaflets twenty-four hours a day. It was a resistance commune. Some of you may know of that. If you don't, our history will tell you. This was a commune of what the Black Panther Party called the white mother radicals, the white Mother Country radicals. They were our back-up and support in the Black Panther Party.

When I came back from Chicago, the imprints of those bullet holes forever remained in my mind. Whatever apprehensions I may have had of becoming a Black Panther were dispelled. I immediately joined the Black Panther Party.

When Safiya asked me to talk today, we spoke briefly about what caused us to go into the party. Mumia went into the party because he had been brutalized and beaten, and I guess Safiya's experience is similar. For me, for so for many of us, it was the violence of the police that forced us to make that ultimate commitment. And I think it is the violence of the police today, as we observe the Battle of Seattle, that will force many of us—especially young whites—to make even more of a commitment now.

It wasn't anarchists that brought down the WTO. It was the unity, the mass struggle of the millions of people who converged on Seattle with an agenda that clearly was an agenda to bring down the WTO. It was the behind-the-scenes meetings of workers, particularly workers of color—those meetings we don't know about, that were not broadcast except on WBAI, where you heard many of those voices. It was the inside goings-on of the African delegation struggling, trying to figure out in which direction they should move and go. When history is written, it will not be the anarchists who brought down the WTO. Mind you, I have nothing against anarchism except I don't want to be ruled by it, in the same way that I don't want to be ruled by a police state.

Brothers and Sisters, as we enter into the new millennium, we have a wonderful opportunity to bring together and to reminisce on the deeds of John Brown, the deeds of Fred Hampton, but also, somehow, the ancestors always place it right before us. Right in our hands, this past week in Seattle, we have the deeds and lessons to learn from the importance of organization, multinational organization. We must clearly understanding the necessity of looking at globalism from the perspective of those who are most hurt and those who are most affected by globalization—the masses of working and oppressed peoples around the world. Today, as we reflect, we would hope that we can use the energy of the Battles of Seattle to extend into New York, to Philadelphia, all over this country. We would hope that those battles will be linked to our calling and demanding an end to one of the most inhumane things that can happen to human beings: when their life is taken away from them when they're murdered by the state.

We must meet and organize and discuss—it's study and practice combined that still allows us to figure out, in traditional Marxist terms, where we go from here—but let us also hope. We're in a crucial period in our history. They are clearly showing us at what level they will go to disrupt. In Seattle, you see, they weren't prepared for our resistance. They clearly were not prepared for that. They underestimated the hostility and the sentiment and the feelings of people all over this world. Next time, mind you, they will be prepared. They're preparing right now to arrest the homeless. Harper's Ferry, West Virginia, Chicago, New York, Seattle. You know we still say it: Same struggle, Same fight! Free Mumia!!

Participant: I've heard that now the police chiefs of all America's major cities, along with the military intelligence via the FBI/CIA, will be working together. It's really like creeping fascism. So we're going to have big battles in the future... Also, what of the situation at "control units"—in Florence, Colorado, and at Pelican Bay in California?

Safiya: Yes, political prisoners are being held indefinitely in Florence. One of our longest held, Ruchell Magee, who became political while institutionalized, has been held in Pelican Bay. They are maximum security institutions, and I think they get a lot of play time in terms of people knowing about them. But there are maximum security institutions all across the country! Every state now has its own form of Florence and Pelican Bay and other institutions like that. New York's is called Southport. Southport is right now on twenty-four-hour lock down, and it's where Robert "Seth" Hayes was. When they created Southport, four or five years ago, it was a regular institution. Then they decided to make it a New York version of the "maxi." Seth Hayes, it's ironic, was the last prisoner sent out of Southport before it became the maxi-max. And now he's back in. He was working in the law library then. And now he's back in...

Participant: I understand in a hell hole like Pelican Bay, I always tend to believe that any prisoner would have all his legal rights to an attorney denied. Do you know about any prisoners in Pelican Bay? Are they given some kind of token?

Safiya: You could be in Rikers Island right there in Queens and if you don't have support on the outside, you may have your legal rights denied! The conditions that can happen to you in Pelican Bay can happen to you right there on Rikers Island. In Atlanta, where Mutulu Shakur and Ray Levasseur are right now, the same conditions apply. Three people in a cell, inmates sleeping on the floor, you've got this happening all over. So to single out Pelican Bay because no one was in touch with prisoners at other places would be wrong. Don't get caught with the hype that it's only happening in those two prisons, just because those are the names you hear.

Laura: Pelican Bay did get somewhat exposed because there was a big lawsuit against it. The thing that is so amazing is that once folks looked at the situation, once it was in the spotlight and in front of a judge, you knew that they were going to say something about it. I think what's really important about all the control units is that, once they're in place, the nature of daily life in the general population of prison also changes. It's sort of like what we've been talking about regarding repression. As soon as COINTELPRO came into being through the FBI, you found local police departments getting more into counterinsurgency. It raises the level of repression everywhere. A lot of the things they do are experimental, so when special rules get put out for control units, they then may change the rules in general population to match. That's why what Safiya is saying is so important, because the nature of life in most prisons across the country has moved so far to the right. People probably know this, but in most prisons there are no programs, people can't go to college. The number of books you're allowed to have has been cut down. And when you talk about access to lawyers or law libraries—if you're not a lawyer and you don't have a lexis nexis, you don't know what case you're looking for. The way they have it set up makes it impossible. It's set up so that they can say "the prisoners have legal rights," but when it comes down to actual practice, those rights do not exist at all.

When Florence just opened, we thought that those people would be there forever. Just like we thought about the Lexington High Security Unit for women. And I think that sometimes what's important about having people move against those high points of repression when they come into being, is that it forces the government to know that people are watching. One of the reasons some of the political prisoners were able to get out of Florence, was that the more political prisoners that were there, the harder it was for the government. The attention and the campaigns and the letters made a difference. As much as we know that there are lots of political prisoners who have languished in prison for twenty years or more without visits, without letters as Safiya was saying in the beginning, there are also social prisoners who are doing life sentences who would kill for a tenth of the mail we got.

The prison population as a whole is cut off. It's a nation within the U.S. It has different laws, it has different customs, everything is different. It is a silenced population. For me, one of the reasons why I say to people, "Look, I just got out of prison. Use me. Bring me to your class. Bring me to your church. I'll talk about prison." Because even if those people aren't going to be the people who do very much for political prisoners, number one, they should know about political prisoners because it exposes the nature of the government. When I sit and tell my experiences, people are horrified. They may not like what I did, they may not like armed struggle, they may not like anti-imperialism, but they still think there should be some level of protection of people's rights. Secondly, I'm a link to those women inside who were stolen from their communities, sent away for longer and longer periods of time, and who don't have a voice. That's just one other reason why political prisoner work is so important.

Rosemari: I would like to just talk to the brother participant briefly… you raised the terminology of creeping fascism. I think the best way to understand fascism as we are experiencing it today is to look at the prison industrial complex. That's the pinnacle. The prison industrial complex is one of the clearest examples of fascism because, first, the control nature of it and, secondly, the global connection that it has to everything else in the world. Look at the importation of prisons to Latin America, or to Africa. In fact, when you look at who is controlling these prisons, you'll see a whole plan where prisons are a part of private capital investment. So when you talk about fascism, it's here.

Elombe said it's not creeping, it's galloping fascism! It's consumed us. Those of us who are working around the issue of political prisoners and the death penalty, I think we can use the example of the prison industrial complex as the clearest example of the fact that fascism, in the contemporary sense, does exist. It's one aspect of how fascism displays itself in U.S. society today. Prisons are like a consolidation of capital, and corporations can now invest in the prison industrial complex.

Elombe: You can rest assured that whenever they organize these police all over the country, that New York City Police Commissioner Howard Safir will be there. Safir has one of the longest records as far as police subterfuge; he will play a major role in anything they do. He didn't want people to see his real history, for folks to see who he really was: he's an intelligence agent.

Rosemari: We've got to look at the way the NYPD is a part of an international complex that's training police all over the world. In Italy, they have contracts. In Latin America, in Haiti. In our work, we have to be able to show our community and the people that we're working with those kinds of links. As Elombe said, it's not just limited to here. These contracts, and relationships, who's going to bid to train a terroristic, antipeople force in South Africa, or anywhere in the world? There are organized bounty hunters; there was a bounty placed on Assata Shakur's head. All you have to do is go on the Internet and look at the bounty hunter organizations! In our organizing work around apartheid in South Africa, we would identify the corporations that were in South Africa and we would target those corporations for sanctions. We have to begin to do the same thing, now around the prison industrial complex and the manifestations of it internationally.

Participant: I came in late and don't know if you've already talked about the various companies of medical, health care products, pharmaceuticals, etc., who have a captured population in prison, that they can try anything out on. Horrible stuff has been done in the prisons. I used to be a social worker at Hodel Hospital many years ago, and we had a man who was hospitalized there and I could never get to the bottom of it. He was a prison guard, and I had a sense that this guy had sort of tried to blow the whistle on what was going on. He was so paranoid about everything, and I suspected that someone had doused him with LSD or whatever else, to make him look insane. A lot of what he said, however, made a lot of sense, and I wondered if you had much experience with people who ended up not in prison but in psychiatric hospitals. It happens a lot in Russia and in other countries...

Safiya: We didn't discuss the medical aspect because this day's panel is basically connecting the movements around those issues of John Brown, Mumia and all political prisoners. Certainly one of those things that we discussed in the midst of this program with the Brecht Forum is our next program here. This is not the end, but the beginning of a round of forums that the Jericho Movement will organize around all these issues.[*]

Participant: Is Mumia's brother active in his case?

Safiya: No. The reason I say no to that is because Mumia's brother is an issue in the case, but the case is not whether or not Mumia's family or Mumia's sister or brother or whoever is doing this work. Our struggle is not to get his family involved. Certainly his sisters and his daughters and his wife and his children are involved. But the struggle around Mumia's case is to get a new trial and to get him off of death row. The persons we're struggling with are not the families who are not doing what they're supposed to do, or not doing what we think they're supposed to do. We're struggling against the state who is out to execute him. I'm not saying this to say your question isn't a legitimate one. I'm saying that right now, on this day, time and place, our struggle for Mumia has to focus on getting a new trial, before we can talk about witnesses. Once we get a new trial, then we'll decide who takes the stand. Because we will win the battle of stopping the execution.

Participant: Laura, could you speak briefly about Marilyn Buck's situation. I understand that she's now in a three-person-to-a-cell situation. That's a very distressing situation to be in.

Laura: Women's prison is different than men's prison. In men's prison, open violence is used as the threat and the way of controlling people. There are no holds barred. If anyone ever watched the documentaries about Marion, you can see it. They come in armed to move you from one cell to another. In women's prisons, they don't do it quite that way—although the threat of violence is always there. They will use violence in a second if they feel they need to. But they're not as scared of us, the way they're scared of men. In the years I was in the prison, I would have to say that those guards were more afraid of me than I was of them. Because they didn't understand me. How could somebody be basically so cheerful about doing all this time? First, I was

---

[*] The second Jericho Movement national forum, held at the Brecht on February 5, 2000, did focus on medical treatment and health issues, and featured Jericho Medical Project coordinator Dr. Barbara Zeller, anti-imperialist former political prisoner Dr. Alan Berkman, and South African physician and ANC activist Dr. Judith van Heerden.

not ashamed of what I had done, I was proud of it. Secondly, they had heard that this little person was a scary terrorist… but they weren't afraid of me or us physically in quite the same way as men. Any of those guards were three times my size, and in a second they could probably have subdued me. The threat of sexual violence is much more an issue. What this means is that they do things to women prisoners that they are afraid to do to men. Not to say that men's prisons aren't overcrowded.

In Dublin, California—the last prison I was in, where Marilyn is—the cells were built for one person. There are now three or four women living—not just staying, it's not temporary—living in those cells. The cell that Marilyn is in now, the way I lived too, the way Linda Evans lives, you have literally one foot—twelve inches of space—between your bed and the other bed. There is one double bunk bed and one cot, and there is one foot of space in between the two. Then there are these little lockers that are as high as a table; they're like half of a high school gym locker. Then there's the sink and the toilet, and that's the cell. Now, if you're in county jail for a few months waiting trial and you live that way, it's one thing. If you're living your life in there, which is what they plan for Marilyn if we don't do something about it, you have absolutely no space. You have no place to write, and as people know, Marilyn has a leg injury so it's hard for her to sit on a bed. I'm sorry, but at our age, you know, my back hurts when I sit on a bed and write. And Marilyn is going to school. She's getting her degree, and she's studying psychology, and trying to do that kind of school work on a cot with nothing to write on. It's hideous.

Gilda: When women go to prison, women do hard time. By that I mean—and this is for all women prisoners—most women don't have anybody who visits them. Husbands forget that they're husbands. The boyfriend takes a hike. If you don't have a mother or a sister who brings your children there to see you, you get cut off from your children. You don't get mail. Like Laura said, there are women in prison who would die to get one-tenth of the mail that some political prisoners do get. Many women prisoners don't get phone calls. Women do hard time.

When men go to prison, girlfriends usually stick around, for five or six years anyway. There are wives who bring the kids and show that somebody is there for them. But for women, most women are doing lonely time in prison, and it's very, very difficult. That whole piece about women in prison needs a whole lot more working attention.

Participant: Since Mumia received a temporary stay of execution, is he still on what they call Phase Two?

Safiya: No, he's not in Phase Two right now. Once he got the stay of execution, he was moved back into regular death row. But he's still on death row! Phase Two is when all his property was taken from him; he was only allowed visits from his immediate family and his attorney. Now he's back in the regular phase, where he can read all the time, and he can make phone calls. I think yesterday he was on a radio station, doing an interview. And he's back doing his regular work, writing his commentaries and everything else he was doing before. He's also getting visits again.

I just wanted to say that this time, when he came off of Phase Two, he said that he wanted to see his reverent supporters, the people who have done the work around him. All other times, he's been told who to visit—the visits were from dignitaries. But now he's asked those of us who are coming to visit him to bring somebody with them who he would not ordinarily have a chance to visit. So my visit comes up soon, and I'll be trying to determine who to take with me, so he can... no, not you! (laughter) We'll do a lottery...

Laura: I just wanted to say one additional thing about Seattle. One thing I've noticed is that right away, the same old comments were coming from a lot of white leftists. This is who I heard it from, so I'm not going to say it came from anyone else. Folks say that the people who broke the windows brought the repression down on everyone else. When we're talking about unity here, I think we do have to have some principles. Yes, we want people to support political prisoners. I say to people, "You don't have to agree with what I did, but you've got to support political prisoners." In the case of Seattle, we're talking about cops who were vamping on the people. We can't blame those who broke some windows.

The WTO was stopped from holding their meeting. They finally had to do their business in twenty-four-hour sessions, because they couldn't get in to their meetings during regular business hours. This wasn't because of a few people who broke the windows; it was because of a movement that the cops were sent to repress. As someone who has always been committed to armed struggle, I know that people will always accuse those who take the most steps forward of bringing down repression.

I think everyone on this panel has said it one way or another today: if you're going to fight the U.S. government, if you're going to fight against colonialism, they're not going to sit by and say "Okay." You're going to be faced with repression. If a movement isn't ready to face this, we should go back to the quote of Frederick Douglass: "You don't get anything without plowing up the soil... Power concedes nothing without a demand."

John Brown 2000:
U.S. Political Prisoner/Prisoner of War Writings on the 200th Birthday of John Brown and Nat Turner

Jericho Movement
Resistance in Brooklyn
2000

John Brown 2000

U.S. Political Prisoner/POW Writings on the 200th Birthday of John Brown and Nat Turner

featuring poetry, prose and commentary by

Mumia Abu Jamal•Sundiata Acoli•Janine Africa•Phil Africa•Herman Bell
Veronza Bowers•Marilyn Buck•Bill Dunne•Linda Evans•Larry Giddings
David Gilbert•Bashir Hameed•Wopashitwe Mondo Eyen we Langa
Jann Laaman•Ray Luc Levasseur•Oscar Lopez Rivera•Jalil Muntaqim
Leonard Peltier•Susan Rosenberg•Maroon Shoats•Nuh Washington

a Jericho Movement & Resistance in Brooklyn/RnB publication

The next selection of writings by 21 U.S. political prisoners was assembled for the
John Brown 2000 Conference in May of that year that brought together antiracists and anti-
imperialists from around the country. Resistance in Brooklyn and the Jericho Movement—then
a new coalition calling for the freedom of all political prisoners—published these materials in
a booklet edited by Matt Meyer and Paulette D'Auteuil, and was distributed both during and
after the conference.

VII.3.A

Alliance Building in the Next Period

Sundiata Acoli

What we're really talking about here is whites building alliances with people of color.

I can't speak for all people of color, but for the Black masses, the main problem is racism—the worldwide system of White Supremacy at home and abroad, headed by U.S. imperialism.

Whites are the main beneficiaries of racism. So the real struggle against racism involves whites giving up the special benefits they derive from racial oppression of people of color, in exchange for joining the rest of humanity in building a better world for all people that we all want.

The key to whites building alliances with the Black masses is to put and keep the issue of racism—the world wide system of white domination, suppression and exploitation of people of color—on the front burner and to fight against racism in all its manifestations at home and abroad.

White alliances with people of color will be more effective in the next period if whites —

1. Recognize that barriers that exist between whites and people of color stem primarily from each side's long history of being on opposite ends of the effect of racism.
2. Since whites are from the side exercising racial domination and privilege, both people of color and whites have to take precautions that these tendencies don't reproduce themselves in alliances.
3. Talk, communicate, exchange views frankly and consult with people of color and their representatives to come up with the best way to form and maintain alliances; also consult with people of color early on when their participation is needed.
4. Follow the lead of people of color and their representatives on issues of main concern to them—or leave it alone.
5. Focus more on organizing in the white community as opposed to preferring to organize in communities of color—unless invited in.
6. Give preference to direct action over rallies, self-defense over nonviolence, and thinking globally, acting locally.

VII.3.B

A Life Lived Deliberately...
and the spiritual grandchildren of John Brown

Mumia Abu-Jamal

I feel privileged to address your chosen theme, not because I'm some kind of avatar, but because a life lived deliberately has been the example of people I admire and respect, such as Malcolm X; Dr. Huey P. Newton, founder of the Black Panther Party; like Ramona Africa, who survived the hellish bombing by police of May 13, 1985; or the MOVE 9, committed rebels now encaged for up to 100 years in Pennsylvania hellholes despite their innocence, solely for their adherence to the teachings of John Africa. These people, although of quite diverse beliefs, ideologies, and lifestyles, shared something in common: a commitment to revolution and a determination to live that commitment deliberately in the face of staggering state repression.

No doubt some of you are disconcerted by my use of the term "revolution." It's telling that people who claim with pride to be proud Americans would disclaim the very process that made such a nationality possible, even if it was a bourgeois revolution. Why was it right for people to revolt against the British because of "taxation without representation" and somehow wrong for truly unrepresented Africans in America to revolt against America? For any oppressed people, revolution, according to the Declaration of Independence, is a right.

Malcolm X, although now widely acclaimed as a Black nationalist martyr, was vilified at the time of his assassination by *Time* magazine as "an unashamed demagogue" who "was a disaster to the civil rights movement." The *New York Times* would describe him as a "twisted man" who used his brains and oratorical skills for "an evil purpose." Today, there are schools named for him, and recently a postage stamp was even issued in his honor.

Dr. Huey P. Newton, Ph.D., founded the Black Panther Party in October of 1966 and created one of the most militant, principled organizations American Blacks had ever seen. J. Edgar Hoover of the FBI targeted the party, using every foul and underhanded method they could conceive of to neutralize the group, which they described as the "number one threat to national security."

This is the transcript of a 13-minute audiotape played at the commencement ceremony at Evergreen State College, a small liberal arts school in Olympia, Washington, on June 11, 1999, attended by 8,000. Mumia's address followed months of student campaigning aimed at spotlighting his case, furiously countered by the Fraternal Order of Police and the Pennsylvania Attorney General. Maureen Faulkner, widow of the police officer Mumia is alleged to have killed, attended as a protest, but the college rejected her demand to speak. One year later, Mumia would similarly address the commencement ceremony at Antioch University, as well as the graduation ceremony at Brooklyn Friends High School.

Sister Ramona Africa of the MOVE organization survived one of the most remarkable bombings in American history, one where Philadelphia police massacred eleven men, women, and children living in the MOVE house and destroyed some sixty one homes in the vicinity. She did seven years in the state prison on riot charges, came out, and began doing all she could to spread the teachings of John Africa, the teachings of revolution, and to free her imprisoned brothers and sisters of MOVE from their repressive century in hellish prison cells.

These people dared to dissent, dared to speak out, dared to reject the status quo by becoming rebels against it. They lived—and some of them continue to live—lives of deliberate will, of willed resistance to a system that is killing us. Remember them. Honor their highest moments. Learn from them. Are these not lives lived deliberately? This system's greatest fear has been that folks like you, young people, people who have begun to critically examine the world around them, some perhaps for the first time, people who have yet to have the spark of life snuffed out, will do just that: learn from those lives, be inspired, and then live lives of opposition to the deadening status quo.

Let me give you an example. A young woman walks into a courtroom, one situated in the cradle of American democracy—that's Philadelphia—to do some research for a law class. This woman, who dreams of becoming a lawyer, sits down and watches the court proceedings and is stunned by what she sees. She sees defendants prevented from defending themselves, man-handled in court, and cops lying on the stand with abandon. She sees the judge as nothing more than an administrator of injustice and sees U.S. law as an illusion. Her mind reels, as she says to herself, "They can't do that," as her eyes see them doing whatever they want to. Well, that young woman is now known as Ramona Africa, who lived her life deliberately after attending several sessions of the MOVE trial in Philadelphia. After that farce she knew she could never be a part of the legal system that allowed it, and she found more truth in the teachings of John Africa than she ever could in the law books which promised a kind of justice that was foreign to the courtrooms she had seen. The contrast between America's lofty promises and the truth of its legal repression inspired her to be a revolutionary, one that America has tried to bomb into oblivion. What is the difference between Ramona Africa and you? Absolutely nothing, except she made that choice.

Similarly, Huey Newton studied U.S. law with close attention when he was a student at Merritt Junior College in West Oakland, California. His studies convinced him that the laws must be changed, and the famous Black Panther Party ten-point program and platform prove, then and now, that serious problems still face the nation's Black communities, such as all the predominantly white juries still sending Blacks to prison, and cops still treating Black life as a cheap commodity. Witness the recent Bronx execution of Ghanaian immigrant Amadou Diallo, where cops fired 41 shots at an unarmed man in the doorway of his own apartment building. Huey, at least in his earlier years, lived his life deliberately and set the mark as a revolutionary. What was the difference between Huey Newton and you? Absolutely nothing, except he made the choice.

Each of the MOVE 9—including the late Merle Africa, who died under somewhat questionable circumstances after nineteen years into an unjust prison sentence—members of the MOVE organization whose trial initially attracted the attention of a young law student named Ramona decades ago, each was a person who came to question their lives as lived in the system. Some were U.S. Marines, some were petty criminals, some were carpenters, but all came to the point of questioning the status quo, deeply, honestly, and completely—irrevocably. One by one, they turned their back on a system that they knew couldn't care less if they lived or died and joined a revolution after being exposed to the stirring teachings of John Africa. They individually chose to live life deliberately and joined MOVE. And although they are individuals—Delbert Africa, Janet Africa, Phil Africa, Janine Africa, Chuckie Africa, Mike Africa, Debbie Africa, and Eddie Africa—they are also united as MOVE members, united in heart and soul. What's the difference between the MOVE 9 and you? Absolutely nothing, except they made the choice.

Now, unless I miss my guess, Evergreen is not a predominantly Black institution, and my choices heretofore given may seem somewhat strange to too many of you, for far too many of you may identify yourselves by the fictional label of "white." In truth, as I'm sure many of you know, race is a social construct. That said, it is still a social reality formed by our histories and our cultures. For those of you still bound by such realities, however, I have some names for you, like John Brown, like Dr. Alan Berkman, Susan Rosenberg, Sue Africa, Marilyn Buck. Each of these people are or were known in America as white. They are all people I know of, who I admire, love, and respect. They all are or were revolutionaries.

John Brown's courageous band's attack on Harper's Ferry was one deeply religious man's strike against the hated slavery system and was indeed considered one of the opening salvos of the U.S. Civil War. Dr. Alan Berkman, Susan Rosenberg, and Marilyn Buck were all anti-imperialists who fought to free Black revolutionary Assata Shakur from an unjust and cruel bondage. They are the spiritual grandsons and granddaughters of John Brown. Dr. Alan Berkman, Marilyn Buck, and Susan Rosenberg were treated like virtual traitors to white supremacy and thrown into American dungeons. Buck and Rosenberg remain so imprisoned today. They lived lives deliberately and chose liberation as their goals, understanding that our freedom is interconnected. They chose the hard road of revolution, yet they chose. And but for that choice they are just like each of you seated here tonight, people who saw the evils of the system and resolved to fight it. Period.

Now, the name Sue Africa may not be known to you. She's what you may call white. Yet when she joined the MOVE organization, the system attacked her bitterly for what was seen as a betrayal of her white-skinned privilege. On

May 13, 1985, she lost her only son because the Philadelphia police bombed the house she was living in. She served over a decade in prison where the guards vilely taunted her in the hours and days after the bombing. When she came out, she went right to work to rebuild the MOVE organization in Philadelphia. She lives her life deliberately by promoting John Africa's revolution each and every day. Except for that choice, she's just like you.

Now, some of you are sure to be wondering, "Well, if this guy's gig is with revolutionaries, why is he saying this to us?" The answer of course is "Why not?" OK, I know you ain't supposed to answer a question with a question, but do I expect you guys and gals who've just received your degrees to chuck it all for so nebulous a concept as revolution? Nope. I ain't that dumb. The great historians Will and Ariel Durant teach us that history in the large is the conflict of minorities. The majority applauds the victor and supplies the human material of social experiment. Now, I take that to mean that social movements are begun by relatively small numbers of people who, as catalysts, inspire, provoke, and move larger numbers to see and share their vision. Social movements can then become social forces that expand our perspectives, open up new social possibilities, and create the consciousness for change. To begin this process, we must first sense that, one, the status quo is wrong, and, 2, the existing order is not amenable to real, meaningful, and substantive transformation. Out of the many here assembled, it is the heart of he or she that I seek who looks at a life of vapid materialism, of capitalist excess, and finds it simply intolerable. It may be a hundred of you, or fifty, or even ten, or even one of you who makes that choice. I'm here to honor and applaud that choice and to warn you that, though the suffering may indeed be great, it is nothing to the joy of doing the right thing. Malcolm, Dr. Huey P. Newton, Ramona Africa, the MOVE 9, Dr. Alan Berkman, Susan Rosenberg, John Brown, Susan Africa, Marilyn Buck, Geronimo ji Jaga, Leonard Peltier, Angela Davis, and others, all of them people just like you, felt compelled to change the conditions they found intolerable. I urge you to join that noble tradition.

I thank you all, and I wish you well. On the MOVE. Long live John Africa. From Death Row, this is Mumia Abu-Jamal.

VII.3.C

LONG LIVE REVOLUTION!
On the MOVE from the MOVE 9!

Janine Africa, Minister of Education,
for the MOVE 9 Prisoners

I want to give thanks to all of you here at this conference and let you know that we appreciate all that you have done in this fight for justice! With all that we of MOVE have been through for telling the truth, confronting this corrupt system, we know the courage it takes to go against this established criminal! So to all of you who have taken that step, we say thank you and keep up the hard work!

It's taken a long time and lots of examples of persecution for all of us to get to this point. It started with the crystallized examples of enslavement, and I'm not just talking about the enslavement of Africans—the Chinese, the Irish protestants, the early Christians, the American Indians and many people all over the world have been and still are being enslaved by some government.

The American Indians are still imprisoned on reservations in this country just because they are Indians. Then we have the examples of the Black Panthers, the SLA, Martin Luther King and his freedom fighters, Mumia and MOVE: not to mention the poor people that are being beat, locked up and killed by the police daily just because they are poor, Black, Puerto Rican or in some other category that those running this government don't respect. We've had these examples for a Millennium and it's past time for something to be done about it! Which is why you all are here at this conference, to put an end to the crimes of this system. We've all been informing people for a long time, the MOVE organization has been putting out the truth to people for over 30 years! So it's not like people don't know what's going on or are confused about the conditions of the world. The only thing holding up Justice now is that the people don't want to get involved and do something. Politicians don't feel they have to stop doing the people wrong, don't see that they have to stop arrogantly slapping us in the face with their crimes or answer to the people for their lawlessness! It's good to have these conferences, but it's time to take this out to the criminals and let them know that we are serious about stopping crime, let them know that we are serious about getting our freedom! If you don't, it will be another Millennium of bloody persecution from this system! These officials let us know everyday that they are serious about hurting us with every unjust beating, jailing and murder of people, so we've got to let them know that we are just as serious about stopping them! And as John Africa has shown MOVE, we do have the power to confront this system and win! People might as well take a stand against this corruption because this system is oppressing and killing you, your children, your grandchildren whether you fight or not. These prisons ain't filled with just revolutionaries. These prisons are overcrowded with the men, women and children of people who believe in this government, people who pay taxes, vote and go to war for this country. There are people in prison who criticize people for going against this government and still think judges are honest.

So you see it's no escaping this disease by being quiet and going along with the program; it's affecting everybody! So if people truly want to be Free and not just live in the illusion of Freedom (going to the movies, living in the suburbs, having a high paying job, etc.) then we are going to have to fight for it! It's no getting around it! We've talked enough, it's time to put our talks into Action!

I'm not telling people to take a stand like MOVE or to do anything they feel they aren't prepared to do. I'm saying it's time to do something! It's time to put these officials on the hot seat! People can flood the television and radio stations with different officials' names and the wrongs they have done or the lives they have ruined; people can go to the public speaking events these politicians have and make them speak to whatever issue it is that they are ignoring. You've got to find ways to embarrass these officials publicly and make them see that if they don't do what they are supposed to do, they will lose their position, which means money. That's what hurts them, that Money, that's their God and they will do anything to get and keep it!

We have to stop letting these judges lock up people for half their lives, for Life, for crimes they didn't commit, or in some cases for crimes that aren't nowhere as bad as the crimes rich people commit and get away with. People need to be at those court cases showing those judges and district attorneys that they are being watched by people demanding Justice! And if you don't get it, expose the case in any way you can! I know it may not sound like much to some of you but you'd be surprised at how effective these things are! My point is that it's time to do! And whatever it is that people can do they've got to be serious about it and committed to it. And don't think it's going to be fast; this fight is a long one! Look at us, the MOVE 9 have been fighting in prison righteously since 1978! And we're still fighting and going to Keep fighting till the day we are no longer on this earth! Long Live Revolution Forever!

This my message to all of you today, if you want to truly get justice and see some justice in this Millennium, it's going to take Action! And the only way this action is going to be effective is with Unity! You've got to leave your Prejudices behind you, no more judging a person by his color or so-called status. John Africa teaches us that prejudice is this system's training that was devised to cause conflict and keep dissension amongst the people so that we would be too busy fighting amongst Ourselves and not have the energy or the direction to fight against the Real enemy, this system! Justice ain't a Black thing, Justice is for *all life!* So if you want justice you have to unite and don't let this system divert you from your aim against prejudice. That's why this system can't stop MOVE. Because of John Africa we are one family, united, our aim is revolution, our target this system and nothing can deter us from this! So be unified and stay unified!

THE POWER OF TRUTH IS FINAL! LONG LIVE REVOLUTION! ON THE MOVE!

VII.3.D
NEED FOR TOTAL REVOLUTION!
Phil Africa

The need for all oppressed people to begin to move out on activities designed to eliminate this system is a must! By now folks should realize they can not buy their way "into this system" or buy their way to so-called "freedom" from it. Folks must be willing to take a stand! Folks must become demanding in dealing with this system. People got the right to demand "true freedom," people got the right to demand "justice," folks got the right to demand that a government that claims to represent them lives up to that responsibility of taking "care" of their needs! People got the right to demand that this government work for them! Ain't that what they pay their taxes for! What folks fought wars for?! These politicians/government is suppose to work for the people, not the people working for these rich-ass racist politicians! Government officials are public servants employed by the "people" to work for the "people," but you see these government officials have flipped the script on the people and have turned things around on people to where they have made slaves of those they "claim" to work for. It's why the few have it all and control the many.

Instead of this rotten system spending hundreds of billions on "space programs," folks must demand these bastards spend that money on building free housing for their citizens, and if they "refuse," then folks need to revolt against them! Folks need to demand that these politicians who be spending all them trillions of dollars on the "military," spend that money on making sure everyone has food to eat in this country, folks must demand this of this government that claims to "represent" them and if these politicians "refuse," folks should revolt against them by stopping their support of this system in every way. People have to make this government be "for the people" or get rid of it through total revolution and that means to stop supporting this system on all levels!

If folks' "religions" don't push for demanding from this system what folks know is right, then people must stop supporting them religions! If the "schools" don't teach the truth about how corrupt and racist this system is, if the schools this system forces you to send your kids to don't teach the truth about all the crimes this system committed and still commits against the poor and those of color, then stop supporting those schools by refusing to send your children to those schools! If the president of this country is supposed to be working for you but makes far more than you, then demand that you get paid the same as he does! What I'm saying ain't crazy, it's the truth. What is crazy, is for people to continue to allow this system to enslave, imprison, murder them by willfully submitting to this "insanity" without rebelling against it! Long live John Africa's revolution and down with this rotten reform world system!!!!

The bottom line is for there to be true, meaningful change, one must be willing to fight as hard for it, in fact harder for it, than those who fight to hold you down do. If people do not build the courage to rebel against the conditions they complain about, then their complaints will always fall on the deaf ears of the system. Folks must become as aggressive in the battle for righteousness as the wicked are in their push for oppression!

There are more black elected officials now than ever before, but if they have positions just to try to "hold on" to them, just to say they got 'em, instead of using those positions to fight this system with, they may as well not have those positions at all. So once elected, they must be pressed to do right by the people or the people need to stop supporting them! This ain't no game we are playing in this struggle. It is a matter of freedom or death! Those who are putting their lives on the line day in and day out, those who are in prison for putting their lives on the line in battle to make a righteous change for all must be supported, must never be forgotten, and those elected officials who do not help in this cause should not be supported! Folks must put those elected officials on the spot to do what they were elected to do and not just let them "ego trip" and "see out" once those positions are gotten. This system responds to one thing—pressure, so we must continue to come up with ways and ideas to keep as much pressure on this system as possible at all times!

People are a powerful force when we are all as one in unity.

That is the key for success for all oppressed peoples—unity! It is what more than anything else must be worked on as the solution to the problems we all face in the times ahead of us. In unity we can be that stampede; the cowboys of this system will be trampled as we move towards freedom! In unity we can be that force that knocks down any dam built up against us by those who would oppress the will to be free! In unity we can build those crime-free communities, nations we all talk about, that are free of racism and hate that destroys so many right now. Unity can force those politicians to bend to the will of "the people"! Unity is the aim we all should set as our goal to help make a change as we move into these times ahead of us in struggle!!!!

On the MOVE!!!! Free the MOVE 9!! Free Mumia Abu-Jamal!! Free all political prisoners!! Long live John Africa's revolution and down with this rotten reform system!!!!

VI.3.E

Expressions of Solidarity

Oscar López Rivera

Compañeros(as),

Thank you for all the support you have given to the Puerto Rican political prisoners. We have witnessed the fruits of your energies with the excarceration of eleven Compañenos(as). Today, thanks to the support they received, they are at home, sharing with loved ones and establishing new roots.

During the Christmas season I heard from many peace, justice and freedom-loving people from different parts of Europe and the U.S. For those of us who are in the gulags, such expressions of solidarity are very important.

For the Puerto Ricans, the issue of Vieques is foremost in our minds and hearts. The governor of Puerto Rico accepted the White House's offer [to hold a referendum on Vieques on whether the Navy should leave, with staying linked to economic aid]. By doing so, the movement of a united Puerto Rico in support of Vieques has been split. That's exactly what the politicians in Washington and the Pentagon wanted. But the majority of the Puerto Rican people have openly stated they want the Navy out of Vieques, and the politicians and the Pentagon can't eradicate such a reality. The acts of civil disobedience will continue. So we can anticipate massive arrests and imprisonment. The government can do that and more. But what Washington and the Pentagon can't do is stop us from continuing struggling until not a bomb or bullet is fired again anywhere in Vieques.

Take good care and let's continue struggling for a world of peace, freedom and justice.

En Resistencia y Lucha,

OLR

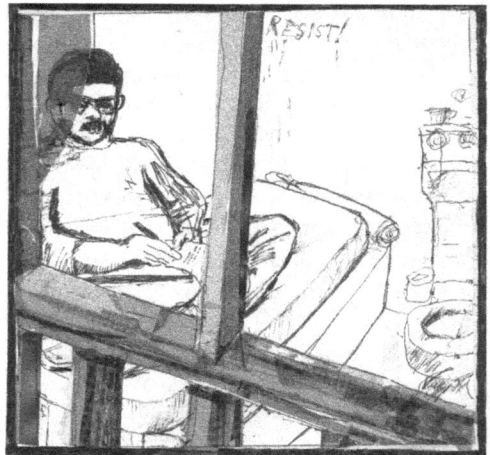

Credit: Elspeth Meyer

VII.3.F

To the John Brown 2000 Conference

Herman Bell

Greetings and solidarity to one and all. We give particular thanks to the memory of John Brown for his unselfish contribution to the abolitionist movement and the uplift of humanity. As a small child I remember the name John Brown was fondly spoken of in many Black households. His name was and continues to be well respected by Blacks who know their history and by people in general who feel inspired by his deeds. In this regard let us give thanks and live up to the sacrifices and expectations of those who came before us. We honor John Brown's legacy by convening this conference in his name so that we might gather our strength and resolve to advance the very ideals that he and so many others before us set out to achieve.

I feel honored by this opportunity to participate in this conference, the purpose for which is to build alliances. There are two kinds of alliances: one is alliance of convenience, which is largely based upon mutual interest of limited duration. The other is based upon commitment, mutual respect and common principles and is far more lasting. Clearly, this conference was convened in the spirit of the latter sense rather then the former. The cover letter requesting my contribution asked: "where do you see our movement(s) headed in this next period?" Over the years I have asked myself many times: do we really have a movement in this country? Others may differ in their assessment but I don't think we do. We have a large progressive community in this country and I believe what's most needed now is that we organize into a national political movement. We witness political actions out there all the time but for the most part they are based upon temporary alliances where one group agrees to support the political actions organized by another and vice versa, which partly explains why the same faces appear and reappear at these events. This is not bad within itself because righteous political actions deserve support. This recurrent tendency, however, seems to suggest a reluctance or inability to reach beyond our immediate political circles.

Lately, though, I feel heartened by what is a new tendency that is growing: an increased activism from our young people. I see larger contingents of them at political events and I read about conferences and activities that they themselves have organized. Their opposition to proposition 21 in California, which proposed to lock juveniles in adult prisons, is one example. Just recently a sizable contingent of them participated in civil disobedience with adults against the WTO meetings in Seattle, Washington. The relatively recent Million Youth March and Critical Resistance conference are further examples of our young people taking on more responsibility for their lives and their future.

Yet, given these various expressions of support and solidarity by these groups and organizations, why is it that little or nothing has been done in the way of organizing them into a National Movement? Fortunately, the Jericho Movement picked up some of the slack and took steps consistent with an emerging national movement in the absence of a real one. But they were just steps and far more needs to be done in this regard.

It seems to me that a National Movement should advocate a select number of well-defined issues that are flexible enough to change as new conditions and circumstances dictate. To call itself progressive is not enough. To declare who we are and what we are about and stand against and seek to inaugurate ought to be a fundamental requirement of a movement. In this regard Jericho was correct to call on national support for PP's/POW's at the demonstration it held in Washington, DC, in '98 (and especially for its support work to save the life of our brother Mumia Abu-Jamal on death row). Jericho also played a key organizing role in the Critical Resistance Conference in Berkeley, California, and is now involved with convening this important John Brown 2000 conference.

In 1997 or there about, comrade Jalil Muntaqim suggested that we, the progressive community, organize a "Poor Peoples' Convention." I thought the suggestion had a great merit for a number of reasons. He thought that the widest range of groups, organizations and special interest people ought to be involved: representatives of the poor, progressive labor unions, welfare mothers, gays, anti-death penalty and prison expansionists, etc. Once convened, he said the delegates should hammer out a national agenda and organize to carry it out. From this he suggested that a national movement could be formed. An intriguing idea. My point here is that we need to take decisive steps to organize and consolidate a national movement. The time is now! We simply have to organize the structure, develop the resources, and hammer out the agenda.

Furthermore, while on the subject of "Agenda," I strongly urge this conference to organize a national amnesty campaign for U.S. PP's/POW's. Practically all of us are doing life sentences with no foreseeable release by the parole boards. We all are considerably older now and some of us are in poor health. Aside from the fact that such a campaign is the right thing to do, it has the potential of revealing to the world much of what goes on in the U.S. that goes largely unreported. I believe this can be done and I feel confident that the progressive international community would support it once it got under way. Given all the national and international support we have successfully organized in support of Mumia, we can successfully organize this campaign as well.

Finally, I would also urge that we work more closely with community-based groups and help them explore new ways to better educate and organize their respective communities. Working with people is what we do and I think we can be far more creative in this regard. For example, these community groups could organize local events with local participation in mind. And once gathered, encourage them to talk. Also ask well-thought-out questions. Learn what they are interested in and would like to do. We organizers should consider what they have to say, rather than rely solely on our own ideas. And when possible, implement those ideas in the form of programs. As regards to education, organization and recruitment, our future is tied to programs to an extent perhaps greater than we currently realize. When we think of catastrophic change, where the old is replaced by the new, this is when the organized forces of resistance fully implement their predeveloped programs because they then have the administrative capacity and resources to put them into effect.

We need to consider new ways to connect with people, and I think developing programs designed to help them help themselves, programs that provide useful services to them is an important first step. For example, consider what we can do to improve health care services? And services that can improve the quality of life for our elders? What about day care/child care programs? And what about developing creative ways to help our people feed themselves and programs that focus on the needs of our young people, on the needs of young mothers, parenting skills, job training, etc. We need to become more involved with the day to day life of the people as a way to help them better organize themselves. It's a great idea to create a pamphlet from the various ideas sent to this conference. I look forward to reading it.

True Freedom Is Seized
And Is Never Granted!!

VII.3.G

John Brown Rises!

Marilyn Buck

On the 200th anniversary of John Brown's birth, I would like to propose that we imagine who John Brown would be were his bones to rise up from the grave today and stand *"Presente!"* Likely, ole JB would reincarnate as a woman picking up where he left off, or rather had fallen short—in his ideological development. Radical as he was, he was a man of his times; he did not give much thought to women as equals. With the exception of Harriet Tubman, that is. She gave him no choice. So ole JB would answer to Johnette perhaps. She would still be of European heritage—white-skinned, but she would be a liberation-minded political activist. Instead of slave catcher brutality and the murder of African slaves, she would be outraged at the police murders, brutality and imprisonment of the descendants of slaves, conquered and colonized Native and Latin Americans, as well as Asians and Pacific Islanders—anyone who can not or would not pass for white. She would have reviewed history and know that despite the Civil War, Black Reconstruction, the antilynching campaign, Civil Rights, Black Power and New Afrikan Independence movements, there is still no equality, no justice and no peace. Global imperialism with its white supremacist culture and social contracts prevail, more brazen and blood-thirsty than ever. A lot yet to be done.

Johnette would be at the protests and the marches; she would join with longtime radicals and activists as well as young folks her age against police brutality—call for cancellation of the foreign debt and reparations to all those peoples and nations raped and pillaged by the nation-state of which she is inescapably a citizen. She would support N'COBRA, Native Americans, as well as the Vietnamese who are asking where are the reparations that were agreed to by the U.S. and never paid. Johnette would march with women and continue to chip away at the dominant male political leadership paradigm. She would have gone to Seattle and would have thought back to her former JB life in Kansas, looking for historical parallels. In Kansas, John had led a guerrilla campaign against the legalized extension of slavery to the Midwestern states. Seattle, Johnette would see as one in a series of global mass actions to hold back the further legalization of global capital's rape, pillage and dismembering of entire nations—the former colonies as well as U.S. internal colonies and the national working classes and reserve armies of labor—a postmodern enslavement with pre-modern dehumanization and dispossession.

The anti-WTO actions in Seattle were quite successful logistically. The transnational corporate plantation summit was effectively disrupted. It is always important to disrupt lines of communication in the enemy's camp. A glimpse of possibility! But Johnette would have considered the debate about violence as somewhat of a red herring. If one wants to effect serious, liberatory social, economic and political change, one must expect that the State will protect and enforce its true interests, not the people's, even white people's interests. She was not shocked by the militarized police response—there are no gentlemen's agreements. Not by the poor white slave catchers for the rich white agribusiness gentlemen; not by the Indian killers and '49ers; not by the Pinkerton guards in labor struggles, nor by the Navy at the Port Chicago explosion. And certainly not around the world. Bombing wars and CIA assassinations. And here—assassinations and incarcerations for those who dared to challenge the State's agenda or its right to exist as the U.S. of A.; no matter whether through civil disobedience like Martin Luther King, Jr. or militant self-determination like Malcolm X and Nat Turner; an Arlington Cemetery full of assassinations and political prisoners who died in detention or of capital punishment.

Johnette might flash back and remember the snapping of her—John Brown's—neck. She would see before her eyes her comrades swinging from the rope at Harper's Ferry and feel mortified that their names were not as well known as hers. There had not been equality, even in death. Damn white supremacy. She would wonder, since she was thinking about actions and demonstrations: had there been a means of retreat in order to have lived to struggle another day? Had it been an error not to have awaited Sis. Harriet Tubman's arrival before the raid? After all, Harriet was a keen strategist and tactician; she was fearless and clear that her troops were precious, not to be squandered. Freedom! Do not turn away from it. To do so extracts a heavy price. Johnette would have heard of Assata Shakur and read her poem, "Carry on the Tradition," and known that she as a white woman had much to learn and that she too must carry on the tradition of fighting white supremacy in the heart of global imperialism.

At Seattle, Johnette would have advanced, hand in hand, with other young folks who had learned from the struggles of their elders some of whom were still present, still strong. The young white comrades—radical, internationalist and antiracist—are those not afraid to challenge their white privilege. They are clear that their interests lie not in white supremacy and capitalism but in alliance with their Black, Latino, Native and Asian-Pacific Islander comrades. Like Johnette they know the system must change. There is no liberation, justice, freedom from fear for some working peoples. They attack the corporations with creativity and an understanding of the power of the State.

Together, these young comrades and Johnette are concerned that many in the white Left, be they environmentalists, labor activists, feminists, anarchists had not fought to include oppressed peoples from inside the U.S. Betita Martínez, in her article, "Where Was the Color in Seattle?" estimated that, including foreign national activists from former and neo-colonial nations, only about 5% of the entire protest was of African, Asian, Latin American or Indigenous heritage. Sis. Martínez, among other comrades, explored why people of color didn't come out from an oppressed peoples' point of view of marginalization, alienation and the results, in Johnette's words, of white supremacy.

The issue is on the table. Along with these conscious comrades she had connected with, Johnette would change the question for white activists: Why was the relationship of the WTO and global imperialism to oppressed peoples inside the U.S. not significantly addressed? Why do white activists support people's struggles against imperialist cannibalization worldwide, but overlook or ignore the same atrocities and conditions inside the U.S.: environmental racism; super-exploitative labor of women, men and youth; wholesale incarceration of a whole generation of labor and culture—postmodern slavery and genocide. Such conditions are not the fault of the targets and victims. It is the responsibility of white activists to stop the U.S. government from its devastation inside the U.S. or outside its borders.

Johnette would be engaged in organizing against the death penalty and to free Mumia Abu-Jamal alongside the growing number of activists from their communities—hiphoppers and antiracist punks, radical rappers, salseros and rockers. She would join the upsurge of resistance and refusal in the face of the increasingly militarized police state. The sights are set on liberation. And they know that there can be no liberation or justice or peace where there is white supremacy, where there is exclusion due to hierarchy, nation, race, class or gender. Johnette and her comrades bring a legacy of courage and creativity.

She would be happy to feel the winds of change even in the stultifying swamp of injustice. Again, in this life she would experience the possibilities of liberation inherent in challenging oppression and in preserving the planet for all peoples and their future generations. She would not be afraid to fight for that future. She might well repeat a slogan she heard from some old Black Panthers: "You're either a part of the problem or part of the solution."

And with some of that old John Brown fire in her eyes, she might ask, "Which side are you on?"

VII.3.H

Toward Building the Future's History

Bill Dunne

For people who aspire to make revolution, assessment & reassessment of their route, vehicle, & destination is always desirable. Under the conditions that presently confront the movement for the most equitable social reality in which all people will have the greatest possible freedom to develop their full human potential—our movement—such analysis is a much-needed necessity. In this morning of a new millennium, we, the people, are confronted by a new world order of rampant capitalism.

Owned & operated by a tiny global elite that recognizes no boundaries to its appropriation of even greater riches & power at the expense of the earth & its people, this instrument of exploitation & oppression is rolling back many of the social, political, & economic gains paid for in sacrifice & blood by previous centuries' revolutionaries. This new incarnation of imperial capital represents an enemy adaptation to past revolutionary theory & practice such that we are losing ground. Hence, it demands of our assessment & reassessment synthesis of the lessons of the past with new & innovative thinking that is the product of our unique times & circumstances toward evolution of our movement.

Evolution of our movement requires that we cling to an ineffective past. Effectiveness demands that we progress to building new structures with new techniques on the foundations previously laid rather than merely rearranging stones already in place with obsolescent methods. It also demands that moribund & declining forms be allowed to wither & die away rather than being artificially sustained on political life support. Given our view of the future a few paces down the road from where yesterday's praxis was vibrant & growing, we can & must replace it with a revitalized vision of where we want to go, the path from here to there, & the means by which we can travel it.

It is not sufficient to be merely anti this or that or even anti every depredation of the ruling class & its agencies of oppression. Nor is it enough to favor reform or even radical change regarding this or that issue or even every injustice wrought by an unjust system. All that leaves us treating symptoms without attacking the disease. Even if we could eliminate the symptoms, the disease would remain to cause new symptoms & leave the body politic weakened & thus prey to parasitic infection by other sicknesses like fascism.

Imperial capital & its class system is the disease of which our revolutionary medicine, the social technology we evolve, must cure humanity. It is a system of socialized production but private ownership. Control of all major elements of social & individual life is concentrated in unaccountable financial centers distant from the overwhelming majority of people in all relevant ways. It institutionalizes an exploitative & oppressive hierarchy in which a small majority claiming ownership of production & the means thereof obscenely squanders the social wealth. The large majority constituting the society that produces the wealth is effectively disenfranchised & left to wallow in the insecurity & privation of an artificially dog-eat-dog paradigm. Its symptoms manifest themselves through the action of its ruling class, which afflicts the society with armed agencies of repression, infects class sisteren & brethren of its opposing class with division & competition, & engages in many other abusive tactics to suppress the social immune response of revolution. We know the disease. And as much as we may elaborate on, lament, or even quell the symptoms, we also know they will continue to crop up in one form or another until we cure the disease.

The cure for imperial capital & its new world order won't come a hand or a foot at a time. History & the increasing integration of the world's people—humanity—tells us that anything short of a complete, systemic cure will leave disease agents lurking to reinfect any part of the organism temporarily liberated from symptoms. For the same reason, the cure is also a socialist one, one that eliminates sick labor & property relationships & the sick social & political relationships spawned from that material base. Hence, we need an all people's (already plural) revolutionary movement that recognizes the human collective & knows no boundaries of gender, race, nation, sect, or other division that depreciate humanity's essential & overwhelming commonality.

That doesn't mean that humanity is a monolith, that we all are or have to be the same, but instead that our differences are inconsequential in comparison to our similarities in nature & needs. And it means that human diversity should not become or remain fault lines between people. Like the tiny amounts of alloying elements that make iron into steel amenable to many uses, our diversity is a strength that can be integrated into a unified movement rather than a gaggle of competitive "identities" that elevate superficial, minor, & artificial differences into rigid barriers through which only distrust & enmity leak. The ruling class is not impeded by such boundaries; indeed, it uses them as instruments of control of its victims—us.

So how do we build such a movement? Collective formation immediately presents itself. Our side of the barricade is, at present, plagued by atomization, lack of resources, & dependence on the exploitative & oppressive system we would overthrow. Activists are, for the most part, forced by circumstances to live in scattered, isolated situations wherein they must organize the resources of both subsistence & struggle around—and despite—selling their labor to the system. That requires an inordinate amount of time that could be more productively used in furtherance of revolution. It also cedes most of the surplus value of our labor to the purpose of exploiting & oppressing class at the expense of our own.

Living & working individually is expensive. It prevents us from taking advantage of economies of scale. It makes getting together for political work costly in time & travel & communication & missed contacts, & risky due to the heavier surveillance of transportation & communication infrastructures by the forces of repression. It ties us to disparate places & jobs & schedules not of our making. It puts us under greater scrutiny whereby absences from those places, jobs, & schedules will be noticed. And it denies us access to means of production that, in addition to paying the bills, would aid in positive practice.

Collectives also diminish the level of scrutiny on their members. Who outside a collective, for example, could certainly say that a member was not toiling in the back room or on an innocuous errand for the enterprise at a time in question? Who within a collective would? Going or coming are minimized & can be done less visibly. And many other material & financial transactions are facilitated &/or shielded from outside eyes by a collective structure, especially with creative use of tax & various registrations & reporting laws… These benefits will be particularly important when the apparatus of repression responds to our movement's increasing effectiveness by criminalization & otherwise attacking legitimate activity.

Collectives not only allow their participants to support themselves, they also give people control of the tools of the trade(s) by which they do so— means of production—that can be pressed into progressive work rather than lying idle under the control of some capitalist when not in use. A truck, for instance, might not only carry people, equipment, supplies to & from a job site: it might do the same for a rally, demonstration, or other event/action. The improved position to render mutual aid applies not only internally, but externally as well, collectives having greater material & personal means to support other forms of organizing, both traditional & experimental. Et cetera. The advantages of collectivity are many & manifest.

Perhaps most importantly, collectives will allow us to prefigure the society we would create as we work towards its realization. We all have been raised in & socially conditioned by an exploitative & oppressive society in which predation on a grand scale is lauded as virtue. As much as we individually may have transcended that programming, we lack the skills of socialism. Developing them includes learning how to handle the obviously material relationships, but also learning how to relate to each other in comradely, non-authoritarian, & nonalienating ways that still allow accomplishment of needful, knowledge too frequently lacking at present. Better to teach ourselves these skills from the bottom, with myriad collective efforts where the occasional dissolution is a relatively minor loss that is the price of knowledge & may be recouped elsewhere. Better that than to plan to impose inadequately tested theory on a large scale where failure would be a cosmic catastrophe that might take generations to repair. Further, the collectives we build & the community of collectives they form would provide working models to validate our theory & practice of social transformation & attract the people we must if we are to make revolution…

Establishing collectives is not the end of this strategy. It is merely a step in constructing an alternative socioeconomic base from & with which to effectively fight the status quo, to wage revolutionary class war. The collectives will generate a full array of exchange & mutual aid links. That will facilitate internal satisfaction of the movement's needs so it will be more independent of manipulation, freeze outs, crises, upheavals, & pressure within the enemy system. Collectivists' mobility will also ensure cross-fertilization, integration, communication, security, & personal component to the external relationships that will stimulate development & improve capacity to resist. As the alternative socioeconomic base expands, collectives will merge into one another's areas & functions & increasingly squeeze out enemy institutions that previously controlled those areas & functions. De facto free zones will emerge. The free zones can follow the same trajectory regionally & globally that collectives & their community of communities follow locally.

Assessment & reassessment of our movement's course based on hard analysis of the current situation is particularly appropriate at this juncture. No common vision of revolutionary theory, practice, & ends appears evident; verily, "identity" & simple issue politics appear ascendant with class struggle relegated to relatively minor, after-thought importance. No political "unified field theory" that ties these & other disparate elements together into a cohesive movement is apparent, leaving our movement at best a collection of "allies" in substrategic struggles.

The currently main or dominant organizational focus seems to be on race & nationalism, to the extent of suggesting white racism is the primary source of the need for revolution & nationalism the primary—indeed, only—strategy for making that revolution. Neither is accurate. The class contradiction is the base source of the multitudinous forms of exploitation & oppression that necessitate revolution. Resolution of that contradiction demands not separate & separatist struggle by people who are & aspire to be no more than fellow travelers in tactical maneuvers. It requires the aforementioned all people's movement that addresses & integrates all of those disparate elements into an effective revolutionary strategy—a house united.

Race is not an inescapable division of humanity into factual subspecies. Race is an artificial construct created by the ruling class to pit the class brethren & sistren of its opposing class against one another & thus divide & well rule them. That the oppressor class has succeeded only too well in erecting that division is evident by the extent to which racial consciousness, racism & notions of racial supremacy have come to pervade the extant society. However, that & the need to resist all forms of racial oppression do not negate the facts that greater differences exist within racial groups than are necessarily found across racial lines, that class comrades of all "races" have much more in common than at odds, & that arbitrary definitions of race fail—especially at the margins. In order to successfully resist—yea, overthrow—ruling class hegemony, domination, exploitation & oppression, we need an all people's movement that works to erase those competitive divisions & recognize, implement, & take advantage of that class commonality in a positive praxis.

Race is not class. The class contradiction is firmly rooted in the material world. Though it plays out in many ways, it is essentially defined by the appropriation by a small minority of exploiters & oppressors of the social wealth created by the large majority of people who are left to subsist by selling their labor. Through that relationship, control of material resources & sociopolitical influence are privatized, redistributed upward & concentrated at the top of a social hierarchy. That power is strategically used to advance the interest of the minority class through a variety of tactics, of which racial division is but one. The exploitation & oppression resulting from this socioeconomic contradiction is what makes revolution necessary.

While members of what are identified as different racial groups may be disproportionately represented on the sides & subdivisions of this class structure, no such group is the exclusive constituency of any of them. Even if the ruling class were exclusively white, white people are not exclusively or majoritively ruling class. Hence, the class divide is an economic, social, & political one that afflicts all groups defined by things other than the determinants of class, even if the hierarchy & its attendant disparities afflict some more than others.

Class privilege is not race privilege. Mistaking race for class also leads to misinterpreting rights as privileges & mistaking class privilege for white privilege. Being free from the abuses we recognize as racism in not a privilege; it is a human right, whether incidentally or deliberately observed or violated. That white people generally are relatively (& only relatively) freer from exploitation & oppression than non-white people generally reflects only less violation of their human rights. And none outside the upper echelons of the bourgeoisie is "proof" against the total disrespect of his or her human rights by the ruling class & its state apparatus that is inflicted on the most oppressed members of society.

Class "privilege" enters at the point at which people usurp greater access to the social wealth than would be theirs in the egalitarian society we would create. If human rights in that society do not include lesser levels of such access currently labeled "privilege," then we need to work on our definition of human rights &/or our social vision. Most whites do not have the above class privilege & some nonwhites enjoy it. Of course there are disparities, privilege or not, in the condition of the most oppressed will of course improve the most toward & until the erasure of any divergence from economic, social, & political parity.

Race is not nation. None of the groups described as racial is so monolithic as to constitute a nation in the usual sense, whether in geographically contiguous areas or across isolated enclaves. That sense itself is problematic, judging from the frequently arbitrary & artificial boundaries drawn as definitions of nations & the upheavals that have resulted from them. Asserting that "races" are so homogeneous as to constitute nations denies reality & is a form of invidious stereotyping.

Moreover, the very notion of nation is fluid: "nations" have risen & fallen & been reconstituted as different nations or parts thereof. Hence, there is no absolute "white" nation, "black" nation. "Latino" nation, "native" nation, "Asian" nation, "queer" nation, etc. While there may be areas populated by people of similar physical characteristics whose right to administer their own affairs has been abrogated by imperialism, that does not necessarily make them nations. Nor is there any reason people not sharing such characteristics cannot share the geography or administration of an area; verily, it must be possible because they already do in many areas.

Nationalism is not the best way forward, despite the great sacrifice, exemplary commitment & s/heroic accomplishment laid down in furtherance of nationalist struggles. Their gains have been illusory & they have failed to realize the full potential of revolutionary struggle. In most cases, the "nations" that have thrown off the physical shackles of occupation & autocratic imperialism have fallen victim to the financial & pseudo-democratic exploitation & oppression of the new world order's neo-imperialism.

The transnational capitalist hierarchy has proven more adept at adapting to, coopting, & diverting nationalist struggles than our side of the barricade has at evolving a new, effective praxis in a dynamic revolutionary movement to carry those gains forward. That was impossible to foretell at the high tide of national revolutions, when imperialist regimes were falling like leaves in what appeared to be the autumn of imperial capital, notwithstanding history's evidence of nationalism' dangers. But hindsight can be 20/20 & should tell us that the strategy of "two, three, many Vietnams" is flawed unless some of those Vietnams are in the imperialist centers & all of their practitioners recognize that capitalism's new world order can't be rolled up only from the edges, can't be defeated without a global revolutionary movement.

Nation states are not the paradigm for global revolution. They imply that there are inherent, significant, unbridgeable differences between humans. They further imply that unfettered association of all groups of humans would damage some of the groups. Intrinsic to that implication is the assumption that either the damaged or damaging groups are inferior or otherwise by nature & thus irremediably bad. Even taking both the implications & the assumption as valid, nation states are no solution: as is obvious from even a cursory analysis; such states are not protected or prevented from exploitation & oppression, either internal or external. And there is no good agreement that either the implication or the assumption is, in fact, valid; verily they are inconsistent with revolutionary principles based on contrary evidence.

Another implication of nation states is that capitalist competition rather than socialist cooperation is the best system of inter-group interaction, also inconsistent with revolutionary principles. Nor is there anything inherent in nationalism that makes it socialist. With a nation state as the primary if not only goal, bourgeois pseudo-democracy, autocracy, monarchy, theocracy, & even fascism are acceptable systems of intra-group interactions. Moreover, imperialism's use of nation states as prisons in which groups of people & their labor power can be locked for competitive exploitation & police suppression of resistance movements while imperial capital recognizes no national boundaries in pursuit of its interests (witness: WTO) exposes nationalism as antipopular & an impediment to real freedom. Hence, a revolutionary movement must seek to break down the boundary walls of nationalism rather than build them up.

Self-determination is not an absolute. Self-determination is a fine slogan, but what does it mean as a goal? In an increasingly global society, it is increasingly necessary to organize the utilization of the world's resources & distribution of its wealth into a sustainable system that serves the needs of all the world's people. Present international law, to the extent it can, given its subordination to imperial power & basis in capitalist ideology, encroaches on self-determination to take some small steps in that direction. But nations of absolute national self-determination & sovereignty render it largely ineffective. And some countries' self-determination is others' subjugation.

A global revolutionary movement would make local & regional autonomy the norm & protect localities & regions from exploitation & oppression through real (as opposed to merely political) democratic centralism. In a rational society, group self-determination is necessarily subject to the constraints of the community of groups as they seek to maximize their freedom by democratically balancing competing interests, just as individual freedom (self-determination) is subject to community constraints. In a revolutionary society, such constraints result in greater freedom for all—which is the point.

Looking at a strategy of revolution through racial nationalism also raises additional concerns of practicality & principle, particularly with respect to what are described as "internal" colonies. Advocating—& practicing—the formation of racially segregated organizations whose goals are intrinsically different & competitive, if not antagonist, cannot benefit the movement.

Trying to stifle the attendant divergence by creating a racial hierarchy is inconsistent with revolutionary principles. And nationalism-based organizations leave many people out in the cold by demanding of them an unmakeable choice.

Geographically separated & culturally diverse enclaves of racial majorities economically dependent on the surrounding areas cannot become viable "nations." Advocating the formation of such nations sets us up for failure. Where a racial group seeks to overcome the difficulties of a nation enclave by asserting a claim to territory in which it is a minority, the disenfranchisement &/or forcible expulsion of the majority requisite to the minority's national supremacy is ethically illegitimate. Further, launching such a struggle would pit a poor & oppressed minority against a more wealthy majority whose members it would be unable to significantly subvert in a contest the former could not win.

Organizing towards one or more such overtly antidemocratic national goals can only alienate a substantial portion of the population that would

531

otherwise be attracted to our revolutionary movement. Since the idea of a race-based nation is inherently racially supremacist, pursuing such goals not only engenders & hardens racial attitudes, it encourages the growth of competitive & negative ones. The U.S. ruling class has demonstrated the efficacy of creating false identity with itself in the mind of many of the exploited & oppressed, especially its tools among them, & using that fallacy to foment & fuel racial divisions that facilitate its social control. Pursuing racial separatist solutions plays into that tactic & inhibits us in creating consciousness of the real identity that exists between the class comrades of all races & the revolutionary action that could & must grow from it. We don't consign all of these potential comrades to enemy status because they are unconscious of the class contradiction. We should be willing to work with them similarly in creating revolutionary consciousness of racial oppression.

Launching one or more such racial nationalist separatist struggles would more than likely elicit a racist reaction, given their underlying assumptions. That reaction would transcend the area of national struggle & lead to pogrom-like atrocities against people of the separatists' racial group(s). They would have no choice in practicality or principle but to resist, & principle would demand that progressive, revolutionary, & antiracist forces of all races join them in that resistance in the spirit of mutual aid. Such an unequal struggle would more likely result in the destruction of the revolutionary movement & strengthening of fascism, if not the hatching of an outright fascist regime, than victory. Making the progressive forces strong enough to be the victors cannot be accomplished by balkanizing them, & especially by segregating the most oppressed & therefore most radical segment of the class from the larger movement. Rather, it requires unifying them in an all-people's movement that leaves the ruling class & its lackeys, lickspittles, minions, & henchpeople the poorer minority.

Of course, none of this means that racism, homophobia, genderism, poverty, & the many other issues that have given rise to various "identities" or have otherwise become the defining foci for people's resistance to imperial capital do not warrant serious struggle. No movement can hope to make real revolution if internally afflicted with &/or unconcerned about the exploitation & oppression represented by those fronts of the class war. Nor can we hope to attract enough people to a movement that does not take an unequivocal & active stand against such violations of human rights external to itself but nevertheless existing within the society in which we must work.

It does mean, however, that we must predicate our program on the application of revolutionary principles to an accurate & pragmatic analysis of our unique times & circumstances. We must also learn to distinguish between people within our movement & the truly free society we would create, the enemy, & the oppressive social order it enforces, & the vast bulk of the people who presently subsist between these poles. Only thus can we avoid rejection of our revolutionary vision because we brought it to people the wrong way.

On the basis thereof, we must prioritize the theory & practice of class war & an all people's revolutionary struggle to win it. That is what will solve the problems we confront, even if through protracted struggle, rather than merely demonstrate fealty to the "proper" positions. If our assessment & reassessment brings us to these conclusions & motivates action thereon, it has done more than well.

VII.3.1

The Struggle Continues

Russell "Maroon" Shoats

I wholeheartedly support the "John Brown 2000" conference. It is fitting that, during the 200th anniversary of John Brown's birth and Nat Turner's 200th birthday, like-minded people would assemble to struggle on how we should honor them by continuing the struggle that they both gave their lives for.

We have our own John Browns and Nat Turners: white anti-imperialists like Marilyn Buck, David Gilbert, the Ohio 7, Linda Evans, Larry Giddings, Bill Dunne and others, as well as Safiya Bukhari, Black Liberation Army combatants, New Afrikan Liberation Front cadre, Assata Shakur and many, many more. All tried and tested veterans.

But like John Brown and Nat Turner we must "never" rest until we get the job done… or until "death surprises us" in our work. Can anyone imagine either John Brown or Nat Turner, giving up their struggle to destroy slavery?!

We must also make a supreme effort to reach out to others who are struggling to stop this monster. We have to broaden our base to include all of those in various communities and organizations who cannot stomach racism, capitalist/imperialist domination and exploitation, cultural destruction and suppression, national oppression, environmental destruction, and all of the other ills that the millions daily try to combat—in their own ways.

We must Network, Network, Network! Not just here in this country, but globally. All the time we must recognize that "we" don't have all of the answers neatly wrapped up in any one of our collective ideological belief systems. If we can go out and make a serious effort to meet others with open minds, it shouldn't take long to identify common problems that are "all" in some way connected. From there we can decide when and how to best attack our problem: Concentration, Accuracy, Timing, and Speed.

I'm encouraged by the upsurge amongst the youth (globally!) over the last few years. Though they are not sure as to what all needs to be done, they still have "Grabbed the Torch!" Let's "network" more with them… our common destinies are Entwined.

VII.3.J

Loving to Be/Struggling to Be Free

Veronza Bowers

A strong, virtuous and industrious young man
  sat contemplative & absorbed at the side of a lake.
Strong body, humble in spirit
with the stillness of the water reflecting the serenity of
his thoughts:
  thoughts of a harvest
      Soon to be gathered,
  thoughts of a gratefulness
      For communal trading & sharing,
  thoughts of our children...
      Our dedicated & nurturing wives,
  thoughts of our loving parents
      Instructing & giving advice,
  thoughts of our people —
      Our beautiful, beautiful, beautiful people
loving to understand & loving to be understood,
loving to help others & loving those who help them,
loving to love & loving to be loved,
loving the freedom of others & longing to be free themselves...

  Then suddenly and imperceptibly
dreams transmitted to nightmares,
tranquility to havoc,
communal serenity to chaos,
and freedom to an inhumane forced servitude
  the likes of which were never Known
    Before or after ------
  Treacherously were we snatched from the place of our birth
  by a man with a plan
calculating our laborious worth.
  Captured, shackled, brought, sold and traded
    By an avaricious incompassion... inhuman, untenable and hatred.
We've been denigrated, debilitated, depreciated and nigger-rated.
We've been desired, denied, deprived, as well as separated.
We've been brutalized, terrorized, dehumanized, and victimized.

Then utilized, vilified and irrevocably criminalized.
We've struggled, fought
  been ridiculed, massacred and died...
  In mutinies, rebellions, protests
  and even freedom rides.
Despised as thieves, yet we continue to be stolen from...
Demeaned as murderers, yet we continue to be slaughtered...
  Incarcerated as Insurgents—We must Continue to Struggle.
We must still love to understand, and love to be understood.
We must still love to help others, and love those who help us.
We must still love to love, and love to be loved in return,
We must still love the freedom of others...

  AND STRUGGLE TO BE FREE OURSELVES.

Veronza Bowers, his daughter and grandchildren

Illegally Imprisoned!

Having been in prison since 1973, Veronza Bowers is one of the longest held political prisoners in the world. After serving his full 30-year term, he was scheduled for Mandatory Release on April 7, 2004. Under pressure from the Fraternal Order of Police, the U.S. Parole Commission blocked this mandatory release. He has been illegally held ever since.

See pages 768-9 for more information about this ongoing travesty of justice.

535

VII.3.K

Alliance Building: Looking Forward, Looking Back

Linda Evans

The need to build antiracist alliances is not at all abstract: today police are on the rampage in the streets of New York, Louisville, and in Angola and Pelican Bay prisons. In order to stop killer cops and win community control of the police, it's urgent that we build the strongest alliances possible between white antiracist and the Black and Latino communities where police kill with impunity. Yet such alliances are increasingly rare. How can effective alliances be built between white antiracists and activists from communities of color? (Comrades outside have urged me to reflect on specific experiences for this essay.)

Some alliances may be built first on individual actions and relationships. In these, most basic is a determination to fight every incidence of racism that we encounter, both institutional and interpersonal. This may be as commonplace as challenging racist language or characterizations whenever they occur in conversations, advertising, or media. A good example of this is the struggle led by the Native Americans against athletic teams' racist names and mascots. It doesn't take long to write a letter to the editor or an e-mail to the public relations department of a product employing racist advertising. Perhaps even more important is confronting racism in employment policies where you work or go to school, or in interpersonal conversations. This may be the first step an individual can take in becoming a dependable ally to people of color in your immediate workplace or neighborhood. Make the fight against racism your own.

Besides exposing and criticizing racism, you can take positive action to impede its development. Antiracist training and political self-education are a good way to start. In prison, for example, racial and national hostilities are encouraged as a means of preventing prisoner unity. For a short period of time, prisoners at F.C.I.-Dublin organized a Council Against Racism. We were disbanded by the prison before we could achieve some short-term goals like directly intervening to resolve conflicts. However, we did accomplish some short-term goals like ensuring the translation of most institutional forms, medical appointments and prisoner orientation sessions into Spanish. We also organized a Multi-Cultural Festival where women prisoners from many different countries performed their nations' music, poetry and dance. Experiencing other cultures and supporting each other's performances markedly lessened racial tension, though the effect was regrettably transitory.

But most of us wanted to organize beyond individual antiracism, to confront institutionalized white supremacy. The next step may be to offer your solidarity by contacting organizations where people of color are addressing

issues that affect their communities: killer cops/police brutality, environmental racism, gentrification, workfare/welfare cuts, prison. Very often
white organizations try to recruit people of color as members, as a way to
"diversify" or "better represent the community as a whole." This approach
ignores the fact that white-dominated structures leave little power for people
of color. Years ago in Austin, a group of white women recognized that our
efforts to include Black and Chicana women in feminist activities were
inevitably mechanistic, even tokenistic, because these women of color did
not choose to belong to white-dominated feminist organizations. We were
antiracist and believed that the women's movement needed to fight for the
demands of Black women and Chicanas. They were involved in organizing
for the survival of their community—specifically against gentrification and
the invasion of white-owned real estate development. In Austin, this invasion had been spearheaded by the takeover of a community lakeside park for
national jet-propelled speedboat competitions. The destruction of the park
had brought an invasion of reckless drunk drivers, property destruction, and
finally a serious hit-and-run injury of a young Chicana. The Black Citizens'
Task Force and the Brown Berets formed an alliance to stop the boat races. We
approached them, pledging to organize white opposition to "boat-racism"
and gentrification. The Black Citizens' Task Force and Brown Berets were
rightfully dubious of our commitment and political perseverance; there had
been little contact or solidarity from the white community since the Civil
Rights movement. Gradually we built trust amongst us through our day-
to-day practice—confrontations with white racists, skirmishes with cops,
arrests, organizing broad support to attend City Council meetings. Fighting
for survival of their community was the first priority of Black and Chicana
women.

Our experience has many parallels in today's struggles: the fight for survival
of ethnic studies and bilingual education, against red-lining and agribusiness
takeovers of Black-owned farms in the South, support of Native American
land and fishing rights. Organizing direct support for the demands of communities of color is a way white activists can fight their own tendencies to
dominate decision-making. We can fight white supremacy and arrogance in
our own practice by relinquishing control.

Another form of organizational alliance-building takes place in campaigns
with a broad, single-issue focus. White antiracists working in the AIDS
movement, for example, struggle for funds to be directed to Black, Native
American, Latino and Pacific Islander organizations, so they can decide how
best to utilize those resources. Only a very few AIDS activists on the outside
have advocated for HIV+ prisoners or prisoners with AIDS—though this is
another important way to fight the white-centeredness of the AIDS movement. Prisoners with AIDS have urgent needs: compassionate release for terminal illnesses, consistent access to new treatments and quality medical care,
programming opportunities equal to those of other prisoners, political and

material support for peer education programs. Responding to the ongoing needs of HIV+ prisoners and their families, political prisoners have founded AIDS education and support—another form of alliance-building inside. At F.C.I. Dublin (then F.C.I. Pleasanton), we initiated the process of forming PLACE (Pleasanton AIDS Counseling and Education) by discussing the idea with Black, Native American and Latina women, approaching individuals and their organizations—the Black Cultural Workshop, Four Winds Group and Latina Club. PLACE was a joint effort from its beginning; its existence represented an important alliance between the diverse communities here. We made consistent efforts to fight racial divisions, translating all our literature and programs into Spanish, co-sponsoring Women's Health Fairs with Black History Month committees, and training women of different ethnic backgrounds to be spokespeople. We directed proceeds from our Prisoners Fight AIDS Walk-a-thons to organizations that focused on the most oppressed and underserved people with AIDS—women, a hospice in the Black community, drug addicts and queers of color—in addition to contributing to a camp for children with AIDS. In this way, PLACE also built an alliance with the communities outside. (PLACE was outlawed by the prison and shut down in 1997.)

Resources and money are often the issue that break alliances apart. White supremacy in our society means that white activists in general have more access to money and resources than our comrades from communities of color. Part of the success of any alliance depends on a commitment to share these resources. Many political relationships have been built specifically to facilitate the acquisition and transfer of resources—solidarity campaigns providing material aid. Fund-raising specifically to finance travel for people of color to national demonstrations or conferences is central to facilitating their participation and should not be limited to just a specific number of scholarships. When these solidarity efforts also organize political action, a transformation occurs—individuals go beyond simply making a donation and are radicalized by joining the resistance struggle.

In alliances between white people and people of color, leadership is also an important dynamic. In the John Brown Anti-Klan Committee (JBAKC), we believed that following the leadership of Black revolutionaries and organizations was the way we could be most effective in fighting white supremacy. We recognized that the people who experience racism most directly are the most knowledgeable about how to best oppose it and that any action taken by white people fighting the KKK, for example, could well have repercussions that would affect the Black community. We built consistent, respectful lines of communication with the Black Citizens' Task Force and the Brown Berets, to ensure that they could contribute meaningfully to our planning process, or veto actions if they felt they were inappropriate or endangered their communities. They, in turn, often asked for us to fulfill specific responsibilities or to organize support in the white community for their campaigns. We learned another lesson about self-determination because of the dynamic between local and national Black organizations. JBAKC nationally was directly responsible to the New Afrikan People's Organization (NAPO), a revolutionary nationalist organization that was struggling for land and independence as the concrete expression of self-determination for the Black nation. In Austin, the Black Citizens' Task Force did not identify their organization as either revolutionary or nationalist—they organized primarily around immediate needs of the local Black community. Members of the Austin chapter of JBAKC initially felt conflicted by these ideological differences, but to intervene in these political differences would have been racist and inappropriate. What was primary was our commitment to antiracist organizing. We soon realized that NAPO's leadership complemented and broadened the perspective of the daily work we did with the BCTF. For example, NAPO's revolutionary political perspective aided us in relating the local struggle against killer cops and the KKK, and for a civilian review board, to nation-wide campaigns. Similarly today, developing relationships with local activists in national Black networks like NAPO, N'COBRA, or the Black Radical Congress can allow white antiracists in local communities to contribute to national campaigns and strategies.

As long as its common goals are kept primary, an alliance benefits from political discussion and struggle. For example, many of us in JBAKC were lesbians; we confronted antigay attitudes among comrades in the BCTF and Brown Berets, as we did in the rest of society. Based in the overriding commitment to our work together, mutual respect enabled us to criticize and struggle with each other in ways that ultimately strengthened our alliance rather than destroying it.

Following the leadership of the Black, Puerto Rican, Native American, Mexican-Chicano organizations does not mean being passive or waiting for direction. A mock lynching occurred just outside East Austin: a black-faced effigy was shot up and hung from a tree, with white supremacist literature scattered nearby. The Black and Chicano communities were prepared for self-defense, but decided not to directly confront the incident. For their white allies, this mock lynching was one more indication that the Ku Klux Klan's paramilitary operations were expanding. We planned out a campaign to oppose and expose the Klan's growth in Texas, consulting with BCTF and Brown Berets as we implemented each step. The KKK was actively recruiting—using community access TV facilities, starting up a chapter of the NAAWP (National Association for the Advancement of White People), using free advertising offered by an alternative community newspaper, publicizing the paramilitary training that they conducted on National Grasslands. We confronted them directly and consistently: making arguments against their access to community resources, threatening a boycott and picket line against the newspaper if they ran the NAAWP ads, holding demonstrations outside TV and radio stations where the Klan was interviewed, going door-to-door with a petition to shut down all their paramilitary training camps.

We talked to hundreds of people face-to-face about the Klan, killer cops, and manifestations of white supremacy internationally in Palestine and South Africa. JBAKC was initiating these antiracist campaigns, but prioritized and maintained communications with NAPO and our Black and Chicano comrades locally. Our own initiatives to fight white supremacy strengthened the alliances we were building with communities of color, both in Austin, statewide, and nationally.

Our resistance to today's white supremacy must be creative and consistent. It's crucial to keep up the pressure to win community control of the police, to stop the murders of people of color by killer cops. The freedom fighters of the Black Liberation Army and Black Panther Party were the first to target police in defense of Black communities across the U.S. Campaigns against killer cops and police brutality should include demands to free Mumia Abu-Jamal and other POW's and political prisoners. The fight for prisoners' human rights exposes the genocidal and white supremacist aspects of mass imprisonment: criminalization of whole communities and especially young people of color, the destruction of families via mass incarceration, the racially selective death penalty and "war against drugs." White prison activists can be more effective by building direct relationships with organizations of prisoners' families and other grassroots prison reform efforts based in communities of color. We must never forget that tens of thousands of white supremacists are active in armed paramilitary organizations: they pose a clear and very present danger and must be exposed and confronted. Activists in the antiglobalization movement should self-consciously build alliances both internationally and locally by working on issues that affect people of color. Their communities have been devastated by economic restructuring, whether through cutbacks in welfare, lost jobs because of runaway shops, homelessness, or cutbacks in public education and health care. It's crucial that we build alliances that connect all these issues, in addition to confronting racist attitudes and institutional practices. Making these alliances a priority will strengthen our ability to effectively fight supremacy and ultimately to build a revolutionary resistance movement.

VII.3.L

Mixed, Like You; Mixed, Like Me

Larry Giddings

As we embark into the 21st, Christian calendar, century we are confronted with immense social and cultural upheaval. The very foundations of political and social analysis evolved from our many origins are called into question. History/Herstory/Ourstory (how social/political/economic evolution is documented and taught) is in great flux. From an "Industrial Age," to an age of "Science and Technology"; and now—we are firmly in the tide of the "Information Age." The numbers of competing histories of social evolution are multiplying—rather than diminishing. The "truthfulness," or "accuracy," of a number of histories are not questioned—by many. Designing a history to meet philosophical-political-religious goals has become easier, rather than more difficult. It is this titanic struggle to define histories, which marks the battle ground of the present.

The study of DNA has fairly well demythologized the belief in "racial" difference. "Race" is a nonstarter. Human beings; regardless of hair, eye or skin variation, belong to the same race: *Homo Sapien Sapien.* The transplanting of organs: hearts, livers, kidneys, corneas, etc. amongst people of all hues has punctuated the DNA research with a solid exclamation point!!

"Nationalism," described by many as a "liberatory" activity, has deteriorated to "tribalism" throughout much of the world. The break-up of Yugoslavia into its tribal/ethnic parts as separate "nation-states," and numerous, previously, "socialist republics," are firm examples of tribalism as the basis of conflict. Postcolonial Africa continues to be driven by tribal/ethnic conflict exacerbated by the colonial experience.

Tribal and ethnic conflict disguised as "nationalist" movements and "civil-class war" are reflected around the globe. They are a human condition. Defining a people, a tribe and its evolution and relations with other tribes is the goal of all history.

What is a "white" person? Is it someone with a light, pale skin color? Or is it someone with blue eyes? Are they defined by "national" origin; were they born in a particular country? As we all know, no definition suffices. Just as there is no single definition of a "Black" person. These appellations are social-political in nature and not merely descriptions of skin-tone and hair, etc.

The gene-pools of the European, Asian and African continents have mixed for untold millennia. Tribal differentiation can and does occur with great rapidity. Cultural diversity occurs even more quickly. The Irish of North America are culturally different from those who remained in Ireland. The examples are endless.

I, as an individual, do not pretend to represent any group, ethnic-genetic-

541

social or otherwise. My study of histories and human geography of "genetic drift" causes me to recognize origins from across the human landscape. There is no mythology strong enough to make me "white." Confronting "reality," revealing "truths," should be what "history" is about. For myself, historian and cultural analyst Jan Carew has been a great example. While politically acknowledged as a Black-Caribbean scholar, he celebrates his diverse ethnic origins. That self-knowledge must be the foundation of my personal journey into the 21st century. How others define themselves, I cannot say. To build a new and hopefully "better" world, I work to allow others to define themselves. I will struggle to expand an understanding of the breadth of human history. Our history did not begin a few hundred years ago, or even a few thousand. The world includes more than Europe, more than Africa, more that the Americas. The future will not be defined by one ethnic enclave or a single individual.

For myself, the building of a movement that recognizes the multiplicity of ethnic-social-genetic origins at work—in each of us—is a constant refrain. As economic globalism explodes alongside information exchange, so must any social movement globalize for any hope of survival. Indigenous "nations" (tribes) have recognized this, from Papua New Guinea to Zapatistas of Chiapas, Mexico. Confronting domination: economic, class, or otherwise, will require an even greater grasp of history. I hope to see this evolve in the years ahead.

John Brown is someone I view as willing to step across the perceived boundaries of "race & class," to create a country without chattel slavery. We, too, can step across boundaries, define who we are, and create an inclusive culture of struggle.

Source: www.radicalgraphics.org

542

VII.3.M

Some Lessons from the 1960s

David Gilbert

The movement of the 1960s showed the potential for positive response from whites to the rise of national liberation struggles, along with a desire for a more humane and cooperative society. It is true that this response came first from elite students, the children of the petty bourgeoisie and professionals. These sectors felt more secure in their privilege and felt less immediately threatened by advances for Black people than did the poorer sectors of whites. Also, students and intellectuals are frequently the group that early on, albeit subjectively, responds to emerging contradictions in a given society. The movement was a real reflection of the objective advance of national liberation and the need to transform U.S. society. As the war in Vietnam dragged on, increasing numbers of working-class youth became involved in the movement.

This fledgling success and glimmer of potential of the '60s also provided some historical lessons that we have not done nearly enough to analyze and codify. The movement involved more than the traditional unrest of students. Broader cultural identification played a major role in generating a larger youth movement. First and foremost it was the impact of Black culture, with its more humane values of social consciousness, emotional expressiveness, and sense of community—primarily through the genesis of rock 'n' roll. The cultural rebellion also importantly involved an opening of sexual expression that challenged the prevailing strait-jacket of repression. Paradoxically, to the grim realities we've come to understand, at that time drugs (particularly marijuana and LSD) were seen as liberation from repressive control and the promotion of antiauthoritarianism.

Civil rights and antiwar activity among whites started mainly on the campuses, and the student movement was a spearhead for political consciousness throughout the '60s. Most white working-class youth were initially indifferent if not downright hostile to these initial stirrings. But over the years there were increasing cultural links that laid the basis for a broader movement.

David writes:"The following is from the concluding section of my 1991 pamphlet, *Looking at the White Working Class Historically*, published by the Cooperative Distribution Service with comments from J. Sakai. The purpose of this section was to assess the 1960s in order to draw out lessons about the potential and terms for future antiracist organizing among white people. Today, we obviously are not in a period of rapid victories for national liberation struggles; it's not even clear precisely what forms of struggle and strategies will lead to revolutionary, humane social change. But the oppression and resistance of people of color—both in the third world and within the U.S.—is still the fundamental social reality. Finding fruitful ways to organize white people against racism continues to be our critical and central responsibility." *Looking at the White Working Class Historically* was subsequently published in pamphlet form by Abraham Guillen Press/Arm the Spirit, and is currently available through AK Press.

For example, white working-class youths who dropped out of the daily work grind and were often into drugs, gravitated to communities near campuses. Antidraft counseling offices brought many into more direct, political contact with the movement. The burgeoning of community colleges meant that more working-class youth were themselves students. By the late 1960s the growing disenchantment and anger about the war in Vietnam provided a unifying focus and sense of identity for all the disaffected. When soldiers in Vietnam started to turn against the war, that added a new dimension to the movement, as well as significantly deepening its class composition.

The main base for the anti-imperialist movement of the '60s was a social movement of youth, heavily impacted and in many ways generated by Black culture. As the movement developed, it involved increasing numbers of working-class youth, who played a major role in the movement's growth and heightened militancy. This extension showed (1) the ability of culture to be a bridge to deepening the class base of a social movement, (2) the increasing ways the draft, in the context of a bloody and losing war, made the interests of some working-class people intersect with those of national liberation, and (3) the contagious effect of victorious revolutions and liberatory vision.

The New Left did have an intelligent strategy for extending the movement and deepening its class base, but abandoned it at the very moment it was achieving stunning success. The Revolutionary Youth Movement (RYM) strategy called for the extension of what had started as a primarily elite student base to a broader, particularly working-class, youth base by doing more work around the draft, with GIs, in community colleges, and among youth in working-class neighborhoods. The movement, still heavily male supremacist, had little sense of the role of women and often lapsed into very negative sexist posturing. However, even here, the freedom, energy, and rhetoric of the movement provided a new opening for women's liberation. Women active in the Civil Rights Movement and in SDS (Students for a Democratic Society) provided a major impetus for the new wave of feminism that emerged in 1967. Unfortunately the reaction of men within the movement was so sexist that it led to what has become an ongoing and destructive stasis that pits anti-imperialism and women's liberation against each other. But RYM did offer a vision extending the movement to involve broader working-class sectors without losing the political focus on antiwar, antiracism and militancy.

Large numbers of working-class youth did get involved in the movement. At the high point, millions took to the streets in the wake of the 1971 invasion of Cambodia and the killing of students at Kent State. This movement was of course not magically free of racism, as painfully illustrated by the failure to make issue of the killing of Black students at Jackson State and of Chicano antiwar activists in Los Angeles. But it was a movement that could, with political leadership, have strong anti-imperialist potential.

SDS, which correctly formulated the RYM strategy in December 1968, was already splintered apart by May 1971. The dissolution of SDS shortly before the triumph of its strategy was not simply a question of stupidity or even just a matter of the pervasive power of opportunism. The student movement had reached a crisis in 1968 because its very successes had moved it from simply "shocking the moral consciousness of America" to realizing it was in fundamental opposition to the most powerful and ruthless ruling class ever. The murderous attacks on the Black movements we supported (dozens of Black activists were killed and a couple of thousand incarcerated from 1968 through 1971) drove the point home graphically at the same time that the dictates of solidarity urgently pressed us to qualitatively raise our level of struggle. The movement went into a crisis in 1968 because it came face to face with the terrifying reality of imperialism's power.

RYM was a creative and realistic strategy to extend the base and power of the movement, although it needed to be joined by an equally strong politics of women's liberation. But for all of its value as a transitional strategy, RYM was of course in itself nowhere near an adequate basis for overthrowing bourgeois power. So, looking for immediate answers in the crisis, the left floundered on the perennial dilemma in white supremacist society. The majority looked for a magic solution to the problem of power by mythologizing the white working class (the majority in the U.S.) as "revolutionary"—in reality this position meant a retreat into white supremacy and away from confronting imperialism. The minority tried to maintain purity around racism and the war by seeing ourselves as exceptional whites, separated from any social base—in reality this position meant abandoning responsibility for building a movement that could sustain militant struggle against imperialism.

While a youth movement in itself can't be sufficient, the promising success of RYM within its realm does suggest some lessons:

1. the role culture can play in building cross-class movements;
2. the value of looking for potential points of intersection of interests of whites with the advance of national liberation—e.g., a) costs of imperialist wars, GIs, the draft, taxes, social priorities, b) situations of common oppression where there is Third World leadership (welfare, prisons, some labor struggles), and c) situations where a vision of a revolutionary alternative can be most readily perceived (youth, women);
3. the likelihood that social movements can play more of a role in involving white working people in a progressive struggle than traditional, direct forms of class organizing. The social movements though—youth, Lesbian-Gay-AIDS, antiwar and antinuclear, ecology, and potentially around housing, health, and education—have typically had a "middle-class' leadership and a primarily middle-class base. ("Middle class" meaning people from college-educated backgrounds—mainly professionals and petty bourgeois).

While the women's movement is usually labeled as a social movement because it is not one of the traditional struggles for state power, it should be more appropriately grouped with national liberation and class as responding to one of the three most fundamental structures of oppression. No movement can be revolutionary and successful without paying full attention to national liberation, class content, and the liberation of women. After the collapse of the antiwar and youth movements in the '70s, the women's movement provided the most sustained and extensive impetus for social change within white America. Like the social movements, the leadership and main active base was middle class. With the ebbing of the radical women's liberation tendency that identified with national liberation, the apparent leadership of contemporary feminism has a more pronounced middle-class character—at the same time that many more working-class women, while eschewing the name "feminism," have actively adopted and adapted the goals and struggles of the movement.

We would argue that the women's movement and the social movements, to be revolutionary, must relate to racism, national liberation, and Third World leadership. But we should add that, as with the youth movement, each should be looking for ways to extend its base into the working class on an antiracist and pro-women's liberation basis.

The Lesbian-Gay-AIDS movement has been of particular urgency, militancy and importance in this period. The struggle around AIDS has pushed the radical sector toward the need to ally with Third World and poor white communities impacted by intravenous drugs and poor health care. The AIDS movement has also provided leadership in breaking through the sterile conservative (cut back services to the poor) versus liberal (defend state bureaucracy) definition of political debate. ACT UP and others have provided an excellent example of mobilization and empowerment from below for self-help while at the same time demanding a redistribution of social resources to meet these social needs.

Peace, ecology, the homeless, health care, education all speak to important pieces that express the inhumanity and ineffectiveness of the whole system. Of course these movements have been, almost by definition, reformist. But that doesn't mean that they have to be under all circumstances: e.g., (1) a deeper crisis in imperialism where it has less cushion from which to offer reforms, (2) a situation where revolutionary alternatives are strong enough to be tangible, (3) a political leadership that pushes these movements to ally with national liberation, promote women's liberation, and deepen their class base, while at the same time drawing out the connections among the different social movements into a more coherent and overall critique of the whole system. Under such circumstances and leadership, the social movements could not only involve far more white working-class people in antisystemic struggles, but would also serve to redefine and revitalize class issues and class struggle itself.

Lessons from the '60s certainly don't offer a blueprint for the '90s, which are a very different decade. Clearly we are not now in a period of progressive social upheaval. Economic dislocation, at least initially, provides fertile ground for white supremacist organizing. National liberation struggles are not at this point achieving a clear path to socialism.

What is certain is that there will be changes, and, at points, crises. We can't afford to repeat the old errors of once again floundering on the dilemma of either "joining" the working class's white supremacy or of abandoning our responsibility to organize a broader movement. While there is no blueprint, the basis for a real starting point is an analysis of actual historical experience.

In sum, revolutionaries must be realistic about the history of white supremacy, the impact of material wealth and dominance, and the mushrooming of job and status differentials among workers, both nationally and internationally. There is nothing approximating the Marxist revolutionary proletariat within white America. At the same time, the distinction between those who control the means of production and those who live by the sale of labor power has not been completely obliterated.

A system of white supremacy that was historically constructed can be historically deconstructed. A key factor for whites is the tangibility of a revolutionary alternative as opposed to the more immediate relative privileges that imperialism has had to offer. In this regard we have no map for what the future will bring. The experience of the '60s does offer some possible lessons for when the system is under stress:

1. Anti-imperialist politics are more important than initial class composition.
2. Culture, especially with ties to Third World people, can be an important force for building progressive cross-class movements.
3. In seeking to extend such movements, revolutionaries should look for intersection points of white working-class interests with the advance of national liberation, such as the draft.
4. Women's liberation must play a central role in all movements we build.
5. The various social movements, if we can fight for an alliance with the national liberation and the presence of women's politics and leadership, can be important arenas for extending the base to include working-class people, mutually redefining class and social issues, and making the connections to an overall antisystemic perspective.

VII.3.N

For John Brown's 200th Birthday, three haiku

David Gilbert
May 9, 2000

Cynosure

John Brown's our North Star
we know of no perfection
only caring and struggle

Embrace

Whites embrace all (and
our) humanity (only)
by fighting racism

Our Politics... in 17 Syllables*

Love for the people
means non-stop struggle against
imperialism

---

* Originally appeared as "Marilyn-David-Laura Haiku," as the "short version" of a
ca. 70,000-syllable political interview (*Enemies of the State,* published by Resistance in
Brooklyn, subsequently republished by Kersplebedeb and available through AK Press), with
Marilyn Buck, Laura Whitehorn, and David.

VII.3.N
Unity of Humanity...
Bashir Hameed

Bismillahir   Rahmanir   Raheem
I am not a statement writer, but I do support the need for building alliances against the reactionary forces aligned against those of us seeking the betterment and unity of humanity.

Those of us who are nationalists or former nationalists were never into any antiwhite nonsense. There are white revolutionaries currently languishing in prisons throughout this country that have sacrificed their lives in the cause of the Black Liberation Movement.

I would like to thank everyone for their efforts on our behalf. I trust this letter is taken in the Spirit that it is sent, which is for us to reflect upon principles and standards that we all should hold dear and be ever vigilant and cognizant of, and that we all stand on.

In Struggle, Bashir

VII.3.O
Reparations...
Jalil Muntaqim

Greetings!
If there is one thing I would like to see come out of the John Brown 2000 conference, it is the building of a reparations movement for the slavery of Africans. I believe it is important for progressives and anti-imperialists in the U.S. to take an active position in the fight for reparations for African slavery. A forward position on this issue in solidarity with New Afrikans' initiative will ultimately raise the issue unto the national debate. It will force America to face the failure to apologize for slavery and make amends, and further expose economic disparity, white privilege, and the need to challenge continuing racist practices. So out of the conference I hope a resolution is made on this extremely important issue in the next century... of course the fight for the release of PP/POW's must be highlighted! Until next time.

Struggle Straight Ahead, Jalil

VII.3.P

About Our Commonalities

Wopashitwe Mondo Eyen we Langa

I joined the Omaha chapter of the Black Panther Party in 1969 and was in the Party in 1970 at the time of my arrest. I joined because I admired the work the Party was doing in standing up for African people against European-supremacist-based police arrogance and because I wanted to be a part of something—whether standing up against police attacks against the African community, feeding African children, exposing the anti-African nature of the U.S. political/economic system, or/and otherwise—through and by which African people were moving forward under our own leadership and for our own collective interests. Though my involvement in this work made me a target for what would turn out to be almost thirty years of false imprisonment thus far, I am proud to have been a Panther and grateful for what the experience did for my growth as an African person.

For a time, our chapter ran what we named the "Vivian Strong Liberation School for Children," where I taught political education and "Black" history. In teaching this history of African people, I was limited in the information and insight I could relay to the young children by my inadequate knowledge of the history of our people beyond the space and time boundaries of the United States of (occupied) America. It wasn't until sometime after I had been locked up that I would become familiar with Yosef ben-Jochannan, John Henrik Clarke, Drusilla Houston, Ivan Van Sertima, Cheikh Anta Diop, and other such African scholars and thinkers and their crucial research on the many aspects of the history of African people.

I wish I would have had the knowledge and insights gained from these scholars when I was teaching the African children back in the day. I wish I would have been able to instill in them more than "Black" pride and give them more than a sense of some "Black" nationalism.

As is now well known, there was conflict between the Black Panther Party national leadership and Maulana Ron Karenga's U.S. organization. U.S. characterized us as being some kind of slaves to the dead Europeans—Marx and Lenin, et al. The Party called U.S. and other cultural nationalist groups "pork chop nationalists" and ridiculed their African dress and talk and so forth as being little more than style, lacking substance. However accurate these characterizations might have been or how off-base, we know what the conflict led to—the FBI's capitalizing on this crack in our movement to assist in the transforming of it into a virtual chasm. We know that people died behind this friction.

There are other things we know: that European (Caucasian) cops have returned to the pre-Black Panther mindset whereby they feel no hesitance

, to treat African people as they feel like. Abner Louima, Amadou Diallo, and Tyisha Miller are but a tiny few of many examples of this. We know that the "nachral" has, for many African girls and women, been replaced by chemically-straightened hair and blond wigs and so forth; that the relative popularity of traditional African garments has given way to an obsession with trendy clothes with the names of European men affixed to them—Tommy Hilfiger, Calvin Klein, et al. We know that "Black" pride has come to be overshadowed by the prevalence of "Jerry Springer people"—males and females who have learned to enjoy being publicly ridiculed and debased for the entertainment of TV audiences. In other words, much of the progress that we, as African people, made during the "Black" liberation movement has eroded.

What we Africans in this country need now is what we needed back in the day of clenched fists and black berets—a strong sense of our African selves: a knowledge and understanding of our pan-African history, traditional cultures and values, and an instituting of programs and systems by which we can operate according to traditional African values, in contexts that are political, economic, social, and so forth.

In the process of this kind of collective and individual rediscovery, we will not only cure the psychic ailments we have contracted from materialism/individualism/European-supremacism-driven U.S. culture but will be enabled to see how much we have in common with the indigenous people of this country, including both the so-called "Indians" and Mexicanos(as)/Chicano(as). Respectfully, I would submit that this rediscovery of the collective self is one needed as much by these populations as it is by Africans. And this commonality I speak of is not merely the obvious one—that of having a shared enemy: the European-supremacist system. It is, more importantly, a matter of shared traditional (before Colon and company) values and outlooks. When we people of color study and grasp an understanding of our respective histories, we uncover the facts that we were, respectively, communal in our relations, that we viewed life holistically, that we saw earth as our Creator's dominion and that we were its caretakers, etc.

As we learn about our commonalities, it will be much easier for us to work together. It will be easier for us to see that the imprisonment of Leonard Peltier is part of the same repression as is the imprisonment of Panthers; that the "Indian" names and mascots of sports teams are symptomatic of the same European-supremacist arrogance as was the creation of "Little Black Sambo" in the past or Budweiser's "whassup" commercial in the present; that our fighting each other over politically generated economic crumbs plays into the hands of those in whose interest it is to keep us in conflict with each other and blind to the efficacy of our allying with each other.

VII.3.Q

To the John Brown 2000 Conference

Jaan Laaman

My friends,

I'd like to begin by sending all you good folks attending this John Brown 2000 conference, as well as everyone else who will be part of the ongoing work from this conference, a very warm and red salute. It goes without saying I'd much rather be there with you. But besides us political prisoners, there should be significant numbers of people this conference can reach and influence.

In this my 16th year of captivity, I'm not going to presume to tell any of you how and where our movement should go. I will share some of my reflections, analysis and practice on John Brown and our work ahead.

As a white person, for many long years I've viewed John Brown as a fine upstanding American. Within the anti-imperialist and antiracist movement and especially among my closest Ohio 7/United Freedom Front comrades, John Brown has always been seen as an admirable figure to be learned from. He not only said the right things, but took bold and militant action on his beliefs. He took up the cause of freedom, by becoming a freedom fighter.

Of course, the mid-19th-century United States, the pre-Civil War times of John Brown, was a world apart from our life today. It's an obvious truism that reality is constantly changing and things must be seen in context of their own conditions, time and place. Looking back as recently as 10 to 20 years ago, we have seen momentous and significant changes in the world. Any understanding of the struggles facing us today have to be rooted in the realities of the present.

As many changes as we have seen since the 1980s, let alone the drastic differences from John Brown's 1850s, a central reality of America remains in effect. The oppression and exploitation of African people has been a fundamental feature, almost since the beginning of European colonization, of America. The principal forms of oppression that Black people have faced have changed over time. In John Brown's day the fundamental issue was actual slavery—human bondage. In the 135 years since the defeat of the Confederate slave states in the Civil War, advances and improvements have been made. Yet today everyone, except maybe a crude white supremacist, would agree that African people still face injustice and oppression throughout life in the U.S.

Historically and presently Black people are not the only victims of oppression and injustice in America. The list is ugly and long and includes: the genocide and land theft committed against Native people; class and economic inequality and the oppression of the landless and poor; political, social, and economic oppression of women; a long list of exploited and discriminated against immigrants (Irish, Chinese, Italians) as well as the historical and ongoing exploitation and oppression of Mexicans and other Latinos; the 100-year colonization of Puerto Rico, etc.... Such injustice has been and remains part of the basic fabric of U.S. reality. Nonetheless, the racism and discrimination against, and the inequality and hyperexploitation of, Black people are a historic and ongoing reality that influences and effects just about everything else in America. This is true on a societal and personal level and affects us in economic, social, and political areas of life. This certainly remains a key issue in the anti-imperialist and revolutionary struggles and, I would argue, in every struggle for social and economic justice.

As a young man John Brown witnessed and examined life around him. He came to an understanding and position, as a human being and as a white man, on the most cutting and conflicting issue in America then, slavery of Africans. He became an abolitionist. He educated others and worked in the Underground Railroad. In time he came to understand that a more active struggle had to be waged by the antislavery movement and particularly by white abolitionists. John Brown stepped forward and took up arms to free slaves and to combat the slave-owning forces. He supported the efforts of Africans and he organized whites and Blacks as guerrilla fighters. Historically John Brown came to be seen as a noble and outstanding figure in the antislavery movement, but often during his life, the more established white forces in the abolitionist movement were critical of him and shied away from him. John Brown not only criticized the shortcomings of moderate white abolitionists, but simultaneously directly acted to liberate Black slaves.

Throughout recent times—the 1960s, '70s, '80s, and '90s—we too have had to examine and take positions on the most crucial issues. A central contradiction throughout U.S. history has been the oppression of African people in this land.

From slavery to sharecropping, lynching, Jim Crow laws, rural and urban poverty and ghetto living, last hired-first fired, to the present-day realities of hugely disproportionate numbers of Blacks in poverty, prison and death row, African people, not only individually but as a group, as a nation, a colonized nation existing within the borders of the U.S.A., face economic, social, and political oppression. The manifestation of the oppression has changed over time, but the reality has not. Any revolutionary or anti-imperialist movement must recognize this core contradiction of America. Any fundamental change, particularly any truly liberating vision of a just, humane and free future, is impossible without a resolution of the oppression of the African nation within America. This struggle remains central to all struggle for revolutionary change in the U.S.

Personally, I don't believe we will ever have revolutionary change in America until the African nation is liberated. Conversely, I don't see any liberation (even a phony, neocolonial type change) of the African nation without

LET FREEDOM RING

an actual social and political revolution in the U.S. Saying this does not mean that there are no other crucial or pressing contradictions within America. I certainly think that there are. I recognize the class contradiction as the principal issue that effects people of all nations and genders within the U.S. But without recognizing that there is a captive Black nation and its right to self-determination, we will not be able to mobilize all the necessary forces that we will need to end imperialism and bring about a new revolutionary future.

I think we, white revolutionary forces, must continue to affirm our full support for the liberation of the African nation. The term that best captures this for me is proletarian internationalism—the revolutionary proletarian class provides international support for the just liberation struggle of the primary colonized nation within the United States.

U.S. imperialism not only holds the African nation in bondage, but also Puerto Rico and Native American nations. U.S. imperialism is also the same system that exploits poorly paid workers here, even while exporting more and more jobs to other countries where even lower wages and harsher exploitation exist. It's the same system that allows the destruction of our environment, usually for corporate superprofits. Meanwhile, the government in Washington uses its superpower to bully countries and to act like the world cop for the likes of the WTO and transnational corporations. These are all interrelated struggles, all contradictions within America that cry out for our attention and work. So I'm not saying it's a question of only working to further the struggle of the African nation, but we must see the core connection that this struggle has to the others.

I do not believe that every Black group or campaign has to be supported. What should be done, particularly by white revolutionary forces, is to extend constant support to the overall revolutionary Black struggle. Based on our particular ideology, communist, anarchist, etc., we may work more closely with different African forces and organizations. The African community has the right and duty to bring forth its own leaders and formations, and as revolutionaries within America we will all link together as we feel most appropriate. As for what the post-imperialist revolutionary America will look like, it clearly is too early to say. The people through struggle will bring about this new positive future. Whether we have one unified revolutionary state, a confederation of allies, a more rearranged geographic map, or a regional or world revolutionary alliance is all yet to be decided. In fact the struggle we are now in and those battles yet to come, particularly those that demonstrate how fully white revolutionary forces join with the struggles of African and other oppressed nations, will have a major influence on how unified we will be after our victory. Just as John Brown fought alongside Africans for the freeing of Black slaves, I urge people to fight with the African nation (also Puerto Rico and Native nations), to overthrow imperialism and clear the way for oppressed nations to exercise self-determination and for the exploited working class to exercise political power.

Our antiracist, anti-imperialist, and revolutionary formations should be unashamed and clear about what we fight for, as well as against. We should be principled and brave. Certainly John Brown, who not only fought himself, but who also brought his family and sons to battle, can guide us in this. Further, I would urge us to be willing and positively oriented to work with other revolutionary and progressive forces. We should maintain our position and line but try to work with other genuine forces. I truly believe our focus should primarily be on the enemy, not on differences among allies.

As political prisoners in the U.S., we, communist, revolutionary nationalists, anarchists, anti-imperialists, have years of experience in working closely together. We do this out of necessity, solidarity, comradeship, and because it makes sense. Likewise we have had years of good working relations with outside formations of anarchists, Trotskyists, environmentalists, feminists and others, as well as our more closely identified allies, revolutionary nationalists, communists—Maoists, and anti-imperialists. In recent years some of our most consistent support, including regular material support, has come from the anarchist ABC Federation and to a lesser degree from the Partisan Defense Committee (a Trotskyist-led formation). I raise this matter to demonstrate that principled working relations among left forces are possible, useful, and often very necessary.

As a final point I do want to say that line and principle are very important. To me it seems impossible to gain a thorough understanding and analysis without utilizing the revolutionary scientific tool of dialectical and historical materialism, the tools of Marxism-Leninism. Without a worked-out political position, we won't be able to grow much or usefully lead and participate in struggles. Without firm revolutionary principles and the willingness and ability to stand on them, we won't even last long. It's also a fact, because of our line and principles, that we won't be able to work in every coalition or campaign, nor should we try to. This also is part of revolutionary struggle, finding those allies and issues that we grow from and advance on. Reaching out, educating, listening, seeking principled unity both on a tactical and hopefully, at least with some others, on a strategic level, should guide our practice.

In closing and as one practical way to act on much of what I've discussed, I urge everyone to put more work into the battle to free Mumia Abu-Jamal. The government is deadly intent on killing this brother. It is heartening to see the movement and momentum to free Mumia, but until this death sentence is off his head and he is free back on the streets, we cannot relax our efforts. This African man, lifelong political activist and longtime political prisoner, must not be allowed to die by the hands of the racist imperialist U.S.A. This battle can be won. He can be freed and we should all do even more now to set him free!

Freedom is a constant struggle!

VII.3.R

John Brown 2000

Ray Luc Levasseur

A day after his capture, John Brown was questioned by several slavery supporting politicians. His responses are instructive. He said he'd answer no questions about others who participated in or supported their attack on the U.S. armory at Harpers Ferry, West Virginia. John Brown refused to cooperate with the enemy.

He said it takes secrecy to succeed in guerrilla operations. John Brown understood the importance of clandestinity.

He said they intended to appropriate weapons from the U.S. armory, and take the property of slave owners. John Brown believed in arming and funding revolutionary forces through expropriation.

He said that his troops received no wages for their services. John Brown and his comrades were not motivated by personal nor material gain.

He said their objective was to free the slaves. John Brown respected the rights of Black people that a racist U.S. supreme court ruled had no rights that whites were bound to respect.

He said, "I feel no consciousness of guilt." John Brown made clear that the principle upon which he based his actions was to aid those suffering a great wrong against them. A great wrong against humanity. John Brown did not need a document of international law to define for him what is a crime against humanity. He was a man of principle who educated, organized and carried out guerrilla operations to the best of his abilities. He was a leader by example.

John Brown was both a model and a military leader. He was a winter soldier—not one to limit his commitment to when the political sun was shining, blessing him with the absolutely correct time, place and conditions to act forcefully against slavery. He was a white abolitionist who could've stayed home behind a white curtain, but instead made the supreme sacrifice on behalf of Black Liberation.

A year before the Harpers Ferry raid, John Brown and comrades adopted a constitution which they intended to serve as a basis for governing the land they had liberated. This constitution defined slavery as "perpetual imprisonment and hopeless servitude" and called for its "absolute extermination." It was their view that there was no course leading from bondage to freedom that did not necessitate the complete destruction of the slave system.

The execution of John Brown and his comrades from the Harpers Ferry raid was a collaborative effort between the United States government and the state of West Virginia. Both governments defended the system of slavery. It wasn't until three years after their execution that President Lincoln issued the Emancipation Proclamation. But this Proclamation only freed slaves in those southern states that were in open rebellion against the federal government and exempted those that weren't. It also allowed individual slaveholders who did not support the Confederacy to keep their slaves. Lincoln wasn't a man of principle—he was a racist opportunist. Slavery wasn't abolished until 1865 when the Thirteenth Amendment was ratified. The intellectual architects of this amendment had the racist foresight to exclude prisoners from this amendment, thereby paving the way for millions of Blacks to be locked into "perpetual imprisonment and hopeless servitude" of American penitentiaries, chain gangs and jails.

In 1868, President Andrew Johnson re-enfranchised confederate rebels, former slave owners, and politicians, issuing them a full pardon and amnesty. Concurrent with this, Black people were being disenfranchised through an apartheid-like system of laws called "black codes" (e.g., one such code prohibited freed slaves from renting or leasing farmland); withdrawal of federal support for Black Reconstruction; and the terror of the Ku Klux Klan. These are the consequences of the federal government's victory in the Civil War. Had John Brown been able to continue marching on from Harpers Ferry, armed former slaves would have decided and defined their terms for Land and Liberty.

Prior to my early twenties, my knowledge of American history was minimal and distorted. I barely knew of John Brown and what I was told was that he was badly in need of a psychiatrist. It was something I read by Malcolm X that got me looking deeper into the life of John Brown. Malcolm, speaking to the issue of what role is there for whites in the Black Liberation Struggle, said look to John Brown for what is to be done. So I did. What I found was a person totally committed to freeing those held in bondage, by any means necessary.

Those who owned and operated the bondage system were his enemies. They were enemies of humanity. He sought neither white skin refuge nor privilege. Nor would he allow his commitment to wither before the racist indifference of a white majority. He didn't sit on his hands while people suffered and died for the profit of others. The principle that all should be free guided his political and military choices.

What I have taken from the life of John Brown and admire of Malcolm X is that if you're for real about revolution then be a stand-up person of principle willing to organize among your own, challenge the opposition and make sacrifices. In terms of moving the freedom train forward, this need hasn't changed in the 200 years since John Brown's birth.

Where do I see the anti-imperialist movement headed in this period? Toward irrelevance unless it's able to recruit. The same is true of any political movement. To recruit we need to put into practice our commitment to serve the people. To serve the people we need to respond to their needs. Their survival, their empowerment, their future. We can talk loud and long, wielding the most political of lines, but few will listen and join unless we accomplish tasks, build solid organizations and blueprint an attainable alternative to capitalism. We are against imperialism and against racism—wouldn't it be useful to outline what we are for and how we intend to get it.

The problems and needs are great: police brutality and killer cops, jails and prisons, violence against women, environmental destruction, substandard housing and homelessness, inadequate health care, drug and alcohol abuse, unemployment and unorganized workers, poverty and racism are its many manifestations. Think globally and act locally. I was struck by the many "local activists" participating in the World Trade Organization protest in Seattle, Washington. They came from villages and cities as far away as Central America and Southeast Asia. They added a substantive credibility and spirit to the resistance. Yet who had heard of them before Seattle? The people in their neighborhoods and workplaces and communities is who! That's the credibility they brought with them. However, while we respect and admire their commitment, we too often do not emulate their example by organizing locally among our own people.

Our willingness and ability to organize locally determines our ability to build alliances with other movements. We must be able to bring something substantive to other movements, whether they be across town or halfway around the world. What can be more substantive than people mobilized for work and action more from the heart than obligation. While ideology lays the foundation of a revolutionary movement, it's organized people in small and large numbers that move it forward, like John Brown. It's time to get moving.

VII.3.S

Honoring the People's Struggle

Leonard Peltier

I am happy to address the conference being held here today because I feel that what you are doing is very important and meaningful. I don't know how to end racism and I do not know where or why imperialism started. I do not have all of the solutions and answers to the many problems we must solve. But, I know enough to know that the most important weapon we hold is the ability to come together and break the pattern of division that conquerors use to maintain their power. That is what you are doing today and I congratulate you.

But, we must remember what we are up against: ruthless and power-hungry forces, like the FBI and police (backed by their judge and prosecutor allies), the CIA, multinational corporations, rich politicians and rich individuals who view the world as their chess game and our lives as pieces to be manipulated for their gains. This frightening realization should be enough to make our differences seem petty and our need to unite an essential tool for survival. It should also remind us that the struggle to end imperialism and racism must be carried out every day of our lives.

Leonard Peltier and other political prisoners and P.O.W.'s at Marion Prison, 1977. Front row, l-r: Armando Miramon, Rafael Cancel Miranda, Leonard Peltier. Back row, l-r: Herman Bell, Stephen Kessler, James "Buffalo" Parker, Shahid Muhammed Faris. *(Source: New Studies on the Left, the Prison Issue)*

Racism has long been used by imperialists to make other people do their dirty work, to refocus the hate and frustration felt by those they already oppress toward others whom they still need to conquer, and they have been very effective in doing it. Just look and examine how they do it today. The media portrays people of color and youth as criminals to be feared, they lock up two million of us; meanwhile the police can get away with shooting people in the street with no repercussions. Laws are being passed that strip away all of our rights, and the public is tightening their own noose with each vote, with each misplaced fear.

Those of the public who know better because they have lived under imperialism, colonialism, and racism need forums where they can tell their stories and let people know that there is more to reality than what the media and politicians tell them. We must build strong coalitions to stop imperialism in very specific ways. We must recognize what imperialism is, how it uses racism, and we must recognize the many forms it takes, from prisons, police abuse, and poverty at home, to slave labor, low-intensity warfare, and CIA abuses abroad. It is the most horrible thing to stand on the land that you know is your home and be treated as an outcast, an enemy, and an outsider, and what is worse, to watch your people disappear. When you go home from this conference please continue to carry out the message and do the work in your own communities. I encourage you to carry on your struggles and I thank you for your dedication and commitment.

IN THE SPIRIT OF CRAZY HORSE
Gwarth-ee-loss

VII.3.T

Reflections on John Brown

Susan Rosenberg

John Brown believed that the tree of liberty must be watered with the blood of tyrants. John Brown believed that there was no greater sin than slavery, and he wanted full equality between whites and blacks. John Brown believed that it would take war to overthrow the tyranny of slavery, and John Brown started one.

When the 54th Massachusetts Regiment, the all-black fighting force in the Union Army, marched into Charleston, with thousands and thousands of fugitive slaves following the liberating army of General Sherman, the song that rang out through the city was "John Brown's Body." At the time of his life and then death, he was judged by those in whose cause he fought to be an avenging angel.

Recently there has been a whole spate of books about John Brown, as people try to deconstruct him and deconstruct what and why race relations are what they are today, searching for answers. Having read these newest accounts and being deeply involved in the discussion of white supremacy and antiracist responsibility I am struck again and again by how John Brown is like the acid test. Because how he is deconstructed is very much defined by the ideological eyes doing the deconstruction. The whole thing in the simplest of terms is whether John Brown was a crazy, fanatical, religious lunatic, or a sane man obsessed and driven by insane inhumanity and barbaric cruelty.

Having said that one's position on John Brown's role and view of his importance is a question of one's ideas about race, let me say mine. I don't think John Brown was crazy. For the last year I have been involved in teaching African-American history in an adult continuing education program for women in prison. As a result of this incredible experience, I have had the occasion to re-look at the 19th century of American history and to the institution of slavery and the movement for abolition. For me there is an irony in this, because John Brown has been a figure of enormous example to me for my life. In fact, I could say that my exposure to an examination of John Brown by Professor Shenton at Columbia University in 1975 is in no small part what led me to become a founding member of the John Brown Anti-Klan Committee in the late 1970s and early 1980s, and then to where I am today. So, having prefaced with all that, I thought I'd submit to this conference a small meditation on John Brown, and how I see him today.

Why such a contested historical figure could possibly hold relevance now, in the 21st century is because his actions took place at the moment when objective and subjective conditions came together and combined in the bloodiest civil conflict to end the systematic practice of human bondage. And it was his very action that helped to create that moment.

John Brown was not a prominent member of the organized abolitionist movement, nor well known for a long time. But his early experience of being witness to the brutal whipping of a slave boy left an indelible impression that he would continue to reference throughout his life. He was always a man of action and he was an active conductor on the Underground Railroad despite the financial strains it put on him. He attended abolition meetings in Ohio and occasionally contributed to abolitionist newspapers. But the decade of the 1850s brought the conflicts of slavery closer to the inevitable clash. As a result of the Compromise of 1850, the fugitive slave law went into effect and the struggle over free state versus slave state intensified: the Supreme Court said a "black man had no rights that a white man was bound to respect," and the movement for abolition grew. And John Brown's revulsion for the system grew as did his radicalism.

One important thing to see from John Brown's raid at Harpers Ferry is that he was not alone. He was not totally isolated, and he certainly was never the object of ridicule or scorn by anyone within the vast span of views that existed within abolition. In fact Nat Turner, Denmark Vesey, and David Walker had all come before. He wanted to end slavery, he believed it would take armed rebellion, he organized support from a small number (who would later be indicted for conspiracy) and was rejected by others, and he went ahead with his plans anyway.

Harpers Ferry announced to the white power structure that there were abolitionists both black and white who would fight and die to end slavery. The fear he struck in their hearts was the harbinger of their secession. As Frederick Douglass said, John Brown was willing to die for black freedom, while others were willing to live for it. And his passionate commitment to that end was in its starkest truth a practice that rarely rises to the surface of our collective consciousness: "no one is free until everyone is free." He was hanged by the very state that less than four years later was forced into fighting on the same side he represented.

I think John Brown was extraordinary, but I think the times were extraordinary too. When over a hundred years later in the 1960s the anti-imperialist left reclaimed John Brown, when the Black nationalist movement redefined him as a hero and ally, it was important because it was an attempt to link the emerging politics with a thread from the past, however slender, not unlike when the post civil rights black movement reclaimed the historical past and forced open the thick walls of white supremacist scholarship and rewrote the history of African-Americans.

And so I bring this meditation to the present. I think we, who are in prison for essentially the politics of solidarity and against white supremacy, are akin to John Brown. But I think those times were so different that beyond the generalization it goes no further. I think that we hoped that first: there was a greater history of antiracist whites, and second: that, inspired by our own example, others in a much larger way would respond to the conditions and oppose white supremacist violence as we did. Were we crazy to want to prosecute an armed resistance to the injustices in our society, however well cloaked they were? I don't think so. But I do think that the metaphor used by many black historians to describe the black freedom struggle as a mighty river is useful here. The river that flowed then was ever-deepening with the blood and sacrifice and work and struggle of thousands and thousands of oppressed people. The range of ideas and methods were all bound together and part of the same forward-moving flow. But a hundred years later without the deeper springs of radical thought and action from which to flow from, we could only be but a small stream. And yet, there is nothing that would make me want to be elsewhere. In the study of this history, I have found that the drama of life is in both victory and defeat. John Brown was defeated and victorious in the same breath.

And in that he was unique, but what goes alongside him were all the other efforts and struggles, and they too are part of the picture, as are we.

VI.3.V

Three Poems of Nuh Abdul-Qayyam

Nuh Washington, New Afrikan Prisoner of War
In Memoriam: February 28, 1941- April 28, 2000

Black
    is a political condition,
    a state of oppression and consciousness
    a nation seeking to become,
       A people who hope.
Liberation
    is freedom from oppression
    freedom to define, to determine one's destiny
    free from despair
       A slave to hope.
Army
    is a politically armed unit
    to defend and preserve
    after it achieves
       Liberation for those who hope.

By Way of Introduction...

Who are you, i am asked
If i give a name
It only tells what i am called
Having had many names
It still does not say
Who or what i am

To the oppressed i am the angel of deliverance
To the oppressor i am the angel of destruction
So who i am

Depends on who you are...

Minutes that are oh so few
Hours that we let slip away
Days that hasten into a future we can't predict
Weeks we count but can't count on
Years that pass and become our past
And all that is left is now
So let us live in these moments
While we've got the time

What can I say to you Nuh? It is impossible to express how much you mean to so many people. It is not enough to speak of your kindness. It is not enough to speak of your gentle strength. You have given so much to our struggle. The few material goods that you possessed in this world, you have shared with generous warmth. You have taught many people, and touched many more. ——Assata Shakur

I was born on a stormy February day in an apartment on Sugar Hill in New York City. My mother said if I had been born a girl she would have named me Gail because of the gale force winds blowing outside. The world was at war and nature was raging. I am a child of the storm. I am the second born and the first to survive. The pattern was set and has been consistent ever since.

Nuh Washington died of liver cancer at the Regional Medical Unit at Coxsackie prison in the early morning hours on April 28, 2000. He is buried in a family plot near Mt. Vernon, New York. His headstone was designed by his dear friends Chango and Safiya Bukhari. It reads: "In Death We Escape to Freedom."

Only the poems on these pages appeared in the John Brown 2000 booklet—all else is excerpted from the book All Power to the People, a memorial tribute to Nuh published jointly by Solidarity and Arm the Spirit in 2002, and distributed by Kersplebedeb.

The Jericho Movement:
Amnesty and Freedom for All Political Prisoners!!!

National Jericho Movement
2000

The Jericho Movement grew out of a call by political prisoner Jalil Muntaqim for a national march on the White House during Spring Break of 1998. The call was made in October of 1996 through the Provisional Government, Republic of New Afrika, and the New Afrikan Liberation Front—but the organizers decided to use this opportunity to jump-start a much-needed movement to build a national support organization for political prisoners in general.

Jericho '98, which was the collective work of over fifty organizations—defense committees and groups, sixty-four Jericho Organizing Committees, Students for Jericho—succeeded in making the issue of Recognition and Amnesty for U.S.-held political prisoners and prisoners of war a national one, with its successful demonstration and rally at the White House. The organizers who made up the Jericho Organizing Committees were/are just as diverse as the demonstrators who came from all across the United States, crossing the spectrum from the El Barrio Defense Committee representing Alvaro Hernandez, a Mexican political prisoner; the Earth First!/Animal Liberation Front of which former political prisoner Rod Coronado is a member; ProLibertad and the National Committee to Free Puerto Rican Political Prisoners and POW's, which supports the Puerto Rican nationalists; Out of Control, which supports the women political prisoners, to the Sundiata Acoli Freedom Campaign, the International Concerned Family and Friends of Mumia Abu-Jamal, the Lincoln Justice Committee working for the freedom of

get on the bus for

Jericho '98

Amnesty and Freedom for All Political Prisoners!
National March on the White House

Friday, March, 27, 1998

Buses leaving 5am from:
- Main Post Office,
  33rd St. & 8th Ave., Manhattan
- Harlem State Office Bldg.,
  125th St. & 7th Ave., Harlem
- St. Mary's Church,
  125th St. & Amsterdam, Harlem
- Union Square Park, SW corner
  14th St. & Univ. Place, Manhattan
- Atlantic & Flatbush Avs., Brooklyn
- 149th & Grand Concourse, Bronx
- D&J Book Distributors,
  Merrick Blvd. & 229 St, Laurelton
- Afrikan Poetry Theater
  17603 Jamaica Av. @ 176 St., Jamaica, Queens

Ticket buyer must choose a site when purchasing ticket. Only advance ticket buyers are guaranteed a seat. Buy your ticket today!

For more info:
Jericho '98 Office • 212-473-4257
http://jericho98.togdog.com

Ticket price $30 rt
Available at:
- Jericho '98 Office-
  c/o Center for Const'l Rights, 666 B'way, NYC, 212-473-4257
- Creative Visions-
  260 W. 125th St., bet. 7/8 Avs., Harlem, 212-662-5518
- Revolution Books-
  9 W. 19th St., @ Fifth Av., NYC, 212-691-3345
- Int'l Action Center-
  39 W. 14th St. #207, @ Sixth Av., NYC, 212-633-6646
- BlackOut Books-
  Avenue B & 4th St., East Village, 212-777-1967
- Brecht Forum-
  122 W. 27 St., NYC, 212-242-4201
- Sista's Place-
  456 Nostrand Av., enter on Jefferson, B'klyn, 718-398-1746
- D&J Book Distributors-
  Merrick Blvd. & 229th St., Laurelton, Queens
- Afrikan Poetry Theater-
  17603 Jamaica Av. @ 176 St., Jamaica, Queens

Mondo Langa and Ed Poindexter, National Refuse and Resist, and the Not on the Guest List Coalition. Besides the march on the White House itself, rallies were held in major cities across the country and in Canada.

The 1998 demonstration was just the beginning of a whole new commitment to supporting these political prisoners and demanding recognition and amnesty for them. There are hundreds of people who went to prison as a result of their work on the Street against oppressive conditions like indecent housing, inadequate and nonexistent medical care, lack of quality education, police brutality and murder, and for independence and liberation. These people belonged to organizations like the Black Panther Party, *La Raza Unida*, FALN, *Los Macheteros*, North American anti-imperialist movements, May 19th, the Plowshares peace movement, American Indian Movement, the Black Liberation Army, etc., and were incarcerated because of their political beliefs and acts in support of and/or in defense of freedom.

The Mission of the Jericho Movement

The issue of whether or not political prisoners and prisoners of war exist inside the borders of the United States of America is one that the government of the United States has successfully been able to refute. They have been able to deny the existence of political prisoners and prisoners of war because we have not taken the battle to them and forced them to address this issue. Over the last thirty years the numbers of political prisoners and prisoners of war languishing within the prisons of the United States of America has grown to enormous and geometric proportions as the struggle for liberation and independence has intensified.

While we have consistently contended that we are involved in a liberation struggle, our approach to winning the freedom of our political prisoners and prisoners of war has not supported our claim. It has also enabled the government of the United States, through its varied police agencies, to criminalize these political prisoners and prisoners of war, try them in their courts, and sentence them to mammoth sentences. It is the mission of the Jericho Movement to raise this issue to the height where the United States will no longer be able to deny the existence of our political prisoners and, by so doing, change the playing field.

We have vacillated too long. On the one hand we say we have political prisoners and prisoners of war, and on the other hand we have not forged a comprehensive approach to freeing them. The mission of Jericho is to bring this issue out into the open and push for the public recognition of the existence of political prisoners and prisoners of war inside the United States. The United States recognizes that if they acknowledge that political prisoners and prisoners of war exist, they implicitly recognize the existence of liberation struggles going on inside this country, because political prisoners and prisoners of war don't come out of a vacuum but are the results of political struggles. We all know that war is politics with bloodshed.

There are four principal issues that the Jericho Movement has decided to address:

1. Building the Amnesty Campaign. A big part of this work is locating political prisoners, compiling dossiers on them, and building the case for amnesty.
2. Continuing the Educational Campaign About the Existence of Political Prisoners inside the U.S.A.
3. Establishing the Jericho Legal Defense Fund, including organizing lawyers and law students to provide legal defense for political prisoners.
4. Establishing the Jericho Medical Project to fight for adequate and quality medical care for political prisoners.

People Can Help By Doing One or Many of the Following:
1. Organize speaking engagements about political prisoners in your church, school, community.
2. Volunteer to work on one of the projects of the Jericho Movement.
3. Organize a Jericho Committee in your area, or get in touch with one of these existing chapters:
4. Make a financial contribution to Jericho.
5. Write to a political prisoner and tell them what you're doing.

Political Prisoners Do Not Come Out of a Vacuum,
But Out of the Struggles of a People to Be Free!!!

Credit: Laura Whitehorn

Picking Up the Work: Health Care in Prison:
A Conversation with Dr. Barbara Zeller

2008

Barbara Zeller: I started getting into the work because I was a physician who was supporting political prisoners in the late 1970s and early 1980s. I was part of the movement where there were grand jury resisters and some of the early Puerto Rican Nationalist political prisoners, and the Black Panther political prisoners. Prisoners' health issues just came up, and I was seen to be a person that they could trust. I was often asked to see people or talk to people in those early years.

Both my husband, Dr. Alan Berkman, and I learned of the need for medical assistance for the American Indian Movement during a solidarity event in New York City in 1973. People came from Wounded Knee, raising support and money around the country. One AIM representative said that what they really needed was medical people, because Wounded Knee was still under siege. Alan and I had just graduated from medical school two years earlier, and we immediately left after this event for Rapid City, South Dakota. We went with as many medical supplies as we could gather in a couple of days. We collected supplies from hospitals and from the community clinic that we were working in at the time. In those days, there were a lot more free and community-based clinics.

By the time we arrived, Wounded Knee was completely under siege by the U.S. government, and they were preventing any material aid from getting into the reservation. So we had to walk overland for about 30 miles, surrounded by small tanks and armored personnel carriers. It took us two days, and we got lost, but finally—after a great deal of anxiety—we managed to get onto the reservation at dawn, under the cover of darkness and dense tree cover. Almost immediately we were needed to help a woman who was in labor. I volunteered, but the husband wanted a "real" doctor, which meant a man. The woman in labor was unfortunately having trouble and was in the second stage of labor. After a number of hours, Alan said that the woman's condition was getting dangerous, and she needed to be hospitalized. It was a very tense situation, because the Native American activists knew that if the husband went along to the hospital, he would be arrested as an AIM leader. She might even be arrested! But there just wasn't any equipment to help the situation. Eventually, we all were able to get an ambulance to take her to the

Rapid City hospital—and she delivered a healthy baby, but he was arrested.

Alan stayed at Wounded Knee for some time and testified at the official hearings about the conditions inside the reservation. It was really one of the first times that there was, in our experience, a high level of medical solidarity needed and successfully delivered. But it was also a time when we could see firsthand the militarized U.S. response to resistance. This was war going on.

When the Chicago-based Puerto Rican activists were arrested in the early 1980s, I was living in Chicago at the time. I saw one of the gentlemen who they thought had appendicitis, and the care in prison was just so poor. I saw Dylcia Pagán at one point as well. The Attica prison uprising, too, saw many people hurt and injured and tortured. And while I wasn't really involved in the Attica rebellion, Alan had been, as one of the health care people, and he ended up testifying to the terrible conditions that the prisoners faced.

Alan was called in again, after Sekou Odinga was tortured following his capture at the time of the 1981 Brink's robbery. Alan testified about Sekou's medical condition, and the fact that he had been burned and had his head put into the toilet and other conditions of outright torture at the time of his arrest. Sekou had abdominal injuries that were very extreme; he was really severely injured. It became important that people both got a reliable medical opinion about their condition and also had someone who could testify if there was a legal case.

Matt Meyer: Not too much later in the decade, six white activists were jailed as part of the Resistance Conspiracy Case—one of whom was Alan. While in prison, Alan himself started getting quite sick. Could you talk a bit about this?

Barbara Zeller: As you know, there are general issues for any prisoner who is ill. Health issues are never a priority for prison officials, and they're also used to further intimidate and frighten people who are trying to resist. In Alan's case, when he self-diagnosed the cancer, there had to be campaigns at every step of his care, including court hearings to get him what he needed.

All medical procedures were done with Alan shackled to the bed, even though he was too weak to move. He was shackled during surgery when he was under anesthesia! The state's desire to hype up the security came first, with no interest in any kind of humane medical care. It took the movement constantly advocating for him to get through. At some point, he was actually asked for political information when he was very ill, with the indication that things would go easier for him if he talked. But Alan could barely breathe and was paralyzed after the results of the chemotherapy.

MM: I've heard it said a few times that Alan would have died if not for the fact that he and his wife were themselves medical doctors.

Barbara Zeller: I think that was absolutely true. Alan first identified the cancer as a lump and advocated for somebody to do something about it and find out what it was. When he was finally diagnosed, and getting chemotherapy in the prison ward of DC General Hospital, they didn't have any of the medicinal agents that help protect your white blood count and reduce your infection risk. So he felt he got a fever and felt that he was going into what is called septic shock. He was getting weaker and weaker and was locked alone with nobody seeing him. He was pretty sure he was dying, so he bit the IV line with his teeth because if your IV line occludes it automatically starts beeping. Finally, the medical staff responded. So that was one instance he did get by because of his own ability to understand his condition and the equipment around him. Septic shock has an almost 50% mortality rate under the best circumstances, and if you're not treated it's really almost 100% mortality.

In addition to that incident, Alan went into shock more than once. The second time, one of his lawyers happened to be visiting, called me immediately. I honestly don't know how I did it, but I got in a car, walked up to the prison ward at 2AM, and just said "I'm Dr. Zeller and I need to get in." And for whatever reason, they let me in. It wasn't visiting hours, and they must have known that I wasn't just visiting as a doctor, but I was able to stay through the night until we could make sure that the right people were called and Alan could get the treatment he needed.

I don't think that Alan would have survived if he didn't have the wherewithal to understand what was going on with him at every point. It's a horrible truth, with a happy ending, but so many of these cases don't have that. It worries me so much about everyone else.

MM: Let's fast forward to 1998, and the founding of the National Jericho Amnesty Movement. Jericho founder Safiya Bukhari was very concerned with the question of medical care for political prisoners.

Barbara Zeller: Yes, Safiya was very, very aware and concerned because so much of this work had been taken care of in a piecemeal fashion for so long. Safiya had such a great heart and a great understanding of all aspects of the prisoner experience. Jericho had a medical component from the beginning, and they knew that they would be doing advocacy work the whole time, while I, and others, could do prison visits as medical personnel.

For people who had been in prison for a long time, for over twenty or thirty years, there is a particular physical vulnerability that one faces. Safiya was on front lines, getting all the phone calls from practically every political prisoner that existed! It was part of her conception of Jericho from the beginning that we'd need to have a built-in component of emergency medical response. There was a particular sense of tragedy around the case of New York 3/Black Liberation Army political prisoner Nuh Washington. His cancer was diagnosed so late and at a point where there was no cure and very

571

little possibility of help. The idea that Nuh would die in prison was, of course, heartbreaking for Safiya and for all of us.

Today, there are still so many instances of poor care and life-threatening medical neglect. Political prisoners do fight for and advocate for themselves, but poor medical treatment in prisons is such a systematic issue. I've been seeing Black political prisoner Robert "Seth" Hayes, who is getting terrible care—or lack of care—for a serious case of diabetes and hepatitis C. And there are many, many cases like that.

For the coming period, I think that one of the urgent tasks is to continue to work with medical groups to see if we can get a broader network of doctors involved. We must have a core of doctors and medical people who are willing to do pro bono work, and go into prisons to serve as advocates for political prisoners. In this case, it's also an instance where the political prisoner movement can help fight for better health care for all prisoners.

Section VIII.

Critical Resistance and the Prisoner Rights Movement

*T*here has always been a creative tension between those working exclusively around freedom for political prisoners and those working with politicized social prisoners or for prisoner rights in general.

Critical Resistance emerged in 1998 as a national organization dedicated to prison abolition, but with clear support of the work around political prisoners and with inclusion of so-called social prisoners as well. This section includes some commentary from political prisoners at the time of the first Critical Resistance conference and a new interview with activist Linda Thurston on the eve of the Critical Resistance 10th anniversary conference.

Criminalization of Poverty in Capitalist America

Jalil Muntaqim
1996

An anonymous poet in the 1700s wrote about crime: "The law will punish a man or woman who steals the goose from the hillside, but lets the greater robber loose who steals the hillside from the goose."[*]

When talking about "the greater robber," it seemed particularly appropriate in the midst of the biggest financial rip-off in the history of this country to think about the billions of dollars the Savings & Loan criminals stole and about how most of them have gotten away with it. I thought about the complete insanity of how this country defines crimes in society. If you steal $5, you're a thief, but if you steal $5 million—you're a financier.

Thirty percent of the wealth of this country is controlled by one-half of 1 percent of the people. Eighty percent of the wealth is controlled by 10 percent of the people. I think that is a crime. In the dictionary, the word "crime" means "an act which is against the law." Crime applies particularly to an act that breaks a law that has been made for public good. Crime in one country, the dictionary continued, "may be entirely overlooked by the law in another country or may not apply at all in a different historical period."

That was interesting. What that really said was that concepts of "crime" are not eternal. The very nature of crime is sociopsychological and defined by time and place and those who have the power to make definitions; by those who write dictionaries, so to speak.

The more I thought about that and about those who write the laws, or at least define what law is, the more profound it became. I believe we all will agree that the United States is a nation of criminals. From its inception as a settler nation, exiled British criminals stole the land and lives from Native Americans and Africans. They justified their actions with making and defining the law of the land, for example defining Africans as 3/5 of a man during slavery. Hence the power to define is an awesome power. It is the power of propaganda. It is the ability to manipulate our ideas, to limit our agenda, to mold how we see, and to shape what we look at. It is the power to interpret

Reprinted from *Schooling the Generations in the Politics of Prisons*, edited by Chinosole (Berkeley, CA: New Earth Publications, 1996).

[*] Taken from an edited version of a speech by Sabina Virgo, given in LA on International Human Rights Day, December 8, 1990.

the picture we see when we look at the world for the American people in general, and New Afrikans, in particular. It is the power to place the picture we see when we look at the world. It is the power to place a frame around the picture, to define where it begins and ends. It is, in fact, the power to define where our vision begins and ends, the power to create our collective consciousness.

That kind of social propaganda is not only tremendously powerful, but it is also mostly invisible. We can't fight what we don't see. Most people accept the images and definitions that we have been taught as true, neutral, self-evident, and for always; so that the power to paint the future, to define what is right and wrong, what is lawful and what is criminal, is really the power to win the battle for our minds. And to win it without ever having to fight it. Simply said, it is hard to fight an enemy who has an outpost in our minds. This indicates the need for revolutionary nationalists to develop a national agitation-propaganda mechanism. Specifically, nationalists need a single national publication and organ that represents the unified development of NAIM (The New African Independence Movement) to which each formation and organization contributes and supports its distribution.

The Social Dynamics of Crime

Though some may question, as did Marx, the system's fairness in applying its rules, today most people don't question the basis of the system itself. That is, people don't question the relationship between those who own and those who don't. Though many people vote every four years on who governs, they never vote on and rarely question what governs. People don't challenge the legitimacy of the system, they accept it. The exception, of course, is when the oppressed rebel in insurrections. But usually we don't step outside of the frame around the picture. We don't disconnect the dots. Emile Durkheim argued that crime is "normal" and necessary social behavior. "According to Durkheim, the inevitability of crime is linked to the differences (heterogeneity) within a society. Since people are so different from one another and employ such a variety of methods and forms of behavior to meet their needs, it is not surprising that some will resort to criminality. Thus as long as human differences exist, crime is inevitable and one of the fundamental conditions of social life."* In this regard, the conservatives' view echoes this sentiment in as much as they seek to establish a genetic trait that explains criminal behavior. They argue, "If liberals have trouble with the idea that people's genes influence their chances of committing crimes, conservatives have trouble with the idea that poverty causes crime. Conservatives do not deny that the poor commit more crimes than the rich. But instead of assuming that poverty causes crime, conservatives usually assume that poverty and crime have a common cause, namely the deficient character or misguided values of the

---

* Quoted from the text, *Criminology*, by Larry Siegel, p. 40.

576

poor." (Jencks, p. 11) Concomitantly, the neo-liberals are essentially giving credence to the conservative's position as it pertains to the "underclass." For instance, sociologist William J. Wilson purports, "The liberal perspectives on the ghetto underclass has become less persuasive and convincing in public discourse principally because many of those who represent traditional liberal views on social issues have been reluctant to discuss openly or, in some instances, even to acknowledge the sharp increase in social pathologies in ghetto communities." (Wilson, p. 6) Needless to say, such ideas as that genetic traits are the cause of crime set a dangerous precedent. Trying to discern the social pathologies of the underclass harbors views that purport the wholesale contamination of entire communities. However, if one were to advocate that criminal behavior, especially of the poor, is either caused by genetic traits and/or born of social pathologies, then indisputably, it must be espoused that much of America suffers from these same causes.

In the March 12, 1993, issue of the *Wall Street Journal* an article entitled "Common Criminals—Just About Everyone Violates Some Laws, Even Model Citizens," byline by Stephen J. Adler and Wade Lambert, stated: "We are a nation of lawbreakers. We exaggerate tax-deductible expenses, lie to customs officials, bet on card games and sports events, disregard jury notices, drive while intoxicated—and hire illegal childcare workers."

The last of these was recently the crime of the moment, and Janet Reno wouldn't have been in the position to be confirmed unanimously as attorney general yesterday if Zoe Baird had obeyed the much-flouted immigration and tax laws. But the crime of the moment could have been something else and next time probably will be.

This is because nearly all people violate some laws, and many people run afoul of dozens without ever being considered, or considering themselves, criminals.

When we look at downtown urban centers, when we look at the lines of humanity waiting for food or a bed at the missions; if we look at the faces of people living in cardboard boxes on the streets of the cities, we must know that a crime has been committed. When we look at the faces of the dispossessed people, we see faces that look like people who lived in California when it was part of Mexico. In Miami we see faces of people whose great-great-grandparents were abducted and brought here from Africa.

In America, in the 1990s, as was the case in England in the 1800s, it is a crime to be poor. The poorer you are, the more criminal you are. If you are so poor that you have no place to live, and you live on the pavement or sleep in a car or in a park, you have committed a crime. It's against the law to sleep on the streets or in a park. If we have no home, it's against the law to sleep anywhere. Walter I. Trattner in *From Poor Law to Welfare State: A History of Social Welfare in America* makes the following observation in opposition to government policies that sought "to dismantle all benefit programs for working-age people except perhaps for unemployment insurance." (p. 335)

577

Indeed, others argued that structural changes in the economy and the erosion in antipoverty programs were the causes of the problem and that a strengthening, not dismantling, of the welfare state was essential in order to solve it. Such was the theme of Michael Harrington's *The New American Poverty* (1984), a depressing sequel-pronouncement, "The poor are still there." They are poor, however, said Harrington, not because of any personal shortcomings or decisions on their part, but because of changes in the international economy, especially the "de-industrialization" of America, and the way in which they have been treated, or mistreated here at home. They are the uprooted and the homeless, products of de-institutionalization, cuts in welfare programs, shortages in low-rent housing, and other social and economic forces over which they have no control; undocumented aliens who have become the new sweatshop laborers; unemployed blue-collar workers victimized by the disappearance of steady and relatively well-paying manufacturing jobs in the "smokestack industries" as a result of technological advances and global competition; white-collar workers who lost their jobs due to reorganization schemes in the name of efficiency, plant closings, or moves to new locations in the so-called Sunbelt; hopeless, uneducated, and untrained young blacks unable to get and hold jobs; families headed by poor, unmarried women; uprooted farmers and farm laborers hurt by the elimination of the subsistence farm and the agricultural depression; and millions of others in unskilled, unsteady (and often part-time), low-wage, dead-end benefitless jobs in the service sector of the economy—cooks in fast food restaurants, dishwashers and chambermaids in hotels and motels, janitors and cleaning women in schools, hospitals, nursing homes, and the like. Harrington and others demand that the government spend billions of dollars on social programs to meet the needs of these "rejects" of society. (p. 336)

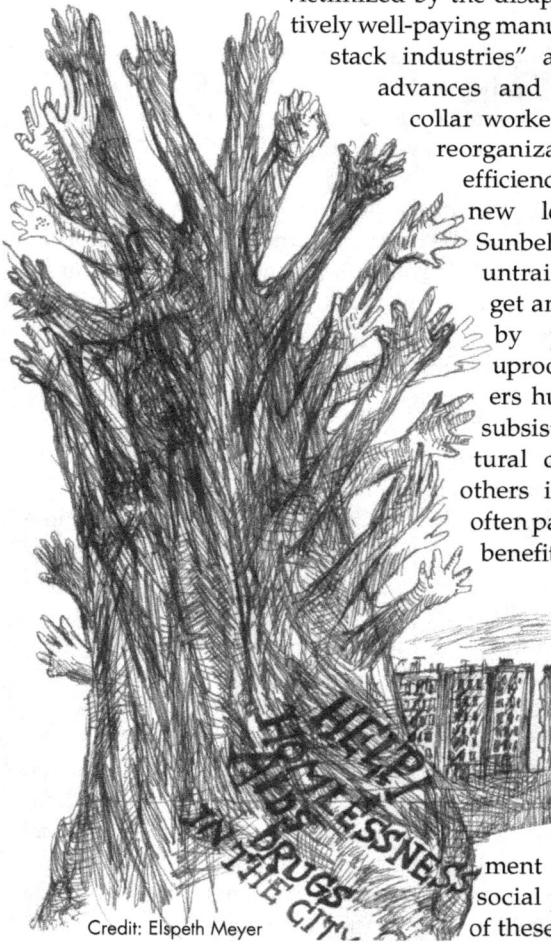

Credit: Elspeth Meyer

578

When the government fails to be responsible to its citizens and ignores the social dynamics of poverty, people are generally forced to seek illegitimate means to eke out an existence. In this case, it is a question of national oppression, whereby the imperialist government maintains exploitative relationships with New Afrikans, Native Americans, Chicanos, and Asians. Too many of these "rejects" of society are caught in the vicious web of the criminal justice system. But the real criminals are those who create the socioeconomic conditions that perpetuate impoverishment. The real criminal is the colonial government itself. It then becomes necessary to assess the pathology of the capitalist and social policy makers that make crime big business and deflect culpability of their criminal behavior.

Crime Is Big Business

The political decisions of the bankers are decisions about who will be poor. Corporate decisions made in the late '50s to remove industry from communities of color were about who would be unemployed. Decisions by developers and bankers about redevelopment (redlining and gentrification) are decisions about who will be homeless. Such decisions affect everyone, but people have no say in the matter. Generally people, especially the poor, have no say in most social and economic decisions that affect their lives. Somehow that is not part of the democratic method of government, and because people have no say in the process, creating homelessness is not criminal, but being homeless is. Runaway plants and plant closures are legal, but vagrancy is a crime. Trattner says:

> Meanwhile the plight of the nation's hungry and homeless worsened. In November, 1984, in a pastoral letter on "Catholic Social Thinking and the U.S. Economy," American Roman Catholic bishops had called poverty in America a "social and moral scandal that must not be ignored," and stated that "works of charity cannot and should not have to substitute for humane public policy.... A little more than a year later, the Physicians Task Force on Hunger in America reported on a two-year nationwide study it had conducted and concluded that, despite fifty-eight continuous months of economic expansion, hunger was more widespread and serious than at any time in the fifteen years (affecting some twenty million Americans), largely, in its words, because of "governmental failure"... (Trattner, p. 337-38)

Hunger and homelessness are deliberately imposed socioeconomic conditions that disenfranchise large numbers of the American population. This is especially significant when consideration is given to the method and means by which the malfeasance of the powers that be operate to ensure that such conditions stay the same. Thus such pathology ensures the rich get richer, while the poor get prison and early death.

Max Weber has argued that society is structured to function in a specific way to ensure its existence, that the social structure is subject to the mechanics of government, and that governing is all important above and beyond the immediate needs of the people. "Weber held that social stratification depends on the distribution of three resources: wealth (economic resources), power (political resources), and prestige (social resources). Thus, in our society wealthy business owners often gain power by contributing to political campaigns and earn prestige by making large donations to charity or to the arts. In other cases, however, the three are not linked. For example, in our society an individual acquires less prestige (in most circles) than someone who acquires comparable wealth by legitimate means. Artists, the clergy, and others may enjoy prestige but not wealth. On occasion people with few economic resources and little social prestige—bureaucrats, for instance—exercise considerable power.... Weber held that because stratification is multidimensional, the formation of groups depends on which interests or identities people choose to emphasize. In capitalist societies, for example, ethnic and national identifications have proved more important than economic or class identification."*

We are able to determine the social and racial implications of certain classes, then, having a vested interest in crime. It can be argued that because an elite class of criminals is in charge, they commit capital crimes, crimes against society and humanity. The jails are overflowing, but that doesn't seem to help—because the real criminals aren't in jail. They're in the board rooms and in the White House. They are the social policy makers that run this country. And today, they are increasing social repression by building more prisons, creating harsher legal sanctions (i.e., 52 death penalty laws, three strikes you're out), and becoming ever more heedless to the social implications of poverty as an impetus to committing crime.

Under their misleadership, over five million people are homeless, 37 million have no health insurance, 30 million are illiterate, 30 million more are functionally illiterate, one million are incarcerated, and 60 million live in poverty and are struggling day to day. But contrast a tiny fraction of the population controls enormous wealth. The median net worth of the top 1% of households is 22 times greater than the median net worth of the remaining 99% of outstanding stocks and shares. The wealth of the richest 5% of the population increased by 37% from 1977 to 1988. The wealth of the richest 1% increased by 74.2%. At the same time, the number of people in poverty increased by one-third.

In this case crime does pay. The U.S. Justice Department's Bureau of Justice Statistics announced on July 15, 1990, the federal, state, and local governments spent $61 billion for civil and criminal justice in 1988, a 34 percent increase

---

* Quoted from *An Introduction to Sociology,* by Michael S. Bassis, Richard J. Gelles, and Ann Levine, pp. 238-39.

since 1985. Other findings in the report were that federal, state, local governments spent $248 per capita: $114 for police, $78 for corrections, $54 for judicial and legal services, and $2 for other items.

Almost half of the nation's justice spending was for police protection. Corrections accounted for almost one-third of justice costs. Spending for corrections grew the most during that period, by 65 percent. Since 1979 state spending for prison construction increased 593 percent in actual (constant) dollars. That's some 2.6 times the rate of spending to operate prison facilities. In October of 1988 the nation's civil and criminal justice system employed 1.6 million persons, and the total October payroll for them was almost $3.7 billion.[*]

Crime is big business in America. Annually the laws are changed to ensure profitability in the industry of crime. Social conditions that serve to maintain levels of poverty, feed the industry of crime, also put stress on the social stratifications of society. Given the fact that America is a nation of criminals as elucidated in the *Wall Street Journal* article, social conflict is inevitable. It then becomes a matter of identifying the real culprits of crime and seeking the means to have them become accountable for their criminal behavior. This may very well include the redistribution of their wealth and the reorganization of the social contract between the government and the governed.

In response to the stratification outlined above, it requires revolutionary nationalist and socialist efforts to formulate a national political agenda and policy that will challenge the prevailing social contract between the oppressed and the oppressor nation. This means revolutionary nationalists and socialists must have a clear and concise mass-line and political program that identifies and explains the nature of poor peoples' oppression, and how they are to be organized to confront their oppression.

Bibliography

Hacker, Andrew. *Two Nations: Black and White, Separate, Hostile, Unequal.* New York: Ballantine Books, 1992.

Jencks, Christopher. *Rethinking Social Policy: Race, Poverty and the Underclass.* New York: HarperCollins, 1992.

Time Magazine. "Lockem Up: Outrage over crime has America talking tough." Feb. 7, 1994.

Trattner, Walter I. *From Poor Law to Welfare State: A History of Social Welfare in America.*, New York: Free Press, 1989.

---

[*] Justice Expenditure and Employment, 1988 (NCJ-124132).

The Prison Industrial Complex and the Global Economy

Eve Goldberg and Linda Evans
1998

Over 1.8 million people are currently behind bars in the United States. This represents the highest per capita incarceration rate in the history of the world. In 1995 alone, 150 new U.S. prisons were built and filled.

This monumental commitment to lock up a sizeable percentage of the population is an integral part of the globalization of capital. Several strands converged at the end of the Cold War, changing relations between labor and capital on an international scale: domestic economic decline, racism, the U.S. role as policeman of the world, and growth of the international drug economy in creating a booming prison industrial complex. And the prison industrial complex is rapidly becoming an essential component of the U.S. economy.

Credit: Eric Drooker (www.drooker.com)

This document was originally published as a pamphlet in 1998 by the Agit Press. It was subsequently republished by a number of organizations, including both Kersplebedeb Publishing and PM Press.

Prisons Are Big Business

Like the military industrial complex, the prison industrial complex is an inter-weaving of private business and government interests. Its twofold purpose is profit and social control. Its public rationale is the fight against crime.

Not so long ago, communism was "the enemy," and communists were demonized as a way of justifying gargantuan military expenditures. Now, fear of crime and the demonization of criminals serve a similar ideological purpose: to justify the use of tax dollars for the repression and incarceration of a growing percentage of our population. The omnipresent media blitz about serial killers, missing children, and "random violence" feeds our fear. In reality, however, most of the "criminals" we lock up are poor people who commit nonviolent crimes out of economic need. Violence occurs in less than 14 percent of all reported crime, and injuries occur in just 3 percent. In California, the top three charges for those entering prison are possession of a controlled substance, possession of a controlled substance for sale, and robbery. Violent crimes like murder, rape, manslaughter, and kidnapping don't even make the top 10.

Like fear of communism during the Cold War, fear of crime is a great selling tool for a dubious product.

As with the building and maintenance of weapons and armies, the building and maintenance of prisons are big business. Investment houses, construction companies, architects, and support services such as food, medical, transportation and furniture, all stand to profit by prison expansion. A burgeoning "specialty item" industry sells fencing, handcuffs, drug detectors, protective vests, and other security devices to prisons.

As the Cold War winds down and the Crime War heats up, defense industry giants like Westinghouse are retooling and lobbying Washington for their share of the domestic law enforcement market. "Night Enforcer" goggles used in the Gulf War, electronic "Hot Wire" fencing ("so hot NATO chose it for high-risk installations"), and other equipment once used by the military, are now being marketed to the criminal justice system.

Communication companies like AT&T, Sprint, and MCI are getting into the act as well, gouging prisoners with exorbitant phone calling rates, often six times the normal long distance charge. Smaller firms like Correctional Communications Corp., dedicated solely to the prison phone business, provide computerized prison phone systems, fully equipped for systematic surveillance. They win government contracts by offering to "kick back" some of the profits to the government agency awarding the contract. These companies are reaping huge profits at the expense of prisoners and their families; prisoners are often effectively cut off from communication due to the excessive cost of phone calls.

One of the fastest growing sectors of the prison industrial complex is private corrections companies. Investment firm Smith Barney is a part owner of a prison in Florida. American Express and General Electric have invested in private prison construction in Oklahoma and Tennessee. Correctional Corporation of America, one of the largest private prison owners, already operates internationally, with more than 48 facilities in 11 states, Puerto Rico, the United Kingdom, and Australia. Under contract by government to run jails and prisons and paid a fixed sum per prisoner, the profit motive mandates that these firms operate as cheaply and efficiently as possible. This means lower wages for staff, no unions, and fewer services for prisoners. Private contracts also mean less public scrutiny. Prison owners are raking in billions by cutting corners, which harms prisoners. Substandard diets, extreme overcrowding, and abuses by poorly trained personnel have all been documented and can be expected in these institutions, which are unabashedly about making money.

Prisons are also a leading rural growth industry. With traditional agriculture being pushed aside by agribusiness, many rural American communities are facing hard times. Economically depressed areas are falling over each other to secure a prison facility of their own. Prisons are seen as a source of jobs—in construction, local vendors, and prison staff—as well as a source of tax revenues. An average prison has a staff of several hundred employees and an annual payroll of several million dollars.

Like any industry, the prison economy needs raw materials. In this case the raw materials are prisoners. The prison industrial complex can grow only if more and more people are incarcerated—even if crime rates drop. "Three Strikes" and mandatory minimums (harsh, fixed sentences without parole) are two examples of the legal superstructure quickly being put in place to guarantee that the prison population will grow and grow and grow.

Labor and the Flight of Capital

The growth of the prison industrial complex is inextricably tied to the fortunes of labor. Ever since the onset of the Reagan-Bush years in 1980, workers in the United States have been under siege. Aggressive union busting, corporate deregulation, and especially the flight of capital in search of cheaper labor markets have been crucial factors in the downward plight of American workers.

One wave of capital flight occurred in the 1970s. Manufacturing such as textiles in the Northeast moved south—to South Carolina, Tennessee, Alabama—nonunion states where wages were low. During the 1980s, many more industries (steel, auto, etc.) closed up shop, moving on to the "more competitive atmospheres" of Mexico, Brazil, or Taiwan where wages were a mere fraction of those in the U.S., and environmental, health, and safety standards were much lower. Most seriously hurt by these plant closures and layoffs were African-Americans and other semiskilled workers in urban centers who lost their decent paying industrial jobs.

Into the gaping economic hole left by the exodus of jobs from U.S. cities has rushed another economy: the drug economy.

The War on Drugs

The "War on Drugs," launched by President Reagan in the mid-eighties, has been fought on interlocking international and domestic fronts.

At the international level, the war on drugs has been both a cynical cover-up of U.S. government involvement in the drug trade, as well as justification for U.S. military intervention and control in the Third World.

Over the last 50 years, the primary goal of U.S. foreign policy (and the military industrial complex) has been to fight communism and protect corporate interests. To this end, the U.S. government has, with regularity, formed strategic alliances with drug dealers throughout the world. At the conclusion of World War II, the OSS (precursor to the CIA) allied itself with heroin traders on the docks of Marseille in an effort to wrest power away from communist dock workers. During the Vietnam war, the CIA aided the heroin producing Hmong tribesmen in the Golden Triangle area. In return for cooperation with the U.S. government's war against the Vietcong and other national liberation forces, the CIA flew local heroin out of Southeast Asia and into America. It's no accident that heroin addiction in the U.S. rose exponentially in the 1960s.

Nor is it an accident that cocaine began to proliferate in the United States during the 1980s. Central America is the strategic halfway point for air travel between Colombia and the United States. The contra war against Sandinista Nicaragua, as well as the war against the national liberation forces in El Salvador, was largely about control of this critical area. When Congress cut off support for the contras, Oliver North and friends found other ways to fund the contra resupply operations, in part through drug dealing. Planes loaded with arms for the contras took off from the southern United States, offloaded their weapons on private landing strips in Honduras, then loaded up with cocaine for the return trip.

A 1996 exposé by the San Jose *Mercury News* documented CIA involvement in a Nicaraguan drug ring that poured thousands of kilos of cocaine into Los Angeles's African-American neighborhoods in the 1980s. Drug boss Danilo Blandon, now an informant for the DEA, acknowledged under oath the drugs-for-weapons deals with the CIA-sponsored contras.

U.S. military presence in Central and Latin America has not stopped drug traffic. But it has influenced aspects of the drug trade and is a powerful force of social control in the region. U.S. military intervention—whether in propping up dictators or squashing peasant uprisings—now operates under cover of the righteous war against drugs and "narco-terrorism."

In Mexico, for example, U.S. military aid supposedly earmarked for the drug war is being used to arm Mexican troops in the southern part of the country. The drug trade, however (production, transfer, and distribution points), is all in the north. The "drug war money" is being used primarily to fight against the Zapatista rebels in the southern state of Chiapas who are demanding land reform and economic policy changes that are diametrically opposed to the transnational corporate agenda.

585

In the Colombian jungles of Cartagena de Chairá, coca has become the only viable commercial crop. In 1996, 30,000 farmers blocked roads and airstrips to prevent crop spraying from aircraft. The Revolutionary Armed Forces of Colombia (FARC) one of the oldest guerrilla organizations in Latin America, held 60 government soldiers hostage for nine months, demanding that the military leave the jungle, that social services be increased, and that alternative crops be made available to farmers. And given the notorious involvement of Colombia's highest officials with the powerful drug cartels, it is not surprising that most U.S. "drug war" military aid actually goes to fighting the guerrillas.

One result of the international war on drugs has been the internationalization of the U.S. prison population. For the most part, it is the low-level "mules" carrying drugs into this country who are captured and incarcerated in ever-increasing numbers. At least 25 percent of inmates in the federal prison system today will be subject to deportation when their sentences are completed.

Here at home, the war on drugs has been a war on poor people. Particularly poor, urban, African-American men and women. It's well documented that police enforcement of the new, harsh drug laws have been focused on low-level dealers in communities of color. Arrests of African-Americans have been about five times higher than arrests of whites, although whites and African-Americans use drugs at about the same rate. And, African-Americans have been imprisoned in numbers even more disproportionate than their relative arrest rates. It is estimated that in 1994, on any given day, one out of every 128 U.S. adults was incarcerated, while one out of every 17 African-American adult males was incarcerated.

The differential in sentencing for powder and crack cocaine is one glaring example of institutionalized racism. About 90 percent of crack arrests are of African-Americans, while 75 percent of powder cocaine arrests are of whites. Under federal law, it takes only five grams of crack cocaine to trigger a five-year mandatory minimum sentence. But it takes 500 grams of powder cocaine—100 times as much—to trigger this same sentence. This flagrant injustice was highlighted by a 1996 nationwide federal prison rebellion when Congress refused to enact changes in sentencing laws that would equalize penalties.

Statistics show that police repression and mass incarceration are not curbing the drug trade. Dealers are forced to move, turf is reshuffled, already vulnerable families are broken up. But the demand for drugs still exists, as do huge profits for high-level dealers in this fifty billion dollar international industry.

From one point of view, the war on drugs can actually be seen as a preemptive strike, the state's repressive apparatus working overtime. Put poor people away before they get angry. Incarcerate those at the bottom, the helpless, the hopeless, before they demand change. What drugs don't damage (in terms of intact communities, the ability to take action, to organize) the war on drugs and mass imprisonment will surely destroy.

The crackdown on drugs has not stopped drug use. But it has taken thousands of unemployed (and potentially angry and rebellious) young men and women off the streets. And it has created a mushrooming prison population.

Prison Labor

An American worker who once upon a time made $8/hour loses his job when the company relocates to Thailand, where workers are paid only $2/day. Unemployed, and alienated from a society indifferent to his needs, he becomes involved in the drug economy or some other outlawed means of survival. He is arrested, put in prison, and put to work. His new salary: 22 cents/hour.

From worker, to unemployed, to criminal, to convict laborer, the cycle has come full circle. And the only victor is big business.

For private business, prison labor is like a pot of gold. No strikes. No union organizing. No unemployment insurance or workers' compensation to pay. No language problem, as in a foreign country. New leviathan prisons are being built with thousands of eerie acres of factories inside the walls. Prisoners do data entry for Chevron, make telephone reservations for TWA, raise hogs, shovel manure, make circuit boards, limousines, waterbeds, and lingerie for Victoria's Secret. All at a fraction of the cost of "free labor."

Prisoners can be forced to work for pennies because they have no rights. Even the 14th Amendment to the Constitution, which abolished slavery, excludes prisoners from its protections.

And, more and more, prisons are charging inmates for basic necessities— from medical care, to toilet paper, to use of the law library. Many states are now charging "room and board." Berks County jail in Pennsylvania is charging inmates $10 per day to be there. California has similar legislation pending. So, while government cannot (yet) actually require inmates to work at private industry jobs for less than minimum wage, necessity forces them to do so.

Some prison enterprises are state run. Inmates working at UNICOR (the federal prison industry corporation) make recycled furniture and work 40 hours a week for about $40 per month. The Oregon Prison Industries produces a line of "Prison Blues" blue jeans. An ad in their catalog shows a handsome prison inmate saying, "I say we should make bell-bottoms. They say I've been in here too long." Bizarre, but true. The promotional tags on the clothes themselves actually tout their operation as rehabilitation and job training for prisoners, who of course would never be able to find work in the garment industry upon release.

Prison industries are often directly competing with private industry. Small furniture manufacturers around the country complain that they are being driven out of business by UNICOR, which pays 23 cents/hour and has the inside track on government contracts. In another case, U.S. Technologies sold its electronics plant in Austin, Texas, leaving its 150 workers unemployed. Six week later, the electronics plant reopened in a nearby prison.

Welcome to the New World Order

The proliferation of prisons in the United States is one piece of a puzzle called the globalization of capital.

Since the end of the Cold War, capitalism has gone on an international business offensive. No longer impeded by an alternative socialist economy or the threat of national liberation movements supported by the Soviet Union or China, transnational corporations see the world as their oyster. Agencies such as the World Trade Organization, World Bank, and the International Monetary Fund, bolstered by agreements like NAFTA and GATT, are putting more and more power into the hands of transnational corporations by putting the squeeze on national governments. The primary mechanism of control is debt. For decades, developing countries have depended on foreign loans, resulting in increasing vulnerability to the transnational corporate strategy for the global economy. Access to international credit and aid is given only if governments agree to certain conditions known as "structural adjustment."

In a nutshell, structural adjustment requires cuts in social services, privatization of state-run industry, repeal of agreements with labor about working conditions and minimum wage, conversion of multi-use farm lands into cash crop agriculture for export, and the dismantling of trade laws that protect local economies. Under structural adjustment, police and military expenditures are the only government spending that is encouraged. The sovereignty of nations is compromised when, as in the case of Vietnam, trade sanctions are threatened unless the government allows Camel cigarettes to litter the countryside with billboards, or promises to spend millions in the U.S.-orchestrated crackdown on drugs.

The basic transnational corporate philosophy is this: the world is a single market; natural resources are to be exploited; people are consumers; anything that hinders profit is to be rooted out and destroyed. The results of this philosophy in action are that while economies are growing, so is poverty, so is ecological destruction, so are sweatshops and child labor. Across the globe, wages are plummeting, indigenous people are being forced off their lands, rivers are becoming industrial dumping grounds, and forests are being obliterated. Massive regional starvation and "World Bank riots" are becoming more frequent throughout the Third World.

All over the world, more and more people are being forced into illegal activity for their own survival as traditional cultures and social structures are destroyed. Inevitably, crime and imprisonment rates are on the rise. And the United States law enforcement establishment is in the forefront, domestically and internationally, in providing state-of-the-art repression.

Within the United States, structural adjustment (sometimes known as the Contract with America) takes the form of welfare and social service cuts, continued massive military spending, and skyrocketing prison spending. Walk through any poor urban neighborhood: school systems are crumbling and after-school programs, libraries, parks, and drug treatment centers are closed. But you will see more police stations and more cops. Often, the only "social service" available to poor young people is jail.

The dismantling of social programs and the growing dominance of the right-wing agenda in U.S. politics have been made possible, at least in part, by the successful repression of the civil rights and liberation movements of the 1960s and '70s. Many of the leaders—Martin Luther King, Jr., Malcolm X, Fred Hampton, and many others—were assassinated. Others, like Geronimo ji Jaga Pratt, Leonard Peltier, and Mumia Abu-Jamal, have been locked up. Over 150 political leaders from the black liberation struggle, the Puerto Rican independence movement, and other resistance efforts are still in prison. Many are serving sentences ranging from 40 to 90 years. Oppressed communities have been robbed of radical political leadership that might have led an opposition movement. We are reaping the results.

The number of people in U.S. prisons has more than tripled in the past 17 years—from 500,000 in 1980 to 1.8 million in 1997. Today, more than five million people are behind bars, on parole, probation, or under other supervision by the criminal justice system. The state of California now spends more on prisons than on higher education and over the past decade has built 19 prisons and only one branch university.

Add to this, the fact that increasing numbers of women are being locked up. Between 1980 and 1994, the number of women in prison increased five-fold, and women now make up the fastest growing segment of the prison population. Most of these women are mothers—leaving future generations growing up in foster homes or on the streets.

Welcome to the New World Order.

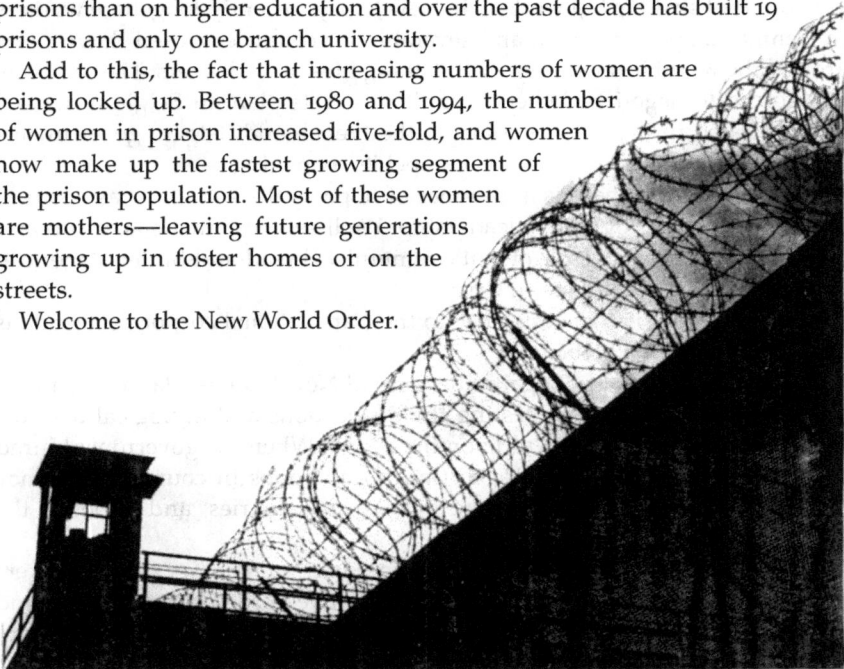

What Is to Be Done?

Prisons are not reducing crime. But they are fracturing already vulnerable families and communities.

Poor people of color are being locked up in grossly disproportionate numbers, primarily for nonviolent crimes. But Americans are not feeling safer.

As "criminals" become scapegoats for our floundering economy and our deteriorating social structure, even the guise of rehabilitation is quickly disappearing from our penal philosophy. After all: rehabilitate for what? To go back into an economy that has no jobs? To go back into a community that has no hope? As education and other prison programs are cut back, or in most cases eliminated altogether, prisons are becoming vast, overcrowded holding tanks. Or worse: factories behind bars.

And, prison labor is undercutting wages—something that hurts all working and poor Americans. It's a situation that can only occur because organized labor is divided and weak and has not kept step with organized capital.

While capital has globalized, labor has not. While the transnationals truly are fashioning our planet into a global village, there is still little communication or cooperation between workers around the world. Only an internationally linked labor movement can effectively challenge the power of the transnational corporations.

There have been some wonderful, shining instances of international worker solidarity. In the early 1980s, 3M workers in South Africa walked out in support of striking 3M workers in New Jersey. Recently, longshore workers in Denmark, Spain, Sweden and several other countries closed down ports around the world in solidarity with striking Liverpool dockers. The company was forced to negotiate. When Renault closed its plant in Belgium, 100,000 demonstrated in Brussels, pressuring the French and Belgian governments to condemn the plant closure and compel its reopening.

Here in the U.S., there is a glimmer of hope as the AFL-CIO has voted in some new, more progressive leadership. We'll see how that shapes up and whether the last 50 years of anticommunist, bread-and-butter American unionism is really a thing of the past.

What is certain is that resistance to the transnational corporate agenda is growing around the globe:

In 1996, the people of Bougainville, a small New Guinea island, organized a secessionist rebellion, protesting the dislocations and ecological destruction caused by corporate mining on the island. When the government hired mercenaries from South Africa to train local troops in counterinsurgency warfare, the army rebelled, threw out the mercenaries, and deposed the prime minister.

A one-day general strike shut down Haiti in January 1997. Strikers demanded the suspension of negotiations between the prime minister and the International Monetary Fund/World Bank. They protested the austerity measures imposed by the IMF and WB, which would mean laying off 7,000 government workers, and the privatization of the electric and telephone companies.

In Nigeria, the Ogoni people conducted a protracted eight-year struggle against Shell Oil. Acid rain and hundreds of oil spills and gas flares were turning the once fertile countryside into a near wasteland. Their peaceful demonstrations, election boycotts, and pleas for international solidarity were met with violent government repression and the eventual execution of Ogoni writer and leader Ken Saro Wiwa.

In France, a month-long general strike united millions of workers who protested privatization, a government worker pay freeze, and cutbacks in social services. Telephone, airline, power, postal, education, health care, and metal workers all joined together, bringing business to a standstill. The right-wing Chirac government was forced to make minor concessions before being voted out for a new "socialist" administration.

At the Oak Park Heights Correctional Facility in Minnesota, 150 prisoners went on strike in March 1997, demanding to be paid the minimum wage. Although they lost a litigation battle to attain this right, their strike gained attention and support from several local labor unions.

Just as the prison industrial complex is becoming increasingly central to the growth of the U.S. economy, prisoners are a crucial part of building effective opposition to the transnational corporate agenda. Because of their enforced invisibility, powerlessness, and isolation, it's far too common for prisoners to be left out of the equation of international solidarity. Yet, opposing the expansion of the prison industrial complex, and supporting the rights and basic humanity of prisoners, may be the only way we can stave off the consolidation of a police state that represses us all—where you or a friend or family member may yourself end up behind bars.

Clearly, the only alternative that will match the power of global capital is an internationalization of human solidarity. Because, truly, we are all in this together.

> International solidarity is not an act of charity. It is an act of
> unity between allies fighting on different terrains toward the
> same objective. The foremost of these objectives is to aid the
> development of humanity to the highest level possible.
>
> Samora Machel (1933-1986)
> Leader of FRELIMO
> First President of Mozambique

591

Capitalism and Crisis: Creating a Jailhouse Nation

David Gilbert
2001

Book Review: Christian Parenti, *Lockdown America: Police and Prisons in the Age of Crisis* (Verso, 1999).

By the time I was captured in 1981, the prologue to a life sentence, I had 20 years of movement experience—both above and underground—under my belt. So I thought I had a good understanding of the race and class basis of prisons. But once actually inside that reality, I was stunned by just how thoroughly racist the criminal justice system is and also by the incessant petty hassles of humiliation and degradation. As political prisoner Mumia Abu-Jamal aptly noted in *Live from Death Row*, there is a "profound horror... in the day-to-day banal occurrences... [the] second-by-second assault on the soul." The 1980s became the intense midpoint of an unprecedented explosion of imprisonment.* Since 1972, the number of inmates in this country, on any given day, has multiplied six-fold to the two million human beings behind bars today.† Another four million are being supervised on parole or probation. The U.S. is the world leader in both death sentences and incarcerations. With just 5 percent of the world's population, we hold 25 percent of the prisoners.

The qualitative political change has been just as stark as the numbers: no politician who hopes to get elected can risk a charge of being soft on crime. Literally thousands of new repressive laws have been passed, and law and order has become the battering ram for a broader right-wing offensive. The political importance of criminal justice is, as we say in prison, "obvious to a duck."

Originally published in *Monthly Review* 52, no. 10, March 2001, this review was subsequently reprinted in *No Surrender: Writings from an Anti-Imperialist Political Prisoner* (Abraham Guillen Press, 2004).

* Most of the data cited in this review comes directly from *Lockdown America*. I've added data based on reports from the U.S. Department of Justice's Bureau of Justice Statistics and from the Sentencing Project.

† The two million figure is for the number of persons behind bars on a given day. Because many people are in and out of county jails in a matter of months or even days, the number of persons in jail or prison over the course of the year would be several times larger than two million.

What is far from obvious—in fact purposely obscured—are the real reasons for these dramatic and ultimately very damaging developments. It certainly isn't a rational response to crime. Consider just a couple of the many telling but rarely mentioned facts: Western Europe and Japan, with about 1/7 our incarceration rate, maintain lower levels of violent crime. Throughout 20 years of mushrooming imprisonment here, U.S. crime rates continued to climb. The marked decline in violent offenses didn't start until 1993—along with the fall in unemployment and the lower percent of males in the high-risk 15- to 24-year-old age group. Wholesale repression and incarceration are emphatically not real solutions. However, the political role of these themes makes them burning issues for everyone concerned about social change.

Christian Parenti's *Lockdown America* is an analytical gem, with many sparkling facets on key developments—from the advent of computerized, nationwide police files to tower guards shooting down unarmed inmates in California. This book does not take on the complex questions of the causes and cures for crime. Instead, its forte is laying bare the driving forces behind the burgeoning of the criminal justice system. Parenti's starting point might seem far removed from police and prisons, but it proves compelling. It is the serious structural crisis of U.S. and world capitalism that emerged in the late 1960s. To put Parenti's much fuller account into a nutshell, the very success of the post-Second World War glory days of capitalist growth proved to be its undoing. The extraordinary investment opportunities in rebuilding the war-ravaged economies of Europe and Japan resulted in highly productive competitors for U.S. industry. These developments ushered in a period of chronic overproduction, in which capitalism tends to produce more goods and services than can be profitably sold (given the limited purchasing power of most people).

Source: www.radicalgraphics.org

At the same time, capital was hit with political changes within the U.S. The examples of civil rights and antiwar activism inspired growing worker militancy, which resulted in rising labor costs, and a new environmental movement, which led to expensive pollution controls. To summarize a complex international and domestic crunch by how it reads on capital's bottom line, average profit rates fell from a peak of almost 10 percent in 1965 to a low of 4.5 percent in 1974. And there was no prospect for a cyclical upswing out of this pit.

Parenti describes two major phases of capital's counteroffensive. The first was the withering attack on radical movements and insurgent communities, including a counterintelligence program resulting, among other things, in the murders of some 30 members of the Black Panther Party. The real motive behind the law and order rallying cry is deftly revealed with a quote from the diary of President Nixon's Chief of Staff H. R. Haldeman:

> [President Nixon] emphasized that you have to face the fact that the whole problem is really the blacks. The key is to devise a system that recognizes this while not appearing to.

The second stage entailed the sweeping economic restructuring that was kicked off by England's Prime Minister Thatcher in 1979. It became the heart of the Reagan Revolution here and is still going strong today. Here's how Thatcher's chief economic advisor, Alan Budd, put it:

> Rising unemployment was a very desirable way of reducing the strength of the working classes.... What was engineered—in Marxist terms—was a crisis in capitalism which re-created a reserve army of labor, and has allowed capitalists to make high profits ever since.

This opening salvo was followed by a raft of measures that could best be summarized as successively gutting the Great Society and New Deal social compacts, leaving labor in a weak bargaining position even in subsequent economic expansions.

These changes severely hurt the inner cities. First, capital, now more globally mobile, shifted some manufacturing to low-wage countries and regions within the U.S., eliminating many of the jobs that had provided at least a measure of stability for Blacks and Latinos. The new, poorly paid service jobs more likely went to immigrant workers, who could be intimidated with the threat of deportation. From the point of view of capitalist production, people in the ghettos and barrios became "surplus population" or "social junk." At the same time, these stressed communities, with a history of militancy, were potentially "social dynamite"—a serious threat located near the city center, headquarters of the most profitable sectors of the new economy such as finance, insurance, real estate, and communications. Parenti sees the core of the anticrime crusade as rooted in capital's acute need to control and contain the ghettos and barrios and to create *cordons sanitaires* around the central business districts.

Second, capital's campaign to wrest away many of the last generation's gains for U.S. workers posed a pressing political problem: the need to deflect rising frustration and anger away from the rulers. To do so, they recharged their "...trusted trope: race spoken through the code of crime and welfare." In short, there is a complete correlation over the past 20 years between the greatest ever recorded shift of wealth from the poor to the rich and our skyrocketing prison population. The dual needs of containment and scapegoating are clearly expressed in the racial character of American justice. For example, African Americans are 13 percent of the illegal drug users but 74 percent of drug prisoners. Overall, the ratio of Black to white incarcerations is seven to one. The U.S. now imprisons Black males at four times the rate of South Africa under apartheid.

Lockdown America describes key aspects of the spectacular expansion of repressive powers over the period, in a writing style that combines analytical clarity with striking examples. Below are some of the areas covered:

- **Police Special Weapons and Tactics (SWAT) teams.** Los Angeles created the first SWAT team in 1966. There are 30,000 such units today. SWAT's serve as the vanguard of militarizing the police, with weapons such as assault rifles, armored vehicles, attack dogs, and helicopters—all too often accompanied by a commando mentality that makes all Black and Latino people the enemy. While providing some grisly examples of overkill, Parenti emphasizes the broader function of intimidating entire communities.
- **Anticrime legislation.** *Lockdown America*'s look at just a few provisions of recent federal laws, just a tiny sampling of the spate of state and federal acts, presents a breathtaking cascade of authoritarian measures that greatly expand police powers and stiffen penalties.
- **The criminalization of immigration.** Parenti calls the new level of cooperation among various law enforcement agencies, and at times the military, at the U.S.-Mexican border "the most aggressive and totalizing police enforcement regime the country has ever seen." The racism is patent to anyone who has gone through an immigration check point. Those with white skin are waved right through while those with brown skin are routinely stopped. The formidable increase in detentions, with people often held under the most wretched conditions, can't begin to stanch the flow of immigration, itself driven by the economic forces of globalization. But the palpable threat of deportation is a powerful cudgel against labor organizing and complaints, while these victims of transnational capital are blamed for the loss of U.S. jobs. So, "...politicians get easy scapegoats; employers get docile labor...."

- **"Quality of Life."** The newest chapter in policing is the highly touted "Quality of Life" and "Zero Tolerance" campaigns. In theory, the thorough crackdowns on minor offenses such as graffiti, open beer cans, and unpaid traffic tickets will nab potential felons and create a climate of compliance with the law. In practice, there have been increased complaints of police brutality as well as widespread ensnaring of young people of color into the justice system. The experiences of abuse and arrest are themselves strong predictors of future felonies. Thus these programs may well generate more crime in the long run, but they are very useful for creating a comfort zone for the higher echelons working in the central business districts.

Each of the above policies leads to more people behind bars. Parenti provides a quality chapter on the growing "prison industrial complex." With about $40 billion per year being spent on building and running prisons, and over 500,000 full-time corrections employees, crime definitely pays for some sectors. Perhaps the most chilling example is the California correctional officers' union. It has become the state's second biggest lobbyist and spends millions on election campaigns. It was the driving force behind "three strikes" and over 1,000 other anticrime measures passed in California since the late 1980s. But Parenti wisely avoids economic reductionism. Corrections budgets are nowhere near those for the military industrial complex and don't play the same strategic role of subsidizing research for high-tech industries. Also, despite the impressive initial spurt of the for-profit sectors of private prisons and corporate use of convict labor, these are still a small fraction of the corrections complex and face major constraints to continued growth. While the pockets of pork-driven prosperity assert some influence, such vested interests are secondary to the needs and strategies of a ruling class responding to structural crisis.

While not attempting a detailed description of prison life, *Lockdown America* spotlights some of its more unsettling aspects, such as gang rivalries and rape. In addition to the horrible direct violence involved, the ever-present dangers and antagonisms prevent inmates from uniting against oppressive conditions, which in turn fuel more frustration and internal violence. The very chaos the institutions create is then used to justify bigger budgets and more repression. The flagship of these trends is the proliferation of super-max prisons and special (or secure) housing units. The rationale is that these are needed for "superpredators," but in practice they are also used against organizers, rebels, and "jailhouse lawyers." These prisons-within-prisons are characterized by 23-hour-a-day lock-ups, intense electronic surveillance, almost no social interaction or programs, and brutal reprisals against defiant inmates. One couldn't consciously design conditions better suited for fostering mental illness and antisocial, violent behavior.

A lot more could be added about the damage being done: severe HIV and hepatitis C epidemics; the high percentage of women prisoners whose problems started with sexual or physical abuse on the outside and who are then placed under the complete domination of male guards; the impact of sentences on convicts' children, who thereby become five times more likely than their peers to eventually land in jail.* At the same time, correctional programs that greatly reduce recidivism—most notably college education—are being dismantled behind the propaganda myth that our prisons are "country clubs."

Meanwhile, the police keep sweeping more young people—whether for "quality of life" misdemeanors or nonviolent drug offenses—into a corrections system primed for chewing up human beings and spitting out violent parolees. While counterproductive, in the long run, against crime, this approach serves capital well. The key, in my view, is the political role of racial scapegoating. Parenti articulates it well:

> As economic contradictions deepen, the racialized class Other—the immigrant, the urban mendicant, the cheats, the dark-skinned, the "thieves," and "predators"—looms larger than ever in the minds of the economically besieged middle and working classes. [Since] the corporate system will not and cannot profitably accommodate the needs of the poor and working majority, [politicians] necessarily turn to crime-baiting and racially coded demonology as a way of inciting, mobilizing, and diverting legitimate political anxieties toward irrelevant enemies.

The U.S. today is criminalizing an ever-widening range of social problems. The government would rather militarize the police and build prisons than provide quality education, good-paying jobs, and a sound public health response to drug abuse. These trends, while ineffective on crime, serve to aggrandize police power. Even more importantly, the law and order mania has become an essential political arena of struggle for the left. Conceding the weight of public opinion to the bandwagon of racial scapegoating would only build the momentum and power of the grand-scale criminals who rule over all of us.

---

* Ann McDiermert, "Programming for Women Offenders and Their Children," *International Association of Residential and Community Alternatives Journal* 3:4 (September 1990) 5.

Prison Abolition, Political Prisoners, and the Building of Critical Resistance: An Interview with Linda Thurston

2008

Matt Meyer: You have a long history of working not just for political prisoners, but for the rights and freedom of prisoners in general, as well as for prison abolition. What motivated you to get involved in this work?

Linda Thurston: In the very beginning it was extremely personal. My first memory in my entire life is of police showing up at my front door and taking my father away when I was four. I remember being very upset that the grownups weren't acting the way grownups usually act. I was upset that these unidentified, unknown, large, loud, white men were taking daddy away. But I had also been freaked out because daddy had been hitting mommy. I was in this situation where my parents were arguing and the police dealt with it by dragging dad away. Everyone was in pain, with screaming, yelling, and chaos.

It was instinctively clear to me at this point that something was desperately wrong. This was not a solution to anything. I think that every single time during my life, when I was working with prisoners, all these issues came up again. I would remember what it felt like and think about the children. It wasn't at that moment that I committed myself to working with prisoners or even to being an activist. I didn't come from an activist family in the sense of people having a political analysis—although we did things in the community and with the local church. But it framed my thinking about imprisonment and police for the rest of my life.

When I was in junior high school, I started doing work through my church with what was euphemistically called The Children's Center in Providence, Rhode Island. It was basically a maximum-security prison for kids, with such horrendous and repressive policies that it was later shut down. It was very interesting to be the same age as those kids, the same look as those kids, the same neighborhood as those kids, the same language as those kids, and be acutely aware that there but for the powers that be go I. Even before I knew how badly the kids were being treated and abused, the entire situation seemed wrong to me.

The next significant moment in my political development regarding prisons was as a college student, running the Black theater group as a Harvard undergraduate. The group was called the Black Community and Student Theater, but given that this was Harvard, many folks had unfortunately forgotten the community piece of it! I remember sitting in a board meeting when a letter came in from one of the prisoner organizations asking if we would please come out and do a play for the prisoners. The entire group swung their heads in my direction, because I was already involved in some political activity on campus. They knew that I'd be interested in doing it. We took a play out to the prison, and I remember being profoundly affected by that experience. I actually ended up working with the "prisoner self-help groups" at Walpole prison outside of Boston, helping with issues involving prisoner mistreatment, use of pepper spray, tear gas, and such.

Coming of age in the late 1970s and 1980s, paying attention to these issues, it was hard not to notice that at one moment there were three hundred thousand prisoners in America, and a moment later there are five hundred thousand. Just a few years later, there were a million prisoners in America and today there are two million people locked up in America. My lifetime has been the period of time when the United States has used prisons as its solution to everything.

MM: You've worked with a number if the key regional and national organizations in this field. Would you share some of those experiences?

Linda Thurston: When I became the director of the New England Criminal Justice Program of the Quaker-based American Friends Service Committee, one of the big issues was a tendency to lock up any prisoners who spoke out on any issues in solitary confinement—sometimes for years. These were clear cases of political repression, locking people up not because they posed any threats but because they were willing to fight for their rights, even as prisoners. Many folks whom I worked with then may not have landed in prison because of political activities, but they certainly got politicized once in prison.

Partly because I was in Boston, where there was a very strong antiapartheid movement and a very strong Central American solidarity movement, I learned about many people doing time because of refusal to cooperate with federal grand jury investigations. At the Red Book Store in Cambridge, I remember meeting some people—like Tommy Manning and Jaan Laaman of the Ohio 7 case—who are still political prisoners to this day. Kazi Toure, now out of prison and the national co-chair of the Jericho Amnesty Movement, was around in those days, along with his brother, Arnie King, who is also still doing time despite an incredible record of community support and work. I think there are some regional cultural differences that have shaped people's political development differently. In New York City, for example, most of the political prisoners came directly out of the local Black Panther Party. But in Boston and later in Philadelphia, with the case of MOVE and the MOVE 9, I had a different framework. While I was working for AFSC, I began to learn more about political prisoners through my own writing and radio projects.

As an AFSC staff person, I was involved in the 200 Years of Penitentiary project, recognizing Philadelphia's Walnut Street Jail as the first prison in the U.S.A. The campaign was a way of doing prison abolition work in the 1980s, and I got to dress up in my Sunday best and speak to all the Quaker groups, and Methodists, and Presbyterians, and United Church folks. From there, I got to work with the National Interreligious Task Force on Criminal Justice. Those networks, with people like Episcopal Minister S. Michael Yasutake (founding chair of the Prisoner of Conscience Project) building bridges between social and political prisoners, helped create lasting relationships and commitments. Fast forward some years, to the early 1990s, and I ended up working with Amnesty International USA on death penalty issues.

I actually had, from the beginning, some very real issues with Amnesty International. In part, this was because Amnesty refused to name Nelson Mandela, or any number of other people, as political prisoners. I didn't understand at that moment the human rights movement's nuanced differences in definition regarding political prisoners, prisoners of war, and prisoners of conscience. Nor did I understand how amazingly egg-headedly legalistic and academistic the whole human rights framework could be. But at that particular moment, between 1994 and 1995, executions in the U.S.A. had almost doubled in one year. It seemed important to do that work with those resources, but it was one of the most frustrating experiences of my life. Amnesty is an organization that grows out of the Cold War mentality. They began as a group that issued bulletins on behalf of prisoners of conscience, one prisoner from the West and one from the Soviet Union, trying to embarrass those governments by bombarding them with letters. While I was there, we did begin trying to get Amnesty to pay attention to the case of Black Panther death row inmate Mumia Abu-Jamal. But I could not stay at Amnesty for long.

The job I had at the Center for Constitutional Rights was coordinator of the Ella Baker Student Program, which I used to refer to as my job of training little "baby radical lawyers." These were young people whom we would recruit from various law schools who thought that they wanted to be "movement" lawyers. Whatever issues they were eventually going to work on, it was crucial that they get an education in the history and the current way of looking at the role of prisons in society and the reality of political prisoners. I remember bringing in Attica prison rebellion survivor and representative Big Black to talk to these law students after we'd shown them the film *Attica*. It was a strong way of educating and radicalizing people who could have a direct effect on the lives of prisoners.

MM: What were and are some of the issues involved in building bridges between the people who do work around political prisoners and those who work around the prison industrial complex or prison abolition?

Linda Thurston: I think there are people who come out of a political context, who make many assumptions about categories such as "social prisoners." Some people who work on political prisoner cases have, in a general theoretical sense, the idea that prisons themselves are bad, but also that prisons are where bad folks are. If you stole something, you're a thief. If you killed somebody, you're a murderer. And that is what you are, that is who you are, and that is all you are. I really have a problem with that idea, maybe coming from my spirituality or maybe just my common-sense political analysis. Nobody is only one thing, and no one is only as bad as the worse thing they ever did. If that were true, we'd all be in big trouble because we're all human. Some people who won't do work around social prisoners or politicized social prisoners have this perspective, and many people who do work with the general prison population do it purely from a social service perspective and aren't interested in working on political prisoner issues. The key is to see the connections between these struggles and not to pit them against one another. We've got lots of work ahead of us.

It also has now gotten way more complicated because more and more political prisoners are spending vast, unbelievable amounts of time in prison and not getting out. Political prisoners are dying in prison, so the issue becomes more urgent, as vastly increased numbers of people are being sent to prison for long periods of time. In countries where the concept of "political prisoner" is recognized as a legal category, there may still be human rights problems and justice issues, but the complications and divisions tend to be easier to deal with. It is agreed that there are political prisoners, and it is agreed that there are major problems in the prison industrial complex (PIC). Here in the U.S. an urgent task of the current political moment is for folks doing political prisoner support work to recognize the broader context of the PIC.

One place where we've seen this take place is around the case of Mumia Abu-Jamal. Mumia's case has brought so many people from different political movements and perspectives together. In general, though, with all the cases, we need to make more opportunities for all kinds of interaction and discussion. Not to be naïve, but these dialogues between those of us doing basically similar work are an urgent necessity. We've got to find greater ways to work together.

MM: You've been active, since the beginning, in the development of Critical Resistance (CR), which in some ways tries to present a new framework about how to do some of this work. And you continue to help bridge the gap between work around prison abolition and around political prisoners. Could you describe the current national scene, around the time of the 10th anniversary of CR, and discuss how things have changed, and how they've stayed the same?

Linda Thurston: It may be a new framework and a new concept in this current iteration, but the notion of prison abolition is much older than the 1998 founding conference of CR. I actually didn't get involved in CR until after that initial national conference in Oakland, but I did attend the conference. There were many folks at the first Critical Resistance gathering who were over-joyed that people were talking about prison abolition again. We didn't know that over a thousand people would show up, with energy to build local and regional chapters. We clearly hit upon a moment when people were ready to work on issues involving the role of prisons in U.S. life.

One issue that we've been dealing with, and need to continue to deal with, is the role of people who have been most impacted by the prison industrial complex. Our organizations can't just be made up of people who want to work on an issue. It has to include people who did time, people whose family members have done time. These folks must be in the leadership of the move-ment and the leadership of the struggle, because in many ways they can best understand and convey the complexities of the system on a local and national level. As we all need to step up and become active when that's needed, we also need to learn to step back and take leadership from the folk who haven't been in leadership. Some of us older folks need to learn that in regard to the youth, too.

Another thing that's fairly unique about CR, in my experience, is the way in which the regional organizations reflect the national program as well as the specific political context in a given region of the country. We've been weaving a sort of web between the local networks and the national group.

There's also a great deal of attention in CR given to political education. Far too often in our movements, we don't find out where people are coming from. If somebody shows up for a meeting, we're so glad that they're there, we'll just give them some things to do and tell them when and where to go for the next meeting. But CR really works to build community. I feel very con-nected to the local folks in the organization, even though I work more with the national. We are in a situation where someone can put a call out and say, "Yo, the sister who was at the meeting last night—her kid just got arrested. Can any of you get to court?" And people do it. It reminds me of working with the groups in Boston when I was younger: that sense of community, of family, of connectedness. That feeling also comes up when I get emails from different political prisoner support groups saying, "So and so on the inside is sick. We've got to jump in here and deal with this."

I guess I've come full circle after all these years, realizing that we need the political analysis, we need the political education, we need the strategizing, we need more bodies, and we need resources. But we also damn sure better remember that we're human beings and we need to support one another on all levels or we're not going to make it. Sometimes our failure is as simple as calling a meeting at dinnertime and not having so much as a pitcher of water at the table. If we're going to survive, if we've going to succeed, if we're going to win, if we're going to free folks, we've got to get better at doing the human piece of building movement by building community.

Section IX.

At War:
The U.S. Government's Illegal and Ongoing War Against the Black Liberation Movement

As the extremes of racism, repression, and imprisonment continue to hit the Black community with particular might, the movement for survival and fightback has taken many forms. This section, in addition to an interview with Assata Shakur, several writings by Jericho founder, San Francisco 8 member, and political prisoner Jalil Muntaqim, and some Jericho documents, also takes up the call to understand the continuing nature of the Counterintelligence Program of advanced assassination. The transcripts of the Washington, DC, hearing convened by then-Congresswoman Cynthia McKinney and former Black Panther leader Kathleen Cleaver make up an important part of this section.

IX.1
An Interview with Assata Shakur

Meg Starr (Free Puerto Rico Committee)
& Matt Meyer (War Resisters League)
1991

At one time labeled "the Most Dangerous Woman in America," Assata Shakur is an uncompromising, broad-minded revolutionary, critical thinker and a clear representation of modern-day resistance. Assata was one of the primary targets of the FBI's counterinsurgency operation, COINTELPRO. On May 2, 1973, Assata, Sundiata Acoli, and Zayd Malik Shakur were attacked by state troopers on the new jersey turnpike. The ambush led to the murder of Zayd and the severe wounding and capture of Assata. Though Sundiata was able to escape capture at the time, he was later arrested and is currently one of Our longest held combatants.

After spending six years in prison, Assata was liberated by New Afrikan and Anti-Imperialist forces in 1979. She received political asylum from the Cuban government and resides there today. A memorable shero of revolutionary struggle, Assata documented the horrendous episode of her "encounter" with the U.S. government, experiences with the Black Panther Party and "coming of age" in amerikkka in her book *Assata* (Lawrence Hill Books).

Having survived COINTELPRO, Assata remains grounded in liberatory principles. As a warrior, teacher, and thinker, Assata brings over 20 years of experience to struggle. Her revolutionary outlook and analysis should be heard, discussed, and critiqued.

This interview first appeared in the Spring/Summer, and Fall 1992 issues of *Crossroad*, the newsletter of Spear and Shield Publications.

Meg Starr: You mentioned you were working on a book, could you tell me something about it?

Assata Shakur: The book is essentially about the ideological development of the Black Liberation Movement, the relationship between the Black Liberation Movement in the united states and world revolutionary movements. It deals, in some parts, with changes in eastern europe—in passing. It also explores some ideas i am currently dealing with in terms of things i think are important for Afrikans living in the united states to think about. These are just some ideas i want to fill out. i am trying to write the book in a way that does not say, "These are the answers; this is the answer." i'm trying to just deal with: This is what i'm thinking at the moment. Hopefully, that will grow. But, these are some things to throw out for people to reflect on and to give me some feedback on. i'm trying to write in a nonarrogant, nonabsolutist way, and i think that's important right now for people interested in making ideological input; to develop a style of writing and a style of work that is contra-arrogant. i think arrogance is one of the things that has really stifled the world revolutionary movement and really hindered communication between people.

M.S.: As you're doing that, I'm sure you are thinking a lot about the '60s and '70s. Do you have any things that you feel were particular lessons? And I know you don't want to put this in dogmatic terms, but any particular lessons from the '60s and '70s that you've been thinking about?

Assata: Well, i think all of us have learned many, many lessons from the '60s and '70s. Those years for me were my political education, my political period of growth and development—the beginning of my political growth and development. i think that one of the things that i learned, or think i learned, is that it's not important so much who directs, who is in the vanguard, it's that people work together wherever they are—whether they're in a union; whether they're in a block committee, whether they're working in a political organization; whatever place they are: to do work; to become active; to become aware; to increase the level of activity rather than to concentrate on being the vanguard, on trying to lead a movement. A lot of times people who were trying to lead didn't know where they were going.

Leadership has to be, in the new sense of leadership, a collective process, and the concept of vanguard has to be collectivized, has to be put in the context of the 1990s and approaching 2000, because people come from many different concepts of freedom. The point is for us to sit down and make some kind of agreement on some basic things and understand that what is going to be freedom to me, is not necessarily going to be freedom for you. Self-Determination must be a very important part of what We're talking about when We talk about political organization—political activity—that has to be underlined, because everybody doesn't have the same dream. So, there has to be room for everybody to attempt to move toward that dream, as long as that dream does not include oppressing other people, exploiting other people.

M.S.: When I was young, my political development was being shaped by the Black Movement in a lot of different ways. (I might now look back on it and say in my consciousness-raising group as a woman, all these terms like stereotype were being used, things that we were getting from the Black Movement, but not knowing we were getting them from the Black Movement.) One of the terms that's come up from the '60s and '70s, in talking about the leadership of the Black Movement, within the movements in the united states, that it had a role in radicalizing lots of other parts of the movement. I wonder how you see that—the leading role of the Black Movement?

Assata: Well, i think it's logical, and i also think it's correct that the people that are most oppressed, in any given country, should have a great deal to say about the direction that a movement must take, should take, etc. Logically, the most oppressed people should have a great deal of influence in what happens. If that doesn't happen, then what you have is a very elitist, racist movement.

So, if the Black Liberation Movement, the Movement for Puerto Rican Independence, the movement of oppressed people in general, the movement for the liberation of the Indigenous people, if these movements are not in first focus, are not up front in the movement as a whole, then something is wrong. i think that necessarily the "working class" movement has to deal with the most oppressed workers, workers who are dealing with an oppression that is much greater. Those workers must be heard. Those workers must have some kind of role in leadership of the movement as a whole. Because without that you have a distortion, you have something that does not reflect the reality. It just disintegrates into something that is arrogant, racist, and eurocentric. i think that for too many years the ideological input into the movement has been eurocentric. The ideas and the revolutionary examples of Third World people have been ignored, minimalized, minimized. The contributions of so many revolutionary people have just been overlooked by the european movement, by the white left in the united states. This has not been studied with any seriousness; that trend must be changed. i think that for a revolutionary ideology to evolve, that is truly scientific in nature, it must come from the experience not of europe, but from all of the world; the experience of Afrikans, the experiences of Asians, Latin Americans, and of europeans. But it must reflect a body of knowledge that comes from the whole world and a theory of history that is based on the experiences of the whole world, not just europe. That is one of the errors that must be corrected at this time.

The bankrupt kind of ideology, the kind of stagnation that has been coming out of the european experience, for the last years, shows that something else must be developed. The most oppressed people in the world right now are Afrikans, Asians, and Latin Americans. So, the ideological input of Afrikans,

Asians, and Latin Americans is not only important, it is essential. It's necessary because imperialism has reached such a state it's really difficult to separate racism from imperialism; eurocentrism from imperialism, because they're connected. Perpetuating an ideology that is eurocentric is also perpetuating an ideological imperialism.

So, in order to destroy imperialism, there must be an ideological movement from the people who are victimized by imperialism. This is not to say that other experiences are not important and not to say the contributions of european revolutionaries—Marx, Engels, Lenin—are not valid, not important. You don't throw them out. But that must be expanded.

A science, to be a science, cannot be stagnant; it has to grow. If it does not grow, then it becomes a dogma. A science must be something that is constantly expanding, constantly growing, and one of the problems has been that there has been no systematic way in which socialist theory could grow because the dogmatism has just dominated—for years—the ideological and, in many ways, practical aspects of the left. That has to be rethought, and those tendencies have to be thrown out the window, because they don't help and they've done a lot to hinder people's freedom.

Matt Meyer: I guess from that, we were wondering if you could speak generally about what you think the role now of north americans or european americans are within the revolutionary process—what can european americans do to be a positive part of the process?

Assata: Well, i think that one thing that needs to be done is education. People really need to educate themselves and to educate other people to communicate with others; to make use of the tremendous amount of technology that is in the hands of white north americans. People have access to computers, have access to videos, have access to all kinds of technology that needs to be exploited. i mean the ideas that some revolutionary people have had to organize people has been prehistoric reality. Somebody has an idea that to organize people is with a leaflet. You go up to somebody and hand them a leaflet and the leaflet says "Workers of the World Unite." This is 1991, going into 1992. You have so many more things at your disposal now.

What needs to be done is to use those things to organize in a creative way; to organize other white people, other people, in some cases Black people. But, i think the principal task of white revolutionaries is to organize white people and to struggle against racism—not only in terms of institutional forms—but in terms of struggling against one's own racism. i think it is dishonest to say that white people living in a racist society, receiving racist education with racist teachers and often with racist parents, reading racist books, looking at racist television, etc., etc., are not affected by racism. Everybody living in a racist society is affected by racism. White people have to deal with racism on two planes. One: on a political level, and two: on a personal level. And that's a lifelong battle for one who's seriously interested in struggling against racism.

In the same way that Black people, who are affected by racism, have to struggle constantly with the feelings of inferiority, which are inflicted by the society on an overall basis—and that's a constant struggle. White people have to struggle against racism in its institutional forms and all of its forms. The struggle against racism and the struggle for a new society is one that is a lifelong process. It has to take many forms. It has many aspects.

Obviously most white people in the united states are not going to feel outraged by extreme poverty; some will, but the majority won't. Most will become involved in issues that are related to the environment, women, etc., etc., etc., so coming from there—whether it's the environment, whether it's women—and relating that to an international system of imperialism, understanding the underlying roots, and understanding that in order to struggle against any form of oppression, one has to go to the source. One must look at the whole system, and it's not just the united states. It's not just the military industrial complex; it's a system of international imperialism that is causing the destruction of the environment, that is causing the oppression of women, that is causing so many ills, that is causing racism, that is causing people to starve in Afrika, that is causing people to be tortured in El Salvador. It is an international system that must be struggled against.

i think that one of the things people who struggle (i don't care who they are) need to be real conscious of right now is that revolutionary movement needs to be internationalized at a much higher level. People really need to do networking, to touch base, not just in their neighborhood, in their city, not just in their state or country, but at an international level.

People who are concerned about the environment need to deal on an international level. People who are struggling to liberate political prisoners should organize on an international level, because this is the only way We're gonna win. What We're struggling against is an international system of imperialism, and those imperialists are organizing very effectively internationally.

So, in order to struggle against that, and to be effective, We've got to make outreach; to not have an exclusionary type of mentality when it comes to approaching other people, but to have an inclusionary type of outreach. Come in, let's get together, what can We agree on, what can We work together on. That has got to go from being just a general idea to a skill that's a well-tooled, well-developed skill.

M.M.: You know, one of the things white folk who have been struggling against racism on both a political and personal level have confronted is contradictions or confusions about what real solidarity means. Solidarity, collaboration, oppressed movements, and then this whole concept about what intervention can mean for white folk with all that technology and all these material resources. Will you speak on the concepts of solidarity and intervention, define them and say what you think true avenues for that could be?

Assata: Okay, i think one of the fundamental things needed for solidarity is respect. The respect of other people's culture, other people's ideas, and respect for Self-Determination. Going back to the experience of eastern europe, on one hand you had Stalinists and the Stalinist model, and in some ways, some very real ways, the Soviet Union lent real help to Third World people who were struggling. In other ways they fell short of that. Many of the eastern european countries, with the exception of those having a [Communist Party] school (having some foreign students there), really showed no true internationalism in the sense of say, a Cuba. Even though Cubans are generally a people who share what they have, Cuba is an underdeveloped country. The sense of imperialism in Cuba is much more highly developed than in any of the european countries. One of the fatal errors of that process was to consider solidarity as simply going to the U.N. and voting with the Soviet Union and not much more. It did not include personal sacrifices; it did not include a much more serious commitment to the liberation of Third World people. And so you have european workers who did not really feel a sense of solidarity with workers in the Third World, but felt a material kind of envy for workers in england, france, and the united states. Workers who shared those kinds of values, the "we want color tv's," and did not really perceive that the reason why the lifestyle of some workers, and i have to emphasize "some" workers, in the developed countries was at a higher level was because those countries were directly involved in sucking the blood of Third World workers—Third World people. Only a country that is involved in this kind of behavior can give some workers a higher standard of living. Solidarity in the sense of many european countries was lip service, was a few gestures, but was not a real gut self-sacrificing solidarity with Third World people. You find a situation now where you have people all throughout eastern europe volunteering to go live in South Africa. You have a situation where europeans are attacking Third World people all over europe and eastern europe, too. Eastern europe, western europe, there is this wave of racism that didn't just come out of nowhere. It is there because there was no real struggle raised against it. There was no real ideological process that took place on any real, in-depth level. So, solidarity meant one thing very superficial. And in addition to that, there was chauvinism. A kind of "we have the answers and all y'all savages gotta listen to us, cause we got Marx and Engels and we know all the answers. And you can make a revolution just the way we think you should make it, and you can just repeat what we say. And if you say anything different from what we say, you're a revisionist."

There's this kind of totally arrogant refusal to listen to anybody else, to learn from the experiences of anybody else, to appreciate the struggle or the culture of anybody else. And i'm not absolutizing because there was some effort in the socialist bloc to struggle against racist ideas, to struggle against eurocentricity, but it was not adequate in dealing with the reality of the Third World. And you had people, from Che Guevara to Nkrumah, who were completely ignored. i mean, nobody studied what Fidel was saying, and Fidel made critical remarks about what was happening in europe dating back to 1968 or before. But nobody listened. He was like, "our boy in Havana"—the revolutionary with the gun rather than anyone who had any ideological input into the world revolutionary movement. The same thing happened all over the world, whether it was with Ho Chi Minh or whoever. The ideological contributions were minimized. Therefore, the doubts and the problems raised in reference to the Third World were minimized. No real solutions, in terms of how do Third World countries free themselves, were looked at. (Not just from the national bourgeoisie, but how do they develop? How do they free themselves from an international system of imperialism, which is much stronger than the national bourgeoisie?) So it was just this kind of chauvinistic outlook that the white left all over the world has been historically guilty of, must take the weight for, and must try to rectify by studying, listening, and learning from Third World people.

They must recognize that logically, the most oppressed people must have a leadership role in any revolutionary process. i mean, that is logical, that is historically valid, and i think that is historically necessary. i don't know if i answered your question.

M.M.: You did. Intervention?

Assata: Intervention can take place, armed intervention, ideological... Intervention is a broad term. If you talk about intervention in terms of the role of the white left in the united states—if that's the context We're using...

M.M.: Yeah. Absolutely.

Assata: What people really have to think about is the work, and the content of that work. And if the content of the work is antiracist, antiarrogant, antiimperialist, then i think that's the important part. i think the most important thing is to commit to an ideology and workstyle that's not arrogant and is anti-imperialist, antiracist, antisexist, etc., etc., etc.

M.S.: Speaking of antisexist, we have a couple of questions relating to women. How were you empowered as a woman—a woman leader in the movement— and what things did you find empowering for yourself? What were some of your experiences with the Black Movement? And here in Cuba, how have you seen women involved in those movements?

Assata: Well, actually, to tell you the truth, i don't feel empowered. i feel that i'm a woman who struggles in a society that is sexist, in a movement that is sexist, and that is an ongoing struggle. i feel that any leadership role that i have played, or may play in the future, has to do with the work i do and

611

the historical role i will play (do play, hopefully). i tend to believe leadership should depend on one's ability, one's work. Period. And that too often, people, men and women, are hung up on the leadership question. i think We should be more hung up on the work question. What is the quality of my work?

But, i think in terms of the women question, women need to be struggled with, to be respected as equals, to be respected as human beings. Women need to struggle to eliminate any phase, all phases, of sexism in the movement and in the society as a whole. i don't think that you can eliminate sexism without eliminating, again, the roots of sexism; without building institutions that permit men and women to have nonsexist relationships. At this time, women are in a hell of a fix. The whole world is experiencing a crisis between men and women. The old way of relationships, the old division of work: men working in the field, women working in the home, is no longer valid. That is no longer real. Men and women have to find new ways to deal with each other that are not based on "me cookin' and you doin' whatever you do in the street." i mean, there's no economic basis for those old relationships. The reality of the modern world is that men and women both have to work in most societies because of economic necessity, because of the objective conditions. Therefore, there must be new relationships between men and women based on equality. And that's gonna be a struggle because men are not going to give up those privileges without a fight. And right now men are privileged. Women have to struggle to take away those privileges, and say, "i'm not gonna deal with oppression. i'm not going to deal with working two jobs, one in the home and one in the street. That's crazy."

The only human way that people can relate is as equals. That has an aesthetic, that has a beauty that no other kind of relationship can offer. The stereotypical, cartoon-type relationships people see repeatedly on television and at the movies and read about in books, that kind of stereotypical, narrow relationship is an impoverished relationship. The only way people can have rich relationships is to have relationships where exploitation is absent. And the only way exploitation is absent is when people say, "Well, We'll change this."

Women have to be at the vanguard of that process, at the head of that process, because We are the most victimized. And men have to work, too! i mean, it's a two-way street. Sexism is something that people must work at. In terms of African-American women and men, Our situation is one of oppression— serious oppression. The only kind of sane relationships We can have are relationships of partners, partnerships in struggle. Any human relationship, any human relationship with any kind of beauty, has to involve changing the definition of what relationships are and change the reality of what We're dealing with in the context of the united states. So, We need to form a new aesthetic on how We relate to each other. We need to go to a new dimension in how We relate to each other out of necessity. Out of pure necessity. Because if We don't, We will be systematically wiped out. That's the reality. And the women question, the issue of the oppression of women, is key to the oppression of Our people as a whole. No kind of movement can be built with a sexist model, because that model is destructive to Us as a people, it's destructive in all senses. In Our movement, the issue of women is even more important. And the issue of struggling against sexism is even more important because We need a model of family, We need a model of relationships, of organizations, that is antisexist. We need that just on pure survival.

M.M.: Base those thoughts on Cuba regarding those questions, any models from Cuba?

Assata: i think Cuba has done a lot in terms of creating institutions that form the material base for sexism to be totally abolished. In terms of child-care centers, in terms of laws that protect women's rights, in terms of laws that protect children's rights, in terms of the family code that all men are supposed to adhere to when they get married, etc. However, there's a lot of machismo that exists in Cuban society. The family code exists, but many men just ignore it. The people who must be at the forefront of this struggle are women. You can't look at Cuba through the eyes of the united states. In the beginning of the revolution, i mean, it was a big struggle for the FMC, the Federation of Cuban Women, just to have women work outside of the home. They had to wage a tremendous struggle because the situation was one where many families could just not conceive of women doing anything but working inside of the home. They had to almost start from scratch. They couldn't talk about equality in the beginning between women and men, or women and men sharing the household chores. They had to first talk about men helping women because that was the only way in which it could be conceived. You cannot leap and step, just make drastic changes that the people don't understand 'cause the people are what it's about. So they had to go from one step to the next step, and now men are able to talk about sharing work. They're able to talk about total equality between men and women. But that was, and is, a process, one that still needs a whole lot of work. But, in terms of the government, and in terms of the revolution's commitment to the equality of women and women's participation, i think Fidel has demanded that the number of women in leadership reflect the population of women in the country—that women play an important role in all aspects of the society and in the leadership of the society. But again, that's a process. And again, it's still something that men struggle against and still try to frustrate.

M.M.: We want to hear a little about how the crisis in socialism has affected Cuba and some of the tasks for solidarity in terms of North Americans and people in the U.S.

Assata: Well, at the present time, there are virtually very few socialist countries left. As you know, most of Cuba's trade was with the Soviet Union and with the eastern european countries. In terms of Cuba, the changes economically have meant the majority of the eastern european countries have not honored any, or most, of the contract agreements and economic treaties that they had with Cuba. So the goods that Cuba was expecting, were planning on, never arrived, haven't arrived, etc. In terms of the Soviet Union, some goods have arrived, but the number is around 30 percent of what was promised, what was agreed on. In different instances, 30 percent, or less, has arrived. The Soviet Union (what was the Soviet Union—now We're dealing with the Commonwealth of whatever) is so unstable that it changes daily, so Cuba cannot really depend on the Soviet Union for anything at this moment. There's an extreme shortage of fuel, wheat, rice, beans... everything that Cuba needs right now is in shortage.

So Cuba's in an extremely difficult situation, between a rock and a hard place. On one hand, Cuba is still suffering the effects of the U.S. blockade, economic embargo, etc. On the other hand, there's a kind of unofficial blockade by the Soviet Union and eastern european countries. Whether that's intentional or unintentional, the result is very real. The reality is that Cuba is, in effect, suffering a double blockade; suffering all kinds of political attacks by the united states—in the media, etc.—constantly. So now, more than any other time in Cuba's history, it's important to support Cuba. This is a crucial time economically, and because of the ideological changes that have swept the world, Cuba cannot be uninfluenced by this. So politically, it is a very sensitive time for Cuba. It's a time where Cuba is analyzing its history to rid itself of the mistakes inherited from europe and the Soviet Union and trying to outline its own path. This is a very difficult thing for an underdeveloped country to do, especially a country that is suffering the kind of blockade that Cuba is suffering.

Right now, Cuba needs people, too; it needs all the solidarity that it can get. It needs people who have appreciated the revolution, who have appreciated the achievements of the revolution, to come out and actively organize on whatever level, to help the revolution to sustain itself, and to go on to a higher level and struggle within the united states to overturn the blockade. There was never any logical reason for the blockade, but even the pretenses are no longer valid. Not at all. No one can be duped at this point into saying that Cuba is a satellite of the Soviet Union. Nobody can be duped anymore into saying that Cuba is a strategic military launching point for the Soviet planes or whatever. If anybody might have been duped in the past, all of that is completely exposed and pure fiction. So there is no reason for the blockade to be maintained.

People in the united states have to point this out and struggle around the issue that Cuba has a right to Self-Determination. People who believe in Self-Determination (whether they believe in socialism or not), who believe that a country has the right to determine what kind of government it has and what kind of system it wants, have to struggle to lift the blockade. The blockade is there for one reason, and one reason only, to prevent Cuban people from determining their own destiny. i think that has to be a focus of the movement, the left or anybody else concerned about Self-Determination and a people's right to freedom, liberty, and justice for all.

M.M.: You've spoken about the need for a whole new work style on the Left; and that presently there are no recipes to follow. Given these two dynamics, what are your thoughts about future work in general: how do we go through the process of figuring out what to do—in that we need to re-haul and there are no recipes to follow?

Assata: Well, i don't think there were ever any recipes to follow. There was an idea and many people went around acting like they had the recipe, acting like socialism was something like red paint. You can just paint on anything and it will come out socialist. Each specific country, each specific situation, each specific people has its own specific needs, requirements, desires, aspirations, etc. that fit into a movement. That's the kind of dialectic between the national reality of people and the international reality of a world revolutionary movement—and the need to struggle against imperialism.

i really don't think there was ever a recipe. It's not like you took two cups of Marx and a cup of Engels, throw in three drops of Lenin, and you've got freedom forever. That's silly. The reality of struggle is that you have to think, invent, and create. You have to work and learn from experience what works and what doesn't, what makes sense and what doesn't. You have to learn to get along. i mean to get along in terms of progressive people working together—whether you agree on everything or not. You have to learn that it's not a luxury to form working unity, it's a necessity. People need to find ways of working around common issues that they share. That's an absolute necessity and simple logic.

It's like, if there were eight monsters attacking me and 20 people in the room. Now, if my attitude is that i'm just gonna fight against these monsters by myself and i'm not gonna try to deal with these 20 other people to help me fight these monsters, then i am not dealing with a sane and rational mind. Then, if i do deal with these 20 other people and i say, "you just do what i say, you listen to me," that is also irrational. Those 20 people might have some very good ideas about how we can deal with these monsters. Let's get together y'all, let's exchange ideas, let's deal with the monsters. As long as We keep the focus on the monsters, We'll be all right.

But i think We've got to get away from the idea that one party is going to be the vanguard to lead us to some salvation. i mean, that does not fit with the reality of the 1990s. It might fit in some places—i don't want to absolutize or apply one experience to everybody. There may be places where one party might lead a people to liberation, but in the majority of situations, especially in multinational places like the united states, that's very unrealistic. So, forming the leadership has to be thought of in collective terms. In order to do this, We have to develop the skills necessary to deal collectively. We have to develop the respect to deal collectively. We have to learn by doing. We're in an electronic age. We have to find new ways of organizing people, new ways of educating people—creative ways. It could be revolutionary folk operas, [laughs] i don't know. We have to find and deal with people where they are— not where We think they should be.

i think a lot of the young rap artists are setting a great example. i think they're more in touch with people and more actively involved in changing people's way of thinking than many of the so-called revolutionaries with long histories, who just talk to themselves. We have to deal with that fact.

It's okay to talk to yourself, and it's okay to talk among yourselves, but when you start doing that exclusively, then you start acting crazy. When all you do is talk to yourself, then you have got a problem. And many revolutionaries have got a problem. They are not only talking to each other—to themselves, but when they deal with people who have nothing to do with their movement, they talk at them. They don't listen to what the people are saying, they don't learn from them. So, it's a problem when you just talk to yourself and talk at people. That, you know, is a category of mental illness! i think that the movement has got to deal with being sane, being logical, being concrete and setting priorities—realistic priorities—not fantasizing, not trying to apply the experiences of other people mechanically. We really have to analyze what damage has been done and make a sincere effort not to repeat those same kind of mistakes.

M.M.: Speaking of future work, you've spoken on the role of guns as almost the least important piece of struggle. Can you share your reflections on this?

Assata: The 1960s were very important in terms of the world liberation movement; in Afrika; in Asia, and in Latin America, there were many processes and people struggling for political independence. They were struggling against colonialism and imperialism. Many of those processes had elements of armed struggle. But in many cases, people romanticized the aspect of armed struggle without understanding that at the same time Vietnam was involved in armed struggle, there was also political struggle, diplomatic struggle, a struggle of the unions… i mean, there was a whole process of struggle that was going on.

Many people conceived of the Cuban revolution, for example, as Fidel, Che, and Raoul going to the mountains. But they did not understand that there was a whole political struggle that had been going on, that continued to go on, all the way back from before Cuba received its "independence." The July 26 movement was a political movement that was waged on campuses, had links with the unions and other leftist movements, and was able to forge unity—a political unity. It wasn't just a simplistic matter of going off into the mountains.

In the 1960s, the whole idea of armed struggle was a romantic one, was prevalent because of the objective conditions during that time. In many countries, whether it was in Brazil, or Uruguay with the Tupamaros, wherever, the revolutionaries were dealing with the idea of urban guerrilla warfare and rural guerrilla warfare. In most cases, there was an emphasis on armed struggle and not on other aspects of the struggle. In most of those cases, there was a failure of people on the left to unify. In the majority of those cases, those movements were destroyed and defeated. i think the reason for the defeat was (a) a lack of unity on the left and (b) many of those movements failed to analyze the objective conditions in their specific countries.

In relation to the united states, obviously revolutionaries in the '60s and early '70s were very much affected by what was going on in Afrika, Asia, and Vietnam; those were very inspiring revolutionary struggles that We were all affected by. In some instances, We tried to apply the experiences of other people mechanically to Our struggle. In the specific case of the Black Liberation Movement in the united states, the question of armed struggle had a very specific and a very important significance. The question of armed struggle took on added significance because all during the civil rights movement—because of direct action and nonviolence—many people interpreted "nonviolence" as the only framework Afrikans in the united states could struggle in, morally, realistically, etc. Instead of being dealt with as a tactic, direct action and nonviolence were dealt with as an ideology. There was a need to combat on different levels: on the level that Afrikans in the united states have the right to self-defense and that that right was an absolute; whether We defended ourselves or not, in a given situation, depended on what We decided—what Our tactics were, what Our strategy was. That was important for Us to deal with as a people.

So, the question of armed struggle within Our movement was even more important because there was a whole national media that was saying "look, you don't have any right to (a) defend yourself and (b) you must struggle under these terms and the terms we dictate. If you go outside of these terms— that framework—then you're crazy, you're terrorists."

So it was important, in terms of the 1960s and '70s, to say (a) We have the right to self-defense, and (b) that We have the right, as Malcolm X said, to struggle "by any means necessary." Those were key ideas that We had to struggle around during that period. And in the course of that struggle, there was an emphasis on armed struggle; an emphasis on self-defense that may have, in some instances, minimized other aspects of the struggle. But that was a necessary time, it was a necessary experience, and it was necessary for Afrikan people to realize that We, as a people, are going to have to free Ourselves. That's a reality. That's an objective reality.

Hopefully We will not have to do it alone. It does not make sense for Us to try to do it alone. For example, the experiences of the Soviet Union clearly shows what happens when different people work together to bring a huge country to a halt. Within that process, there were different people with different goals, different ideas of what Self-Determination is, but only by bringing the monster down is Self-Determination possible.

Now, i'm not equating bringing down the united states monster with the bringing down of the Soviet Union. One is/would be a revolutionary process, as in the context of the united states. In the context of the Soviet Union, i don't know what the hell that is. i mean, there were people who sincerely wanted to reform socialism, who wanted to make it better, more human. There were other people who wanted to destroy it. Within the whole process of Glasnost and Perestroika, you have people who were interested in making socialism better, others who were purely interested in personal power. That's my analysis. And it remains to be seen whose ends those changes are going to serve. Right now, it looks like the workers are the people who are going to suffer the most. i think it's a shame that the conditions of Stalinism and the kind of model that was constructed by Stalin were so negative that many people are manipulated by it today.

But there is a lesson to be learned for anybody in what looks like a huge, great power; in that that huge, great power can be broken down to obtain Self-Determination—not by one people, but by many people who are struggling within that structure to gain Self-Determination. It would be very difficult for Us to determine Our destiny without bringing the united states down, without a true revolution—and it doesn't have to be a violent revolution, it just has to be a change; a total change by a variety of people because revolutionary change now can happen in any way. There's no formula for it, and the reality is Our politics have to say that We don't like violence. Anybody whose politics say, "I love violence, I like to kill"—i mean, that's a crazy person. Our politics have to be, i hate violence, i don't want to deal with it. If i am forced to deal with it, if there's no other way around it, i will be violent against those who are violent against me. But clearly, the question of armed struggle, the question of, can it be an isolated thing, there cannot be any such thing as a narrow arrow type of struggle that is just armed struggle. In every political process, there must be struggle on all fronts—whether it's in the electoral arena, on a community grassroots level, in a union level, political parties... whatever. There must be coordinated political struggle on all levels involving different groups of people: students, workers, farmers, what have you. You have to deal with all kinds of elements of society that are experiencing oppression. And that's a lesson that just has to be learned.

M.S.: What do you think about the over 100 political prisoners and prisoners of war held in the united states? What do you think the Left should be doing about their cases right now?

Assata: What do i think about…?

M.M.: The first tribunal, the first tribunal…

Assata: i think it's a damn shame, that's what i think about it!

i think it's horrendous. The fundamental reason there are so many political prisoners in the united states is because the united states government's policy is to destroy anybody who poses a threat to the policies of its government. There's a secondary reason why those political prisoners are still in prison, why so many political prisoners are still in prison. There are a lot of people in the united states who are brainwashed; there are a lot of people on the left who are brainwashed and who claim to understand that COINTELPRO was real and that COINTELPRO under another name, whatever they call it now, is still real. Even though people claim that they understand the history of the united states, that they understand McCarthyism, the problem of AIDS, the repressive role of the FBI, the police agencies, etc., there still seems to be a kind of mind warp in terms of supporting and freeing political prisoners. Because a lot of people, even though they claim to understand all that, they claim to see all that, but they are not actively supporting political prisoners.

There's this kind of double psychology, "they must have done something." i think it has to do with the way that many of us are not conscious to the extent that the media shapes and forms the way We conceive of a given event. So you have 100, and i don't know how many, political prisoners—some of whom have been in prison for more than 20 years—and you have a left that claims to be opposed to government repression, but has not done the job it should have been doing to free political prisoners.

You have the case of Dhoruba Bin-Wahad who, after 19 years in prison, the government finally admitted that they played with the evidence, withheld evidence that would have served to free him and proved his innocence. And after 19 years, the government said, "yeah, well, you know…" Can We deal with a reality where those who are victimized by the government are going to have to go to the government files to prove that the government victimized them? And when that same government, through the Freedom of Information Act, sends blank pages, half or three-quarters of all of the pages blank, now how can you prove—how can political prisoners be forced to prove their innocence? How can they prove that their acts are political acts made in the valid struggle for Self-Determination and the liberation of their people?

i think that the only way We can principally deal with the question of political prisoners and prisoners of war in the united states is to demand amnesty for all political prisoners and struggle around that. It's important to work in defense committees, but as a movement, We have got to make decisions. We have to agree on certain basic things: (a) that oppressed people have the right to struggle for their liberation, to struggle to end their oppression, and they need to be supported—whether We agree with their particular line, organization, whatever; and (b) that it is in fact true that the united states government frames people, sends them to prison, kills people, etc., and We have to be conscious that anybody who poses a threat, imagined or real, is subject to that kind of repression.

So it is key to not deal with the specifics of the cases, but to demand amnesty for all political prisoners, period. And also to realize, as political activists, if i do not struggle to liberate those who have been in prison for so long, then i am creating a situation where the government feels freer and freer to come after me.

If We do not struggle to liberate those political prisoners who have been in prison since the '60s, since the beginning of 1970, then what are We saying to our youth? Are We saying, "Alright, you struggle, if the FBI frames you, well, it's your problem. We're not going to defend you, We're not going to fight for your liberation. We accept the propaganda. We accept the right of the poor to be used as a repressive instrument, We accept that. We accept the position of the government; We accept the accusations of the government." Is that what Our movement is truly about? Whose definitions are We willing to accept?

And, the facts in the particular cases, say in the case of Geronimo Pratt, the New York 3, the Queens Two, i mean, the facts are overwhelming. The government actively conspired, is actively conspiring, to imprison activists. So, i mean, it's a question of unbrainwashing ourselves, and unracisizing ourselves. Because part of the reason, i think, so many Afrikans and Third World people have been in prison so many years is also due to racism on the left. If white people want to know what they can do in terms of struggling, one of the things they can do is struggle on a much more intense level to liberate political prisoners.

Source: www.assatashakur.org

What the Corporate Media Didn't Tell You: An Interview with Ramona Africa

Hans Bennett
2003

Ramona Africa is the sole adult survivor of the May 13, 1985, massacre of 11 members of the MOVE organization. The FBI and the City of Philadelphia dropped a C4 bomb on MOVE's 6221 Osage Avenue home in West Philadelphia. Carrying the young Birdie Africa (the only other survivor) with her, Ramona dodged gunfire and escaped from the fire with permanent scarring from the burns.

After surviving the bombing, she was charged with conspiracy, riot, and multiple counts of simple and aggravated assault. Subsequently Ramona served seven years in prison. If she had chosen to sever her ties with MOVE, she could have been released far earlier. Even in the face of this, she held true to her revolutionary beliefs and was uncompromising in the face of state terror. Since her release from prison, Ramona has tirelessly worked as the MOVE Minister of Communication on behalf of the MOVE 9, Mumia Abu-Jamal, and all political prisoners and prisoners of war.

The May 13 assault was the culmination of many years of political repression faced by the mostly black revolutionary and back-to-nature organization at the hands of Philadelphia authorities. In the 1970s, MOVE took up arms in response to extensive police brutality that included the murder of the young Life Africa as well as the provocation of several miscarriages. On August 8, 1978, the police attacked their Powelton Village home, and in the process, police officer James Ramp was shot by a bullet, traveling in a downward trajectory, as he was laying down facing the MOVE home. Despite the physical impossibility of MOVE firing the bullet at that angle from their position in the basement, nine MOVE members were convicted for his murder and were given 30- to 100-year sentences still being carried out today. In 1985, organizing to free the MOVE 9 was at the forefront of MOVE political activities.

A few months ago, I rode my bike out to see 6221 Osage Avenue for the first time since I moved to Philadelphia. Upon arrival I was shocked to find "Permit Parking for Phila. Police Civil Affairs" posted directly in front of the 6221 lot. I later verified that 6221 Osage is now an actual police station. Particularly striking is the presence of Civil Affairs, Philly's political police.

This article was published in *Dissident Voice*, May 24, 2003.

As Ramona Africa talks about in the interview, Civil Affairs played a key role on May 13 as the official diplomats.

This May, I spoke with Ramona about 6221 today. "Ever since they rebuilt the houses out there, they never intended to sell 6221. They made it a police station with police present around the clock, 24/7." Ramona does feel insulted by the police station there, but says that it "is indicative of this system. On May 13, 1995, councilwoman Jamie Blackwell (whose district includes 6221 Osage Avenue) introduced a resolution to make May 13 "kiss a cop day." Why May 13 of all possible days? That is the mentality of these people and we don't expect anything different from them."

Things were tense when last September, New Jersey judge Shelly Robbins New reversed an earlier decision granting supervised visits to John Gilbride for his son Zachary Africa, who was under the full-time custody of his mother, Alberta Africa (a MOVE member). Because of past psychological and physical abuse, Zachary Africa had told the previous judge that while he loved his father he was afraid to be alone with him and, subsequently, only wanted to be with his father if his mother was with him also.

Seeing Judge New's decision as illegitimate, Alberta and MOVE said that they would not hand Zachary over for unsupervised visits and boarded up the windows of their Kingsessing headquarters in West Philadelphia because of the threat of a police assault.

While the Philadelphia PD officially stated that they were giving MOVE their space and did not want any confrontations, their actions showed otherwise. During the nights that I spent with MOVE, late at night while they were on 24-hour watch at their front gate, I observed an unusually large number of police cars passing by. Besides this harassment, there were two major incidents at this point.

On the night of September 11, 2002, the police made an aggressive act in front of MOVE's Kingsessing home. As a group of MOVE supporters was backing their car out the driveway following their visit, a police car drove up and blocked them (almost causing a collision). The MOVE supporters were suspicious of the police motives, and when the cops demanded they leave their car without giving any reason for it, the driver hit the horn to alert MOVE inside the house.

When Ramona Africa and others came out of the house and confronted the police, the cops claimed to not have known that it was the MOVE home. The police claimed that the MOVE supporters' car with Virginia plates fit the profile of a vehicle suspected of kidnapping a young child nearby. During a September 20 press conference at MOVE's house, I asked Civil Affairs Captain Fisher about the September 11 incident, and he denied that it ever happened, despite the numerous neighbors that witnessed the police cars there that night.

On September 13, four cops came to the MOVE house to get Zack, even though the court order specified that the first unsupervised visit would be the upcoming Friday (September 20). According to MOVE, the police claimed to have a court order saying that Gilbride would have custody, but when MOVE demanded to see it, they explained that Gilbride himself had it, so they could not show them. This supposed court order is also suspect because if he had one, Alberta Africa should have been given one also. However, Alberta and MOVE said they hadn't gotten anything of the sort.

On September 27, Gilbride was shot dead in his car by what looked to be a professional hit. While there was an initial fear that the police would blame MOVE for the murder, the police officially didn't suspect MOVE and the murder remained unsolved.

Last month when 7-year-old Zachary Africa and a friend were in Alberta Africa's backyard in Cherry Hill, NJ, they spotted a man wearing all black with dark paint on his face. Given the recent events with Alberta and Zachary Africa, it appeared as if this may have been related. While concerned about who was in their backyard and why, Ramona was unsure about it. "We really don't know whether it was the government, grandparents, or some nut. We just keep a close eye on our kids. That's all we can do."

Hans: Can you please talk about the weeks leading up to May 13, 1985?

Ramona Africa: Things were relatively quiet. The biggest thing that happened was on April 29. We heard our dogs barking and upon checking it out, we saw cops out back that were counting the dogs or something. We knew they were up to something sneaky, so we turned on our loudspeaker. Note that we didn't have our speaker on 24/7 like the media attempts to portray.

With the loudspeaker, we let the neighborhood know that there were cops in the back of our house, and we didn't know what they were up to, but we knew it was no good and we didn't trust them. We weren't going to let them sneak in and attack MOVE people without the neighborhood knowing what was going on.

Civil Affairs cops (the official diplomats) like George Draper, Ted Vaughn, and others came to our home that day and knocked on the front door. My sister Theresa Africa and I came out and talked to them at length—with them standing right on the steps of our house for at least a half hour. We explained to them why we turned on the loudspeaker. That's all that happened that day.

Two weeks later, on Saturday, May 11, DA Ed Rendell got officer Ted Vaughn to charge us with terroristic threats, disorderly conduct, and nonsense like that stemming from April 29. Rendell then had the arrest warrants approved by Judge Lynne Abraham (now Philadelphia's DA), who was acting as the emergency judge for that Saturday. Based on the events of April 29, Abraham signed warrants for myself and three others.

People need to understand that this incident happened two weeks prior. How in the hell can it be an emergency if it waited two weeks? Second, if we were guilty of terroristic threats and officers Vaughn and Draper felt threatened by us, why would they talk to us on our steps for over a half hour. It's nonsense, but that's the excuse they used for the warrants, because they had absolutely nothing else to use.

The City of Philadelphia tells people that there were complaints from neighbors about us. That may very well be true, but they've never been able to verify for us who complained and what they specifically complained about. Even if this is true, you explain to me when this government ever cared about black people's neighborhood complaints. Since when is it such an issue that the FBI and the Justice Department get involved in something like that?

If the government is saying that their solution to a neighborhood dispute is to bomb the neighborhood and burn it down, then there wouldn't be a single neighborhood standing. All neighborhoods have disputes, but they aren't bombed. Look at 8th and Butler here in Philadelphia—a known drug area. The residents of that area have demonstrated, sat out in the middle of the street, and stormed City Council representatives' offices demanding some kind of relief from the drug trafficking. It is so bad that if you pull up at a red light in that area, people will come up to your car to try and sell you drugs. Parents say that they're upset because in the summer they can't even let their kids play outside because they're afraid of a shooting. You don't see any bombings in that neighborhood. You don't see cops en masse coming out to that neighborhood.

In our case, they claim that the bombing was a response to a handful of black people's complaints. Anybody with half a brain cell has to know there's something wrong with that. People also need to understand that when I went to court after the bombing, every charge listed on Rendell and Abraham's May 11 warrant was dismissed. During the pretrial motion, trial judge Michael Stiles was forced to dismiss every single charge. This means that they had no valid reason to even be out there.

They did not dismiss the charges placed on me as a result of what happened *after* they came out. This is illegal, and an inconsistency, because if the police had no valid reason to be out there, that should mean that anything coming after that would also be invalid. They wouldn't drop the other charges because I would have been released. People's emotions were so high at that time after May 13, they were not about to put me back out in the streets.

You can see how this was nothing but a setup. Meanwhile, the media sat back and did everything possible to justify what this government did. They had warrants for four adults, but they knew there were many children in the house. On the morning of Sunday, May 12, one of our supporters (Gloria) went to the Italian market for us and took a couple of our children with her. By the time she came back, they had cordoned off the street. But when Gloria pulled her car up, the Civil Affairs cops (including George Draper) looked in the car (seeing Gloria and the children) and let them through the barricade to return to MOVE's home.

They let the children back into the house knowing what they were getting ready to do. All that nonsense about looking for every opportunity to remove the children from the situation is a bold-faced lie. They're aim was to kill everybody in that house—particularly the children. According to Police Commissioner Sambor at the time, they saw MOVE children as being as much, if not more, of a threat than the adults. So, we understand why they let the children back into the house.

In terms of what led up to May 13, we feel it was simply a matter of the government looking for an excuse to attack MOVE again. For over a year they tried to come up with a plan of action to do it. On August 8, 1984, they sent hundreds of cops out to Osage without actually doing anything. This was just a drill while they were putting together a plan. All of this came out in the Commission that Wilson Goode put together.

Anybody can see that their aim, very simply, was to kill MOVE people—not to arrest anybody. They had overwhelming opportunity to arrest MOVE people if that's what they wanted to do. They knew our schedule as well as we did. They would follow us around when we left the house. I walked the streets by myself and would often stop and speak to the Civil Affairs cops. They could have snatched me up anytime.

Hans: Could you please give your personal account about what happened inside 6221 Osage on May 13?

Ramona Africa: There's unfortunately not a whole lot I can say because I was in the basement with the children the whole time. When it had begun to get dark at around 8 or 9 Sunday night, we saw cops in houses across the street, and we knew they were set to attack us. In response, we took the kids to the basement, and after a while down there water started pouring in from the hoses. Then the tear gas came. They said that they used explosives to blow three-inch diameter holes in the wall to insert tear gas. But photos show that the whole front of the house was blown off. The police estimate shooting over 10,000 rounds of bullets into the house during the first 90 minutes. They said they used all of the ammunition they had brought and had to get more from the armory. I did hear a lot of gunfire. Then for a pretty long time things were pretty quiet. It was then that they dropped the bomb without any warning.

At first, those of us in the basement didn't realize that the house was on fire because there was so much tear gas that it was hard to recognize smoke. After a while it seemed to be getting hotter and the smoke was thickening and choking us. That's when we started realizing that it was more than just tear gas. Conrad opened the door and we started to yell that we were coming out with the kids. The kids were hollering, too. We know they heard us but

625

The 1985 bombing of MOVE by the Philadelphia police

the instant we were visible in the doorway, they opened fire. You could hear the bullets hitting all around the garage area. They deliberately took aim and shot at us.

I personally tried to get out with some of the kids at least twice before the last time when it was so hot with the flames everywhere. After I escaped with Birdie, they immediately took both of us into custody. I didn't realize how badly I was burned when they threw me onto the ground and handcuffed me.

On the 13-minute police video given to us in court, they were across from us on Osage and you could hear the cops talking in the background. There was a shot where you could see the house fully engulfed in flames and you can hear the cops talking and laughing in the background. You can hear them say: "That's the last time they'll call the commissioner a -----." It shows you their mentality. This wasn't about an arrest.

Hans: In their coverage of the May 13 bombing, the A&E television show *American Justice* argued that Mayor Goode's physical safety was threatened by a letter signed by you. What did this letter say?

Ramona Africa: First, as I explained it court, I didn't write that letter. Someone from another chapter probably wrote the letter and signed my name to it, as was usually done because I was the Minister of Communications.

Second, after reading the letter in court after it was entered in as evidence, I didn't see anything threatening Wilson. I did see the tone of the letter being

626

"if you come at us, you can expect us to defend ourselves." This government blames the victim. They are brutal and vicious towards you and then accuse you of being vicious and violent. They're saying that a letter was sent to Goode, but he dropped a bomb on us. That went past words, didn't it?

If we wanted to attack Goode, we knew where he worked every day and could have done it. That's not how we do things and this government knows that. Cops have trampled a three-week-old MOVE baby to death. Police have beat, stomped, and kicked pregnant MOVE women into miscarriage. They've beaten MOVE men and locked up innocent MOVE people. When did you ever see us go out and try and shoot a cop? Absolutely never.

If we didn't do it then why all of a sudden would we want to go and attack Goode? It doesn't make any sense.

Showing who Goode was really afraid of, he wrote in his later book (*In Good Faith*) that he didn't come out to 62nd and Osage because police had threatened his life and subsequently he felt that his life was in danger.

Hans: The corporate press often reports that MOVE was shooting guns at the Fire Department as well as the police. What evidence was presented in court in regards to MOVE firing weapons from their house?

Ramona Africa: I don't recall them presenting anything other than saying that MOVE shot at them with automatic weapons and that they heard it. But then they got messed up because after digging through all of the rubble, they couldn't find a single automatic weapon. Then they said they found a handgun and some type of shotgun or something. I've never seen a gun in a MOVE house. Not in the Osage house or any other. That's all I can say about that. After digging through the rubble with those big claws, who knows where that came from? Even if those were our weapons, that couldn't have created automatic weapon fire.

During the later civil trial, two or three firefighters said they never heard or saw MOVE people shooting at them at all. They said they did hear automatic weapon fire but that it was from the police. The fire commissioner tried to say that he didn't fight the fire out of fear of putting firemen in danger. Meanwhile when the whole thing started, he had four huge hoses on our home for over an hour. If they weren't in danger then, why couldn't they do it later when the house and block was on fire?

By their own admission, they're saying that MOVE gunfire was a response to the use of explosives to blowholes through the walls of our house. Even if that were true, you're blowing up a house and then you have a problem when someone defends their home?

They will wreak havoc all over the world. They will beat you, kill you, lock you up, shoot at you, bomb you, and do all this crazy stuff to you, but they want to be seen as respectable and righteous. They will say that what they do is in defense of freedom, justice, or national security.

Meanwhile, the right of self-defense is lost when cops attack an individual like they did to Amadou Diallo or Abner Louima in New York, or that brother Thomas Jones here in Philadelphia. We're just supposed to accept whatever this government and the kill-crazy, blood-thirsty cops do. You're supposed to accept that as necessary and righteous. In other words, it's acceptable for the government to turn guns on people, but its never acceptable to turn guns on this government. MOVE is saying that the instinct of self-defense is just that: it's instinctive. It's god-given and comes from mother nature. There is not a species alive walking this earth that doesn't defend itself when attacked. Humans are no different.

This government cannot explain how you are wrong to defend yourself. In fact, you are wrong if you refuse to defend yourself, because that is violent because it endorses and encourages violence. It makes you suicidal. MOVE is not suicidal or masochistic. We do believe in defending ourselves, no question. This government is never going to take that away from us and will never convince us that we are criminal and wrong for that.

What the hell do they say this country was founded on? Every 4th of July these motherfuckers celebrate the so-called "American Revolution." They say that these founding fathers were courageous and brave men who defied legality and went to war against cops called "red coats" and the government of King George. They said "give me liberty or give me death" and went to war. Every day these people are celebrated and applauded in second and third grade history classes and beyond. What makes Nathan Hale a "freedom fighter" for defying legality in favor of what is right but makes Mumia Abu-Jamal, Leonard Peltier, or Delbert Africa or any other MOVE prisoner a "criminal"?

I've heard that Police Commissioner Sambor made an announcement before the May 13 assault saying "Attention MOVE! This is America!" If this was 1776 and he was a British soldier saying to Nathan Hale or Patrick Henry, "Attention! This is an English colony and you have to abide by the laws of England," what do you think would have happened to him? He'd be a dead man right about now and the person who killed him would be celebrated as a hero for over 200 years. But he's going to stand in front of our house and say that.

Hans: It seems that some are willing to support Mumia, Leonard Peltier, and the MOVE 9 because the evidence available strongly suggests that they are innocent of the crime they are accused of. Unfortunately there seems to be less support for political prisoners and prisoners of war like Ruchell "Cinque" Magee, Assata Shakur, or Russell "Maroon" Shoats, who were forced to break the law in order to protect themselves from their oppressor.

Ramona Africa: There is no way in the world that this government, with the blood of Leonard Peltier's ancestors on their hands, is going to convince us to see him as a murderer. We don't care what happened on the Pine Ridge reservation because it isn't the issue. The very people that dropped a bomb on my family and burned babies alive are going to convince me to see Leonard or Mumia as a murderer?

To make it clear, I do believe that both Leonard and Mumia are innocent, but people are confused and misled by this system. With issues like Mumia, Leonard, or MOVE, the government tries to convince people that the issue is whether or not they actually pulled the trigger and killed somebody. Mumia and Leonard are not in prison for the accusation of murder, but rather because of who they are and because they dared to stand up.

If murder was truly the issue, it would be applied across the board. If it was about murder, they'd have to charge with murder and imprison those who murdered my family, who murdered Thomas Jones, Amadou Diallo, and Winston Hood back in the '60s. Why aren't they, if murder is the true issue? Anytime you don't apply the same principle across the board, you're not talking about equality and justice.

Hans: What do you think were the facts presented in the later civil trial that most convinced the jury to decide in your favor?

Ramona Africa: The point that we made in that civil suit was that, first of all, this was not an accident that got out of control. This was a planned murder and wasn't an isolated incident. I had to go to war with the attorneys representing me on this case. I told them that we had to deal with August 8, 1978 (when hundreds of cops conducted the raid), and with the unjust imprisonment of our family because it was the root of our protest prior to May 13.

The lawyers didn't want to deal with it because a police officer had been shot and they didn't want to prejudice the jury by bringing that up. I said, "The hell with that! They attacked my family that day. They destroyed the house, the evidence; they know my family is innocent, and that is what we were protesting. They wanted to stop the protest and shut us up permanently. Also, this isn't an isolated incident, but an ongoing problem of police attacking MOVE and killing their babies." I felt that the jury needed to get the clear picture and entire history.

We showed a video of the August 8, 1978, beating of Delbert Africa and the city just went crazy. They did not want that in. When I testified, I talked about the history of MOVE with this system and I think the jury didn't have a choice because we made clear that all of the charges justifying the May 11 warrants had been dismissed.

There was nothing the city could say to justify the assault. That jury did not want to find in my favor. Besides an Asian man and a black woman on the jury, the rest were white suburbanites. It took them about five days to come to a verdict. They were in there battling. In fact, a white man got discharged during the deliberations. He just couldn't take it. We know they didn't want to find in my favor, because they just ordered police commissioner Sambor and fire commissioner Richmond to each pay me one dollar a week for 11 years. That was their penalty. The jury decided the City of Philadelphia had to pay me $500,000. Especially after paying my legal fees, that wasn't much money. A woman got a one million dollar award for spilling hot coffee on herself at McDonald's.

To add insult to injury, the judge comes back after the jury arrived at their verdict and overrules them in regards to Sambor and Richmond (granting them immunity). The judge never expected the jury to find Sambor and Richmond liable, even for that insulting fine. He was willing to take the chance of finding the city liable. The City of Philadelphia is a faceless entity. They had already given Wilson Goode and many others in the city immunity.

This judge was an old white man. He didn't relate to me, but rather to Sambor and Richmond, and he never expected the jury to find them individually liable, but they did. In justifying his move, the judge said that he believed Commissioner Sambor's statement that he had never given the order to let the fire burn.

Hans: Is there anything else you'd like to add?

Ramona Africa: People had better wake up for their own protection, because where this government is heading and what it's involving itself in is very dangerous and a threat to all of us. People need to wake up and start taking charge of their own lives and make their own decisions, because that's the only way all of this insanity can be stopped. Those running this country are completely out of control. Taking control isn't easy. It takes a lot of commitment and hard work, but when you look at the alternative there is no choice and that's the bottom line.

Ramona Africa

Adding Insult to Injury:
Media Bias Against Dhoruba Bin-Wahad and Other Political Prisoners

Bob Lederer
1992

While the corporate (and white-controlled) media often renders people of color either invisible or criminal, the coverage of imprisoned political activists of color intensifies these distortions. Were such people jailed in any other country, the U.S. media would correctly consider them—convicted on either fabricated allegations or "criminal" charges for clearly political acts—to be political prisoners.

According to the New York-based Center for Constitutional Rights, there are currently more than 100 U.S. political prisoners, the majority Black, Puerto Rican and Native American. Only occasionally are their cases covered even minimally (usually just upon conviction), and the rare, hard-hitting investigative stories face strong right-wing attacks. Consider, for example, the case of Dhoruba Bin-Wahad (formerly Richard Moore), a Black activist imprisoned in New York from 1971 to 1990.

A vitriolic *Wall Street Journal* editorial (2/7/92) endorsed several Republican Senators' attack on the Public Broadcasting System (PBS) for its "stream of left-wing documentaries... with such suggestive and compelling titles as 'An Act of War: The Overthrow of the Hawaiian Nation' or 'Warrior: The Case of Leonard Peltier'" (a Native American political prisoner whose release has been advocated by 50 U.S. Congresspeople and Amnesty International). Exhibit A, excoriated no less than three times in the editorial, was "Citizen Dhoruba," which the *Journal* labeled "a documentary extolling the virtues of a former Black Panther convicted of shooting two New York policemen." (The editorial sarcastically noted that the Republican assault on independent journalists "of course, has raised cries and screams of censorship"!) A similar PBS-bashing column by the Heritage Foundation's Laurence Jarvik, also citing "Citizen Dhoruba," appeared in the *Los Angeles Times* (4/6/92).

In reality, this documentary—not even completed yet—will tell the story of how Bin-Wahad's 1973 conviction (in his third trial) was based on perjury

This is a longer version of an article published under the title"U.S. Political Prisoners Face Media Silence"in the September 1992 issue of *Extra!*, the magazine of Fairness and Accuracy in Reporting (FAIR). Research assistance was provided by FAIR associate Sam Husseini.

by government witnesses, prosecution coercion of an unbalanced associate of Bin-Wahad's, and withholding of major evidence from the defense.

The latter fact—uncovered through relentless Freedom of Information Act litigation by Bin-Wahad, while serving 19 years of a 25-years-to-life sentence, together with his pro bono attorneys—persuaded a New York State judge to overturn the conviction and release Bin-Wahad in March 1990. The documentary also places the government's manhunt and arrest of Bin-Wahad in the context of the FBI's massive, illegal campaign called COINTELPRO (Counterintelligence Program) to destroy radical political groups, especially the Black Panther Party. FBI documents list Bin-Wahad as a key COINTELPRO target.

The 1970s criminal trials of Bin-Wahad and other Panthers still imprisoned on similar charges all got massive, pro-prosecution publicity. But their two decades of struggle for vindication and release—cases that have drawn substantial community support and that have been likened to that of South Africa's Nelson Mandela—have hardly merited a word from the corporate media.

On December 19, 1991, the New York State Court of Appeals, by a 4-3 vote, reinstated Bin-Wahad's conviction, insisting that to void his conviction, he must prove that the evidence withheld by the prosecution was crucial. The *New York Times* article the next day, "State Appeals Court Narrows Right to a New Trial When Evidence Is Withheld" (12/20/91), covered the decision almost exclusively in terms of the narrow legal issue involved—indisputably important and precedent-setting—with no reference to COINTELPRO's involvement in the case.

But after that decision, nearly all mainstream coverage of the case ceased. While Bin-Wahad continued seeking legal redress as prescribed by the Appeals Court, the Manhattan District Attorney sought Bin-Wahad's reincarceration, despite two years of law-abiding behavior and appearance at his hearings. On February 6, 1992, a lower court judge scheduled a hearing on this request, over the objections of Bin-Wahad and his lawyer, who had a schedule conflict that day. Over 80 supporters packed the court, and at the last minute the judge postponed the hearing for a week.

The only media coverage of this was a tiny article in *New York Newsday* ("Ex-Panther No-Show," 2/7/92), highlighting Bin-Wahad's nonappearance without explaining that he would have been forced to proceed without a lawyer. The report sensationally declared, "Bin-Wahad's absence prompted speculation that he intends to flee the country and will not appear for a newly scheduled date in Manhattan Criminal Court next week." A brief letter to the editor published 2/12/92 attempted to correct the record, noting that "nowhere in your three-sentence account is it mentioned that Dhoruba is challenging his conviction as a political frame-up" and adding, "Recall that none other than Nelson Mandela, on his 1990 visit to New York City, embraced [Bin-Wahad] on the dais as a political prisoner of the U.S." (Tellingly, just as Bin-Wahad was about to speak that day, the live ABC coverage cut to a commercial break, which lasted through his remarks and the Mandela embrace.)

But neither *Newsday* nor any other corporate media covered Bin-Wahad's appearance in court the following week—in which the judge rejected the prosecutor's request and allowed Bin-Wahad to remain free without bail, as 300 supporters rallied in front of the court. Only alternative Pacifica radio station WBAI and the Black weekly *Amsterdam News* covered the story ("Defiant Dhoruba scores big victory in the courts," 2/26/92). Contrast this mainstream media boycott to the front-page *New York Daily News* story (5/18/92),"Rally Round the Don; 700 Demand New Gotti Trial," about a demonstration supporting a more well-connected prisoner, Mafia leader John Gotti.

On March 25, 1992, the *New York Times*, ABC's *Nightline,* and other major media gave prominent (and much deserved) coverage to the case of two Black men in California who had been released after spending long terms in prison, falsely convicted of murder. While referring several times to the frequency of such incidents of police frame-ups, there was no mention—much less separate coverage—of the almost identical cases of Bin-Wahad and other former Black Panthers accused of shooting police. Among these are Geronimo ji Jaga Pratt (now 21 years into a life sentence in California, a case adopted by numerous Congresspeople and Amnesty International), the New York 3 (also 21 years into life sentences and pursuing court proceedings to overturn their convictions), and Mumia Abu-Jamal (the first U.S. political activist since the Rosenbergs facing execution after his 1982 conviction by a nearly all-white jury in a Philadelphia trial with many prosecutorial irregularities).

The corporate media's exclusion of Black political prisoners, and more generally, grassroots African American voices, became especially glaring in the coverage of the Los Angeles and other urban uprisings after the Rodney King police beating verdict. On May 1, 1992, the *Phil Donahue Show* had a panel discussion on the verdict's aftermath. Bin-Wahad, one of several Black community spokespeople on the panel, cogently explained the basis for Black rage. Yet never in any of the other numerous TV panel discussions or news programs was Bin-Wahad or anyone else with his radical, grassroots perspective asked to appear. Whatever critique of media narrowness can be made in "normal" times takes on much greater urgency when cities are burning. The public deserves and needs to hear the voices of those who can personally explain the origins of the rage that spawned one of the largest U.S. uprisings in this century.

Life: A Political Prisoner's Journey in the U.S. Prison System

Jalil Muntaqim
2005

After the illegal NYC NEWKILL conviction of killing two police officers in 1975, I was transferred back to San Quentin prison in California to complete the sentence for which I was originally captured on August 28, 1971, in a shoot-out with San Francisco police (it was alleged that my codefendant, Albert "Nuh" Washington, and I attempted to assassinate a police sergeant in retaliation for the August 21, 1971, assassination of comrade George Jackson). Once again held in the infamous S.Q. Adjustment Center, locked in a cell between Brother Ruchell Magee and Charles Manson, I received a leaflet from Sister Yuri Kochiyama of the National Committee in Defense of Political Prisoners (NCDPP) informing me of an initiative to build international support for U.S. political prisoners. In response, I wrote an outline to petition the United Nations in support of U.S. political prisoners. I gave the outline to Ruchell, who thought it was very good, and then passed it along to Geronimo ji Jaga (Pratt), who also approved. I then rewrote the outline into a proposal and sent it to Yuri for consideration. Unfortunately, NCDPP did not act on the proposal. Then, in late 1976, I met a white guy named Commie Mike, and he introduced me to the United Prisoners Union (UPU). He explained that UPU may be willing to implement my proposal to petition the U.N. in support of U.S. political prisoners. A young UPU activist white woman named Pat Singer came to visit me and brought my proposal to the group, which eventually agreed to support this national campaign. The campaign in early 1977 had grown beyond what UPU could handle alone, and the Prairie Fire Organizing Committee (PFOC) joined in the campaign, which was facilitated by China Brotsky. A young lawyer from Amnesty International was recruited to represent the petition at the United Nations, while at the same time, UPU and PFOC organized a signature petition gathering 2500 signatures from prisoners across the country. In fact, we had affiliate cadres in state and federal prisons in 25 U.S. states, with communications with prisoners in parts of Europe.

In 1977, the attorney presented our petition to a special subcommittee of the United Nations in Geneva, Switzerland. This was the very first time U.S. political prisoners had a petition submitted and recorded at a United Nations subcommittee pertaining to racism and the conditions of political prisoners in the U.S. penal system. (See: U.N. document E/CN.4/SUB.2/NGO/75.) As the petition campaign was being organized, Comrade Sundiata Acoli in New Jersey agreed to assist with organizing a march in support of the petition to the United Nations. The march and demonstration was held in front of the Harlem State Office Building, an initiative that Sister Bibi Angola ensured would be successful. This campaign was responsible for former U.N. Ambassador Andrew Young being fired from his post at the U.N. by then President Jimmy Carter. What happened was that PFOC informed me that they knew a reporter that would be in Paris, France, when Andrew Young would be visiting, and asked what he could do in support of our campaign. I suggested the reporter ask Ambassador Andrew Young the single question "are there political prisoners in the United States?" When Andrew Young answered, "perhaps thousands," right-wing political forces and the media had a field day rebuking and attacking him, resulting in him being fired from his U.N. post.

This campaign was so successful that UPU and PFOC had communications in prisons across the country. We organized the first demonstration in front of San Quentin on August 21, 1977, initiating the first of what would become a Black August tradition. By September 19, 1977, I was paroled and transferred from San Quentin back to New York City and held in isolation at Rikers Island for 58 days. I was held in isolation because I was supposed to have been transferred to federal authorities in accordance with the stipulations for parole from San Quentin, but instead I was taken to New York City. When New York City and State officials recognized their error, they decided to keep me in New York State, or otherwise possibly lose future custody of me. Eventually, I was transferred to Sing-Sing, enroute to Clinton Correctional Facility for orientation. I stayed at Clinton until December 29, 1977, and was then transferred to Attica.

In the 11 months I stayed at Attica, I eventually inherited the position of chairman of the Lifers' Committee, an inmate organization working to win lifers' "good time" off the minimum sentence for good behavior as is given to all other classes of prisoners in New York State. At a community forum sponsored by the Attica Lifers' Committee, former U.S. Attorney General Ramsey Clark attended and made a presentation. I originally met Ramsey Clark when waiting on trial in the Tombs Correctional Facility; he and his father came on a tour, and I made it a point to speak to both of them. One of the things I said to Mr. Clark was to be sure to tell the people the truth about what is happening in this government. At any rate, at the forum in Attica, he remembered that brief conversation and told people attending that he would help me get out of prison. Unfortunately that has not happened, but he has been a staunch advocate of human rights around the world. After the 1971 insurrection in Attica, prison guards were still treating prisoners abusively, as they do now, and eventually I was accused of organizing what had been called "The Attica Brigade," a group of prisoners allegedly prepared to retaliate against prison guards' brutality. I was held for 60 days in the Special Housing Unit (SHU), accused of being the leader of the Attica Brigade. The Attica prison administrators sought to keep me in Administrative Segregation after the 60 days was terminated, but when that failed, I was transferred to Auburn. My nine-month stay at Auburn in 1979 was uneventful until there was a fight between two prisoners in the Mosque. The prison authorities decided to take the Mosque from the Muslims and make them conduct their Friday prayer in the Christian chapel. The Muslims rebelled and decided to conduct their Friday prayers in the exercise yard. At the time, praying in the yard was against the rules, and for that act several prisoners were transferred out of Auburn. Again, I was accused of being a ringleader of the Muslims, but was not officially charged with a disciplinary report.

I was transferred to Green Haven Correctional Facility from Auburn in July 1980. Green Haven was found to be one of the most corrupt prisons in New York State. At Green Haven, I became the executive director of the inmate organization Creative Communications Committee (CCC). Essentially, the CCC operated as a lifers' group seeking to influence and change state penal and prison laws. Initiatives were being organized to win lifers' "good time." Also, under my direction, CCC sponsored a class action lawsuit challenging the clause in the 13th Amendment of the U.S. Constitution that held prisoners are slaves of the state. The lawsuit was supported by a petition that was submitted to the United Nations arguing that the 13th Amendment was in violation of international laws governing human rights. The CCC sponsored community forums inviting New York State legislators, community representatives, and other notables to discuss issues of penal reform. However, in the three-year period from 1977-1980, there had been three escapes from Green Haven; drugs, prisoner rapes, and extortion were rampant in the prison. Members of CCC sought to curtail a number of these activities, especially in terms of preventing gang violence due to drugs and extortions. There was a growing base of support and respect from the prisoners for CCC commitment and work. This was noted in Albany, when the chairman of the CCC, Ralph "Ratton" Hall, was permitted to give a presentation to a Legislative Assembly Committee.

When the last escape occurred from the visiting room at Green Haven, the authorities decided to revamp and restrict visiting. The series of new regulations were implemented to restrict visiting and prisoners' movement in the prison. In response, the various prisoners' organizations, including the Inmate Liaison Committee (ILC) and Inmate Grievance Resolution Committee (IGRC), which had been officially created as a result of the demands from the 1971 Attica insurrection, met to discuss a prisoner response. At the meeting, it was decided to gauge the extent of prisoners' support for any future action by conducting a one-day hunger strike. If the prison population supported the strike, then other decisions would be made to ensure prisoners' concerns were heard and considered by the prison authorities.

When 98% of the entire prison population did not attend any meals in the mess hall, the next day prisoners met to discuss what issues would be brought to the prison administrators and how they would be delivered. The prison administration and commissioners from Albany wanted to meet with the prison representatives, first calling the ILC and IGRC reps to discuss the problems. However, the ILC and IGRC members informed the prison administrators that they did not represent the population in the hunger strike, claiming that the various inmate organizations must meet and elect representatives to discuss the issues with the prison administrators. Of course, the ILC and IGRC members had been previously instructed on what to say when called by the administrators, several of them being CCC members. The prison administrators permitted the leaders of the inmate organizations to meet, and it was decided that 40 prisoners would meet with the prison authorities, and I would be the spokesperson for the group.

The 40 prisoners met with the Green Haven executive team and commissioners from Albany, and I presented the prisoners' grievances. Essentially I informed them that corruption in the prison administration was the cause for the trouble in the prison, and the restrictions being implemented would cause further upheaval. When the meeting began, we asked that it be recorded and that the tape be played on the institutional radio so the entire population could hear what happened and know they had been adequately represented. At first the prison administrators refused to record the meeting. I then turned to face the prisoners who were seated behind me. They stood in unison, prepared to exist the meeting. At that point, the administrators relented and recorded the entire meeting; it was played back that evening on the institutional radio. At the conclusion of the meeting, it was negotiated and agreed that there would be no retaliation or transfers for those prisoners who had attended the meeting, especially since the prison administrators had asked for the meeting in the first place.

The next day, the superintendent of Green Haven was transferred, the prison was placed on total lockdown for a general shake-down search, and they began transferring prisoners. Three days after transfers began, guards came to my cell claiming I was being transferred. However, I was assaulted by the six guards after I had been stripped naked. After a struggle, I was handcuffed, and they put my pants on. Barefooted and bare-chested, I was moved to another housing block and beaten along the way. Then I was transferred to Down State Correctional Facility where I was placed in the SHU and given a disciplinary report that I assaulted one of the guards who came to escort me to be transferred.

At the preliminary disciplinary hearing conducted at Down State, I refuted the charges, and the lieutenant conducting the hearing changed the charges in order to defeat my defense against the bogus charge of assault. The next day, I was handcuffed and transferred to Comstock Correctional Facility, roughed-up, and placed in the SHU. There I was put in a cell that was completely enclosed with a quarter-inch sheet of plexiglass covering the front bars. The sheet of plexi-glass has small holes drilled at the bottom to permit air inside the cell. I was kept in that cell for nearly two weeks. In the daytime, the temperature in the cell reached 100 degrees in the middle of July. I would have to lie on the ground for hours to get fresh air and breathe. Today plexi-glass covered cells are being used throughout New York State SHU's.

In Comstock, they completed the disciplinary hearing, in violation of all their rules governing such hearings, and gave me six months in the SHU, losing all privileges. I appealed the decision to the Director of SHU in Albany, who summarily affirmed all charges and sanctions. I then filed an Article 78 petition with the courts, and within a month of filing the petition, Albany reversed all charges, making the petition before the court a moot point, and I was released into the general population at Comstock. However, prior to being released to the general population, I was taken out of the plexiglass cell in the SHU and placed in a regular cell in the SHU. Many of the prisoners were being abused in the SHU, and the guards permitted a snitch trustee to spray a high-powered fire hose on several prisoners. One in particular was a close friend who was crippled as a result of a stab wound he'd suffered in Green Haven. To protest the abuse, several prisoners decided to go on a hunger strike. After the fifth day, only five of us stood strong, and on the seventh day we were escorted to the hospital. In the hospital, guards tried to intimidate one of the younger hunger strikers, and a more seasoned prisoner, the only white guy in the group, jumped in the officer's face and took the beat-down for this young Black kid. We were then placed in isolation cells in the hospital, and after the 11th day living on nothing but water, the prison administrators relented, got rid of the trustee, and assured us changes would be made in the SHU. We were then escorted back to the SHU and given a meal with no disciplinary report for the protest. I had spent nearly four months in the SHU for having been assaulted by Green Haven prison guards and having been lied to by prison administrators that there would be no retaliation for meeting with them. Subsequently, the 40 prisoners that were transferred filed and won a lawsuit against Green Haven and New York State Department of Correctional Services; a suit called the "Green Haven 40."

During the Green Haven lawsuit, then DOCS Commissioner Thomas A. Coughlin testified that I was the leader of a prison take-over at Green Haven, that CCC had become a Black Liberation Army front operation, and that I had established BLA cadres throughout the prison engaged in drug sales, extortion, and intimidation to control the prison. Of course, the jury in the Green Haven 40 lawsuit refuted the commissioner's allegations, especially after the tape from the meeting, which we had prisoners in the radio room make a copy of and send to a lawyer in the streets for safekeeping, was brought to court and played. This happened right after the commissioner testified he knew nothing about a tape having ever been made.

While in Comstock, I was able to prevent a riot in the mess hall and was given a commendation. But within the four months in Comstock general population, I saw that prisoners were regularly being brutalized by prison guards. This eventually led to a sit-down strike in the prison yard, and, once again, I was accused of being the organizer and ringleader. I was then transferred back to Auburn, placed in the SHU, and charges with various rule violations. Again, after four months in SHU, all charges were dismissed after filing an Article 78 petition in the Court. I was then released to the general population at Auburn, where I stayed for three years without incident until transferred in the middle of the day to Clinton Correctional Facility general population. Subsequently, it was later learned that I was transferred because someone claimed I was planning an escape from Auburn, which proved untrue. After a three-year stay at Clinton without incident, I was transferred back to Green Haven, where I stayed for four years, becoming the chairman of Project Build prisoners' organization. During this time at Green Haven, I received another commendation for preventing a riot in the auditorium and received awards from various prisoners' organizations for my participation and leadership in programs. Also during the period, I drafted a legislative bill to win lifers good time. The bill was submitted by New York State Assembly representatives, and was adopted by then Assemblyman Arthur O. Eve, and submitted to the Committee on Corrections. I taught Black history, trained boxers in the gym, and initiated research for the filing of a lawsuit to win prisoners the right to vote. After four years in Green Haven, and before I could complete my research for the lawsuit, I was transferred to Eastern Correctional Facility. But I only stayed eight months because my codefendant, Herman Bell, wanted to enter the college master's program at Eastern, and DOCS would not permit us to be held in the same prison. So, DOCS made a switch, and he was brought to Eastern from Shawangunk, and I was taken to Shawangunk.

At Shawangunk, I continued to teach Black/African studies, as I had done while at Green Haven. I also established the first Men's Group in a prison in the entire country. I completed a double-major degree, receiving a Bachelor of Science in Psychology and Bachelor of Arts in Sociology, *summa cum laude*. At the same time, I completed the research on the prisoners' right to vote, and in 1994, I filed the lawsuit in the federal Northern District Court. Yet Shawangunk also proved to be a prison where guards rigidly exercised their authority, regularly abusing prisoners. Originally, Shawangunk was constructed to be a maxi-max prison to hold the most incorrigible New York State prisoners. Many of the guards maintained that kind of attitude despite the prison operating as a regular maximum security institution. While there, I worked as the clerk in the grievance office and was able to get a good feel of the atmosphere and sentiments of the prison population. Again, unrest eventually reached a nodal point, and prisoners started a work strike in response to a number of restrictions being arbitrarily implemented after an attempted escape. Once again, I was transferred, this time back to Attica and held in the SHU for 11 days, when charges of leading the strike were down-graded to simply participating in the strike.

While at Attica in 1996, I became the Imam of the Muslim community. Soon into my six-month stay, DOCS began to implement a statewide policy of double-bunking a number of prisoners due to overcrowding in the sytem. Across New York State, prisoners protested this policy, and in Attica, prisoners locked themselves in their cells on a work strike. The work strike, in my opinion, was poorly organized. Because Attica is divided into four sections, with little interaction between prisoners in the different housing areas, it was difficult to organize the strike. Unfortunately, due to the lack of proper communications, some members of gangs supporting the strike would retaliate against prisoners who went to the mess hall to eat, not staying in their cells. This was not a hunger strike, and it could not be expected that prisoners without food in their cells would stay in their cells and not eat. As the Imam of the Muslims, I asked for several representatives of groups to come to the yard to resolve this problem, essentially to stop the prisoner on prisoner violence. The position of the Muslims were that we would support anything that the majority of prisoners decided to do to protest the double-bunking policy, but we were not going to engage in prisoner on prisoner violence to enforce the strike.

In the prison yard, with a number of prisoners, I explained that no one could prevent a prisoner from going to the mess hall to eat, unless they intend to feed those hungry prisoners. Because I was vocal and adamant about this position, prison guards in the gun towers took it upon themselves to interpret that I was instructing prisoners on how to conduct the strike. Once again, I was taken to the SHU and given a disciplinary report of leading a prison strike. At the hearing, I was found guilty, and given two years in the SHU. I appealed the sanctions to Albany, which modified them to nine months, and I was transferred to Elmira Correctional Facility SHU.

Elmira SHU is essentially a sensory deprivation cell block, where for 23 hours a day a prisoner is held in a cell completely enclosed by concrete walls for the exception of a small door opening facing a wall. The only time a prisoner sees another person is when he is going to one-hour recreation or to and back from a shower three times a week. Food is served through a tray opening in the door. Speaking to another prisoner has to be through a crack at the bottom of the door; however yelling to other prisoners is not permitted, and if caught doing so it could result in additional time in the SHU. During the nine months spent in SHU, I was able to complete the editing of my book, *We Are Our Own Liberators!* with the assistance of Bonnie Kerness. I also worked with Herman Ferguson and the New Afrikan Liberation Front (NALF) lobbying the Congressional Black Caucus (CBC) to reopen COINTELPRO hearings. After nine months in SHU, the Deputy Superintendent of Security personally gave me an ultimatum: either go into a double-bunk cell in the general population or remain in the SHU. I laughed at him, but he told me to give him my answer the next day. After consulting a very close friend of mine who was in the SHU (he was permitted to sweep and mop during the day), I was advised that the policy had been fully implemented, and many prisoners were asking to go into double-bunk with their friends. He explained that I needed to get back in direct communications with family and friends on the streets, and that my own isolation in SHU would be for nothing. I agreed to be released, and after one week in Elmira general population, one morning at 3AM I was awakened by guards and transferred back to Eastern Correctional Facility.

I stayed at Eastern this time for three years, teaching prisoners computer literacy, and in 1997, with the support of Herman Ferguson and my dear comrade Sister Safiya Bukhari, founded and initiated the Jericho '98 March on the White House. This campaign brought over 6,000 activists and supporters of U.S. political prisoners to Washington, DC, of which forged into existence the Jericho Amnesty Movement. The time spent in Eastern was without incident, and on May 6, 1999, at 4AM, I was awakened and transferred back to Auburn. No reason was given, but within six months at Auburn I was placed in the SHU subject to confidential informant's statements that I was organizing a strike. Originally, I was being held in administrative segregation pending charges, and when the confidential informant's statements proved unreliable, my personal property was searched. Hence, they found some literature pertaining to explosives that had been sent to me in the mail while I was in

Flier for Jericho '98 March on the White House, initiated by Jalil Muntaqim, with help from Safiya Bukhari and Herman Ferguson, in 1997.

Eastern and was permitted to receive. In fact, the cell has been searched two other times and the literature was not seized. But this time I was charged with having contraband literature and kept in SHU for 90 days. While in the SHU, prisoners throughout New York State were protesting the implementation of the death penalty without providing "good time" for lifers. These were called the "Y2K strikes," allegedly being organized from Sing-Sing prison with the assistance of outside activists. As a pre-emptive measure, I was taken out of the population by Auburn prison administrators to prevent the possibility of a strike at the premier prison where prisoners' labor produces

Safiya Bukhari and Paulette D'Auteuil with the author, prisoner of war Jalil Muntaqim

license plates. After 90 days in the SHU, I was released back into the general population and continued to be confronted with harassment by prison guards. Ironically, the deputy superintendent of security who gave me the ultimatum at Elimira was promoted and is now the superintendent at this prison, so you can imagine....

I have now been in Auburn for six years, and for three of those years I was the chairman of the Lifers' Committee. In that position, I facilitated the teaching of a Sociology class, and submitted several proposals to the prison administration including raising funds for the victims of 911, the establishing of a parenting class for young fathers, and a pre-release program to prepare prisoners for parole. Presently I am facilitating a poetry class and a legal research and discussion class. Having twice been denied release on parole, although scheduled to appear before the parole board in July '06, I am challenging the parole denial in the Court via an Article 78 petition. Also, I continue to litigate the prisoners' right to vote lawsuit that is on appeal in the U.S. Court of Appeals for the 2nd Circuit, with oral arguments calendared for June 22, 2005. Plus, I have two other legal matters pending in the Court, while at the same time, I continue to seek the means to build progressive support for U.S. political prisoners through the Jericho Amnesty Movement.

This is an abbreviated history of my three-decade experience in the U.S. prison system. To be more detailed would result in a voluminous biographical journey that I am not now prepared to write. However, I sincerely hope what is here elucidated offers insights as to what this political prisoner has suffered and endured. I am certain many others have more horrendous experience indicting inhume prison conditions, abuse, and brutality, underscoring what happened in Abu Graib by American prison personnel in Iraq.

Human Rights in the U.S.: The Unfinished Story of Political Prisoners and Victims of COINTELPRO

Human Rights Research Fund
2000

The FBI kept its COINTELPRO Program (COunterINTELligence PROgram), which served to disrupt and destroy the Black liberation movement and many progressive organizations in the U.S., a secret, but Senate investigations exposed it during 1975.

Conducted by the Church Committee, as the Senate Select Committee to Study Governmental Operations with Respect to Intelligence Activities became known, the hearings led to a final report that was published in 1976. Despite widespread recognition of the limitations of the Church Committee, attempts to have the congressional investigations reopened have been frustrated for decades. However, on September 14, 2000, Representative Cynthia McKinney (D-GA), who sits on the Human Rights Subcommittee of the House International Affairs Committee, convened a forum to examine these issues. It was held during the Congressional Black Caucus's Legislative Conference, an annual event that hosts workshops, panel discussions, and other social events to highlight significant concerns among the constituents. The title of the panel McKinney convened was "Human Rights in the United States: The Unfinished Story of Political Prisoners/Victims of COINTELPRO."

Six panelists, all deeply engaged in seeking the release of unfairly imprisoned freedom fighters, presented information on COINTELPRO and its relevance to the cases of the approximately 100+ political prisoners in U.S. custody at this moment. Some of these men and women have been imprisoned for more than 30 years; all have served excessively long sentences. While the U.S. government denies that it holds any political prisoners, the role COINTELPRO operations have played in the arrests, trials, and convictions of these prisoners indicates otherwise.

Several current and past political prisoners, most notably Jalil Muntaqim (Anthony Bottom), Dr. Mutulu Shakur, and released political prisoner

This text was adapted from the transcript of the September 14, 2000, forum that
Rep. Cynthia McKinney (D-GA), hosted during the Congressional Black Caucus's legislative
weekend in Washington, DC. It was initially published in pamphlet form in 2001 by the
Human Rights Research Fund (founded by activist attorneys Kathleen Cleaver and Natsu
Saito) in collaboration with Release 2001.

Herman Ferguson have consistently urged that the illegalities committed under COINTELPRO be examined further and that compensation be made to the victims of these acts. The panel presentations excerpted below all point to the necessity of such an examination—and of releasing all of the U.S.-held political prisoners in order to redress the crimes committed against progressive political movements under the aegis of COINTELPRO and other FBI counterintelligence programs.

The forum was held in Room 2200 of the Rayburn House Office Building, a room where committee hearings are held. The tremendous crowd that gathered and participated in the discussion following the presentations demonstrated the significance of this human rights problem to the Black community. Below, the presentations given at the three-hour-long program are excerpted.

Rep. Cynthia McKinney introduced the panel by saying

> This discussion of COINTELPRO and political prisoners in the U.S. is our initial contribution to a long-standing struggle that we will be a part of for as long as we are in Congress. This is not going to be a one-time thing. When we began to plan this panel, I didn't realize the full extent of how important this issue is to individuals, to our community as a whole. Trying to give relevance to my tenure in Congress, I originally chose to dedicate my service to human rights issues around the world. But it became patently clear to me that there is a big, gaping hole in our human rights approach, because we dare not mention human rights at home. And once we begin to talk about this issue, human rights in the United States, a whole lot of folks become uncomfortable. We intend to broaden the definition of human rights to include human rights at home, and this panel discussion is our opening shot.

Nkechi Taifa: I am going to give a very brief sketch of what COINTELPRO was and how it worked. In the FBI's own words:

> The purpose of this new counterintelligence endeavor [code named COINTELPRO] is to expose, disrupt, misdirect, discredit, and otherwise neutralize the activities of black nationalist organizations and groupings and their leadership, spokesmen, membership, and supporters.

Never meant to be disseminated to the public, millions of pages of FBI internal documents reveal a coordinated national program of war against the movement.

An FBI memorandum described the goals of COINTELPRO. First, "to prevent the coalition of militant black nationalist groups." FBI director J. Edgar Hoover wrote, "An effective coalition of black nationalist groups might be the first step toward a real Mau Mau in America." The second goal was "to prevent the rise of a messiah who could unify and electrify the militant black nationalist movement." On this point, Hoover said:

> Malcolm X might have been such a messiah. Martin Luther King could be a very real contender for this position, should he abandon his supposed obedience to white liberal doctrines, nonviolence, and embrace black nationalism. Stokely Carmichael has the necessary charisma to be a real threat in this way.

Goal three was "to prevent violence on the part of black nationalist groups," and I'll just stop right there, because we have to remember that it was actually the FBI who was fomenting the violence.

Number four: "Prevent militant black nationalist groups and leaders from gaining respectability." The FBI was very specific. They said,

> You must discredit these groups and individuals to, first, the responsible Negro community. Second, they must be discredited to the white community, both the responsible white community and to the "liberals": political, religious and civics groups and individuals who have vestiges of sympathy for militant black nationalist groups simply because they are Negroes. Third, these groups are to be discredited in the eyes of the Negro radicals, the followers of the movement.

Another goal was to prevent the long-range growth of militant Black nationalist organizations among the youth. The FBI said that specific tactics were needed for this. And as we look at the drug trade—crack and heroin—I think that they have been very successful with respect to some of these tactics.

According to the Senate Select Committee on Intelligence, which investigated activities of the FBI in the '70s, COINTELPRO was an illegal and unconstitutional abuse of power by the FBI. Now, that is not Kathleen or Geronimo saying this; this was the Senate Select Committee on Intelligence, chaired by Frank Church, in the '70s that said it was an illegal and unconstitutional abuse of power by the FBI.

The committee said, "COINTELPRO is the FBI acronym for a series of covert programs directed against domestic groups. Many of these techniques would be intolerable in a democratic society even if all the targets had been engaged in violent activity," but COINTELPRO, the Senators said, went far beyond that. The bureau conducted a sophisticated vigilante operation aimed squarely at preventing the exercise of First Amendment rights of speech and association, allegedly to protect the national security and deter violence.

One word that comes up again and again in the FBI documents is "neutralization." That is a military term, a war term. They were talking about war against people who were simply trying to exercise rights and stand up for justice. The targets included such groups as the Southern Christian Leadership Conference, the Revolutionary Action Movement, the Deacons for Defense, the Black Panther Party, Students for a Democratic Society, the Nation of Islam, the Republic of New Afrika, and the National Lawyers Guild.

The FBI organized a vast network of political spies who infiltrated thousands of organizations and trained and coordinated similar operations by other law enforcement agencies at every level of government. The information gathered by informants was augmented by illegal wiretaps, letter openings, burglaries of homes and offices, secret examination of bank records, physical surveillance, and arranged murders.

By 1969 the Black Panther Party had become a primary focus of the program and was ultimately the target of 233 of the total 295 authorized black nationalist COINTELPRO operations. Although the claimed purpose of the bureau's COINTELPRO action was to "prevent violence," many of the FBI's tactics were clearly intended to foster violence. Some of these were assassinations, false imprisonment, and provocateur activities. Such actions demonstrate that the chief investigative branch of the federal government, which was charged by law with investigating crimes and criminal conduct, itself engaged in lawless tactics and responded to deep-seated social problems by fomenting violence and unrest.

Many organizations and individuals did not survive the FBI neutralization program. Some were destroyed; some, seriously weakened and destabilized. Many people were unjustly imprisoned; others were driven underground. Some were outright murdered. The only two FBI officials ever convicted for COINTELPRO abuses, Mark Felt and Edward Miller, were pardoned by Ronald Reagan before they even began to serve their sentences.

We need to reopen the Church Committee hearings of the 1970s. Although that congressional committee rightly condemned the FBI's counterintelligence program as an illegal and unconstitutional abuse of power by the FBI, they failed to establish remedies for those who were victims of COINTELPRO.

(Source: Agents of Repression: The FBI's Secret War Against the Black Panther Party and the American Indian Movement, Ward Churchill and Jim Vander Wall, South End 1990)

Kathleen Neal Cleaver: Much of what we are talking about today—the United States human rights record, COINTELPRO, political prisoners—has roots in the social uprisings that wracked this country in the wake of the Vietnam War. Most of us were students at that time, and we began to understand how intolerant this country is toward human rights. That is when we formed our commitment to the human rights struggle.

Nineteen sixty-seven was the year of uprisings—the government called them riots, we called them rebellions. There were 150 across the country, most notably in Detroit and Newark.

The United States Government convened the National Advisory Commission on Civil Disorders (the Kerner Commission) to study this phenomenon, determine its causes, and decide how to prevent future disorders. The commission stated that the cause of these disturbances was white racism and its attendant ills of unemployment and distress. But when it came to what should be done, one clear conclusion was a call for more sophisticated police tactics to suppress the disorders.

One of the report's recommendations was a training program for intelligence officers, to use undercover police and more reliable informants. And so you can see the genesis of COINTELPRO in this very liberal and supposedly enlightened report on how this country can handle civil disorder.

When it came out, I wasn't reading the Kerner Report. In 1967 I went out to California to join the Black Panther Party. We were reading things like Fanon's *The Wretched of the Earth* and Malcolm X—texts that would help us understand and further what we saw as the revolutionary opportunity to transform this country. That same summer of 1967, J. Edgar Hoover was articulating his counterintelligence program and identifying his targets: Stokely Carmichael, the head of the organization I had been a part of, SNCC; Southern Christian Leadership Conference, led by Martin Luther King; Elijah Muhammad; Revolutionary Action Movement, led by Max Stanford; and many others—all parts of the upheaval, the challenge. As we thought, "This is our chance, we will transform this country, we will make a difference." We all were targets of COINTELPRO.

When I first arrived in California, a man named Earl Anthony came with Eldridge Cleaver, whose car was in the shop, to pick me up at the airport. Earl Anthony was a COINTELPRO agent. Of course, I didn't know that at the time. But from the beginning of my connection with the Black Panther Party in California, COINTELPRO was there.

I moved to California and joined the BPP full-time because Eldridge called me and said, "You've got to come back out and help us. Huey Newton has been arrested. He's charged with murder. He's facing the gas chamber." Usually in that time we would hear reports, "Black man killed by police. Justifiable homicide." No one ever heard a report that said, "Policeman killed by black man." That we never heard. When we did, it was a murder charge.

So my full-time involvement with the Black Panther Party began with working around a prisoner, working around a case. And what we saw in this charge of murder was an effort to destroy our movement, to destroy our leader.

In those years, we saw an enormous number of cases arising out of battles in which members of the Black Panther Party became political prisoners. It is my pleasure to be here today with my brother Geronimo. The last time I was at the Congressional Black Caucus Legislative Weekend, I was on a panel talking about his case and how he was set up by the FBI and how to free him. Now he is here.

There are others, like Romaine Fitzgerald, who after 30 years is still serving time in California for killing a policeman—and it is known that he did not do the shooting. He is very ill. We have Mumia Abu-Jamal. We have Eddie Conway in Baltimore. This government says there are no political prisoners, that these are all criminals. But when you look at what the people did, what Mumia, Marilyn Buck, and Mutulu Shakur did, you will know that there was a revolutionary movement. These are people who dedicated their lives to the transformation of this country, who put the benefit of their communities ahead of themselves, who believed that transformation was not only possible but was worth dying for, to end brutality, racism, economic discrimination, imperialism, war. And when you hear their stories and know who they are, then you know that the sanitized version of the civil rights movement is not the whole story. Fabrication of evidence, perjury, the deceit that was used to put people away—that is another story that you have to know.

This country stands in violation of international treaties that the United States has signed, but when we raise the issue of human rights, we are told, "You are criminals. Your issues are criminal. It has to be handled by the criminal courts." Mumia Abu-Jamal had absolutely nothing that even begins to resemble a fair trial. When you challenge his conviction and say he was framed and given the death penalty because of his earlier membership in the Black Panther Party, the government comes back with "he's a criminal." If you go back through Black history, back to Marcus Garvey or even as far as Nat Turner, you see our history progressing through similar trials. I remember in my own history when we would say, "Free Angela," "Free Bobby," "Free all political prisoners." We are still trying to free all political prisoners.

Our fight for human rights continues today. This is what was starting back in Alabama, continuing with the Black Panther Party, continuing into the black liberation movement. The issue was always human rights. The government tried to redefine our struggle for us, to minimize the international, broad concept of human rights that motivated us and turn it into something smaller and less threatening.

We have to get this story told, have a clear understanding of where we are, who we are, know our own human rights struggle, and move to bring these prisoners and these freedom fighters out of the dungeons.

Michael Tarif Warren: The counterintelligence program involves institutions that interact and relate to each other for one purpose: to oppress communities of color and poor communities in this country and to make sure that a vanguard never succeeds in liberating those people.

A number of institutions carry out counterintelligence. I'm going to talk mostly about the role of courts. The courts take political activists and fighters for justice and criminalize them. They take freedom fighters from our communities and call them criminals. But in many ways the most important institution that carries out this process is the so-called private—really state-controlled—media. The media function as a propaganda organ of the state, coloring the political prisoners as criminals, when in fact they are valiant revolutionary soldiers fighting on behalf of oppressed people. It is necessary for the media to paint these people as criminals because political prisoners have the ability to tell the truth and expose this system. It is in the state's interest to silence political prisoners, to prevent the public from listening to their words and understanding their actions.

The political prisoner, once arrested, is treated unlike any other prisoner, because the political prisoner is more dangerous to the system than any other type of prisoner. Many of them, even those with no prior arrest record, receive no bail and are held in preventive detention. In many cases, this means that political prisoners who have no prior arrest record are held without bail.

Many political prisoners are thrown into isolation, thrown into the hole right away. Often they stay there for long periods of time with the ultimate purpose of attempting to break their spirits.

Dr. Mutulu Shakur is a political prisoner who is housed in the federal prison in Atlanta, Georgia. Dr. Shakur is a brilliant acupuncturist, studied in China, very dedicated to his community. He worked at Lincoln Hospital in the Bronx where he helped to develop the use of acupuncture to treat drug addiction. Later he operated a community acupuncture center in Harlem. But once he was arrested and charged with expropriation of funds for revolutionary purposes, as well as participation in the liberation of Assata Shakur from prison, all of Dr. Shakur's activities were portrayed in the media and the court as part of a "criminal enterprise." People involved with the clinic were swooped up, put in jail, and stigmatized for months in the media to ensure that prospective jurors remember these people not as individuals who struggled on behalf of their community but as criminals. So, by the time they reached the trial stage, they didn't have a snowball's chance in hell. And that is the anticipated outcome of the counterintelligence program. Consequently, Dr. Shakur, who was arrested in California back in 1986, stood trial in 1987, and was basically convicted on the testimony of one confidential informant. That is all the government really had, one confidential informant.

In the case of Dr. Shakur and the others charged in this case—his co-defendant Marilyn Buck, as well as Sekou Odinga and Silvia Baraldini—much of the counterinsurgency program was implemented by the Joint Terrorism Task Force (JTTF). The JTTF consists of federal and local law-enforcement agents. One of their primary objectives is to entrap people who struggled on behalf of their communities and to make sure they are isolated, arrested, prosecuted to the fullest extent, and imprisoned for a very long time. The Joint Terrorist Task Force has repeatedly, in numerous cases, employed all the techniques developed through COINTELPRO.

After Dr. Shakur was sentenced (to 60 years), he was sent immediately to an underground maximum security prison in Marion, Illinois, where the prisoners have very little contact with each other. They are kept in a cell for 23 hours a day, only getting out one hour for exercise.

So the judiciary becomes a fifth column in this counterintelligence program. It's not just the FBI and the Joint Terrorist Task Force. They are merely the front lines.

One other judicial aspect of counterintelligence is the grand jury system. The government uses the grand jury as a tool of oppression. And I know because I have represented people who were arrested in sweeps.

For example, in Dr. Shakur's case, Fulani Sunni Ali, who is here today, was arrested and separated from her children (and she was pregnant at the time of her arrest) on a subpoena to a federal grand jury. The government used that grand jury to fact-gather, based on their need for more evidence against Dr. Shakur, Sekou Odinga, Marilyn Buck, and Silvia Baraldini. All they had was the word of a snitch; they needed more.

The grand jury serves another purpose, too: it criminalizes all the friends and associates of the people who are on trial in the case in question. Many grand jury resisters are required to spend up to 18 months in prison for contempt, based on their refusal to obey a grand jury subpeona. Consequently the state vicitimizes these individuals as well and destroys their political organizations.

Bruce Ellison: I will share with you today my continued efforts to expose what the FBI has done out in my part of the country. I was raised to believe in the importance of justice for all people, in the importance of our democracy and our fundamental rights to free speech, freedom of association, and freedom to seek redress of grievances. From what I have seen over the last 25 years, Native Americans have many legitimate grievances, as do others in this country, that are never redressed.

Educated as a lawyer, I was taught that our courts exist to promote and preserve justice, our Congress to enact responsible legislation, and our executive branch to enforce the laws of our country. What I have experienced in representing Leonard Peltier and other Native Americans has shocked, amazed, and terrified me as a citizen of this country.

FBI documents and court records in the thousands, together with eyewitness accounts, show clearly that beginning in the late 1960s the FBI began a campaign of disruption of the American Indian Movement. FBI operations were directed toward the destruction of AIM and its grassroots supporters in the urban and reservation communities. Operations began with surveillance of peaceful demonstrations calling for the enforcement of treaty rights, for human rights, for equal opportunities for jobs and housing and medical care, and for justice in America's courts. It soon led to the infiltration of agents provocateurs, to the manipulation of our criminal justice system, and ultimately to state-sponsored terrorism in Indian communities. Particular emphasis was directed toward the descendants of the Lakota, who stopped General George Armstrong Custer and who now reside on the Pine Ridge Indian Reservation.

During the antiwar days, we used to talk about "bringing the war home." I think the FBI thought that was a good idea and tried out many of the tactics they used in Indochina and Central America on the Pine Ridge Reservation.

Claiming that AIM members were engaging in acts of sedition, the bureau sought to arrest hundreds after the 71-day siege at Wounded Knee in 1973. It soon concluded that this approach was insufficient.

The FBI then began to fund and arm a group of more western-oriented Lakota who called themselves the Guardians of the Oglala Nation, or the "goon squad." As many as 60 men, women, and children, out of a population of 11,000, were killed in the political violence that followed. These were mostly members of AIM, their families, and supporters. I remember staying in homes in Pine Ridge during this period where men felt compelled to keep

Leonard Peltier when he was held at the Marion Control Unit (1983)

651

loaded weapons nearby while they and their families, including children and elders, slept, fearful of the real and immediate danger of an attack by the goon squad in the night.

One instance I personally witnessed involved FBI agents and a Bureau of Indian Affairs SWAT team escorting carloads of goon squad members and their weapons out of the community after a day and night of armed attacks on the community. This resulted in the ambush murder of a young AIM member, and the burning and shooting up of several homes.

The FBI acted as if making bridges across barriers of color and ethnicity was terrifying. Many of the documents we obtained under the Freedom of Information Act talk about Wounded Knee, and the firefight in Oglala, of the connections between the American Indian Movement and the Black Panther Party.

I represented a young mother and AIM member named Anna Mae Pictou Aquash on weapons charges. She told me after her arrest that the FBI threatened to see her dead within a year unless she cooperated against AIM In an operation previously used against the Black Panther Party, the FBI began a rumor that she was an informant. Six months later her body was found on the reservation. The FBI said she died of exposure. They cut off her hands, claiming this was necessary to identify her, and buried her under the name of Jane Doe.

A second, independent autopsy revealed that someone had placed a pistol to the back of her head and pulled the trigger. When I asked for her hands after the second autopsy, because she was originally not buried with her hands, an FBI agent handed me a box, and with a big smile on his face he said, "You want her hands? Here."

The firefight near Oglala was preceded by FBI documents declaring AIM to be one of the most dangerous organizations in the country and a threat to national security. It followed by two months the issuing of a position paper entitled "FBI Paramilitary Operations in Indian Country," a how-to plan of dealing with AIM on the battlefield. It used such terms as "neutralization," which it defined as "shooting to kill." Leonard Peltier and other AIM members from outside the reservation had come to join local AIM members because the violence on the reservation had gotten so intense. Three young men lost their lives that day, two FBI agents and one AIM member. The FBI considered that only two men died, their own agents. No one has ever been prosecuted for the killing of AIM member Joe Stuntz.

The FBI eventually charged four AIM members, including Leonard Peltier, with the killing of the agents. Two of Peltier's codefendants were acquitted on self-defense grounds by an all-white jury in the conservative town of Cedar Rapids, Iowa—truly a remarkable thing. The FBI analyzed why these long-haired, militant men were acquitted and at a meeting in Washington, DC, decided to "put the full prosecutive weight of the Federal Government" against Leonard Peltier.

The government argued that Peltier personally shot the agents. The U.S. Attorney's Office has now admitted in court that it had no credible evidence Leonard Peltier killed the agents and speciously claimed it never tried to prove it did. The FBI still withholds thousands of pages in this case, claiming that disclosure would compromise national security. In the absence of such disclosure, no further efforts toward a new trial are possible.

Citing the case of Leonard Peltier as an example, Amnesty International has called for an independent inquiry into the use of our criminal justice system for political purposes by the FBI and other intelligence agencies in this country. Amnesty cited similar concerns for other members of AIM and other victims of COINTELPRO-type operations by the FBI

Under our system, if there is a reasonable doubt, then Leonard Peltier is not guilty. Yet he has been in prison for nearly 25 years for a crime he did not commit. On behalf of Leonard Peltier, I urge a full congressional investigation and the granting of executive clemency to those activists from the '70s, '80s, and '90s who have yet to gain their freedom.

Geronimo ji Jaga: This panel has established important truths already today, but there is one thing that has been omitted: the activists of the '60s who were killed by COINTELPRO. What it boils down to is murder. That is something that we have been trying to get established since I have been out of prison. We are trying to get hearings into actual murder cases. And here's how it would work. When you would have everyone together, like we are all together right herd, we all say, "Okay, we are all going to not disrespect each other," and everybody agrees. But then the FBI sends someone in who stirs things up, tells lies and causes us to begin to disrespect each other. So one may begin to disrespect another one, and then another one stabs him and he is dead, and then you have the murderers in the background boasting and bragging about it. COINTELPRO came in so many forms. But the first thing I would think of is these murders. When you have beautiful sisters and brothers such as Fred Hampton, who was shot and killed; you have Robert Wells, put in a sleeping bag

FREE GERONIMO PRATT!

Poster From Free Geronimo Campaign
(Source: New Studies on the Left: The Prison Issue)

and thrown off a freeway, killed in New York City, still unsolved. All of these cases I am talking about are clear COINTELPRO murders. Fred Bennett, who was killed in San Francisco. Franco Diggs. John Huggins. Bunchy Carter.

They Were Victims. They Were Murdered.

All of the names I have mentioned are victims of COINTELPRO. They were murdered. Their murderers have never been brought to justice. So this is where we need to begin. We are dealing with straight-up murderers who turn around and call me a murderer and put me in prison for 27 years, when I murdered no one. These murderers are running around. They still are practicing their art of murder, outright murder. *[Audience begins to call out names.]* John Clark. Watature Pope.

These brothers and sisters were murdered. Mark Clark. Twyman Meyers. *[Geronimo: Come on with some more.]*

John Africa. Kombora. Komboze. Tracy. Kayatta. Ralph Featherstone.

That's very true. There is Malik el Shabazz. And we can continue to call names. This is how important and serious this is to us.

These brothers and sisters we have mentioned, they were family members. They were mothers, they were fathers, they were sisters, they were brothers. And they are dead. They were murdered. It was done by the U.S. government. They have admitted it.

You have brothers like Mutulu—and myself when I was in, and others—who call ourselves prisoners of war. We say political prisoners, okay. And you try to understand, what are you talking about? This war continues. It is an actual war against our people. And it should be handled just as they handled the trials in Nuremburg.

So I want to urge everyone to support and put muscle behind this effort that will expose the true murderers and let the victims out. What is Sundiata Acoli doing in prison? Ruchell Magee. Yogi Pinell. Chip Fitzgerald. There are so many.

We can't allow that to happen. These hearings will make it very clear, and then these brothers and sisters will be released out of these prisons.

COINTELPRO didn't stop at the Black liberation movement—we all should study this—but it went into every movement that was involved in liberation. This is why Laura Whitehorn spent so much time in prison; why Marilyn Buck and Susan Rosenberg and so many who are victims of COINTELPRO continue to languish.

Laura Whitehorn: I think these hearings are significant because COINTELPRO continues. Even though that particular FBI program with that particular name was supposedly stopped in '72, it continues in other forms. Until all the political prisoners are out, COINTELPRO continues. About a week ago, the Bureau of Indian Affairs apologized for the genocide against the Native American people—but Leonard Peltier is still in prison. The U.N. definition of genocide includes the destruction of political movements and leadership. So genocide—including COINTELPRO—continues against the Native American peoples.

I was a political prisoner for a little over 14 years, in a case called the Resistance Conspiracy case. The U.S. government said we were guilty of "conspiring to protest, change and oppose policies and practices of the United States government in domestic and international affairs through violent and illegal means." And we said the domestic and international policies and practices of the United States government were violent and illegal. [Interrupted by applause.] For example, the overthrow of the democratically elected government of Grenada, in this hemisphere, not coincidentally the first socialist African government in this hemisphere. And the shelling of the people of Beirut, Lebanon, at the same time. And the use of low-intensity counterinsurgency warfare against the liberation struggles in Central America.

Most political prisoners were born around the same time as me, in the '40s and '50s, and we grew up in the era of national liberation and struggles for human rights. It was going to be the era of international law. Nazi Germany wasn't going to happen again. As a child, I was taught that there were human rights that were so important that if your government stopped those rights, you had a responsibility to take action against that government. And I believe that to this day. [Applause] That is what every political prisoner, I believe, stands for.

As a child I was moved by the civil rights movement. The courage of the people who were standing up was inspiring to me and, I think, to a whole generation. I moved to Chicago in 1968 and worked to support the Black Panther Party and got to know Fred Hampton. He was the chairman of the Illinois chapter of the Black Panther Party. He was about 20 years old—and a danger to the United States government, if the United States government was afraid of the rise of a Black messiah, because Fred had the ability, like Malcolm X, to articulate the aspirations of an entire people. Anyone who was in Chicago in those days remembers people of all ages coming out to hear Fred.

In 1969 he was murdered, along with another Black Panther Party member, Mark Clark. The Chicago police, who carried out the assassination, claimed there had been a shootout. It took a long time, but it was proven that not a single shot was fired from inside Fred's apartment; every bullet was fired by the police. Eventually it came out that the murder had been well planned by the Illinois State Attorney's Office, the Chicago Police, and the FBI. An FBI informant named William O'Neal was infiltrated into the Panther environment, and he gave the police a map of Fred's apartment, drugged the food of Fred and the rest of the Panthers that night, and then the murder could take place.

That told me that we could not be confined by the laws of this country, because it was a war. It was a war declared by the FBI and the law enforcement agencies, and backed by the U.S. government, against the Black nation,

Native American nations, and the colonized nation of Puerto Rico. And if there was going to be justice, we would have to fight for it.

I wasn't a victim of COINTELPRO. But I took those actions, and did time in prison for them, because COINTELPRO convinced me we had to fight. Eventually, I ended up with 23 years, which was a fortunate sentence.

That might sound like a terrible thing to say, but when you look at Marilyn Buck with 80 years and Mutulu Shakur with 60 years, and Sundiata Acoli having already served nearly 30 years, you realize that 23 years is a very fortunate sentence.

The day I got out of prison was the happiest day of my life—and the saddest, because I left behind Marilyn Buck, Linda Evans, Carmen Valentín, Lucy and Alicia Rodríguez, and Dylcia Pagán. They were in the prison I was in. I have no choice but to fight for their freedom and for the freedom of all political prisoners. A month after my release, Carmen, Lucy, Alicia, and Dylcia were released when President Clinton gave the 11 Puerto Rican political prisoners clemency. I watched from the beginning the campaign for the freedom of the *independentistas*. When they were arrested in 1980, the slogan was, "They are freedom fighters, not terrorists." And the nation of Puerto Rico took up that slogan and said, "They are our freedom fighters. They are not terrorists."

We need to wage a campaign like that for all of the political prisoners. Otherwise, they will not be free. And that is simply unacceptable. It is a matter of human rights and justice.

Conclusion

To close the discussion, Rep. McKinney commented:

> The testimony here today has deepened my commitment to making sure that we get to the bottom and go all the way up to the top, in order to make sure that we get justice, justice for our people and justice for the survivors of COINTELPRO.

We need to support her efforts and organize many more federal, state, and local legislators and politicians to do the same.

Since the panel discussion last September, one more political prisoner has died in prison: Teddy Jah Heath died of cancer in New York State's Coxsackie Prison on January 21, 2001. Jah was a member of the Black Panther Party in New York City in the 1970s, and he never stopped struggling for human rights. His arrest in 1973 stemmed from his attempt to stop the influx of drugs into the Black community. He had been turned down for parole in 1998, despite a perfect prison record and despite having served 28 years for a case in which there was no injury to any person.

His name joins the long list of those whose lives have been taken as a result of COINTELPRO and political repression.

Call for COINTELPRO
Congressional/CBC and TRC Hearings

National Jericho Amnesty Movement
2007

Dear Sisters and Brothers,

In January 2007, Congressman John Conyers will become the new chair of the United States House of Representative Committee on the Judiciary. The House Committee on the Judiciary jurisdiction includes the following areas: (1) the judiciary and judicial proceedings, civil and criminal; (2) civil liberties; (3) claims against the United States; (4) national penitentiaries and (5) revision and codification of the Statutes of the United States.

Herman Ferguson, on behalf of the Jericho Movement, has written a letter to Congressman Conyers requesting that he schedule hearings on "COINTELPRO: Its Legacy and Continuing Impact." A copy of Herman's letter is below.[*] It is our hope that these hearings, if held, will not only further expose the FBI and local law enforcement crimes against the Black Liberation Movement and many of those involved in it, but also result in legislation addressing some of these injustices.

Of particular concern to the Jericho Movement is the release and treatment of our political prisoners. Though the United States steadfastly denies it, presently there are many political prisoners in the United States, the majority of them Black/New Afrikans who were targets of the COINTELPRO "Black Nationalist Hate Groups" program. Many of these brothers and sisters have been incarcerated for decades.

For example, Jalil Abdul Muntaqim has been incarcerated since 1971; Sundiata Acoli and Herman Bell, since 1973. It is critical that the human rights and constitutional violations surrounding their arrests, trials, sentencing, conditions of their confinement and continuing incarceration because of their political histories—all were members of the Black Panther Party—and continuing commitment to the liberation of Black/New Afrikan people be brought to the wider attention of the public. Sundiata Acoli, now 70 and with a near exemplary record, has twice been denied parole.

If nothing else, congressional hearings on "COINTELPRO: Its Legacy and Continuing Impact" would go a long way toward achieving this result.

To this end, we are calling on all supporters of political prisoners—defense

---

* See IX.6.A on page 659.

committees; revolutionary nationalist, radical, and progressive organizations; elected officials; community, religious, spiritual leaders; etc.—to write, fax, or call Congressman Conyers to urge that he schedule hearings on COINTELPRO.

Your support of Jericho's call will help ensure that it becomes a reality. Forward, download, copy, and distribute this letter and Jericho's call to as many people as possible. Please mail or e-mail copies of your letters to Herman Ferguson care of National Jericho Movement.

Thank you in advance for your support of this effort. Please also do not hesitate to contact Herman or us if you have any questions about this campaign.

In solidarity,

Joan P. Gibbs, Esq.

Mani Gilyard
Chair, Malcolm X Commemoration Committee

IX.6.A

Dear Congressman Conyers...

Herman Ferguson
National Jericho Amnesty Movement
2007

Dear Congressman Conyers:

Congratulations on your pending ascendancy to the chair of the House Committee on the Judiciary. We write to request that you schedule hearings on "COINTELPRO: Its Legacy and Continuing Impact." For more than a decade, many of us have been requesting hearings on COINTELPRO and, hopefully, legislation that begins to address some of the injustices committed against the Black movement and activists as a result of COINTELPRO. We hope that one of your acts as the new chair of the Judiciary Committee will be to schedule these hearings.

As I am sure you are aware, COINTELPRO is an acronym for a series of FBI counterintelligence programs against, *inter alia*, the Communist party and so-called "Black Nationalist Hate Groups." The August 1967 FBI memorandum announcing the Black Nationalist Hate Group program describes its goals as:

1. Prevent a coalition of militant black nationalist groups;
2. Prevent the rise of a messiah who could unify and electrify the militant nationalist movement;
3. Prevent violence on the part of the black nationalist groups;
4. Prevent militant black nationalist groups and leaders from gaining respectability by discrediting them;
5. Prevent the long-range growth of militant black nationalist organizations especially among youth.

The targets of the Black Nationalist Hate Group program included a wide array of Black organizations and individuals, among them the Southern Christian Leadership Conference (SCLC), the Student Nonviolent Coordinating Committee (SNCC), the Revolutionary Action Movement, the Republic of New Afrika, Reverend Martin Luther King, Jr., Kwame Toure, formerly known as Stokely Carmichael, and countless others.

Though the Black Panther Party (BPP) was not among the original targets of the program, in September 1968, then FBI Director J. Edgar Hoover labeled the BPP "the greatest threat to the internal security of the country." Thereafter, the BPP became the primary focus of the program and was ultimately the target of 233 of the believed total authorized "Black Nationalist" COINTELPRO actions.

As the Final Report of the 1976 Select Committee to Study Government Operations With Respect to Intelligence Activists states: "Although the claimed purpose of the Bureau's COINTELPRO tactics was to prevent violence, some of the FBI's tactics against the BPP were clearly intended to foster violence, and many others could reasonably have been expected to cause violence."

In its pursuit of the BPP, the FBI, often together with local law enforcement officials, knew no bounds. BPP members and supporters were not only spied on and harassed but, in blatant violation of the both the United States Constitution and International law, falsely accused of crimes that they had not committed. Many were wounded and murdered by police and FBI.

December 4, 2006, marked the thirty-eighth anniversary of the assassination of Fred Hampton, one of the leaders of the Chicago chapter of the BPP, by local Chicago police thanks to information from an FBI informant, while he slept in his bed. Hampton was shot twice in the head, once in the arm and shoulder; while three other people sleeping in the same bed escaped unharmed. Mark Clark, sleeping in a living room chair, was also murdered while asleep. Hampton's wife, who was eight months pregnant, was also shot but survived. Four Panthers sleeping in the apartment were also wounded, while one escaped injury. Fred Hampton was 21 years old when he was assassinated; Mark Clark was 17.

While the true impact of the COINTELPRO Black Nationalist Hate Group Program on the Black Liberation Movement will probably never be known because the FBI never recorded all of its activities, has destroyed many of its files, and many of the architects and participants are now deceased, it is crucial that the impact and continuing legacy of this program be investigated and remedies developed to repair the damage it has done. This is particularly true with respect to the many members of the Black Panther Party, the Republic of New Afrika, and other organizations who today languish in jail as a result of their having been targeted by the FBI and local law enforcement officials as part of the counterintelligence programs.

We urgently request that you schedule hearings on "COINTELPRO: Its Legacy and Continuing Impact" in the near future. Thank you in advance for your prompt attention to this matter. We expect that you will give our request the serious attention that it deserves.

Section X.
The Struggle Continues

It is clear from all that has come before that *La Lucha Continua* is more than just a rhetorical rallying cry. While the majority of political prisoners and prisoners of war buried in the government's dungeons have been locked away for decades, political internment continues to hang like a sword of Damocles over the heads of activists from yesterday and today. No collection of documents regarding political prisoners could be complete or acceptable without mention of the watershed case of the current period—that of the framed San Francisco 8, former members and associates of the Black Panther Party rounded up after 30 years to send a message that no new movements should even think about rising up. Along with some basic information on that case, this section includes a look at these issues post-September 11, 2001. In addition, the cases of Chicano/Mexicano activist Alvaro Luna Hernandez, the Cuban Five, the Green Scare environmental/ animal rights prisoners, Black activists Kamau Sadiki and Imam Jamil Al-Amin, Arab and Muslim activists such as Sami Al-Arian, and the Iraq Veterans Against the War military resisters are noted to remind us that political prisoners don't just come out of any one or two movements, nations, or communities. As the imperial government tries to destroy any effort potentially threatening to its global domination plans, political imprisonment will continue. People's movements, if we are to present a real challenge to the machine, must reach through the walls, break the chains, and build resistance. There must be many forms, but one, united struggle. Rebuild.

X.1

A Moment of Silence

Emmanuel Ortiz
2002

Before I begin this poem, I'd like to ask you to join me in a moment of silence in honor of those who died in the World Trade Center and the Pentagon on September 11th, 2001.

I would also like to ask you to offer up a moment of silence for all of those who have been harassed, imprisoned, disappeared, tortured, raped, or killed in retaliation for those strikes, for the victims in Afghanistan, Iraq, in the U.S., and throughout the world.

And if I could just add one more thing…

A full day of silence… for the tens of thousands of Palestinians who have died at the hands of U.S.-backed Israeli forces over decades of occupation.

Six months of silence… for the million and-a-half Iraqi people, mostly children, who have died of malnourishment or starvation as a result of a 12-year U.S. embargo against the country.

…And now, the drums of war beat again.

Before I begin this poem, two months of silence… for the Blacks under Apartheid in South Africa, where "homeland security" made them aliens in their own country

Nine months of silence… for the dead in Hiroshima and Nagasaki, where death rained down and peeled back every layer of concrete, steel, earth and skin, and the survivors went on as if alive.

A year of silence… for the millions of dead in Viet Nam—a people, not a war—for those who know a thing or two about the scent of burning fuel, their relatives bones buried in it, their babies born of it.

Two months of silence… for the decades of dead in Colombia, whose names, like the corpses they once represented, have piled up and slipped off our tongues.

Before I begin this poem,
Seven days of silence… for El Salvador
A day of silence… for Nicaragua
Five days of silence… for the Guatemaltecos
None of whom ever knew a moment of peace in their living years.
45 seconds of silence… for the 45 dead at Acteal, Chiapas…
1,933 miles of silence… for every desperate body
That burns in the desert sun
Drowned in swollen rivers at the pearly gates to the Empire's underbelly,
A gaping wound sutured shut by razor wire and corrugated steel.

25 years of silence… for the millions of Africans who found their graves far deeper in the ocean than any building could poke into the sky.
For those who were strung and swung from the heights of sycamore trees
In the south… the north… the east… the west…
There will be no DNA testing or dental records to identify their remains.

100 years of silence… for the hundreds of millions of indigenous people
From this half of right here,
Whose land and lives were stolen,
In postcard-perfect plots like Pine Ridge, Wounded Knee, Sand Creek,
Fallen Timbers, or the Trail of Tears
Names now reduced to innocuous magnetic poetry on the refrigerator of our consciousness…

From somewhere within the pillars of power
You open your mouths to invoke a moment of our silence
And we are all left speechless,
Our tongues snatched from our mouths,
Our eyes stapled shut.

A moment of silence,
And the poets are laid to rest,
The drums disintegrate into dust.

Before I begin this poem,
You want a moment of silence…
You mourn now as if the world will never be the same
And the rest of us hope to hell it won't be.
Not like it always has been.

...Because this is not a 9-1-1 poem
This is a 9/10 poem,
It is a 9/9 poem,
A 9/8 poem,
A 9/7 poem...
This is a 1492 poem.
This is a poem about what causes poems like this to be written.

And if this is a 9/11 poem, then
This is a September 11th 1973 poem for Chile.
This is a September 12th 1977 poem for Steven Biko in South Africa.
This is a September 13th 1971 poem for the brothers at Attica Prison,
New York.
This is a September 14th 1992 poem for the people of Somalia.
This is a poem for every date that falls to the ground amidst the ashes of
amnesia.

This is a poem for the 110 stories that were never told,
The 110 stories that history uprooted from its textbooks
The 110 stories that that CNN, BBC, The New York Times, and Newsweek
ignored.
This is a poem for interrupting this program.

This is not a peace poem,
Not a poem for forgiveness.
This is a justice poem,
A poem for never forgetting.
This is a poem to remind us
That all that glitters
Might just be broken glass.

And still you want a moment of silence for the dead?
We could give you lifetimes of empty:
The unmarked graves,
The lost languages,
The uprooted trees and histories,
The dead stares on the faces of nameless children...

Before I start this poem we could be silent forever
Or just long enough to hunger,
For the dust to bury us
And you would still ask us
For more of our silence.

So if you want a moment of silence
Then stop the oil pumps
Turn off the engines, the televisions
Sink the cruise ships
Crash the stock markets
Unplug the marquee lights
Delete the e-mails and instant messages
Derail the trains, ground the planes.
If you want a moment of silence, put a brick through the window
of Taco Bell
And pay the workers for wages lost.
Tear down the liquor stores,
The townhouses, the White Houses, the jailhouses, the Penthouses
and the Playboys.

If you want a moment of silence,
Then take it
On Super Bowl Sunday,
The Fourth of July,
During Dayton's 13 hour sale,
The next time your white guilt fills the room where my beautiful brown
people have gathered.

You want a moment of silence
Then take it
Now,
Before this poem begins.
Here, in the echo of my voice,
In the pause between goosesteps of the second hand,
In the space between bodies in embrace,
Here is your silence.
Take it.
Take it all.
But don't cut in line.
Let your silence begin at the beginning of crime.

And we,
Tonight,
We will keep right on singing
For our dead.

X.2

We Will Rise Again

Alvaro Luna Hernandez
1997

If you believe that there exists true Justice in this country for Chicanos/
Mexicanos, this pamphlet is not intended for your eyes. It is aimed at
those willing to shake off the yoke of mental conditioning and recognize
that inherent injustices of the current system; who consider themselves
oppressed, treated as second-class citizens, and victims of the brutal legacy
of white power rule. It is for those who have experienced the pain, the
humiliation, the suffering, and who understand the necessity of struggle
to change their condition, for a fair redistribution of wealth, justice and
power. The present hypocritical and unjust system which oppresses us
cannot continue.

This writing is for the eyes and hearts of the poor, the voiceless, the dispossessed, the imprisoned—the real victims. I am not a historian, scientist, nor
writer. I have no formal education, nor degree. My education is self-taught.
My thoughts come from the heart, from a prophecy to be fulfilled. My recent
trial in Odessa, Texas, June 2-9, 1997, on two counts of aggravated assault on
a sheriff and a city police officer must be placed in its proper perspective. The
historical foundation, the police conspiracy and the system's web of lies and
contradictions must be exposed.

This pamphlet is but the start of a series of writings to be consolidated into
a future book. It is my sincerest wish that my testimonial experiences and
confrontations with the system will serve to awaken and inspire *Raza*, not
only in Alpine, Texas, where I lived and was arrested, but throughout the
Southwest, to stand up, to assert their humanity, and to struggle against the
gross injustices occurring daily to *Raza*, from the police house to the courthouse, to the White House.

No Choices

Some of us have no "choices". We are born into a life of poverty and oppression unable to escape the cycle because of many social factors. Conditions of
life are even worse in rural areas such as in West Texas.

Common in oppressed barrios throughout the Southwest, in my native
hometown of Alpine, are racist, corrupt and brutal police who continue to
rule with an iron fist. From a notorious murderous, anti-Mexicano Sheriff who
ruled Alpine with terror for more than 30 consecutive years to a racist judicial

system to hate groups who committed unpunished crimes against *Raza* to an economy controlled by the gringo elite to a community which today still suffers the vestiges of a segregated society—this is the order of things in Alpine today. It is humiliating. It is painful. It is unjust. It is criminal. Those are daily realities for Mexicanos in Alpine, who ironically constitute approximately 50 percent of the county's population.

Despite overwhelming numbers, Mexicanos have no voice and are excluded in the management decisions of daily government, civic and economic affairs, yet their sweat, blood and labor build the physical buildings that house the institutions now oppressing them. In the truest sense of the term, they are victims of taxation without representation. Economic development monies are always destined for dregs north of the Southern Pacific railroad tracks, but never to the south where *Raza* is concentrated, but forced to remain silent to outright injustices otherwise they will find themselves without a job in the gringo controlled economy.

The stark differences can be seen in the quality of community life and development, the public parks, public streets and in the social services that only trickle down to the barrio as miserable crumbs after the fat cats, the gringo power structure, has eaten up all of the tax revenues of the social and economic development pie to better the lives of their own. The Mexicano populace, in particular youth, are caught up in the never-ending cycle of white economic power servitude, dire poverty, institutionalized racism, violence, crime, oppression and death. From the womb to the tomb of its segregated cemeteries, *Raza* pass away not knowing true freedom and justice. "Hispanic" *vendido* politicians are content with only crumbs, and defend the status quo. Mexicano traditional institutions such as the Catholic Church ignore these injustices and contradictions.

Consciousness

There is no genuine grass-roots community-based organizations promoting justice or the betterment of poor *Raza*. The time has arrived to come to terms with these realities. Despite "civil rights" laws, we are the most discriminated against, exploited, marginalized and oppressed sector of United States society. The media daily reports another police murder, or brutality; another Mexicano maimed or killed by *La Migra* or the U.S. military on the border; another anti-Mexicano government law or policy; another city curfew to harass our youth and on and on.

Historical, sociological myths that have served to degrade, to condition us, to make us feel inferior before the gringo, must be challenged. Those myths have served the interests or our oppressors, "Lazy," "Meskin," "gardeners," "maids," "wetbacks," "gangbangers," "treacherous" and "criminals" are but a few stereotypes. It is only when our rich culture, heritage customs and traditions serve the commercial interests of the mighty white American dollar that it is acceptable to our oppressors.

Universal consciousness will help us to liberate ourselves, from such socio-logical, psychological slavery and genocide. We must control the politics of our barrio. Our traditional institutions must promote human rights and jus-tice for our *Raza* and be accountable to our people and not to the status quo. We must enrich and empower our souls and our families with true awareness and knowledge. Knowledge is power and power is knowledge. The racist educational systems must be replaced with our own cultured institutions for a higher learning. It is only through such an empowerment that we can become truly independent, become self-sufficient, achieve true happiness and social justice for our people.

A Crossroads

We are at a crossroads in history. We either choose to accept our present misery, or we chart a new path of unity, reconciliation, healing, justice, lib-eration, and self-determination. Power has never yielded to anything without a demand. The seasons—the moon, the sun, the skies are all signaling the fulfillment of our prophecy. Let future generations look at our generation through the eyes of pride, respect and glory, and not through the eyes of shame and cowardice. We owe it to our elders, our daughters and sons. We must create a united voice, a united political movement, a barrio force to be reckoned with. Let our oppressors tremble in fear at the thought of waking up tomorrow without their class privileges of white ruling power and feeling the sting of our rage and retribution in their behinds and heels. Our oppres-sor needs to be freed from his greed, arrogance and sickness, His sickness has condemned poor people to a life of slavery, oppression and death not only within the internal colonies of the United States, but throughout the world. Their imperialism is the enemy of the human species. It must be overthrown. *Raza*, we are fulfilling a prophecy!

Let us learn from our past historical movements—Crystal City, Texas, Brown Berets and other formations for political self-determination that spread like prairie fires throughout our barrios in the occupied territories of our homeland, Aztlán, from Tejas to Califas, from Denver to Chiapas. History will repeat itself. But this time we will master "history" and not allow our oppressor to make it "his story" of falsehoods and trickery to justify their genocide war against our *Raza*. Ethics, morals and righteousness are on our side. Our nationalism will unify us—our indigenous blood, our *Mexicanidad*, our *Chicanismo*, our *carnalismo*, our spriitualism, our *Zapatismo*.

Let us reignite in the hearts of our barrio warriors, our soldiers, the burning flames of *Raza* pride, courage, spiritual rebirth and liberation; of our righteous duty to rebel against tyranny; to make revolution. We are becoming a majority in the occupied territories. The recent passing of a bright flame in the night sky is the signal that the prophecy written in the codices of our ancestors in Tenotchitlan will be fulfilled in the 21st century... we will rise again!

Uprising

If my message, my testimony, will have served to reach and touch even one lost soul, I will have considered my mission accomplished.

Although totally innocent of the false charges, I was unjustly sentenced to prison for 50 years for defending myself against a police conspiracy and for resisting armed attacks by a racist, corrupt, and arrogant policy army who initially set out to outlaw me from Alpine or to kill me. They won a battle, but will not win the war. I will rise again!

White police critic Fred Vogt recently wrote a letter published in the local newspaper complaining about the Alpine police department: "Will people be thrown in Jail falsely? Searched without a warrant? Harassed?"*

It's been happening to Mexicanos in Alpine for years, Mr. Vogt. Open your eyes and ears and look to the South, across the railroad tracks that have always divided and excluded Mexicanos in Alpine. Mexicanos do exist and live to the South of your narrow tunnel vision, your white privileged world. It is not human, not wise to live in a glass house, in a glass world.

A special heart-felt thanks to all the *linda Raza* that supported me during my trial, my family, my friends, especially our youth, our future.

From the ashes of the birth cradle of Tenotchitlan, we will fulfill our prophecy. We will rise again!

VIVA LA RAZA!
TIERRA Y LIBERTAD!
EL BARRIO UNIDO, JAMAS SERA VENCIDO!

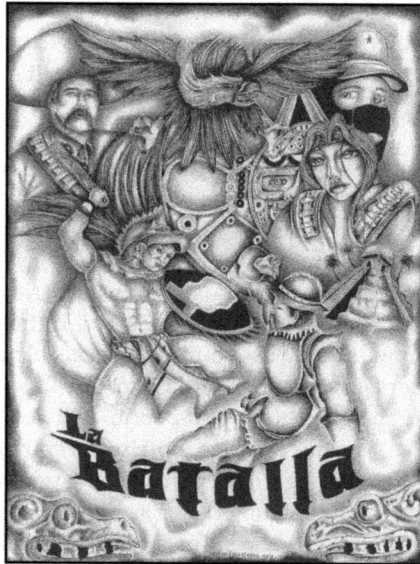

"La Batalla" by Alvaro Luna Hernandez

---

* *Alpine Avalanche,* May 1, 1997

"Please Accept Our Appeal"

Release 2000 Campaign
2000

Dear President Clinton:

Please accept our appeal to you on behalf of 12 imprisoned women and men serving exceptionally long sentences that arose from their politically motivated actions. As attorneys, we have devoted years of pro bono service to human rights and politically charged cases. We have volunteered our expertise to these prisoners who are jointly applying for executive clemency. A brief profile of each prisoner is attached to this letter.

Around the world, the dawning of a new millennium traditionally leads to grants of amnesty or clemency to people whose imprisonment resulted from conflicts with their government. In Northern Ireland, Israel and Palestine, pardons in the cause of peace have led to the release of many prisoners whose actions were motivated by larger social and political objectives or responses to broader civil strife. In Italy, a pardon was extended to the Turkish national, Mehmet Ali Agca, by Italian President Carlo Azeglio Cianipi after he was convicted of attempting to assassinate the Pope. In South Africa, Nelson Mandela's ascendance to the Presidency came after his release from a prison sentence imposed for revolutionary actions in support of African self-determination. Today, South Africa's "truth and reconciliation" process has provided an ongoing opportunity for healing by making honest dialogue and leniency a central part of that nation's new course. America stands in dire need of a process of healing that would enable us to benefit from talented people working together for the future instead of remaining behind prison walls.

We ask that you formally extend the olive branch of forgiveness to these men and women as we set out on a new millennium. Like those fighters pardoned in other lands, these prisoners were also highly committed to movements that sought justice during an era marked by war, racial violence and political assassinations. In an act of courage and compassion, you granted the release of the Puerto Rican political activists last year. In this same spirit, we ask that you examine the plight o these petitioners and grant their release.

In some instances, their illegal actions were taken in response to severe legalized repression and government misconduct. Some convictions arose

Release 2000 was an attempt, at the end of the Clinton Administration, to increase pressure for general amnesty of all long-held political prisoners in federal custody.

directly from the "targeting" of activists under secret, illegal government "counter-intelligence" actions committed under the infamous COINTELPRO program, and similar initiatives. COINTELPRO was investigated by the Senate Select Committee to Study Governmental Operations with Respect to Intelligence Activities (popularly known as the "Church Committee"), which submitted a final report in 1976. "The origin of COINTELPRO demonstrated that the Bureau adopted extralegal methods to counter perceived threats to national security and public order because ordinary legal process was believed to be insufficient to do the job. There were innocent people who were victimized by COINTELPRO. In essence, the Bureau took the law into its own hands, conducting a sophisticated vigilante operation against [perceived] domestic enemies.'" This is a wrong that must be condemned and corrected. The Church Subcommittee concluded that many of the actions carried out by the government against these social activists could only be described as "abhorrent in a free society."

Other individuals fell victim to a justice system that failed to keep its promise of fairness and due process. Still others sought to defend themselves or their communities from continued attack or otherwise responded to a unique period of civil strife that engulfed our nation during the 1960s, 1970s and beyond.[†]

The United States stands virtually alone in its growing imposition of sentences in excess of 20 years, regardless of the offenses involved. These prisoners, whose convictions reflect ongoing and unresolved justice issues affecting all of us, have served longer sentences than they would have in any other industrialized nations. Many sentences were improperly motivated by "political" factors, either because prosecutors were permitted to multiply charges growing out of one set of actions, and/or because the defendants' militant trial stance led judges to impose terms that were grossly disproportionate to those given for comparable crimes under different circumstances. Some of these prisoners received lengthy prison terms that would not be permitted under the new law establishing strict federal guidelines to eliminate sentencing disparities, while others have been denied parole based on their political views or the politically motivated nature of their offenses, despite meeting traditional parole criteria.

By now, many of these applicants for clemency are aging behind prison walls. They face the future without adequate medical care or other minimal human rights guarantees given to prisoners in most other "civilized" countries and required by international law and treaties. Many of the prisoners

---

* Church Committee Report, p. 27.
† In contrast to the plight of political prisoners, government officials involved with Watergate, Irangate, and military offenders implicated in atrocities such as My Lai have been pardoned, and the only two FBI agents, W. Mark Felt and Edward Miller, convicted for COINTELPRO activities were immediately pardoned by President Reagan before they began to serve their sentences.

have been subjected to inhumane conditions, including long years in solitary confinement or maximum control units, and harsh separation from family and loved ones. In some cases, permanent mental and/or physical harm has resulted from these conditions of confinement.

All of these men and women have served substantial prison time. All of them can make significant contributions to their communities upon release, as documented by many of their efforts behind bars to lead, teach and serve others despite their difficult circumstances. The people whose imprisonment arose from similar convictions who have already gained their release have made significant contributions to society. For example, the contributions made by the Petitioners' codefendants, spouses and comrades include the following: Dr. Alan Berkman is the Medical Director of Highbridge Woodycrest Center, a long-term care facility for adults and children with AIDS, located in the Bronx, New York. He is also an Assistant Professor of Clinical Psychiatry at Columbia University and a Medical Specialist for the HIV Center for Clinical and Behavioral Studies at the New York State Psychiatric Institute and Columbia University. Jamal Joseph, now known for his extraordinary work with youth arts programs and as a filmmaker, teaches screenwriting at the Film Division of Columbia University's Graduate School of the Arts. His script credits include television and feature films, and he has won numerous awards, including a Director's Fellowship at Sundance. After many years as the artistic director of Citykids, Joseph and veteran theatre producer Voza Rivers founded Impact Repertory Theatre in Harlem. Joseph, as artistic director, serves as mentor, counselor and teacher in the creative and leadership training for young people, including his own three children in addition to his full schedule of writing and teaching. Barbara Curzi Laaman is employed by a law firm in Boston. Patricia Levasseur is currently employed as a paralegal at a law firm in New York City. Prior to this she worked for five years for the Center for Constitutional Rights. She has three daughters who are attending college. Carol Manning lives in Maine and is employed as a supervisor in a local electronics manufacturing firm. She also works as a personal trainer. Donna Wilmott lives with her family in San Francisco. She has worked for four years at Legal Services for Prisoners with Children as an advocate for women prisoners, where she is now Litigation Coordinator. Dr. Imari Abubakari Obadele earned his Ph.D. at Temple University in 1985, and is today an Associate Professor at Prairie View A&M University located in Texas. Laura Whitehorn, released one year ago, is now an Assistant Editor at *POZ Magazine*, a national monthly magazine about HIV and AIDS. Safiya Bukhari is the Director of Administration at Brooklyn Legal Services Corp.

The prisoners who seek your grant of clemency would similarly devote their talent to socially creative work upon returning to their families and loved ones. We call upon you as a man of power and a man of faith to continue to honor the democratic ideal and promise of this troubled nation. As you so eloquently stated during the recent Democratic National Convention,

"...we're not just better off, we're also a better country—more decent, more humane, more united." We agree and believe that this truth can best be demonstrated by granting clemency to Silvia Baraldini, Hanif Shabazz Bey (Beaumont Gereau), Veronza Bowers, Marilyn Jean Buck, Bill Dunne, Larry Giddings, Ray Luc Levasseur, Jaan Karl Laaman, Tom Manning, Jalil Abdul Muntaqim (Anthony Bottom), Sekou Odinga and Mutulu Shakur, as well as Linda Evans, Leonard Peltier and Susan Rosenberg who have pending Executive Clemency petitions.

Respectfully yours,

Robert Boyle, Esq.
Kathleen Cleaver, Esq.
L. King Downing, Esq.

J. Soffiyah Elijah, Esq.
Charles J. Ogletree, Esq.
Nkechi Taifa, Esq.
Michael Tarif Warren, Esq.

Political Prisoners and 9/11:
The Reality of Political Prisoners in the United States: What September 11 Taught Us About Defending Them

J. Soffiyah Elijah[*]
2002

Prior to September 11, 2001, there were nearly 100 political prisoners and prisoners of war incarcerated in the United States.[‡] Political prisoners are men and women who have been incarcerated for their political views and actions. They have consciously fought against social injustice, colonialism, and/or imperialism and have been incarcerated as a result of their political commitments. Even while in prison, these men and women continue to adhere to their principles. This definition of the term "political prisoner" is accepted throughout the international community.

Political prisoners have always been an especially vulnerable and abused subset of the American prison population.[§] Now, in the wake of September 11, these prisoners and their lawyers have been targeted for renewed abuse.

A. Political Prisoners in the United States: A Brief History
Many of today's political prisoners were victims of an FBI counterintelligence program called COINTELPRO.[¶] COINTELPRO consisted of a series

Originally published in *Harvard BlackLetter Law Journal,* Vol. 18, 2002.

[*]   Clinical Instructor, Criminal Justice Institute, Harvard Law School. The views and opinions expressed herein are those solely of the author and are not necessarily reflective of the position held by Harvard Law School or the Criminal Justice Institute.

[‡] After September 11 hundreds of immigrants, mostly of Middle Eastern descent, were rounded up and interned in a manner reminiscent of American treatment of Japanese people during World War II. (For a description of this treatment, see Korematsu v. United States of America, 323 U.S. 214 (1944)). Just weeks after September 11, the Department of Justice admitted it had detained over 1,000 immigrants, none of whom had it charged with participation in any terrorist activity. Many of the detainees were held for extraordinary periods of time. Amy Goldstein, et al.,"A Deliberate Strategy of Disruption," *Washington Post,* Nov. 4, 2001, at A1.

[§] Despite their prevalence in United States society, U.S. Government officials have long denied the very existence of political prisoners. When Andrew Young, the former U.S. ambassador to the United Nations, publicly acknowledged the existence of over 100 political prisoners in his country, he was swiftly removed from office.

[¶] COINTELPRO was created in 1956 by J. Edgar Hoover, then the director of the Federal Bureau of Investigation, as a result of Hoover's increasing frustration about rising political dissent in the country and the response of the Supreme Court that limited the government's power to proceed overtly against dissident groups. Final Report of the Select Committee

of covert actions directed against domestic dissident groups, target-
ing five perceived threats to "domestic tranquility." These included the
Communist Party USA (1956-71), the Socialist Workers Party (1961-69), White
Hate Groups (1964-71), Black Nationalist Hate Groups (1967-71) and the
New Left (1968-71).* People viewed as dissidents, Communists, or antiestab-
lishment were at risk of prosecution, persecution or both:

> In these programs, the Bureau went beyond the collection of intel-
> ligence to secret action designed to "disrupt" and "neutralize" target
> groups and individuals. The techniques were adopted wholesale from
> wartime counterintelligence, and ranged from the trivial (mailing
> reprints of *Reader's Digest* articles to college administrators) to the
> degrading (sending anonymous poison-pen letters intended to break
> up marriages) and the dangerous (encouraging gang warfare and
> falsely labeling members of a violent group as police informers).†

In response to pressure from a broad spectrum of the American public, a congressional subcommittee, popularly known as the Church Committee, was
formed to investigate and study the FBI's covert action programs. In its report,
The Church Committee concluded that the FBI had "conducted a sophisticated vigilante operation aimed squarely at preventing the exercise of First
Amendment rights of speech and association, on the theory that preventing
the growth of dangerous groups and the propagation of dangerous ideas
would protect the national security and deter violence."‡ It went on to report
that "[m]any of the techniques used would be intolerable in a democratic society even if all of the targets had been involved in violent activity...."§

In fact, before COINTELPRO was laid to rest, it was responsible for maim-
ing, murdering, false prosecutions and frame-ups, destruction, and mayhem
throughout the country. It had infiltrated every organization and association
that aspired to bring about social change in America whether through peaceful or violent means. Hundreds of members of the Puerto Rican independence
movement,¶ the Black Panther Party (BPP), the Young Lords,** the Weather

---

to Study Governmental Operations With Respect to Intelligence Activities (Apr. 23, 1976)
[hereinafter Church Committee Report]. The Committee was chaired by Senator Frank Church
of Idaho.
* The COINTELPRO initiative formed part of the long history of domestic surveillance of U.S.
citizens, a history dating at least as far back as the beginning of the twentieth century.
† The Church Committee Report, supra note 3.
‡ Id.
§ Id.
¶ Between 1960 and 1971 there were at least thirty-seven actions authorized and "aimed at
militant groups which sought Puerto Rican independence." Church Committee Report, supra
note 3, at 14 n.59.
** The Young Lords were primarily a Puerto Rican liberation organization headquartered in
New York City.

Underground, Students for a Democratic Society (SDS), the Republic of New Afrika (RNA), the Student Non-Violent Coordinating Committee (SNCC), members of the American Indian Movement (AIM), the Chicano movement, the Black Liberation Army (BLA), environmentalists, the Revolutionary Action Movement (RAM), peace activists, and everyone in between were targeted by COINTELPRO for "neutralization."

In 1969 the FBI and local Chicago police agents were responsible for the pre-dawn assassination of Fred Hampton and Mark Clark as they lay asleep in their beds. Hampton and Clark were the leaders of the Chicago office of the Black Panther Party.* Among Hoover's other targets were Leonard Peltier of AIM; the Rev. Dr. Martin Luther King of the Southern Christian Leadership Conference (SCLC); El-Hajj Malik Shabazz (Malcolm X); Kwame Ture (Stokely Carmichael) of SNCC; Huey Newton (leader of the BPP); and Rev. Philip Berrigan and his brother Rev. Daniel Berrigan, peace activists who challenged the Vietnam War and the U.S. military-industrial complex.†

Prosecutor's offices and the courts were complicit in the destruction meted out by the FBI. Prosecutors routinely withheld exculpatory evidence as was evidenced in the cases of Geronimo ji Jaga Pratt, Dhoruba Bin-Wahad, and Mumia Abu-Jamal.‡ Although Pratt and Bin-Wahad were eventually exonerated after serving twenty-seven and nineteen years respectively for crimes they did not commit, requests by Peltier and Abu-Jamal for new trials have been frustrated at every turn by law enforcement and the prosecution.§

Many of today's political prisoners were incarcerated as a direct result of COINTELPRO's activities. They were targeted because of their political beliefs and/or actions. Unlike those convicted and sentenced for similar crimes, they

---

* The FBI created a plan of attack on the Chicago BPP headquarters where Hampton resided. They planted an informant, William O'Neal, in the Chicago BPP who was to become the local chief of security. O'Neal became Hampton's bodyguard and quickly secured measures in the house to follow through with the FBI plan. He provided the FBI with detailed floor plans of the BPP apartment complex including the location of Hampton's bed and closet areas and on what side Hampton's wife slept. A wiretap was placed on the phones in the BPP apartment as well as on the phone of Hampton's mother in February of 1968. In May of 1968, Hampton's name was placed on the FBI's "Agitator Index." The FBI and local law enforcement set the date for the raid on the BPP apartment for December 4, 1969, at 4am Hampton v. Hanrahan, 600 F 2d 600 (7th Cir. Ct. App. 1979).

† In March 1971, the FBI resident agency in Media, Pennsylvania, was burglarized. The documents seized from the office were widely distributed and published by the press. The resultant concern led to the termination of COINTELPRO for "security reasons" the following month. Many believe that its operations were continued under another name. The Church Committee was able to determine the continued existence of at least three COINTELPRO-type operations after 1971. Four months after the official termination of COINTELPRO, "information on an attorney's political background was furnished to friendly newspaper sources under the so-called "Mass Media Program," intended to discredit both the attorney and his client." Church Committee Report, supra note 3, at 13.

‡ Personal communication with counsel.

§ Personal communication with counsel.

were given much harsher sentences and routinely denied parole. Black Panther Party member, Sundiata Acoli (f.k.a. Clark Squire), the codefendant of Assata Shakur,* was sentenced to life plus thirty years for the death of a New Jersey State Trooper. He was eligible for parole after twenty years. After serving twenty-two years, however, the New Jersey parole board denied him parole and gave him an unprecedented twenty-year set-off. Susan Rosenberg was sentenced to fifty-eight years for possession of explosives and denied parole despite her exemplary prison record.† Geronimo ji Jaga Pratt was denied parole at least seven times although he was innocent of the charges for which he was serving time.‡

B. Facing Renewed Abuse:
The Post-September 11 Treatment of Political Prisoners

In concluding its review of COINTELPRO, the Church Committee wrote: "The American people need to be assured that never again will an agency of the government be permitted to conduct a secret war against those citizens it considers threats to the established order."§ Just over twenty-five years later, the American people are again in need of such assurance. In the wake of the attacks on the World Trade Center and the Pentagon on September 11, 2001 the use of the nation's jails and prisons for political repression was renewed. Within hours of the attacks, several of the political prisoners were rounded up and put in administrative segregation, generically known as the hole.¶ No charges or allegations were levied against them. Some of them were told that they were being placed in the hole for their own safety. They were held in solitary confinement and restricted to their cells twenty-three or twenty-four hours a day. Some, like Marilyn Buck, Sundiata Acoli** (both represented by

---

* Shakur, formerly known as Joanne Chesimard, escaped from a New Jersey state prison in 1979. Years later she was granted political asylum in Cuba, where she continues to reside. The state of New Jersey has offered a reward of $100,000 for her capture. The United States Congress passed a resolution in 2000 demanding the return of Shakur and several other exiles living in Cuba. H. Con. Res. 254.

† She was released in January 2001 pursuant to a commutation granted by President Clinton at the end of his term of office.

‡ For a detailed discussion of Mr. Pratt's ordeal, see generally Jack Olsen, *Last Man Standing: The Tragedy and Triumph of Geronimo Pratt* (2000).

§ Church Committee Report, supra note 3, at 77.

¶ The political prisoners who were rounded up were Sundiata Acoli, Carlos Alberto Torres, Phil Berrigan, Marilyn Buck, Antonio Camacho Negrón (released from prison in May 2002 after serving thirteen years), Yu Kikumura, Ray Levasseur, Tommy Manning, and Richard Williams. There is no discernable connection between these political prisoners. During the time that some of them were held incommunicado, their lawyers had no way of verifying if they were still in the facilities to which they had previously been designated. There was a total Bureau of Prisons blackout of information concerning them. Conversations with anonymous BOP representatives during the period between September 13 and November 17, 2001.

** Sundiata Acoli was not returned to general population until January 3, 2002.

the author), and Richard Williams,* were held incommunicado for weeks without access to legal counsel.† Other prisoners were told that they were to have no contact of any kind with Marilyn Buck once she was thrown in administrative segregation "for her own safety." Numerous requests to arrange for legal visits and phone calls with these prisoners were flatly refused by administrators of the Bureau of Prisons (BOP). All legal mail was suspended; no letters were allowed out of the prison and legal mail that was mailed in was neither given to the prisoners nor returned to the attorneys. From September 11 to October 24, 2001, Sundiata Acoli was not allowed any access to his lawyers. Social visiting, mail, and phone calls were suspended for many of these prisoners. The actions of the Bureau of Prisons were so unusual that initially the BOP General Counsel denied that any prisoners were being refused access to their lawyers. The Bureau continued to put forward this position as late as February of this year.‡ Yet on September 26, 2001, the Warden of U.S.P. Allenwood, where Mr. Acoli was being held, wrote to the author to inform her that he was "denying her request to allow Inmate Squire (Acoli's former name) a legal telephone call."§

Between September 11 and 17, 2001, the restrictions placed on the prisoners were in flux, and it seemed clear that the individual prison authorities were trying to determine exactly what the directions from Washington contemplated. But on or about September 17, Attorney General John Ashcroft issued a memorandum to the Bureau of Prisons directing them to terminate all communications, both social and legal, for certain prisoners.¶ Some have posited that the memo left the discretion to the prison wardens. Others believe that Ashcroft determined who should be held incommunicado.** No matter who had the final discretion, the result was the same for the prisoners; they were in the hole and some had no access to the outside world.

C. The War on Terrorism: Targeting Attorneys

Political prisoners have not suffered alone; their attorneys have proven equally vulnerable to political abuse. Defending the "unpopular client," the client who

---

* Richard Williams was not returned to general population until February 11, 2002. The next day he suffered a minor heart attack. On April 30, 2002, he was sent back to the hole. Again, the isolation was not the result of any disciplinary infraction.

† All information concerning Buck and Acoli comes from the author's personal representation of Buck and Acoli. All information concerning Williams comes from the author's personal communications with counsel for Williams.

‡ Anne Marie Cusac, "You're in the Hole: A Crackdown on Dissident Prisoners," *Progressive*, Dec. 2001, at 34.

§ See letter dated September 26, 2001, from Warden Jake Mendez to Jill Elijah regarding Sundiata Acoli, f.k.a. Clark Squire (on file with author).

¶ Anonymous communications from various Bureau of Prisons officials (2001-02).

** The lawyers for the prisoners thrown in the hole formed an ad hoc committee to try to gather information about what was happening to our clients and to share the information with each other. It is in this context of discussing the information that we all speculated about the reasons that these things were being done to our clients.

has been targeted by the government as a terrorist, a cop killer, a bank robber, a revolutionary, or "the sole white member of the Black Liberation Army" does not get you nominated to the list of American's 100 Most Influential Lawyers. Such professional endeavors usually find the lawyer on the receiving end of constant harassment from prison and jail officials, federal marshals, court personnel and prosecutors.* Nonetheless, the Constitution and accepted ethical and criminal procedure norms guarantee that every defendant is entitled to legal counsel and zealous advocacy.

That's what is taught in law school, but is that what is meant? Recent legislation has raised serious doubts as to whether we can continue to take these principles for granted. How else can we explain the recent unprecedented arrest and indictment of New York lawyer Lynne Stewart, a zealous advocate well respected amongst members of the bar and the bench?† Ms. Stewart has represented numerous "unpopular" clients, some of whom have clear political ideologies, such as David Gilbert, who was charged as a former member of the Weather Underground with the 1981 Brink's armored car robbery in Nyack, New York; Bilal Sunni-Ali, a member of the Republic of New Afrika also charged in the 1981 Brink's case in a federal prosecution; and Richard Williams, who was alleged to have conspired with members of the Ohio 7 to blow up several military buildings and offices of major corporations.‡

Ms. Stewart has been a thorn in the side of prosecutors for over two decades. It seems that the time for revenge has arrived. The U.S. Attorney General boldly announced at a press conference following her arraignment that the federal government had been monitoring conversations between Stewart and her client, Sheikh Omar Abdel-Rahman, from at least as far back as May of 2000. Even the most conservative observer would concede that the USA PATRIOT Act was not signed into law until October 26, 2001. Even had it been operational at the time Ms. Stewart's communications were monitored, a scrupulous review of its provisions will reveal no specific reference to monitoring of attorney-client communications. Upon what authority did the

---

* See Deborah L. Rhode, "Terrorists and Their Lawyers," *New York Times*, Apr. 16, 2002, at A27.

† Sadly this is not the first time that Ms. Stewart has been used as a test case by the government in unprecedented interference in the attorney-client relationship. Back in 1989, the Manhattan District Attorney's office, led by Robert Morgenthau, attempted to undermine Ms. Stewart's representation of her client, Dominick Maldonado, by having unauthorized communications with him and convincing him to cooperate. This led him to participate in a scheme concocted by the DA's office that ultimately led to felony charges being lodged against Ms. Stewart for contempt of court. She refused to testify before a grand jury investigating the source and amount of funds paid to her and other lawyers in the case. Mr. Maldonado was charged with participation in a heroin ring. The charges against Ms. Stewart were ultimately reduced. Her client committed suicide after being sentenced to 100 years and realizing that he had been misled and used as a pawn to destroy her career.

‡ Gilbert and Williams were convicted in 1983 and 1986 respectively and remain incarcerated today as political prisoners. Sunni-Ali was acquitted in an emotional and political upset for the U.S. Attorney's office for the Southern District of New York. At that time, the office director was none other than Rudolph Giuliani.

government rely in determining that it could monitor undisputed attorney-client communications in May of 2000?*

Prior to October 30, 2001, the Bureau of Prisons regulations on institutional management authorized the Bureau to impose special administrative measures, including the monitoring of certain inmate communications, with respect to specified inmates. The imposition of these administrative measures had to be based on information provided by senior intelligence or law enforcement officials, where it was determined to be necessary to prevent the dissemination of either classified information or that could endanger the national security or other information that could lead to acts of violence and terrorism.† It was not contemplated by these regulations, however, that the privileged communications between an inmate and his or her attorney were to be subject to such monitoring.

On October 30, the Department of Justice instituted new regulations amending certain key provisions. In addition to extending the time during which a prisoner could be subjected to special administrative measures from 120 days to up to one year, the new regulations provide,

> In any case where the Attorney General specifically so orders, based on information from the head of a federal law enforcement or intelligence agency that reasonable suspicion exists to believe that a particular inmate may use communications with attorneys or their agents to further or facilitate acts of terrorism, the Director, Bureau of Prisons, shall, in addition to the special administrative measures imposed under paragraph (a) of this section, provide appropriate procedures for the monitoring or review of communications between that inmate and attorneys or attorneys' agents who are traditionally covered by the attorney-client privilege, for the purpose of deterring future acts that could result in death or serious bodily injury to persons, or substantial damage to property that would entail the risk of death or serious bodily injury to persons.‡

---

* Attorney General Ashcroft shamelessly admitted that Ms. Stewart's conversations with her client were surreptitiously wiretapped during a prison visit that took place two years ago.
† 28 CFR pts. 500-501.
‡ 28 CFR 501.3 (d).
   1. The certification by the Attorney General under this paragraph (d) shall be in addition to any findings or determinations relating to the need for the imposition of other special administrative measures as provided in paragraph (a) of this section, but may be incorporated into the same document.
   2. Except in the case of prior court authorization, the Director, Bureau of Prisons, shall provide written notice to the inmate and to the attorneys involved, prior to the initiation of any monitoring or review under this paragraph (d). The notice shall explain:
      i. That, notwithstanding the provisions of part 540 of this chapter or other rules, all communications between the inmate and attorneys may be monitored, to the extent determined to be reasonably necessary for the purpose of

It is alleged *inter alia* in Ms. Stewart's federal indictment that she violated the Special Administrative Measures that have been in place since 1997 with respect to Sheikh Omar Abdel-Rahman by facilitating communications between him and members of the so-called Islamic Group.* The Islamic Group is described in the indictment as an "international terrorist group dedicated to opposing nations, governments, institutions and individuals that did not share its radical interpretation of Islamic law." The government's indictment of Ms. Stewart is based on the monitoring of communications between lawyer and client. This monitoring appears to have been illegal at the time it took place. Although the October 2001 amendments to the Bureau of Prisons regulations may permit the government's conduct under limited conditions now, there appears to have been no authority for their actions prior to that date.

As the nation begins to accept greater infringements on civil liberties, it seems that lawyers are amongst the first to feel the effects on their profession. Indeed, Ms. Stewart believes that she is being used as an example to deter others from representing controversial figures and causes.† If she is right, hers

---

deterring future acts of violence or terrorism;

ii.   That communications between the inmate and attorneys or their agents are not protected by the attorney-client privilege if they would facilitate criminal acts or a conspiracy to commit criminal acts, or if those communications are not related to the seeking or providing of legal advice.

3.   The Director, Bureau of Prisons, with the approval of the Assistant Attorney General for the Criminal Division, shall employ appropriate procedures to ensure that all attorney-client communications are reviewed for privilege claims and that any properly privileged materials (including, but not limited to, recordings of privileged communications) are not retained during the course of the monitoring. To protect the attorney-client privilege and to ensure that the investigation is not compromised by exposure to privileged material relating to the investigation or to defense strategy, a privilege team shall be designated, consisting of individuals not involved in the underlying investigation. The monitoring shall be conducted pursuant to procedures designed to minimize the intrusion into privileged material or conversations. Except in cases where the person in charge of the privilege team determines that acts of violence or terrorism are imminent, the privilege team shall not disclose any information unless and until such disclosure has been approved by a federal judge.

* 02 Crim. 395 SDNY Paragraph 16.

† But history is instructive here. In 1991, around the same time that Lynne Stewart was having her difficulties with the Manhattan DA's office, attorney Linda Backiel was being targeted by the U.S. Attorney's office in Philadelphia for her refusal to testify before a federal grand jury about communications she had with Elizabeth Ann Duke, a client who was believed to have jumped bail. Ms. Duke was an admitted revolutionary who had been indicted on weapons and explosives charges. Ms. Backiel, like Ms. Stewart, had represented a number of "politically unpopular" clients such as Kathy Boudin, who was charged as a member of the Weather Underground with the 1981 Brink's armored car robbery in Nyack, New York, and Antonio Camacho Negrón, who was charged with conspiracy in the 1983 Wells Fargo $7.1 million robbery in West Hartford, Conn. Mr. Camacho was a Puerto Rican *independentista* and alleged to be a member of Los *Macheteros*. Ms. Backiel spent six months in jail for civil contempt before the grand jury disbanded.

is a case of over-deterrence if ever there was one. How do we explain the fact that the Arabic-speaking court-certified interpreter was also indicted along with Ms. Stewart? What was his crime? Interpreting documents into English for Ms. Stewart and her client? If the interpreter's prosecution is allowed to go forward, it will be nearly impossible for attorneys representing "unpopular" clients to hire someone to translate for them during prison visits and phone calls. There seem to be no limits to the possible abuses. The net has been cast far too wide. Many would argue that the net should not have been cast at all.

So the message is clear. Attorneys who believe that they are obligated to follow the Code of Professional Responsibility and "not decline representation because a client or cause is unpopular or community reaction is adverse"[*] are at risk of being targeted for character assassination and prosecuted to the full extent of, and in some instances beyond, the law.

Conclusion

The full ramifications of the political climate that followed September 11 remain to be seen. It is clear that the post-September 11 rollback on civil liberties did not stop at the restrictions placed upon political prisoners and their attorneys. On October 12 Attorney General Ashcroft issued another memorandum, this time urging all federal agencies to resist requests filed pursuant to the Freedom of Information Act seeking information and documents.[†] There was very little media attention given to this maneuver, but the ramifications for the American public were substantial. Daniel J. Metcalfe, co-director of the Justice Department's Office of Information and Privacy, explained that "[t]he Ashcroft memorandum places more emphasis on an agency being careful, on giving full and careful consideration of the interests that are being protected under the FOIA exemptions. That's its primary focus."[‡]

---

[*] The ABA Model Code states that regardless of personal feelings, "a lawyer should not decline representation because a client or cause is unpopular or community action is adverse." *Model Code of Professional Responsibility EC 2-27* (1980).

[†] According to the Department of Justice Office of Information and Privacy, "In replacing the predecessor FOIA memorandum, the Ashcroft FOIA Memorandum establishes a new 'sound legal basis' standard governing the Department of Justice's decisions on whether to defend agency actions under the FOIA when they are challenged in court. This differs from the 'foreseeable harm' standard that was employed under the predecessor memorandum. Under the new standard, agencies should reach the judgment that their use of a FOIA exemption is on sound footing, both factually and legally, whenever they withhold requested information." FOIA Post at www.usdoj.gov/oio/foiapost/2001foiapost19. In Attorney General Ashcroft's words, "[w]hen you carefully consider FOIA requests and decide to withhold records, in whole or in part, you can be assured that the Department of Justice will defend your decisions unless they lack a sound legal basis or present an unwarranted risk of adverse impact on the ability of other agencies to protect other important records." Memorandum for Heads of All Federal Departments and Agencies (Oct. 12, 2001).

[‡] See Ellen Nakashima, "Bush View of Secrecy Is Stirring Frustration; Disclosure Battle United Right and Left," *Wash. Post*, Mar. 3, 2002, at A04.

This is small consolation to most Americans. Because of the Freedom of Information Act, we eventually learned the truth behind the Bay of Pigs invasion, Watergate, Contragate, and so many other questionable government operations. In the years to come, we must rely upon the Freedom of Information Act to ascertain the truth about the government's targeting and persecution of politically unpopular prisoners and their lawyers.

The increasing numbers of FOIA-related lawsuits regarding the withholding of previously available government information testify to the fact that our civil liberties are under attack. In New York and around the country, defense lawyers watch apprehensively as the wheels of "justice" turn slowly over Lynne Stewart and her codefendants. And from California to Massachusetts, from behind prison bars, prisoners are watching to see if the days of confidential communications with their counsel are gone forever.

Who Are the Cuban Five?

National Committee to Free the Cuban Five
2007

The Cuban Five are five Cuban men who are in U.S. prison, serving four life sentences and 75 years collectively, after being wrongly convicted in U.S. federal court in Miami, on June 8, 2001. They are Gerardo Hernández, Ramón Labañino, Antonio Guerrero, Fernando González and René González.

The Five were falsely accused by the U.S. government of committing espionage conspiracy against the United States, and other related charges. But the Five pointed out vigorously in their defense that they were involved in monitoring the actions of Miami-based terrorist groups, in order to prevent terrorist attacks on their country of Cuba. The Five's actions were never directed at the U.S. government. They never harmed anyone nor ever possessed nor used any weapons while in the United States.

For more than 40 years, anti-Cuba terrorist organizations based in Miami have engaged in countless terrorist activities against Cuba, and against anyone who advocates a normalization of relations between the U.S. and Cuba. More than 3,000 Cubans have died as a result of these terrorists' attacks. Terrorist Miami groups like Comandos F4 and Brothers to the Rescue operate with complete impunity from within the United States to attack Cuba—with the knowledge and support of the FBI and CIA.

Therefore, Cuba made the careful and necessary decision to send the Five Cubans to Miami to monitor the terrorists. The Cuban Five infiltrated the terrorist organizations in Miami to inform Cuba of imminent attacks. The aim of such a clandestine operation by the Cuban Five—at great personal risk—was to prevent criminal acts, and thus protect the lives of Cubans and other people.

But instead of arresting the terrorists, the FBI arrested the Cuban Five *anti*terrorists on September 12, 1998. The Five were illegally held in solitary confinement for 17 months in Miami jail. The trial began in November 2000. With the seven-month trial based in Miami, a virtual witchhunt atmosphere existed. Defense attorneys' motions for a change of venue were denied five times by the judge, although it was obvious that a fair trial was impossible in that city. In a blow to justice, the Cuban Five were convicted June 8, 2001 and sentenced to four life terms and 75 years in December, 2001.

This is edited from an article on the National Committee's website, www.freethefive.org, followed by a June 2008 update compiled from various sources.

On August 9, 2005, after seven years of unjust imprisonment, the Cuban Five won an unprecedented victory on appeal. A three-judge panel of the 11th Circuit Court of Appeals overturned the convictions of the Cuban Five and ordered a new trial outside of Miami.

However, in an unexpected reversal on Oct. 31, 2005, the 11th Circuit Court vacated the three-judge panel's ruling and granted an *en banc* hearing before the full panel of 12 judges. Exactly one year after the victory that granted the Five a new trial, in August 2006, the panel voted 10 to 2 to deny the Five heroes a new trial, and instead affirmed the trial court. Nine remaining issues of appeal [remained] before the three-judge panel [including the trial judge's rulings on the suppression of evidence from searches conducted under the Foreign Intelligence Surveillance Act, flawed discovery procedures and jury selection, prosecutorial and witness misconduct, jury instructions, sufficiency of the evidence to support their convictions, and sentencing flaws].

This case is a political case and the Cuban Five are political prisoners. Their freedom will depend not only on the arduous work of the defense team but just as importantly on the public support that can be organized. Over 250 committees have been established in the United States and around the world, demanding immediate freedom for Gerardo, Ramón, Antonio, Fernando and René.

Important declarations have been made by hundreds of parliamentarians in Britain, Italy, and the European and Latin American Parliaments. The U.N. Working Group on Arbitrary Detentions, with five judges, ruled that there were irregularities in the Five's trial and arrest, effectively denying them a fair trial and calls on the U.S. government to remedy this injustice.

In the United States, the National Committee to Free the Cuban Five is working very hard to build broad support for these antiterrorist heroes, with forums and video showings, media and publicity work, and a march that was held on Sept. 23, 2006 in front of the White House.

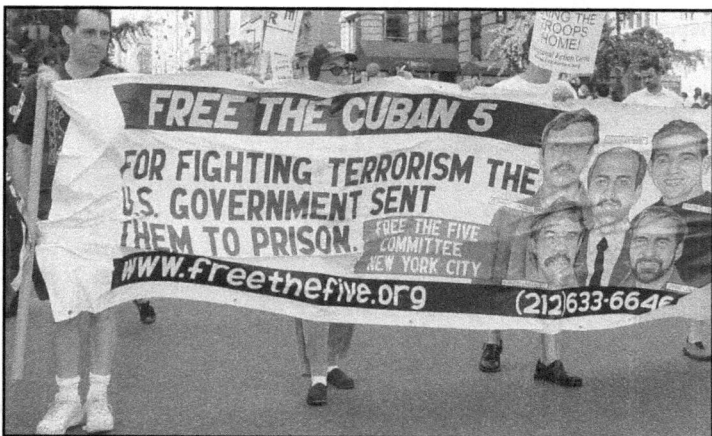

Case of Cuban Five Takes Stage in Nairobi

NAIROBI, JAN. 23—The case of the imprisoned Cuban Five, which has held space for eight years in World Social Forums, was again defended Wednesday by solidarity organizations at the seventh World Social Forum (WSF) in Nairobi, Kenya.

Organizations in favor of freeing the five antiterrorists made a call to other progressives to join the fight for their release, and denounced the treatment Washington gives the topic.

At the initiative of the Kenya-Cuba Friendship Association, an activity was held to denounce the terrorist acts against the Cuban people and their leaders, as well as to obtain support for release of the Cuban Five.

Antonio Guerrero, Fernando González, Gerardo Hernández, Ramón Labañino and René González were sentenced to long terms in prison for fighting terrorism.

Kenyan Pro-Liberation Committee chairman Rajan highlighted that his organization held several press conferences, meetings, and festivals with Cuban music and films before the WSF in order to sensitize local public.

World Forum Supports Cuban 5

NAIROBI, JAN. 25—The Cuban crusade for the release of five Cuban antiterrorist fighters imprisoned in the U.S. over eight years ago was openly backed by the 7th World Social Forum (WSF), concluding in this capital Thursday.

The support was revealed in a proposal presented by Cubans Lourdes Cervantes and Jose Miguel Hernandez, as one of the 21 issues of the meeting.

Cervantes, an official from the Organization of Solidarity with the Peoples of Africa, Asia and Latin America, told *Prensa Latina* that the motion was entitled "Release for the five Cubans imprisoned in the United States." That was part of the map of proposals and actions by participants in the 7th WSF, stated Cervantes.

The Five, as Antonio Guerrero, Fernando González, Gerardo Hernández, Ramón Labañino and René González are universally known, are serving harsh sentences for defending their country from violent actions by anti-Cuban groups settled in that northern nation.

Prensa Latina is the official Cuban international press agency, which maintains a large English-language section, including a webpage with in-depth coverage of the Cuban Five case (www.antiterroristas.cu). These two articles are reprinted from dispatches dated January 23 and January 25, 2007 editions respectively. They are merely a tiny sample of the vast international campaign that has won broad support for the freedom of the Cuban Five.

X.5.A

Response to Court Ruling on Cuban Five Appeal

International Committee for the Freedom of the Cuban Five
2008

On Wednesday June 4, 2008, the 11th U.S. Circuit Court of Appeals announced its ruling in the appeal case for the Cuban Five. In the 99-page opinion, the three-judge panel unanimously upheld the convictions against the Five Cuban Patriots. The court also upheld the sentences given to René González (15 years) and Gerardo Hernández (two life sentences plus 15 years).

The court's ruling on Gerardo's sentence, however, was not unanimous: 2 to 1. On page 16 of the written opinion, Judge Phyllis Kravitch states that the government did not present sufficient evidence to convict Gerardo of conspiracy to commit murder.

The sentences of Ramón Labañino (life plus 18 years); Fernando González (19 years) and Antonio Guerrero (life plus 10 years) were returned to Judge Joan Lenard's Florida court for re-sentencing. Lenard will need to call for a hearing to issue the new ruling—this is the same judge who imposed the excessive and unjust sentences in 2001.

The Atlanta Appeals Court's written opinion, which employs startling political rhetoric, states that the defense's arguments lacked merit and clearly favors the government. The court's ruling exposes various contradictions between the opinions of two of the justices and the author of the opinion, Judge William H. Pryor, an ultraconservative appointed to the bench with the help of Republican John McCain despite opposition from the Senate.

The defense attorneys, Weinglass, McKenna and Horowitz, ensured they will continue the legal battle that began in December 2001 when they were unjustly sentenced. There are still some legal avenues open.

Given the United States government's legal ploys to expand the sentences of our Five Brothers, we are not surprised by the judicial ruling. On the contrary, it reaffirms our need to continue fighting tirelessly to denounce this colossal injustice.

Exposed once again is the contempt of the United States government, which yesterday, in another U.S. city, defended the criminal Luis Posada Carriles [the CIA counterrevolutionary terrorist who, according to FBI evidence, planned from Venezuela the bombing of a Cuban airline in 1976, killing 73 civilians, and has been linked to 1997 hotel bombings in Cuba]. A man who, rather than fittingly declaring him a terrorist for his crimes against humanity and

---

This statement by the Cuba-based International Committee is reprinted from *Daily Granma*, the Cuban Communist Party newspaper, of June 5, 2008. In the days that followed, protest demonstrations were held in 11 U.S. cities, as well as in Canada, Argentina, Peru, Britain, Scotland, Spain, Belgium, Ukraine, and New Zealand.

extraditing him to Venezuela where the government has declared Carriles a fugitive and repeatedly demanded his extradition, the U.S. government has granted him full liberty.

Gerardo is not surprised by the ruling. "This is the same system that has unjustly incarcerated Mumia for more than 20 years along with Leonard Peltier and the Puerto Rican political prisoners," he said today. "We will endure as many years as necessary, 30, 40, whatever it takes. As long as one of you is resisting, we will also resist until there is justice." Gerardo has asked that we communicate his confidence to all of you, "For anyone who asks, tell them I am fine, strong and always looking forward."

Along with all of our friends around the world we call for mobilizations beginning on the morning of June 6, in front of all headquarters of the terrorist U.S. government —in Europe, Latin America and the U.S.—which holds our Five Brothers imprisoned.

Only solidarity, constant condemnation and international mobilization will secure freedom for the Five.

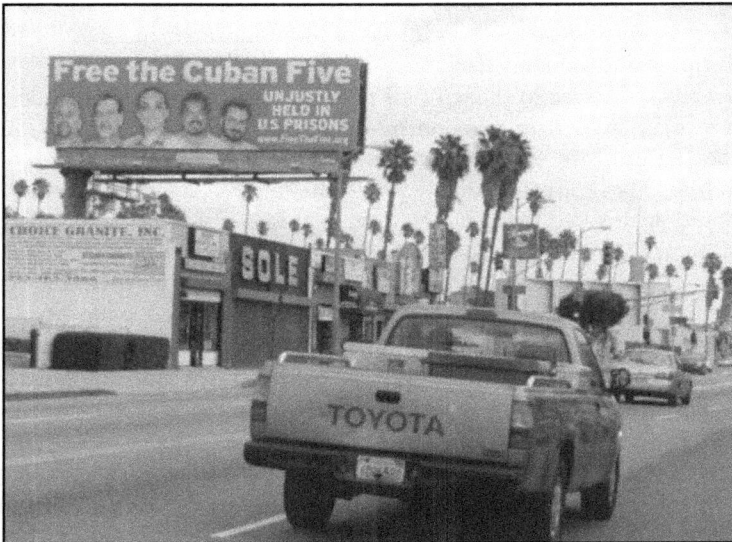

X.5.B

Nobel Prize Winners and World Intellectuals
Sign New Call for the Release of the Five

Granma Internacional
2007

The Cuban chapter of the Defense of Humanity Network announced in Havana a new call for the release of the five antiterrorist Cubans incarcerated for nine years with heavy sentences hanging over them.

Poet and novelist Roberto Fernández Retamar, president of *Casa de las Américas,* presented the document to the national and foreign press. It has already been signed by more than 245 public figures, including Nobel Literature Prize winners Wole Soyinka of Nigeria and Nadine Gordimer of South Africa; Nobel Peace Prize winner Adolfo Pérez Esquivel of Argentina; and Nobel Physics Prize winner Zhores Alfiorov of Russia; as well as artists and intellectuals, including 20 who are outstanding in U.S. political and cultural life.

"The Five," states the document, "have remained isolated in maximum security prisons under cruel conditions of imprisonment, in violation of their human rights and U.S. law itself."

"We add our voices to those of all people in the world who are demanding an immediate end to this enormous injustice. We must not give up our undertaking until the truth is heard and these men return to their country and their families," it concludes.

It should be recalled that a panel of three judges from the Court of Appeals in Atlanta unanimously declared invalid the rigged trial to which they were subjected in Miami and stated that the sentences should be revoked.

Subsequently that ruling was overturned in a divided vote by the full Court, and the result of the appeal on that decision is awaited.

The detention of the Five, who helped to monitor acts of terrorism organized against Cuba by ultra-right Cuban groups in Florida, was described as unjust by the U.N. Working Group on Arbitrary Detention.

Relatives of the Five present at the meeting urged the international press to circulate the call. Maria Eugenia, the sister of Antonio Guerrero, affirmed that the wall of silence surrounding them is an additional sentence.

Granma Internacional is the weekly edition of the daily *Granma* newspaper, published in English, French, Portuguese, German and Italian. The English-language website is www.granma.cu/ingles. This article appeared in the October 13, 2007 edition.

X.5.C

Freedom for the Five Cubans Imprisoned in the United States!

2007

For more than nine years now, five Cubans have remained imprisoned in the United States. On their shoulders rest lengthy convictions, resulting from a politicized trial held in the city of Miami. The Five were helping monitor the terrorist plans orchestrated against Cuba from Florida by far right-wing Cuban groups.

The Working Group on Arbitrary Detentions, attached to the U.N.'s former Commission on Human Rights, declared their detention to be arbitrary, and a three-judge panel, tasked with examining the case at the Atlanta Appeals Court, unanimously agreed to nullify the trial and instructed that the sentences delivered in Miami be repealed. Afterwards, in a split vote, the Court dismissed that decision; and the case is still going through the appeal process.

The Five have remained in isolation in maximum security prisons, under ruthless conditions of seclusion, in violation of their human rights and of the very laws of the United States. Two of them have been deprived of the right to be visited by their wives.

We join our voices to all those in the world that call for the immediate end to this enormous injustice. We must not give up on this endeavor until truth prevails and these men return to their homeland and to their families.

Initial signatures (partial list):

Mumia Abu-Jamal, U.S.;
Zhores Alfiorov, Russia;
Tariq Ali, Pakistan;
Alicia Alonso, Cuba;
Medea Benjamín, U.S.;
Roy Brown, Puerto Rico;
Rafael Cancel Miranda, Puerto Rico;
Manu Chao, France;
Noam Chomsky, U.S.;
Ramsey Clark, U.S.;
Miguel D'Escoto, Nicaragua;
James Early, U.S.;
Roberto Fernández Retamar, Cuba;
Danny Glover, U.S.;
Nadine Gordimer, South Africa;

Eduardo Galeano, Uruguay;
Marta Harnecker, Chile;
Gloria La Riva, U.S.;
Juan Mari Bras, Puerto Rico;
Istvan Meszaros, Hungary/
United Kingdom;
Danielle Mitterrand, France;
Evo Morales, Bolivia;
Adolfo Pérez Esquivel, Argentina;
Silvio Rodríguez, Cuba;
Cindy Sheehan, U.S.;
Wole Soyinka, Nigeria;
Alice Walker, U.S.;
Lucius Walker, Jr., U.S.;
Howard Zinn, U.S.

The Green Scare and Eco-prisoners: A Brief Synopsis

Brendan Story and Margie Lincita
2008

The future of life on Earth is in danger. Human activities, including industrial development and the consequences thereof, have already driven countless species to extinction. Tragic destruction of the ecological balance and sustainable indigenous cultures is found all over the globe, and the process is only accelerating. This increasingly dire ecological crisis became more apparent, to people both in the U.S. and around the world, as global capitalism and industrialization continued to advance and expand into the 1980s and 1990s. This realization, coupled with the growing awareness of violence and torture perpetuated against animals in captivity, gave rise to increased political activity in the United States. As aboveground political action increased, but continued to fail to stop the dangers and consequences of increasing ecological destruction and cruelty, an underground movement developed to sabotage the businesses and industries perpetuating the issues.

For decades, the Earth Liberation Front (ELF) and the Animal Liberation Front (ALF) have employed tactics, including liberations, property destruction, and arson, to seriously disrupt businesses engaged in the decimation of ancient forests, habitat infringements, and genetic engineering as well as animal testing and captivity. The ALF and ELF were founded in '76 and '92, respectively. The ELF guidelines define the actions as economic sabotage to educate the public, while taking "all necessary precautions against harming any animal, human and nonhuman."[*] This organizing strategy, common to both the ALF and the ELF, codifies an anarchist ethic: the name provides only a framework for conducting actions, rather than constituting a formal clandestine organization. Any act consistent with the guidelines can be claimed in the name of the ALF or the ELF. The similar guidelines and complementary politics have led to several acts of arson and vandalism being claimed as joint ALF/ELF attacks.

The decentralized nature of ALF and ELF structure brought about a new response from the aboveground: the formation of "press offices." Serving in these self-appointed roles, public activists with no connection to the underground publicize, contextualize, and vocally support the clandestine work. While underground groups have always publicized their actions, and aboveground supporters have amplified their publicity, the respective ALF and ELF press offices have formalized this process through established representa-

---

[*] See www.satyamag.com/mar04/elf.html

tives. As a result, these activists have found themselves facing repression in the form of routine police raids on their homes, surveillance, and being subpoenaed to testify in front of grand juries.

Government Repression: The "Eco-terrorism" Label and the Green Scare
Predictably, companies that profit from ecological destruction and animal cruelty, along with the legislators they support, have been a powerful influence on the U.S. government, particularly in the Pacific Northwest. Especially noteworthy is the development of legislation meant to empower the FBI, as well as the judicial system, to deliver harsh retribution on the radical environmental and animal rights movements. As the confrontation between radical environmentalists and timber companies over old-growth logging intensified in the Pacific Northwest through the 1980s and 1990s, a new threat to national security emerged: "eco-terrorism." Executive vice-president of the Center for the Defense of Free Enterprise and author of *EcoTerror* Ron Arnold claims he coined the term "eco-terrorism" in 1982.* In 1990, Rep. Denny Smith (R-OR) deployed the term in a stage-managed White House meeting to lobby against stricter environmental legislation in the Pacific Northwest. Industry advocates and critics of the environmental movement clamored not only for the imprisonment of activists carrying out these actions but also for an aggressive campaign of disruption and repression to eradicate movements and intimidate those who might be inspired by their legacy. Ron Arnold was quoted in a 1991 article saying, "Our goal is to destroy, to eradicate the environmental movement. ... We're mad as hell. We're not going to take it anymore. We're dead serious— we're going to destroy them." By May 2001, then-FBI director Louis Freeh told Congress that the ELF and the ALF represented "the most active extremist elements in the United States." With CIA director George Tenet sitting by his side, Freeh noted that "some special interest extremists, most notably within the animal rights and environmental movements" were turning "increasingly toward vandalism and terrorist activity in attempts to further their causes."†

Industries and government agencies incensed by radical activity, gained great momentum soon after the Al-Qaeda terrorist attacks of September 11, 2001. Ramifications of this attack on U.S. state and economic power included a huge shift in the political climate of the United States, which enabled legislation granting the FBI and local law enforcement generous funding and liberties in combating "terrorism." The Earth and Animal Liberation Movements, despite their activity having virtually nothing in common with the events of September 11, were included in the targets. Simultaneously, similar U.S. government offensives were launched against the legacy of the Black Liberation Movement and the Puerto Rican Independence Movement, as well as the rights of immigrants and the right to dissent and speak freely in America. In 2005, FBI deputy assistant director John Lewis would tell Congress that "the

---

* See www.indypendent.org/2007/10/05/1299
† See www.fbi.gov/congress/congress01/freeh051001.htm

693

No. 1 domestic terrorism threat [in the United States] is the eco-terrorism, animal-rights movement."*

The "Green Scare" is a term popularized by environmental activists to refer to the ongoing period of backlash and repression on the part of the U.S. government against the radical earth and animal liberation movements. The spring 2002 edition of the prisoner support newsletter, *Spirit of Freedom*, defined the term as "the tactics that the U.S. government and all their ten-tacles (FBI, IRS, BATF, Joint Terrorism Task Force, local police, the court system) are using to attack the ELF/ALF and specifically those who publicly support them." The term alludes to a similarity between the government's recent response to these movements and their response in the Red Scares of the early half of the 20th century, which were periods of backlash and repression of communist, anarchist, labor, and class-struggle agitation in U.S. society. Movements targeted by the Green Scare include Earth Liberation, Animal Liberation, and Green Anarchism, as well as the campaign against Huntingdon Life Sciences' use of animal testing.

The Initial Cases
In September 1998, a federal grand jury indicted Peter Young and Justin Samuel each on four charges of "Extortion by Interfering with Interstate Commerce" and two charges of "Animal Enterprise Terrorism." While Samuel was arrested and agreed to cooperate with the government by implicating Young in exchange for a reduced sentence in 1999, it was not until March of 2005 that Young was apprehended. Many of his initial charges (that would have warranted an 82-year sentence) were dropped, and he pleaded guilty to "conspiracy to release mink from 6 fur farms in South Dakota, Wisconsin, and Iowa; and the actual release of 2,400 mink from a farm in Wisconsin."† He was sentenced to two years in federal prison; 360 hours of community service at a charity "to benefit humans and no other species"; $254,000 in restitution; and one-year probation. He was released from prison on February 1, 2007. Noteworthy aspects of this case are the use of the Animal Enterprise Terrorism Act and the pressure exerted on Young to provide information about people he knew (not just about other underground actions).

In June 2001, 23-year-old forest defense activist Jeffrey "Free" Luers was convicted by a judge (rather than a jury) and sentenced to 22 years and 8 months for the burning of three Sport Utility Vehicles (SUV's) at a dealer-ship in Eugene, Oregon, and another attempted arson at Tyree Oil. Luers and his codefendant in the SUV arson case, Craig "Critter" Marshall, had done the arson to raise awareness about global warming and the role that SUV's play in that process. An arson specialist at trial confirmed that the action did not pose any threat to people based on its size and distance from any fuel source;

---
* See www.fbi.gov/congress/congress05/lewis051805.htm
†"Animal activist to plead guilty and serve two years", Associated Press, August 31, 2005.

however, Luers's sentence was considerably longer than those convicted of murder, kidnapping, and rape in Oregon. Marshall was also convicted and sentenced to four and a half years due to a noncooperating plea deal that was never offered to Luers because of his involvement in the attempted arson at Tyree Oil. On February 28, 2008, Luers received his long-awaited, appealed sentence of 10 years and could be released in December of 2009.

Grant Barnes was arrested in March of 2006 and pleaded guilty to one count of using an incendiary device and one count of second-degree arson for firebombing SUV's in the Denver area. He is now serving a 12-year sentence.

Operation Backfire
On December 7, 2005, federal and local law enforcement began the largest roundup of environmental and animal liberation activists in American history. That day, the FBI arrested six people in four different states and issued grand jury subpoenas to several others. Over the next few months, the number of arrests, indictments, and subpoenas would mount in what the government called "Operation Backfire." On January 20, 2006, Attorney General Alberto R. Gonzales, with FBI Director Robert S. Mueller III announced a sweeping 65-count indictment, including two conspiracy charges, against 11 individuals relating to 17 different incidents in Oregon, Washington, Wyoming, Colorado, and California. The indictment charged various defendants in Oregon and Washington with arson, attempted arson, and using and carrying a destructive device. The destructive device charge carries a 30-year mandatory sentence, with a mandatory life sentence for a second conviction of this charge. The government used this charge, and the conspiracy charge, to coerce individuals to become informants by threatening them with multiple life sentences for acts of property destruction that caused no injuries. Nine dishonorable people sided with the government and cooperated in the prosecution of others, and four people who were indicted have yet to be arrested and are considered fugitives. Bill Rodgers committed suicide in his jail cell on Winter Solstice 2005.

Political prisoners who took noncooperating plea deals in the Oregon case are Nathan "Exile" Block, Daniel McGowan, Jonathan Paul, and Joyanna "Sadie" Zacher. Despite the strong arguments of defense lawyers, Judge Ann Aiken ruled on May 21, 2007, that the terrorism enhancement was applicable in each case except for Paul's and that a federal crime of terrorism does not require a substantial risk of injury, gravely expanding the existing scope of this terrorist label.

In Washington on March 6, 2008, a federal jury found Briana Waters guilty of two counts of arson relating to ELF actions that took place in 2001. Waters is a mother and known for directing a documentary in 2001 entitled *Watch,* which tells the story of a peaceful campaign that built a coalition between environmentalists, loggers, and the residents of Randle, Washington, to save the old-growth forest on Watch Mountain. She maintains her innocence; sen-

695

tencing had been been postponed indefinitely because of concerns over the credibility of one of the cooperating witnesses (Jennifer Kolar). She faced a mandatory five-year minimum prison term, subject to an enhancement of up to 20 years, and was sentenced to six years.

Civil Liberties at Stake
In a case against free speech and association with a campaign against animal testing, the Stop Huntington Animal Cruelty (SHAC) 7 were found guilty of multiple federal felonies on March 2, 2006, for advocating the closure of the notorious animal-testing lab Huntingdon Life Sciences. Political prisoners include Jacob Conroy, Darius Fullmer (released 2007), Lauren Gazzola, Joshua Harper, Kevin Kjonaas, and Andrew Stepanian. All of the defendants were charged with conspiracy to violate the Animal Enterprise Protection Act, a never-before-applied 1992 statute. Kjonaas, Gazzola, Conroy, and Harper were also charged with conspiracy to harass using a telecommunications device (sending black faxes). Kjonaas, Gazzola, Conroy, and SHAC USA were charged with conspiracy to commit interstate stalking and three counts of interstate stalking via the Internet. The defendants are not actually accused of having personally engaged in terrorist or threatening acts. Instead, the government's case centers around the idea that aboveground organizers of a campaign are responsible for any and all acts that anyone engages in while furthering the goals of the organizers. In this case, the claim is that the defendants should be imprisoned because they were alleged to have been connected to the SHAC website or to have known people who were underground activists who took illegal actions against companies with ties to Huntingdon Life Sciences.

Eric McDavid was arrested in Auburn, California, on January 13, 2006, along with Zachary Jenson and Lauren Weiner, and all three were charged with "conspiracy to destroy property by means of fire or explosives." Both Jensen and Weiner testified against McDavid and were promised shorter sentences in return. The government's case against McDavid was largely based on the word of a single FBI informant who was paid over $75,000 to fabricate a crime and implicate a group of activists. The group never made more than vague plans to target anything in particular, but the FBI did provide funds to purchase materials that the group understood would be sufficient to manufacture an explosive device. This case is considered to be an alarming development in the erosion of civil liberties in the Green Scare, as it allows the FBI to use entrapment and the courts to convict on alleged conspiracies for political actions that never actually took place. McDavid was sentenced to 19 years and 7 months and is currently appealing the ruling.

Rod Coronado, a Yaqui Indian eco-anarchist, animal rights activist, and father, was arrested in February of 2006 on a felony charge of demonstrating the use of an incendiary device at a public gathering in San Diego. An advocate and former activist for the ALF and a spokesperson for the ELF, he now supports nonviolent direct action.

Coronado was jailed in 1995 in connection with an ALF arson attack on research facilities at Michigan State University. Some alternative media sources say Coronado was simply exercising his constitutional right to freedom of speech at the event in San Diego when he "responded to a question from an audience member... and explained how he had constructed a nonexplosive, incendiary device out of a plastic jug filled with gasoline to commit a past arson for which he had long since been sentenced and done his time." Coronado pleaded guilty to one count of "distribution of information related to the assembly of explosives and weapons of mass destruction" and is now serving a one-year sentence.

Currently Unfolding

Three concrete trucks owned by Ross Island Sand & Gravel were destroyed by fire in April of 2001. Less than two months later, two Schoppert logging trucks were also destroyed by fire. Jacob Sherman, a 21-year-old university student was subsequently arrested by the FBI and interrogated on four separate occasions. Sherman was under a great deal of FBI pressure. This, in addition to his knowledge of the case of Jeffery "Free" Luers, who received over 22 years for burning three SUV's, led Sherman to name others who had participated in the crimes and later offer the name of an individual whom he said was the mastermind behind these arsons: Tre Arrow. Arrow was a well-known and high-profile environmental activist involved in a number of tree sit campaigns and ran for Congress as a member of the Pacific Green Party, receiving over 15,000 votes. Environmental journalist Tim Ream wrote in reference to Arrow's case, "If you garner increasing popular support, you are a threat to everything the state stands for. You must be stopped." After his indictment was made public, Arrow headed to Canada for asylum. On March 13, 2004, he was arrested in Victoria, B.C., held for being in the country illegally, and awaited a possible extradition to the United States. Arrow was extradited in March of 2008, and his trial is set for July 8. Arrow cites the recent convictions of Eric McDavid and Briana Waters, as well as "the risk of potentially being convicted and spending the rest of my life in prison" as reasons why he decided to accept a noncooperation plea agreement that will see him spend no more than six and a half years in prison, including the time he already spent detained in Canada.

On March 10, 2008, four people were indicted on charges relating to actions claimed by the ELF in Michigan in 1999 and 2000. The charges could result in up to 20 years in prison. Stephanie Fultz, Aren Burthwick, and Frank Ambrose of Detroit and Marie Mason of Cincinnati were each charged with one count of arson and one count of conspiracy to commit arson. Ambrose and Mason were also charged with two additional counts of arson. Almost immediately, Ambrose signed an unconditional plea agreement to fully cooperate with the government in this and any other investigation, in exchange for the dismissal of the three arson charges against him and a reduced sentence. Burthwick and Fultz were released on bail, and Mason is currently under house arrest and awaiting her trial, which is tentatively set for August 12, 2008. Mason is a longtime environmental and social justice activist and mother of two. The Midwest case has several similarities to Operation Backfire: the investigation of an ELF action, the intimidation and persecution of aboveground environmental activists and communities, a clear intention to prosecute the actions as "terrorism," a press conference politicizing the arrests before the national media, and a defendant assisting the government's investigation.

On March 16, 2008, 17-year-old Michael Sykes was arrested for allegedly torching two newly constructed homes in order to call attention to the problem of urban sprawl. Sykes was charged as an adult, has pled not guilty, and may be considering a plea deal. He is being held in Monroe County Jail in lieu of $1 million bond.

While it may be the government's most dramatic and heavy-handed use of repression to date against the countercultural, anarchist milieu that came of age over the past 10 years, the Green Scare is neither something new, nor is it something that has run its course. Rather, it represents the same kind of intimidation, dirty tricks, and political imprisonment that have long been used against liberation movements in the United States, most notably those of Black, Chicano, Puerto Rican, and Indigenous people. Indeed, the experiences of other liberation movements show that the government is easily able and willing to go to great lengths if it feels that becomes necessary in its struggle to maintain its power and prerogatives.

What's new about the Green Scare is the sheer volume of tax-financed legislation, surveillance, grand juries, Joint Terrorism Task Forces, and other mechanisms that have come down quite openly and legally against a marginal community within U.S. borders. Without a threat of popular insurrection that existed during the Red Scares or during the 1960s, the state has nonetheless taken harsh and aggressive action against dissent, and it has done so openly, without needing a secret operation like COINTELPRO. Though this round of activity may have only affected the radical environmental, Earth and Animal Liberation, and anarchist communities directly, the offensive occurred in tandem with similar renewed activity against immigrant communities and against the legacies of Black and Puerto Rican Liberation struggles. All signs indicate that this is not something that has run its course— that without a large and effective showing of unity and solidarity across movements to defend our right to resist and exist, this era of repression will continue to seek out new targets in its endeavor to bury dissent.

Ongoing as it is, the Green Scare serves as a bitter reminder of the relevance of organizing against political repression, COINTELPRO, and its spawn, not simply as a matter of justice to those who struggle today or who struggled yesterday, but also as a matter of protection and security for those who will struggle tomorrow.

Analysis of Green Scare Repression:
For Those Who Came In Late...

CrimethInc. Workers' Collective
2008

At the end of 2005, the FBI opened a new phase of its assault on earth and animal liberation movements with the arrests and indictments of several current and former activists. This offensive, dubbed Operation Backfire, was intended to obtain convictions for many of the unsolved Earth Liberation Front arsons of the preceding 10 years. Of those subpoenaed and charged, eight ultimately cooperated with the government and informed on others in hopes of reduced sentences: Stanislas Meyerhoff, Kevin Tubbs, Chelsea Dawn Gerlach, Suzanne Savoie, Kendall Tankersley, Jennifer Kolar, Lacey Phillabaum, and Darren Thurston. Four held out through a terrifying year, during which it seemed certain they would end up serving decades in prison, until they were able to broker plea deals in which they could claim responsibility for their actions without providing information about others: Daniel McGowan, Jonathan Paul, Exile (aka Nathan Block), and Sadie (aka Joyanna Zacher). Briana Waters is standing trial as this goes to print, while Joseph Dibee, Josephine Overaker, Rebecca Rubin, and Justin Solondz have been charged but not found. One more defendant, William Rodgers (aka Avalon), tragically passed away in an alleged suicide while in custody shortly after his arrest.

The months following the launch of Operation Backfire saw an unprecedented increase in government repression of anarchist environmental activists, which came to be known as the Green Scare. Longtime animal liberation activist Rod Coronado was charged with a felony for answering a question during a speaking appearance and faced potentially decades in prison. Six animal rights activists associated with SHAC, the campaign against animal testing corporation Huntingdon Life Sciences, were sentenced to several years in prison, essentially for running a website. Animal liberationist Peter Young, who had spent seven years on the run from the FBI, had finally been captured and was being threatened with double jeopardy. Tre Arrow, famous for surviving a 100-foot fall when police and loggers forced him out of a forest occupation, was fighting extradition from Canada to the United States to face arson charges. Innumerable people were subpoenaed to grand juries, and

This text first appeared in *Rolling Thunder* #5 Spring 2008; it is available online at http://www.crimethinc.com/texts/rollingthunder/greenscared.php

some did jail time for refusing to cooperate. Perhaps most ominously of all, three young people were set up by an agent provocateur and arrested on conspiracy charges without having actually done anything at all. Two of them, Zachary Jenson and Lauren Weiner, pled guilty and became government informants; the third, Eric McDavid, who has contracted life-threatening health problems as a consequence of being denied vegan food by his jailers, was recently found guilty and awaits sentencing.

This phase of the Green Scare seems to be drawing to a close. Most of those apprehended in Operation Backfire are now serving their sentences. The first of the SHAC defendants has been released from prison. Peter Young has been out of prison for a year and is doing speaking tours. Rod Coronado's trial ended in a deadlock, and he took a plea in return for a short sentence when the government threatened to bring further charges against him. It's been months now since a new high-profile felony case was brought against an environmental activist, though federal agents have been poking around in the Midwest. It's time to begin deriving lessons from the past two years of government repression, to equip the next generation that will take the front lines in the struggle to defend life on earth.

Distinguishing Between Perceived and Real Threats

In some anarchist circles, the initial onset of the Green Scare was met with a panic that rivaled the response to the September 11 attacks. This, of course, was exactly what the government wanted: quite apart from bringing individual activists to "justice," they hoped to intimidate all who see direct action as the most effective means of social change. Rather than aiding the government by making exaggerated assumptions about how dangerous it is to be an anarchist today, we must sort out what these cases show about the current capabilities and limits of government repression.

The purpose of this inquiry is not to advocate or sensationalize any particular tactic or approach. We should be careful not to glorify illegal activity—it's important to note that most of even the staunchest noncooperating defendants have expressed regrets about their choices, though this must be understood in the context of their court cases. At the same time, federal repression affects everyone involved in resistance, not just those who participate in illegal direct action; the Green Scare offers case studies of the situation we are all in, like it or not.

Case Study in Repression: Eugene, Oregon

Operation Backfire took place against a backdrop of government investigation, harassment, and profiling of presumed anarchists in the Pacific Northwest. It is no coincidence that Eugene, Oregon was a major focus of the Operation Backfire cases, as it has been a hotbed of dissent and radicalism over the past decade and a half—although repression and other problems have taken a toll in recent years. We can't offer a definitive analysis of the internal dynamics of the Eugene anarchist community, but we can look at how the authorities went about repressing it.

One useful resource for this inquiry is "Anarchist Direct Actions: A Challenge for Law Enforcement," an article that appeared in *Studies in Conflict & Terrorism* in 2005, authored by Randy Borum of the University of South Florida and Chuck Tilby of the Eugene Police Department. According to Jeff "Free" Luers, Tilby was one of the cops who surveilled Free and his codefendant, Critter, on the night of their arrest in June 2000. Tilby has given presentations on the "criminal anarchist" movement to law enforcement groups and was intimately involved in the Operation Backfire cases, even making statements to the media and providing a quote to the FBI press release at the end of the Oregon federal prosecution.

Surprisingly, the article does not explicitly reference Eugene, Oregon, at all. Besides Tilby's byline at the beginning, there's no indication that the paper was co-written from Eugene. All the same, the article provides several important clues about how the government proceeded against the Oregon defendants and those who were perceived to support them.

The authors centralize the importance of intelligence and informants for repressing criminal "anarchists," while acknowledging the difficulty of obtaining them. In the case of grand jury subpoenas, anarchists regularly fail to comply, and support groups are often set up for those targeted; one of the more recent examples of this was Jeff Hogg, who received a grand jury subpoena while the Backfire prosecutions were under way and was jailed for nearly six months in 2006 as a result. The authors warn that "investigators and law enforcement officers should be cautious during questioning not to divulge more to the subject about the case (via questions), than is learned through their testimony." Indeed, questions asked by grand juries turned up more than once in the pages of the *Earth First! Journal*, which was edited from Eugene for a time. It is extremely important to support those under investigation and keep abreast of investigators' efforts. Some believe that the Backfire investigation only arrived at a position of real strength once such support started to weaken in Oregon.

Regarding infiltration, "Anarchist Direct Actions" advises that:

> Infiltration is made more difficult by the communal nature of the [anarchist] lifestyle (under constant observation and scrutiny) and the extensive knowledge held by many anarchists, which require a considerable amount of study and time to acquire. Other strategies for infiltration have been explored, but so far have not been successful. Discussion of these theories in an open paper is not advisable.

What we know of the early Backfire investigation points to a strategy of generalized monitoring and infiltration. While investigators used increasingly focused tools and strategies as the investigation gained steam—for example, sending "cooperating witnesses" wearing body wires to talk to specific targets—they started out by sifting through a whole demographic of counter-cultural types. Activist and punk houses as well as gathering spots such as bars were placed under surveillance—anarchists who drink should be careful about the way alcohol can loosen lips. Infiltrators and informants targeted not only the most visibly committed anarchists, but also bohemians who inhabited similar cultural and social spheres. Police accumulated tremendous amounts of background information even while failing to penetrate the circles in which direct action was organized. The approximately 30,000 pages of discovery in the Oregon cases contain a vast amount of gossip and background information on quite a few from the Eugene community.

A similar profiling methodology appears to have been used in nearby Portland, Oregon. In March 2001, for example, a large-scale police raid was carried out on a house party attended by Portland punk rockers. The attendees were photographed and questioned about the Earth and Animal Liberation Fronts. Some were arrested and charged with kidnapping and assault on an officer—a standard over-charging which eventually led to plea deals. The defendants from the raid were videotaped at their court appearances by officers later identified as Gang Enforcement Unit members. In the aftermath of this raid, cops routinely harassed punks on the street, demanding to be told whether they were anarchists.

In retrospect, it seems likely that such efforts were not meant simply to intimidate Portland's punks, but to uncover information relevant to the anarchist and ALF/ELF cases of the time.* This may have been a wrong step in the Backfire investigation; right now there's no way to know. We do know, however, that "wide net" approaches by the state can be effective at stifling socially aware subcultures, even when they uncover no real links to radical action. Fortunately, in Portland those affected by the raid came together in response, aiding each other, limiting the damage done, and taking advantage of the situation to draw attention to police activity.

Another point of speculation is the degree to which authorities fostered division and infighting within radical circles in Eugene. This was a common COINTELPRO tactic and is probably still in use. Borum and Tilby hint at this in the final section of their paper, "Law Enforcement Strategies/ Implications":

> Internal conflicts are another major source of vulnerability within the movement. The DoT ["Diversity of Tactics"] debate has already been addressed, but the movement also is struggling with a perceived lack of power among women, and the lack of inclusion of ethnic minorities. This kind of conflict occurred three decades ago within the leftist revolutionary movement in the United States.

---

* For information on this incident in Portland, see Kristian Williams's "The Criminalization of Anarchism, Part Two: Guilt by Association, Questionable Confessions and Mandatory Minimums," reprinted in *Confrontations: Selected Journalism* by Tarantula Publications.

For those familiar with Eugene radical circles, this brings to mind the heated conflicts over gender and feminism within that community. There is no concrete evidence that government operatives were involved in escalating such debates, and we should be careful not to jump to conclusions; such speculation can only assist the state by propagating paranoia. However, law enforcement from local to federal levels must have been aware of the vulnerabilities that opened up when real debates turned to groupthink and factionalism in Eugene. Tilby and his cohorts must have used such insights to their advantage as they devised antianarchist strategies. By the time Operation Backfire grand juries began following up on real leads in Eugene, many who could have come together to oppose them were no longer on speaking terms. While this does not justify the lack of integrity shown by those who assisted grand juries, it does offer some context for why the grand juries weren't resisted more effectively.

Borum and Tilby close their paper by urging investigators to display "patience and persistence"—and indeed, patience and persistence ultimately paid off in Operation Backfire. This is not to lend credibility to the notion that "The FBI always gets their man." The investigation was riddled with errors and missteps; plenty of other actions will never be prosecuted, as the authorities got neither lucky breaks nor useful cooperation. But we must understand that repression, and resistance to it, are both long-term projects, stretching across years and decades.

According to some accounts, one of the most significant leads in Operation Backfire came from a naïve request for police reports at a Eugene police station. According to this version, the police deduced from this request that they should pay attention to Jacob Ferguson; Ferguson later became the major informant in these cases. It is less frequently mentioned that the police were accusing Ferguson of an arson he did not participate in! With Ferguson, the unlikely happened and it paid off for the authorities to be wrong. Later on, when agents made their first arrests and presented grand jury subpoenas on December 7, 2005, two of those subpoenaed were wrongly assumed to have been involved in attacks. Their subpoenas were eventually dropped, as the authorities gained the cooperation of more informants and eventually made moves to arrest Exile and Sadie instead.

The investigation was not as unstoppable and dynamic as the government would like us to think, although the prosecution gathered force as more individuals rolled on others. The authorities spent years stumbling around, and they continued to falter even when prosecution efforts were under way—but they were tenacious and kept at their efforts. Meanwhile, radical momentum was less consistent.

Let's review the arc of radical activity in Eugene over the past decade. The anticapitalist riot of June 18, 1999 in Eugene led to jubilation on the part of anarchists, even if one participant spent seven years in prison as a result. The participants in the June 18 Day of Action had put up a fight and fucked up some symbols of misery in the town, catching the police unprepared. The pitched battles on the streets of Seattle later that year at the WTO meeting only reinforced the feeling that the whole world was up for grabs. Most of the active anarchists in Eugene had never lived through such a period before. Despite the paltry demands and muddled analysis of much of the official "antiglobalization" movement, there was a sense that deeper change could be fought for and won. Being an anarchist seemed like the coolest thing you could be, and this perception was magnified by the media attention that followed. The ELF was setting fires all over the region at the time.

A series of reversals followed. In June 2001, Free received his initial sentence of 22 years and eight months. The following month, Carlo Giuliani was murdered on the streets of Genoa during protests against the G8 summit in Italy. While both of these tragedies illustrated the risks of confronting the capitalist system, Free's sentence hit home especially hard in Eugene. In the changed atmosphere, some began dropping away and "getting on with their lives"—not necessarily betraying their earlier principles, but shifting their focus and priorities. This attrition intensified when American flags appeared everywhere in the aftermath of September 11, 2001. Anarchist efforts did not cease, but a period of relative disorientation followed. A year and a half later, the invasion of Iraq provided another opportunity for radicals to mobilize, but some consistency had been lost in the Eugene area. And all the while, FBI employees and police kept their regular hours, day in and day out.

Law enforcement received its most significant breakthrough in the Backfire cases—even though it started as an incorrect hypothesis—just before Free's sentencing, in the period between anarchist jubilation and the shift to the defensive. The same fires that were incorrectly linked to Ferguson were used to justify Free's stiff sentence, which intimidated some anarchists out of action. There was not enough reevaluation, learning, and sharpening of skills, nor enough efforts at conflict resolution; the retreat occurred by default. What would have happened if the Backfire investigation had continued under different circumstances, while radicals maintained their momentum? That would be another story. Its conclusion is unknown.

Putting Up a Fight

Repression will exist as long as there are states and people who oppose them. Complete invulnerability is impossible, for governments as well as their opponents. All the infiltrators and informants of the Tsarist secret police were powerless to prevent the Russian revolution of 1917, just as the East German *Stasi* were unable to prevent the fall of the Berlin Wall even though they had files on six million people. Revolutionary struggles can succeed even in the face of massive repression; for our part, we can minimize the effects of that repression by preparing in advance.

For many years now, anarchists have focused on developing security culture, but security consciousness alone is not enough. There are some points one can never emphasize too much—don't gossip about sensitive matters, share delicate information on a need-to-know basis,* don't surrender your rights if detained or arrested, don't cooperate with grand juries, don't sell other people out. But one can abide by all these dictums and still make crucial mistakes. If antirepression strategies center only on what we should not talk about, we lose sight of the necessity of clear communication for communities in struggle.

State disruption of radical movements can be interpreted as a kind of "armed critique," in the way that someone throwing a brick through a Starbucks window is a critique in action. That is to say, a successful use of force against us demonstrates that we had pre-existing vulnerabilities. This is not to argue that we should blame the victim in situations of repression, but we need to learn how and why efforts to destabilize our activities succeed. Our response should not start with jail support once someone has been arrested. Of course this is important, along with longer-term support of those serving sentences—but our efforts must begin long before, countering the small vulnerabilities that our enemy can exploit. Open discussion of problems—for example, gender roles being imposed in nominally radical spaces—can protect against unhealthy resentments and schisms. This is not to say that every split is unwarranted—sometimes the best thing is for people to go their separate ways—but that even if that is necessary, they should try to maintain mutual respect or at least a willingness to communicate when it counts.

Risk is relative. In some cases, it may indeed be a good idea to lay low; in other cases, maintaining public visibility is viewed as too risky, when in fact nothing could be more dangerous than withdrawing from the public eye and letting momentum die. When we think about risk, we often picture security cameras and prison cells, but there are many, more insidious threats. The Operation Backfire defendants ended up with much shorter sentences than expected; as it turned out, the most serious risk they faced was not prison time, after all, but recantation and betrayal—a risk that proved all too real. Likewise, we can imagine Eric McDavid, who currently awaits sentencing on conspiracy charges, idly discussing the risk factor of a hypothetical action with his supposed friends—who turned out to be two potential informants and a federal agent provocateur. Unfortunately, the really risky thing was having those discussions with those people in the first place.

Preparing for the Worst
Conventional activist wisdom dictates that one must not mix public and clandestine activity, but Daniel McGowan's case seems to contradict this.

---

* It does appear that Operation Backfire defendants could have done better at limiting the flow of information inside their circles. Rather than organizing in closed, consistent cells, the defendants seem to have worked in more fluid arrangements, with enough crossover that once a few key participants turned informant the government had information about everyone.

McGowan was not brought to trial as a result of investigations based on his public organizing, but rather because he had worked with Jacob Ferguson, who turned snitch under police pressure. Though the government was especially eager to convict him on account of his extensive prisoner support work and organizing against the Republican National Convention, McGowan received tremendous public support precisely because he had been so visible.* Had he simply hidden in obscurity, he might have ended up in the same situation without the support that enabled him to weather it as successfully as he did—and without making as many important contributions to the anarchist movement.

Considering how many years it took the FBI to put together Operation Backfire and the prominent role of informants in so many Green Scare cases, it seems like it is possible to get away with a lot, provided you are careful and make intelligent decisions about who to trust. McGowan's direct action resumé, as it appears in the government arguments at his sentencing, reads like something out of an adventure novel. One can't help but think—just seven years, for all that!

The other side of this coin is that, despite all their precautions, the Green Scare defendants did get caught. No matter how careful and intelligent you are, it doesn't pay to count on not getting caught; you have to be prepared for the worst. Those who are considering risky direct action should start from the assumption that they will be caught and prosecuted; before doing anything, before even talking about it, they should ask themselves whether they could accept the worst possible consequences. At the same time, as the government may target anyone at any time regardless of what they have actually done, it is important for even the most law-abiding activists—not to mention their friends and relatives—to think through how to handle being investigated, subpoenaed, or charged.

The Green Scare cases show that cooperating with the government is never in a defendant's best interest. On average, the noncooperating defendants in Operation Backfire are actually serving less time in proportion to their original threatened sentences than the informants, despite the government engaging the entire repressive apparatus of the United States to make an example of them. Exile and Sadie were threatened with over a thousand years in prison apiece and are serving less than eight; if every arrestee understood the differ-

---

* This is not to say that all visibility is good visibility. Media attention was a significant factor in the conflicts that wracked Eugene. Such visibility can divide communities from within by creating the appearance that spokespeople have more power than everyone else, which provokes jealousy and stokes ego-driven conflicts whether or not what's on the screen reflects reality on the ground. Those who fall prey to believing the media hype about themselves become dependent upon this attention, pursuing it rather than the unmediated connections and healthy relationships essential for long-term revolutionary struggle; the most valuable visibility is anchored in enduring communities, not media spectacles. There are reasonable arguments for using the media at times, but one must be aware of the danger of being *used by* it.

ence between what the state threatens and what it can actually do, far fewer would give up without a fight.

In the United States legal system, a court case is essentially a game of chicken. The state starts by threatening the worst penalties it possibly can, in hope of intimidating the defendant into pleading guilty and informing. It is easier if the defendant pleads guilty immediately; this saves the state immense quantities of time and money, not to mention the potential embarrassment of losing a well-publicized trial. Defendants should not be intimidated by the initial charges brought against them; it often turns out that many of these will not hold up and are only being pressed to give the state more bargaining power. Even if a defendant fears he won't have a leg to stand on in court, he can obtain some bargaining power of his own by threatening to put the state through a costly, challenging, and unpredictable trial—to that end, it is essential to acquire the best possible legal representation. When a defendant agrees to cooperate, he loses all that leverage, throwing himself at the mercy of forces that don't have an ounce of mercy to offer.

As grim as things looked for Sadie, Exile, McGowan, and Jonathan Paul through most of 2006, they looked up when McGowan's lawyer demanded information about whether prosecutors had used illegal National Security Agency wiretaps to gather evidence against the defendants. The government was loath to answer this question, and for good reason: there had just been a public scandal about NSA wiretaps, and if the court found that wiretaps had been used unconstitutionally, the entire Operation Backfire case would have been thrown out. That's exactly why so many members of the Weather Underground are professors today rather than convicts: the FBI botched that case so badly, the courts had to let them go free.

No matter how hopeless things look, never underestimate the power of fighting it out. Until Stanislas Meyerhoff and others capitulated, the linch-pin of the federal case in Operation Backfire was Jacob Ferguson, a heroin addict and serial arsonist. Had all besides Ferguson refused to cooperate and instead fought the charges together, Operation Backfire would surely have ended differently.

On Informants

If becoming an informant is always a bad idea, why do so many people do it? At least eleven high profile defendants in Green Scare cases have chosen to cooperate with the government against their former comrades, not including Peter Young's partner, who informed on him back in 1999. These were all experienced activists who presumably had spent years considering how they would handle the pressure of interrogation and trial, who must have been familiar with all the reasons it doesn't pay to cooperate with the state! What, if anything, can we conclude from how many of them became informants?

There has been quite a bit of opportunist speculation on this subject by pundits with little knowledge of the circumstances and even less personal experience. We are to take it for granted that arrestees became informants because they were privileged middle class kids; in fact, both the cooperating and noncooperating defendants are split along class and gender lines. We are told that defendants snitched because they hadn't been fighting for their own interests; what exactly are one's "own interests," if not to live in a world without slaughterhouses and global warming? Cheaper hamburgers and air conditioning, perhaps? It has even been suggested that it's inevitable some will turn informant under pressure, so we must not blame those who do and instead should avoid using tactics that provoke investigations and interrogations. This last aspersion is not worth dignifying with a response, except to point out that no crime need be committed for the government to initiate investigations and interrogations. Whether or not you support direct action of any kind, it is never acceptable to equip the state to do harm to other human beings.

Experienced radicals who have been snitched on themselves will tell you that there is no surefire formula for determining who will turn informant and who won't. There have been informants in almost every resistance movement in living memory, including the Black Panther Party, the Black Liberation Army, the American Indian Movement, and the Puerto Rican independence movement; the Green Scare cases are not particularly unusual in this regard, though some of the defendants seem to have caved in more swiftly than their antecedents. It may be that the hullabaloo about how many eco-activists have turned informant is partly due to commentators' ignorance of past struggles.

If anything discourages people from informing on each other, it is blood ties. Historically, the movements with the least snitching have been the ones most firmly grounded in longstanding communities. Arrestees in the national liberation movements of yesteryear didn't cooperate because they wouldn't be able to face their parents or children again if they did; likewise, when gangsters involved in illegal capitalist activity refuse to inform, it is because doing so would affect the entirety of their lives, from their prospects in their chosen careers to their social standing in prison as well as their neighborhoods. The stronger the ties that bind an individual to a community, the less likely it is he or she will inform against it. North American radicals from predominantly white demographics have always faced a difficult challenge in this regard, as most of the participants are involved in defiance of their families and social circles rather than because of them. When an ex-activist is facing potentially decades in prison for something that was essentially a hobby, with his parents begging him not to throw his life away and the system he fought against apparently dominating the entirety of his present and future, it takes a powerful sense of right and wrong to resist selling out.

In this light, it isn't surprising that the one common thread that links the noncooperating defendants is that practically all of them were still involved in either anarchist or at least countercultural communities. Daniel McGowan was ceaselessly active in many kinds of organizing right up to his arrest; Exile and Sadie were still committed to life against the grain, if not political activity—a witness who attended their sentencing described their supporters as an otherworldly troop of black metal fans with braided beards and facial piercings. Here we see again the necessity of forging powerful, long-term communities with a shared culture of resistance; dropouts must do this from scratch, swimming against the tide, but it is not impossible.

Healthy relationships are the backbone of such communities, not to mention secure direct action organizing. Again—unaddressed conflicts and resentments, unbalanced power dynamics, and lack of trust have been the Achilles heel of countless groups. The FBI keeps psychological profiles on its targets, with which to prey on their weaknesses and exploit potential interpersonal fissures. The oldest trick in the book is to tell arrestees that their comrades already snitched on them; to weather this intimidation, people must have no doubts about their comrades' reliability.

"Snitches get stitches" posters notwithstanding, anarchists aren't situated to enforce a no-informing code by violent means. It's doubtful that we could do such a thing without compromising our principles, anyway—when it comes to coercion and fear, the state can always outdo us, and we shouldn't aspire to compete with it. Instead, we should focus on demystifying snitching and building up the collective trust and power that discourage it. If being a part of the anarchist community is rewarding enough, no one will wish to exile themselves from it by turning informant. For this to work, of course, those who do inform on others must be excluded from our communities with absolute finality; in betraying others for personal advantage, they join the ranks of the police officers, prison guards, and executioners they assist.

Those who may participate in direct action together should first take time to get to know each other well, including each other's families and friends, and to talk over their expectations, needs, and goals. You should know someone long enough to know what you like least about him or her before committing to secure activity together; you have to be certain you'll be able to work through the most difficult conflicts and trust them in the most frightening situations up to a full decade later.

Judging from the lessons of the 1970s, drug addiction is another factor that tends to correlate with snitching, as it can be linked to deep-rooted personal problems. Indeed, Jacob Ferguson, the first informant in Operation Backfire, was a longtime heroin addict. Just as the Operation Backfire cases would have been a great deal more difficult for the government if no one besides Jake had cooperated, the FBI might never have been able to initiate the cases at all if others had not trusted Jake in the first place.

Prompt prisoner support is as important as public support for those facing grand juries. As one Green Scare defendant has pointed out, defendants often turn informant soon after arrest when they are off balance and uncertain what lies ahead. Jail is notorious for being a harsher environment than prison; recent arrestees may be asking themselves whether they can handle years of incarceration without a realistic sense of what that would entail. Supporters should bail defendants out of jail as quickly as possible, so they can be informed and level-headed as they make decisions about their defense strategy. To this end, it is ideal if funds are earmarked for legal support long before any arrests occur.

It cannot be emphasized enough that informing is always a serious matter, whether it is a question of a high profile defendant snitching on his comrades or an acquaintance of law-abiding activists answering seemingly harmless questions. The primary goal of the government in any political case is not to put any one defendant in prison but to obtain information with which to map radical communities, with the ultimate goal of repressing and controlling those communities. The first deal the government offered Peter Young was for him to return to animal rights circles to report to them from within: not just on illegal activity, but on all activity. The most minor piece of trivia may serve to jeopardize a person's life, whether or not they have ever broken any law. It is never acceptable to give information about any other person without his or her express consent.

Regaining the Initiative

We must not conceptualize our response to government repression in purely reactive terms. It takes a lot of resources for the government to mount a massive operation like the Green Scare cases, and in doing so they create unforeseen situations and open up new vulnerabilities. Like in Judo, when the state makes a move, we can strike back with a countermove that catches them off balance. To take an example from mass mobilizations, the powers that be were eventually able to cripple the so-called antiglobalization movement by throwing tremendous numbers of police at it; but in the wake of lawsuits subsequently brought against them, the police in places like Washington, DC, now have their hands tied when it comes to crowd control, as demonstrated by their extreme restraint at the IMF/World Bank protests in October 2007. We're in a long war with hierarchical power that cannot be won or lost in any single engagement; the question is always how to make the best of each development, seizing the initiative whenever we can and passing whatever gains we make on to those who will fight after us.

There must be a way to turn the legacy of the Green Scare to our advantage. One starting place is to use it as an opportunity to learn how the state investigates underground activity and make sure those lessons are shared with the next generation. Another is to find common cause with other targeted communities; a promising example of this is the recent connection between animal liberation activists in the Bay Area and supporters of the San Francisco 8, former members and associates of the Black Panther Party who are now being charged with the 1971 murder of a police officer.

Postscript: Cowards...

I find it ironic that you support victimized women, yet in your communiqués you verbally victimize those with whom you disagree. I wonder if you ever called scholars in the Northwest about how to be effective and take positive action. Like the professors who wrote letters to the court on your behalf, most professors are incredibly generous with their ideas. I've learned a lot in my years on the bench... seen it all... it's called the human experience. Take off the masks until the real Daniel McGowan is revealed... be the change you truly want to be. Don't use Gandhi just when it's convenient. I hope you'll go back to your website and tell who you were, what you did. You may not be as popular, but... change your website. Denounce, renounce and condemn. If you really mean it, it shouldn't be hard. To the young people, send the message that violence doesn't work. If you want to make a difference, have the courage to say how the life you lived was the life of a coward.... It is a tragedy to watch these extremely talented and bright young people come in and do damage to industries. It's not okay to put people in fear doing what they need to do to survive. Take off the hoods, sweatshirts, and masks and have a real dialogue.

> Judge Aiken in sentencing Daniel McGowan to
> seven years in prison with a terrorism enhancement[*]

In reflecting on Judge Aiken's sentencing, let us put aside, for the time being, the question of whether executives who profit from logging, animal exploitation, and genetic engineering are "doing what they need to do to survive." Let's allow to pass, as well, the suggestion that those who run these industries are more likely to enter into a "real dialogue" with environmentalists if the latter limit themselves to purely legal activity. Let's even reserve judgment on Aiken's attempt to draw parallels between domestic violence and sarcastically worded communiqués—which parallels the prosecutors' assertion that the ELF, despite having never injured a single human being, is no different from the Ku Klux Klan.

There is but one question we cannot help but ask, in reference to Judge Aiken's rhetoric about cowardice: if she found herself in a situation that called for action to be taken outside the established channels of the legal system, would she be capable of it? Or would she still insist on due process of law, urging others to be patient as human beings were sold into slavery or the Nazis carted people off to Dachau? Is it fair for a person whose complicity in the status quo is rewarded with financial stability and social status to accuse

---

[*] Notes taken by Gumby Cascadia.

someone who has risked everything to abide by his conscience... of coward-ice? Perhaps Aiken would also feel entitled to inform John Brown that he was a coward, or the Germans who attempted to assassinate Hitler?

Once this question is asked, another question inexorably follows: what qualifies as a situation that calls for action to be taken outside the established channels of the legal system, if not the current ecological crisis? Species are going extinct all over the planet, climate change is beginning to wreak seri-ous havoc on human beings as well, and scientists are giving us a very short window of time to turn our act around—while the U.S. government and its corporate puppeteers refuse to make even the insufficient changes called for by liberals. If the dystopian nightmare those scientists predict comes to pass, will the refugees of the future look back at this encounter between McGowan and Aiken and judge McGowan the coward?

We live in a democracy, Aiken and her kind insist: bypassing the estab-lished channels and breaking the law is akin to attacking freedom, commu-nity, and dialogue themselves. That's the same thing they said in 1859.

Those who consider obeying the law more important than abiding by one's conscience always try to frame themselves as the responsible ones, but the essence of that attitude is the desire to evade responsibility. Society, as represented—however badly—by its entrenched institutions, is responsible for decreeing right and wrong; all one must do is brainlessly comply, argu-ing for a change when the results are not to one's taste but never stepping out of line. That is the creed of cowards, if anything is. At the hearing to determine whether the defendants should be sentenced as terrorists, Aiken acknowledged with frustration that she had no control over what the Bureau of Prisons would do with them regardless of her recommendations—but washed her hands of the matter and gave McGowan and others terrorism enhancements anyway. Doubtless, Aiken feels that whatever shortcomings the system has are not her responsibility, even if she participates in forcing them on others. She's just doing her job.

That's the Nuremberg defense. Regardless of what she thinks of McGowan's actions or the Bureau of Prisons, Aiken is personally responsible for send-ing him to prison. She is responsible for separating him from his wife, for preventing him from continuing his work supporting survivors of domestic violence. If he is beaten or raped while in prison, it is the same as if Aiken beat or raped him. And not just McGowan, or Paul, or Sadie or Exile, but every single person Aiken has ever sent to prison.

But Aiken and her kind are responsible for a lot more than this. As the polar icecaps melt, rainforests are reduced to pulp, and climate change inflicts more and more terrible catastrophes around the planet, they are responsible for stopping all who would take direct action to avert these tragedies. They are responsible, in short, for forcing the wholesale destruction of the natural environment upon everyone else on earth.

Aiken might counter that the so-called democratic system is the most effective way to go about halting that destruction. It sure has worked so far, hasn't it! On the contrary, it seems more likely that she cannot bring herself to honestly consider whether there could be a higher good than the maintenance of law and order. For people like her, obedience to the law is more precious than polar icecaps, rainforests, and cities like New Orleans. Any price is worth paying to avoid taking responsibility for their part in determining the fate of the planet. Talk about cowardice.

...and Heroes

So—if McGowan and the other noncooperating Green Scare defendants are not cowards, does that mean they are heroes?

We should be cautious not to unthinkingly adopt the inverse of Aiken's judgment. In presenting the case for the government, Peifer described the Operation Backfire defendants' exploits as "almost like Mission Impossible." It serves the powers that be to present the defendants as superhuman—the more exceptional their deeds seem to be, the further out of reach such deeds will feel to everyone else.

Similarly, lionizing "heroes" can be a way for the rest of us to let ourselves off the hook: as we are obviously not heroes of their caliber, we need not hold ourselves up to the same standards of conduct. It is a disservice to glorify McGowan, Exile, Sadie, Peter Young, and others like them; in choosing anonymous action, they did not set out to be celebrated, but to privately do what they thought was necessary, just as all of us ought to. They are as normal as any of us—any normal person who takes responsibility for his or her actions is capable of tremendous things.

This is not to say we should all become arsonists. There are countless paths available to those who would take responsibility for themselves, and each person must choose the one that is most appropriate to his or her situation. Let the courage of the noncooperating Green Scare defendants, who dared to act on their beliefs and refused to betray those convictions even when threatened with life in prison, serve as reminders of just how much normal people like us can accomplish.

Kamau Sadiki: Injustice Continues...

Safiya Bukhari
2002

Sitting in a cell in the Fulton County Jail in Atlanta, Georgia, under the name of Freddie Hilton is Kamau Sadiki. Kamau is awaiting trial on a 30-year-old murder case. A Fulton County police officer found shot to death in his car outside a service station. A case that they refused to try 30 years ago because they didn't believe they could win it. The question is, "Why him? Why now?"

Kamau Sadiki is a former member of the Black Panther Party. At the age of 17 he dedicated his life to the service of his people. He worked out of the Jamaica office of the Black Panther Party. Having internalized the 10 Point Program and Platform, the 3 Main Rules of Discipline and 8 Points of Attention, Kamau used his knowledge to guide his organizing efforts within the Black Community.

He worked in the Free Breakfast Program, getting up every morning, going to his designated assignment and cooking and feeding hungry children before they went to school. When the Free Breakfast Program was over for the day, he reported to the office, gathered his papers and received his assignment for the day, and went out into the community to sell his papers. While selling his papers, he continued to educate the people, organizing tenants, welfare mothers, whomever he came in contact with. At the end of the day, he reported to the office. He wrote his daily report and attended political education classes.

Kamau Sadiki was one of the thousands of young Black men and women who made up the Black Panther Party. The rank-and-file members of the Party who made the Black Panther Party the international political machine it was. While the media followed Huey Newton, Bobby Seale and others, the day-to-day work of the Party was being carried out by these rank-and-file brothers and sisters, the backbone of the Black Panther Party. They were the

---

This statement was circulated on behalf of the Jericho Movement as part of Safiya's diligent campaign to free Kamau Sadiki. In October 2003, three months after her passing, Kamau was convicted of the 1971 murder of the Fulton County, Georgia, police officer and the next month sentenced to life plus 10 years. In his sentencing statement, Kamau said (in part):"My joining the Black Panther Party and consequently the Black Liberation Army was a response to the oppressive climate that existed in America at the time....Now, do I regret some of the actions and tactics of the BLA? Of course....Because of my change as a human being, I regret the loss of any human life....[But] I maintain my innocence."

nameless and faceless, tireless workers who carried out the programs of the Black Panther Party, without whom there would have been no one to do the work of the Free Health Clinics, Free Clothing Drive, Liberation Schools, and Free Breakfast for Children Program. It was to these brothers and sisters that the people in the Black community looked when they needed help and support.

It was because of this tireless work in the community that J. Edgar Hoover, the then FBI director, declared the Black Panther Party to be the greatest threat to national security and sought to destroy it. It was not because we advocated the use of the gun that made the Black Panther Party the threat. It was because of the politics that guided the gun. We had been taught that politics guide the gun, therefore our politics had to be correct and constantly evolving. We had to study and read the newspapers to keep abreast of the constantly changing political situation. But this was not the image that the government wanted to portray of the Black Panther Party. It preferred the image of the ruthless gangster, [the] racist, gun-toting thug. Every opportunity that came up to talk or write about the Black Panther Party was used to portray this image.

When the opportunity didn't arise on its own, they created situations and circumstances to make the claim. An all-out propaganda war was waged on the Black Panther Party. Simultaneously, a psychological and military campaign was instituted. The government's war of terror against the Black Panther Party saw over 28 young black men and women of the Black Panther Party killed over a period of less than four years, hundreds more in prison or underground, dozens in exile and the Black Panther Party in disarray. Even though the Black Panther Party, as an entity, had been destroyed, the government never ceased observing those Panthers who were still alive. Whether or not others believed it, the government took seriously that aspect of the Black Panther Party's teaching that included the 10-10-10 Program.

If one Panther organized ten people, those ten people organized ten people, and those ten people organized ten people exponentially we would organize the world for revolution. The only way to stop that was to weed out the Panthers. Not only must the Black Panther Party be destroyed, but all the people who were exposed to the teachings must be weeded out and put on ice or destroyed. During this turbulent time, Kamau had been among the members of the Party who had gone underground. He was subsequently captured and spent five years in prison. While he was on parole, he legally changed his name from Fred Hilton to Kamau Sadiki.

About eighteen months ago, a story appeared in the *Daily News* in New York about a former Panther being arrested and charged with child sexual abuse. The newspaper identified the former Panther as Freddie Hilton. The first thing that comes into the minds of most people when such an allegation is read in the newspaper is that it must be true. We, in the Black Panther Party, have been taught from day one the adage, "No investigation, no right to speak." In a case like this, a political case, it's extremely important to get to the bottom of such an allegation as quickly as possible. Part of the pattern of COINTELPRO has been to demonize individuals, destroy their credibility, and discredit their character, thereby making them vulnerable to the enemy because their base of support has been eroded.

It appears that the charge was brought against Kamau by the woman he had been living with for a number of years to get him out of the house. Kamau had been, and still is, very sick and suffering from sarcoidosis, cirrhosis of the liver and hepatitis C. He had been out of work sick for an extended period. Everyone believed he was going to die. However, he didn't die. He went into remission, got better and returned to work. The problem was his woman friend had moved on with her life and wanted him out of the way. She told the police that he had abused her daughter three years earlier. When that didn't stand up to scrutiny, they were told he had a gun in the house and where it could be found and that he was a former Black Panther, etc.

Even though the government did not initiate this arrest, they seized the opportunity, based on today's climate, to get Kamau off the street. A domestic dispute was handled in an incorrect manner and a man's reputation and character have been sullied and destroyed. People are more interested in the fact that this allegation was made than they are about the fact that he is going on trial for the murder of a police officer. Says Kamau, "All I have is my name and my honor. They can't be allowed to take that away from me." The molestation charge was dropped, and Kamau pled guilty to a disorderly conduct charge. While he was serving his sentence, the warrant from Georgia was issued.

The damage had already been done. A seed had been planted in the minds of the people. While the story of the charge being made had appeared in the newspaper, there was no story of the disposition of the case. Kamau Sadiki had never, at any time, molested any child.

While the people who would normally come to his defense were still reeling from these charges and being told not to make a big deal out of it, the state was using this time to put pressure on Kamau. Knowing that he suffers from hepatitis C, cirrhosis of the liver and sarcoidosis, they told him that unless he helped them capture Assata Shakur, he would "die in prison." They told him that if he worked with them and got Assata to leave Cuba and go to some other country where they could apprehend her, they would not prosecute on the police killing. This seemed to be the right time to play this card. So many different forces were congealing in the world that had changed the mood of the country in favor of mania and fear. The conflict in the Middle East had heightened the stakes with 9/11. The PATRIOT Act had been passed, giving new meaning to what it meant to be patriotic and making disagreeing with or not going along with the policies of the government unpatriotic.

Police and other uniformed personnel were heroes/heroines and above the law... untouchables. What would not have been able to be prosecuted thirty years ago was now, in this climate, possible. Then, too, Kamau has not been in the spotlight in the last twenty-five years. What people don't know is, he never was. After being released from prison, he went to work. Having two daughters and himself to support, he went to work. He worked for the telephone company in New York for over eighteen years. Both of his daughters finished college and are now married with families of their own. No, Kamau wasn't out beating the drums; he was being the quiet warrior that he is. He is a Muslim. Another liability in these United States, where the term is almost synonymous to terrorist now.

There are many lies and distortions of the truth that come to play in this case. The most glaring and insidious is that Freddie Hilton had been in hiding under the name Kamau Sadiki and that's why it has taken so long to find and indict him. A bald-faced lie. The entire five years Kamau spent in prison, he wrote and signed all his mail under the name Kamau Sadiki. All of his mail was censored. When he was released from prison, he was on parole and while he was on parole he had his name legally changed to Kamau Sadiki. His parole officer was aware of this. When he went to work, he didn't obtain a new social security number under Kamau Sadiki, but his name was changed on his old card to Kamau Sadiki. There was never an attempt to hide from anything. How could he? One of his daughters was also the daughter of Assata Shakur, and he couldn't hide from that. He was always under the scrutiny of the federal government, if for this reason alone.

Kamau Sadiki did not "come to the attention" of the police because of the molestation charge, but the charge was a convenient way to arrest him and keep him in jail while they attempted to use him. They knew who he was and where he was all the time. What they didn't have was a convenient excuse to arrest him that wouldn't get everyone up in arms. Once in jail, they knew they didn't have a lot of time because the molestation charge would not hold up. So they placed the warrant from Georgia on him to give them additional time to put pressure on him.

New evidence?! No. No new evidence. The same old story from the '70s that was supposedly told to them by Sam Cooper. The same old story that was not enough to indict at the time of the death of the police officer in 1972 is now enough to indict in 2002. Thirty years later, they are able to find independent witnesses to corroborate Sam Cooper's story. It boggles the mind that they have found a way to make memories that usually fade over time, reverse themselves and grow stronger.

We have long held that there is a diabolical scheme going on in the minds of those who run this government. It is not something that started yesterday or the day before. It is not something that will end tomorrow or the day after. This scheme is to rid the world of those who disagree with the politics of the United States. The Black Panther Party was such an entity, and it no longer exists. It was systematically and meticulously destroyed almost thirty years ago. But the effort to destroy the legacy of the Black Panther Party continues.

Books are continually written attacking the Party. Daily, articles still appear in newspapers and periodicals redefining the work of the Black Panther Party. Panthers are still in prison and still going to prison from cases dating back to the '60s and '70s.

The further we get away from the '60s and '70s, the more likely that people will forget what happened and what we were really about. When issues are taken out of their historical place and placed into another day and time, people tend to get confused. The government banks on that. Historically, it has worked for them. In this new day and time. In the shadow of 9/11, in Atlanta, Georgia, one of the greatest historical figures of the Civil Rights/Black Power era was convicted and sent to prison for life without the possibility of parole. The response of the community was, "We told you we were capable of convicting him." This gave impetus to the government's plan to clean up the streets of dissent. In 1967 it was disclosed that one of the goals of COINTELPRO was to "expose, disrupt, misdirect, discredit, or otherwise neutralize... no opportunity must be missed to exploit through counterintelligence techniques ... for maximum effectiveness ... long range goals are being set... prevent [them from] gaining respectability ... and a final goal should be to prevent the long range growth of militant black organizations, especially among youth."

COINTELPRO didn't go away. It continues today. This case, as well as the cases of Mumia Abu-Jamal and Imam Jamil Abdullah Al-Amin, are prime examples of the existence of COINTELPRO and its agenda. We have a tendency to forget and think that things have changed. The enemy doesn't forget. They maintain files and lists. They maintain think tanks and, when it is convenient and at the proper time, they move. The movements of the 60s caught them by surprise. They rushed to catch up and won the first skirmish. We still have casualties. While we were busy they were preparing so they wouldn't be caught off guard again. This round of activity on the part of the state is their effort to clean up the books. We must not allow them to do this. We must defend Kamau Sadiki. We must push back the state. We must not allow them to use Kamau as a scapegoat... we must Free Kamau Sadiki and all Political Prisoners.

Kamau Sadiki with his granddaughter

Imam Jamil Al-Amin (the former H. Rap Brown) Moved to the Stateside Guantánamo

International Committee to Support Imam Jamil Al-Amin
2008

Imam Jamil Al-Amin, the former H. Rap Brown, is approaching his eighth year of political internment: A conspicuous stop for driving while Black during the spring of 1999, a court closing due to a snowstorm in January 2000, a bench warrant for nonappearance at that court date, a shooting incident and a rush-to-judgment accusation on March 16, 2000, an unjust arrest, a forced conviction, and the inhumane sentence of life without parole plus 35 years in March 2002.

After being forced to serve five and a half years in administrative segregation—23-hour-per-day lockdown, no human contact—at the notorious K-Block in the state prison at Reidsville, Georgia, Imam Jamil Al-Amin was transferred in August 2007 to the maximum security federal prison at Florence, Colorado, known as the Supermax. His housing conditions remain 23-hour lockdown, no human contact, silence, five social visits per month, two phone calls per month and denial of all media requests for interviews.

Although he has no contact with them, he is joined in Florence by many other political prisoners who are well-known Muslim leaders, as well as leaders in the struggle for self-determination: Dr. Mutulu Shakur, Imam Malik Khaba (Jeff Fort), Brother Sekou Odinga, Larry Hoover, leader of Growth and Development (formerly the Gangster Disciples) and Dr. Malakai Z. York, to name just a few. Due to all these leaders representing legitimate "people's struggles," Florence Supermax is being referred to as the stateside Guantánamo.

Imam Jamil Al-Amin's transfer into federal custody and to the Supermax

---

In the late 1960s, H. Rap Brown became well-known as the Chair of the Student Nonviolent Coordinating Committee (SNCC) and later Minister of Justice of the Black Panther Party. As a result, he became a target of COINTELPRO. For years he was harassed, arrested and repeatedly jailed. In 1971 Brown converted to Islam and changed his name to Jamil Abdullah Al-Amin. He later started a mosque and helped build a large Muslim community in Atlanta's West End neighborhood. After the 1993 bombing of the World Trade Center, Imam Jamil was hauled in, interrogated and released under heavy and continuous surveillance despite the absence of any evidence connecting him to the bombing. In March 2000, Imam Jamil was framed and later convicted of the murder of one Fulton County (Atlanta) sheriff and the wounding of another—although no physical or scientific evidence linked him to the scene.

comes on the heels of some hard-won victories: 1) the 11th Circuit Court of Appeals ruling in Imam Jamil's favor against the prison at Reidsville in regard to a suit filed to disallow them from continuing to open his legal mail, 2) the groundswell of support for the Imam developing into phone call-ins and postal and e-mail write-ins, bringing the offices at Reidsville Prison and the Department of Corrections to a virtual standstill, along with the periodic protest demonstrations that would cause Reidsville, the town and the prison to shut down.

Support must continue. Write to:

Imam Jamil Al-Amin, # 99974-555
U.S.P. Florence Admax
P.O. Box 8500
Florence, CO
81226.

Depositions relating to his Habeas Corpus hearing are being prepared. Being housed at Florence Supermax makes it additionally difficult for lawyers, family and the Imam to jointly work on his appeal. Financial contributions should be made to the Justice Fund, P.O. Box 98963, Atlanta, GA 30377.

Free Imam Jamil! Free all political prisoners!

Imam Jamil Al-Amin

X.10.A

"Once Upon a Time, They Called Me a Terrorist, Too"

Naji Mujahid and Ryme Katkhouda
2005

On Thursday, December 8, 2005, TransAfrica Forum hosted a press conference to give voice to three former Black Panther Party members. Hank Jones, John Bowman, and Ray Boudreaux came to Washington, DC, to discuss their current struggle with the San Francisco Police Department. They were joined on the panel by Danny Glover, famous actor and Chairman of the Board, TransAfrica Forum; Professor Charles Ogletree, Founder and Executive Director of the Charles Hamilton Houston Institute for Race and Justice at Harvard Law School; Ron Daniels, Executive Director, Center for Constitutional Rights; and Bill Fletcher, President, TransAfrica Forum.

Over the past few months, several former members of the Black Panther Party were held in contempt and jailed for refusing to testify before a San Francisco grand jury investigating a police shooting that took place in 1971. The 34-year-old case evolves from an incident in which two men armed with shotguns attacked the Ingleside Police Station resulting in the death of Sgt. John V. Young, 45, and injuring a civilian clerk. Law enforcement authorities have always assumed that black radical groups were involved.

In 1973 when 13 alleged "Black militants" were arrested in New Orleans, some of them—John Bowman, Ruben Scott, and Harold Taylor—were tortured for several days by law enforcement authorities in striking similarity to the methods used on detainees in U.S. prisons at Guantánamo Bay and Abu Ghraib. San Francisco Police Department Inspector Frank McCoy and Ed Erdelatz were on site at the New Orleans police department for the interrogation and torture of the arrested men. Some of the torture methods used included

- Stripping them naked and beating them with blunt objects
- Blindfolding them and throwing wool blankets soaked with boiling water over their bodies
- Placing electric probes on their genitals and other body parts
- Inserting an electric cattle prod in their anus
- Punching and kicking
- Slamming them into walls while blindfolded
- This process lasted for several days until the detectives got the confessions they wanted.

In 1974, a court in Los Angeles ruled that the San Francisco and New Orleans police had engaged in what amounted to torture to extract a confession from one of the men and threw out the tortured statement. In 1975, a San Francisco grand jury indicted three suspects, all of whom had been tortured in New Orleans, in connection with the 1971 shooting. However, in 1976, a San Francisco judge dismissed the indictments, finding that the prosecution had failed to tell the grand jury that the men's confessions had been coerced.

Defense sources state that while these confessions were suppressed, it appears that this is the basis for the previous and current grand jury investigations. Inspectors McCoy and Erdelatz have returned from retirement and have been deputized as federal agents for the current investigation.

Speaking about McCoy and Erdalatz, John Bowman says, "The same people who tried to kill me in 1973 are the same people who are here today, in 2005, trying to destroy me. I mean it literally. I mean there were people from the forces of the San Francisco Police Department who participated in harassment, torture, and my interrogation in 1973. [It is] these same people I have to come in contact with, I have to go before courts in front of [those] who are asking me the same questions that they interrogated and tortured me for. I have to be confronted with these people, and none of these people have ever been brought to trial. None of these people have ever been charged with anything. None of these people have ever been questioned about that!"

The former Black Panthers have determined that though they remained silent about the interrogation and torture 34 years ago, they will not make the same mistake twice. With the counsel of J. Soffiyah Elijah—Harvard University Law professor—they have formed the "Committee for the Defense of Human Rights." Among other things, they want to tell the world how torture has been used often by the U.S. administration to oppress and repress opposition and dissent, as well as coerce information. They say that what allowed such torture to happen was the lack of transparency and accountability the government had under Hoover, which is exactly the secrecy that the USA PATRIOT Act calls for today.

"This is a broad general investigation going on under the current COINTELPRO grown up into the USA PATRIOT Act, ... an extension of what was going on back then," says Hank Jones. "The same violations of our human and constitutional rights, totally unjust, done in secret and quietly. We've chosen not to be quiet about this." The broader implication of this case they say, is that other organizations will be targeted as potential terrorists, so they want to educate as many people as soon as possible as to what happened with them and the Black Panthers. "They are destroying democracy with this PATRIOT Act activity," adds Jones, "It's not just confined to us, and it's other activist organizations as well. And it was back then, under COINTELPRO, [that] all the major civil rights organizations were under surveillance. The Black Panther Party became a target under J. Edgar Hoover and designated 'The Greatest Threat of National Security to the Nation.'"

"When I watched on TV the Twin Towers come down, deep in my heart, I knew that someone will come by and visit me as soon as they can get it organized, and they did," says Ray Boudreaux, "because once upon a time, they called me a terrorist, too. To expedite something in the system, they put the 'Terror' tag on it and it gets done," adds Boudreaux. "Terror means money. These people have a budget and they are working it."

"What we hope to accomplish with the Committee for the Defense of Human Rights is to educate, inform, and try to move people to action against the policies that are in effect in the country today," concludes Hank Jones. "The same fear climate, the same tactics that were going on in the '60s are prevalent today. ... We claim that we don't torture in this country. I bring some of our slave ancestors here today, they can tell you things that would curl your hair about torture, ... not just physical, but psychological. What's happening to us today is akin to that. Dr King described Black Folks' existence in this country as tiptoed stance, always on-guard. I want to see this does not happen again, to me, or us or anybody. This is why we are speaking out and addressing this today."

"It is ironic," said Bill Fletcher, "that instead of having a press conference in which apologies are being offered to the individuals here and to many, many others who were victims of COINTELPRO, that instead we are to call attention to the prosecution of people who were freedom fighters and continue to be."

According to Ron Daniels, the President of the Center for Constitutional Rights, "The antiwar movement and the civil rights movement had effectively checked the national security state in relationship to surveillance, intrusive... it had blunted it. And many of the forces, particularly on the extreme right, had been bristling and eager for an opportunity to impose new measures. The USA PATRIOT Act had already been on the drawing board. The terrorist attacks provided an opportunity for them to impose them." Daniels adds that "Former Attorney General Ashcroft before he left issued a broad-ranging edict that all the cases that involved any incident where a police officer had been killed and the case had been closed be re-opened. ... And if these men and women can be indicted or harassed, it sends a chilling effect. It's the Lynne Stewart effect: if you engage in this, this is what can happen to your life," referring to the guilty verdict given to the "radical" human rights attorney Lynne Stewart, who represented Sheikh Abdel-Rahman, accused of bombing the World Trade Center in 1993.

These men have spent their lives trying to help others like you and I; we all now have an opportunity to reciprocate their efforts. In so doing we may help to prevent a similar fate from befalling others or even ourselves. "These gentlemen, Ray Boudreaux, Hank Jones, and others have been victims of the most vicious forms of American terrorism and torture," says Professor Ogletree. "It takes a village to protect its Elders, [...and] the East Coast through people like Ron Daniels in New York, and myself and Soffiyah Elijah in Boston, we tell them today, through our presence here and through our commitment that we will provide a protective blanket over them. They will not come in this village and take these elders, except over our dead bodies."

X.10.B

Former Black Panthers Arrested and Indicted in 1971 Homicide: Charges Based on Evidence Obtained Through Torture

Center for Constitutional Rights
January 23, 2007

NEW YORK—Authorities in San Francisco announced the arrests and indictments of former Black Panthers in the 1971 killing of police officer Sgt. John V. Young despite the use of torture to obtain confessions. Attorneys with the Center for Constitutional Rights (CCR) compared the documented torture by law enforcement of Black Panthers arrested in New Orleans in 1973 to the documented torture the U.S. government has practiced recently at Abu Ghraib and Guantánamo.

CCR Legal Director Bill Goodman said, "The case against these men was built on torture and serves to remind us that the U.S. government, which recently has engaged in such horrific forms of torture and abuse at places like Bagram, Abu Ghraib, and Guantánamo, has a history of torture and abuse in this country as well, particularly against African Americans."

CCR Attorney Kamau Franklin said, "These indictments are an attempt to rewrite history—the history of the Black Panthers, the history of COINTELPRO, and the history of the Civil Rights Movement."

In 1973, New Orleans police employed torture over the course of several days to obtain information from members of the Black Panthers who were stripped naked, beaten, blindfolded, covered in blankets soaked with boiling water, and had electric probes placed on their genitals, among other methods. A court ruled in 1974 that both San Francisco and New Orleans police had engaged in torture to extract a confession, and a San Francisco judge dismissed charges against three men in 1975 based on that ruling. Two years ago, a grand jury convened in San Francisco to reopen the case, but several of the men involved felt they were being wrongly compelled to testify and refused to attend the proceedings. CCR represents victims of torture by the U.S. at Guantánamo, Abu Ghraib, and Bagram Air Base in Afghanistan, a well as Canadian rendition victim Maher Arar. In addition, CCR has filed suit against the NSA for the warrantless domestic spying program authorized by President Bush; the COINTELPRO program illegally spied on Black activists in the Sixties and Seventies and engaged in numerous unconstitutional acts against Civil Rights organizations.

X.10.C

Interview with Richard Brown of the San Francisco 8

Revolution Newspaper
2007

Revolution: Could you tell me about the charges against you and the other defendants who make up the San Francisco 8?

Richard Brown: We're being charged with the 1971 Ingleside Station attack where a police sergeant by the name of John Young was murdered. Because we were Panthers, we are being charged with that murder and conspiracy to murder police officers and commit certain crimes. This was brought up for the first time in the 1970s. When the case was taken to court, the three people charged, John Bowman, Ruben Scott, and Harold Taylor, all stated that they were tortured and forced to confess. Because of that and the fact that they were questioned without any attorney being present in New Orleans, the court threw the so-called "admission of guilt" and the case out.

In January of this year, 2007, they rearrested eight of us for the same crime and the same charges, and as far as we can tell from what we've heard in court they plan to use the same "confessions" that were ruled illegal in the first place. If you go according to what they said in court, what they've presented so far, they don't even have any new evidence. We are being recharged with the same thing again which was already stated as illegal back in the 1970s.

Since then, I might add, a lot of things have changed because of the PATRIOT Act and Homeland Security and the environment of the country, a period where they feel that they can come back and use what they couldn't use before because it's not so clear whether [the torture] is illegal or not.

Revolution: Could you give people a picture of the torture that took place in New Orleans?

Richard Brown: Three members of the Black Panther Party—John Bowman, who was a San Francisco Panther; Ruben Scott, who was a San Francisco Panther; and Harold Taylor, who was a Panther from Los Angeles—were arrested in New Orleans in 1973. Actually they arrested 13 Panthers.

They were separated and for days they were tortured. They were stripped naked, handcuffed, isolated, repeatedly beaten, denied sleep, food, and all that type of stuff. They were beaten around the stomach and back. They used slapjacks on their shins and legs, where torturers are trained to beat people so the

The following interview first appeared in the December 23, 2007, edition of *Revolution* (#113), the newspaper of the Revolutionary Communist Party.
It is available online at http://revcom.us/a/113/sf8-interview-en.html

wounds don't show. They used what is called waterboarding now. Technically what they were using were hot and wet blankets. Also plastic bags were placed over their heads until the point where they would pass out. They used electrical cattle prods to their private parts and to their anus. Their treatment was so inhumane, it's hard to even describe, let alone endure. And my friends who had to endure this, I see how this has affected them. How they look when they describe it. It's horrifying and it's hard for me to even talk about it, honestly and truly. It's horrible for human beings to treat someone else like that for days. They tortured them like that for three or four days.

Revolution: There were two San Francisco police who participated in the torture in New Orleans. What's their role?

Richard Brown: Ed Erdelatz and Frank McCoy were San Francisco homicide detectives and had run-ins with the Panthers long before the Ingleside case. In 1973, they were in New Orleans. Their part was that they never actually touched them. They would come into the room along with the detectives from New York, Los Angeles, and the FBI. They would come in and ask questions and if the questions weren't answered to their satisfaction, they would leave the room, and the New Orleans Police Department would come in and they would start the torture. Actually the torture started before the questioning even started. They arrested them, took them in, stripped them, isolated them, and just started beating them. They just enjoyed torture. They would do a job on them and then leave and tell them "we'll be back." Then the detectives would come in and start asking questions. First they would try and tell the detectives that they were being tortured and then the detectives would get up and walk out of the room and the New Orleans police would come in. This went on for days. They would keep them up at night, not allow them to sleep. Wake them up every hour or so. Throw water-soaked blankets on them, scalding hot water so they couldn't breathe. This is the treatment that they had to endure for days.

Ed Erdelatz and Frank McCoy were the ones who in 2005 came knocking on people's doors during the grand jury investigation asking, "Do you remember me?" and giving us subpoenas to appear before a grand jury. They were brought out of retirement and deputized by Homeland Security in order to do these cold case things [opening previously closed cases involving the Black Panther Party] that were going on nationwide.

Revolution: What happened with the grand jury investigation?

Richard Brown: When they first came and wanted to talk to us, we were told that they wanted to question us about white people that we knew. But once they started asking questions, it was clear that they were interested in Black people's role in the Ingleside attack. They had made up their minds already that the Panthers had to be responsible for this. It was a situation where they were trying to make the evidence fit the theory, and they've been trying to do that ever since then.

In 2005 we all refused to testify before the grand jury. Five of us were held in contempt of court: Hank Jones, Ray Boudreaux, Harold Taylor, John Bowman (now deceased), and myself. We were held in contempt of court and locked up until the grand jury expired. We were released on October 31, 2005.

Revolution: How long were you locked up for?

Richard Brown: I was locked up for about a month. People were locked up at different times depending on when we were called in front of the grand jury for questioning. I think Hank Jones was first and he was in the longest. John Bowman was the last and he was only locked up for eight or nine days. I think Hank did something like two and a half months. We weren't guilty of any crime. We were just standing on the Fifth Amendment, and because of that I was taken away from my family, locked up. I was transferred all around. Nobody actually knew where I was, including my attorney. It would take days for them to find me and then when they did find me, I'd be transferred to another place. They just messed with us as usual to put pressure on us or to just be vindictive, whatever motive people like that have, that's what they were doing. I'm sure they always have some motive in their twisted mind about why they torture people or why they lie about people or why they kill people, why they lock people up for life knowing that they are innocent. They can obviously justify that shit in their mind because they do it and they're still here and they continue to do it. I find it difficult to see and understand, though.

Revolution: Could you speak a little more about why you decided not to cooperate with the grand jury?

Richard Brown: First of all, because they're trying to convict me of something that I am innocent of. The grand jury is trying to go along with this story that was concocted in New Orleans by the conglomerate of agencies that were there, putting together a case involving torture that was targeting me and saying that I was a part of it. And now you ask me to go before a grand jury and participate and say something so that it can be used against me. I know that as a Black man in America and as a Panther, I have not been treated fairly by the judicial system in the courts. Every time I have gone to court, I have never seen justice, so why would I? And we're talking about a murder, a homicide, and they want me to cooperate with them? And I know from the facts that all this is bullshit; they are trying to convict me of something that I am not guilty of.

Even if you could get past all that, these same people, Ed Erdelatz and Frank McCoy, the police departments, and the FBI and the rest of them tortured my friends. It's pitiful. I truly will never get over that, what they've done to my friends. I will never, ever cooperate with people like that. I will have no respect for them. I don't like them. I think they should be arrested and held accountable for the crimes that they committed back then. Until that happens, they can forget about me even having a decent word to say to them. I don't want to have nothing to do with them, and I'm sure the rest of the people share that. I will never cooperate with them, I didn't then and I never will.

The things that were done to the Black Panther Party by COINTELPRO and by the local police departments all across the country and the way I was treated every time I went to court, I have nothing but disdain for them. Even if there was something to cooperate about, they couldn't get it from me.

Revolution: You started talking about COINTELPRO, and we were talking about it a little earlier. A big part of the background to this case is COINTELPRO, the Counterintelligence Program by the FBI that targeted the Black Panther Party. Could you speak to what COINTELPRO was and what it did, both any personal experience you have as well as its overall role?

Richard Brown: What they did overall was destroy the Black Panther Party as it was. Their job as the Counterintelligence Program was to destroy the movement, period, all of the progressive political movements that were going on at that time. If I'm not mistaken at that time [FBI Director J. Edgar] Hoover declared the Black Panther Party the greatest threat to the nation's internal security. And we in the Panthers, even at the time he was saying that, had no idea, I actually don't even remember him saying that. I was too busy as a Panther trying to do something to serve my community. I was a young Black man in a community of Black people. And Black people at that time were in a world of trouble—actually today we still are. We had nothing in the world going for us. The government didn't represent us at all. They weren't doing anything for us. The only thing we saw every day was repression from the police department as an occupying force in our community, trying to keep us in line or intimidate us from doing anything against the other parts of society. We were the lowest on the totem pole. We didn't have decent housing, we didn't have decent food, we didn't have decent schools, we didn't have decent jobs—we had no jobs. So when the Black Panther Party came along and said we can do all this stuff for ourselves, people like me and hundreds of other young people joined the Party in order to serve the Black community and to help the people. We were interested in feeding children, getting people to organize, to unify, to bring about the vote so that we could control the politicians in our community, to putting together schools for our children, clinics—all of the things that the government had failed to do for us we were willing to do for ourselves and we were beginning to do that.

For this the Counterintelligence Program deemed us the number one threat in the United States and focused on us with an intensity that I, to this very day, find astonishing. I didn't believe it at all back then. None of us believed that the FBI and the Counterintelligence Program and all of these agencies were spending all this money, going through all these tricks, doing everything they could to undermine our efforts to help our people—framing us, using up all our resources by taking us to jail every other day, falsifying documents and evidence to send people to jail for life to get rid of them and destroy our leadership, torture and even murder. It has been proven that they were guilty of all of that. We honestly did not know that they would do something like this, that they were doing it. I'm still finding out things that the COINTELPRO did today.

In the 1970s the Senate's Church Committee investigation found that the Counterintelligence Program was illegal and unconstitutional. A couple of agents were even found guilty of some charge, but they never did any time because their sentence was commuted by the president. He decided that we should forgive and forget. But here I am, almost 40 years later, not forgiven and forgotten—and I'm not even guilty! These people were guilty of those crimes.

Revolution: This case goes back more than 35 years. Why do you think they are bringing it back now?

Richard Brown: Number one, they want to legalize torture. They felt this would work for them, because we are all Black people and it's easier to find Black people guilty than it is to find white people or anyone else guilty. It's a ready-made case for them. They thought they would be able to turn the public against us because a police officer lost his life, especially with eight Black men accused. They want to see if this case will fly because of the new laws and the doing away with of certain constitutional rights that we used to have. They call it "relaxation," that they've temporarily taken them, but we don't have them any more. They feel that if they can do it with us and get away with it, then they can push it forward and take it nationwide to anyone and everyone who is opposing and will oppose them because of the direction that this country is going in. They are alienating all of the masses and they have to find some way to keep them in line and intimidate people so that they know that "if you go against us, we ain't going to never let it go. We'll come back at you time and time again. You will suffer. So you better think twice."

Revolution: Two of your codefendants, Herman Bell and Jalil Muntaqim, have been in jail for the last 30 years. I know you wanted to speak about their situation.

Richard Brown: Them and all political prisoners who are still suffering behind the Counterintelligence Program or COINTELPRO. It has been proven beyond a shadow of a doubt that people were framed, that evidence was manufactured, that people were paid to lie, they withheld evidence that could prove people was innocent. The case of Geronimo ji Jaga who was framed and did 27 years before the government was forced to admit that they knew he didn't do it. They withheld the evidence that could prove that he was somewhere else when the crime was committed. These types of things are what I would really like America to understand and take a good hard look at. Not only does it affect us, Black people at this particular time—and most of the political prisoners, though not all, are Black. But I would like all of the political prisoners' cases to be reopened. I would like everyone who was touched by the Counterintelligence Program in any way, for their cases to be revisited and for something to be done in order to remedy the situation.

You have people still to this day, like Herman and Jalil, who are locked up only because of the participation of the Counterintelligence Program and how they went about conducting their business over the years.

I was framed, just blatantly framed, given a case. At the time I was raising nine children in the same house. And they took me away from my family for over two and one-half years behind that crap. I still say I was fortunate because I didn't have to stay in for 27 years or 35 years like some of my other comrades who are still locked up today. And I could have been in prison much longer if it hadn't been for the attorneys who were able to legally get me out and prove that I was innocent.

This has to change. We have to do something. We have hundreds and hundreds of people all over this nation who are locked up in prison and who it appears have no chance of ever coming home because of the Counterintelligence Program and what it did to them. The masses are not in charge of when they come home or don't come home. This fascist government is still saying we deem these people a threat just like they deemed me a threat for trying to feed children in the Black community. And they're not going to release them, and that is one of the biggest crimes being committed by this government.

Revolution: What gives you the strength to carry on the struggle?

Richard Brown: The love for my great-grandchildren, my grandchildren and my children, my love for the people. The fact that I'm just not the type of person who's just going to lie down and take anything. You hit me, I hit back. I believe in people. That's another thing that the Party taught me, that true power comes from the people. I love the masses. I actually love America and I love the American people. There's a difference now. I'm not talking about the American so-called government. The so-called president and his administration, if you go by the definition of what a president is, he doesn't fit that. He fits more of the definition of a dictator and therefore he's in charge of a regime. It has nothing to do with the American people. I believe that the majority of the American people are decent people who believe in freedom, justice and equality for all, who truly want this to be "the land of the free and the home of the brave." It is not that, but it can be that, and I have faith that it will be if we continue to try and bring forth the contradiction, which is what I'm doing, and educate people to get them to understand the true picture of what's going on so that things will be better, not just for my grandchildren and great-grandchildren, but for everybody's children.

I can't stop. If the people understand and take control like they can, they can turn this around and they will. As long as I can be effective and as long as I can try to continue to do that, I'm going to be working toward that. I guess I'm doing this out of love for the people and love for peace and freedom. And until we get it, I'm going to continue to fight.

Revolution: Anything else that you want to add?

Richard Brown: Again, political prisoners and prisoners of war. Honestly and truly, I want people to understand and take a good look at that. We started the Committee for the Defense of Human Rights, that's what the SF8 has started. And out of this we want to reopen an investigation of the Counterintelligence Program. It's kind of silly to think that the government is taking freedom and constitutional rights away from us, and we're talking about investigating an agency that did the same thing that the government is doing now. It's in order to get the people of the United States to understand what's truly going on, and until we paint a clear picture of what happened and what is happening now, political prisoners don't have a chance of coming home. We not only want them to come home, we want people who are guilty of these crimes against them and against all of us to be held accountable.

Honestly and truly, when I think of Jalil and Herman and other political prisoners, I feel real, real, real bad. I feel like I'm not doing enough. You asked me what keeps me going. The love that I have for those brothers, who gave so much because of their love of the people, and who're suffering like they are. And I want to stop that.

X.10.D

Joint Statement from the San Francisco 8

Herman Bell, Ray Boudreaux, Richard Brown,
Hank Jones, Richard O'Neal, Harold Taylor,
Francisco Torres, Jalil Muntaqim
2007

We, the San Francisco 8, would like to send this joint statement extending our heartfelt gratitude and appreciation to all our friends and supporters. As many of you know, this COINTELPRO persecution has been ongoing for nearly 36 years. However, in the last few years, in accord with the implementation of the PATRIOT Act, state and federal authorities initiated plans to stifle political dissent, particularly targeting young activists. Similarly, COINTELPRO's objective was to "... expose, disrupt, misdirect, discredit, or otherwise neutralize the activities of Black nationalist, hate type organizations and groupings, their leadership, spokesmen, membership, and supporters, and to counter their propensity for violence and civil disorder..." (COINTELPRO memo of August 25, 1967).

The FBI not only targeted the Black Panther Party, but according to this COINTELPRO memo: "Intensified attention under this program should be afforded to the activities of such groups as the Student Nonviolent Coordinating Committee, the Southern Christian Leadership Conference, Revolutionary Action Movement, the Deacons for Defense and Justice, Congress of Racial Equality, and the Nation of Islam. Particular emphasis should be given to extremists who direct the activities and policies of revolutionary or militant groups such as Stokely Carmichael, H. 'Rap' Brown, Elijah Muhammad, and Maxwell Stanford." By March 4, 1968, COINTELPRO was in full operation leading to directing its full attention to the Black Panther Party to prohibit the BPP from developing durable, long-term political and organizational relationships with various segments of the Black community.

This case represents the continuation of that COINTELPRO objective, to further indicate how the government will persecute today's activists. The government is seeking to rewrite the history of struggle as exemplified by the BPP, venomously trying to define that legacy of struggle as a "terrorist" movement.

We vehemently reject that labeling, as the government attempts to characterize the San Francisco 8 as "terrorists," "criminals," and "wanton killers." They will never say the SF8 were political activists and progressive civil/human rights organizers. They will never say they sought to relieve the community of all forms of state-sponsored terrorism that is often found in Black, Asian and Latino communities today. They will never admit to the unconstitutional practices of the FBI COINTELPRO activities, despite the 1974 Senate Church Committee findings condemning those practices. Furthermore, they will never seek to establish remedies for those who are victims of the illegal FBI and local police actions under COINTELPRO, and now under the PATRIOT Act, if we don't demand they do so.

It is with this understanding that the SF8 are issuing this joint statement, calling for friends and supporters to organize a national determination to ensure our victory. Ours will be a victory against fear and state terrorism; it will be a defeat against state torture tactics, threats and coercion.

This case and our call for action will teach today's activists what to expect from the state in its efforts to suppress dissent and protest of government repression. Indeed, this task will forward a broader understanding of what happened in the Movement of the 60s and 70s, and how COINTELPRO disrupted and destroyed the most viable Black political party that emerged out of the civil rights movement. Ultimately, what is here proposed will tell of a youth movement and how the government sought to undermine and destroy it. The proposal will expose how the government seeks to retaliate because those youth (who are now Elders) did in fact challenge the system of racist oppression. They not only challenged oppressive conditions in our collective communities, but also worked to support all oppressed peoples fighting against colonialism and imperialism at that time.

This case evolves out of a history of political struggle in this country, and it is our duty to fulfill that mission by expressing what happened then and COINTELPRO's negative impact on today's social movements. Therefore, while we engage in a legal battle in the courtroom, it is imperative we urge our friends and supporters to extend the political front in the various communities. We must reach out to the various street organizations and youth groups, the animal and earth liberation groups, women's rights and LGBT forums, the immigration rights struggles, and the many ethnic communities who are struggling for a better life in this country.

Hence, the course of the overall struggle to win the release of the San Francisco 8 requires a broad political determination, reaching beyond the important legal issues of the case. For example, the question of torture, COINTELPRO, and matters of reconciliation are essential to this case. Therefore, a successful national campaign in support of the SF8 requires friends and supporters to achieve the following objectives:

1. Antitorture Legislation:

In 1909, the Niagara Movement evolved into the NAACP, led by W. E. B. Du Bois. The principal platform of the NAACP at that time was a struggle to forge an antilynching movement. Today, torture in its many forms has become a scourge in America: there is the inhumane use of restraint chairs in jails and prisons, an especially despicable device reminiscent of medieval torture mechanisms; there has been an increase in use of the taser as a weapon to induce confessions and control prisoners, resulting in many deaths, another inhumane torture device. In the case of the SF8, law enforcement officers employed similar torture techniques, including those used in Vietnam and in Abu Ghraib by U.S. military personnel. The use of torture permeates all facets of the so-called "criminal justice system."

Obviously, like the old antilynching platform of the NAACP, the San Francisco 8 call for a national campaign demanding antitorture legislation on local levels (city councils and state legislatures). The SF8 hold that any form of interrogation that employs the use of waterboarding, simulated drowning techniques, cattle prods, tasers, restraint chairs, physical beatings, sensory and sleep deprivation, and psychological coercion must be deemed inhumane and criminal. Therefore, the San Francisco 8 call for all progressive and peace loving people to join in a national campaign on city, state and congressional levels for proclamations and legislation outlawing all forms of torture.

2. Reopen COINTELPRO Hearings:
It is well known that the FBI targeted the Black Panther Party for annihilation under the secret counter-intelligence program (COINTELPRO). The FBI COINTELPRO effort resulted in the assassination, criminalization, vilification, and the splitting of the BPP leading to its destruction, with many BPP members today languishing in prisons. The FBI COINTELPRO actions worked in alliance with police departments across the country, and today, the PATRIOT Act has legalized much of what were illegal COINTELPRO practices. In 1974, the Senate Church Committee investigating the illegal FBI COINTELPRO activities declared such practices unconstitutional. However, the Senate Church Committee failed to create remedies for those who suffered from the unconstitutional practices of the FBI and police departments.

Subject to that reality, the San Francisco 8 hereby call for a national movement for the reopening of COINTELPRO hearings. We, the SF8, urge friends and supporters to phone/fax/write to John Conyers, Chair of the Judiciary Committee in Congress, and appeal for him to conduct public hearings on why victims of COINTELPRO languish in prison over 30 years after it was declared unconstitutional. We, the SF8, ask friends and supporters to contact your congressional representative, Congressional Black Caucus members and other elected officials urging them to enable John Conyers to reopen COINTELPRO hearings.

3. Truth and Reconciliation Commission:
At the conclusion of hostilities in the struggle to end apartheid in South Africa, many progressive forces took a path to resolve potential antagonisms subject to racial, socioeconomic and political strife during the decades of apartheid. That path led to the creation of the Truth and Reconciliation Commission, principally led by the Honorable Bishop Desmond Tutu.

In the United States, people of Afrikan descent suffered the trauma of chattel slavery, Black Codes, Jim Crow segregation laws, political repression and state terrorism under the auspices of COINTELPRO. However, unlike South Africa, at no time has there been a national determination to resolve political, social or economic antagonisms born out of centuries/decades of racial strife. In recent years, as a result of the reparations movement, some corporations, cities and states have issued apologies for having been involved in the Atlantic slave trade. Despite these apologies, the systemic inequities prevail with devastating consequences on every vestige of life confronting the majority of people of Afrikan descent in America.

The San Francisco 8 understand that these historic dynamics perpetuate social-cultural determinants that inhibit the necessary psychological inducements toward self-reliance and self-determination. Therefore, we are calling for progressive peoples to open dialogue and begin the process towards organizing a national Truth and Reconciliation Commission to address these inequities. We believe such a Commission could serve as a catalyst to forge substantial resolutions to heal America's racial trauma.

In conclusion, it is these three areas of concern we jointly agree will empower a national campaign to virtually expose the negative impact of both COINTELPRO and the PATRIOT Act. We call for all progressive peoples in support of the San Francisco 8 and all U.S. political prisoners to find the means to organize committees and coalitions to implement this proposal on local and national levels.

Again, we, the San Francisco 8, extend our heartfelt appreciation for your solidarity and support. Let us, together, build a sustainable and durable initiative that redresses civil and human rights violations, as we organize to win the freedom of the San Francisco 8.

Free All U.S. Political Prisoners!

X.10.E

International Call on the San Francisco 8

Initiated by
Archbishop Desmond Tutu and Mairead Corrigan Maguire
2007

Given our commitment to and history in the global justice and human rights movements,

Given our commitment to reconciliation between peoples and governments,

Given that the U.S. government and Federal Bureau of Investigation has been shown, through past U.S. Congressional hearings and legal proceedings, to have been involved in illegal policing activities against civil and human rights organizations;

Given that these illegal activities, epitomized by the FBI Counter Intelligence Programs (COINTELPRO), targeted the Black Panther Party, and appears to have an ongoing presence;

Given that eight former Black Panthers—men now all in their fifties, sixties, and seventies—were arrested on January 23, 2007;

Given that these arrests were based on charges related to a 1971 murder, a murder investigated and brought to court in 1975 with the charges dismissed;

Given that no new evidence has been uncovered, and that the alleged evidence in the 1973 investigation was thrown out of court due to a judicial finding that statements were made under conditions of extreme torture, including: electric shock, cattle prods, beatings, sensory deprivation, plastic bags and hot, wet blankets for asphyxiation; and

---

* At a November 30, 2007, press conference, World Council of Churches representative Lois M. Dauway officially released the International Call on the San Francisco 8. The document was drafted to bring the attention and the solidarity of the global peace and human rights community to the case. It was initiated by two Nobel Peace laureates and signed by a third, as well as by two activists in leadership positions with Nobel Peace Prize-winning organizations. Dauway stated:"The time has come to set free those who have been bound. The case of the San Francisco 8 requires all of us to come together and take an active stand for justice for all U.S. political prisoners." Interest in the Call has been generated amongst the founders of the Nobel Women's Initiative, in academic circles, and in key constituencies across three continents.

Given that these new charges amount to little more than continued governmental harassment, violating basic principles set forth in the Universal Declaration of Human Rights and the United Nations Convention against Torture;

We call on all appropriate legal and governmental authorities to:

- investigate and end all incidents of torture within the U.S. criminal justice system;
- drop all current charges for all eight men in question, namely: Herman Bell, Ray Boudreaux, Richard Brown, Henry W. (Hank) Jones, Jalil Muntaqim (Anthony Bottom), Richard O'Neal, Harold Taylor, and Francisco Torres;
- convene official investigations into the ongoing legacy and possible continued operation of COINTELPRO and similar programs, with an eye toward true reconciliation and human rights based on internationally recognized standards and principles; and
- release immediately, on humanitarian grounds, Herman Bell and Jalil Muntaqim (Anthony Bottom)—each of whom have served over thirty years of disproportionately long sentences based on the COINTELPRO criminalization of the Black Panther Party and the U.S. civil rights movement.

The Most Rev. Dr. Desmond Mpilo Tutu,
Archbishop Emeritus of Cape Town,
Primate of the Church of the Province of
Southern Africa;
Nobel Peace Laureate 1984

Mairead Corrigan Maguire,
Community of Peace People,
Northern Ireland;
Nobel Peace Laureate 1976

Betty Williams,
Community of Peace People,
Northern Ireland;
Nobel Peace Laureate 1976

Darryl Jordan,
Director,
American Friends Service Committee
Third World Coalition

William Wardlaw,
Executive Director's Leadership
Council, Amnesty International/USA[†]

Marie Dennis,
Co-President, Pax Christi International
Director-Maryknoll Office
for Global Concerns

Lois M. Dauway,
Women's Division, Global Ministries,
United Methodist Chuch;
Central Committee member,
World Council of Churches

---

[*] AFSC received the Nobel Peace Prize in 1947.
[†] Amnesty International received the Nobel Peace Prize in 1977.

U.S. Government Persecution of Arabs and Muslims Pre- and Post-9/11

Bob Lederer and Ryme Katkhouda
2008

For more than two decades, Arab and Muslim communities in the U.S. and abroad have seen escalating attacks on their leadership and communities. In the early 1980s, the Reagan administration drafted a secret plan for a massive roundup and detention of Arabs around the U.S. In 1987, immigration officials jailed and tried to deport the "LA 8," seven Palestinian activists and a Kenyan arrested for their alleged political beliefs and activities supporting Palestinian national liberation, an attack which was finally defeated after 20 years of struggle. What followed was an escalating, official agenda of demonization, criminalization, and deportation against Arab and Muslim immigrants. Aided by "antiterrorism" and immigrant-crackdown laws and executive orders passed in the Clinton era, this policy took a quantum leap after the September 11, 2001, attacks. Under the cloak of "the war on terror," illegally installed "President" Bush pushed the so-called PATRIOT Act and one repressive bill after another through a compliant Congress. Meanwhile, the Bush administration embarked on evermore audacious assaults on the First, Fourth, and Fifth Amendments, including flagrant violations of longstanding statutes and court orders, not to mention international humanitarian law. (For a good summary, see Stephen Lendman's lengthy December 2007 article "Police State America—A Look Back and Ahead," available at www.globalresearch.ca.)

In addition to the well-publicized torture and other outrages at the U.S.'s widely condemned Guantánamo Bay detention center, this policy has produced a massive increase in immigrant incarcerations within the U.S.—with many cases of verbal and physical abuse and even some deaths—and deportations by the dreaded ICE (Immigration and Customs Enforcement) bureau of the Department of Homeland Security. In the immediate weeks after 9/11, according to a two-part *Washington Post* investigative report published on June 12 and 13, 2005, "768 suspects were secretly processed on immigration charges. Most were deported after being cleared of connections to terrorism." By assembling large amounts of data about individual cases, the report's authors determined that in the two years since ICE's creation, 500 mainly Arab and Muslim immigrants were charged in relation to "terrorism" investigations—yet just 39 were convicted of crimes related to "terrorism." Some were acquitted, and most of the rest were convicted of minor offenses totally unrelated to terrorism—like making false statements or violating immigration laws. (Not surprisingly, all these cases were handled by the same FBI/police "Joint Terrorism Task Forces" that have relentlessly persecuted Black, Puerto Rican, and white anti-imperialist radicals for over two decades.)

Few cases are more chilling in their intimidating "message" than that of Tashnuba Hayder, a 16-year-old Muslim girl living in Queens, NY, summarily deported in 2005 to a Bangladesh she had left at age 5. Tashnuba was held for six weeks at a Pennsylvania detention center, where as many as three agents at a time grilled her about her friends, her notes and essays for school—even the way she decorated her bedroom. All this simply because FBI monitoring had found her writing to an online chat room also visited by a fiery Muslim imam during a high school research project on terrorism she was conducting with another Muslim teenager, Adama Bah, also detained by the FBI for six weeks.

The dragnet has extended beyond immigrants to include Arab and Muslim U.S. citizens and is now intersecting with evermore aggressive raids on workplaces of exploited, primarily Latino immigrant workers—leading to further jailings, deportations, family breakups, and heart-wrenching suffering. All of these attacks have given rise to growing resistance movements by people from these communities, along with all too few allies, demanding respect for human rights and justice. The following article by Stephen Lendman exposes one of the most nakedly political of the many U.S. government attacks of recent years.

X.11.A
Police State America: Sami Al-Arian's Long Ordeal
Stephen Lendman
2008

Sami Al-Arian is a political prisoner in Police State America....Because of his faith, ethnicity and political activism, the Bush administration targeted Al-Arian for supporting "terrorism." In fact, he's a Palestinian refugee, distinguished professor and scholar, community leader and civil activist.

Nonetheless, the FBI harassed him for 11 years, arrested him on February 20, 2003, and falsely accused him of backing organizations fronting for Palestinian Islamic Jihad—a 1997 State Department-designated "Foreign Terrorist Organization (FTO)."

A week later, in spite of his many awards, impeccable credentials and tenured status, University of South Florida president Judy Genshaft fired him under right wing pressure.

Since February 20, 2003, Al-Arian has been imprisoned—first at Tampa, Florida's Orient Road jail, then on to more than a dozen different maximum and other federal prison facilities. He's currently on hunger strike at Warsaw, Virginia's Northern Neck regional jail after being transferred back March 18 from Butner, North Carolina's medical prison.

Originally published by the website of the Centre for Research on Globalization at www.globalresearch.ca on March 24, 2008. Also included are excerpts of an earlier article by Mr. Lendman, "The Long Ordeal of a Political Prisoner / Sami Al-Arian—Civil and Human Rights Advocate," published by the Centre on April 4, 2007.

Al-Arian's trial began in June 2005 and was a travesty. It lasted six months, cost an estimated $50 million, and the prosecution called 80 witnesses, including Israeli intelligence agents and victims of suicide bombings to prejudice the jury. It introduced portions of hundreds of wiretapped phone calls from over a half million recorded; "evidence" from faxes, emails and what was seized from his home; quotes from his speeches and lectures; conferences, events and rallies he attended; articles he wrote; books he owned; magazines he edited; and various publications he read—all legal and in no way incriminating unless falsely twisted to appear that way.

After years of effort and millions spent, Al-Arian was exonerated. On December 6, 2005, after 13 days of deliberation, the jury acquitted him of all (eight) "terrorism" charges. They were deadlocked 10—2 for acquittal on nine others. All of them were false and unjust.

Nonetheless, within days, the Justice Department said it would retry him on the lesser charges. His lawyers called it legal but a highly unusual move. At the same time and in secret, a plea bargain deal was struck. It stipulated that:

- Al-Arian neither engaged in nor had any knowledge of violent acts;
- he would not be required to cooperate further with prosecutors; and
- he would be released on time served and deported voluntarily to his country of choice.

In the meantime, Al-Arian remained in custody pending sentencing and deportation on May 1, 2006. He expected to be free and his ordeal ended. Instead, the presiding judge changed the deal. He sentenced Al-Arian to the maximum 57 months, gave him credit for time served, and ordered him held for the remaining 11 months, after which an April 2007 deportation would follow. Now it's extended, as explained below.

In October 2006, assistant prosecutor Gordon Kromberg violated plea bargain terms by subpoenaing Al-Arian before a grand jury. His defense attorneys tried to block it by citing his "no-grand jury cooperation" provision to prevent DOJ from springing a perjury-obstruction trap. Defense's motion was denied, and on November 16 Al-Arian refused to testify and was held in contempt.

A month later, the grand jury expired, a new one was convened, and Al-Arian was again subpoenaed to testify. He continued to refuse, was held in contempt, and had his sentence increased without mitigation to April 7, 2008.

On March 3, 2008, Kromberg subpoenaed Al-Arian before still another March 19 grand jury, three weeks before his scheduled release and deportation. On the same day, Al-Arian began a hunger strike against the government's continued harassment. It's his third one but is life-threatening for a man in his condition. He's diabetic and needs regular sustenance to avoid serious health problems. His January through March 2007 strike depleted one-fourth of his body weight, gravely harmed him and ended only at the urging of his family.

He's now 20 days into his latest fast, lost 30 pounds, is weakening, and his life is endangered. On March 12, Al-Arian was transferred to the Butner, North Carolina, medical facility where treatment is poor, the staff indifferent, and in Al-Arian's case hostile to a designated enemy of the state. On March 18, he was returned to Warsaw, Virginia's Northern Neck regional jail ahead of his third grand jury appearance. Again, he refused to testify, so he'll likely face new contempt charges and continued confinement.

George Washington University Law School professor Jonathan Turley heads up Al-Arian's legal team. On March 3, he released the following statement:

> On behalf of Mr. Olson and Mr. Meitl and the entire legal team, (we are greatly disappointed by) the Justice Department('s) continu(ing)... effort to mete out punishment that it could not secure from a jury. Having lost (its) case, (it's) openly sought to extend (Al-Arian's) confinement by daisy-chaining grand juries. As in other cases, the government has given Dr. Al-Arian the choice of an obvious perjury trap or a contempt sanction. (Either way assures his imprisonment. This) choice... is obnoxious to our legal system and contrary to any standard of decency. The mistreatment of Dr. Al-Arian remains an international symbol of how the Bush Administration has discarded fundamental principles of fairness in a blind pursuit of retribution against this political activist. We stand committed to fighting this great injustice and hopefully reuniting Dr. Al-Arian with his family and friends.

In the meantime, his long ordeal continues at a time when lawlessness prevails over justice, and we're all Sami-Al-Arians in America's "war on terrorism."

June 2008 Update: On April 29 after 57 days, Sami Al-Arian suspended the hunger strike he began to protest his continued confinement and harassment. At its end, he lost over 40 pounds, and his blood sugar and pressure were at dangerously low levels.

On April 7, he was scheduled to be released. Yet he remains in "total segregation" under harsh conditions, is allowed no visitors and is given only two phone calls a month.

There's no legal basis for confining Al-Arian. He was exonerated on major charges, a 10-2 hung jury on lesser ones, and his plea bargain said he'd be released on time served and wouldn't have to cooperate further with the government—meaning testify before grand juries where clever questioning could entrap him in perjury. He now faces an unending catch-22: Refuse to testify and be held in contempt or do it and be charged with perjury. Either way, remain incarcerated.

And he's innocent of all charges and a glorious human being.

On June 15 in Santa Clara, California, the American Muslim Alliance and Citizens' Committee for Equal Justice held a Civic Forum on "The Deepening Civil Rights Crisis." It included a status report on Al-Arian's confinement. Prominent figures like Ramsey Clark participated to highlight the threat to everyone.

Background on Sami Al-Arian

Sami Al-Arian is one of many dozens, likely hundreds, of political prisoners in the U.S. today but is noteworthy because of his high-profile status and as an especially egregious example of persecution and injustice in post-9/11 America with its climate of state-induced fear and resulting repression, with special targeting of Latino immigrants and all Muslims characterized as "Islamofascists" because of their faith and ethnicity. One of them is Dr. Sami Al-Arian—Palestinian refugee, scholar, academic, community leader, civic activist and advocate for freedom and justice for his people—imprisoned since February 2003 on trumped-up charges ...

Al-Arian is a Kuwaiti-born son of Palestinian refugees forced to flee Palestine during the 1948-49 *Nakba* catastrophe when the new state of Israel's "War of Independence" ethnically cleansed and willfully slaughtered 800,000 Palestinians, desecrated their sacred holy sites and seized their lands. The final master Plan D (Dalet) was for a war without mercy against defenseless people in which unspeakable atrocities were committed while destroying 531 Palestinian villages; 11 urban neighborhoods in cities like Tel Aviv, Haifa and Jerusalem; thousands of homes; and vast amounts of crops. Al-Arian's parents were lucky to escape the carnage and destruction alive.

Al-Arian came to the U.S. in 1975, was denied citizenship, and taught computer science as a distinguished professor at the University of South Florida (USF) from 1986 until the worst of his ordeal began in February 2003. It was because of his public, passionate and effective advocacy for human and civil rights and the liberation of his people long oppressed for six decades.

Al-Arian is a man of great distinction. He's a devout Palestinian Muslim, imam of the Islamic Community of Tampa, and a respected and admired man of principle who helped empower the Muslim community through his dedicated hard work and personal relationships with other civic, political and religious leaders in Florida and across the country in spite of having to do it in a post-9/11 environment when all Muslims became suspect and were viewed as possible "terrorists."

Post-9/11, USF president Judy Genshaft consorted with Florida Governor Jeb Bush, suspending Al-Arian on September 28 with pay on phony grounds of campus safety. She then tried firing him, falsely claiming he supported terrorists and damaged the university's reputation, even though he was a respected award-winning tenured professor guilty of no crime but his faith, ethnicity and courageous activism encouraging other Muslim Americans to act likewise.

Earlier in August 1996, USF placed Al-Arian on paid leave pending the outcome of an FBI investigation into whether organizations he was involved with fronted for terrorist groups, allowing him to resume teaching two years later when it uncovered nothing.

Days before his arrest, indictment and imprisonment in February 2003, sensing what was to come after months of rumors, Al-Arian wrote: "I am crucified today because of who I am: a stateless Palestinian, an Arab, a Muslim and an outspoken advocate for Palestinian rights, but more a persistent defender for civil and constitutional rights on the home front." This was from a man *Newsweek* magazine called the premier civil rights activist in America for his efforts to repeal the use of secret evidence that became HR 2121, which only got as far in the 109th Congress as a favorable vote in the House Judiciary Committee; it's now up to the 110th Congress to take further action.

Earlier, Al-Arian cofounded the Tampa Bay Coalition for Justice and Peace, a local organization opposing unconstitutional use of secret evidence and other civil rights violations as well as slanderous media attacks against Muslims and Arabs. He also cofounded the National Coalition to Protect Political Freedom, the nation's leading organization challenging the use of secret evidence serving as its first president in 2000. Because of his efforts, Al-Arian advised members of Congress and was invited to briefing meetings at the White House, personally meeting Presidents Clinton and Bush.

Context: Al-Arian—Just One of Many Muslims
and Arabs Targeted by U.S. Government
[Another recently jailed Muslim political prisoner] is Dr. Rafil Dhafir, a Muslim American of Iraqi descent and practicing oncologist until his license was suspended. He was convicted in a politically motivated Department of Justice (DOJ) "kangaroo court" trial of violating the Iraqi Sanctions Regulations (IEEPA) using his own funds and what he could raise through his Help the Needy charity to bring desperately needed essential-to-life humanitarian aid to Iraqi people unable to get it because of the U.S./U.N.-imposed punitive sanctions from 1990-2003. For his "Crime of Compassion"*, he was convicted of violating the sanctions and a total of 59 of 60 trumped up charges, including tax fraud, money laundering, and mail and wire fraud, resulting in a 22-year prison sentence he's currently serving in Terre Haute far from his family in Syracuse, New York. He wasn't charged with or convicted of "terrorism" or any act of violence, is not a "high-security risk" and yet is being treated like one because he's a Muslim. He's also, like Sami Al-Arian, a "trophy" in the Bush administration's phony "war on terrorism" against Muslims demeaned and persecuted everywhere because of their faith and ethnicity.

---

* See dhafirtrial.net, by Katherine Hughes.

...In the wake of 9/11, all Muslims have been in the Bush administration crosshairs, targeted with abusive harassment and persecution, including mass roundups, detentions, prosecutions and deportations, in an age of state-induced phony terror to scare the public enough to allow the government to get away with anything. It took full advantage and continues doing it today with a greatly enhanced Department of Homeland Security/Immigration and Customs Enforcement (DHS/ICE) campaign going after vulnerable undocumented Latino workers along with targeted Muslims and others, designated threats to national security in an age when anyone is suspect if federal agencies say so. Who'll object if it's in the interest of "national security."

It began shortly after the 9/11 attacks with the Bush administration declaring a permanent state of preventive war against claimed threats to national security, especially targeting Muslims abroad and at home. It resulted in two wars of illegal aggression without end and mass witch-hunt roundups at home in which constitutional and international laws are flaunted along with fundamental principles of human rights and civil liberties. In an atmosphere of state-induced fear trumpeted by the dominant media, the FBI swung into action in mass sweeps and detentions affecting many thousands of mainly Muslim immigrants, citizens and visitors picking the wrong time to be here.

Even before 9/11, the Clinton administration and Republican-controlled Congress legalized these activities in the 1996 Immigrant Responsibility Act (IIRAIRA) and Antiterrorism and Effective Death Penalty Act (AEDPA). They're harsh repressive laws denying targets their rights of due process and judicial fairness. Today they allow DHS/ICE agents the right to conduct wiretaps and searches (the Bush administration does without required warrants), conduct proceedings in secret courts with permanently sealed rulings, detain immigrants and other targets called "terrorists," deny them bail, deport them without discretionary relief, restrict their access to counsel, deny their right to appeal, and throw the book at them even for minor offenses.

The consequences for those targeted are devastating.

It affected 5,000 Muslims in the immediate aftermath of 9/11, with only three of them being charged with an offense and not a single "terrorist" nabbed to show for it, even the 9/11 (whitewash) Commission admitted.

Yet, those swept up then and now are generally detained on noncriminal administrative charges, often without their families' knowledge. They're kept in degrading and inhumane conditions—locked in cells 23 hours a day where lights never go off, kept in hand and leg shackles whenever outside them, harassed and abused without redress, and denied telephone calls and family visitations.

Many are dragged from their homes in the middle of the night or before dawn in paramilitary-style raids, while others get picked up in the wrong place at the wrong time or for willingly coming forward as aliens when asked to and being punished for it. In the case of Rafil Dhafir, his door was broken down about 6AM, February 26, 2003, when 85 law enforcement agents showed up to arrest him including 15 from the FBI, five of whom held guns menacingly to his wife Priscilla's head, traumatizing her from the experience as it would anyone. This is how things are done in a police state where victims have no choice but take the punishment or get shot or pummeled "resisting."

Innocent people like these undergo unspeakable humiliations and treatment even though most committed no crimes and the few who have only get charged with minor offenses. ...Virtually no one's been found guilty of terrorist-related offenses or violence, yet those rounded up are forced to undergo degrading indignities like strip searches and are beaten and sexually abused for their race, faith, country of origin and immigration status. They're Muslims or impoverished Latinos here for jobs in an age when the rule of law is null and void and human rights and civil liberties are just artifacts from another era.

Early on, the Justice Department boasted it successfully deported hundreds of targeted individuals connected to 9/11 investigations. Estimates since from human rights groups, Muslim community leaders and organizations, peace groups and lawyers show the numbers skyrocketed, amounting to many thousands more plus tens of thousands of others fleeing the country in fear after having been surveilled, interrogated and detained or arrested in a systematic reign of state terror pattern of abuse leaving scars that won't ever heal. Those here only as visitors won't ever return or have faith in this country again. All affected are devastated by the experience. It harms individuals, communities and families, tearing them apart and leaving them to wonder how they'll recoup after being through so much. This is the state of America today, with horrific cases like Sami Al-Arian's and Rafil Dhafir's highlighting it.

A New Generation of War Resisters in Military Jails

Matt Meyer
2008

As the war in Iraq, and war in general, is resisted by an increasing number of people, the role of active duty soldiers and veterans takes on increasing importance. Like the Vietnam War resistance of a previous generation, the strategic significance of a U.S. military force that refuses to participate in imperialist design cannot be stressed enough. Unlike the previous generation, without a draft to rouse the ranks of noncombatents, the focus on war resisters has been reserved for those active duty objectors who face time not in U.S. courts and jails, but in military court martial and prison. A coordinated movement has centered around the Iraq Veterans Against the War <*www.ivaw.org*>, with support from a wide variety of peace movement groups. For general antiwar resistance and the movement to close the U.S. prison at Guantánamo, see the War Resisters League <www.warresisters.org> and Witness Against Torture <www.witnesstorture.org>.

The following statements are from Iraq Veterans Against the War members who have served, are serving, or face jail time for their refusal to support the war:

Specialist Suzanne Swift
The following is an excerpt taken from a statement written by Spc. Swift's mother, Sara Rich.

> It has now been 60 traumatic days since my daughter—who signed up with the Army as an MP, and after bravely serving one tour in Iraq, chose to go AWOL rather than engage in the two more tours to Iraq that awaited her—was forcibly taken from our home in handcuffs. Like many soldiers, she was suffering from Post-Traumatic Stress Disorder. What we didn't know, what she couldn't tell us, is that she was also suffering Military Sexual Trauma. Late the evening of Sunday June 11, 2006, Spc. Suzanne Swift was taken to the county jail, where she was strip-searched and orifice-checked.... She sat in that cell for two and a half days, a veteran of Iraq combat, terrified that she may be sent back. ...

In the meantime, we wait. We wait for the Army to decide what to do with my daughter. Perhaps they are waiting for us to break down emotionally, mentally and financially so that we will give up. They wait for our support to dwindle so they can do something unethical to Suzanne and get rid of her. I trusted the Army once before and was severely let down. But I wholeheartedly want to believe that the Army will do the right thing.

Spc. Swift is currently on active duty at Ft. Lewis, Washington, waiting for a decision on her discharge or possible court martial. Go to www.suzanneswift.org to find out how you can support Spc. Swift and also find information and resources on military sexual trauma.

Lieutenant Ehren Watada

The war in Iraq violates our democratic system of checks and balances. It usurps international treaties and conventions that by virtue of the Constitution become American law. The wholesale slaughter and mistreatment of the Iraqi people with only limited accountability is not only a terrible moral injustice, but a contradiction to the Army's own Law of Land Warfare. My participation would make me party to war crimes.

Normally, those in the military have allowed others to speak for them and act on their behalf. That time has come to an end. I have appealed to my commanders to see the larger issues of our actions. But justice has not been forthcoming. My oath of office is to protect and defend America's laws and its people. By refusing unlawful orders for an illegal war, I fulfill that oath today.

Lt. Watada is currently facing charges on seven counts, including missing movement, contempt toward officials, and conduct unbecoming an officer and gentleman. If convicted, Lt. Watada faces over eight years in prison. Political charges of "contempt toward the president" have been dropped, but four years of prison are still possible for political speech critical of the Iraq War. The trial date is not yet set, but is expected early 2007. Find out more about Lt. Watada and how you can support this IVAW member at www.thankyoult.org.

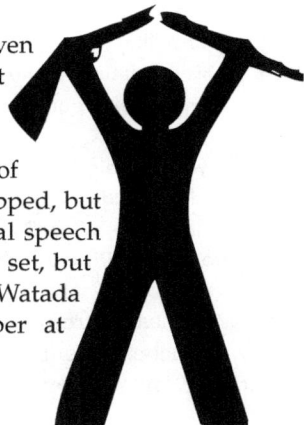

Sergeant Ricky Clousing

In Iraq, I operated as an interrogator and was attached to tactical infantry units during daily patrol operations. As an interrogator, I spoke to Iraqis each day. This gave me an idea of what local civilians thought of coalition forces. Throughout my training, very appropriate guidelines for the treatment of prisoners were set. However, I witnessed our baseless incarceration of civilians. I saw civilians physically harassed. I saw an innocent Iraqi killed before me by U.S. troops. I saw the abuse of power that goes without accountability.

Being attached to a tactical infantry unit and being exposed to the brutalities of war, I began to doubt and reconsider my beliefs. I thought about these experiences and what they meant each day I was deployed and until I was back in garrison at Fort Bragg in April of 2005. My convictions, spiritually and politically, began to make me call into question my ability to perform day-to-day functions as a soldier. I finally concluded after much consideration that I could not train or be trained under a false pretense of fighting for freedom.

After 14 months being AWOL, Sgt. Clousing turned himself in to authorities at Ft. Lewis, Washington, and is currently facing charges for desertion. Find out more about IVAW member Sgt. Clousing at www.couragetoresist.org.

Specialist Mark Wilkerson

There were many experiences that I had in Iraq that made me question my mission and also made me change the way I viewed spirituality, relationships, our government, and my life in general. It was a complete life turn-around, which allowed me to come to the conclusion that military service was no longer the correct path for me to take. This revelation led me to apply as a Conscientious Objector, or C.O., immediately upon return from Iraq in March 2004.

My C.O. claim was denied in November, so I applied for a rebuttal and was told it wouldn't be considered until my return from Iraq, more than a year away. So I made the difficult decision to go AWOL, for political, spiritual, and personal reasons.

Mark was released from a five-month incarceration on July 13, 2007, and is currently a college student and Colorado Springs chapter president. Read more about IVAW member Spc. Mark Wilkerson at markwilkerson.wordpress.com.

In Closing

Afterword
Lynne Stewart
2008

Thirty-five years after I first defended persons who had been criminalized by the State, I see even more clearly that our duty is not only to constantly champion them but to set them free. All that we believed but
couldn't necessarily prove is now abundantly clear—revealed, without
shame or blame or fear of reprisal by a vicious and oppressive government.
Torture??? I saw David Gilbert's black eyes and battered face in Rockland
County in 1981 and heard from him how the FBI broke Sam Brown's neck to
force him to identify other comrades. I heard Sekou Odinga reveal to a jury
the truth of the waterboarding he had endured in a Queens, New York, police
precinct.

When Richard Williams was transported to New Jersey from Ohio, the
troopers told him he was going get a real "ass whipping," which was prevented only by disclosure to the press. We have had "Guantánamos" in these
United States for decades.

The police state has now arrived, as predicted by my Brother and Friend Bill
Kunstler. Racially motivated murder in the streets and in the prisons. Callous
disregard by prosecuting authorities and the Judicial system. Immigrants are
now being sentenced to jail as the system makes it illegal to earn a living for
a suffering third world. And it all feeds an oppressive and ever-ravenous law
enforcement/prison system that Corporate Capitalism relies upon in more
ways than only the obvious.

What to do? I only know the old ways, enhanced by modern electronics.
Build Solidarity with these true heroes and heroines behind the walls!! Speak
up!! Organize !!! Write!! Email!! Blog!! Web Cast!!! Attend Rallies/Events and
bring people, especially the Youth, with you!!! Tell their stories. How these
true freedom fighters fought the system for the love of freedom and the people.
Our duty now is to set them free by all means possible and necessary.

After the Afterword:
America Means Prison
Ashanti Omowali Alston
2008

Dear to our hearts: the political prisoners. In fact, not just dear to our hearts, but—in the words of New Afrikan People's Organization founder Ahmed Obafemi—they are the heartbeats of our movements. They are the red ink dripping on the pages of our ongoing, unfolding stories of liberation within the confines of this prison called the United States of America.

Whether we are talking about Leonard Peltier of the American Indian Movement or the Black/New Afrikan liberation fighters, the Chicano/Atzlan liberation fighters or the *independentistas* of Puerto Rico, the white anti-imperialists or the earth/animal liberation fighters, we are essentially raising up the very foundational horrors of the American Empire. It's a fact that nothing can be truly done about changing our world or creating a new one without acknowledging and joining with these representatives who stood up to resist.

Land? "Free Leonard!" is also about coming to terms with the theft of this land and continuing genocide of the Indigenous peoples. "Free the San Francisco 8!" is also about coming to terms with the kidnapping, enslavement, and *continuing* judicial and social mass confinement of people of African descent. "Free Alvaro Luna Hernandez!" is also about coming to terms with the U.S. war on Mexico, the theft and incorporation of Mexican lands into the present-day U.S. You've heard the slogan: "We didn't cross the border, the border crossed us!"

"Free Oscar López Rivera!" is about coming to terms with the 1898 U.S. war with Spain, taking as its spoils the islands of Puerto Rico—still a colony to this very day. "Free Marilyn Buck!" is about coming to terms with revolutionary white folks who are not only post-modern-day Jane and John Browns giving unconditional support to folks of color liberation struggles, but who totally understand that their own humanity and liberation is tied to their frontline sacrifices. And "Free the SHAC 7!" is about coming to terms with new generations of folks who link their vision for nonoppressive, liberatory relations between human beings with *all* living things and the very planet. We have here the most ancient messages and wisdoms. Think of this, these political prisoners and their visions—their political vision quests—in light of all that is going on in the U.S. and the world empire today. In spite of how bad it looks, folks come forward to act. How can we not support them and work for their total freedom from judicial confinement?

Movements today extend from our political prisoners. Antiwar activists, do you know David Gilbert and the Vieques political prisoners? Environmental and animal rights activists, do you know Rod Coronado and Lauren Gazzola? Do you know the MOVE 9? Cop-watch activists, do you know Abdul Majid and Bashir Hameed, the Queens Two? Do you know Chip Fitzgerald? International solidarity supporters, do you know Leonard Peltier? You, who feed the hungry, demand housing for the homeless, and work for the best and free treatments for those with HIV/AIDS, do you know who came before you?

The political prisoners tell us by their very presence that the Empire will not disappear or give in. It will not even compromise. Whatever it offers as a solution will only "fix it" to last a little longer. Those crumbs will solve or resolve nothing. Yet the political prisoners say that "Power to all the Peoples" is the only solution. And victories, real victories, can only happen when those who came before us are put on the top of our agendas. We cannot just fight for the future. We must fight for the past, present, and future.

We must figure out how to bring it all together. This issue is not just about freedom for the confined revolutionaries. It is about freedom with dignity for all of us that can only come about through rejuvenated struggle. Freedom for the political prisoners can only come about when grassroots movements are organized for our lives and use the act of putting political prisoners on the top of our agendas as a momentous and monumental seizing of hearts from judicial confinement. This issue is for communities and for the people's institutions in our communities. It is for the revival of dignity amongst the Elders. It is for nurturing a dignified and righteous anger amongst the young. At the bottom line, we are at war!

We are at war, and they are closing in on us. They are using all the mechanisms at their disposal: the prison-industrial complex, the continued segregation and militarization of the police, the increased police occupation and murder of our communities, the underground drug economy's use as mass social control, and the increasing distance put between people and formal mechanisms of power. We are living under a system that has no more need for Black, Asian, Latin@, and Indigenous peoples and poor Whites. It is a system that criminalizes youth, hip-hop culture, attempting to unravel any hope for self-determination. It is a system that uses the "drug war," the "war against terrorism," and the PATRIOT Act to stimulate fear of so-called dangerous people. It is obvious that one key function of the democratic fascist state is to *pre-empt* revolutionary consciousness and organizing from gaining any ground. And one key to turn this back has to be *free all political prisoners*.

Free those whose armed points-of-entry into the brain of the Monster in the 1960s and 1970s led directly to their political confinement. They gave their all to struggle, to glorious revolution, to (as the Indigenous Elders would say) the next seven generations still unborn. We must fight aggressively for their total freedom, as powerful, organized grassroots movements!

In asking you to join us, we are asking you also to reclaim the honor of the phrase "revolutionary" for yourself. We must join together as revolutionaries who still believe in the dreams of our peoples. Our peoples... with many dreams flowing like rivers. We are asking that you not only be able to envi-

756

sion wonderful "after" scenarios, but that you also envision ourselves as daring to take on this Monster empire more assertively, more daringly. We are about reclaiming our lives, reclaiming the desire to live dignified lives. We are diverse peoples, respectful of each other and all living things. That's all, that's all. But to be willing to resist like a Geronimo, Harriet Tubman, John Brown, Brad Will, Richard Williams, Nuh Washington, Safiya Bukhari, Judi Bari, Filiberto Ojeda Ríos is a way of honoring those who sacrificed so much to prepare the way. To be willing to sacrifice like an Assata Shakur is a way of preparing your way, preparing our ways.

Thus we say that revolution ain't over, that no empire is invincible, and that the final determinator of all social dreams is the people, *__all the people__*.

**FREE THE POLITICAL PRISONERS,
BECAUSE WE WANT OUR HEARTS BACK.**

**FREE ALL THE POLITICAL PRISONERS,
BECAUSE WE WANT TO NOURISH OUR DREAMS.**

**FREE ALL THE POLITICAL PRISONERS,
BECAUSE WE ARE STILL EXCITED ABOUT THE NEW WORLDS.**

WE WILL CREATE ON THE ASHES OF IMPERIAL EVIL.

THE STORY CONTINUES... WE WILL WIN!

Appendix I.

Contributor Profiles

*T*hese profiles were compiled and condensed from a very wide range of sources, in some cases written by the person her/himself, in other cases not. Unfortunately, due to time constraints, we could not contact current political prisoners/POWs to review their profiles or solicit new biographical material (the exception being Bill Dunne, as he was already contributing new material for this volume). Any errors are the responsibility of the editor, Bob Lederer. The ages of the current political prisoners are included to remind readers of the advanced ages of many, and thus—especially given the purposeful denial of medical care by the prisons that hold them—the increasing urgency of working toward their immediate release.

Please note that prisoners' addresses can change periodically, so always check the websites at the top of the Political Prisoner Support Organization (page 808) section before writing a letter or circulating an address.

Mumia Abu-Jamal (formerly Wesley Cook), 54, is a renowned journalist from Philadelphia who has been in prison since 1981 and on death row since 1982 for allegedly shooting to death Philadelphia police officer Daniel Faulkner. He is known as the "Voice of the Voiceless" for his award-winning reporting on police brutality and other social and racial epidemics that plague communities of color in Philadelphia and throughout the world.

Mumia Abu-Jamal was serving as the president of the Association of Black Journalists at the time of his arrest. He was a founding member of the Philadelphia chapter of the Black Panther Party as a teenager. Years later he began reporting professionally on several radio stations, including affiliates of National Public Radio (NPR), and was the news director of Philadelphia station WHAT. Much of his journalism called attention to the blatant injustice and brutality he watched happen on a daily basis to MOVE, a revolutionary organization that works to protect all forms of life—human, animal, plant— and the earth as a whole.

Late at night on December 9, 1981, while driving a taxi to supplement his income, Mumia saw his brother being beaten by police officer Daniel Faulkner. He stepped out of his cab to intervene, at which point both he and Faulkner were shot. Although several witnesses claim they saw others flee the scene, Mumia was charged with Faulkner's murder. At Mumia's trial, Judge Albert Sabo denied him the right to have an attorney of his choosing (MOVE founder John Africa) and also denied Mumia the right to defend himself, even removing him from the courtroom during most of the proceedings. Witnesses heard Judge Sabo, notoriously eager to send people to the electric chair, utter racial slurs and a commitment to "fry" Mumia, and the prosecutor, in violation of Supreme Court rulings, used Mumia's Black Panther past as an argument for the death penalty.

A broad international movement has formed in support of Mumia. Celebrities such as Danny Glover, Susan Sarandon, and the late Ossie Davis; world leaders like Nelson Mandela, Danielle Mitterrand (former First Lady of France), and Fidel Castro; and governing bodies such as the Japanese Diet, 22 members of the British Parliament, and the European Parliament have all recognized the blatant injustice in this case and have called for a new trial at the very least. Millions of people throughout the world have taken to the streets to protest his unjust imprisonment.

In 1995, Mumia had a post-conviction review hearing before the same blatantly biased judge, Albert Sabo, who had presided over his original trial. Sabo refused to overturn his decision, and the Pennsylvania Supreme Court rejected Mumia's appeal. In 2001, U.S. District Court Judge William Yohn affirmed Mumia's conviction but voided his death sentence, citing "irregularities" in the original sentencing. The judge converted the sentence to life without parole and gave the prosecution the option to conduct a new sentencing hearing to determine whether Mumia would be sentenced to death. Both sides appealed. In March 2008, a three-judge panel of the U.S. Court of Appeals in Philadelphia affirmed Judge Yohn's decision upholding Mumia's conviction and denying him a new trial – despite clear evidence of many violations of his constitutional rights by prosecutors and Judge Sabo. The panel also affirmed Judge Yohn's decision overturning Mumia's original death sentence.. In July 2008, the full Third Circuit refused to rehear Mumia's appeal, and his attorney announced that he will seek review by the U.S. Supreme Court. If the prosecution continues to fight for execution, it could either ask the Supreme Court to reverse the voiding of Mumia's death sentence or it could insist on a new jury hearing on that issue, and there is a possibility that such a jury could reimpose the death sentence. For now, Mumia remains on death row.

From death row, Mumia has continued to speak out for all who are oppressed through his journalism. He has published five books, which have sold over 150,000 copies, and several have been translated into nine languages: *Live From Death Row* (Addison-Wesley, 1995, republished by HarperCollins, 1996),

All Things Censored (Seven Stories Press, 2000—Noelle Hanrahan, ed.), *Death Blossoms: Reflections from a Prisoner of Conscience* (Addison-Wesley, 1997; republished by South End Press, 2003), *Faith of Our Fathers: An Examination of the Spiritual Life of African and African-American People* (Africa World Press, 2004), and *We Want Freedom: A Life in the Black Panther Party* (South End Press, 2004). In addition, he has written for many publications, including the *Nation* and the *Yale Law Review*. His weekly columns are published throughout the world, and his frequent radio essays continue to air on stations of the Pacifica Radio Network and its affiliates—after a contract to broadcast them on NPR was abruptly canceled in 1994 under political pressure. Many of Mumia's recorded radio essays are available at www.prisonradio.org.

> Mumia Abu-Jamal
> AM 8335
> SCI-Greene
> 175 Progress Drive
> Waynesburg, PA 15370

See also Mumia Abu-Jamal Support Organizations under Support Organizations.

Sundiata Acoli (formerly Clark Squire), 71, is, after 35 years behind bars, one of the longest-serving political prisoners in the United States. Born and raised in Texas, he graduated from Prairie View A & M College of Texas in 1956 with a B.S. in mathematics. For the next 13 years, he worked for various computer-oriented firms, mostly in the New York area.

During the summer of 1964, he did voter registration work in Mississippi. In 1968 he joined the Harlem Black Panther Party and did community work around issues of schools, housing, jobs, child care, drugs, and police brutality. In 1969 he and 13 others were arrested in the Panther 21 conspiracy case (they were charged with plotting to bomb major New York City department stores), part of the FBI's COINTELPRO campaign to destroy the party. He was held in jail without bail and on trial for two years before being acquitted, along with all other defendants, by a jury deliberating less than two hours. Upon release, he found that FBI intimidation of potential employers shut off all employment possibilities in the computer profession, and stepped-up COINTELPRO harassment, surveillance, and provocations soon drove him underground.

In May 1973, while driving on the New Jersey Turnpike, Sundiata and two of his comrades were ambushed by New Jersey state troopers. One of them, Zayd Shakur, was killed, and another, Assata Shakur, was wounded and captured. One state trooper was killed and another wounded, and Sundiata was captured days later. After a highly sensationalized and prejudicial trial, he was convicted of the death of the state trooper and of Zayd Shakur and was sentenced to life plus 30 years. (Assata was convicted in a separate but equally unfair trial; see also profile of Assata Shakur.)

Upon entering Trenton State Prison, he was confined to a new and specially created Management Control Unit solely because of his political background. Let out of the cell only 10 minutes a day for showers and two hours twice a week for recreation, he was held for almost five years. In September 1979, the *International Jurist* interviewed Sundiata and subsequently declared him a political prisoner. Days later, prison officials secretly transferred him to the federal prison system, where he was placed in the harsh, 23-hour-a-day-locked-down Marion (Illinois) Control Unit. He remained there for eight years. In 1992 he was denied parole. Among the Parole Board's stated reasons were Sundiata's pre-arrest membership in the Black Panther Party and the BLA and the board's receipt of hundreds of "Free Sundiata" form letters that characterized him as a New Afrikan Prisoner of War. The courts rejected his appeal of that decision. In 2004, the Parole Board again turned down his application. Sundiata is the author of the articles "A Brief History of the New Afrikan Prison Struggle" (1992) available at www.prisonactivist.org/pubs/brief-hist-naps.html, and "A Brief History of the Black Panther Partyand Its Place in the Black Liberation Movement" (1995), available at www.hartford-hwp.com/archives/45a/004.html. He also wrote a eulogy published in *Kuwasi Balagoon: A Soldier's Story* (Kersplebedeb, 2003). A documentary feature film about Sundiata's life, *A Power Sun*, is in development by Field Up Productions. For more information about the project and how to donate to it, visit www.fieldup.com/power_sun.htm.

> Sundiata Acoli #39794-066
> FCI Otisville, P.O. Box 1000
> Otisville, NY 10963

See also Sundiata Acoli Freedom Campaign under Support Organizations.

Janine Africa (formerly Janine Phillips), 52, is one of the MOVE 9 political prisoners (the other eight are Charles Sims Africa, Debbie Sims Africa, Delbert Africa, Edward Goodman Africa, Janet Holloway Africa, Merle Austin Africa, Michael Africa, and William Phillips "Phil"Africa) who have been held for 30 years. The MOVE 9 are innocent men and women who have been in prison since August 8, 1978, following an assault by 600 heavily armed police on MOVE Headquarters in PoweltonVillage, Philadelphia (seven years before the city government—with FBI support—dropped a bomb on MOVE, killing 11 people, including 5 children). The 1978 military assault was conducted under the direction of then-mayor and former police commissioner Frank Rizzo—well known for his history of abuse of communities of color—following a one-year siege of MOVE's house and years of police brutality against the organization. (For example, in March 1976, police beat and fractured the skulls of six MOVE men; when Janine Africa tried to protect her husband, Phil, a cop threw her to the ground with three-week-old Life Africa in her arms. The cop stomped them until Janine was nearly unconscious, crushing the skull of the baby, who died. Police denied the attack and even claimed that no such baby had ever been born, but MOVE members displayed the body to city councilmembers willing to view it.)

During the 1978 assault, police moved in while SWAT teams staked out every possible exit. MOVE members retreated to the basement, where they withstood fire hoses and water deluge guns. As the basement flooded, they held children and dogs above the rising water. Suddenly shots rang out and bullets immediately filled the air as police throughout the area opened fire, ultimately discharging over 2,000 rounds. Officer James Ramp was struck and killed by a single bullet.

MOVE adults came out of the house carrying their children through clouds of tear gas and were immediately taken into custody. MOVE never fired any shots, and no MOVE members were arrested with any weapons. All were viciously beaten. TV cameras filmed police brutally beating and kicking Delbert Africa (three of the four police officers were brought to trial and acquitted despite irrefutable photographic evidence). The city bulldozed and leveled the house immediately that day, thereby destroying evidence.

The MOVE 9 were sentenced in 1980 to 30 to 100 years each, allegedly for the death of Officer Ramp. Autopsy reports show clearly that the bullet that hit Ramp traveled in a *downward* direction; MOVE members were in the basement of their house *below* the street, making it ballistically imposssible for them to have fired the shot. In reality, the MOVE 9 were sentenced because they were MOVE members. When Judge Edward Malmed was a guest on a radio show a few days later, journalist Mumia Abu-Jamal called in to ask him who killed Ramp. Malmed replied, "I haven't the faintest idea." He said that since "they call themselves a family, I sentenced them as a family."Three other adults who were in the house on August 8 did not get the same treatment as those that the government knew were committed MOVE members.

Merle Africa died of cancer in prison in 1998. The other eight remain in prisons across the state of Pennsylvania. In April 2008, the three surviving MOVE women (Debbie, Janet, and Janine Africa) were denied parole by the state parole board, which claimed that the women minimized or denied the nature and circumstances of the offense, refused to accept responsibility, and lacked remorse and that MOVE members act outside the "law." In fact, it's the parole board that is "acting outside the law" by demanding that any inmate say that they are guilty when they are not. Mike and Eddie Africa were similarly denied parole in May 2008, as were Phil and Del Africa in June 2008. Chuck Africa's parole hearing is scheduled for October 2008.

Janine Africa has written: "I'm Janine Africa, Minister of Education for the MOVE Organization. I've been in MOVE since 1973. I'm one of the MOVE 9. If I have to be in prison for the rest of my life, I will still stay committed to JOHN AFRICA's Teaching because of all JOHN AFRICA is doing for me. I met MOVE people when I was 17 years old. They were having a demonstration and I just happened to be passing by. I stopped to see what was going on, I listened to them speak, and what really caught my attention was the strength, confidence, and assertiveness of the MOVE women. They were everything I wasn't and all I could think about was that I wanted to be like them. After the demonstration, I approached some of the MOVE women and asked who they were. They told me they were the MOVE Organization and explained to me what the organization's belief is. They invited me to come to their weekly study sessions they held to teach people about JOHN AFRICA's Teaching. I started going to these study sessions regularly and listening to the information from MOVE's Guidelines, and I could hear that what JOHN AFRICA teaches is the truth, is right. JOHN AFRICA's Teaching is what I've been looking for because I was just like everybody else in the system, unhappy, riddled with problems, and desperately looking elsewhere for the solution to these problems. My search stopped with JOHN AFRICA."

> Janine Phillips Africa #006309
> SCI-Cambridge Springs
> 451 Fullerton Avenue
> Cambridge Springs, PA 16403-1238

See also the MOVE organization under Support Organizations.

Phil Africa (formerly William Phillips). Phil, 52, has written: "My name is Phil Africa, a revolutionary disciple of MOVE's revered founder, John Africa, and one of the 'MOVE 9.' Since August 9, 1978, eight of my MOVE sisters, brothers, and myself have been unjustly imprisoned, framed for the death of a cop who was killed while he participated in a vicious racist genocidal system that directed attack on our family at our Philadelphia headquarters, in this rotten system's ongoing attempts to stop John Africa, a wise righteous powerful strategic Black man who generates the MOVE organization." In June 2008, he was denied parole. (For more details about the MOVE 9 case, see Janine Africa above.)

> William Phillips Africa #AM-4984
> SCI-Dallas
> 1000 Follies Road
> Dallas, PA 18612

See also the MOVE organization under Support Organizations

CONTRIBUTOR PROFILES

Ramona Africa is the sole adult survivor of the May 13, 1985, massacre of 11 members of the MOVE organization. The FBI and the city of Philadelphia dropped a C4 bomb on MOVE's 6221 Osage Avenue home in West Philadelphia. Both Ramona (then 30) and Birdie Africa (then 13, whom Ramona carried to safety) later reported that as the MOVE family attempted to escape their burning home, they were met with massive rounds of automatic gunfire, forcing 11 human beings to be burnt alive. Ramona dodged gunfire and escaped from the fire with permanent scarring from the burns.

After surviving the bombing, she was charged with conspiracy, riot, and multiple counts of simple and aggravated assault. Subsequently Ramona served seven years in prison. If she had chosen to sever her ties with MOVE, she could have been released far earlier. In the face of this, she held true to her revolutionary beliefs and was uncompromising in the face of state terror.

Despite two grand jury investigations and a commission that found that top city officials were negligent in the murderous 1985 bombing, no government leaders or employees were ever charged with any crimes. In 1996, in a civil suit brought by Ramona, a jury found the police and fire commissioners and the city of Philadelphia liable for the MOVE bombing, and Ramona was awarded $500,000 for pain and suffering and for disfigurement.

Since her release from prison, Ramona has tirelessly worked as the MOVE minister of communication on behalf of the MOVE 9, Mumia Abu-Jamal, and all political prisoners and prisoners of war. She has spoken at numerous colleges and universities throughout the U.S. and abroad.

Ashanti Omowali Alston is an anarchist activist, speaker, and writer and former member of the Black Panther Party. He was also a member of the Black Liberation Army, and spent over 14 years in prison as a result of his political activism. Ashanti is a former northeast coordinator for Critical Resistance, currently co-chair of the National Jericho Movement (to free U.S. political prisoners), a member of the pro-Zapatista, people-of-color, U.S.-based *Estación Libre*, and a member of the Malcolm X Grassroots Movement in New York City. His website is www.anarchistpanther.net.

Kuwasi Balagoon (1946-1986) was a staunch advocate of liberation for the New Afrikan nation (colonized Black people in the U.S.) and the eradication of capitalism, as well as an anarchist and a participant in armed struggle. In the late 1960s, serving a stint in the U.S. Army in Germany, he and other Black GIs formed a clandestine direct action group called De Legislators, which set out to punish racist soldiers with beatings or worse. Upon his return to the U.S., he became involved with the Black Panther Party in New York City. Kuwasi was one of the Panther 21, whom the government attempted (unsuccessfully) to frame in 1969. Many of his earliest writings can be found in the collective autobiography of the Panther 21, *Look for Me in the Whirlwind*. As the Party disintegrated due to outside pressure from the police and FBI as well as internal conflicts, Kuwasi went underground, joining the part that became the Black Liberation Army (BLA), a formation that engaged in armed confrontation with the state, breaking comrades out of prison, attacking the police, and carrying out expropriations against capitalists.

Captured and convicted of various crimes against the state, he spent much of the 1970s in prison, escaping twice. After each escape, he went underground and resumed BLA activity. In search of theoretical grounding, he began reading anarchist work and embraced anarchism while retaining his unbending support for New Afrikan independence. Kuwasi was captured again in January 1982, charged with participating in a Brink's armored car expropriation in West Nyack, New York, in October of the previous year. In that failed action—carried out by the Revolutionary Armed Task Force, an alliance of the BLA and white activists—two police officers and a money courier were killed. Tried on felony murder

765

charges along with white anti-imperialists David Gilbert and Judy Clark, he took a position as a POW and was convicted and sentenced (along with them) to 75 years to life. A bisexual man, he died in prison of complications of AIDS in December 1986.

A collection of writings by and about Balagoon, *Kuwasi Balagoon, A Soldier's Story*, was published by Solidarity in 2001, and subsequently republished by Kersplebedeb in 2003. (See ad at end of book.) Kersplebedeb also maintains a series of web pages about Balagoon at http://www.urbanguerilla.org/kuwasibalagoon.html

Herman Bell, New Afrikan political prisoner, 60, was born in Mississippi and moved to Brooklyn, New York, as a boy. He was a talented high school football player and won a football scholarship to the University of California in Oakland. While in Oakland, Herman joined the Black Panther Party and became active around human rights issues in the Black community. In 1971, he went underground because of relentless FBI attacks on Black activists, in particular the Black Panther Party. In September 1973 he was captured in New Orleans and extradited to New York on charges of having killed two New York City police officers in 1971—a case for which his comrades Jalil Muntaqim and the now-deceased Nuh Washington *(see also profiles of them)* were already jailed awaiting trial, in the case that came to be called the "New York 3."

Herman has written: "In the aftermath of the murders of Malcolm X, Medgar Evers, Dr. King, Fred Hampton, and Mark Clark, to name a few, coupled with the Civil Rights Movement, the burgeoning Black consciousness movement, and the antiwar movement of the 1960s and 1970s, the tone and spirit of those times can be described as highly charged and volatile. And in the wake of what had been perceived as an unambiguous racist policy of police malevolence, willful brutality, excessive use of deadly force and general disrespect of Black people's rights, scores of policemen at that time were seriously injured or fatally shot in the Black community. I come out of that time period.

"In 1975, after two trials [the first resulted in a hung jury], I was convicted (along with my two codefendants) of having killed two New York City policemen, to which we all pled not guilty. No eyewitness identified me as one of the assailants. Coerced witnesses, manufactured and circumstantial material evidence, along with prosecutorial and judicial misconduct are what persuaded the jury to convict at the end of the second trial."

Also, despite the secret involvement of the FBI and Nixon's White House in efforts to secure a conviction, the trial judge refused to allow testimony about the infamous COINTELPRO program. All of the New York 3 were sentenced to 25 years to life. Years and years of state and federal appeals have been unsuccessful. Yet during one appeal hearing, a federal judge found that a New York City detective perjured himself about ballistics evidence at the original trial. The government illegally destroyed all ballistics evidence during the appellate process.

Since his conviction, Herman has been a prison activist who has coached sports teams and counseled countless others to complete their education. He earned both his bachelor's degree in psychology and sociology and his master's degree in sociology while in prison. In 1995, he met two environmental activist farmers from Maine, and together they created the Victory Gardens Project. The project brought people together from diverse lifestyles and remote locations—the urban-rural connection—to plant, grow, tend, harvest, and then distribute free food to various communities. This project enjoyed eight successful seasons, with Herman as an active participant via his outreach and writings. In 2002, Herman joined with other U.S. political prisoners in a pen-pal dialogue with homeless children in New York City, which was made into a booklet for free distribution. From 2002 on, Herman has been instrumental in the production of an annual political prisoner calendar with the help of Montreal activists. This extremely educational item, *Certain Days* has been distributed internationally, documenting the historic and current struggles and sacrifices of our imprisoned activists. The proceeds have consistently been dedicated to the support of various community groups.

Now, after nearly 35 years of imprisonment, Herman faces new charges. He and seven other Elder Black activists and former members and associates of the Black Panther Party (including his codefendant Jalil Muntaqim) were falsely charged in January 2007 with conspiracy in a police killing that took place nearly 40 years ago in San Francisco (see also the San Francisco 8 profile). Jalil Muntaqim and Herman were extradited to California to stand trial, but as of July 2008, they are seeking to return to New York State for their parole hearings in the New York 3 case, after which the state will transport them back to California.

Herman Bell, #2318931
850 Bryant Street
San Francisco, CA 94103

See also Committee for the Defense of Human Rights under Support Organizations.

Hans Bennett is a prison-abolitionist, an independent multimedia journalist, and co-founder of Journalists for Mumia, www.Abu-Jamal-news.com. His website is insubordination.blogspot.com.

Dan Berger is a Philadelphia-based activist and author of *Outlaws of America: The Weather Underground and the Politics of Solidarity* (AK Press, 2006). He is the coeditor (with Chesa Boudin and Kenyon Farrow) of *Letters From Young Activists* (Nation Books, 2005) and of the forthcoming anthology *70s Confidential: Hidden Histories from the 60s Second Decade*. His articles have appeared in *Monthly Review*, the *Nation*, the *Philadelphia Inquirer*, *Z magazine*, and elsewhere. Dan is currently working on a project about prison struggles in the 1970s. Politicized as a teenager in the mid-1990s, he was the founding coeditor of the anarchist newspaper *Onward*, which came out of the global justice movement. Currently he is part of the anti-imperialist collective Resistance in Brooklyn, works with Critical Resistance, and serves on the advisory board to the anticapitalist journal *Upping the Anti*. His writings and work can be found online at www.danberger.org.

Dhoruba Bin-Wahad (formerly Richard Moore) was born in the South Bronx in 1944. He joined the Black Panther Party in New York City in 1968 and organized chapters along the Eastern Seaboard while working with tenants in Harlem and on drug rehabilitation in the Bronx. He was arrested in 1969 as part of the New York Panther 21 conspiracy case (charged with conspiring to blow up department stores, subway stations, and police stations). While free on bail, and after receiving numerous death threats, Dhoruba fled to Algeria, but returned to New York in May 1971 following the full acquittal of all Panther 21 defendants. A month later, he was indicted for the shootings of two cops guarding the district attorney's home and the shooting deaths of two cops in a Harlem housing project. He maintained his innocence. The first trial ended in a hung jury. Following a second mistrial in 1973, he was convicted and sentenced to 25 years to life. Dhoruba appealed his conviction and over years of struggle forced the FBI to release thousands of classified documents proving that he had been framed as part of a massive COINTELPRO operation. This finally forced a New York State judge to overturn his conviction in 1990, leading to his release after 19 years of false imprisonment—seven of those years in solitary confinement. The state prosecutors appealed but ultimately lost. Dhoruba later sued the state and in 2000 won a large settlement on the eve of the trial.

For several years, Dhoruba has lived in Ghana, where he has run a nongovernmental organization (NGO) that coordinated expatriate expertise to evaluate policies from a grassroots

Pan-African perspective and also edited an e-newsletter, *African Chronicles*. He has worked with scores of civil war refugees in West Africa seeking asylum in the United States and elsewhere. On several occasions, Dhoruba has appeared before the United Nations Commission on Human Rights and the U.N. Decolonization Committee as an NGO representative. He has participated in and organized several international forums and tribunals on political prisoners and human rights violations in the United States. He has also acted as an unpaid consultant to various grassroots Civil Rights campaigns in the U.S.

Dhoruba's writings have appeared in numerous publications from *Covert Action Information Bulletin* to various anthologies of African-American activist writers. His work has been published in *The Black Scholar* and various African and Middle-Eastern journals. He continues to write for various Black publications. He collaborated with Mumia Abu-Jamal and Assata Shakur on the book *Still Black, Still Strong* (Semiotext(e), 1993; now distributed by AK Press). Dhoruba's experiences were featured in two award-winning film documentaries *Framing the Panthers in Black & White* and *Passin' It On*. As a contributing correspondent from Africa to Pacifica Radio station WBAI's *Afrikaleidoscope* program (hosted by Elombe Brath—see profile), Dhoruba has provided timely insight into current affairs on the African continent from the point of view of a Pan-African. Dhoruba currently lives in the U.S. and West Africa.

Terry Bisson is a Hugo Award-winning science fiction author who, back in the day, was an activist in the anti-imperialist movement associated with the Weather Underground, at which time he did most of what was expected of him, and little that wasn't. He was imprisoned for three months in 1985 for refusing to testify before a federal grand jury investigating the anti-imperialist movement. His 1988 novel about John Brown, *Fire on the Mountain*, will be reprinted by Red Sea Press in the fall of 2008. Among many other works, Terry is also the author of *On a Move: The Story of Mumia Abu-Jamal* (Plough Publishing, 2001).

B♀ (rita d. brown) is a 60-year-old white working-class butch dyke lesbian antiauthoritarian anti-imperialist ex-political prisoner who has done nine years in federal prison. The first one was as a social prisoner in 1971 and the other eight as a political prisoner in the 1980s for several bank robberies in Oregon claimed by the George Jackson Brigade, an independent underground cell operating out of Seattle, Washington. She has been a prison abolitionist for more than 30 years. B♀ is also a founding mother of Out of Control: Lesbian Committee to Support Women Political Prisoners and also works regularly with All of Us or None, as well as the Prison Activist Resource Center in Oakland, California, where she lives and spends a lot of time on the phone talking with prisoners' families. All of this grassroots work is volunteer and solely motivated by the need to create real change and real community where children will matter and prisons will not seem to be so damn necessary and will not be such an incredible source of income for the ruling class. Writings by and about B♀ and the George Jackson Brigade are available at www.gjbip.org.

Veronza Bowers, Jr., 62, is one of the longest-held political prisoners in U.S. history. In the late 1960s, Veronza was one of the principal organizers of the Black Panther Party chapter in Omaha, Nebraska. In 1973, as part of the FBI's infamous COINTELPRO against the Panthers, Veronza was tried and convicted of the murder of a U.S. park ranger on the word of two government informers, both of whom received reduced sentences for other crimes by the federal prosecutor's office. There were no eyewitnesses and no evidence independent of these informants to link him to the crime. At his trial, Veronza offered alibi testimony, which was not credited by the jury, nor was testimony of two relatives of the informants who insisted that they were lying. The informants had all charges against them in this case dropped, and one was given $10,000 by the government, according to the prosecutor's post-sentencing report. Veronza was sentenced to 30 years, but has consistently proclaimed his innocence of the crime he never committed—even at the expense of having his appeals for parole denied.

In the 35 years of his confinement, Veronza has become a "model" prisoner. He is an author, musician, student of Asian healing arts, and practitioner of Buddhist meditation. Veronza is also an honorary elder of the Lompoc Tribe of Five Feathers, a Native American spiritual and cultural group. He is a mentor and founder of the All-Faith Meditation Group, a nondenominational spiritual organization devoted to healing meditation using the traditional Japanese shakuhachi flute.

Veronza was scheduled for mandatory parole on April 7, 2004. Mandatory parole is a requirement by statute after a prisoner has completed his full sentence if there is a record of positive institutional behavior and if one cannot consider the inmate a "threat to society" upon release. Four different Parole Examiners, as well as the U.S. Parole Commission (USPC) itself, the most powerful parole authority in the nation, agreed that Veronza had complied with these prerequisites. Despite this, just minutes before his scheduled release, the USPC rescinded his parole at the request of a powerful law enforcement lobby group known as the Fraternal Order of Police (FOP), which claimed to have evidence that Veronza had violated prison rules.

At a later hearing, the court dismissed FOP claims as unsubstantiated, and a new parole date was set. But the FOP then successfully lobbied then-U.S. attorney general Alberto Gonzales to intervene. On October 6, 2005, the U.S. Parole Commission upheld Gonzales's request to deny Veronza parole and keep him indefinitely in prison. The truth of the matter is that Veronza has served his full sentence under law plus, as of 2008, more than four years of illegal detention.

> Veronza Bowers, Jr. #35316-136
> USP Atlanta
> P.O. Box 150160
> Atlanta, GA 30315

See also Veronza Bowers, Jr. Legal Defense Fund under Support Organizations.

Francis A. Boyle is professor of international law at the University of Illinois, Champaign. He received a J.D. degree magna cum laude and A.M. and Ph.D. degrees in political science from Harvard University. Professor Boyle is a widely respected authority who has advised numerous international bodies in the areas of human rights, war crimes and genocide, nuclear policy, and biowarfare.

He was responsible for drafting the Biological Weapons Anti-Terrorism Act of 1989, the U.S. implementing legislation for the 1972 Biological Weapons Convention. He served as legal advisor to the Palestinian Delegation to the Middle East Peace Negotiations from 1991 to 1993, served on the Board of Directors of Amnesty International (1988-1992), and represented Bosnia-Herzegovina at the World Court. He has written and lectured extensively in the United States and abroad on the relationship between international law and politics. He has represented national and international bodies including the Blackfoot Nation (Canada), the Nation of Hawaii, and the Lakota Nation, as well as numerous individual death penalty and human rights cases. He was special prosecutor at the International Tribunal of Indigenous Peoples and Oppressed Nations in San Francisco in 1992.

Professor Boyle is the author of numerous books, including *Defending Civil Resistance Under International Law* (Translational Publishers, 1987), *The Criminality of Nuclear Deterrence* (Clarity Press, 2002), *Palestine, Palestinians and International Law* (Clarity

Press, 2003), and *Destroying World Order: U.S. Imperialism in the Middle East Before and After September 11th* (Clarity Press, 2004). His *Protesting Power: War, Resistance and Law* (Rowman & Littlefield, 2007) has been used successfully in antiwar protest trials. His latest book is *Breaking All the Rules: Palestine, Iraq, Iran and the Case for Impeachment* (Clarity Press, 2008).

Patrick Braouezec is the former mayor of Saint-Denis, France, and is currently president of the Community of 12 Suburban Cities, including Saint-Denis. He is an elected representative to the National Assembly of France. He is a member of the French Communist Party and has been active in a range of progressive issues, including opposition to the death penalty in the U.S. and support for the case of Mumia Abu-Jamal.

Elombe Brath is a lifelong Pan-African activist, journalist, and educator. He has been host for years of the weekly public affairs program, *Afrikaleidoscope* (about African struggles worldwide) on WBAI/Pacifica Radio in New York. In 1956, Elombe cofounded the African Jazz-Art Society & Studios, a jazz concert series and cultural and political forum to discuss the exploitation of Black people. He later worked for 37 years at ABC-TV as a graphic artist and videotape librarian, 10 years as shop steward, and 17 years as African affairs consultant at *Like It Is*, a Black public affairs program produced and hosted by Gil Noble, an award-winning television producer at WABC-TV, Channel 7 (still on the air). He cofounded the Patrice Lumumba Coalition in 1975 and remains its chair. During the 1990s, Elombe worked with the U.N. Special Committee Against Apartheid and the U.N. Commission on Namibia and was invited to join a team of international monitors for the first nonapartheid election in South Africa in 1994. Elombe served as the cochair and moderator of a Harlem reception for Nelson Mandela in 1990 and was the moderator for a reception for President Fidel Castro at Abyssinian Baptist Church. For years, his Harlem forums provided community residents and activists with direct reports from African and Caribbean heads of state and national liberation movement leaders. When it comes to Africa and the history of Black struggle in the U.S. or elsewhere, Elombe has been considered the "Walking Encyclopedia." His knowledge of the history of Black people has caused him to be a favorite for information for students, journalists, and world leaders alike. He has also been a consistent supporter of freedom for U.S. political prisoners.

Richard Brown, 65, has worked for decades in San Francisco on issues affecting poor people such as affordable housing. Employed for 20 years as a program coordinator at the Ella Hill Hutch Community Center, he's also a founding member of the African American Police Community Relations Board and several other neighborhood organizations. He has also been a community court judge arbitrator working with the San Francisco District Attorney's office. He was arrested in the San Francisco 8 case in January 2007 and finally freed on bail in August 2007. He is currently awaiting trial.

See also **San Francisco 8** *in this section. For Richard's address and other support information, see* Committee for the Defense of Human Rights *under* Political Prisoner Support Organizations.

Dennis Brutus, distinguished poet, writer, educator, and activist, was born in 1924 in Zimbabwe and educated in South Africa. Known as the "singing voice of the South African Liberation Movement," Dennis was involved in political campaigns that led to his being banned from all political, social, and literary activity and his arrest in 1963 and incarceration on Robben Island, where he served time with such leaders as Nelson Mandela, Walter Sisulu, and Robert Sobukwe. When Dennis was released from prison in 1966, he traveled across Africa before making his way to the United States, where in 1983, after a long struggle, he won political refugee status and resumed his career as a poet and antiapartheid campaigner. He helped secure South Africa's expulsion from the Olympics in 1970. In the U.S. Dennis has held appointments at several universities. He is currently professor emeritus of African studies and African literature at the University of Pittsburgh and a professor at the University of KwaZulu-Natal in South Africa, to which he recently returned. He has lectured worldwide as well as in South Africa and is the recipient of several awards.

Following the transition to democracy in South Africa, Dennis remained active with grassroots social movements in his home country and internationally. In the late 1990s, he became a pivotal figure in the global justice movement and a featured speaker each year at the World Social Forum. In the antiracism, reparations, and economic justice movements, he continues to serve as a leading strategist, working closely with the Center for Economic Justice, 50 Years Is Enough! and the Jubilee antidebt movement. In South Africa, he is a key figure in the Social Movements Indaba, the coalition of progressive activists who marched more than 25,000 people against the World Summit on Sustainable Development in 2002. He is the author of several books of poetry. His work has been collected in *Poetry & Protest: A Dennis Brutus Reader*, edited by Lee Sustar and Aisha Karim (Haymarket Books, 2006). His website is www.dennisbrutus.com.

Marilyn Buck, 60, is an anti-imperialist political prisoner, imprisoned for actions supporting national liberation, women's liberation, and social and economic justice. In the 1960s, Marilyn participated in protests against racism and the Vietnam war and joined Students for a Democratic Society. She joined a radical filmmaking collective and participated in international solidarity groups supporting the Vietnamese, the Palestinians, and the Iranian struggle against the Shah. She worked in solidarity with the Native American, Mexicano, and Black liberation struggles.

In 1973, she was arrested and convicted of buying two boxes of bullets. Accused of being a member of the Black Liberation Army, she was sentenced to 10 years, the longest sentence ever given for such an offense at the time. In 1977 she was granted a furlough and did not return to prison. In 1985 she was captured and faced four separate trials. She was convicted of conspiracy, including the successful liberation of Assata Shakur from a New Jersey prison. Marilyn and her codefendants, Dr. Mutulu Shakur and Sekou Odinga, were also convicted of conspiracy to commit "armed bank robbery" in support of the New Afrikan independence struggle. In 1988 she was one of those charged in the Resistance Conspiracy case. In 1990, Marilyn, with Laura Whitehorn and Linda Evans, pled guilty to parts of the indictment (including the bombing of the U.S. Capitol) in exchange for the dropping of charges against three other codefendants: Alan Berkman, Tim Blunk, and Susan Rosenberg (particularly out of concern for Alan, then seriously ill), all already serving lengthy sentences for related cases. Marilyn's total sentence is 80 years. She is scheduled for release in 2011.

In the Dublin, California, federal women's prison, Marilyn is deeply involved in cultural and educational activities for prisoners and translates for Spanish-speaking women prisoners. She participated in the call by political prisoners to organize for Mumia Abu-Jamal's life and contributed to Art and Writings Against the Death Penalty. She writes poetry; in 2001 she won the PEN Prison Writing Program poetry prize. She has written numerous articles for progressive books, magazines, and journals. In prison Marilyn has earned B.A. and M.S. degrees and has written, "I am deeply interested in the psychology of repression and resistance, and the psychological results of both state and self-censorship. I intend to use my skills to help explain and transform prison conditions and existence."

In 1998, *Enemies of the State*, a collection of interviews with Marilyn and others, was published by Resistance in Brooklyn (later republished separately by Abraham Guillen Press and Kersplebedeb). A collection of Marilyn's poems, *Rescue the Word*, was published in 2001 (available from AK Press). In 2004 the Freedom Archives released a CD, "Wild Poppies,"featuring more than 20 poets reading 46 poems, most written by Marilyn. In 2008, Marilyn's translation of the poetry of Uruguayan political exile Cristina Peri Rossi, *State of Exile* (City Lights Press) was published, with an introduction by Marilyn. Poetry and other writings by Marilyn are available at www.prisonactivist.org/pps+pows/marilynbuck.

In Marilyn's words:"Just because we are prisoners does not mean that we have lost our reasoning, analytical powers. We still have a worldview based on long years of experience. Too many, even in our political movements, would prefer to relegate us to museum pieces, objects of campaigns perhaps, but not political subjects and comrades in an ongoing political struggle against imperialism, oppression, and exploitation. The state tries to isolate us, true; that makes it all the more important not to let it succeed in its proposition. We fight for political identity and association from here; it is important that political forces on the outside not lose sight of why the state wants to isolate and destroy us, and therefore fight to include us in political life, [including] ideological struggle. Don't lock us into roles as objects or symbols."

Marilyn Buck #00482-285
Unit B, 5701 8th Street, Camp Parks
Dublin, CA 94568

See also Friends of Marilyn Buck under Support Organizations.

Safiya Bukhari (1950-2003) had a long history of revolutionary struggle. She was a deep-thinking and brilliant sister, a grassroots organizer, a political strategist, and a unifier around principled positions. Joining the Black Panther Party (BPP) around 1969, when the state was doing everything it could to destroy the Party, Safiya later joined the Black Liberation Army (BLA). Safiya was devastated by the loss of her comrades, as one after another revolutionary was murdered by the police or captured and incarcerated. Ultimately, she, too, spent close to nine years in prison, during which time she managed to make a daring escape (though she was captured and locked up again). When released, Safiya immediately threw herself into political prisoner support work, dedicating herself to the freedom of all political prisoners, not just those from her own organizations. She felt very strongly that we could never build a movement, could never expect people to make the sacrifices that needed to be made in a revolution, if we weren't there to support each other (and each other's families) when we were caught, incarcerated, or died. She followed every appeal, every parole hearing, and all of the prisoners' health conditions. She wrote prolifically about individual cases, designed and made political prisoner T-shirts, buttons, bumper stickers, mouse pads, and fact sheets.

Safiya was an anchor of the campaign to free the New York 3 and founded the Free Mumia Abu-Jamal Coalition in New York City in 1992, establishing it as a significant force in the movement to free Mumia, as well as in the overall struggle to free political prisoners. She cochaired it until her passing. In 1998 she, along with others, founded the Jericho Movement to free all U.S. political prisoners and served as national cochair until her passing. She also served as vice president of the Provisional Government of the Republic of New Afrika, an organization working toward the formation of a separate Black nation comprised of five southern states that were built on the backs of enslaved Africans. In her later years, Safiya took Islam as her religion and found great strength in the spirituality it embodied.

Chrystos, born off-reservation in San Francisco to a Menominee father and a Euro-immigrant mother, is a self-educated writer, artist, and activist who identifies as an Urban

Indian. From a feminist and lesbian perspective, Chrystos uses her poetry and activism to explore issues of class, genocide, colonialism, and gender and how these affect women and Indian peoples. Her work as a Native land and treaty rights activist has been widely recognized, and politics are an essential part of her writing, though she refuses to be taken as a "voice" of Native women or as a "spiritual leader." She worked toward freedom for imprisoned Indian activist Norma Jean Croy and continues to work for the freedom of Leonard Peltier. The other dominant aspect of her work is her identity as a lesbian, which she is outspoken about and personalizes in her love-and-lust poems. She is the author of the poetry books *Not Vanishing* (1988), *Dream On* (1991), *In Her I Am* (1993), *Fugitive Colors* (1995), and *Fire Power* (1995). Her work has also appeared in such anthologies as *This Bridge Called My Back: Writings by Radical Women of Color* (1981) and *Living the Spirit: A Gay American Indian Anthology* (1988). She was the winner of the Audre Lorde International Poetry Competition in 1994 and of the Sappho Award of Distinction from the Astraea National Lesbian Action Foundation in 1995.

John Henrik Clarke, Ph.D. (1915-1998), historian, Black nationalist, and Pan-Africanist, was a pioneer in the formation of African heritage and Black studies programs around the United States. Principally a self-trained historian, Dr. Clarke dedicated his life to correcting what he argued was the prevailing view that people of Africa and of African decent had no history worthy of study. Over the span of his career, he became one of the world's most respected historians of African and African American history. Dr. Clarke was also known for his influence on several generations of African American leaders. Among his many scholarly titles, he was the first president of the African Heritage Studies Association and was a founding member of the Black Academy of Arts and Letters and the African American Scholars' Council. He received over a dozen citations for excellence in teaching and served as chair and later professor emeritus of African world history in the Department of Africana and Puerto Rican Studies at Hunter College in New York.

Dr. Clarke's political and community activism began in the 1930s with his opposition to the Italian invasion of Ethiopia and his membership in the Universal Ethiopian Students Association. A personal friend of Malcolm X, who paid tribute to his encyclopedic knowledge of Africa, he was instrumental in drafting the charter of the Organization of Afro-American Unity.

A prolific writer, he was the author and editor of more than 20 books and wrote over 50 articles. Even though he had been legally blind since the mid-1980s, Dr. Clarke wrote and read daily with the aid of a computerized reading machine. His more recent publications were *New Dimensions of African History* (Africa World Press, 1991), *African People in World History* (Black Classic Press, 1993), and *Malcolm X: The Man & His Times* (Africa World Press, 1991). His most ambitious work was *Africa at the Crossroads: Notes for an African-World Revolution* (Africa World Press, 1992), a collection of political essays and commentary. For an anthology of some of his writings, see *Pan African Nationalism in the Americas: The Life and Times of John Henrik Clarke*, edited by James L. Conyers, Jr., and Julius Eric Thompson (Africa World Press, 2005). For more on Dr. Clarke's life and work, go to www.africawithin.com/clarke/dr_clarke.htm.

Kathleen Cleaver has spent most of her life participating in the human rights struggle. She dropped out of Barnard College in 1966 to work full time with the Student Nonviolent Coordinating Committee (SNCC). From 1967 to 1971, Kathleen served as the communications secretary of the Black Panther Party the first woman on their Central Committee. After sharing years of exile with her former husband, Eldridge Cleaver, she returned to the United States and earned her B.A. in history from Yale College and a J.D. from Yale Law School. Professor Cleaver has taught at several universities, including the Cardozo

School of Law in New York, the Graduate School at Yale University, and Emory University School of Law in Atlanta, where she teaches currently. She has served as a board member of the Atlanta-based Southern Center for Human Rights and was the cofounder of the International Black Panther Film Festival. She devoted many years to the defense of Geronimo ji Jaga, a former Black Panther Party leader who won his habeas corpus petition in 1997 after spending 27 years in prison for a murder he did not commit. She has also contributed to the efforts to free Mumia Abu-Jamal.

Professor Cleaver is the coeditor, with George N. Katsiaficas, of *Liberation, Imagination and the Black Panther Party: A New Look at the Panthers and Their Legacy* (Routledge, 2001) and the editor of *Target Zero: A Life in Writing*, a collection of essays by Eldridge Cleaver (Palgrave Macmillan, 2006). She wrote the introduction to *We Want Freedom: A Life in the Black Panther Party*, by Mumia Abu-Jamal (South End Press, 2004). Her writing has appeared in numerous magazines and newspapers, including *Ramparts, The Black Panther*, the *Village Voice*, the *Boston Globe*, and *Transition*, and she has contributed scholarly essays to the books *Critical Race Feminism, Critical White Studies*, and *The Black Panther Party Reconsidered*. The Schomburg Center for Research in Black Culture and the Center for Scholars and Writers of the New York Public Library gave her fellowships to complete the book of memoirs that she is working on, *Memoirs of Love and War*.

Mark Cook was born and raised in Seattle, growing up in a poor family and moving frequently from school to school. At the age of 17, he was arrested and sent to a state mental hospital, where he was subsequently abused by the facility staff. While attending college, his frustration with not being able to find steady work led to his committing robberies, which resulted in convictions and long periods of incarceration. While in prison, he realized that the denial of labor rights was more severe in prison than the denial of labor rights in the outside world regarding nonunion workers. This awareness attracted him to the Black Panther Party; he cofounded a chapter at Walla Walla State Penitentiary and became lieutenant of information.

Upon his release in 1972, Mark founded Convention '73, an organization demanding labor rights and franchise rights for prisoners and ex-prisoners. He led forums in 1973, '74, and '75 which grew in participation (from multiple progressive sectors) and public respect—while also attracting attention and surveillance by the Seattle Police Department's Intelligence Unit. In 1976, he was arrested and convicted of both federal and state charges of conspiracy to rob banks and aid in prisoner escapes, actions that were claimed by the George Jackson Brigade. The Brigade was a group of revolutionaries operating in the Northwest, engaging in armed attacks to support the struggles of workers, prisoners, and Indigenous people, especially during the siege of Wounded Knee. Mark was convicted primarily on the testimony of two paid informers, one of whom was his former companion.

After doing 24 years in various cells throughout the prison-industrial complex, Mark was finally paroled on April 4, 2000. An oral history interview with him by the Seattle Black Panther Party History and Memory Project is available at http://depts.washington.edu/civilr/cook.htm.

Edwin Cortés was born in Chicago, Illinois, in 1955; he was one of 15 children. As a student leader, he participated in struggles in support of the Iranian and Palestinian people. Edwin was one of the founders of the Union for Puerto Rican Students, an organization that defended student rights, promoted the history and culture of Puerto Rico, and organized support for Puerto Rican independence. In 1978, Edwin graduated from the University of Illinois, Chicago Circle Campus, receiving a bachelor's degree in political science. Edwin was also active in community struggles, particularly on the south side of Chicago, where he was born and raised. He helped found the Pedro Albizu Campos Collective, a group of independence activists who organized community and youth programs. He later helped establish the Latino Cultural Center.

In June 1983, Edwin was arrested along with two other comrades (Alejandrina Torres and Alberto Rodríguez), accused of participation in the *Fuerzas Armadas de Liberación Nacional* (FALN) and charged with seditious conspiracy. During their trial, all three asserted their position as anticolonial prisoners of war (POW's) resisting the illegal U.S. occupation of their homeland. All were convicted and sentenced to 35 years. In prison, Edwin maintained his involvement in the independence movement through his writing, ceramics, and input into discussions. He was also involved in the creation of cultural and social programs for prisoners. During his 16 years of incarceration, he endured many violations of his human rights, including being held in isolation for his first 10 months in prison and later denials of needed medical care. Edwin was one of the 11 Puerto Rican political prisoners granted clemency by President Clinton in September 1999.

Since his release, Edwin has lived in Aguadilla, Puerto Rico. He processes and tracks medical billing for physicians, coaches a youth basketball team, cares for his aging parents and father-in-law, and works actively advocating the release of the remaining Puerto Rican political prisoners.

Angela Davis is known internationally for her ongoing work to combat all forms of oppression in the U.S. and abroad. Over the years she has been active as a student, teacher, writer, scholar, and activist/organizer. Professor Davis's political activism began when she was a youngster in Birmingham, Alabama, and continued through her high school years in New York. But it was not until 1969 that she came to national attention after being removed from her teaching position in the Philosophy Department at UCLA as a result of her social activism and her membership in the Communist Party USA. In 1970 she was placed on the FBI's Ten Most Wanted List on false charges and was the subject of an intense police search that drove her underground and culminated in one of the most famous trials in recent U.S. history. During her 16-month incarceration, a massive international "Free Angela Davis" campaign was organized, leading to her acquittal in 1972.

Professor Davis's longstanding commitment to prisoners' rights dates back to her involvement in the campaign to free the Soledad Brothers (Black Panther leader George Jackson, John Clutchette, and Fleeta Drumgo, falsely charged with killing a prison guard), which led to her own arrest and imprisonment. Today, she remains an advocate of prison abolition and has developed a powerful critique of racism in the criminal justice system. She is a member of the Advisory Board of the Prison Activist Resource Center. In 1997, Professor Davis helped found Critical Resistance, a national organization dedicated to dismantling the prison-industrial complex (PIC), a concept she developed.

During the last 25 years, Professor Davis has lectured in all of the 50 United States, as well as in Africa, Europe, the Caribbean, and the former Soviet Union. Her articles and essays have appeared in numerous journals and anthologies, and she is the author of eight books, including the feminist classic, *Women, Race & Class* (Vintage Books, 1983); *Angela Davis: An Autobiography* (International Publishers, 1989); and *Blues Legacies and Black Feminism: Gertrude "Ma" Rainey, Bessie Smith and Billie Holiday* (Vintage, 1999). *The Angela Y. Davis Reader* (Blackwell Publishing), a collection of Professor Davis's writings that spans nearly three decades, was published in 1998.

Former California governor Ronald Reagan once vowed that Davis would never again teach in the University of California system. From 1994 to 1997, she held the honor of an appointment to the University of California Presidential Chair in African American and Feminist Studies. Today, she is a tenured professor in the History of Consciousness Department at the University of California, Santa Cruz.

Susie Day is a freelance writer living in New York City. She contributes a humor column to feminist and gay publications and became involved in support of political prisoners when she first interviewed Marilyn Buck, Laura Whitehorn, and other defendants in the Resistance Conspiracy case in Washington, DC, in 1988. She has written about Mumia Abu-Jamal, the death penalty, the Lexington High Security Unit for Women, and other prison and labor issues. She thinks her girlfriend, Laura Whitehorn, is hot stuff. Links to many of her pieces can be found at mrzine.monthlyreview.org/day031207.html.

Dave Dellinger (1915-2004) was a longtime pacifist revolutionary and former political prisoner who frequently committed civil disobedience in opposition to U.S. militarism, beginning with resisting U.S. involvement in World War II, for which he spent three years in prison. After the war, Dave cofounded *Direct Action* magazine with two other Christian pacifists, A. J. Muste and Dorothy Day. His first editorial criticized the dropping of the atomic bombs on Hiroshima and Nagasaki. He edited or published a number of magazines, most notably *Liberation*, which ran for 20 years.

In the late 1960s, Dave was the chief architect of the major coalitions against the war in Southeast Asia, including the Mobilization Committee to End the War and the People's Coalition for Peace and Justice, both of which brought together national activist organizations with burgeoning youth and student antiwar efforts. He was one of the main organizers of the demonstrations in Chicago at the 1968 Democratic Convention and then became famous as a member of the Chicago Eight charged with conspiracy to riot at that convention—even though, in fact, a Presidential Commission concluded that it was a "police riot." During the trial, Black Panther Bobby Seale was jailed on contempt charges (later voided) and severed from the case. The remaining seven were ultimately acquitted of the conspiracy charges, but Dave and five others were convicted of crossing state lines to incite a riot and sentenced to five years, convictions that were later overturned on appeal.

After the war ended, Dave was one of a handful of activists who continued his solidarity with the Vietnamese people, traveling to the region many times. In the late 1970s, he also helped found the multi-issue Mobilization for Survival. In 1986 he moved to Vermont, where he founded the progressive magazine *Toward Freedom*. He maintained solidarity work with U.S. political prisoners, particularly Leonard Peltier, and participated in several long fasts for Indigenous rights and for Leonard's release.

Dave was a member of the War Resisters League for much of his life and in the 1940s and '50s was a member of its Executive Committee. His last appearance at a League action was at the 1998 Day Without the Pentagon civil disobedience, where he was arrested with members of the Resistance in Brooklyn affinity group, linking the issues of U.S. militarism with U.S. imperial ambitions in Puerto Rico.

His autobiography, *From Yale to Jail: The Life Story of a Moral Dissenter* , was published by Pantheon in 1993.

Michael Deutsch has been a lawyer since 1969, representing political activists and victims of police and government civil rights violations. He has tried tens of civil and criminal cases in federal and state courts and has written and argued numerous appeals, including several in the United States Supreme Court. Michael was one of the lawyers for the Attica prisoners and helped to obtain an $8 million settlement for their class-action suit resulting from New York State officials' violations of their civil rights (Al-Jundi v. Mancusi, et al.). For many years, he has been with the People's Law Office in Chicago. He was also a past legal director of the New York-based Center for Constitutional Rights.

Michael has represented many political prisoners and POW's, including the Puerto Rican Nationalist Party prisoners (Lolita Lebrón, Irvin Flores, Rafael Cancel Miranda, Oscar Collazo, and Andrés Figueroa Cordero), William Morales and the other Puerto Rican FALN prisoners,

Puerto Rican *Machetero* militants accused of the Wells Fargo depot robbery, Puerto Rican grand jury resister José López, Mexicano grand jury resister Ricardo Romero, anti-imperialist activists Claude Marks and Donna Wilmott, death row prisoner Zolo Agona Azania, Palestinian activist Muhammad Salah, and political prisoners who were imprisoned at the Marion Prison Control Unit, including Leonard Peltier, Herman Bell, and Raul Salinas.

Bill Dunne has been a prisoner of war—of class war, the war from which all other struggles arise—for almost 30 years. He has written: "I was made a prisoner of the state on October 14, 1979 in Seattle Washington. Late that evening, I was picked up by paramedics while under the influence of police bullets near a shot-up and wrecked car containing some weapons and a dead jail escapee. According to the ensuing state and federal charges, I and a codefendant and unknown other associates of a San Francisco anarchist collective had conspired to effect a comrade's armed liberation from a Seattle jail and attempted to execute the plot on October 14, 1979. The charges further alleged the operation was financed by bank expropriation and materially facilitated by illegal acquisition of weapons, explosives, vehicles, ID, and other equipment. After long subjection to atrocious jail conditions and three sensationalized trials, I got a 90-year sentence in 1980. I subsequently got a consecutive 15 years as a result of an attempted self-emancipation in 1983. The aggregate 105 years is a 'parole when they feel like it' sort of sentence."

Dunne's fifth U.S. Parole Commission hearing is scheduled for January 2009.

Dunne has maintained and developed his revolutionary principles while in prison. In 1982, he was banished into internal exile in the federal prison system from the Washington State system for editing and writing for the *Washington Prison News Service*. In 1985, he was relegated to the notorious control unit prison of U.S.P. (United States Penitentiary) Marion. Early in his decade there, he initiated an edited the important newsletter, *The Marionette*, which exposed destructively oppressive conditions at the prison. *The Marionette* later became a section of the more broadly focused *Prison News Service*, which Dunne also inaugurated and edited. *The Marionette* ceased publication after Dunne was transferred from Marion to USP Terre Haute, though the *Prison News Service* continued for a few more editions. Dunne has been transferred several times since then. Over the years, he has assisted other prisoners in political, legal actions and vocational education.

During his time in prison, Dunne has written a number of analytical, political essays beyond the WPNS and *Marionette*/PNS. He has written, "I am a happily atheist, antisexist, antiracist, globalist, antiauthoritarian, environmentalist, democratic (little d), socialist, socialist, socialist, partisan of class war, wherein the world proletariat necessarily seeks to (and does!) overthrow the world bourgeoisie. None of those adjectives, however, sufficiently characterize my politics over the others that I can define myself by any of them alone. Rather than a gaggle of competitive identities, my vision of the road to revolution encompasses all of the fibers of a diverse humanity, as inherently synergistic strands we must weave into a new social fabric."

Responsibility to those politics and having fallen as the result of an armed confrontation with agents of the state in furtherance of class war leads Dunne to assert prisoner of war status rather than ceding that status and thus strategic primacy to national (as opposed to all people's) liberation movements, where it is claimed that only nationals fallen in their movement's armed struggle can attain that status, and where armed struggle is claimed to be the highest expression of struggle.

Bill Dunne #10916-086
USP Big Sandy
P.O. Box 2068
Inez, KY 41224

J. Soffiyah Elijah is the deputy director of the Criminal Justice Institute at Harvard Law School, where she teaches and oversees the day-to-day operation of institute. She has a distinguished career as an attorney and law professor. She has represented a number of political prisoners and activists in the U.S., including Kwame Turé, Marilyn Buck, and Sundiata Acoli. She serves as a legal advisor to the San Francisco 8, eight former members and associates of the Black Panther Party facing 36-year-old murder and conspiracy charges. The prosecution is based on tortured confessions extracted from some of the defendants in 1973.

Professor Elijah has also done extensive research on the U.S. criminal justice and prison systems and on the Cuban legal system. In 2006 she coauthored the National Lawyers Guild's *amicus curiae* ("friend of the court") brief in support of Mumia Abu-Jamal's appeal.

Bruce Ellison is a South Dakota criminal defense attorney who represented Leonard Peltier for many years. Bruce left New York City in the 1970s to join the Wounded Knee Legal Defense Committee, a group of legal workers defending Native activists persecuted on the Pine Ridge Indian Reservation. Witnessing the Pine Ridge "Reign of Terror" and representing several Native activists unfairly targeted for crimes (including Leonard), Bruce gained firsthand knowledge of a justice system that operates under a double standard, failing to treat Native people equally. He has researched, studied, and documented the FBI's involvement on Pine Ridge and the FBI's activities against the American Indian Movement.

Elizam Escobar, Puerto Rican former political prisoner, is considered one of the island's most illustrious revolutionaries, poets, and painters. He was born in Ponce, Puerto Rico, in 1948. Elizam received a bachelor's degree in fine arts from the University of Puerto Rico (where he became active in the militant, pro-independence Puerto Rican Socialist League) and continued his studies in New York City at the City University, *El Museo del Barrio*, and the Art Students League. During 1979-80, Elizam was part of the faculty of *El Museo del Barrio*'s Art School.

On April 4, 1980, Elizam was arrested along with 10 comrades, all charged with seditious conspiracy for membership in the Puerto Rican clandestine independence organization *Fuerzas Armadas de Liberación Nacional* (FALN). They took a position as anticolonial prisoners of war resisting the illegal U.S. occupation of their homeland. All were convicted and Elizam was given a 68-year sentence.

During 19 years and five months of prison, Elizam continued painting and writing. He published his poetry and theoretical essays in magazines and anthologies in Puerto Rico, the United States, Latin America, and Europe. His work was exhibited in New York, Chicago, San Francisco, San Juan, Toronto, Anchorage, Edinburgh, Madrid, Havana, Managua, and other Latin American cities. Elizam was one of the 11 Puerto Rican political prisoners granted clemency and released by President Clinton in September 1999. He returned to live in Puerto Rico. His release coincided with the publication of his book *Los ensayos del artificiero: mas allá del postmodernismo y lo político-directo* (Isla Negra/Sopa de Letras). He later received the PEN Club first prize for best creative essay. In 2002, *Dobles de Elizam Escobar, with an essay by Joserramon Melendes* (Libros Libres) addressed a thematic-structural aspect of his plastic work. The Puerto Rican Institute of Culture published *Elizam Escobar: Cuadernos de cárcel*, a selection of drawings from his prison sketchbooks, in 2006. His essay "Art of Liberation: A Vision of Freedom" appeared in *Art on the Line: Essays by Artists about the Point Where Their Art & Activism Intersect*, Jack Hirschman, ed. (Curbstone Press, 2002).

Elizam has had numerous exhibits of his work since his release from prison, both in Puerto Rico and the U.S. His works are included in several private and public collections in both countries. He is currently teaching in the Painting Department of the School of Plastic Arts in San Juan, having served as director of the department for three years.

Linda Evans was a political prisoner for 16 years because of her anti-imperialist activities. In the 1960s, Linda was a regional organizer for Students for a Democratic Society (SDS), working to end the Vietnam War and to support Black liberation. She was arrested in 1970 for conspiracy and crossing state lines to incite riot while organizing with SDS in Chicago for the National Action (Days of Rage), and for conspiracy/transportation of weapons and explosives in Detroit. These charges were eventually dropped because of illegal wiretaps used to collect evidence. Linda later became active in the women's liberation movement and the lesbian community, all the while organizing support for Black and Chicano/Mexicano grassroots organizations in Texas. She became a national leader of the John Brown Anti-Klan Committee, which fought against white supremacy and the KKK, forced sterilization, and killer cops. She was also active in building solidarity for South African, Palestinian, and Central American national liberation struggles and opposition to U.S. intervention. She also organized support for Black/New Afrikan, Native and Puerto Rican political prisoners/POW's. Linda began working with others to develop a clandestine resistance movement to change government policies.

Linda was arrested in 1985 and charged with acquisition of weapons, ID, safe houses, finances, political and military training, and actions to bring the war against U.S. imperialism home, later indicted with others in the "Resistance Conspiracy" case. She received a 40-year sentence, which was commuted by President Clinton on his last day in office, January 20, 2001 (at the same time he commuted codefendant Susan Rosenberg's sentence).

While in prison she was a founding member of Pleasanton AIDS Counseling and Education, an inmate-to-inmate AIDS peer counseling organization, and of the Council Against Racism, an inmate organization that worked against institutional racism and to lessen racial tensions inside the prison. She also helped to initiate an art show by political prisoners in support of Mumia Abu-Jamal.

Linda is currently an organizer with All of Us or None (www.allofusornone.org), a national organization of prisoners, formerly incarcerated people, and families. All of Us or None is fighting the many forms of discrimination people face because of past imprisonment or a conviction history. Linda lives with her partner, Eve Goldberg.

Chaka Fattah is a Democratic member of the U.S. House of Representatives first elected in 1994. He represents the Second Congressional District of Pennsylvania, which includes parts of Philadelphia. He had served as a representative in the Pennsylvania House of Representatives from 1983 to 1988 and a state senator from 1988 to 1994. Born and raised in Philadelphia, Chaka Fattah was influenced by the community activism of his parents, Queen Mother Falaka Fattah and David Fattah, who cofounded the House of Umoja, a residential program for teenaged boys aimed at reducing gang violence. As a congressmember, Chaka Fattah played a leading role in organizing members of the Congressional Black Caucus to issue public statements in 1995 and 1999 supporting a new trial for Mumia Abu-Jamal. In 2006, after announcing his (ultimately unsuccessful) candidacy for Philadelphia mayor, he came under fire from the Fraternal Order of Police (FOP) for his stand. Later that year, when House Resolution 1808, which condemned the town of St. Denis, France for renaming a street after this alleged "cop-killer," Congress member Fattah was publicly threatened on the FOP's unofficial website, saying they would be present at the vote and watching carefully how he voted. He abstained.

Herman Ferguson, chairman emeritus of the Malcolm X Commemoration Committee, a long-distance runner in the battle for national liberation, has been a judge and district representative of the Republic of New Afrika, a nation striving for self-determination and sovereignty within the borders of these united states. A member of the Organization of Afro-American Unity (OAAU) founded by Malcolm X in 1964, Baba Herman was chairman of that organization's Education Committee, which organized Liberation Schools for the OAAU.

As a part of the legacy left us by Brother Malcolm, Baba Herman organized the Black Brotherhood Improvement Association. He held street-corner rallies and political education classes and formed the Jamaica Rifle and Pistol Club, Inc. He became a target of the U.S. government's Counterintelligence Program (COINTELPRO). He was arrested in 1967 and (together with activist Arthur Harris) convicted by an all-white, all-male jury of various made-up charges, including conspiracy to assassinate leaders of the NAACP and the National Urban League. Both men were sentenced to three and a half to seven years. They appealed, arguing that they had been targeted and entrapped by the FBI because of their association with radical organizations. While out on appeal, Baba Herman, who continued to work as a public school educator, became active in the struggle for community control of schools. He became a mentor to many of the young people who became leaders of the New York City Chapter of the Black Panther Party. Following the exhaustion of their appeals in 1970, Baba Herman and Arthur Harris went into exile. Baba Herman spent 19 years in Guyana and Arthur continued on to Sweden. Eventually Baba Herman joined the Guyana Defense Force (GDF), and when he retired he held the rank of lieutenant colonel.

In 1989, Baba Herman voluntarily returned to the united states and was immediately remanded to prison. Upon his release in 1996 (pursuant to an order by famed progressive New York City Judge Bruce Wright), he continued his work within the nationalist community. He formed the Malcolm X Commemoration Committee, along with friends and associates of Brother Malcolm, Yuri Kochiyama, Jean Reynolds, Butch Alexander, and Preston Wilcox. He also became a leader of the Free Mumia Abu-Jamal Coalition, along with Safiya Bukhari. In 1998, he became a founding member, along with Safiya Bukhari and Jalil Muntaqim, of the Jericho Movement and remains active in that work today. He was publisher of the New Afrikan Liberation Front's quarterly digest, *Nation Time*, and has served as cochair of the Queens, New York, chapter of the National Coalition of Blacks for Reparations in America (N'COBRA).

Elizabeth Fink has been a Brooklyn-based civil rights attorney for more than two decades. For 25 years, she was one of the lead attorneys in the class action suit by 1,281 former Attica prisoners tortured and/or shot by New York State authorities during the murderous 1971 assault (Al-Jundi v. Mancusi, et al.), ultimately resulting in an $8 million settlement in 2000. She also led the legal battle that shut down the federal Lexington (KY) Women's Control Unit in 1988. She was also one of the two attorneys (with Robert Boyle) who won the release of Dhoruba Bin-Wahad in 1990 after 19 years of unjust imprisonment. In 1999, Liz successfully concluded negotiations with the U.S. and Italian governments that allowed Silvia Baraldini, an Italian national held as a political prisoner in the U.S., to be returned to Italy. She has also represented the Ohio 7, Catherine Wilkerson, and numerous grand jury resisters. More recently, she represented Lynne Stewart and the activists who were mass-arrested at the Republican National Convention protests in New York City in 2004, and currently represents David Gilbert.

Joan P. Gibbs is a longtime activist, attorney, and teacher who lives and works in Brooklyn, New York. Joan was born in Harlem but spent her growing years in Swan Quarter, North Carolina, a small town on the eastern coast, where she witnessed the violence and segregation that accompanied Jim Crow. She first became involved in the movement for peace and social and economic justice in 1968, as a high school student. Joan received her J.D. from Rutgers University School of Law in Newark, New Jersey, in 1985. She is presently the general counsel of the Center for Law and Social Justice at Medgar Evers College, City University of NewYork, and the project director of the Medgar Evers College Immigration Center. Prior to joining the staff of CLSJ, Joan was a staff attorney at the Center for Constitutional Rights and the ACLU Women's Rights Project and was the Marvin Karpatkin Fellow in American Civil Liberties in the national office of the ACLU.

As a lawyer, Joan has devoted herself to the defense of political activists, victims of discrimination on the basis of race, gender, and sexual orientation. Over the years, her clients have included Herman Ferguson, Sundiata Acoli, ACT UP (an AIDS activist group), Dignity (a Catholic gay rights group), and many others fighting for freedom and justice. She was one of the prosecutors at the International Tribunal on Hurricanes Katrina and Rita held in New Orleans in 2006.

Joan is also a writer and a poet. Her articles, stories, and poems have appeared in a number of publications, among them the *Iowa Review*, *Social Policy*, *Journal of Community Advocacy and Activism*, *Our Times Press*, *The Final Call*, and *Daily Challenge*. Joan was the founding editor of *Azalea*, the first magazine published in the U.S. by and for Lesbians of Color.

Larry Giddings, an antiauthoritarian former POW/political prisoner, was born in 1952 and has been an anarchist revolutionary for his entire life. In August 1971, Larry was wounded during a shoot-out and arms expropriation with four other comrades in Los Angeles. He was arrested and served seven years in jail. After he was set free, Larry lived in a food and prisoner support collective in the Bay Area and soon resumed clandestine activities with the aim of helping to liberate jailed comrades. On October 14, 1979, Larry was again wounded and captured, along with comrade Bill Dunne, during the liberation of a comrade from a Seattle jail. Larry was convicted of aiding an escape, the shooting of a police officer, conspiracy, and bank robberies (to garner funds for clandestine activities). While in prison, Larry contributed paintings to Art and Writings Against the Death Penalty project, which raised funds and awareness for Mumia Abu-Jamal's legal defense. He also continued his contributions to the anarchist/antiauthoritarian movement. In addition, he completed B.A. degrees in sociology and psychology. He was released on parole in 2004. Larry is the author of the essay/pamphlet *Why Anti-Authoritarian?*

An account of his activities and political development as an anarchist is available at www.spunk.org/texts/misc/sp000124.txt

David Gilbert, 64, anti-imperialist political prisoner for 27 years, was born in 1944. He has written: "The starting point for me is identifying with other people. That solidarity, that tenderness, mandates standing with the oppressed—the vast majority—against the power structure. The 50 percent of children in sub-Saharan Africa suffering from severe malnutrition, the women and girls sold into sexual bondage in Thailand, the homeless kids scavenging in the streets of São Paulo, the prisoners with AIDS locked in isolation cells in Alabama… they are all precious human beings whose lives matter.

"Reality burst into my consciousness when I was 15, with the Greensboro sit-ins of February 1960. I guess I had been unusually naive in that I fervently believed in America's rhetoric about democracy and equality. This promise was totally belied by the patent racism, as well as by the U.S. practice of imposing brutal dictators on third world nations around the globe. The Civil Rights Movement also showed me more of a sense of humanity and nobility of purpose than I found in the white suburbs where I had grown up. In 1962 I joined the Congress of Racial Equality, and in 1965 I started the Committee Against the War inVietnam at Columbia University. I was one of the founding members of the SDS

(Students for a Democratic Society) chapter there, and in 1967 I wrote the first national SDS pamphlet that named the system as 'U.S. Imperialism.' I participated in the Columbia strike of 1968. The rise of the Women's Liberation Movement and determined efforts by women comrades showed me the importance of struggling against sexism and of striving to live our humanist values in our personal relationships.

"In response to the murderous government assault on the Black Liberation Movement and the unending, massive bombing of Vietnam, the Weather Underground formed in the early 1970s. I spent 10 years in underground resistance. On October 20, 1981, I was captured when a unit of the Black Liberation Army and allied white revolutionaries attempted to take funds from a Brink's truck, with the unfortunate result of a shoot-out in which a guard and two policemen were killed. Mtayari Shabaka Sundiata was subsequently killed by police, while numerous other comrades were captured and given long sentences. I was sentenced under New York State's 'felony murder law' (even with no allegations of doing any shooting, a participant in the robbery can be given full legal responsibility for all deaths) to 75 years to life, which makes my earliest parole eligibility in 2056.

"Kathy Boudin and I have a thoughtful, magnificent, loving son, Chesa Boudin. I also am very fortunate to have many fine friends and family who have stood by me. In prison, I have tried to continue to contribute through political writings. In addition, after my codefendant Kuwasi Balagoon died of AIDS on December 13, 1986, I became intensely active as an advocate and educator around AIDS in prison."

A collection of David's political essays, interviews, and children's stories, *No Surrender*, was published by Abraham Guillen Press in 2004. David is also the author of a number of essays, many of which have been published as booklets. His expose of the racist and far-right underpinnings of many conspiracy theories about AIDS was published as *AIDS Conspiracy Theories—Tracking the Real Genocide* by Cooperative Distribution Service in 1997 (later by Kersplebedeb in 2001). In 1998, a booklet of interviews with David and his comrades Marilyn Buck and Laura Whitehorn, titled *Enemies of the State*, was published by Resistance in Brooklyn (later separately republished by Solidarity, Abraham Guillen Press and Kersplebedeb). A DVD of a 1998 interview, "David Gilbert: A Lifetime of Struggle," is available from the Freedom Archives (www.freedomarchives.org).

David Gilbert #83A6158
Clinton Correctional Facility,
Box 2001,
Dannemora, New York, 12929

Mani Gilyard is chair of the Malcolm X Commemoration Committee. He has a long history of tenants' organizing and support for political prisoners.

Eve Goldberg has worked as a filmmaker and writer for over 20 years. Her credits include *Cover-Up: Behind the Iran-Contra Affair* (writer/editor) and *Dorothy Healey: An American Red* (producer/director). She is the partner of Linda Evans.

Bashir Hameed (formerly James York), 67, a Black Liberation Army political prisoner, was born and raised in New Jersey. In 1968, Bashir joined the Black Panther Party (BPP) while residing in Oakland, California. Once he returned to New Jersey, he became deputy chairman of the New Jersey Chapter of the BPP. FBI documents obtained during the 1970s reveal that during this time, Bashir became a COINTELPRO target. By 1971, COINTELPRO operations succeeded in dividing the BPP into two, effectively destroying its ability to perform community-based public work.

Bashir continued in the spirit of the BPP throughout the 1970s, spending some time in prison as a result of political activity. Bashir worked in rural areas of the South, organizing unions and for better overall conditions for Black people to defend themselves against racist attack.

In 1982, Bashir and a former BPP comrade, Abdul Majid (formerly Anthony LaBorde), were charged and later convicted of the murder and the attempted murder of two police officers, a case known as the Queens Two. These convictions came as a direct result of their political activity. Bashir and Abdul were tried three times. Their first trial ended in a hung jury, divided along racial lines. The second trial was declared a mistrial by the judge immediately after the jury rendered a decision that acquitted Bashir on the murder charge. At a third trial, they were eventually convicted of murder. Bashir is currently serving a sentence of 25 years to life.

Since his incarceration, Bashir, a devout Muslim, has applied his religious and political principles to struggle against injustice and racism behind the walls, gaining wide respect among prisoners. In 1987, Bashir was thrown into solitary confinement for three years, falsely targeted for allegedly organizing a strike—but actually due to his political and religious beliefs. Because of frequent false charges of involvement in actions wherever he is incarcerated, he has been repeatedly transferred and harassed by prison guards. He has had serious medical problems in prison, and in 2006, after considerable outside pressure, he underwent triple bypass open heart surgery. At this time, obtaining proper health care remains an ongoing struggle for him with prison authorities.

Bashir Hameed #82-A-6313
Great Meadow Correctional Facility
Box 51
Comstock, NY 12821

For updated information and support, see New York Jericho under Support Organizations.

Alvaro Luna Hernandez, 56, is a Chicano Mexicano political prisoner. In 1976, Alvaro was sent to prison (narrowly dodging the death penalty) in Texas for a murder he did not commit, a fact exposed by various media outlets, leading to his eventual release. In the 1980s, Alvaro was brutally beaten by police in Alpine, Texas. He responded by successfully suing the Sheriff's Department and began a career as an activist. Alvaro became an organizer with the Prisoners Solidarity Committee, Stop the Violence Youth Committee and National Movement of *La Raza*. In the 1990s, Alvaro was the national coordinator of the defense committee that successfully led the struggle to free Mexican national Aldape Guerra from Texas' death row; Guerra had been framed by Houston police for allegedly killing a cop. Alvaro was a public speaker invited by many colleges, universities and conferences. In 1993, as a nongovernmental-organization delegate before the United Nations Human Rights Commission in Geneva, Switzerland, he condemned the U.S. government's human rights violations against political prisoners. His human rights work has been recognized in Italy, France, Spain, Switzerland, Mexico and other countries.

As an anti-police brutality and prison abolition activist, Alvaro was a popular target of police in west Texas. In July 1996, a sheriff attempted to arrest Alvaro at his home without a warrant. When Alvaro questioned the legality of the arrest, the sheriff drew his gun. The unarmed Alvaro successfully disarmed the sheriff and fled. Several days later, police found Alvaro at his mother's house. Without identifying themselves, they opened fire on the house and refused to accept Alvaro's attempts to surrender for several hours. A police officer was wounded by a ricocheting police bullet. In June 1997, Alvaro was convicted of "threatening" the sheriff, but acquitted of shooting the police officer. The trial evidence

clearly showed Alvaro was the victim of a police-orchestrated conspiracy to frame or eliminate him, and a judge later dismissed the original robbery charge for which the sheriff had
attempted to arrest him. Nonetheless, Alvaro was sentenced to 50 years. He is appealing
his conviction.

> Alvaro Luna Hernández, #255735
> Hughes Unit, Rt. 2, Box 4400
> Gatesville, TX 76597

See also Committee to Free Alvaro Luna Hernandez under Support Organizations.

Lennox S. Hinds, a professor of law and former chair of the Administration of Justice
program at Rutgers Law School, is the permanent representative of the International
Association of Democratic Lawyers to the United Nations. He is best known for serving
as legal counsel to Nelson Mandela and the African National Congress, and his numerous
radical clients have included Angela Davis and the Black Panther Party, members of the
Palestine Liberation Organization, and the Liberation Movement for Angola. His outspoken defense of Assata Shakur after her conviction, when he represented her in suits against
prison mistreatment, led to a legal disciplinary motion, which he defeated. He has worked
for the American Civil Liberties Union, heading up their project for defending the civil
and human rights of prisoners around the United States. Later he became director of the
National Conference of Black Lawyers, which describes itself as"the legal arm of the Black
Liberation Movement."

An expert in international law, he was (along with Jan Susler) a prosecutor at the 1990
Special International Tribunal on Violations of Human Rights of Political Prisoners and
Prisoners of War in United States Prisons and Jails; helped organize (along with Richard
Harvey) the team of judges for the 1997 People's International Tribunal for Justice for
Mumia Abu-Jamal, held in Philadelphia; was a prosecutor at the 2001 International War
Crimes Tribunal on U.S. Crimes in Korea, also held in NewYork; drafted the charter of the
World Tribunal on Iraq, which reviewed war crimes allegations from 2003-5; and was one
of the judges at the 2005 International People's Tribunal in the Philippines that indicted
President Gloria Macapagal-Arroyo for human rights violations.

Jean Hughes, OP, an Adrian Dominican sister, lived, learned, and worked in Latin America
for 15 years. She also learned, worked, and was inspired at 8th Day Center for Justice,
a coalition of Catholic religious communities advocating and organizing around justice
issues in Chicago for 12 years. During the 1980s, she was an activist in the Central America
Pledge of Resistance and the Sanctuary Movement. For the past 14 years she has lived,
loved, learned, and worked at St. Leonard's Ministries, a residential transitional program
for formerly incarcerated men and women attempting to rebuild their lives.

Rev. C. Nozomi Ikuta became active in the antinuclear weapons movement during her
seminary years. In the 1990s, while working for the national offices of the United Church
of Christ, her focus shifted toward racial justice and the self-determination of oppressed
groups, working closely with the campaign for the release of the Puerto Rican political prisoners and prisoners of war. She continues to serve as cochair of the Interfaith Prisoners of
Conscience Project and is currently pastor of the Denison Avenue United Church of Christ,
an urban congregation in Cleveland, Ohio. She is married and the mother of two grown
children and practices tai chi and taiko drumming.

Geronimo ji Jaga (formerly Elmer Pratt) is a former New Afrikan prisoner of war. In 1968, Geronimo returned to the U.S. as a decorated war veteran after three years in Vietnam. Originally from Louisiana, he moved to Los Angeles, enrolled at UCLA, and joined the Black Panther Party. Because of his effectiveness as a community leader, the FBI and police created a "Geronimo Pratt Squad," whose objective was to "get Geronimo" by hook or by crook. As a result he was framed for the senseless murder of a white schoolteacher on a Santa Monica tennis court in 1968. At the time of this killing, Geronimo was attending a weeklong Black Panther Central Committee meeting 400 miles away in Oakland, California. While the FBI had Geronimo and the Panther leadership under constant surveillance, the government claimed to have mysteriously "lost" their records for this period. He remained imprisoned for 27 years for this crime the FBI knew he did not commit.

Geronimo was never paroled, despite the fact that at the time of his conviction, most murderers served average sentences of 10 years. Instead, Geronimo was released from prison in 1997 through the tireless organizing that occurred around his case and the ongoing work of his attorneys, including Johnnie Cochran and Stuart Hanlon. Geronimo won a writ of habeas corpus in an Orange County Superior Court that threw out his conviction. The judge ruled that prosecutors had withheld vital evidence regarding a witness who could have cleared Geronimo of the charges. Later, Geronimo, again represented by Cochran, won a $4.5 million settlement of his civil rights suit against the FBI and the city of Los Angeles. Since his release, Geronimo has spread the message about the need to struggle against all forms of racist oppression and to fight for the release of all political prisoners.

Ryme Katkhouda is the founding director of the People's Media Center in Washington, DC. An Arab Muslim woman who grew up in Lebanon during the Israeli invasion, Ryme is committed to giving people a voice. So she cofounded the dcradiocoop.org—a cooperative of progressive radio producers—and wbix.org—an Internet radio network that broadcast 24/7 for the year of 2001, when there was a coup at Pacifica station WBAI in New York. She also teaches media all over the U.S., including students at New York's School of Visual Arts, news directors from Portland to Palestine, and some 500 journalists across the world. She has been a senior producer and news editor at Pacifica Radio/WPFW in Washington, DC, since 2003 and is the executive producer of the weekly news magazine *Voices with Vision*, airing Thursdays at 11AM at 89.3FM in DC and WPFW.org. She is also a national correspondent with Free Speech Radio News (www.fsrn.org) and works with Atlantic TV Network.

Jaan Laaman is an anti-imperialist political prisoner. Jaan, 60, was imprisoned for being a member of the United Freedom Front (which carried out armed actions against apartheid, imperialism, and war in the 1980s), involvement in firefights with police forces, and weapons charges.

In the 1960s Jaan had worked in Students for a Democratic Society, fought against the war and racism, and did labor and community organizing. This included organizing youth along with the Black Panther Party and Young Lords (a revolutionary Puerto Rican organization). Jaan also worked with the underground revolutionary forces. In 1972, he was charged with bombing Nixon's reelection headquarters and a New Hampshire police station. He was sentenced to 20 years. After winning an appeal and getting some of his sentence cut, he was released in 1978. In 1979, he and his comrade Kazi Toure helped to organize the Amandla Festival of Unity to support freedom in Southern Africa, which featured Bob Marley. This activity, along with the antiracist and community security work he was doing, led to increased police and Klan harassment, so Jaan went underground and joined the armed clandestine movement. He was captured in 1984 with other members of the Ohio 7, and charged with seditious conspiracy. His sentence totals 98 years.

He is currently the editor of *4strugglemag: Views, Thoughts, and Analysis from the Hearts and Minds of North American Political Prisoners and Friends*. The magazine's archives are at www.4strugglemag.org.

> Jaan Karl Laaman, #W 87237
> MCI Cedar Junction
> Box 100
> South Walpole, MA 02071-0100

See also 4strugglemag under Support Organizations.

Wopashitwe Mondo Eyen we Langa (formerly David Rice), 59, has been a political prisoner in the Nebraska State Penitentiary for 38 years. Mondo was born in Omaha in 1949, graduated from Creighton Preparatory School, and took courses at Creighton University. He wrote for the local underground paper from 1969 to 1970 and joined Omaha's Black Panther chapter called the National Committee to Combat Fascism, and became its minister of information. Caught up in the then-secret FBI COINTELPRO operation against the Black Panthers, Mondo and fellow Panther Ed Poindexter were convicted in 1970 and received life sentences for the bombing murder of Omaha policeman Larry Minard. Both have consistently denied any connection with the crime, and the confessed bomber got off with a reduced charge. Amnesty International, after reviewing the many inconsistencies in the trial transcript, as well as FBI files obtained through the Freedom of Information Act, has called for either a new trial or immediate release.

In the years since his conviction, Mondo has continued his education, and is a mentor and exemplar to young inmates coming into the system. He has created many works of art (many of which can be viewed at www.mondo.info), has written short stories, poetry, and journalistic pieces. He had five books of poetry published between 1973 and 1978 and has contributed poems and stories to such literary journals and magazines as *Prairie Schooner, The Black Scholar, ARGO, Black American Literary Forum, Shooting Star Quarterly Review, Pacific Review, Obsidian, Black Books Bulletin,* and many others. His poem "Great Babaleur" was featured in *Malcolm X: By Any Means Necessary*, by Walter Dean Myers (Scholastic, 1993). Two of Mondo's plays, *Different Dances* and *We Dance in Our Neighborhood*, were performed by Ujima Youtheatre in Nebraska, as well as in New York City.

Mondo is one of several coauthors (including Yosef ben-Jochannan, John Henrik Clarke, and others) of *The Race: Matters Concerning Pan Afrikan History, Culture, and Genocide* (Native Sun Publishers, 1992). He is a contributor to *Nebraska Voices*, an anthology commissioned by the Nebraska Humanities Council. In 2007, he published *The Black Panther Is an African Cat—Poems of Exploration and Testimony* (House of August Press). In that book, Mondo writes: "As David Rice, I was proud of being a Panther then and, as Wopashitwe Mondo Eyen we Langa, I am proud now that I was a Panther…. The poems and raps I selected for this book express what it means to me to be an African and how the meaning of this influences how I see and interpret things. At the same time, though, I'm an African who was born and brought up in the U.S. and continues to be influenced by its institutions, and I'm an African who's been locked up."

> Mondo we Langa (David Rice), #27768
> Nebraska State Penitentiary
> P.O. Box 2500
> Lincoln, NE 68542

See also Nebraska's Two Political Prisoners (website) under Support Organizations.

Bob Lederer is a longtime antiracist, anti-imperialist, and lesbian/gay/bisexual/transgender (LGBT) liberation activist and also a health journalist, program host, and board member of WBAI/Pacifica Radio. From 1977 to 1992, he was a member of the Free Puerto Rico Committee, a North American solidarity organization. In 1985, he served three months in federal prison for refusing to collaborate with a grand jury investigating North American anti-imperialist organizations. In 1992, Bob became a cofounder, and remains a member today, of the anti-imperialist collective Resistance in Brooklyn. From 1988 to 2000, he was an active member of ACT UP, the AIDS Coalition to Unleash Power, and participated in several acts of civil disobedience. From 2000 to 2002, he was an organizer with the successful campaign to reclaim the Pacifica Radio Network from Democratic Party/neoliberal forces. Bob is a cofounder of the WBAI Justice & Unity Campaign, which seeks to elect antiracist, progressive candidates to the WBAI board. He continues to be active in communications and media work in support of Mumia Abu-Jamal and other U.S. political prisoners, as well as advocacy of integrative/holistic health strategies and community health empowerment. His life partner and inspiration is John Riley, a continuing ACT UP member, gay liberationist, WBAI producer, and political prisoner supporter.

Stephen Lendman is a retired, Wharton-educated small business guy who lives in Chicago. He was always concerned about the state of things, but who never got super-charged until after his retirement when by accident he became a writer. Since then he has devoted his time and efforts to the progressive causes and organizations he supports, all involved in working for a more humane and just world for all people everywhere, but especially for the most needy, disadvantaged, and oppressed. His efforts have included some writing on the various issues of most concern to him like war and peace; social, economic, and political equity for all; and justice for all the oppressed peoples of the world like the long-suffering people of Haiti and the Palestinians. In 2007, he became an accidental host of a weekly online radio program. He now cohosts *The Global Research News Hour* with Michel Chossudovsky; the program podcasts on RepublicBroadcasting.org Mondays from 11AM to 1PM Central Time. Stephen's blog is sjlendman.blogspot.com, and many of his articles are published at www.globalresearch.ca.

Raymond Luc Levasseur, anti-imperialist former political prisoner, was born in Maine in 1946 to French-Canadian parents. He writes:"In 1967 I did a tour of duty in Vietnam where I was deeply affected by the devastation of the war on the Vietnamese people and their country. In 1968 I began my first political activism with the Southern Student Organizing Committee in Tennessee. Our work centered on bringing an end to the war, supporting the formation of labor unions, and support work for Black liberation. Police repression ensued, and from 1969 through 1971 I spent most of my time in segregation cells of the Tennessee State Penitentiary. When released in 1971 I became a state organizer for Vietnam Veterans Against the War (VVAW). In 1973 I left VVAW and began working with prisoners, ex-prisoners, and their families. I became an organizer with a [Maine] community-based group called SCAR (Statewide Correctional Alliance for Reform)... In 1974 I was involved with the formation of the Red Star North bookstore, which also operated a free books-to-prisoners program. In late 1974 I went underground became of my commitment to building a revolutionary movement that could grow, sustain, and defend itself at each stage of its development. In 1974 police repression had reached intolerable levels.

"In 1984 I was captured by agents of the federal government [along with others in a case that became known as the Ohio 7]. In 1985 I was tried and convicted of bombings against U.S. military facilities, military contractors, and corporations doing business in South Africa. I received a 45-year sentence. In 1986, I was indicted with seven others for seditious conspiracy and RICO (Racketeering Influenced Corrupt Organizations). The indictment charged me with membership in the Sam Melville-Jonathan Jackson Unit and the United Freedom Front. These groups carried out a series of actions from 1976 through 1984 in support of Puerto Rican Independence; freedom struggles in Southern Africa; 'for the Sufferers—the Homeless—the Unemployed—the Hungry—the Imprisoned—those who die in the streets of amerikkka;' and in opposition to U.S. war crimes in Central America. In what became the longest sedition trial in the history of the U.S., I was acquitted of seditious conspiracy. The jury deadlocked on the RICO charges and the government was forced to dismiss them. Following our victory in this trial, I was sent directly to the control unit at Marion, Illinois. In 1995 I was transferred to the government's highest security prison—Administrative Maximum, Florence, Colorado. I stayed there until 1999, when I was transferred to U.S. Penitentiary, Atlanta."

Ray was released in 2004. Upon his release, he wrote, "Take heart with my release. There are those who opposed my excarceration and wished me dead in prison but I prevailed. I came home. I believe that all our political prisoners are coming home. I believe so because I believe in the righteousness of our cause and that struggle brings results. Keep hauling up the morning—it's the best way to live."

In January 2008 Ray became a cofounder of the Maine Prisoner Advocacy Coalition, the first statewide group in many years to be devoted to prisoner issues. Ray was the co-editor, with Tim Blunk and the editors of Jacobin Books, of *Hauling Up the Morning/Izando la Manana—writings and art by political prisoners and prisoners of war* (Red Sea Press, 1990).

Margie Lincita assists in providing financial and material aid to political prisoners and prisoners of war, as well as raising awareness of issues surrounding imprisonment, through the In Our Hearts Anarchist Network and the New York City Anarchist Black Cross Federation.

José López has written extensively on the political and social reality of Puerto Ricans in the United States while serving as a founding member and executive director of the Juan Antonio Corretjer Puerto Rican Cultural Center (PRCC) in Chicago since 1973 and teaching at Northeastern Illinois University, Columbia College, and the University of Illinois at Chicago. With its motto of "To Live and Help to Live," the PRCC has sponsored a wide variety of community services, such as a licensed day care facility, a literacy program for single mothers, an alternative high school, a bilingual AIDS prevention program, and a monthly community newspaper. The PRCC has had a tremendous influence on the life, thought, and development of the Puerto Rican community in Chicago.

For over 35 years, José has been a leading member of the Puerto Rican independence movement. In 1977, he refused to collaborate with a federal grand jury investigating the Puerto Rican independence movement and served seven months in prison. He also served from 1977-1994 as a leading member of the *Movimiento de Liberación Nacional*, a national political organization that organized for the independence of Puerto Rico and the reunification of Mexico, and was composed of Puerto Ricans and Chicano/Mexicanos. He also sits on the Advisory Board of the Boricua Human Rights Network, formerly the National Committee to Free Puerto Rican Prisoners of War and Political Prisoners, which has played a leading role in many of the struggles that led to the release of the five Puerto Rican Nationalists and other Puerto Rican political prisoners. In his role as educator/activist, he has been invited to speak at over 50 colleges and universities in the United States, Mexico, Canada, and Puerto Rico as well as in international forums such as the United Nations Decolonization Committee.

As a professor, José has been a leading figure in the struggle for Puerto Rican human rights and in the construction of a Latino Agenda in the United States and throughout the Americas. He has articulated numerous theories regarding the impact and intersection of racism, globalization, colonialism, the prison-industrial complex, and gentrification on oppressed communities in the United States. He edited *Puerto Rican Nationalism, A Reader* (Editorial El Coquí Publishers, 1975) and contributed chapters to *USA on Trial* (Alejandro Luis Molina, Ed., Editorial El Coquí, 1996), *Can't Jail the Spirit* (Editorial El Coquí, 1996), *The Criminal Injustice System* (Elihu Rosenblatt, Ed., South End Press, 1998), and *States of Confinement* (Joy James, ed., South End Press, 1999).

Oscar López Rivera, 65, Puerto Rican prisoner of war, was born in San Sebastian, Puerto Rico, in 1943. He moved to Chicago with his family at the age of 12, where he experienced racism in the schools and on the street. He was drafted into the army in 1967 and spent a year in Vietnam. Oscar was transformed by this experience and by the Chicago Puerto Ricans' resistance against police brutality, which was fueled by the Puerto Rican Riots of 1966. Oscar became involved in many struggles around welfare rights, bilingual education, unemployment, housing, political representation, and police brutality. He helped to found a Puerto Rican alternative school now known as Dr. Pedro Albizu Campos High School, and the Juan Antonio Corretjer Puerto Rican Cultural Center, and he participated in the Committee to Free the Five Puerto Rican Nationalists during the '70s.

In 1981, Oscar, accused of participation in the *Fuerzas Armadas de Liberación Nacional* (FALN), was arrested and convicted of seditious conspiracy, armed robbery, and lesser charges. As with his colleagues arrested earlier, during his trial, he asserted his position as an anticolonial prisoner of war (POW) resisting the illegal U.S. occupation of his homeland. He was convicted—not of any specific act of violence, but for his political beliefs—and received a disproportionately long sentence of 55 years in prison. In 1988, Oscar was convicted of conspiracy to escape and sentenced to another 15 years. After much hard work and struggle by Puerto Rican activists and supporters, Oscar was offered a limited clemency by President Clinton in 1999 (requiring 10 more years in prison), along with 11 other Puerto Rican political prisoners. Oscar rejected the offer because it would leave other Puerto Rican political prisoners behind and because he would have to renounce his political beliefs. His projected release date is 2027.

From 1987 to 1999, in Marion, Illinois, and the Administrative Maximum (ADX) unit in Florence, Colorado, Oscar withstood 12 years of psychological torture, locked in his cell in complete isolation for 22 and a half hours per day. Despite the harsh and inhuman conditions endured, he remains a man of dignity, hope, and aesthetic sensibility. In 2005-6, Oscar and political prisoner comrade Carlos Alberto Torres contributed their art work to a touring exhibit called Not Enough Space; it showcased how both have discovered art as a means for their self-development and self-expression from their conditions of confinement.

Oscar López Rivera #87651-024
FCI Terre Haute
P.O. Box 33
Terre Haute, IN 47808

See also Puerto Rican Support Organizations in the section Support Organizations.

Mairead Corrigan Maguire founded the Community of Peace People (www.peacepeople.com) in Belfast in 1976 along with Betty Williams and Ciaran McKeown. Mairead was the aunt of the three Maguire children who were hit by a getaway car after its driver was shot by a soldier. The deaths prompted a series of marches throughout Northern Ireland and further afield, all demanding an end to the violence. Mairead and Betty went on to win the Nobel Peace Prize in 1976. She was also one of the co-founders of the Committee of the Administration of Justice, a nonsectarian group heavily involved in the debate over changes in the legal system in Northern Ireland. In 2006, she was one of six Nobel Peace Laureates who founded the Nobel Women's Initiative to work for peace, justice, and women's rights worldwide. In 2007, while participating in a protest against the construction of the West Bank barrier outside the Palestinian village of Bil'in, Israeli security forces intervened and Mairead was hit by a rubber-coated steel bullet and inhaled tear gas, requiring medical attention.

Rosemari Mealy is a freelance radio journalist, essayist, poet, author, and teacher. She is also a facilitator and trainer in media analysis, conflict resolution, and youth empowerment. A former Black Panther, Rosemari has lived and worked in Cuba, where she collaborated with Assata Shakur on several projects in support of U.S. political prisoners. She is also an activist in the international human rights and political prisoner movements. Her current efforts are focused on contributing to the organizing campaigns to win freedom for Mumia Abu-Jamal. She has been honored for her community involvement on numerous occasions and was the recipient of the prestigious Claudia Jones Fellowship in the African New World Studies Program at Florida International University (Miami), where she taught Critical Race Theory Analysis. She has also taught at several schools of the City University of New York.

Rosemari is the author of *Fidel and Malcolm X—Memories of a Meeting* (Ocean Press, 1993) and *Lift These Shadows from Our Eyes* (West End Press, 1978). Her works have appeared in numerous publications, including *Confirmation: An Anthology of African American Women Writers*, edited by Amiri and Amina Baraka (Quill-William Morrow, 1983).

Rigoberta Menchú Tum, Nobel Peace Prize laureate, was born into poverty in a small Guatemalan village. Rigoberta's father, Vicente, was one of the first in their region to seek justice and a better life for Indigenous people. He began a struggle to improve the conditions of the peasant workers and was burned to death during a protest. Her mother was killed a few weeks later by the government. Rather than destroying her, these atrocities strengthened Rigoberta Menchu's resolve to win freedom for her people. Self-educated, she became an active political worker in labor, campesino, and human rights groups. In 1983, her testimonial book, *I, Rigoberta Menchú: An Indian Woman in Guatemala*, was published (Verso), followed by various of her texts and poems. Rigoberta Menchú's work has focused on the promotion of the defense of human rights, peace, and Indigenous peoples' rights. She received the Nobel Peace Prize in 1992, becoming not only the youngest recipient ever, but also the first Indigenous person to ever receive the Peace Prize. She is also the author of *Crossing Borders: An Autobiography* (Verso, 1998).

Pablo Marcano García is a former Puerto Rican political prisoner and renowned artist. Pablo, together with Nydia Cuevas Rivera, took over the Chilean Consulate in Puerto Rico on July 4, 1978, demanding freedom for the five Puerto Rican Nationalist political prisoners, cancellation of the U.S. "Independence Day" celebrations in Puerto Rico, and an end to the Chilean dictatorship of General Augusto Pinochet. No one was injured in their 22-hour action. They were convicted of taking hostages and sentenced to 12 years in prison. While in prison, Pablo was initiated into the art of drawing and painting by Puerto Rican graphic artist Carlos Irizarry and African American artists Jamil (Bryson Harris) and Rashid Wright. Since his release in 1985, Pablo has been part of several collective and individual exhibitions in Puerto Rico and abroad. His critically acclaimed paintings can be seen in important private and public collections in Puerto Rico and abroad. Together with singer Danny Rivera, Pablo heads the International Institute of Fine Arts and Music in Cuba and the Dominican Republic. For more about Pablo's art, go to www.marcanogarcia.com.

Matt Meyer, the editor of this volume, is a former chair of the War Resisters League, founding chair of the Peace and Justice Studies Association, and founding member of Resistance in Brooklyn. He is coauthor with Bill Sutherland of *Guns and Gandhi in Africa: Pan-African Insights on Nonviolence, Armed Struggle and Liberation* (Africa World Press, 2000), and the author *of Time Is Tight: Urgent Tasks for Educational Transformation—Eritrea, South Africa, and the USA* (Africa World Press, 2007). Matt is also editor of *Seeds of New Hope: Pan-African Peace Studies for the 21st Century* (Africa World Press, 2008), and the editor and author of numerous academic articles and news reports. Through Resistance in Brooklyn, the War Resisters League, the Free Puerto Rico Committee (until its dissolution in 1992), and other organizations, Matt has for many years been dedicated to campaigns to free U.S. political prisoners and end the U.S. occupation of Puerto Rico, including major involvement in several International Tribunals and organizing of petitions by Nobel laureates seeking amnesty for political prisoners. The educational director of a small, alternative high school based in Manhattan, Matt's political work—in addition to all of the above and the work noted in this volume—revolves around the care and upbringing of his two fabulous children, Michael Del and Molly Soo. Matt can be contacted at mmmsrnb@igc.org or c/o the War Resisters League, 339 Lafayette Street, New York, NY 10012.

Betsy Mickel joined Resistance in Brooklyn, an anti-imperialist collective, shortly after its formation in 1992. Her political work began in 1970 with the Women's Bail Fund, a project to raise funds and awareness for women prisoners in New York City. Her activism continued through work in the late '70s and early '80s with the Committee for the Suit Against Government Misconduct, a group of former Weather Underground activists who successfully sued the FBI for violating their rights and exposed COINTELPRO tactics against themselves and Black liberation activists. She was active in the successful campaign in the late '80s to close the Lexington Control Unit for women. She was also a member of the Free Puerto Rico Committee for several years until it disbanded in 1992. For more than a decade, Betsy has been active in the Free Mumia Abu-Jamal Coalition in New York City. She has been a copy editor for over 40 years.

Naji Mujahid is an inheritor of the Black Liberation struggle, and it is from this prospective that he approaches all of his work. He was born in Washington, DC, in 1981. His youth was troubled because of his natural inclination toward challenging authority, but as an adult that characteristic has become one of his greatest assets. In the tradition of Mumia Abu-Jamal, he fights with the media on one front of the struggle. A member of the DC Radio Co-op (media production and training), he is the cohost/producer of *Voices with Vision*, a weekly radio news magazine on WPFW-Pacifica; he reports regularly from Capitol Hill for Free Speech Radio News and does freelance reporting. Naji is also the cofounder and chairman of the Black August Planning Organization, which works to propagate the plights of political prisoners and share the histories of the Black Liberation struggle. He lives in Washington, DC, with his two daughters.

Jalil Abdul Muntaqim (formerly Anthony Bottom), 57, is a former member of the Black Panther Party who has been a political prisoner and prisoner of war for 37 years; he is one of the longest held in the U.S. Born in 1951, Jalil spent his early years in San Francisco. He participated in NAACP youth organizing during the civil rights movement, and in high school he became a leading member of the Black Student Union. After the assassination of Dr. King, Jalil began to believe a more militant response to racism and injustice was necessary. He began to look toward the Black Panther Party (BPP) for Self-Defense for leadership and joined at age 18. On August 28, 1971, Jalil was captured along with Albert "Nuh" Washington in a midnight shootout with San Francisco police. It was alleged that Jalil and

Nuh had attempted to assassinate police in retaliation for the assassination of George Jackson a week earlier. When Jalil was arrested, he was a 19-year-old high school graduate, employed as a social worker. Jalil and Nuh were later charged with a host of revolutionary underground activities, including the assassination of two New York City police officers, for which they, along with Herman Bell (thus the case known as "the New York 3") were sentenced to life in prison. (Nuh died of liver cancer in prison in 2000.)

In 1976, Jalil launched the National Prisoners Campaign to Petition the United Nations to recognize the existence of U.S. political prisoners. Progressives nationwide joined this effort, and the petition was submitted in Geneva, Switzerland. This led to Lennox Hinds and the National Conference of Black Lawyers having the United Nations International Commission of Jurists tour U.S. prisons and speak with specific political prisoners. The International Commission of Jurists then reported that political prisoners did in fact exist in the U.S.

Jalil put out the call for the Jericho March on Washington in spring 1998, demanding recognition of and amnesty for U.S. political prisoners; he became a cofounder, along with Herman Ferguson and Safiya Bukhari, of the National Jericho Movement. He was also instrumental in the formation of the New Afrikan Liberation Front.

In 1994, Jalil received a B.S. in psychology and a B.A. in sociology. He has worked as an educator of other inmates and practices organizing and advocacy to ensure humane treatment for all people. He has filed numerous lawsuits on behalf of prisoners. He has been repeatedly punished for these activities, through physical abuse, formal discipline, and numerous prison transfers. Jalil wrote and submitted a New York State legislative bill for prisoners with life sentences to receive good time off their minimum sentences.

Since his incarceration, Jalil has authored numerous essays of analysis and strategy concerning the Black Liberation Movement. He established the first revolutionary prisoners' national newspaper called *Arm the Spirit* and wrote an unpublished novel and teleplay. He is the author of the book *We Are Our Own Liberators* (Abraham Guillen Press, 2003). He is the subject of the DVD *Jalil Muntaqim—Voice of Liberation*, based on a 2000 interview, available from the Freedom Archives (*www.freedomarchives.org*). Many of his writings can be found at www.freejalil.com. During his imprisonment, Jalil has become a father and a grandfather.

Now, after more than 35 years of imprisonment, Jalil faces new charges. He and seven other elder Black activists and former Panthers (including his codefendant Herman Bell) were falsely charged in January 2007 with conspiracy in a police killing that took place nearly 40 years ago in San Francisco *(see also the San Francisco 8 profile)*. Jalil and Herman were extradited to California to stand trial, but as of July 2008, they are seeking to return to New York State for their parole hearings in the New York 3 case, after which the state will transport them back to California.

Jalil Muntaqim (Anthony Bottom), #2311826
850 Bryant Street
San Francisco CA 94103

See also Free Jalil and the Committee for the Defense of Human Rights under Support Organizations.

Luis Nieves Falcón, Ph.D., is a distinguished Puerto Rican educator, lawyer, sociologist, author, and human rights activist. He was born in Bayamón, Puerto Rico, and obtained a master's degree in sociology, a law degree, and a doctorate in sociology. At the University of Puerto Rico, Dr. Nieves Falcón has held the positions of director of the Educational Research Center, director of the Social Sciences Research Center, and director of the

Institute of Caribbean Studies and is professor emeritus in social sciences. He was a distinguished visiting professor at City University of New York and visiting professor at the University of Wisconsin and at the Sorbonne, Paris, France. He has been a member of the Advisory Committee to the Education and Culture Committee of the Puerto Rican House of Representatives and a board member of the *Ateneo de Puerto Rico* (Puerto Rican Atheneum, the island's premier cultural institution) and of the (U.S.-based) Council on Interracial Books for Children. Dr. Nieves Falcón has published 18 books and dozens of articles in publications both in Puerto Rico and internationally.

For many years, Dr. Nieves Falcón has been dedicated to the struggle for the human rights of political prisoners, seniors, people of color in the United States, and human rights in general. He has been president of the PEN Club of Puerto Rico (an international organization of poets, essayists, and novelists) and president of the Puerto Rico National Chapter, International League for the Rights and Liberation of Peoples. He coordinated the Permanent Peoples'Tribunal Session on Puerto Rico, held in Barcelona, Spain, in 1989; the Special International Tribunal on Violations of Human Rights of Political Prisoners and Prisoners of War in United States Prisons and Jails, held in New York City in 1990 (see Section Two); and, the International Tribunal on Human Rights Violations in Puerto Rico and Vieques, held in San Juan and Vieques in 2000 (see Section Four). As founder and coordinator of the Human Rights Committee of Puerto Rico, he led a decade-long organizing campaign on the island, and played an important role in parallel work in the mainland U.S. and internationally, that led to the release of 11 Puerto Rican political prisoners by President Clinton in 1999. Currently, Dr. Nieves Falcón continues his role with the Human Rights Committee and serves as chair of the Nilita Vientós Gastón Foundation, which pursues a program of cultural affirmation and defense of Puerto Rico's right to self-determination and independence.

Emmanuel Ortiz is a third-generation Chicano/Puerto Rican/Irish-American community organizer and spoken word poet. He is the author of a chapbook of poems, *The Word Is a Machete* (self-published, 2003), and coeditor of *Under What Bandera?: Anti-War Ofrendas from Minnesota y Califas* (Calaca Press, 2004). He is a founding member of Palabristas: Latin@ Word Slingers, a collective of Latin@ poets in Minnesota. Emmanuel has lived in Minneapolis, Minnesota; Oakland, California; and the Arizona/Mexico border. He currently lives in Fort Wayne, Indiana, the "buckle of the Bible Belt," with his two dogs, Nogi and Cuca. In his spare time, he enjoys guacamole, soccer, and naps.

Leonard Peltier, 64, a great-grandfather, artist, writer, and Indigenous rights activist, is a citizen of the Anishinabe and Dakota/Lakota Nations who has been unjustly imprisoned since 1976. A participant in the American Indian Movement, in the mid-70s he went to assist the Oglala Lakota people on the Pine Ridge Reservation—facing intense persecution orchestrated by the FBI's COINTELPRO—where a tragic shootout occurred on June 26, 1975. Accused of the murder of two agents of the Federal Bureau of Investigation (FBI), Leonard fled to Canada believing he would never receive a fair trial in the United States. On February 6, 1976, Peltier was apprehended. The FBI knowingly presented the Canadian court with fraudulent affidavits, and Peltier was returned to the U.S. for trial.

Key witnesses were banned from testifying about FBI misconduct, and testimony about the conditions and atmosphere on the Pine Ridge Reservation at the time of the shoot-out was severely restricted. Important evidence, such as conflicting ballistics reports, was ruled inadmissible. Still, the U.S. prosecutor failed to produce a single witness who could identify Leonard as the shooter. Instead, the government tied a bullet casing found near the bodies of their agents to the alleged murder weapon, arguing that this gun had been the only one of its kind used during the shoot-out and that it had belonged to Leonard.

Later, Leonard's attorneys uncovered, in the FBI's own documents, that more than one weapon of the type attributed to him had been present at the scene and the FBI had intentionally concealed a ballistics report that showed the shell casing could not have come from the alleged murder weapon. Other troubling information emerged: the agents undoubtedly followed a red pickup truck onto the land where the shoot-out took place, not the red and white van driven by Leonard, and compelling evidence against several other suspects existed and was concealed. At the time, however, the jury was unaware of these facts. Peltier was convicted and sentenced to two consecutive life terms.

For more details of the government's abusive tactics against Leonard, see "The American Indian Movement" section of the article, "The Real Dragons: A Brief History of Political Militancy and Political Incarceration, 1960s to 2000s," in this book.

The campaign for Leonard's freedom has gained the support of numerous political, religious, and social leaders and millions of individuals worldwide. Amnesty International has written that it "considers Leonard Peltier to be a political prisoner whose avenues of redress have long been exhausted.... Amnesty International recognizes that a retrial is no longer a feasible option and believes that Leonard Peltier should be immediately and unconditionally released." While his legal appeals have been rejected in the courts, a major organizing campaign for Presidential clemency almost succeeded in January 2001, but at the last minute Clinton caved in to pressure from FBI agents who mobilized to block it. A model prisoner, Leonard continues to maintain his innocence and has consequently been denied fair consideration for parole.

Leonard has won several human rights awards and in 2008, for the fifth consecutive year, was nominated for the Nobel Peace Prize.

Leonard has played a key role in getting people from different tribes with a history of animosity to come together in peace. He advocates for peaceful resolution of all Native American issues and respect for the rights of others. He has worked on a pilot program on the Rosebud Reservation to document needs and requirements for health care and delivery, as well as a program to stimulate reservation-based economics and investments in Native American business enterprises. In 1992, Leonard established a scholarship at New York University for Native American students seeking law degrees. He also was instrumental in the establishment and funding of a Native American newspaper by and for Native young people in Washington State. He serves on the Board of the Rosenberg Fund for Children.

Leonard began working with pastels in 1983, and his spirit began to know a freedom he had never before experienced. Although limited by the prison environment, Leonard has emerged as a master of Indigenous art. In 1986, Leonard suffered a stroke and lost about 80 percent of his sight in his left eye. He has written: "My eye problem has slowed me down considerably, but I am still inspired." Leonard Peltier donates his artwork to several human rights and social welfare organizations to help them raise funds. He also has worked to develop prisoner art programs.

Leonard's book, *Prison Writings: My Life Is My Sun Dance* (Griffin Trade Paperback, 2000), was met with critical acclaim. He has written: "Doing time creates a demented darkness of my own imagination; doing time does this thing to you. But of course, you don't do time. You do without it. Or rather, time does you. Time is a cannibal that devours the flesh of your years day by day, bite by bite."

Leonard Peltier #89637-132
USP-Lewisburg
P.O. Box 1000
Lewisburg, PA 17837-1000

See also Leonard Peltier Defense Offense Committee under Support Organizations.

Adolfo Pérez Esquivel, the recipient of the 1980 Nobel Peace Prize, was born in 1931 in Buenos Aires, Argentina. He studied architecture in the National School of Bellas Artes and in the University of La Plata; he later worked as a teacher, and in 1971 he began to get involved in movements that fought for justice and peace. In 1973, he founded the newspaper *Paz y Justicia* (Peace and Justice) that soon after turned into the peak of the movement and defense for human rights in Latin America and became the *Movimiento Ecuménico Paz y Justicia* (Ecumenical Movement for Peace and Justice), along with some Christian groups. Two years later, he participated in the creation of the Permanent Assembly for Human Rights. In 1976 he traveled the world and designed programs meant to develop and help Indigenous communities in Latin America, working-class movements, and other groups in need. During 1977 and 1978, he was imprisoned in Argentina by the military dictatorship headed by President Videla, and during this period he received the Juan XXIII Memorial Peace Prize granted by International Pax Christi. In 1980 he won the Nobel Peace Prize for his fight for human rights, and soon after he was designated as member of the executive committee of the United Nations' Human Rights Permanent Assembly. He has contributed to numerous international missions like the Ship for Peace to Nicaragua, Ship for Solidarity to Poland, and campaigns for resolution of conflicts in South Africa, Afghanistan, the Middle East, and Tibet, among others.

Among his literary highlights is *Caminando Junto al Pueblo* (Walking with the People) (1995), where he describes his experiences in the struggle for the ideal of nonviolence in Latin America. Today, he commits his time to the *Fundación Servicio, Paz y Justicia* (SERPAJ—Service, Peace and Justice Foundation) and to the Village of Children for Peace Project that helps numerous minors in social-risk conditions.

Alberto Rodríguez, former Puerto Rican political prisoner, was born in 1953 in the Bronx, New York, and was raised in Chicago. While he was in high school, he became part of a new generation of Puerto Ricans in the United States who demanded that their history and culture be recognized. He joined the national liberation struggle, becoming part of a group of Latino students who, using the tactics of sit-ins and civil disobedience, forced the Chicago Board of Education to be more responsive to the needs of Latino students. Alberto entered the University of Illinois in 1972 and immediately became involved in the struggle for a Latin American studies program and for recruitment of Latino students. Upon graduation in 1976, he began to work for community programs that provided opportunities for working adults to pursue educational goals. He also worked in various community organizations such as the Workers Rights Center, *El Comite Pro-Orientación Comunal*, *El Desfile del Pueblo*, the Latino Cultural Center, the Committee to Stop the Grand Jury, the Committee to Free the Five Nationalist Prisoners, and the National Committee to Free Puerto Rican Prisoners of War.

In June 1983, when he was working as an academic counselor at Northeastern Illinois University and completing his thesis requirements for a graduate degree from Governor's State University, Alberto he was arrested along with two other comrades (Alejandrina Torres and Edwin Cortés). They were accused of participation in the *Fuerzas Armadas de Liberación Nacional* (FALN) and charged with seditious conspiracy. During their trial, all three asserted their position as anticolonial POW's resisting the illegal U.S. occupation of their homeland. All were convicted and sentenced to 35 years. During Alberto's 16 years of incarceration, he faced many violations of his human rights. His first 10 months in prison were in solitary confinement, where, he has written,"I had to search within myself to find the spiritual strength to persevere."

Alberto was one of the 11 Puerto Rican political prisoners granted clemency by President Clinton in September 1999. Alberto has lived in Chicago since his release. After working for seven years as a paralegal at the People's Law Office, he left to help raise his young son and work with his wife's wedding photography business (www.photographybylin.com). He also helps care for his aging parents.

Ninotchka Rosca, who grew up in the Philippines, is a writer and an internationally known activist for human rights. She has been involved in the Philippine national democratic movement since the 1960s. A political prisoner under the Marcos regime, she was forced into exile when threatened with a second arrest and is currently a New Yorker. She was a founder and the first national chair of Gabriela, the preeminent women's rights organization of the Philippines, and cofounded Gabriela Network U.S.A., a Philippine-U.S. women's solidarity organization, and the Philippine Workers Support Committee. She is the international spokesperson for Gabriela's Purple Rose Campaign against the trafficking of women, with an emphasis on Filipinas. She has participated in numerous world forums and conferences for human rights. She serves on the board of the Survivors Committee, a network of former political prisoners and human rights activists. She has also been in leadership positions with Amnesty International and the PEN American Center. She considers the issues of freedom of expression, women's rights, and human rights as crucial to the struggle against neocolonialism and certainly crucial to the advancement of humanity.

Ninotchka is the author of six books: her short story collections include *Bitter Country* and *Monsoon Country;* her two novels are *State of War* (Simon & Schuster, 1990) and *Twice Blessed* (WW Norton & Co., 1992), and her books of nonfiction are *Endgame: The Fall of Marcos* (Franklin Watts, 1987) and *Jose Maria Sison: At Home in the World—Portrait of a Revolutionary* (Open Hand Publishing, 2004). Her short stories have been included in several anthologies, and she is a frequent contributor to numerous periodicals. She is a two-time recipient of the New York Foundation for the Arts Fellowship and has received numerous awards for literature, including the American Book Award. Her blog is www.ninotchkarosca.blogspot.com.

Susan Rosenberg, born in 1955 in New York City, is a former political prisoner. While still in high school in the early 1970s, she worked with and was greatly influenced by the Black Panther Party and the Young Lords Party (a Puerto Rican independence organization). She later worked in support of political prisoners, against COINTELPRO, and in support of national liberation movements in Africa and Latin America. In the mid-1970s, she worked at Lincoln Hospital in the Bronx with the first U.S.-based acupuncturists led by members of the Black liberation movement. She received her acupuncture doctorate from the Montreal Institute of Chinese Medicine.

Targeted by the FBI, Susan went underground in 1982 rather than face a biased community in defending against federal RICO conspiracy charges. Arrested and charged with weapons possession in New Jersey in November 1984 along with activist Tim Blunk, the two were sentenced to 58 years in federal prison, the longest sentence in U.S. history (at the time) for weapons possession. The judge cited their political ideology as the reason for the lengthy prison term. Charges against her for the 1981 Brink's robbery by the Revolutionary Armed Task Force and the 1979 escape from prison of Assata Shakur were dropped for lack of evidence. In 1990, charges were also dropped in the "Resistance Conspiracy" case (for conspiring to oppose U.S. foreign and domestic policy through violence). Susan was one of three women political prisoners (along with Alejandrina Torres and Silvia Baraldini) placed in the Lexington (Kentucky) High Security Unit in 1986. With broad community and legal support, they successfully fought against the psychological torture of this experimental unit. In over 10 years of isolation and maximum-security conditions, Susan continued to organize, teach, and write. She obtained her master's degree in writing from Antioch in 2000 and worked as an HIV/AIDS prisoner peer-educator.

After 16 years in prison, Susan received clemency (along with former codefendant Linda

Evans) from President Clinton on his last day in office, January 20, 2001. An international human- and prisoner-rights activist since her release, she has written a memoir, has taught literature at the John Jay School of Criminal Justice, City University of New York, and is working for an international development organization.

Suzanne Ross has been an anti-imperialist/antiracist activist since the mid-'60s, deeply involved in the Vietnam solidarity movement and in antiracist work as a psychologist and educator. She considers herself a "hardcore internationalist" and has participated in many international solidarity movements. Since the early 1990s, she has concentrated on the campaign to free Mumia Abu-Jamal and other political prisoners, is co-chair of the Free Mumia Abu-Jamal Coalition (New York City) and has become very committed to fighting and dismantling the prison system, the embodiment and end point of white supremacy in this country.

The San Francisco 8—Herman Bell, Ray Boudreaux, Richard Brown, Henry (Hank) Jones, Jalil Muntaqim, Richard O'Neal, Harold Taylor, and Francisco Torres. In January 2007, the FBI dredged up a 35-year-old unsolved murder of San Francisco police Sergeant John V. Young (and various other "conspiracy" charges) and arrested eight former members and associates of the Black Panther Party—two of them (Jalil Muntaqim and Herman Bell) already in prison for over 30 years on other political charges. In 1973, New Orleans police had arrested 13 alleged Black Panthers; over the next several days, three of them, including Harold Taylor, were tortured, Abu Ghraib-style—stripped naked, beaten, blindfolded, covered in blankets soaked with boiling water, and endured placing electric probes on their genitals, among other horrors. The next year, a judge threw out charges based on "confessions" made under this torture. But in recent years the FBI has dusted off these old, coerced confessions and is determined to use them to make examples out of these Black men, who are now aged 55 to 72 and respected community leaders. The San Francisco 8 now face many years in prison, and a strong defense campaign is under way.
See also Committee for the Defense of Human Rights under Support Organizations.

Jane Segal is a lifelong activist. For the past 20 years, her political work has focused on women political prisoners and the prison-industrial complex. She along with Bø (rita d. brown), Jay Mullins, and Judith (Mirk) Mirkinson founded Out of Control Lesbian Committee to Support Women Political Prisoners. She lives in San Francisco and is an educator, a mother, an artist and a dog lover. Jane loves California landscapes, the outdoors, listening to live jazz and playing with her dog.

Assata Shakur, (formerly Joann Chesimard), a 61-year old African woman, is a social justice activist, a poet, a mother, and a grandmother. She has written: "I am a 20th-century escaped slave. Because of government persecution, I was left with no other choice than to flee from the political repression, racism, and violence that dominate the U.S. government's policy toward people of color. I am an ex-political prisoner, and I have been living in exile in Cuba since 1984.

"I have been a political activist most of my life, and although the U.S. government has done everything in its power to criminalize me, I am not a criminal, nor have I ever been one. In the 1960s, I participated in various struggles: the Black liberation movement, the student rights movement, and the movement to end the war in Vietnam. I joined the Black Panther Party. By 1969 the Black Panther Party had become the number one organization targeted by the FBI's COINTELPRO program. Because the Black Panther Party demanded the total liberation of Black people, J. Edgar Hoover called it the 'greatest threat to the internal security of the country' and vowed to destroy it and its leaders and activists."

In May 1973, while Assata and two companions were traveling on the New Jersey Turnpike, state police spotted and identified them as people they believed to be members of the Black Panther Party and the Black Liberation Army, and proceeded to ambush them. When the smoke cleared, one police officer and one of Assata's companions, Zayd Shakur, lay dead. Assata, shot with her hands in the air and dragged from the car, lay wounded. Only belatedly taken to the hospital, Assata was then chained to her bed, tortured, and questioned while injured. In fact, she never received adequate medical attention even though she had a broken clavicle and a paralyzed arm. Nonetheless, she was quickly jailed, prosecuted, and incarcerated over the next few years for the series of trumped up cases. In five separate trials, and with majority-white juries, where charges were not dismissed due to lack of evidence, she was repeatedly found not guilty of charges ranging from bank robbery to murder. As the manager of one bank said at trial, "She is just not the one who robbed my bank." In the final trial in 1977, where she was charged with the Turnpike killings, she was found guilty by an all-white jury. This, even though forensic evidence taken that day showed that she had not fired a weapon. She was sentenced to life plus 33 years in prison. (Sundiata Acoli was tried separately, convicted of killing the policeman, and sentenced to life plus 30 years.)

Assata has written: "In 1979, fearing that I would be murdered in prison and knowing that I would never receive any justice, I was liberated from prison, aided by committed comrades who understood the depths of the injustices in my case and who were also extremely fearful for my life." Later she emerged in Cuba where she applied for and received political asylum. Since being in Cuba, she has continued her college education, published an autobiography (see below), and writes on global issues facing women, youth, and people of color.

During the late 1990s, rightist politicians and police organizations, in conjunction with conservative members of the Cuban-American community, reinvigorated their attempts to pursue Assata. Linking "fear of crime" rhetoric with anti-Cuban sentiment, New Jersey governor Christine Todd-Whitman placed a bounty on her head—ultimately $1 million—announcing her bounty on Radio Martí, the U.S. government radio station that beams anti-Castro propaganda into the Caribbean. The goal was to put Assata in danger, encouraging any opportunist to kidnap and/or kill her for pay. In addition, in 1998, Congress members Franks and Menendez from New Jersey and Ros-Lehtinen and Diaz-Balart of Florida introduced and got passed House Resolution 254, which calls for the Cuban government to extradite Assata Shakur as a condition to normalizing U.S.-Cuba relations.

A shero of revolutionary struggle, Assata documented the horrendous episode of her "encounter" with the U.S. government, experiences with the Black Panther Party, and "coming of age" in this country in her book *Assata* (Lawrence Hill Books, 1987; second edition, 1999). Besides her autobiography, Assata has written many poems and articles on a variety of topics. Many of her writings and more background on her struggles are available at the New York Hands Off Assata Coalition website, www.handsoffassata.org. She is the subject of the film documentary, *Eyes of the Rainbow*, by Gloria Rolando, (available from www.happybirthdayassata.org) and an interview about her mistreatment in jail is included in *Still Black, Still Strong* (Semiotext(e), 1993—distributed by AK Press).

Mutulu Shakur, D.Ac. (formerly Jeral Wayne Williams), 58, a lifelong activist in the New Afrikan (Black) independence movement and a Doctor of Acupuncture, has been a political prisoner since 1986.

In the mid-1960s, as a junior high school student in Queens, New York, Mutulu worked with Sekou Odinga (then a Black Panther, now a prisoner of war) to form a student organization that demanded inclusion of Black history in the curriculum. At age 15, Mutulu met Black revolutionary educator Herman Ferguson, a junior high school principal who was to have a major influence on the city's Black youth. As a teenager, Mutulu had already concluded that the number one priority for Black people in the U.S. was the struggle for self-determination—total control over every aspect of their lives. He believed they were owed land and reparations for 250 years of slavery and another 100 years under a white supremacist social and political system. He became a cofounder of the Provisional Government of the Republic of New Afrika in 1968 and later worked with the New Afrikan People's Organization to pursue the goals of establishing an independent Black nation in the southern United States.

In 1970, Mutulu was asked to teach political education to clients of the Lincoln Hospital Detoxification Program, a program founded by Black and Latino revolutionary youth in the South Bronx, New York. Shortly after starting there, two of his children were badly injured in an auto accident. Looking for alternative treatment, he approached activists of the *I Wor Kuen*, a revolutionary Chinese organization that ran a health service for the older Chinese community. An Asian woman acupuncturist cured his children using Traditional Chinese Medicine. Discussions with the Chinese and sessions with addicts at Lincoln Detox showed Mutulu similarities between the struggles of China against addiction to opium, which had been brought there by the British colonizers, and the struggles in the Black community against the genocidal drug traffic recently revealed to have been orchestrated by the CIA. Mutulu attended classes at the Quebec Acupuncture Association, where he obtained a doctorate in acupuncture. He used his skills to treat narcotics addiction and eventually became director of the Lincoln Detox Acupuncture Research Unit.

After losing a legal battle with the New York City Health and Hospitals Corporation over the control of the project, Dr. Shakur and several other acupuncturists were transferred out of the Lincoln Hospital Detoxification Program. Today the treatment of addiction with acupuncture continues at several public hospital sites in New York City, but—as is common—the names of the radical pioneers are not mentioned in the official history. Dr. Shakur and several comrades later founded the Harlem Institute of Acupuncture, where community residents received holistic health care and students were trained in acupuncture and other healing arts and sciences.

Dr. Shakur's contributions were not limited to health care. He also supported tenant housing, fought alongside parent organizations for control of their children's educational destiny, and participated in every significant struggle in the Black community. He was also a cofounder and director of the National Task Force for COINTELPRO Litigation and Research, which investigated, exposed, and sued the FBI and other law enforcement agencies for criminal acts, domestic spying, dirty tracks, and repression against the Black liberation movement and its allies.

As a freedom fighter targeted by the FBI's COINTELPRO, Dr. Shakur was captured by the Joint Terrorism Task Force in 1986 and was placed on trial along with anti-imperialist Marilyn Buck. Both were charged with being part of an armed underground unit that conspired to free Assata Shakur from prison and with conspiring to carry out several armored car and bank "robberies" (or revolutionary expropriations), the proceeds of which, the governments alleged, were used to support political activities. Both were convicted under questionable circumstances, and Dr. Shakur was sentenced to 60 years in federal prison. His revolutionary nationalist spirit remains strong despite continuing efforts by prison official to crush him.

Dr. Shakur is the father of six children. The Federal Bureau of Prisons made every effort to keep him separated from his son, legendary rapper Tupac Shakur, who was assassinated in 1996. He has solid evidence that the murder was a continuation of COINTELPRO.

Dr. Shakur has worked to promote education among other prisoners and has participated in efforts to promote unity between prisoners from different regions and religious, ethnic and cultural affiliations. He was a key organizer of the historic gang truce between the Bloods and the Crips at Lompoc Penitentiary. At each institution where Dr. Shakur has been incarcerated, he has worked with other prisoners, staff, and community artists, activists, and intellectuals to create educational and cultural programs to encourage positive development for the incarcerated, particularly Black and Latino youth.

In 2002, the Parole Commission denied parole to Dr. Shakur. In 2004, his attorneys filed a habeas corpus petition to challenge the six-year delay in his parole hearing, but his appeals lost at each level, and the U.S. Supreme Court declined to hear the case in 2006. He was again denied parole in January 2008. His release date is 2017.

> Mutulu Shakur #83205-012
> USP Florence ADMAX
> PO Box 8500, Florence, CO 81226

See also Family and Friends of Dr. Mutulu Shakur under Support Organizations.

Gilda Sherrod-Ali a graduate of the Rutgers University School of Law, is an attorney who has practiced criminal and family law for many years in Washington, DC. She has served as the cochair of the Criminal Justice Conference of the National Conference of Black Lawyers and was for several years director of the Jericho Legal Defense Fund working for amnesty for U.S. political prisoners. She has worked on the cases of political prisoners Mutulu Shakur and Robert "Seth" Hayes. She also does defense work in mass protest cases with the National Lawyers Guild, and represented activists arrested in the Supreme Court civil disobedience in 2000 in support of Mumia Abu-Jamal.

Russell "Maroon" Shoats, New Afrikan political prisoner of war, 66, was a dedicated community activist and founding member of the Philadelphia-based organization Black Unity Council, which in 1969 merged with the Black Panther Party. In 1970, Maroon and five other activists were accused of an attack on a police station during which an officer being killed. This attack was carried out in response to the rampant police brutality in the Black community. For 18 months Maroon functioned underground as a soldier in the Black Liberation Army. In 1972 he was captured and convicted for the attack on the police station and was sentenced to multiple life sentences. Twice he escaped—once in 1977 and again in 1980—but both times he was recaptured. Most of his time in prison—including today—has been spent in control units in which he is locked in his cell for 22 to 24 hours a day. has written: "I remain a committed New Afrikan freedom fighter, who will not rest until the New Afrikan peoples are free from oppression and a free and self-governing nation."

An extensive interview with Maroon, as well as his essays *Black Fighting Formations, Twenty First Century Political Prisoner: Real and Potential,* and *Liberation or Gangsterism: Freedom or Slavery,* has been published by South Chicago ABC Zine Distro. His short texts *Death by Regulation* and *Message from a Death Camp* have been published by Kersplebedeb in 2008, as has his essay *The Real Resistance to Slavery in North America.*

> Russell "Maroon" Shoats #AF-3855
> SCI-Greene
> 175 Progress Drive
> Waynesburg, PA 15370

See also Russell Maroon Shoats Support under Support Organizations.

Meg Starr is an educator, author, founding member of the antiracist, anti-imperialist collective Resistance in Brooklyn, and active member of the group's women's caucus that organizes an annual women-only cultural event. She was a solidarity activist with the Free Puerto Rico Committee from 1982 until its dissolution in 1992 and has also been active in women's movements against misnamed "welfare reform." Meg has been part of many campaigns to free U.S. political prisoners and was one of the main organizers of the John Brown 2000 Conference organized by Resistance in Brooklyn and other groups. She has written and spoken extensively on issues of self-determination, white supremacy, and the role of women in revolutionary struggle. An early childhood education specialist, she is author of the popular children's book *Alicia's Happy Day* (Star Bright Books, 2001), and has designed workshops and teacher training courses for City College of the City University of New York and Touro College.

Lynne Stewart, 69, has been a criminal defense lawyer for over 30 years. In addition to representing many people marginalized by the criminal justice system and victims of the war on drugs and the prison-industrial complex, she has represented such well-known political prisoners as David Gilbert, Richard Williams, and Sekou Odinga, as well as Larry Davis (an African American man acquitted in 1988, based on self-defense, of attempted murder of nine New York policemen) and Sheik Abdel Rahman (an exiled Egyptian cleric convicted in 1995 of "seditious conspiracy" for allegedly planning never-implemented bombings of New York City landmarks).

Lynne Stewart was arrested on April 9, 2002, along with paralegals and translators Mohammed Yousry, Ahmed Sattar, and Yassir al-Sirri, after their indictment on charges of "materially aiding a terrorist organization"—in Lynne's case, through a press conference and allowing access by others as part of her representation of Sheik Rahman. The indictments were trumpeted in a press conference by then-attorney general John Ashcroft. In July 2003, Federal District Court judge John Koeltl dismissed the most serious charges as "unconstitutionally void for vagueness." Four months later, Lynne and two of her codefendants (al-Sirri's case was dismissed) were reindicted on five counts of aiding and abetting a terrorist organization under the 1996 Antiterrorism Act.

Lynne and her codefendants had a nine-month trial in which prosecutors used the most inflammatory "evidence," including irrelevant videos of Osama Bin Laden, and painted Lynne as a traitor with "radical" views supporting armed revolution. On February 10, 2005, all four defendants were convicted on all counts. Lynne thus became the first lawyer in the United States to be convicted of aiding terrorism; she was automatically disbarred. Prosecutors asked for a 30-year sentence. Nationally, many defense attorneys—along with thousands of supporters—rallied to Lynne's cause. Hundreds wrote the judge, decrying the injustice of the charges and testifying to her dedication to representing society's most persecuted. On October 16, 2006, Judge Koeltl sentenced Lynne to 28 months in prison, a major defeat for the feds. Lynne remains free pending appeal, which was argued before the Second Circuit Court of Appeals on January 29, 2008. Since her conviction, Lynne has struggled with breast cancer, which fortunately was successfully treated, and has continued to tirelessly campaign not only for justice in her case but also for freedom of all U.S. political prisoners.

By targeting and indicting Lynne Stewart, the U.S. Justice Department hopes to make an example of an attorney with a long history of progressive political beliefs as well as a reputation for vigorously advocating on behalf of those whose lives have been entrusted to her. Her prosecution is meant as a signal to the defense bar to cease and desist zealous representation of persons criminalized by the government. (See X.4 "The Reality of Political Prisoners in the United States: What September 11 Taught Us About Defending Them" on page 675.)

See also Lynne Stewart Defense Committee under Support Organizations.

Brendan Story moved to Brooklyn in 2003 and went to work editing for the argentina autonomista project, writing for queeringdiabetes.org, and organizing letter-writing sessions to political prisoners and prisoners of war. The letters led to some activists participating in emergency campaigns, primarily for New Afrikan POW's. Threats of eroding health care at the day job eventually propelled him into labor organizing with the New York City Industrial Workers of the World. Once his friend Daniel McGowan was arrested by federal marshals in late 2005, Brendan found himself devoting more and more time to prisoner support. Now he's part of the Family and Friends of Daniel McGowan as well as the New York City Anarchist Black Cross Federation and is trying to set aside more time to write fiction, read, and practice karate.

Jan Susler is a partner with the People's Law Office (PLO) in Chicago, which she joined in 1982 after a six-year stint at Prison Legal Aid, the legal clinic at Southern Illinois University's School of Law. Her long history of work on behalf of political prisoners and prisoners' rights includes litigation, advocacy, and educational work around Marion Federal Prison and the Women's High Security Unit at Lexington, Kentucky. Her practice at PLO focuses, in addition, on police misconduct civil rights litigation. For several years she was an adjunct professor of criminal justice at Northeastern Illinois University and has also taught at the University of Puerto Rico. Representing many of the Puerto Rican political prisoners for over two decades, she served as lead counsel in the efforts culminating in the 1999 presidential commutation of their sentences. She continues to represent two of those who remain imprisoned, Oscar López Rivera and Carlos Alberto Torres.

Nkechi Taifa has played a major role as an attorney in raising the visibility of issues involving unequal justice. She has been widely published on issues involving sentencing and justice reform. She is an adjunct professor at Howard University Law School, teaching a seminar on "Racial Disparities in the Criminal Justice System." She has served as the director of the Equal Justice Program at Howard University School of Law, legislative counsel for the American Civil Liberties Union, public policy counsel for the Women's Legal Defense Fund, and staff attorney for the National Prison Project. She also spent many years as a criminal defense attorney in private practice.

Professor Taifa serves on the board of several organizations, including the Washington Council of Lawyers, the Bureau of Rehabilitation, and DC Prisoner Legal Services, Inc. She is an active member in several associations, including the American Bar Association's Race and Racism Committee, the National Association of Blacks in Criminal Justice, the National Conference of Black Lawyers, the National Bar Association, and the Washington Bar Association. Currently she is a senior policy analyst in the Washington Office of the Open Society Institute (OSI). In this role, she works to advance reforms in the areas of law enforcement, sentencing, prison conditions, and reentry.

Professor Taifa has worked on issues involving COINTELPRO and political prisoners since 1975. She has been the cochair of the Legislative Commission of NCOBRA (National Coalition of Blacks for Reparations in America). She is the coauthor (with Imari A. Obadele and Chokwe Lumumba) of *Reparations Yes!: The Legal and Political Reasons Why New Afrikans, Black People in the United States, Should Be Paid Now for the Enslavement of Our Ancestors and for War against Us after Slavery* (House of Songhay, 1995) and coeditor (with Chokwe Lumumba and Viola Plummer) of *De-Colonization U.S.A.: The Independence Struggle of the Black Nation in the United States Centering on the 1996 United Nations Petition* (House of Songhay, 1997).

Linda Thurston, a radical activist from an early age, has worked for three decades to abolish the prison-industrial complex, sparked by her experience doing theater in Walpole State

Prison in Massachusetts in 1978. Linda is a founding member of International Concerned Family and Friends of Mumia Abu-Jamal and has fought for the lives of death-row prisoners in many states, losing friends and comrades to the executioner's chair and struggling not to lose more to the exhaustion of carrying on in the struggle. In the 1980s and early 1990s, she coordinated the New England and National Criminal Justice Programs at the American Friends Service Committee, working with prisoner and community organizations to fight brutal conditions and repressive prison policies and to fight for alternatives to the relentless expansion of the prison and jail system. Linda has worked with Boston and New York Jericho and with Critical Resistance, including work on the campaign for amnesty for prisoners of Hurricane Katrina. Her work currently focuses on sharpening the use of Internet communications in these struggles and urging activists to remember when it's time to step away from the computer and into the streets. Linda currently works as the office coordinator at the War Resisters League in New York City.

Archbishop Desmond Tutu. As general secretary of the South African Council of Churches from 1978 to 1985, Bishop Tutu led a formidable crusade for justice and racial conciliation in South Africa. His tireless work was recognized in 1984, when he was awarded the Nobel Peace Prize. Then, following a short stint as the bishop of Johannesburg, he was elected archbishop of the Church of the Province of Southern Africa in 1986, an office he held until his retirement in 1996. Once the African National Congress and other political organizations were unbanned, Bishop Tutu became a key mediator and conciliator in the difficult transition toward democracy. In 1996, he was appointed by President Nelson Mandela to chair the Truth and Reconciliation Commission, the body set up to probe gross human rights violations during apartheid. Following the presentation of the commission's report to the president in 1998, Bishop Tutu has been visiting professor at several overseas universities, and has published several books, the latest of which is *God Has a Dream*. For more on Bishop Tutu, go to www.tutufoundationuk.org.

Michael Tarif Warren, as a college student in the 1960s, led an organization called Unity for Unity, which was a Student Nonviolent Coordinating Committee (SNCC) affiliate. Graduating from law school in 1973, he worked for five years in Washington, DC, before coming to New York. Tarif has served as legislative aide to Congressman Louis Stokes; associate director of the National Conference of Black Lawyers' Juvenile Defense Project; assistant general counsel for the NAACP Special Contributions Fund; and staff attorney for the National Committee Against Discrimination in Housing. He is currently in private practice in Brooklyn, specializing in criminal, police misconduct, and human rights cases.

Tarif has represented numerous political prisoners and currently represents Dr. Mutulu Shakur, a longtime activist in the New Afrikan liberation movement. He also served on the defense team in the 2002 capital murder trial of Jamil Abdullah Al-Amin (formerly H. Rap Brown) in Atlanta. In 1984, he represented the family of Michael Stewart, a young Black man murdered by the New York Police. He represented rapper Tupac Shakur in 1994, served as lead counsel in the 1998 Million Youth March case in Harlem, and was lead counsel in the "Central Park Five" case in which the 1990 convictions of five young men wrongfully convicted of raping the "Central Park Jogger" were set aside. He also was involved in the People's International Tribunal for Justice for Mumia Abu-Jamal in Philadelphia in 1997 and has spoken for Mumia's freedom in Europe. In December 2003, he served on the prosecution team at the International Criminal Tribunal for Afghanistan in Tokyo, where evidence was presented against George W. Bush and the U.S. government for the illegal bombing and use of depleted uranium weapons in Afghanistan.

Albert "Nuh" Washington (1941-2000), New Afrikan prisoner of war, was a freedom-loving freedom fighter. Nuh died in prison of liver cancer after fighting a courageous battle with this disease. He was determined that the effects of the disease on his system would not compromise his integrity, self-respect, or humanity. His life and death leave a rich legacy to be learned from and cherished.

Nuh was a teacher, friend, loyal comrade, leader, spiritual advisor, father figure, and much more. Nuh was exposed to international politics early in life through meeting some immigrants from Africa who rented rooms from his grandmother. In 1969, he joined the Denver, Colorado, Chapter of the Black Panther Party, working with the Free Breakfast Program. By 1971, the year of the "split" in the party, Nuh was working out of the party's San Francisco Branch. During this time he, along with many other San Francisco party members, went underground as soldiers of the Black Liberation Army (BLA) and formed a network of underground cells.

Shortly before Nuh's passing, Mumia Abu-Jamal wrote, "Nuh (the Arabic form of Noah) was a committed member of the Black Panther Party and later, after the notorious FBI-engineered East Coast-West Coast split, worked with the Black Liberation Army (BLA) in defending the lives and dignity of black folk. Back in the 1970s, Nuh was shot and captured with another Panther, Jalil Muntaqim, and was later charged and convicted of murder along with Jalil and Herman Bell (the New York 3). Evidence has since surfaced strongly suggesting the three men were unjustly convicted in this case. For over 28 years, Nuh has been held in California and New York gulags and repeatedly punished for his political ideas."

When Nuh was diagnosed with terminal cancer, he was devastated. He never envisioned dying behind the walls. He always believed he could win his freedom. While accepting the diagnosis, he still fought until the end, but he sought to put his house in order, so to speak. He made arrangements to see people that he needed to see in order to resolve any contradictions and not to leave this world with any animosity in his heart toward anyone on personal levels. Those he couldn't see in person, he spoke with on the phone. His final days were spent doing this to the best of his ability.

In 2003, Solidarity and Arm The Spirit, two Canadian collectives, co-published a book of writings by and about Nuh, as a tribute to his memory. This book, *All Power to the People*, is currently available from Kersplebedeb.

Linn Washington, Jr., is an award-winning columnist for the *Philadelphia Tribune* and free-lance journalist for publications nationwide. He writes extensively on matters involving the criminal justice system and racism. An associate professor in the Journalism Department at Temple University in Philadelphia, he holds a master's degree from Yale Law School and a B.S. in communications from Temple University.

He has covered Philadelphia's persecution of the MOVE organization since the 1970s. Washington has written: "When you look at the media coverage of MOVE, everything that was perceived as MOVE doing something wrong, was publicized. In contrast, the attacks on MOVE, the injustices, and the deprivations that they endured never found any coverage in the mainstream media." He has extensively covered the case of Mumia Abu-Jamal from the day of Mumia's arrest in December 1981 (when he was a reporter for the *Philadelphia Daily News*) to the present.

Laura Whitehorn became politically active in the 1960s, in solidarity with the Civil Rights Movement and, later, the Black power movement, Puerto Rican Independence Movement, and the Vietnamese fight for independence. She was part of the worldwide uprising in those years against colonialism and for socialism. In the '70s and early '80s she organized in support of political prisoners, against white supremacy and Zionism, for women's and gay liberation, and in support of prisoners' rights.

Laura was arrested in 1985 and charged, with five codefendants, with "conspiring to influence, change and protest domestic and internal policies and practices of the U.S. government by violent and illegal means," including bombings against government and military targets such as the U.S. Capitol and the New York City Patrolmen's Benevolent Association; no one was injured in any of the actions. This became known as the "Resistance Conspiracy" case. In 1990, Laura, along with codefendants Linda Evans and Marilyn Buck, pled guilty to two counts of the indictment in exchange for the dropping of charges against their three other codefendants: Alan Berkman, Tim Blunk, and Susan Rosenberg (particularly out of concern for Alan, then seriously ill), all of whom were already serving lengthy sentences for related charges. Laura was sentenced to a total of 23 years.

In prison, Laura worked on HIV/AIDS peer education. She helped organize a series of art shows to raise support for Mumia Abu-Jamal (Art and Writings Against the Death Penalty/ Free Mumia Abu-Jamal). She also contributed writings and artwork to various progressive publications and art exhibitions. She served her time in a variety of federal prisons, including the Marianna, Florida, control unit for women, and appreciated the support of a wide variety of progressive activists across the country.

In 1999 Laura was released from prison after a little more than 14 years—the maximum proportion of her original sentence then required to be served. She currently lives in New York City with her lover, the writer Susie Day, and organizes in support of those political prisoners still incarcerated. She is an editor at *POZ*, a national magazine for those affected by HIV. Laura is the subject of the documentary film, *OUT: The Making of a Revolutionary* (Third World Newsreel, 2000).

Rev. Seiichi Michael Yasutake, Ph.D. (1920-2001), a second-generation Japanese American, was born and raised in Seattle, Washington, becoming an Episcopal priest and moving to Chicago in 1950. He carried out a ministry of peace, justice, and reconciliation for over 50 years, working extensively in the fields of civil rights, racial justice, and sovereignty of Indigenous peoples, and the rights of political prisoners and prisoners of conscience.

Mike had been interned with his family in U.S. concentration camps for Japanese Americans during World War II. He became a conscientious objector during that war and was an advisor to conscientious objectors during the Vietnam War era. From 1983 until his death, he was executive director of the Interfaith Prisoners of Conscience Project (IPOC), which he founded with the purposes of mobilizing support in church and society for the release of political prisoners in the United States and monitoring prisons on human rights concerns. IPOC is sponsored by the National Council of Churches of Christ, USA. To broaden his work internationally, he founded the United States-Japan Committee for Racial Justice in 1984.

In a 1996 tribute, the Chicago-based Committee to End the Marion Lockdown wrote, "Mike is now 'retired' and in this capacity he does as much as 100 people.... He fights against all persecution of political prisoners and in this capacity has likely visited more U.S. political prisoners than any other person.... Mike is also the motivating force behind the book *Can't Jail the Spirit* [Committee to End the Marion Lockdown, fifth/final edition: 2002], which contains the biographies and autobiographies of many of the political prisoners caged by the United States."

In the late 1970s after a hiatus of 53 years, he took up kendo again for exercise and discipline and achieved the rank of 5th degree black belt when he was 73 years old.

A fuller biography can be found in the Archives of the Episcopal Church, under www.episcopalarchives.org/yasutake.html.

Barbara Zeller, M.D., graduated from the Columbia University College of Physicians and Surgeons in 1971 and completed a residency in primary care internal medicine. She was one of the first to serve as a medical volunteer during antiwar and antiracist protests and demonstrations. She went with a medical team that traveled overland to reach Wounded Knee through the government's military lines during the siege in 1973. In the late 1970s, Dr. Zeller worked in two free clinics in New York City that provided health care to women. In 1977 she volunteered with the Community Acupuncture Clinic at Lincoln Detox in the South Bronx (see profile of Mutulu Shakur, D.Ac. for more information) and provided support and solidarity to the Black and Latino leadership who developed community-controlled care and then founded the first community acupuncture school in the city.

During these years, Dr. Zeller began to provide medical consultation and advocacy to political prisoners. This has continued for over 30 years and has included being the medical advisor for the Jericho Movement. As a medical advocate she has visited Dylcia Pagán, Mumia Abu-Jamal, Bashir Hameed, "Seth" Hayes, Nuh Washington, David Gilbert, Laura Whitehorn, and Marilyn Buck, among many others. When her husband, political prisoner Dr. Alan Berkman, developed a deadly cancer in prison, she spearheaded the campaign that was required to save his life. In the 1990s, she visited a prison in El Salvador and helped to prepare a U.N. report on conditions there. Since the early 1990s, Dr. Zeller has provided care to people with HIV/AIDS as medical director of a residence for formerly homeless people with AIDS in the Bronx. She has also been a consultant for a class action suit brought by HIV-positive prisoners in New York State against the Department of Corrections to force a change in conditions and quality of care.

Political Prisoner
Support Organizations

The following list includes many organizations and websites in support of U.S. political prisoners and prisoners of war. It was compiled by Bob Lederer with assistance from Sara Falconer. Undoubtedly we omitted some about which we were not aware; for that, we apologize. In addition to those currently functioning, descriptions are included of defunct organizations that authored pieces in this book. This list will be maintained and updated at www.thejerichomovement.com. If you have changes or new organizations to add, please email nationaljericho@gmail.com.

* Indicates committees/websites that are supporting specific political prisoner(s) who are included in the Contributor Profiles section.

Writing the prisoners directly is a concrete way of showing support and involving these activists in the continued dialogue of the movements for radical change. For the names and addresses of current U.S. political prisoners, go to the lists maintained by:

National Jericho Movement
www.thejerichomovement.com/prisoners.html

Anarchist Black Cross Federation
www.abcf.net/abcf.asp?page=prisoners

Prison Activist Resource Center:
www.prisonactivist.org/pps+pows/pplist-alpha.shtml
(which also has profiles of released prisoners and those who have died).

Note that these lists may not be complete and may use slightly different definitions of the term political prisoner from each other. Also be aware that prisoners' addresses can change periodically, so always check these lists before writing a letter or circulating an address.

Autobiographical essays by many of the U.S. political prisoners held as of 2002 are contained in *Can't Jail the Spirit*, published by the (now defunct) Committee to End the Marion Lockdown, but still available from Kersplebedeb Publishing and Distribution in Montreal (info@kersplebedeb.com or www.kersplebedeb.com).

To get the latest news on U.S. political prisoners, you can subscribe to the excellent e-newsletter "Political Prisoner News," available from Freedom Archives at www.freedomarchives.org.

For information on how to contact your federal, state, and local elected officials to urge them to take action on political prisoners, go to www.congress.org, where you can input your zip code and get a list of email and postal mail addresses for all officials who "represent" you.

GENERAL SUPPORT

National Jericho Movement
P.O. Box 1272, New York, NY 10013
nationaljericho@gmail.com • www.thejerichomovement.com

Jericho is a movement with the defined goal of gaining recognition of the fact that political prisoners and prisoners of war exist inside of the United States, despite the United States government's continued denial, and winning amnesty and freedom for these political prisoners. The Jericho Movement grew out of a call for a national march on the White House during Spring Break of 1998 by political prisoner Jalil Muntaqim. The call was made in October of 1996 through the Provisional Government-Republic of New Afrika and the New Afrikan Liberation Front, but the organizers decided to use this opportunity to jump-start a much-needed movement to build a national support organization for political prisoners in general. Jericho98 was the collective work of over 50 organizations, defense committees and groups, 64 Jericho Organizing Committees, and Students for Jericho, making the issue of recognition and amnesty for U.S.-held political prisoners and prisoners of war a national one with its successful demonstration and rally at the White House.

Some of the Jericho Organizing Committees that came into being around this work continue working as chapters educating people about the existence of political prisoners. Then, too, Jericho is working with local defense committees to bring the cases of individual political prisoners to the public. Building a bond across organizational lines is what Jericho is about… that's where our strength lies.

Local chapters:

Boston Area Jericho Movement
P.O. Box 301057, Jamaica Plain, MA 02130
617-830-0732 • jericho_boston@yahoo.com
www.jerichoboston.org

Jericho Amnesty Coalition LA
c/o ARA, PO Box 1055, Culver City CA 90232
310-495-0299 • antiracistaction_la@yahoo.com
www.geocities.com/jerichoamnestycoalitionla

New Jersey Jericho Movement
T.J Whitaker, 973-229-3069 • newjerseyjericho@riseup.net
www.myspace.com/newjerseyjericho

New York City Jericho Movement
P.O. Box 1272, New York, NY 10013
Paulette D'Auteuil, 718-853-0893 • nycjericho@gmail.com
www.jerichony.org

Philadelphia Jericho Movement
c/o The A-Space, 4722 Baltimore Ave., Philadelphia, PA 19143
215-605-1759 (leave message) • PhillyJericho@riseup.net

San Francisco Bay Jericho Movement
P.O. Box 3585, Oakland, CA 94609
510-667-9293 • 510-595-1653 • www.prisonactivist.org/jericho_sfbay

Syracuse Jericho Movement
P.O. Box 35677, Syracuse, NY 13235
315-396-1600 • syracusejericho@riseup.net
www.myspace.com/syracusejerichomovement

Western Pennsylvania Jericho Chapter
c/o Kareem Howard, P.O. Box 2305, Pittsburgh, PA 15230
412-261-1086 • NCUPJ@aol.com

Wisconsin Jericho Movement
c/o Ifama Jackson, 4227 N. 18th Street, Milwaukee, WI 53209
Ifama4maat@earthlink.net

Anarchist Black Cross Federation
Los Angeles ABCF
P.O. Box 11223, Whittier, CA 90603
562-214-1554 • la@abcf.net • www.abcf.net

Making sure political prisoners and Prisoners of War are a part of their own support is crucial and one of the greatest strengths of the Federation. We directly communicate with as many PP/POW's as we can. A large part of this communication is working together with them to find out what they need and how we can practically provide this support. A Prisoners' Committee made up of five PP/POW's who have shown the most interest in our work and helping it grow serve on the ABCF's Federation Council. Members of the Prisoners' Committee rotate yearly.

As part of working with the prisoners, the ABCF works to build alliances with the communities and the movements the prisoners participated in prior to the arrests. Through these alliances we work toward increasing the awareness about various liberation movements and the political prisoners associated with the movements. It is through these coalitions that we continue to ensure that imprisoned comrades are not forgotten by their movements as well as our own.

Other chapters:

Jacksonville ABCF
P.O. Box 350392, Jacksonville, FL 32235-0392
jax@abcf.net

Montreal ABCF
P.O. Box 42053, Succ. Jeanne Mance, Montreal, QC, H2W 2T3 Canada
montrealabcf@gmail.com

New Jersey ABCF
nj@abcf.net

New York City ABCF
P.O. Box 110034, Brooklyn, NY 11211
nycabc@riseup.net • myspace.com/nycanarchistblackcross

Philadelphia ABCF
P.O. Box 42129, Philadelphia, PA 19101
timabcf@aol.com

Toronto ABCF
P.O. Box 97048, RPO Roncesvalles Avenue, Toronto, ON, M6R 3B3 Canada
torontoabcf@gmail.com

Books Through Bars Philadelphia
4722 Baltimore Avenue, Philadelphia, PA 19143
215-727-8170 • info@booksthroughbars.org • www.booksthroughbars.org/pbp

We send quality reading material to prisoners and encourage creative dialogue on the criminal justice system, thereby educating those living inside and outside of prison walls. Books Through Bars has created an interactive map showing prison book programs in the U.S. and Canada, including contact information. Check it out, and get involved with a prison book program near you! Note: The prison book programs listed on this map are not affiliated with, and operate independently of, Books Through Bars Philadelphia.

Break the Chains.info
www.breakthechains.info

Break the Chains.info is a news and discussion forum for supporters of political prisoners, prisoners of war, politicized social prisoners, and victims of police and state intimidation. This blog is organized and updated autonomously of the disbanded Break the Chains Prisoner Support Network formerly based in Eugene, Oregon. While this online project shares several of the same concerns as the old Break the Chains collective, no formal organization exists behind the current web presence.

Can't Jail the Spirit
c/o Portland Victory Gardens Project, 207-761-1504 • pvg@riseup.net
www.cantjailthespirit.org

This was launched as a website devoted to art and writing by and about political prisoners. This website features an online gallery, links to other political prisoner artists' websites and political prisoner support groups, and downloadable writings and art with Tom Manning's works alongside work by other political prisoners. It was designed and hosted by the TUG Initiative at the People's Free Space in Portland, Maine. We are looking for more submissions for this website, so any support committees of political prisoner artists and writers can get in touch with us to submit art and writing.

Can't Jail the Spirit was organized by the Portland Victory Gardens Project. The Project uses the process of growing and distributing food to raise awareness about the urgent need for the liberation of U.S. political prisoners, community self-reliance, ecological sustainability, and social change. Portland VGP grows food in Portland, teaches girls and women about medicinal herbs, and organizes events in support of political prisoners. Portland VGP is inspired by and collaborates with the original Victory Gardens Project, which was started by three Maine farmers and Black Panther political prisoner Herman Bell. Since 1995, the Athens VGP has grown tons

811

of organic vegetables in the community of Athens, Maine. The project has distributed these free and healthy vegetables to local community members, urban neighborhoods, and activists.

Center for Constitutional Rights
666 Broadway, 7th Floor, New York, NY 10012
212-614-6464 • www.ccrjustice.org

The Center for Constitutional Rights is dedicated to advancing and protecting the rights guaranteed by the United States Constitution and the Universal Declaration of Human Rights. Founded in 1966 by attorneys who represented civil rights movements in the South, CCR is a nonprofit legal and educational organization committed to the creative use of law as a positive force for social change. Among many other areas of work, CCR represents demonstrators who have been wrongfully arrested and movements that have been infiltrated and spied on. CCR's website contains various fact sheets, booklets, and other information on repressive legislation and practices by the U.S. government.

Certain Days: Freedom for Political Prisoners Calendar
c/o QPIRG Concordia, 1455 de Maisonneuve Boulevard O.,
Montreal, QC H3G 1M8, CANADA
info@certaindays.org • www.certaindays.org

The calendar is a joint fund-raising and educational project between outside organizers in Montreal and Toronto and three political prisoners held in maximum-security prisons in New York state: Herman Bell, David Gilbert, and Robert "Seth" Hayes. The initial project was suggested by Herman and has been shaped throughout the process by all of our ideas, discussions, and analysis. All of the members of the outside collective are involved in day-to-day organizing work other than the calendar, on issues ranging from refugee and immigrant solidarity to community media to prisoner justice. We work from an anti-imperialist, antiracist, anticapitalist, feminist, queer, and trans positive position.

Critical Resistance
National Office
1904 Franklin Street, Suite 504, Oakland, CA 94612
510-444-0484 • crnational@criticalresistance.org
www.criticalresistance.org

Northeast Regional Office
976 Longwood Avenue, Bronx, NY 10459
718-676-1660 • crne@criticalresistance.org

Southern Regional Office
930 N. Broad Street, New Orleans, LA 70119
504-304-3784 • crsouth@criticalresistance.org

Also has chapters in Baltimore, Chicago, Gainesville (Florida), Los Angeles, New Orleans, Tampa/St. Petersburg (Florida), and Washington, DC.

Critical Resistance seeks to build an international movement to end the prison industrial complex by challenging the belief that caging and controlling people makes us safe. We believe that basic necessities such as food, shelter, and freedom are what really make our communities secure. As such, our work is part of global struggles against inequality and powerlessness. The success of the movement requires that it reflect communities most affected by the PIC. Because we seek to abolish the PIC, we cannot support any work that extends its life or scope.

4strugglemag: Views, Thoughts and Analysis from the Hearts and Minds of North American Political Prisoners and Friends
P.O. Box 97048, RPO Roncesvalles Avenue, Toronto, ON M6R 3B3 Canada
jaanlaaman@gmail.com • www.4strugglemag.org (all issues available online)

This magazine, edited by Ohio 7 political prisoner Jaan Laaman and members of Toronto Anarchist Black Cross Federation, focuses the insights and experiences of U.S. political prisoners on major issues of the day. While a lot of the writing is by political prisoners, other activists, allies, revolutionaries, and insightful outside voices are included. 4strugglemag is an independent, nonsectarian revolutionary voice. We are unapologetically anti-imperialist and solidly in support of progressive National Liberation, especially the struggles of New African/Black, Mexicano/Chicano, Puerto Rican, and Native American Nations presently controlled by U.S. imperialism. Reflecting the work and principles of political prisoners held by the United States, 4strugglemag advocates for Justice, Equality, Freedom, Socialism, Protection of Our Mother Earth, Human Rights, and Peace.

Hard copies are available (free to prisoners, $5 an issue for people outside). We encourage readers to respond, critique, and carry on discussions in the magazine.

Freedom Archives
522 Valencia Street, San Francisco, CA 94110
415-863-9977 • info@freedomarchives.org • www.freedomarchives.org

Freedom Archives is a nonprofit educational media archive dedicated to the preservation and dissemination of historical audio and video documenting progressive movements from the 1960s to the present. The Archives offers a youth development program that encourages engagement with these historical materials and offers media production training. Freedom Archives regularly produces original documentaries and educational media for use within schools and organizations as tools for community building and social justice work. Productions (available for purchase) regarding political prisoners include: a CD about the murder of George Jackson and the Attica Rebellion; a CD of the poetry of Marilyn Buck; a DVD of interviews with the late Nuh Washington, Jalil Muntaqim, and David Gilbert; a DVD ("Legacy of Torture") about the San Francisco 8 case; a DVD about "COINTELPRO 101"; and a DVD about the late prison activist Charisse Shumate and the struggles of women in prison. The Archives also edits an e-newsletter, "Political Prisoner News."

Kersplebedeb Publications
CP 63560, CCCP Van Horne, Montreal, Quebec, Canada, H3W 3H8
info@kersplebedeb.com • www.kersplebedeb.com
Political prisoner/POW page: www.kersplebedeb.com/mystuff/powpp.html

Dozens of books and pamphlets by and about political prisoners, prisoners of war, and the movements from which they came—both in the united states and around the world. Write for a free catalog.

Prison Activist Resource Center
P.O. Box 70447, Oakland, CA 94612
510-893-4648 • info@prisonactivist.org • www.prisonactivist.org
Political prisoner/POW page: www.prisonactivist.org/pps+pows

PARC is a prison abolitionist group committed to exposing and challenging the institutionalized racism of the prison industrial complex. We are also committed to developing and practicing antioppression as individuals and in our organization. PARC believes in strategies and tactics that build safety in oppressed communities without reliance on the police or the prison-industrial complex. We produce a directory that is free to prisoners upon request and seek to work in solidarity with prisoners, formerly incarcerated people, their friends and families. We also work with teachers and activists on prison issues. This work includes building action networks and materials that expose human rights violations. PARC's website also has a section devoted to U.S. political prisoners.

Prison Radio
P.O. Box 411074, San Francisco, CA 94141
info@prisonradio.org • www.prisonradio.org

Prison Radio's mission is to challenge mass incarceration and racism by airing the voices of men and women in prison by bringing their voices into the public dialogue on crime and punishment. Our educational materials serve as a catalyst for public activism. Prison Radio produces radio essays and commentaries by political prisoners Mumia Abu-Jamal, Herman Wallace and Albert Woodfox of the Angola 3, and Lori Berenson (U.S. solidarity activist imprisoned in Peru), among others.

Resistance in Brooklyn (RnB)
c/o WRL/Meyer, 339 Lafayette Street, New York, NY 10012
mmmsrnb@igc.org

Resistance in Brooklyn is an affinity group that came together in 1992 to combine political action, study, and a sense of community. We have been active in anti-imperialist work, including in Puerto Rican, Central American, African, and Black liberation solidarity movements; we've been involved in groups doing antimilitarist, antinuclear, anti-Klan, prisoner support, women's liberation, pro-feminist men's, AIDS, and LGBT liberation work. We prioritize work to free U.S. political prisoners and currently participate in such organizations as the National Jericho Movement, Free Mumia Abu-Jamal Coalition, Lynne Stewart Defense Committee, Friends of Marilyn Buck, and Friends of David Gilbert, among others. We sponsor an annual Political Prisoner Card-Writing Party, have presented workshops on political prisoners at numerous conferences, and have published booklets about particular political prisoners and the struggle against white supremacy, including *Enemies of the State: Interviews with Marilyn Buck, David Gilbert and Laura Whitehorn* (1998), later republished separately by Abraham Guillen Press and Kersplebedeb, and currently available from AK Press.

Safiya Bukhari—Albert "Nuh" Washington Foundation
P.O. Box 690458, Hillside Station, Bronx, NY 10469
info@safiyanuhfoundation.org • www.safiyanuhfoundation.org

The Foundation is a nonsectarian grantmaking organization whose founders, officers, advisors, members, supporters, associates, volunteers, and staff are all individuals who have come together to provide unbiased assistance to the numerous families and groups who work on behalf of United States-held political prisoners and prisoners of war. Additionally, we provide similar services to the survivors and families of political prisoners, POW's, and activists who have died in service of all oppressed peoples' struggles inside the U.S. Both Safiya Bukhari and Albert "Nuh" Washington were U.S.-held political prisoners and noted members of the original Black Panther Party who selflessly sacrificed their lives for the self-determination and ultimate liberation of Black and oppressed people. Thus, it is in their names that this foundation is dedicated to continuing the work to gain amnesty and freedom for U.S.-held political prisoners and POW's. One of the Foundation's projects, the Janet Cyril Justice Fund, has been established to help political prisoner and POW supporters and family members in providing those held captive with needed commissary access as well as assistance in securing unbiased, and/or alternative, humanitarian medical services for their loved ones.

South Chicago ABC Zine Distro
P.O. Box 721
Homewood, IL 60430
anthonyrayson@hotmail.com

Publishes and distributes writings by political prisoners, POWs and politicized social prisoners.

Turning the Tide: Journal of Anti-Racist Action, Research & Education
c/o ARA, P.O. Box 1055, Culver City, CA 90232
310-495-0299 • antiracistaction_la@yahoo.com
www.aratoronto.org (archive of recent issues)

Turning the Tide is an independent, grassroots journal of antiracism, anticolonialism, and anti-imperialism produced by Anti-Racist Action Los Angeles/People Against Racist Terror (ARA-LA/PART). There is frequent coverage of U.S. political prisoners. The newspaper has been published for 20 years without partisan subsidies, foundation grants, corporate money, or government funds. It is distributed free to prisoners and antiracist activists and at shows, schools, protests, and other activities. One-year subscriptions in the U.S. (6 bimonthly issues) are $18 for individuals and $28 for institutions or international subscribers (payable to Anti-Racist Action).

Committee to End the Marion Lockdown (Defunct)
The Committee to End the Marion Lockdown (CEML) was founded in 1985 to fight against the brutality of the lockdown at Marion Federal Penitentiary. The lockdown, which began in 1983, transformed the whole prison into a "control unit" where the prisoners were kept in tiny cells for 22-23 hours per day and are under total physical control. CEML made a point of saying that unless Marion was stopped, control unit prisons would proliferate across the United States. Unfortunately we were correct. We were unable to stop Marion and since then control unit prisons (often referred to as "supermax" prisons) modeled on Marion have proliferated

throughout the state prison systems so that today almost every state has such a prison. CEML was committed to exposing the racist nature of imprisonment. This racism can be expressed in many different ways: for example, a Black person is more than eight times more likely to go to prison than a white person in the U.S. Though these facts are an outrage, they are still not widely known within the progressive community. CEML worked to create awareness among progressive people of prisons as an attack on people of color. Our work involved collecting and disseminating information, organizing letter campaigns and so on, but we also believe in direct, visible action and organized, with other groups such as the National Committee to Free Puerto Rican Political Prisoners and POW's, numerous demonstrations in Chicago, Marion, and around the country. (CEML functioned until 2000. For history and documents, visit www-unix.oit.umass.edu/~kastor/ceml.html.)

BLACK/NEW AFRIKAN/MOVE POLITICAL PRISONERS

*International Concerned Family and Friends of Mumia Abu-Jamal
P.O. Box 19709, Philadelphia, PA 19143
215-476-8812 • icffmaj@aol.com
www.freemumia.com

The International Concerned Family and Friends of Mumia Abu-Jamal (ICFFMAJ) dates back to the incarceration of Mumia Abu-Jamal on December 9, 1981. It is the leading international organization that fights for Mumia's freedom. With the help of many other organizations nationwide and worldwide, ICFFMAJ has organized major demonstrations in Philadelphia, Harrisburg, New York, San Francisco, and even France. ICFFMAJ has either led or sent delegations to international tribunals and conferences in Philadelphia, Paris, Durban (South Africa), Athens (Greece), England, Spain, Cuba, and Puerto Rico. ICFFMAJ regularly confronts the Philadelphia and Pennsylvania powers responsible for Mumia's frame-up and continued incarceration on death row. The organization also hosts international delegations that come to Philadelphia to pressure city and state officials to remedy the injustice of his conviction and treatment. Pam Africa, the head of the organization, is recognized around the world for her 25+ years of fighting for Mumia's freedom and against all forms of injustice nationally and internationally. She has been Mumia's "feet on the street" and has traveled extensively in response to calls for her presence and fiery speeches. ICFFMAJ is convinced that Mumia is innocent but will also work with whoever supports Mumia's right to a new, fair trial—whether based on opposition to the death penalty, a view that Mumia's constitutional rights were denied, support for political prisoners, or opposition to police brutality, misconduct, and terrorism.

*Free Mumia Abu-Jamal Coalition (New York City)
P.O. Box 16, College Station, New York, NY 10030
212-330-8029 • info@FreeMumia.com • www.freemumia.com

The Free Mumia Abu-Jamal Coalition (FMAJC)'s primary goal is to fight for Mumia's freedom. We believe that Mumia is innocent and should be released immediately, but that at the very least he is entitled to a new and fair trial. All are welcome to join the Coalition regardless of their feelings about Mumia's innocence, if they support the idea that Mumia was denied justice and minimally deserves a new trial. Those who choose to work with us can limit their work to this aspect alone of our work, as we also work to free all our political prisoners and prisoners of war, to abolish the death penalty, to abolish the prison-industrial complex, and to oppose police brutality, misconduct, and rising terroristic and fascistic practices—all aspects of Mumia's incarceration and death sentence. We also support efforts to stop the U.S. wars in Iraq and Afghanistan, as well as other imperialist interventions, and see ourselves as part of the anti-imperialist/antiracist movements. We work very closely with the International Concerned Family and Friends of Mumia Abu-Jamal and recognize it as the leadership of the international movement to free Mumia. We also communicate directly with Mumia. The FMAJC works democratically with accountability to collective process and decision-making. It is actively engaged in a range of activities from confrontations and demonstrations to educational and cultural events, campaigns, and international collaboration. The FMAJC is committed to a diverse membership and thus is multi-ethnic and cross-generational in its composition.

*Mobilization to Free Mumia Abu-Jamal
P.O. Box 10328, Oakland, CA 94610
510-268-9429 • alerts@freemumia.org or jmackler@lmi.net
www.freemumia.org

The Northern California-based Mobilization to Free Mumia Abu-Jamal was formed in 1995 as a broad-based coalition of organizations and individuals fighting for the freedom of innocent death row inmate, African-American political prisoner, and award-winning journalist Mumia Abu-Jamal. The Mobilization has focused on organizing broadly sponsored periodic mass demonstrations for Mumia's freedom, including the San Francisco protest in 1999 of 25,000. Mobilization activities include the organization of an International Tribunal to judge the case of Mumia, several dozen mass educational rallies featuring prominent figures in public life, teach-ins, regional and national conferences, tours of leading civil and democratic rights advocates, and fund-raising efforts that have contributed over $500,000 to Mumia's legal and political defense. The Mobilization maintains a comprehensive website and publishes a newsletter and other educational literature. Mumia T-Shirts, videos, CDs, and buttons are available. The Mobilization was a key initiator of the annual Michael Franti "Power to the Peaceful" concert a decade ago. Beginning with 5,000 people in 1997, the September 2007 concert attracted an audience of 120,000 in San Francisco's Golden Gate Park, with Mumia speakers prominently featured. The Mobilization collaborates closely with the International Concerned Family and Friends of Mumia Abu-Jamal in the organization of coordinated national demonstrations, conferences, and tours.

Millions for Mumia
c/o International Action Center, 55 W. 17 St., Suite 5C, New York, NY 10011
212-633-6646 • iacenter@action-mail.org
www.millions4mumia.org

Millions for Mumia is an international grassroots campaign launched in 1999 to demand freedom and a new trial for Mumia Abu-Jamal. Hip-hop artists, prominent political figures, and religious leaders came together with constituent-based coalitions such as Asians for Mumia, Youths and Students for Mumia, Latin@s for Mumia, Rainbow Flags for Mumia, and Labor for Mumia in an effort to make Mumia a "household name." On April 24, 1999 – Mumia's birthday – 50,000 people participated in demonstrations in Philadelphia and San Francisco. Since then, countless events and demonstrations have been organized across the country and around the world demanding freedom for Mumia Abu-Jamal. Today, Millions for Mumia is an anti-death penalty project of the International Action Center that fights for the freedom of all U.S. political prisoners and against the prison-industrial complex.

* Educators for Mumia Abu-Jamal
www.emajonline.com
Tameka Cage, cage@pitt.edu
Johanna Fernandez, johanna_fernandez@baruch.cuny.edu
Mark Taylor, mark.taylor@ptsem.edu

Educators for Mumia Abu-Jamal (EMAJ) is a network of teachers and educators who have advocated and organized for Mumia Abu-Jamal since 1995. Its members have participated in numerous fund drives, campus teach-ins, educational events and protest actions. The purpose of EMAJ is to mobilize educators into the broad public movement seeking freedom and justice for Mumia, doing all we can as teachers (1) to educate about Mumia's case, (2) to stop all plans to execute Mumia, and (3) to overturn Mumia's conviction, whether this comes about through a judicial mandate for his immediate release, through an evidentiary hearing, or through a new trial.

*Journalists for Mumia Abu-Jamal
P.O. Box 30770, Philadelphia, PA, 19104
Michael Schiffmann: mikschiff@t-online.de • www.againstthecrimeofsilence.de
Hans Bennett: hbjournalist@gmail.com • insubordination.blogspot.com
www.abu-jamal-news.com

Journalists for Mumia has been formed to challenge the long history of media bias against Abu-Jamal's case for a new trial. Through our website and print newspaper, we are providing independent, nonsectarian, up-to-date news about the case.

*Sundiata Acoli Freedom Campaign
P.O. Box 1959, Newark, NJ 07102
www.myspace.com/freesundiata

The Campaign helps raise public awareness, mobilizations, and material aid to bring about the freedom of Sundiata Acoli.

*SundiataAcoli.org
www.sundiataacoli.org

This website is a project of the Talking Drum Collective (www.thedrum.org), a collective of organizers and website owners who have come together in the spirit of unity for the upliftment of Afrikan People. The site contains much information about, and writings by, Sundiata.

International Committee to Support Imam Jamil Al-Amin
547 West End Place, SW, Atlanta, GA 30310
917-645-3822 • defendingthepoor@yahoo.com
www.myspace.com/FreeTheImam • www.geocities.com/icsijaa

National Coalition to Free the Angola Three
c/o Kings Freelines, 2008 New York Avenue, #B, Austin, TX 78702
512-473-0680 • kingsfreelines@gmail.com
www.angola3.org

Thirty-six years ago, deep in rural Louisiana, three young Black men—Herman Wallace, Albert Woodfox, and Robert King Wilkerson—were silenced for trying to expose continued racial segregation, systematic corruption, and horrific abuse in the biggest prison in the U.S., an 18,000-acre former slave plantation called Angola. In the early 1970s, nonviolent hunger and work strikes organized by inmates caught the attention of Louisiana's first Black legislators and local media. Legislative leaders and the governor called for investigations into the extraordinarily cruel treatment commonplace in the prison. In 1972 and 1973, prison officials—determined to put an end to outside scrutiny—charged these three men with murders they did not commit and threw them into six-by-nine-foot solitary-confinement cells, keeping them there for decades. Despite this, each has remained principled and politically active. Robert King was released in 2001 after a judge overturned his conviction. In July 2008, Albert Woodfox's sentence was overturned, yet he remains imprisoned, as does Herman Wallace. The website includes details and updates about the Angola Three and links to pages on facebook.com and myspace.com.

No Death Penalty for Zolo (Azania) Committee
P.O. Box 478314, Chicago, IL 60647
crsn@aol.com
www.zoloazania.org • www.prairiefire.org/Zolo/support.html
www.thejerichomovement.com/zoloazania.html

Zolo Azania is one of the numerous African-Americans who await execution as a result of a racist criminal justice system. He is a politically conscious activist, who at the time of his arrest in 1981 for allegedly murdering a police officer was actively involved in the movement for the self-determination of African-American people. This directly influenced the way the police, the prosecution, and the Indiana courts denied him a fair trial and fanned the flames of prejudice to obtain the death penalty. Twice he has been sentenced to die, and twice the death sentence has been reversed on appeal due to unconstitutional suppression of favorable evidence by the prosecution, ineffective assistance of counsel, and systematic exclusion of Blacks from the jury pool. Zolo did not receive a fair trial and has always maintained his total innocence of any involvement in the crime. The Indiana courts have set a new date for a trial before a jury on the sole issue of Zolo's sentence, which could be the death penalty, on October 20, 2008. Zolo is a prolific writer and an accomplished artist whose work has been exhibited in many places around the country (the first website above has a gallery of his work). His writing and his art reflect who he is: A man who lives his political convictions.

The stakes are high for this next step in Zolo's more than quarter century of fighting for justice, for his freedom, and for his very life. Those who oppose the death penalty need to continue to get the word out that Zolo is a wonderful person who has contributed much to the lives of others and still has much to contribute. The government should not be allowed to put him to death.

LET FREEDOM RING

*Family and Friends of Veronza Bowers, Jr.
www.veronza.org

Website contains personal and legal information about Veronza, writings and poetry by him, and how people can help obtain his release.

*Veronza Bowers, Jr. Legal Defense Fund
c/o M. M. Garfield, 2500 Barton Creek Boulevard, #1509, Austin, TX 78735

Raises funds for the team fighting for the freedom of this political prisoner incarcerated for 34 years – and still held more than four years after his mandatory release date.

*Collective Press - Support for Veronza Bowers, Jr.
904-824-8526 • veronza@collectivepress.org
www.collectivepress.org

The Collective Press is a not-for-profit publication based in, but not confined to, St. Augustine, FL. Its purpose is to provide an independent alternative to mainstream money-driven news sources, while fostering a greater sense of community among its readers and contributors. Their website gives the background on the injustices of Veronza's case. Also on the site are T-shirts and CDs of Veronza's music for sale.

Partnership for Social Justice (Support for Eddie Conway)
c/o AFSC, 4806 York Road, Baltimore, MD 21212
443-570-4830 • dominique@psjustice.org
www.freeeddieconway.org

The Partnership for Social Justice (PSJ) originated to free Marshall "Eddie" Conway, a political prisoner serving his 35th year in a Maryland prison. In 1970, Eddie was charged with killing a Baltimore police officer, convicted, and sentenced to life plus 30 years in prison. Like so many other victims of the FBI's COINTELPRO, Eddie, a former leader of the Baltimore Black Panther Party, was targeted for his political and social activism. PSJ members are currently lobbying the Congressional Black Caucus to call for a congressional investigation of COINTELPRO. PSJ also regularly organizes fund-raisers and rallies to heighten community awareness around Eddie's case and fund the campaign to win a new trial for him. PSJ also offers support to local community efforts that aim to bring justice to Baltimore, including such issues as the criminal in-justice system, housing, education, and health care.

Committee to Free Chip Fitzgerald
629 Main Street No.195, Watsonville, CA 95076
831-254-2580 • freechipfitzgerald@yahoo.com
www.freechip.org

Romaine "Chip" Fitzgerald joined the Southern California chapter of the Black Panther Party in early 1969 as a teenager. In September of that year, after the murders of several other LA Panthers by police or FBI agents operating as part of COINTELPRO's campaign to destroy the party, Chip was involved in a shootout with Los Angeles police and sustained a gunshot wound to the head. He survived this attack, only to be arrested later and charged with assault on police and the murder of a security guard. He was convicted and sentenced to death. In 1972, when the California Supreme Court declared the death penalty unconstitutional, his sentence was one of scores commuted to life with the possibility of parole. (Most of the other surviving inmates who were on death row at the time have since been freed.) In prison for 39 years now, he is the longest-held political prisoner in the United States. In 1998, he suffered a massive stroke and was denied proper medical care for both this and a degenerative spinal condition. Chip's dedication to the liberation of Black and all oppressed people has not wavered through his long, brutal incarceration. In July 2008, Chip was denied parole and required to wait one more year for a new hearing. Chip was first eligible for parole in 1976. Since then, he has not been charged with any prison violations sufficient to justify this denial.

Information about Seth Hayes
info@sethhayes.org • www.sethhayes.org
www.thejerichomovement.com/seth.html

Robert "Seth" Hayes is one of the longest-held political prisoners in the U.S. Born in the Bronx in 1948, Seth was imprisoned due to his activity in the Black Panther Party. Seth has struggled for years to receive adequate treatment for type II diabetes and hepatitis C. While in prison, Seth continues to work for the betterment of the community in which he lives. He has participated in programs with the NAACP, the Jaycees, and other organizations and has worked as a librarian, prerelease advisor, and AIDS counselor. He is also a longtime advisor and collaborator in the annual Certain Days: Freedom for Political Prisoners Calendar project. Imprisoned now for 34 years, Seth will be going before the parole board for the sixth time in September 2008. At each of Seth's previous parole hearings, he was denied release due to the serious nature of the crime he was convicted for and given another two year hit. The refusal of parole for the serious nature of the crime is contrary to the spirit of the law, for it is something that a prisoner can never change, and the giving of parole is supposed to be based upon the prisoner's behavior while behind bars.

It's About Time Committee: Black Panther Party Legacy & Alumni
www.itsabouttimebpp.com

The It's About Time Committee is committed to preserving and promoting the legacy of the Black Panther Party (BPP) and its programs of community survival pending social change. We will commemorate the historic legacies of the BPP as well as the many sacrifices and constructive contributions that all of us made while serving the people body and soul. We have the responsibility to place our own experiences into historical context; otherwise, the legacy of the Black Panther Party will be ignored, dismissed, and distorted by today's commentators and tomorrow's historians. We will maintain a network of Black Panther Party alumni and supporters for the purpose of providing educational information to community groups or the public at large regarding issues of social justice. We will support other community organizations who promote social justice issues. We commemorate the sacrifices of those who fell in body and spirit to the prevailing internal and external forces of those times. We must continue to bring attention to the plight of the many political prisoners and exiles who were victims of the government repression that contributed to the Party's demise. The website contains a wealth of documents about former Black Panther political prisoners.

*John Africa's MOVE Organization—Support for the MOVE 9
P.O. Box 19709, Philadelphia, PA 19143
610-499-0979 • onamovellja@aol.com
www.onamove.com • www.move9parole.blogspot.com

The MOVE Organization was founded by John Africa in Philadelphia in the early 1970s. MOVE is a revolutionary organization that fights to protect all life. They are characterized by dreadlocks, the last name "Africa," and an uncompromising commitment to their belief: LIFE. The system pollutes the air, poisons the water, contaminates the soil, and causes weakness and sickness. MOVE is about getting rid of the system and living by natural law, in harmony with life. MOVE confronts the system through information and demonstrations. MOVE exposes politicians who serve industry and greed. For these reasons, they have been consistently harassed and attacked by the Philadelphia police, including the massive shoot-in in 1978 and the bombing in 1985 that killed 11 MOVE members, including five children and John Africa.

Almost 30 years after the 1978 police attack that led to the unjust conviction and 30- to 100-year sentences for the MOVE 9, MOVE continues to organize for the freedom of the eight survivors (Merle Africa died in prison of cancer in 1998), who became eligible for parole in 2008. As of July 2008, seven had been denied parole. Charles Sims Africa will come before the parole board in October 2008. John Africa taught that there is no justice in this system. But MOVE is still urging people to write to the parole board to challenge its unjust decisions to keep innocent people in prison and to demand parole for Charles. MOVE is also asking supporters to contact the media. On the move9parole website, videos about the MOVE 9 are available featuring Ramona Africa (the sole adult survivor of the 1985 police bombing of MOVE headquarters) and Mike Africa, Jr. (the son of MOVE 9 prisoners Debbie and Mike Sr.).

Malcolm X Commemoration Committee
P.O. Box 340084, Jamaica, NY 11434
718-949-5153 • mxcc519@aol.com
www.malcolmxcommemorationcommittee.com

The Committee was formed in 1992 by a small group of former members of the two organizations founded by Malcolm X after his expulsion from the Nation of Islam in 1964, the Organization of Afro-American Unity and the Muslim Mosque, Inc. The Committee is committed to revealing to the legions of Black people who have no direct knowledge of Malcolm the true legacy of this great warrior. The Committee joins with the Sons and Daughters of Africa to conduct an annual pilgrimage to Malcolm's gravesite on his birthday (May 19). In 1996 our group began to sponsor an annual tribute dinner for the families of political prisoners in the New York, New Jersey, and Pennsylvania area as a demonstration of our sympathy and understanding of the suffering they were enduring along with their loved ones behind the bars. All proceeds from that dinner go into the commissary account of the freedom fighters whose families are present at the dinner. The committee has launched a campaign to organize their families into a potent force to give a human face to the political prisoners and in the process offset the criminalization and dehumanizing effect of the media and prison authorities who want them locked away forever.

Malcolm X Grassroots Movement

National office: (toll free) 877-248-6095 • www.mxgm.org
Local chapters in Jackson, MS; Birmingham, AL; Oakland, CA; Atlanta, GA; New York, NY;
and Washington, DC

The Malcolm X Grassroots Movement is an organization of Afrikans in America/New Afrikans whose mission is to defend the human rights of our people and promote self-determination in our community. While organizing around our principles of unity, we are building a network of Black/New Afrikan activists and organizers committed to the protracted struggle for the liberation of the New Afrikan Nation—By Any Means Necessary!

The Movement asserts that it is an exercise of one's human right to engage in acts of resistance against oppression and domination. It is in the spirit of the tradition of Afrikan resistance that we work to free all political prisoners and prisoners of war and that we encourage those committed to the ideals of freedom to join us in the struggle. The website has information on many present and former political prisoners, as well as on how to support them.

The New York State Task Force on Political Prisoners is an ad hoc group of former political prisoners, attorneys, and activists dedicated to providing legal, organizing, and technical support to political activists incarcerated in New York State. All but one of these seven prisoners are past members of the Black Panther Party and Black Liberation Army and have spent about 30 years in prison. The Task Force includes representatives of the Malcolm X Grassroots Movement and other organizations and individuals.

*Jalil Muntaqim Support—The Plaid Dragon Collective

718-853-0893 • info@freejalil.com
www.freejalil.com

Multimedia site with timely updates about Jalil's parole efforts and the case of the SF8. Features video, audio, and writings by Jalil on a diverse range of topics, from analysis of the "Black bourgeoisie" to poetry. The Plaid Dragon Collective along with Raven's Shadowrunners are a collective of warriors of all colors who are too dark, too light, too tall, too fat, too young, too old, too gay, too straight, too crazy. But we are committed to Rising-Up-Angry in defense of people both inside and outside the wall constructed by: racism, sexism, classism, elitism, capitalism, and imperialism. We believe in taking an offensive position of struggle, organizing, and education that will lead to and support a future world without borders for the individual or the state.

Nebraska's Two Political Prisoners

www.n2pp.info

The website has in-depth information on the cases of former Black Panthers Mondo we Langa and Ed Poindexter, framed for murder and imprisoned since 1971.

Mondo's Art Gallery

www.mondo.info

Art produced in prison by political prisoner Mondo we Langa.

Hugo Pinell—Information and Support
kiilu2@sbcglobal.net • gingersyrup@hotmail.com • dbwall@earthlink.net
www.hugopinell.org

Hugo, nicknamed Yogi Bear, has been in California prisons since age 19, when he was jailed on a disputed assault charge. Politicized in the late 1960s by revolutionary prisoners like George Jackson, he became part of the Black Liberation Movement formed in resistance to the deplorable conditions and unspeakable brutality exacted on prisoners, especially Blacks. Born of an African-Nicaraguan father, Hugo resisted the segregation of Blacks from Latinos mandated by prisons at that time, i.e., he refused to disassociate from Black prisoners. That plus being bilingual made him even more of a target and a threat as someone who worked toward unity. In August 1971, George Jackson was murdered on the yard at San Quentin in what prison officials described as an escape attempt, but many activists believe was a setup based on earlier attempts on his life. Six prisoners were later put on trial for the murders and assaults of three guards and two inmate trustees during that incident. Of the three convicted, Hugo is the only one who remains in prison, although he was only convicted of assault. Now 63, he has spent 42 years in California prisons, the last 36 in solitary confinement, including 16 in the windowless, high-tech SHU (Security Housing Unit). He was denied parole for the eighth time in 2006. His supporters continue to campaign for his release, publishing updates and analysis on his website.

Friends and Family of Kamau Sadiki
www.helpkamau.blogspot.com

The website has background and updates on the case of this former Black Panther and Black Liberation Army member. The group also raises funds for Kamau's needs in prison. Funds can be sent to: Bradley Greene, 8239 N. Williams Avenue, Philadelphia, PA.

*San Francisco 8 Support: Committee for Defense of Human Rights
P.O. Box 90221, Pasadena, CA 91109
415-226-1120 • freethesf8@riseup.net • www.freethesf8.org

The Committee for Defense of Human Rights was formed in the wake of a 2005 grand jury by five Black activists who resisted it. That state grand jury was the precursor to the charges in the San Francisco 8 indictment of 2007. CDHR was organized to draw attention to human rights abuses perpetrated by the U.S. government and police agencies that were carried out through COINTELPRO in an effort to destroy progressive organizations and individuals—particularly the Black Panther Party. CDHR also addresses the history of torture, false imprisonment, and ongoing repression in the San Francisco 8 case.

*New York Hands Off Assata (Shakur) Coalition
www.handsoffassata.org

The New York Hands Off Assata Coalition is a collective comprised of activists, artists, scholars, elected officials, students, parents, attorneys, workers, clerics, and concerned community members who are standing in solidarity against the latest attack on Assata Shakur. We know that Assata is not a terrorist and contest the use of that term by the government to denounce people who are not terrorists but who stand in opposition to U.S. policies. Demanding a halt to the $1 million bounty placed on her head, along with the removal of her name from the U.S.

government's federal terrorist list, this broad coalition has taken shape and gained momentum by the love of its members for Assata Shakur, the Black Liberation Movement, the Cuban Revolution, and other international struggles.

*Hands Off Assata Campaign
www.assatashakur.org

The Hands Off Assata Campaign is a coming together of organizations and individuals who are outraged by the heightened attempts by the federal government, congress of the united states and the state of new jersey to illegally force thru kidnapping a return of Assata Shakur from Cuba to the plantation United States. We know that Assata Shakur is a bona fide political exile living in the island nation of Cuba. She was persecuted for her political beliefs and tortured while in prison. We support the international human rights and Geneva conventions, which enabled her to seek and secure political asylum in Cuba, and we support the right of the Cuban people to grant it to her. The website is a project of the Talking Drum Collective, www.thedrum.org.

*Family and Friends of Dr. Mutulu Shakur
P.O. Box 3171, Manhattanville Station, New York, NY 10027
347-221-4333 • mutulushakur@hotmail.com • www.mutulushakur.com

The task of Family and Friends of Dr. Mutulu Shakur is at least twofold: (1) to provide moral, material and legal support to win his release from a blatantly unjust incarceration; and (2) to keep alive Dr. Shakur's longstanding passion for innovative healing and social justice. One method for advancing the latter is an annual fund-raising dinner presenting health activist awards. The website includes information about the case, downloadable flyers, essays by Dr. Shakur on reparations and other subjects, music videos and CDs featuring Dr. Shakur's son Mopreme, student Zayd, and godson Tupac Shakur.

*Russell "Maroon" Shoats Support
www.myspace.com/freerussellshoatz

Updates on Maroon's situation including his ongoing struggle to receive medical treatment for heart problems.

Free Gary Tyler
info@freegarytyler.com
www.freegarytyler.com • www.jerichony.org/garytyler.html

Gary Tyler has spent 32 of his 48 years in jail for a crime he did not commit. In 1975, Gary, a Black teenager, was wrongly convicted by an all-white jury for the murder of a 13-year-old white youth killed during a white mob's attack on a bus filled with Black high school students in Destrehan, Louisiana. Gary's trial featured coerced testimony, planted evidence, judicial misconduct, and an incompetent defense. He was sentenced to death at age 17. A federal appeals court found that he was "denied a fundamentally fair trial" but refused to order a new one. The Louisiana death penalty was then ruled unconstitutional, and Gary was resentenced to life. Today, far too few people are aware of Gary's case, which in the mid-1970s mobilized thousands across the country for his freedom and led Amnesty International to declare him a political prisoner.

*Research Committee on International Law and Black Freedom Fighters in the United States (Defunct)
The purpose of the Research Committee, active in the 1980s and early 1990s, was to increase awareness of the relevance of international law to the situation of Black political prisoners and prisoners of war in the U.S. Several of those prisoners, as well as outside attorneys and activists, contributed to the research and writings by this committee.

INDIGENOUS POLITICAL PRISONERS

Information about Eddie Hatcher
www.eddiehatcher.blogspot.com

Eddie Hatcher is a Native American political prisoner known worldwide for his February 1988 armed takeover (along with fellow Tuscarora activst Timothy Jacobs) of the offices of *The Robesonian* newspaper in Lumberton, North Carolina, in a desperate attempt to focus attention on corruption in Robeson County. Eddie demanded investigation of: local and state officials' involvement in major drug trafficking; over two dozen unsolved murders, mostly of Natives and Blacks; and the death of a young Black man in jail under suspicious circumstances. The takeover last 10 hours and ended peacefully. Eddie was acquitted of federal kidnapping charges and then convicted on state charges. He was recognized as a political prisoner by the National Council of Churches and Amnesty International. He served seven years in prison. In 1998, after his release and completion of parole (that required him to leave Robeson County for a year), Eddie again became vocal in local politics, even contemplating running for office. The next year he was rearrested, accused of a killing a man in a drive-by shooting with a high-powered rifle, even though his right arm is permanently disabled and there was no ballistics match. Yet Eddie was convicted of murder and sentenced to life without parole. The website, though outdated, contains prison writings from Eddie, who is currently struggling with AIDS in the hospital section of a prison in Raleigh, North Carolina.

*International Indian Treaty Council
Information Office
2390 Mission Street, Suite 301, San Francisco, CA 94110
415-641-4482 • iitc@treatycouncil.org
www.treatycouncil.org

The International Indian Treaty Council (IITC) is an organization of Indigenous Peoples from North, Central, and South America and the Pacific working for the Sovereignty and Self-Determination of Indigenous Peoples and the recognition and protection of Indigenous Rights, Treaties, Traditional Cultures, and Sacred Lands. The IITC was founded in 1974 at a gathering by the American Indian Movement in Standing Rock, South Dakota, attended by more than 5,000 representatives of 98 Indigenous Nations. The IITC supports grassroots Indigenous struggles through information dissemination; networking; coalition building; technical assistance; and organizing and facilitating the effective participation of traditional Peoples in local, regional, national, and international forums, events, and gatherings. In 1977, the IITC became the first organization of Indigenous Peoples to be reorganized as a Non-Governmental Organization (NGO) with Consultative Status to the United Nations Economic and Social Council. The IITC also focuses on dissemination of information regarding the U.N. and opportunities for involvement to grassroots Indigenous communities and works to educate and build awareness about Indigenous struggles among non-Indigenous Peoples and organizations.

*Leonard Peltier Defense Offense Committee
P.O. Box 7488, Fargo, ND 58106
701-235-2206 • contact@whoisleonardpeltier.info
www.whoisleonardpeltier.info

The concepts of justice and good government require that the tragic errors of the past be set right. We know that Leonard Peltier is an innocent man. Our mission is to educate the public about Leonard Peltier's wrongful conviction and illegal imprisonment and build widespread support for his freedom. Join with us and numerous internationally recognized human rights organizations, including Amnesty International, and civil rights leaders who have called for the immediate release of Leonard Peltier.

Oso Blanco Information and Support
www.osoblanco.org

Byron Shane Chubbuck is a wolf clan Cherokee/Choctaw raised in New Mexico. His Indian name is Oso Blanco and he became known by the authorities as "Robin the Hood" after the FBI and local gang unit police officers learned from a confidential informant that Oso Blanco was robbing banks to send thousands of dollars worth of supplies to the Zapatista rebels of Chiapas on a regular basis during 1998 and 1999. He is serving 80 years for bank robbery and a firearms violation. This site is for rising up true warriors who will truly fight for the people of the EZLN communities and to rise up the Mexica and Indigenous of Aztlán, North America and Canada.

PUERTO RICAN POLITICAL PRISONERS

Comité Familiares y Amigos de Avelino González Claudio
(Committee of Family and Friends of Avelino González Claudio)
Apartado Postal #22282, San Juan, PR 00931-2282
avelinogonzalezclaudio@yahoo.com

In February 2008, Avelino González Claudio, a 65-year-old Puerto Rican *independentista*, was arrested in Manati, Puerto Rico. He was one of those indicted in 1985 for the 1983 operation carried out by the *Macheteros* to secure $7 million from a Wells Fargo armored truck in Hartford, Connecticut. Many have been the trenches of struggle of this well-known leader of our people's movement for national liberation for the past 50 years. Following the arrests in 1985, Avelino became part of the struggle of our people as "José Ortega." For 22 years he eluded the enemy and was able to participate not only in the liberation struggle but also as a computer teacher. Avelino has been transferred to a state prison in Hartford to await trial. He is being held there in "maximum security": 23 hours a day in isolation with no access to his family and no phone communication with his family, lawyers, or friends. The prosecutors plan to try him, as they have his comrades, far away from his Puerto Rican homeland. Avelino has demand that the U.S. government recognize his status as a fighter for independence and a political prisoner.

Hostos Grand Jury Resistance Campaign
718-559-9276 • resistgrandjury@gmail.com
www.geocities.com/resistgrandjury

The campaign is a coalition of progressive and community organizations, artists, educators, community and religious leaders, and organizers that was formed in response to the repression present in the round of subpoenas served on January 11, 2008, by FBI agents on Puerto Rican pro-independence human rights activists and artists to appear before a grand jury investigating the Puerto Rican independence movement (as of July 2008, five people have been served). The campaign's objectives are to denounce the use of the federal grand jury as an instrument of political internment and repression against the Puerto Rican community by organizing demonstrations and press conferences on court dates; to bring awareness that the federal grand jury is used as a "fishing expedition" and is the continuation of COINTELPRO and surveillance of the Puerto Rican Independence Movement started in the 1930s; to educate through literature, lectures, conferences, community meetings, and speak-outs about how to protect yourselves, your family, and your community from FBI intrusions, intimidations, illegal searches and seizures, and intelligence-gathering by utilizing the political principle of "noncollaboration" and building a Wall of Resistance—Do Not Speak to the FBI (educational pamphlet on the website); and to support grand jury resisters and families politically, economically, and socially.

*National Boricua Human Rights Network
2739 W Division Street, Chicago, IL 60622
773-342-8023 • info@boricuahumanrights.org
www.boricuahumanrights.org

The National Boricua Human Rights Network (NBHRN) is an organization composed of Puerto Ricans in the U.S. and their supporters that educates and mobilizes the Puerto Rican community, the broader Latin American community, and other people of conscience regarding issues of justice, peace, and human rights. Our priorities include: (1) the decontamination, development, and return of the island of Vieques to its people; (2) the release of the remaining Puerto Rican political prisoners; and (3) an end to the continuing political repression and criminalization of progressive sectors of the Puerto Rican community. *La Red* is the monthly newsletter of the NBHRN. It is available through the Network's website as individual posts of articles or as a downloadable document. The site also has links to galleries of the artwork of political prisoners Oscar López Rivera and Carlos Alberto Torres.

*ProLibertad Freedom Campaign
718-601-4751 • prolibertad@hotmail.com • www.prolibertadweb.com
To join listserv: ProLibertad-subscribe@yahoogroups.com

The ProLibertad Freedom Campaign is an organization composed of individuals and organizations who work together on a broad and unitary basis, accepting differences of ideological and political position, but sharing the responsibility to support the Puerto Rican political prisoners and prisoners of war who have been imprisoned for their political convictions and activities in the cause of Puerto Rico's ongoing struggle for independence and right to self-determination. The ProLibertad Freedom Campaign has been working for the release of the Puerto Rican political prisoners and prisoners of war for over 10 years. Through a comprehensive regimen of public educational programs and events, ongoing lobbying efforts, public pressure work and related initiatives like our website and *El Coquí Libre*, ProLibertad's newsletter, it is our goal to secure the freedom of these brave patriots whose only"crime" has been the unconditional love of their homeland, Puerto Rico. Currently, ProLibertad works for the freedom of Carlos Alberto Torres, Haydée Beltrán Torres, Oscar López Rivera, and Avelino González Claudio.

*Puerto Rican Freedom Album
freedomalbum@gmail.com • www.prfreedomproject.org

The Welfare Poets, Boricuation, and other concerned organizations and individuals have come together to collaborate on a fund-raising project to directly aid the current Puerto Rican political prisoners and prisoners of war incarcerated for fighting for the independence and self-determination of Puerto Rico. The Freedom Album will be a musical CD/compilation dedicated to the welfare of our political prisoners. We have united under the name The Puerto Rican Freedom Project Committee. Additionally, we also want this album to assist past political prisoners and prisoners of war who have been freed and are now attempting to survive in a system where many channels have been closed to them, and even possibly aid future political prisoners and prisoners of war.

CHICANO/MEXICANO POLITICAL PRISONERS

*Committee to Free Alvaro Luna Hernandez
John S. Dolley, Jr., Central Campaign Coordinator
ABC/PLS, P.O. Box 7187, Austin, TX 78712
512-478-7666 • twitchon@hotmail.com
www.freealvaro.org

The Committee to Free Alvaro Luna Hernandez encourages human rights and prison support communities to step up the work on behalf of political prisoner Alvaro Luna Hernandez and all prisoners of political repression, targeted for their prison activism. While his case is on appeal, a legal defense fund has been established to solicit funds for appeal costs, and organizing materials have been made available, including Alvaro's writings, recordings and artwork. If you're interested in the case, offering promotions, support, or starting a local support chapter, please email us. If you want to distribute literature in your area, you can download PDFs on our website.

CUBAN POLITICAL PRISONERS IN THE U.S.

*National Committee to Free the Cuban Five
2489 Mission Street, #24, San Francisco, CA 94110
415-821-6545 • www.freethefive.org

In September 2006, a historic march was held through the streets of Washington, DC, from the Justice Department to the White House. In February 2008, a billboard was unveiled in Hollywood, California, demanding the freedom of the Cuban Five. Visit the website for updates, photos, audio, and transcripts and to contact 19 local chapters and dozens of international support groups.

ARAB AND MUSLIM POLITICAL PRISONERS

*Sami Al-Arian Support Committee
c/o Tampa Bay Coalition for Justice and Peace
tampabayjustice@yahoo.com • www.freesamialarian.com
e-newsletter subscription:
tampabaycoalitionforjusticeandpeace-subscribe@yahoogroups.com

Press releases, case history, writings from Sami Al-Arian, and a petition to support him.

Muslim American Society Freedom
1050 17th Street, NW, Suite 600, Washington, DC 20036
202-496-1288 • mas4freedom@aol.com
www.masnet.org

MAS Freedom, the civic and human rights advocacy entity of the Muslim American Society (MAS), supports the rights of detained activists and religious leaders. MAS Freedom Executive Director Mahdi Bray has worked tirelessly on the cases of imams arrested by U.S. Immigration and Customs Enforcement (ICE) officials. It is often the support of family and community members that makes a difference in the successful outcome in arrests of this nature.

EURO-AMERICAN POLITICAL PRISONERS

*Friends of Marilyn Buck
c/o Legal Services for Prisoners with Children
1540 Market Street, #490, San Francisco, CA 94102
fombuck@yahoo.com • www.marilynbuck.com

Friends of Marilyn Buck, NY
mbuckny@gmail.com

Friends of Marilyn Buck supports her political and creative work. We work toward her release in the context of freedom for all political prisoners. We provide material support and help to distribute writings and recordings by and about her.

*Information on Bill Dunne
www.prisonactivist.org/pps†pows/bill-dunne

*Friends of David Gilbert
P.O. Box 7326, Capitol Station, Albany, NY 12224
freedavidgilbert@gmail.com • www.freedavidgilbert.org

Friends of David Gilbert is an organization of his friends and family working to coordinate communication with and about David, to support him in prison, to distribute information about his life and work, and to campaign to win his freedom.

*Free Jaan Laaman!
www.freejaan.com • www.freejaan.podomatic.com

Here you will find info about the ongoing struggle for the freedom of U.S. anti-imperialist political prisoner Jaan Laaman, as well as another Ohio 7 defendant, Tom Manning, and all political prisoners, prisoners of war, and prisoners of conscience. Includes a link to a site with audio commentaries by Jaan on current issues, featured on Kansas City Black Liberation Radio (www.kcblr.org).

Friends of Tom Manning
dec16th@hotmail.com • www.geocities.com/capitolhill/parliament/3400/

Tom Manning is a Vietnam veteran, working-class revolutionary, and U.S. political prisoner. He militantly struggled against the war in Vietnam and supports the right of self-determination of all oppressed peoples. Tom Manning was captured in 1985 and sentenced to 53 years in federal prison for a series of bombings carried out as "armed propaganda" against apartheid and U.S. imperialism. He tirelessly fought against racist, genocidal capitalism in the U.S.A. Tom Manning was also wrongly sentenced to 80 years in prison for the self-defense killing of a New Jersey state trooper. Tom Manning has been subject to human rights violations that include physical abuse, lock-down, and solitary confinement.

*Lynne Stewart Defense Committee
350 Broadway, Suite 700, New York, NY 10013
212-625-9696—Pat Levasseur • info@lynnestewart.org
www.lynnestewart.org

The Lynne Stewart Defense Committee has a speakers bureau made up of attorneys and activists able to speak at an event in your area. Also, if you are interested in setting up a forum in your community, we can help with suggestions of people knowledgeable about Lynne's case and issues related to the decline in civil liberties since 9/11 and the Patriot Act.

ENVIRONMENTAL AND ANIMAL RIGHTS POLITICAL PRISONERS

Tre Arrow Defense Committee
250-361-1876 • tre@riseup.net
www.trearrow.org

Environmentalist and political prisoner Tre Arrow has been incarcerated in Canada and the U.S. since March 2004. For almost four years, Tre was imprisoned while contesting extradition to the United States. Like the 125,000 American draft refusers who came to Canada between 1964 and 1977, Tre came to Canada hoping to escape persecution in the United States. This became Tre's only option when his life in Portland, Oregon, was unjustly turned upside down in the summer of 2002. The U.S. government is laying charges that could see him locked up for the rest of his life if convicted. After working tirelessly for years to protect some of the only ancient forests left in the Northwestern U.S., Tre had become an extremely well-known and important organizer. Like other peaceful organizers, Tre found himself at the forefront of an environmental movement that successfully interfered with industrial powers; he therefore became a target.

Support for Rod Coronado
P.O. Box 732, Tucson, AZ 85702
info@supportrod.org • www.supportrod.org

On February 22, 2006, Native American environmental activist and former Animal Liberation Front (ALF) prisoner Rodney Adam Coronado, 39, was indicted in California on one felony charge of demonstrating how to use a destructive device. In 2007, Coronado stood trial in San Diego on charges related to his speech in 2003 in Hillcrest. After two days of deliberations, the jury remained deadlocked in his favor, and on September 19, 2007, Judge Jeffrey Miller declared a mistrial. Coronado subsequently entered a guilty plea, accepting a deal for a one-year prison term, as a result of which he was sentenced in March 2008 to one year and one day.

He is an advocate and former activist for the Animal Liberation Front and a spokesperson for the Earth Liberation Front. He is also a former crew member of the Sea Shepherd Conservation Society and was a member of the editorial collective of the *Earth First!* Journal

Earth Warriors Are OK
fightthegreenscare@riseup.net
www.midwestgreenscare.org

The EWOK! (Earth Warriors are OK!), formerly the Twin Cities Eco-Prisoner Support Committee, formed in 2006 to provide support to people who are accused or convicted of actions taken in defense of the Earth and its inhabitants. Actions, accusations, or convictions that would warrant support would include: Earth and animal liberation activity (regardless of whether the "ALF" or "ELF" claimed responsibility), road resistance, communities fighting development, indigenous resistance, antifascist, and prisoners from the MOVE family.

GreenScare.org
greenscare@mutualaid.org • www.greenscare.org

The term Green Scare refers to the federal government's expanding prosecution efforts against animal liberation and ecological activists, drawing parallels to the "Red Scares" of the 1910s and 1950s. A 2002 edition of a prisoner support zine, *Spirit of Freedom*, defined the Green Scare as "the tactics that the U.S. government and all their tentacles (FBI, IRS, BATF, Joint Terrorism Task Forces, local police, the court system) are using to attack the ELF/ALF (Earth Liberation Front and Animal Liberation Front) and specifically those who publicly support them." The term has now been widely used to describe an early 2006 sweep of arrests, convictions, and grand jury indictments of alleged ELF/ALF activists on charges relating to acts of property damage, conspiracy, arson, and use of destructive devices dubbed "Operation Backfire"; the cases of the SHAC 7, Eric McDavid, and Rod Coronado; and recent repressive legislation such as the Animal Enterprise Terrorism Act, which attempts to turn activists into "terrorists." The site includes news, updates, addresses and links on the cases of Green Scare political prisoners.

Friends of Jeffrey Free Luers (and Free's Defense Fund)
info@freejeffluers.org • www.freefreenow.org
www.myspace.com/freefreenow

In June 2001, 23-year-old forest defense activist Jeffrey "Free" Luers was sentenced to 22 years and 8 months in prison for the burning of three sport utility vehicles (SUVs) in Eugene, Oregon. To make a statement about global warming, Jeff and his codefendant, Craig "Critter" Marshall, set fire to the three sport utility vehicles at a Eugene car dealership. Their stated purpose was to raise awareness about global warming and the role that SUVs play in that process. No one was hurt in this action nor was that the intent. An arson specialist at trial confirmed that the action did not pose any threat to people based on its size and distance from any fuel source. Despite the fact that this action hurt no one, it caused only $40,000 in damages, and the cars were later resold, Jeff was sent to prison for a sentence considerably longer than those convicted of murder, kidnapping, and rape in Oregon state. The Court of Appeals unanimously ruled that Jeff's case be reversed, and a resentencing hearing finally took place on February 28, 2008, in Lane County Circuit Court, which reduced Jeff's sentence to 10 years. He could be released by December 2009.

Friends and Family of Eric McDavid
info@supporteric.org • www.supporteric.org

Eric McDavid was arrested in Auburn, California, on January 13, 2006, as part of the government's ongoing Green Scare campaign. He was convicted of "conspiracy to destroy property by means of fire or explosives," despite no crime actually taking place. Eric was sentenced to 19 years and seven months imprisonment. He was arrested along with Zachary Jenson and Lauren Weiner. The government's case is based on the word of a single FBI informant who was paid over $75,000 to fabricate a crime and implicate the trio. Both of Eric's codefendants have since caved under the threat of being imprisoned for 20 years and pled guilty to a lesser charge. In doing so, they also agreed to testify against Eric and cooperate in every way possible, including testifying in front of secret grand jury proceedings. Eric has been repeatedly denied bail. For over two years, he has only been allowed to leave his cell for a few hours per week and receives very little contact with the outside world. He needs your support now more than ever, as he prepares to appeal this outrageous conviction.

Family and Friends of Daniel McGowan
c/o Lisa McGowan, PO Box 106, New York NY 10156-106
friendsofdanielmcg@yahoo.com • www.supportdaniel.org
www.myspace.com/danielmcgowan

Daniel McGowan is an environmental and social justice activist from New York City. He was charged in federal court on counts of arson, property destruction, and conspiracy, all relating to two actions in Oregon in 2001. Until recently, Daniel was offered two choices by the government: cooperate by informing on other people, or go to trial and potentially spend the rest of his life in prison. His only real option was to plead not guilty until he could reach a resolution of the case that permitted him to honor his principles. As a result of months of litigation and negotiation, Daniel was able to admit to his role in these two incidents, while not implicating or identifying any other people who might have been involved.

Family and Friends of Daniel McGowan raises funds to pay his legal defense, sets up public events about the Green Scare, and provides financial, logistical, legal, and emotional support to Daniel. He will be earning a master's degree and will hopefully complete a book about his experience while imprisoned.

North American Earth Liberation Prisoners Support Network
naelpsn@mutualaid.org • www.ecoprisoners.org

The NA-ELPSN is part of the Earth Liberation Prisoners Support Network (ELP), an international network of groups that support people who are accused or convicted of actions taken in defense of the Earth and its inhabitants. Such actions, accusations, or convictions that would warrant support by ELP would include: Earth and animal liberation activity (regardless of whether the "ALF" or "ELF" claimed responsibility), anti-nuclear activity, communities fighting development, peace action, indigenous resistance, anti-fascist, and prisoners from the MOVE family. Simply, we are a prisoner support network. Although our acronym "ELP" resembles the name of the international direct action movement, "ELF", we have no connection to this movement other than our ideological support for actions taken by individuals operating under the ELF banner. Our support of prisoners is of a wholly separate, legal and aboveground manner. Please send us any updated prisoner addresses, new photos, news items related to prisoners we support, information on federal and state grand juries, tips, advice or stamps. To receive e-mail updates, write to elp4321@hotmail.com.

Friends of Jonathan Paul
PMB 267, 2305 Ashland Street, Suite C, Ashland, OR 97520
friendsofjonathanpaul@yahoo.com • www.supportjonathan.org

Jonathan has been an animal and environmental activist since the 1980s and a vegan for 25 years. He and his wife live with five companion animals off the grid, powering their home with solar panels. Jonathan is currently serving a 51-month sentence in federal prison in Phoenix, Arizona, for his role in the 1997 arson of the Cavel West horse slaughterhouse in Redmond, Oregon. Jonathan has dedicated his life to protecting the earth and alleviating the suffering of animals, human and nonhuman. From 1999 until the time he reported to prison in October of 2007, Jonathan served his community as an emergency medical technician and volunteer firefighter. Jonathan has received numerous awards for his community service.

SHAC 7 Support Fund
740A 14th Street, #237, San Francisco, CA 94114
info@shac7.com • www.shac7.com

The SHAC7 are six activists and a corporation, Stop Huntingdon Animal Cruelty USA Inc., that have been found guilty of multiple federal felonies for their alleged role in simply campaigning to close down the notorious animal testing lab, Huntingdon Life Sciences. Five of the individuals are currently in federal prison (the sixth, Darius Fullmer, has been released, after completing his one-year sentence). They are not accused of actually smashing windows, liberating animals, or even attending demonstrations, rather reporting on and encouraging others to engage in legal demonstrations and supporting the ideology of direct action. After being found guilty, they are beginning their appeal. Unfortunately this appeal will be done from prison.

Support Briana Waters
c/o Eric Waters, P.O. Box 1689, Old Chelsea Station, New York, NY 10113
donate@supportbriana.org
www.supportbriana.org

Briana Waters is a devoted and loving mother of her three-year-old daughter. She is a professional musician and violin teacher based in Oakland, California. On March 15, 2006, she was falsely accused of participating in a politically motivated arson that took place at the University of Washington in May 2001. Briana steadfastly maintains her innocence. She is a peaceful woman who believes in nonviolence. In 2001, she directed a documentary, entitled *Watch*, which tells the moving, true story of a peaceful campaign that built a coalition between environmentalists, loggers, and the residents of Randle, Washington, to save the old-growth forest on Watch Mountain. Briana's family, friends, and supporters were heartbroken and left in disbelief when a federal jury found her guilty of two counts of arson on March 6, 2008. She is currently detained while awaiting sentencing. She faces a mandatory five-year minimum prison term, potentially subject to an enhancement of up to 20 years.

WAR RESISTERS

*Courage to Resist
484 Lake Park Avenue, # 41, Oakland, CA 94610
510-488-3559 • www.couragetoresist.org
www.myspace.com/couragetoresist

Courage to Resist is a group of concerned community members, veterans, and military families that supports military objectors to illegal war and occupation and the policies of empire. Our People Power strategy weakens the pillars that maintain war and occupation in Iraq, Afghanistan, and elsewhere by supporting GI resistance, counter-recruitment, and draft resistance, which cuts off the supply of troops. We are autonomous from and independent of any political organization, party, or group. Our activities include reaching out to troops; supporting individual resisters; building national and international support networks; promoting People Power antiwar strategies; and organizing visibility and resistance in streets and public places. Also has bimonthly e-newsletter.

Jonah House: Community—Nonviolence - Resistance
1301 Moreland Avenue, Baltimore, MD 21216
410-233-6238 • www.jonahhouse.org

Jonah House is a longtime nonviolence resistance community. The website includes large amounts of information and updates on Plowshares anti-nuclear and other anti-militarism and anti-war direct actions, as well as on political prisoners from those movements, including their letters from prison. See also www.plowsharesactions.org for a chronology of Plowshares actions through 2004.

LET FREEDOM RING

The Nuclear Resister
P.O. Box 43383, Tucscon, AZ 85733
520-323-8697 • nukeresister@igc.org
www.serve.com/nukeresister

Occasional newspaper and website offering information about and support for imprisoned anti-nuclear and antiwar activists.

*War Resisters League
339 Lafayette Street, New York, NY 10012
212-228-0450 • wrl@warresisters.org • www.warresisters.org

The War Resisters League (WRL), founded in 1923 as a secular group committed to nonviolent social change, has been the leading consistent support organization for over four generations for U.S. draft resisters, registration resisters, draft evaders fleeing to Canada and elsewhere, and—currently—for active-duty GI military resisters, working closely with the Iraqi Veterans Against the War. WRL has always gone beyond counseling and supporting potential conscientious objectors and has actively advocated resistance both to and within the armed forces. WRL has publicly aided and abetted these resisters, as well as war tax resisters, an act that often carries legal penalties similar to the acts of resistance themselves. In addition, WRL is the U.S. affiliate of the War Resisters International, together promoting December 1 as an annual, international Prisoners for Peace Day.

LESBIAN/GAY/BISEXUAL/TRANSGENDER SUPPORT FOR POLITICAL PRISONERS

*Out of Control: Lesbian Committee to Support Women Political Prisoners
3543 18th Street, P.O. Box 30, San Francisco, CA 94110
www.prisonactivist.org/ooc

Out of Control is a Bay Area group of lesbians that formed 20 years ago to educate in our community about women in prison, with a focus on women political prisoners. In addition, we work at exposing the criminal (in)justice system and the U.S. "prison-industrial complex" for what it is: a racist, sexist, homophobic system with horrendous medical care and unspeakable conditions. Our primary educational tool is our newsletter, *Out of Time*. Currently we send *Out of Time* to over 600 women inside. In addition, over 1,500 readers receive our newsletter on the outside, separately or in combination with *Ultra Violet*, the publication of Lesbians and Gays Against Intervention (LAGAI-Queer Insurrection). The newsletter is FREE to all. *Out of Time* articles focus on prison-related issues, the cases and struggles of women political prisoners (in the U.S. and elsewhere). We also provide information about women social prisoners, battered women locked up for defending themselves, and lesbian, gay, and transgender prisoners.

Rainbow Flags for Mumia
RF4Mumia@gmail.com
www.workers.org/2008/us/lgbt_0424

Rainbow Flags for Mumia, a project of the International Action Center, is a coalition of lesbian, gay, bi and trans people and organizations that came together in 1999 to demand a new trial for Mumia Abu-Jamal. Despite the racist, anti-LGBT oppression we face, it is because of our movement's rich history of resistance, from the Stonewall Inn to the Compton Cafeteria in California, that we continue to fight for equality and social justice today. It is with that same righteous rage against injustice that we as LGBT peoples demand the immediate freedom of the Jersey 4 and continue to fight for the freedom of Mumia Abu-Jamal. Historically, LGBT activists and groups have been integral to the Mumia solidarity movement worldwide. We have mobilized 1000-strong Rainbow Flags for Mumia contingents in Philadelphia, led feeder marches through the Castro in San Francisco and organized highly successful fundraising campaigns for his defense.

*QUISP (Queers United in Support of Political Prisoners) (Defunct)

According to a QUISP brochure: "QUISP is a collective of lesbians and gay men committed to building support for political prisoners in the U.S. and educating the lesbian and gay community at large about them. We do this work knowing that our liberation as lesbians and gay men will not occur without the liberation of all oppressed peoples." Originally called Lesbians and Gay Folks Supporting Political Prisoners, the group operated in New York City from 1990 to 1996. It hosted many educational forums and video showings about the cases of particular political prisoners, both straight and gay/lesbian; raised funds to support legal and political defense of political prisoners; organized queer contingents in political prisoner demonstrations and did a lesbian political prisoner visibility action in the 1992 New York Lesbian and Gay Pride March; supported activist campaigns by queers of color; participated in coalitions working against police violence; and distributed literature and audiovisual materials, including the booklet *Dykes and Fags Want to Know*, 1991 interviews with lesbian political prisoners Linda Evans, Laura Whitehorn, and Susan Rosenberg, as well as an audiocassette of Dhoruba Bin-Wahad's rousing speech at the group's forum on the case of Mumia Abu-Jamal in 1991.

When the prison doors are opened
the rea dragon will
fly out

Elspeth Meyer

Index

C

G

H

J

K

L

M

N

Anti-Arab 182, 739–740, 741–747
anti-Latino 740, 746, 747
Islamophobia 144, 739–740, 741–747, 830
Radio Martí 798
Rage Against the Machine 407
Rahman, Abdel 801
Rainbow Flags for Mumia 385, 390, 393, 408, 836
Ramos, Jovelino 161
Ramos-Horta, José 335, 341
Ramp, James 10, 621, 763
Rangel, Charles 417
Rape 352, 748. *See also* PRISON: SEXUAL ASSAULT/CAVITY SEARCHES/STRIP SEARCHES; *See also* PRISON: RAPE
Rashid, Ali 163
Raven's Shadowrunners 823
La Raza Movement 25, 240, 783
Reagan Administration 7, 61, 77, 584, 594, 646, 672, 739
Reagan, Ronald 775
Ream, Tim 697
Reasons to Fear: The Cultural Defense of Hooty Croy (film) 299
Rebel Diaz 409
Red Army Faction 32, 189
Red Book Store (Cambridge, MA) 599
The Red Dragon (newspaper) 119
Red Guerrilla Resistance 29, 30, 387, 388. *See also* RESISTANCE CONSPIRACY CASE
Red Star North bookstore 787
Redwood Summer 38
Reel, Dawn 393
Refuse and Resist 407, 408, 409, 436, 567
Reidsville Brothers 191
Release 2000 Campaign 671–674
Release 2001 643
Rendell, Ed 623
Reno, Janet 407, 415, 577. *See also* CLINTON ADMINISTRATION
Republican Party 342, 444, 496, 631, 688, 706, 746. *See also* NIXON ADMINISTRATION; *See also* REAGAN ADMINISTRATION; *See also* BUSH ADMINISTRATION (43); *See also* BUSH ADMINISTRATION (41)
Republic of New Afrika (& Provisional Government) 7, 8, 168, 179, 223, 566, 646, 659, 660, 677, 680, 772, 780, 799, 809

Research Committee on International Law and Black Freedom Fighters in the United States 52–53, 68, 68–88, 826
Resistance Conspiracy Case 30, 54–62, 159, 210, 372, 377, 388, 418, 570, 655, 771, 776, 779, 796, 805
Resistance in Brooklyn 336–338, 341, 409, 433, 435, 441–442, 476, 479, 499, 508, 767, 771, 776, 787, 791, 800, 814
Revolutionary Action Movement 3, 168, 646, 647, 659, 677, 733
Revolutionary Armed Forces of Colombia 152, 586
Revolutionary Armed Task Force 6, 796. *See also* BRINK'S ROBBERY: (NYACK, NY 1981)
Revolutionary Communist Party 726
Revolution (newspaper) 726–732
Reynolds, Jean 780
Ricardo Aldape Guerra Defense Committee 25
Rice, David. *See* LANGA, WOPASHITWE MONDO EYEN WE
Richards, Ann 495
Richardson, Bill 428
Richardson, David 404
Rich, Sara 748–749
RICO. *See* CRIMINAL JUSTICE SYSTEM: RACKETEER INFLUENCED AND CORRUPT ORGANIZATIONS LAW
Ridge, Tom 404, 407, 413, 423, 424, 445
Ridley-Thomas, Mark 163
Riegle, Mike 372
Riley, John 389, 436, 787
Ríos, José 7
Rivera, Carmen 162
Rivera, Danny 790
Rivera, Dennis 408
Rivera, Héctor 334
Rivera, Nydia Cuevas 137, 790
Rivers, Voza 673
Rizzo, Frank 10, 11, 422, 498, 763
Robideau, Bob 14, 235
Robinson, Mary 428
Rockefeller, Nelson 9, 95, 192
Rodgers, Bill 695, 699
Rodriguez Diaz, Esdras 161
Rodríguez, Alberto 19, 165, 201, 225, 251–254, 323, 326, 418, 775, 795

Sweden 590, 780
Swift, Suzanne 748–749
Sykes, Michael 698
Symbionese Liberation Army 40–41, 514

T

Taifa, Nkechi *644–646*, 674, 802
Taiwan 119, 584
Talking Drum Collective 818, 825
Tampa Bay Coalition for Justice and Peace 745
Tanaka, Toshi Yuki 213
Tankersley, Kendall 699
Taylor, Donald 193
Taylor, Harold 40, 722, 726, 728, 733–736, 738, 797
Taylor, Mark 405
Taylor, Robert 7, 165
Teheran Proclamation (1968) 353
Tenet, George 693
Terrorism 185, 687, 693, 723, 740
 definitions 185
 "eco-terrorism" 690, 693, 832
 smear 39, 60, 67, 183, 190, 374, 679–683, 698, 739, 741, 742, 801
Thatcher, Margaret 367, 594
The Other Economic Summit (TOES) 318
Third World Resurgence *356*
Thomas, Andres 162
Thomas, Piri 148
Thompson, Bennie G. 417
Thompson-El, Richard 96
Thoreau, Henry David 331, 475
Thornburgh, Richard 166
Through the Wire (film) 211
Thurston, Darren 699
Thurston, Linda 428, 598–602, 802
Tijerina, Reies López 23
Tilby, Chuck 701–703
Tipograph, Susan 387
Todd-Whitman, Christine 798
Toineeta, Sammy 326
Tokyo War Crimes Tribunal 227
Tolen, Aaron 335

The Torch (newspaper) 119
Torres, Alejandrina xxvi, 19, 43, 50, 59, 65, 83, 92, 102, 158, 165, 177, 184, 189, 201, 202, 203, 205, 206, 207, 208, 209, 225, 242, 256, 274, 277, 323, 326, 327, 342, 342–344, 344, 394–396, 395, 442, 775, 795, 796
Torres, Carlos Alberto 19, 165, 201, 202, 204, 326, 343, 357–358, 678, 789, 802, 828, 829. *See also* NOT ENOUGH SPACE ART EXHIBIT
Torres, Christopher 359
Torres, Francisco 40, 733–736, 738, 797
Torres, Haydée Beltrán. *See* BELTRÁN, HAYDÉE
Torres, José Alberto 163
Torresola, Griselio 15
Torture 123, 173–174, 197, 637, 724, 730, 734–735, 753, 824, 825. *See also* PRISON: ISOLATION; *See also* PRISON: SEXUAL ASSAULT BY STAFF/STRIP SEARCHES/ CAVITY SEARCHES
 by police 6, 7, 18, 722–723, 725, 726–727, 728, 753, 797, 798. *See also* POLICE: VIOLENCE
 sensory deprivation 82–85, 90, 174, 202, 207–209, 231, 342, 640, 735
 sleep deprivation 232, 342, 357, 735
Toure, Kazi 31–32, 165, 197, 599, 785
Toure, Kwame. *See* CARMICHAEL, STOKELY
Toward Freedom (magazine) 776
Towns, Edolphus 415
TransAfrica Forum 722
Trattner, Walter I. 577
Tre Arrow Defense Committee 831
Treaty of Guadalupe-Hidalgo (1848) 284, 291, 296
Treaty of Paris 328
Treaty of Tlatelolco 319
Trials 171–173. *See also* COURT DECISIONS; *See also* CRIMINAL JUSTICE SYSTEM; *See also* POLITICAL INTERNMENT
 attacks on lawyers 172, 187, 679–683
 denial of proper venue 14–13, 173, 230, 319, 827
 disproportionate sentencing 61, 159, 173, 187, 192–193, 230–231, 233, 324, 332, 340, 356, 357, 417, 477, 672, 695, 738, 777, 782, 785, 789, 799
 intimidation of jurors 14, 55, 171–172, 185–186, 229, 233

V

Y

Z

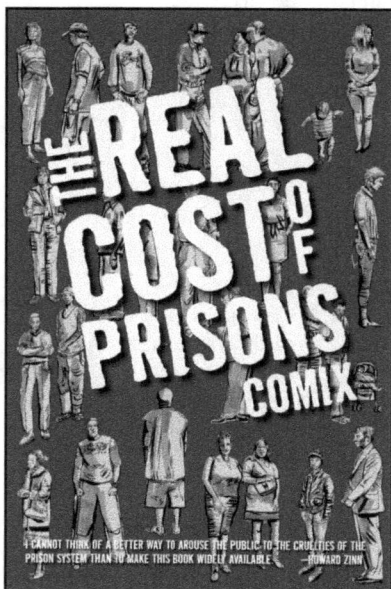

The Real Cost of Prisons Comix

"I cannot think of a better way to arouse the public to the cruelties of the prison system than to make this book widely available."
—Howard Zinn

Edited by Lois Ahrens
PM Press 2008
ISBN 978-1-60486-034-4
96 pages paperback

$12.95

One out of every hundred adults in the U.S. is in prison. This book provides a crash course in what drives mass incarceration, the human and community costs, and how to stop the numbers from going even higher. This volume collects the three comic books published by the Real Cost of Prisons Project: *Prison Town: Paying the Price, Prisoners of the War on Drugs, Prisoners of a Hard Life: Women and Their Children*.

The stories and statistical information in each comic book is thoroughly researched and documented.

Over 125,000 copies of the comic books have been printed and more than 100,000 have been sent to families of people who are incarcerated, people who are incarcerated, and to organizers and activists throughout the country. The book includes a chapter with descriptions about how the comix have been put to use in the work of organizers and activists in prison and in the "free world" by ESL teachers, high school teachers, college professors, students, and health care providers throughout the country. The demand for them is constant and the ways in which they are being used is inspiring.

PM PRESS, PO Box 23912, Oakland, CA, 94623
www.pmpress.org

The Angola 3: Black Panthers and the Last Slave Plantation

Narrated by Mumia Abu-Jamal, featuring interviews with former Panthers, political prisoners and revolutionaries, including the Angola 3 themselves, and Bo Brown, Geronimo ji Jaga (Pratt), Malik Rahim, Yuri Kochiyama, David Hilliard, Rod Coronado, Noelle Hanrahan, Kiilu Nyasha, Marion Brown, Luis Talamantez, Gail Shaw and many others.

Produced by Scott Crow and Ann Harkness
PM Press · ISBN 978-1-60486-020-7
DVD 109 minutes
$19.95

THE ANGOLA 3: BLACK PANTHERS AND THE LAST SLAVE PLANTATION

THE
ANGOLA 3
BLACK PANTHERS AND THE LAST SLAVE PLANTATION

TRUTH

NARRATED BY MUMIA ABU-JAMAL

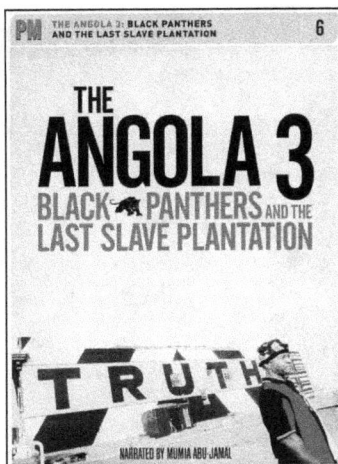

The Angola 3 are Robert King, Herman Wallace and Albert Woodfox, men who have endured solitary confinement longer then any known living prisoner in the United States. Politicized through contact with the Black Panther Party while inside Louisiana's prisons, they formed one of the only prison Panther chapters in history and worked to organize other prisoners into a movement for the right to live like human beings. This feature length movie explores their extraordinary struggle for justice while incarcerated in Angola, a former slave plantation where institutionalized rape and murder made it known as one of the most brutal and racist prisons in the United States.

In a partial victory, the courts exonerated Robert King of the original charges and released him in 2001. In July 2008, Albert Woodfox's sentence was overturned, yet he remains imprisoned, as does Herman Wallace.

From the Bottom of the Heap: The Autobiography of Black Panther Robert Hillary King

Robert Hillary King | 240 pages | $24.95
PM Press 2008 | ISBN 978-1-60486-039-9

Prior to having his conviction overturned in 2001, the author was one of the longest held political prisoners in the Unites States, having survived 31 years of imprisonment and abuse—29 of of them in isolation in a six by nine foot cell. This is his story, from his childhood in Louisiana, to his traveling to Chicago as a 15-year-old hobo, to the prison that would claim over three decades of his life.

RECOMMENDED FROM KERSPLEBEDEB

KER
SPL
EBE
DEB

Since 1998 **Kersplebedeb** has been an important source of radical
literature and agit prop materials, with over five hundred button
designs in English and French, as well as dozens of t-shirts
and a challenging selection of revolutionary literature.

The project has a non-exclusive focus on anti-patriarchal
and anti-imperialist politics, framed within an anti-capitalist
perspective. A special priority is given to writings regarding
armed struggle in the metropole, and the continuing
struggles of political prisoners and prisoners of war.

check it out on the web, or write for a free catalog:

KERSPLEBEDEB PUBLISHING AND DISTRIBUTION
CP 63560, CCCP Van Horne, Montreal, Quebec, Canada, H3W 3H8
http://www.kersplebedeb.com • info@kersplebedeb.com

PM

PM Press was founded in 2007 as an independent publisher with offices in
the US and UK, and a veteran staff boasting a wealth of experience in print
and online publishing. We produce and distribute short as well as large run
projects, timely texts, and out of print classics.

We seek to create radical and stimulating fiction and non-fiction books, pamphlets, t-shirts, visual and audio materials to entertain, educate and inspire
you. We aim to distribute these through every available channel with every
available technology - whether that means you are seeing anarchist classics
at our bookfair stalls; reading our latest vegan cookbook at the café over
(your third) microbrew; downloading geeky fiction e-books; or digging new
music and timely videos from our website.

PM Press is always on the lookout for talented and skilled volunteers, artists,
activists and writers to work with. If you have a great idea for a project or
can contribute in some way, please get in touch.

PM Press . PO Box 23912 . Oakland CA 94623
510-658-3906
www.pmpress.org

www.ingramcontent.com/pod-product-compliance
Lightning Source LLC
Chambersburg PA
CBHW071411290326
41932CB00047B/2484